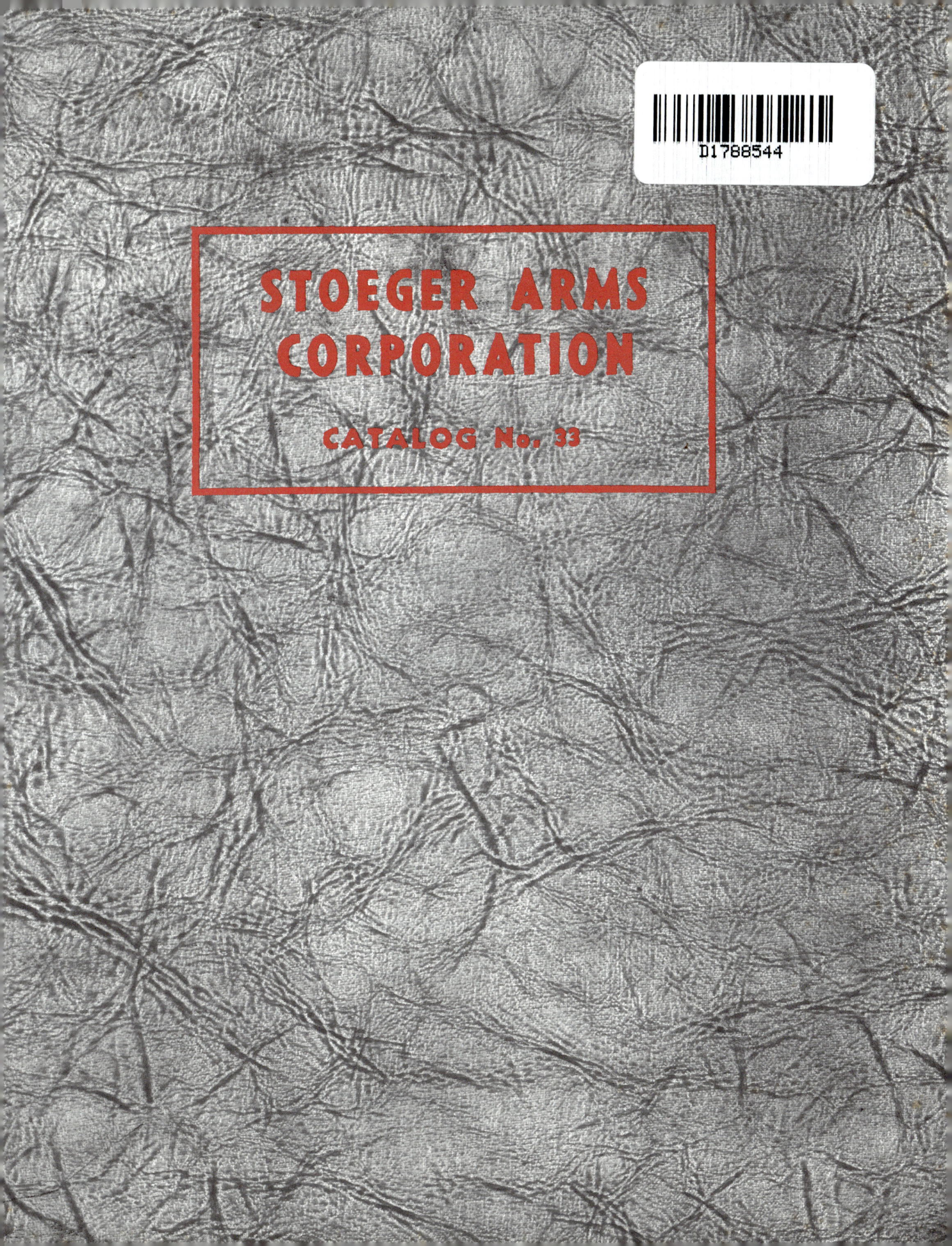

STOEGER ARMS CORPORATION

CATALOG No. 33

HEADQUARTERS FOR

In the heart of New York's famous Fifth Avenue shopping district Stoeger Arms Corporation exhibits the most complete collection of American and imported guns and accessories shown anywhere in the world. These sales and display rooms, illustrated above, are headquarters for the largest organization in the United States devoted exclusively to guns and shooting equipment. When you are in New York you are cordially invited to our store. The Stoeger offices have become a mecca for shooters, hunters, gun authorities and hunters from all over the world.

Our entire effort is devoted to the gun lover. Our own experts buy, both here and abroad, so that you may have the finest equipment available. Our master gunsmiths are at your service to repair, inspect or give advice.

SHOW THIS CATALOG TO YOUR FRIENDS

Cover Design and Photo: Ray Wells • Copyright © 1940 by Stoeger Publishing Company. All rights reserved. No part of this book may be reproduced or transmitted in any form or by any means, electronic or mechanical, including photocopying, recording, or by any information storage and retrieval system, without permission from the Publisher. • Published by Stoeger Publishing Company, 55 Ruta Court, South Hackensack, New Jersey 07606

AMERICAN SHOOTERS!

Our store, like this catalog, is a source for complete, accurate information on all types of guncraft. In both you can compare and inspect the leading makes of guns, examine all accessories and acquire knowledge concerning all phases of shooting.

Every product sold by Stoeger Arms Corporation must measure up to the strictest standards of fine quality. That is why the name Stoeger has always been associated with something better than just ordinary guns and equipment. Our nation-wide reputation assures you satisfaction, quality merchandise, fair dealing, and courteous, helpful service.

Your order will receive prompt attention. Shipments are made direct from our store at 507 Fifth Avenue, New York City.

THEY TOO WILL WANT TO OWN A COPY

ISBN: 0-88317-154-6 • Manufactured in the United States of America. Distributed to the book trade and the sporting goods trade by Stoeger Industries, 55 Ruta Court, South Hackensack, New Jersey 07606. • In Canada, distributed to the book trade and to the sporting goods trade by Stoeger Canada, Ltd., Unit 16, 1801, Wentworth Street, Whitby, Ontario L1N 5S4.

BEHIND THE

★ EXPERT REMODELING

A Stoeger specialty. Illustration above shows special form-cutter of milling machine removing ears from receiver of Enfield rifle. While a single cut would suffice, we take three cuts to assure smoother finish.

★ RESTOCKING

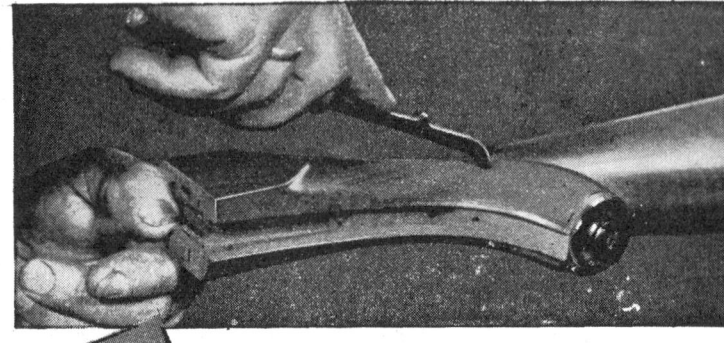

Checkering pistol grip on a shotgun stock. This is an operation which requires considerable experience, a steady hand, and sharp eye. All restocking work is done by experts of long experience.

★ REBLUEING

The method of blueing with our "Black Diamond Lightening Bluer" is illustrated above. This is the bluer used in all our military remodeling and wherever there are no soldered parts. In the blueing of fine shotguns and other pieces with soldered parts the old-fashioned acid and rust process in combination with the steam cabinet illustrated, at right, is used. In this process our "Gunsmiths' Bluer" is generally employed.

★ BUFFING

After the barrel has been allowed to rust in the steam cabinet and subsequently boiled, the artificial rust is buffed off with a fine wire brush. This completes the blueing operation.

★ THREADING BARREL

In fitting a new barrel it is of utmost importance that the barrel be exactly threaded to fit perfectly to the receiver. This is an operation requiring considerable skill and experience.

★ GRINDING STEEL BUTT

The over-sized steel butt plate is attached to the unfinished stock and is ground to conform to the stock dimensions. The right equipment and a skilled hand are required for Stoeger custom finishing.

SCENES

★ WELDING

A gunsmith shop is complete without a welding outfit. Welding is one of the most important operations in gun work and one which must only be undertaken by experts because if done carelessly the work becomes porous and brittle. Done by a Stoeger expert with modern equipment, the two pieces become as one and a perfect, unseen weld is effected.

★ BAND-SAWING

When a customer requires a special stock, the rough outlines are traced on the block of walnut and roughed out to fairly close tolerances on a band-saw, after which the work is completed entirely by hand.

★ DRILLING

This illustration shows receiver of a small bore rifle being drilled for the attachment of telescope sights. The solid base assures perfect alignment and a permanent and satisfactory job.

★ ADJUSTING TRIGGER PULL

The adjusting of the trigger pull is of greatest importance to all shooters and a matter given the most careful attention. A good job requires greatest patience and careful and exact stoning of the necessary parts.

★ FITTING NEW BARRELS

The simple looking tool illustrated at left is a costly precision instrument. The permanent part has special blocks to conform to the barrel and the special lever has special blocks for the various receivers so that the receiver may be attached or detached without marring the gun or straining the parts.

★ MILLING

This illustration shows the heavy type of milling machine required in the milling of Enfield receivers. Because of the exceptional hardness of these receivers a lighter machine would go to pieces under the strain.

★ INLETTING

The inletting of a rifle stock must not only be neat and clean of appearance but it must also be exact since a high power rifle will crack the stock if the fitting is not perfect. Stoeger inletting is your insurance against this danger.

AMERICAN GAME AND CONSERVATION

BUFFALO. AMERICAN BISON. Tens of millions lived on the Great Plains of the West, the last wild buffalo being killed by hide-hunters late in the last century.

COTTONTAIL RABBIT. The most common game animal of the United States. The cottontail is at home on farms and thrives with civilization if the brushy, marshy spots are not "cleaned up."

This article has been contributed to this catalog through the courtesy of the National Wildlife Federation, Investment Building, Washington, D. C., from whom the illustrations on these pages may be had in beautiful natural colors in sheets of 100 at the price of $1.—Every Dollar sent to the National Wildlife Federation means an increase of game and sport in America.

One of the greatest advances in conservation thinking has been the growing realization by nature lovers, sportsmen, farmers, and citizens generally that the fundamental materials of conservation—soils, waters, vegetation and wildlife—are so interrelated that it is impossible to influence one without inevitably affecting all the others. For example, when forests, woodlands, grasses— the protective cover of vegetation —are removed from the soil, erosion begins. A larger and larger proportion of rainfall runs off the slopes into the streams, and a smaller proportion of moisture is retained in the soil, or filters through to ground water level. Consequently this ground water level, the water table, is lowered; sometimes as much as thirty to forty feet. Springs and wells go dry; the remaining vegetation dies. Wildlife disappears, since it must have vegetation to furnish it food and protection. Streams silt up because of the soil which washes into them. Game fish disappear when the silt covers the productive stream bottoms which provide food for the plants and animals of the streams. Result: A man-made biological desert!

To restore the resources of such man-made deserts, it is necessary for us to consider the whole chain of life which leads from simple plant forms to the higher animals. To re-

MOOSE. The biggest of the deer tribe. In summer, gets much of its food from water plants. Moose are found in wooded country of the north and west, the very largest being in Alaska.

ELK OR WAPITI. Once plentiful in wooded country from Pennsylvania to the Rocky Mountains. The elk has suffered from settlement and civilization even more than the buffalo.

BLUEBILL. SCAUP. Has many other names in various parts of the country. The big bluebill, or broadbill frequents the larger bodies of water and is almost identical in everything except size.

BIG HORN. ROCKY MOUNTAIN SHEEP. Once very plentiful in the foothills, now making its stand in the high mountain country. Believed to have the best eye-sight of any game animal.

PRONG HORN ANTELOPE. Dweller on the plains. Depends on speed for safety. Twenty years ago, the antelope were rapidly disappearing. Now the antelope is "coming back" in many states.

CANADA GOOSE. Found throughout North America in migration. Has resumed nesting in some of its former breeding grounds in the United States. Perhaps the wariest of our waterfowl.

HELP RESTORE OUR WILDLIFE

store bobwhite quail to a depleted area we must do more than simply buy or raise birds and release them. There are definite reasons why the quail have become scarce. It may be overhunting that is responsible; if so, the obvious remedy is to regulate shooting so that the annual take is less than the annual increase of the quail. More often the difficulty is lack of adequate food or cover, or both. When this is the case, the quail released in excess of the carrying capacity of the range will die of starvation or exposure. It is clear, then, that the food and cover of the range must be improved until the range is capable of supporting a larger number of birds. The same principles apply to all forms of wildlife. We must make sure that mammals, birds, and fish have adequate food, homes, and protection. Generally, to provide food and cover we must restore vegetation. To restore vegetation we shall have to restore soils and waters. We cannot restore only a single resource, for the woods, waters, and wildlife are interdependent.

Fundamentally, the National Wildlife Federation works to coordinate the power of the various conservation organizations so that real achievement can be made in a broad and comprehensive program. To accomplish this, it is necessary that accurate information concerning the problems of conservation be available to interested groups, individuals, and the public schools. The money raised by the Federation from the sale of Wildlife Conservation Stamps is used primarily for this purpose of education, since only an informed citizenry can be expected to make intelligent use of its renewable outdoor resources—woodlands, vegetation, soils, waters, and wildlife.

The Federation now maintains a Servicing Division, set up in answer to the many requests for information from all over the United States.

GRIZZLY BEAR. The real "king of beasts." A big grizzly weighs more than twice as much as a lion. Once grizzlies were plentiful in the west and were really dangerous to hunt with muzzle-loading guns.

BEAVER, whose dams and ponds are helpful in wildlife restoration. Beaver fur, used in making high hats two hundred years ago, started the exploration and conquest of the northwest.

CHINESE PHEASANT. RING-NECK PHEASANT. Brought into the United States in 1882 and let go in Oregon. This beautiful bird is wise and hardy and does well in settled country.

CANVASBACK. Favorite of gunners on big, open water. With other species, nesting in the Canadian prairie provinces, the canvasback has suffered acutely from the deadly combination of drouth and drainage.

BOB-WHITE. QUAIL. One of America's best loved birds. Bob-white make their homes close to man, and are reared and released by tens of thousands in many states.

RUFFED GROUSE, PARTRIDGE. In the South, "pheasant". Called "King of upland game birds." The ruffed grouse is subject to cycles of scarcity, a mystery despite much scientific research.

MALLARD DUCK. Ancestor of the domestic duck. The best known of all waterfowl. The black duck of the eastern United States is a close cousin of the mallard.

JACKSNIPE. WILSON'S SNIPE. The snipe, with its long bill, catches worms and insects in the bogs and marshes. Drainage has greatly cut down the number of snipe.

HOW TO ORDER FROM THIS CATALOG
IMPORTANT NOTICE

Sales are subject to the following understanding: Title to firearms, ammunition and kindred articles remains in the seller until delivery to the buyer. If application to purchase firearms, ammunition or kindred articles is made through the medium of the mail or telegraph, the prospective buyer must state if he or she is a minor. It is not the intention of the seller to pass title to firearms, ammunition or kindred articles to persons under age. The filling of all orders for firearms, ammunition or kindred articles is subject to such laws as may apply at the time thereof.

Due to present unstable and fluctuating conditions, all prices in this catalog are subject to change or correction without notice. Merchandise will be charged for at the prevailing established prices.

NO ORDER FOR LESS THAN $1.00 CAN BE SHIPPED
Look through Index in back of catalog before you finish your order

GENERAL INSTRUCTIONS
1. Write plainly, or better yet, print name and address. Illegible signatures delay shipments.
2. Give all specifications and description and catalog numbers, etc., or article ordered. Be sure to state: number of catalog from which ordering; as full a description of item as possible, including any numbers given in catalog.
3. Specify whether goods are to be shipped by truck, freight, express or parcel post.

PAYMENTS
Payments should be made by postal money order, express money order, U. S. Postage stamps, or check, made payable to Stoeger Arms Corporation. If ordering prepaid, please include shipping charges and insurance.

DELIVERY
In order to assure the promptest dispatch of your order, we carry an exceptionally large and varied stock on hand and can, therefore, ordinarily make quick shipment. Since, however, it is practically impossible to have on hand at all times every item, particularly Sights and Parts, our delivery on such items as we may be temporarily out of stock of, is dependent upon the manufacturers' ability to deliver. In no case will there be a delay on our part and where a delay is unavoidable, you will be immediately notified and may rest assured that everything possible is being done to give you the very best service obtainable anywhere.

PISTOLS AND REVOLVERS
Pistols and revolvers cannot be sent through the mails except to bona fide firearms dealers; therefore they will have to be shipped to all others by express.

MINIMUM SHIPPING ORDER $1.00
Because of the large amount of clerical and detail work connected with the handling and filling of each mail order, regardless of the value of the order we have found it impossible to continue filling mail orders for less than $1.00 because each such order represents a direct loss, and since the enormous quantity of such orders, mostly for small parts, overburdens all normal facilities, thereby slowing down the general efficiency and service on all orders.

We sincerely trust that our customers will appreciate the difficulties which force us to this move, but to bear in mind that thru this new policy all orders can be given better and prompter service.

Surely a perusal of this catalog will show some additional item or items sufficient to bring the total value of the order to $1.00.

AMMUNITION AND POWDER
Ammunition can be shipped only by express or freight, and regulations require wooden cases. Freight is used only for large orders.

All ammunition including primers, smokeless and semi-smokeless powder cannot be shipped by parcel post and will therefore be shipped by express. Black powder can only be shipped by freight.

Freight represents a saving only on large shipments because the minimum freight charge amounts to approximately $2.50.

CORRESPONDENCE
While we are at all times glad to give any special or additional information, we have tried to make this catalog complete enough so that a careful study of same will undoubtedly produce the desired data.

When writing for information, it is of much help to us, due to the great and varied correspondence, if letters are held short, clear, concise, and to the point.

SHIPMENTS
Goods other than pistols and revolvers or ammunition, may be shipped by parcel post or express. Shipments can be made by parcel post C.O.D., but they are more expensive than if prepaid. If shipment C.O.D. is desired, deposit of at least 20 per cent of the total amount should accompany order. You will be credited for this amount and merchandise will be shipped C.O.D. for the balance.

Consult the table at the bottom of this page for parcel post charges and include insurance charges in payments at the rate of 5c for $5.00 value, 15c for $50.00 value, and 25c for $100 value.

All parcel post shipments are privately insured, no insurance marks appear on package. In case shipment does not reach you notify us, we will submit our insurance form for your signature and duplicate shipment will be made upon receipt of form properly signed.

CLAIMS
We are not responsible for loss or damage sustained in transit. Shipments are insured by the carrier and therefore claims for loss or damage in transit should be promptly made by customer against transport company.

All merchandise we ship is in good order as represented, carefully packed for shipment. If for any reason you wish to make returns, ask for our consent as otherwise we cannot accept goods.

For goods returned with our consent, we will issue credit memorandum good for other merchandise of equal value. Merchandise made to customer's own special order cannot be returned.

PRICES IN THIS CATALOG ARE SUBJECT TO CHANGE WITHOUT NOTICE, NOT RESPONSIBLE FOR TYPOGRAPHICAL ERRORS

SHIPMENTS: Parcel post and express rates show shipping charges on catalog items to be very little.

PARCEL POST RATES FROM NEW YORK CITY

Wght. in lbs.	Local	1st Up to 50 miles	2nd 50 to 150 miles	3rd 150 to 300 miles	4th 300 to 600 miles	5th 600 to 1000 miles	6th 1000 to 1400 miles	7th 1400 to 1800 miles	8th over 1800 miles	Wght. in lbs.	Local	1st Up to 50 miles	2nd 50 to 150 miles	3rd 150 to 300 miles	4th 300 to 600 miles	5th 600 to 1000 miles	6th 1000 to 1400 miles	7th 1400 to 1800 miles	8th over 1800 miles
1	$0.07	$0.08	$0.08	$0.09	$0.10	$0.11	$0.12	$0.14	$0.15	11	$0.12	$0.19	$0.19	$0.29	$0.45	$0.64	$0.82	$1.04	$1.25
2	.08	.10	.10	.11	.14	.17	.19	.23	.26	12	.13	.21	.21	.31	.49	.70	.89	1.13	1.36
3	.08	.11	.11	.13	.17	.22	.26	.32	.37	13	.13	.22	.22	.33	.52	.75	.96	1.22	1.47
4	.09	.12	.12	.15	.21	.27	.33	.41	.48	14	.14	.23	.23	.35	.56	.80	1.03	1.31	1.58
5	.09	.13	.13	.17	.24	.33	.40	.50	.59	15	.14	.24	.24	.37	.59	.86	1.10	1.40	1.69
6	.10	.14	.15	.19	.28	.38	.47	.59	.70	16	.15	.25	.25	.39	.63	.91	1.17	1.49	1.80
7	.10	.15	.15	.21	.31	.43	.54	.68	.81	17	.15	.26	.26	.41	.66	.96	1.24	1.58	1.91
8	.11	.16	.16	.23	.35	.49	.61	.77	.92	18	.16	.27	.27	.43	.70	1.02	1.31	1.67	2.02
9	.11	.17	.17	.25	.38	.54	.68	.86	1.03	19	.16	.28	.28	.45	.73	1.07	1.38	1.76	2.13
10	.12	.18	.18	.27	.42	.59	.75	.95	1.14	20	.17	.29	.29	.47	.77	1.12	1.45	1.85	2.24

APPROXIMATE RAILWAY EXPRESS RATES FROM NEW YORK

CITIES	3 lbs.	5	10	25	50	100	150	CITIES	3 lbs.	5	10	25	50	100	150
Akron, Ohio	$0.30	$0.35	$0.50	$0.96	$1.81	$3.41	$5.22	Indianapolis, Ind	$0.35	$0.45	$0.65	$1.12	$2.14	$4.07	$6.21
Buffalo, N. Y.	.25	.30	.40	.78	1.45	2.70	4.15	Jacksonville, Fla.	.35	.45	.65	1.27	2.44	4.68	7.12
Bangor, Maine	.30	.35	.50	.87	1.64	3.08	4.72	Kansas City, Mo.	.35	.50	.70	1.52	2.94	5.67	8.61
Baltimore, Md.	.25	.25	.30	.56	1.01	1.82	2.83	Los Angeles, Cal.	.49	.75	1.40	3.33	6.56	12.92	19.48
Boston, Mass.	.25	.25	.31	.61	1.12	2.04	3.16	Madison, Wis.	.35	.45	.65	1.20	2.30	4.40	6.70
Chicago, Ill.	.35	.45	.65	1.15	2.19	4.18	6.37	Minneapolis, Minn.	.35	.45	.70	1.55	2.99	5.78	8.77
Dallas, Texas	.35	.50	.85	1.96	3.82	7.43	11.25	Nashville, Tenn.	.35	.45	.65	1.25	2.39	4.57	6.96
Denver, Colo.	.40	.60	.96	2.24	4.37	8.53	12.90	Philadelphia, Pa.	.25	.25	.30	.50	.90	1.60	2.50
Des Moines, Iowa.	.35	.50	.70	1.42	2.74	5.28	8.02	Spokane, Wash.	.45	.69	1.27	3.01	5.91	11.61	17.52
Grand Rapids, Mich.	.30	.35	.50	1.09	2.08	3.96	6.04	New Orleans, La.	.35	.50	.70	1.59	3.07	5.94	9.01

FREIGHT—Shipment by freight takes longer and rates vary over different railroads. Your local freight agent can, however, furnish the rate per pound from New York City to your Station. NOTE: We are not responsible for change in rates, or errors.

MINIMUM SHIPPING ORDER, NOT LESS THAN $1.00

YOU CAN NOW BUY STOEGER MERCHANDISE ON TIME PAYMENT

A $5.00 DEPOSIT WILL OPEN YOUR ACCOUNT
NO FURTHER PAYMENT FOR 30 DAYS

Now Stoeger Arms Corporation makes it easy to purchase all arms and accessories listed in this catalog in the same convenient way as you have been able to purchase a car. No need to wait until you have the cash, the SPORTSMAN'S TIME PAY PLAN enables you to purchase several items at one time and pay for them in small monthly payments designed to fit your income.

We have made special arrangements with one of the leading finance companies in the United States to place their services at the disposal of our customers. This service, embracing most towns in the 32 states listed at foot of opposite column is available to all regularly employed persons except enlisted personnel of the army and navy.

Applications from customers residing in states not listed or in districts not covered within the states listed, cannot be considered. For these, as well as soldiers and sailors we recommend our special "Put-Away Plan".

HERE ARE THE DETAILS

1. **TIME PAY PLAN** applies to purchasers residing in the United States only
2. **Minimum Order $30**
3. **$5 must accompany order as a deposit**
4. **No further payment for 30 days**
5. **There are no unnecessary details**
6. **All information held in strictest confidence**
7. **If for any reason your application is not acceptable, your deposit will be immediately refunded**
8. **Fill out the special Time Pay Application Order Form in center of book and send in with your $5 deposit**

Amount of Purchase	5 Monthly Payment Plan	8 Monthly Payment Plan
$30	$6.55	$—.—
35	7.64	—.—
40	8.73	5.70
45	9.83	6.41
50	10.92	7.12
55	12.01	7.84
60	13.10	8.55
65	14.19	9.26
70	15.28	9.97
75	16.38	10.60
80	17.47	11.40
85	18.56	12.11
90	19.65	12.82
95	20.74	13.53
100	21.84	14.25
110	24.00	15.66
120	26.16	17.06
130	28.31	18.46
140	30.46	19.85
150	32.60	21.24
160	34.75	22.62
170	36.89	24.00
180	39.02	25.38
190	41.15	26.76
200	43.28	28.14
250	53.95	35.00
300	64.57	41.86

Amount of monthly payments may be further reduced by extending time of repayment up to 20 months.

Example— $50 PURCHASE. You send $5 as a deposit with your application—using time order-form. A balance of $45 remains to be paid. If you indicate repayment in 5 months, you pay $9.83 a month for 5 months. First payment 30 days after date of order.

*Terms Differ Slightly in Various States

STOEGER RECOMMENDS THE
"Put-Away Plan"
Without Interest or Carrying Charges

For our customers who would prefer not to pay interest and carrying charges, or who do not live in one of the 32 states listed below, Stoeger offers the "Put-Away Plan". With this method of payment you may send any amount with your order, and at convenient intervals of your own choosing send additional payments until the entire amount is covered. Or, if you prefer, we will send the merchandise upon request, C. O. D. for the balance due, at any time. You will find this method of payment extremely adaptable to your own budget and offers incentive for you to "put-away" the money for the gun or accessory which you want, without having to pay additional handling charges.

States in Which Our Regular Financing is Available

Arizona	Maine	Oregon
California	Maryland	Pennsylvania
Colorado	Massachusetts	Rhode Island
Connecticut	Michigan	Tennessee
Florida	Missouri	Utah
Illinois	Nebraska	Vermont
Indiana	New Hampshire	Virginia
Iowa	New Jersey	Washington
Kansas	New York	West Virginia
Kentucky	Ohio	Wisconsin
Louisiana	Oklahoma	

Use Special Time Payment Application Order Blank In Center of Book
BUY NOW! Pay In Small Monthly Installments

THE RIFLE

Rifling, a word derived from the old German word "Rifflen," meaning to groove, is the term used to designate the spiral grooves of the inside of a gun barrel which impart a rotary motion to the projectile as it proceeds down the barrel and which is maintained during flight. This equalizes irregularities of bullet shape and in addition, cuts down the air resistance and thereby adds immensely to the velocity, accuracy and efficiency of a bullet.

The credit for the invention of rifling is usually assigned to Gaspard Kollner, a Viennese gun maker in the 15th Century but, others credit Augustus Kotter of Nueremberg in the year 1520. Rifling has been practiced in many different styles such as straight, parallel, half round and with the number of grooves ranging from 3 to 12 and the twists varying accordingly.

Although a Hessian Prince in the year 1631 had a number of men equipped with rifles and others were used in Bavaria about 10 years later, the rifle as a military weapon did not really become popular until the middle of the 19th Century. It had in the meantime, however, been highly developed by some of the early Pennsylvania colonists who used these most effectively at 150 yards against the British during the Revolution, whose gun the "Brown Bess," a smooth bore, had an effective range of but slightly over 60 yards. The muzzle loading hunting rifle reached its highest point of perfection just before the Civil War when a rifle was produced which was quite accurate up to 500 yards.

In the Tower of London is a breech loading weapon of the year 1537 but, breech loading guns for sporting rifles had not become common until about the middle of the 19th Century. A number of them being used in the Civil War. The Henry lever action repeater was the first popular rifle of this type and the predecessor of the modern lever and slide action rifles.

The bolt action rifle which is today the most popular and practical of the high powered rifles found had its origin in the old Prussian needle gun which was used so successfully in the Franco-Prussian War.

The most recent type of gun is the semi-automatic rifle, which is, nevertheless, about 40 years old but, only very recently, has been developed for a really high powered cartridge. It is a particular pleasure for us in this catalog to introduce and place on the market for the first time in America a semi-automatic gas operated rifle capable of firing any rimless high powered cartridge including the popular cal. .30-06 Government. In closing this brief introduction on the History and Development of rifles, we should like to state that the semi-automatic high power rifles such as shown on page 53 of this catalog represents the gun of the future.

Game rifles in a broad way are classified as small game, medium size game, and large game rifles. Large game rifles are again divided into two classes, for large North American game and those for large African and Indian game.

The small game rifle usually has a caliber from .22 to .25; the medium game usually has a caliber from .25 to .30; the large game rifle depending upon the power of the cartridge, runs from .25 caliber up to caliber .600 Nitro Express.

Our catalog lists a great many different models chambered for numerous different cartridges, for all game shooting purposes.

Without a doubt, the .22 Long Rifle Rim Fire Cartridge enjoys the greatest popularity. This cartridge can be used in the well-known slide action or pump action repeating rifle, bolt action, single shot, lever action, and automatic rifle. During the last two or three years the .22 rim fire cartridge has been manufactured and offered in a strong brass alloy case and should not be used in old guns. This strong case permits high breech pressure which in turn almost doubles the power of the ordinary .22 Long Rifle cartridge. Accordingly using a modern .22 rifle and high speed cartridge, the hunter may kill small game up to 200 yards. This cartridge is also supplied in a hollow point lead bullet which has a tremendous shocking power and has been known to kill woodchucks at 200 yards.

Target shooting in matches with the well-known .22 caliber rifle is becoming more and more popular. For this style of shooting, if one is to be outstandingly successful, a gun weighing 8 pounds or more should be used having micrometer receiver sights and globe front sight installed. In addition to this, many matches allow rifles with target telescopes. The rifle target telescope has many advantages; through it, one can easily see the bull's eye, the shots may be easily spotted and the eye strain is less. It is not necessary to have an expensive rifle. We list all kinds of target rifles and the light weight target rifle, a single shot or repeating bolt action model performs very well and is widely used in camps and for practice wherever one chooses.

The medium game rifle from caliber .25 to caliber .30 is used for game ranging in size of a woodchuck up to and including small size deer. A variety of cartridge loads and styles of bullets is available for the medium game rifle.

The large game rifle ranging in caliber from .25 up to .405 Winchester may be had in a large variety of cartridges and loads.

This rifle is used for game ranging in size from medium size deer up to and including the Alaskan Kodiak bear and also the American grizzly. One of the very most popular calibers is the caliber .30-06 Military cartridge for sporting bolt action rifles. However, there are many other cartridges which will suffice if one does not care for the bolt action style of rifle and such a large cartridge.

For African big game hunting we recommend the .350 Rigby, .375 Magnum, .416 Rigby, .404 or .500 Jeffery where a bolt action is desired. Many other calibers which have specific purposes may also be used suitably. In this catalog will be found the most complete listing of bolt action rifles including those made by concerns with such worldwide reputations as Holland & Holland, John Rigby, W. J. Jeffery and others.

For the largest and most dangerous thick skinned game we particularly recommend the double barrel rifle which has a distinct advantage over every other type in that it is, for practical purposes, two rifles built in one and the failure or breakage of one part of the mechanism will not cause the weapon to be useless. The double barrel rifle offers two shots as quickly as the automatic rifle and does not require any shifting of the hands for making ready for the second shot and is so heavily constructed that it is possible to shoot cartridges with bullet weights up to 900 grains and developing an energy of 7590 foot seconds.

AMERICA'S GREAT GUN HOUSE

With Courtesy of The Winchester Rptg. Arms Company

The first rifle to bear the name Winchester appeared in 1866. It was the product of the newly incorporated Winchester Repeating Arms Company, founded by Oliver F. Winchester, one time lieutenant governor of Connecticut.

Appearing right at the close of the Civil War and at the dawn of the era of great development of the American West, this eminently successful repeater came into widespread use and popularity. It played a vital part in the opening-up of the great West and the building of the transcontinental railroads, particularly in the Model 73, the second of the Winchesters, which became the dependable companion of the pioneers and the famed rifle of "Buffalo Bill." On the foundation of these two successful rifle developments the three quarters of a century of success, during which Winchester arms and ammunition have become world famous, has been built.

Precision manufacture, rugged durability, de-dependability and the finest shooting qualities have been family traits of Winchesters throughout their notable history.

Winchester world leadership has come from progressive, precision quality manufacture. Working in finely equipped laboratories, Winchester engineers have enlisted the services of the most expert producers of raw materials. Searching laboratory tests of these materials determines that Winchester's rigid requirements are met and maintained.

Relentless gauging, testing and checking insure that your rifle or shotgun will, when assembled, be an arm fully up to Winchester standards.

When fully assembled your Winchester is thoroughly tested for smooth, dependable operation and for accurate targeting or patterning. When you receive it from your dealer it bears the well known Winchester Proof-Mark. This assures you that it operates and shoots correctly and that it has been fired with test charges far in excess of any commercial loads for which it is designed and has come through without sign of flaw or defect.

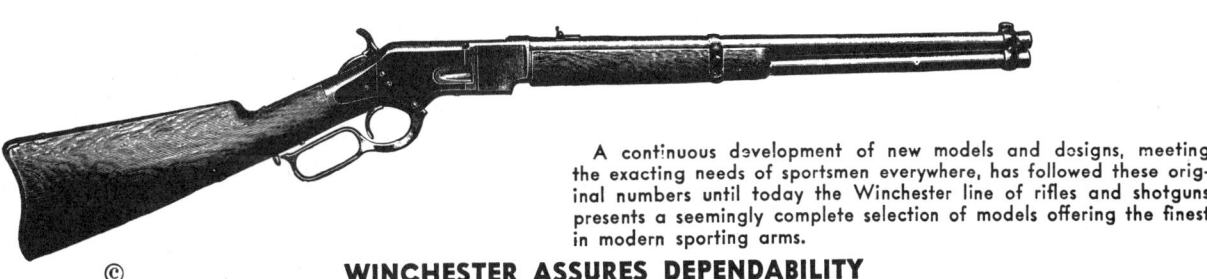

A continuous development of new models and designs, meeting the exacting needs of sportsmen everywhere, has followed these original numbers until today the Winchester line of rifles and shotguns presents a seemingly complete selection of models offering the finest in modern sporting arms.

WINCHESTER ASSURES DEPENDABILITY

The WINCHESTER Model 70
TRADE MARK

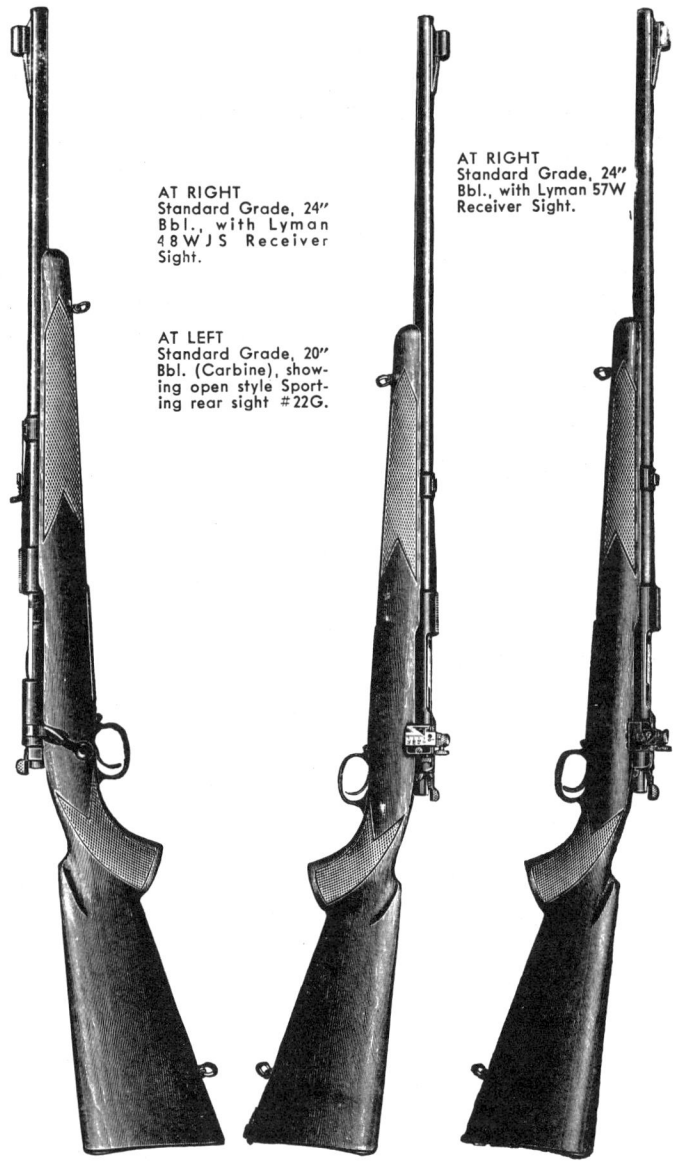

AT RIGHT
Standard Grade, 24"
Bbl., with Lyman
48 WJS Receiver
Sight.

AT LEFT
Standard Grade, 20"
Bbl. (Carbine), showing open style Sporting rear sight #22G.

AT RIGHT
Standard Grade, 24"
Bbl., with Lyman 57W
Receiver Sight.

The Winchester Model 70 is especially well adapted for long range work and for hunting where strength, accuracy and durability are required. It is available in a selection of calibers suitable for any big game in the world. The gun is simple, graceful and well-balanced, following the lines of a fast-handling modern shotgun. The Winchester 70 standard is a particularly superior sporting firearm which adapts itself perfectly to all modern requirements.

Round tapered barrel of Winchester proof-steel. Pistol grip N.R.A. type walnut stock with full, well shaped fore-end. Grip and fore-end checkered. Length of pull 13½"; drop at comb 1⅝"; drop at heel 2⅝". Bead front sight on ramp base with sight cover. Winchester 22G open sporting rear sight, round top. Flat top rear sight substituted, if specified. For flat top sight add letter "F" to symbol as shown below. New Winchester design safety, operating in horizontal plane. 5 cartridge (4 in .300 and .375 H. and H. Magnum calibers) magazine with hinged floor plate. Weight about 8¼ lbs.

Magazine floor plate is hinged, giving quick easy access to empty or clean magazine.

Front sight is forged integral with barrel, and ramp is matted to prevent glare. Spring steel sight cover is quick-detachable.

MODEL 70 BOLT ACTION REPEATING RIFLE—Standard Grade
For .22 Hornet, .250-3000 Savage, .270 Winchester, .30 Govt. M/06, 7 m/m, .257 Roberts, and .375 H.H. Magnum, with 24" barrel.
For .220 Swift, .300 H. H. Magnum with 26" barrel.
Price $61.80
Without sights 24" barrel 30-06 caliber, $59.63

MODEL 70 BOLT ACTION with Lyman 48 WJS Receiver Sight
With Wind Gauge Receiver Sight in place of Winchester 22-G open sporting Rear Sight.
Price $73.51

MODEL 70 BOLT ACTION with 20" Round Barrel
For .22 Hornet, .250-3000 Savage, .270 Winchester, .30 Govt. M/06, 7 m/m, .257 Winchester Roberts.
Price $61.80

MODEL 70 BOLT ACTION with 20" Round Barrel and Lyman 48 WJS Receiver Sight.
Price $73.51

MODEL 70 FOR ACCURACY AND DURABILITY

HIGH POWER BOLT ACTION RIFLES

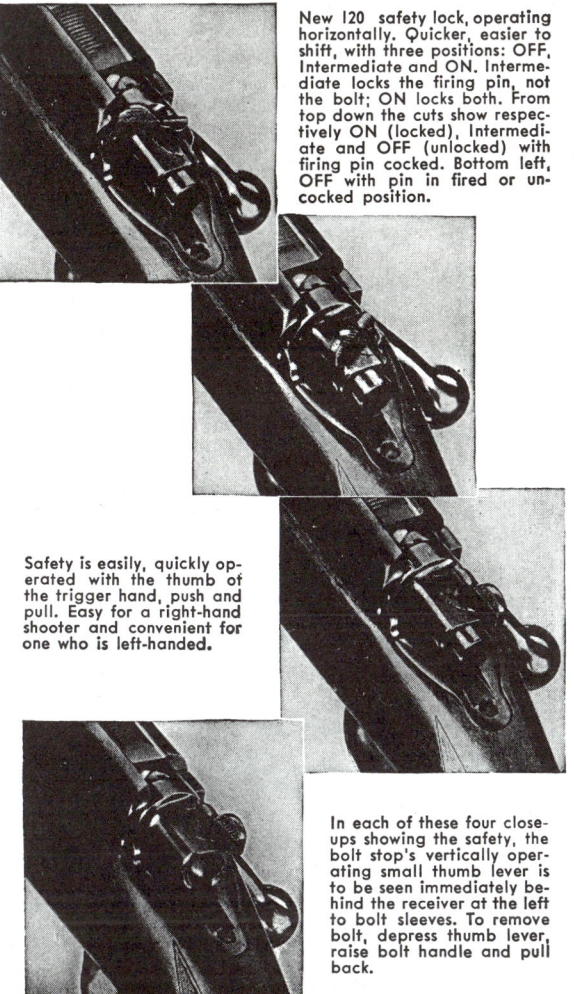

New 120 safety lock, operating horizontally. Quicker, easier to shift, with three positions: OFF, Intermediate and ON. Intermediate locks the firing pin, not the bolt; ON locks both. From top down the cuts show respectively ON (locked), Intermediate and OFF (unlocked) with firing pin cocked. Bottom left, OFF with pin in fired or uncocked position.

Safety is easily, quickly operated with the thumb of the trigger hand, push and pull. Easy for a right-hand shooter and convenient for one who is left-handed.

In each of these four close-ups showing the safety, the bolt stop's vertically operating small thumb lever is to be seen immediately behind the receiver at the left to bolt sleeves. To remove bolt, depress thumb lever, raise bolt handle and pull back.

This is a Winchester proof-steel rifle, all major parts being made of special heat-treated alloy steel. This has among other advantages, higher tensile strength, elastic limit and resistance to erosion. The Winchester Model 70 Super can withstand any standard charge of American rifle powder used with a normal bullet. Each rifle has been tested to insure a breech pressure from 30 to 45% higher than the regular service load. The stock is made of selected black walnut of the improved Winchester type, and has greatly improved handling feel due to considerably more wood forward, with balance maintained.

Round, tapered barrel of Winchester proof-steel. American walnut stock with cheek piece. Pistol grip and fore-end fancy checkered. Length of pull, 13½"; drop at comb, 1⅝"; drop at heel, 2⅝". Redfield full gold bead front sight on ramp with sight cover. Winchester 22G open sporting rear sight, round top. Flat top rear sight substituted if specified. For flat top sight add letter "F" to symbol shown below. New Winchester design safety operating in horizontal plane. 5 cartridge (4 in .300 and .375 H. and H. Magnum calibers) magazine with hinged floor plate. N. R. A. ⅞" leather sling strap attached by quick detachable swivels. Weight about 8¼ lbs.

Model 70 Standard Rifle—With Lyman 57W Receiver Sight
For .22 Hornet, .250-3000 Savage, .270 Winchester, .270 Winchester, .30 Govt. M/06, 7m/m, 257 Roberts............Price $67.40
With 20" Barrel................Price $67.40

MODEL 70 STANDARD
(With Lyman #57W Receiver Sight)

Model 70 Bolt Action Repeating Rifle— Super Grade
For .22 Winchester Hornet, .250-3000 Savage, .270 Winchester, .30 Govt. M/06, 7m/m, .257 Roberts, .375 H.H. Magnum with 24" barrel.
For .220 Winchester Swift and .300 H.H. Magnum with 26" barrel.......Price $86.17

MODEL 70 SUPER GRADE
(Standard Sights)

Model 70 Bolt Action Repeating Rifle— Super Grade with Lyman #48WJS Receiver Sight—Solid Frame
Same specifications as Standard Model. Price $97.87

MODEL 70 SUPER GRADE
(With Lyman #48WJS Receiver Sight)

KEEP UP TO DATE WITH STOEGER

WINCHESTER Model 70 Match Rifles

NATIONAL MATCH
(Weight 9½ Lbs.)

TARGET
(Weight 10½ Lbs.)

The new Winchester Model 70 target rifles, three in number, have been developed to meet the requirements of all long-range high power target shooting, and also to give service in long-range shooting at small game. All three have the same target start, differing only in the barrels.

All are characterized by a specially designed one-piece target stock of solid, close-grain selected black walnut—ample in size and weight, with large butt-stock, well rounded comb, large full pistol grip, curving close to the guard, target butt plate and long, wide beaver-tail forestock. A new improvement is an adjustable forestock base for the forward sling swivel, which provides for adjustment to suit the shooter's reach. A sling accessory located here, bakelite hand-rest, raises the sling and avoids pinching the hand.

For .22 Win. Hornet, .250-3000 Savage, .270 Win., .30 Govt. M/06, 7 M/M, .257 Win. Roberts,—with 24" barrel. For .220 Win. Swift, .300 H. & H. Magnum with 26" barrel.

MODEL 70—NATIONAL MATCH RIFLE

24" round Winchester Proof Steel barrel, floating type. Marksman design stock with full pistol grip and full fluted comb. Length of pull, 13¼"; drop at comb, 1 9/16"; drop at heel, 1⅞"; pitch down, 3"; Lyman No. 77 front sight on forged ramp sight base. Lyman No. 48WH receiver sight. Telescope mount bases. 1¼" leather Army type tan sling strap.

PRICE: Super grade with Lyman 48WJS sights
With Lyman 77 and 48WH........................$96.86

MODEL 70—TARGET

Medium weight Winchester Proof Steel barrel. Marksman design stock with full pistol grip and full fluted comb. Length of pull, 13¼"; drop at comb, 1 9/16"; drop at heel, 1⅞"; pitch down, 3". Lyman No. 77 front sight, Lyman No. 48WH receiver sight. Telescope mount bases. 1¼" leather Army type tan color sling strap.

PRICE: With Lyman 77 and 48 WH......................$104.43
Without sight, 30-06 caliber, $88.89

MODEL 70—BULL GUN, HEAVY BARREL
(Weight 13¼ Lbs.)

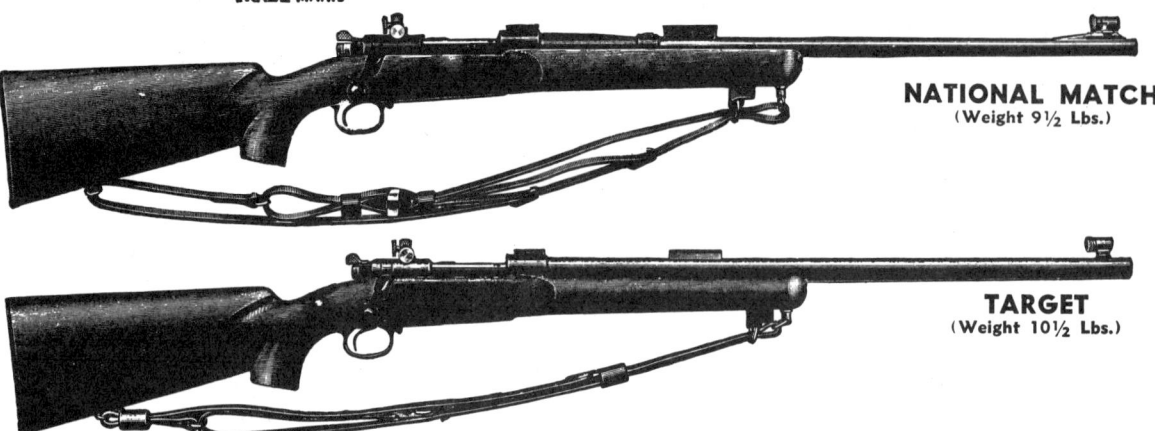

At left: new angle low shoulder bolt handle operates freely with above scope sight and mounting. Bolt shown fully raised.
At bottom of page is shown side view of rifle with scope mounted over receiver sight.

28" heavy Winchester Proof Steel barrel, floating type. Marksman design stock with full pistol grip and full fluted comb. Length of pull, 13¼"; drop at comb, 1 9/16"; drop at heel, 1⅞"; pitch down, 3". Lyman No. 77 front sight, no ramp. Lyman No. 48WH receiver sight. Telescope mount bases. 1¼" leather Army type tan color sling strap. For .30 government M/06, and .300 H & H magnum, with 28" R. D. barrel.

PRICE: With Lyman 77 and 48WH....$115.03

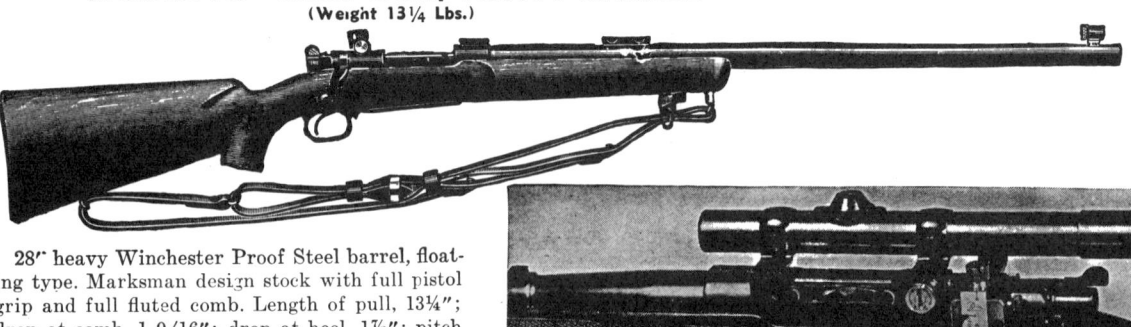

MINIMUM SHIPPING ORDER $1.00

WINCHESTER Lever Action and Self-Loading Rifles

MODEL 71
For Big Game Hunting
Standard barrel, length 20 or 24" only. State length when ordering. A Supreme American Hunting Rifle Achievement.
CALIBER .348

MODEL 07 SELF-LOADER
For Deer and Smaller Game
Shoots .351 Winchester self-loading center fire cartridges.

MODEL 71—LEVER ACTION REPEATING RIFLE

SOLID FRAME ONLY.

This model offers new advantages for big game hunters. The gun is built for its own high efficiency cartridge—the Winchester Model 71 with the new 86 Golden-Jubilee action. The gun is single calibre and has a cartridge which combines greater ballistic efficiency, broader adaptability, higher velocity with medium to abundant bullet weight, with flat trajectory. Increased killing power is obtained with balanced increase of bullet speed, weight & diameter; reducing loss of triple gain.

Winchester Proof Steel barrel. Sporting type pistol grip walnut stock with semi-beavertail fore-end. Bead front-sight on ramp-sight base. Removable sight cover. Winchester rear peep sight No. 98A. Option of Winchester 22K sporting rear sight instead of 98A. N.R.A. leather gun sling, 1" wide. Weight about 8 lbs.

PRICES:

Model 71 Rifle with Bead front sight and Winchester 22K sporting rear sight, as illustrated	$58.27
Model 71 Rifle with Bead front sight and Winchester 98A peep sight, as illustrated	58.27
Model 71 Rifle without checkering, gun sling and swivels with Winchester 22K sporting rear sight	50.40
Model 71 Rifle without checkering, gun sling and swivels with Winchester 98A peep sight	50.40

MODEL 07—SELF-LOADER

TAKE-DOWN.

With its lightning-fast self-loading action and stationary barrel, fine shotgun handling feel, and powerful cartridge, this is a very popular deer rifle in many fine hunting sections. Especially in thick covers in some parts of the South and in correspondingly difficult scrub-oak or popple ranges in the North, where quick shots are the rule. Has fewer working parts than any other self-acting deer rifle—no projecting moving parts, no pins or screws that will shake loose. Trigger lock—safe to carry loaded and cocked. Walnut stock of shotgun style, hard rubber butt plate, pistol grip. Deep U-shaped walnut forearm, giving comfortable, secure hand grasp. Round barrel, 20 inches. Sporting blade front sight; rear adjustable with sliding elevator. Standard five-cartridge box magazine. One cartridge in barrel makes this a six-shot gun. Extra magazines, capacity five or ten shots, are extra. Weight approximately 7¾ lbs. Takedown only.

Model 07	$67.91
Model 07 with 10-shot magazine	69.42
Extra 5-Shot Magazine	2.50
Extra 10-Shot Magazine	4.00

BIG GAME HUNTERS FAVORITES

WINCHESTER
Trade Mark

MODEL 65

For Small Game

SOLID FRAME — **LEVER ACTION REPEATING**

Light and Fast!

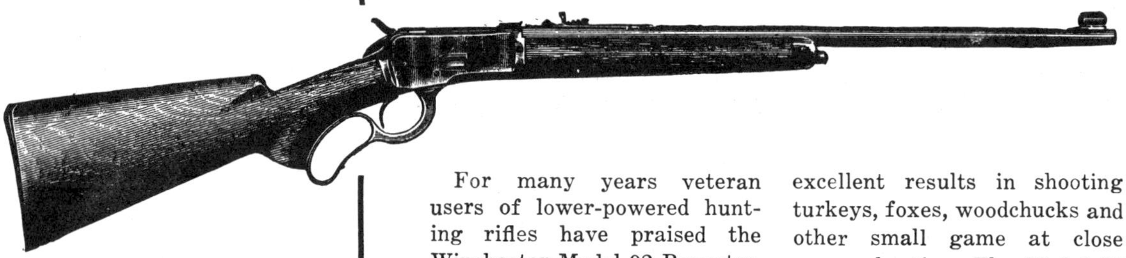

22" round, tapered barrel. Pistol walnut stock and forearm. Bead front sight on ramp with sight cover. Winchester number 22H open, rear sporting-sight. Magazine holds seven cartridges. Weight about 6½ pounds. For .25-20 Winchester and .32 Winchester.

PRICE $40.11

For many years veteran users of lower-powered hunting rifles have praised the Winchester Model 92 Repeater. Taking the basic principles of this model, Winchester has developed a new type. These improvements involve the entire rifle and to the average shooter they show up immediately because of the increased accuracy of shooting. The general design has been refined, and the action has been made smoother and easier. New sighting equipment has been added. It is especially lightweight and is sure to get excellent results in shooting turkeys, foxes, woodchucks and other small game at close range shooting. The Model 65 has a specially designed stock, shotgun butt, with checkered steel butt plate, full comb and pistol grip. Round 22 inch barrel with graceful taper and ramp front sight base. Solid frame. Light trigger pull Lyman gold bead front sight. Rockey mountain type rear sight, with sliding elevator. Half magazine, holding seven cartridges.

Superior Shooting!

.218 BEE — **LEVER ACTION REPEATING**

A Beauty!

24" round, tapered barrel of Winchester proof-steel. Pistol grip walnut stock and forearm. Bead front sight on ramp, with sight cover. Winchester No. 98C peep sight mounted on rear portion of the bolt. Half magazine only, holds 6 cartridges. Weight about 6¾ pounds. For .218 Winchester Bee.

PRICE $44.55

The Model 65, .218 Bee uses the new Super Speed Winchester Bee cartridge with a velocity of 2860 foot seconds, which outranges all others in the low price field. Especially adapted for shooting woodchucks, bobcats, foxes, and coyotes at average range. This rifle has a 24" tapered barrel with Gold bead front sight, detachable cover and a peep sight especially developed for Winchester lever action rifles. The magazine capacity is six cartridges with one in the chamber, it becomes a seven-shot repeater. The approximate weight is 6¾ pounds.

IDEAL GUNS FOR SHOOTING SMALL GAME

WINCHESTER
TRADE MARK

MODEL 64

With the world famous lever action!

MODEL 64—LEVER ACTION REPEATING RIFLE

Solid frame only—two-thirds magazine

24" or 20" round barrel tapered. Shotgun butt, pistol grip stock. Bead front sight on ramp with sight cover. Winchester No. 22H open sporting rear, round top. Flat top furnished if specified. Add letter "F" to symbol below. 5-shot magazine. Weight about 7 lbs.

For .25-35 Winchester, .30 (.30-30) Winchester, .32 Winchester Special, with 24" barrel; For .25-35 Winchester, .30 (.30-30) Winchester, .32 Winchester Special, with 20" barrel.

Model 64 rifle with 20" barrel is also furnished with Lyman No. 56 receiver sight in place of Winchester rear sight as follows: For .25-35 Winchester, .30 (.30-30) Winchester, .32 Winchester Special, with 20" barrel.

PRICE: With 20 or 24" barrel $47.37

With Lyman No. 56 Receiver Sight (20" barrel only) $55.14

This is an all-round, lightweight game rifle, perfectly adapted for deer, black bear, or any other medium sized game. It is dependable, beautifully made, light, and handles accurately and quickly. This is one of the most popular hunting rifles ever produced by Winchester. It was developed from the famous Model 74, which more than a million shooters have bought. It has improved NRA type stock—shot gun butt of selected walnut, with wide full comb and full pistol grip. The steel butt plate is checkered and has plenty of pitch. The frame is solid and the 24" barrel is round tapered. The 2/3rds magazine holds five cartridges—one in each chamber, which makes a 6 shot repeater. Mechanism refinements given even smoother operation, and lighter trigger pull. Improved sights: Front, long matted ramp, with hunting bead; rear, new quick-elevating Rocky Mountain type with adjusting slide. Tang is tapped for Lyman tang peep sight. Weight approximately 7 lbs.

The DeLuxe Rifle for Deer Hunters!

MODEL 64—DEER RIFLE— LEVER ACTION REPEATING

Solid frame only—two-thirds magazine

24" or 20" round barrel, tapered. Pistol grip stock with rubber pistol grip cap, shotgun butt; semi-beavertail forearm, stock and forearm checkered; 1" leather sling strap with quick detachable swivels. Sights as on Standard Model 64.

For .30 (.30-30) Winchester, .32 Winchester Special, with 24" barrel.
For .30 (.30-30) Winchester, .32 Winchester Special, with 20" barrel.

PRICE: $58.27

Rifle with 20" barrel and Lyman 56 Receiver Sight

For .30 (.30-30) Winchester, .32 Winchester Special, with 20" barrel.

PRICE: $66.04

This is a rifle which is designed especially for particular deer hunters. It has a wide, semi-beaver tail, handsomely checkered forearm; full comb stock—well pitched at the heel—with checkered steel butt plate and checkered full pistol grip; an added sling-strap with quick detachable swivels, which is helpful both in shooting and in resting on the stand or trailing.

This gun is of course not just for deer, but equally important in hunting any game which requires use of a powerful rifle. The same basic specification for the Standard Model 64 apply to this model. Stock and forearm of selected walnut, both finely checkered; grip with hard rubber cap. The combination of well-pitched broad butt with checkered steel butt plate, full style well rounded comb, and pistol grip, is valuable in snap shots and rapid fire. Solid frame. Weight (strap included) approximately 7¾ lbs.

STOEGER ARMS CORPORATION, 507 FIFTH AVENUE, NEW YORK, N. Y.

Model 64
WITH WORLD FAMOUS WINCHESTER LEVER ACTION

Flat Trajectory, Quick Handling
Lightweight, Six Shots
Moderate Cost

3,390 FEET PER SECOND WITH 46-GRAIN BULLET

Price $51.81

For .219 Winchester—
Center Fire Cartridges.
With Winchester 98A Peep Sight.
Price $51.81
With Winchester 22H—Sporting Rear Sight with Elevator.
Price $48.43

The WINCHESTER
TRADE MARK
.219 ZIPPER
HIGH VELOCITY REPEATING RIFLE

Research and development have stimulated great advance in high velocity rifle shooting. The Winchester .219 Zipper rifle, with its 3390 f.s. velocity, provides advanced performances in lever action. The .219 Zipper is an adaptation of the popular Winchester Model 64, but has been redesigned for quicker, more accurate handling. Its improved stock has plenty of pitch so that it will hold to the shoulder in rapid fire, and in snap shooting will not cause shooting high. The forearm is ample is proportions and modern instyle, with a good grasp which aids accuracy. The solid frame is another important improvement. The Winchester rear-peep sight, mounted on the bolt, gives maximum sighting radius. The .219 has 2″ more barrel length than the standard Model 64 hunting rifle, but handles like a shotgun.

SUPER SPEEDED LEVER ACTION
SPECIFICATIONS

BARREL—26-inch round, tapered, with ramp front sight base.
STOCK—N.R.A. Type pistol grip stock of selected walnut. Shotgun butt with metal butt plate.
SIGHTS—Bead front mounted on ramp with sight cover and Winchester No. 98A Peep Sight mounted on the rear portion of the bolt.
MAGAZINE—Two-thirds magazine. Six shots, five in the magazine and one in the chamber. Model 64 Zipper Rifle furnished in two-thirds magazine only.
WEIGHT—About 7 lbs.

MODEL 94 LEVER ACTION REPEATING RIFLE
"America's Favorite Deer Rifle"

CAL. 30/30 AND .32 SPECIAL
CARBINE MODEL $30.27

This dependable, light, rugged Carbine has been popular for many years throughout Western mountain and plain areas as a saddle gun. It is reknown as a trappers and prospectors firearm and is used on my timber hunting or back-packing trips. This model has been a leader in the Winchester field for more than forty years. Strong, smooth-working, fast action, 20″ round barrel with integral ramp front sight base. New straight-grip shotgun type butt plate. Carbine-type walnut forearm with barrel band. Full magazine—holds six shots, which with one in the chamber, makes the Carbine a seven-shot repeater. Bead sight on integral ramp, with quick-detachable steel cover. The open sporting rear-sight is mounted on the barrel. Weight about 6¼ pounds.

Special model 94 Carbine, chambered to handle 25/35 ammunition. Specifications same as .30 W.C.F. and .32 Winchester Special..................$30.27

A NEW GUN CARRIES A FACTORY GUARANTEE

AMERICA'S GREAT GUN HOUSE

WINCHESTER MODEL 52 SPORTING RIFLE
TRADE MARK
The .22 Rim Fire Rifle De Luxe!

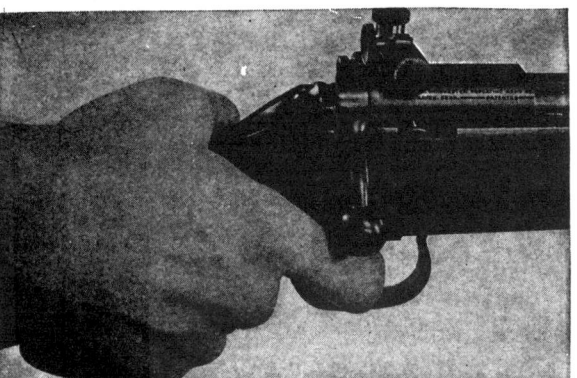

The famous accuracy of the Winchester Model 52 Target rifle is made available for hunting in this distinctive, supremely fine sporting arm. It has the same bolt action with lightening Speed Lock and the same controlled straight line loading, "bank-lock" accuracy in the breeching, and close fitting of the head space. Adjustable trigger pull.

24" round lightweight tapered barrel with ramp front sight base, integral with barrel. New sporting design selected walnut stock with cheek piece, pistol grip and fore-end fancy checkered. Length of pull, 13½"; drop at comb, 19/16"; drop at heel, 2½". Leather gun sling. Redfield 5/64" full length gold bead front sight with Winchester detachable sight cover. Weight about 7¼ lbs.

FOR TARGET AND SMALL GAME SHOOTING

Price as Illustrated With Lyman 48-F
$90.10

G5272R (Without Sights)			$75.68
Front Sights	**Rear Sight**	**Receiver Sight**	
G5252R Redfield 5/64" full gold bead	None	Lyman 48-F	90.10
G5262R Redfield 5/64" full gold bead	None	Lyman 57-FH	84.00
For stock without cheek piece, add			5.55

EXTRAS *for Winchester Rifles*

Making stocks of special dimensions, either straight or pistol grip (except for Models 52 and 70)	$15.14
Changing standard dimension stock from straight to pistol grip (pistol grip rubber cap not included)	5.20
Making stock and forearm of specially selected walnut to standard dimensions, either pistol grip or straight grip, with or without pistol grip cap (except Models 07, 52 and 70)	15.14
Making stock and forearm of specially selected walnut as above for Model 07	19.17
Plain checking stock and forearm, except Models 52, 64, 70, 71 and 07, which take fancy checking price	2.77
Fancy checking stock and forearm	5.85
Full nickel plating	8.43
Nickel plated trimmings	5.65
Gold plated trigger	2.93
Rubber pistol grip cap (except Models 52 and 70)	2.27
Rubber pistol grip cap fitted to Models 52 or 70	2.93
Checking triggers	2.27
Recoil pads fitted to rifles with shotgun butt stocks. (See detail under recoil pads.)	
Telescope sight mount bases	1.77
Blank piece to fill rear sight slot	.55
Attaching screw eyes for sling strap	.55
High polished finish on stock and forearm	5.65
Parts necessary to change from single trigger to double set triggers on Models 64, 64 Deer and 65	8.98

RECOIL PADS (When attached to guns)

Winchester large pad—1" thick	$3.33
Winchester small pad—1" thick	3.33
Noshoc pad—1" thick	3.33
Hawkins pad—1 1/16" thick—large size	5.55
Hawkins pad—1" thick—medium size	3.33
Hawkins pad—¾" thick—medium size	3.33
Jostam Hy Gun pad—1 1/16" thick	5.55
Jostam Anti-Flinch pad—1" thick	5.55
Jostam Air Cushion pad—15/16" thick	5.55
Jostam Sponge Rubber, 1-ply pad, black—15/16" thick	5.55
Jostam Sponge Rubber, 2-ply pad, black—1¼" thick	5.55
Jostam Sponge Rubber, 3-ply pad, black—1⅝" thick	5.55
Leather facing for any of the above Recoil Pads	.81

MINIMUM SHIPPING ORDER $1.00

SUPREME LEADERSHIP EVER SINCE 1919 IN SMALL BORE TARGET RIFLES HELD BY WINCHESTER MODEL 52

TWO MAIN TYPES—THREE STYLES
Choice of Twenty Different Sight Combinations

Model 52 Bull Gun with Waver No. 35 Mielt extension receiver sight, and Waver W11AT front sight.

Model 52, Heavy Barrel Target Rifle with Lyman No. 48FH rear sight, and Lyman No. 77 front sight.

Model 52 Standard Weight Target Rifle with Lyman No. 57FH rear sight, Lyman No. 17A front sight.

FEATURES OF MODEL 52

RECEIVER AND ACTION: Stiffness and strength of the receiver is an important advantage of the Model 52. The breeching shoulders have been increased in area. The receiver is deeply recessed to admit the front end of the bolt. It has a rounded top and a special sand-blasted, browned finish which prevents light refraction. Jerking and slamming is eliminated by the smooth working cams for both initial extracting and final closing movements. Twin extractors give controlled straight-line loading from chamber to magazine. The firing pin has simplicity and dependability. Efficient bolt operation and coordinating magazine make this rifle suitable for rapid fire.

SPEED LOCK: Speed Lock is distinguished for short, quick firing-pin throw, uniform engagement of the sear with the firing pin until the trigger is pulled, and for dependable trigger engagement and pull-off adjustment. Crisp let-off without trigger take-up. Reduced vibration because of weight reduction of moving parts. Improved trigger support. Sear is large with two springs.

PATENTED ADJUSTABLE TRIGGER: The trigger pull in the Winchester Speed Lock permits adjustment to a reasonable degree with the assurance that once set it will remain without variation. It is scored to prevent finger slip.

SAFETY: This is a Winchester triple-locking development, which positively locks the firing mechanism.

MAGAZINE: A standard detachable box-type five-cartridge magazine, and also a single-shot adaptor are available. The Model 52 magazine is completely enclosed and dependable for handling .22 long rifle rim fire cartridges, and single loading is convenient.

BARRELS: The variation allowed by the maximum and minimum gauges used for diameters of both bore size and groove size is but .0005". Actual lead tests detect as little as 1/20,000 of an inch variation throughout the length of the barrel.

TELL OTHERS ABOUT STOEGER'S CATALOG

AMERICA'S GREAT GUN HOUSE

WINCHESTER MODEL 52
TRADE MARK

COMES IN THESE STYLES

Standard Weight Target Rifle—Bolt Action Box Magazine with Winchester Speed Lock

28 inch standard weight round barrel, tapered, of Winchester Proof-Steel. Telescope sight bases spaced 7.2" center to center. These barrels have a ramp (lug) front sight base forged on the barrel.

Pistol grip target stock of walnut with a chromium plated, satin finish metal forearm adjustment base and a composition hand support, located on the underside of the front portion of the forearm.

This stock is used with standard height sight combinations. Standard dimensions are:

Length of pull, 13¾"; Drop of stock from center of nore, (at comb) 63", (at heel) 98"; Drop of stocks from line of sights with sights set for 25 yards, (at comb) 1¹⁵⁄₁₆, (at heel) 2"; Down pitch, 3". Convenient triple locking safety. Weight, approximately 10 pounds.

PRICES
(Please Order By Symbol Number)
FLAT TOP RECEIVER

Symbol	Front Sight	Rear Sight	Receiver Sight	Price
*G5217R	None	None	None	$47.12
G5207R	Winchester 93-B	Win. 82A	None	53.02
G5237R	Lyman 17-A	Win. 82A	None	55.44
G5269R	Lyman 17-AG	None	Vaver WS2 Lt. Ext. Marble Goss MG52	66.54
G5279R	Lyman 17-A	None	Ext. Low Base	63.21

*Front sight cut in barrel filled with blank piece.

ROUND TOP RECEIVER

†G5210R	Lyman 17-A	None	Lyman 57-F	56.55
G5209R	Winchester 93-B	None	Lyman 48-F	60.24
G5239R	Lyman 17-A	None	Lyman 48-F	62.66
G5289R	Lyman 17-A	None	Lyman 52-F Ext.	64.32

†Will be furnished if order does not specify sight combination desired.

Any of above rifles may be had with heavy weight Marksman type stock on special order at an additional charge of **$5.50**.

Heavy Weight Target Rifle—Bolt Action Box Magazine with Winchester Speed Lock

BARREL—28 inch heavy weight, round, tapered of Winchester Proof Steel. New type barrel band. Telescope sight bases spaced 7.2" center to center. STOCK—Marksman stock of selected walnut with full pistol grip, full fluted comb and wide beavertail fore-end. Chromium plated, satin finish metal forearm adjustment base and a composition hand support, located on the under side of the front portion of the forearm.

STOCK DIMENSIONS

Length of Pull ....13¼"   Drop at Heel ....1⅞"
Drop at Comb ....1⁹⁄₁₆"   Pitch ....3"
Drop of stock from center to bore .50" at comb and .83" at heel.
Steel butt plate checked. WEIGHT—About 12 lbs. Other details same as described for Standard Weight Barrel model.

PRICES
(Please Order By Symbol Number)
28" RD. HEAVY WEIGHT BARREL
Marksman No. 1 Stock (High Comb) High Sights

Flat Top Receiver Symbol	Front Sight	Rear Sight	Receiver Sight	Price
G5245R	None	None	None	$54.69

No receiver sight cut in stock. Receiver drilled and tapped on left side, holes filled with plug screws. Front sight filled with blank piece. Win. 82A Rear Sight Seat Cut (Dovetail) on Receiver, filled with blank piece. Winchester Comb. Telescope Sight Bases attached.

G5264R	Vaver 36 F.S. with 35E Barrel Band	None	Vaver 35 Mielt Ext.	80.22
G5274R	Lyman 77	None	Marble Goss M.G.—52 M.S.—Ext.	72.45
†G5225R	Lyman 77	None	None	59.13
†G5235R	Redfield 63	None	None	58.57

†Win. 82A Slight Cut on Receiver filled with blank piece.

28" HEAVY WEIGHT BARREL

G5255R	None	None	None	54.69

No receiver sight cut in stock. Receiver drilled and tapped on left side, holes filled with plug screws. Front sight filled with blank piece. Winchester Comb. Telescope Sight Bases attached.

†G5265R	None	None	None	54.69

†No receiver sight cut in stock. No sight cut on barrel or receiver, except disc clearance cut on rear of receiver. Receiver drilled and tapped on left side, holes filled with plug screws. Winchester Comb. Telescope Sight Bases attached.

*G5234R	Lyman 77	None	Lyman 48 F.H.	71.89
G5284R	Lyman 77	None	Lyman 52 F.H. Ext.	73.56
G5294R	Vaver W11AT	None	Vaver R5237—Ext.	78.00

*Will be furnished if order does not specify sight combination desired.

MODEL 52 BULL GUN
Extra heavy barrel (without sights) 64.78

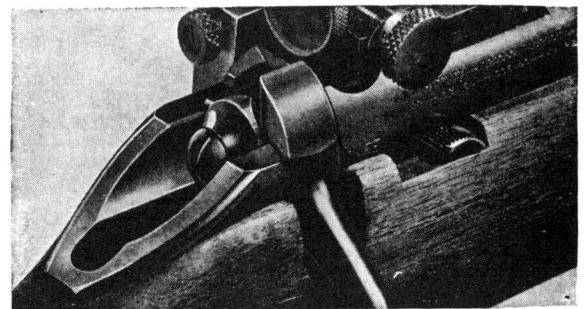

Thumb-lever safety. Firing pin uncocked, thumb lever forward, safety inactive.

Forearm of Marksman stock, showing new adjustable barrel band (adjustable screw on right side, not shown), and adjustable hand support and sling swivel.

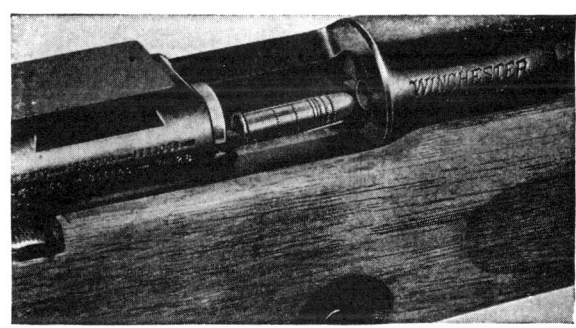

Showing how receiver is stiffened by additional steel at left side of leading well. Does not interfere with convenient hand loading. Cartridge is shown on tray of single-shot adaptor.

Bolt closed, firing pin cocked, safety in rear or safe position, triple locking the action.

A NEW GUN GIVES NO REGRETS

"RARIN' TO GO!" Winchester 75 SPORTER

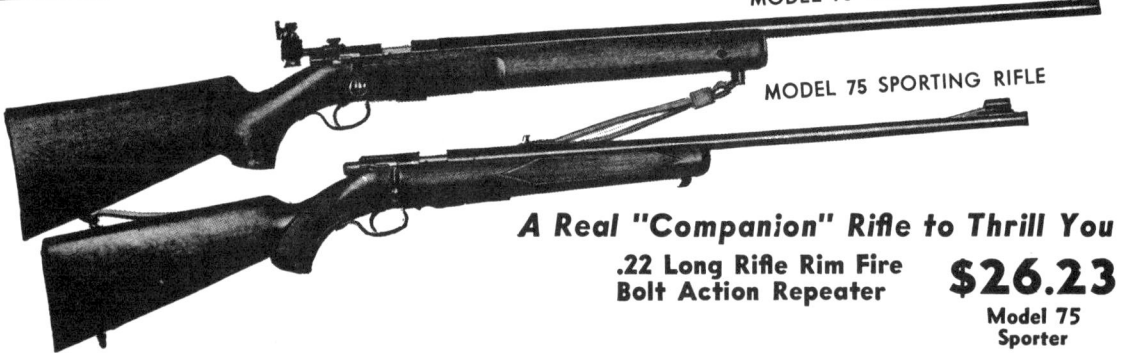

MODEL 75 TARGET RIFLE

MODEL 75 SPORTING RIFLE

A Real "Companion" Rifle to Thrill You

.22 Long Rifle Rim Fire
Bolt Action Repeater

$26.23
Model 75
Sporter

Every shooter admires a beautiful fire-arm. The Model 75 Sporting Rifle strikes you with its beauty immediately. It will stop any shooter, anywhere, and tempt him to handle it—even fondle it!

Take a good look at this gun. The more you know about guns and the more you examine it, the more you will like it. Considering the moderate price, it is truly a "honey"! It is handsomely stocked, excellently barreled—in fact it is a rare combination of mechanical and artistic superiority. It is the ideal gun to tuck under your arm when you intend to ramble in the wood for a day of sport.

Although full-sized the Model 75 Sporting Rifle is light and handy, and will thoroughly live up to its good looks in giving you all-round satisfaction. See specification on following page.

The New Model 75
A MAN-SIZED RIFLE!

The Winchester Model 75 is built man's size with the same length barrel and the same length of trigger pull as the model 52. It is, however, 22 ounces lighter than the Standard grade Model 52.

The action is military type, developed especially for this rifle. A thumb-type lever safety is conveniently placed on the right side. The Standard target clip box type magazine holds five .22 long rifle rim fire cartridges. The barrel is 28" long, with a diameter at the shoulder of approximately 1". At the muzzle it measures approximately 11/16". It comes equipped with the Winchester No. 99A telescope height sight, with quick detachable, covered front sight and interchangeable target post and aperture inserts. The stock is sturdy, one-piece American black walnut.

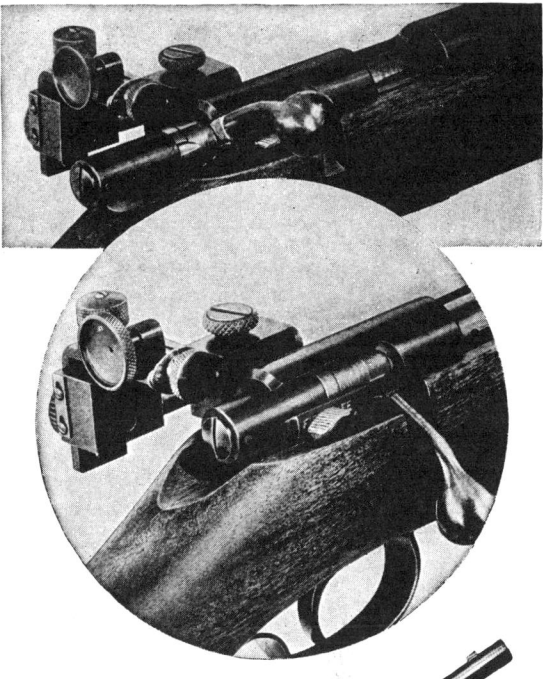

SPECIFICATIONS

New design pistol grip target stock with semi-beavertail fore-end. High comb. Length of pull, 13¼"; drop at comb, 1⅝"; drop at heel, 2¼"; pitch down, 3". Bolt action with speed lock. Locks on opening of the bolt. New Winchester 99A telescope height front sight with post and extra aperture. Sight cover. New Winchester 84A extension rear peep with quarter minute clicks for windage and elevation. New type slide lever safety. 5-shot magazine. Adjustable sling swivel base. 1¼" Army type leather sling strap. Weight about 8 lbs. 10 oz.

At top, bolt retracted, showing high back wall of receiver loading well. Below, closeup of Safety thumb lever and Receiver Sight.

DEPENDABLE ACCURATE SHOOTING!!

Target Model 75 As Illustrated But Without Scope
$25.63

Extra for 8 Power Scope
$9.50

Standard Rifle with 99A front and 84A rear sights, including leather sling.

$30.22

ADDITIONAL PRICES

G7521R—Rifle with scope bases for new Winchester 8 power telescope sight (no iron sights) $25.63
Winchester 8 power telescope for above...... 9.50
G7525R—Rifle without any sight equipment..... 25.17
G7527R—Rifle with Vaver No. 1175 front and Vaver No. 3875 receiver sight 37.94
G7537R—Rifle with Lyman No. 77 front and Lyman No. 58E receiver sights............. 37.28
G7547R—Rifle with Redfield No. 63 front and Redeld No. 5HW receiver sights 37.94

Showing magazine release and another view of Receiver sight.

Look at These Model 75 Advantages!
Adjustable Trigger Pull
Special Metallic Sights
Adjustable Sling Swivel Base
Adjustable-Tension Barrel Band
Model 52 Self Loader
Accurate, Precision Shooting

SEE PAGE 8, "HOW TO ORDER"

WINCHESTER MODEL 61

$24.87 With 24" Round Barrel

THE ACE OF .22's

1. Finely balanced, gracefully tapered 24" Winchester proof steel barrel.
2. Man size genuine black walnut stock with well shaped pistol grip.
3. Shotgun butt with slightly curved, checkered, steel butt plate.
4. Bead front and Winchester quick elevating sporting rear sight. Tang has screw holes for mounting Lyman tang peep sight.
5. New design of semi-beavertail slide handle, gracefully modeled to give a most satisfying grip because of its broad under surface. Admirably fits the shape of the hand.
6. Closed-in breech, hammerless slide action—simple in construction, surprisingly fast in action, sure in functioning.
7. Sturdy breech construction that makes this rifle safe for use with any of the .22 high power rim fire cartridges of standard manufacture.
8. No extractor cuts extending into the chamber.
9. Hammer cannot fall when gun is not breeched.
10. Cannot be jammed with a cartridge by partial movement of the action.
11. Cartridge in action can be seen.
12. Slide action lock is in safe and convenient position. Trigger lock locks directly under nose of sear.

A Hammerless Repeater to Kindle The Enthusiasm of All Gun Lovers

The Model 61—an all around hammerless slide action .22 repeater—presents a fast finely balanced arm that combines the Winchester gun design with the famed selection of high quality materials and precision workmanship. This takedown model presents the most modern development of the popular closed-in breech type of rifle.

G6101R—.22 Short, .22 Long and .22 Long Rifle (24" round barrel) ... **$24.87**
G6102R—.22 Short only (24" octagon barrel) **26.13**
G6104R—.22 Long Rifle only (24" octagon barrel) **26.13**
G6105R—.22 W. R. F. only (24" octagon barrel) **26.13**
G6116R—.22 Long Rifle shot (miniature target boring) **28.40**

MODEL 62
The Repeater for All-Around .22 Shooting

Throw It to Your Shoulder —Let It Tell You Its Own Story!

AS ILLUSTRATED ONLY $18.01

Winchester MODEL 62 Take-down

Here are a few of the features which make Model 62 a rifle for the discriminating shooter who seeks an all round slide action hammer repeater:

1. Round 23-inch tapered barrel, Winchester proof marked, carefully proportioned for the accuracy and balance of the arm.
2. Bead front sight with new Winchester quick elevating sporting open rear sight.
3. Smooth, sure-functioning Winchester slide action developed from the standard action that has served with such unfailing satisfaction in more than 1,500,000 Winchesters.
4. New design slide handle, admirably formed to fit the hand.
5. Full-sized genuine black walnut straight grip stock.
6. Shotgun butt with slightly curved butt plate.
7. Extra large capacity magazine—holds 20 Shorts or 16 Longs or 14 Long Rifles.

Its gracefully tapered, round 23-inch barrel is of a length adroitly calculated to secure perfect balance and at the same time attain full accuracy and high velocity in every shot.

Every man who wants a moderate priced dependable rifle, or every boy who yearns for a repeater with a man-sized stock for .22 shooting, target or small game, will find the Model 62 Winchester an arm that will give him "full measure" and a quality of construction and design that he would not expect to find in anything but a higher priced rifle.

G6201R—For .22 Short, .22 Long and .22 Long Rifle (23" round barrel) . **$18.01**
G6202R—For .22 Short only (23" round barrel) **18.01**

CAREFUL ATTENTION AND SAFE DELIVERY OF YOUR ORDER

AMERICA'S GREAT GUN HOUSE 25

MODEL 74 *Provides* REAL SHOOTING ENJOYMENT!

Above, Model 74's cross-gun safety. Upper right, the action slide. Below, the new Winchester No. 88A peep rear sight, specially developed for Model 74 and furnished on one of the three styles as listed above. Vertical adjustment only. Mounted on bolt stop plug.

Model 74 has the same straight-feed tubular type magazine which has always been used in Winchester .22 Automatic rifles. Simple, dependable, convenient. To load, turn knurled head of magazine to unfasten it, withdraw tube part way and insert cartridges through loading port in right side of butt stock.

No matter what your shooting experience may be you will be sure the minute you take the Model 74 in your hand that here, at a surprisingly convenient price, is a Winchester automatic .22 that you are going to enjoy. This is the ideal rifle for a lot of shooting at a low cost. It has lightning fast automatic reloading, husky sporting target stock, styles to balance perfectly. The action is up-to-the-minute in design, convenience, fit, quick pointing, and accuracy. The gun shoots the popular, inexpensive .22 short rim fire cartridge, both regular and high speed. In standard rifle, with magazine capacity of 20 cartridges and choice of two different styles of rear sight.

SPECIFICATIONS

The newest in the famous family of Winchester .22 rim fire automatics. 24 inch round tapered barrel. Chambered for .22 Short rim fire or .22 Long Rifle Rim fire cartridges. Standard rifle and gallery special has capacity of 20 .22 Shorts; Standard .22 Long Rifle has capacity of 14 .22 Long Rifle cartridges. Sporting type pistol grip stock with semi-beavertail fore-end. Checkered steel butt plate. Length of pull, 13 7/16"; drop at comb, 1½"; drop at heel, 2 5/8". New type horizontally operating safety. Sights—Winchester bead front with open sporting rear or specially designed elevating peep sight located on bolt stop at rear of receiver. Over-all length, 43¾ inches. Weight about 6¼ lbs.

.22 CALIBER AUTOMATIC

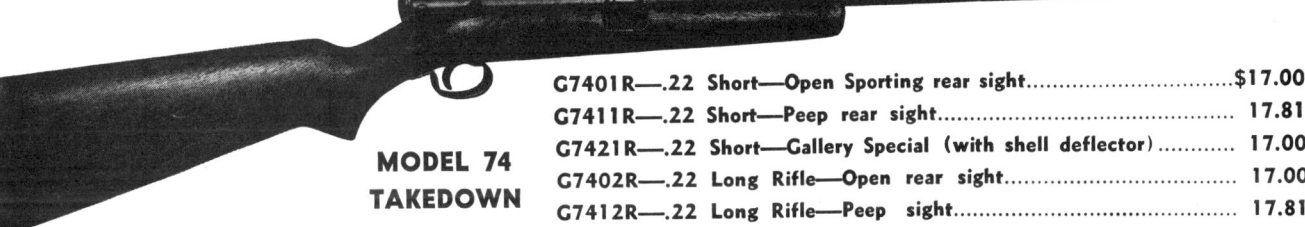

MODEL 74 TAKEDOWN

G7401R	—.22 Short—Open Sporting rear sight	$17.00
G7411R	—.22 Short—Peep rear sight	17.81
G7421R	—.22 Short—Gallery Special (with shell deflector)	17.00
G7402R	—.22 Long Rifle—Open rear sight	17.00
G7412R	—.22 Long Rifle—Peep sight	17.81

The Winchester Speed King
MODEL 63 AUTOMATIC—.22 CALIBER

- GREATER POWER!
- LONGER RANGE!
- MORE SPEED!
- ACCURACY!

$33.25
TAKEDOWN

SPECIFICATIONS

23" round tapered barrel. American walnut pistol grip stock and forearm. Bead front and Winchester 32B sporting rear sight. 10 cartridge magazine. Weight about 5½ lbs.

IDEAL LOW COST SHOOTING

That's what you get in the Winchester Speed-King. Approximately 33% higher velocity and 50% more energy, than the former world-renowned Winchester Model 103 Automatic. The same superior design, materials and manufacture. The same super accuracy of barrel, super speed and dependability of action, and matchless proportions. Improved by restyling for even better handling, and by rebuilding to shoot faster and flatter traveling ammunition. A rim fire .22 rifle for the shooter whose heart is set on speed shooting, who values fine equipment and who is interested in economy in ammunition without sacrifice of performance.

PRICES

G6302R—Rifle, 23" round barrel; designed expressly for .22 Long Rifle Super Speed and Super-X .. 33.25
Barrel reflector .... .50

Winchester .22 Bolt Action

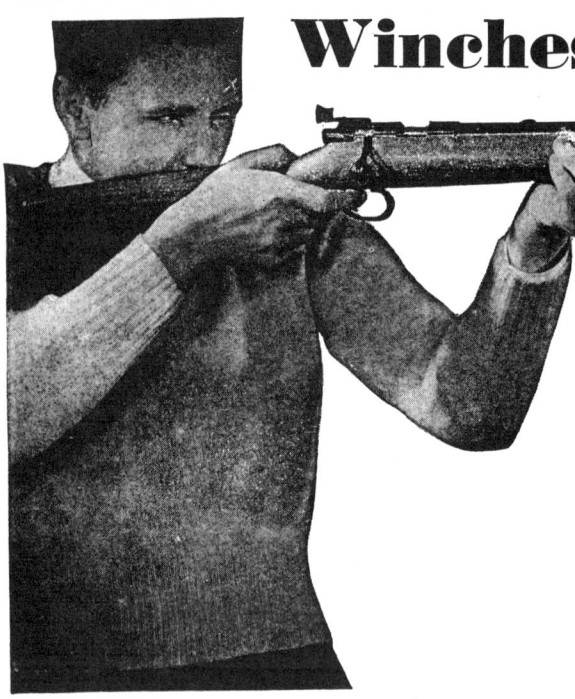

MODEL 72 WITH *Tubular Magazine*

If your choice inclines toward a sporting type bolt action tubular magazine .22, look Model 72 over carefully. Size up it's general design. You'll find it attractive, clean, finely balanced and easy to handle. Heft the good weight in the 25-inch barrel, and note its pleasing straight taper. Examine the black American walnut one-piece sporting stock. You have an extensive choice of eight different Model 72 rifles equipped with sights ranging from open sporting metallic sights to a 5-power Winchester telescope sight with extra low mounting.

SPECIFICATIONS
For .22 Short, .22 Long and .22 Long Rifle Rim Fire Cartridges Interchangeably

25-inch round barrel, tapered and crowned at the muzzle. Sporting type pistol grip walnut stock with semi-beavertail fore-end. Length of pull, 13½"; drop at comb, 1 9/16" (with open rear sight) or 1⅝" (with peep sight); drop at heel, 2 9/16" (with open sight) or 2 11/16" (with peep sight). Winchester 75C front sight and No. 32B open sporting rear. Also furnished with 97B front, on ramp with sight cover, and Winchester 80A peep rear. Magazine holds 20 Short, 16 Long or 15 Long Rifle cartridges.

- Sporting Target Design
- Rim Fire Repeater
- Eight Styles

$14.83 with open rear sight

PRICES
Price with peep rear sight and ramp front sight	$14.83
with open rear sight—no ramp	14.08
with Winchester 2¾ X Telescope	add 4.90
with Winchester 5 X Telescope	add 6.40
Model 72 with 5 X Telescope and no iron sights	21.69
Model 72 with 2¾ X Telescope and no iron sights	19.43

MODEL 69 A MODERN, ALL-ROUND .22 REPEATING RIFLE

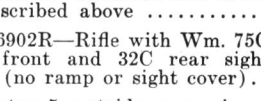

This is another Winchester contribution to good shooting that is strictly in step with the times. It is modern in design, appearance, performance, popularity and *price*. The Model 69 has all the vital features that shooters want in a general-purpose, low-priced .22 caliber rim fire bolt action repeater. When you buy Model 69 you get a rifle that is Winchester through and through. It will give you more all-round rifle service for your dollar!

PRICES
G6901R—Standard rifle as described above	$11.00
G6902R—Rifle with Wm. 75C front and 32C rear sight (no ramp or sight cover)	10.54
Extra 5 cartridge magazine	1.00
Extra 10 cartridge magazine	1.25

MODEL 69 SPECIFICATIONS
BARREL: 25 inches. Round, tapered with crowned muzzle. Chambered for .22 Short, .22 Long and .22 Long Rifle rim fire cartridges—regular, Super Speed or Super-X.
STOCK: American walnut. Full-size, one-piece sporting type with correctly shaped pistol grip and amply deep and rounded long semi-beavertail forestock. Overall length 27½ inches. Composition butt plate.
ACTION: Military type with up-turn and pull-back breech bolt. Safety firing pin; position of safety lock instantly indicated by both sight and touch. Firing pin cocks as bolt is closed.
SIGHTS: Front: Winchester sporting type with bright, non-tarnishing metal bead, mounted on low, non-glare ramp base. Slip-on spring steel sight cover. Rear: (1) latest Winchester peep sight with finger-controlled fine adjustments for both elevation and windage, mounted on receiver bridge or (2) rear open sporting sight with sliding elevator.
MAGAZINE: Detachable box type, inserted from below, removable by spring latch on side of stock. Two 5-cartridge magazines supplied, one for .22 Long and .22 Long Rifle, the other for .22 Short. Five-shot and ten-shot magazines also available as extras.
SIZE: Overall length 42 inches. Takedown length 29½ inches.

**Low in Cost!
Inexpensive to Shoot!**

SEE PAGE 8 "HOW TO ORDER"

WINCHESTER BOLT ACTION—SINGLE SHOT RIFLES

Whether you are a beginner or a seasoned shot, your Model 67 Winchester has an unexpected thrill for you when you try it out. You'll be surprised at the sure, easy way it mounts to your shoulder, points and aims. You can be proud of Model 67's all-round superior materials, workmanship, appearance and shooting. It shoots not only regular .22's but powerful long-range cartridges.

The Winchester Model 67 boasts these features: proof-marked barrel, popular sporting rear sight, patented sporting front sight, short compact bolt with pear shaped bolt handle, safety firing pin, military style firing pin safety-lock, automatic ejector, walnut sporting stock, deep semi-beavertail forearm, take-down screw countersunk in forearm.

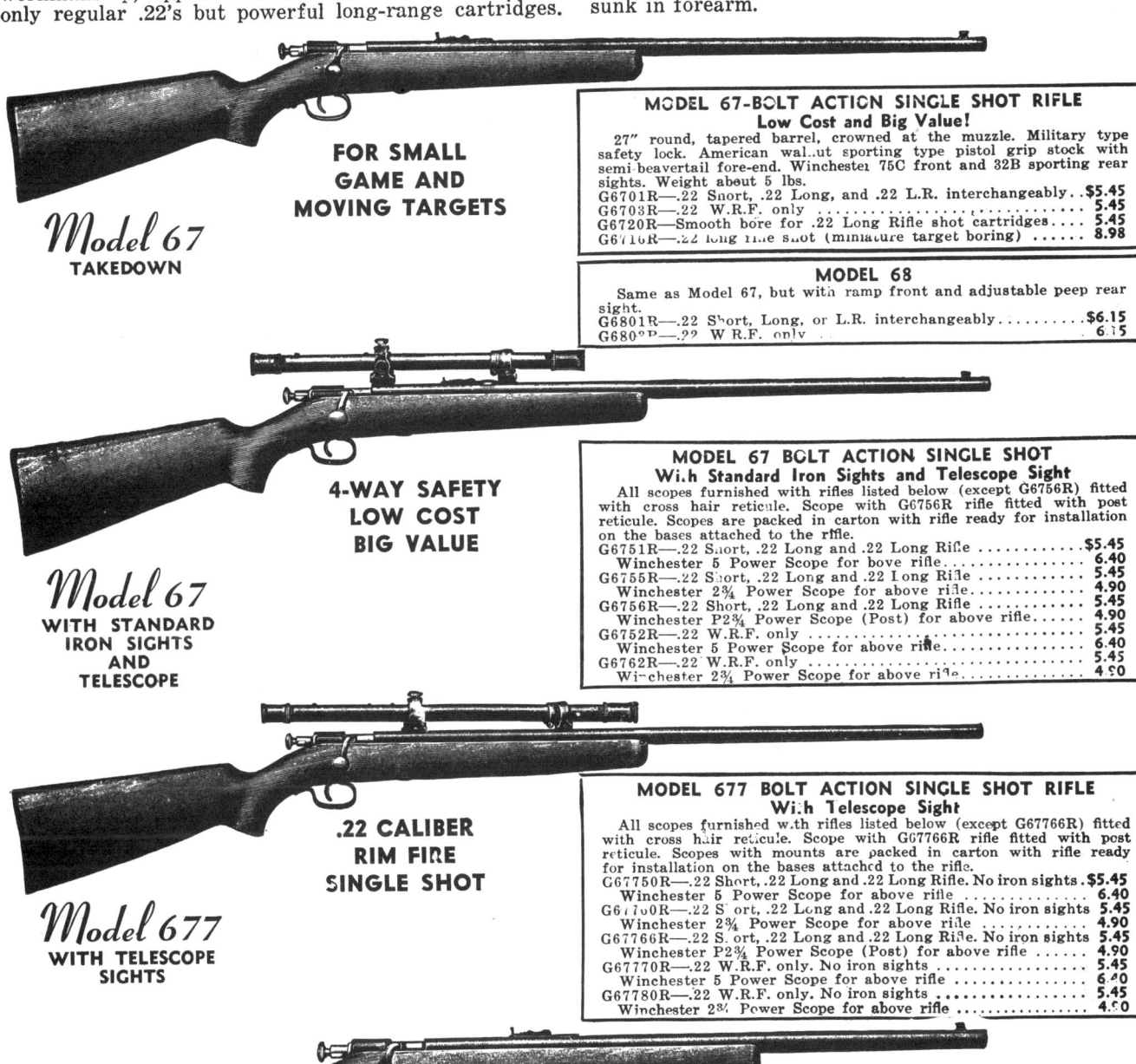

Model 67 TAKEDOWN — FOR SMALL GAME AND MOVING TARGETS

MODEL 67-BOLT ACTION SINGLE SHOT RIFLE
Low Cost and Big Value!

27" round, tapered barrel, crowned at the muzzle. Military type safety lock. American walnut sporting type pistol grip stock with semi-beavertail fore-end. Winchester 75C front and 32B sporting rear sights. Weight about 5 lbs.

G6701R—.22 Short, .22 Long, and .22 L.R. interchangeably..$5.45
G6703R—.22 W.R.F. only 5.45
G6720R—Smooth bore for .22 Long Rifle shot cartridges... 5.45
G6716R—.22 long rifle shot (miniature target boring) 8.98

MODEL 68
Same as Model 67, but with ramp front and adjustable peep rear sight.
G6801R—.22 Short, Long, or L.R. interchangeably..........$6.15
G6803R—.22 W.R.F. only 6.15

Model 67 WITH STANDARD IRON SIGHTS AND TELESCOPE — 4-WAY SAFETY LOW COST BIG VALUE

MODEL 67 BOLT ACTION SINGLE SHOT
With Standard Iron Sights and Telescope Sight

All scopes furnished with rifles listed below (except G6756R) fitted with cross hair reticule. Scope with G6756R rifle fitted with post reticule. Scopes are packed in carton with rifle ready for installation on the bases attached to the rifle.

G6751R—.22 Short, .22 Long and .22 Long Rifle $5.45
  Winchester 5 Power Scope for bove rifle.................. 6.40
G6755R—.22 Short, .22 Long and .22 Long Rifle 5.45
  Winchester 2¾ Power Scope for above rifle.............. 4.90
G6756R—.22 Short, .22 Long and .22 Long Rifle 5.45
  Winchester P2¾ Power Scope (Post) for above rifle...... 4.90
G6752R—.22 W.R.F. only 5.45
  Winchester 5 Power Scope for above rifle............... 6.40
G6762R—.22 W.R.F. only 5.45
  Winchester 2¾ Power Scope for above rifle............. 4.90

Model 677 WITH TELESCOPE SIGHTS — .22 CALIBER RIM FIRE SINGLE SHOT

MODEL 677 BOLT ACTION SINGLE SHOT RIFLE
With Telescope Sight

All scopes furnished with rifles listed below (except G67766R) fitted with cross hair reticule. Scope with G67766R rifle fitted with post reticule. Scopes with mounts are packed in carton with rifle ready for installation on the bases attached to the rifle.

G67750R—.22 Short, .22 Long and .22 Long Rifle. No iron sights.$5.45
  Winchester 5 Power Scope for above rifle 6.40
G67760R—.22 Short, .22 Long and .22 Long Rifle. No iron sights 5.45
  Winchester 2¾ Power Scope for above rifle 4.90
G67766R—.22 Short, .22 Long and .22 Long Rifle. No iron sights 5.45
  Winchester P2¾ Power Scope (Post) for above rifle 4.90
G67770R—.22 W.R.F. only. No iron sights 5.45
  Winchester 5 Power Scope for above rifle 6.40
G67780R—.22 W.R.F. only. No iron sights 5.45
  Winchester 2¾ Power Scope for above rifle 4.90

Model 67 Junior — IDEAL SIZE for Younger Shooters — REAL VALUE! **$5.45**

MODEL 67 BOLT ACTION SINGLE SHOT RIFLE

In learning to shoot it is of great importance to have a rifle that you can hold and aim comfortably. Here is a junior size that is adapted for and fits younger shooters. This rifle is the same in action and sight equipment as the regular Model 67 but is made with 20" barrel and a stock 1³⁄₁₆" shorter and with an overall length of only 34½". It is designed especially for youngsters who hope to become expert shooters.

G6738R—For .22 Short, .22 Long and .22 Long Rifle rim fire cartridges interchangeably ....Only $5.45

Remington
REG. U.S. PAT. OFF.

"The Master Line"

The beginning of the Remington Arms Company goes back more than 120 years, the day when Eliphalet Remington Jr. asked his father, a smith, for money to buy a rifle and met with his refusal. Undaunted, the youth collected scrap iron, welded it carefully into a gun barrel, and the first Remington gun was born.

Friends and neighbors seeing his finished sample liked it and first orders for Remington guns were placed. His father supported his son, and the business outgrew the little shop and a large farm was purchased which is still the site of the Remington plant at Ilion.

In 1845 the Government expecting trouble in Mexico looked about for firearms. A contract was placed with Amos & Company of Springfield, Mass., for the William Jencks carbine was turned down by this concern and Eliphalet Remington purchased the contract and made his first sale of firearms to the Government. When the Civil War broke out the Government again called on Remington and in 1856 the firm of E. Remington & Sons was formed.

The founder of the concern died on August 12th, 1861. Four years later the partnership of E. Remington & Sons was succeeded by a corporation of the same name. The Remington plant also became the birthplace of the first typewriter. However, the business became stranded in 1885 through several financial reverses and was taken over in March 1888 by Marcellus Hartley and Malcolm Graham of New York.

Mr. Hartley formed the Union Metallic Cartridge Company in 1867 from the purchase of two small cartridge companies;—the Crittenden, Tibbals Mfg. Company of South Coventry and the business of C. D. Lett of Springfield. At the beginning this company manufactured rim fire cartridges, percussion caps and shotguns.

Another step forward was made by the new invention of Colonel Berdan of the new type primer permitting the production of the first center-fire cartridges.

In 1873 the business of C. D. Wells of Springfield was purchased. Mr. Wells developed the manufacture of paper shells for shotguns. Mr. Marcellus Hartley Dodge, Mr. Hartley's grandson, took over the leadership of the company when the latter died in 1902.

In 1912 Mr. Dodge brought about the merger of the U. M. C. and Remington Arms Company resulting in today's Remington Arms Co., Inc. At this time the size of the plant at Bridgeport, consisted of 101 buildings with a total floor area of 16 acres. The outstanding land-mark was the Shot Tower in which 150 tons of metal can be daily converted into 1,200,000,000 shot pellets.

During the World War both plants at Bridgeport and Ilion were expanded considerably from a peace time total of 4,500 men to about 20,000 men. In 1933 a controlling interest was purchased by E. I. DuPont de Nemours & Company, Inc. In 1933 the Chamberlin Cartridge and Target Company was taken over. In 1934 the Peters Cartridge Company and the Charles Parker Company of Meriden, makers of the famous Parker shotguns, were taken over.

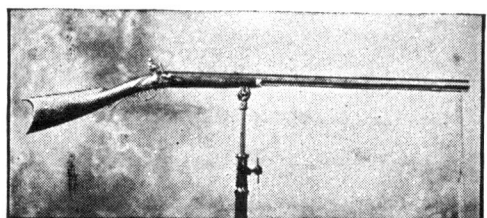

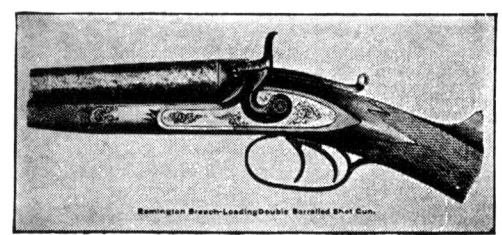

TELL OTHERS ABOUT THE STOEGER CATALOG

AMERICA'S GREAT GUN HOUSE

REMINGTON BOLT ACTION AND REPEATING RIFLES
For Big Game Shooting

MODEL 30A AND 30R

For Big Game   Caliber U. S. 30/06 Springfield Only

Unsurpassed accuracy—the result of carefully selected barrels, bored and rifled to exact standards; superb balance and beauty of line—the outcome of traditional Remington engineering and craftsmanship; dependable, smooth working mechanism—due to Remington precision production and absolute synchronization of working parts.

OUTSTANDING FEATURES OF THE MODEL 30 RIFLE

When bolt is pulled back it is stopped by a bolt stop—not on the sear or trigger as in most other bolt action rifles. Detachable magazine bottom for cleaning. Safety is positive and conveniently located for quick operation. Durable American walnut stock and fore-end, both checkered. Floating barrel to give maximum accuracy. Barrel is not attached to forestock. Uplift of bolt permits proper fitting of telescope.

No. 30A—"Standard" Grade, 22-inch barrel $60.49
No. 30R—"Carbine," 20-inch barrel (not checkered) 55.44

SPECIFICATIONS 30A
No. 30A "Standard" Grade, 22-inch barrel; American walnut stock, half pistol grip and fore-end finely checkered. Rifle style steel butt plate, grooved to prevent slipping. Rifle cocks on opening movement of bolt. Top of receiver matted. Short, snappy, light, single trigger pull. Thumb-operated safety. Buckhorn adjustable rear sight with gold bead front sight. Receiver drilled and tapped for Lyman No. 48R micrometer windgauge sight. Magazine holds 5 cartridges. Length over all 42¾ inches. Weight, about 7¼ pounds.

SPECIFICATIONS 30R
No. 30R Carbine. Same as 30A "Standard" Grade except that barrel is 20 inches long. Stock furnished without checkering. Shotgun style steel butt plate. Weight, about 7 pounds.
⅞-inch Sling Strap (leather, Whelen type); with hooks, extra $2.02

MODEL 30SL

For Big Game

MADE IN 30/06 SPRINGFIELD AND .257 REMINGTON-ROBERTS (.25 ROBERTS) CALIBERS WITH 24-INCH BARREL

SPECIFICATIONS 30S

Note the design of stock and fore-end of Model 30S embodying the best ideas of many of America's foremost sportsmen; the full pistol grip, capped; the double trigger pull of military type; the matted front sight ramp, with removable guard; the modern Lyman receiver sight; the steel butt plate; the handsome checkering and the facility with which telescope can be mounted and used.

Model 30S "Special" Grade; made in .30 Springfield '06, and .257 Remington-Roberts (.25 Roberts) calibers with 24-inch barrel. Carefully bored and rifled for extreme accuracy; special high comb stock of American walnut, checkered; long, full forestock; steel butt plate; Lyman No. 48 windgauge receiver full pistol grip with rubber cap; shotgun style sight; gold bead front sight mounted on a matted ramp with removable guard; double trigger pull of the military type (option of single pull); wide screw eyes for quick release swivels (option of regular screw eyes). Rifle cocks on opening movement of bolt. Top of receiver matted. Thumb-operated safety. Magazine holds 5 cartridges. Weight, about 8 pounds.

No. 30SL—"Special" Grade with Lyman No. 48 sight $73.61
No. 30SR—"Special" Grade with Redfield No. 102R receiver sight 65.48
No. 30SX—"Special" Grade without receiver sight but with step adjustable open rear sight on barrel 60.49
No. 30SM—"Special Grade with Marble Goss receiver sight 73.61
⅞-inch Sling Strap (leather, Whelen type); with hooks, extra 2.02
⅞-inch Sling Strap (leather, Whelen type); with quick release swivels, extra 4.44

THE GAMEMASTER MODEL 141

HIGH POWER SLIDE ACTION REPEATING RIFLES
New Stock—Semi-beavertail Fore-end—Longer Barrel—New Front Sight Ramp
Made in .30 Rem., .32 Rem., and .35 Rem. calibers.
All Center Fire and Rimless

The "Gamemaster" is the choice of big game hunters who appreciate the advantages of the slide action type of firearm. It is the same as the famous Model 14, but with important new improvements. It has a longer barrel, larger stock, semi-beavertail fore-end, and a new front sight ramp. The fast, smooth, dependable action, perfect balance, and suitability for all North American big game are outstanding features.

SPECIFICATIONS

"Gamemaster" No. 141A "Standard" Grade. Slide action, takedown, hammerless, solid breech; 24 inch barrel; American walnut stock with half pistol grip and shotgun style steel butt plate, checkered to prevent slipping. Semi-beavertail fore-end. Step adjustable rear sight. White metal bead front sight mounted on matted ramp, integral with barrel. Magazine hold five cartridges which, with one in the chamber, gives a capacity of six shots. Cross bolt safety. Length over-all 42¾ inches; taken down 29½ inches. Weight, about 7¾ pounds.

No. 141A "Standard" Grade .... $54.44   No. 141F "Premier" Grade 286.76
No. 141B "Special" Grade .... 63.72   No. 141R "Carbine" (same as No. 141A
No. 141D "Peerless" Grade .... 149.13   but with 18½-inch barrel) .30 and .32 calibers only $54.44
⅞-inch Sling Strap (leather, Whelen type) with hooks and eyes, extra 2.22

SEE INSIDE FRONT COVER "HOW TO ORDER"

REMINGTON AUTOMATIC AND REPEATING RIFLES

"SPEEDMASTER" Model 241
TAKE DOWN

For Small Game — For Plinking

SHOOTS .22 SHORT ONLY OR .22 LONG RIFLE ONLY, ORDINARY OR HI-SPEED

If YOU seek a light, graceful, fast-shooting, hard-hitting rifle for all 'round use—ridding the world of vermin pests, for "plinking" or for small game in season—the Model 241 Autoloader is made to order" for you.

It fires as fast as you can work your trigger finger. It is operated by the recoil which ejects the empty cartridge, puts in a new one and cocks the action. Autoloading—but reliable.

Accuracy? All you'd expect of a Remington. Finest barrels, rifled the Remington way; good sighting equipment; careful fitting of parts and that silky smooth action to rattle out the shots without disturbing your aim. No other .22 repeater can give such results.

Convenience? Model 241 takes down in a jiffy and stores in suitcase or dufflebag; the breech block removes for cleaning without tools; you can buy ammunition for the Model 241 at any crossroad store.

Model 241SA is chambered for the regular or Hi-Speed .22 Short; the Model 241LA for regular or high speed .22 Long Rifle cartridges. Not interchangeable. The magazine is in the stock and is easily loaded.

SPECIFICATIONS OF NO. 241 STANDARD GRADE

Hammerless, take-down, solid breech; 24 inch round, gracefully tapered barrel. Full-sized half pistol grip and semi-beavertail fore-end of genuine American walnut. Shotgun style steel butt plate, corrugated to prevent slipping. Chambered for .22 Short cartridge only or .22 Long Rifle cartridge only. Hi-Speed and regular. (When ordering specifically mention caliber wanted, either .22 Short or Long Rifle). .22 Short magazine holds 15 cartridges. .22 Long Rifle magazine holds 10 cartridges. Step adjustable sporting rear sight. White metal bead front sight. Length over-all 41½ inches. Length taken down 24 inches. Weight about 6 pounds.

No. 241SA or 241LA. "Standard" Grade	$ 33.25
No. 241SC or 241LC. "Special" Grade	42.53
No. 241SD or 241LD. "Peerless" Grade	88.24
No. 241SE or 241LE. "Expert" Grade	124.86
No. 241SF or 241LF. "Premier" Grade	150.39
⅞" Leather Sling straps with hooks and eyes	2.22

"FIELDMASTER" Model 121
TAKE DOWN

MOST MODERN SLIDE-ACTION .22 REPEATING RIFLE
Made for .22 Short, .22 Long, .22 Long Rifle or .22 Rem. Spec. Cartridges

New Grooved Semi-Beavertail Fore-End • New Shotgun Style Butt Plate • New Half-Pistol Grip Stock • Increased Magazine Capacity • Longer, Heavier Barrel • Easy Takedown • Excellent Accuracy • Solid Safety Breech

Always a step ahead in gun design. Remington offers the "FIELDMASTER" with its long, semi-beavertail fore-end, properly shaped pistol grip, and shotgun style butt plate. These features permit quick aiming, fast firing, and straight shooting from any position. The fore-end fits man or boy and is grooved to prevent slipping. The barrel is longer, heavier and more accurate. With magazine capacity greatly increased the "FIELDMASTER" holds 20 Short, 15 Long or 14 Long Rifle cartridges which may be used interchangeably without adjustment. Rifles especially chambered for the .22 Rem. Special Cartridge have a 12 shot magazine capacity. Its easy takedown feature is popular everywhere for it packs conveniently in a suitcase. A cross bolt safety available for either left or right handed shooters is easily operated with the trigger finger.

The sights are white metal bead front and step adjustable rear. For all-round easy handling, light weight, straight and fast shooting the "FIELDMASTER" is in a class by itself.

SPECIFICATIONS
The "FIELDMASTER" Model 121A

"Standard" Grade. Takedown, hammerless, solid breech; 24-inch round barrel; American walnut pistol grip stock with shotgun style steel butt plate; grooved semi-beavertail fore-end; chambered for .22 Short, Long and Long Rifle cartridges which may be used interchangeably without adjustment. Magazine holds 20 Short, 15 Long or 14 Long Rifle Cartridges, Rear Sight with adjustable step for elevation; white metal bead front sight; length taken down 27½ inches. Weight, about 6 pounds.

MODEL 121S—"Remington Special" Grade Same as 121A, except it is chambered for .22 Rem. Special (.22 W.R.F.) cartridges only. Magazine holds 12 cartridges.

No. 121A "Standard" Grade	$ 24.87
No. 121S "Remington Special" Grade	24.87
No. 121B "Special" Grade with selected American Walnut stock and fore-end checkered	34.15
No. 121D "Peerless" Grade	80.17
No. 121E "Expert" Grade	116.79
No. 121F "Premier" Grade	142.27
No. 121SB "Standard" Grade (smooth bore, shotgun bead front sight, no rear sight)	26.89

WOODMASTER MODEL 81
TAKEDOWN

AVAILABLE IN
- .30 Remington
- .300 Savage
- .32 Remington
- .35 Remington

Built to withstand hard service this hard hitting, big game rifle has the most rapid operation with the least disturbance of any rifle made. This high-power autoloader shoots as fast as the trigger can be pulled and released for each shot. Loading, cocking, and ejecting are all done by recoil. The "Woodmaster" is the only high-power autoloading rifle made in this country that locks the cartridge in the chamber until the bullet has left the muzzle. This prevents loss of killing power—delivers the full energy of the cartridge and provides the utmost safety, yet it is under the shooter's control at all times for the trigger must be pulled and released for each shot. Other important safety features include two lugs on the bolt which lock in the barrel extension, and the thumb safety, conveniently located for quick operation. Cartridges may be loaded singly or with a clip into the box magazine which is permanently attached and cannot be lost. When the last shot is fired the action remains open ready for reloading. The "Woodmaster" in .35 caliber is powerful enough for the largest North American big game.

SEMI-BEAVERTAIL FORE-END

Made full and well-rounded to fit the palm of the hand, this comfortable fore-end holds steadily and does not cramp the fingers. It withstands the hardest knocks of hunting and facilitates fast handling for quick shots at running game. Made long and rounded in front for those who hold far out in the fore-end.

HALF-PISTOL GRIP PROPERLY SHAPED

Designed to permit a better control over each shot fired, this new pistol grip fits the hand and gives a firm hold on the stock. The hand and trigger finger remain in place and are not disturbed by recoil. It places the finger well forward around the trigger.

SHOTGUN STYLE STEEL BUTT PLATE

Speeds up sighting on quick shots and is checkered to prevent slipping. It's wider and longer to give a greater bearing surface that reduces the effect of recoil. Aids in steady holding and comes quickly to the right place on your shoulder from any position.

Specifications of the "Woodmaster" Model 81A

"Standard" Grade. Takedown, hammerless, solid breech; 22-inch barrel, American walnut pistol grip stock fitted with shotgun style steel butt plate. Trigger pull exceptionally light. Semi-beavertail fore-end. Step adjustable rear sight, white metal bead front sight. Magazine holds 5 cartridges. Length taken down, 23 inches. Weight, about 8 pounds. Made for .30, .32, and .35 Remington Center Fire cartridges, also .300 Savage. Length over-all 41½ inches.

No. 81A "Standard" Grade	$ 70.58
No. 81B "Special" Grade	79.86
No. 81D "Peerless" Grade	165.98
No. 81E "Expert" Grade	232.57
No. 81F "Premier" Grade	299.17

A NEW GUN CARRIES A FACTORY GUARANTEE

A Precision Rifle for Champions!

THE NEW REMINGTON 1940 "RANGEMASTER"
MODEL 37—BOLT ACTION TARGET RIFLE
.22 Long Rifle Caliber Only

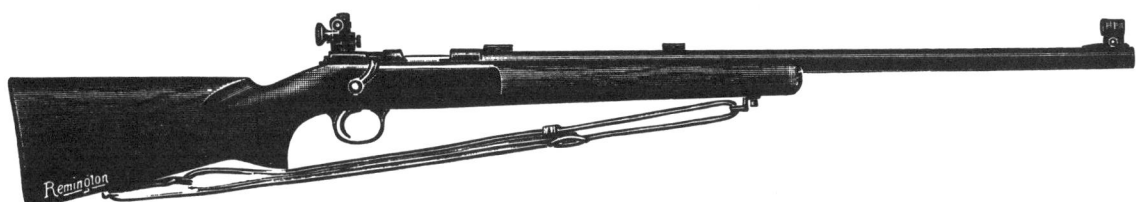

BARREL. Specially rifled for unsurpassed accuracy. 28 inches. Heavy. Semi-floating. Double countersunk at muzzle.

SPEED ACTION. Smooth operation. Heat treated wearing surfaces to insure minimum head space. Double locking lugs. Double extractors. Shrouded bolt. Remington milled steel patented loading platform for single loading. Interchangeable 5-shot clip magazine. Positive thumb safety.

STOCK. New design. Lacquer finish. Higher, thicker comb for better sighting. Close pistol grip for sensitive control of trigger finger. Wider, longer beaver-tail fore-end for steady holding. Sharply checkered shotgun style steel butt plate. Carney shooting sling of heavy leather. Adjustable front sling swivel, properly positioned for long or short armed shooter.

TRIGGER. Remarkable new trigger mechanism. Smooth, sharp, crisp, lightning fast let-off. No back lash. No perceptible movement. No drag or creep. Quickly adjustable for pull.

SIGHTS. Remington micrometer target rear sight with six-hole eyepiece. ¼ minute clicks. Redfield globe front sight with seven interchangeable inserts. Both sights removable without changing setting. Iron sights and telescope on same sighting plane. Adjustable extension mounting block supplied with rear sight. Standard telescope blocks.

WEIGHT. Approximately 12 pounds. Over-all length, 46½ inches.

No. 37AR complete with Remington receiver sight and Redfield front sight (Furnished unless otherwise specified)	$72.60
No. 37AS complete, but without sling strap	71.18
No. 37AF without rear sight but with Redfield front sight	59.83
No. 37AX without front and rear sights	57.06
No. 37AV with Wittek Vaver receiver sight and Redfield front sight	76.48
No. 37AM with Marble-Goss receiver sight and Redfield front sight	73.15
Oil finishing stock, extra	5.55
Selected figured American walnut stock, extra	4.84
Remington rear sight adapter for Redfield, Lyman, Marble-Goss, Pacific, and Merit discs, extra (not taxable)	.50

REMINGTON MICROMETER REAR SIGHT
Quickly removable with changing setting. Large adjusting knobs. ¼ minute clicks. Six-hole eyepiece. Line of sight same with peep or telescope.

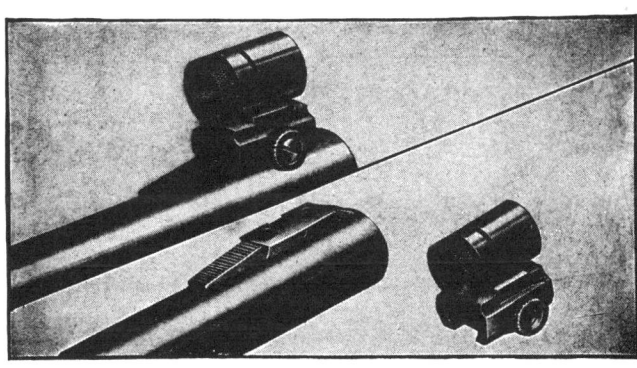

REDFIELD FRONT SIGHT
Mounted on special base. Easily attached or removed. Seven interchangeable inserts.

SPECIALLY RIFLED FOR UNSURPASSED ACCURACY

REMINGTON
Bolt Action .22 Caliber
RIFLES

"SPORTSMASTER" No. 341P

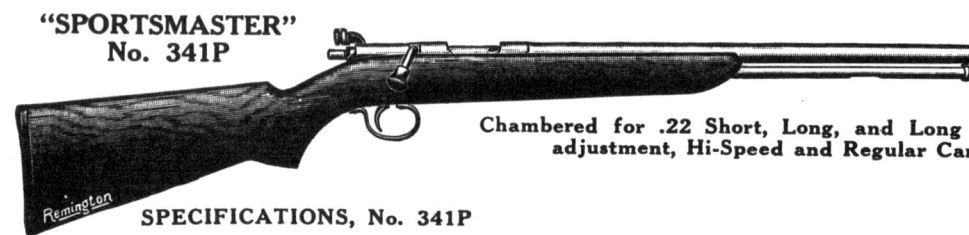

Chambered for .22 Short, Long, and Long Rifle, without adjustment, Hi-Speed and Regular Cartridges

SPECIFICATIONS, No. 341P

"Sportmaster" No. 341P. Takedown. Heavy 24-inch round tapered barrel, crowned at muzzle. Automatic ejector. Polished non-friction bolt. Magazine holds 22 Short, 17 Long, 15 Long Rifle cartridges. One piece genuine American walnut stock and fore-end. Semi-beavertail fore-end. Composition shotgun style butt plate, checkered to prevent slipping. Military type thumb safety. Remington receiver peep sight, closer to the eye. Hooded front sight. Length over-all, 42 inches; taken down, 30¾ inches. Weight, about 6 pounds.

No. 341P $14.83
⅞" Sling Strap (Leather, Whelen type) with hooks and eyes, extra.. 2.22

SPECIFICATIONS, No. 341A

"Sportmaster" No. 341A. Same as "Sportmaster" No. 341P, except fitted with step adjustable sporting rear sight instead of Remington peep sight. White metal bead instead of hooded front sight. Weight, about 6 pounds.

No. 341A $14.08
No. 341SB, with smooth bore barrel for use with shot cartridges.... 14.08

"TARGETMASTER" No. 510A

Chambered for .22 Short, Long, and Long Rifle, without adjustment, Hi-Speed and Regular Cartridges

SPECIFICATIONS, No. 510A

The "Targetmaster" Model 510A bolt action single shot rifle cal. 22 has a 25 inch long tapered barrel, crowned at muzzle, carefully rifled and chambered. Bolt and bolt handle are case hardened for strength. A new loading platform makes loading easy and gives straight line cartridge feed, eliminating shaved bullets. An exclusivee new sear insures crisp trigger pull. Trigger is corrugated to prevent slipping. Stock is of genuine American walnut, with pistol grip, shotgun style checkered butt plate, and semi-beavertail fore-end. Sights are of latest Remington design with long sighting redius. Low up-turn of bolt handle permits low mounting of telescope. Exclusive new features include double locking lugs, double extractors, streamlined self-cocking bolt with double cams, for easy cocking, firing pin safety indicator, that shows red when cocked. Thumb safety is easy to operate, goes on automatically when cocking rifle, locks trigger, shows red dot when ready to fire. Receiver is heavy for extreme strength. Bolt head is encased for additional safety, and accuracy. Automatic ejector. Simple takedown. Rifle length overall, 43 inches, taken down 31 inches. Weight about 5¾ pounds.

Price $5.45
No. 510SB Grade, with smooth bore barrel for use with shot cartridges.
  Open sights 5.45
⅞" Leather Sling Strap, Whelen type, with hooks and eyes extra..... 2.22

SPECIFICATIONS, No. 510P

"Targetmaster" No. 510P. Same as "Targetmaster" No. 510A except fitted with "Point-crometer" receiver peep sight with two interchangeable discs and with Patridge type blade front sight mounted on non-glare ramp.

Price $6.15

"SCOREMASTER" No. 511A

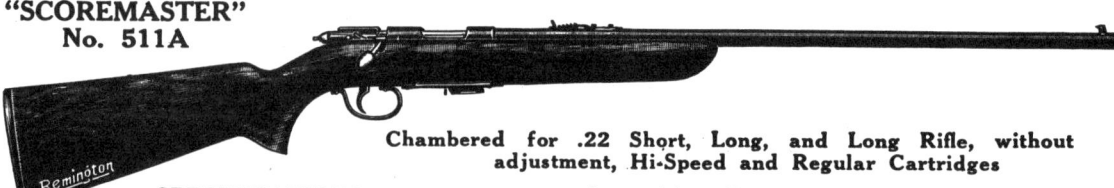

Chambered for .22 Short, Long, and Long Rifle, without adjustment, Hi-Speed and Regular Cartridges

SPECIFICATIONS, No. 511A

The "Scoremaster" Model 511A bolt action .22 caliber repeating rifle has double locking lugs, double extractors, streamlined bolt and bolt handle, and self-cocking bolt with double cams for easy cocking are the same as on the model 510. Cocks on opening movement of bolt. Accuracy features include the 25 inch tapered barrel, crowned at muzzle, carefully chambered and rifled, case hardened bolt and bolt handle, crisp trigger pull, and corrugated trigger. Safety features are the firing pin safety indicator that shows a red warning dot, the easily operated, silent thumb safety showing a ready to-fire red warning dot, the encased bolt head, and receiver of heavy milled steel. Fitted with Remington step adjustable rear sight. Concealed dovetail slot for other sights if desired. White metal bead front sight. Magazine capacity is 6 shots. Additional cartridge in chamber gives total capacity of 7 shots. Handles .22 short, long, and long rifle cartridges. Magazine is quickly detached for reloading by pressing magazine thumb catch. Simple take-down. Automatic ejection. Length over-all, 43 inches, taken down, 31 inches. Weight, about 5¾ pounds.

Price $10.54
No. 511SB Grade, with smooth bore barrel for use with shot cartridges
  open sights 10.54
Additional interchangeable 6-cartridge box magazines, each extra.... 1.00
⅞" Leather sling strap, Whelen type, with hooks and eyes, extra..... 2.22

SPECIFICATIONS, No. 511P

"Scoremaster" No. 511P. Same as "Scoremaster" No. 511A except fitted with "Point-crometer" receiver peep sight with two interchangeable discs and with Patridge type blade front sight mounted on non-glare ramp.

Price $11.00

REMINGTON MATCHMASTER

REMINGTON MODEL 513 TARGET AND SPORTING RIFLES
BOLT ACTION BOX MAGAZINE REPEATERS

.22 Long Rifle Caliber Only
No. 513T "Target" Grade

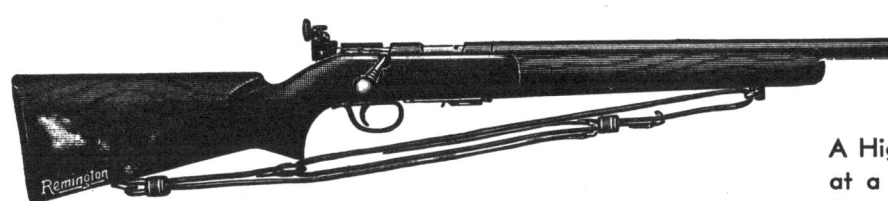

HEAVY, 27 - INCH SEMI - FLOATING BARREL, double countersunk at muzzle, carefully bored and rifled for fine accuracy. Self-cocking bolt. Adjustable trigger stop. Smooth, crisp, short trigger pull. Short, fast firing pin travel. Corrugated trigger. Double extractors. Double locking lugs. Firing indicator. Positive side lever type safety. Detachable magazine box holds six cartridges which, with one in chamber, gives total capacity of seven shots. Length over-all, 45 inches; taken down, 33 inches.

No. 513T "TARGET GRADE. American walnut lacquer finished stock with close pistol grip and high, thick comb. Long, wide beavertail fore-end. Sharply checkered steel butt plate. Redfield Globe front sight with seven interchangeable inserts. Redfield No. 75 Micrometer rear sight with ¼ minute clicks. Barrel drilled and tapped for scope blocks. Adjustable front sling swivel. 1¼-inch government type sling of high grade leather. Weight, including sling strap, 9 pounds.

A High Grade 9-Pound Target Rifle at a Moderate Price—Complete in Every Detail—Ready for Immediate Use—Exceptionally Fine Accuracy—New Style Stock of Accepted Design—Adjustable Swivel—Redfield Precision Sights—Short, Crisp Trigger Pull—Fast Lock Time—Double Locking Lugs—Firing Indicator—Every Desirable Feature for Match Shooting in All Positions.

No. 513TR "Target" Grade, complete as described $30.22
No. 513TX "Target" Grade, without any sights 25.17

No. 513S "Sporter" Grade

No. 513S "SPORTER" GRADE. Tapered barrel. Streamlined lacquer finished sporting stock of American walnut, with grip and fore-end checkered. Sharply checkered steel butt plate. Front and rear screw eyes for sling swivels. Patridge type frontsight, mounted on non-glare ramp. Step adjustable sporting rear sight. Dovetail slots concealed under front and rear sights to permit fitting of special sights. Receiver drilled and tapped for Redfield No. 75 Micrometer rear sight. Length over-all, 45 inches; taken down, 33 inches. Weight, about 6¾ pounds.

A Smart, Racy Sporting Rifle of Top-Notch Quality for General Use—Outstanding Performance—Streamlined—Sporting Stock—New Style Bolt Handle—Distinctive—Incomparable at This New Low Price.

No. 513SA "Sporter" Grade, complete as described $26.23
⅞" Leather Sling Strap, Whelen type, with hooks on, "Sporter" Grade 2.22
Oil finishing stock, extra 5.55
Selected figured American walnut stock, extra 4.84

EXTRAS FOR REMINGTON RIFLES

Checkering Standard Grade Stock and fore-end, Extra (Excepting where regular) $4.44
Soft rubber recoil pad fitted, Extra (Excepting where regular) 5.55
Full pistol grip with rubber cap on Models 141A, 141C, 30A, 81A, 81C, Extra 4.44
Full pistol grip with rubber cap on Models 121A, 121S, 241A, 241C, 341, 41, Extra 3.33
Nickel plated trimmings (receiver, trigger guard and butt plate) on Models 121 and 241, Extra 8.32
Full nickel plating on Models 121 and 241, Extra (All exterior metal parts) 10.29
Oil finishing stock and fore-end A-B-C Grades, Extra 5.54
Checkering Trigger, Extra (Standard on Model 30) 1.11
Reversing safety for left-handed shooter on all Models, except Models 30, 341, 41 and 81 .... No extra charge

Rear sight slot on Models 241, 121, 341A, 341P, 41A, 41P, or front sight slot on Models 341P, 41P 2.22
Gold Name Plate inlaid in stock, Extra (Excepting on F Grade) 8.88
Silver Name Plate inlaid in stock, Extra (Excepting on E and F Grades) 6.66
Base blocks for Lyman No. 438 or No. 5A telescope (not fitted), Extra 1.10
Fitting base blocks for Lyman No. 438 or No. 5A telescope, Extra. (Price of base block should be added) 2.77
Drilling and tapping .22 caliber rifles for Weaver No. 344 scope, when telescope is not ordered .... .25
Special sights (Lyman, Marble, etc.) fitted on rifles, Extra (Manufacturer's List) .... Net
(No allowance made for regular sights.)

A NEW GUN CARRIES A FACTORY GUARANTEE

HISTORY OF THE SAVAGE ARMS CORPORATION

On April 5, 1894 Arthur W. Savage formed the Savage Repeating Arms Company at Utica, New York. The company was organized to manufacture a hammerless, repeating high power rifle invented by Mr. Savage.

The rifle is a lever action, hammerless design and was at once accepted by sportsmen as an outstanding improvement in firearms design, and the Savage Rifle became world famous for its safety and reliability. The rifle was designated as Model 99 Savage High Power Rifle, and although advances have been made in the power and pressures of high power cartridges, the original design—with but a few refinements, continues to be sold today in increasing volume.

Following the introduction of the Model 99 High Power Rifle, the Savage Arms Corporation began a series of experiments on cartridges of small caliber and high velocity, which resulted in the introduction of the revolutionary .22 Hi-Power and .250/3000 Savage Cartridge. These developments further increased the reputation of the Savage Arms Corporation for maintaining leadership in the origination and development of sporting arms and ammunition.

New models were gradually added to the company's products, until 1915, when the company was manufacturing in addition to its high power rifles, and ammunition, several .22 caliber rifles and an automatic pistol. The Savage Automatic Pistol was sold in large quantities at export for several years but has now been discontinued.

In 1915 the Savage Arms Company was purchased by the Driggs-Seabury Ordnance Company for the production of the Lewis Machine Gun, and Mr. Savage retired from the business. The manufacture of domestic arms was practically discontinued during the period of the World War, the plant facilities were greatly enlarged and a large quantity of Lewis Machine Guns was produced for the United States Government.

Following the War, the new Management resumed the production of Savage High Power Rifles; engineers developed the famous .300 Savage Cartridge and several new models were introduced into the line.

In 1864 Joshua Stevens built the first Stevens Rifle in a little frame building in Chicopee Falls, Mass. It was a good rifle. The barrel had been so precisely bored and rifled that it performed with a degree of accuracy never before attained in a sporting arm. Stevens rifles had become world famous, so the merging of the Savage and Stevens companies in 1920 gave the Savage Arms Corporation the most complete line of firearms manufactured by one concern in the United States.

The Stevens Arms Company purchased several small competing companies. In 1926 the Page Lewis Company was purchased, and in 1930 the Davis-Warner Arms Corporation was taken over. In 1931 the Crescent-Firearms Company of Norwich, Conn. was acquired. In the meantime, the Savage Arms Corporation had purchased, in 1930, the famous A. H. Fox Gun Company and moved the entire equipment and many of the skilled personnel to their plant at Utica, New York.

For the past ten years, the Savage Arms Corporation has maintained a position of leadership in the origination and development of sporting arms and ammunition. Each rifle, shotgun and cartridge that bears the Savage or Stevens name, fills a very definite need in the big, medium or small game field. Each is the result of expert engineering skill, accurate workmanship and careful selection of high grade materials. Savage arms are made of the finest materials procurable and exemplify the advanced state of the gun-making art.

SAVAGE COMBINATION RIFLES AND SHOTGUNS

The Savage Arms Corporation has filled herewith a long felt demand for a low priced combination of High powered Rifle and Shotgun for those who cannot spend a great deal of money for more expensive equipment of such design. Construction of these guns is modern and of the best in material and expert workmanship such as the name Savage stands for.

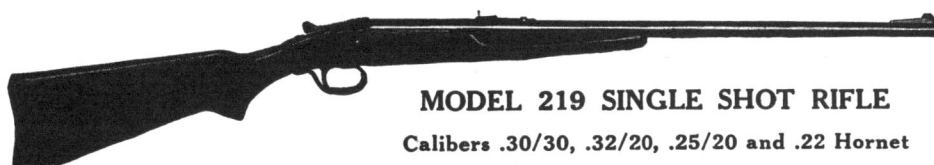

MODEL 219 SINGLE SHOT RIFLE

Calibers .30/30, .32/20, .25/20 and .22 Hornet

Tapered, medium weight, round barrel with raised ramp front sight base, length 26 inches. Proof tested. Barrel and lug forged in one piece. Hammerless action with Automatic Top Tang Safety. Automatic ejector, insuring positive extraction and ejection. Polished and blued frame. Barrel bolted to frame with large beveled locking bolt. Forearm fastens with tension of heavy steel spring against hinge pin and forearm barrel lug. Both features designed to automatically take up wear. Selected American Walnut stock and forearm, full pistol grip stock with fluted comb. Hard rubber butt plate. Sights, adjustable flat top rear sight. Bead front sight. Weight about 6 pounds.

Model 219 .... Price **$15.00**

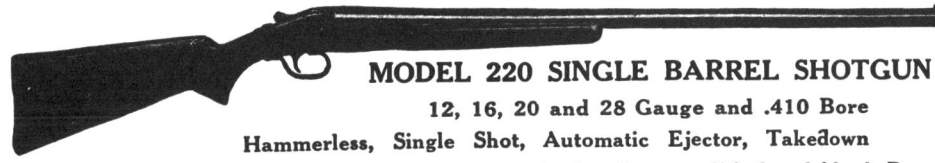

MODEL 220 SINGLE BARREL SHOTGUN

12, 16, 20 and 28 Gauge and .410 Bore

Hammerless, Single Shot, Automatic Ejector, Takedown

Barrel made of selected forged gun barrel steel. Proof tested. Barrel and lug forged in one piece. Full choke. Barrel lengths: 12 gauge, 28, 30, and 32 inch (50 cents extra for 34 and 36 inch); 16 gauge, 28, 30 and 32 inch; 20 gauge, 26, 28, 30 and 32 inch; 28 gauge, 28 and 30 inch; .410 bore, 26 and 28 inch. Hammerless action with Automatic Top Tang Safety. All working parts made of long wearing special alloy steel and operated by strong coil springs. Automatic ejector is ½ inch wide, insuring positive extraction and ejection. Frame polished and blued. Barrel bolted to frame with large beveled locking bolt. Forearm fastens with tension of heavy steel spring against hinge pin and forearm barrel lug. Both features designed to automatically take up wear. Walnut stock and forearm, stock full pistol grip and forearm large wide design. Hard rubber butt plate. Weight about 6 lbs.

Model 220 .... Price **$11.10**

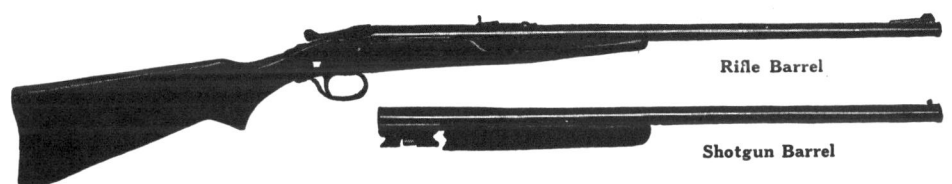

SAVAGE UTILITY GUN RIFLE and SHOTGUN

Model No.	Rifle-Barrel	Shotgun Barrel		Model No.	Rifle Barrel	Shotgun Barrel	
221	.30/30 caliber	12 gauge	30″	227	.22 Hornet	12 gauge	30″
222	.30/30 caliber	16 gauge	28″	228	.22 Hornet	16 gauge	28″
223	.30/30 caliber	20 gauge	28″	229	.22 Hornet	20 gauge	28″

THE SAVAGE UTILITY GUN is made up of the Model 219 Rifle described below and a shotgun barrel and fore-end carefully fitted to the rifle frame. Packed complete as a single unit, one in a box.
Price **$19.50**

THE SAVAGE UTILITY GUN will be furnished on special order in other combinations; the Model 919 Rifle in the orders listed above, and any gauge Model 220 Shotgun barrel at the following additional charge over the regular price of the Utility Gun.
Price **$3.30**

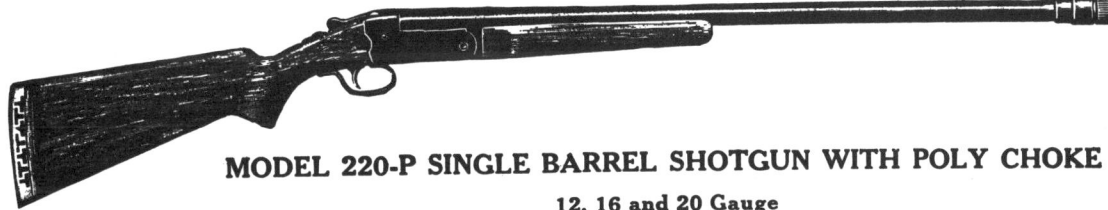

MODEL 220-P SINGLE BARREL SHOTGUN WITH POLY CHOKE

12, 16 and 20 Gauge

Same specifications as Model 220 above with following extras:
 Special Poly Choke built integral with barrel.
 Metal Bead front sight.
 Special Recoil Pad.

Barrel lengths: 12 ga., 30″; 16 ga., 28″; 20 ga., 28″.
The Poly Choke is a device at the muzzle of barrel with finger adjustable sleeve so the shooter can instantly change to any choke desired. Nine distinct adjustments can be obtained from cylinder to full choke.
Price **$16.15**

SAVAGE MODEL 99 HIGH POWER RIFLES

This is the famous repeating rifle that first introduced the hammerless, solid breech design and rotary type magazine. Its popularity in every hunting field is tremendous—for it embodies all the technical superiority and mechanical perfection of tested Savage methods.

An extra margin of safety is built into the Model 99 mechanism. The breech bolt has an unusually large locking area, wedging solidly against the receiver. The cycle of operation is quick and positive—permitting easy firing from the shoulder. All Savage Model 99 rifles are made with barrels of "Hi-Pressure" steel, especially adapted to modern smokeless powder high power cartridges. Sportsmen around the world know the Savage reputation for barrel accuracy.

GENERAL SPECIFICATIONS

Hammerless, solid breech, lever action. Hi-Pressure steel barrel, polished breech bolt, case hardened lever, blued receiver. Varnished American Walnut stock and forearm. Steel butt plate. White metal bead front sight on raised ramp base and adjustable semi-buckhorn sporting rear sight. Six shots, magazine capacity five cartridges. Magazine rotary box type with numerical indicator. Hammer indicator showing automatically cocked or fired position of hammer. Made in 8 styles and 5 calibers.

CALIBERS OF THE 99 MODELS

.22 Savage Hi-Power—Accurate at long ranges. The ideal cartridge for use on small and medium game, from woodchucks to wolves. For use in Savage Rifles: Models 99-E, 99-F, 99-G and 99-K.

.30-30 Savage Hi-Power—Extremely popular throughout the country, this cartridge is standard for deer and similar game at moderate ranges. Possesses splendid accuracy. For use in Savage Rifles: Models 99-A, 99-B, 99-E, 99-F, 99-G, 99-K, 99-H Carbine.

.303 Savage Hi-Power—Famous for over twenty-five years for its deadly accuracy and hard hitting. Dependable for deer, caribou and black bear. A fine cartridge in timbered country. For use in Savage Rifles: Models 99-F, 99-G, 99-EG, 99-K, 99-R, 99-T and Model 99-H Carbine.

.250-3000 Savage Hi-Power—Noted for its high speed and accuracy, this cartridge is powerful enough for any animal in North America. Excellent for mountain sheep, goats, deer, etc. For use in Savage Rifles: Models 99-F, 99-EG, 99-G, 99-K, 99-R, 99-RS, 99-T.

.300 Savage Hi-Power—For biggest American game, this is a super-modern cartridge, similar in ballistics to the .30 Springfield-Government Cartridge. Ideal for Alaskan bear, moose, and elk. For use in Savage Rifles: Models 99-F, 99-EG, 99-G, 99-K, 99-R, 99-RS, 99-T.

MODEL 99-F

FOR BIG GAME

CALIBERS: Model F, .22 Hi-Power, .30-30, .303 and .250-3000 with 22 in. barrel. .300 with 24 in. barrel.

Model 99-F. Takedown. Tapered round barrel. Raised ramp front sight base. Shotgun butt. Weight about 7½ pounds.

Model 99-F Takedown is the featherweight design, so called, because the shorter barrel and straight stock with shotgun butt plate makes this rifle, which is chambered for the most powerful cartridges, quick handling and easy to carry. Stock dimensions, 1⅞ x 2⅝ x 13 inches. Butt plate 1½ x 4⅞ inches. Matted trigger.

Model 99-F, Takedown $53.50

MODELS 99-G & EG

FOR BIG GAME

CALIBERS: .22 Hi-Power, .30-30, .303 and .250-3000 with 22 inch barrel. .300 with 24 inch barrel.

Model 99-G. Takedown. Tapered round barrel. Raised ramp front sight base. Shotgun butt, full pistol grip, checkered stock and forearm, checkered trigger and corrugated steel butt plate. Matted trigger. Weight about 7¾ pounds.

The Savage Model 99, Style G is our most popular rifle and is selected by sportsmen who desire a rifle of moderate weight, fine finish and extreme efficiency. Especially adapted to high concentration cartridges because of the exceptional strength and safety of the action. Ideal for all American game.

Model 99-EG is same as the Model 99-G, but solid frame and without checkering.

Model 99-G, Takedown $55.25
Model 99-EG, Solid Frame—No Checkering 47.40

MODEL 99-T—FEATHERWEIGHT

FOR BIG GAME

CALIBERS: .22 Hi-Power, .30-30, .303 and .250-3000 with 20 inch barrel. .300 with 22 inch barrel.

Model 99-T. Solid Frame. Featherweight. Tapered, light weight, round barrel with raised ramp front sight base. Barrel length 20 inches for .250/3000, .303, .30/30 and .22 Hi-Power cartridges; 22 inch barrel for .300 Savage cartridges. Sights: red bead front, new semi-buckhorn rear, without sighting notch. Light weight full pistol grip stock and large wide forearm of selected walnut, oil finished. Forearm dimensions: 10½ inches long, 1½ inches wide and 2 inches deep. Stock dimensions 1⅞ inches drop at comb, 2⅝ inches drop at heel, 13 inches long. Butt plate 1½ x 4⅞ inches. Matted trigger. Weight 7 pounds.

Model 99-T, Solid Frame $53.50

.410 BORE SHOTGUN BARREL FOR MODEL 99 TAKEDOWN RIFLE

.410 Bore Auxiliary Shotgun Barrel—Interchangeable with all caliber rifle barrels on Savage Model 99 Takedown Rifles. Rifle should be sent to factory for necessary fitting or adjusting to the receiver. For 2½" .410 gauge shells only. Shells do not function through magazine. In ordering, specify style, caliber and serial number of rifle. Weight about 2 pounds. Length 22 or 24 inches.

Price $7.10

A NEW GUN CARRIES A FACTORY GUARANTEE

SAVAGE MODEL 99 HIGH POWER RIFLES

MODEL 99-H CARBINE

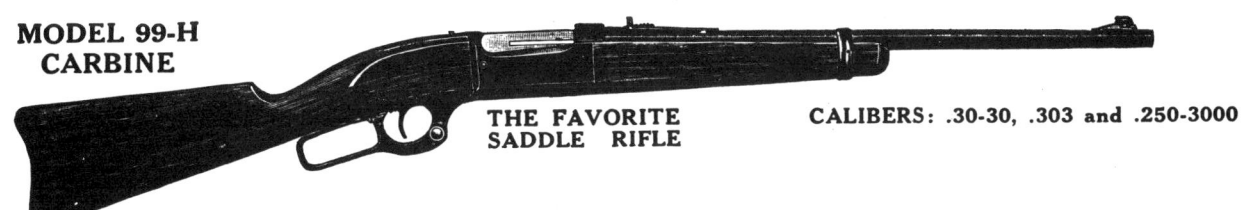

THE FAVORITE SADDLE RIFLE

CALIBERS: .30-30, .303 and .250-3000

Model 99-H Carbine—Solid Frame. 20-inch special medium weight barrel. Walnut carbine stock and forearm. Steel butt plate. Adjustable semi-buckhorn rear sight and bead front sight. Weight 6½ pounds. Matted trigger.

The Savage Carbine has been designed for men who require a compact, sturdy, well-balanced rifle, for use in the saddle or in thickly timbered country. A rifle that is light and fast in action, but which packs a blow with sufficient power for big game.

Note its clean-cut lines, not an extra ounce of weight anywhere, and it holds firm and steady. Its barrel is made of the same "Hi-Pressure" steel that goes into all other Savage Model 99 barrels and is rifled and chambered in accordance with the exact Savage standards. These features combine to make this rifle admirably suited for guides, trappers and sportsmen desiring a sturdy rifle for rough, exacting service at a low price.

Model 99-H Carbine—solid frame **$45.40**

MODEL 99-R

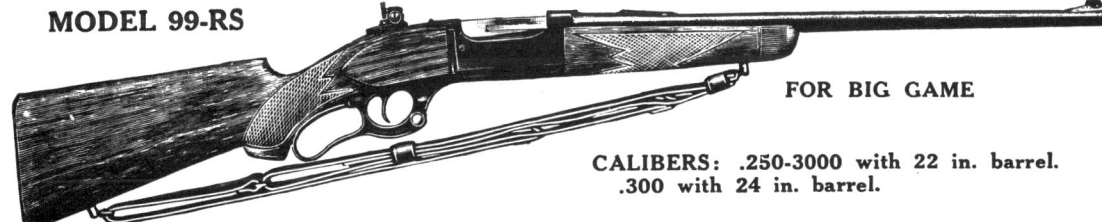

THE IDEAL DEER RIFLE

CALIBERS: .250-3000 and .303 with 22 in. barrel. .300 with 24 in. barrel.

Model 99-R—Solid Frame. Tapered medium weight round barrel. Raised ramp front sight base. Special large stock and forearm of selected walnut, oil finish, corrugated steel butt plate of shotgun design. Full pistol grip stock. Fine checkering on grip and forearm. Adjustable Semi-Buckhorn rear sight and gold bead front sight. Matted trigger. Weight about 7¼ pounds.

The Model 99-R has been designed to meet the demands of expert riflemen requiring a solid frame rifle of extreme accuracy. An ideal deer rifle.

Model 99-R, solid frame **$54.00**

MODEL 99-RS

FOR BIG GAME

CALIBERS: .250-3000 with 22 in. barrel. .300 with 24 in. barrel.

Model 99-RS. Solid Frame. Same specifications as Model 99-R with following refinements: Lyman windgauge and elevation adjustment rear peep sight, Lyman folding leaf middle and gold bead front sight. Also equipped with ⅞ inch combined adjustable leather sling and carrying strap with quick release swivels and screw studs. Weight about 7½ pounds.

The Model 99-RS is the same rifle as the Model 99-R, with additional equipment consisting of special sights, with accurate windage and elevation adjustments and a sling strap, which is provided for ease in carrying and as an aid to steady holding.

Model 99-RS, solid frame **$64.60**

MODEL 99-K

FOR BIG GAME

CALIBERS: .22 Hi-Power, .30-30, .303 and .250-3000 with 22 inch barrel. .300 with 24 inch barrel.

Model 99-K—Take-down. Same specifications as Model 99-G with following refinements: Selected American walnut stock and forearm—special fancy hand checkering on forearm, panels and grip. Receiver and barrel artistically engraved. Action carefully fitted and stoned. Lyman rear peep sight, folding middle sight and gold bead front sight. Matted trigger.

The Model 99-K is our finest grade rifle and is a beautiful specimen of the gunmaker's art. The checkering and engraving are unusually attractive.

Model 99-K, Takedown **$85.75**

ALL SHIPMENTS ARE INSURED

SAVAGE BOLT ACTION SMALL AND LARGE BORE RIFLES

A rifle that American sportsmen have craved for years—embodying many features heretofore found only in expensive, imported rifles. Chambered for such outstanding cartridges as the famous .30-'06 Springfield and .30-30, .250-3000 and .300 Savage, the Sporter Rifle is a quality arm at a remarkably low price.

The bolt is completely housed in against dirt, snow, etc. The ignition is exceptionally rapid, the firing pin having only ⅜-inch stroke. Another feature is the hunter's ability to insert a fresh magazine while the bolt is closed and a loaded cartridge is in the chamber.

BOLT ACTION CALIBERS

.22 HORNET—This cartridge is the most accurate small bore, high speed cartridge yet developed. Ideal for target shooting or for small and medium game. For use in Savage Model 23-D Sporter, and Model 19.

.25-20 and .32-20 SAVAGE HI-POWER—For all small game up to fox or wolf, these are splendid medium power cartridges. For use in Savage Rifles, Models 23-B and 23-C Sporters.

.250-3000 SAVAGE HI-POWER—Noted for its high speed and accuracy, this cartridge is powerful enough for any animal in North America. Excellent for mountain sheep, goats, deer, etc. For use in Savage Rifles, Models 40 and 45 Super-Sporter.

.30-30 SAVAGE HI-POWER—Extremely popular throughout the country, this cartridge is standard for deer and similar game at moderate ranges. Possesses splendid accuracy. For use in Savage Rifles, Models 40 and 45 Super-Sporter.

.300 SAVAGE HI-POWER—For biggest American game, this is a super-modern cartridge, similar in ballistics to the .30 Springfield-Government Cartridge. Ideal for Alaskan bear, moose and elk. For use in Savage Rifles, Models 40 and 45 Super-Sporter.

.30-'06 SPRINGFIELD—For years, an outstanding all-round cartridge in this popular caliber. Suited to every type of American big game hunting. For use in Savage Super-Sporter Rifles, Models 40 and 45.

MODEL 40 Standard Grade

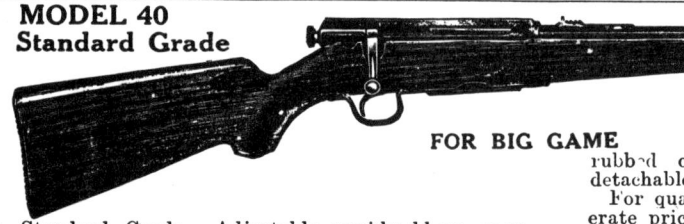

FOR BIG GAME

CALIBERS: .30-30 and .250-3000 Savage with 22 inch barrel. .300 Savage and .30-'06 Springfield with 24 inch barrel.

Model 40—Standard Grade. Adjustable semi-buckhorn rear sight; white metal bead front sight.

SPECIFICATIONS—Bolt action, solid frame repeating rifle. Tapered round barrel with raised ramp front sight base. One-piece walnut stock with pistol grip and British type forestock, rubbed oil finish; corrugated steel butt plate. Four-shot, detachable magazine, 3-shot capacity. Weight about 7½ pounds.

For quality of materials, excellence of workmanship and moderate price, the Super-Sporter equals the best commercial arms. Our technical staff has put the fruit of its many years of experience into the design and manufacture of this fine rifle—and the hunter who owns one will find years of satisfactory service built into it.

Model 40—Super-Sporter (Standard Grade).....................$45.05

MODEL 23-D

FOR SMALL GAME

CALIBER: .22 Hornet

Model 23-D—.22 Hornet Bolt Action Repeating Rifle. High-speed lock. Five-shot detachable magazine. Hi-Power smokeless steel 25-inch barrel. New design, large size, one-piece pistol grip stock and forearm of selected walnut, oil finish. Flat top, adjustable sporting rear sight and gold bead front sight. Weight about 6½ pounds.

New High-Speed Lock—The speed of the new lock is less than 2-1000 of a second. This speed eliminates shift in aim between release of trigger and ignition.

The trajectory is extremely flat and a trained rifleman can make sure hits on small game and vermin up to 200 yards.

The .22 Hornet will be found the most satisfactory small game, woodchuck and target rifle. With it the skill of any rifleman should be increased and more satisfactory results secured.

Model 23-D—.22 Hornet Sporter Rifle........................$32.70
Extra Magazine 1.10
Extras for the above rifle can be had as follows:
⅞-inch leather sling strap 1.90
1¼-inch leather sling strap 2.20

MODELS 23-B & 23-C

FOR SMALL GAME

CALIBERS: .25-20 and .32-20

Model 23-B—.25-20 Caliber Repeating, Bolt Action Rifle. 25-inch round barrel, one-piece walnut stock, full pistol grip. Four shot detachable box type magazine. Weight 6½ pounds.

Model 23-C—.32-20 (.32 Winchester) Repeating, Bolt Action Rifle. Same specifications as above.

In the introduction of the Models 23-B and 23-C Sporter Rifles, sportsmen were offered at a moderate price a bolt action rifle for small and medium game designed to handle the efficient .25-20 and .32-20 cartridges.

The barrels are made of Hi-Pressure steel and are carefully made to insure extreme accuracy. The pistol grip stock was carefully designed to give perfect balance and to maintain the attractive appearance which characterizes Savage Rifles. The loading is quick and positive—detachable box magazines are interchangeable, allowing loaded magazines to be carried and quickly changed. Safety in rear of receiver can be operated by the hand in firing position.

Model 23-B—.25-20 caliber Sporter Rifle.....................$32.70
Model 23-C—.32-20 caliber Sporter Rifle..................... 32.70

MODEL 29

.22 Caliber, Hammerless, Takedown Repeating, Slide Action Rifle

Selected walnut stock, full pistol grip, checkered. Hard rubber butt plate. Extra long checkered walnut fore-end. Tubular magazine, capacity 20 short, 17 long or 15 long rifle cartridges.

Takedown receiver, one-piece bolt easily removed for cleaning. Short fore-end stroke ejects and loads; positive operation. Push button type safety in rear of trigger guard. Adjustable flat top sporting rear sight, gold bead front sight. Stock tang drilled and tapped for all standard aperture sights, and especially for Savage No. 30 Rear Peep sight. Weight about 5¾ pounds.

Chambered for .22 long rifle rim fire cartridges. Will also function and shoot without adjustment, .22 long or .22 short rim fire cartridges. Suitable for use with either "high speed" or "regular" cartridges. 24 inch octagon barrel of selected barrel steel, rifled with same four groove system used in Model 19 Target Rifle.

Model 29—(As described above)..............................24.05
Model 29-S—Same specifications as Model 29 except equipped with Savage No. 30 rear peep sight and Savage No. 31 folding middle sight.... 26.60

A NEW GUN CARRIES A FACTORY GUARANTEE

SAVAGE SMALL BORE .22 CALIBER RIFLES

MODEL 19
TARGET RIFLE

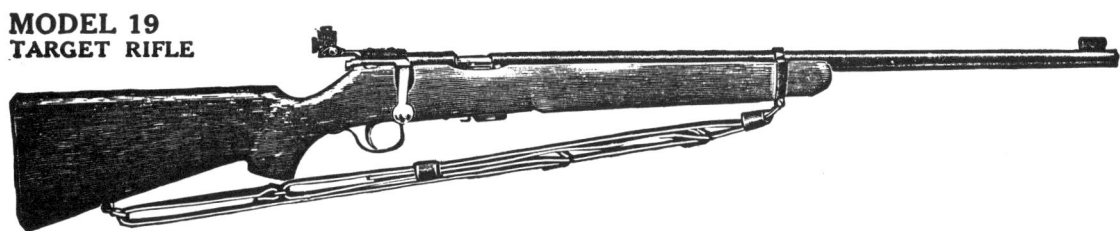

Model 19—.22 caliber repeating bolt action rifle (new design). Caliber—.22 long rifle, rimfire, suitable for use with all "high-speed" and "regular" cartridges. Stock—one-piece, oil finished, walnut, pistol grip with beaver-tail forearm full 2 inches wide, checkered steel butt plate. Drop at heel 1⅞ inches, drop at comb 1⅝ inches, length 13½ inches, butt plate 1⅝ inches wide, 5⅛ inches long, over all length stock 32 inches. Barrel—heavy 25-inch barrel, 31½ inches over all sighting radius. Magazine—5-shot, curved, detachable; positive loading; a spring snap lock at rear functions easily and locks securely. Bolt action—2 locking lugs. New high-speed lock—the speed of the new lock is less than 2/1000 of a second. Open loading port—the large loading port will be appreciated whenever rifle is used in single shot firing. Sights—New design, No. 15 Savage aperture extension rear sight with click adjustments for elevation and windage. Hooded front sight with 5 inserts. Drilled for telescope sight blocks. Weight—about 8 pounds. Equipped with 1¼ in. leather sling strap; front swivel 16½ in., forward of trigger.

Model 19-M—Heavy Barrel Target Rifle, cal. .22 Long Rifle, weight 9¼ lbs. Barrel: Extra heavy (13/16" diameter at muzzle) 28" long, 34" overall Sighting radius. Fitted with Telescope sight blocks. Sights: No. 15 Savage extension rear sight. Hooded front sight with removable hood. Adjustable trigger pull.

Model 19-H—.22 Hornet. Same sights, stock and barrel specifications as standard Model 19. Barrel is high-pressure smokeless steel. Loading port, magazine and bolt mechanism same as Model 23-D. Chambered for the sensational Hornet Cartridge. Barrel drilled for telescope sight blocks. The straight stock makes this the ideal arm to equip with telescope for target practice or precise small game and vermin shooting.

Model 19—target rifle, .22 long rifle..................$29.75
Model 19-M—heavy barrel target rifle, cal. .22 long rifle......... 36.30
Model 19-H—target rifle, .22 Hornet...................... 36.30
Model 19—less sights................................... 24.70

MODEL 23AA
GAME RIFLE

FOR SMALL GAME   **CALIBER: .22 Long Rifle**

Model 23AA—.22 caliber repeating bolt action rifle. Barrel—23-inch round; tapered. Chambered for .22 short, .22 long and .22 long rifle, regular and high speed cartridges. Action—polished bolt, double locking lugs. New high-speed lock—the speed of the new lock is less than 2-1000 of a second. This speed eliminates shift in aim between release of trigger and ignition. Lever type safety. Magazine—5-shot, detachable, curved design. Spring catch lock. Stock—One-piece stock and forearm of selected American walnut, full curve pistol grip, rubbed oil finish. Sights—white metal bead front and flat top elevator adjustment rear sight. Receiver tapped for new No. 10 Savage aperture rear sight. Weight—about 6½ pounds.
Model 23-AA—.22 caliber Sporter Rifle $23.95

MODEL 3
GAME RIFLE

FOR SMALL GAME   **CALIBER: .22 Long Rifle**

Model 3—.22 caliber bolt action single shot rifle, take-down. Barrel—26-inch round, tapered. Chambered for .22 short, long and .22 long rifle, regular or high-speed cartridges. Action—chromium plated bolt and trigger. Stock—one-piece full pistol grip stock and large forearm of selected walnut, finger grooves in forearm, steel butt plate 1⅜ x 4½ inches. Forearm 1⅜ inches wide at take-down screw, stock length 28¼ inches. Overall length 43 inches. Sights—gold bead front sight and adjustable flat top rear sight. Receiver drilled and tapped for telescope sight. Weight—about 5 pounds.
Model 3—single shot bolt action rifle $5.45
Model 3-S—Specifications—Same as Model 3 Rifle shown above, except equipped with hooded front sight with 3 interchangeable inserts and receiver rear peep sight; with elevation and windage adjustments and sighting disc with three sizes of aperture openings—large, medium and small.
Price $6.15

MODEL 4
GAME RIFLE

FOR SMALL GAME   **CALIBER: .22 Long Rifle**

Model 4—.22 caliber bolt action repeating rifle, take-down. Barrel—tapered, round, 24-inch, with crowned muzzle, for .22 long rifle, .22 long or .22 short, regular or high-speed cartridges, 5-shot detachable clip magazine. Action—all parts finely polished, self-cocking, bolt action with independent safety, chromium plated bolt and trigger. Stock—one-piece full pistol grip stock and large forearm of selected walnut, rubber butt plate. Sights—gold bead front and sporting rear with elevation adjustment. Receiver drilled and tapped for telescope sight. Weight—about 5½ pounds.
Model 4—bolt action repeating rifle.....................$10.05

Model 4-S—Specifications—Same as Model 4 Rifle shown above, except equipped with hooded front sight with 3 interchangeable inserts and receiver rear peep sight; with elevation and windage adjustments and sighting disc with three sizes of aperture openings—large, medium and small.

Price $10.70
Extra Magazine .... .65

SAVAGE AUTOMATIC AND BOLT ACTION .22 RIFLES

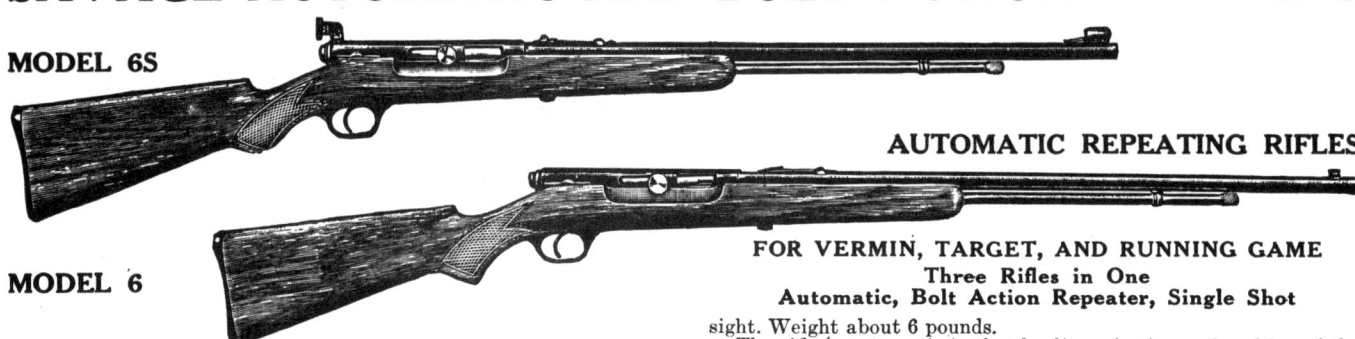

MODEL 6S

MODEL 6

AUTOMATIC REPEATING RIFLES

FOR VERMIN, TARGET, AND RUNNING GAME
Three Rifles in One
Automatic, Bolt Action Repeater, Single Shot

Model 6—.22 Caliber Automatic Rifle—Takedown. As automatic ... use .22 Long Rifle cartridges, regular or high speed, with lubricated bullets; capacity 15 cartridges. As manually operated repeater or single shot rifle ... use .22 Long Rifle or .22 Long or .22 Short cartridges; capacity 15 .22 Long Rifle, 17 .22 Long or 21 .22 Short cartridges.
24 inch tapered round barrel with crowned muzzle.
Chrome molybdenum alloy steel used in high shock parts; specially selected steels throughout; scientifically heat-treated. Cross bolt lock for use as single shot or repeater. Action easily disassembled without tools for cleaning. Convenient independent safety. Hammer release mechanism allows the firing of one shot only with each pull of the trigger.
One piece full pistol grip stock with fluted comb and large forestock of selected walnut. Checkered grip. Hard rubber butt plate.
Gold bead front and sporting rear sight, with elevation and windage adjustments. Receiver tapped for mounting Weaver telescope sight. Weight about 6 pounds.

The rifle is automatic in that loading, ejecting and cocking of the action are accomplished by the force of recoil. It is absolutely necessary to pull and release the trigged for each shot fired. If the trigger is pulled and held back only one shot will be fired. The ability to fire successive shots rapidly, increases the chance to take fast moving game usually hunted with a shotgun.
The Model 6 Rifle can be operated by hand as a single shot or as a repeater, if desired, by simply pushing in on the bolt handle.
The left side of the receiver is ventilated to allow gas and powder residue to escape. A thousand shots may be fired before cleaning is necessary.
Price $16.40

Model 6-S—Same as Model 6 Rifle except equipped with hooded ramp front sight with three interchangeable inserts. Receiver rear peep sight with elevation and windage adjustments and two sighting discs; folding middle sight.
Price $17.15

Model 602—.22 Short only $16.40

MODEL 7S

MODEL 7

AUTOMATIC REPEATING RIFLES

FOR VERMIN, TARGET, AND RUNNING GAME
Three Rifles in One
Automatic, Bolt Action Repeater, Single Shot

Model 7—.22 Caliber—Automatic Action Repeating Rifle—Takedown—Clip Magazine.
24-inch round, tapered barrel with crowned muzzle. Chambered for .22 Long Rifle, regular or high speed cartridges with lubricated bullets. Also can be used as a hand operated repeater or Single Shot using .22 Long Rifle, .22 Long or .22 Short cartridges. Chrome-molybdenum alloy steel used in high shock parts; specially selected steels throughout. Scientifically heat-treated. Cross bolt locks for use as single shot or repeater. Action easily disassembled without tools for cleaning. Convenient independent safety. Hammer release mechanism allows the firing of one shot only with each pull of the trigger.
Full pistol grip stock and large forestock of selected walnut, oil finish. Checkered grip. Hard rubber butt plate. 5-shot detachable clip magazine. Gold Bead Front and Sporting Rear Sight, with elevation and windage adjustment. Receiver tapped for mounting Weaver Telescope Sight. Weight about 6 pounds.

The rifle is automatic in that loading, ejecting and cocking of the action are accomplished by the force of recoil. It is absolutely necessary to pull and release the trigger for each shot fired. If the trigger is pulled and held back only one shot will be fired. The ability to fire successive shots rapidly, increases the chances to take fast moving game usually hunted with a shotgun.
The Model 7 Rifle can be operated by hand as a single shot or as a repeater, if desired, by simply pushing in on the bolt handle.
The left side of the receiver is ventilated to allow gas and powder residue to escape. A thousand shots may be fired before cleaning is necessary.
Price $14.40

Model 7-S—Same as Model 7 Rifle except equipped with hooded ramp front sight with three interchangable inserts. Receiver rear peep sight with elevation and windage adjustments and two sighting discs; folding middle sight.
Price $15.15

MODEL 5

TUBULAR MAGAZINE REPEATING RIFLE
FOR TARGET AND SMALL GAME

Model 5—.22 Caliber Tubular Magazine Repeating Rifle—Takedown. Fitted with 24 inch tapered, round barrel with crowned muzzle, for .22 long rifle, .22 long or .22 short, "regular" or "high speed" cartridges. Tubular magazine, capacity: 15 .22 Long Rifle, 17 .22 Long or 21 .22 Short cartridges. Self cocking bolt action with independent safety. Chromium plated bolt and trigger. All parts finely polished.

Full pistol grip checkered stock with fluted comb and large broad forestock of selected walnut. Hard rubber butt plate.
Gold bead front and sporting rear sights with elevation and windage adjustments. Weight about 6 pounds. Length over all 43½ inches. Drilled and tapped for Weaver telescope sights.
Price $13.45

Model 5-S—Same as Model 5 Rifle except equipped with target sights same as Model 6-S.
Price $14.25

AMERICA'S GREAT GUN HOUSE

Definite proof loads developing breech pressures of 17,800-18,000 pounds per square inch is the exacting test every Marlin shotgun must pass.

Painstaking attention to the smallest detail of manufacture is an established principle in the making of a Marlin gun.

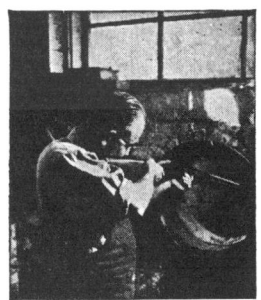

The Model 90 shotgun must also undergo a strength test. When this test is safely passed, it receives further firing tests for positive, easy action.

Small parts are machined and gauged to a thousandth of an inch. Every part must fit perfectly, for each Marlin gun is precision made.

THE MAKING OF THE MARLIN GUN

In New Haven, Connecticut, a history-making business was started in 1870 by J. M. Marlin, who began in a small shop, making single shot pistols and revolvers and the BALLARD single shot rifle under the brand "J. M. Marlin." The MARLIN-BALLARD single shot rifle became the world's outstanding target arm, because of its simple, strong action—and above all for the remarkable shooting qualities of the barrel. Its deep-cut Ballard rifling greatly increased accuracy, and is still unsurpassed.

In 1880 Marlin perfected repeating lever action rifles, a specialty of the plant ever since. Ten years later, Marlin introduced its solid-top, side-ejection construction, a notable contribution to safety and convenience. John Marlin's lever action magazine repeating rifle created a sensation. Sturdy yet light, this arm was amazingly simple and practical in design and a reliable, accurate repeater. Marlin's famous Model 39-A .22 caliber lever action repeater is today the only take-down rifle exposing all working parts for cleaning and oiling—with the turning of a single hand-operated screw!

Many have been the inventions, improvements and refinements, in the making of Marlin guns, but the basic features established by John M. Marlin 70 years ago still remain. Safe, sturdy, simple construction—positive, reliable action—fast, easy handling and high accuracy are distinguishing qualities of firearms bearing the Marlin name today.

Chambering a rifle is an exact science because a ringed chamber means a jammed cartridge. This work calls for special tools and machines, operated by carefully trained, experienced workmen.

How long wear, safety and reliable performance are built into Marlin guns is illustrated by these pictures of Marlins in the making. Hand craftsmanship has always entered largely into their manufacture. Many Marlin gunmakers have been working at their craft 30 years or more. As the guns move through the plant they are subjected to continual testing, gauging and inspecting. The infinite care which goes into the making of Marlin firearms is responsible for the easy handling, straight shooting qualities for which the guns are famous.

When you buy a gun, you want a trustworthy firearm which will give you a lifetime of safe, dependable, accurate service. The making of fine guns demands long experience and genuine craftsmanship. Marlin has made firearms continuously since 1870. Many an old-time sportsman treasures and uses the same Marlin gun he had as a youth.

One of the important tests for a repeating rifle is running dummy cartridges through the magazine. It is then loaded with regular live cartridges, fired, sights adjusted and targeted for accuracy.

MARLIN GUNS ARE OUTSTANDING FIREARMS

MARLIN BOLT ACTION AND AUTOMATIC .22 RIFLES

MODEL 80B

8 SHOT
.22 Caliber Clip Magazine Rifle

Remarkable bolt action repeater of simple, dependable design and fine accuracy. NEW features include: walnut finish, military type full pistol grip, man-size stock—"non-slip" shaped, rubber butt plate—positive thumb-controlled safety—flush take down screw—modern plastic trigger guard.

24" round tapered blue steel barrel, crowned muzzle, Ballard rifling, chrome-plated bolt assembly and trigger. Sporting adjustable rear sight, silver bead front sight. Removable bolt, automatic side ejector, self-cocking action, take down. Shoots .22 short, long and long rifle cartridges—regular and high speed, without adjustment.

Overall length 42½"; weight about 6 lbs.
NEW—Barrel Bores are specially treated with a process to impede rust or corrosion.
Model 80B $9.48

MODEL 80BE

Same specifications as Model 80B, but with special Marlin receiver peep sight, adjustable for windage and elevation, furnished with hunting and target discs. Globe target front sight, silver bead, quick detachable hood.
Model 80BE $10.19

MODEL 81B

25-SHOT
.22 Caliber Tubular Magazine Rifle

This strong, reliable, bolt action repeater features a number of important improvements. 24" round tapered blue steel barrel, crowned muzzle, Ballard rifling. NEW unique feeding mechanism, of simple, positive action, chrome-plated bolt assembly and trigger. Man-size, walnut finish, military type full pistol grip stock, hand-rubbed oil finish. Sporting adjustable rear sight, silver bead front sight. NEW positive thumb-controlled safety. Removable bolt assembly, NEW flush take down screw, automatic side ejector, self-cocking action. NEW "non-slip" shaped, rubber butt plate, NEW modern plastic trigger guard. NEW quick release trigger. Shoots .22 short, long and long rifle; regular or high speed without adjustment. Magazine holds 25 short, 20 long, 18 long rifle cartridges. Overall length 42½"; weight about 6¼ lbs.
NEW—Barrel Bores are specially treated with a process to impede rust or corrosion.
Model 81B $12.07

MODEL 81BE

Same specifications as Model 81B but equipped with Marlin special receiver peep sight, adjustable for windage and elevation, furnished with hunting and target discs. Globe target front sight, silver bead, quick detachable hood.
Model 81BE $12.77

MODEL A1-E
With Target Sights

6 SHOT AUTOMATIC
Shoots All .22 Cal. Long Rifle Without Adjustment

SPECIFICATIONS—MODEL A1-E

24" round tapered blued steel barrel with famous Ballard type rifling, crowned muzzle. Take down. Shoots .22 long rifle cartridges only, regular or high speed without adjustment. New designed large walnut finish, military type pistol grip stock. New "nonslip," unbreakable flexible rubber buttplate. New modern plastic trigger guard. New flush take-down screw. Automatic ejection. New independent thumb operated safety. Shoots as fast as you can pull the trigger. Exclusive marlin receiver peep sight, adjustable for windage and elevation—furnished with hunting and target discs. Globe target front sight, silver bead, quick detachable hood. Length overall 41". Weight about 6 lbs.
Price $13.42
Extra Magazine 1.20

SPECIFICATIONS—MODEL A1

Same specifications as Model A1-E but with Sporting Adjustable rear sight. Silver bead front sight.
Price $12.72

MODEL 100

SINGLE SHOT
Shoots All .22 Cal. Short, Long, & Long Rifle

24" round tapered blued steel barrel with famous Ballard type rifling. Crowned muzzle. Take down. Shoots all .22 short, long, and long rifle, regular or high speed cartridges. New designed large walnut finish military type, pistol grip stock. New "nonslip" unbreakable, flexible rubber buttplate. Chromium plated bolt assembly and trigger. New designed steel trigger guard. New flush take-down screw. Automatic ejection. Removable bolt assembly—gives quick access to action and permits cleaning barrel from breech end. New designed cocking knob. Rebounding safety striker. New Patridge type front and rear sights. Length overall 40½". Weight about 4½ lbs.
Price $5.35

TELL OTHERS ABOUT STOEGER'S CATALOG

MARLIN LEVER ACTION .22 AND HIGH POWER RIFLES

MODEL 39-A

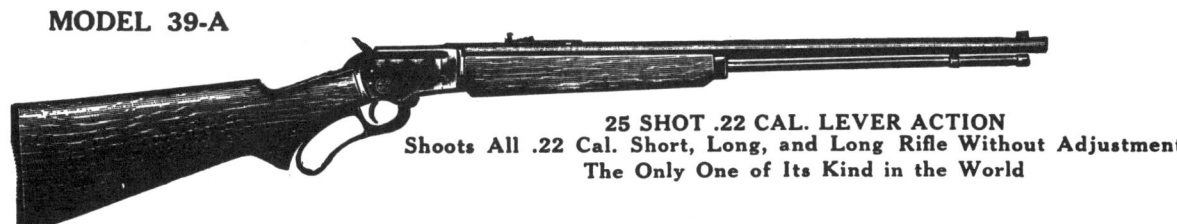

25 SHOT .22 CAL. LEVER ACTION
Shoots All .22 Cal. Short, Long, and Long Rifle Without Adjustment
The Only One of Its Kind in the World

SPECIFICATIONS—MODEL 39-A

Take down. 24½" semi-heavy round, tapered, blued steel barrel with unsurpassed famous Ballard type rifling. Crowned muzzle. Full magazine. Holds 25 short, 20 long or 18 long rifle cartridges Shoots all .22 short, long and long rifle cartridges, both regular and high speed without change or adjustment. Solid top, case hardened, receiver. Side ejection. New designed pistol grip buttstock of genuine American walnut. New large corrugated buttplate of light, unbreakable material. New designed long semi-beaver tail forearm. The only take down rifle exposing all working parts for cleaning and oiling. Barrel can be cleaned from breech end. Silver bead front sight. Flat top Rocky Mountain rear sight drilled and tapped for tang peep sight. Length overall 41 inches. Weight about 6½ lbs.

Price $29.77

MODEL 36 CARBINE

FULL MAGAZINE—7 SHOTS
Available in .30-30 and .32 Special Calibers
Suitable for All North American Big Game

SPECIFICATIONS—MODEL 36 CARBINE

Lever action, repeater with solid frame, 20" round tapered barrel of special smokeless steel. Proof tested, crowned muzzle. Famous Ballard type rifling. Solid top receiver, an original Marlin invention. Side ejection. Receiver and finger lever case hardened. Visible hammer. Genuine American walnut pistol grip buttstock. Length about 13¼". Drop at comb about 1⅛". Drop at heel about 2⅞". Checkered unbreakable buttplate. "Sure Grip" semi-beaver tail forearm of American walnut. Silver bead front sight. Flat top Rocky Mountain rear sight, excellent for quick, accurate shooting. Drilled and tapped for tang peep sight. Length overall 38". Weight about 6½ lbs.

Price $28.76

SPORTING CARBINE MODEL 36

⅔ MAGAZINE—6 SHOTS
Available in .30/30 and .32 Special Calibers
Ideal For Hunting in Rough Country

SPECIFICATIONS—MODEL 36 SPORTING CARBINE

Same general specifications as the 36 Carbine except steel forearm tip, new "Huntsman" non-glare ramp front sight with silver bead and quick detachable hood. Weight about 6¼ lbs.

Price $28.76

MODEL 36-A RIFLE

⅔ MAGAZINE—6 SHOTS
Available in .30/30 and .32 Special Calibers
An All Around Hunting Rifle

SPECIFICATIONS—MODEL 36 RIFLE

Same general specifications as the 36 Carbine except 24" barrel, steel forearm tip, new "Huntsman" non-glare ramp front sight with silver bead, quick detachable hood. Length overall 42". Weight about 6¼ lbs.

Price $31.29

A NEW GUN GIVES NO REGRETS

SPRINGFIELD
AUTOMATIC RIFLES
Shoot AS FAST AS YOU CAN PULL THE TRIGGER!

Try **speed shooting** with a Springfield Automatic .22 Rifle. Hit game or vermin on the run. Test your skill hitting several targets in rapid succession. Enjoy a whole new world of real sport. The Springfield Automatic is really three rifles in one—can be used as automatic, or hand operated bolt action repeater, or single shot. The rifle is automatic only in that loading, ejecting and cocking are accomplished by the force of recoil. The trigger must be pulled and released for each shot, but if the trigger is pulled and held back only one shot will be fired.

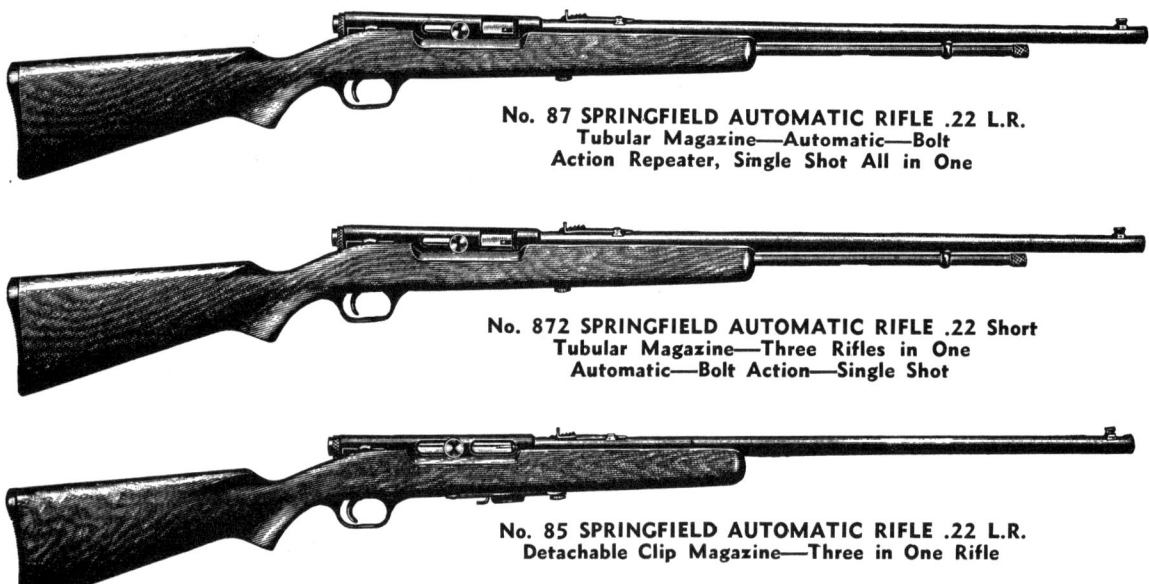

No. 87 SPRINGFIELD AUTOMATIC RIFLE .22 L.R.
Tubular Magazine—Automatic—Bolt
Action Repeater, Single Shot All in One

No. 872 SPRINGFIELD AUTOMATIC RIFLE .22 Short
Tubular Magazine—Three Rifles in One
Automatic—Bolt Action—Single Shot

No. 85 SPRINGFIELD AUTOMATIC RIFLE .22 L.R.
Detachable Clip Magazine—Three in One Rifle

No. 87 Springfield Automatic—Operates as an AUTOMATIC Rifle with .22 long rifle cartridges, regular or high speed, with lubricated bullets. Hammer release mechanism allows the firing of one shot only at each pull of the trigger. Magazine capacity 15 .22 long rifle cartridges.

Operates as a **single shot** or **bolt action repeating rifle** with .22 long rifle, .22 long or .22 short cartridges. Pressing cross bolt to the left when action is closed locks the action and adapts the rifle to use as a single shot or repeater. Magazine capacity 15 .22 long rifle, 17 .22 long or 21 .22 short cartridges.

Tubular magazine. Takedown. 24 in. barrel with crowned muzzle. Walnut finish pistol grip stock. Hard rubber butt plate. Equipped with gold bead front and sporting rear sight with elevation adjustment. Action easily disassembled for cleaning without the use of tools. Receiver tapped for Weaver telescope sight.................$14.85

No. 087—.22 Long Rifle—Same as No. 87 except equipped with hooded front sight with three interchangeable inserts, rear peep sight with two sighting discs and folding flat top middle sight.................$15.50

No. 087C—.22 Long Rifle—Same as 087 except fitted with cheek-piece stock.................$15.80

No. 872 Springfield Automatic—.22 Short—Operates as an AUTOMATIC Rifle with .22 SHORT cartridges, with lubricated bullets, regular or high speed.

Operates as a SINGLE SHOT or BOLT ACTION REPEATING Rifle with .22 short cartridges, lubricated or unlubricated, regular or high speed. Tubular magazine, capacity 21 .22 short cartridges.

Other specifications same as No. 87 Rifle.........$14.85

No. 85 Springfield Automatic Rifle—**.22 L.R.**—Operates as an AUTOMATIC Rifle with .22 long rifle cartridges, regular or high speed with lubricated bullets. Hammer release mechanism allows the firing of one shot only at each pull of the trigger.

Operates as a SINGLE SHOT or BOLT ACTION REPEATING Rifle with .22 long rifle, .22 long or .22 short cartridges. Pressing cross bolt to the left when action is closed locks the action to use as a single shot or repeater.

Detachable clip magazine, capacity 5 .22 long rifle cartridges. Takedown. 24 in. barrel with crowned muzzle. Walnut finish pistol grip stock. Hard rubber butt plate. Equipped with gold bead front sight and sporting rear sight with elevation adjustment. Action easily disassembled for cleaning without the use of tools. Receiver tapped for Weaver telescope sight................$12.75

No. 085 Springfield Automatic Rifle—**.22 L.R.**—Same specifications as No. 85 except equipped with hooded ramp front sight with three interchangeable inserts, removable hood, folding sporting middle sight and receiver peep sight with two sighting discs.........................$13.40

FAST, ACCURATE SHOOTING WITH SPRINGFIELD

AMERICA'S GREAT GUN HOUSE

The 4 Newest Models of a Maker Famous Since "Schutzen" Club Days

STEVENS "WALNUT HILL"

Down through the past 70 years STEVENS has clung faithfully to the ideals and high standard established by its founder. How much so, is exemplified by these four latest Stevens Models Nos. 417, 417½, 418 and 418½ ... developments and modernization of famous Stevens rifles that made many world records and were the choice of experts in the days of the "Schutzen" rifle clubs and famous shooting matches.

NO. 417
for Target Shooting

STEVENS "WALNUT HILL" HEAVY TARGET RIFLE

For HiSpeed or regular cartridges. BARREL—28 inch heavy, round, tested for accuracy. FRAME—Casehardened. ACTION—Original Stevens "Ideal" Breech Block. Automatic Ejector, Lever Action, Short, Fast Hammer Fall. STOCK—American Walnut 13½-inch, Oil Finish, High Comb, Full Pistol Grip Target Model Stock and Forearm, Fitted with 1¼-inch military Style, Neatsfoot Oil Treated Sling Strap, Shotgun Butt with Steel Butt Plate. SIGHTS—Standard Equipment Lyman No. 17A Front, Telescope Blocks, Lyman No. 48L Receiver Sight. WEIGHT—about 10½ pounds. AMMUNITION—.22 Long Rifle

No. 417-0, fitted with Lyman No. 52L Extension Sight. **$55.85**
No. 417-1, fitted with Lyman No. 48L Sight......... **54.35**
No. 417-2, fitted with Lyman No. 144 Sight in place of No. 48L **48.45**
No. 417-3, without front or rear sights **43.00**
Extra heavy 29 inch barrel add to above prices $25.00

NO. 417½
for Small Game

STEVENS "WALNUT HILL" HEAVY "WALNUT HILL" RIFLE

For HiSpeed or regular cartridges. BARREL—28 inch, Tapered Round, Light Weight, Tested for accuracy. FRAME—Casehardened. ACTION—Original Stevens "Ideal" Breech Block, Positive Extractor, Short, Fast Hammer Fall, Independent Safety Notch on Hammer, Lever Action. STOCK—American Walnut, Oil Finish, High Comb, Full Pistol Grip Stock and Sporting Forearm, Fitted with 1¼ inch Military Style, Neatsfoot Oil Treated Sling Strap, Shotgun Butt with Steel Butt plate. SIGHTS—Lyman No. 28 Gold Bead 3/32 inch Front, Single Folding Leaf Middle, and Lyman No. 144 Tang Peep Sight with Click Adjustment for Elevation and Windage Barrel Tapped for Telescope Blocks. WEIGHT—About 8¼ to 8½ pounds. AMMUNITION—.22 Long Rifle, Regular or High Speed. .22 W.R.F. Regular or High Speed. .25 Stevens R.F. **$43.00**

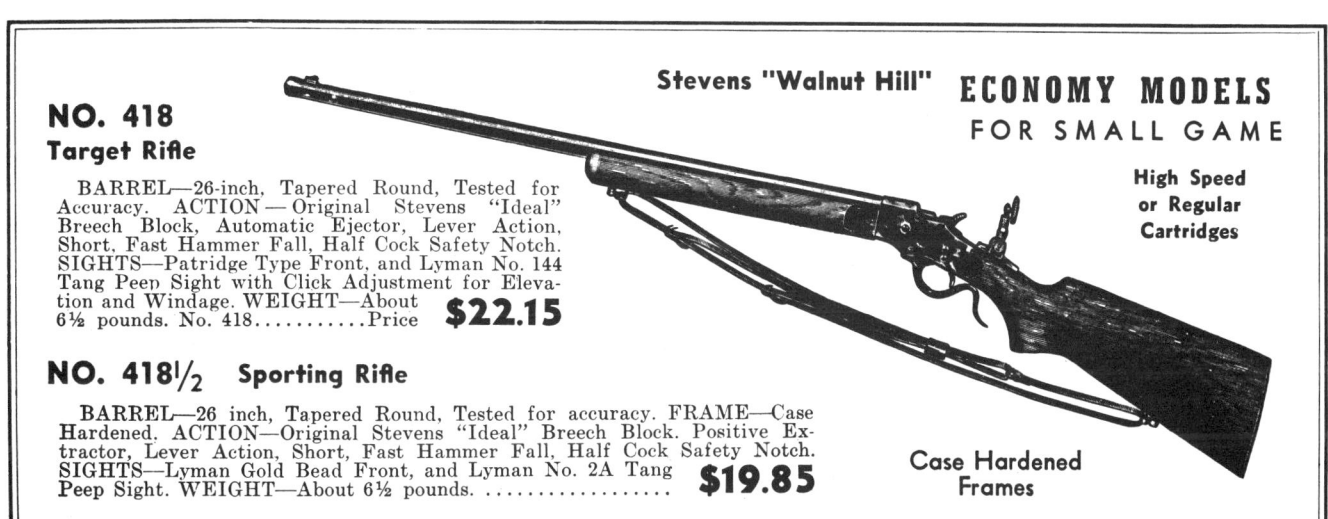

Stevens "Walnut Hill" ECONOMY MODELS FOR SMALL GAME

High Speed or Regular Cartridges

Case Hardened Frames

NO. 418
Target Rifle

BARREL—26-inch, Tapered Round, Tested for Accuracy. ACTION—Original Stevens "Ideal" Breech Block, Automatic Ejector, Lever Action, Short, Fast Hammer Fall, Half Cock Safety Notch. SIGHTS—Patridge Type Front, and Lyman No. 144 Tang Peep Sight with Click Adjustment for Elevation and Windage. WEIGHT—About 6½ pounds. No. 418..........Price **$22.15**

NO. 418½ Sporting Rifle

BARREL—26 inch, Tapered Round, Tested for accuracy. FRAME—Case Hardened. ACTION—Original Stevens "Ideal" Breech Block. Positive Extractor, Lever Action, Short, Fast Hammer Fall, Half Cock Safety Notch. SIGHTS—Lyman Gold Bead Front, and Lyman No. 2A Tang Peep Sight. WEIGHT—About 6½ pounds. **$19.85**

STEVENS RIFLES ARE MODERN RIFLES

STEVENS BUCKHORN RIFLES

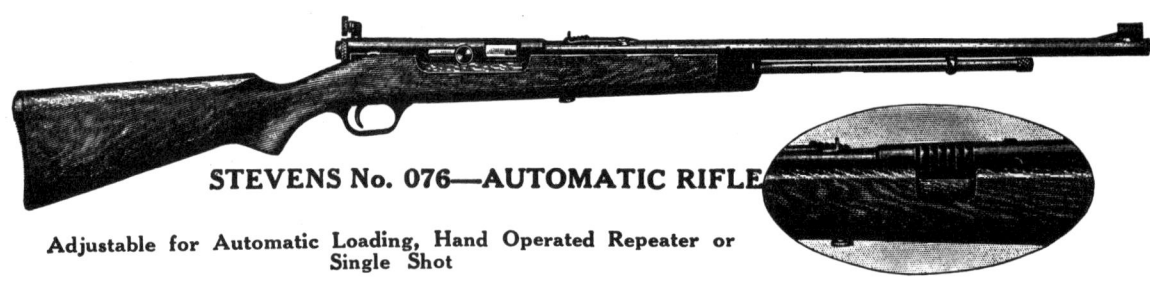

STEVENS No. 076—AUTOMATIC RIFLE

Adjustable for Automatic Loading, Hand Operated Repeater or Single Shot

These rifles are the latest in .22 caliber bolt action. The appearance shows the stock is the right shape with full forearm nicely finished with a black forend tip. The action is safe and stands all low pressure and high speed cartridges. The barrel gives accurate performance as expected of the famous Stevens make. The sights are adjustable and come with inserts for Game and Target shooting.

TUBULAR MAGAZINE—15 .22 Long Rifle, regular or high speed with lubricated bullets for automatic loading. For use as a single shot or bolt action repeater with .22 short, long or long rifle cartridges.

TAKEDOWN—24-inch tapered round barrel with crowned muzzle. Cross bolt locks for use as single shot or repeater. Independent safety. Hammer release mechanism allows the firing of one shot only at each pull of the trigger. Stock: Full pistol grip, American walnut, hard rubber butt plate. Equipped with hooded front sight with three interchangeable inserts, receiver rear peep sight with 2 sighting disc. and folding flat top middle sight. Weight about 6 lbs.

No. 076 .... Price **$16.55**
No. 76—Same as above except equipped with gold bead and open rear sights .... Price **15.80**
No. 762—.22 short only .... Price **15.80**

MODEL 053

FOR TARGET SHOOTING AND SMALL GAME

Caliber .22 Long Rifle, .22 W. R. F. or .25 Stevens R. F.

Single Shot. Chambered for .22 long rifle, .22 W.R.F. or .25 Stevens R.F. regular and high-speed cartridges. The .22 L.R. will also shoot .22 long and .22 short. The .25 short may be used in place of .25 Stevens R.F. Barrel: 24 inch, round, tapered, rifled for supreme accuracy. Crowned muzzle. Take-down. Bolt action with independent safety. Stock: Large size, broad forearm, full pistol grip. Walnut stock with Black Tip and Rubber Butt Plate. Sights: Hooded Ramp Front Sight with three interchangeable inserts, Removable Hood; Folding Sporting Middle Sight and Receiver Rear Sight with Three Aperture Sighting Disc. Weight: About 5½ pounds. Length: 41¼ inches.
Price **$6.15**

No. 53—Same as 053 except fitted with Gold Bead front sight and sporting rear sight with elevation and windage adjustment.
Price **$5.45**

MODEL 056

FOR TARGET SHOOTING AND SMALL GAME

Caliber .22 Long Rifle.

6-Shot Repeater. Chambered for .22 long rifle regular and high-speed cartridges. Will also shoot .22 long and .22 short. Barrel: 24 inch, round, tapered, bored and rifled for supreme accuracy. Crowned muzzle. 5-shot detachable clip magazine. Bolt Action: Independent safety. Stock: Large, broad forearm, full pistol grip. Walnut stock with Black Tip and Rubber Butt Plate. Sights: Hooded Ramp Front Sight with three interchangeable inserts, Removable Hood; Folding Sporting Middle Sight and Receiver Rear Sight with Three Aperture Sighting Disc. Weight: About 6 pounds. Length: 43½ inches.
Price **$10.25**

No. 56—Same as 056 except fitted with Gold Bead front sight and sporting rear sight with elevation and windage adjustment.
Price **$9.60**

MODEL 066

FOR TARGET SHOOTING AND SMALL GAME

Caliber .22 Long Rifle.

Tubular Magazine Repeater. Chambered for .22 long rifle regular and high-speed cartridges. Will also shoot .22 long and .22 short. Barrel: 24 inch, round, tapered, bored and rifled for supreme accuracy. Crowned muzzle. Magazine: Capacity—Twenty-one .22 short; seventeen .22 long, or fifteen .22 long rifle cartridges. Bolt Action: Independent safety. Extra large, "heavy-duty" bolt. Stock: Full size, broad forearm, full pistol grip. Walnut stock with Black Tip and Rubber Butt Plate. Sights: Hooded Ramp Sight with three interchangeable inserts, Removable Hood; Folding Sporting Middle Sight and Receiver Rear Sight with Three Aperture Sighting Disc. Weight: About 6 pounds. Length: 43½ inches.
Price **$13.40**

No. 66—Same as 066 except fitted with Gold Bead front sight and sporting rear sight with elevation and windage adjustment.
Price **$12.60**

CAREFUL ATTENTION AND SAFE DELIVERY OF YOUR ORDER

STEVENS-SPRINGFIELD BOLT ACTION .22 CALIBER RIFLES

MODEL 416-2 STEVENS TARGET RIFLE

For .22 R. F. Long Rifle Cartridges

A NEW MATCH RIFLE
Fully Equipped—Guaranteed Accuracy

This new rifle represents the most recent offering in the .22 target line and is a genuine contribution by the Stevens factory to the small bore shooter. For the first time a really substantial, well proportioned match rifle with proper weight, balance, trigger pull, target sights and great accuracy is available at a price within reach of many who formerly had to content themselves with inferior rifles.

No. 416-2 Specifications:
Barrel—26-inch. Heavy Tapered Round, .22 Long Rifle. A five shot machine rest group with each rifle guarantees extreme accuracy.
Action—Bolt Action, Five Shot Clip Magazine, Speed Lock, Adjustable Trigger Pull, Bolt Handle of design to permit telescope sight in low position giving same sighting plane as regular sights, Independent Safety with Red Dot Indicator.
Stock—American Walnut, Oil Finish, Adjustable Front Sling Loop, Fitted with 1¼-inch Neats-foot Oil Treated Leather Sling, Checkered Steel Butt Plate.
Sights—New Stevens No. 25 Hooded Front Sight with Five Removable Inserts, and No. 106 Peep Sight, Telescope Blocks.
Weight—With Sling Strap about 9½ pounds.
Ammunition—.22 Long Rifle Regular or High Speed.

No. 416-2 ....$29.80
No. 416-3 (without sights) 25.00

MODEL 083

FOR SMALL GAME AND TARGET

Caliber .22 Long Rifle, .22 Long, .22 Short, .22 W. R. F., or .25 Stevens R. F.

Barrel—24-inch Round, Tapered with Crowned Muzzle for .22 L. R., .22 L. or .22 S. and .22 W. R. F., Regular or High Speed Cartridges.
Action—Fast Bolt Action, Self Cocking with Safety Firing Pin prevents accidental discharge. Chromium plated bolt and trigger.
Stock—Full size, Oval Military Style, Full Pistol Grip, Walnut Finish, Rubber Butt Plate, Large Take-down Screw.
Sights—Hooded Ramp, Removable Hood, Front Sight with three interchangeable inserts and receiver rear with three sighting discs. Also folding sporting middle sight.
Weight—About 5 lbs. Take-down. Length over all 41¼ inches.
Price $5.65
Price Model 83 Open Sights........................ 5.00

MODEL 084

FOR TARGET SHOOTING AND SMALL GAME

Caliber .22 Long Rifle, .22 Long and .22 Short

Barrel—Tapered, Round, 24-inch, with Crowned Muzzle for .22 L. R., .22 L. or .22 S., Regular or High Speed Cartridges, Take-down, 5 shot Detachable Clip Magazine. Action—Self Cocking, Bolt Action with Independent Safety, Chromium Plated Bolt and Trigger. Stock—Full size, Oval Military Style, Full Pistol Grip, Walnut Finish, Rubber Butt Plate.
Sights—Hooded Ramp Front sight with removable hood and three interchangeable inserts. Receiver rear with three sighting discs, also folding sporting middle sight. Ammunition—Any .22 L. R., .22 L., or .22 S., High Speed or Regular Cartridge.
Weight—About 6 pounds. Length over all, 43½ inches. $9.65
Price Model 84 Open Sights........................ 9.00

MODEL 086

FOR TARGET SHOOTING AND SMALL GAME

Caliber .22 Long Rifle, .22 Long and .22 Short

Barrels—24-inch, Round, Tapered. Take-down. The rifle has a tubular magazine with capacity of fifteen .22 long rifle, seventeen .22 long, or twenty-one .22 short, High Speed or Regular Cartridges.
Action—Self Cocking, Bolt Action, with Independent Safety, Chromium Plated Bolt and Trigger.
Stock—Turned, Walnut Finish. Rubber Butt Plate.
Sights—Hooded Ramp Front Sight with three interchangeable inserts. Receiver rear sight with sighting disc, also folding sporting middle sight. Weight—5½ pounds. Length over all, 41½ inches.
Price $12.10
Price Model 86 Open Sights........................ 11.45

STOEGER ARMS CORPORATION, 507 FIFTH AVENUE, NEW YORK, N. Y.

MOSSBERG

"Perfection in Reflection"

RIFLES TELESCOPES SHOTGUNS

"The Mossberg plant was supervised, until his recent death by Oscar F. Mossberg, a man who lived gun design and manufacturing from the day he landed as a Swedish emigrant in 1886. The heritage is now in the hands of his son, whose 25 year training began with the manufacture of pistols in an old barn. Mossberg has established a reputation of "firsts". They gave the first ramp and peep sights as standard equipment on popular priced rifles; first rifles designed for scope sight-shooting and drilled and tapped to take scope mounts; first popular type target rifles; first true left-hand rifles for the "forgotten man"; first telescope sights at reasonable prices; first sight equipment for combination use of open, peep and scope sight shooting. Below is listed an array of outstanding and exclusive Mossberg features in models now available.

LOOK AT THESE EXCLUSIVE FEATURES

1—New Mauser-type bolt handle which lays close to stock and does not interfere with low mounted scope sights when raised.

2—Streamlined magazine bar fills opening between barrel and magazine.

3—Ramp front sight with removable hood, and instant selection of 4 inserts that are permanently fastened.

4—Custom built type check-piece—an exclusive feature of Mossberg Arms.

5—1¼" screw-in type" swivels fitted on front and butt of stock.

6—1¼" quick detachable swivels—fitted on stock and fore-end—a great convenience for every shooter.

7—Open Rear sight with knurled screws for making instant elevation and windage adjustments. Elevation screw has graduations equivalent to approximately one minute, or a change in bullet impact of 1" at 100 yards.

8—Only high grade peep sights which actually swings out of the way, so that open sights or a scope can be used without removing any part of the sight. Micrometer click adjustments equivalent to ⅛" change at 100 yards. Also allows removal of bolt without losing sight adjustment. Equipped with No. 4D single aperture disc.

9—Adustable trigger pull—nothing at all to change your trigger pull from 2½ to 5 pounds.

10—Moulded streamlined trigger guard with finger grooves.

11—Grooved trigger—a feature found only in high priced guns.

12—Flush take down screw—a simple innovation that not only adds streamlined effect but avoids catching on clothing and brush. The disappearing lever enables you to tighten screw more securely than any thumb screw.

13—Safety cover plate—probably one of the most practical of recent gun improvements. Attached directly to the bolt, it covers ejection port-hole when action is closed and slides back with bolt when action is open. It also keeps dirt from getting into the action.

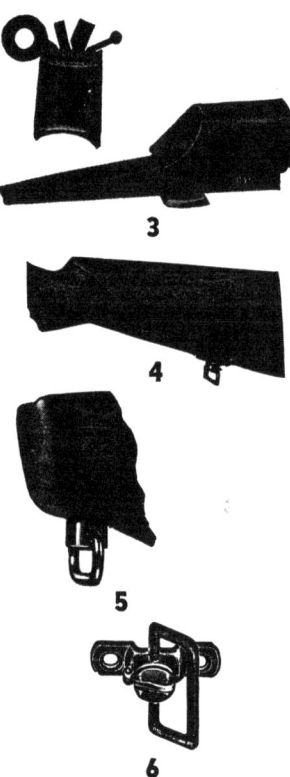
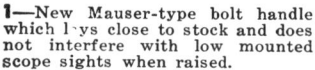

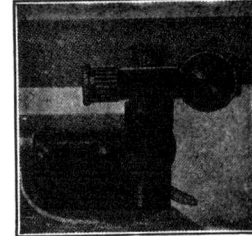

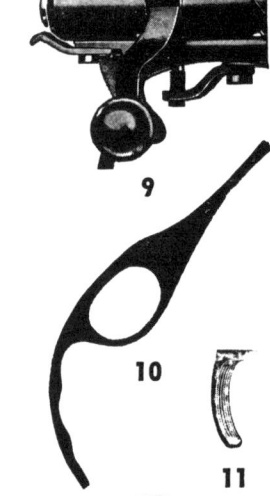

Model No.	1	2	3	4	5	6	7	8	9	10	11	12	13
26B			✓	✓			✓	✓		✓		✓	
26C							✓			✓		✓	
42B	✓	✓		✓			✓	✓	✓	✓	✓	✓	✓
42C	✓						✓			✓	✓	✓	✓
42M	✓	✓	✓	✓		✓	✓	✓	✓	✓	✓	✓	✓
44B	✓		✓	✓		✓	✓	✓	✓	✓	✓		✓
45B	✓	✓		✓		✓			✓	✓	✓		✓
46B	✓	✓	✓	✓		✓	✓	✓	✓	✓	✓		✓
46M	✓		✓	✓		✓	✓	✓	✓	✓	✓		✓
50							✓			✓	✓		
51M			✓	✓		✓	✓	✓		✓			

"PERFECTION IN REFLECTION"

AMERICA'S GREAT GUN HOUSE

MOSSBERG RIFLES

Here is a line of guns of outstanding features and remarkable values. These rifles are fitted with stocks of the latest creation for the target shooter with pistol grip allowing a hold in comfortable position and large forearm as desired. The actions on these rifles are the latest word, just drop your cartridges in and the bolt will do the rest. The self-cocking is on the forward stroke. No chance of blow backs to your face. The actions are all nicely finished. The bolt and lever are Chrome plated. All rifles are tapped and drilled for Mossberg telescopes and are equipped with sights of Mossberg's own design. Nothing has been overlooked to give you a complete rifle for the lowest price.

MODEL 26 B

Model 26 B $6.35

A single shot .22 bolt action rifle of the latest design. The barrel is 26-inch tapered, chambered for .22 short, long and long rifle cartridges, standard or high speed, equipped with Mossberg No. 1A hooded Ramp sight with 4 selective posts, new No. 2A open sporting rear sight and No. 4 micrometer click adjustment peep sight. Drilled and tapped for all Mossberg side mounting scopes. Rifle has oil finished stock with pistol grip and swivels. The action is self-cocking with safety. Total length overall 41¾ inches. Weight: 5½ pounds.

Model 26 C $5.25

The same as Model 26 B, has only hooded gold bead front sight and No. 2A open rear sight with 24-inch barrel. No swivels.

MODEL 42 B

Model 42 B $10.25

A newly designed bolt action 5 shot repeater built on the Mossberg "Master" action. Working surfaces are hardened, self-cocking bolt, lever and trigger and chrome plated with self-indicating safety. Very important is the straight line feed into the chamber, preventing deformation of the bullet. Barrel is 24-inch long for cal. .22 short, long and long rifle or high speed. Drilled and tapped for Mossberg side mounting scopes, equipped with the No. 1A Hooded Ramp sight, No. 2A open rear sight and No. 4 peep sight. The Walnut stock is designed for target shooting with the new trigger guard curved to fit the pistol grip; fitted with 1¼-inch swivels, oil finished.

Model 42 C $9.35

The same as Model 42 B without No. 4 peep sight, no swivels and hooded flat top gold bead front sight instead of No. 1A ramp sight.

MODEL 44 B

Model 44 B $16.45

A fine target rifle weighing 8 pounds with Walnut stock, large beavertail forearm and cheek piece and 26-inch heavy barrel for cal. .22 long rifle and 7 shot clip. The action has speed lock, thumb safety, grooved trigger and adjustable trigger (minimum 2½ pounds). Stock has corrugated steel butt plate and 1¼ detachable swivels with selection of 4 different positions of the front swivel. Sight equipment consists of the No. 1A front sight and No. 4 peep sight with No. 4A peep sight disc. Rifle is tapped and drilled for all Mossberg side and well as top mounting scopes.

MODEL 45 B

Model 45 B $12.25

The action of this bolt action rifle uses the tubular magazine for Cal. .22 short, long and long rifle standard or high speed. The Walnut stock is nicely shaped with pistol grip and butt plate with new flush type take down screw. The barrel is 24 inches long. The magazine holds .22 short, .18 long or .15 long rifle cartridges. Length overall of rifle is 41½ inches. Weight: 6¼ pounds.

MODEL 46 B

Model 46 B $14.25

This rifle is the most popular of the Mossberg line. A tubular magazine repeater with 26-inch barrel, equipped with ramp front sight, open rear sight and No. 4 peep sight with selective disc. Trigger pull is adjustable from 2½ to 5 pounds. Drilled and topped for Mossberg side mounting scopes. The rifle has a solid finished Walnut stock with cheek piece with full pistol grip, molded butt plate and detachable swivels. Length overall 43¾ inches. Weight: 7 pounds.

Mossberg True Left Hand Rifle.

Model L42A (not illustrated) a 8 shot clip repeater............ $13.35

PERFECTION IN REFLECTION

MOSSBERG AUTO RIFLES AND BOLT ACTION SHOTGUNS

MODEL 51M AUTOMATIC RIFLE

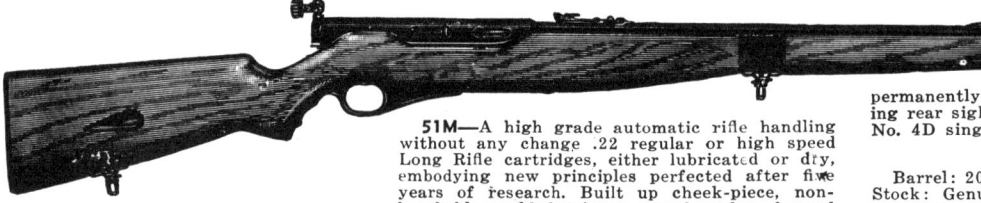

51M—A high grade automatic rifle handling without any change .22 regular or high speed Long Rifle cartridges, either lubricated or dry, embodying new principles perfected after five years of research. Built up cheek-piece, non-breakable molded trigger guard and a formed steel buttplate, quick detachable swivels, red and green "traffic light" safety indicators, chrome trigger, No. 1A hooded ramp front sight with four permanently attached inserts, No. 2A open sporting rear sight, No. 4 microclick peep sight with No. 4D single aperture disc.

SPECIFICATIONS
Barrel: 20" round tapered with crown muzzle. Stock: Genuine American walnut, oil finished, two piece custom type. Magazine: Holds 15 Long Rifle cartridges. Length: 40". Weight: 7 lbs.

Price.......................... **$17.95**

MODEL 50 AUTOMATIC RIFLE

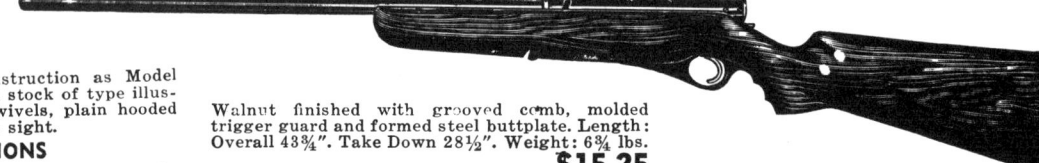

50—Same mechanical construction as Model 51M but with walnut finished stock of type illustrated, no cheek-piece, no swivels, plain hooded front sight and without peep sight.

SPECIFICATIONS
Barrel: 24" tapered with crown muzzle. Stock: Walnut finished with grooved comb, molded trigger guard and formed steel buttplate. Length: Overall 43¾". Take Down 28½". Weight: 6¾ lbs.

Price.......................... **$15.25**

MODEL 46M TUBULAR REPEATER

46M—Genuine walnut, oil finished stock with custom design cheek-piece and grooved comb also new "Safety Cover Plate," safety indicators, chrome-plated trigger, streamlined molded trigger guard with finger grooves, molded buttplate, flush take down screw, detachable swivels, new "Mauser" type bolt handle, hooded ramp front sight with 4 permanently attached inserts, No. 2A rear sight, No. 4 Micro click peep sight, adjustable trigger pull.

SPECIFICATIONS
Barrel: 23" tapered—Crown muzzle chambered for .22 short, long and long rifle regular or high speed ammunition. Stock: Genuine American walnut, oil finished, 2-piece custom design. Magazine: Holds .22 short, 18 long or 15 long rifle cartridges. Length: 40". Weight: 7 lbs.

Price.......................... **$15.95**

MODEL 42M TUBULAR REPEATER

42M—This rifle has all the features of the 46M and differs only that it is a clip magazine repeater with detachable clip of Double Duty type as illustrated and described on page 4. Magazine holds 7 shots and one in chamber. An added feature though is the "trap door" buttplate and cut out stock in which we insert an extra clip.

SPECIFICATIONS
Barrel: 23" tapered—Crown muzzle chambered for .22 short, long and long rifle regular or high speed ammunition. Stock: Genuine American walnut, oil finished, 2-piece custom design. Length: 40". Weight: 6¾ lbs.

Price.......................... **$13.95**

MODEL 83B .410 GAUGE BOLT ACTION REPEATER

410 gauge four shot repeater chambered for 2½" and 3" factory loaded shells.
Full choke 24" barrel.
Fixed type top-loading magazine holds 3 shells and 1 in chamber.
Length 43½". Weight 4¾ lbs.

Price.......................... **$10.75**

MODEL 85B .20 GAUGE BOLT ACTION REPEATER

New molded butt plates, streamlined trigger guards with finger grooves in grip, flush type take down screws, new streamlined stocks flush with bottom of magazines, self-cocking actions on upstroke of levers, selective visible safeties. 20 gauge 3 shot repeater chambered for 2½" and 2¾" factory loaded shells. Double-locking bolt and closed top receiver. Detachable type clip magazine holds 2 shells and one in chamber.
Full choke 26" barrel.
Length 47½". Weight 6¼ lbs.

Price.......................... **$11.95**

SENSATIONAL AMERICAN MADE RIFLES

A. F. STOEGER GUNS

MODEL 256
Price $350

MODEL 256L
With Lightweight
Dural Action
$385.00

MUZZLE VIEW

**HAND BUILT
OVER & UNDER
RIFLE AND SHOTGUN**

Barrels genuine Krupp steel, suitable for nitro powder, double locking extension ribs, Greener cross bolt and double underbolt, side clips, safety on neck of stock, signal pins to show if gun is cocked; checkered patent snap fore-end, checkered pistol grip, dark walnut stock, horn heel plate, very handsome engraving, high grade finish. Shooting qualities, fitting and balance are perfect. Shot barrel full or modified choke or cylinder bore, 12, 16 or 20 Gauge, rifle barrel underneath with express boring for .30-30, .25-35, .22 Hornet, or other calibers; length of barrels, 26, 28 or 30 inches.

MODEL 259
Price $485

MODEL 259L
With Lightweight
Dural Action
$535.00

MUZZLE VIEW

**HAND BUILT
OVER & UNDER
DOUBLE RIFLE
AND SHOTGUN**

This model has all the advantages of the ordinary combination Over and Under rifle and shotgun with the added advantage of a third small bore barrel which may be chambered for the .22 L. R. or even the .22 Hornet.

No. 300
Price $800.00

MUZZLE VIEW

**HAND MADE
FOUR BARREL GUN**

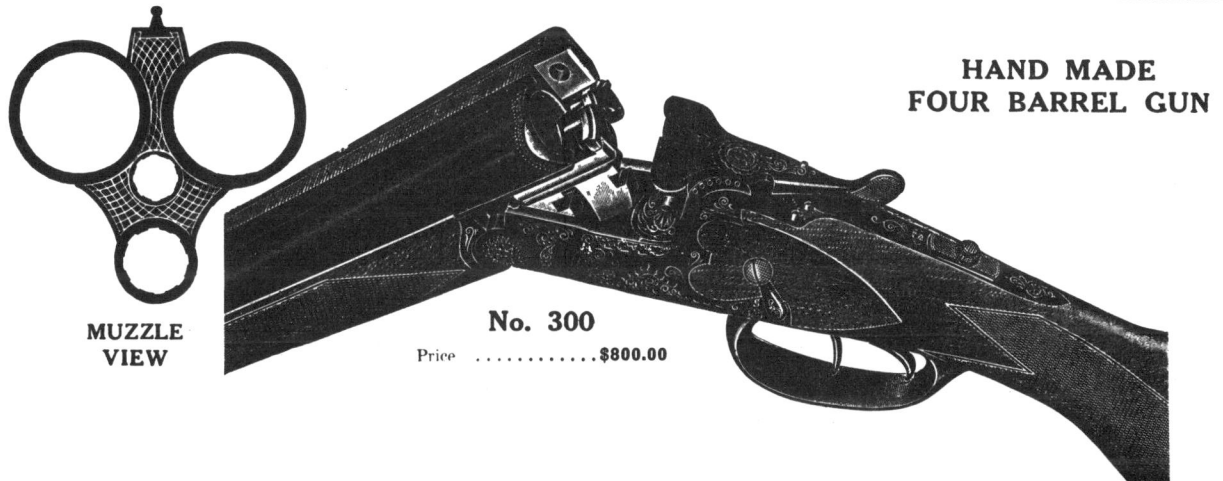

Anson & Deeley System Hammerless 4-Barrelled Gun (Vierling). This gun has 2 shot barrels side by side, 12, 16 or 20 gauge, one rifle barrel in between for .22 Hornet and one rifle barrel underneath for .30-30 or .25-35 caliber. Barrels genuine **Krupp Steel,** suitable for nitro powder, left barrel full choke, **right** modified choke, **rifle barrels** with express boring, matted extension rib, Greener side safety also a special safety upon neck of stock for rifle barrels, adjustable rear sight. Checkered pistol grip and patent snap fore-end, dark walnut stock, fine English style or hunting scenes engraving. Length of barrels 28 inches. Weight above 8½ to 9 pounds.

THE PRINCIPAL FOREIGN PROOF MARKS

We present on this page, for the first time in any American catalog an illustrated list of the principal foreign proof marks with which every owner of an imported arm is acquainted, but in most cases ignorant of their purpose or meaning.

The arms industry of Europe is far different from that in the United States. In the U. S. A. naturally the entire arms industry is in the hands of less than a dozen very large responsible manufacturers. In each of the principal European sporting arms manufacturing countries there exist hundreds of makers, from shops employing two or three skilled workmen to factories employing thousands. In order to protect both the manufacturer and the public every arm must be thoroughly examined and proof tested at an official government proof house, with an excessive load, whereupon it is re-examined and the appropriate mark stamped. Gun barrels are usually proof fired at least twice, once in the unfinished state before being fitted to the stock and action, then again when finished.

The proving of firearms has been compulsory in England and Belgium since 1672, the English standards being the highest. In 1892 Germany adopted the English standards, refusing to accept the Belgian proof, whereupon Belgium raised its standards to the same level. Today the English, German and Belgium proof marks command the highest recognition.

While there are a variety of proof marks not listed here, those not shown are for the most part obsolete, and we have compiled herewith nearly all those proof marks in common use today.

GERMAN PROOF MARKS

 1st Proof

 N Nitro — Smokeless Powder Proof

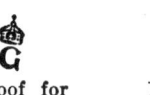 2nd Proof and Examination

 B Proof for Guns Which are Only Tested Once (Foreign Arms)

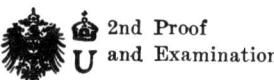

G Proof for Rifles   **R** Proof for Repairs   **S** Proof for Shot Guns   **W** Proof for Choke Barrels

Austrian-Hungarian-Tschechoslovakian

 Ferlach   Prag   Weipert   Wien    Budapest

NOTE: First Line Indicates the First Proof; Second Line Indicates Smokeless Proof.

FRENCH PROOF MARKS

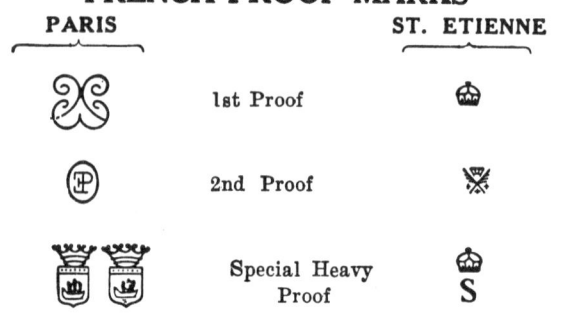

PARIS		ST. ETIENNE
	1st Proof	
	2nd Proof	
	Special Heavy Proof	

ITALIAN PROOF MARKS

P.N. (2)	FINITO	2nd Black Powder Proof
P.N. (2)		Final Black Powder Proof
PSF (2)		Smokeless Proof for Shot Guns
P.D. (2)		Smokeless Proof for Rifles and Pistols

ENGLISH PROOF MARKS

LONDON

 1st Proof

 Indicates Gauge in Shot Guns

 2nd Proof

P.N. with Sword Arm above Indicates Smokeless Powder. 577 Ex., etc., Denotes Caliber in Express Rifles

BIRMINGHAM

 1st Proof

 Proof for Single Barrel Guns With Crown Smokeless Proof

BP BV With Crown 2nd Proof

NP Shot Gun Gauge Shown Same as London

BELGIAN PROOF MARKS

Preliminary Proof

 Final Proof

Proof For Rifles

P. V. Smokeless Powder Proof (P.V.=Poudre Vive—X Proof Powder)

E. C. Smokeless Powder Proof (E.C=E.C. English Powder)

SPANISH PROOF MARKS

Eibar   Barcelona — Mark of the Proving Station (on Barrel and Action)

 Black Powder Proof

 Smokeless Powder Proof

 For All Arms

This Proof Mark Is used with Letter "R" in Circle for Revolvers, with Letter "P" for Automatic Pistols, or with Letter "E" for Foreign Arms.

Light Rifles and Pistols

SEND YOUR GUN TO STOEGER FOR EXPERT REPAIRING

THE SHOTGUN

This article is written to assist the sportsman in the choice of a shotgun to suit his needs. Space does not permit and it is not our purpose at this time, to go into lengthy technical details. We are sure however, that the novice and perhaps some others will find the following remarks helpful.

First of all, anyone starting out to purchase a shotgun after consulting his friends who may claim to be experts, will frequently find that each friend has opposite ideas regarding the specifications and make. In spite of the advice of well meaning friends, one must decide for himself about the make, the specifications and the cost of the gun which will best suit his needs. It is not difficult for the beginner to choose the proper gun. Three things must be considered; the amount to be spent, the kind of game which will be hunted and the specifications, which include the dimensions of the stock, length of barrel, choke of barrels, the weight, etc. We illustrate, describe and price many shotguns, including the single barrel, double barrel, repeating slide action, automatic, over and under and the drilling models (the conventional single or double barrel shotgun with one or more rifle barrels).

The next thing to be considered is the gauge, this means the inside diameter of the barrel tube. A glance at our ammunition pages will show shotgun gauges from the newly popularized 3 inch .410 gauge to the 10 gauge, shooting from ¾ ounces of shot to 1⅝ ounces of shot. We consider the popular gauges to be 12, 16, 20 and the new 3 inch .410 gauge. Those who wish a light weight gun should use a 20 or .410 gauge. Those who prefer a heavier gun shooting a powerful load, should choose a 12 gauge. It may be added that there are light and heavy shell loads available for each gauge. See ammunition pages.

After the gauge has been decided upon, the next matter to take up is the length of barrels and kind of choke desired. Short barrels are desirable for brush shooting, also lightness and handiness. As the barrel length increases up to about 32 inches, the velocity and consequently the power of the load are slightly increased because the powder has an opportunity for fuller combustion. For long range shooting a 30 inch or 32 inch barrel should be chosen.

The "choke" of a gun refers to the diameter of the barrel at the muzzle compared to diameter of the barrel tube. Where the diameter at the muzzle is the same as in the barrel tube, it is known as cylinder bore. If it is smaller, it is "choked" and the amount of this choke is termed, improved cylinder, modified or full choke. A cylinder bore barrel groups about 45 per cent of its shot load in a 30 inch circle at 40 yards; a full choke barrel groups about 75 to 80 per cent. It will be readily understood that the narrower muzzle bunches the shot more compactly in passing, and this compactness of the shot group gives it added range.

In double barrel shotguns the first trigger usually fires the right hand barrel, the rear trigger the left barrel. For this reason the right barrel should always have the smaller amount of choke, the left barrel the greater, because the first shot is usually shot at closer range whereas when the second shot is fired the game is usually further. Again, if small game is hit at close range with a full choke charge, it will likely be shot to pieces and so full of lead as to make it useless for food purpose. An easy way to think of the effect of choke boring on the shot string, is to visualize the shot as coming out in funnel shape, the width of the funnel being reduced the greater the choke. This matter could be discussed at great length but for all practical purposes it is enough to say that guns are usually made with 26 inch barrels in cylinder or improved cylinder choke; 28 inch barrels are usually modified or full choke; 30 inch barrels are usually made in modified or full choke. Of course on special order one may have any length of barrel from 26 inches to 32 inches bored to suit one's requirements.

For field shooting the usual choice is 26 inch barrels, cylinder or improved cylinder choke. Any gauge gun to these specifications will be found suitable for rabbits, pheasants, quail, etc., shot within 20 to 35 yards. For game to be shot up to 45 yards one should have improved cylinder and modified choke with a 28 inch barrel. For duck shooting one should have a 28 inch or 30 inch full choke shotgun, shooting two or more shots and use a powerful shell.

We are frequently asked "What is the all around shotgun?" Our advice is that a 12 gauge shotgun, shooting two or more shots should have a barrel length of 28 inches, bored modified or full choke. With such a gun one may take game in the field using No. 8, 9 or 10 shot up to 40 yards. When it comes to shooting ducks or game where the range will be from 50 to 75 yards, one can take a powerful load of No. 4, 5 or 6 shot and kill ducks in some instances up to 75 yards.

For extremely long ranges, one should use a shotgun with 30 or 32 inch barrels and bored with what manufacturers call their long range boring. Using the most powerful shells available in No. 4, 5 or 6 shot one can frequently kill ducks at 85 yards. It should be remembered that the range of a shotgun is determined by the load of the shell, the size of shot, the length and choke of the barrel. State your requirements and we shall be pleased to assist you in the choice of a shotgun.

Shotgun stock dimensions will of course vary with the individual. It has however come to be accepted that a good shot can make a credible performance using a gun of our average stock dimensions which are: length of stock, 14 inches; drop at comb, 1⅝ inches; drop at heel, 2⅝ inches. Models will often vary an ⅛-inch from the above drops and ¼-inch more or less in the length of stock. Above all, a gun should feel "natural" and comfortable to the shooter.

Shotguns may be had in most any price range. One may buy a cheap and also an expensive model and find that they each shoot about the same range. The more expensive models have more hand work and hand fitting throughout. Gun making is still an art and in the finer shotgun one will find better materials, finish, balance and beauty. Most sportsmen are particular about these matters and demand a gun which will be a lasting pride and satisfaction.

Of recent years the new game of "Skeet" has become increasingly popular. It is not only an exciting sport but it closely approximates shooting conditions in the field. It is an all year sport which enables the shooter to improve his ability in the field. Skeet shotguns usually have barrel lengths of 26 inches and are bored cylinder and improved cylinder. Although recently manufacturers have adopted a new boring for this game known as "Skeet Choke." We list skeet guns, traps and other equipment.

In shooting a shotgun it is well to remember that a natural and easy style should be acquired. Most of the best shots, shoot with both eyes open. They have become so accustomed to their gun that the aiming, leading and firing is instinctive. Shotgun shooting, as most sports, requires practice to become proficient. Skeet shooting is particularly recommended because it duplicates field shooting so closely and one may practice on the difficult shots until one becomes expert.

A study of our shotgun and ammunition pages will clear up many foggy points regarding shotguns and their use.

BROWNING AUTOMATIC SHOTGUNS

The shooting advantage of the Automatic shotgun as compared to other types are well known. After loading it is necessary only to pull the trigger for each shot. The operation of the smooth action of the Genuine Browning Automatic ejects the empty shell and reloads automatically. There are many reasons for Browning superiority which we know are deciding factors with sportsmen all over the world. A few of these outstanding reasons are: Browning's long and successful experience in gun building; perfectly balanced guns; the recoil operation which absorbs the "kick" because of the ingenious Browning Shock Absorber; the Browning system of chocking which evenly distributes the shot pattern, etc. The Browning automatic has stood the test of time—almost a generation—and because of constant research and improvements, based on experience, it is the leading and most popular Automatic Shotgun.

NOTE: Available also in a 3-shot model. The 3-shot model has a more compact magazine assembly, with shorter forearm.

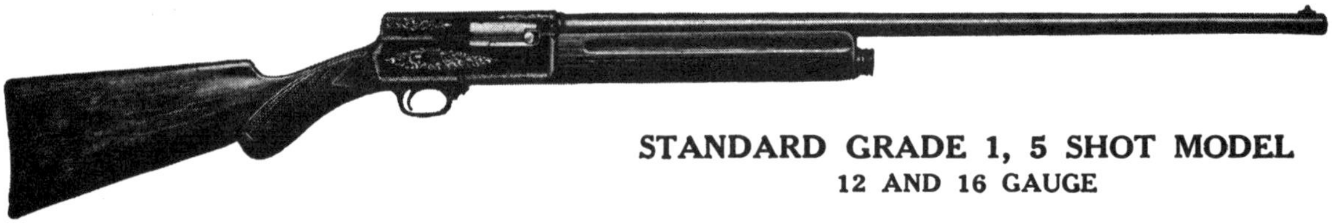

STANDARD GRADE 1, 5 SHOT MODEL
12 AND 16 GAUGE

STANDARD SPECIFICATIONS—3 and 5 shot Model

In design, material quality of workmanship and hand engraving, the 12 and 16 gauge Browning Automatics are identical—both have walnut stocks and forearms, hand finished and hand checkered—both have the same specially prepared steel barrel and hand-fitted action parts. The only differences are in size and weight. The 16 gauge is chambered for shells up to 2 9/16 inches. Weight about 7¼ lbs. The 12 gauge is chambered for shells up to 2¾ inches. Weight about 8 lbs. Stock specifications both 12 and 16 gauge are—half pistol grip—drop at comb 1⅝ inches—drop at heel 2½ inches—length 14¼ inches.

Barrel Lengths: 12 gauge, full choke, 30 inches standard, optional, 28 and 32 inches. Modified choke, 28 or 30 inches. Improved cylinder, 26 or 28 inches. Special skeet boring, 26 or 28 inches. Cylinder bore, 26 or 28 inches.

Barrel Lengths: 16 gauge, full choke, 28 inches standard, optional, 30 inches. Modified choke, 28 or 28 inches. Improved cylinder, 26 or 28 inches. Special skeet boring, 26 inches. Cylinder bore, 26 or 28 inches.

When ordering be sure to give the Grade, Gauge, Barrel Length, Choke or Bore and whether 5 or 3 shot desired. Standard length, choke and 5 shot supplied unless otherwise specified. Extra charges for changes that differ from standard specifications. Read specifications when ordering.

The difference in prices of Standard Grade 1, Browning Special, Grades 3 and 4 (both 12 and 16 gauge) is due to extra finish, selected wood, extra hand fitting, extra hand engraving and Green and Yellow Gold inlay.

Prices for the Browning Automatic Shotgun are:

STANDARD GRADE 1—Hand engraved, either gauge 5 or 3 shot without rib	$51.75
BROWNING SPECIAL—Either gauge, 5 or 3 shot with raised matted hollow rib	59.75
BROWNING SPECIAL—Either gauge, 5 or 3 shot, with ventilated rib	65.85
GRADE NO. 3—Either gauge, 5 or 3 shot, without rib	148.50
GRADE NO. 4—Either gauge, 5 or 3 shot, without rib	235.25

EXTRA barrel without rib:

STANDARD GRADE 1	19.85
BROWNING SPECIAL	19.85
GRADE NO. 3	32.70
GRADE NO. 4	43.25

EXTRA

for raised matted hollow rib, any grade	$8.00
For ventilated rib, any grade	14.10
For Beavertail forearm on new gun	6.35
For Standard Grade American Walnut stock made to special dimensions on new gun, in any grade	15.65
For high grade curly selected American Walnut stock made to special dimensions on new gun, any grade	23.30
For Circassian Walnut stock made to special dimensions on new gun, any grade	35.65

THE BROWNING "SWEET 16" GAUGE

(Not Illustrated)

Special lightweight Automatic Shotgun about 6¾ lbs. The "Sweet 16" has been produced to meet the demand of skeet and field shooters who want a lighter weight, finely finished gun—outstanding and attractive—at a moderate price. All seven exclusive Browning features in regular weight guns are in this gun, plus the additional distinctive features of lighter weight; gold-plating on trigger, safety and safety latch; special conventional foliage design, hand engraving and neat, narrower raised matted hollow and ventilated ribs. Guns without rib have striped matting on barrels.

STANDARD SPECIFICATIONS
5 and 3 shot "Sweet 16" Gauge

Barrel lengths, full choke, 28 inches, modified choke, 26 or 28 inches. Cylinder bore, 26 inches, Improved cylinder, 26 or 28 inches. Special Skeet boring, 26 inches. Matted receiver. Good quality Walnut stock and forearm, all hand-finished and hand-checkered. Specially prepared steel barrel and action parts. Stock Specifications: Half pistol grip, length 14¼ inches, drop at comb 1⅝ inches, drop at heel 2½ inches. Chambered for shells up to 2-9/16 inches. Weight about 6¾ lbs. without rib. Raised matted hollow and ventilated rib guns weight slightly more.

Price Sweet 16 without rib but with striped matting	$67.75
Price Sweet 16 with raised matted hollow rib	71.75
Price Sweet 16 with ventilated rib	77.85
EXTRA barrel without rib but with striped matting on barrel	24.60
For raised matted hollow rib	8.00
For ventilated rib	14.10

BROWNING OVERUNDER SHOTGUNS

MIDAS GRADE

The Midas Overunder startles even the connoisseur of fine arms with the richness and artistry of its embellishments. The subjects are gold pigeons with spreading wings in relief, one on trigger guard and on each side of receiver. Heavy lines of gold form a conventional foliage design around birds and receiver, extending on to trigger guard and continuing on top of barrel. The receiver is rich blue-black, furnishing a fitting on top of barrel, contrast for the gold. Stocks of choice selected walnut, finely hand checkered. Metal polishing and blueing are of the highest quality. Firing pins, ejector hammers and trip rods are gold plated.

Price with level matted rib	$285.00
Price with ventilated rib	305.00

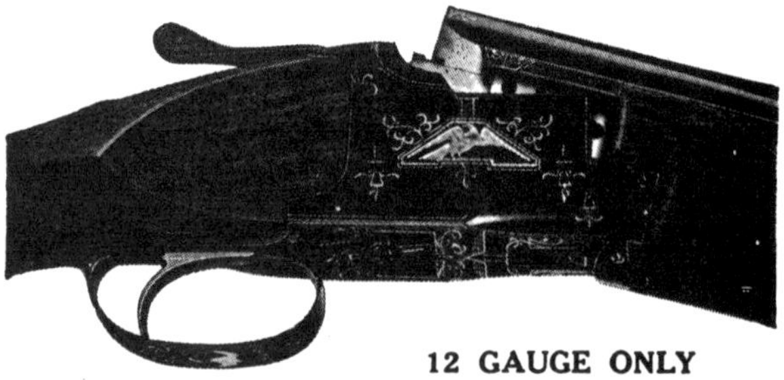

12 GAUGE ONLY

BROWNING OVERUNDER SHOTGUNS

The Browning Overunder shotguns are today the favorite of the hunter and skeetshooter. Their fine construction, under the exclusive Browning patents, excellent workmanship are recognized as a standard feature with all Browning guns. The Browning Overunder is all hand fitted and all hand finished. All Browning Overunder guns are equipped with single selective trigger and automatic selective ejectors and are hand engraved.

GRADE 1. "LIGHTNING MODEL"

12 GAUGE ONLY

The new "Lightning Model" Browning Overunder shotgun weighs only 6¾ lbs. The upper barrel has matted line and gun can be had with 26, 28 and 30 inch barrels and with the following standard choke combinations.
(c) Under barrel modified choke, over barrel full choke (d)

Under barrel improved cylinder, over barrel modified choke (e) Special skeet boring both barrels. Extra charge will be made for changes that differ from the standard specifications. All guns come with nice selected walnut stocks with pistol grip and full forend checkered. Standard dimensions are 1⅝ x 2½ x 14⅛ inches.
Price $75.80

Grade 1 Lightning Model equipped with ventilated rib, specially recommended for Skeet shooting. Weight 6⅞ lbs.
Price $89.90

GRADE 1. "STANDARD MODEL"

12 GAUGE ONLY

This particular model weighs about 7½ lbs. with 28" barrels. Same can be had with 28, 30 and 32 inch barrels with level Matted Rib. Field stock with pistol grip and forearm checkered. Not available without rib. Standard choke combinations are (a) Both barrels full choke (b) Under barrel modified, over barrel full choke. All frames on Browning guns are hand engraved.
Price $79.80

Grade 1 Standard Model with ventilated rib recommended for Trapshooting comes only with 30 and 32 inch barrels. Standard choke combinations are (a) Both barrels full choke (b) Under barrel improved modified choke, over barrel full choke. Weight about 7¾ lbs.
Price $89.90

PIGEON GRADE

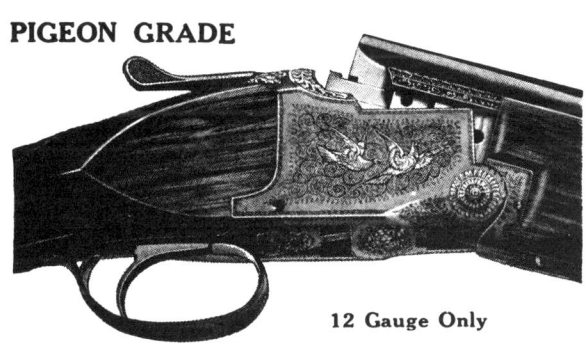

12 Gauge Only

A finely engraved and distinctive high grade gun. The receiver is finished in a rich light steel gray color, thus bringing out the finest lines of the hand engraved design of lifelike pigeons surrounded by scroll work and covering the sides and bottom of receiver. Oak leaves are artistically carved in bold relief on the top curves of the receiver. Fine line conventional designs and borders cover joints, screws and pins. Selected walnut stocks, finely hand checkered with high lustre finish.

Price with level matted rib.................$143.00
Price with ventilated rib.................... 158.00

NOTE: Available in Lightning and Standard Models, Specifications same as Grade 1 Guns.

DIANA GRADE

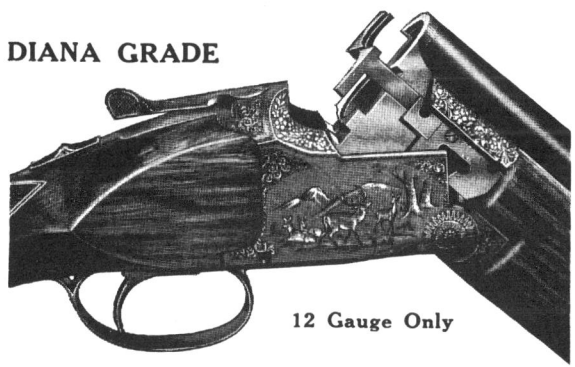

12 Gauge Only

The receiver of the Diana Grade is also finished in a rich light steel gray color, accentuating the elaborate though fine artistic hand engraved scenes of deer on one side and wild boars on the other with appropriate scenic backgrounds; pheasant subjects on both sides of receiver available, if desired, without extra charge. Flowers, etc., are hand carved in bold relief on the curves of the standing breech. We believe sportsmen will enjoy this departure in engraving from more conventional designs. Special subjects and designs supplied on special orders at additional price quoted upon request. The firing pins, ejector hammers and trip rods are gold plated. High quality selected walnut stocks, fine hand checkering.

Price with level matted rib.................$200.00
Price with ventilated rib.................... 218.00

NOTE: Available in Lightning and Standard Models, Specifications same as Grade 1 Guns.

BE SURE TO VISIT OUR SHOWROOMS

PARKER SHOTGUNS

PARKER V. H. E.

Hand-fitted, hand-finished, and made to customer's exact specifications throughout. Stock and fore-end of selected American walnut, hand checkered. German silver name shield inlaid in stock. Stock dimensions, unless otherwise specified, 14 inches long, 2½ inches drop at heel, 1⅝ inches drop at comb. Stocks made to order with lengths from 13½ to 14½ inches, and with drops from 2 to 3¼ inches without extra charge. Full pistol grip with cap, option of straight or half pistol grip. Hard rubber butt plate. Line engraving. Ivory sights if desired. Automatic ejectors. Any boring of barrels.

"V. H. E." Grade with double triggers $140.25
"V. H. E." Grade with selective single trigger 169.11

Raised ventilated rib, extra 27.75
Soft rubber recoil pad, extra 5.55
Skeleton steel butt plate, extra 8.88
Oil finishing stock and fore-end, extra 8.88
Stock outside of prescribed limits 15.14
Extra set of interchangeable barrels 72.65

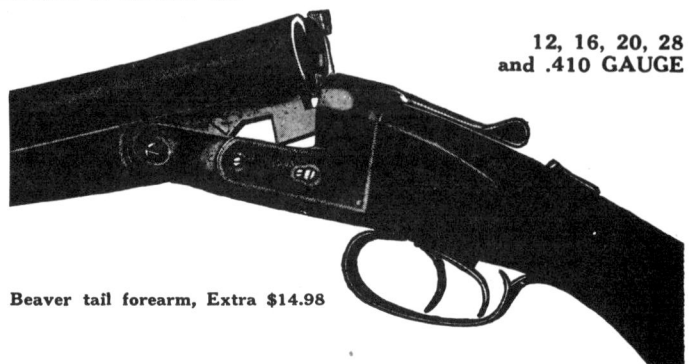
12, 16, 20, 28 and .410 GAUGE
Beaver tail forearm, Extra $14.98

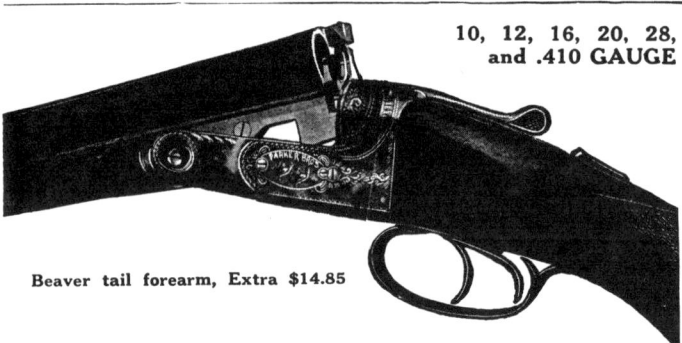
10, 12, 16, 20, 28, and .410 GAUGE
Beaver tail forearm, Extra $14.85

PARKER G. H. E.

Figured American walnut stock and fore-end, selected for natural beauty. Nicely hand checkered. German silver name shield inlaid in stock. Stock dimensions, unless otherwise specified, 14 inches long, 2½ inches drop at heel, 1⅝ inches drop at comb. Stocks made to order with lengths from 13½ to 14½ inches and with drops from 2 to 3¼ inches without extra charge. Full pistol grip with cap. Option of straight or half pistol grip. Hard rubber butt plate. Game birds and scroll engraving. Ivory sights if desired. Automatic ejectors. Any boring of barrels.

"G. H. E." Grade with double triggers $160.43
"G. H. E." Grade with selective single trigger 189.29
Beavertail fore-end, extra 14.98
Raised ventilated rib, extra 27.75
Soft rubber recoil pad, extra 5.55
Skeleton steel butt plate, extra 8.88
Oil finishing stock and fore-end, extra 8.88
Stock outside of prescribed limits 15.14
Extra set of interchangeable barrels 83.75

PARKER D. H. E.

Stock and fore-end of fancy walnut, finely hand checkered. Sterling silver name plate inlaid in stock. Stock custom-built to any specifications desired without extra charge, including cheek piece, Monte Carlo or cast off, and any style of grip. Rubber recoil pad or skeleton steel butt plate. Engraving is game scenes and scroll. Nickel plated triggers. Ivory sights if desired. Automatic ejectors. Any boring of barrels.

"D. H. E." Grade with double triggers $196.76
"D. H. E." Grade with selective single trigger 229.04
Raised ventilated rib, extra 30.27
Extra set of interchangeable barrels 110.99

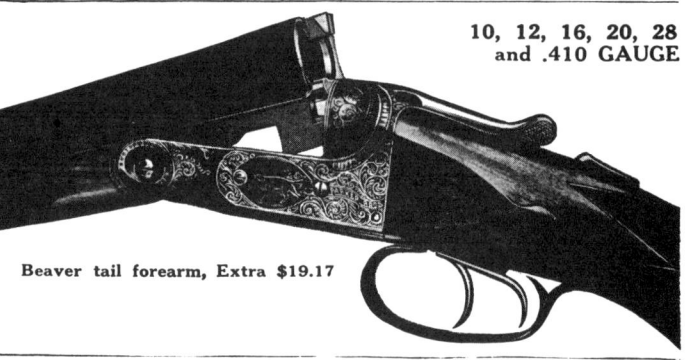
10, 12, 16, 20, 28 and .410 GAUGE
Beaver tail forearm, Extra $19.17

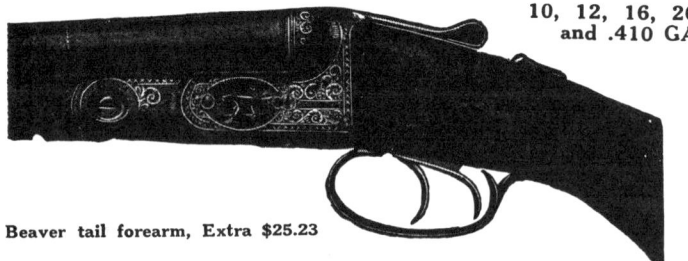
10, 12, 16, 20, 28 and .410 GAUGE
Beaver tail forearm, Extra $25.23

PARKER C. H. E.

Selected high grade walnut stock and fore-end, handsomely checkered. Sterling silver name plate inlaid in stock. Stock with any specifications desired including cheek piece, Monte Carlo or cast off, and any style of grip. Rubber recoil pad or skeleton steel butt plate. Engraving is game scenes and scroll. Nickel plated triggers. Ivory sights if desired. Automatic ejectors. Made in 10, 12, 16, 20, 28, and .410 gauges. Any boring of barrels.

"C. H. E." Grade with double triggers $292.61
"C. H. E." Grade with selective single trigger 324.90
Raised ventilated rib, extra 35.22
Extra set of interchangeable barrels 149.33

PARKER B. H. E.

Stock and fore-end of high grade walnut with fine grain and beautiful figure. Handsomely checkered. Mounted with solid gold name plate in stock or in pistol grip cap. Custom-built stock to any measurement desired, including cheek piece, Monte Carlo or cast off, and any style of grip. Rubber recoil pad or engraved skeleton steel butt plate. Scroll engraving and life-like hunting scenes. Nickel plated triggers. Ivory sights if desired. Automatic ejectors. Made in 10, 12, 16, 20, 28, and .410 gauges. Any boring of barrels.

"B. H. E." Grade with double triggers $393.51
"B. H. E." Grade with selective trigger 425.80
Raised ventilated rib, extra 35.32
Extra set of interchangeable barrels 176.58

10, 12, 16, 20, 28, and .410 GAUGE
Beaver tail forearm, Extra $29.26

PARKER SHOTGUNS

PARKER A. H. E.

Specially selected high grade figured walnut stock and fore-end, beautifully checkered. Solid gold name plate inlaid in pistol grip cap or in stock, engraved with name or monogram. Any stock measurements, including any style of grip, cheek piece, Monte Carlo or cast off. Rubber recoil pad or engraved skeleton steel butt plate. Tastefully applied engraving. English scroll or game scenes and scroll, as desired. Nickel plated triggers. Hinged front trigger. Ivory sights if desired. Automatic ejectors. Made in 10, 12. 16, 20, 28, and .410 gauges. Any boring of barrels.

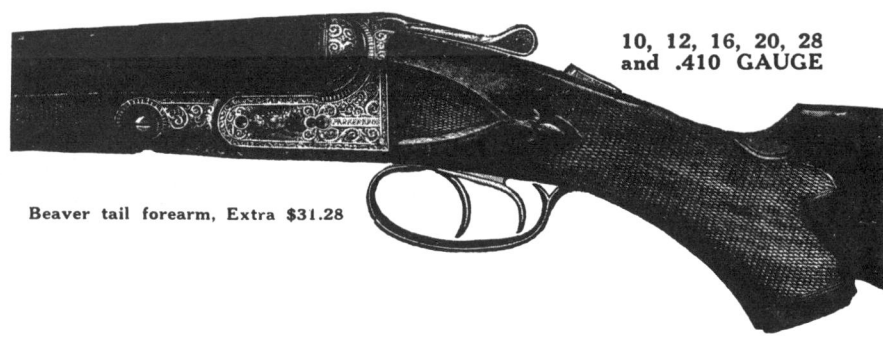

10, 12, 16, 20, 28 and .410 GAUGE

Beaver tail forearm, Extra $31.28

"A. H. E." Grade with double triggers $534.77
"A. H. E." Grade with selective single trigger 567.06
Raised ventilated rib, extra 35.32
Extra set of interchangeable barrels 227.03

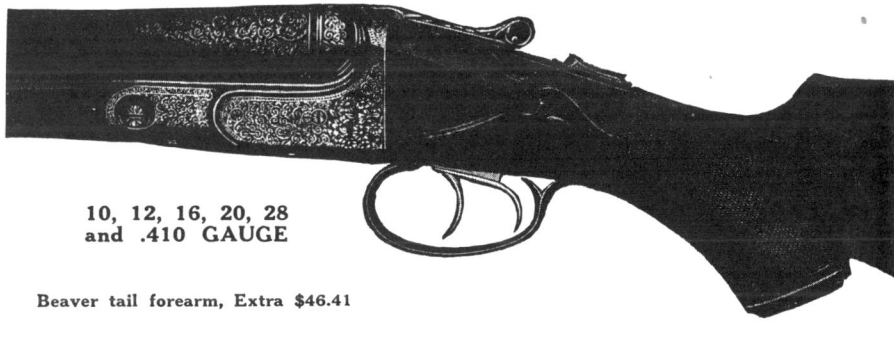

10, 12, 16, 20, 28 and .410 GAUGE

Beaver tail forearm, Extra $38.34

PARKER A. A. H. E.

Beautifully figured selected curly walnut stock and fore-end, expertly fitted and shaped by hand to customer's individual needs. Artistically hand checkered. Solid gold name plate inlaid in pistol grip cap or in stock with engraved name or monogram. Any stock dimensions including cheek piece, Monte Carlo or cast off, and any style of grip. Choice of recoil pad or engraved skeleton steel butt plate. Highest quality engraving on barrels and frame—either scroll or a combination of game scenes and scroll. Silver plated triggers. Hinged front trigger. Ivory sights if desired. Automatic ejectors. Made in 10, 12, 16, 20, 28, and .410 gauges. Any boring of barrels.

"A. A. H. E." Grade with double triggers $756.75
"A. A. H. E." Grade with selective single trigger. 798.62
Raised ventilated rib, extra 46.41
Extra set of interchangeable barrels 325.91

PARKER A-1 SPECIAL

Made to order individually. Finest obtainable specially selected curly walnut stock and fore-end. Elaborate hand checkering. Any stock dimensions, including Monte Carlo, cheek piece or cast off, and any style of grip desired. Choice of recoil pad or engraved skeleton steel butt plate. Barrels and frame extensively engraved. Gold inlay if desired. Triggers gold plated. Hinged front trigger. Solid gold name plate inlaid in pistol grip cap or in stock with owner's name or monogram. Ivory sights if desired. Automatic ejectors. Made in 10, 12, 16, 20, 28, and .410 gauges. Any boring of barrels.

"A. 1. SPECIAL" Grade with double triggers $898.01
"A. 1. SPECIAL" Grade with selective single trigger 950.48
Raised ventilated rib, extra 46.41
Extra set of interchangeable barrels..... 393.51

10, 12, 16, 20, 28 and .410 GAUGE

Beaver tail forearm, Extra $46.41

PARKER SKEET GUNS

All double barrel PARKER guns from the "V. H. E." Grade up are furnished in Skeet models. These guns are built to the customer's individual specifications. They are thoroughly tested to insure the finest shooting qualities at Skeet ranges.

Made in 12, 16, 20, 28, and .410 gauges, 26-inch barrels. Bored for Skeet shooting. Right barrel marked "SKEET-OUT" for first shot at outgoing target. Left barrel marked "SKEET-IN" for incoming target. Option of any other barrel length and boring. Automatic ejectors. Non-automatic safety. Option of automatic safety. Selective single trigger. Ivory bead front and rear sights. Red bead front sight if desired. Beavertail fore-end. Stock dimensions, unless otherwise specified, 14 inches long, 2¼ inches drop at heel, 1½ inches drop at comb. Checkered butt on "V. H. E." and "G. H. E." grades. Skeleton steel butt on "D. H. E." to "A. 1. SPECIAL" grades. Straight grip. Option of full pistol grip with cap or half pistol grip. Stock measurements and other specifications will be varied in accordance with descriptions and prices given under separate grades. Quality of walnut, type of engraving, and other features correspond with respective

This Illustration Shows The "V. H. E." Grade Skeet Gun

grades. Also supplied with raised ventilated rib at the extra charge.

"V. H. E." Grade Skeet Gun........................$182.45
"G. H. E." Grade Skeet Gun......................... 202.45
"D. H. E." Grade Skeet Gun......................... 246.00
"C. H. E." Grade Skeet Gun......................... 347.00
"B. H. E." Grade Skeet Gun......................... 451.00
"A. H. E." Grade Skeet Gun......................... 593.00
"A. A. H. E." Grade Skeet Gun...................... 829.50
"A. 1. SPECIAL" Grade Skeet Gun.................... 988.00

H. & R. SINGLE BARREL SHOTGUNS

H. & R. FOLDING SINGLE GUN

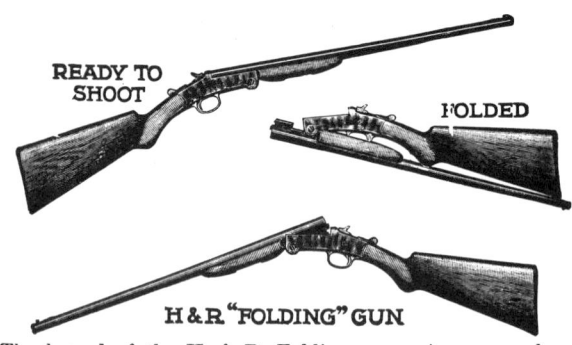

H & R "FOLDING" GUN

The barrel of the H. & R. Folding gun swings around against the stock without becoming detached from it.

AMMUNITION
Standard factory loads, black or smokeless powder.

Light Frame	SPECIFICATIONS		Heavy Frame
.410—12 M/M	22-inch Barrel	12 Gauge	26-inch Barrel
14 M/M	Weight, about	16 Gauge	Weight, 5¾ to
28 Gauge	4½ pounds	20 Gauge	6½ pounds
		28 Gauge	
		.410—12 M/M	

Price Light or Heavy Frame with Automatic Ejector............$12.00

H. & R. "Heavy Breech" Single Gun

WITH AUTOMATIC EJECTOR

No. 6

For those who wish a heavier gun than our Standard Model, either for trap shooting or to reduce the recoil of heavy loads, we offer H. & R. Heavy Breech Model.

In this gun a larger frame increases the weight to 7 or 7¼ pounds, but due to the distribution of this added weight, the balance of this model is exceedingly fine.

AMMUNITION
Standard factory loads, black or smokeless powder.

LENGTHS OF BARRELS		Prices
10 gauge, 30, 32, 34 or 36 inch	12, 16, or 20 gauge......	$11.55
12 gauge, 30, 32, 34 or 36 inch	10 gauge...............	11.55
16 gauge, 30 or 32 inch	**EXTRA LENGTH BARRELS**	
20 gauge, 28 inch	34-inch Barrel	$.50
Stock, fine black walnut, flexible hard rubber butt plate.	36-inch Barrel	1.00

H. & R. "Heavy Breech" Single Gun

WITH AUTOMATIC EJECTOR

No. 8

The H. & R. Standard Single gun is made in the regulation three piece take-down construction with a snap-on fore-end. It can be furnished either automatic or non-ejecting as desired.

LENGTHS OF BARRELS SUPPLIED

12 Ga. Stl. Bbl., 28, 30 or 32 in.	28 Ga. Stl. Bbl., 26, 28 or 30 in.
16 Ga. Stl. Bbl., 26, 28, 30 or 32 in.	.410—12 M/M Stl. Bbl., 26 or 28 in.
20 Ga. Stl. Bbl., 26, 28, 30 or 32 in.	
24 Ga. Stl. Bbl., 26, 28, or 30 in.	Weight, 5½ to 6½ pounds, according to gauge and length of barrel.

Price $11.10

BAY STATE SINGLE BARREL SHOT GUN

WITH AUTOMATIC EJECTOR

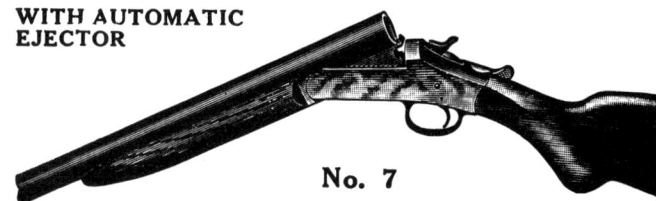

No. 7

Weight 5¼ to 6½ pounds according to gauge and length of barrel.

12 gauge, length of barrel 28, 30 and 32 inch; 16 gauge; length of barrel, 28 and 30 inch; 20 gauge; length of barrel, 28 inch; .410-12 mm; length of barrel, 26 inch.

.410 gauge is now chambered for the new 3" .410 gauge shell with which remarkable patterns are obtained.

Price $9.75

H. & R. "Hammerless" Single Gun

WITH AUTOMATIC EJECTOR

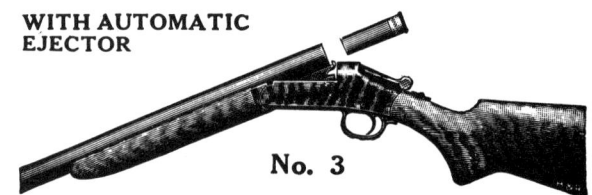

No. 3

Instead of a heavy, slow swinging hammer, a light military type striker is used, which travels less than ¼ of an inch, thus making the action the fastest used on any shotgun.

SPECIFICATIONS	LENGTHS OF BARRELS
Length of stock.......13¾ inch	12 Gauge, 28, 30, and 32 inches
Drop at heel..........2¾ inch	16 Gauge, 28, 30, and 32 inches
Weight ......6½ to 7¼ pounds according to gauge and length of barrel.	20 Gauge, 28 inches only
	.410—12M/M, 26 inches only

Price $12.20

H. & R. "Standard" Light Weight

WITH AUTOMATIC EJECTOR

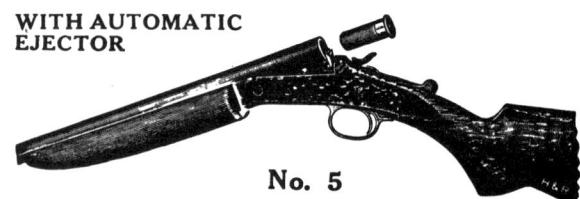

No. 5

With the more general use of small gauge loads—24, 28, and .410—we were asked to furnish a single barrel shotgun especially designed for this ammunition.

The H. & R. Light Weight Single Gun weighs 4 to 4¾ pounds and its slender attractive lines make it pleasing to users of the small bore.

AMMUNITION
Standard factory loads, black or smokeless powder.

.410—12 M/M Chambered for 3-inch shells. Will also take .44 W. C. F. Shot cartridges and .44 XL, .44 Game Getter Shot cartridges, and .410 and .44 Game Getter with round ball.

LENGTHS OF BARRELS

24 Gauge, 26 or 28 inch	.410—12M/M 26 or 28 inch
28 Gauge, 26 or 28 inch	14M/M 26 or 28 inch

Price $11.10

HISTORY OF THE L. C. SMITH SHOTGUN

The L. C. Smith gun has been manufactured continually since 1880 and in the present factory at Fulton, New York, since 1888 when the Hunter Arms Company bought it from the L. C. Smith Company of Syracuse, New York.

At that time the Hammer gun was still very popular, while the hammerless gun was just beginning to assume the popularity which it so justly deserves. The Hunter Arms Co., Inc. no longer manufacture hammer guns although in those days it was made in several different grades, the more expensive grades being elaborately engraved.

During the early years Smith guns were furnished with various varieties of Damascus steel barrels. This type of barrel proved to be more or less of a fad, as the popular demand for them has almost entirely died out. This is consistent as they are not equal to the high grade steel barrels now used exclusively with modern high velocity loads.

First manufactured by the L. C. Smith people was the old three-barrel Baker gun with rifle barrel. This was made before the L. C. Smith gun was designed, was obsolete years ago, and was never built in the Hunter Arms Company factory. This gun is of particular interest to collectors because of the peculiar mechanism. There was no lever on the gun—you pushed the front trigger forward to fire the rifle barrel which was hammerless and triggerless. Just ahead of the front trigger was a little checkered rocker. You cocked the right lock first, then shoved the rocker forward and the rifle barrel was ready to fire. All Baker models were discontinued after the Smith people bought out the L. C. Smith gun.

One of the strongest features of the L. C. Smith gun is its bolting device which has always been guaranteed "Never to Shoot Loose". A 1900 Smith gun was advertised as being shot over two hundred thousand times and as being as tight at the end of this period as at the first shot.

The first Grand American Handicap was won in 1900. Since that time this gun has won many more of the Grand American Handicaps as well as a large percentage of the other big shoots.

In 1904 the Hunter Arms Co. brought out the famous Hunter One Trigger which has since so ably proven its worth in the hands of thousands of satisfied shooters.

In 1905 the Hunter Arms Co. was awarded a gold medal, the highest award at the Lewis & Clark Centennial Exposition at Portland, Oregon, for the Smith Hammerless and the Hunter One Trigger.

The 20-gauge gun was introduced in 1907. Up to this time the Smith gun was made in 10, 12 and 16 gauge only. In order to produce a 20 gauge gun of perfect proportions it was necessary to build a complete new gun, frame, and other parts as well as different barrels. This was called the Featherweight model, as distinguished from the original, or regular model. The Featherweight model is a Smith gun in every detail, the proportions of the gun being lighter, but of equal strength, to give the same perfect balance in a 20 gauge that the Regular model gave to the 12 and 10 gauges. This Featherweight model was also used for 16 and 12 gauge guns, which made it possible to furnish a perfectly balanced gun in weights ranging from five and three-quarter pounds in a 20 gauge to ten pounds in a 10 gauge. The 16 and 20 gauge guns are now made in the Featherweight model exclusively, while the 12 gauge gun is made in both the Regular and Featherweight. The 10 gauge is, of course, almost obsolete and is no longer manufactured by the Hunter Arms Co. Inc. The 410 gauge can be furnished in all of the various grades and is especially popular among the skeet shooters.

In 1916 the L. C. Smith One Barrel Trap gun was developed on the same principles as the double barrel gun. This gun at once met with great favor, and in 1919 won first and second places in the Grand American Handicap and in 1920, second and third places in this event, as well as first place in the Grand Canadian Handicap.

Later, in 1921, the Hunter Arms Company gave the shooting world the double barrel trap gun fitted with their special Beavertail forend. This forend is considerably larger than the regular forend, blanketing both the barrels and affording a solid grip without the danger of burning the hand from barrels overheated from excessive shooting.

With the development of high Velocity powder for shotguns, a demand was created for a gun to handle this heavy load in a 12 gauge gun to equal, or better, the performance of the old 10 gauge. To meet this demand the L. C. Smith Long Range Wild Fowl gun is built from the regular model L. C. Smith and is designed to handle the heavy charge of modern propellent powders, giving an increased effective range of from fifteen to twenty-five yards of extensive velocity and penetration. With this gun some truly wonderful patterns have been made.

Included in more recent developments of the Hunter Arms Co. Inc. is the L. C. Smith Ventilated Rib Double Barrel Gun for trap and field use. This design embodies all the features of the single barrel gun, making it possible for the trapshooter to sight a double gun along a single plane and giving the added advantage of one gun for double and single targets. The Ventilated rib is of equal advantage for field and marsh shooting for the sportsman has at all times a clean vision of the "mark". The ventilated rib is used almost entirely in conjunction with the Beavertail forend, the Hunter One trigger, and the Automatic Ejector.

The raw material which goes into the making of the L. C. Smith gun comes from widely different parts of the world. For instance, the Circassian Walnut Stocks used on the higher grades come from North Shores of the Black Sea; while the horn for the Buttplates used on these guns, comes from India. Practically all of the barrels are imported from Belgium in a forged and rough condition. The Sir Joseph Whitworth Fluid Steel barrels, which are the very best barrels obtainable and used only on very high grade guns, are obtained from England.

The majority of the stocks are American Walnut and some of the most beautiful stocks are from this material which is purchased in blocks with the ends dipped in paraffine to prevent checking. These blocks must be thoroughly air dried from two to three years so that there will be no possible chance of their shrinking after they are fitted to the guns.

The barrels, after being cut to the desired length, are reamed and choke bored before the tubes are brazed together with the lug and extension. The choke of the gun is the most important part from the shooting standpoint, as this determines entirely the pattern which the guns will make. The top rib and bottom rib are soldered to the barrels and after the other machine operations are completed they are given the gun metal finish which is a chemical oxidizing process.

All the main parts of the gun such as frame, forend, lock plates, toplever, etc. are made from forgings. These forgings require anywhere from 25 to 150 machine operations. Other parts such as the bridles, ejector, guide blocks, safety parts, etc., are made from sheet metal or bar stock, while for the smaller parts—drill rod, screw stock, clock spring steel, music wire and special drawn shapes are used.

Manufacture of the L. C. Smith gun is divided into two main departments. The Production Dept. furnishes all the parts completely machined and ready for the Assembly Department. It is in the Assembly Dept. that the skilled labor is employed which is necessary to produce a high grade gun.

To give the best satisfaction a shotgun must fit the person using it. For this reason a large portion of L. C. Smith guns are built to special order. Variations of $\frac{1}{16}$ of an inch in the comb or heel drop of a gun in the hands of an experienced shooter may make a material difference in the results of the shooting.

The engraving on all of the guns is done entirely by hand, and the higher grade guns with their gold inlay are truly works of art. Incidentally, the man who does all the fine engraving and gold inlay work on Crown, Monogram, DeLuxe, and Premier guns has been at it for fifty years in our factory.

L. C. SMITH SHOTGUNS

IMPROVED FIELD GRADE

In its price class, this staunch and dependable model continues to reign as the favored selection of double gun users throughout the world. It is every inch an L. C. Smith from its perfectly coordinated Armour Steel Barrels down over the sturdy beauty of its selected walnut stock and matching forend, to its genuine hard rubber butt plate and grip cap; it has the same sleek lines, polished smoothness, true balance and sure aim of its more elaborate custom-made brothers; yet, amazingly enough, it is priced within everyone's reach.

For rough work in timber and brush, for the strain of incessant shooting on the skeet field and over the traps, for long range and "to bring 'em down"—an L. C. Smith *Improved* Field Grade! Complete with the SINGLE SIGHTING PLANE rib.

Price	$49.00
With Automatic Ejectors (E)	63.15
With Non-selective Hunter One-trigger (N)	60.00

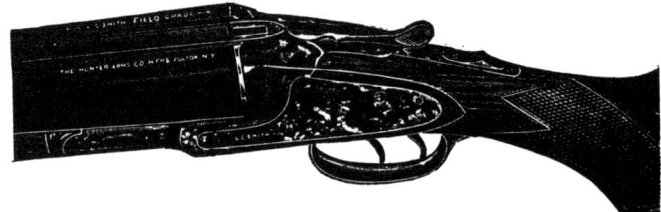

Grip: Full pistol regular, half or straight to order. Barrels: 26, 28, 30 and 32-inch Armour Steel only, bored to order from full choke to cylinder. Gauge: 12, 16, 20, and .410-caliber. Weights: 12-gauge, 6 lbs., 8 ozs., to 8¼ lbs.; 16-gauge, 6¼ to 7 lbs.; 20-gauge, 5¾ to 6½ lbs.; .410-caliber, 5¼ to 5½ lbs.

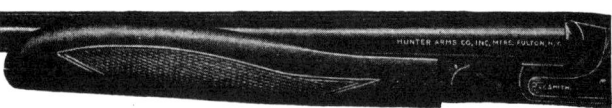

SKEET SPECIAL

Skeet shooting demands a combination of quick thinking, fast action and a light, true-shooting, perfectly balanced gun. The L. C. Smith Skeet Special is just that kind of a gun! Custom-built to any reasonable dimensions, it assures perfect fit. Bored Skeet No. 1 and No. 2, it guarantees an ideal skeet pattern. Equipped with Hunter One-trigger, it assures infallible operation on doubles without interruption of aim. Fitted with Streamline Beavertail Forend, it lends itself perfectly to the precision required of the shooter.

In answer to the squad hustler's call, go to your position with a Skeet Special ... the gun you will shoot with a new assurance and pride. With Automatic Ejectors, Non-selective Hunter One-trigger, Streamline Beavertail Forend and checkered Butt.

Price	$95.45
Price with Selective Single Trigger	109.70

Gauge	Weights	Barrels
12, 16 or 20 .410-caliber		26, 27 or 28-inch London Steel, proof tested.
12-gauge	7 to 7¼ lbs.	Grip
16-gauge	6 lbs. 10 oz. to 7⅛ lbs.	Made on special order in various combinations. Furnished with straight, full or half pistol grip.
20-gauge	6 lbs. 6 oz. to 6¾ lbs.	
.410-caliber	6 lbs. 2 oz. to 6½ lbs.	

IDEAL GRADE

A real custom-built gun without the additional expense that is usually involved. The perfect fit which is the assurance of every special order gun, plus the beauty of selected first-class walnut stock and matching forend, is in keeping with the quality of the fine London Steel Barrels. Lock-plates and frame tastefully engraved with a simple oak leaf design. In all combinations of gauges and barrel lengths.

With two triggers	$63.90
With Automatic Ejectors (E)	78.05
With Automatic Ejectors and Selective Hunter One-trigger (EO)	103.30

Gauge	Barrels
12, 16 or 20 .410-caliber	26, 28, 30 or 32-inch London Steel, proof tested, bored to order from full choke to cylinder, .410-caliber, 26 and 28-inch only.

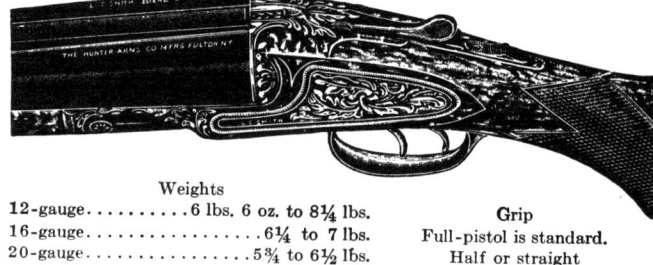

Weights		Grip
12-gauge	6 lbs. 6 oz. to 8¼ lbs.	Full-pistol is standard. Half or straight to order.
16-gauge	6¼ to 7 lbs.	
20-gauge	5¾ to 6½ lbs.	
.410-caliber	5½ to 5⅞ lbs.	

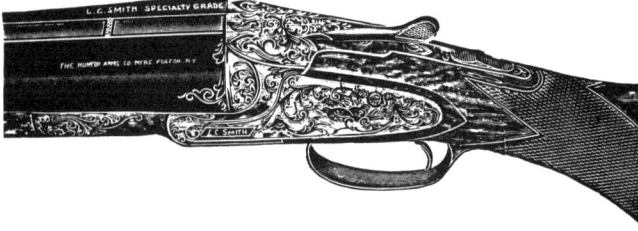

SPECIALTY GRADE

A prize to possess ... a privilege to shoot. Superior in every way to the ordinary firearm. Lock-plates finely engraved, oil-finished, selected walnut stock and hand-checkered forend, Nitro Steel Barrels renowned for positive strength. A representation of beauty and quality to the highest degree.

With two triggers	$106.00
With Automatic Ejectors (E)	124.70
With Automatic Ejectors and Selective Hunter One-trigger (EO)	155.70

Gauge	Barrels
12, 16 or 20 .410-caliber	26, 28, 30 or 32-inch Nitro Steel, proof tested, bored to order from full choke to cylinder, .410-caliber, 26 and 28-inch only.

Weights		Grip
12-gauge	6 lbs. 6 oz. to 8¼ lbs.	Full-pistol is standard. Half or straight to order.
16-gauge	6¼ to 7 lbs.	
20-gauge	5¾ to 6½ lbs.	
.410-caliber	5½ to 5⅞ lbs.	

Single Sighting Plane Rib

THE SINGLE SIGHTING PLANE RIB is a new development of the Hunter Arms Company embodying a type of raised solid broad rib for use on double barrel shotguns. When sighting over a gun so equipped, only the rib is seen—the single sight plane. In this manner the same effect is attained with the double barrel as with the pump over-under automatic. Thus the general conceded superior balance of the double shotgun is maintained without its disadvantages.

REGULAR and FEATHER weight Models

All L. C. Smith 12 gauge shotguns are made both in FEATHER weight and REGULAR weight, making possible a perfectly balanced gun ranging from 6 lbs., 6 oz. to 8¼ lbs.

The REGULAR weight models, available in 12 gauge only, have a longer frame, wider lug, and are designed for heavy use as in trap and duck shooting. The FEATHER weight embodies a narrow frame, lighter weight, better balance, and faster handling. FEATHER weight is standard in all gauges.

SEE PAGE 8, "HOW TO ORDER"

L. C. SMITH SHOTGUNS

"CROWN GRADE"

The L. C. Smith Royal Family of custom-built shotguns is perfectly represented by the Crown Grade. A small gold crown on the top-lever is symbolic of the beauty and quality of the complete gun. Selected walnut stock rich in finish, figure, color; fine, neat, hand-checkering; strong Nitro Steel Barrels carefully selected. Unsurpassed for artistic appointments. Delicately engraved hunting dogs on the lock-plates. Mechanical perfection. For the man of unusual discrimination.

With two triggers $255.55
With Automatic Ejectors and Selective Hunter One-trigger (EO).... 307.60
With Automatic Ejectors, Selective Hunter One-trigger, Beavertail
   Forend, Ventilated Rib (EOBV) 371.25

Gauge	Barrels
12, 16 or 20	26, 28, 30 or 32-inch Nitro Steel, proof tested, bored to order from full choke to cylinder. .410-caliber, 26 and 28-inch only.
.410-caliber	

Weights	Grip
12-gauge..........6 lbs. 6 oz. to 8¼ lbs.	Full-pistol is standard.
16-gauge................6¼ to 7 lbs.	Half or straight
20-gauge................5¾ to 6½ lbs.	to order.
.410-caliber............5½ to 5⅞ lbs.	

Custom-built to incorporate your personal requirements ... engraved to attest our engravers' skill ... monogrammed in gold to certify your ownership. Carefully shaped Circassian Walnut Stock of satin smoothness and beautiful curly grain. Exquisite engraving and a remarkable combination of English Scroll Work and Teutonic Relief. Barrels are of Sir Joseph Whitworth Fluid Steel ... superior in hardness, tensile strength, and fine finish. A connoisseur's choice.

With two triggers $500.00
With Automatic Ejectors, Selective Hunter One-trigger (EO)..... 554.60
With Automatic Ejectors, Selective Hunter One-trigger, Beavertail
   Forend, Ventilated Rib (EOBV) 637.45

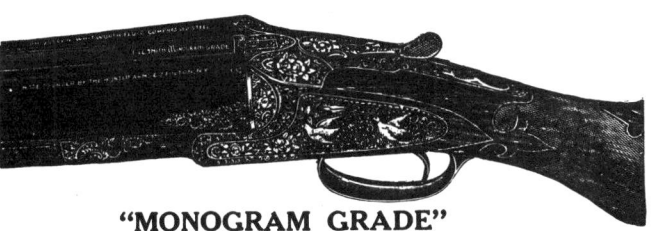

"MONOGRAM GRADE"

L. C. SMITH PREMIER GRADE

A quiet elegance surrounds the serene splendor of the L. C. Smith Premier. Its hand-worked Circassian Walnut Stock and skillfully hand-checkered matching forend are perfectly accentuated by the delicate engraving and hunting dogs depicted in gold on both lock-plates. Sir Joseph Whitworth Fluid Steel Barrels. A gold monogrammed seal inlet in the stock consummates a crowning achievement ... a genteel work of the gun maker's art. Custom-made to any gauge, barrel length, grip, and stock specifications.

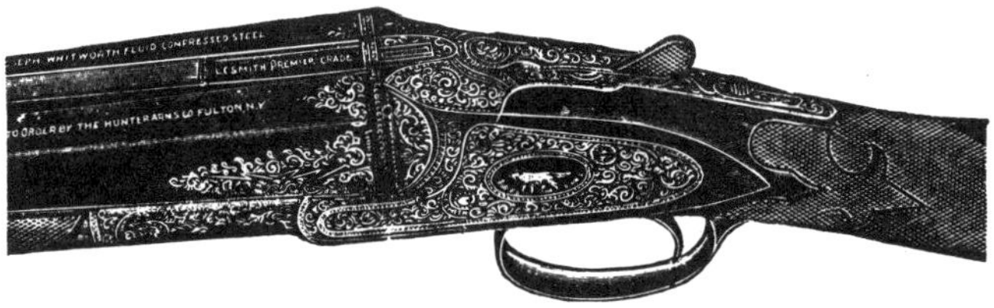

With two triggers $825.25
With Automatic Ejectors, Selective Hunter One-trigger, Beavertail
   Forend, and Ventilated Rib (EOBV) 965.70
De Luxe Grade (Not Illustrated) 1,212.00

DETAILS FOR THE MONOGRAM, PREMIER, AND DE LUXE

Gauge	Barrels
12, 16 or 20	26, 28, 30 or 32-inch Whitworth Fluid Steel, proof tested, bored to order from full choke to cylinder. .410-caliber, 26 and 28-inch only.
.410-caliber	

Weights	Grip
12-gauge..........6 lbs. 6 oz. to 8¼ lbs.	Full-pistol is standard.
16-gauge................6¼ to 7 lbs.	Half or straight
20-gauge................5¾ to 6½ lbs.	to order.
.410-caliber............5½ to 5⅞ lbs.	

SINGLE BARREL TRAP GUN

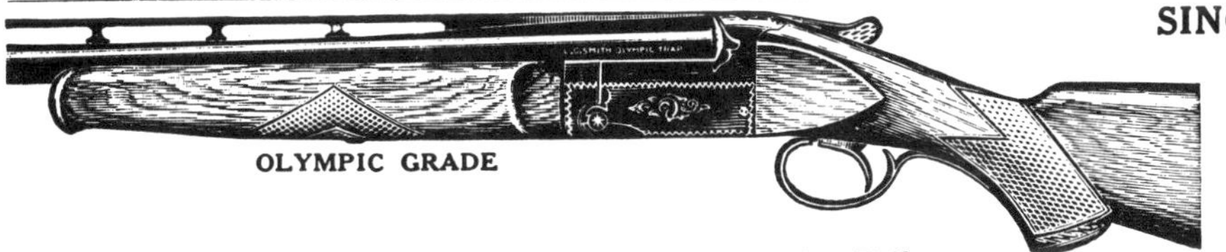

PRICES

Olympic	$115.15
Specialty	154.55
Crown	287.85
Monogram	476.20
Premier	793.85
De Luxe	1,190.25

OLYMPIC GRADE

Stock and fore-end from especially selected walnut. Grip: Full pistol, half pistol or straight. Barrels: 12 gauge, 30, 32 and 34 inches, Nitro steel, bored by the Smith system for perfection in trap shooting. Trigger Position: Rear, unless otherwise specified. The Olympic single-barrel is manufactured and sold only in the one standard stock dimension, 14½—1½—1⅞, full pistol grip, while the Specialty and better grades can be had in any reasonable stock dimensions and in the different style pistol grips. Recoil pad and Lyman sights included as regular equipment on all Smith single barrel trap guns.

EXTRA EQUIPMENT

If the combination you want is not listed on these pages, it may be made up from the prices shown below of the two trigger gun without ejector. the extra price of the features desired. Price combinations must be on the same grade. To obtain the price of any type combination on any L. C. Smith gun, add to the base price.

AUTOMATIC EJECTOR
Field, Skeet and Ideal—E $14.15
Trap, Specialty and Crown—E 18.70
Monogram, Premier and De Luxe—E 21.25

SELECTIVE HUNTER ONE-TRIGGER
Field Skeet and Ideal—O $25.25
Trap and Specialty—O 31.00
Crown, Monogram, Premier and De Luxe—O 33.35

NON-SELECTIVE HUNTER ONE-TRIGGER
Field, Skeet and Ideal—N $11.00
Specialty—N 15.50
Crown, Monogram, Premier and De Luxe—N 18.20

BEAVER TAIL FORE-END
Ideal—B $15.75
Specialty—B 21.70
Crown—B 30.30
Monogram—B 49.50
Premier—B 52.50
De Luxe—B 60.60

LONG RANGE WILD FOWL GUN
12 Gauge Only
All Grade—L $5.05

VENTILATED RIB
Including Recoil Pad and Two Ivory Sights
Specialty—V $28.00
Crown, Monogram, Premier and De Luxe—V 33.35

ACCESSORIES
Recoil Pad (and grade) $5.05
Leather Covered Recoil Pad 6.05
Checkered Trigger (and grade) 2.05
Checkered Butt (except on Skeet) 3.55
Ivory Sights (per pair) 1.00
Chambering for 3" Shells (any grade) 3.05
Oil Finished Stock (Field, Skeet Special, Ideal) ... 4.05

FOX SHOTGUNS

FOX MODEL B

The new Fox Model B has the features of light weight, streamline design, perfect balance and superior shooting qualities.
ACTION—Two trigger, extractor type. Lightning-fast coil spring, hammer and sear design.
BARRELS—Alloy forged steel, proof tested. Chambered for 2¾" shells, except .410 bore which is chambered for 3" shells. 12 gauge 26", 28" and 30" barrels; 16 gauge 26" and 28" barrels; 20 gauge 26" and 28" barrels; .410 bore 26" barrels. Barrels bored right modified choke, left full choke, except .410 bore, which are both full choke. Other standard borings furnished to order at no additional charge.
STOCK—American walnut, stream-line design. Checkered pistol grip. Fluted comb. Length about 14"; drop at heel about 2¾". Hard rubber butt plate.
FRAME—Black gun-metal finish. Shock-proof bolting.
WEIGHT—12 gauge, 7¼ to 7½ lbs. 16 gauge, 6¼ to 6½ lbs. 20 gauge, 6 to 6¼ lbs. .410 bore, 5¾ to 6 lbs.
Price $26.00

STERLINGWORTH GRADE

Owing to the simplicity of mechanism, all superfluous metal in frame is eliminated, giving the gun a perfect balance and at the same time leaving plenty of metal in barrels, where strain is the greatest. The Fox system of boring is responsible for uniform pattern and maximum penetration attained in all Fox guns.

Special alloy forged steel Barrels, adapted to smokeless or black powders, American Walnut stock; full pistol grip; genuine hard rubber butt plate. Any other barrel borings if desired at no extra charge.
Without Automatic Shell Ejector $48.95
With Automatic Shell Ejector 61.80
STERLINGWORTH DE LUXE, fitted with Jostam Anti-Flinch Recoil Pad and two Lyman ivory bead sights. Made in 28, 30 or 32 inch barrels. Any boring at no additional charge. Barrels regularly furnished bored right modified and left full choke.
Non-Ejector price $52.00
Sterlingworth Deluxe with Ejector 65.00

Weight 12 Gauge	Weight 16 Gauge	Weight 20 Gauge	Barrel Length	Boring of Barrels		Length Stock	Drop Stock
				Right	Left		
7¾ to 8¼ lbs.	6½ to 7 lbs.	6¼ to 6¾ lbs.	32"	Full	Full	14"	2¾"
7¼ to 7¾ lbs.	6½ to 6¾ lbs.	6¼ to 6½ lbs.	30"	Mod.	Full	14"	2¾"
7 to 7½ lbs.	6¼ to 6½ lbs.	6 to 6¼ lbs.	28"	Mod.	Full	14"	2¾"
6⅞ to 7¼ lbs.	6 to 6¼ lbs.	5¾ to 6 lbs.	26"	Cyl.	Mod.	14"	2¾"

STERLINGWORTH SKEET AND UPLAND GAME GUN

To meet the demand for a moderately priced skeet and upland game double gun we have produced the famous Fox-Sterlingworth gun in this new straight grip model with 26 or 28 inch barrels bored: right, skeet cylinder; left, quarter choke. This is a standard stock model possessing the features of skeet boring and stock design, heretofore available only in custom-built guns.
BARRELS—Special alloy forged steel; boring, right barrel, skeet cyl.; left barrel, mod. choke.
STOCK—American walnut, straight grip. Length 14 inches, drop at heel 2⅝ inches.
FRAME—Forged ordnance steel; case hardened finish; ornamented with fine line engraving.
ACTION—Two trigger, extractor type.
WEIGHT—12 gauge about 7 pounds. 16 gauge about 6 pounds. 20 gauge about 5¾ pounds.
Sterlingworth Skeet and Upland Game Gun $54.00
With Automatic Ejectors 67.00
Full Beaver-Tail Forend, extra 11.10
Fox-Kautzky Selective Single Trigger, extra 21.20
Recoil Pad, extra 3.55
Ivory Bead Sights, extra 1.10

SP GRADE

BARRELS: Special alloy forged steel, proof-tested, guaranteed for shooting qualities. 26 inch barrels regularly bored right cylinder and left modified; 28 and 30 inch barrels, right modified and left choke; 32 inch barrels both full choke. Any other borings furnished at no additional charge. Frame: Forged ordnance steel. Stream line. Black gun metal finish.
STOCK: Selected American Walnut with checkered cap full pistol grip, oil finished. Length 14 inches, drop at heel 2¾ inches. Forend: Selected American Walnut finely checkered special design. Made in 12, 16, 20 gauge.
Grade SP $64.00
Grade SPE with Automatic Ejectors $77.75

A NEW GUN CARRIES A FACTORY GUARANTEE

THE FOX SHOTGUN
A SUPREME ACHIEVEMENT IN SHOTGUN BUILDING

It has been said that to the true lover of the beautiful in a gun, there is nothing more beautiful in all the realm of mechanics than the rhythmic speed and action of a perfectly designed gun lock.

From the old flint lock, down through the muzzle-loaders and the breech-loader with external-hammers, to the present highly developed "hammerless," the lock has always been a subject of keen interest to the true sportsman.

In spite of some popular belief to the contrary, the tendency has been toward a steady simplification in design. For instance, the flint lock contained twenty-two parts, including lock plate. The muzzle-loading lock consisted of fifteen parts. The breech-loading hammer gun lock contains seventeen parts.

The Fox Lock, simplest gun-firing mechanism ever devised, contains but *three principal working parts*—the coil spring, the one-piece hammer, including as part of it the firing pin, and the sear. No other gun made operates so simply or with so few parts. In some cases the firing pin is still a separate part from the hammer, which alone adds several extra delicate parts, such as bushings, etc., to the lock. In other cases as high as ten or fifteen additional parts are required to do no more than is accomplished by the wonderful simplicity of the Fox Lock.

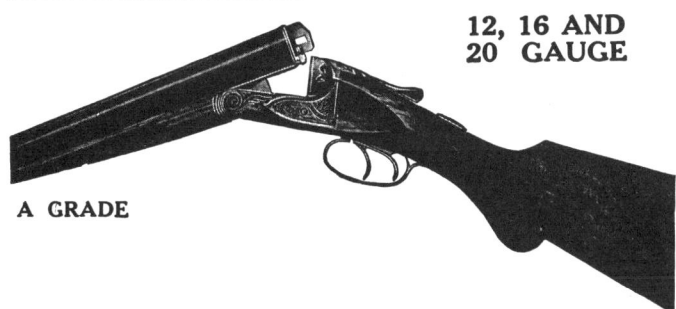

12, 16 AND 20 GAUGE

A GRADE

SPECIFICATIONS

Barrels, high quality alloy forged steel, adapted to smokeless or black powders. Selected walnut stock; checkered and engraved; half pistol grip; 12, 16 and 20 gauge: 26, 28, 30 and 32 inch barrels. Full pistol or straight grip to order at no extra charge. Weight, 12 gauge, 6⅞ to 8 pounds; 16 gauge, 6 to 7 pounds; 20 gauge, 5¾ to 6¾ pounds; various drops and lengths of stocks.

Grade A $64.00
A.E. with Selective Automatic Ejectors 77.75

The Super Fox HE Grade is built especially for long range shooting. When used with long range shells loaded with progressively burning powder, it gives patterns never before attained at forty, fifty and sixty yards.

The standard gun is chambered for 2¾ inch shells and will be chambered for 3 inch shells if so ordered. All stock HE Grade guns are bored both barrels full choke.

BARRELS—Special alloy forged steel, proof-tested and guaranteed for any factory loaded shells. STOCK AND FOREND—Selected walnut, artistically checkered. ENGRAVING—Fine line work around frame and guard. SPECIFICATIONS—Regularly equipped with automatic ejectors: 12 gauge, 30 or 32 inch barrels, weight, 8¾ to 9¾ pounds.

Both barrels bored full choke. Any other boring at no extra charge. Standard stock half pistol grip, 14⅛ inches long with 2⅝ inch drop at heel.

HE GRADE

12 GAUGE ONLY

LONG RANGE GUN

Any length and drop of stock or style of grip furnished at no extra charge.
Price $80.75

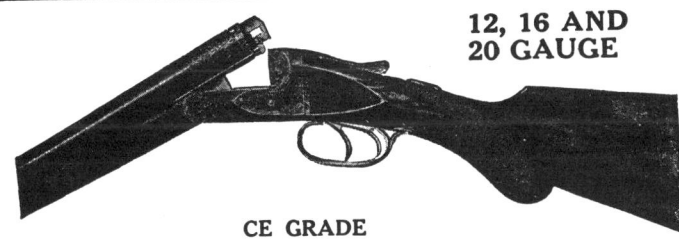

12, 16 AND 20 GAUGE

CE GRADE

This is the grade that is making good everywhere. In every respect it is unusual—a high grade gun—at a very modest price. It's a beauty in looks and finish. No gun will stand up better to hard work. Its every detail is perfect. And at the price it is in a class absolutely by itself.

High Quality, alloy forged Steel Barrels, figured and dark finished, selected walnut stock; artistic engraving, well covered with scroll and picture work. Half pistol grip; made in 12, 16 and 20 gauge; 26, 28, 30 and 32 inch barrels. Full pistol or straight grip to order at no extra charge. Weight, 12 gauge, 6⅞ to 8 pounds; 16 gauge, 6 to 7 pounds; 20 gauge, 5¾ to 6¾ pounds.
CE with Automatic Shell Ejector $126.00

High quality alloy forged Steel Barrels, especially bored and tested by hand for evenness of pattern for trap shooting. Stock of beautifully figured Walnut straight, half or full pistol grip, all at the same price. Beautiful engraving of new style. Equipped with Silver's Recoil Pad, Automatic Ejector and Lyman sights. Weight, 12 gauge, 6⅞ to 8 pounds; 16 gauge, 6 to 7 pounds; 20 gauge, 5¾ to 6¾ pounds. Barrels 26, 28, 30 and 32 inch.

Grade XE $212.00
Grade DE 323.00
Grade FE 570.00

(Any extras may be had on FE Grade at no extra cost.)

12, 16 AND 20 GAUGE

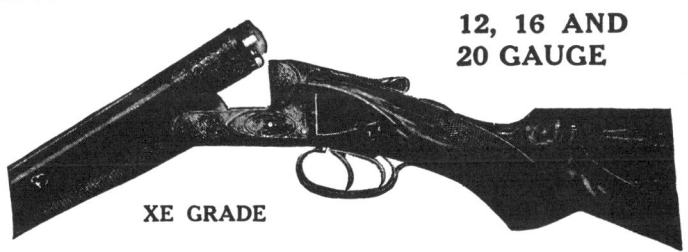

XE GRADE

EXTRAS, FITTED TO NEW GUNS

Fox-Kautzky Selective Single Trigger..... $21.20	Set of Ivory Bead Sights—any grade..... $1.10	Beavertail Forend—CE Grade........... $20.20
Ventilated Rib—any grade............... 34.80	Soft Rubber Recoil Pad—any grade..... 3.55	Beavertail Forend—A, AE, or HE Grade. 13.60
Cast-off Stock, Extra.................. 5.00	Beavertail Forend—DE Grade.......... 26.25	Beavertail Forend—SP or SPE Grade.... 13.60
Monte-Carlo Stock, Extra.............. 7.50	Beavertail Forend—XE Grade......... 21.35	Beavertail Forend—Sterlingworth 11.10

FOX GUNS ARE TRADITIONALLY FINE

STEVENS SHOTGUNS

STEVENS No. 22-410

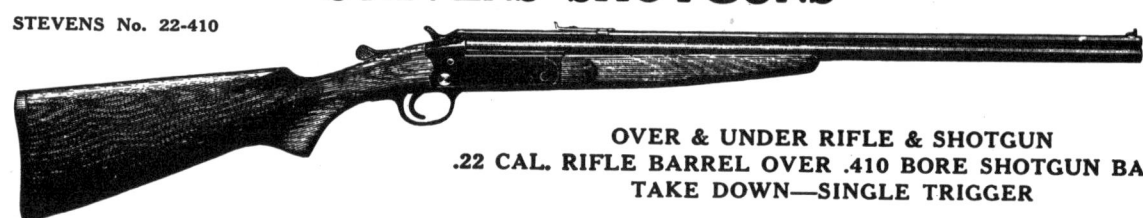

OVER & UNDER RIFLE & SHOTGUN
.22 CAL. RIFLE BARREL OVER .410 BORE SHOTGUN BARREL
TAKE DOWN—SINGLE TRIGGER

This Over & Under Gun has a .22 Long Rifle caliber barrel over a .410 bore shotgun barrel. An easily operated button on the right side of the frame instantly selects barrel to be fired. Ideal for vermin and small game.

SPECIFICATIONS

Barrels: Length 24". Rifle barrel "precision" rifled for accuracy. Shotgun barrel bored full choke. New combination rifle and shotgun stainless steel bead front sight and adjustable rear sight. Take-down.

Stock: Tenite. Pistol grip. Fluted comb. Hard rubber butt plate.

Fore-end: Tenite. Equipped with special fastening which positively prevents gun from shooting loose.

Action: Single trigger. Low rebounding hammer. Separate extractors. Top lever operates either to the right or left to open action.

Frame: Handsome case-hardened finish. Slide button on right side for instant selection of barrel to be fired.

Weight: About 6 lbs.

Ammunition: Top barrel, .22 short, long, and long rifle, regular or high speed lower barrel, .410 bore, chambered for 3" shells.

Price $15.10
No. 240—410-410 26" barrel, 3" chamber................. 15.10

STEVENS No. 530M

DOUBLE BARREL SHOTGUN WITH THE
EPOCH MAKING NEW "TENITE" STOCK AND FOREARM
AVAILABLE IN 12, 16, 20, AND .410 GAUGE

"TENITE" STOCK AND FORE-END

TENITE is an ideal material for gunstocks. It is of hornlike hardness, is chip-proof and crack-proof, and has great resistance to breakage. It is absolutely weather-proof and withstands moisture, heat and cold without swelling, shrinking or warping. Its rich, lustrous, permanent burled finish resists scratching. Its uniform weight assures perfect balance.

SPECIFICATIONS

Barrels: Blued forged steel with matted rib, fitted with two white bead Colasta sights. Lengths: 12 ga., 28, and 30"; 16 ga., 28"; 20 ga., 28". Barrels bored right modified and left full choke. Chambered for 2¾ in. shells.

Stock: Tenite. Rich burl walnut appearance. Checkered full pistol grip, capped. Fluted comb; paneled sides. Length 14", drop 2¾".

Fore-end: Tenite. Checkered. With special fastening which positively prevents gun from shooting loose.

Action: Hammerless. Rugged lock-up. Coil springs. Fast hammer fall. Positive extraction. Design of frame prevents powder residue from blowing back into action.

Frame: Handsome case-hardened finish.

Weight: 12 gauge, about 7½ lbs.; 16 gauge, about 7 lbs.; 20 gauge, about 6½ lbs.

Price 22.95
Price with single trigger................................ 26.25

BOLT ACTION 20 GAUGE. BLACK TIP REPEATING SHOTGUN

Model 258

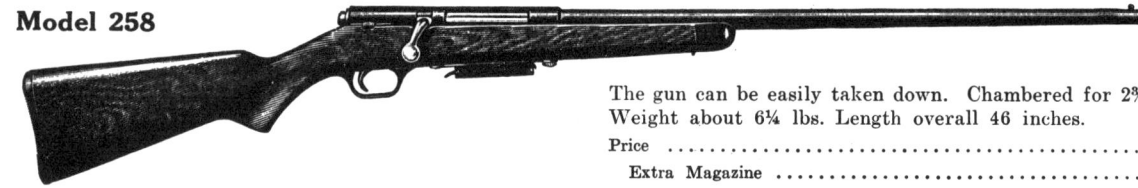

A new design in a 20 Gauge repeater for those preferring bolt action. These guns have a magazine capacity of 3 shots, 2 in detachable clip magazine, self cocking and independent safety. The stock is one piece American walnut with full pistol grip, black tip forearm and hard rubber butt plate. The gun is fitted with a round 26 inch tapered barrel full choke crowned muzzle. The gun can be easily taken down. Chambered for 2¾ inch shell. Weight about 6¼ lbs. Length overall 46 inches.

Price $12.60
Extra Magazine 1.00

Model 58 is of the same design as model 258 but made for 410 Gauge and comes with 24 inch barrel full choke. This gun is a 4 shot repeater and takes a 3 shot clip detachable magazine for the 3 inch shell. Weight about 5½ lbs.

Price $11.35
Extra Magazine 1.00

BOLT ACTION 410 GAUGE REPEATING SHOTGUN

Model 59

This model is of the latest design using a tubular magazine. An advantage over the clip loader you will recognize readily, taking 6 shots, 5 in the magazine and one in the chamber, doing away with the loss of magazine clips. Of bolt action construction with all the features of the models 258 and 58. Handling the 410 Gauge 2½ and 3 inch shell. Weight about 6 lbs. Length overall 44 inches.

Price $13.35

ALL SHIPMENTS ARE INSURED

MARLIN OVER-UNDER AND COMBINATION GUNS

MODEL 90
STANDARD

Price $40.27

FOR FIELD AND GENERAL USE
12, 16, and 20 GAUGE

Standard Barrel Lengths: 12 Ga. 26" and 30"; 16 and 20 Ga. 26" and 28". Boring: 26". Top Barrel Modified Choke, Bottom Barrel Improved Cylinder; 28" and 30". Top Barrel Full Choke, Bottom Barrel Modified Choke. Take Down. Hammerless. Matted Top Barrel. Single Sighting Plane. Special Steel Barrels Chambered for 2¾" Shells. Double Trigger—Front trigger fires bottom barrel, Rear trigger fires top barrel. Frame Attractively Engraved on both sides. Positive Automatic Safety (Independent Safety on order). Retracting Strikers. Rubber Recoil Pad. Easy, Smooth Cocking—Strikers smoothly and automatically cocked when gun is opened. Short snappy Striker travel prevents misfiring and reduces "lock time." Special Extra Large Locking Lug on breech of barrels. Direct Line

Locking. Straight Line Recoil. Action easily accessible for Cleaning and Oiling by removing Buttstock. One Piece Frame. No bothersome top lever "Trip." Strikers can be lowered without snapping by first opening the gun, pushing the Safety Button forward; partially close Gun while holding back triggers; release the triggers and finish closing gun. Genuine American Walnut Buttstock and Forearm. Buttstock dimensions: Full Pistol Grip, length about 14", drop at comb about 1⅝", drop at heel about 2¼". Forearm Large, Hand-filling and designed to protect the hand from heat of barrels. Buttstock and Forearm Checkered on Order. Weight—12 Ga. about 7½ lbs., 16 & 20 Ga. about 6¼ lbs.

Extra Barrel & Forearm.....................................$20.18

MODEL 90
"SKEETKING"

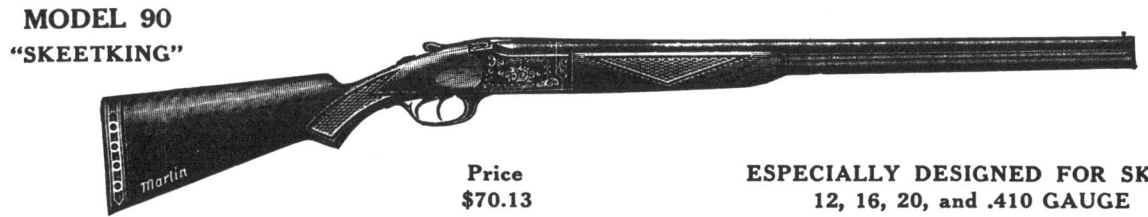

Price $70.13

ESPECIALLY DESIGNED FOR SKEET
12, 16, 20, and .410 GAUGE

CUSTOM BUILT To Give the Exact SPECIFICATIONS you want, in 12, 16 & 20 Gauge and .410 Bore. Special Attention to Details of "Fit," "Balance," and Boring will Give you Results Never Before Possible.

HIGHEST QUALITY Throughout, Correctly Designed and Beautifully Finished.

STOCK & FOREARM of Selected Fancy Figured Walnut, Hand Rubbed Finish and Finely Checkered.

ENGRAVING Hand Engraved in a Neat Design.

UPLAND GAME. Although Designed Epecially for Skeet Shooting, they are equally as effective in the quest of Upland Game.

SPECIFICATIONS 12, 16 & 20 Gauge and .410 Bore. Barrels— 26 inches—Option of 28 inches in 12-16-20 Ga. All Proof Tested with Excessive Proof Loads. Ivory Bead Sight—Matted Top Barrel —Full Pistol Grip—Option Half Pistol or Straight Grip. Hand Filling Semi-Beaver Tail Forearm—Recoil Pad on 12, 16, 20 gauges —Option Hard Rubber Buttplate. Any Reasonable Comb & Heel

Drop, Stock Length, Pitch, etc., etc. Automatic Safety—Option Independent Safety. Double Trigger. Approximate Weights: 12 Ga. 7¼ lbs., 16 & 20 Ga. 6¼ lbs., .410 Bore 5¾ lbs.

BORING-TARGETING. Each Barrel Has its Choke or Constriction adjusted so as to give the best potential Target Breaking Spread of Shot at 20 yards for the Bottom Barrel and 30 yards for the Top regardless of the amount of choke resulting.

REMEMBER, Custom Made Guns do not go thru regular production line and are worked on only by the most experienced gunmakers, therefore 4 to 6 weeks after receipt of order are required to build and such orders are NOT SUBJECT TO CANCELLATION.

Prompt shipment can be made on "SKEETKINGS," all custom made, of the following Specification: 26 inch Barrels. Buttstock; Length 14"—Drop at Comb 1⅝"—Drop at Heel 2¼" with Recoil Pad on 12, 16, 20 gauges.

Extra Barrel & Forearm.....................................$28.25

MODEL 90
COMBINATION

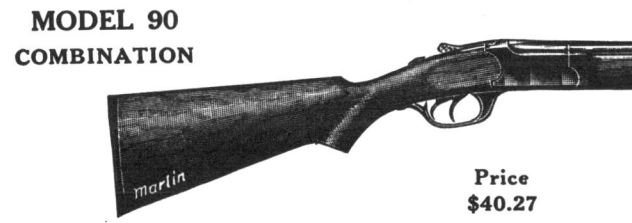

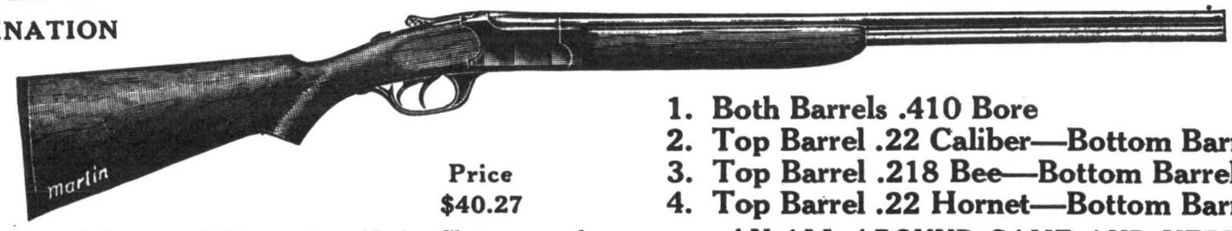

Price $40.27

1. Both Barrels .410 Bore
2. Top Barrel .22 Caliber—Bottom Barrel .410 Bore
3. Top Barrel .218 Bee—Bottom Barrel .410 Bore
4. Top Barrel .22 Hornet—Bottom Barrel .410 Bore

AN ALL AROUND GAME AND VERMIN GUN.

With the addition of the new .410 bore Over-Under Shotgun, and the new .22 Caliber—.410 Bore combination Marlin has the only complete line of Over-Unders. With the Splendid Reputation and Following of the Model 90 Over-Under in the 12, 16 & 20 gauges and the Great Sensation it has Created, these new additions should prove extremely Popular Numbers.

These will be built along the same general specifications as the 12, 16 & 20 gauges but proportionately smaller. The .410 Bore will be chambered for 3 inch shells and the .22 Caliber for Short, Long

and Long Rifle Cartridges. A Rubber Buttplate will be Standard Equipment. Recoil Pad will be furnished on Special Order. The frame will be plain with a high polished blue finish. It will be furnished with 26 inch barrels only. The .410 will be Bored: Top Barrel Full Choke; Bottom Barrel Modified Choke. The lower barrel on the .410-.22 combination will be bored Full Choke. Weight about 5¾ lbs.

Extra Barrel & Forearm.....................................$20.18

BE MODERN WITH AN OVER-UNDER

IVER JOHNSON SHOTGUNS

SKEET-ER MODEL

(Showing Straight Grip)

DOUBLE BARREL HAMMERLESS

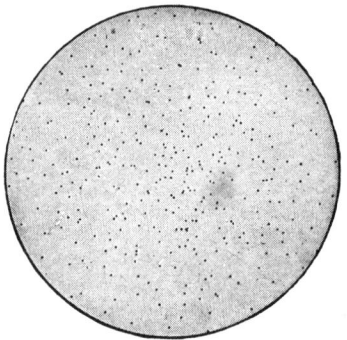

Actual photograph of pattern made with SKEET-ER, using 3 inch .410 long shells, No. 9 C shot. Reverse barrel boring furnished as option.

This is a Championship Gun specially built with an advanced system of boring which gives amazing results at Skeet Shooting.

SPECIFICATIONS

Stocks are of selected fancy figured walnut beautifully hand-checkered. 14⅛ in. in length with drop of 2¾ in. at heel. The 12, 16, 20 and 28 gauges have forged steel frame, full pistol grip rubber capped with option of straight grip; the .410 straight grip with option of full pistol grip. The .410 is chambered to take the long 3 in. shells. Regular boring right barrel choked and left barrel open. Large hand-protecting forend with D. & E. fastener. Blued frame and parts. Lyman No. 10 Ivory front sight. Hard rubber butt plate.

We can supply, at no extra cost but subject to delay, variations in stock dimensions and barrel borings. We can also equip with the Miller Single Trigger, either Non-Selective or Selective type and Jostam Anti-Flinch Recoil Pad at extra charge listed below.

PLAIN EXTRACTOR			AUTOMATIC EJECTOR		
No. 512	12 Ga.		No. 612	12 Ga.	
No. 516	16 Ga.	$55.30	No. 616	16 Ga.	$65.35
No. 520	20 Ga.		No. 620	20 Ga.	
No. 528	28 Ga.		No. 628	28 Ga.	
No. 541	.410 Bore		No. 641	.410 Bore	
28 inch Barrels. (Option 26 inch)			28 inch Barrels. (Option 26 inch)		

Right barrel, 338 shot in 30 inch circle at 30 yards.
Left barrel, 347 shot in 30 inch circle at 20 yards.

Extras: Miller Single Trigger Non-Selective, **$14.00**; Miller Single Trigger Selective, **$17.50**; Jostam Anti-Flinch Recoil Pad, **$1.50**. Additional Ivory Sight, **$.50**.

FOR TRAP SHOOTING

A brand new trap gun of exceptional merit, correctly designed and beautifully finished. New and improved straightline ventilated rib breaks up heat waves and makes clear vision for accurate shooting.

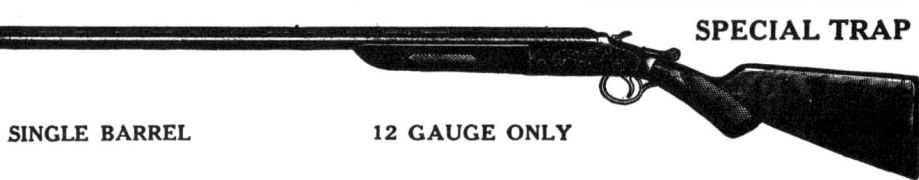

SPECIAL TRAP

SINGLE BARREL   12 GAUGE ONLY

SPECIFICATIONS

No. 26—12 gauge, 32 inch barrel with ventilated matted top rib, fitted with two Lyman Ivory Sights. Automatic ejector. Length of stock 14½ inches; drop at comb 1½ inches, drop at heel 2 inches. Weight, approximately 7 pounds, 6 ounces. (Jostam Anti-Flinch Recoil Pad $1.50 extra) .... Price, **$18.10**

HERCULES GRADE

FOR UPLAND GAME AND DUCKS   12, 16, 20, .410 (3 INCH) WITH AND WITHOUT EJECTOR

Stock and forend of selected black walnut finely hand checkered with flexible hard rubber butt plate. Lightning locks. Easy cocking. The automatic ejector mechanism is housed in the forend (D. & E. fastener) and will eject either one or both shells at option. Both barrels on the 12 gauge 32 inch and the .410 are full choke, and the .410 has straight grip. With these exceptions all others have full pistol grip capped with right barrel modified and left full choke. Both models beautifully finished and of high quality.

SPECIFICATIONS—HAMMERLESS DOUBLE BARREL

PLAIN EXTRACTOR				AUTOMATIC EJECTOR			
NO.				NO.			
812	12	26, 28, 30, 32 (Reg. 30)		912	12	26, 28, 30, 32 (Reg. 30)	
816	16	26, 28, 30 (Reg. 28)	$35.20	916	16	26, 28, 30 (Reg. 28)	$42.25
820	20	26, 28 (Reg. 28)		920	20	26, 28 (Reg. 28)	
841	.410	26, 28 (Reg. 26)		941	.410	26, 28 (Reg. 26)	

The weight of Plain Extractor Guns 5¾ to 7½ pounds, and the Automatic Ejector 6 to 7¾ pounds, according to gauge and barrel length.

EXTRAS, BOTH MODELS

Jostam Anti-Flinch Recoil Pad	$1.50
Lyman Ivory Sights, each	.50
Swivels	1.00
Miller Single Trigger Non-selective	14.00
Miller Single Trigger Selective	17.50

SPECIFICATIONS

Has improved straightline ventilated rib. Stock and forend of handsome selected walnut hand checkered. Made only in 12 gauge, 32 inch barrels, both full choke. Two Lyman Ivory Sights and Jostam Anti-Flinch Recoil Pad. Full pistol grip, rubber capped. Beaver tail forend with D. & E. fastener. Drop at comb 1½ inches, and at heel 2 inches. Automatic Safety, with option of Independent Safety. Weight about 8½ pounds. This gun is designed for trap shooting, and is also unequaled for game.

Price **$49.80**

12 GAUGE ONLY

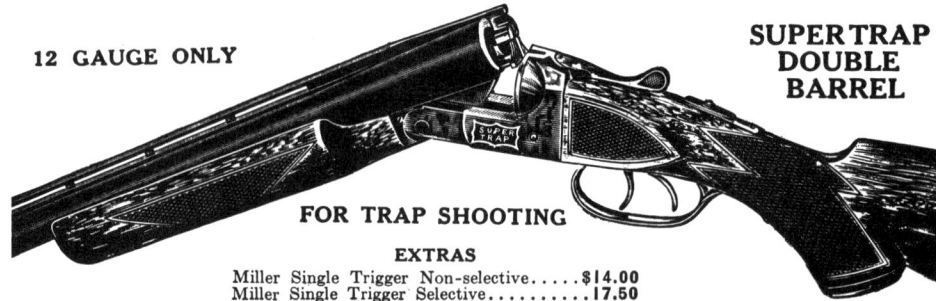

SUPER TRAP DOUBLE BARREL

FOR TRAP SHOOTING

EXTRAS

Miller Single Trigger Non-selective **$14.00**
Miller Single Trigger Selective **17.50**

A NEW GUN CARRIES A FACTORY GUARANTEE

IVER JOHNSON, FULTON, & HUNTER SHOTGUNS

12, 16, 20, 28 AND .410 Gauge

IVER JOHNSON CHAMPION GRADE
WITH AUTOMATIC EJECTOR

Three piece take-down gun with real Black Walnut Trap Style Forend and Stock with full pistol grip and flexible hard rubber Butt Plate. Made in Automatic Ejector and Plain Extractor. When not otherwise specified, Automatic Ejector will be sent. The .410 is chambered for 3 in. shells.

FOR FIELD AND DUCK SHOOTING

SPECIFICATIONS

No.	Gauge	Barrel Lengths
312	12	28, 30, 32 in. (Reg. 30")
316	16	28, 30, 32 in. (Reg. 30")
320	20	28, 30 in. (Reg. 28")
328	28	26, 28 in. (Reg. 28")
341	.410	26, 28 in. (Reg. 26")

Price, Automatic Ejector.....................$9.00
Weights from 5¾ to 6½ pounds, according to gauge and barrel length.

EXTRAS

Brazed Swivels, all gauges	$1.00
Hard Rubber Cap on Pistol Grip	.40
Checkered Stock and Fore-end	.50
Jostam Anti-Flinch Recoil Pad	1.50
34 in. Barrel on Nos. 312 and 316	.50
36 in. Barrel on Nos. 312 and 316	1.00
Band Swivels on Nos. 312, 316, 320	.50

12, 16, 20 & .410 Gauge

IVER JOHNSON MATTED TOP RIB
WITH AUTOMATIC EJECTOR

Three piece take-down gun with a finely Matted Top Rib extending full length of barrel. Has Black Walnut Trap Style fancy forend and stock with full pistol grip capped. Both forend and stock are beautifully hand checkered. Flexible hard rubber Butt Plate. The .410 is chambered for 3 inch shells.

FOR FIELD AND DUCK SHOOTING

SPECIFICATIONS

No.	Gauge	Barrel Lengths
412	12	28, 30, 32 in. (Reg. 30")
416	16	28, 30, 32 in. (Reg. 30")
420	20	28, 30 in. (Reg. 28")
441	.410	26, 28 in. (Reg. 26")

Price, Automatic Ejector.....................$12.60
Weights from 6¼ to 6¾ pounds, according to gauge and barrel length.

EXTRAS

Jostam Anti-Flinch Recoil Pad	$1.50
Lyman Ivory Sights fitted, each	.50
34 in. Barrel on Nos. 412 and 416	.50
36 in. Barrel on Nos. 412 and 416	1.00
Brazed Swivels	1.00

FULTON

This is an exceptionally well made gun built by the well known Hunter Arms Company to meet the demand for low priced Shot Guns which carry their name and guarantee. It is a reliable box frame gun capable of the most satisfactory shooting results. In finish, style and balance it outranks its price. Satisfies the demand for which it is built and is deservedly popular.

SPECIFICATIONS

To be had with 26, 28, 30 and 32-inch barrel, in 12, 16 and 20 gauge, except that the 32 and 30-inch barrels are furnished only in 12 gauge guns.

12, 16 AND 20 Gauge

Price.........$29.95
With Non-Selective Hunter Single Trigger $36.70

Price........$35.10
With Non-Selective Hunter Single Trigger $41.75

THE HUNTER SPECIAL

This is a new gun produced by the makers of the famous L. C. Smith and utilizes the same rotary bolt giving assurance against shooting loose. It is a fast handling, true shooting and perfectly balanced gun, very serviceable, sturdy, and dependable, and its exceptionally low price places it within the range of everyone. It is equipped with checkered full pistol grip, and in various combinations of choke.

SPECIFICATIONS

Gauge	Barrels	Weight	Stock
12	26", 28", 30"	6¾ to 7¼ lb.	14" long
16	26", 28", 30"	6⅝ to 7 lb.	2¾" drop
20	26", 28", 30"	6½ to 6⅞ lb.	Full Pistol Grip

ALL SHIPMENTS ARE INSURED

HISTORY OF LEFEVER AND ITHACA GUN CO.

HISTORY OF LEFEVER GUNS

Among names famous in the gunmakers' art, not one is more resplendent with brilliant success than that of the late Dan Lefever, affectionately known to thousands of sportsmen as Uncle Dan Lefever.

Dan Lefever learned his trade as a gunsmith in Rochester, N. Y. That was about 80 years ago. In 1861, when the Civil War broke out, this great gunsmith had a little shop in Canandaigua, N. Y., and there he made superior rifles for some of the sharpshooters in the Northern army. A few years later he moved to Auburn, N. Y., where he did high class gunsmithing, also making a few shotguns on special order, all handwork. Occasionally he converted a muzzle loader into a high class breech loader and that is a mighty hard thing to do. The Lefever was the first double breech loading hammerless gun made in America.

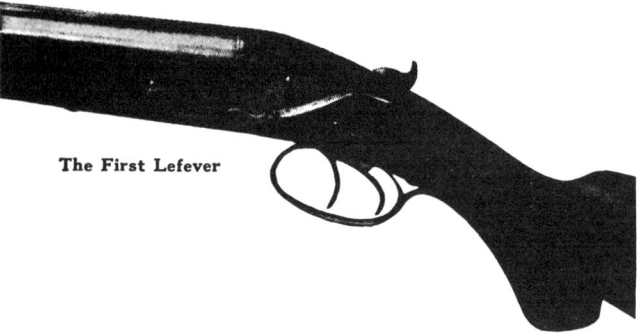

The First Lefever

This original breech loading Lefever hammerless was cocked by a side lever, which the shooter pushed down directly after firing the gun in order to cock it so it could be loaded and fired again. A little later a change was made so that when the gun was opened in order to put the shells in the barrels, the opening of the gun cocked both hammers so the side lever cocking mechanism was dispensed with.

Patents on the first Lefever hammerless were issued in 1872.

From Auburn Uncle Dan Lefever moved to Syracuse, where he went into the extensive manufacture of shotguns bearing the name Lefever and for many years he superintended the building of his famous line of guns.

A few years before his death Uncle Dan Lefever sold his interests in the Lefever Arms Co. of Syracuse and moved to Ohio, where he started another factory under the name of D. M. Lefever & Son. The Ohio plant was hardly going smoothly when Uncle Dan Lefever lay down for his last long sleep—the sleep that send a man to the Happy Hunting Ground and soon thereafter the Ohio factory was closed.

About twenty years ago the Lefever Arms Co. of Syracuse was sold to the Ithaca Gun Co. of Ithaca, N. Y., and the plant was moved to Ithaca and has since operated as The Lefever Arms Co., a branch of the Ithaca Gun Co.

Today the Lefever Arms Co. of Ithaca, N. Y. builds three grades of medium priced double guns in .410, 20, 16 and 12 gauge with or without the inexpensive single trigger, guns designed for skeet and game shooting. It also builds an inexpensive hammerless single gun for field and trapshooting and the single gun with the extra features, which make it an exclusive gun for trapshooting, a single barrel trap gun selling for less than forty dollars.

HISTORY OF ITHACA GUN CO., Ithaca, N. Y.

In the year 1880 the Ithaca Gun Co. started building guns in a small wooden building which is still standing on the bank of Fall Creek from which the Ithaca Gun Co. gets its inexpensive water power and around that original small wooden building, which is still kept in good repair for sentimental reasons, has grown a much larger Ithaca plant of modern construction.

One of the founders, the late L. H. Smith, was the oldest of the five Smith brothers, who eventually became known the world over as manufacturers of sporting firearms and typewriters bearing the family name.

George Livermore, a brother-in-law of L. H. Smith, who is still hale and hearty at the ripe old age of 92, worked with L. H. Smith to build the Ithaca plant up to the point where it has an annual capacity of over 52,000 double and repeating game, skeet and trap guns.

Today the first, second and third generation of the Smith and Livermore families are actively engaged in the manufacture and marketing of Ithaca guns.

From a humble beginning the Ithaca Gun Co. struggled along for years before its output was ten guns per day and year by year Ithacas have become more and more popular until the Ithaca plant has grown to the point where the output has been over 52,000 guns in one year. During the 58 years since its conception, the Ithaca Gun Co. has absorbed several gun plants including the Syracuse Arms Co., the Lefever Arms Co., Union Fire Arms Co., Wilkes-Barre Gun Co. and others.

Ithaca guns have won the championship of about every civilized country in the world where trapshooting is carried on and Ithaca guns are used by game hunters in every country on the face of the globe.

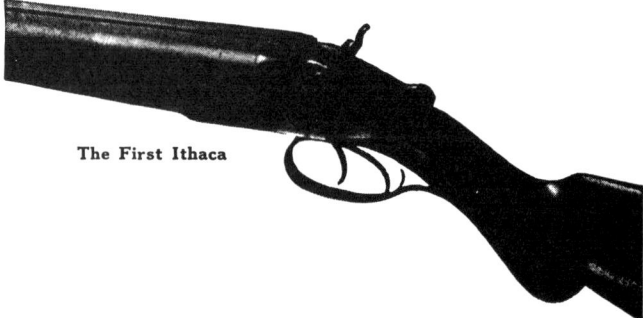

The First Ithaca

Ithaca game and trap guns in both doubles and repeaters can be had at prices ranging from about $43.00 to $1,000.00.

The first Ithaca gun was a double barrel 12 gauge hammer gun. The second double hammerless built in America was an Ithaca and it followed closely after the advent of the Lefever double hammerless which was the first of its kind made in America.

Today Ithacas are built in .410, 28, 20, 16, 12 and 10 gauge, the Magnum 10 gauge being the gun designed and built to handle the 3½ inch Magnum shell with a 2 ounce shot load.

Gun lovers who want to see how guns are built, are always welcome at the Ithaca plant.

UNITED STATES STATE DEPARTMENT ARMS AND AMMUNITION CONTROL, REGISTRATION NO. 18.

ORDER FORM

69

FEDERAL FIREARMS ACT
MANUFACTURER'S LICENSE
NO. 176
3RD DISTRICT, NEW YORK

Order to

STOEGER ARMS CORPORATION
America's Great Gun House
507 FIFTH AVENUE
NEW YORK, N. Y.

TELEPHONE:
MUrray Hill 2-7848

CABLE ADDRESS
STOEGER NEW YORK

Print or Write Plainly. Ask Questions on Separate Sheet.
Write for anything you are interested in, not shown in catalog.

No. of Catalog............... Date...............
Name ....
Street Address or R. F. D...........................
Post Office ....State..........
Express Office Station................How Ship.........

Pistols, Revolvers and Ammunition Can only Be Shipped by Express

AMOUNT SENT	
Draft or Check	
Post Office or Express Order	
Cash	
Stamps	
TOTAL	

ALL FIREARMS ARE SOLD SUBJECT TO THE FOLLOWING UNDERSTANDING: TITLE TO FIREARMS, AMMUNITION AND KINDRED ARTICLES REMAINS IN SELLER UNTIL DELIVERY TO THE BUYER. IF APPLICATION IS MADE TO PURCHASE FIREARMS, AMMUNITION OR KINDRED ARTICLES THROUGH THE MEDIUM OF THE MAIL OR TELEGRAPH, A PROSPECTIVE BUYER MUST STATE IF HE OR SHE IS A MINOR, AS IT IS THE INTENTION OF THE SELLER NOT TO PASS TITLE TO THE GOODS KNOWN AS FIREARMS, AMMUNITION OR KINDRED ARTICLES TO PERSONS UNDER AGE, OR CONTRARY TO LAW.

Page	Quan.	Name and Number of Article	Each	Total

ON ORDERS FOR ARMS AND AMMUNITON, FORM ON REVERSE SIDE OF THIS ORDER MUST BE FILLED IN

PURCHASE APPLICATION FORM

To accompany all orders for firearms, and pistol or revolver ammunition, except .22 cal. r.f. ammunition

INSTRUCTIONS TO APPLICANT

To aid both the seller and the purchaser of firearms and ammunition to comply with the Federal Firearms Act, you are required to fill out such portion of the application form that applies to you. If you believe you are exempt from the provisions of the Act, excerpts from which are printed on the back inside cover of this catalog, you merely fill in the first part. If you do not claim exemption you must fill in the second part and if you live in certain states and wish to purchase a pistol or revolver you must in addition comply with the requirements of the third part. If a dealer Part IV must be filled in.

PART I

Exemption from the provisions of the Federal Firearms Act is claimed by reason of the fact that the purchaser is:

....

....
(State buyer's official position or business which entitles exemption)

....
Signature

PART II

Full Name..Sex..............................

Residence...

....

Business Address..

....

Occupation..

I hereby certify that I have never been convicted in any court of the United States, the several states, territories, possessions (including the Philippine Islands) or the District of Columbia, for commission of a crime of violence as defined in the Federal Firearms Act; nor am I now under indictment in any such court for such a crime; nor am I a fugitive from justice as defined in said act.

I further certify that I do not believe that I am under any such legal disability that would prohibit the Stoeger Arms Corporation from selling and shipping to me the firearms and ammunition I am ordering on the order form attached to and made a part of this application.

....
Signature

PART III

For purchasers who reside in states that require purchase permits, or licenses, to buy the types of firearms ordered herewith, the license to purchase issued by the proper State authorities must be enclosed.

See front inside cover. You can learn what your state's firearms purchase permit or license requirements are by inquiring of your local police chief.

I am enclosing necessary permit herewith.

....
Signature

PART IV

For Dealers Only

Dealers are required to be licensed to receive any firearms whatsoever as well as pistol and revolver ammunition except Cal. .22 Rimfire Cartridges.

This order is placed by a (manufacturer) (dealer) licensed under the Federal Firearms Act,

License Number...

....
Signature

ITHACA FEATHERLIGHT REPEATING SHOTGUNS

ITHACA MODEL 37 STANDARD REPEATING GUN *Featherlight*

ITHACA FEATHERLIGHT STANDARD GRADE REPEATER
MODEL 37

12, 16, and 20 gauge only. 12 gauge 26, 28, 30, and 32 inches. 16 gauge 26, 28, and 30 inches. 20 gauge 26 and 28 inches. These are Featherlight guns and may be had as light as 6½ pounds in the 12 gauge, 6 pounds in the 16 gauge, 5¾ pounds in the 20 gauge, AND every gun is thoroughly proof-tested with loads far more powerful than any available on the market. The light weight of this model as compared with other repeaters of the same and even smaller gauges makes it extremely popular for use in the field where a heavy arm is burdensome. Any choke. Five shot capacity—a plug is furnished to conform to the 3 shot Federal Migratory Bird Law. Chamber length 12, 16, and 20 gauge, 2¾ inches. Stock 14 inches. Drop 1⅝ inches at comb and 2¾ inches at heel. Full pistol grip with gripcap. Hand checkered stock and forend. Waterfowl scene on one side of receiver shows three ducks in natural setting. The other side has an equally pleasing hunting scene featuring a bird dog with two rising ringneck pheasants.

Price of Standard Grade Repeater................................$43.90
Extra barrel for Model 37 (must be fitted at factory)............. 18.83
Special drop other than standard................................. 5.64
Ithaca Recoil Pad.. 2.51
Stock shorter than standard...................................... 3.38

ITHACA MODEL 37 REPEATING SKEET GUN

ITHACA SKEET GRADE REPEATER
MODEL 37S

12, 16, and 20 gauge only. 12 gauge 26 and 28 inches. 16 gauge 26 and 28 inches. 20 gauge 26 and 28 inches. Weight about 7 pounds in the 12 gauge, about 6¾ pounds in the 16 gauge, about 6½ pounds in the 20 gauge. Skeet choke standard, but any choke available. Stock 14 inches. Drop 1½ inches at comb and 2½ inches at heel. Ventilated rib, same type as on Ithaca one barrel trap guns; no dips, no sway, AND NO RAMP (an exclusive Ithaca feature); absolutely unobstructed sighting plane. Lyman ivory sights, front and rear. Large skeet type forend. Stock and forend amply hand checkered. Full pistol grip with gripcap. Attractive game scenes on sides of receiver. Five shot capacity—plug furnished to conform to 3 shot Federal Migratory Bird Law. Chamber length 12, 16 and 20 gauge, 2¾ inches. The RAMPLESS ventilated rib, natural "feel," and effortless handling make this gun a real "pointer." That means more dead "targets and more successful field shots. This makes an excellent upland game gun as well as skeet gun.

Price of Skeet Grade Repeater.................................$67.96
Extra barrel with ventilated rib on Model 37S (must be fitted at factory) 39.37
Special drop other than standard................................. 10.07
Ithaca Recoil Pad on Model 37S................................... 2.51
Stock shorter than standard...................................... 3.38

ITHACA MODEL 37 REPEATING TRAP GUN

ITHACA TRAP GRADE REPEATER
MODEL 37T

12, 16, and 20 gauge only. 12 gauge 30 and 32 inches. 16 gauge 26 and 28 inches. 20 gauge 26 and 28 inches. Full choke standard, but any choke furnished. Weight about 7½ to 7¾ pounds in the 12 gauge, about 6¾ to 7 pounds in the 16 gauge and about 6½ to 6¾ pounds in the 20 gauge. Stock 14½ inches. Drop 1½ inches at comb and 1⅞ inches at heel. Ithaca Soft Rubber Recoil Pad is standard equipment. Five shot capacity—plug furnished to conform to 3 shot Federal Migratory Bird Law. Chamber length 12, 16, and 20 gauge, 2¾ inches. The large, trap type forend and beautiful walnut stock of selected, figured wood are both elaborately hand checkered. Ithaca type RAMPLESS ventilated rib, the same type as chosen by EIGHT Grand American Handicap winners. Lyman front and rear ivory sights. Wild life settings on sides of receiver. This gun is as good for waterfowl and other game as it is for trap shooting.

Price of Trap Grade Repeater..................................$90.11
Extra barrel with ventilated rib (must be fitted at factory)....... 39.37
Special drop other than standard................................. 10.07
Stock shorter than standard...................................... 3.38
Model 37R (with solid rib)....................................... 51.95

ALL THREE models of Ithaca Repeaters have the following features: Quick takedown (no tools needed); shot oil-smooth forend stroke; shells fed in straight line into chamber; handy action release for removing shells; handy crossbolt safety (furnished reversed for left-handed shooter if wanted); receiver with solid top AND SIDES for safety; bottom ejection (protects your face and arm from brass, burned powder residue, shot, or gas blown back from a defective shell. Safe for left-handed shooter. Shells not ejected in face of man beside you. Rain, sleet, snow, or dirt cannot fall into receiver to clog action).

Every gun made in Ithaca is thoroughly prooftested with loads developing 7½ tons pressure each! Far more powerful than any load available on the open market.

WINCHESTER SLIDE ACTION REPEATING SHOTGUNS

MODEL 12
STANDARD GRADE

FOR SKEET AND UPLAND GAME
FOR TRAPSHOOTING AND DUCKS

Made in 12, 16, 20 and 28 gauges. Take down.

Above everything else, Model 12 is known for its close, hard shooting—which accounts for its great popularity for wild fowl and pheasant hunting and for trap shooting. Quail, ruffed grouse and skeet shooters find it fast, have popularized it for their use. In short, so well does this gun shoot, handle and work that for years critical experts representing all branches of shotgun shooting have pronounced it "The Perfect Repeater." It has fine balance, comes up, points and swings with ease for quick, accurate shooting under all conditions. Superior finish, one-piece receiver, closed at the rear—not simply on the top. Short solid breech bolt. Easy dependable action. Positive cross-wise safety trigger lock, in front of trigger guard. Quick, easy takedown. Handsome walnut stock with full pistol grip, full rounded comb, rubber butt plate; walnut action slide handle. Barrel length, 26, 28, 30 or 32 inches in 12 gauge, 26, 28, 30 in 16 or 20 gauge. 26 and 28 inches in 28 gauge. Boring, full choke, improved modified, modified, improved cylinder or cylinder bore. The Winchester special, skeet chokes, Nos. 1 and 2, as introduced in the Model 21 skeet gun, can be furnished on special order at no extra charge. 28 gauge in full, modified and cylinder bore with skeet choke on special order. 12, 16 and 20 gauges chambered for 2¾-inch shells. 28 gauge for 2⅞-inch shells. Interchangeable barrels can be furnished, but must be fitted at factory. Five-shot magazine—with shell in chamber fires six shots. Weight—12 gauge approximately 7¼ pounds; 16, 20 or 28 gauge approximately 6¼ pounds.

PRICES

Standard Grade, 12, 16, 20 and 28 Gauge.................$43.64
Standard Grade, with Solid Raised Matted Rib 51.71
Standard Trap Grade with Solid Raised Matted Rib, Pistol Grip or Straight Grip, 12 Gauge only 63.31
Pigeon Grade with Solid Raised Matted Rib, Stock to Customer's Dimensions without engraving 108.72
Riot Gun, 12 Gauge, 20 inch barrel 43.64

EXTRAS FOR MODEL 12—Add to Price of Gun
STANDARD GRADE

Interchangeable Barrel $22.20
Interchange Barrel with Raised Matted Rib............... 30.27
Making Stock to Customer's Dimensions of Standard Wood.. 15.14
Checking Stock Only, Plain.............................. 1.51
Cutting off Stock to Shorten 3.38
Bending Shank to Change Drop 5.65

PIGEON GRADE

Interchangeable Barrel, matted rib without engraving.......$36.73

MODEL 12
VENTILATED RIB

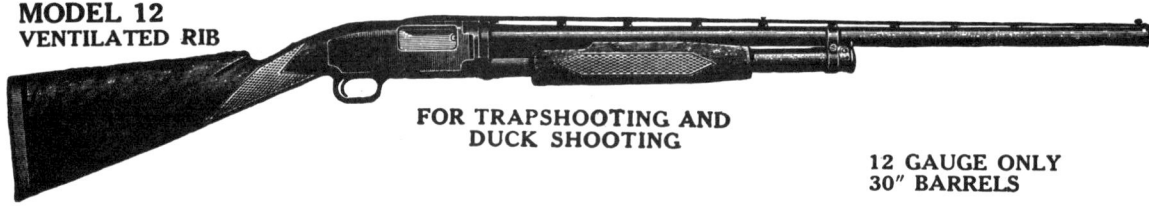

FOR TRAPSHOOTING AND DUCK SHOOTING

12 GAUGE ONLY
30" BARRELS

The Model 12 shotgun as built with the scientifically designed Winchester raised ventilated rib, gives the shooter a sighting plane free from heat waves and a clear, steady path of vision. Sliding connections between rib and barrel allow independent expansion and contraction from the heat of continued shooting, preventing warping of the rib. The Winchester ventilated rib is supplied on the Trap or Pigeon Grade Model 12 in 12-gauge, 30-inch barrel only. Guns regularly are full choke; option of improved modified or modified choke, improved cylinder, cylinder, or skeet bore. Other specifications the same as for corresponding grades without ventilated rib.

PRICES FOR MODEL 12 VENTILATED RIB

Standard Trap Grade with Extension Slide Handle..............$93.58
Pigeon Grade with Extension Slide Handle without engraving....138.99
Interchangeable Barrel, Pigeon Grade without engraving........ 67.00
Pigeon Grade B engraved on receiver, matted rib barrel........128.90
Pigeon Grade C engraved on receiver, barrel and trigger guard, matted rib barrel 169.26
For ventilated rib (in 12 gauge only, 30" or 26¾" only) add to any of the above prices 30.27

MODEL 12
SKEET GUN

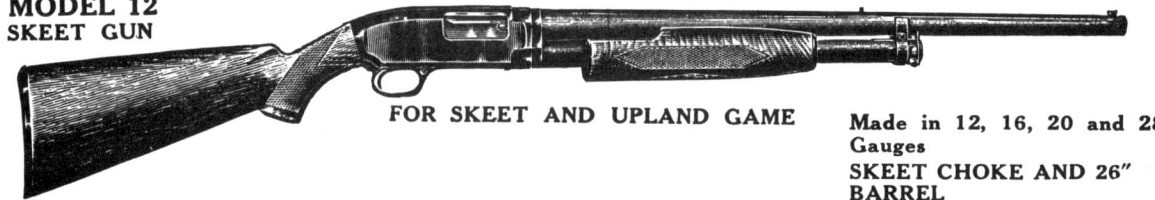

FOR SKEET AND UPLAND GAME

Made in 12, 16, 20 and 28 Gauges
SKEET CHOKE AND 26" BARREL

This finely styled gun, a great favorite with and meeting every demand of the most exacting skeet-shooters, is also extensively used for upland shooting. Barrel length: 26 inches.

Raised solid matted rib. Can also be had with plain barrel. Winchester special skeet choke, as introduced in the Model 21 skeet gun. 12, 16 and 20 gauges chambered for 2¾-inch shells. 28 gauge for 2⅞-inch shells. Walnut stock with checkered pistol grip, carefully finished. Extension slide handle, checkered. Standard rubber butt plate. Front and middle sights. Magazine holds five shells—one in chamber gives six-shot repeating. Approximate weight, 12 gauge, 7¾ pounds; 16, 20 or 28 gauge, 6¾ pounds.

STANDARD GRADE, 12, 16, 20 and 28 Gauge, 26 inch Skeet Choke. Solid Raised Matted Rib Barrel, New Design Pistol Grip Stock and Extension Slide Handle Checkered, Take-Down............$60.74
Same but with plain barrel, except 28 Gauge.................. 52.67

WINCHESTER MODEL 42 SLIDE ACTION SHOTGUNS

MODEL 42
STANDARD GRADE

FOR SKEET AND UPLAND GAME

.410-bore, chambered for 3-inch shells

New, light, racy, entirely in a class by itself! The super .410—the first .410-bore shotgun in the world to achieve what it does with its remarkable new 3-inch shell, produced especially for it. And a beauty! With its powerful load of progressive-burning powder—new and never before used in any shotgun—and ¾-ounce charge of shot—exactly *double* the usual .410 charge—what does it do? In full choke with 26-inch barrel it puts *more* shot in a 20-inch circle at 30 yards than you can find in the usual 2½-inch .410 shell with shot of same size. In short, at longer range than a great deal of small game is killed, this new Winchester actually *patterns* more than the entire charge of other .410 guns. At 30 yards will kill rabbit, quail, snipe, dove, pigeon, pheasant, duck or crow stone dead. Breaks all Skeet targets neatly, also 16-yard targets in trap shooting. The best of guns for sport and practice at clay birds, thrown with a hand trap. Walnut pistol grip stock and walnut slide handle. Barrel, 26 inches, full choke. Options: modified choke, skeet choke or cylinder bore, or 28-inch barrel with same choice in boring. Weight approximately 5⅞ pounds. Length of pull, 13¾ inches; drop at comb, 1½ inches; drop at heel, 2¼ inches; pitch, 1 inch. Light enough for any boy or woman shooter, yet full size for men.

MODEL 42 STANDARD GRADE

Barrel Length	Choke	Price
26″	Full Choke	$35.77
26″	Modified Choke	
26″	Cylinder Bore	
26″	Skeet Choke	
28″	Full Choke	
28″	Modified Choke	
28″	Cylinder Bore	

MODEL 42 STANDARD GRADE WITH MATTED RIB

Barrel Length	Choke	Price
26″	Full Choke Matted Rib	$43.84
26″	Modified Choke Matted Rib	
26″	Cylinder Bore Matted Rib	
26″	Skeet Choke Matted Rib	
28″	Full Choke Matted Rib	
28″	Modified Choke Matted Rib	
28″	Cylinder Bore Matted Rib	

EXTRAS FOR MODEL 42 ADD TO PRICE OF GUN

	Price
Interchangeable regular barrel with regular slide handle	$14.08
Interchangeable matted rib barrel with regular slide handle	22.15
Interchangeable regular barrel with extension slide handle	17.86
Interchangeable matted rib barrel with extension slide handle	25.93
Checkered stock, straight or pistol grip with checkered extension slide handle of standard wood of standard dimensions	5.30
Special Dimension Stock	15.14

MODEL 42
SKEET GUN

FOR SKEET AND UPLAND GAME

.410-bore, chambered for 3-inch shells

Built especially for Skeet, but is besides an exceptionally fast, hard-hitting light field gun which will give the finest satisfaction in close-range shooting at most upland small game. Steps up .410 Skeet scores remarkably. Special Skeet stock, forend and boring. Chambered for the same new world-beating 3-inch Winchester Repeater Super Speed Shells as the Standard Model 42. Shoots exactly the same shot charge of ¾-ounce which used to be regular for all light 20-gauge guns, and gives a smaler, denser and more uniform pattern. Its new progressive-burning powder load knows how to handle this heavy shot charge, does it with very moderate report and recoil, yet with ample penetration. This model is ideal for every beginner in wing shooting, particularly a boy, girl or woman. Handles as easily as a fine light man-sized .22 rifle, and the extension action slide handle suits any reach. Straight grip stock same dimensions as Standard gun and slide handle of selected walnut, grip and handle nicely checkered. Barrel 26 inches, with Skeet boring. Options: Full choke, modified choke or cylinder bore; or 28-inch barrel with same full choice in boring. Weight, 6 pounds to 6⅛ pounds, according to barrel length.

Barrel	Choke	Price
26″	Skeet Choke	$41.07
26″	Skeet Choke Matted Rib	49.14

MODEL 12
HEAVY DUCK GUN

FOR DUCK AND LONG RANGE SHOOTING

30″ or 32″ Full Choke Only
Weight 8½ Lbs.
Chambered for 3″ shells only

Shooters who want a gun ideally designed for duck and similar long range shooting will find the special features of this new Winchester admirably suited for this purpose. It is specially chambered to shoot the heavy loads available in 3 inch shells, has a barrel expressly designed and bored for this type of shooting and is materially heavier than the standard gun of this gauge. In providing this additional weight, particular attention has been given to maintaining the excellent balance for which the Winchester Model 12 has always been famous. This new duck gun has its extra weight so distributed that it will be found to balance as beautifully and so to point as well as the standard "Perfect Repeater". Furnished with Winchester Recoil Pad.

Price, with Plain Round Barrel	$49.19
Price, with Solid Raised Matted Rib Barrel	57.26

MODEL 97 REPEATER

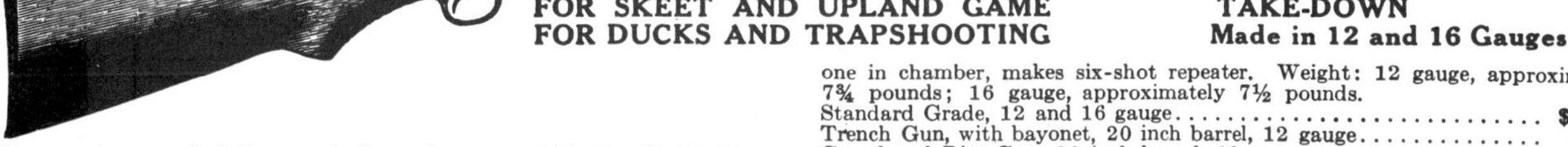

FOR SKEET AND UPLAND GAME
FOR DUCKS AND TRAPSHOOTING

TAKE-DOWN
Made in 12 and 16 Gauges

No other gun has equalled the popularity and success which the Model 97 Winchester achieved in both hunting and trapshooting during its first 15 years. What is more, despite the arrival on the scene then of the Winchester Model 12, the Model 97 has kept right on showing other guns how to shoot—is still today a popular wild fowl and trap gun. Another reason is the fact that it is a hammer gun. With hammer at safety half cock, gun is locked against opening. Same choice in barrel length and boring as in Model 12 of same gauges. Similar stock and slide handle; standard dimensions: length of pull, 13⅞ inches; drop at comb, 1¾ inches; drop at heel, 2⅝ inches. Chambered for 2¾ inch shells. Five shells in magazine, one in chamber, makes six-shot repeater. Weight: 12 gauge, approximately 7¾ pounds; 16 gauge, approximately 7½ pounds.

Standard Grade, 12 and 16 gauge	$34.05
Trench Gun, with bayonet, 20 inch barrel, 12 gauge	60.59
Guard and Riot Gun, 20 inch barrel, 12 gauge	34.05
Interchangeable barrel. Standard grade	19.98

EXTRAS FOR MODEL 97—Add to Price of Gun

Matting Barrel	$6.71
Cutting Off Stock to Shorten Length	3.38
Bending Shank to Change Drop at Heel	5.65
Making Stock to Customer's Dimensions	15.14
For Specially Selected Walnut Stock and Slide Handle of Standard Dimensions Not Checked	15.14

A NEW GUN CARRIES A FACTORY GUARANTEE

WINCHESTER DOUBLE and SINGLE BARREL SHOTGUNS

MODEL 21
STANDARD GRADE

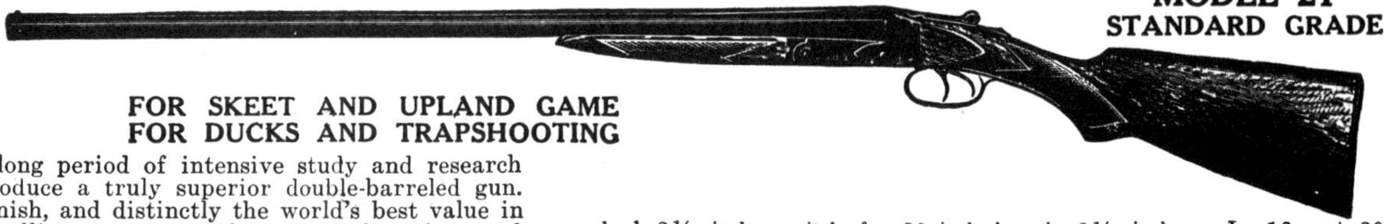

Made in 12, 16 and 20 Gauges

FOR SKEET AND UPLAND GAME FOR DUCKS AND TRAPSHOOTING

The product of a long period of intensive study and research by Winchester to produce a truly superior double-barreled gun. New from start to finish, and distinctly the world's best value in all-around design, handling ease, operation, strength, safety and shooting ability. Barrels interlock mechanically—no brazing; no extension rib—the gun locks properly without need of one. Result, better shooting. Because barrel chambers are not warped by brazing, they retain true concentricity and alignment. Breech is built scientifically to precision fitting, instead of by obsolete cut-and-try, rule-of-thumb methods.

New Winchester method of choke reaming improves pattern. New steel give barrels of double usual strength, frame of triple strength. Will not shoot loose. Remarkably easy to open and close. An exceptionally hard-shooting gun, giving the finest uniformity of pattern. Single or double trigger with or without selective ejection. Choice in barrel lengths: 12 gauge—32, 30, 28 or 26 inches; 16 and 20 gauges—30, 28 or 26 inches. All barrels furnished in full, improved modified or modified choke, improved cylinder or cylinder bore; usual combinations. Other combinations to special order at no extra charge. Winchester special Skeet chokes, No. 1 or No. 2, introduced on Winchester Model 21 Skeet Gun, can be furnished on special order at no extra charge. Walnut stock with fluted, well-rounded comb and checkered pistol grip; hard rubber butt plate. Walnut checkered fore-end. Standard dimensions—12 gauge—length 14 inches, drop at comb 1 9/16 inches, drop at heel 2½ inches, pitch for 30-inch barrels 2½ inches. In 16 and 20 gauge, same except drop at comb is 1½ inches and at heel on 16 gauge is 2$\frac{7}{16}$ inches and on 20 gauge drop at heel is 2⅜ inches. Winchester 81A front sight with option of 81D with 94B middle sight. Extra set of barrels and fore-end can be furnished. Weight with 30-inch barrels; 12 gauge—approximately 7½ pounds; 16 and 20 gauges—approximately 6½ pounds.

MODEL 21 STANDARD GRADE, 12, 16 and 20 GAUGES

12 Gauge, 32, 30, 28, 26-inch Barrels. Usual Choke Combinations:

Double Trigger, Non-Selective Ejection	$78.15
Double Trigger, Selective Ejection	91.92
Single Trigger, Non-Selective Ejection	91.92
Single Trigger, Selective Ejection	105.69

EXTRAS add to price STANDARD GRADE

Stock to customer's dimensions	14.00
Extra set of Barrels without fore-end, purchased with a new gun:	
Non-Selective Ejection	44.40
Selective Ejection	55.50
Extra fore-end—purchased with new gun:	
Regular shape—Non-Selective	10.09
Selective	14.63
Beaver-tail—Non-Selective	18.97
Selective	23.50
Chambering for 3-inch Shell	5.55
Beavertail fore-end instead of regular fore-end, add	8.27

MODEL 21
SKEET GUN

Made in 12, 16 and 20 Gauges

FOR SKEET AND UPLAND GAME

Designed especially for the fascinating and fast growing sport of Skeet shooting—and giving at the same time the best of service for the fastest upland game shooting. Furnished in Standard, Trap or Custom Built Grade, including specifications of those grades, with its own special Skeet specifications. All Model 21 Winchesters are specially bored, by a new Winchester method of true radius choke reaming. The Skeet Gun has, besides, its own special new chokes. These Winchester Skeet Chokes, No. 1 in the right barrel, and No. 2 in the left, give the most consistently satisfactory skeet patterns, and the best for brush and short range field shooting. Skeet Gun specifications, all three gauges, are: Length of barrels, 26 inches. Straight grip (checkered) walnut stock with checkered wood butt (no plate or pad), 14″ x 1½″ x 2″, with 1″ pitch. Pistol grip 14″ x 1 9/16 x 2½″ with 1⅝″ pitch. Walnut beavertail forend, handsomely checkered. Single trigger, selective ejection, non-automatic safety. Boring as mentioned above.

MODEL 21 SKEET "STANDARD" GRADE

12, 16 and 20 Gauge, Straight or Pistol Grip Stock $117.30

MODEL 21 SKEET "TRAP" GRADE

12, 16 and 20 Gauge, Straight or Pistol Grip Stock $117.30

MODEL 21 "CUSTOM BUILT" GRADE

Strictly to customer's specifications desired. State wishes and quotation will be furnished.

MODEL 24
TAKE DOWN

DOUBLE BARREL HAMMERLESS

12 GA., 26″, 28″, OR 30″ BBL.
20 OR 16 GA., 26″ OR 28″ BBL.

This new Winchester double barrel shotgun represents a remarkably sturdy and efficient double at an extremely low price. A distinctive feature of this new Winchester is the special streamline design of both metal and wood parts which give a pleasing and graceful appearance and practical and satisfying balance and feel. Among the features of this new model, the following will commend themselves strongly to shotgun lovers: Frame made from solid forging—extra strong; sturdy forged cocking levers which are readily accessible in take down position to release top lever; forged top lever, firing pins retracted by first opening movement of the top lever, thereby preventing gun from sticking due to firing pin indent in primers. Speed lock firing pin giving exceedingly fast lock time.

Price $29.72

MODEL 37 "STEELBILT"
SINGLE SHOT SHOTGUN

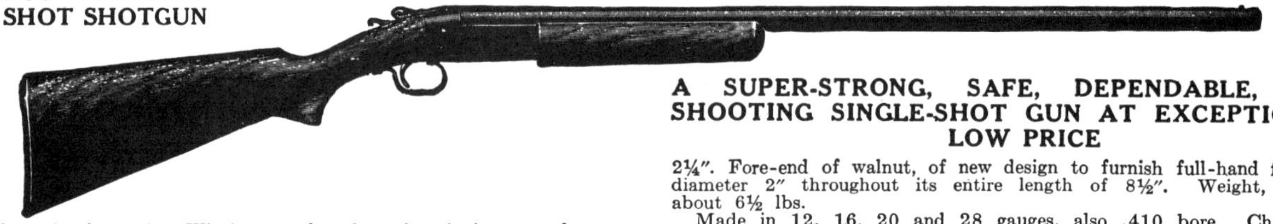

A SUPER-STRONG, SAFE, DEPENDABLE, HARD-SHOOTING SINGLE-SHOT GUN AT EXCEPTIONALLY LOW PRICE

Frame formed of genuine Winchester-selected steel. Action, top lever breakdown with semi-hammerless rebounding lock, safety cocking lever on tang. Positive automatic ejection. Barrel sturdy steel with extra large main lug and brazed fore-end lug. Full choke, designed to give patterns of approximately 70%. Stock of genuine American walnut, with pistol grip and composition butt plate; length 14″, drop at comb 1½″, drop at heel 2¼″. Fore-end of walnut, of new design to furnish full-hand fitting grip, diameter 2″ throughout its entire length of 8½″. Weight, 12 gauge, about 6½ lbs.

Made in 12, 16, 20 and 28 gauges, also .410 bore. Chambered in 12, 16 and 20 gauges for 2¾ inch shells; in 28 gauge for 2⅞″ shells, in .410 bore for 3″ shells. Shoots all standard shotgun loads. Barrel lengths furnished: 12 ga.—28, 30 and 32 in. 16, 20 and 28 ga.—28, 30 and 32 in. In .410 bore with 26 or 28 in. barrel.

Price $8.98

WINCHESTER
Model 40 Automatic (Self-Loading) Shotguns
Streamlined for Natural Pointing

Field Gun

$52.42

MODEL 40 FIELD GUN

This handsomely streamlined completely new design represents the latest development of the Winchester Automatic (self-loading) gun principle. It includes a number of new features that combine to make it an outstanding gun, with smoothness of operation, balance and handling feel, and mechanical precision.

Chambered for 2¾" shells. Pistol grip stock of standard grade American walnut. Stock and forearm not checkered. Dimensions: Length of pull, 14". Drop at comb, 1½". Drop at heel, 2½". Pitch down 2". Stock to special dimensions can be furnished at extra charge on special order only. Plain barrel of Winchester proof-steel in lengths and chokes as listed below. Magazine capacity of four shells. Furnished with wooden magazine plug to reduce capacity to three shots where required and desired. Hard rubber, checkered butt plate. Weight approximately eight pounds. Solid raised matted rib and ventilated rib barrels cannot be furnished.

	Barrel Length	Choke	Price
G4006S	30 inches	full	$52.42
G4008S	30 inches	modified	52.42
G4003S	28 inches	full	52.42
G4005S	28 inches	Modified	52.42

MODEL 40 SKEET GUN
(With Cutts Compensator Attached)

You will find the Winchester Model 40 skeet gun a handsome, well balanced standard skeet gun. Replacing no other skeet model, this gun is introduced to give skeet shooters a gun of the automatic or self-loading type with the same superior type provided in Winchester double barrel and slide-operated repeater types of special skeet guns.

The Model 40 has a plain barrel with forged muzzle shoulder and Cutts compensator attached. Besides the compensators spreader tube for skeet there is a .705 full-choke tube which interchanges with the spreader, and a special wrench for seating the tubes. Overall length of barrel with choke tube attached is 25⅝ inches. Regular stock dimensions are: Length of pull 14"; drop at comb 1⅝"; drop at heel 2⅜"; pitch down, 2". The forearm is full, round, semi-beavertail, about 2" wide and 10⅜" long. Weight, approximately 8 pounds.

		Price
G4011S	Steel Compensator	$78.30
G4012S	Aluminum Compensator (bright)	78.30
G4013S	Aluminum Comp. (blacked)	78.30

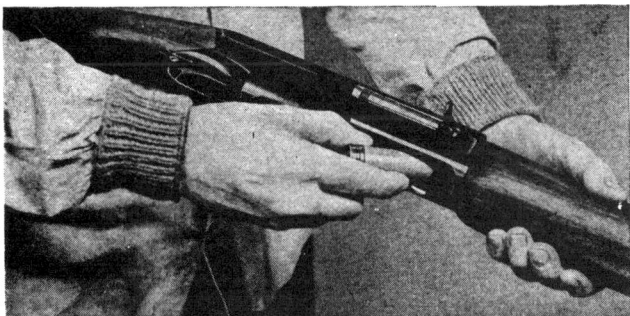

Better balance, from improved distribution of receiver's weight. Note too, both hands in the same horizontal plane, which helps shooting speed and accuracy.

You can load the magazine of Model 40 with one hand. To unload just press down the shell carrier with your thumb, catch each shell with thumb and take them into your hand.

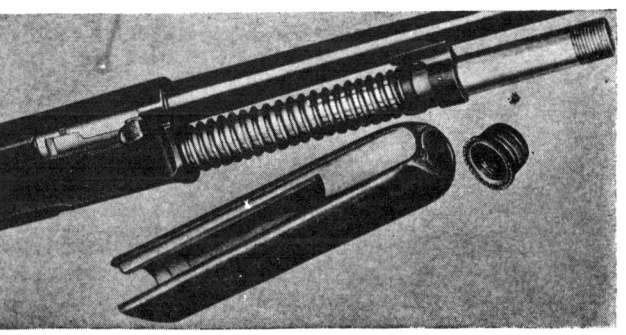

MODEL 40 IS AN OUTSTANDING GUN

SAVAGE AUTOMATIC SHOTGUNS

SAVAGE "UPLAND SPORTER"
12 and 16 Gauge—3 Shots

MODEL 726

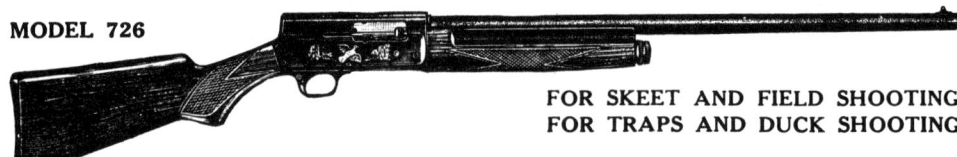

FOR SKEET AND FIELD SHOOTING
FOR TRAPS AND DUCK SHOOTING

The Upland Sporter is a new three-shot automatic especially designed for field shooting. It is light to carry, fast in action and easy to point. The receiver is artistically decorated and this with the special checkering on stock and forearm combine to make an attractive arm for field use. It excels in ease of operation, shooting qualities and all-around dependability.

MODEL 726

Plain round barrel.
BARRELS—12 gauge, 26, 28, 30 and 32-inch lengths; 16 gauge, 26, 28 and 30-inch lengths. Full, modified or cylinder bore.
STOCK—Selected American walnut. Full pistol grip checkered on grip and forestock. Push-button type safety in rear of trigger guard. Magazine capacity two shells, with one in chamber, giving three shots. Receiver channeled and matted in line of sight. Friction ring adjustment for light and heavy loads. Receiver artistically decorated. Weight, 16 gauge, about 7½ pounds; 12 gauge, about 8 pounds.
Price $46.85
(Model 720, similar to Model 726 but 5 shot capacity available at same price.)

MODEL 727
With solid raised matted rib. Same specifications as Model 726. Raised rib on barrel gives a flat line of sight from receiver to end of barrel.
Price $54.70
(Model 721, similar to Model 727 but 5 shot capacity, available at same price.)

MODEL 728
With ventilated raised rib. Same specifications as Model 726.
Price $60.75
(Model 722, similar to Model 728 but 5 shot capacity, available at same price.)

EXTRA BARRELS FOR AUTOMATIC SHOTGUNS
Plain round barrel $18.65
With raised matted rib...26.50
With ventilated raised rib..32.55

SAVAGE AUTOMATIC SHOTGUN WITH CUTTS COMPENSATOR

MODEL 720-C—5 shot Model 720-C..$65.55
MODEL 726-C—3 shot Model 726-C..65.55

Same specifications as Models 720 and 726 as described above except as follows: 20-inch Special Barrel with Cutts Compensator attached furnished with two choke tubes. Spreader tube making barrel length overall 24⅝ inches. No. 705 Full Choke Tube making barrel length overall 26¼ inches. Modified choke tube will be substituted if specified.

MODEL 740-C—3 shot Skeet Model

With Cutts Compensator and two tubes as above. With special large Beavertail forearm and selected American walnut stock both elaborately checkered and oil finished. Receiver artistically decorated on sides, channeled and matted in line of sight. Friction ring adjustment for light and heavy loads. Weight about 8½ pounds.
Price $71.10

SAVAGE AUTOMATIC SHOTGUNS WITH POLY CHOKE

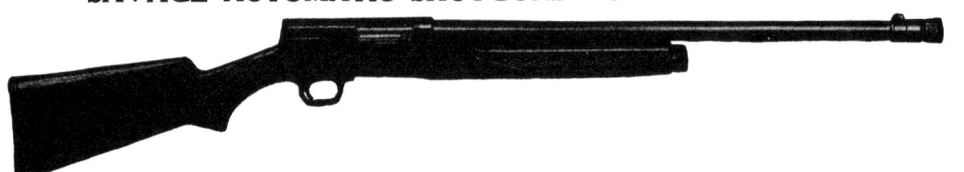

MODEL 720-P—5 shot Model 720-P..$55.90
MODEL 726-P—3 shot Model 726-P...55.90

Same specifications as Models 720 and 726 except as follows: Barrel equipped with Poly Choke—26-inch standard length. Any standard barrel length for this model on special order.

MODEL 740-P—3 shot Price........$59.50
(not illustrated)

Skeet Model. Of the same specifications and finish as Model 740-C except with Poly choke. Special barrel equipped with Poly choke. Barrel length 26 inches overall. Weight about 8½ pounds.

A NEW GUN CARRIES A FACTORY GUARANTEE

SAVAGE OVER AND UNDER SHOTGUNS

MODEL 420
MODEL 430

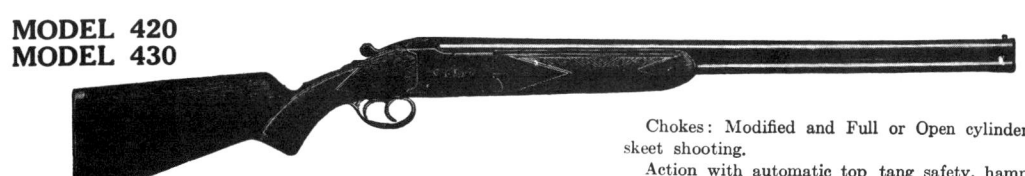

The Savage Over-and-Under Double has filled the long felt demand for such a gun. It is beautifully designed, of safe construction and has fine balance, especially recommended for Field and Skeet shooting. Once you use one of these new Over-and-Under guns you will find a different reaction of the recoil; no side whip, therefore much faster to fire your second shot. For the hunter used to shooting a rifle it will appeal instantly, doing away with the side by side vision always found to interfere with the sighting of a double barrel shotgun.

Model 420—Hammerless, Takedown made in 12, 16 and 20 Gauge.
Stock of selected oil finished walnut with full pistol grip. (No checkering.)

Barrels to be had 12 and 16 Gauge in 26 inch, 28 inch and 30 inch length and in 20 Gauge, 26 inch and 28 inch.

Chokes: Modified and Full or Open cylinder and Improved cylinder for skeet shooting.
Action with automatic top tang safety, hammerless with unbreakable coil springs, all working parts are made to give long wearing service. The front trigger fires the lower barrel and the rear trigger the upper barrel.
Stock dimensions on all guns are 14 inch length, drop at heel 2¾ inch, at comb 1⅝ inch.
Weight—12 Ga./28 inch about 7 lbs. 12 oz.
Weight—16 Ga./28 inch about 7 lbs. 6 oz.
Weight—20 Ga./28 inch about 6 lbs. 13 oz.
Price $35.30
Model 430—Hammerless, Takedown made in 12 16 and 20 Gauge. Same specifications as Model 420 with following extras:
Barrel with matted side line on top barrel.
Stock of selected Fancy Crotch Walnut with full pistol grip beautifully checkered and fitted with Jostam Anti-Flinch Recoil Pad.
Price $39.85
Extras for Models 420 and 430:
   Non-selective Single Trigger..................Price 9.60
   Extra set of barrels for Model 420.................. 17.65
   Extra set of barrels for Model 430.................. 20.20

STEVENS REPEATING SHOTGUNS

MODEL 620

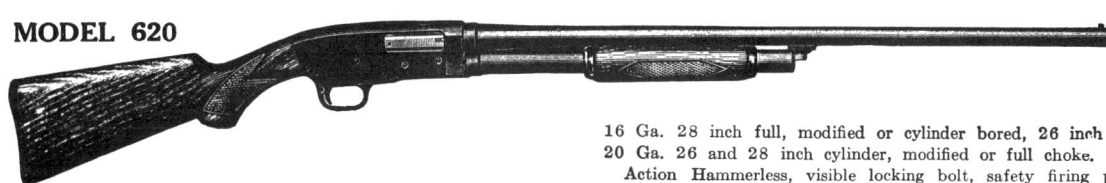

This gun has many features well liked by those who have used it. The take-down is one of the simplest ever constructed and is based on the Browning patents. This gun will stand heavy loads when used for Field shooting or in the Duck blind, and when given proper care it will last a life time. As a Riot gun it is used for guard duty and stands rough handling. In price it is the cheapest, but in quality it counts among the best.

Model 620 Repeating Shotgun to be had in 12 Ga. 28, 30 and 32 inch full choked, 28 and 30 inch modified, 26 and 28 inch cylinder bored; 16 Ga. 28 inch full, modified or cylinder bored, 26 inch cylinder bored; 20 Ga. 26 and 28 inch cylinder, modified or full choke.
Action Hammerless, visible locking bolt, safety firing pin, independent safety side ejection, take down and solid breech drop forged.
Stock of American walnut with checkered full pistol grip and checkered slide handle, rubber buttplate. Length 13¾ inches. Drop at heel 2¾ inches.
Weight: 12 Ga., about 7¾ lbs., 16 Ga. 7¼ lbs., 20 Ga. about 6 lbs.
Magazine capacity—Six Shots. A plug is furnished to cut down magazine capacity to 3 shots to conform with Government regulations on migratory birds.
Model 620 .... $36.60
Model 620P—Same as above but equipped with Poly-Choke. Barrel 12 Gauge, 28" or 30"; 16 or 20 Gauge, 28" only.............. 41.65
Model 621 the same as Model 620 with raised matted solid rib..... 40.10

STEVENS DOUBLE BARREL HAMMERLESS SHOTGUNS

MODEL 530

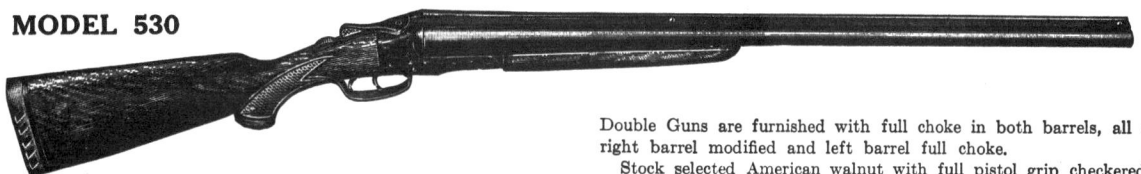

The Stevens factory has been making shotguns for a good many years and knows how to make them to stand up under any and all conditions. Here is a model designed according to the most modern ideas, nothing forgotten to make these guns as wanted by the shooter for field and skeet.

Model 530 comes with blued compressed forged steel barrels tested with Nitro Powder. Length: 12 Ga. 26, 28, 30 and 32 inches; 16 Ga. 26, 28 and 30 inches; 20 Ga. 26 and 28 inches; 410 Ga. 26 inches with matted rib and 2 Lyman ivory bead sights. All 12 Ga. 32 inch and 410 Ga.

Double Guns are furnished with full choke in both barrels, all others have right barrel modified and left barrel full choke.
Stock selected American walnut with full pistol grip checkered and fitted with Jostam Anti-flinch recoil pad. Length 14 inches, drop about 2¾ inches. Frame is polished and case hardened. Action is hammerless with coil springs of new design.
Weight: 12 Ga. 7½ to 8 lbs., 16 Ga. 7 to 7½ lbs., 20 Ga. 6½ to 6¾ lbs., 410 Ga. 5¾ to 6 lbs.
Price $24.25
Model 530ST Same specifications as Model 530 except fitted with non-selective single trigger.
Price $27.60

REMINGTON REPEATING SHOTGUNS

MODEL 31A
TAKEDOWN

For Skeet and Upland Game
For Trapshooting and Ducks

The reception by outstanding upland game and duck shooters, and its selection by so many seasoned Skeet enthusiasts, proves that Remington craftsmen have produced, in the Model 31 a repeating shotgun that meets *every requirement* for supreme speed, ease of handling and perfect balance,—also fast, smooth operation.

Another attribute that is generally conceded is the ease and speed with which it takes down, and the interchangeability of its barrels. For, with the Model 31, you have your choice of any standard barrel length, any boring, cylinder, modified or full choke, 12, 16 or 20 gauges, with least monetary outlay. And, whether you use the Model 31 for upland game, or for high flying water fowl,—or at trap or on the Skeet field, rest assured this repeater will function perfectly, deliver uniform patterns at the longest possible range, as will no other gun of its type marketed today at anywhere near its modest price.

Its supremely smooth action, with extremely short stroke ... its superb balance, makes it lightning fast and easy to point. In addition, it takes down easily and quickly, and the fact that the barrel is removed as a separate unit is a decided advantage for the man who wishes an extra barrel of another length and boring for different kinds of game. It is unnecessary to buy an extra magazine tube and fore-end with an extra barrel.

Here's a repeater that you can hold in any position with the action open and a shell cannot fall out if the fore-end is slightly advanced. And you can have it in 12, 16 and 20 gauges, with barrels from 26 to 32 inches, cylinder, modified or full choke.

SPECIFICATIONS

No. 31A Standard Grade. Chambered for 2¾-inch shells. Side ejection, hammerless, solid breech, take-down, 3 or 5-shot. Cross bolt safety; 26, 28, 30 or 32-inch barrel—full choke, modified choke or cylinder bore. Top of receiver matted. American walnut stock and fore-end, both handsomely checkered. Regular stock dimensions, 14 inches long, 2½ inches drop at heel and 1⅝ inches drop at comb; half pistol grip. Bakelite butt plate. Weight, 12 gauge, about 7½ pounds; 16 gauge, about 6¾ pounds; 20 gauge, about 6½ pounds.

Selection of Standard Barrel Lengths and Borings
Any boring not listed in lengths shown will be furnished at extra charge

12 GAUGE

	PLAIN BARRELS	SOLID RIB BARRELS
Full Choke	28, 30, 32 inch	28, 30, 32 inch
Modified Choke	26, 28, 30 inch	28, 30 inch
Cylinder or Imp. Cyl.	26, 28 inch	26, inch

16 GAUGE

Full Choke	26, 28, 30 inch	28, 30 inch
Modified Choke	26, 28 inch	28 inch
Cylinder or Imp. Cyl.	26, 28 inch	26 inch

20 GAUGE

Full Choke	26, 28, 30 inch	26, 28, 30 inch
Modified Choke	26, 28 inch	26, 28 inch
Cylinder or Imp. Cyl.	26, 28 inch	26 inch

No. 31A—"Standard" Grade (without checkering)	$43.64
Extra barrel	18.87

Standard dimensions of stock, 14 inches long, 2½ inches drop at heel, 1⅝ inches drop at comb. Half pistol grip. Any other length or drop of stock made to order at an advance of........ **15.14**

No. 31R—"Riot" Grade (without checkering)	43.64
No. 31B—"Special" Grade	52.92
Extra barrel	18.87

Standard dimensions of stock same as 31A. Any other stock dimensions subject to an additional charge of................ **15.14**

No. 31D—"Tournament" Grade	137.32
Extra barrel	27.75
No. 31E—"Expert" Grade	206.09
Extra barrel	35.52
No. 31F—"Premier" Grade	274.95
Extra barrel	42.18

Nos. 31D, E and F supplied with any grip, length or drop desired without additional charge.

Raised solid matted rib, extra	8.07
Special Long Range Choke (12 ga. only, 30″), extra	4.44
Checkering on A or R Grade	4.44

MODEL 31TC
TARGET GRADE

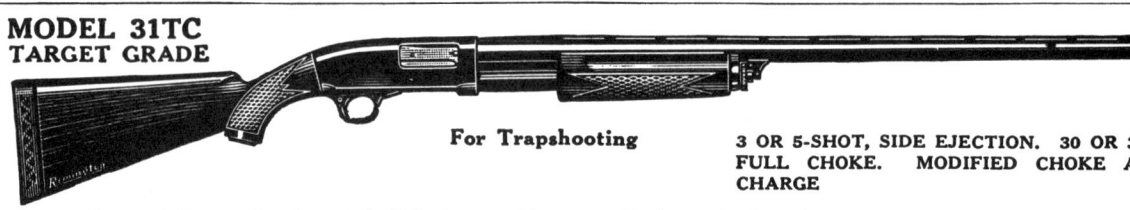

For Trapshooting

3 OR 5-SHOT, SIDE EJECTION. 30 OR 32 INCHES. FULL CHOKE. MODIFIED CHOKE AT EXTRA CHARGE

Whether a man shoots at live or clay targets he'll just naturally revel in this popular Remington ... its remarkably fast, easy action,—the result, in large measure, of the shorter fore-end stroke—the way it handles ... the absence of barrel whip ... the light, snappy, trigger pull.

Of course, the confirmed trap shooter will want, in addition, a raised, ventilated rib, to provide the desired sighting plane, a modern recoil pad, and finely checkered stock and fore-end to give a firm grip and insure steady holding.

In the Model 31TC "Target" Grade, Remington has achieved all this, and more. The result is *the finest trap gun ever offered at a moderate price*—a strong statement, but one that careful comparison of values quickly substantiates.

When making this comparison, note how, in the Model 31TC the ventilated rib is made in one piece, integral with the barrel ... the specially designed fore-end, with its short stroke ... the easy loading feature. Observe that coil springs are used throughout —you'll never know a broken spring with your Model 31TC. An important safety feature is that constant pressure on trigger when closing the action will not fire the gun.

SPECIFICATIONS

Model 31TC "Target" Grade. Chambered for 2¾-inch shells; 3 or 5-shot capacity. Ventilated ribbed barrel; barrel length 30 or 32 inches. Full choke; modified choke at extra charge. Front and rear sights. Fore-end as illustrated, regularly furnished. Long extension Beaver Tail fore-end same as on Model 31 "Skeet" grade furnished on special order without extra charge. Hawkins recoil pal. Checkered stock and fore-end of selected high-grade walnut. Standard stock dimensions, 14⅜ inches long over all, 1⅞ inches drop at heel, 1½ inches drop at comb. Full pistol grip with rubber cap; option of straight grip. Will furnish made-to-order lengths from 13½ to 15 inches without extra charge. Weight, about 8 pounds, in 12 gauge only.

No. 31TC—"Target" Grade with ventilated rib	$88.44
Extra barrel with ventilated rib	39.45
Shortening regular stock up to 1 inch, No. 31TC, extra	4.44
Stock with dimensions outside of prescribed limits, extra	15.14
Modified choke boring, 30-inch barrel, extra	4.44

AMERICA'S GREAT GUN HOUSE

REMINGTON PUMP GUNS
MODEL NO. 31—SKEET GUN—5-SHOT—Side Ejection—12, 16 AND 20 GAUGES

The popular choice among Skeet shooters who prefer slide action. Many field hunters use this gun at Skeet. The smooth action with short fore-end stroke is lightning fast to operate, and absolutely dependable.

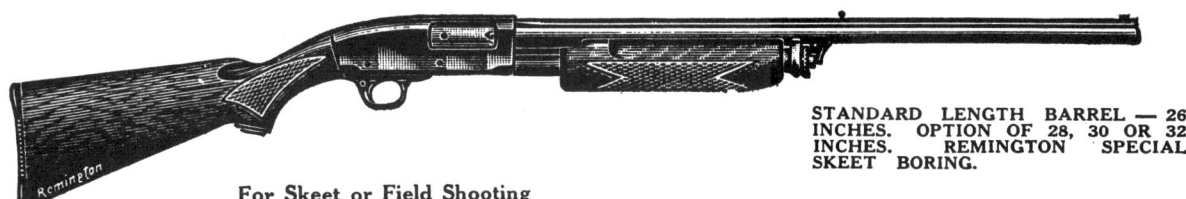

For Skeet or Field Shooting

STANDARD LENGTH BARREL — 26 INCHES. OPTION OF 28, 30 OR 32 INCHES. REMINGTON SPECIAL SKEET BORING.

SPECIFICATIONS

Model 31 "Skeet" Grade. Side ejection, hammerless, solid breech, takedown. Chambered for 2¾ inch shells. Raised solid ribbed barrel. Top of receiver matted. Cross bolt safety. American walnut stock and fore-end, both handsomely checkered. Full pistol grip with rubber cap. Walnut colored Bakelite butt plate. Lyman ivory bead front sight. White metal bead rear sight on ribbed barrels only. Long extension Beaver Tail fore-end. 5-shot capacity. A 3-shot magazine plug at no extra charge. Weight, 20 gauge, about 7 pounds; 16 gauge, about 7¼ pounds; 12 gauge, about 8 pounds.

No. 31. "Skeet" Grade with raised solid matted rib (Furnished unless otherwise specified) $60.74
No. 31. "Skeet" Grade with raised ventilated rib (12 Ga. only) 73.25
No. 31. "Skeet" Grade with plain barrel 52.67

MODEL 31S 12 GAUGE

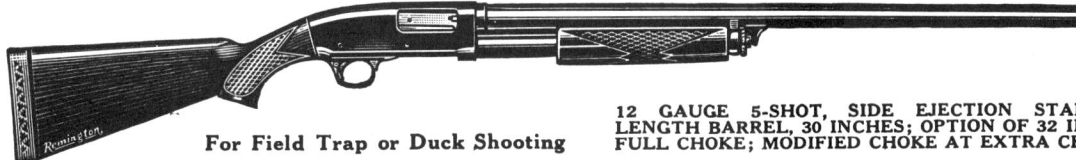

For Field Trap or Duck Shooting

12 GAUGE 5-SHOT, SIDE EJECTION STANDARD LENGTH BARREL, 30 INCHES; OPTION OF 32 INCHES. FULL CHOKE; MODIFIED CHOKE AT EXTRA CHARGE.

It was to be expected that the factors that have endeared the famous Model 31 side-ejection pump gun to so many field shooters, since its inception, should strike a responsive chord with trap shooters.

All barrels are carefully bored to give uniform, evenly distributed patterns, so necessary to prevent targets getting through when the shooter is dead on the target.

Whether a man shoots at live or clay targets he'll just naturally revel in this popular Remington . . . its remarkably fast, easy action,—the result, in large measure, of the shorter fore-end stroke—the way it handles . . . the absence of barrel whip . . . the light, snappy, trigger pull.

SPECIFICATIONS

Model 31S "Trap Special" Grade. 5-shot capacity. 3-shot magazine plug at no extra charge. Raised solid matted ribbed barrel (option of matted top surface of barrel). 30 or 32 inch barrel. Full choke. Modified choke at extra charge. Front and rear sights. Hawkins recoil pad. Checkered stock and fore-end of American walnut. Standard stock dimensions, 14⅜ inches long over-all, 1⅞ inches drop at heel, 1½ inches drop at comb. Half pistol grip—option of straight grip. Weight, about 8 pounds.

No. 31S. "Trap Special" Grade with Raised Solid Rib or matted top surface of barrel $63.31
Extra barrel, matted or with Raised Solid Rib 26.94

Standard stock dimensions, 14⅜ inches long including Hawkins recoil pad, 1⅞ inches drop at heel, 1½ inches drop at comb. Half pistol grip; option of straight grip. American walnut stock and fore-end.
Shortening regular stock up to 1 inch, on 31S, extra $4.44
Special drop or greater length of stock, on 31S, extra 15.14
Modified choke boring, 30 inch barrel only, extra 4.44

EXTRAS SUPPLIED ON REMINGTON SHOTGUNS
SPECIAL WORK OF THIS KIND ENTAILS SOME DELAY

Soft rubber recoil pad fitted, extra (excepting where regular) $5.55
Full pistol grip with rubber cap on Models 11A, 11B, Sportsman (A&B), 31A, 31B, 31S, 32A, 32S, extra 4.44
Cutting off regular stock up to 1 inch, extra (Shotguns only) 3.00
Long Extension fore-end on Model 31 (excepting where regular), extra 8.07
Beavertail fore-end on Sportsman, extra (excepting on "Skeet" Grade) 4.44

Beaver Tail fore-end on Model 32, extra (excepting where regular) $3.03
White metal bead rear sight on shotguns (ribbed barrels only), extra .... .55
Ivory bead front sight on shotguns, extra 1.11
Ivory bead rear sight on shotguns (ribbed barrels only), extra ..... .55
Gold Name Plate inlaid in stock, extra (excepting on F Grade) 8.88
Silver Name Plate inlaid in stock, extra (excepting on E and F Grades) 6.66

SPECIAL LONG RANGE BARRELS

Distance is annihilated with the new, especially bored, Remington Long Range Barrels.
Trapshooters—an extra advantage on double targets and handicap shooting. Especially designed for Remington Trap Load and Remington Handicap Trap Load Coppered Shot.
Duckshooters—will bring down their game at ranges heretofore impossible for the ordinary 12-gauge gun.

For all long range shooting—closer patterns and greater effectiveness are obtainable than with the standard full choke barrel. Especially bored for Nitro Express and Arrow Express Loads.
Price, extra (add to price of gun or extra barrel) $4.44
SUPPLIED IN 12 GAUGE ONLY—BARREL LENGTHS 30 AND 32 INCHES ONLY—FOR ALL REMINGTON 12 GAUGE SHOTGUNS EXCEPT MODEL 32.

CAREFUL ATTENTION AND SAFE DELIVERY OF YOUR ORDER

REMINGTON OVER AND UNDER SHOTGUNS

MODEL 32A 12 GAUGE

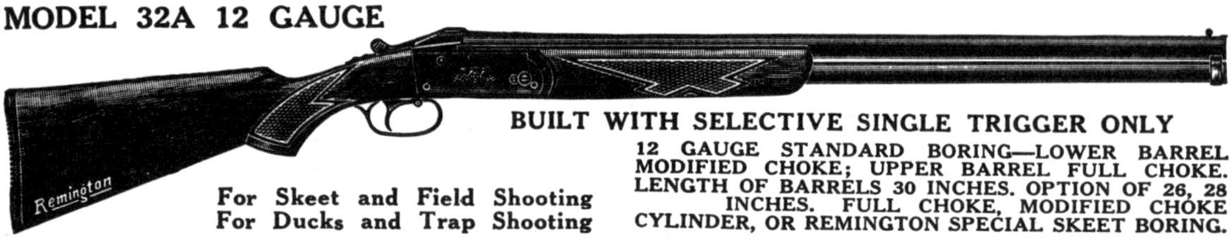

For Skeet and Field Shooting
For Ducks and Trap Shooting

BUILT WITH SELECTIVE SINGLE TRIGGER ONLY

12 GAUGE STANDARD BORING—LOWER BARREL MODIFIED CHOKE; UPPER BARREL FULL CHOKE. LENGTH OF BARRELS 30 INCHES. OPTION OF 26, 28 INCHES. FULL CHOKE, MODIFIED CHOKE CYLINDER, OR REMINGTON SPECIAL SKEET BORING.

The first American-made Over-and-Under gun. No finer or stronger gun of this type available. Has exclusive features not found in imported Over-and-Under guns at considerably higher prices. Its attractive appearance, smooth graceful lines and superb balance will appeal to discriminating sportsmen. Smaller, stronger and better looking frame. Simple but sturdy construction. Upper and lower tangs made in one piece with frame. Special mounting of barrels to allow for uneven expansion and to insure shooting on center. Absence of side ribs eliminates heat waves and permits better pointing. Mechanism readily accessible. Automatic ejectors. Selective three-way safety—automatic, manual or inoperative. Heat treated frame for greater strength. Both sides of frame handsomely decorated. Grip and fore-end beautifully checkered.

One barrel above the other gives the advantage of a single sighting plane; straight line recoil reduces recoil and whip of gun. Simple take-down. Narrow-grip—more natural. Ideal for Trap and Skeet shooting, especially on doubles.

SPECIFICATIONS

No. 32A Standard Grade. Take-down, hammerless, automatic ejectors, 12 gauge only. Standard length barrels 30 inches; also furnished in 26, 28, inches. Full choke, modified choke, improved cylinder or true cylinder bore. Option of any combination desired. Selective single trigger. Walnut pistol-grip stock and fore-end, both handsomely checkered. Top of main bolt is matted and both sides of frame are decorated. Regular stock dimensions 14 inches long, 2½ inches drop at heel, and 1⅝ inches drop at comb. Bakelite butt plate. Weight about 7½ lbs.

No. 32A—"Standard" Grade	$127.13
Extra pair of barrels	60.54
*Standard stock dimensions, 14 inches long, 2½ inches drop at heel, 1⅝ inches drop at comb. Half pistol grip. Any other dimensions, subject to extra charge of	15.14
No. 32D—"Tournament" Grade	278.99
No. 32E—"Expert" Grade	329.44
No. 32F—"Premeir" Grade	415.20

Nos. 32D, E, F also supplied with any grip, length or drop desired without additional charge.

Raised solid matted rib, extra 8.07

MODEL 32 SKEET GUN

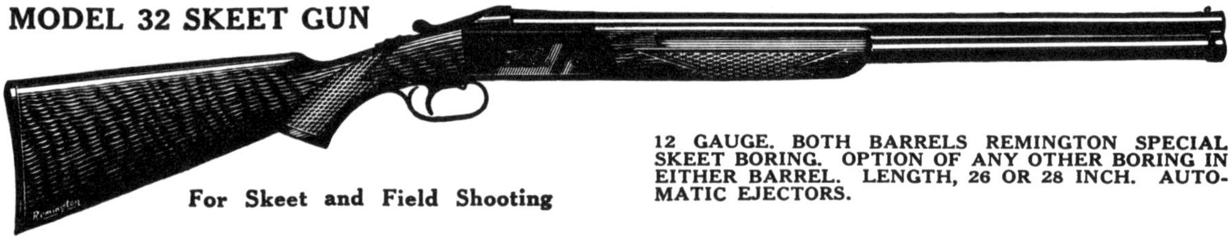

For Skeet and Field Shooting

12 GAUGE. BOTH BARRELS REMINGTON SPECIAL SKEET BORING. OPTION OF ANY OTHER BORING IN EITHER BARREL. LENGTH, 26 OR 28 INCH. AUTOMATIC EJECTORS.

This is the coming gun for Skeet shooting. Its popularity is rapidly increasing. Particularly fine on Skeet "doubles" shots. Straight line recoil of lower barrel leaves the shooter ready without disturbance for his second shot immediately after breaking the first target. Single sighting plane permits the most accurate pointing. Perfect balance. Remington Selective Single Trigger absolutely dependable. Remington Special Skeet Boring in both barrels assures well distributed shot patterns at all Skeet ranges. Lower barrel is marked "out" for use on outgoing target. Upper barrel is marked "in" for use on incoming target.

SPECIFICATIONS

No. 32 Skeet Grade (26-inch barrels). Take-down, hammerless, automatic ejectors, 12 gauge only. Standard length barrels 26 inches; also furnished in 28, inches. Standard boring, both barrels Remington Special Skeet Boring. Lower barrel marked "out" for use on outgoing target, upper barrel marked "in" for incoming target. Option of any other combination of borings desired. Single trigger. Selected, high-grade walnut pistol-grip stock and fore-end, both handsomely checkered. Top of main bolt is matted and both sides of frame are decorated. Regular stock dimensions 14 inches long from front trigger, 2½ inches drop at heel, and 1⅝ inches drop at comb. Bakelite butt plate. Weight about 7½ pounds. Half pistol grip. Beaver tail fore-end.

No. 32. "Skeet" Grade with plain barrel	$130.16
No. 32. "Skeet" Grade with raised solid rib	138.23
No. 32. "Skeet" Grade with ventilated rib	150.74
Shortening regular stock up to 1 inch, extra	4.44
Special drop or greater length of stock, extra	15.14

MODEL 32TC 12 GAUGE
WITH VENTILATED RIB

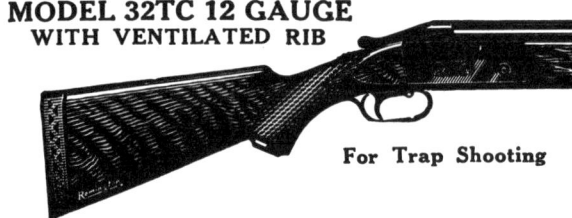

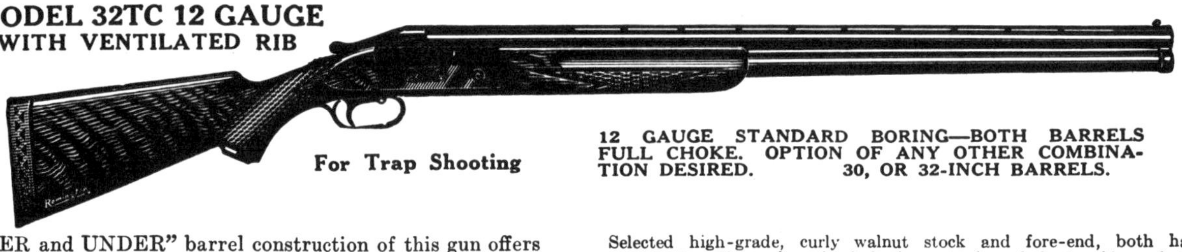

For Trap Shooting

12 GAUGE STANDARD BORING—BOTH BARRELS FULL CHOKE. OPTION OF ANY OTHER COMBINATION DESIRED. 30, OR 32-INCH BARRELS.

The "OVER and UNDER" barrel construction of this gun offers a single sighting plane which permits more accurate pointing. Straight line recoil of the lower barrel eliminates barrel whip. Special features for the trapshooter include the raised ventilated rib which is integral with the barrel, the stock and fore-end which are especially designed for trapshooting, the full pistol grip, soft rubber recoil pad, and Remington Selective Single Trigger.

Selected high-grade, curly walnut stock and fore-end, both handsomely checkered. Top of main bolt is matted and both sides of frame are decorated. Standard stock dimensions 14⅜ inches long over all, 1⅞ inches drop at heel and 1½ inches drop at comb. Full pistol grip with rubber cap; option of straight grip. Will furnish made-to-order lengths from 13½ to 15 inches without extra charge. Weight about 8¼ pounds.

No. 32TC—"Target" Grade with Ventilated rib, Selective Single Trigger and Beaver Tail Fore-end (as illustrated) $156.29

Stock with dimensions outside of prescribed limits, No. 32T, extra . 15.14

SPECIFICATIONS

Model 32TC Target Grade with raised ventilated matted rib. Take-down, hammerless, automatic ejectors, 12 gauge only. Choice of 30 or 32-inch barrels. Standard boring—both barrels full choke. Option of any other combination desired. Front and rear sights. Hawkins recoil pad.

NOTE—Only Regular dimensions carried in stock. Special stocks require from five to eight weeks to make and orders for such are POSITIVELY NOT SUBJECT TO CANCELLATION.

REMINGTON AUTOLOADING SHOTGUNS
3-SHOT—12, 16 AND 20 GAUGES

"SPORTSMAN" TAKEDOWN

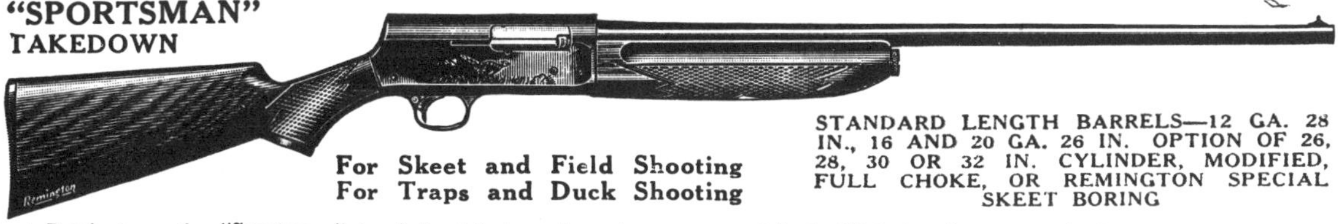

For Skeet and Field Shooting
For Traps and Duck Shooting

Like most Remingtons, the "Sportsman" is of the takedown type, hammerless, with solid breech. It has what is admitted to be the most effective, positive safety feature of any gun—the Cross Bolt Safety, which is conveniently located in rear of the trigger guard for quick operation.

Beyond any shadow of doubt the "Sportsman" has the fastest action of any shotgun ever built.

The strong action and recoil springs prolong the life of the gun and reduce recoil.

There is a special friction ring device to reduce recoil of heavy loads to the very minimum; a fibre cushion is located at the back of the receiver to absorb the shock of recoiling parts. Additional features that further endear this "aristocrat of shotguns" to gun connoisseurs in particular, are the reinforced fore-end, locked breech to give maximum shooting qualities, barrel guide ring with long bearing surface to prevent buckling, loading or unloading of magazine without removing shell from the chamber—or removal of loaded shell from the chamber without disturbing those in the magazine.

The Sportsman A—"Standard" Grade	$52.42
Extra barrel	19.98

*Standard dimensions of stock, 14 inches long, 2½ inches drop at heel, 1⅝ inches drop at comb. Half pistol grip. Any other length or stock made to order subject to additional charge of | 15.14

The Sportsman B—"Special" Grade	57.26
Extra barrel	19.98

*Stock dimensions same as 11A.
*Standard dimensions of stock, 14⅜ inches long, 2¼ inches drop

STANDARD LENGTH BARRELS—12 GA. 28 IN., 16 AND 20 GA. 26 IN. OPTION OF 26, 28, 30 OR 32 IN. CYLINDER, MODIFIED, FULL CHOKE, OR REMINGTON SPECIAL SKEET BORING

at heel, 1½ inches drop at comb. Straight grip option of half pistol grip. Any other length or drop of stock made to order subject to additional charge of $15.14

The Sportsman D—"Tournament" Grade	147.82
Extra barrel	26.64
The Sportsman E—"Expert" Grade	214.41
Extra barrel	35.52
The Sportsman F—"Premier" Grade	281.01
Extra barrel	42.18

Grades D, E and F also supplied with any grip, length or drop desired without additional charge.

Raised solid matted rib, extra	8.07
Raised ventilated rib, extra	14.43
Remington special long range choke boring (12 ga. only 30 or 32 ins.) extra	4.44

SPECIFICATIONS

The Sportsman. Take-down, hammerless, solid breech; 12, 16 and 20 gauges, 3 shots (2 in the magazine and 1 in the chamber). Cross bolt safety (reversed for left-handed shooters at no extra charge) 26, 28, 30 or 32-inch barrel; cylinder, modified or full choke. Top of receiver matted and both sides handsomely decorated. American walnut pistol grip stock and fore-end, both finely checkered. Barrel and receiver in rich, glossy black finish. Stock dimensions, 14 inches long, 2½ inches drop at heel, 1⅝ inches at comb. Weight, 20 gauge, about 6¾ pounds; 16 gauge, about 7 pounds; 12 gauge, about 7¾ pounds.

MODEL 11A TAKEDOWN
5-SHOT—12, 16 AND 20 GAUGES

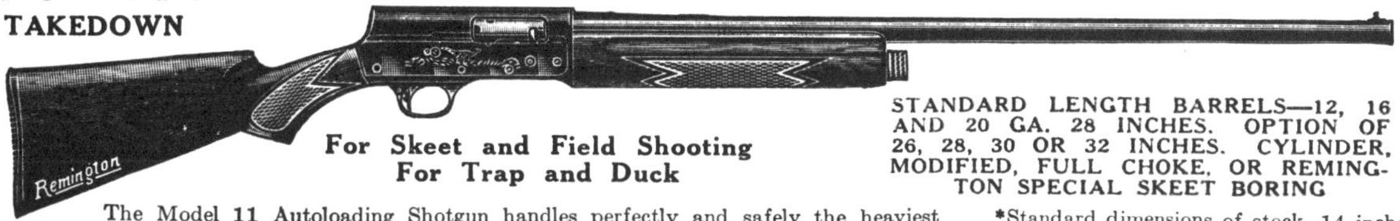

For Skeet and Field Shooting
For Trap and Duck

The Model 11 Autoloading Shotgun handles perfectly and safely the heaviest long range loads. It has a friction ring device to reduce the recoil of the heavy loads, after the fashion of the shock absorbers on automobiles. A fibre cushion at the back of the receiver still further takes up the shock and makes for durability and long life in the gun.

A decided advantage in this Remington Autoloader is the fact that a loaded shell may be removed from the chamber without disturbing shells in the magazine. Furthermore, the magazine may be filled or unloaded without removing shell from the chamber.

In the Model 11 there is no loss of power of the shot charge in the operation of the mechanism. The barrel and the breech bolt are locked together until after the shot leaves the muzzle; the gun being full recoil operated.

Heavy action and recoil springs materially prolong gun life and reduce recoil. The fore-end is reinforced; the solid breech provides added protection. The barrel guide ring has long bearing surface to prevent buckling.

The Remington Model 11 and "Sportsman" are the only autoloaders, made in 16 gauge to take the Kleanbore Auto Express load in 2¾-inch shell. This splendid 16-gauge load gives 12 gauge results because it exceeds 3¼ drams of progressive burning powder and 1⅛ ounces of shot.

SPECIFICATIONS

No. 11A "Standard" Grade. Chambered for 2¾-inch shells. Take-down, hammerless, solid breech; 12, 16 and 20 gauges, 5 shots. 3-shot magazine plug at no extra charge. Cross bolt safety; 26, 28, 30 or 32-inch barrel, cylinder, modified or full choke. Top of receiver matted. American walnut pistol grip stock, and fore-end, both finely checkered. Regular stock dimensions 14 inches long, 2½ inches drop at heel, 1⅝ inches drop at comb. Weight, 12 gauge, about 7¾ pounds; 16 gauge, about 7 pounds; 20 gauge, about 6¾ pounds.

No. 11R—"Riot" Grade, 20-inch barrel	$52.42
No. 11A—"Standard" Grade	52.42
Extra barrel	19.98

STANDARD LENGTH BARRELS—12, 16 AND 20 GA. 28 INCHES. OPTION OF 26, 28, 30 OR 32 INCHES. CYLINDER, MODIFIED, FULL CHOKE, OR REMINGTON SPECIAL SKEET BORING

*Standard dimensions of stock, 14 inches long, 2½ inches drop at heel, 1⅝ inches at comb. Half pistol grip. Any other length or drop of stock made to order subject to additional charge of $15.14

No. 11B—"Special" Grade	57.26
Extra barrel	19.98

*Stock dimensions same as 11A.
*Standard dimensions of stock, 14⅜ inches long, 2¼ inches drop at heel, 1½ inches drop at comb. Straight grip, option of half pistol grip. Any other length or drop of stock made to order subject to additional charge of 15.14

No. 11D—"Tournament" Grade	147.82
Extra barrel	26.64
No. 11E—"Expert" Grade	214.41
Extra barrel	35.32
No. 11F—"Premier" Grade	281.01
Extra barrel	42.18

Nos. 11D, E and F also supplied with any grip, length or drop desired without additional charge.

Raised solid matted rib, extra	8.07
Raised ventilated rib, extra	14.43
Remington special long range choke boring, (12 ga. only 30 or 32 ins.) extra	4.44

*Note—Only Regular dimensions carried in stock. Special stocks require from five to eight weeks to make and orders for such are POSITIVELY NOT SUBJECT TO CANCELLATION.

"SPORTSMAN" SKEET GUN 3-SHOT—12, 16, AND 20 GAUGES

The "Sportsman" is the ideal gun for Skeet. Nothing so attests the fine performance of the "Sportsman" as its popularity in the hands of the great army of Skeet shooters. The "Sportsman" is the main reliance of a great many expert Skeet shots. Easy to load, easy to operate, light in weight, perfectly balanced, this three-shot autoloader combines greater accuracy with faster handling, less recoil. Remington special skeet boring assures well distributed shot patterns at all skeet ranges. The shot spreads sufficiently for the close incoming targets and holds together uniformly for the speedy outgoers.

SPECIFICATIONS: Sportsman "Skeet" Grade, Takedown, hammerless, solid breech. Chambered for 2¾ inch shells. Cross bolt safety. Top of receiver matted and both sides decorated. Raised ventilated rib. American walnut stock and fore-end, both finely checkered. Full pistol grip with rubber cap. Walnut colored Bakelite butt plate. Lyman ivory bead front sight. White metal rear sight on ribbed barrels only. Beaver Tail fore-end. Weight, 20 gauge, about 7 pounds; 16 gauge, about 7½ pounds; 12 gauge, about 8¼ pounds. Standard length barrel, 26 inches. Option of 28, 30, or 32 inches. Remington Special Skeet Boring. Option of any other boring desired.

The Sportsman "Skeet" Grade, with ventilated rib (standard)	$74.16
The Sportsman "Skeet" Grade, with raised solid rib	67.80
The Sportsman "Skeet" Grade, with plain barrel	59.73

CUTTS COMP AND SUPER POLY CHOKE

Furnished for 12, 16, 20, 28 or .410 Gauge single barrel shotguns of the single shot, repeating and auto-loading types. The compensator produces more hits, lessens the recoil, and eliminates the tendency to flinch. Takes the punishment out of shooting. Especially desirable for shooters desiring to wear minimum clothing in hot climates. Pattern control tubes distribute the uniform pattern, free from breaks or blows.

After deducting from the Compensator the weight of the section of barrel removed, there is but little increase in muzzle weight and with the aluminum compensator the balance is not disturbed at all.

The results of recent tests clearly indicate that an uncompensated shotgun with a trap load has 34% more recoil than a compensated gun. Using maximum high velocity loads this difference is 43%. Users of compensated guns readily appreciate these reductions in recoil.

Recommended for traps, field shooting, or skeet. Reduces Recoil, Gives Uniform Patterns, makes One Gun Good for Many purposes—Features different chokes by using different tubes, easily changed.

CUTTS COMP furnished as set comprising body, two tubes, carrying case for tubes, cleaning brush, wrench and metal bead front sight. Supplied regularly made from SPECIAL STEEL.

Now also available made from ALUMINUM ALLOY metal, weighing 1/3 of steel. Aluminum Comp used with light finish—Steel Comp has popular gun metal finish.

Pattern Tubes made for Cutts Comps cover the wide conditions under which shotguns are used. Cut shows various tubes available for Comps on 12 ga. guns.
Tube No. 680. Intended to be used at ranges 40-65 yds. with the heavy loads and large shot.
Tube No. 690. Similar to No. 680 tube except will give a little more open pattern.
Tube No. 705. Full Choke, corresponds in general pattern percentage to what is known as Full Choke.
Tube No. 725. Modified Choke. Corresponds in general pattern percentage to what is known as modified choke.
Tube No. 755. Popular general purpose tube. Much used by skeet and field shooters. This tube supersedes the No. 740 general purpose tube as originally furnished.
Spreader Tube. This tube of special design is recommended for close range shooting of 30 yds. and under using small shot in standard loads. The tube gives even spread of pattern over 30" circle at 25 yds. and is ideal for Brush and Skeet Shooting.
Note: In ordering tubes specify by number. Spreader and Modified Tubes are supplied in the set unless specified.

Cutts Comps

Reduce Recoil—Takes the punishment out of shooting by reducing recoil by approximately 1/3. This is appreciated by shooters who are competing or who desire to wear light clothing in warm climates.

Give Uniform Patterns—"Blown" patterns unknown when Cutts Comps are used. Even distribution over entire pattern gives shooter most uniform results.

One Gun for Many Purposes

The interchangeable pattern control tubes makes one gun adapted to all kinds of shooting. There are six tubes for 12 ga. guns and 3 tubes for each 16, 20, 28, and .410 ga. guns.

Fitting Cutts Comp

The fitting of a Cutts Comp should be undertaken only by a skilled gunsmith thoroughly familiar with this special work.

Since such facilities are usually not available, we strongly urge all our customers to send in their complete guns to be properly fitted by our competent and experienced gunsmiths.

Prices

Comp, two tubes, wrench, brush, metal front sight, wooden carrying case for tubes $18.50

Pattern control tubes only (see centre column) each $3.00

Labor charge in attaching compensated shotgun $3.50

AERO-DYNE SUPER POLY CHOKE

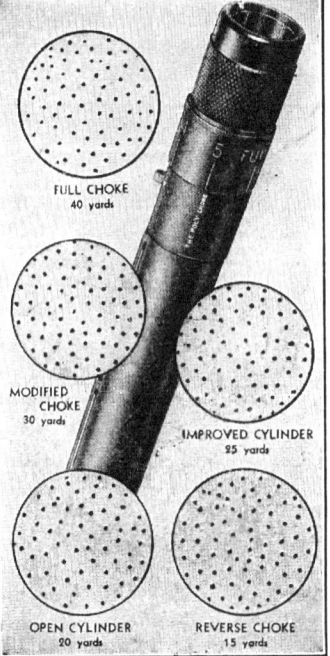

No compromise is necessary when your gun is equipped with a SUPER POLY CHOKE as not only can the proper choke for the various ranges be easily obtained, but whatever choke is required to give maximum results with different sizes of shot is available INSTANTLY!

The SUPER POLY CHOKE was evolved to give a multiplicity of chokes which could be changed from one degree of choke to another almost instantly, thereby doing away with the necessity of extra barrels.

Thus, in an average day's hunt, one hour you may be after woodcock in bushes as thick as the hair on a dog's back, and a wide-open gun is the thing. Another hour, after quail, where the average shot is 20 to 25 yards, an improved cylinder is best. Another time, a full choke is the one to use at some passing crows or ducks. When your gun is equipped with a SUPER POLY CHOKE, and you have selected your shells, patterned the gun, in changing from one choke to another, there is no change in the weight, feel, balance, or center of impact of the gun. This is of very great importance, because success in shotgun shooting is largely the result of having a gun that fits you and with the weight, feel, and balance of which you are familiar.

Instantaneous Adjustment of Choke

With a SUPER POLY CHOKE, your gun is right for either skeet or trap shooting during the summer and equally correct for hunting, and it comes up just as naturally and feels just as good in all shooting. The SUPER POLY CHOKE makes it a truly UNIVERSAL GUN!

The SUPER POLY CHOKE is made from electric furnace chrome nickel steel properly heat treated to give a tensile strength many times greater than the barrel itself. No POLY CHOKE has ever worn out.

The SUPER POLY CHOKE, which comes in 12, 16, and 20 gauge sizes only, is very light and small—about 2¼ inches long, weighs approximately 2½ ounces, and is about 1/8 inch larger in diameter than the gun barrel. Usually we cut off about one ounce of barrel weight, *leaving a net increase of approximately 1½ ounces*—a negligible quantity which does not noticeably affect the balance of the gun; in fact, it helps to steady the swing. The SUPER POLY CHOKE can be attached to either plain, matted, or ventilated rib barrels, and it is beautifully finished a gun-barrel blue. It adds decidedly to the beauty of the gun!

SAVE POSTAGE—SEND BARREL ONLY

Price, Installed $14.75

ALL SHIPMENTS ARE INSURED

WEAVER CHOKE

Makes Your Shotgun an All-Around Gun

Weaver Choke complete with any 2 choke tubes

$9.75

Attaching at Factory Extra $2.50

Although choke boring has improved patterns, the regular shotgun does not always shoot even and true. Occasionally there are "blown" patterns. These may have large holes in the center or the shot may be so scattered that game could be easily missed even with a perfect hold.

The **Weaver-Choke** was developed to eliminate "blown" patterns, to adapt one gun for 20 to 70 yard shooting, and to reduce recoil.

The **Weaver-Choke** is made with a series of baffles in the bore designed to catch the rushing powder gases. These baffles divert much of the gas out through the numerous vents. This gas is released before the shot leaves the muzzle, reducing the pressure on the shot column and reducing the muzzle blast. This, in turn, reduces the disturbance to the shot and it continues on its way as directed by the choke, resulting in even and uniform patterns.

Any degree of Choke from the wide even 20 yard Skeet pattern to Extra Full Choke pattern deadly to 70 yards.

Reduced recoil.

Reduced muzzle blast.

Dependable, uniform distribution of pellets, no blown patterns.

HOW TO ORDER

The **Weaver-Choke** is available in 12, 16, and 20 ga. It is adapted to all autoloading, pump, and single barrel shotguns, either plain or ribbed. It can be attached by any good gunsmith or in our factory. An overall barrel length or 28" to 32" with the XFC Choke is recommended, then with the S Choke the overall length will be 26" to 30".

When ordering give the make and model of your gun, or preferably the outside diameter of the barrel a few inches from the muzzle. Shotgun barrels vary in size and the **Weaver-Choke** is made in two different thread sizes.

EXTRA CHOKES—EACH $1.50

Each individual choke is separate allowing the exact length, boring, shape, and taper for best results.

XFC *(Extra Full Choke)* For extra long range shooting.
FC *(Full Choke)* About like the standard full choke gun.
3/4 *(Three-quarter Choke)* For small game to 40 or 45 yards.
1/2 *(One-half Choke)* For general shooting to about 35 yards.
1/4 *(One-quarter Choke)* Wide pattern for short ranges.
S *(Skeet or Scatter)* For Skeet, also single ball loads.

Note the baffle rings and gas vents in this cutaway view of the WEAVER CHOKE. Rushing gases strike these rings and tend to pull the gun forward, thereby lessening rearward recoil. Gases are released through vents, BEFORE shot leaves barrel, reducing the muzzle blast and preventing scattered shot.

Check These Weaver Features
Uniform Killing Patterns at ALL Ranges
Reduced Recoil and Muzzle Blast
No "Blown" Patterns   Any Degree of Choke

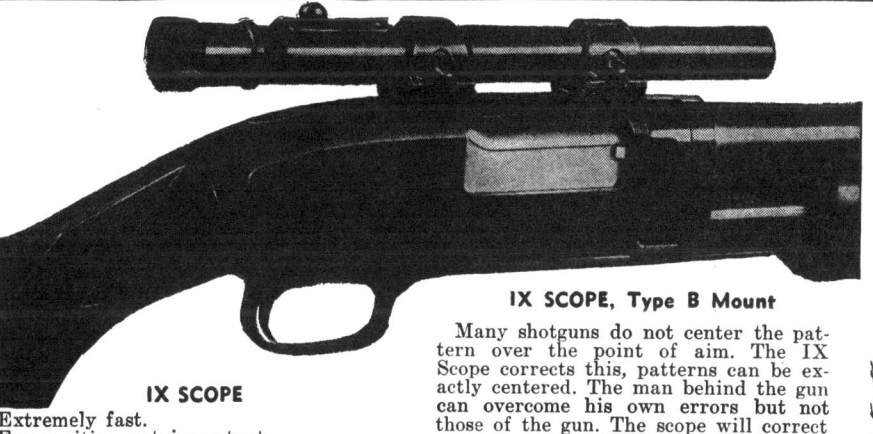

WEAVER SHOTGUN SCOPE
Fastest Sight Ever Made

IX SCOPE
Extremely fast.
Eye position not important.
One conspicuous aiming point or sight.
Neither the sight nor target is blurred.
Two eye shooting simplified.
Exact leads on cross flying game.
Scope adjustable to strike exact center.
Price, Complete with B Mount..$22.50
Price, Complete with T Mount.. 19.00

IX SCOPE, Type B Mount

Many shotguns do not center the pattern over the point of aim. The IX Scope corrects this, patterns can be exactly centered. The man behind the gun can overcome his own errors but not those of the gun. The scope will correct gun error and help the man correct his.

SPECIFICATIONS
Field of View........................75 feet
Eye Relief..........4½ inches (3¼" - 7")
Length............................9½ inches
Weight with Mount.......About ½ pound
Magnification....................Natural size
Illumination............................120
Adjustments, Internal, windage and elevation

MAKE YOURS AN ALL PURPOSE GUN

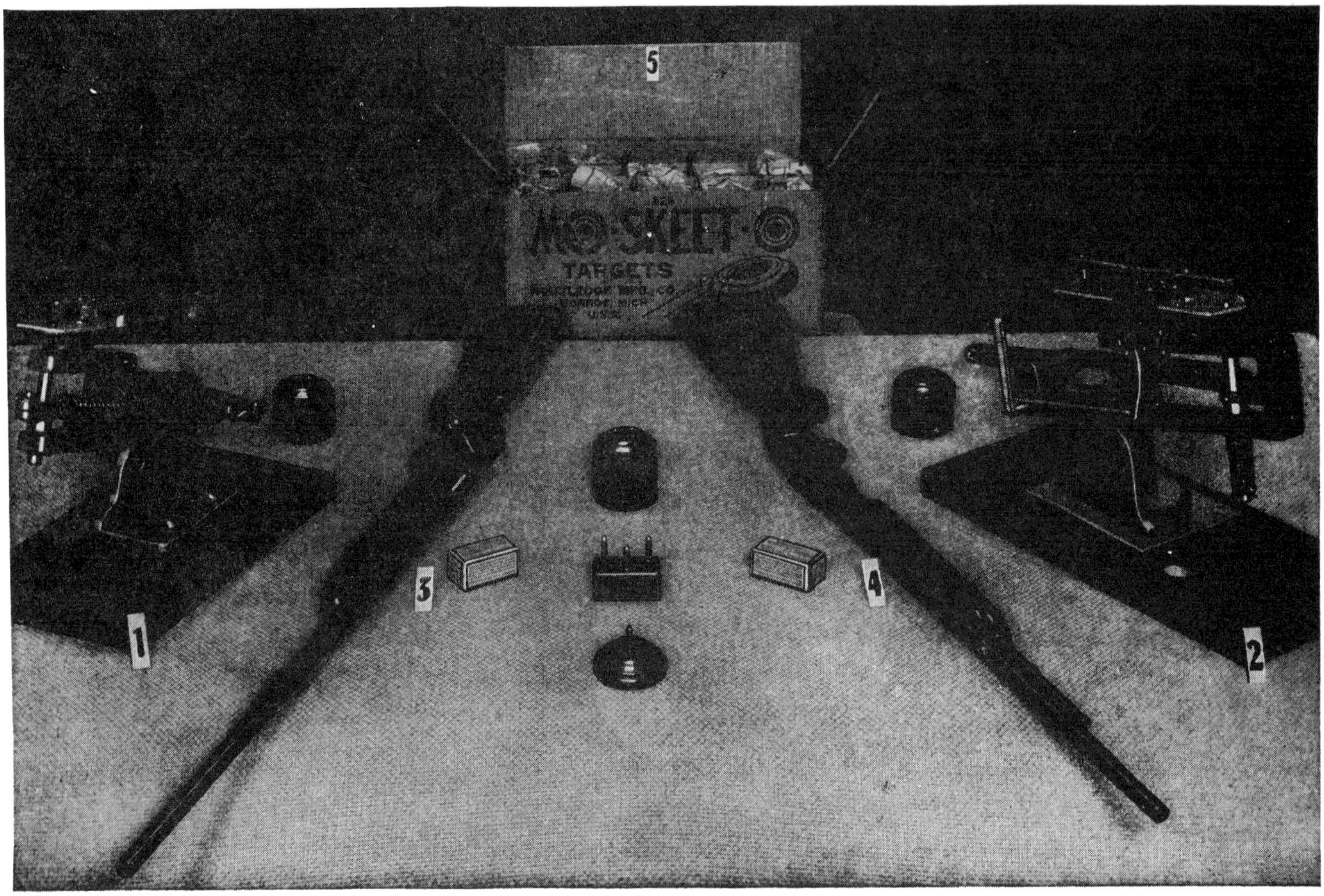

Complete MO-SKEET-O Equipment
All the Thrills of Trap and Skeet Shooting at Small Cost

The new shooting game—MO-SKEET-O—makes the learning of shot-gun shooting as easy as A B C. It also proves fascinating to the most expert shot-gun pointer. The MO-SKEET-O game can be used indoors or outdoors, either in the form of Skeet or Trapshooting. Although MO-SKEET-O made its first appearance at the 1938 "Grand American", it was not in production until the beginning of 1939. Then it made its bow before the crowds at the International Sportsmen's Show at Chicago, where it made such a hit, it immediately grew by leaps and bounds.

The possibilities for economical, enjoyable shooting are unlimited. A complete outfit of trap and special gun can be purchased as low as $25.50, and the ammunition used is the 22 caliber shot shell, which is comparatively inexpensive. The space required for a range is small and the danger zone of the gun is limited; consequently a range can be set up in a few minutes and operated in places that would be out of the question with any other firearm. With MO-SKEET-O you get all the thrills and practice of shooting clay targets without the large cost of regulation trap and skeet shooting.

MO-SKEET-O shooting can be done very well day or night, indoors or outdoors. For night shooting two 150-watt spots give ample lighting effect.

The complete absence of recoil from the MO-SKEET-O guns makes this game very desirable for ladies and children to learn to shoot. Expert shooters know that the recoil from larger guns is a great interference to learning.

No. 1 on the display above is light weight (Model 66) trap. This trap has an elevation adjustment, and main spring tension adjustment $14.00

No. 2 on the display is the regular trap (Model 14) built to give long service and fast operation. This trap has a swivel type base for throwing angles. Also an elevation, and main spring tenson adjustment $23.00

Model 14 trap with 6 volt electric pull suitable for skeet shooting (less battery and wire). Additional....$7.00

6 volt dry cell or auto battery will operate these pulls.

No. 3 is the single shot bolt action Mo-Skeet-O gun. Weight about 5¼ lbs. $11.50

No. 4 is the repeating type Mo-Skeet-O gun necessary for the skeet type of shooting to take care of the doubles. This gun is also entirely satisfactory for trap shooting. Weight about 6 pounds...$30.50

No. 5 is the target carton. The targets are wrapped in packages of 15 and placed in the partitioned carton which holds 15 packages (225 targets). We pack four cartons in one large container for shipping. Shipments of targets must be in multiples of 900 targets. These large cartons weigh about 55 pounds. Cartons of 900 targets........$4.50

Targets furnished white over entire upper surface. Per carton $5.40

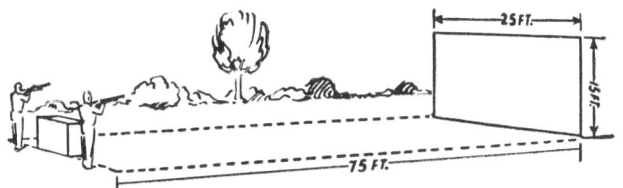

ENJOY SKEET AT FRACTIONAL COST

TARGO

Low Cost Trap Shooting Everyone Can Enjoy!

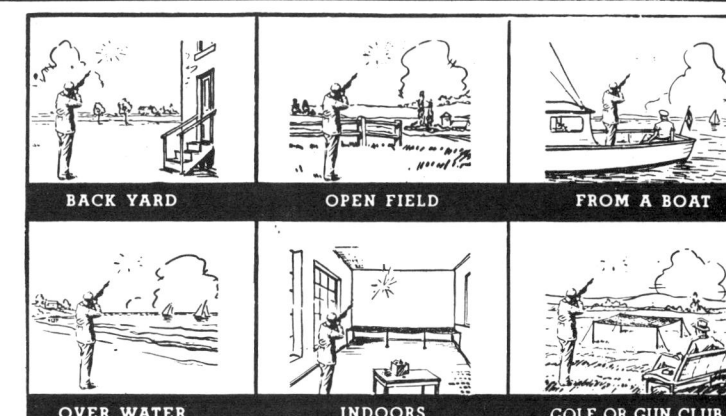

Targo is the grandest fun in the world. Perhaps, until now, you've never had the fun of trap shooting because of the expense involved and because it was all pretty complicated and involved. If so, here's MOSSBERG'S answer! For, in Targo you don't need the great open spaces, nor bulky, heavy, expensive equipment. You, yourself, work the trap that throws the targets, so you can shoot alone or with friends.

COMBINATION TRAP GUN AND RIFLE
Model 42TR

.22 cal. Repeater
$11.75

TARGO TRAP

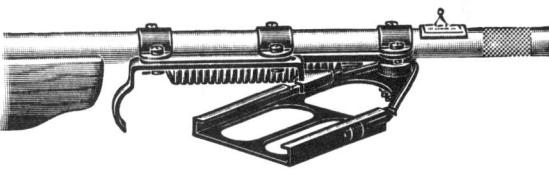

.22 cal. streamlined, smooth bore, bolt action, 8 shot clip repeater, built on our famous "Master" action, walnut finish stock with molded trigger guard with finger grooves and molded butt-plate. Beautifully designed, nicely balanced with or without the trap. Uses standard and easily obtainable .22 cal. long rifle (scatter) SHOT shell containing 120-130 tiny pellets. Breaks TARGO targets up to 50 feet. Barrel has silver bead detachable hooded front and adjustable sporting rear sights for use with Rifle Adapter. 22" Round, smooth-bore barrel fitted with 8" Targo tube that gives even distribution of pattern and eliminates shot from balling thereby preventing slugs. Targo tube is interchangeable with #RA1 Rifle Adapter. Length overall 43½". Weight about 5½ lbs.

Model 42TR (without trap).....................$11.75

This small compact trap that weighs only 14 ounces fits onto the barrel of the Targo gun—or most any single barrel .22 cal. smooth bore or .410 bore shotgun—and throws the Targo Target when you pull the trap trigger. It is cleverly "spring balanced" to prevent whip. When sprung, the throwing arm comes immediately to rest, without vibration, underneath the barrel. An adjustment on the spring permits you to vary the flight of the targets, making the shooting either easy or difficult, as you like. The trap is of the finest all-steel, heat-treated construction, channeled and ribbed for light weight strength. Included with each trap are 5 non-breakable "practice targets" of semi-hard rubber.

Targo trap (as illustrated) $7.45

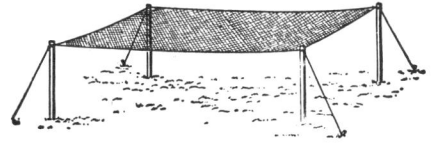

TARGO NET
This net 20 x 20 feet made of a substantial white seine twine will pay for itself in short time by allowing you to retrieve and save "missed" targets, same as they do at most skeet fields. Supplied with 12 foot lengths of manila cords on each corner so you can easily set it up on poles. Weight 2¼ lbs.
Targo Net.........................$5.95

TARGO TARGETS
Targo Targets are scientifically designed to be fragile enough to break upon the impact of the tiny .22 cal. shell pellets, up to 50 feet, yet sturdy enough to permit salvage of most of those missed in shooting over reasonably soft ground, sand or grass. Packed 200 to the box.
Price, Per 1M.................$6.50 F.O.B. New York

MAKES TWO GUNS IN ONE

EQUIPMENT FOR TRAP AND SKEET SHOOTING
REMINGTON CHAMBERLAIN TRAPS

BLUE ROCK TRAP

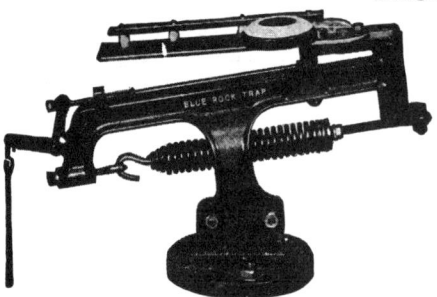

The Blue Rock Trap is especially adaptable for use by small clubs and private estates, or for backyard shooting where the area is large enough to avoid the danger of shot pellets injuring anyone. The Blue Rock Trap will throw either double or single targets, and with a few minutes adjustment can be changed to throw Skeet targets.
Price $20.00

EXPERT TRAP

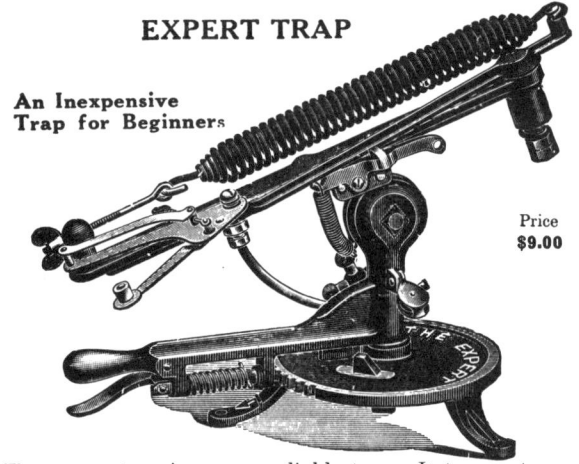

An Inexpensive Trap for Beginners

Price $9.00

The expert trap is a very reliable trap. It is easy to operate, throws birds the regulation distance and is easily installed.

BLUE ROCK TARGETS

Packed in cartons, are easily stored and shipped. Breakage is practically eliminated. Per double carton 270 .... $2.95

REMINGTON AUTOMATIC HAND TRAP

THE REMINGTON AUTOMATIC HAND TRAP

Light, compact, perfectly balanced, designed to produce the widest variety of shots with the least possible effort. The automatic feature eliminates maximum effort and allows the most difficult targets to be tossed with a mere swing of the body. The weight of the target itself does the trick! So finely balanced that once the carrier is "off center" the powerful spring automatically leaps forward to do the rest. Yet it can be cocked with the little finger. Shipping weight 1½ lbs.
Price $2.95

CHAMBERLAIN SINGLEVER SKEET OUTFIT

Note Singlever Control

The Chamberlain Singlever Skeet Outfit including Wonder Traps is unsurpassed for speed, economy of operation and accuracy of targets thrown. Their much greater weight means added stability, ruggedness and uniform operation. The selection is real economy in the long run. For individual use, for private estates or clubs where speed in operation is not so essential BLUE ROCK SINGLEVER Skeet Equipment is a good buy.
Price $90.00
Blue Rock Singlever Skeet Outfit (same as above, except with Blue Rock Traps) 50.00

REMINGTON-LEGGETT TRAP

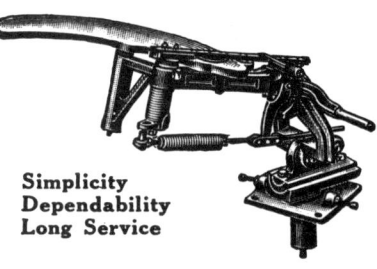

Simplicity Dependability Long Service

The experienced trapshooter will recognize this quickly when he focuses his attention on the following important features:

1. When single targets are thrown the left quartering bird will be at the same elevation as the straight-away or right quartering targets. No high left or low right targets with this trap.

2. All targets travel the same speed, rotation and distance. That means the right quartering bird *does* travel the same distance as the left.

3. Double targets are the bane of the trapshooter. Remington-Leggett traps are the solution because the left and right quartering birds travel in the same elevation—no high left and no low short range right targets

4. Whether singles or doubles the Remington-Leggett trap projects each target straight as an arrow the whole distance. There's no curl in any target thrown by this trap.

5. Whether the winds blow from North, South, East or West the elevating and special leveling devices employed in this new trap are positive adjustments to insure perfect target flight.

Price $80.00

PORTABLE DUVROCK TRAP

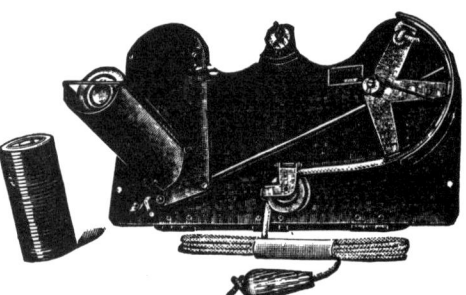

Easily carried. Targets and trap can be taken with you to the field. Can be used with all gauges. Repeating and adjustable.

Duvrock Trap, price $10.00
Duvrock Targets, price per 1000 .... 7.50
Duvrock Targets, price per 500 .... 3.75

SEND YOUR GUN TO STOEGER FOR EXPERT REPAIRING

AMERICA'S GREAT GUN HOUSE

Skeet & Trapshooting Equipment

Left: Throwing White Flyer Targets with the Western Hand Trap from the deck of a cruiser.

Right: Entertain house-party guests with the Western Hand Trap and White Flyer Targets.

WESTERN McCREA MASTER TRAP

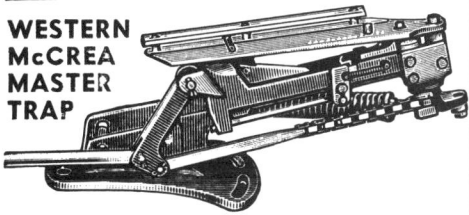

Throws equally satisfactory single or double targets. Simple to install, easy to load and operate. No additional parts needed for doubles. Angles may be changed by varying target position on carrier. Without an equal in its price range. Shipping weight, 99 lbs. Price, (F. O. B. East Alton, Ill.)....$40.00

WESTERN MASTER SKEET TRAPS

So finely engineered, so dependable in operation, they provide freedom from trap trouble and delays. Their ruggedness and simplicity insure maximum operating economy. Throw satisfactory targets under any and all weather conditions. The most inexperienced individual can release perfect "doubles".

Positive target stop will not permit targets to slip at high angles of elevation—assuring level, satisfactory targets—never throws an outlaw. Safety device prevents firing of trap until cocking lever is returned to the release position, protecting trap boy against accident. Location of cocking lever in relation to trap operator removes all danger from overthrow of carrier. Electric or wire release.

Mechanically operated outfit consists of two traps, pull-stand, without variable delay, and wire release. Shipping weight, 186 lb. Price, **$68.20** F. O. B. East Alton, Ill.

Two traps, wire release and mechanical Skeetimer. Price, **$100.00** F. O. B. East Alton, Ill.

Electric release outfit includes two traps with hand-cocking lever and electro-magnetic release mounted on each trap, delay timer, necessary wire and connections, a wire release which may be put into service in the event of power failure. 110-volt, 60-cycle A. C. Price, **$125.00** F. O. B. East Alton, Ill. 110-volt, 25-cycle A. C. Price, **$136.35** F. O. B. East Alton, Ill. Shipping weight, 292 lbs. 6-volt D. C., Battery not included. Price, **$125.00** F. O. B. East Alton, Ill. Shipping weight, 262 lbs.

SELF-ANGLING WHITE FLYER TRAP

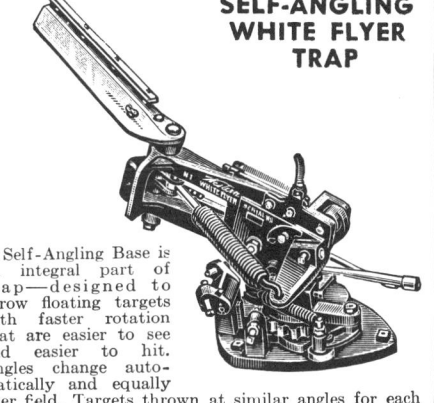

Self-Angling Base is an integral part of trap—designed to throw floating targets with faster rotation that are easier to see and easier to hit. Angles change automatically and equally over field. Targets thrown at similar angles for each shooter without having to rely upon trap boy to follow satisfactory sequence. Quickly changed from singles to doubles. Heavy and durable. Withstands prolonged operation. Target trajectory consistently regular over entire shooting arc. Shipping weight, 178 lbs. Price, (F. O. B. East Alton, Ill.).......**$68.50**

STANDARD WHITE FLYER TRAP

Rugged wear-resisting parts, efficiency, simplicity, safety and dependability combine to make an ideal trap. Differs from the Self-Angling White Flyer Trap only in the base unit. Shipping weight, 160 lbs. Price, (F. O. B. East Alton, Ill.).........**$52.50**

WESTERN MECHANICAL SKEETIMER

Designed for Western Master Skeet Traps. Can also be used with earlier Western Skeet Traps, and most other traps slightly modified. Can be adjusted to vary from instantaneous to the maximum delay selected—less than one second, three seconds as prescribed by the Skeet rules, or any intermediate delay. No trouble due to power failure—no batteries to run down—no fuses to blow out —no power line service charge. Functions so easily, a small boy can operate it for hours, keeping score at same time. Shipping weight, 90 lbs. Price, (F. O. B. East Alton, Ill.). **$38.65**

WESTERN PRACTICE TRAP

Simple, compact, light. Throws targets which imitate the flight of game birds, as well as very acceptable regulation targets. Ideal for practice during the closed season, or where an inexpensive Skeet layout is wanted. Shipping weight, 21 lbs. Price, (F. O. B. East Alton, Ill.) **$9.00**

WESTERN HAND TRAP

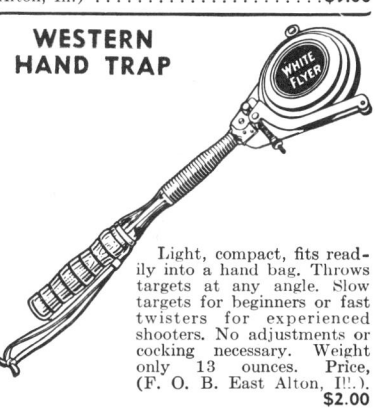

Light, compact, fits readily into a hand bag. Throws targets at any angle. Slow targets for beginners or fast twisters for experienced shooters. No adjustments or cocking necessary. Weight only 13 ounces. Price, (F. O. B. East Alton, Ill.) **$2.00**

You Get the B-r-e-a-k-s With WHITE FLYER TARGETS

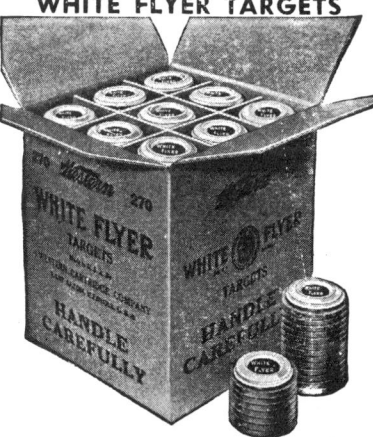

Price per carton of 270, as illustrated..**$2.95**

REAL SPORT ON YOUR OWN PREMISES

ZEPHYR SHOT GUNS

The Zephyr shotgun is the result of our many years of experience in development of a high quality, hand finished shotgun at a price within the reach of the average shooter. This gun was first introduced by us several years ago and was an immediate success, combining as it does all the features of the very highest grade hand built English shotguns together with perfect proportion and balance at a price of less than half that of competitive guns of comparable quality.

The Zephyr shotgun is produced to meet the exacting demands of experienced shooters who demand a light weight, well balanced shotgun for skeet or field shooting. The barrels are carefully bored and consistently even patterns are the result.

In construction, the well known Anson & Deeley box lock system has been used in connection with the excellent Purdy style top lock which is not only neat, clean and effective, but also makes insertion and extraction of shells easier. The forend which is of English style is released by means of the Purdy style push button. The ejectors are of the Southgate type. The rib is flat and matted to prevent glare. The safety is automatic. The triggers are checkered to prevent slipping of the finger even when gloves are worn, and is carefully chromium plated to prevent rust.

In addition to the checkering of the pistol grip and forearm, the cheeks of the stock are carefully checkered in the form of a shield extending out into a diamond shape inlay of genuine black Buffalo horn. The action itself, which is made with integral side clips to prevent any possibility of looseness is supplied with artistic light scroll engraving. The trigger guard is also neatly engraved with scroll work and a flying partridge and extends, in guns with pistol grip, all the way to the horn pistol grip cap with which it cuts off flush. The stock is of selected French Walnut and has an oval silver name plate imbedded. Instead of a butt plate, the butt end is tastefully checkered.

All Zephyr guns have Automatic Ejectors.

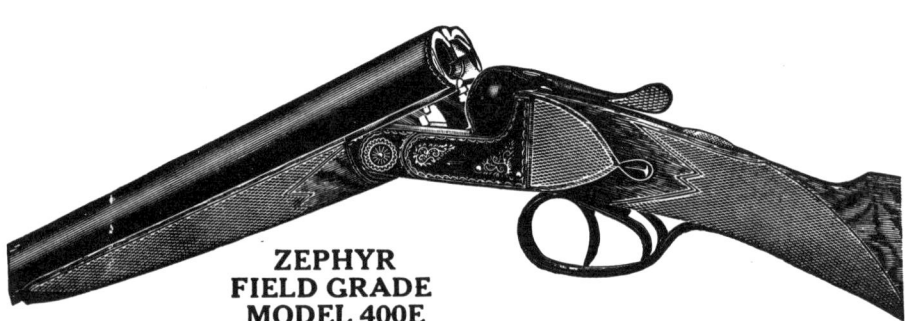

ZEPHYR FIELD GRADE MODEL 400E

The Field Grade is available in 12, 16, 20, 28 and .410 ga. with barrel length of from 25" to 30" in various weights, chokes and stock dimensions. However, this model is regularly made in very light weights; the .410 ga. weighs about 4½ lbs., the 28 ga. about 5 lbs., the 20 ga. 5½ lbs., the 16 ga. 5¾ lbs., and the 12 ga. 6¼ lbs. This gun may also be had on special order with almost any specifications at no extra charge; delivery time about four months.

Zephyr, Field Grade, 12, 16 or 20 gauge..$115.00
Zephyr, Field Grade, 28 or .410 gauge... 125.00
Extra for Selective Single Trigger....... 35.00

The Zephyr Skeet Grade is about the same as the Field Grade except that it is supplied with Beaver Tail forend and on special order with selective or non-selective single trigger. The Zephyr Skeet gun is available in all gauges from .410 to 12 ga. with barrel length varying from 25" to 28". The Beaver Tail forend, itself, is of excellent design and has enjoyed great popularity on the Skeet fields. It is specially bored for skeet shooting.

Zephyr, Skeet Grade, 12, 16 or 20 gauge..$137.50
Zephyr, Skeet Grade, 28 or .410 gauge.... 147.50
Extra for Selective Single Trigger........ 35.00
Extra for Non-Selective Single Trigger.... 27.50

ZEPHYR SKEET GRADE MODEL 401E

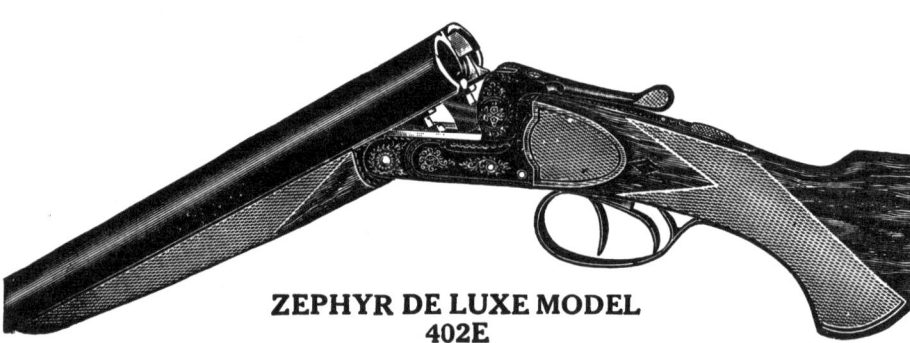

ZEPHYR DE LUXE MODEL 402E

The Zephyr De Luxe Grade was built to satisfy the demand of those who wish a gun of even finer appearance and still smoother workmanship. The De Luxe Grade is basically the same as the Field Grade except that the entire action is specially carefully hand honed for the greatest possible smoothness. The engraving through-out is more elaborate. The checkering is of particularly pleasing effect and the walnut of exceptional quality and beauty.

Zephyr, De Luxe Grade, 12, 16 or 20 gauge $150.00
Zephyr, De Luxe Grade, 28 or .410 gauge 160.00
Extra for Selective Single Trigger... 35.00

SEND YOUR GUN TO STOEGER FOR EXPERT REPAIRING

ZEPHYR SHOTGUNS

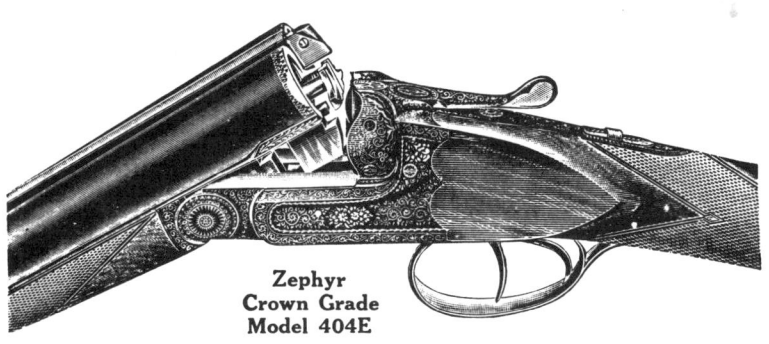

Zephyr Crown Grade Model 404E

ZEPHYR CROWN GRADE

The Zephyr "Crown Grade" is a weapon of superior quality and particularly pleasing appearance. A gun available in all calibers and weights to meet any requirements. It is built on the well-known Anson & Deeley system and will find approval among those accustomed to seeking this quality of gun only in weapons of a much higher price.

Zephyr, Crown Grade, 12, 16 and 20 Ga............$175.00
Zephyr, Crown Grade, 28 or .410 Ga................ 190.00
Extra for Selective Single Trigger.................... 35.00

ZEPHYR PREMIER GRADE

The Zephyr "Premier Grade" is of the same quality as the "Crown Grade" although built on slightly different lines including side plate thus allowing a large field for engraving for those who desire a gun embodying not only quality but extremely smart appearance as well. This gun, too, is available in a variety of calibers, barrel lengths, etc.

Zephyr, Premier Grade, 12, 16 or 20 Ga............$195.00
Zephyr, Premier Grade, 28 or .410 Ga.............. 210.00
Extra for Selective Single Trigger.................... 35.00

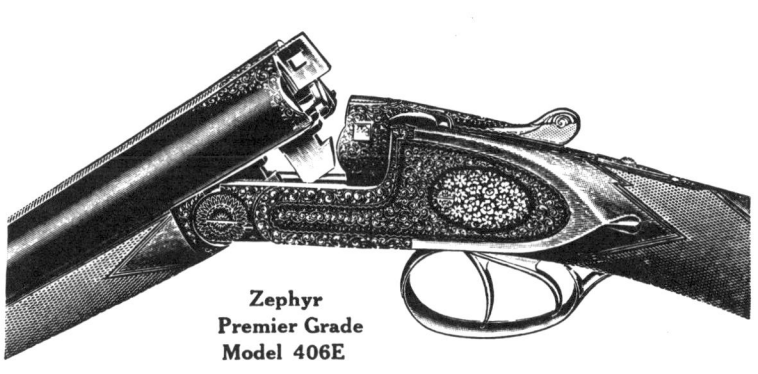

Zephyr Premier Grade Model 406E

ZEPHYR ROYAL GRADE

The Zephyr "Royal Grade" has been built to satisfy the demands of the most discriminating shooters and those who have been accustomed to only the very finest in shotguns. The "Royal Grade" is a truly first quality gun built along the lines of the finest English first quality guns with which the "Royal Grade" compares most favorably although at but a fraction of the cost. The gun has genuine side locks, is of extremely smooth operation and perfect balance, made through-out of the best materials, and the engraving is of the finest English scroll type. This gun will bear comparison with guns selling at $1,000.00 and more.

Zephyr, Royal Grade, 12, 16 and 20 Ga............$395.00
Zephyr, Royal Grade, 28 or .410 Ga................ 415.00
Extra for Selective Single Trigger.................... 50.00

Zephyr Royal Grade Model 410E

ZEPHYR DOUBLE RIFLES

ZEPHYR DOUBLE BARREL

To meet the demand for a really first quality double rifle at a fairly reasonable price, we offer the Zephyr "Double" which is patterned after the finest English double rifles and is more carefully built and executed in the very best of material, assuring easy and certainty of operation as well as ruggedness and high accuracy. This gun will be found dependable even under the most adverse and vigorous conditions. It is built only to order and may be had for any big game cartridge.

Zephyr Double Rifle...........................$475.00

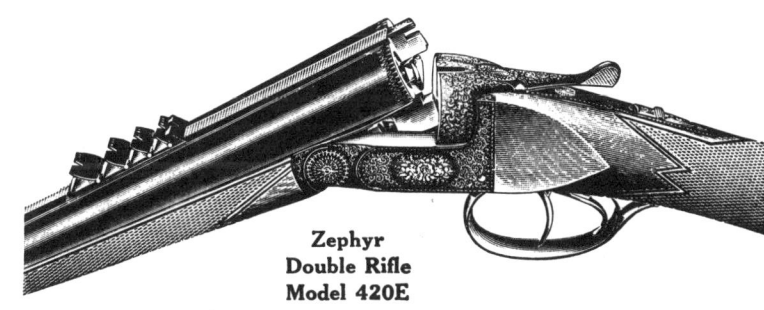

Zephyr Double Rifle Model 420E

POWELL SHOTGUNS

Established in 1802, the business has been carried on by generation after generation of Powells on the old painstaking lines, and by the personal and active participation of the members of the firm in the production of guns, all built without any possibility of deterioration by resorting to cutting of cost. This explains why POWELL guns made thirty to forty years ago are still in use and likely to be for some time to come, whilst those now being manufactured on the most sound methods will still be going strong thirty to forty years hence.

The number of discriminating sportsmen, following in the steps of their fathers and forefathers, who patronize these guns, is substantial and ever increasing. The firm of Powell has been described as the Purdey of Birmingham. This reputation, though it suffers from a suggestion of plagiarism, is highly prized, since it ably expresses the care and thought devoted to the effort to realize perfection. The firm of Powell whilst recommending the "best" quality of gun to all who can see their way to pay the necessary price, recognize nevertheless that when a lower price is required, resort must be made to the Anson & Deeley type of mechanism. Messrs. Powell have devoted particular attention to this model, seeking, they believe with considerable success, to apply to its construction and regulation, the tests which have become routine in their ordinary work.

The Powell No. 1, "Best" Hammerless Ejector is a side lock gun, perfectly balanced, highly finished and engraved and perfectly adjusted in every detail, possessing remarkable properties of endurance, making it a joy to possess and use. Only the finest steel barrels with solid lumps are used. The exquisite detail and smoothness of action is a result of the most painstaking effort on the part of master gunsmiths accustomed to work only on the finest guns. The outward appearance of such a gun can be reproduced by those who are not masters of the entire art, and therefore at the finish the definition rests upon the reputation which has been earned by the several makes of best guns. Powell's best gun can appeal confidently to such a test.

Built to order without extension rib or if desired with trebel bolt and dolls head extension if desired. The 12 bore usually weighs from 6 to 6½ pounds and all specifications of stock, barrel length and bore may be carried out to satisfy the users special wishes and requirements. This model may also be had at an extra charge, equipped with new self-opening action which makes operation still easier and eliminates shooting fatigue.

POWELL No. 1
BEST GRADE

Price in England........£94/10/0
With self opening Action......£105
Price in U. S. A..........$700.00
With self opening Action...$835.00

POWELL No. 2
BEST GRADE, PLAIN FINISH

Price in England............£84
Price in U. S. A.........$620.00

The highest quality throughout, same as the Powell No. 1, but finished plain without engraving. We make any length of barrels, but have preference for 28 in. as being the happy medium conducive to handiness and perfect balance, and shooting equally well at any distance as the old standard 30 in.

POWELL No. 6
CROWN GRADE, HIGHEST QUALITY BOX LOCK

Price in England............£63
Price in U. S. A.........$465.00

Best Quality Hammerless Ejector Gun, with Anson & Deeley Locks. Perfect balance.

This pattern can be produced at less cost than the high grade Side-lock. It is strong and durable and keeps well to its work, in fact may be termed to have everlasting wear. We are continually meeting with these models that have been used for upwards of thirty years, little the worse for wear and tear. Constructed with the finest materials and best finish.

Weight in 12 gauge—6¼ lbs. to 6½ lbs. according to length of barrels.

Made exclusively for the U.S.A.

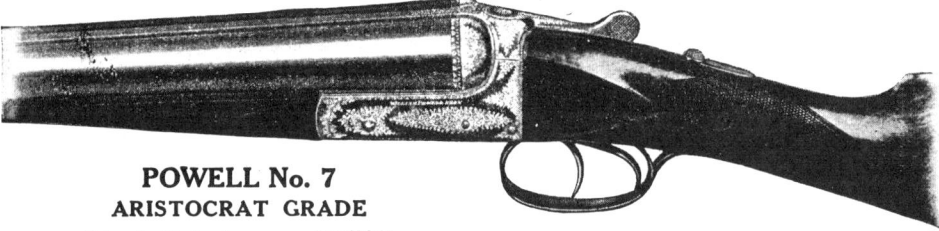

POWELL No. 7
ARISTOCRAT GRADE

Price in England........£52/10/0
Price in U. S. A.........$385.00

A very popular number, a gun of fine balance and feel, a real product of English guncraft. Specially designed for Field work. Strong hand finished action and barrels, with selected walnut stock, with best locks and ejector mechanism. Built to all specifications.

A FINE GUN IS A JOY FOREVER

POWELL SHOTGUNS AND DOUBLE RIFLES

Chambered for the new 2-inch 12 gauge shells.
Anson & Deeley locks, Southgate ejector. Weight 5¼ pounds.
Ideal for ladies and elderly sportsmen.
Lighter and more effective than a 20 bore.
Fine quality and well finished.

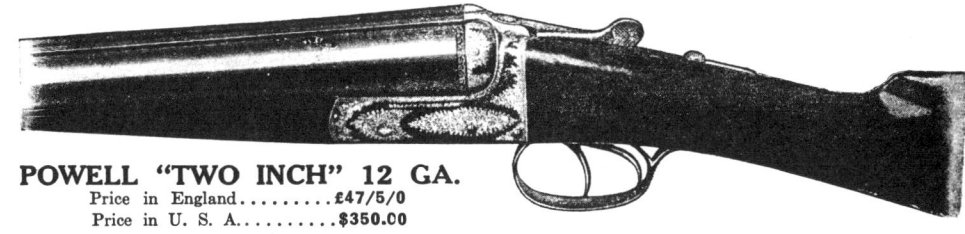

POWELL "TWO INCH" 12 GA.
Price in England........£47/5/0
Price in U. S. A.........$350.00

POWELL'S PIGEON AND WILDFOWL GUN
Price in England......£42/0/0
Price in U. S. A......$315.00

A handsome fine quality gun, 30-inch steel barrels, both full choke, chambered for 2¾-inch or 3-inch cartridges and specially bored to give dense patterns, dead level flat file cut rib, Anson & Deeley locks, treble grip with strong square concealed cross bolt and side clips. Half pistol grip stock. Handsomely engraved and finished. Weight 7½ pounds to 8 pounds.

A plain well made Hammerless Ejector of the Anson & Deeley type, constructed under our personal supervision. English steel barrels, carefully bored, and shooting powers equal to the best productions. Well adapted for hard wear and Colonial use.

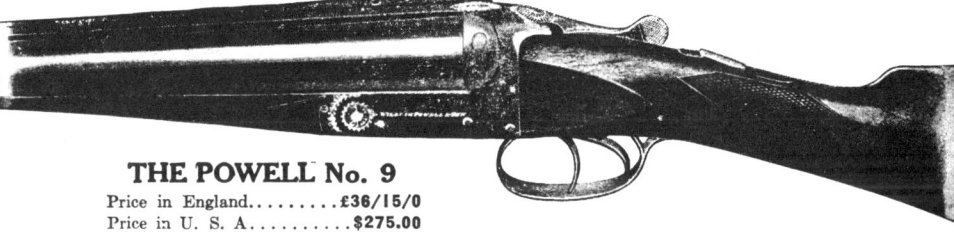

THE POWELL No. 9
Price in England........£36/15/0
Price in U. S. A..........$275.00

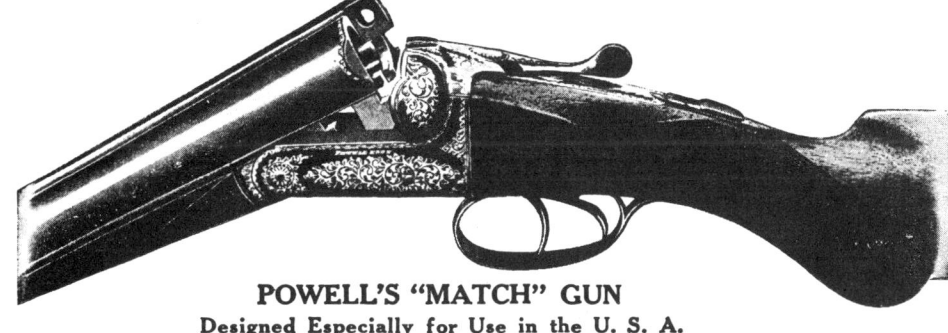

POWELL'S "MATCH" GUN
Designed Especially for Use in the U. S. A.

A sound well-made gun, 30-inch or 32-inch steel barrels, both full choke, chambered for 2¾-inch or 3-inch cartridges, flat file cut rib, Anson & Deeley locks, treble grip, concealed cross bolt, side clips. Half pistol grip stock. Engraved and well finished. Weight in 12 gauge, 7½ pounds to 8 pounds.
Price $275.00

POWELL DOUBLE RIFLES

AVAILABLE ON ORDER IN ALL CALIBERS FOR THE HEAVIEST GAME

Double barrel Hammerless Ejector, High Velocity. Best quality. Plain finish as illustrated. Made in all calibers to the individual requirements and specifications of the user.

Price in England..........£84
Price in U. S. A.......$620.00

CAREFUL ATTENTION AND SAFE DELIVERY OF YOUR ORDER

ZEPHYR LIGHTWEIGHT OVER & UNDERS

In order to meet the requirements of a high class Over & Under shotgun of medium price, we have made a careful study of the European markets and have been successful in having built several models of Over & Under shotguns all of which have been carefully designed for the American market and built strictly in accordance with the wishes of the American shooting public. We feel that in offering this line of Over & Unders, we are offering values which cannot be duplicated elsewhere. Prices on all models include automatic ejectors.

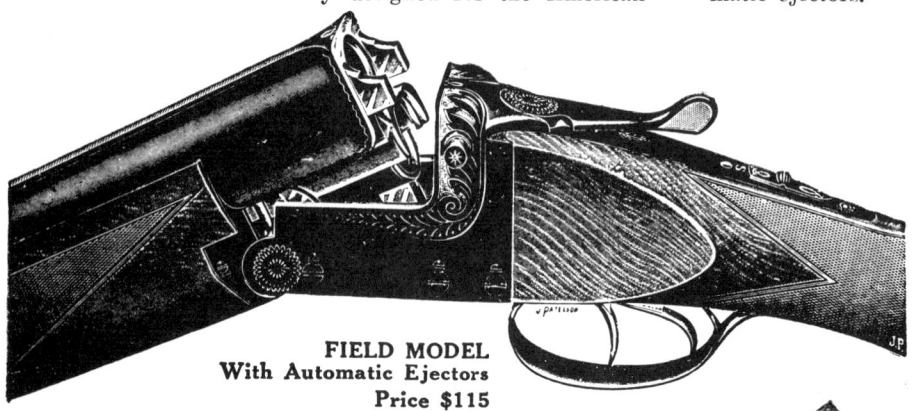

FIELD MODEL
With Automatic Ejectors
Price $115

This gun has been selected by us as the lowest priced imported Over & Under of sufficiently high quality to bear our name and will be found to compare very favorably with every Over & Under gun up to 50% higher in price. The gun is a modification of the well known Anson & Deeley system with double Purdy type extension rib. The gun is supplied with finely matted top rib and carefully checkered forearm and pistol grip. The barrels are of first quality Belgium steel fully proof tested by the government proof house. The stock is of good quality French Walnut oil finished and the action is lightly engraved as indicated. This gun is regularly available in 12, 16, and 20 gauge with a variety of barrel lengths, chokes and stock specifications. It may also be built to order at no extra cost.

Model No. 1 represents a gun of a very distinctive class in that it is the lowest priced Over & Under on the market which has absolutely straight firing pins and under locking lugs. It should be borne in mind that in the average Over & Under with under locking lugs, the firing pin of the lower barrel protrudes at such an angle as to make opening sometimes very difficult. In other words, this gun is of the same type as the higher grade German Over & Under shown elsewhere in this catalog. This gun is made with divided forearm, well seasoned select quality French Walnut stock, very pretty English engraving and scalloped frame. In this gun particular attention has been placed in ease of operation. This gun is designed to meet the requirements of the more discriminating shooter and is available in 410, 28, 20, 16, and 12 gauge.

ZEPHYR MODEL 1
With Automatic Ejectors
Price $175
Extra for .410 or 28 ga., $15

ZEPHYR MODEL 2
With Automatic Ejectors
Price $200
Extra for .410 or 28 ga., $15

This model is similar in construction to the Model No. 1 but is made with side plates which are preferred by many as they are not only decorative but also serve the primary purpose of adding considerably to the strength of the stock. In this model, only a very select Walnut is used, checkering is particularly well worked out and the action is particularly smooth. As in Model No. 1 the forearm is divided which eliminates the danger of the forearm cracking which is the case with the necessarily fragile forearm which is indicated where the forearm is of one piece. This gun is built to order in all specifications and may be had in a variety of gauges from 12 to 410 gauge. It may also be built to order at no extra charge.

Model No. 3 is similar to Model No. 2 except that it has a particularly fine finish and exceptionally fine oil finished French stock. The engraving as will be noticed from the illustration is a combination of fine English scroll together with 3 figures on each side of the gun of dogs and birds. In this gun is offered a weapon which is not only substantially and well built but will meet the requirements of those who appreciate the artistic in the execution of a fine shotgun. The gun is exceptionally light and well handling and a delight to every lover of a fine gun. This model may be had in all gauges from 410 to 12 gauge and with a variety of stock measurements, barrel lengths and chokes. It may be built to the customer's own specifications at no extra charge.

ZEPHYR MODEL 3
With Automatic Ejectors
Price $225
Extra for .410 or 28 ga., $15

A NEW GUN CARRIES A FACTORY GUARANTEE

AN INTRODUCTION TO MUZZLE LOADERS

By Judge Roy S. Tinney

The guns of a century or more ago have allure peculiarly their own; they are the answer to a guncrank's prayer. The old front-fed, loose-loaders stand for romance, adventure and re-enacted history. They enable the shooter, with his own hands and a few simple tools, to evolve, produce and apply no end of useful gadgets for the fabricating of ammunition on the firing line, as-and-when needed. Our great-great-grandsires were the original re-loaders, for 'twas then a case of reload or stop shooting. And it is the safest shooting known if one will strictly observe this simple rule: NEVER USE SMOKELESS POWDER. Always load the old guns with the propellent for which they were designed, black or semi-smokeless powder. It is a game where the human element plays a predominant part. A carefully systematic loader can and frequently does defeat a far better shot who is neither exact nor methodical while recharging his gun. Also, such firing gives the marksman an understanding of the basic principles of the science of ballistics he can acquire in no other way.

While Rapid Fire is "out," loading the old guns is not by any means the slow, laborious operation most imagine. On the contrary the greased patch in which the ball is wrapt makes loading a pleasant ritual, it is done so easily the standard Slow Fire rule, "One minute per shot" can be calmly accepted. One afternoon I saw a friend fire 25 shots in 14 minutes with a duelling pistol without making the slightest effort to speed-up the proceeding.

Another pleasant surprise is the way the old guns behave; the black powder recoil is merely a firm push, not at all like the bruising kick delivered by smokeless powder. This is particularly noticeable when firing cap-and-ball revolvers or duelling pistols. Most of the old duellers weigh less than the .38 "Official Police" or the .45 Service revolvers and the Army Auto. They fire round balls ranging from .44 caliber running 50 to the pound and each weighing 140 grains up to the really big appointment-guns who toss a .68 caliber ball, 14 to the pound, weight 500 grains. Yes, we of the Sword and Pistol Club actually fire 500-grain bullets successfully and pleasantly from a pistol— one of a pair of smoothbore, percussion English duellers made a century ago. We often use them in Parallel Duelling events where the two contestants stand side by side at "Lower Pistol" firing "On Command" at two silhouette man targets "according to the code."

Captain Dillin of Media, Pa., has a flintlock Kentucky rifle made in 1750 that is still both accurate and serviceable, only requires "a man behind it" to win matches. At Fortyrod (220 yards) the heavy barrel percussion rifles of the type used by Berdan's Sharpshooters during the Civil War, "slug-guns" using conical bullets, will give the modern rifles a run-for-their-money. "Possibles" on the four-inch tenring of the Standard N.R.A. 200-yard decimal targets are not at all impossible, occur quite frequently. While the "round-ball-rifles," both flint and percussion, make creditable scores at fifty and a hundred yards on the Standard N.R.A. small bore targets used for the Dewar Course.

The first chokebore shotguns were muzzle loaders, their virtues being discovered and made known by Fred Kimble some seventy years ago. He is still alive and a most interesting first-hand account of his findings is presented in the November and December, 1936, issues of THE AMERICAN RIFLEMAN. At various times I have been permitted to test a few of those early shotguns and in each instance they delivered patterns that in closeness of pattern, count, evenness of distribution (density) and penetration in every respect equalized the patterns delivered by the best of our modern shotguns.

Shooting at live birds or clay pigeons with a flintlock is a real experience, one you will never forget. The "flash-lag-boom" of the stone-age ignition requires one to "carry through," keep on aiming after the trigger has functioned. The "firelock" with its delayed-action-ignition also plays havoc with the current generation of pistoleers, producing scores to weep-over or laugh-at, depending on whether you chance to be the shooter or the kibitzer. We regard it as keen sport, a real test of a man's ability to hold well under trying circumstances and the man who can't "take it" has no place on our firing line.

Over a thousand shooters are burning black powder in the old muzzle loaders; rifles, pistols and shotguns; on outdoor ranges scattered from Maine to California. Twenty-odd regional matches are held twixt spring and fall; with the big National Muzzle Loading match at Dillsboro, Ohio, each October. If you are a dyed-in-the-wool guncrank, a man more interested in the game than the medals that decorate the expert minority, one who loves to burn powder with a minimum of expense and a maximum of pleasure, by all means take up the muzzle loaders. You will not be disappointed and in the doing meet many kindred spirits and have one whale of a good time.

Courtesy, H. Nicolas, St. Ouen, France

NO. 2 ENGLISH STYLE FLINTLOCK

The lock shown above is approximately half size and is complete and ready for installation and includes flint. This was one of the most popular styles in colonial days.
Price .... complete **$6.00**

POWDER FLASKS

The flask illustrated measures somewhat over 4" over all and is designed for use with a pistol.

It is an extremely handy flask which fits easily into the pocket, indispensable to muzzle loading shooters.

It is made entirely of metal of exceptionally good construction and is equipped with powder measure which can be altered to suit any required load.
Price **$3.50**
Larger flasks for rifles, according to condition and pattern .... **$5.00** to **$10.00**

NO. 3 FRENCH STYLE FLINTLOCK

The above illustrated lock enjoyed great popularity in former days. It represents a very excellent value. It is polished and finished, complete with flint.
Price **$6.00**

SEE PAGES 414 AND 415 FOR ADDITIONAL PARTS

MUZZLE LOADING PERCUSSION & FLINT LOCK GUNS

For hundreds of years the Flint Lock and Percussion Cap guns were the only type known, in fact, there are still many old-time shooters who were brought up on the percussion type gun and in whose memory this type of weapon still holds an honored place. Many of these Percussion Cap guns are still in use.

The Flint Lock gun is of course, of far older development, having directly superseded the old wheel-lock guns. Interest in Flint Lock guns has been greatly revived of late and throughout the country many matches are being held with this ancient type of weapon. One of the difficulties to the sport of shooting with Flint Locks has been the inability of the shooter to purchase such guns on the open market. As a result of an increasing demand, we have felt it not only advisable but of popular interest to include within the covers of this catalog a fairly complete line of both Flint and Percussion type guns.

All of the Flint Lock and Percussion arms shown have been fully approved and tested with black powder loads at the proof house in Liege and all bear the official Liege black powder proof marks. For the benefit of those who desire to get the best shooting results we have procured from the Birmingham Proof House in England, the officially suggested black powder loads for the various gauges as a guide.

Many sportsmen will also find these guns decorative and ornamental as well as actually useful for the hunting lodge. Over an open fireplace no more fitting adornment can be found. In spite of the novelty of these guns and their decorations the prices are exceedingly reasonable, ranging from $10.00 for the plainest to $100.00 for the most ornate and within this price range every sportsman will be able to find a piece to suit his particular requirements.

MODEL 21
Price $10.00

A plain but serviceable percussion single barrel gun, part octagon and part round barrel, 44 gauge with 32-inch barrel. Has damascus finish, straight English style stock with iron butt plate and ram rod. Polished fittings and brown walnut varnished stock.

MODEL W24
Price $10.00

This gun is similar in style to the No. 21 except that it has a Military style stock with swivels, partially checkered, forearm and round barrel.

MODEL 7
Price $14.00

This model Percussion gun is of the type usually referred to as a "trade gun" and is particularly made for use by the African natives. The stock is brightly colored, the gun has polished brass mountings, a ram rod and some engraving. It is supplied in 44 gauge with 32-inch barrel and weighs less than 4 pounds.

MODEL 109
Price $27.50

This is a very well built single barrel Percussion gun, 32 gauge with 32-inch barrel, weighing about 3¾ pounds with damascus finished barrel, ram rod, checkered pistol grip, engraved action, walnut stock with brass cartridge percussion cap, storage box neatly inlaid as shown in the illustration.

MODEL 73
Price $35.00

This is a very ornate single barrel Percussion gun of French pattern with head carved into the stock, fancy checkering and elaborate engraving. The barrel is of damascus finish and the gun is supplied with ram rod. The stock has pearl forend tip with silver inlaid into the grip and forend, part octagon barrel, engraved with oak leaves. A piece of exceptional beauty.

TRY A MUZZLE LOADER FOR A NEW SHOOTING THRILL

DOUBLE MUZZLE LOADING GUNS

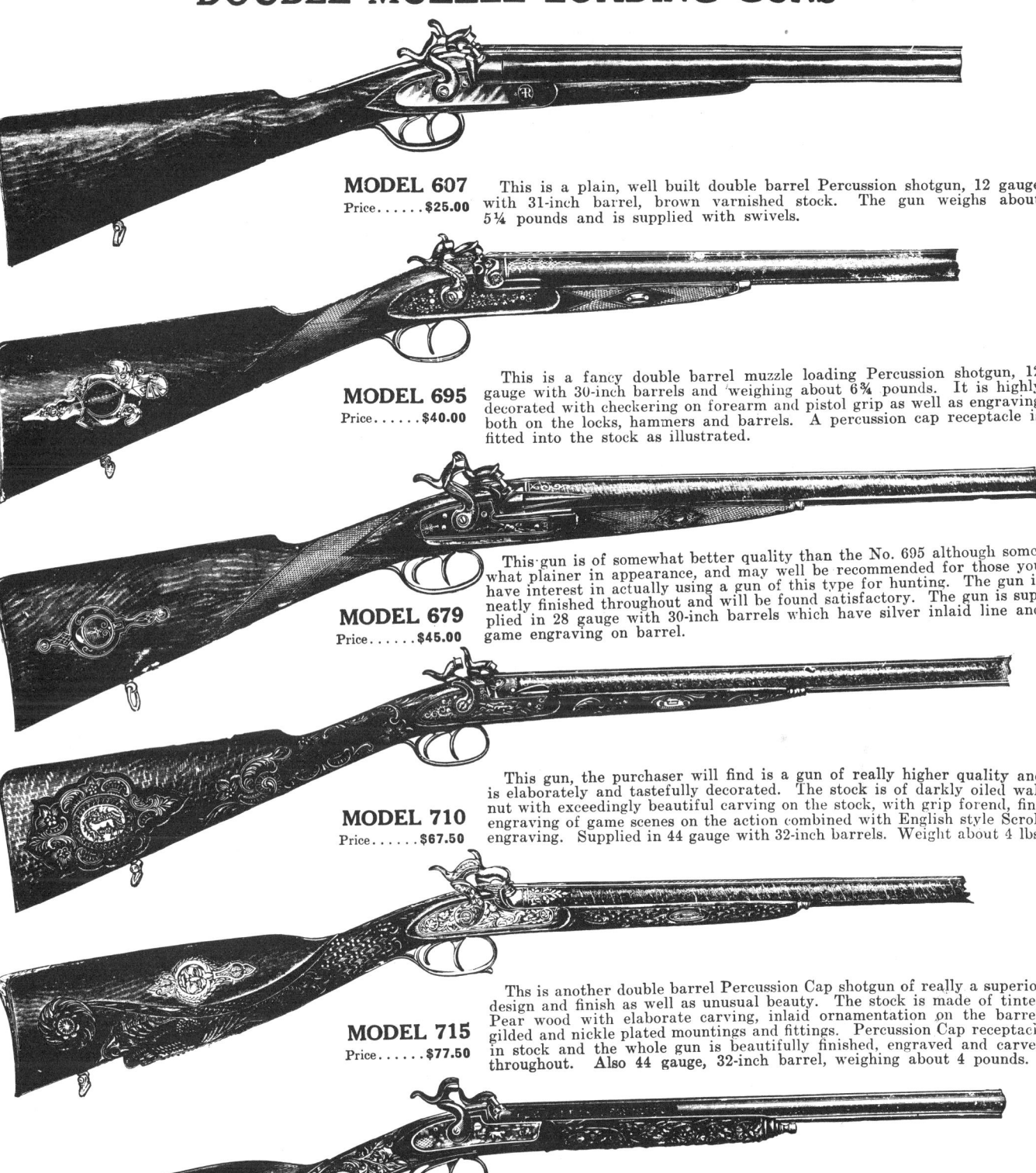

MODEL 607
Price.....$25.00

This is a plain, well built double barrel Percussion shotgun, 12 gauge with 31-inch barrel, brown varnished stock. The gun weighs about 5¼ pounds and is supplied with swivels.

MODEL 695
Price.....$40.00

This is a fancy double barrel muzzle loading Percussion shotgun, 12 gauge with 30-inch barrels and weighing about 6¾ pounds. It is highly decorated with checkering on forearm and pistol grip as well as engraving both on the locks, hammers and barrels. A percussion cap receptacle is fitted into the stock as illustrated.

MODEL 679
Price.....$45.00

This gun is of somewhat better quality than the No. 695 although somewhat plainer in appearance, and may well be recommended for those you have interest in actually using a gun of this type for hunting. The gun is neatly finished throughout and will be found satisfactory. The gun is supplied in 28 gauge with 30-inch barrels which have silver inlaid line and game engraving on barrel.

MODEL 710
Price.....$67.50

This gun, the purchaser will find is a gun of really higher quality and is elaborately and tastefully decorated. The stock is of darkly oiled walnut with exceedingly beautiful carving on the stock, with grip forend, fine engraving of game scenes on the action combined with English style Scroll engraving. Supplied in 44 gauge with 32-inch barrels. Weight about 4 lbs.

MODEL 715
Price.....$77.50

Ths is another double barrel Percussion Cap shotgun of really a superior design and finish as well as unusual beauty. The stock is made of tinted Pear wood with elaborate carving, inlaid ornamentation on the barrel, gilded and nickle plated mountings and fittings. Percussion Cap receptacle in stock and the whole gun is beautifully finished, engraved and carved throughout. Also 44 gauge, 32-inch barrel, weighing about 4 pounds.

MODEL 718
Price.....$100.00

This gun represents the best that is available today in double barrel percussion cap shotguns. It is similar to Model 715, but all details and workmanship are carried out with even greater care. For the collector wishing the best in double barrel percussion guns we can strongly recommend our No. 718. Supplied in 44 gauge with 32-inch barrel, and weighing about 4½ pounds.

EVERYTHING IN MUZZLE LOADERS

SINGLE BARREL MUZZLE LOADING FLINT LOCK GUNS

MODEL 1303
Price $10.00

A plain, but well made flint lock gun, 24 ga. with 34" barrel with brown walnut stock, polished iron fittings, black barrel and iron ram rod. This gun is built for service but is also well suited for decorative purposes. Weight about 6¾ lbs.

MODEL 1257
Price $12.50

French pattern, flint lock gun, 12 ga. with 36" barrel and weighing about 8¼ lbs., made of good quality walnut witth iron ram rod.

MODEL 1355
Price $15.00

This gun is of somewhat better construction with a small amount of engraving and fancy carving. The gun is supplied in 30 ga. with 39" barrel, weighs about 5¼ lbs., has varnished stock with brass mountings and is supplied with ram rod.

"ELEPHANT FLINT LOCK GUN"

MODEL 1495
Price $20.00

This is the model which is still used extensively today for use against dangerous game by natives in the Belgian Congo. It is 4 ga. with 34" barrel and weighs about 9½ lbs. The barrel is heavily constructed for using almost any kind of slugs.

MODEL 1235
Price $20.00

This is an unusually well built flint lock gun, 22 ga. with 45" barrel and weighing about 8¾ lbs. The gun has half stock and swivels, ram rod, checkering, steel butt plate, walnut stock, varnished brown and brass fittings and should be particularly welcomed to any lover of flint lock guns.

"BUCCANEER" GUN

MODEL 1213
Price $22.50

This is a large 11 bore flint lock gun with 51" barrel and weighing approximately 10 lbs., has a black walnut stock with brass fittings and is supplied witth wooden ram rod.

EVERYTHING IN GUNS UNDER ONE COVER

FLINT AND PERCUSSION GUNS AND PISTOLS

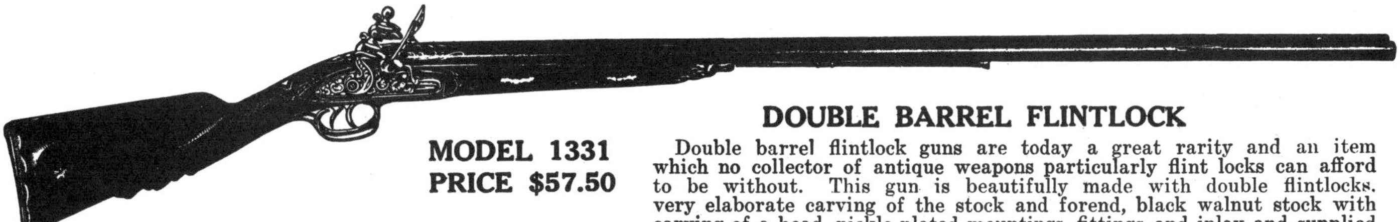

MODEL 1331
PRICE $57.50

DOUBLE BARREL FLINTLOCK

Double barrel flintlock guns are today a great rarity and an item which no collector of antique weapons particularly flint locks can afford to be without. This gun is beautifully made with double flintlocks. very elaborate carving of the stock and forend, black walnut stock with carving of a head, nickle plated mountings, fittings and inlay and supplied with ram rod. An exceedingly beautiful piece. Supplied in 22 gauge weighing about 6¾ pounds.

PERCUSSION CAP PISTOLS

In addition to the line of antique shotguns and rifles we have had call for, the old-fashioned type of Percussion Cap Duelling Pistol has come into popularity and we are, therefore, offering four types as illustrated below.

These pistols are made in 36 cal. with 8-inch barrel. The general style and workmanship is better illustrated than can be described verbally.

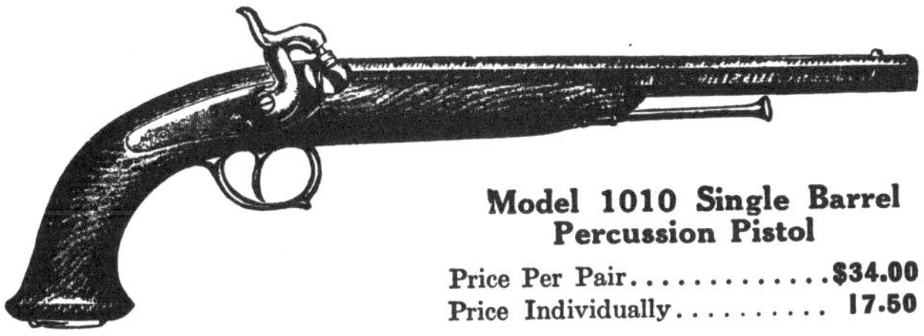

Model 1010 Single Barrel Percussion Pistol

Price Per Pair............. **$34.00**
Price Individually.......... **17.50**

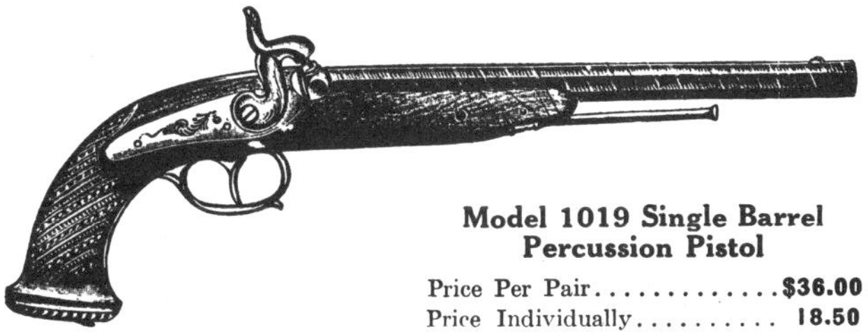

Model 1019 Single Barrel Percussion Pistol

Price Per Pair............. **$36.00**
Price Individually.......... **18.50**

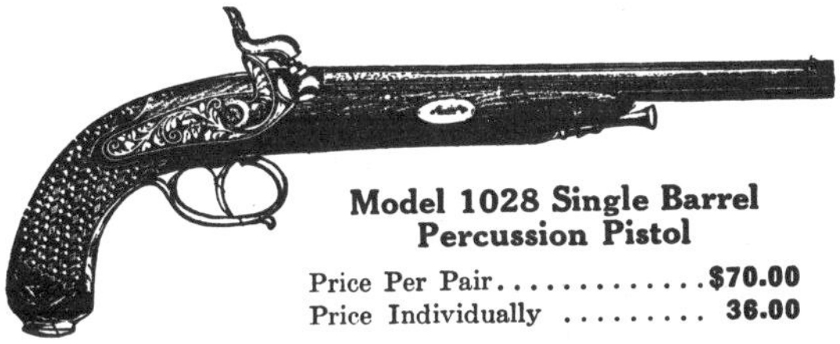

Model 1028 Single Barrel Percussion Pistol

Price Per Pair............. **$70.00**
Price Individually **36.00**

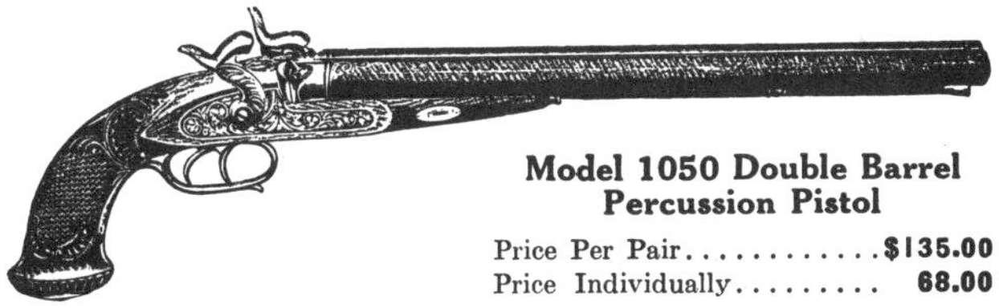

Model 1050 Double Barrel Percussion Pistol

Price Per Pair........... **$135.00**
Price Individually......... **68.00**

BLACK POWDER CHARGES FOR MUZZLE LOADERS

The following charges are those given in an extract of rules and regulations, made in the month of February, 1896, by the Gunmakers' Company and the Guardians of the Birmingham Proof House, under authority of the Gun Barrel Proof Act of 1886.

NUMBER OF GAUGE	SERVICE CHARGE			
	grains.	drs.	grains.	oz.
4	273	10	1531	3½
5	213	$7\frac{25}{32}$	1217	$2\frac{25}{32}$
6	179	$6\frac{17}{32}$	1025	$2\frac{11}{32}$
7	154	5⅝	889	$2\frac{1}{32}$
8	135	$4\frac{15}{16}$	793	$1\frac{13}{16}$
9	122	$4\frac{15}{32}$	725	$1\frac{21}{32}$
10	109	4	656	1½
11	96	3½	574	$1\frac{5}{16}$
12 to 13	89	3¼	547	1¼
14 to 15	82	3	492	1⅛
16 to 18	75	2¾	437	1
19 to 21	68	2½	383	⅞
22 to 30	55	2	328	¾
31 to 40	41	1½	246	$\frac{9}{16}$
41 to 50	27	1	164	⅜

FLINTLOCK PARTS

Two Piece Lock **$6.00**
Filed Hammer **6.00**
Large Spring **1.25**
Small Spring **1.25**
Flints .... 6 for **.75**
each **.25**

PERCUSSION LOCK PARTS

Complete lock with foreward mechanism **$5.00**
Complete lock with rear mechanism .... 1st quality **4.50**
Complete lock with rear mechanism .... 2nd quality **3.50**
Filed Hammer with rear mechanism **1.25**

MOULDED ROUND LEAD BALLS

These balls are moulded to a close tolerance and are free of the deformities common to ordinary drop shot.

We recommend these balls to the muzzle loading enthusiast who wishes to attain the highest possible degree of accuracy.

Regular drop and chilled shot will be found described on page 310, and may be had in any size at $1.00 per 5 Lb. Bag.

	Dia. in In.	Dia in m/m	No. in Lb.	No. in Box	Price Per Box	Price Per 1000
.44 Game Getter	.425	10.79	60	50	**.35**	**6.40**
.44 S. & W Russian Gallery	.428	10.87	58	50	**.35**	**6.50**
.45-5 Armory Practice	.452	11.48	50	50	**.40**	**7.25**
½				50	**.50**	**9.00**
28 Gauge	.510	12.95	35	25	**.50**	**9.25**
24 Gauge	.542	13.76	29½	25	**.60**	**10.50**
20 Gauge	.545	13.84	28½	25	**.60**	**11.00**
16 Gauge	.610	15.49	20½	25	**.75**	**13.85**
12 Gauge	.645	16.38	17	25	**.90**	**16.25**
10 Gauge	.710	18.03	13½	25	**1.10**	**20.50**
.410 Gauge				50	**.35**	**5.10**

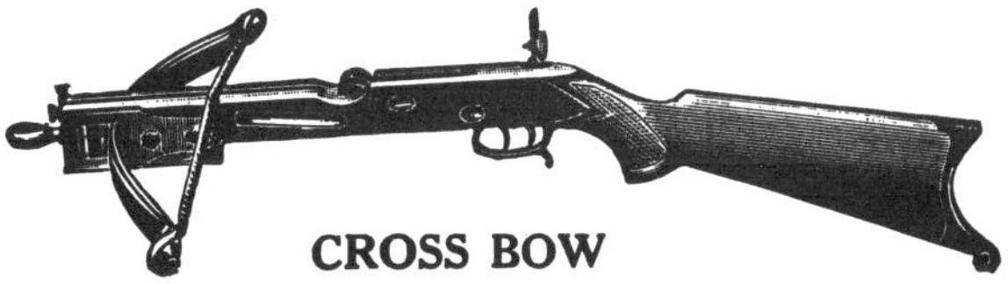

CROSS BOW

Made of selected walnut with double steel bow spring. Adjustable sights, hair trigger, and target style steel butt plate. This Cross-Bow is of heavy construction and requires the use of a special cocking lever which is supplied with it. Accurate up to 40 yards. Supplied with three special precision steel pointed darts. Weight, about 7 pounds.

Price **$85.00**
Extra Darts .... Each **1.00**

PISTOL AND REVOLVER SHOOTING

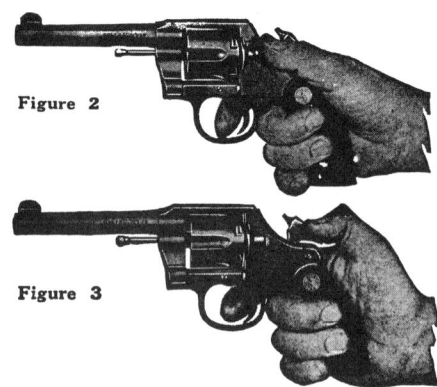

Figure 2

Figure 3

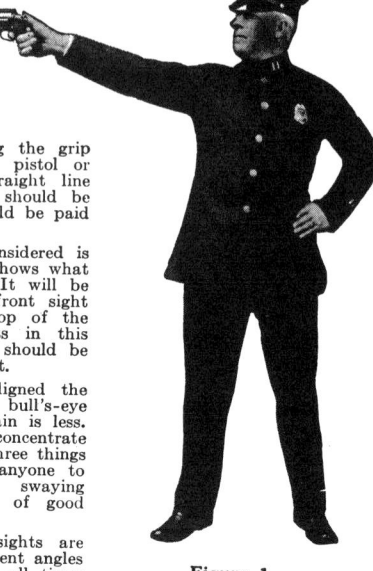

Figure 1

Pistol and revolver shooting is becoming increasingly popular. Today one usually finds an up to date and practical shooting range in most communities throughout the United States. Officials, as a rule, approve and encourage this fascinating indoor and outdoor sport. The National Rifle Association and the United States Revolver Association have for years conducted matches and encouraged the art of skillful shooting.

We have devoted this space for the beginner who wishes to improve his marksmanship but for one reason or other does not have the facilities of a shooting club at hand and a competent instructor. With a reasonable amount of intelligent practice, continued at regular intervals, the beginner may expect to develop into a good average pistol or revolver shot. The following remarks apply particularly to revolver shooting.

The illustrations on this page show in general correct form, hold of the pistol and the proper way to align the sights. These and other fundamentals must be mastered if continued improvement is to be expected. Practically all top notch shooters have acquired a style of their own after many years of practice. Most of the best shots agree that fundamentals should be acquired in the beginning. This will prevent the breaking into bad habits which may slip unnoticed into shooting form.

Figure 4

Position is important, see Figure 1. The weight should be distributed evenly on both feet, the body and feet faced slightly to the left of the target, for right handed persons. Head and shoulders should be erect without restraint. In other words the individual should be comfortable and feel at ease. The arm should be straight, with the hand slightly higher than the shoulder. The left hand may be placed on the hip or in a pocket.

Other details are very well shown from the illustration which is an example of perfect form.

The proper grip hold is very important, see Figure 2. The grasp should not be so tight as to cause tremor but should be firm enough to avoid loosing the grip when a shot is fired. The pistol or revolver should be in a straight line with the arm. The thumb should be relaxed and no attention should be paid to it while firing.

The next matter to be considered is the aiming point. Figure 4 shows what is known as "six o'clock". It will be noted that the top of the front sight is even or level with the top of the rear sight. With the sights in this position all of the bull's-eye should be seen just over the front sight.

If after the sights are aligned the shooter will concentrate on the bull's-eye he will find that the eye strain is less. It is easier for the eye to concentrate on one thing rather than on three things at once. It is difficult for anyone to hold this position without swaying slightly. This is the secret of good target shooting.

It will appear that the sights are crossing the bull's-eye at different angles and that perfect alignment at all times is impossible. This fault is practically overcome provided the trigger is squeezed. Trigger squeezing is the process of slowly pressing or squeezing (requiring several seconds) very slowly only when the sights are aligned. If this process is kept up it can be readily seen that the shot will be fired during perfect alignment, and a perfect shot will often be the result. Trigger squeezing can be mastered and rapid shots can be fired by this method in a fraction of a second. It requires much patient practice.

Figure 3 shows the method of cocking the revolver hammer with one hand. This method is used by most Police Department instructors.

Care should be taken that the finger does not press on the trigger while cocking the hammer.

ILLUSTRATIONS FROM BAIR'S MANUAL OF POLICE REVOLVER INSTRUCTION

 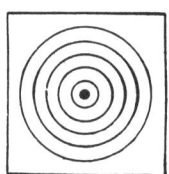

The above illustration shows correct sight alignment, resulting in a perfect shot. This style of sight alignment should be acquired.

The above illustration shows front sight too high and to the right, resulting in shots high and to the right.

 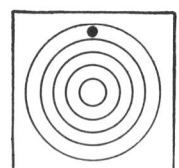

The above illustration shows too high or too much front sight, resulting in high shots.

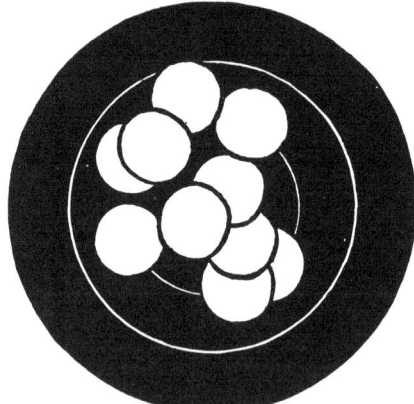

The above illustration shows a "possible" of ten shots fired from a revolver at 20 yards. The illustration is actual size.

 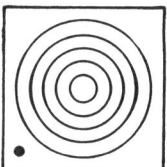

The above illustration shows front sight and pistol canted to the left, resulting in a low left shot.

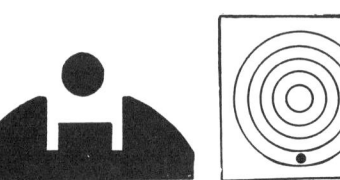

The above illustration shows too low or too little front sight, resulting in a low shot.

The above illustration shows front sight to the left, resulting in a shot to the left.

 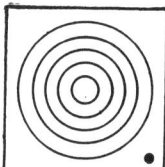

The above illustration shows front sight to the right and pistol canted to the right, resulting in a low right shot.

Sight alignment illustrations are reprinted here by the kind permission of Mr. R. M. Bair.

KEEP IN PRACTICE WITH STOEGER TARGETS

A CENTURY OF ACHIEVEMENT
1836—COLT—1936

The Colt's Patent Fire Arms Mfg. Co., can proudly look back to a century of achievements outstanding in the fire arms industry of this country. Samuel Colt, the founder, was born in Hartford, Conn., July 18, 1814. As a youngster on board a sailing ship bound for Calcutta he completed a working model of the revolving Colt pistol. In the year of 1835 he patented his revolving arm in England and received his first patent in this country in February 1836, and immediately plans were laid for what proved to be the beginning of one of America's industrial giants.

In the same year a small factory was established at Paterson, N. J., for the manufacture of the first Colt revolvers. Frontier conditions in Texas and the Seminole Indian wars in Florida did much to test the value of the Colt revolvers used for the first time in the defense of United States territory. The so-called "Texas-Pistol" used in these wars showed its superiority over the regular clumsy old-fashioned regulation ordnance and the young officers of the army particularly demanded the Colt to be supplied for their troops. Through the influence of General Zachary Taylor the first order for one thousand Colt's was placed with the young concern, and his revolving pistol was now firmly established.

In addition to revolvers, the Paterson plant produced revolving rifles and shotguns in various calibers and models. One of the most debated subjects is the "Walker" Model. This was a heavy .44 caliber six-shooter provided with an attached lever for ramming the bullets into the chamber of the cylinders.

In 1848 Samuel Colt produced a new .31 caliber model and others. The cylinder was removable for loading and later a rammer was added. Among them was the noted "Wells Fargo" model. Other models followed such as the Dragoon Models, adapted officially by the U. S. Government for both mounted and unmounted troops. In 1855 Colt had established mass production methods. In May, 1855, the Colt's Patent Fire Arms Co., was chartered and he established contact with every foreign nation.

Shortly thereafter a new design in revolver construction was developed. This was the jointless frame with top straps to which the barrel was firmly attached and in which the cylinder was inclosed. New models of revolvers and rifles followed in quick succession right up to the outbreak of the Civil War. During this period Colt produced in 1861–69655; in 1862–111676; in 1863–136579 and during 1864 and 1865–69107 pieces. After a hard struggle and achieving great success Samuel Colt passed away on January 10th, 1862.

However, the great business he had established was kept up under the leadership of his faithful associates. With the invention of the metallic cartridge the reloading problem was solved and "rapid fire" made possible. This revolutionized the making of firearms and a full line of new Colt revolvers was produced. In 1873 the famous "Peacemaker" was introduced. This same six-shooter was also produced in .44 and .44-40 calibers and became famous as the Colt "Frontier" revolver.

A unique type of gun introduced in this period was known as the Deringer. The first Deringer introduced by Colt's and National were short, all-metal, single-barreled pistols using .41 caliber, rim-fire cartridges. A second type known as the "No. 2" Deringer using the same caliber cartridge and with wood stocks was later produced by both Colt's and National, which was followed by the third Deringers often referred to as the New Type Deringer. These third Deringers were introduced by Colt's in the late "Seventies" and were furnished with two types of stocks. They used .41 caliber, rim-fire cartridges and were manufactured until about 1912 when the models were discontinued.

During this period (1870–1872) the Colt Company manufactured 40,000 .42 caliber Berdan Breech-loading Military rifles for the Russian Government using for the first time a metallic cartridge having a "Bottle-necked" case, reducing the diameter of the bullet and increasing the powder space. These arms were produced in both musket and carbine types.

The year of 1877 marks the advent of the Double Action revolver. Another advancement was made in 1887, the lateral swinging cylinder with simultaneous ejection. The Bisley model was introduced in 1897, followed shortly by the Bisley Target model. With the turn of the century a new idea in pistols was conceived, a .38 automatic magazine pistol operated by the recoil. During the decade of 1900–1910 automatics of various styles, weights and calibers were made. In 1909 the Army adopted the .45 caliber New Service revolver and in 1911 the U. S. War Department adopted the Colt Automatic pistol as its official arm.

Each year has ushered in some improvement to enchance the efficiency or accuracy and safety of the Colt. Scientific invention marches on. You may obtain a copy of the Colt's book "A Century of Achievement" from us at the price of 25 cents or a de Luxe edition at the price of $1.00.

COLT AUTOMATIC PISTOLS

ACE .22 AUTOMATIC PISTOL CAL. .22 LONG RIFLE

The ACE is designed especially for shooters of the Government Model and Super .38 Automatic Pistols—and has also been in demand by shooters for all around service. Built on the same frame as the Government Model and has the same safety features. Special super-precisioned barrel and hand finished target action. Exceptionally smooth operation and unusually accurate. Rear sight is of target design with adjustments for both elevation and windage. Allows economical target practice for military men, using .22 caliber ammunition in an arm of the same design as the regular military model. For Regular and High Speed Greased Cartridges.

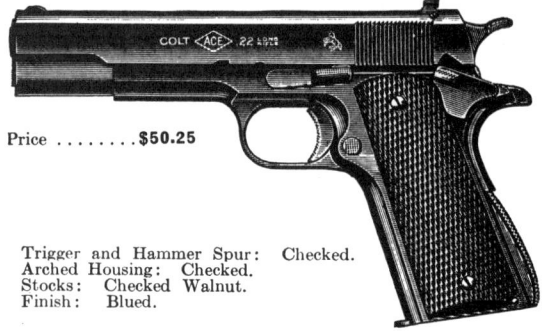

Price $50.25

SPECIFICATIONS

Ammunition: .22 Long Rifle Greased cartridges. Regular or High Speed.
Magazine Capacity: 10 cartridges.
Length of Barrel: 4¾ inches.
Length Over All: 8¼ inches.
Action: Hand finished.
Weight: 38 ounces.
Sights: Front sight fixed. Rear sight adjustable for both elevation and windage.
Trigger and Hammer Spur: Checked.
Arched Housing: Checked.
Stocks: Checked Walnut.
Finish: Blued.

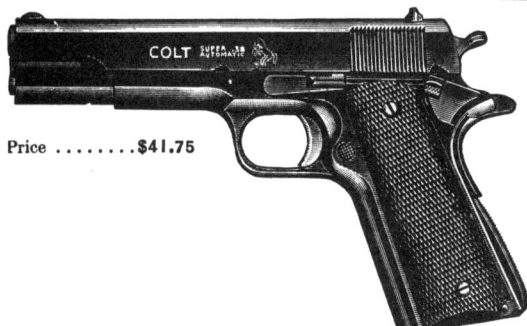

Price $41.75

SUPER .38 AUTOMATIC PISTOL CALIBER .38

For the big game hunter, and the lover of the outdoors, the Super .38 offers an arm of unsurpassed power and efficiency. It is built on the same frame as the Government Model and has all of the safety features found in this famous gun. It is especially popular because of the powerful Super .38 cartridges which it handles—having a muzzle velocity of approximately 1300 foot seconds. Will stop any animal on the American continent and is a favorite for use as an auxiliary arm for big game hunting trips. Magazine holds 9 cartridges.

SPECIFICATIONS

Sights: Fixed Patridge type.
Trigger and Hammer Spur: Checked.
Arched Housing: Checked.
Stocks: Checked Walnut.
Finish: Blued. Nickel Finish at extra cost of $5.00.
Ammunition: .38 Automatic cartridges.
Magazine Capacity: 9 cartridges.
Length of Barrel: 5 inches.
Length Over All: 8½ inches.
Weight: 39 ounces.

The Colt Arched Housing is illustrated above—used on all heavy frame Colt models. It provides a more secure and more comfortable grip.

GOVERNMENT MODEL AUTOMATIC PISTOL CAL. .45

The Colt Government Model is the most famous Automatic Pistol in the world. It has for years been the Official side arm of the United States Army, Navy and Marine Corps, as well as the military organizations of many foreign countries. Extremely powerful and absolutely dependable. Magazine holds seven cartridges and magazines can be replaced with great speed. Rugged and simple, it has withstood the most rigorous tests by the United States Government and proved itself unsurpassed in reliability and efficiency.

Price $41.75

SPECIFICATIONS

Ammunition: .45 Automatic cartridges.
Magazine Capacity: 7 cartridges.
Length of Barrel: 5 inches.
Length Over All: 8½ inches.
Sights: Fixed Patridge type.
Weight: 39 ounces.
Trigger and Hammer Spur: Checked.
Arched Housing: Checked.
Stocks: Checked Walnut.
Finish: Blued. Nickel Finish $5.00 extra.

Price $50.00

DOUBLE ADJUSTABLE REAR SIGHT AND A RAMP TYPE FIXED FRONT SIGHT WITH SERRATED FACE

Here is a beautiful and efficient new rear sight for the Colt National Match and Super Match Automatic Pistols. It is designed especially for these two arms, constructed with precision, and adjustable for both windage and elevation. Take a close look at the illustration. Note the simplicity of this new sight, how extremely easy it is to adjust and to set accurately. It's just the finest hand gun sight ever made. And we mean just that. A host of shooters are going to like the new ramp type rugged sight out front, too. All of which means cleaner definition, higher and more consistent scoring.

COLT NATIONAL MATCH CALIBER .45

The regulation Government Model side arm perfected for match competition. Identical in size and operation, but with velvet-smooth hand-honed target action and a super-precisioned match barrel. Full grip, fine balance, three safety features. Now with adjustable rear sight and ramp type front sight, Colt's National Match brings you accuracy, power and smoothness never before equalled in a caliber .45 automatic pistol.

COLT SUPER MATCH CALIBER .38

With the exception that it is chambered for the high-powered .38 automatic cartridge, the Super Match Automatic Pistol is identical in every way with the National Match Model. It has the same velvet-smooth action, precision match barrel, same dependable safety features, same checked arched housing, same firm non-slipping grip. Accuracy, of course, is further increased by the new sights now available; ramp type front and adjustable rear. The Colt Super Match answers every demand in a caliber .38 automatic for competitive shooting—and possesses tremendous power for the big game hunter.

Prices: National Match and Super Match with adjustable sight $50.25
National Match and Super Match with fixed sights 45.25

SPECIFICATIONS

Ammunition: .38 Automatic cartridges.
Magazine Capacity: 9 cartridges.
Length of Barrel: 5 inches.
Length Over All: 8½ inches.
Weight: 39 ounces.
Action: Hand honed, velvet-smooth.
Stocks: Checked Walnut.
Sights: Adjustable rear, with Adjustments for elevation and windage. Ramp front sight.
Trigger and Hammer Spur: Checked.
Arched Housing: Checked.
Finish: Blued. Can be furnished in nickel finish at extra cost of $5.00.

ADJUSTABLE SIGHTS ON OLDER PISTOLS

You don't have to buy a new gun to enjoy the truly remarkable advantages of this new rear sight. For seven dollars and seventy-five cents, we will equip your Government Model and Super .38, as well as your National Match Model, or your Super Match, with this new sight combination. This includes the cost of the sight, recutting the sight slide cut, labor and targeting. It's a lot of value for **$7.75**.

SEND YOUR GUN TO STOEGER FOR EXPERT REPAIRING

COLT SERVICE MODEL ACE AND .22-.45 CONVERSION UNIT

SERVICE MODEL ACE
Cal. .22 L.R. with floating chamber. A .22 with 4 times the kick. .45 practice at 1/7 the cost.

Price $60.00

DUPLICATES IN SIZE, SHAPE, BALANCE, AND FEEL, THE FAMOUS GOVERNMENT MODEL CALIBER .45 AUTOMATIC

Except for difference in caliber, the new SERVICE MODEL ACE and the Government Model .45 are practically twins. They are so near alike that you can switch from one to the other and hardly notice the difference. The Service Ace saves REAL money and pays for itself in a very short time. It provides accurate, economical target shooting for Service men—members of National Guard, Reserve Officers, and individual shooters of the .45 Caliber Automatic Pistol ... at one-seventh the cost of .45 automatic cartridges. A feature of the Service Ace is its ingenious floating chamber which amplifies the ordinary recoil of a .22 four times, and provides positive functioning under all conditions. According to Colonel J. S. Hatcher in his article in the American Rifleman magazine, "the floating chamber practically quadruples the recoil power of the .22 long rifle cartridge, producing a recoil that sufficiently simulates the action of the .45 so that the gun must be re-aligned on the target after each shot, thus making it possible to obtain extremely effective rapid fire practice. Also it gives sufficient reserve power to insure certainty of functioning, even with old or inferior ammunition. The Service Model Ace offers a most effective method of training for proficiency with the Service pistol, and such an economical one that the amount saved on ammunition in just a few days' practice will pay for the gun."

SPECIFICATIONS
Ammunition .22 Long Rifle, Regular or High Speed. Magazine capacity 10 cartridges. Length of barrel: 5 in. Length overall: 8½ in. Action: Hand Finished. Weight: 42 ounces. Sights: Fixed ramp front sight. Rear sight adjustable for both elevation and windage. Trigger and Hammer Spur checked.

.22–.45 CONVERSION UNIT—Price $34.00

You can now shoot your service arm at 1/7th the cost of .45 ammunition ... thus allowing you hours of additional target practice at small cost.

The .22-.45 Conversion Unit comes equipped with the Colt FLOATING CHAMBER producing a recoil approximately four times the recoil of an ordinary .22.

The Unit consists of the slide assembly as shown above, complete with barrel and floating chamber, extractor, bushing, recoil spring, recoil spring guide, plug and sights. The rear sight is adjustable for both elevation and windage. These parts are interchangeable with similar parts on the .45 caliber pistol and fitted without tools in a very few seconds.

It will save its price in ammunition costs in almost no time.
Price $34.00

.45–.22 CONVERSION UNIT—Price $23.70

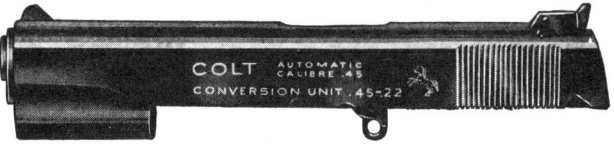

The .45-.22 Conversion Unit converts the recently developed .22-Cal. Service Ace (with floating chamber) to calibre .45. By simply interchanging the component parts of the Unit with the corresponding parts of the Service Ace, the shooter may shift from .22 calibre ammunition to .45 Automatic cartridges in a very few minutes. The .45-.22 is composed of Match Grade slide, equipped with fixed front sight and Stevens adjustable rear sight; selected Match barrel with bushing; recoil spring; recoil spring guide and plug, magazine and slide stop. This Unit makes it possible for you to secure maximum pleasure from your Colt Service Ace.

Price $23.70

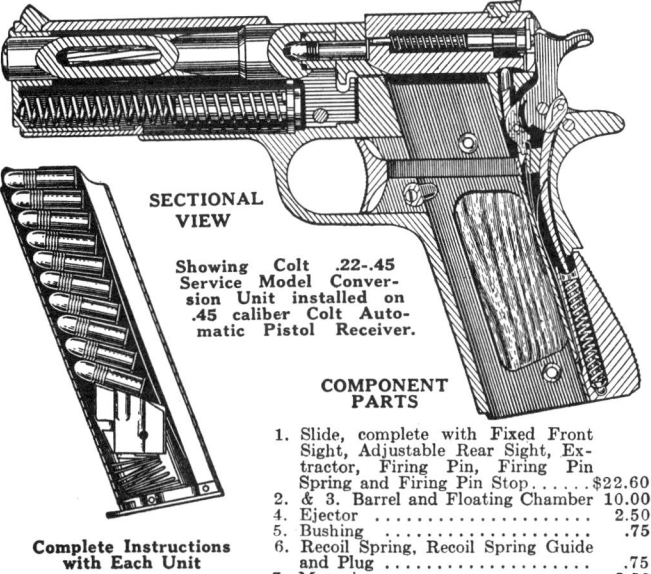

SECTIONAL VIEW

Showing Colt .22-.45 Service Model Conversion Unit installed on .45 caliber Colt Automatic Pistol Receiver.

COMPONENT PARTS

1. Slide, complete with Fixed Front Sight, Adjustable Rear Sight, Extractor, Firing Pin, Firing Pin Spring and Firing Pin Stop......$22.60
2. & 3. Barrel and Floating Chamber 10.00
4. Ejector 2.50
5. Bushing .... .75
6. Recoil Spring, Recoil Spring Guide and Plug .... .75
7. Magazine 3.50
8. Slide Stop 1.20
Other parts same as regular .45 Automatic

Complete Instructions with Each Unit

Pays for Itself in Ammunition Saving

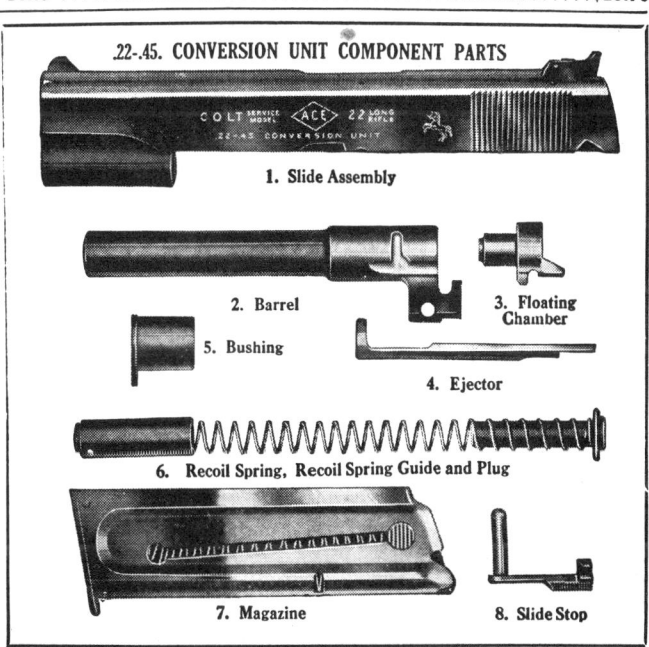

.22-.45. CONVERSION UNIT COMPONENT PARTS

1. Slide Assembly
2. Barrel
3. Floating Chamber
4. Ejector
5. Bushing
6. Recoil Spring, Recoil Spring Guide and Plug
7. Magazine
8. Slide Stop

COLT AUTOMATIC PISTOLS

In every part of the world Colt Automatic Pistols are known and used. The speed with which they may be fired, their power and dependability, have made them popular for every type of service requiring an arm of absolute dependability and complete safety. Colt Automatic Pistols are equipped with both manual and automatic safety features—they are the safest automatic pistols that can be purchased. There is a Colt model for every purpose.

WOODSMAN TARGET MODEL
CALIBER: .22 Long Rifle
6½ Inch Barrel

The Colt Woodsman Model is the most popular .22 Caliber automatic pistol ever produced. Thousands of shooters have found it ideal for all around shooting—and for target shooting. Graceful in appearance and beautifully finished. It is furnished with an unusually comfortable grip that fits the hand snugly and securely. Checked walnut stocks make slipping impossible. Fast and certain action—a trigger pull that is smooth and crisp. Ten shot magazine, and slide lock safety. Target sights, either Bead or Patridge.

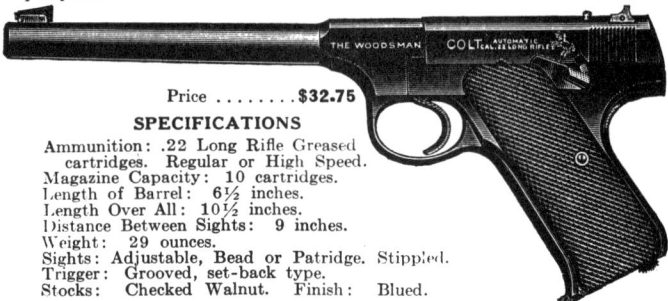

Price $32.75

SPECIFICATIONS
Ammunition: .22 Long Rifle Greased cartridges. Regular or High Speed.
Magazine Capacity: 10 cartridges.
Length of Barrel: 6½ inches.
Length Over All: 10½ inches.
Distance Between Sights: 9 inches.
Weight: 29 ounces.
Sights: Adjustable, Bead or Patridge. Stippled.
Trigger: Grooved, set-back type.
Stocks: Checked Walnut. Finish: Blued.

Price $32.75

SPECIFICATIONS
Ammunition: .22 Long Rifle Greased cartridges. Regular or High Speed.
Magazine Capacity: 10 cartridges.
Length of Barrel: 4½ inches.
Length Over All: 8½ inches.
Distance Between Sights: Fixed Front sight—7½ inches. Adjustable front sight—7 inches.
Weight: 27 ounces.
Stocks: Checked Walnut.
Sights: Front sight fixed, ramp type with serrated face, or adjustable front sight. Rear sight adjustable for windage. Both stippled.
Trigger: Grooved, set-back type. Finish: Blued.

WOODSMAN SPORT MODEL
CALIBER: .22 Long Rifle
4½ Inch Barrel

The same as the standard model described above, except for length of barrel. It can now be furnished with either fixed or adjustable front sight. Ramp type front sight is sturdy and rugged, built to stand up under hard service and abuse. Adjustable type front sight is same as on target model. Rear sight is adjustable for windage. This model was produced for use in the woods and on the trail, where compactness is essential. Unusually accurate and a thoroughbred Colt in every way. Uses either Regular or High Speed cartridges, including hollow point type. Ten shot magazine.

WOODSMAN HIGH SPEED MAIN SPRING HOUSING

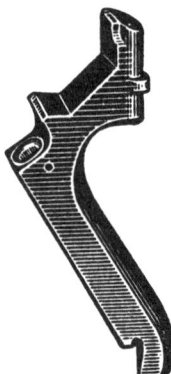

The new Main Spring Housing, built of hardened steel and adapting the Woodsman for use with the new High Speed Cartridges.

Those who may wish to change over their present Woodsman to handle the High Speed Cartridges need simply replace their old housing with the new type.

Price $2.00

POCKET MODEL AUTOMATIC PISTOL
CALIBER: .25

The .25 Caliber Colt Automatic Pistol is designed for personal protection. Because of its small size and light weight it can be easily carried in vest pocket or ladies hand bag. Shoots the hard-hitting .25 Automatic cartridge, with magazine having six shot capacity. Makes a beautiful gift when finished in nickel with pearl or ivory stocks. Three safety features make it absolutely safe to handle.

SPECIFICATIONS
Ammunition: 25 Automatic cartridge. Magazine Capacity: 6 cartridges. Length of Barrel: 2 inches. Length Over All: 4½ inches. Weight: 13 ounces. Stocks: Checked Walnut. Finish: Blued or Nickel.

Price $20.75

Colt Grip Safety and Magazine Disconnector

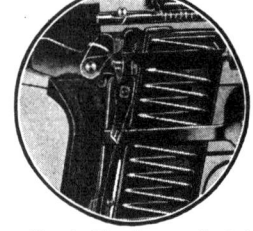

To doubly insure absolute safety in handling Colt Automatic Pistols, all models (with the exception of the Woodsman Model) are fitted with the world famed Colt Grip Safety—in addition to the Slide Lock Safety. The Colt Grip Safety operates automatically and requires the grip safety to be squeezed simultaneously with pulling the trigger in order to discharge the Arm. The arm cannot be fired by simply pulling the trigger.

Colt Automatic Pistol models in calibers .32, .380 and .25 are also equipped with the Colt Magazine Safety Disconnector.

Price $24.25

This is the favorite model for personal and home protection. Ready always for instant action.

POCKET MODEL AUTOMATIC PISTOL
CALIBERS: .32 and .380

This pocket model Automatic Pistol can be furnished in either .32 or .380 caliber. Large magazine capacity, powerful, rugged and dependable. Flat construction takes up minimum room in pocket, bag or dresser drawer. Three safety features, both manual and automatic.

SPECIFICATIONS
Ammunition: .32 Automatic cartridge. .380 Automatic cartridge.
Magazine Capacity: .32 caliber, 8 cartridges. .380 caliber, 7 cartridges.
Length of Barrel: 3¾ inches. Length Over All: 6¾ inches.
Weight: 24 ounces. Stocks: Checked Walnut.
Finish: Blued or Nickel.

NEW STYLE ARCHED MAIN SPRING HOUSING

For Colt Automatic Caliber .45.
Price $1.50

NEW STYLE SHORT CHECKERED TRIGGER

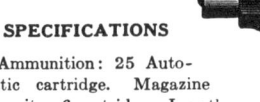

For Colt Automatic .45 or .38.
Price $1.50
Old Style Trigger, Colt Automatic Caliber .45 or .38.
Price .... each $1.50

STOEGER'S 25-SHOT MAGAZINE

Made for the Government Model .45 Automatic Pistol. Fits this model pistol without any alterations. Can be easily loaded by hand. Invaluable for Police, Riot Duty.

This item discontinued

America's Great Gun House 103

COLT MATCH TARGET WOODSMAN
Cal. .22 Long Rifle
NEW 6½″ HEAVY BARREL AND LONGER STOCKS

**NEW STRAIGHTER TRIGGER
... FREE FROM BACKLASH**

The new Woodsman trigger is of straighter design—full width and deeply grooved the entire length to prevent slipping. The backlash has been removed and the trigger travel is so slight as to be hardly noticeable. The new trigger gives the expert shooter a sure, easy, comfortable squeeze.

SPECIALLY DESIGNED LONGER STOCKS

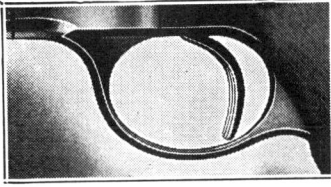

The stocks are constructed in a single piece fitting over the front strap and extending down well beyond the bottom strap. A comfortable, natural shooting grip. Securely attached, thoroughly checked, and non-slipping. Made of selected walnut.

**FIXED FRONT SIGHT ...
RUGGED 2-WAY ADJUSTABLE REAR SIGHT**

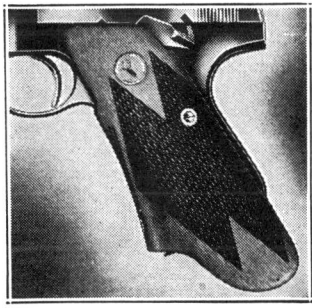

The new Woodsman has a perfect set of sights. The front sight is fixed Kelly type with full face and completely stippled.

The rear sight is NEW with adjustments for both elevation and windage. Both front and rear sights are exceptionally strong and rugged.

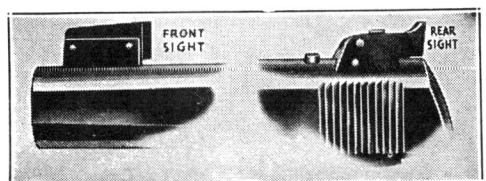

SPECIFICATIONS

Ammunition: .22 Long Rifle Greased Cartridges, Regular or High Speed • Magazine Capacity: 10 cartridges • Action: Hand finished. Velvet smooth • Barrel: Of special weighted design. Slightly tapered, with flat sides • Length of Barrel: 6½ inches • Length over All: 11 inches • Distance Between Sights: 9¼ inches • Weight: 36 ounces • Sights: Front fixed sight. Rear sight adjustable, with adjustments for both elevation and windage • Trigger: Grooved. Of special design, with excess travel and backlash removed • Stocks: Checked Walnut. Specially designed to cover front strap and extend below bottom strap • Finish: Blued. Top of barrel, receiver and slide stippled. Rear of slide and receiver also stippled.

Price $41.75

So perfectly has this new Woodsman been designed, that it is hard to believe that seven full ounces have been added to its weight. The balance is absolutely perfect, with the weight in just the proper spot to boost timed and rapid fire scores. It's a streamlined job ... thoroughly modern in every way.

The muzzle of the barrel is flat, with a slight tapering toward the rifling such as found on the most expensive rifles. To eliminate glare and light reflection the top of the barrel, receiver, and slide, as well as both sights have all been stippled to a fine dull finish. So has the rear of the slide and receiver.

The action of this new Match Target Woodsman is super smooth, and has been hand-honed to a velvet finish that only Colt craftsman could produce. The pull is smooth as glass ... the let-off quick, sharp and without creep. Even the backlash has been removed. It's the smoothest thing out in .22 pistols.

No expense has been spared to make this the World's Finest Target Pistol ... the arm that has been designed BY Expert Shooters FOR Expert Shooters.

IMPROVE YOUR SCORE WITH STOEGER'S TARGETS

COLT REVOLVERS

The name "Colt" has for nearly a century been the symbol of quality, efficiency and dependability in firearms. Colt Revolvers and Automatic Pistols have been selected by thousands of shooters in every part of the world, for personal protection, police and military service, target shooting and for use in the outdoors. Their ruggedness, accuracy and absolute dependability have stamped them as the standard by which all other firearms are measured. There is nothing finer than a COLT.

POLICE REVOLVERS

The most important item in the equipment of a police officer, sheriff or guard is his service revolver. It must be dependable beyond the shadow of a doubt—and ready for efficient and effective action on a moment's notice. These rigid requirements explain in large measure why Colts have been selected by so many thousands of officers throughout the country—hundreds of whom have told us that the Colt, ready at their side for instant duty, makes it easier to face the dangers so common to the modern peace officer.

OFFICIAL POLICE REVOLVER

CALIBERS:
.22 Long Rifle
.32-20 (.32 Winchester)
.38 Special

Price $33.25

SPECIFICATIONS: Calibers .38 and .32-20

Ammunition: .32-20 (.32 Winchester) .38 Short Colt; .38 Long Colt; .38 Colt Special; .38 S. & W. Special (full and mid-range loads); .38 Colt Special High Speed; .38 S. & W. Special High Speed and .38-44 S. & W. Special cartridges in .385 special model.
Lengths of Barrel: 2, 4, 5, 6 inches.
Length Over All: With 6 inch barrel, 11¼ inches.
Weight: With 6 inch barrel, 34 ounces.
Sights: Fixed type, stippled
Trigger and Hammer Spur: Checked. Stocks: Checked Walnut.
Finish: Blued or Nickel. Top of frame matted to prevent light reflection.

The COLT Official Police Revolver is without any question the world's outstanding police arm. This popular service model is famous for its ruggedness, and its ability to stand up under the severe abuse it receives at the sides of police officers the world over. Built on the .41 caliber frame it has ample strength to meet any requirements—and the .38 Special cartridges for which it is chambered offer sufficient power to meet any emergency. The Official Police is furnished with the Colt Positive Safety Lock—which makes accidental discharge impossible. Full size grip, perfect balance, special matted top. Also chambered for .22 Long Rifle cartridges to allow police officers, economical target practice with a small caliber model that is otherwise identical with their regular service arm.

SPECIFICATIONS: Caliber .22

Ammunition: .22 Long Rifle cartridges. Regular or High Speed.
Length of Barrel: 6 inches only.
Length Over All: 11¼ inches.
Weight: 38 ounces.
Sights: Fixed type, stippled.
Cylinder: Embedded Head Type.
Stocks: Checked Walnut.
Finish: Blued only.
Top of frame matted to prevent light reflection.
Trigger and Hammer Spur: Checked.

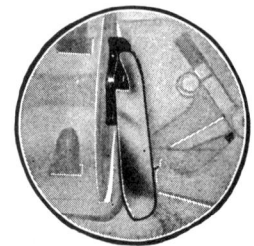

Colt "Two Point" Hand

You have possibly often wondered what device was used in Colt Revolvers to hold the cylinder chamber and the barrel so rigidly and so perfectly in line. This result is obtained through the use of the Colt "Two Point" Hand found only in Colt Revolvers.

POLICE POSITIVE SPECIAL REVOLVER

The Police Positive Special Model is a medium weight police arm—the standard service revolver of many large police departments in this country and abroad. It is chambered for the powerful .38 Special cartridges and furnished with a grip that is secure and comfortable. The Colt Positive Safety Lock is a feature that prevents accidental discharge. *Colt Police Revolvers cannot be fired unless the trigger is intentionally pulled.* This model is ideal for unmounted police officers, as well as for personal and home protection.

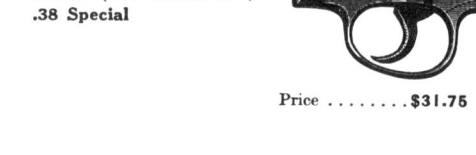

CALIBERS:
.32-20 (.32 Winchester)
.38 Special

Price $31.75

The patented Colt matted frame top. Prevents light reflection and aids in sighting.

SPECIFICATIONS

Ammunition: .32-20 (.32 Winchester). .38 Short Colt; .38 Long Colt; .38 Colt Special; .38 S. & W. Special (full and mid-range loads); .38 Colt Special High Speed; .38 S. & W. Special High Speed and .38-44 S. & W. Special cartridges.
Lengths of Barrel: 4, 5, 6 inches.
Length Over All: With 4 inch barrel, 8¾ inches.
Weight: With 4 inch barrel, 22 ounces.
Sights: Fixed type, stippled.
Trigger and Hammer Spur: Checked.
Stocks: Checked Walnut.
Finish: Blued or nickel. Top of frame matted to prevent light reflection.

SEE PAGE 8 "HOW TO ORDER"

COLT REVOLVERS

DETECTIVE SPECIAL

The Colt Positive Safety Lock makes accidental discharge of a Colt Police Revolver absolutely impossible. The illustration above shows the solid bar of steel, 1/10 of an inch thick, which rests between the hammer and frame at all times except when trigger is intentionally pulled.

The Detective Special is exactly the same as the Police Positive Special Revolver, except that it has been finished with the short 2 inch barrel. This model is designed especially for pocket use, and has been adopted by large police departments for use by detectives, special investigators and plain clothes men. It handles the same ammunition as the Official Police Model, making it the most powerful arm of its size and weight available. Unusually accurate at short range, and absolutely reliable. Equipped with Colt Positive Safety Lock. Weighs only 21 ounces.

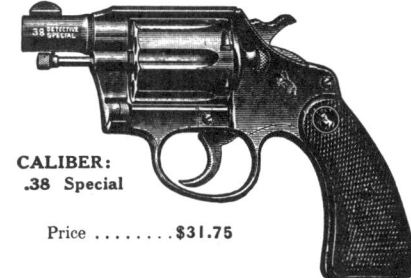

CALIBER:
.38 Special

Price $31.75

SPECIFICATIONS

Ammunition: .38 Short Colt; .38 Long Colt; .38 Colt Special. .38 S. & W. Special (full and mid-range loads); .38 Colt Special High Speed; .38 S. & W. Special High Speed and .38-44 S. & W. Special cartridges.
Length of Barrel: 2 inches.
Length Over All: 6¾ inches.
Weight: 21 ounces.
Sights: Fixed type, stippled.
Trigger and Hammer Spur: Checked.
Stocks: Rounded, checked Walnut.
Finish: Blued or nickel. Top of frame matted to prevent light reflection.

POLICE POSITIVE REVOLVER

CALIBERS:
.32 Police Positive (New Police)
.38 Police Positive (New Police)

For police officers, bank guards and messengers who require a powerful arm, yet one that can be easily concealed, the Colt Police Positive Revolver is recommended. This model is smaller and lighter than the Police Positive Special Revolver, but otherwise has the same characteristics. Chambered for both the .32 and .38 Police Positive (New Police) Cartridges, which are popular for police and guard service in all parts of the country. This model is also adapted for home protection and can be easily and safely carried in pocket, holster or car. Furnished with the Colt Positive Safety Lock.

Price $30.75

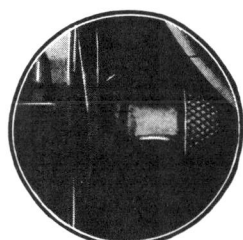

The Colt Rearward action, safety type cylinder latch guards against the possibility of the cylinder being accidentally opened by forward pressure from the thumb. The Colt latch can only be operated by a deliberate rearward motion.

SPECIFICATIONS

Ammunition: .32 Police Positive (New Police) .32 S. & W. Short; .32 S. & W. Long (Regular and Sharp Shoulder) in .32 Caliber model.
.38 Police Positive (New Police) and .38 S. & W. cartridges in .38 caliber model.
Lengths of Barrel: .32 caliber, 2½, 4, 5, 6 inches; .38 caliber, 4, 5, 6 inches.
Length Over All: With 4-inch barrel, 8½ inches.
Weight: With 4-inch barrel, .38 cal. 20 ounces; 32 cal. 22 ounces.
Sights: Fixed type, stippled.
Trigger and Hammer Spur: Checked.
Stocks: Checked Walnut.
Finish: Blued or Nickel. Top of frame matted to prevent light reflection.

BANKERS' SPECIAL REVOLVER

CALIBERS:
.22 Long Rifle .38 Police Positive (New Police)

The .38 caliber Colt Bankers' Special Model has been a great favorite for use by bank messengers, tellers, guards and plain clothes men. It is compact, absolutely dependable and powerful. Easily carried and concealed in pocket or shoulder holster. The new .22 Caliber model uses the regular or high speed .22 Long Rifle cartridges—including the hard-hitting, hollow point. It is in great demand as an arm to be carried at all times, ready for any emergency. Except for caliber, both guns are identical. Both models have COLT POSITIVE SAFETY LOCK.

Price $30.75

Price $30.75

SPECIFICATIONS
.22 Caliber Model

Ammunition: .22 Long Rifle cartridges, Regular or High Speed, including Hollow Point.
Length of Barrel: 2 inches.
Length Over All: 6½ inches.
Sights: Fixed type, stippled.
Cylinder: Embedded Head Type.
Stocks: Rounded, checked Walnut.
Weight: 23 ounces.
Finish: Blued or Nickel. Top of frame matted to prevent light reflection.
Trigger and Hammer Spur: Checked.

SPECIFICATIONS
.38 Caliber Model

Ammunition: .38 Police Positive (New Police) and .38 S. & W. cartridges.
Length of Barrel: 2 inches.
Length Over All: 6½ inches.
Sights: Fixed type, stippled.
Weight: 19 ounces.
Stocks: Rounded, checked Walnut.
Finish: Blued or Nickel. Top of frame matted to prevent light reflection.
Trigger and Hammer Spur: Checked.

COLT REVOLVERS

POCKET POSITIVE REVOLVER

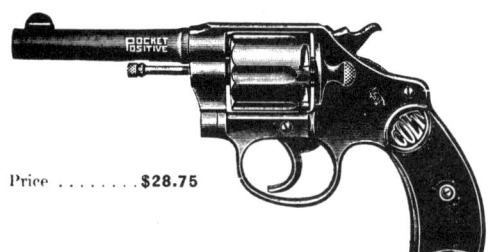

Price $28.75

This model is furnished with the COLT POSITIVE SAFETY LOCK — making it absolutely safe for use by ladies and those not accustomed to handling firearms.

CALIBER: .32 Police Positive (New Police)

The Pocket Positive is an unusually compact revolver, small in size and light in weight. Designed to be carried in pocket or small hand bag and having ample power to make it an ideal arm for personal protection. Small, snug grip with checked rubber stocks. Popular for home protection.

SPECIFICATIONS

Ammunition: .32 Police Positive (New Police); .32 S. W. Short; .32 S. & W. Long (Regular and Sharp Shoulder)
Lengths of Barrel 2, 2½, 3½, 6 inches.
Length Over All: With 2½ inch barrel, 6½ inches.
Weight: With 2½ inch barrel, 16 ounces.
Sights: Fixed type, stippled.
Hammer Spur: Checked.
Stocks: Checked black rubber.
Finish: Blued or Nickel. Top of frame matted to prevent light reflection.

The checked hammer spur used on Colt Revolvers makes possible a firm, sure grip and speeds up cocking for rapid firing.

NEW SERVICE REVOLVER

CALIBERS: .38 Special
.357 Magnum
.38-40 (.38 Winchester)
.44 Special
.44-40 (.44 Winchester)
.45 Colt
.45 Automatic
.455 Eley

Price $37.75

SPECIFICATIONS

Ammunition: .38 Short Colt; .38 Long Colt; .38 Colt Special; .38 S. & W. Special (full and midrange loads); .38 Colt Special High Speed; .38 S. & W. Special High Speed and .38-44 S. & W. Special cartridges in .38 caliber model.
.357 Magnum.
.38-40 (.38 Winchester).
.44 Special. .44-40 (.44 Winchester).
.45 Colt.
.45 Automatic. .455 Eley (English).
Lengths of Barrel Calibers .38 and .357 Magnum, 4, 5, 6 inches. Other calibers, 4½, 5½, 7½ inches.
Length Over All: With 4½-inch barrel, 9¾ inches. .38 caliber with 6-inch barrel, 11¼ inches.
Weight: 45 caliber, with 4½-inch barrel, 39 ounces. .38 caliber, with 6-inch barrel, 43 ounces.
Sights: Fixed type, stippled.
Trigger and Hammer Spur: Checked.
Stocks: Checked Walnut. Either Round or Square. Specify type desired. Lanyard Loop can be furnished for .38 and .357 caliber models on request, at no extra cost. Standard in other calibers.
Finish: Blued or nickel. Top of frame matted to prevent light reflection.

This is the heaviest service revolver made and has been adopted by many large police departments who require a service arm chambered for heavy caliber ammunition. Chambered for a wide variety of cartridges. Either square or round type butt can be furnished for this model on request, at no extra cost. Perfectly balanced, and extremely rugged. This is the standard arm of the Royal Canadian Mounted Police. A favorite for big game hunting. Has Colt Positive Safety Lock.

SINGLE ACTION ARMY REVOLVER

This is the Colt that played so famous a part in the winning of the West and is still extremely popular in many sections of the country. Its dependability and ruggedness have earned the confidence of shooters for over sixty years. It is popularly known as the "Colt Frontier Model," or Colt Six Shooter. The shape and size of the grip adapt this model to the largest and brawniest hands. Single action, with rod ejection.

CALIBERS: .32-20 (.32 Winchester)
.357 Magnum
.38 Special
.38-40 (.38 Winchester)
.44 Special
.44-40 (.44 Winchester)
.45 Colt

"Frontier" Six Shooter Model

Price $37.75

Ammunition: .32-20 (.32 Winchester).
.38 Short Colt; .38 Long Colt; .38 Colt Special; .38 S. & W. Special (full and mid-range loads); .38 Colt Special High Speed; .38 S. & W. Special High Speed and .38-44 S. & W. Special cartridges in .38 caliber model.
.357 Magnum
.38-40 (.38 Winchester).
.44 Special. .44-40 (.44 Winchester).
.45 Colt.

SPECIFICATIONS

Lengths of Barrel: 4¾, 5½, 7½ inches.
Length Over All: With 4¾ inch barrel, 10¼ inches.
Weight: .45 Caliber, with 4¾ inch barrel, 36 ounces.
Sights: Fixed type.
Hammer Spur: Checked.
Stocks: Checked black rubber.
Finish: Blued, with case hardened frame, or Nickel.

A NEW GUN CARRIES A FACTORY GUARANTEE

AMERICA'S GREAT GUN HOUSE

COLT TARGET REVOLVERS

Only the most carefully designed and perfectly manufactured target arm can hold its own on the modern target ranges of America—and it must be designed to meet the rigid requirements for accuracy demanded by today's highly skilled target shooters.

Colt target revolvers have been designed by experts and are flawlessly manufactured by skilled workmen, who thoroughly understand the needs and desires of the modern shooter. Their graceful lines, perfect balance, comfortable grip and super accuracy have earned the confidence of target shooters everywhere. Their match winning ability is being proven on target ranges constantly in every part of the country.

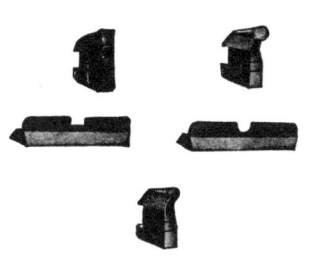

The standard sight equipment of Colt Target Arms—New Service Target, Shooting Master, Officer's Model Target and Police Positive Target Revolvers, "Camp Perry" Model Cal. .22 single shot Target Pistol and "Woodsman" and "ACE" .22 caliber Automatic Pistols are the square or "Patridge" front and square cut rear as shown in the accompanying illustrations. Regulation Bead sights will be supplied on any of these models (except "ACE") when so specified, at no extra cost. Ivory Bead or Gold Bead front sights may be had at an extra cost of $1.00. Unless otherwise specified, the square or "Patridge" sights will be fitted to all Target Arms ordered.

OFFICERS' MODEL TARGET

The Colt Officers' Model Target Revolver is recognized as America's premier target arm—combining perfect balance, smooth, fast action and full, comfortable grip—making possible higher and more consistent scores, for beginners and experts alike. It is the arm chosen by leading target shooters everywhere—the target revolver that makes champions!

SPECIFICATIONS: .32 Police Positive and .38 Special Model

Ammunition—.32 Caliber Model: .32 Police Positive (New Police); .32 S. & W. Short; .32 S. & W. Long (Regular and Sharp Shoulder). .38 Caliber Model: .38 Short Colt; .38 Long Colt; .38 Colt Special; .38 S. & W. Special (full and mid-range loads); .38 Colt Special High Speed; .38 S. & W. Special High Speed; .38-44 S. & W. Special cartridges.
Lengths of Barrel: Caliber .38, 4, 4½, 5, 6, 7½ inches. Heavy barrel, 6 inch length only. Caliber .32, heavy barrel, 6 inch only.
Length Over All: With 6 inch barrel, 11¼ inches.
Weight: Caliber .38, with 6 inch Standard barrel, 34 ounces; with 6 inch heavy barrel, 36 ounces. .32 caliber, 6 inch heavy barrel, 37 ounces.
Sights: Adjustable, Bead or Patridge. Stippled.
Back Strap: Checked.
Stocks: Checked Walnut.
Trigger and Hammer Spur: Checked.
Finish: Blued. Top and back of frame stippled to prevent light reflection.

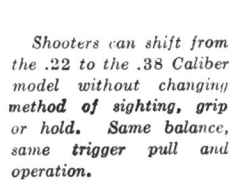

Shooters can shift from the .22 to the .38 Caliber model without changing method of sighting, grip or hold. Same balance, same trigger pull and operation.

CALIBERS: .22 Long Rifle; .32 Police Positive (New Police) .38 Special

This is the model that target shooters depend on for serious target shooting. It is built on a .41 caliber frame with its medium weight perfectly distributed. Equipped with adjustable Bead or Patridge target sights, both stippled to prevent light reflection. Flat type top of frame, stippled. Back strap is checked to provide firm grip and stocks are checked walnut. Trigger and hammer spur are checked and non-slipping. Furnished with five lengths of barrel and in two calibers. The .22 Caliber model is furnished with 6 inch barrel only, and has the new Colt Embedded Head Cylinder, making this model safe for use with high speed or regular ammunition.

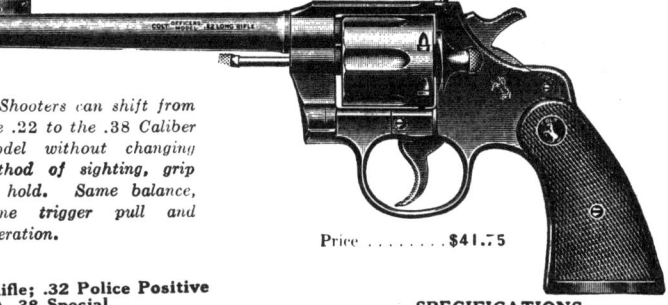

Price $41.75

SPECIFICATIONS: .22 Caliber Model

Ammunition: .22 Long Rifle cartridges. Regular or High Speed.
Length of Barrel: 6 inches only.
Length Over All: 11¼ inches.
Weight: 38 ounces.
Sights: Adjustable, Bead or Patridge. Stippled.
Cylinder: Embedded Head Type.
Stocks: Checked Walnut.
Back Strap: Checked.
Trigger: Checked.
Hammer Spur: Checked.
Finish: Blued. Top of frame stippled to prevent light reflection.

Price $41.75

SPECIFICATIONS

Shown above.

OFFICERS' MODEL TARGET
WITH HEAVY BARREL

CALIBER: .38 Special

An important change was made some time ago in the Colt Officers' Model by furnishing this world famous target revolver with a heavy barrel—similar in design and weight to the barrel used in the Shooting Master Revolver. This heavy barrel adds two ounces to the weight of the gun, steadying it for rapid fire shooting and balancing the arm perfectly. Shooters have already recorded a number of World's Records with the new Officers' Model. Both standard and heavy barrel models are now available at the same price.

POLICE POSITIVE TARGET REVOLVER

CALIBERS:
.22 Long Rifle
.32 Police Positive (New Police)

The Police Positive Target Model is lighter in weight than the Officers' Model, being built on a .38 Caliber frame. Its grip is smaller and is ideal for those with small hands as well as for ladies. This model has all target refinements, including hand finished action, adjustable target sights, stippled frame top and deeply checked trigger. Can be furnished with either Bead or Patridge sights. The action of this model is smooth and fast and the trigger pull crisp and clean. Furnished with Colt Embedded Head Cylinder, in .22 Long Rifle Model, for use with high speed or regular ammunition.

Ammunition—.22 Caliber Model: .22 long Rifle cartridges. Regular or High Speed.
.32 Caliber Model: .32 Colt Police Positive (New Police); .32 S. & W. Short; .32 S. & W. Long (Regular and Sharp Shoulder).
Sights: Adjustable, Bead or Patridge Stippled.
Length of Barrel: 6 inches only.
Length Over All: 10½ inches.
Weight: .22 Caliber, 26 oz.; 32 Caliber, 23 oz.
Action: Hand finished.
Sights: Adjustable, Bead or Patridge. Stippled.
Back Strap: Checked.
Stocks: Checked Walnut.
Cylinder: Embedded Head Type. (.22 L.R. model.)
Trigger and Hammer Spur: Checked.
Finish: Blued. Top of frame stippled to prevent light reflection.

Price
$36.25

COLT TARGET REVOLVERS

CALIBER: .22 Long Rifle
         8 Inch Barrel
         Short Hammer Fall

CAMP PERRY MODEL

Price $41.75

The new Colt Camp Perry Model is the most accurate arm of its type ever perfected and incorporates features that were designed with the aid of expert shooters throughout the country. It is furnished with a new type Kelly front sight blade that gives maximum definition and stands out clearly against the target. The hammer fall has been shortened and the action thereby speeded up approximately 50%. A new type trigger, designed after exhaustive experiments is exceptionally comfortable. When the arm is cocked the trigger is in the same position as on the Officers' Model, thus allowing interchangeability of these two models without changing style of grip. The entire back and top of frame are stippled to prevent light reflection and the sights have also been sand blasted. Furnished with super-precisioned barrel, eight inches in length, including chamber. The new Camp Perry Model is perfectly balanced and is furnished with an action that is exceptionally smooth and fast.

SPECIFICATIONS

Ammunition: .22 Long Rifle cartridges, Regular or High Speed.
Length of Barrel: 8 inches, including chamber.
Length Over All: 12 inches.
Weight: 34 ounces.
Back Strap: Checked.
Special Trigger: Checked.
Hammer Spur: Checked.
Sights: Adjustable, Bead or Patridge.
Chamber: Embedded Head Type.
Stocks: Checked Walnut.
Finish: Blued. Top and back of frame stippled to prevent light reflection.

NEW SERVICE TARGET REVOLVER

CALIBERS: .44 Special
         .45 Colt
         .45 Automatic

Showing deep type checking on back strap of New Service Target and Shooting Master.

The New Service Target Revolver is designed for shooters with large hands who desire a real "he-man's" target revolver. This model is also a favorite for big game hunting. Furnished with smooth, hand-finished action and a barrel that is unusually accurate. Adjustable target sights, either Bead or Patridge. Either square type butt as illustrated or round type butt as on Shooting Master. Built on the .45 Caliber frame and perfectly balanced with either 6 inch or 7½ inch barrel.

Price $52.75

SPECIFICATIONS

Ammunition: .44 Special; .45 Colt, .45 Automatic.
Lengths of Barrel: 6 or 7½ inches.
Length Over All: With 7½ inch barrel, 12¾ inches.
Weight: .45 caliber, 42 ounces.
Sights: Adjustable, Bead or Patridge. Stippled.
Trigger and Hammer Spur: Checked.
Straps: Both front and back straps deeply checked.
Stocks: Checked Walnut.
Finish: Blued. Top of frame stippled to prevent light reflection.

SHOOTING MASTER - - De Luxe Revolver

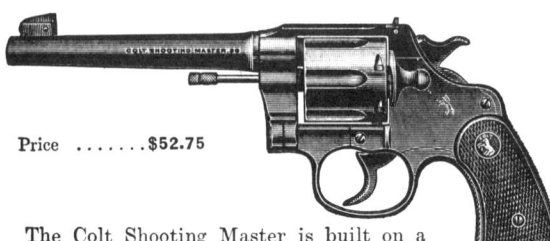

Price $52.75

The Colt Shooting Master is built on a .45 Caliber frame and can be furnished with either the round or square type grip. Its super-precisioned barrel is slightly tapered and perfectly balances the arm for target shooting. This model is a de luxe revolver, having every target refinement known. Equipped with full face Kelly type front sight and adjustable rear sight, both sand blasted. The action of the Shooting Master is velvet smooth and the trigger pull is clean and fast. Stocks are of selected walnut, carefully checked. Both front and back straps are deeply checked.

CALIBERS: .38 Special
         .357 Magnum
         .44 Special
         .45 Colt
         .45 Automatic

SPECIFICATIONS

Ammunition: .38 Short Colt; .38 Long Colt; .38 Colt Special; .38 S. & W. Special (full and mid-range loads); .38 Colt Special High Speed; .38 S. & W. Special High Speed and .38-44 S. & W. Special cartridges in .38 caliber model.
.357 Magnum.
.44 Special.
.45 Colt; .45 Automatic.
Length of Barrel: 6-inch only.
Length Over All: 11¼ inches.
Weight: .38 caliber, 44 ounces.
Sights: Adjustable, Bead or Patridge. Stippled.
Trigger and Hammer Spur: Checked.
Straps: Front and back straps deeply checked.
Stocks: Selected checked Walnut.
Finish: Blued. Top and back of frame stippled to prevent light reflection.

The Shooting Master stippled top and back of frame prevents light reflection.

ENGRAVED COLT REVOLVERS AND PISTOLS

Illustrations below present 3 styles of engraving which can be had at an extra additional cost in 3 grades A, B, and C. In addition Colt guns can also be furnished with Pearl or Ivory grips plain or carved as illustrated and listed. A Colt finished in any of these 3 designs will always be a highly valued arm to the owner. We recommend them for match prizes or for presentation purposes. Such guns must be ordered specially as it will take several weeks to finish them.

Grade C $45.00

Grade B $25.00

Grade A $15.00

Engraving may be had in any one of the 3 grades illustrated in the models shown above. The grade refers only to the amount of engraving desired, "A" representing the minimum, "B" medium grade and "C" the most ornamental. The quality of the work is the same in all cases and performed by the same experts.

Also we can furnish Colt Arms with any special design desired, with full gold or silver plating or inlaid State or National seals, etc. The work is performed by highly skilled craftsmen only, who have had years of experience in this painstaking and beautiful designing. Estimates are furnished upon request.

COLT FANCY PEARL AND IVORY GRIPS

All genuine Colt Pearl or Ivory stocks are identified by the rampant Colt medallion. Whether for presentation purposes, as special match prizes or the favorite Arm of a shooter, Colts may be had in almost any special finish or decoration desired. We have always taken special pride and given the greatest attention to such ornamented Arms. A Colt of any model (except .22 Automatic Pistol) may be fitted with select stocks in choice Pearl or Ivory (either carved or plain). All genuine Colt Pearl or Ivory stocks are identified by the rampant Colt Medallion. Special price list of the Fancy Stocks follow.

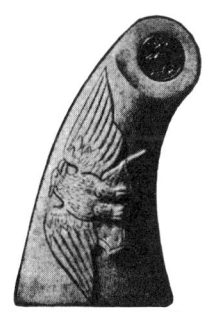
Carved Ivory Eagle

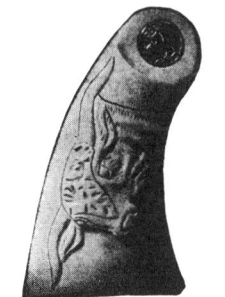
Carved Ivory Steer's Head

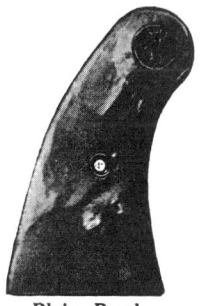
Plain Pearl

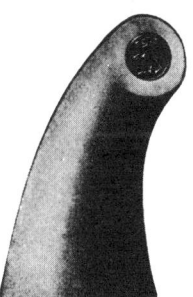
Plain Ivory

	PEARL		IVORY	
	Plain	Carved	Plain	Carved
*New Service, New Service Target, Shooting Master	$18.75	$22.50	$10.50	$19.50
Officers' model target, Official Police	11.50	15.25	9.00	17.75
Police Positive Special, *Detective Special, Police Positive, *Bankers Special, Police Positive Target	8.00	11.75	8.75	17.50
Pocket Positive	6.25	10.00	8.75	17.50
Single Action Army	17.25	21.00	12.50	21.25
Single Shot Pistol (Camp Perry)	11.50	15.25	9.00	17.75
.45 Automatic Pistol (Govt. Model), "National Match" (Govt. Model), Super .38 Automatic Pistol and "Super Match" .38	15.00	**	8.50	17.25
.32 and .380 Automatic Pistols	7.50	11.25	8.00	16.75
.25 Automatic Pistol	6.00	9.75	6.25	15.00
"Woodsman" .22 Auto Pistol (Target and Sport Model)	**	**	**	**
"Ace" .22 Automatic Pistol	15.00	**	8.50	17.25

* These models furnished with both round and square type stocks. Specify type required.
**Not furnished.

Prices do not include U. S. Excise Tax. Tax does not apply when stocks are ordered separately, but must be added when stocks are fitted to a new arm.

YOU ARE CORDIALLY INVITED TO VISIT OUR SHOWROOM

HISTORY OF SMITH & WESSON

Daniel Baird Wesson and Horace Smith began manufacture of the famous Volcanic Action repeating pistol in Norwich, Conn., 1854. In 1856 patents were released to Oliver Winchester and others, resulting in the formation of the Winchester Repeating Arms. Co. Manufacture of the first revolver to employ self-contained ammunition began in a Market Street livery stable at Springfield, Mass. with 25 employees. In 1859 the first building in the present plant location was erected.

With the advent of the Civil War, Government orders expanded the business to 600 employees, and hundreds of thousands of arms were produced.

In 1870 Smith & Wesson designed the famous .44 Russian Model for the Russian Imperial Army and delivered huge numbers of them.

In 1875 the .45 Schofield Model was adopted by the United States Cavalry. It is reliably reported that General Custer used this model in his historic "Last Stand", at the Battle of Little Bighorn.

In 1880 the double action type of revolvers were introduced and the .44 caliber became immensely popular with Western peace officers.

In 1887 the Safety Hammerless was brought out. This arm was and is distinguished by its absolute safety from accidental discharge.

The Military & Police swingout cylinder solid frame model followed in 1902, and with refinements, continues to the present time.

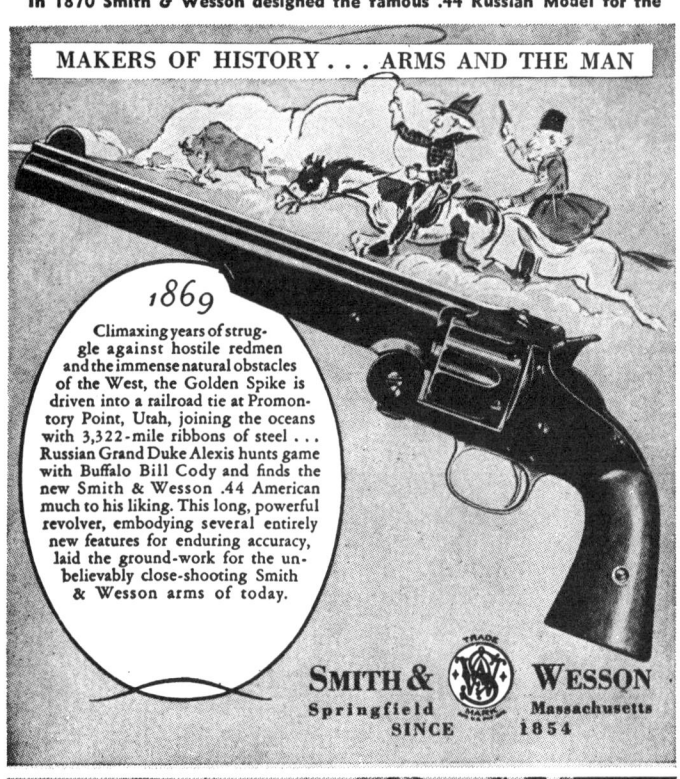

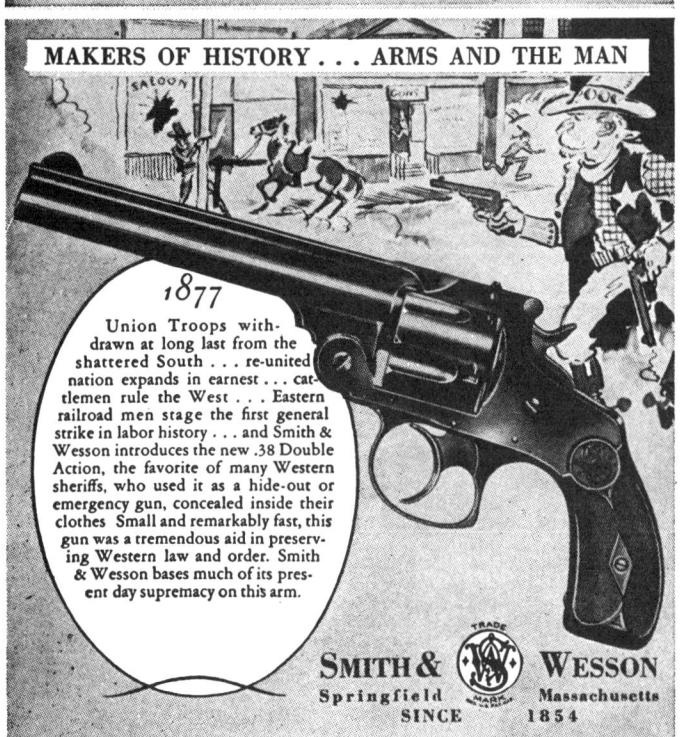

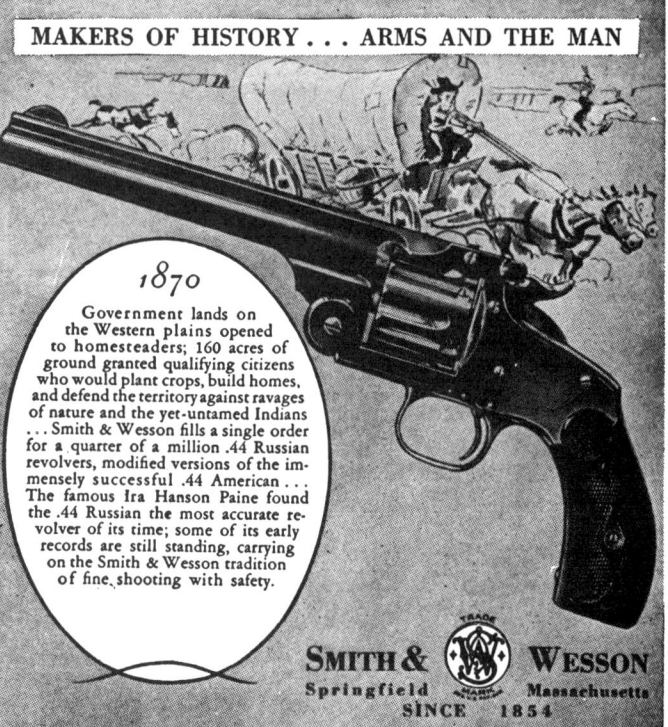

No Guns Nor Parts Thereof Illustrated Above Now Available

SMITH & WESSON

The .32 Hand Ejector

$30.00

Here is the revolver for the man who wants a small, light gun with round handle, which has all the features that were first worked out so successfully in the Military and Police Model.

The .32 Hand Ejector has the same kind of action and sights as the large gun.

Up to 50 yards, the little arm gives very accurate results and is extremely pleasant to shoot. The round handle makes the arm less bulky, so that it may easily be carried without a holster.

SPECIFICATIONS
CALIBER: .32 S & W
NUMBER OF SHOTS: 6
BARREL: 3¼, 4¼ or 6 inches
LENGTH OVER ALL: With 4¼-inch barrel, 8¼ inches
WEIGHT: With 3¼-inch barrel, 18 oz.; 4¼-inch barrel, 18½ oz.; 6-inch barrel, 19¼ oz.
SIGHTS: Fixed, 1/10-inch service type front; square notch rear
STOCKS: Black rubber with S & W Monograms
FINISH: S & W Blue or Nickel
This model is not made with adjustable target sights
AMMUNITION
.32 S & W   .32 S & W Long
.32 Colt New Police

The S & W .38/32
2 inch

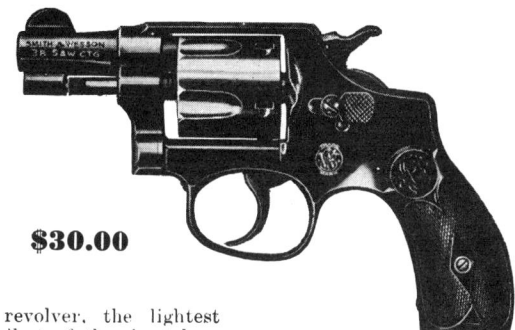

$30.00

This revolver, the lightest and smallest of the short barreled type, is chambered for the .38 S. & W. cartridge which, while having ample power and shock at close range (745 ft. sec., 180 ft. lbs., with 146 grain bullet), is comfortable to shoot and does not produce an excessive recoil. It has all the features of workmanship, material, and finish that distinguish Smith & Wesson arms; while small it has a most comfortable grip and allows ample room between the trigger guard and front strap of the stock.

SPECIFICATIONS
CALIBER: .38 S & W
NUMBER OF SHOTS: 5
BARREL: 2 inches
LENGTH OVER ALL: 6¼ inches
WEIGHT: 17 ounces
SIGHTS: Fixed, 1/10-inch service type front; square notch rear
STOCKS: Checked walnut with S & W monograms (or hard rubber)
FINISH: S & W Blue or Nickel
AMMUNITION
.38 S & W   .38 S & W Super Police

.32 and .38 Safety Hammerless

.32 CAL. $28.00

.38 CAL. $31.00

The .32 and .38 Safety has for years been the favorite arm of the greatest detective agencies and plain clothes men; it is always dependable and cannot jam.

A distinct pause occurs when the hammer has reached full cock position, and before it is released to fire the cartridge.

SPECIFICATIONS

.32 Cal.
LENGTH OF BARREL: 2" or 3"
FINISH: Blue or Nickel
WEIGHT: 14¼ ounces.
LENGTH OVER ALL: 6¾ inches
STOCK: Black rubber with monogram, also Pearl at $4.95 extra
NUMBER OF SHOTS: 5
SIGHTS: Fixed, part of barrel and barrel catch forgings
AMMUNITION
.32 S & W

.38 Cal.
CALIBER: .38 S & W
NUMBER OF SHOTS: 5
BARREL: 2, 3¼ or 4 inches
LENGTH OVER ALL: With 3¼-inch barrel, 7½ inches
WEIGHT: With 3¼-inch barrel, 18¼ oz.; 4-inch barrel, 18¾ oz.
SIGHTS: Fixed, part of barrel and barrel catch forgings
STOCKS: Black rubber with S & W monograms
FINISH: S & W Blue or Nickel
AMMUNITION
.38 S & W   .38 Colt New Police

The .38 Military and Police

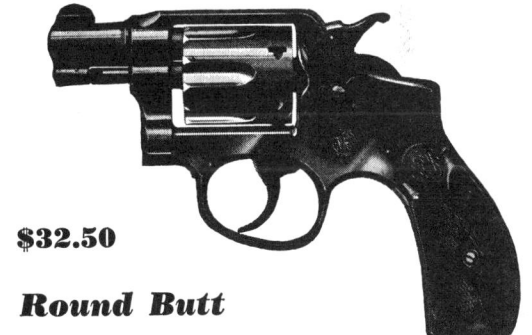

$32.50

Round Butt

Patridge type sights (square section front and flat top square notch rear).

The rebounding hammer is locked in half cock position by two steel blocks which make forward motion of hammer impossible, except when trigger is pulled fully.

Drop forged frame, barrel and working parts. Swing-out, heat treated chrome nickel steel cylinder, locked in perfect alignment in firing position by hardened steel bearings at both front and rear.

SPECIFICATIONS
CALIBER: .38 S & W Special
NUMBER OF SHOTS: 6
BARREL: 2, 4, 5 or 6 inches
LENGTH OVER ALL: With 6-inch barrel, 10⅞ inches
WEIGHT: With 4-inch barrel, 28¾ oz.; 5-inch barrel, 29½ oz.; 6-inch barrel, 30½ oz.
SIGHTS: Fixed, 1/10-inch service type front; square notch rear
STOCKS: Black rubber with S & W monograms
FINISH: S & W Blue or Nickel
This model is not made with adjustable target sights

SMITH & WESSON

The ".357" Magnum*

1512 foot-seconds muzzle velocity! Faster by far than the speed heretofore attained by even the fastest of the small caliber, light weight bullets shot from foreign automatic pistols. *802 foot-pounds muzzle energy!* No hand arm cartridge ever manufactured has developed within hundreds of pounds of this terrific impact. And with this speed and power, *accuracy.* Never, but for those made by other Smith & Wesson revolvers, have there been published machine rest groups made by a large caliber hand arm that can in any way compare with those made with the S. & W. ".357" Magnum* cartridge. While its square-shouldered Sharpe-type lead bullet will shoot through steel plates that are but dented by other cartridges that have heretofore been considered powerful, the S. & W. ".357" Magnum* bullet will upset to .50 caliber in 8 inches of soft paraffin; other bullets pass through practically unchanged in form. Its penetration in boards is but slightly greater than the .38/44 S. & W. Special, but here again the blasted wood and the condition of the recovered bullet tells of the power actually delivered. THE S. & W. ".357" MAGNUM* HAS FAR GREATER SHOCK POWER THAN ANY .38, .44 or .45 EVER TESTED. And with this power it produces machine rest groups at 20 yards (the standard indoor target range) of less than 1 inch! At 100, 200, 500 yards, and even beyond, the inherent power and accuracy continues to exist.

While this revolver is chambered especially for the long S. & W. ".357" Magnum* cartridge, it accuracy and effectiveness with all the various loads for the .38/44 and .38 S. & W. Special is actually amazing, which makes it the greatest all-purpose hand arm ever to be developed. It must be remembered the extremes in muzzle velocity are the greatest ever tested in one revolver; a complete triumph for the Smith & Wesson system of chambering and rifling. A most interesting fact disclosed by the machine rest groups at 50 to 75 yards is that at these distances the size of the groups does not increase in proportion to the range; the groups actually averaging at 50 yards 1.83 inches and at 75, 2.59 inches.

$60.00

SPECIFICATIONS

CALIBER: ".357" (Actual bullet diameter .38 S & W Spec.)
NUMBER OF SHOTS: 6
BARREL: 3½, 5, 6, 6½, 8⅜ inches
LENGTH OVER ALL: With 6-inch barrel, 11¼ inches
WEIGHT: With 8⅜-inch barrel 47 oz.; 6½-inch barrel, 44½ oz.; 6-inch barrel, 44 oz.; 5-inch barrel, 42½ oz.; 3½-inch barrel, 41 oz.
CYLINDER: Heat-treated chrome-nickel steel. Recessed head space and patented burnished chamber walls

STOCKS: Choice of S & W Magna or square stocks
FINISH: S & W Blue or Nickel
FRAME: ".357" Magnum, with finely checked top strap matching barrel rib. Front and rear straps, S & W grooving
HAMMER: Full surface of thumb piece checked to prevent slipping in rapid fire. Concentric relief cuts on sides. Hammer fall weighed and timed for uniform ignition and least disturbance of arm

SIGHTS: Choice of any standard target sights
TRIGGER: S & W grooving. Glass-hard point engaging hammer notch
TRIGGER PULL: Single action, **3 to 4 lbs.** Double action, 10 lbs.

AMMUNITION
S & W .357 Magnum
.38/44 S & W Special
.38 S & W Special Hi-Velocity
.38 S & W Special
.38 S & W Special Super Police
.38 S & W Special Mid Range

The .38/44 Outdoorsman
With Reinforced Frame

Due to the weight and balance of the .38/44 OUTDOORSMAN'S Revolver, it will be found that the high velocity obtained with this new ammunition will be accompanied with practically as little recoil as that of the .38 S. & W. Special Cartridge when shot in the revolvers for which it is designed, and is, in fact, less noticeable than the standard 44's or 45's.

A most convenient feature of these two cartridges is that at twenty yards no readjustment of sights is required when changing from one to the other. At longer ranges, however, it will be found that decidedly less elevation is needed when using the .38/44 S. & W. Special due to its tremendous velocity.

SPECIFICATIONS
CALIBER: .38 S & W Special
NUMBER OF SHOTS: 6
BARREL: 6½ inches only
LENGTH OVER ALL: 11¾ inches
WEIGHT: 41¾ ounces
SIGHTS: 1/10 or 1/8-inch Patridge front; square notch rear adjustable for windage and elevation
STOCKS: Magna checked walnut with S & W monograms (or regular S & W checked walnut) Grooved tangs and trigger
FINISH: S & W Blue only

AMMUNITION
.38 S & W Special Mid Range
.38 S & W Special
.38 S & W Special Super Police
.38/44 S & W Special or Hi-Speed

$45.00

SMITH & WESSON

The .38 Military and Police Target

Continued experiment may develop a finer Smith & Wesson, but except in minor details this arm is the same as when the most expert revolver shots first called it "the finest revolver ever built."

Target arms are used for slow fire with a prolonged trigger squeeze, and best results are obtained when a loose but non-slipping grip is maintained.

For these reasons a special type of trigger pull is desirable—not by any means simply a very light pull, but one having the peculiar quality termed "short and crisp" by shooters. This requires not only a special type of notch and trigger point, but a different adjustment of the working parts of the action as well.

SPECIFICATIONS
CALIBER: .38 S & W Special
NUMBER OF SHOTS: 6
BARREL: 6 inches only
LENGTH OVER ALL: 11⅛ inches
WEIGHT: 32¼ ounces
SIGHTS: 1/10 or ⅛-inch Patridge front; square notch rear adjustable for windage and elevation. Other types of target sights available
STOCKS: Checked walnut with S & W monograms (or Magna stocks at no extra charge) Grooved tangs and trigger
FINISH: S & W Blue only

AMMUNITION
.38 S & W Special .38 Short Colt
.38 Special Super Police .38 Colt Special
.38 S & W Special Mid Range

$38.00

The K-32 Target

Model K-32 Target is a new addition to the famous line of S & W Target revolvers. It follows in every respect the same specifications as the well known model K-22 Masterpiece and also Military and Police K model cal. .38 Special. It has less recoil than the cal. .38 and is allowed in all Police Matches. Especially recommended for rapid fire shooting. If you want to be in the front line you cannot afford to be without one of these "Score-Makers."

SPECIFICATIONS
CALIBER: .32 S & W
NUMBER OF SHOTS: 6
BARREL: 6 inches only
WEIGHT: 34 ounces
SIGHTS: 1/10 or ⅛-inch Patridge front; square notch rear adjustable for both windage and elevation
STOCKS: Checked walnut with S & W monograms (or Magna stocks at no extra charge) Grooved tangs and trigger
FINISH: S & W Blue only

AMMUNITION
.32 S & W Long .32 S & W Short
.32 Colt New Police
.32 Mid Range Sharp Shoulder

$38.00

The .38/44 Heavy Duty

Produced specifically to meet the requirements of severest usage in Police and other public safety work, represents the highest point of accuracy, efficiency, and ability to withstand hard usage.

Its weight of 40 ounces, due to the .44 frame and re-enforced barrel, makes for ease of shooting, either with the .38 S & W Special or the .38 S & W Special Super Police Cartridge; its accurate Smith & Wesson quality of workmanship and finish guarantees its smooth and long lasting action; while its design and finish combine to make it one of the most handsome guns.

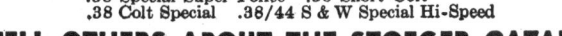

SPECIFICATIONS
CALIBER: .38 S & W Special
NUMBER OF SHOTS: 6
BARREL: 4 and 5 inches
LENGTH OVER ALL: With 5-inch barrel, 10⅜ inches
WEIGHT: With 5-inch barrel, 40 ounces
SIGHTS: Fixed, 1/10-inch service type front; square notch rear
STOCKS: Magna checked walnut with S & W monograms (or regular S & W checked walnut)
FINISH: S & W Blue or Nickel

AMMUNITION
.38 S & W Special Mid Range .38 S & W Special
.38 Special Super Police .38 Short Colt
.38 Colt Special .38/44 S & W Special Hi-Speed

$37.50

SMITH & WESSON

The 1917 Army

The 1917 Model was the Smith & Wesson chosen by the Government for use by American troops and in a Government test it gave greater velocity, greater penetration and greater accuracy than any other gun tested. So satisfactory were the results given by this gun that the demand has continued for it, so that it is still made to the same specifications as those accepted by the Government.

The 1917 Model is not a long range target arm—the cartridge is not designed for such shooting—it is a very powerful, fast handling gun for practical shooting from 25 to 100 yards.

Without doubt the 1917 Model is the fastest loading, safest, most powerful and accurate arm made for the Service Cartridge—it is ideal for men needing maximum shocking power at ordinary range.

SPECIFICATIONS

CALIBER: .45
NUMBER OF SHOTS: 6
BARREL: 5½ inches
LENGTH OVER ALL: 10¾ inches
WEIGHT: 36¼ ounces
SIGHTS: 1/10-inch service type front; square notch rear
STOCKS: Magna checked walnut with S & W monograms (or regular S & W checked walnut) Swivel in bottom of butt
FINISH: S & W Blue only

$37.50

The 1926 Model .44 Target

Whether you use it in the field or at regulation paper targets—there's a pleasure in placing a big bullet accurately that you never get in shooting a small calibre gun.

Of the big guns the .44 Special is, in our opinion, the finest of them all—its big 246 grain bullet develops an energy of 322 ft. pounds and it is surprisingly accurate up to a full 300 yards. For target shooting the sharp shoulder bullet is ideal and cuts a clean hole that is easily seen at 25 yards.

The S & W 1926 Model .44 Calibre Target is the big bore shooter's pet—its action is wonderfully smooth—its sights are strong and easily adjusted and the grip gives one a feeling of confidence.

SPECIFICATIONS

CALIBER: .44 S & W Special
NUMBER OF SHOTS: 6
BARREL: 5 and 6½ inches
LENGTH OVER ALL: With 6½-inch barrel, 11¾ inches
WEIGHT: With 6½-inch barrel, 38 ounces
SIGHTS: Fixed, 1/10-inch service type front; square notch rear
STOCKS: Magna checked walnut with S & W monograms (or regular S & W checked walnut)
FINISH: With 5-inch barrel, S & W Blue only; 6½-inch barrel, S & W Blue or Nickel
AMMUNITION
.44 S & W Special   .44 S & W Russian
Also available chambered for .455 Colt and .455 Eley, for the British and Canadian Service

$45.00

The 1926 Model .44
With Reinforced Frame

The Smith & Wesson Model 1926 Cal. .44 Revolver represents one of the most popular guns among sheriffs and prison guards for heavy duty. The .44 cartridge adapts itself easily to hand loading and for this reason has always proven a very popular number. The gun is built on a heavy reinforced frame to avoid possible bending. The Magna Grip allows a perfect hold.

The Military Model chambered for the .44 Special is in our opinion the finest large calibre revolver, however, its power is practically the same as that of the .45, and its accuracy and ranging power very much greater.

The action of the Military Model is identical with that of the Military and Police except for size and needs no detailed description.

SPECIFICATIONS

CALIBER: .44 S & W Special
NUMBER OF SHOTS: 6
BARREL: 4, 5, 6½ inches
LENGTH OVER ALL: With 5-inch barrel, 10⅜ inches
WEIGHT: With 5-inch barrel, 38¾ ounces
SIGHTS: 1/10-inch service type front; square notch rear
STOCKS: Magna checked selected walnut with S & W monograms (or regular S & W checked selected walnut on request)
FINISH: S & W Blue or Nickel
AMMUNITION
.44 S & W Special   .44 S & W Russian

Fixed Sights
$37.50

STOEGEROL KEEPS YOUR GUN IN ORDER

AMERICA'S GREAT GUN HOUSE 115

SMITH & WESSON

The K-22 Masterpiece

This .22 caliber, heavy frame revolver makes its bow to the hand gun fraternity as a worthy successor to the world famous S & W K-22 Target revolver. A replica of that favorite the .38 M & P Target Revolver, the S & W Masterpiece embodies all the time-proved, sure-shooting features of the K-22 plus unique improvements that make for greater accuracy, speed and ease of handling.

SPECIFICATIONS
CALIBER: .22
NUMBER OF SHOTS: 6
BARREL: 6 inches only
LENGTH OVERALL: 11⅛ inches
WEIGHT: 35 ounces
SIGHTS: 1/10 or 1/8 inch Patridge front; S & W Micrometer rear (patents pending) adjustable for windage and elevation. Other types of target sights available.
STOCKS: Checked walnut with S & W monograms (or Magna stocks at no extra charge) Grooved tangs and trigger
FINISH: S & W Blue only
FRAME: .38 M & P target

$40.00

The .22/32 Target

The .22/32 is a man's gun, the stock fills the hand, and permits the loose yet firm grip so necessary for good shooting, the 6 inch barrel and full size Patridge sights make sighting easy, while the weight makes the gun hang steadily.

For the fancy shot, sportsman or target marksman, the .22/32 is without an equal. Its accuracy is proven by the fact that the "Any Revolver" Match of the United States Revolver Association has been won with it several times as well as making the record high score.

SPECIFICATIONS
CALIBER: .22
NUMBER OF SHOTS: 6
BARREL: 6 inches
LENGTH OVER ALL: 10½ inches
WEIGHT: 23 ounces
SIGHTS: 1/10 or 1/8-inch Patridge front; square notch rear adjustable for windage and elevation
STOCKS: Special Target model, checked walnut with S & W monograms
FINISH: S & W Blue only
AMMUNITION: Any .22 caliber R. F. cartridge

$35.00

The .22/32 Kit Gun

The Kit Gun is designed for the man who loves the woods and streams. While compact for easy carrying in the pocket or kit bag, the barrel is long enough to give ample sight base for accurate shooting and to develop effective speed with the modern cartridges.

The adjustable target sights permit the use of different cartridges without the necessity of holding off the mark to compensate for varying points of impact.

In the illustration we show the round butt stock, as this is the most compact, and yet allows a comfortable hold with sufficient room between the front of the stock and rear of the trigger guard for the middle finger.

SPECIFICATIONS
CALIBER: .22
NUMBER OF SHOTS: 6
BARREL: 4 inches
LENGTH OVER ALL: With round butt stocks, 8 inches
WEIGHT: 21 ounces
SIGHTS: Adjustable target, rear; 1/10-inch Patridge or U.S.R.A. Pocket Revolver, front
STOCKS: Checked walnut with S & W monograms (round butt, as illustrated, small square butt, or large square butt target)
FINISH: S & W Blue or Nickel
AMMUNITION: Any .22 caliber R. F. cartridge

$35.00

Accessories

WESSON GRIP ADAPTER
for Better Hold

The Adapter is of simple construction: two plates, two screws, and a rubber filler block. The installation takes but a moment and requires no change or alteration of the arm. Fits the .38 M&P, .38/44, .45 caliber Hand Ejector Models; also the K-22, K-23 and the Magnum. Includes longer stock screw to allow for the extra thickness.
Price $2.50

S & W "HUMP BACK" HAMMER
for Rapid Fire Speed

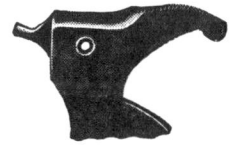

Affords a constant or increasing leverage as the spring tension increases and the power of the thumb lessens. Renders cocking far easier than the conventional hammer. The "Hump Back" Hammer is supplied on the larger models on request at no extra charge. It will be installed on used arms only when sent into us for fitting.
Price, including installation $3.50

A FINE GUN IS A GOOD INVESTMENT

SMITH & WESSON

.38 Military and Police

This arm has established a reputation in all parts of the world for quality, accuracy, and dependability. It is used by the police departments too numerous to mention, and due to its extraordinary accuracy it is also the favorite arm of target experts.

Except for the shape of the handle, it is exactly like the round butt model, uses the same cartridges and has the same smooth action and safety devices.

Made throughout from drop forgings, with chrome nickel steel heat treated cylinder, and ground and polished working parts. It has a fine full grip, beautifully tapered barrel and is finished in heavy nickel or deep blue black.

Square Butt

SPECIFICATIONS
CALIBER: .38 S & W Special
NUMBER OF SHOTS: 6
BARREL: 2, 4, 5 or 6 inches
LENGTH OVER ALL: With 6-inch barrel, 11⅛ inches
WEIGHT: With 6-inch barrel, 31 ounces
SIGHTS: Fixed, 1/10-inch service type front; square notch rear
STOCKS: Checked walnut with S & W monograms (or Magna stocks at no extra charge)
FINISH: S & W Blue or Nickel
AMMUNITION
.38 S & W Special
.38 Short Colt
.38 Special Super Police
.38 Colt Special

$33.00

The .32 Regulation Police

This arm was brought out to meet the demands of one of the greatest police departments for the lightest, absolutely dependable revolver that would shoot the powerful .38 S & W Cartridges accurately. (Does not take the .38 S & W Special Cartridge.)

The practical value of the strength of drop forged parts and a heat treated alloy steel cylinder is shown in this model, as, while having a large surplus strength, it weighs 18 ounces.

Being designed principally for police work, this arm has several features that are of especial interest to anyone needing an arm for personal protection.

SPECIFICATIONS
CALIBER: .38 S & W
NUMBER OF SHOTS: 5
BARREL: 4 inches only
LENGTH OVER ALL: 8¼ inches
WEIGHT: 18 ounces
SIGHTS: Fixed, 1/10-inch service type front; square notch rear
STOCKS: Checked walnut with S & W monograms
FINISH: S & W Blue or Nickel
AMMUNITION:
.38 S & W
.38 S & W Super Police
.38 Colt New Police

$32.00

The .38 Regulation Police

This is a finely proportioned and exceedingly beautiful arm.

Like the Military and Police, this arm is made from drop forgings, has a heat treated alloy steel cylinder held in perfect alignment by front and rear bearings, while gas leakage is reduced to a minimum by close fitting and the elimination of end play of the cylinder by non-wearing hardened steel collars.

The barrel is taper bored to exceedingly close limits, which, with the close chambering, accurate alignment and minimum of space between barrel and cylinder, produces an accuracy which is entirely satisfactory to the most expert.

SPECIFICATIONS
CALIBER: .32 S & W
NUMBER OF SHOTS: 6
BARREL: 3¼, 4¼ or 6 inches
LENGTH OVER ALL: With 4¼-inch barrel, 8½ inches
WEIGHT: With 3¼-inch barrel, 19 oz.; 4¼-inch barrel, 18½ oz.; 6-inch barrel, 19¼ oz.
SIGHTS: Fixed, 1/10-inch service type front; square notch rear
STOCKS: Checked walnut with S & W monograms
FINISH: S & W Blue or Nickel
AMMUNITION:
.32 S & W
.32 S & W Long
.32 Colt New Police

$32.00

SEE STOEGER FOR THE BEST IN GUNS

WALTHER PISTOL PARTS

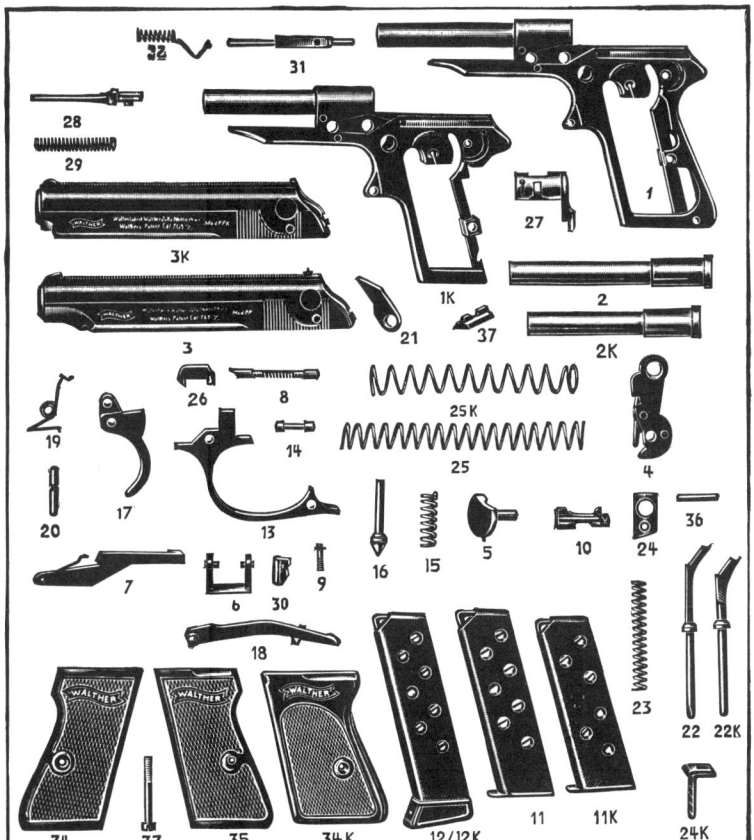

List of spare parts for WALTHER police pistols PP and PPK.

Order No. for the PP Model	Order No. for the PPK Model	Description	Price
1	1 K	Body complete (without barrel)	$12.00
2	2 K	Barrel	7.50
3	3 K	Slide	9.00
4	4	Hammer, complete	2.75
5	5	Hammer axle	.75
6	6	Cocking piece	2.75
7	7	Ejector with spring	3.00
8	8	Extractor pin with spring	2.00
9	9	Locking piece spring with covering disc	.75
10	10	Magazine catch with spring	1.60
11	11 K	Magazine	3.50
12	12 K	Magazine with extension	4.00
13	13	Trigger guard	2.75
14	14	Trigger guard pin	.50
15	15	Trigger guard spring	.50
16	16	Trigger guard spring pin	.50
17	17	Trigger	2.25
18	18	Sear	2.25
19	19	Trigger spring	.85
20	20	Trigger pin	.50
21	21	Relaxing piece	1.00
22	22 K	Hammer bar	2.00
23	23	Hammer bar spring	1.25
24	24 K	Hammer spring base	1.00
25	25 K	Recoil spring	1.50
26	26	Extractor	1.25
27	27	Safety lever	2.75
28	28	Firing pin	2.25
29	29	Firing pin spring	1.00
30	30	Locking piece	1.00
31	31	Signal pin	1.00
32	32	Signal pin spring	.50
33	33	Butt plate screw	.50
34	—	Right butt plate	1.35
35	—	Left butt plate	1.35
—	34 K	Butt plate	2.50
36	—	Hammer spring base pin	.50
37	—	Sight	1.25

Example for ordering: Slide Nr. 3 K for Walther Police Pistol 7.65 calibre Model PPK.

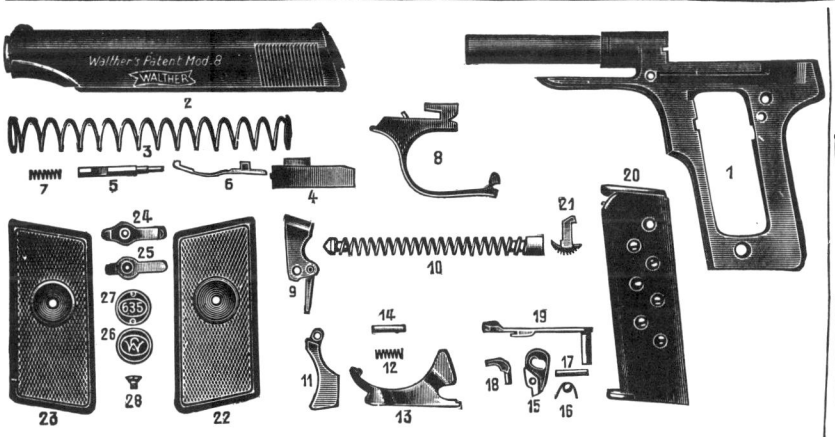

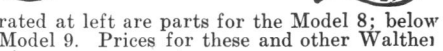

PARTS

Illustrated at left are parts for the Model 8; below for the Model 9. Prices for these and other Walther Models given upon request.

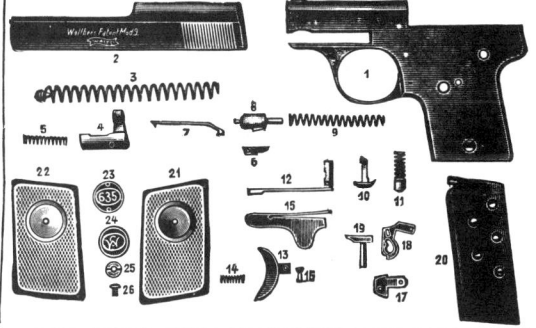

PRINCIPAL PARTS FOR FOREIGN PISTOLS

Listed below are the principal foreign pistols which are not specifically described in this catalog. As there are a number of these pistols in the United States, we supply the principal parts from stock and are in position to secure other parts upon special order.

Magazine	Grips	Firing Pin	Firing Pin Spring	Recoil (Main) Spring
$3.50	$3.50	$2.75	$1.25	$1.50

No.
1 Bayard caliber 6.35, Old Model.
2 Bayard caliber 6.35, Model 1923.
3 Bayard caliber 7.65.
4 Bayard caliber 9 m/m short.
5 Browning caliber 6.35 (Dreyse 6.35).
6 Browning caliber 7.65 and 9 m/m 1912, also D. W. M.
7 Browning caliber 7.65 Old Model (Dreyse 7.65).
8 Browning caliber 9 m/m Police Model 1922.
9 Browning caliber 9 m/m War Model.
10 Dreyse caliber 6.35 (Browning 6.35).
11 Dreyse caliber 7.65 (Browning 7.65 O. M.)
12 Frommer Stop, caliber 7.65.
13 Kommer Model II, caliber 6.35, 7 shot.

No.
14 Kommer Model, 3 caliber. 6.35, 9 shot, also Walther 7-6.35.
15 Lignose Model II and IIa, caliber 6.35.
16 Lignose Model III and IIIa, caliber 6.35.
17 Liliput, caliber 4.35.
18 Mann caliber 6.35.
19 Mann caliber 6.35 and 9 m/m.
20 Ortgies caliber 7.65 and 9 m/m.
21 Ortgies caliber 6.35.
22 Sauer caliber 7.65.
23 Sauer caliber 6.35.
24 Sauer W. T. P. caliber 6.35.
25 Schmeisser model II caliber 6.35.
26 Schmeisser model I caliber 6.35.
27 Simson caliber 6.35.

No.
28 Stenda caliber 7.65; also Menta and Beholla.
29 Steyr caliber 6.35.
30 Stock caliber 6.35.
31 Stock caliber 7.65.
32 Stock-Target Pistol caliber .22.
33 Vesta caliber 6.35.
34 Vesta caliber 7.65.
35 Walther model V cal. 6.35 (Zehna 6.35).
36 Walther model VII cal. 6.35 (Kommer III).
37 Walther model IV caliber 7.65.
38 Walther model VIII caliber 6.35.
39 Walther model IX caliber 6.35.
40 Walther Target Pistol cal. 22.
41 Zehna caliber 6.35 (Walther V.)
42 Pieper caliber 6.35.
43 Pieper caliber 7.65.

TENITE SPECIAL GRIPS

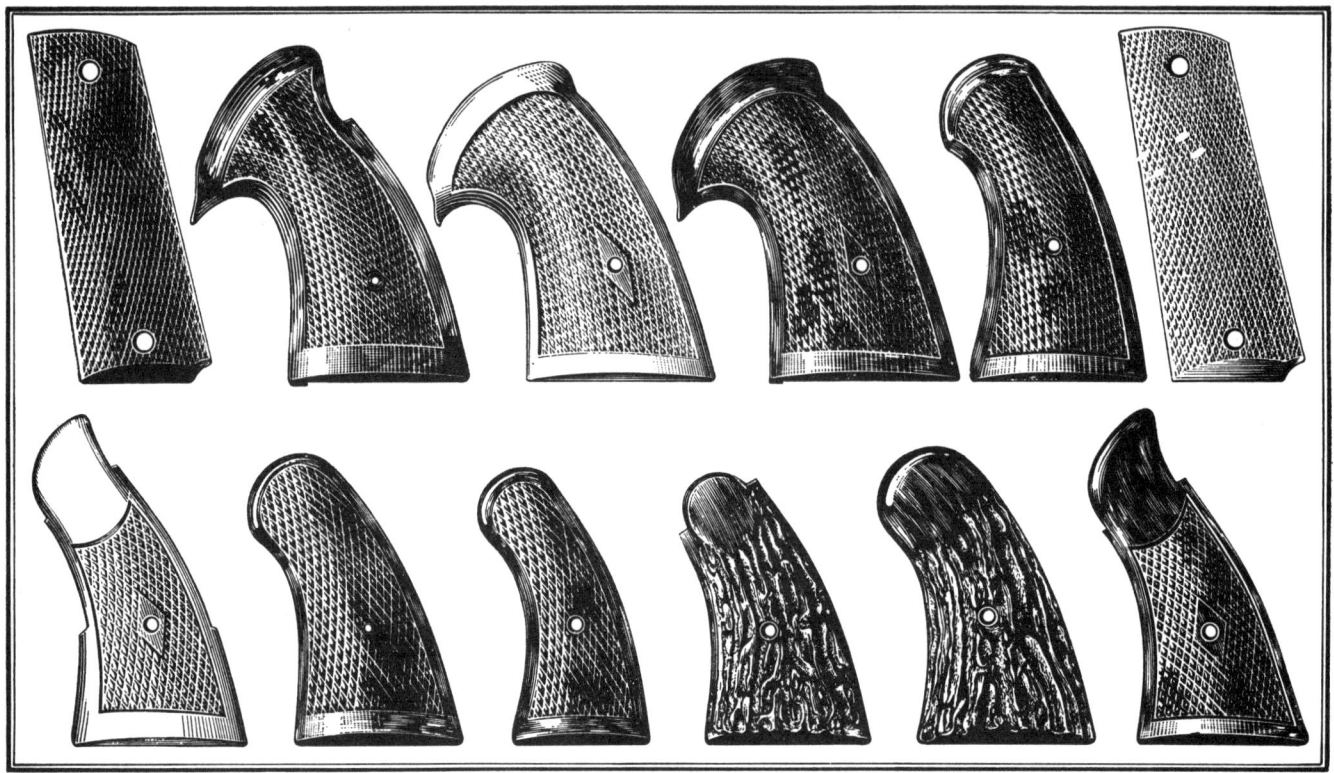

These grips are made from Tenite, a new and tough Plastic. They make the best revolver and pistol grips, they will not break or chip and the checking will not wear off as on wooden grips.

Type S44 and C55 come up high on the frame and have a built in Adapter; they are larger and fill the hand, so revolver will not slide from the recoil and makes it easy to cock. Adapters keep muzzle up and gives better control of the trigger. These handles were originally made to order for some of the best shooters in the country.

SMITH & WESSON

S-0	S&W M&P Stag	$2.00
S-1	S&W 32 also 38/32	1.60
S-2	S&W Reg. Police	2.00
S-3	S&W M&P Rd. Butt	2.00
S-4	S&W M&P Sq. Butt	2.00
S-5	S&W Rd. Butt to Sq.	2.50
S-6	S&W M&P Magna Style	2.20
S-7	S&W Heavy Duty Frame	2.20
S-8	S&W Heavy Duty Magna Style	2.50
S-44	S&W M&P With Built in Adapter	3.50

HI STANDARD

H-1	Hi Standard Model A, D, & C	2.50
H-2	Hi Standard Model B & C	2.00
H-3	Hi Standard With Left or Right Hand Thumb Rest	3.50

ORTGIES

O-1	Ortgies Auto 25 (6.35m/m)	1.80
O-2	Ortgies Auto 32 (7.65m/m)	1.80

COLT

C-0	Colt O. P. Stag	$2.00
C-1	Colt Pocket Positive	1.80
C-2	Colt Police Positive	2.00
C-3	Colt Police Positive Spec.	2.00
C-4	Colt Detective Spec.	2.00
C-5	Colt Official Police or Officers Model	2.00
C-6	Colt Official Police Magna	2.20
C-7	Colt New Service	2.20
C-8	Colt Single Action	2.20
C-9	Colt Bisley	2.50
C-55	Colt Official Police With Built in Adapter	3.50
C-60	Colt Officers Model With Thumb Rest	4.00
C-10	Colt Auto 25 cal.	1.80
C-11	Colt Auto 32 & 380	1.80
C-12	Colt Auto 38, 45 also Ace	2.00
C-13	Colt Auto 22 Woodsman	2.00
C-14	Colt Auto 22 Woodsman With Left or Right Hand Thumb Rest	3.50

LUGER

L-1	Luger 7.65 or 9m/m	3.00

A COMFORTABLE GRIP IMPROVES YOUR SCORE

FINEST QUALITY PEARL, IVORY AND STAG GRIPS

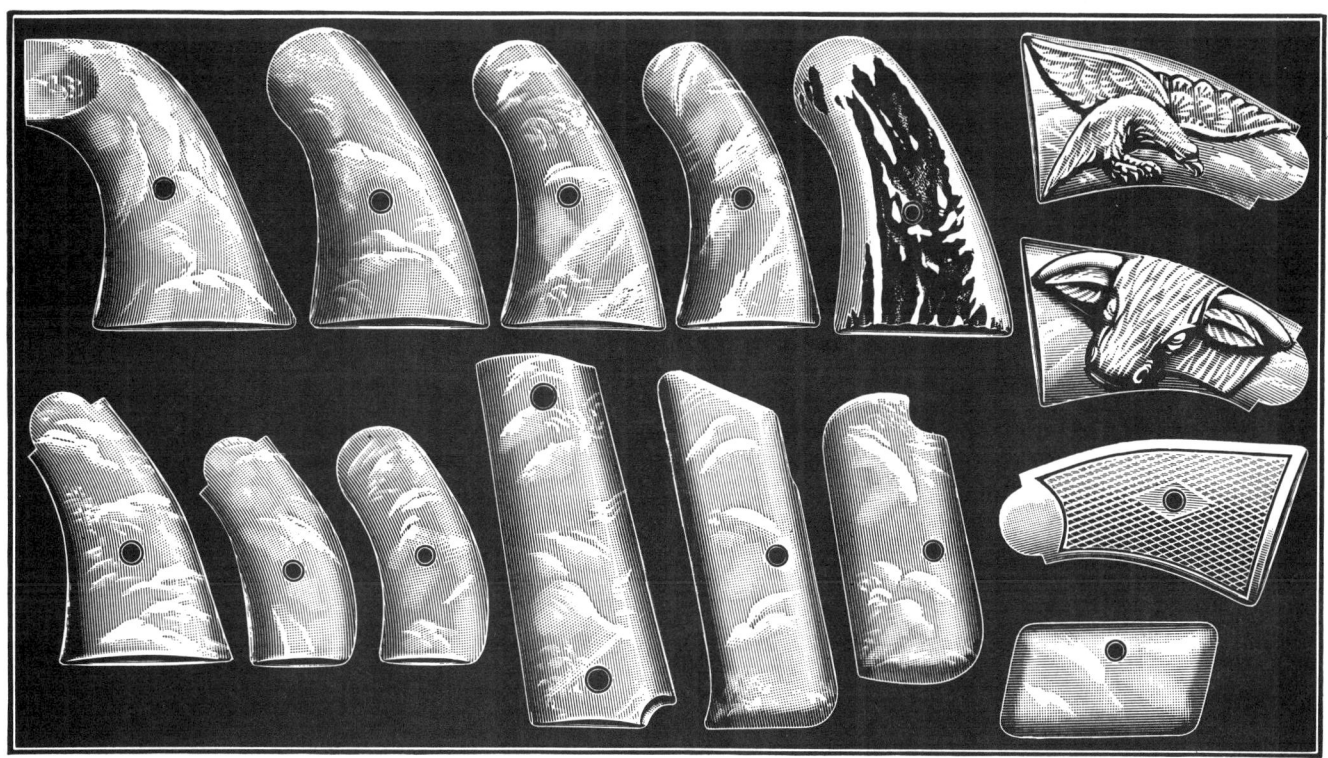

Our grips are superior in quality and workmanship. We only use finest raw material money can buy. We also make grips for antique revolvers and pistols on special order. For special grips, it is always necessary to send in either the entire gun or the frame to insure perfect fitting. All our grips are full bodied and there is no skimping on material or workmanship.

FOR COLT	Pearl	Ivory	Stag	†Arthorn
Single Action Army	$11.00	$9.00	$8.00	$5.00
New Service	10.00	8.00	7.00	4.50
Official Police (formerly Army Special)	6.50	6.30	6.00	3.50
Officer's Model	6.50	6.30	6.00	3.50
Pocket Positive	2.50	2.50	2.25	1.75
Police Positive and Police Positive Special	5.00	5.00	4.50	3.50
Police Positive old Model (Narrow Butt)	4.50	4.50	3.80	3.30
Auto. Military .45 and Super .38	11.00	10.00	7.50	5.00
Pocket Auto. .32 and .380	5.30	5.00	4.50	3.50
Auto. Pocket .25	2.50	2.50	2.20	2.00
Auto. Target .22 Woodsman	10.00	10.00	8.50	6.00
Bisley Model	14.00	14.00	12.00	9.00
FOR SMITH & WESSON				
New Departure .32 or .38 Caliber	1.80	1.80	1.80	1.70
Hand Ejector .32 Caliber Model 1903	1.80	1.80	1.80	1.70
Hand Ejector Model .44 Caliber, Model 1908 and Outdoorsman 38/44	5.50	5.50	5.00	3.50
Military and Police, .38 Caliber (Round Butt) Model 1902	4.00	4.00	3.50	3.00
Military and Police, .38 Caliber (Square Butt) Model 1905 and K22	5.00	5.00	5.00	3.50
Regulation Police	7.50	7.50	7.50	6.50
Target .22/32 Heavy Frame	16.00	16.00	14.00	11.00
Model 1917 .45 Army S. & W.	6.50	6.50	5.50	4.00
Magna	12.00	11.00	7.00	5.00
WE ALSO SUPPLY GRIPS FOR:				
Baby Hammerless	1.50	1.50	1.50	1.00
Remington Double Derringer	2.30	2.30	2.30	2.00
Luger	16.00	15.00	15.00	12.00
Harrington & Richardson* or Iver Johnson*	1.80	1.80	1.80	1.70

* Prices are for grips, which just cover the frame, same as regular grips as on H. & R. Model 6. Target Grips for these models vary from **$7.50** to **$12.50**.

SPECIAL CARVING

Carving of Steer or Eagle Head	$5.00
Monogram in Block Letters filled in black or blue enamel Per Letter	1.00
Full Flying Mexican or American Eagle	9.00

Hand Checkered Pearl or Ivory Grips, extra..............$5.00–$12.50

We also can engrave any design as per your own drawing. Only the finest artistic workmanship. Estimates given on request. We also will make up grips for antique revolvers. Write in and send frame for estimate.

† Arthorn grips are made of composition similar to ivory, but may also be had in imitation tortoise or in colors. Unless otherwise requested, we supply the imitation ivory when Arthorn is ordered.

ORDER BLANK IN MIDDLE AND INDEX IN BACK OF CATALOG

HIGH STANDARD AUTOMATIC PISTOLS

GENERAL SPECIFICATIONS

The High Standard .22 calibre Automatic Pistol is of modern construction and design. It has all the features desired by the target shooter and sportsman. This pistol comes now in 6 different styles giving the shooter a selection never had before. This pistol can be taken down for cleaning very easily without using any tool whatsoever. All models will take low pressure as well as all standard makes of high speed ammunition.

Manufactured by gun mechanics who have had a lifetime of experience in producing firearms. Carefully inspected and tested. Guaranteed to be reliable and accurate.

These new models are, undoubtedly, the last word in modern construction and design of a .22 automatic. Features never before given to the shooters are now available at a remarkably low price.

HAMMER MODELS "H"

There are some shooters who have always handled a revolver that have become used to an outside hammer and who would have changed to an automatic pistol except that all .22 caliber automatic pistols have formerly been of the hammerless type. With this in view we have brought out a line of visible hammer pistols. There is a little shorter hammer fall and a trigger pull that will show less variation with continued shooting. This is brought out by the fact that one of the most prominent shooters in the country states that in five thousand rounds his trigger pull has not changed more than 4 ounces which he considers is remarkable by comparison with some of the other pistols on the market. These new models with the exception of changes made necessary by the outside hammer follows closely the appearance, weight and balance of our popular hammerless models. We believe that the Models H-D and H-E are the last word in fine target pistols.

HAMMERLESS

MODEL B .22 L.R.
MODEL C .22 SHORT
(Model B with 4½" or 6¾" Bbl.)
Model C with 6¾" Bbl. only
MODEL S-B .22 L.R. SHOT
(Smooth Bore)
Price, any one $22.00

HAMMER

MODEL H-B .22 L.R.
Barrel 4½" or 6¾"
Price $22.00

MODELS B, H-B, C, AND S-B

There is not a pistol on the market that can equal the High Standard Model "B" at the same price. The reputation of the manufacturers has been built up on the workmanship and quality of material that goes into this fine pistol plus accuracy excelled by none. An automatic for $22 that will handle both low pressure and high speed ammunition. Buy one, and see for yourself the pleasure and enjoyment you can get with this fine pistol using the inexpensive .22 caliber long rifle rimfire cartridges. Powerful enough for small game and sufficiently accurate for fine target work.

Model C is identical to model B, but for .22 shot only; Model S-B is identical to Model B but has smooth bore and intended for use with .22 L.R. shot cartridges.

SPECIFICATIONS

Calibre .22 Long Rifle, barrel 6¾" or 4½", with fixed Patridge sights, magazine capacity 10 shot. Comes with black hard rubber grips, checkered. Comes with heavy barrel, small bore, deep rifling for extreme accuracy penetration and long wear. Weight: 31 oz.

Model B with 6¾" barrel, cal. .22 L.R., price $22.00
Model B with 4½" barrel, cal. .22 L.R., price 22.00
Model C with 6¾" barrel, cal. .22 short 22.00
Model H-B with 6¾" barrel, cal. .22 L.R., price 22.00
Model H-B with 4½" barrel, cal. .22 L.R., price 22.00
Model S-B with 6¾" barrel, cal. .22 L.R., shot, price 22.00

MODELS A AND H-A

The High Standard Manufacturing Company were the first to bring out the new .22 caliber automatic long handle pistols. Realizing that the grip on the .22 automatic was too short for the average hand we spent a great deal of time and money in developing our new long handle models and at the same time added new features such as the automatic slide lock, adjustable rear sight and walnut grips. The Model "A" is practically the same as the Model "B" with the exception of the features mentioned above. It has the same barrel. The automatic slide lock holds the action open when the last cartridge has been fired from the magazine. The adjustable rear sight is positively locked in position and cannot shoot loose. This pistol is recommended to the shooters who want something a little better than the Model "B" and with additional features.

SPECIFICATIONS

Barrel—Small bore deep rifling for extreme accuracy, penetration, and long wear.
Sights—Patridge front with wide blade and special adjustable rear.
Safety—Positive.
Grips—Walnut, finely checkered.
Finish—Blued.
Takedown—Slide removed without the use of any tools for inspection and cleaning of barrel from the breech end. No loose parts, pins or screws to fall out.
Weight of pistol—Model A 36 oz.

HAMMERLESS

MODEL A .22 L.R.
with adjustable
Rear Sight
Price $28.50

HAMMER

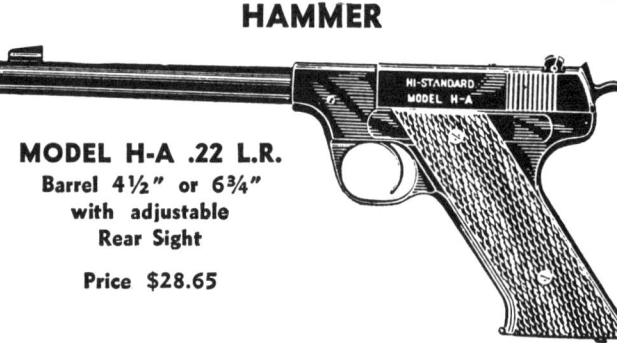

MODEL H-A .22 L.R.
Barrel 4½" or 6¾"
with adjustable
Rear Sight
Price $28.65

STOEGEROL KEEPS YOUR GUN IN CONDITION

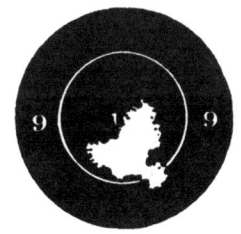

HIGH STANDARD AUTOMATIC PISTOLS

SPECIAL FEATURES OF MODELS A, D & E

New Long Handle

We have felt that the shooter wants more room for the grip on an automatic, and have developed a longer grip that provides more room for the hand. The grips are of walnut, nicely shaped, and finely checked.

NEW AUTOMATIC SLIDE LOCK
A Double Feature

We have provided an automatic lock to lock the action open when the last cartridge has been fired from the magazine. This also operates as a lock on the action when the magazine is empty, and holds the slide open when the pistol is used at the target as a single shot.

HAMMERLESS

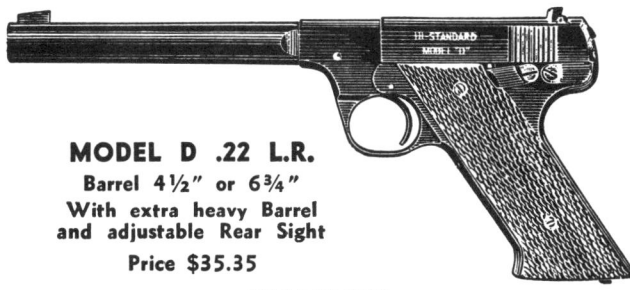

MODEL D .22 L.R.
Barrel 4½" or 6¾"
With extra heavy Barrel
and adjustable Rear Sight
Price $35.35

HAMMER

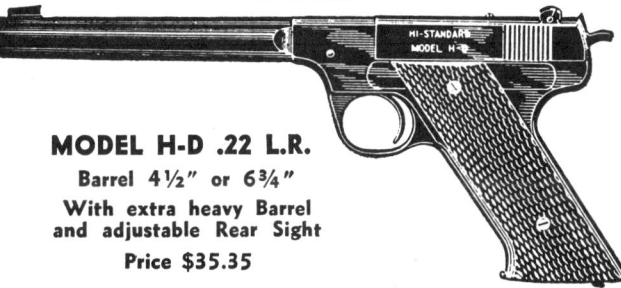

MODEL H-D .22 L.R.
Barrel 4½" or 6¾"
With extra heavy Barrel
and adjustable Rear Sight
Price $35.35

MODELS D AND H-D

The target shooters have long wanted a heavier barrel on a pistol and in designing our new long handle we had particularly in view the fact that we would need additional weight in the handle to balance the additional weight of the barrel. We therefore have gone to the extra expense of getting out new forging dies so that the metal in the handle would come all the way to the bottom, instead of making a long handle by building a hollow shell of wood that could not put the weight where it belonged. The result was most gratifying and we have plenty of weight in the handle to balance the heavier barrel. The Model "D" has a barrel of medium weight, an adjustable rear sight, automatic slide lock, and trigger pull that undoubtedly will satisfy the most exacting requirements. Regular model has straight grip but can be fitted with thumb rest for the target shooter on special order and at an extra cost.

SPECIFICATIONS

Barrel—Heavy barrel weighing 4 ounces more than on the model A.
Sights—Patridge front with wide blade and special adjustable rear sight.
Safety—Positive.
Grips—Walnut, finely checkered.
Finish—Blued.
Takedown—Slide removed without the use of any tools for inspection and cleaning of barrel from the breech end. No loose parts, pins or screws to fall out.
Weight of Pistol—40 oz.

MODELS E AND H-E

With the same qualifications as to smoothness of operation and trigger pull as the Model "D" but with an extra heavy barrel, this Model "E" is built to meet the demand from that class of shooters who want all the weight possible in a pistol. Here again the long metal handle, extending all of the way to the bottom of the grip provides the necessary weight for a perfect balance. The Model "E" as well as the Model "D" is highly recommended by experts and its users number some of the best nationally known shooters. Regularly furnished with thumb rest grip that is said to be one of the best ever designed for average shooters.

SPECIFICATIONS

Barrel—Extra heavy, barrel, slide and frame giving a straight line effect along the entire top of the pistol.
Sights—Patridge front with wide blade and special adjustable rear sight.
Safety—Positive.
Grips—Full walnut grips with thumb rest, finely checkered.
Finish—Blued.
Takedown—The same as model A or D.
Weight of Pistol—42 oz.

HAMMERLESS

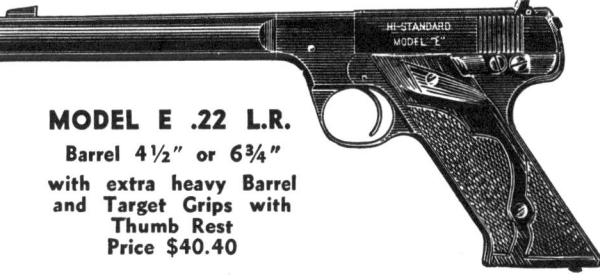

MODEL E .22 L.R.
Barrel 4½" or 6¾"
with extra heavy Barrel
and Target Grips with
Thumb Rest
Price $40.40

HAMMER

MODEL H-E .22 L.R.
Barrel 4½" or 6¾"
with extra heavy Barrel
and Target Grips with
Thumb Rest
Price $40.40

FOR HUNTING AND TARGET SHOOTING

HARRINGTON AND RICHARDSON

H & R .22 "Special" Heavy Frame
No. 944 $17.55

The .22 Special is a heavy frame, 9 shot, fixed sight revolver for which any one of the 11 Sportsman stocks can be supplied. The H & R Safety Cylinder is used, making the arm safe with either high speed or regular ammunition.

Break open type—automatic extractor. Ammunition: .22 Short, Long or Long Rifle.

SPECIFICATIONS
BARREL LENGTH: 6 inches
OVERALL LENGTH: 11 inches
WEIGHT: 23 oz.
FINISH: Blue
SIGHTS: Notched rear and gold front
CYLINDER CAPACITY: 9 shots
AMMUNITION
.22 Short, Long or Long Rifle

H & R 922 SHOT CALIBER Large Frame
No. 922 $11.10

The "922" Model is a medium weight solid frame revolver with a safety cylinder permitting the use of high speed ammunition. The cylinder holds 9 cartridges.

The front sight and lettering on the barrel are in gold. A special stock of checked walnut permits a correct high position of the hand. This is a most satisfactory though low priced revolver.

SPECIFICATIONS
LENGTH OF BARREL: 6 inches
WEIGHT: 21¾ oz.
OVERALL LENGTH: 10½ inch
FINISH: Blue
SIGHTS: Notched rear and gold front
CYLINDER CAPACITY: 9 shots
AMMUNITION
.22 Short, Long or Long Rifle

H & R MEANS QUALITY AND VALUE

HARRINGTON & RICHARDSON REVOLVERS

EUREKA
No. 196
PRICE $30.50

HAMMER
Easy Cocking.
Extra wide cocking spur makes cocking easy.

CYLINDER
Minimum bullet jump.
Cartridge same length as cylinder.

The New EUREKA No. 196 brings us still nearer the aim of producing a Perfect Target Revolver. It embodies improvements on the justly famous H & R Sportsman and is the latest and best thought as to what a Perfect Target Revolver should be.

The New EUREKA No. 196 is equipped with a short cylinder, just long enough to carry the 22 cal. long rifle cartridge thus eliminating any "wandering" of bullet between cylinder and barrel.

The New EUREKA No. 196 has a short and very fast hammer throw.

The New EUREKA No. 196 carries six 22 cal. Long Rifle, Long or Short cartridges and safely handles any standard factory loaded ammunition.

The New EUREKA No. 196 has an entirely new action—very smooth and fast and will give the shooter years of excellent service.

The New EUREKA No. 196 may be had equipped with different size and shaped stocks to perfectly fit the individual shooters hand.

SPECIFICATIONS
Barrel Length—6¼ inch
Overall Length—11 inch
Weight—32 oz.
Finish—Blue
Sights—Patridge, adjustable front and rear
Cylinder Capacity—9 Shots
Ammunition—.22 Short, Long or Long Rifle

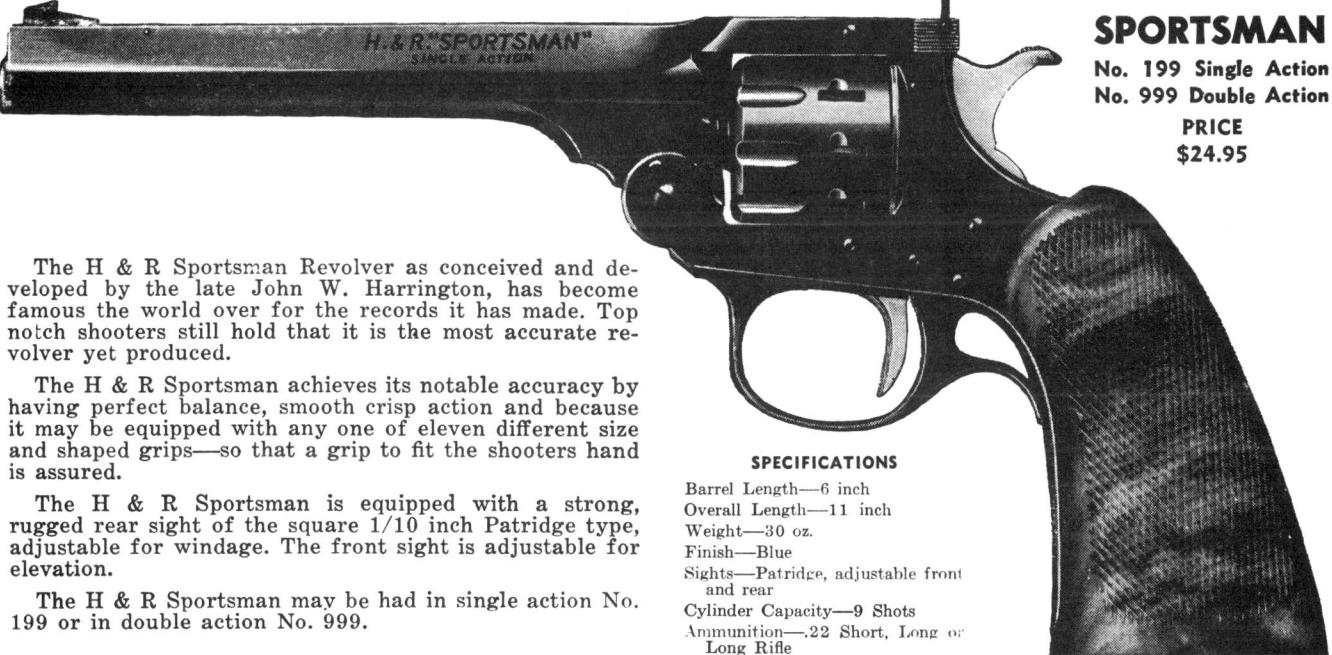

SPORTSMAN
No. 199 Single Action
No. 999 Double Action
PRICE $24.95

The H & R Sportsman Revolver as conceived and developed by the late John W. Harrington, has become famous the world over for the records it has made. Top notch shooters still hold that it is the most accurate revolver yet produced.

The H & R Sportsman achieves its notable accuracy by having perfect balance, smooth crisp action and because it may be equipped with any one of eleven different size and shaped grips—so that a grip to fit the shooters hand is assured.

The H & R Sportsman is equipped with a strong, rugged rear sight of the square 1/10 inch Patridge type, adjustable for windage. The front sight is adjustable for elevation.

The H & R Sportsman may be had in single action No. 199 or in double action No. 999.

SPECIFICATIONS
Barrel Length—6 inch
Overall Length—11 inch
Weight—30 oz.
Finish—Blue
Sights—Patridge, adjustable front and rear
Cylinder Capacity—9 Shots
Ammunition—.22 Short, Long or Long Rifle

No. 1—For small or thin hands.	No. 2—Like No. 1 except thicker and more rounding.	No. 3—Same as No. 2, but with lip at top.	No. 4—Frontier type. No. 4-O—Same shape but thicker.	No. 4TR Thumb Rest.	No. 5—Free Pistol type. No. 5-O—Same shape but thicker.

No. 4, 4-O 5, 5-O may be had with Thumb rest Feature.

Choice of any of above stocks on Eureka, Sportsman, .22 "Special," and U. S. R. A. Single shot. Price of any stock, when purchased separately $2.20

HARRINGTON & RICHARDSON REVOLVERS

H. & R. "TRAPPER MODEL"

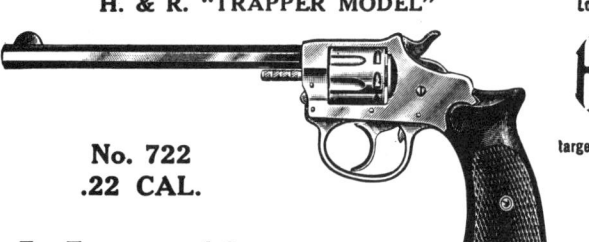

Look for the  target trade-mark

No. 722
.22 CAL.

For Trappers and Campers

Cal.	Shot	Weight	Barrel
.22 R. F.	7	12¼ oz.	6"

Shoots .22 Long Rifle, .22 Long or .22 Short Cartridges. 6 inch barrel for accurate shooting. Checkered Walnut Grip. Blued finish. Gold Front Sight. Weight 12¼ ounces.
Each $10.65

THE "YOUNG AMERICA"

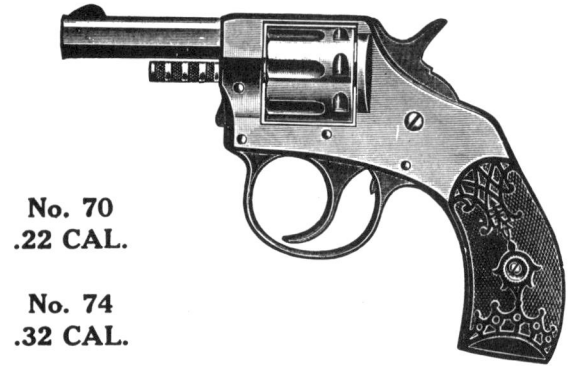

No. 70
.22 CAL.

No. 74
.32 CAL.

No. 70. Young America, 22 Cal., R F., 22 Short & Long. Length of barrel, 2 inches. Nickel or Blue.

2 inch barrel	Price $7.85
4¼ inch barrel	Price 8.35
6 inch barrel	Price 8.85

No. 74. Young America, 32 Cal., C. F., 32 S. & W. Length of barrel, 2 inches. Nickel or Blue.

2 inch barrel	Price $7.85
4½ inch barrel	Price 8.35
6 inch barrel	Price 8.85

H. & R. "VEST POCKET"

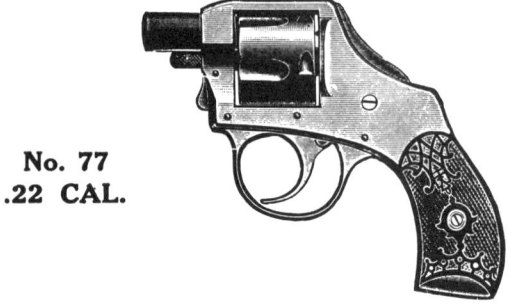

No. 77
.22 CAL.

Blue or Nickel Finish. 1⅛ inch bbl. Cal. .22 R. F. 7 shots. Weight 8½ oz.

Price $7.85
Loading Gate, Extra .... .50

THE AMERICAN DOUBLE ACTION

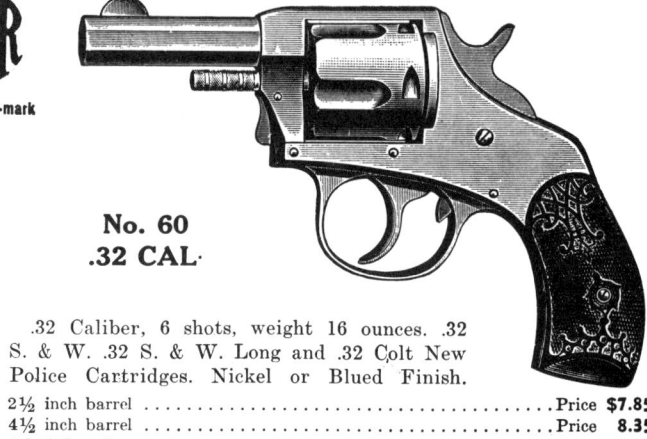

No. 60
.32 CAL.

.32 Caliber, 6 shots, weight 16 ounces. .32 S. & W. .32 S. & W. Long and .32 Colt New Police Cartridges. Nickel or Blued Finish.

2½ inch barrel	Price $7.85
4½ inch barrel	Price 8.35
6 inch barrel	Price 8.85

H. & R. MODELS 4 AND 5

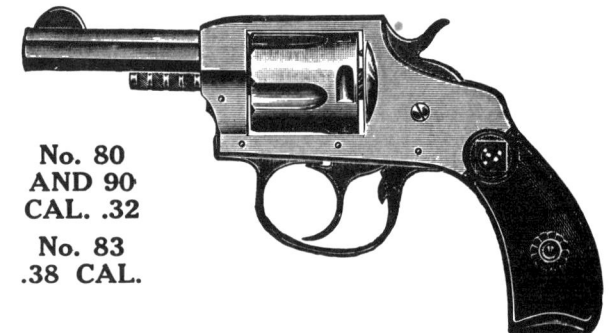

No. 80 AND 90 CAL. .32
No. 83 .38 CAL.

No. 80. 32 Cal. Shoots 32 S. & W.—32 S. & W. Long—32 Colt New Police. H & R Double Action Model 4. Nickel or Blue. Heavy frame.
No. 80. 2½" Bbl. $8.30

No. 83. 38 Cal. Shoots 38 Cal. S. & W. and 38 Colt New Police. H & R Double Action Model 4. Nickel or Blue.
No. 83. 2½" Bbl. $8.30
No. 83. 4½" Bbl. 8.80
No. 83. 6 " Bbl. 9.30

No. 90. 32 Cal. Shoots 32 S. & W. H & R Double Action Model 5. Nickel or Blue. Light frame.
No. 90. 2½" Bbl. $8.30
No. 90. 4½" Bbl. 8.80
No. 90. 6 " Bbl. 9.30

H. & R. MODEL 6

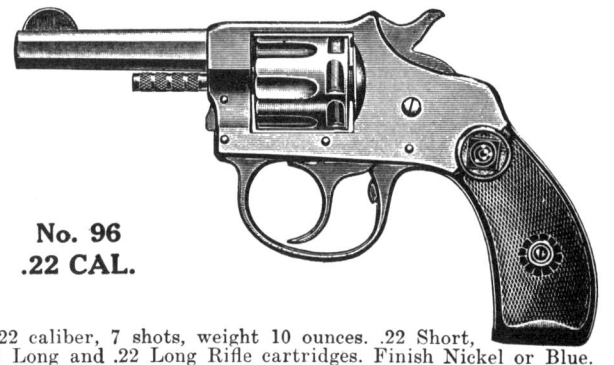

No. 96
.22 CAL.

.22 caliber, 7 shots, weight 10 ounces. .22 Short, .22 Long and .22 Long Rifle cartridges. Finish Nickel or Blue.

2½ inch barrel	Price $8.30
4½ inch barrel	Price 8.80
6 inch barrel	Price 9.30

SEND YOUR GUN TO STOEGER FOR EXPERT REPAIRING

HARRINGTON & RICHARDSON REVOLVERS

H. & R. AUTOMATIC EJECTING

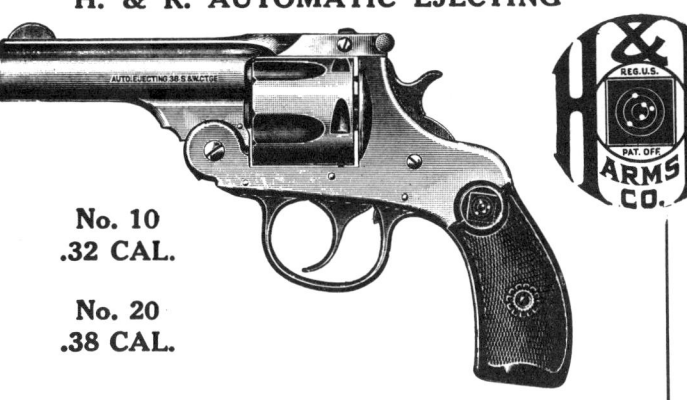

No. 10
.32 CAL.

No. 20
.38 CAL.

The H. & R. Automatic Ejecting Model is an efficient pocket revolver with an outside hammer, and therefore, may be shot either single or double action as desired. Empty shells are automatically ejected when the revolver is opened for reloading.
"Target Grip" (hard rubber) and "Checked Walnut Target Grip" supplied at extra cost.
AMMUNITION: The .32 caliber arm shoots the .32 S. & W., .32 S. & W. Long, and .32 Colt New Police. The .38 caliber arm shoots .38 S. & W. and .38 Colt New Police.
SPECIFICATIONS: Length of barrel, 3¼, 4, 5, and 6 inch; Number of shots, .32 caliber 6, .38 caliber 5; Weight, .32 caliber 16 ounces, .38 caliber 15 ounces; Finish, either nickel or blue.

Model 10 or 20 with 3¼" barrel	$15.70
Model 10 or 20 with 4" barrel	16.20
Model 10 or 20 with 5" barrel	16.45
Model 10 or 20 with 6" barrel	16.70

U. S. R. A. MODEL SINGLE SHOT PISTOL

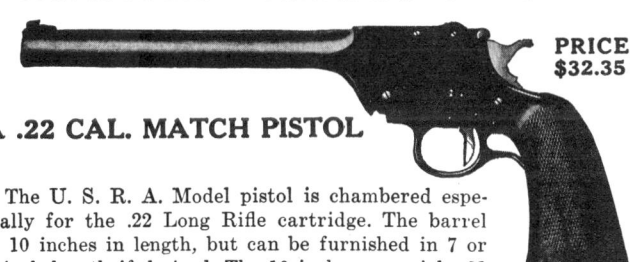

PRICE $32.35

A .22 CAL. MATCH PISTOL

The U. S. R. A. Model pistol is chambered especially for the .22 Long Rifle cartridge. The barrel is 10 inches in length, but can be furnished in 7 or 8 inch length if desired. The 10 inch arm weighs 31 ounces, the 7 inch, 28 ounces. Front sight, 1/10 inch undercut patridge, with detachable guard. Rear sight, with screw adjustment for windage and elevation. This gun has a speed action. Trigger pull is exceptionally clean and sharp. The trigger pull is adjustable and seven different stocks can be supplied for this gun. Fine blued finish.

H. & R. SELF LOADING PISTOL

SPECIFICATIONS

WEIGHT OF PISTOL: 22 ounces
LENGTH OF PISTOL OVERALL: 6½ inches
LENGTH OF BARREL: 3½ inches
CAPACITY OF MAGAZINE: 8 cartridges
AMMUNITION, Colt .32 Auto.

PRICE $16.50

The H. & R. self loading pistol is the result of many years of experience. It is thoroughly well made of forged parts, rugged, accurate, hangs well in the hand, has both manual and grip safety. It is easily taken down and spare parts available.

H. & R. HAMMERLESS

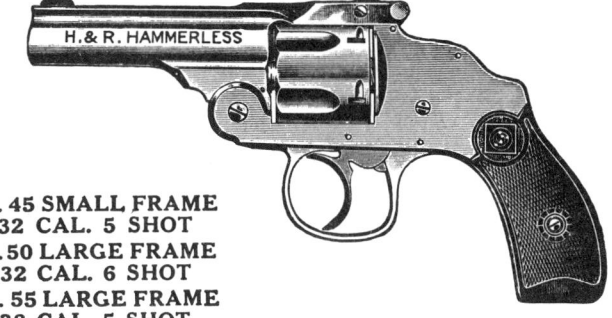

No. 45 SMALL FRAME
.32 CAL. 5 SHOT
No. 50 LARGE FRAME
.32 CAL. 6 SHOT
No. 55 LARGE FRAME
.38 CAL. 5 SHOT

No revolver so perfectly meets the requirements for a satisfactory pocket arm as well as the Hammerless Model. This revolver can be supplied with "Checked Walnut Target Grip" at an extra cost.
AMMUNITION: The No. 45 .32 caliber, 5 shot uses the .32 S. & W. cartridge. The No. 50 .32, 6 shot, shoots .32 S. & W., .32 S. & W. Long and .32 Colt New Police. The No. 55 .38 caliber arm shoots .38 S. & W. and .38 Colt New Police.
SPECIFICATIONS: Length of barrel, small frame, 2, 3, 4, 5, and 6 inch; Number of shots, .22 caliber 7; .32 caliber 5; Weight, either caliber, 13 ounces; Finish, either nickel or blue.
Length of barrel, large frame, 3¼, 4, 5, or 6 inch; Number of shots, .32 caliber 6, .38 caliber 5; Weight, .32 caliber 18 ounces, .38 caliber 17 ounces; Finish, either nickel or blue.

Model 45, with 2" or 3" barrel	$15.70
Model 50, or 55 with 3¼" barrel	15.70
Model 45, 50, or 55 with 4" barrel	16.20
Model 45, 50, or 55 with 5" barrel	16.45
Model 45, 50, or 55 with 6" barrel	16.70

H. & R. PREMIER

No. 30
.22 CAL.

No. 35
.32 CAL.

The H. & R. Premier Model is a small frame outside hammer pocket revolver with an automatic shell ejector. Due to the outside hammer it may be fired either double or single action and on account of its small size and light weight it may be easily carried in the pocket.
"Checked Walnut Target Grip" supplied at extra cost.
AMMUNITION: .22 caliber Premier shoots .22 Short, Long, and Long Rifle cartridges. The .32 caliber arm shoots the .32 S. & W. cartridge.
SPECIFICATIONS: Length of barrel, 2, 3, 4, 5, and 6 inch; Number of shots, .22 caliber 7; .32 caliber 5; Weight, .22 caliber 13 ounces, .32 caliber 12 ounces; Finish, either nickel or blue.

Model 30 or 35 with 2 or 3" barrel	$15.70
Model 30 or 35 with 4" barrel	16.20
Model 30 or 35 with 5" barrel	16.45
Model 30 or 35 with 6" barrel	16.70

RUBBER or CHECKED WALNUT TARGET GRIPS
PRICE $1.00

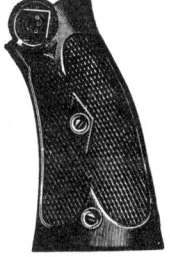

Target grips, as illustrated herewith are available for various H. & R. revolvers whereby a pocket revolver may be transformed into a target arm. These grips are available either in hard rubber or walnut. Both are carefully checkered and afford an excellent hold for target purposes. These grips are available only for the following models: Automatic ejecting, No. 20 only; Hammerless No. 45, 50, and 55; Premier No. 30, and 35, also Models 4 and 5, No. 80, No. 90 and 83; and Model 6 No. 96.

IVER JOHNSON REVOLVERS

.22 PROTECTOR SEALED EIGHT

22 SUPERSHOT SEALED EIGHT

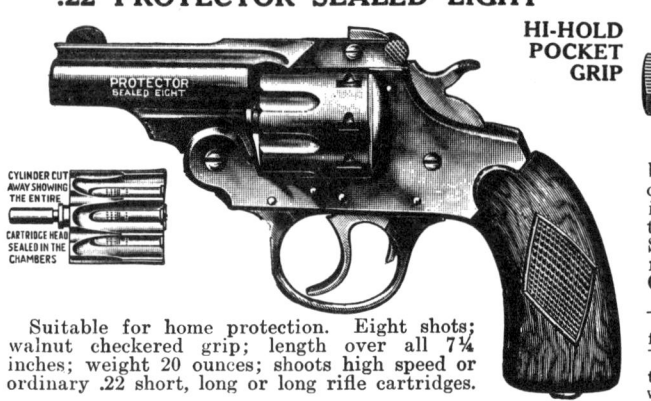

HI-HOLD POCKET GRIP

HI-HOLD GRIP

WITH ADJUSTABLE FINGER REST

SPECIFICATIONS: Counterbored chambers and extractor; 6 inch barrel with special target sights as above. Gold lettering. Blued finish. De Flex rib for better sighting. Scored trigger. One-piece walnut Hi-Hold grip, hand checkered. Shoots all .22 long rifle, .22 long and .22 short rim fire cartridges. Length over all 10¾ inches. Weight 24 ounces. Cellophane wrapped.
No. 834 .... $20.60

Suitable for home protection. Eight shots; walnut checkered grip; length over all 7¼ inches; weight 20 ounces; shoots high speed or ordinary .22 short, long or long rifle cartridges.
Price $17.45

.22 Supershot Sealed Eight: Same as above, but without special sights and finger rest. No. 88 .... $17.45

.22 Supershot 9 Shots: This model does not have the special cylinder with the Counterbored Chambers, and is made in 9 shots. The specifications otherwise are similar to No. 88.
No. 90 .... $16.60

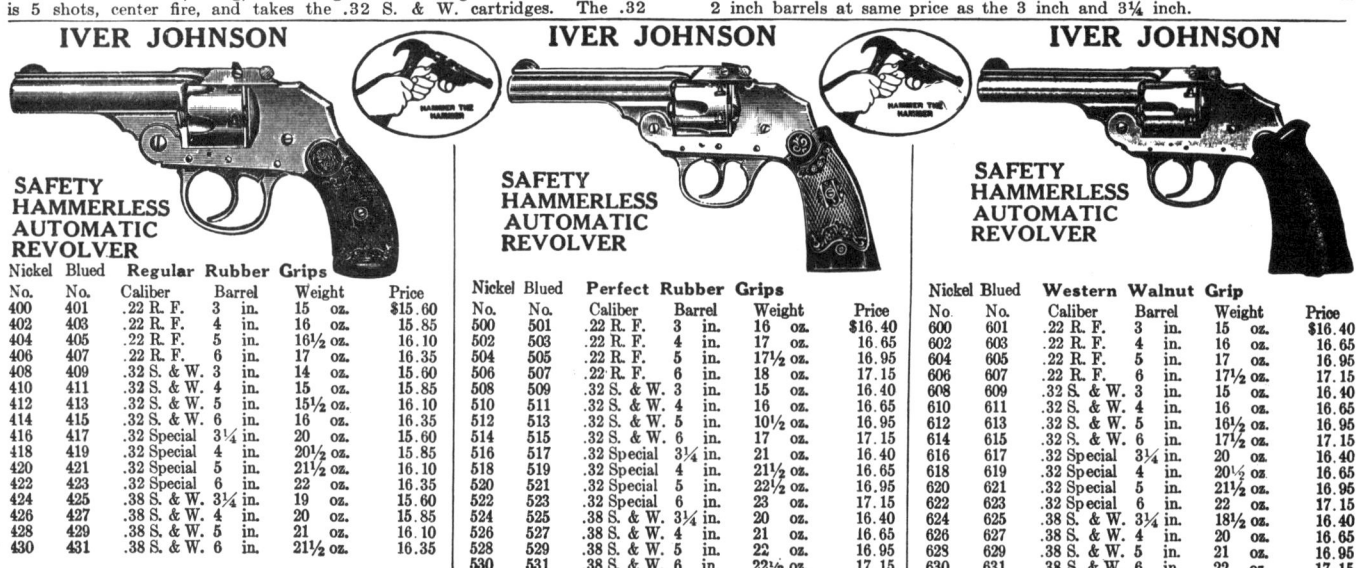

IVER JOHNSON — SAFETY HAMMER AUTOMATIC REVOLVER

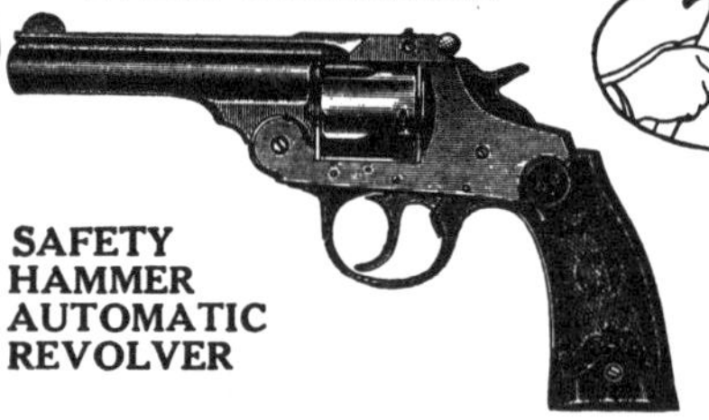

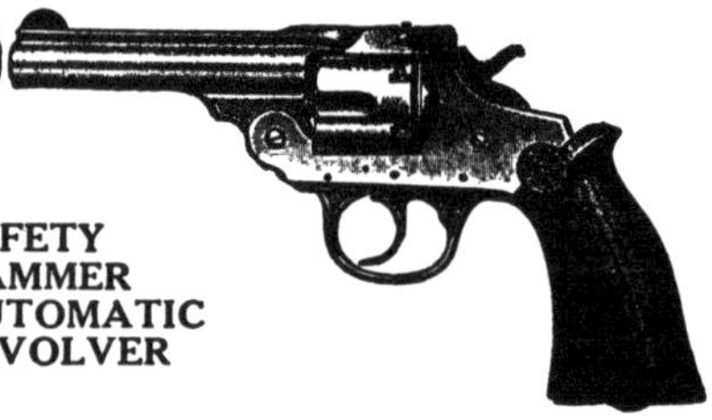

Regular Rubber Grips

Nickel No.	Blued No.	Caliber	Barrel	Weight	Price
100	101	.22 R. F.	3 in.	14 oz.	$15.60
102	103	.22 R. F.	4 in.	15 oz.	15.85
104	105	.22 R. F.	5 in.	16 oz.	16.10
106	107	.22 R. F.	6 in.	16½ oz.	16.35
108	109	.32 S. & W.	3 in.	14 oz.	15.60
110	111	.32 S. & W.	4 in.	15 oz.	15.85
112	113	.32 S. & W.	5 in.	15½ oz.	15.10
114	115	.32 S. & W.	6 in.	16½ oz.	16.35
116	117	.32 Special	3¼ in.	19 oz.	15.60
118	119	.32 Special	4 in.	19½ oz.	15.85
120	121	.32 Special	5 in.	20½ oz.	16.10
122	123	.32 Special	6 in.	21 oz.	16.35
124	125	.38 S. & W.	3¼ in.	17½ oz.	15.60
126	127	.38 S. & W.	4 in.	19 oz.	15.85
128	129	.38 S. & W.	5 in.	20 oz.	16.10
130	131	.38 S. & W.	6 in.	21 oz.	16.35

Perfect Rubber Grips

Nickel No.	Blued No.	Caliber	Barrel	Weight	Price
200	201	.22 R. F.	3 in.	15 oz.	$16.40
202	203	.22 R. F.	4 in.	16 oz.	16.65
204	205	.22 R. F.	5 in.	17 oz.	16.95
206	207	.22 R. F.	6 in.	17½ oz.	17.15
208	209	.32 S. & W.	3 in.	15 oz.	16.40
210	211	.32 S. & W.	4 in.	16 oz.	16.65
212	213	.32 S. & W.	5 in.	16½ oz.	16.95
214	215	.32 S. & W.	6 in.	17½ oz.	17.15
216	217	.32 Special	3¼ in.	20 oz.	16.40
218	219	.32 Special	4 in.	20½ oz.	16.65
220	221	.32 Special	5 in.	21½ oz.	16.95
222	223	.32 Special	6 in.	22 oz.	17.15
224	225	.38 S. & W.	3¼ in.	18½ oz.	16.40
226	227	.38 S. & W.	4 in.	20 oz.	16.65
228	229	.38 S. & W.	5 in.	21 oz.	16.95
230	231	.38 S. & W.	6 in.	22 oz.	17.15

Western Walnut Grip

Nickel No.	Blued No.	Caliber	Barrel	Weight	Price
300	301	.22 R. F.	3 in.	15 oz.	$16.40
302	303	.22 R. F.	4 in.	16 oz.	16.65
304	305	.22 R. F.	5 in.	17 oz.	16.95
306	307	.22 R. F.	6 in.	17½ oz.	17.15
308	309	.32 S. & W.	3 in.	15 oz.	16.40
310	311	.32 S. & W.	4 in.	16 oz.	16.65
312	313	.32 S. & W.	5 in.	16½ oz.	16.95
314	315	.32 S. & W.	6 in.	17½ oz.	17.15
316	317	.32 Special	3¼ in.	20 oz.	16.40
318	319	.32 Special	4 in.	20½ oz.	16.65
320	321	.32 Special	5 in.	21½ oz.	16.95
322	323	.32 Special	6 in.	22 oz.	17.15
324	325	.38 S. & W.	3¼ in.	18½ oz.	16.40
326	327	.38 S. & W.	4 in.	20 oz.	16.65
328	329	.38 S. & W.	5 in.	21 oz.	16.95
330	331	.38 S. & W.	6 in.	22 oz.	17.15

(.38 cal. and .32 Special have Hi-Hold Grip uncheckered.)

All Iver Johnson Safety Revolvers both Hammer and Hammerless, are equipped throughout with finest heat-treated open wound piano wire springs and the Iver Johnson patented Safety Device, which makes accidental discharge impossible. The .22 caliber is 7 shots, rim fire, and takes the .22 Short, Long, and Long Rifle cartridges. The .32 caliber is 5 shots, center fire, and takes the .32 S. & W. cartridges. The .32 Special is 6 shots, center fire, built on heavy frame, and takes the .32 S. & W., .32 S. & W. Long and .32 Colt New Police cartridges. The .38 caliber is 5 shots, center fire, and takes the .38 S. & W. cartridges. Always use greased bullets.

Note—ALL IVER JOHNSON REVOLVERS can be furnished with 2 inch barrels at same price as the 3 inch and 3¼ inch.

IVER JOHNSON — SAFETY HAMMERLESS AUTOMATIC REVOLVER

Regular Rubber Grips

Nickel No.	Blued No.	Caliber	Barrel	Weight	Price
400	401	.22 R. F.	3 in.	15 oz.	$15.60
402	403	.22 R. F.	4 in.	16 oz.	15.85
404	405	.22 R. F.	5 in.	16½ oz.	16.10
406	407	.22 R. F.	6 in.	17 oz.	16.35
408	409	.32 S. & W.	3 in.	14 oz.	15.60
410	411	.32 S. & W.	4 in.	15 oz.	15.85
412	413	.32 S. & W.	5 in.	15½ oz.	16.10
414	415	.32 S. & W.	6 in.	16 oz.	16.35
416	417	.32 Special	3¼ in.	20 oz.	15.60
418	419	.32 Special	4 in.	20½ oz.	15.85
420	421	.32 Special	5 in.	21½ oz.	16.10
422	423	.32 Special	6 in.	22 oz.	16.35
424	425	.38 S. & W.	3¼ in.	19 oz.	15.60
426	427	.38 S. & W.	4 in.	20 oz.	15.85
428	429	.38 S. & W.	5 in.	21 oz.	16.10
430	431	.38 S. & W.	6 in.	21½ oz.	16.35

Perfect Rubber Grips

Nickel No.	Blued No.	Caliber	Barrel	Weight	Price
500	501	.22 R. F.	3 in.	16 oz.	$16.40
502	503	.22 R. F.	4 in.	17 oz.	16.65
504	505	.22 R. F.	5 in.	17½ oz.	16.95
506	507	.22 R. F.	6 in.	18 oz.	17.15
508	509	.32 S. & W.	3 in.	15 oz.	16.40
510	511	.32 S. & W.	4 in.	16 oz.	16.65
512	513	.32 S. & W.	5 in.	10½ oz.	16.95
514	515	.32 S. & W.	6 in.	17 oz.	17.15
516	517	.32 Special	3¼ in.	21 oz.	16.40
518	519	.32 Special	4 in.	21½ oz.	16.65
520	521	.32 Special	5 in.	22½ oz.	16.95
522	523	.32 Special	6 in.	23 oz.	17.15
524	525	.38 S. & W.	3¼ in.	20 oz.	16.40
526	527	.38 S. & W.	4 in.	21 oz.	16.65
528	529	.38 S. & W.	5 in.	22 oz.	16.95
530	531	.38 S. & W.	6 in.	22½ oz.	17.15

Western Walnut Grip

Nickel No.	Blued No.	Caliber	Barrel	Weight	Price
600	601	.22 R. F.	3 in.	15 oz.	$16.40
602	603	.22 R. F.	4 in.	16 oz.	16.65
604	605	.22 R. F.	5 in.	17 oz.	16.95
606	607	.22 R. F.	6 in.	17½ oz.	17.15
608	609	.32 S. & W.	3 in.	15 oz.	16.40
610	611	.32 S. & W.	4 in.	16 oz.	16.65
612	613	.32 S. & W.	5 in.	16½ oz.	16.95
614	615	.32 S. & W.	6 in.	17½ oz.	17.15
616	617	.32 Special	3¼ in.	20 oz.	16.40
618	619	.32 Special	4 in.	20½ oz.	16.65
620	621	.32 Special	5 in.	21½ oz.	16.95
622	623	.32 Special	6 in.	22 oz.	17.15
624	625	.38 S. & W.	3¼ in.	18½ oz.	16.40
626	627	.38 S. & W.	4 in.	20 oz.	16.65
628	629	.38 S. & W.	5 in.	21 oz.	16.95
630	631	.38 S. & W.	6 in.	22 oz.	17.15

(.38 cal. and .32 Special have Hi-Hold Grip uncheckered.)

I. J.—STEVENS—MARBLE

I. J. TARGET SEALED 8
.22 Caliber Double Action   Counterbored Chambers
HI-HOLD GRIP

Extra Heavy Solid Frame Two Barrel Lengths 8 Shots

Cartridges are Safety Sealed. Of high grade construction throughout with quick, smooth and positive action. Especially designed for target practice, Campers and Trappers.

SPECIFICATIONS: Has Counterbored Chambers and shoots the .22 Long Rifle, Long and Short Rim Fire Cartridges. Scored Trigger, Blued Finish with Gold Front Sight and Lettering. De-Flex Sighting Plane. One piece Hi-Hold Walnut Grip, hand checkered. Weight, 6 inches, 24 ounces; 10 inches, 27 ounces. Cellophane wrapped.

No. 68—6 inch Barrel ...$10.60   No. 68—10 inch Barrel ...$11.10

I. J. TARGET 9 SHOTS—Does not have the Counterbored Chambers, and is made in 9 Shots. The specifications otherwise are the same as the Sealed 8.

No. 69—6 inch Barrel ...$10.60   No. 69—10 inch Barrel ...$11.10

I. J. CHAMPION .22 TARGET SINGLE ACTION
MODEL 822

Price $21.25

Barrel, frame and action of new and original design, made extra heavy, and with a very light trigger pull without creep. This revolver is a marvel of precision sighting and accurate shooting.

SPECIFICATIONS: Single action. 8 shots. 6 inch barrel with non-glare rib. Blued finish. Counterbored chambers and extractor. Two Patridge type adjustable sights. Hammer and scored trigger of highly polished steel. Special Hi-Hold walnut grip, beautifully hand checkered. Adjustable finger rest. Proof tested and then targeted. Weight 28 oz. Length overall 10¾ inches, shoots the .22 Long, Rifle Long, and Short rim fire cartridges. This revolver does not have the "Hammer the Hammer" safety device.

STEVENS "OFF-HAND"

SINGLE SHOT TARGET PISTOL

This pistol is an excellent hand gun for the beginner, easy to operate, simple.

SPECIFICATIONS: Sights—.22 caliber; adjustable flat top rear, and bead front. Stock—Selected black walnut. Weight—.22 caliber, 6-inch, 24 ounces; 8-inch, 28 ounces. Barrel—Round with octagon breech. Blued. Length—.22 caliber, 6-inch, 8-inch and 12¼-inch. Action—Single shot. Stevens famous tip-up frame blued, positive extractor.

No. 35—.22 Long Rifle, 12¼-inch .Price $12.10
No. 35—.22 Long Rifle, 8-inch....Price 12.60
No. 35—.22 Long Rifle, 6-inch....Price 13.10

I. J. TRIGGER COCKING

with Counterbored Chambers and Extractor

.22 Single Action Target Eight Shots

One easy pull on trigger cocks the revolver ready to fire—the second pull releases the hammer. This operation of cocking and firing is almost automatic and is accomplished easily without changing position of hand.

This patented construction enables the shooter to do rapid fire target work at a speed heretofore impossible.

SPECIFICATIONS—.22 caliber on heavy frame, Adjustable Finger Rest. 3/32" Patridge type sights with TWO-WAY rear sight adjustable for elevation and windage. One piece walnut grip beautifully hand checkered. Blued finish. Barrel 6". DeFlex Rib. Length overall 10¾". Wt. 24 oz. Shoots all factory loaded .22 Long Rifle, Long and Short rim fire cartridges. Shells are automatically ejected.

Model 36T $20.65

I. J. MODEL 1900

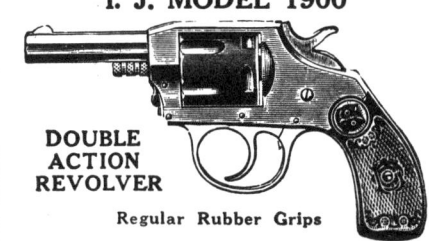

DOUBLE ACTION REVOLVER

Regular Rubber Grips

Nickel No.	Blued No.	Caliber	Barrel	Weight	Price
700	701	.22 R. F.	2½ in.	11 oz.	$7.75
702	703	.22 R. F.	4½ in.	12 oz.	8.00
704	705	.22 R. F.	6 in.	13 oz.	8.25
706	707	.32 S. & W.	2½ in.	12 oz.	7.75
708	709	.32 S. & W.	4½ in.	13 oz.	8.00
710	711	.32 S. & W.	6 in.	14 oz.	8.25
7066	7076	.32 S. & W. (6 Shots)	2½ in.	18 oz.	7.75
7086	7096	.32 S. & W. (6 Shots)	4½ in.	19½ oz.	8.00
7106	7116	.32 S. & W. (6 Shots)	6 in.	20½ oz.	8.25
712	713	.38 S. & W.	2½ in.	18 oz.	7.75
714	715	.38 S. & W.	4½ in.	19 oz.	8.00
716	717	.38 S. & W.	6 in.	20½ oz.	8.25

For Target Rubber Grips add $0.80

MARBLE'S GAME GETTER

"2 Guns in 1"
.22 Rifle and .410 Shotgun

Complete with Leather Holster
Price $24.00

18" Barrel

A Sidearm for the Fisherman, Trapper, and Big Game Hunter

Ideal for Collectors for Museums

The upper barrel is a ".22 Rifle", the lower is a ".410 Shotgun". Either barrel is used without change or adjustment of sights ... A push on the striker sets hammer for either firing pin. The stock folds for compactness in carrying. The gun gives very slight recoil as the grip is large and at right angle to the shooter's arm.

Upper barrel is chambered for .22 short, long and long-rifle.

Lower barrel smooth bore for .410 gauge 2½ inch paper shot or ball shells.

Marble's Rear Sight on this gun gives three combinations: Folding Leaf with small U notch ... Stationary Buck-horn with large U notch ... Folding Peep with 3-32 inch aperture. (Folding leaves are quickly turned up or down with thumb). Front sight is Marble's 1-16 Gold Bead.

BLANK PISTOLS, REVOLVERS, AND CANNON

MINIATURE DOUBLE ACTION REVOLVER

CAL. 2 MM.
Actual Size

This revolver is a genuine work of art and highly interesting for any lover of guns and is furnished with all parts gold plated, finely engraved, and with mother-of-pearl grips, in attractive plush-lined case. Cal. 2 m/m rim fire; weight ½ oz.; 6 shot, double action. Makes an ideal watch charm. Shoots ball or blank ammunition, cal. 2 m/m. (.08).

Price with De Luxe Case, Loader and Ejector	$35.00
2 m/m R. F. Ball Ammunition, per 100	1.00
2 m/m R. F. Blank Ammunition, per 100	.75

KAYBEE .22 BLANK AUTOMATIC

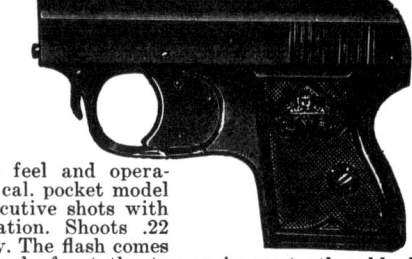

Price $7.50

In appearance, size, feel and operation, a replica of a .25 cal. pocket model automatic. Seven consecutive shots with a single loading operation. Shoots .22 cal. crimped blanks only. The flash comes out of the muzzle instead of out the top as in most other blank guns, giving the gun an entirely realistic effect. Weight 9 oz. Recommended for stage plays.

Practical for dog training, starting races, etc. Small in size, 4⅛" overall, 2⅞" depth, ⅝" thickness, it may readily be carried inconspicuously in vest pocket.

Price, extra magazine	$1.00
.22 cal. crimped blanks, per 100	.75

.22 CAL. STARTER REVOLVER

MODEL 180
9 SHOT

FOR INDOOR USE

Shoots Standard American 122 Blanks

Price $8.75

.22 Blank Cartridges
Price per 250 ......82¢

.32 CAL. STARTER REVOLVER

MODEL 160
6 SHOT

FOR OUTDOOR USE

Shoots Standard .32 S. & W. Blanks

Price $8.75

.32 S. & W. Blank Cartridges
Price per 100 ......$1.51

GENERAL SPECIFICATIONS

This revolver is identical in construction and operation to that of a regular solid frame double action revolver with loading gate. The modifications which make it useable exclusively for starting purposes consist of a special short cylinder, suitable only for blank cartridges, and a solid barrel with pointed extension toward the cylinder. This rear barrel extension serves the double purpose of preventing the accidental use of regular ammunition and also breaks up and disintegrates the wad, thus assuring maximum safety.

Both models are built on the same frame, and are identical except in caliber and capacity. Weight, 16 oz.; overall length, 6½"; finish, nickel or blue.

This Blank Revolver is an American product and it will be of interest to the owner to know this gun will be serviced at a small charge at any time in case it needs repair. This is good news particularly for professionals, stage hands, field trial and race starters.

BREECH LOADING CANNON, 10 GAUGE

The Winchester cannon supplies a general demand for a low-priced breech-loading cannon possessing safety, simplicity of construction, and ease of manipulation. All these desirable features are combined in this gun. In it can be used either paper or brass shells, and we recommend our 10-gauge Winchester blank shells, loaded with 8 drams of black powder, with two Black Edge and one Card wad, to produce the loudest report. This cannon has so few parts that it cannot readily get out of order or cause any trouble in its operation. It can be easily dismounted, if necessary. This cannon will be found satisfactory for Fourth of July and other celebrations, and for saluting on yachts. The shells used in it are not expensive.

Description: The cannon is furnished in two styles differing only in finish, and in the type of wheels. No. G9802S is chromium plated throughout and is equipped with large rubber tired wheels. No. G9801S has a blued barrel and breech closure and nicely japanned carriage and wheels.

The carriage is shapely and substantially built. The barrel is twelve inches long, tapered and cylinder bored.

The barrel and breech closure are proved and tested to withstand a much greater pressure than can be developed by any charge of black powder that can be loaded in a 10 gauge shell.

The length of the cannon overall is 17 inches, its height, 7¼ inches, and its width, 7 inches. Weight, about 14½ pounds.

Operation: The cannon is opened by (1) pushing down the hammer, (2) pulling up the breech bolt handle, and (3) letting down the breech bolt thus exposing the chamber. The shell can then be inserted and the gun closed in the reverse order. The breech bolt is so constructed that the gun cannot be fired until it is locked, thus insuring its safety. To fire the gun, the hammer is pulled forward by a quick pull on a cord which is passed through the hole in the rear of the hammer, drilled for that purpose.

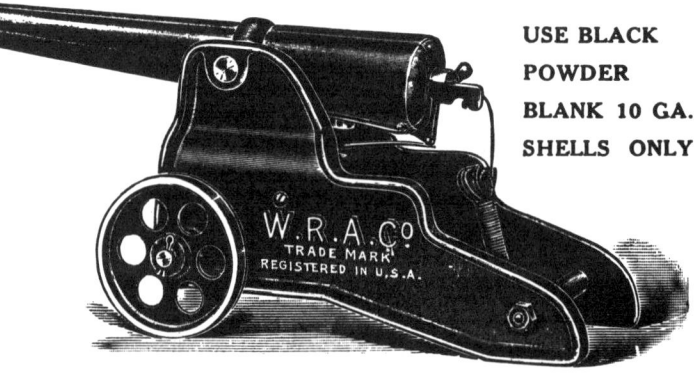

USE BLACK POWDER BLANK 10 GA. SHELLS ONLY

A proper extractor is provided for extracting the fired shell. The mainspring has sufficient strength to avoid mistakes. The barrel can be raised or lowered by an elevating screw placed underneath it.

Winchester Breech Loading, black finish	$19.98
Winchester Breech Loading, chromium finish	38.80
Blank cartridges per 100	4.78

BERLOQUE MINIATURE BLANK PISTOLS

MODEL 100
Natural Size

"Kobold Model 100." The smallest blank pistol made for the 2 mm. rimfire cartridge, of neat appearance, heavy nickle plated, well made and reliable, giving a surprisingly loud report. The pistol is packed in a neat carton together with ejecting rod to dislodge empty cartridges.
Price $1.25

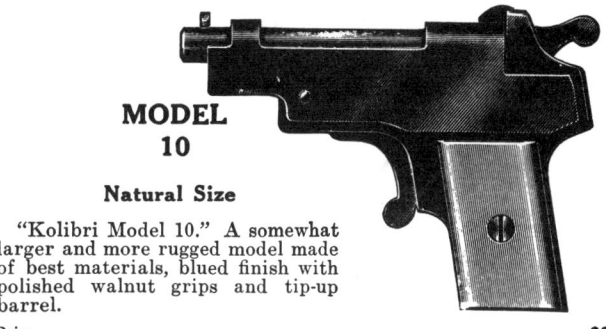

MODEL 10
Natural Size

"Kolibri Model 10." A somewhat larger and more rugged model made of best materials, blued finish with polished walnut grips and tip-up barrel.
Price $2.50

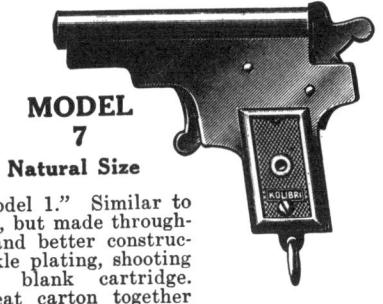

MODEL 7
Natural Size

"Kolibri Model 1." Similar to the Model 100, but made throughout of steel and better construction, best nickle plating, shooting the 2 mm. blank cartridge. Packed in neat carton together with ejector rod.
Price, with engraved German Silver Grips......................$2.00
Price, with engraved Gold Plated Grips..........................2.25

MODEL 500
Length 4¼"

"Flobert Model 500." This little Flobert Blank Pistol is especially constructed for the .22 cal. American Blank Cartridge and is one of the oldest and best liked types. The metal is neatly nickled, the gun well and carefully built, and supplied with checkered grips.
Price $3.25

MODEL 3
Natural Size

MODEL 3
Opened

"Kolibri Model 3." Best grade with tip-up barrel, especially well finish, shooting the 2 mm. blank cartridge. Packed in particularly neat carton with ejector rod.
Price, with engraved silver grips..................................$2.25
Price, with engraved gold plated grips............................2.50
Price, with pearl grips, gold plated................................3.50

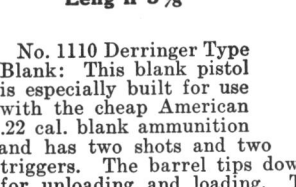

MODEL 1110
Length 3⅞"

No. 1110 Derringer Type Blank: This blank pistol is especially built for use with the cheap American .22 cal. blank ammunition and has two shots and two triggers. The barrel tips down for unloading and loading. The pistol is neatly blued and the grips are of walnut.
Price $3.75

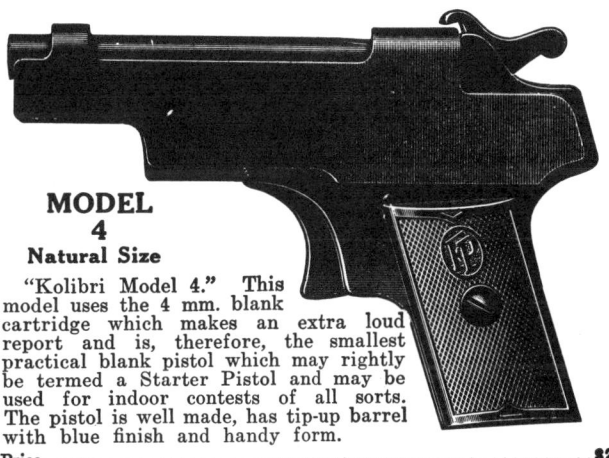

MODEL 4
Natural Size

"Kolibri Model 4." This model uses the 4 mm. blank cartridge which makes an extra loud report and is, therefore, the smallest practical blank pistol which may rightly be termed a Starter Pistol and may be used for indoor contests of all sorts. The pistol is well made, has tip-up barrel with blue finish and handy form.
Price $2.75

AMMUNITION
	Price Per 100
2 mm Rim Fire Blanks	$.75
4 mm Rim Fire Blanks	.75
.22 Rim Fire Blanks	.25

GENUINE MAUSER TWENTY SHOT 7.63 M/M PISTOL

THE PERFECT POLICE ANTI-BANDIT GUN WITH INTERCHANGEABLE 10 AND 20 SHOT MAGAZINES

ACCURATE RANGE 1100 YARDS

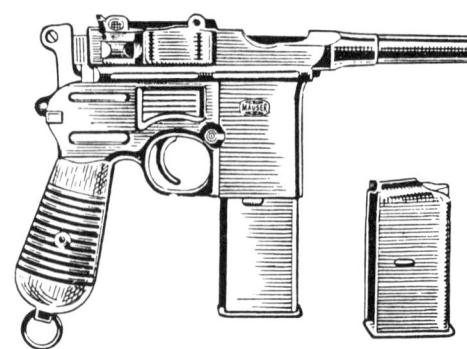

MODEL 712

Illustration shows pistol with twenty shot magazine inserted. Shown outside is the ten shot magazine.

The Mauser Works now present their new autoloading pistol, Caliber 7.63 m/m (.30 Caliber) which permits *twenty consecutive shots* to be fired with one loading. It possesses the further novelty of uniting in the same weapon the Mauser "Clip" and "Detachable Magazine" systems of loading.

This arm occupies a very prominent part in the pistol world, being used for various purposes, such as a military arm used by Germany, Russia, Italy, Turkey, Finland, China, etc., as an efficient police weapon (regulation German police gun), as a target pistol and hunting arm. Special attention is called to its light weight, compactness, high degree of reliability and safety in handling. The weight of the pistol is only 2.79 pounds, and the length of the pistol is only 11.3 inches. This makes an ideal weapon to carry around for hunting, being slipped into the coat pocket. It is used by many sportsmen all over the world for hunting game such as deer, wild boar, wolves, bear, moose, etc. The Mauser is world famed for its great accuracy, hitting power and long range. It is considered the STRONGEST HITTING and FARTHEST SHOOTING pistol in the world with a maximum range of about 2,200 yards. Supplied with ten and twenty shot magazines.

In its essential structural features the new arm is identical with the universally known and reputed Standard Mauser auto-pistol Cal. 7.63 m/m, whose absolutely characteristic points of superiority have assured its sweeping success and unique reputation in all parts of the world.

GENERAL—The new arm integrally embodies the salient characteristics of the Standard Mauser Pistol, namely:
1.—Total avoidance of pins and screws in working parts.
2.—Complete enclosure of mechanism in body.
3.—Grouping of working parts in self-contained assemblies.

thereby not only affording the most complete protection against corrosive gases, dust, snow and foreign bodies generally, but greatly facilitating cleaning, stripping and maintenance.

The chief parts subjected to severe stress have been considerably reinforced, enabling the arm to stand up without reserve to the racking stresses set up in quick fire.

MAGAZINE.—The arm is regularly equipped with a detachable 10-round magazine, which can be interchanged at will with a "long" magazine holding 20 rounds.

MAGAZINE CHANGING is exceedingly simple and certain. The empty magazine is released by pressing a stud on the right hand side of body, then inserting and securing the full one in place by a single motion. Any number of spare magazines can be carried in leather cases on the belt.

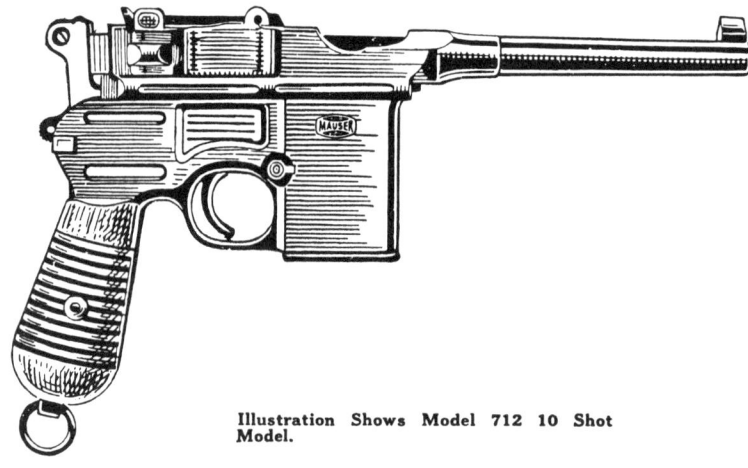

Illustration Shows Model 712 10 Shot Model.

LOADING—Cock hammer and fully retract bolt, in which position it is then held by hammer. Smartly insert full magazine into arm, so that it snaps into place. Ease hammer, releasing bolt, which flies forward, carrying the topmost cartridge into chamber. The arm is now ready to fire.

On firing last cartridge, bolt is held back in its rearmost ("open") position by a projecting stud on carrier, leaving arm ready to reload, and giving the firer unmistakable warning that this is necessary.

RELOADING,—when a fresh loaded magazine is not available, is accomplished—without removing empty magazine—by refilling with two successive clips of 10 cartridges, a valuable advantage in emergency.

UNLOADING — Release and remove magazine and eject cartridge in chamber by gently retracting bolt. Release bolt and lower hammer, if cocked, by pulling trigger.

UNIVERSAL SAFETY LOCK —The arm is provided with the new "Universal" safety lock by means of which the arm can not only be rendered "safe" whether cocked or uncocked, but—safety "on"—the hammer is lowered with one hand and without the slightest risk by simply pulling trigger.

RELIABILITY — Apart from its unconditional reliability under the worst service conditions, the Original Mauser Quickfiring Pistol has been fully tried out by the severest possible tests with a large number of rounds, without loss of accuracy, malfunction of any kind or ascertainable wear. It is offered in complete confidence as an absolutely first rate automatic arm, fulfilling to the last iota the most exacting demands which a responsible War, Gendarmerie, Police or Customs Department can require in a weapon for the equipment of its officers and subordinates.

The original Mauser Auto-pistol Caliber 7.63 m/m alone combines unique structural superiority with the extreme accuracy of workmanship necessary to meet without reserve the most difficult and refined arms-technical problems arising in the functioning of automatic arms. It can be recognized by the Mauser trade-mark on left side of frame and marking on top of barrel and right side of frame: Waffenfabrik Mauser, Oberndorf a. Necker.

Mauser Pistol with interchangeable 10 and 20 shot magazines	$110.00
Extra 10 Shot Magazine	5.00
Extra 20 Shot Magazine	10.00

NUMERICAL DATA OF MODEL 712

Caliber	0.300 in.
Total length	11.3 in.
Length of barrel with chamber	5.20 in.
Length of line of sight	9.05 in.
Weight of pistol with 10 shot magazine	2.79 lbs.
Ditto with 20 shot magazine	2.90 lbs.
Muzzle velocity (vo)	1392 f.s.
Muzzle energy (Ve)	366 ft. lbs.
Spread of 10 shots:	
at 50 m ....vertical	5.9 in.
horizontal	4.3 in.
at 100 m ....vertical	9.8 in.
horizontal	7.9 in.
at 200 m ....vertical	17.7 in.
horizontal	14.2 in.
at 500 m ....vertical	59 in.
horizontal	49 in.
Rear sight graduated to	1000 m; 1100 yds.
Extreme range	2000 m; 2200 yds.
Penetration in pine:	
at 50 m	8 to 9 in.
at 100 m	6.3 in.
at 200 m	4.9 in.

A NEW GUN CARRIES A FACTORY GUARANTEE

MAUSER PISTOL PARTS
COMPONENT PARTS OF THE MAUSER 7.63 MM PISTOLS

The parts listed and illustrated below are for the standard Mauser 7.63 m/m pistol, the sale of which we have discontinued. These parts are also interchangeable with the Military Model 9 m/m Mauser pistols of identical appearance used during the World War.

Parts for the new Model 712 *Twenty Shot* 7.63 Pistol are practically alike, the chief differences lying in the magazine frame. In ordering, be sure to specify for which model the parts are desired.

Since we have had many requests for twenty-shot magazines for use in the standard Mauser 7.63 pistol of which there are thousands in America, we wish to advise that these older pistols can positively not be altered to use the new magazines, which are adapted *only* to the new Model 712.

1	Bbl. with Bolt Casing 5⅛ inches	$17.50
2	Bolt Lock	4.40
3	Bolt Spring	1.25
4	Bolt Spring Stop	4.40
5	Striker	4.40
6	Striker Spring	.50
7	Extractor	3.75
8	Bolt	9.25
9	Lock Frame	11.25
10	Hammer	5.00
11	Hammer Axle	3.75
12	Safety	4.40
13	Sear	3.75
14	Hammer Lock. Lever	4.40
15	Main Spring	1.25
16	Spring Bolt	3.75
17	Rocker Plunger	4.40
18	Coupling	3.75
19	Lock Stop	3.75
20	Frame	17.50
21	Magazine Platform	5.00
22	Magazine Spring	3.75
23	Magazine Bottom	4.40
24	Magazine Plunger	3.75
25	Trigger	3.75
26	Trigger Spring	3.75
27	Handle Shell, Pair	5.00
28	Handle Shell Screw	.50
29	Handle Shell Nut	.50
30	Washer	.50
31	Sight Leaf	5.00
32	Sight Spring	.75
33	Sight Slide	4.40
34	Slide Spring	.50
35	Slide Catch	3.75

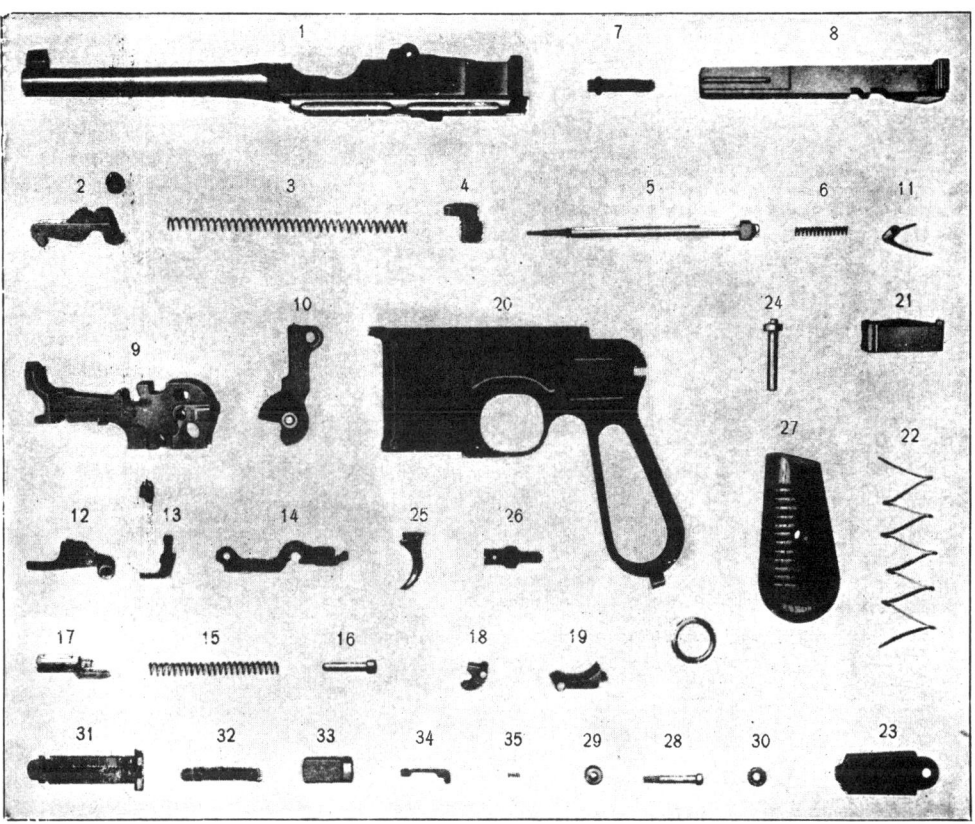

PARTS OF THE MAUSER VEST POCKET PISTOL (W. T. P.) cal. 6.35 mm (.25″)

1	Breech	$5.50	17	Interruptor	$1.50
2	Barrel	6.00	18	Safety	1.50
3	Frame	6.50	19	Barrel Holder	1.50
4	Striker	2.50	20	Barrel Holder Spring	1.50
5	Indicator	1.25	21	Magazine Holder	1.75
6	Indicator Bearing	1.25	22	Handle	2.50
7	Extractor	2.00	23	Handle Screw	.50
8	Extractor Pin	.50	24	Recoil Spring Guide	.75
9	Ejector	1.65	25	Recoil Spring	1.25
10	Cocking Piece	1.25	26	Striker Spring	1.25
11	Interruptor Spring	.75	27	Safety Spring	.75
12	Cocking Piece Spring	.75	28a	Magazine Body	.75
13	Trigger Lever	1.75	28b	Elevator	.75
14	Sear	2.00	28c	Elevator Spring	.75
15	Trigger	1.65	28d	Bottom Plate	.75
16	Trigger Pin	.50	29	Magazine, complete	3.50

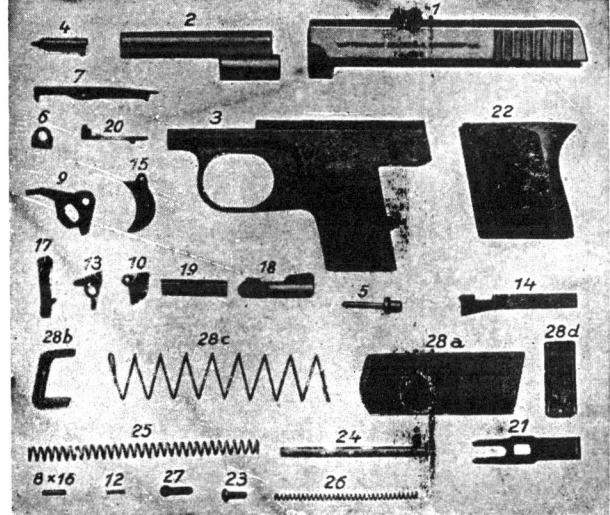

NOTE: The illustration and parts shown here represent the now discontinued Old Vest Pocket Model, which is somewhat larger than the New Model Vest Pocket Model described in this catalog. An illustration of the New Vest Pocket Model parts was not yet available when this catalog went to press, but the parts are similar and the prices correspond. In ordering Mauser Vest Pocket repair parts, please be sure to specify Old or New Model.

SEND YOUR GUN TO STOEGER FOR EXPERT REPAIRING

GENUINE LUGER BARRELS AND H. & R. FLARE PISTOL

PRICES OF LUGER BARRELS WITH FRONT SIGHT

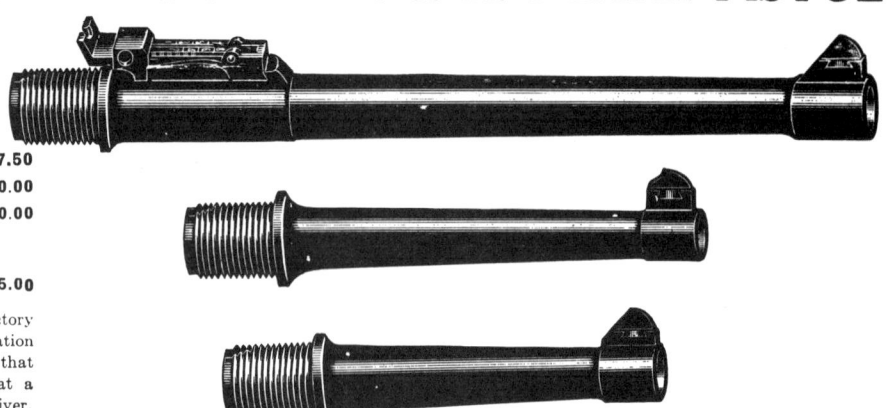

Caliber 7.65 m/m, 3⅝ inch (98 m/m) Barrel.....$7.50
Caliber 9 m/m, 4 inch (100 m/m) Barrel........20.00
Caliber 7.65 m/m, 4½ inch (118 m/m) Barrel....20.00
Caliber 9 m/m, 8 inches (200 m/m) Barrel, including tangent curve sight graduated up to 800 meters (880 yards)..........................25.00

Note: We have specially imported genuine Luger factory barrel removing and fitting machines, and as this operation is sometimes very difficult otherwise, we recommend that pistol be sent to us for fitting, which we undertake at a charge of $1.00. Any barrel complete with receiver, extra $16.00

RECONDITIONED LUGERS

Because of the thousands of re-built and refinished Luger Pistols which have flooded the market and many of which have been spuriously offered as new merchandise at prices actually less than factory new cost, we have decided to offer herewith a line of reconditioned Lugers. We offer these for those who are desirous of obtaining the benefits of the Luger Pistol, but are not in a position to pay the present very high price which present factory costs, import duties, excise and other taxes make necessary.

All Luger Pistols offered by us are thoroughly inspected by experts and tested, thus giving the purchaser assurance of a satisfactory weapon.

The 7.65 mm Pistols are furnished only with 98 mm (3⅝ inch barrel) and the 9 mm only with 100 mm barrel (3¾ inch barrel).

The following pistols are available in either caliber 7.65 mm or 9 mm as indicated.

Luger pistols, Grade 1, refinished, reblued, new grips, new barrels, same as new. Cal. 7.65 mm, Price, $37.50. Cal. 9 mm, Price....$45.00
Luger pistols, Grade 2, slightly used, but in first-class mechanical condition, barrels very good. Price, 7.65 mm only.............. 30.00
Luger pistols, Grade 3, in good serviceable condition. Price, Cal. 7.65 mm or 9 mm.... 27.50

IMPROVED CARTRIDGES FOR LUGER

The German D. W. M. ammunition company has perfected a new speedy and powerful 7.65 m/m Luger Cartridge. Loaded with 5.4 grains of (.35 grams) Rottweiler smokeless powder and with a bullet of 9.2 grains, jacketed with an alloy which prevents metal fouling and increases the velocity, this cartridge has attained results unexcelled by any others. The muzzle velocity has been increased from 1148 feet per second to 1208 feet per second and the muzzle energy from 271 foot pounds to 300 foot pounds. The 7.65 m/m and 9 m/m caliber Luger cartridges fit the same magazine. Both cartridges are the same length but the difference is in the weights of the bullets and powder. The 9 m/m bullet weighs 125 grains.

BALLISTICS OF THE LUGER PISTOL

The ballistics of the Luger pistol as printed below are official figures furnished by the Luger factory. We are unable to give ballistics other than those here listed as these are never made public by the factory.

	7.65	9.00	9.00
Caliber in millimeters............	7.65	9.00	9.00
Length of barrel in inches........	4¾	4	6
Muzzle velocity in foot pounds....	1138	1010	1056
Muzzle energy in foot pounds....	267.84	280.14	307.95
Maximum range in feet..........	5850	4875	5200
Penetration in inches at..........	55 yds.	55 yds.	110 yds.
Pinewood	6⅛	5½	5⅞
Beechwood	2½	2	2¼
Spread in in. at 55 yds., in height.	4	5⅛	4¾
in width.	2¾	3½	3⅛
Spread in in. at 110 yds., in height.	10	12	7½
in width.	7	8½	7
Spread in in. at 220 yds., in height.	26	31	17
in width.	20	23	15
Spread in in. at 330 yds., in height.	—	—	30
in width.	—	—	24

H. & R. FLARE PISTOL SET

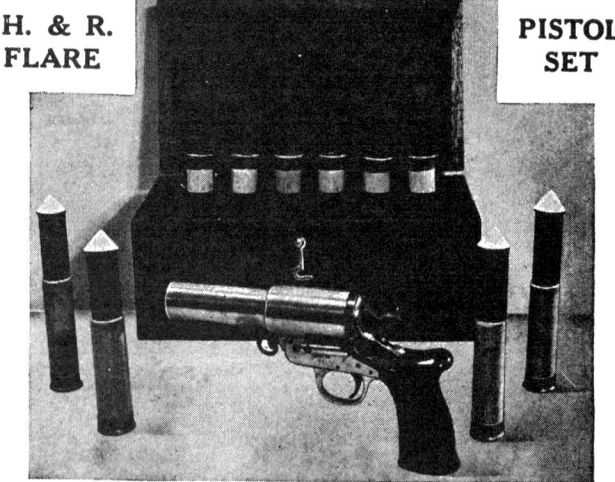

This set contains the following items and is furnished in a well constructed solid wooden box.
One H. & R. brass Very pistol   Two parachute flares, white
Six Single ball flares, red   Two parachute flares, red.
This flare set is an absolutely essential part of the equipment of every yacht, motor boat, airplane, or any other type of expedition or hunting party where its use is often the only means of procuring necessary assistance when lost, injured or in unfamiliar territory.

The elevation of the parachute flares is approximately 150 feet, giving a candle power of 750 feet. The red single ball flares' elevation is about the same and burns red from the moment it leaves the muzzle of the pistol. These single ball flares are also furnished in white and/or green.
Price, Complete Set..$33.75
Also sold individually, as follows:
H. & R. Flare (Very) pistol only.......................$25.00
H. & R. Flare Pistol, special lightweight, weight only 19 ozs...... 20.00
Single Ball Flares, red, white or green, per doz................. 3.00
Parachute Flares, red or white, each......................... 1.75

GENUINE LUGER PARTS AND REPAIRING

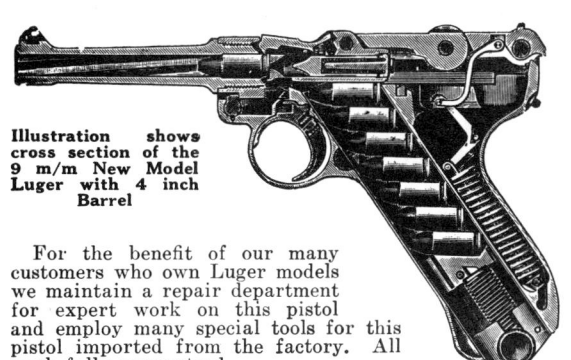

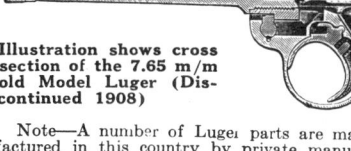

Illustration shows cross section of the 9 m/m New Model Luger with 4 inch Barrel

In ordering Parts, be sure to state whether for old or new model

Parts for 7.65 m/m and 9 m/m are identical

Illustration shows cross section of the 7.65 m/m old Model Luger (Discontinued 1908)

For the benefit of our many customers who own Luger models we maintain a repair department for expert work on this pistol and employ many special tools for this pistol imported from the factory. All work fully guaranteed.

Note—A number of Luger parts are manufactured in this country by private manufacturers. These are without exception grossly inferior, and in most cases the pistol will not function with them. This applies especially to magazines. Our parts are all imported and original. Our genuine imported Luger Magazines are the only dependable and satisfactory ones offered to the public. The imitations offered by others at a cheaper price usually jam the pistol, and cannot be relied upon in emergencies.

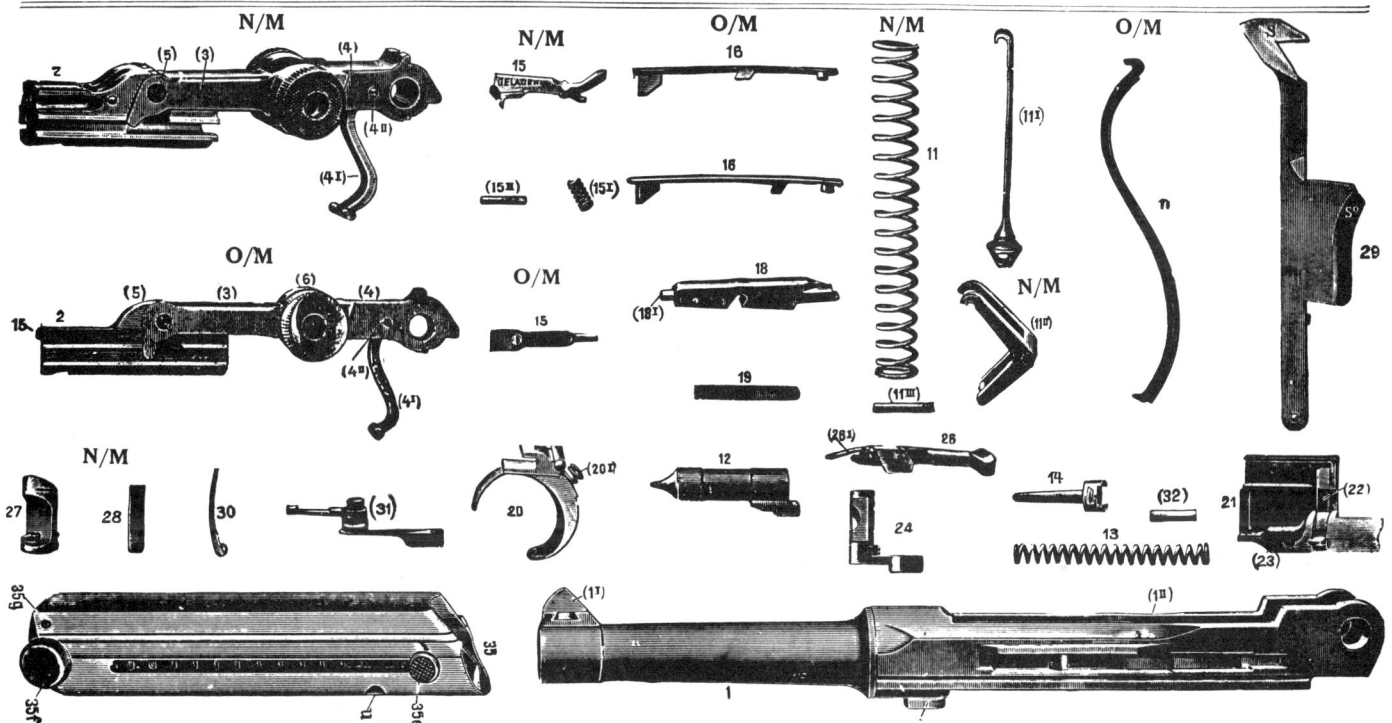

NOTE—N/M—New Model.   O/M—Old Model

Number		Old Model	New Model
1"	Receiver	$17.50	$16.00
1'	Front Sight	1.00	1.00
2	Breech Block	6.50	6.50
3	Forward Link to Toggle Joint	3.00	3.00
4	Rear Link of Toggle Joint	4.00	4.00
4"	Coupling Link	1.75	1.75
4"'	Coupling Link Pin	.50	.50
5"	Connecting Pin, between Breech Block Forward Link	.50	.50
6	Connecting Pin, between Forward and Rear Link	.50	.50
6'	Connecting Pin Rivet	None	.50
7	Connecting Pin, between Rear Link and Receiver	1.00	1.00
8	Retaining Catch on Rear Link	1.00	None
9	Retaining Catch Spring	.50	None
11	Recoil and Rivet, S shaped	3.50	None
11	Recoil Spring, Spiral Shape. When ordering state 7.65 or 9 m/m	None	1.75
11'	Recoil Spring Lever Bar	None	2.50
11'"	Recoil Spring Lever Pin	None	.25
12	Firing Pin	3.00	3.00
13	Firing Pin Spring	1.25	1.25
14	Breech Block End Piece	3.00	3.00
15	Extractor	2.50	2.50
15'	Extractor Spring	None	.50
15"	Extractor Rivet	None	.50
16	Ejector	2.50	2.50
17	Steel Stock (Frame)	15.00	15.00
17'	Catch	.75	None
17"	Sling Swivel	1.50	1.50
17'"	Breech Block Catch Link Rivet	.50	.50
18'	Trigger Bar Spring Stud		
18"	Trigger Bar Spring Stud Spring	$3.50	$3.50
18'"	Trigger Bar Rivet		
18	Trigger Bar		
19	Trigger Bar Spring	.50	.50
20	Trigger	2.50	2.50
20'	Trigger Spring	.50	.50
21	Trigger Plate	3.50	3.50
22	Trigger Lever	1.00	1.00
23	Trigger Lever Pin	.50	.50
24	Locking Bolt	2.50	2.50
25	Locking Bolt Spring	.50	.50
26'	Breech Block Catch Link Spring		
26	Breech Block Catch Link	3.50	3.50
27	Magazine Holder Catch	1.75	1.75
28	Magazine Holder Catch Spring	.50	.50
29	Safety Sear	4.00	4.00
30	Safety Sear Spring	.50	.50
31	Safety Catch	3.00	3.00
32	Safety Catch Pin	.50	.50
33	Butt Plates, per pair	3.50	3.50
34	Butt Plate Screws	.50	.50
35	Magazines, Complete (See Note)	4.00	4.00
35a	Magazine Frame	1.50	1.50
b	Magazine Cartridge Feeder Spring	.50	.50
c	Mag. Cartridge Feeder	.50	.50
d	Mag. Cart. Feeder Pressure Knob	.50	.50
e	Mag. Cart. Feeder Guide Knob	.75	.75
f	Magazine Bottom Piece	.75	.75
g	Magazine Connecting Pin	.50	.50

MAUSER AUTOMATIC POCKET PISTOLS

THE ORIGINAL MAUSER SELF LOADING AUTOMATIC POCKET PISTOL

COMPACT, ACCURATE, SAFE, AND TRUE WEAPONS OF DEFENSE
Pocket Models—25 cal. (6.35 MM), 10 shot; 32 cal. (765 MM), 9 shots

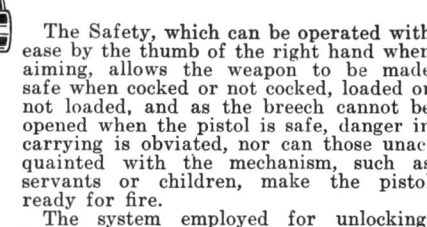

Standard Uses .25 and .32 Cal. Auto. Cartridges.

PRINCIPAL FEATURES

1. Ten, nine and eight shots respectively.
2. Solidity and simplicity of construction.
3. Perfect workmanship.
4. Great accuracy, increased by special length of barrel.
5. Reliability and safety.
6. The state of the pistol, viz., cocked or not, is apparent externally.
7. Considerable penetrative power.
8. Substantial grip and good balance.
9. Ease of taking apart for cleaning.
10. Attractive appearance, absence of projecting parts, flat shape and consequent absence of bulge when carried in the pocket.

The component parts of the Mauser pistols are simple and strong and only the highest quality of materials and best workmanship are used in their manufacture which is based on the same methods and principles to which Mauser constructions owe their world wide reputation.

Magazine Capacity. As the magazine of the 6.35 MM pistol holds nine and that of the 7.65 MM holds eight cartridges, the pistol can be made to hold ten and nine shots respectively.

Security in Handling. The shooter can tell when aiming or in the dark by touch, whether the pistol is cocked or not—when cocked, the rear end of the striker is visible at the back of the breech. This is a most valuable feature, as the absence on other pistols of devices clearly showing the state of the weapon, has led to fatal accidents.

The pistol cannot be fired when the magazine is wholly or partly withdrawn. Accidents due to presumption that there was no cartridge in the barrel after withdrawing the magazine are thus made impossible.

The breech remains open after firing the last cartridge, but closes automatically as long as there is a cartridge in the magazine. This gives greater security in handling.

The Safety, which can be operated with ease by the thumb of the right hand when aiming, allows the weapon to be made safe when cocked or not cocked, loaded or not loaded, and as the breech cannot be opened when the pistol is safe, danger in carrying is obviated, nor can those unacquainted with the mechanism, such as servants or children, make the pistol ready for fire.

The system employed for unlocking. i. e., releasing the safety, prevents the safety from being unlocked while carrying the pistol in, or drawing it out of, the pocket. The involuntary firing of more shots than intended, commonly known as "Maximing" is absolutely prevented by the interceptor which disconnects the trigger from the sear while the breech is in motion and makes it necessary to pull the trigger for each shot. No firing can take place unless the breech is entirely closed, even though one should forget to release the trigger after firing.

The Pistol is perfectly balanced, and its substantial and comfortable grip contributes greatly to the accuracy of shooting which is further increased by the comparatively great length of the barrel, and line of sight.

No. 700—Cal. 25, Ten Shot..............Price $25.00
No. 701—Cal. 32, Nine Shot..............Price $28.00

THE NEW MAUSER VEST POCKET PISTOL

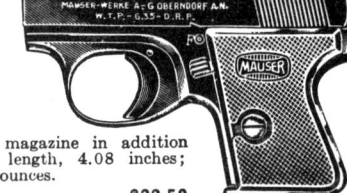

This is one of the smallest serviceable pistols in the world, ruggedly constructed and designed for hard use. In construction it is similar to the earlier model Vest Pocket Pistol which has been discontinued, but smaller in size, and particularly designed to lie comfortably in the hand. Holds six shots in the magazine in addition to one in the chamber. Total length, 4.08 inches; depth, 2¾ inches; weight, 9½ ounces.
Price $22.50

COMPONENT PARTS LIST OF MAUSER POCKET MODEL

No.	Article	Price
1.	Barrel	$6.00
2.	Barrel Holder	2.25
3.	Barrel Holder Catch	1.25
4.	Striker (Firing Pin)	2.75
5.	Striker Spring	1.25
6.	Barrel Holder Guide	1.25
7.	Interceptor	1.00
8.	Rear Sight	1.25
9.	Extractor	2.50
10.	Breech	7.50
11.	Recoil Spring	1.25
12.	Ejector	3.00
13.	Double Action Spring	.75
14.	Grip Cover Plate	2.75
15.	Frame	7.50
16.	Magazine	3.50
17.	Trigger Complete	3.00
18.	Trigger Spring	.75
19.	Grip Cover Plate Screw, left	.50
20.	Grip Cover Plate Screw, right	.50
21.	Safety Locking Spring	1.50
22.	Trigger Catch Spring	.65
23.	Trigger Catch Pin	.50
24.	Trigger Catch	1.50
25.	Magazine Platform	.75
26.	Safety	3.00
27.	Sear	3.00
28.	Magazine Bottom Plate	.50
29.	Magazine Holder	2.50
30.	Magazine Spring	1.25
31.	Side Plate	3.00

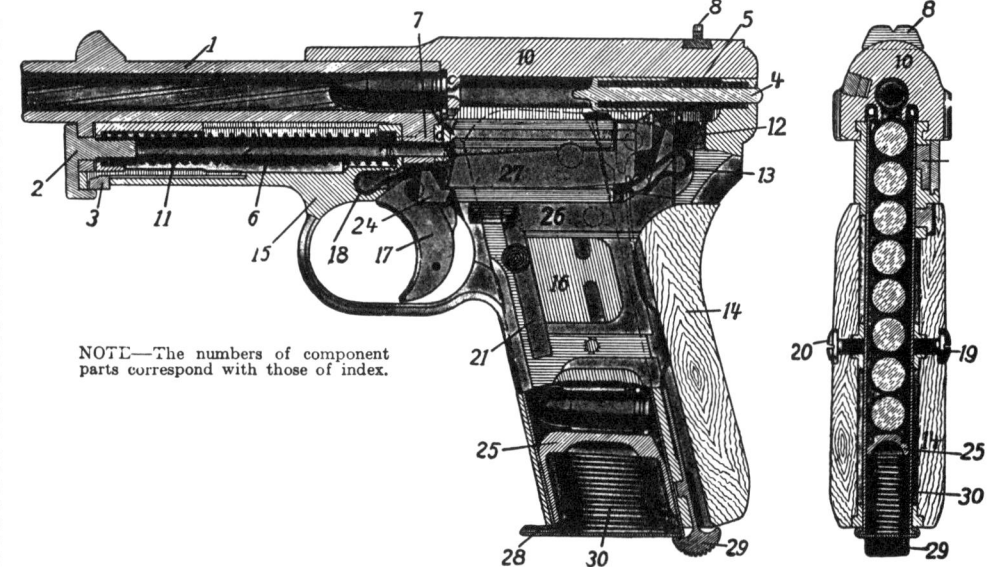

NOTE—The numbers of component parts correspond with those of index.

ALL SHIPMENTS ARE INSURED

ORTGIES—SPANISH—MISCELLANEOUS PISTOLS

ORTGIE PARTS

No.		Price	No.		Price
1	Frame	$6.50	15	Magazine Complete	$3.50
2	Slide	5.50	16	Recoil Spring	2.25
3	Extractor	2.00	17	Firing Pin Spring	1.25
4	Firing Pin	2.75	18	Safety Spring	.50
5	Barrel	6.00	19	Mag. Holder Spring	.50
6	Safety	3.75	20	Sear Spring	.75
7	Safety Button	1.75	21	Extractor Spring	.50
8	Grip Holder	1.75	22	Trigger Spring	.50
9	Sear	2.50	23	Intercepter Spring	.50
10	Intercepter	1.00	24	F. P. Spring Guide	.75
11	Trigger	2.50	25	Safety Pin	.50
12	Magazine Holder	2.25	26	Extractor Pin	.50
13	Left Grip-plate	1.50	27	Trigger Pin	.50
14	Right Grip-plate	1.50	28	Magazine Holder Pin	.50

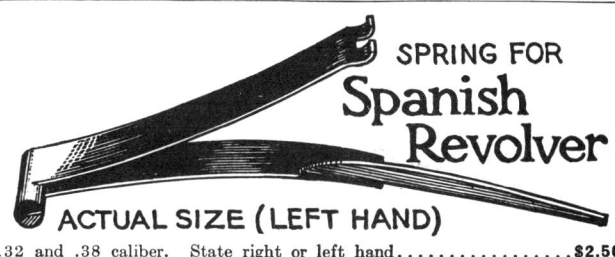

SPRING FOR Spanish Revolver

ACTUAL SIZE (LEFT HAND)

.32 and .38 caliber. State right or left hand.................$2.50

SPANISH PARTS

We carry a great number of assorted Spanish parts. In ordering, it is always necessary to send broken sample, due to the fact that Spanish parts are not always interchangeable. The magazines supplied by us require no further fitting, but the hammers and firing pins sometimes require a gunsmith. We do not supply other Spanish parts than those listed below:

Spanish Automatic Magazines $3.50
Spanish Automatic Firing Pins 2.50
Spanish Automatic Firing Pin Springs 1.00
Spanish Automatic Firing Pin Guides .... .75
Spanish Revolver Hammers 3.50
Grips, as per sample, in Ivory or Pearl, only 2.50up

GEHA BOLT ACTION 2 SHOT GUN

Stock (slightly used)	$7.50	Firing Pin	$3.50
Barrel and Receiver	7.50	Bolt Head	3.00
Stock (slightly used)	10.00	Other parts on request.	

RHEINMETALL 16 GAUGE AUTO. SHOTGUN

Fore-end	$7.50	Carrier Dog	$2.50
Stock	20.00	Breech Block	
Barrel (round only) complete (28, 30, and 32 inch)	20.00	Breech Bolt Forend	Cannot be furnished.
Friction rings (bronze or steel)	1.00	Other parts on request.	

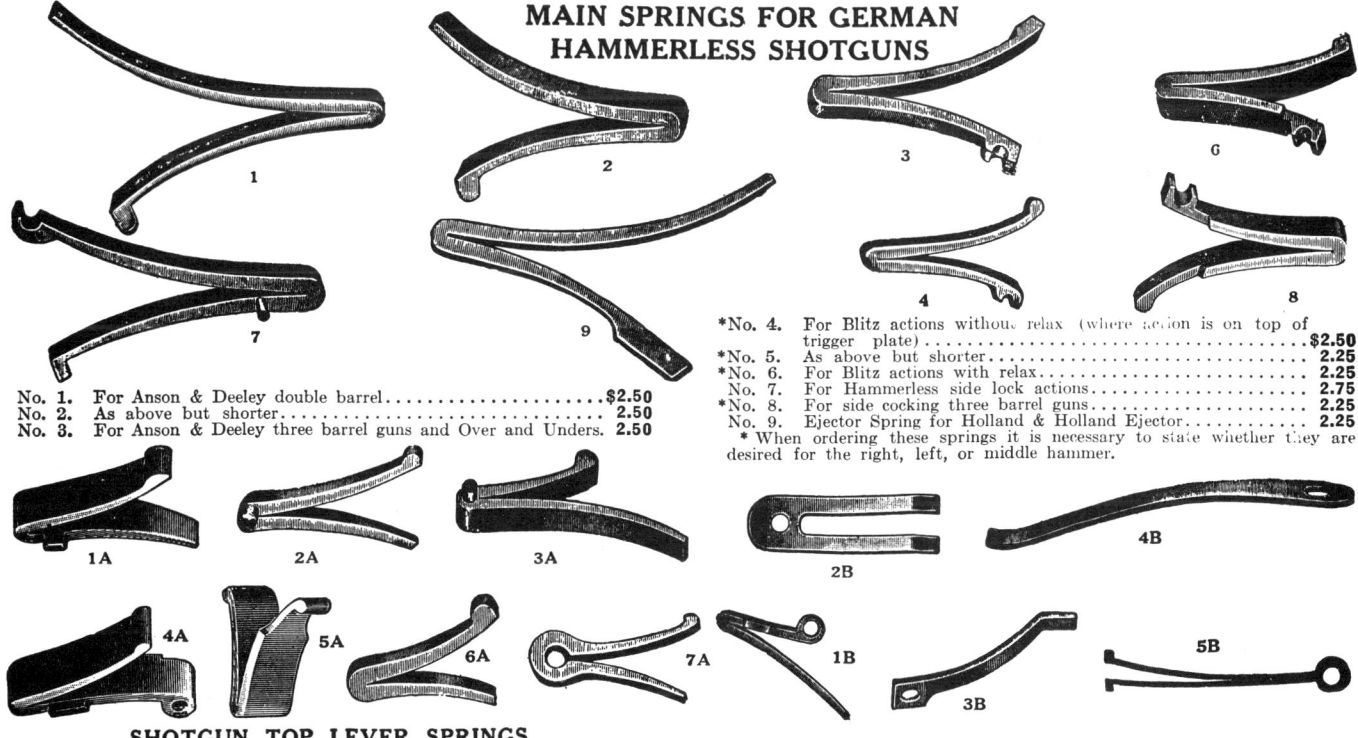

MAIN SPRINGS FOR GERMAN HAMMERLESS SHOTGUNS

No. 1. For Anson & Deeley double barrel.....................$2.50
No. 2. As above but shorter................................. 2.50
No. 3. For Anson & Deeley three barrel guns and Over and Unders. 2.50
*No. 4. For Blitz actions without relax (where action is on top of trigger plate)..$2.50
*No. 5. As above but shorter................................ 2.25
*No. 6. For Blitz actions with relax........................ 2.25
No. 7. For Hammerless side lock actions..................... 2.75
*No. 8. For side cocking three barrel guns.................. 2.25
No. 9. Ejector Spring for Holland & Holland Ejector......... 2.25

* When ordering these springs it is necessary to state whether they are desired for the right, left, or middle hammer.

SHOTGUN TOP LEVER SPRINGS

1A. With Lug for forearm for Scott Top Lever.................$1.50
2A. As above but with lug at end............................. 1.50
3A. Same as above, Belgian Model............................. 1.50
4A. Top Lever Spring with hole............................... 1.75
5A. Top Lever for three barrel guns with hammer and ROUX lock. 1.25
6A. Top Lever Spring without pin for hammer three barrel guns with Scott Top Lock.. 1.25
7A. Top Lever Spring with circular end....................... 1.75

VARIOUS SPRINGS FOR SHOTGUNS

1B. Sear Spring for Hammer locks.............................$1.75
2B. Safety Slide Spring for Hammerless shotguns.............. 1.00
3B. Switch Spring for three barrel guns...................... 1.00
4B. Patent Snap Spring for forends........................... 1.00
5B. Trigger Spring for Hammer shotguns....................... 1.00

POLICE, RIOT AND GAS EQUIPMENT

SHOULDER GAS GUNS

1. TO DISLODGE ARMED CRIMINALS AND VIOLENTLY INSANE PERSONS from Barricaded Buildings, without jeopardizing the lives of officers. (Use Shell No. 212, 214, or 216.)
2. TO PROTECT LIVES AND PROPERTY by Controlling Rioters and Mobs during Strikes and Civil Disorders. (Use Shell No. 212, 214, 216, and 218.)
3. TO CONTROL PRISONERS during Uprisings and to Prevent Jail Breaks. (Use Shell No. 212, 214, 216, and 218.)
4. TO ILLUMINATE AREAS AT NIGHT for Searching Parties when flood lights are not available. (Use Shell No. 220.)
5. TO SIGNAL DISTRESS AT SEA and also for Signal use in Military Operations. (Use Shell No. 220 or 222.)

"MILITARY TYPE" GAS MASKS

Precision Made, Strongly Constructed and Perfectly Balanced. Single Action with *Visible Hammer*, Fast Loading, Automatic Ejection. A dependable Gun. Rapid Fire 20 Shots a Minute.

MODEL "H" LONG RANGE GAS GUN

Single Action • Hammer • Rapid Fire
Standard Police Equipment

SPECIFICATIONS

Calibre: 37 m/m or 1½ inch.
Length: 27 inches.
Barrel: Blued Steel.
Stock: Walnut with Recoil Pad.
Firing Mech.: Single Action Visible Hammer.
Weight: 7 lbs.
Barrel: 10½ inches.
Grip: Semi-pistol.
Extraction: Automatic.
Price: $50.00 each.

MODEL "S" LONG RANGE GAS GUN

Double Action • Hammerless • Rapid Fire
PRICE $50.00

Model S LONG RANGE GAS GUN is chosen by officers who prefer Double Action *Hammerless* Weapons. Light in weight, Accurate, Fast Loading, Automatic Ejection. Both Model H and Model S are easily operated and require no special training for use. Either Gun should be Standard Equipment in all Modern Police Departments. Rapid Fire 20 Shots a Minute.

SPECIFICATIONS

Calibre: 37 m/m or 1½ inch.
Length: 27 inches.
Barrel: Blued Steel.
Stock: Walnut.
Firing Mech. Double Action-Hammerless.
Weight: 6½ lbs.
Barrel: 10½ inches.
Grip: Aluminum, Pistol.
Extraction: Automatic.

Model "P" TEAR GAS PISTOL
Fast Firing, Fast Loading, Fast Ejecting

"A Hand Cannon"

THE HAND CANNON has no equal for close range use. It can "GAS OUT" a 25,000 cubic foot area in Seconds. Has a range of 30 feet in still air and an extra wide Spread. Indispensable for Enforcement and Prison Problems. Thousands in use PROVE their value.

SPECIFICATIONS

Calibre: 25 m/m or 1 inch.
Length: 9½ inches.
Barrel: Steel.
Firing Mech.: Double Action, Hammerless. Positive Safety.
Ejection: Automatic.
Weight: 23 ounces.
Barrel: 4 inches.
Grip: Hard Rubber.
Price: $20.00 each.

25 m/m Tear Gas Shells—All Metal—1x4 inches—Price $30.00 dozen.

Gas Cartridge Revolver

For Detectives, Plain Clothesmen, Police, and Law Enforcement Officers

Made in 38 Cal. only. So constructed that ball cartridges cannot be used in the arm. Nickel finish only. 5 Shot.

MODEL 150 PRICE $8.95

for Protection Against
TEAR GAS, SICKENING GAS,
and
ALSO SPECIAL CANNISTERS
for Protection from DEADLY COMMERCIAL GASES

GAS MASKS have become one of the Most Important and Indispensable forms of Police, Prison and Enforcement equipment, when entering buildings into which Gas has been projected and to Protect Officers against other Gases encountered in cases of asphyxiations, attempted suicides, ammonia leaks, fires, etc. American Masks fit perfectly, are light in weight and do not tire the wearer. Equipped with Full View. NON-FOGGING, SHATTER-PROOF lenses. Canister is carried in canvas case at left hip according to U. S. Army Regulations.

SPECIFICATIONS

M 50 Protects against Tear Gas, Sickening Gas and Chemical Smoke.
M 80 Protects against Organic Vapors, Acid Gases, Ammonia and Smoke.

Price $25.00 each, complete with canister and carrying case. Extra Canisters—Price $5.00 each.

(M 80 Canisters can be furnished to fit M 50 Masks).

SOLD ONLY ON OFFICIAL ORDERS

POLICE, RIOT AND GAS AMMUNITION

Gas and Smoke HAND GRENADES

SURE ACTION TIME FUSE

FAST • SAFE
AUTOMATIC • POSITIVE
ACCURATE TIMING

THESE HAND GRENADES are non-explosive, simple in operation and easily handled. Military firing mechanism operates 2½ seconds after leaving the hand and is too fast to allow Grenade to be picked up and thrown back. American Grenades are used when it is desirable to Arm large numbers of men to cover a large Front or Area. Furnished with Four Loadings.

1. TEAR GAS   Price $90.00 Dozen.
2. TEAR AND SICKENING GAS COMBINED   Price $96.00 Dozen.
3. SICKENING GAS   Price $108.00 Dozen.
4. CHEMICAL SMOKE   Price $84.00 Dozen.

SPECIFICATIONS
Size: 2⅝ x 5 Inches
Material: All Metal
Firing Mech.: Military Automatic
Weight: 18 oz.
Timing: 2½ Seconds
Action: Non-Explosive

37 m/m AMMUNITION for all makes of 37 m/m Guns

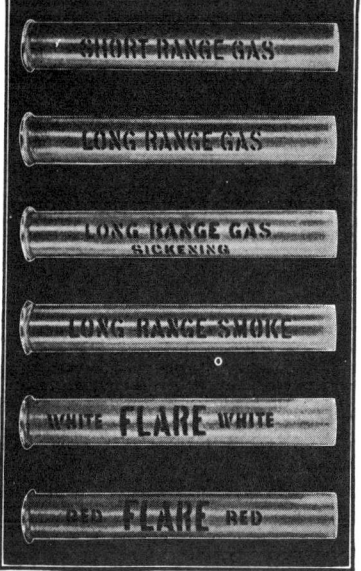

No. 212—SHORT RANGE SHELL shoots a terrific blast of Tear Gas in a "V" shape beginning right at the muzzle of the gun and reaches 50 feet *instantly*. Use for all "Close up" GAS requirements. Price $54.00 dozen.

No. 214—LONG RANGE TEAR GAS SHELL shoots a time fused projectile or TEAR GAS capsule to a range of 200 yards. Develops a high concentration of TEAR GAS for a 200 foot circle and then drifts down-wind, affecting an area of several thousand feet. Projectile penetrates glass windows and is *Instantly effective against barricaded criminals or insane persons*. Price $84.00 Dozen.

No. 216—LONG RANGE SICKENING GAS SHELL is identical to No. 214 except it is loaded with a NEW GAS which produces nausea and stomach sickness besides having the effects of TEAR GAS which are temporary blindness, violent weeping and copious tears. This is the *Most Powerful GAS Shell available* and is used in all cases requiring the most severe measures short of gun fire. Price $96.00 Dozen.

No. 218—LONG RANGE SMOKE SHELL is identical to No. 214 in action, but is loaded with *non-irritating and harmless Chemical Smoke*. This shell is used for Screening purposes to approach barricaded buildings and also to disperse women and children from mobs, before using Tear or Sickening Gas. Price $60.00 Dozen.

No. 220—ILLUMINATING PARACHUTE FLARE is shot into the air igniting a magnesium charge at 150 foot altitude which *illuminates a 600 foot circle with 30,000 candle power*. Used to locate criminals hidden in fields; to assist searching parties at night when illumination is necessary and no flood lights available. Also used for signal purposes on land and at sea. Price $54.00 Dozen.

No. 222—RED PARACHUTE FLARE is identical to No. 220, but is loaded with a Red flare *used for Signal Purposes* in many Military operations and as a Distress Signal at Sea. No. 220 and 222 are Approved by the U. S. Bureau of Navigation. Price $54.00 Dozen.

SPECIFICATIONS
Calibre: 37 m/m or 1½ inch. (Fits All Makes of 37 m/m Guns)
Length: 10 inches.
Weight: 8 Oz. to 22 Oz., depending on Load.
Seal: Air Tight.
Material: All Metal.
Primer: Non-Corrosive.

TEAR GAS CARTRIDGES
FOR ALL STANDARD SIZE GUNS—*Regardless of Make*

Standard size Tear Gas Cartridge Prices:
38 Cal. Tear Gas Cartridges for Revolver or Fountain Pen	Doz.	$4.00
45 Cal. Tear Gas Cartridges for Revolver	Doz.	4.80
405 Cal. Tear Gas Cartridges for Fountain Pens	Doz.	6.00
410 Gauge Tear Gas Shells for Fountain Pens	Doz.	9.60
20 Gauge Tear Gas Shells for Billy Clubs, Shot Guns, etc.	Doz.	12.00
16 Gauge Tear Gas Shells for Shot Guns	Doz.	13.20
12 Gauge Tear Gas Shells for Billy Clubs, Shot Guns, etc.	Doz.	16.00
25 m/m Tear Gas Shells for Riot Gas Pistols, etc.	Doz.	30.00

37 m/m Shells. See Prices in lower right hand column.

NEW—SNEEZING GAS

SNEEZING GAS is a NEW DEVELOPMENT for GASSING OUT a room or premises to PREVENT re-occupation for a period several hours to days. Causes rapid and UNCONTROLLED SNEEZING which affects a person for Several Hours, *but is harmless, SAFE, and leaves no after effects*. Furnished in following Shells:

410 Gauge for Fountain Pen or Shot Gun	Doz.	$12.00
20 Gauge for Shot Gun or Billy Club	Doz.	18.00
12 Gauge for Shot Gun or Billy Club	Doz.	24.00
25 m/m for Model P. Pistol	Doz.	40.00
37 m/m for Any Make Shoulder Gas Gun	Doz.	84.00

An Indispensable Policeman's or Guard's Companion

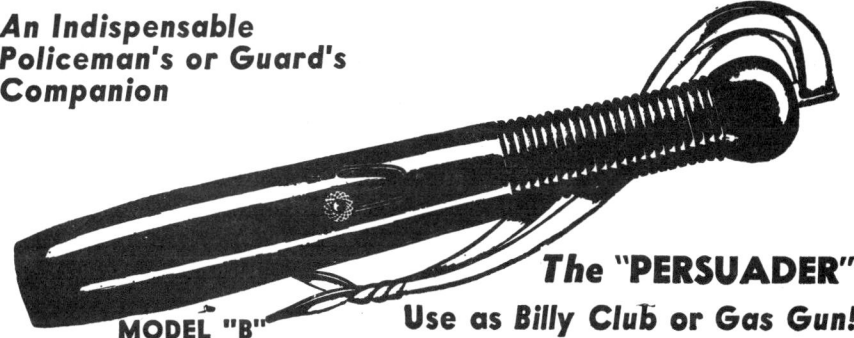

The "PERSUADER"
Use as *Billy Club* or *Gas Gun!*
MODEL "B"

The PERSUADER should be in every officer's hand when questioning suspicious persons on the street or in automobiles. It looks like an ordinary night stick, but *instantly* becomes a real defensive Weapon. When the trigger is pulled, it shoots a Terrific, Wide Spreading Blast of GAS to a range of 15 Feet. It gives the officer a "BREAK" for his life until he can draw his pistol. All persons in front of the officer and within range will be Instantly over-come, whether they number TWO or TEN.

SPECIFICATIONS:
Calibre: 12 Gauge.
Length: 11 Inches.
Finish: Permalite-Jet Black
Weight: 16 ounces.
Material: Duralumium.
Price: $20.00 each.

12 Gauge Shells—All Metal—Generates 12,000 cu. ft. GAS. Price: $16.00 Dozen.

SOLD ONLY ON OFFICIAL ORDERS

REGULATION POLICE EQUIPMENT

Regulation Sam Browne Belt
This is the standard military Sam Browne Belt, suitable for army officers, American Legion and other military organizations.
Made of best grade cowhide, mahogany or black finish. Sizes 32 to 50.
Price $6.30

Police Sam Browne Belt
Black bridle cowhide, regulation construction. Solid brass colonial type hardware, hook buckle. Four dee rings placed so that shoulder strap can be worn on either side. Quarter lined with full grain russet cowhide. Sizes 32 to 50.
Price $4.50

TOWER'S POLICE CLUBS
Cocobolo

16"	$1.15
18"	1.20
20"	1.25
22"	1.35

TOWER'S COCOBOLO BILLETTS

	With Swivel and Strap	With Strap Only
8"	$1.15	$0.90
10"	1.20	.95
12"	1.25	1.00
13"	1.35	1.10
14"	1.55	1.20

LOCUST SERVICE CLUB
Fluted

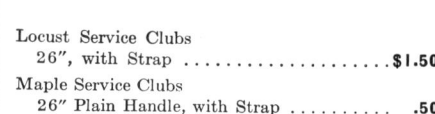

Locust Service Clubs
  26", with Strap $1.50
Maple Service Clubs
  26" Plain Handle, with Strap .... .50
  26" Fluted Handle, with Strap .... .60

POLICE BILLIES

No. 0
0—9-oz. Black Calf and Latigo, 8 plait, California latigo hand loop, select goods..$1.65
2—9-oz. Black and Russet Leather, Fancy, 6 plait, latigo hand loop............ 1.32

No. 10
10—8-oz. Brown Calf Leather, 8 plait, latigo loop, Spring Handle............$2.00
20—10-oz. Brown Calf Leather, 8 plait, latigo hand loop, Spring Handle........ 2.20

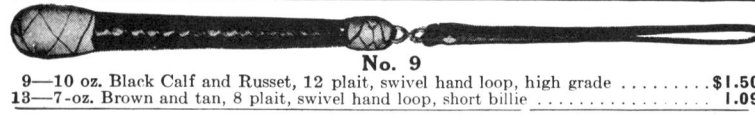
No. 9
9—10 oz. Black Calf and Russet, 12 plait, swivel hand loop, high grade $1.50
13—7-oz. Brown and tan, 8 plait, swivel hand loop, short billie 1.09

No. 8
6—6-oz. Russet Leather, hand sewed, sliding loop, sleeve Billie..............$1.13
8—8-oz. Black and Brown Leather, hand sewed and plaited, Spring Handle, Sliding loop, sleeve Billie... .98
12—8-oz. Fancy Colored Leather Parts, hand sewed, 6 plait, Sand Loaded, slide loop, Spring Handle.. 1.46
14—8-oz. Best Grade 8 plait, slide loop, hand sewed, Spring Handle, Black Calfskin. 1.78

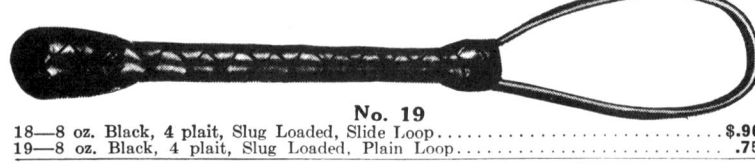
No. 19
18—8 oz. Black, 4 plait, Slug Loaded, Slide Loop........................$.90
19—8 oz. Black, 4 plait, Slug Loaded, Plain Loop......................... .75

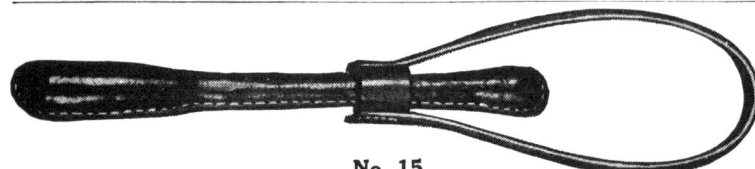
No. 15
15—12 oz. Russet Cowhide, Spring Grip, Slide Loop. A real Police Club........$1.80

Nos. 3 or 4
3—9-oz. Plain Black, shot loaded.........................$1.00
4—7-oz. Plain Russet, machine sewed, shot loaded........ .84
5—6-oz. Plain Russet, machine sewed, slug shot, shot loaded .84

No. 24
1—9-oz. Black Cowhide Leather, shot loaded, sewed loop.$1.25
24—14-oz. Black Cowhide Leather, shot loaded, spring grip, stationary loop 6.67

No. 16

No. 17
16—Metropolitan Police Club, rubber, latigo hand loop....$1.50
17—Metropolitan Police Club, rubber, latigo swivel loop... 2.00

No. 25
Made of several layers of heavy cowhide strongly cemented and stitched. 11" long, ⅜" thick. Large end loaded with lead slug. Weighs about 7 ozs. each.
Price $1.50

SPECIAL QUOTATIONS TO POLICE DEPARTMENTS

AMERICA'S GREAT GUN HOUSE

REGULATION POLICE EQUIPMENT

TOWER'S ADJUSTABLE DOUBLE LOCK HANDCUFFS

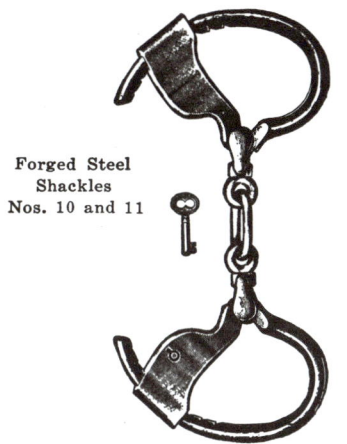

Forged Steel Shackles
Nos. 10 and 11

The Genuine Double Lock Handcuff. Made with two tumbler locks, one self-locking, the second locked with key. Tumblers cannot be picked.
No. 10—Polished $12.80
No. 11—Nickel Plated 14.00

TOWER'S PATENT DOUBLE LOCK LEG-IRONS

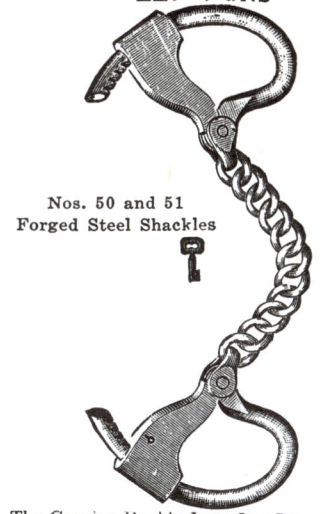

Nos. 50 and 51
Forged Steel Shackles

The Genuine Double Lock Leg-Iron. Made with two tumbler locks, one self-locking, the second locked with key. Tumblers cannot be picked. Length of chain 14".
No. 50—Polished $17.00
No. 51—Nickel Plated 18.20

TOWER'S PERFECT TWISTERS

Interlocking handles, can be used from either side. Weight 3 oz.
Price .... $.90

With the Patent Stop. Nos. 20 and 21.
The Patent Stop prevents locking by accident. To enter bow in lock depress patent stop.
No. 20—Polished, Price $13.30
No. 21—Nickel Plated, Price 14.50

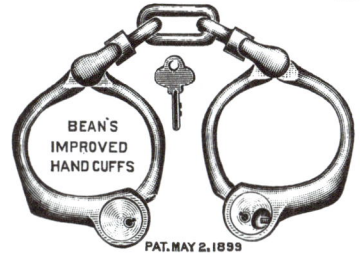

Bean's Improved Hand-Cuffs $5.85
Extra for Nickel Plating .... .50
Cuff Case, Leather 1.25

Bean's Twisters $1.00
Leather Twister holder, each ...... .25

FLASH LIGHT CARRIER

No. 6—Made of Black Strap Leather with Loop on back to wear on belt $1.20
No. 7—Plain Black Leather with Loop for Flashlight with Leather Loop for Belt .... .30

No. 5 COMBINATION CARTRIDGE and TWISTER CARRIER

5—Black Cowhide Leather. All calibers, 6 loops, snap fastener holds twisters. Popular Police Equipment $1.00

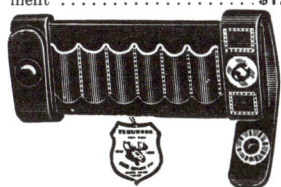

No. 3 CARTRIDGE CARRIER

"Snap-Off" Cartridge Carrier. Made of Black or Brown color leather for any size cartridges or belt.
To hold 6 Cartridges .. $1.13
To hold 12 Cartridges .. 1.50

BEAN'S IMPROVED LEG IRONS

Leg Irons $8.15
Ex. for Nickel ..... .50
Cuff Case Leather .. 1.25

H. & R. SUPER HAND-CUFFS

H. & R. Super Hand-Cuffs are of superior strength, most rigid with welded joints with special fool-proof locking, very comfortable to carry.
Price, Nickel Finish $10.00
Price, Parkerized 10.50

CARTRIDGE CARRIER

1—Made of Russet and Black Color Leather, to fit 1½ to 2½ inch belts, has three loops on back to slide belt through. Made in all calibers. 12 Loops ..... $.70

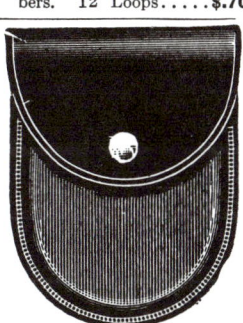

HANDCUFF CASES

1—Good Quality Brown Leather or Black, with flap and snap button fastener for Handcuffs. Belt Loop on back.
Price $1.17
3—Same as No. 1 blocked to fit Peerless Handcuffs.
Price $1.50

TELL AND HAENEL AIR PISTOLS

TELL MODEL 3

TELL MODEL 3

PRICE $15.00

The TELL Air Pistol resembles as to size, general shape and weight the known Luger military pistol.

A great advantage of the Tell Air Pistol over other models simplicity and ease of operation. The gun is cocked by tipping down the barrel, whereupon the pellet is inserted directly into the breech, the barrel closed and the gun is ready to shoot.

The distribution of weight is very favorable and assures a firm and comfortable hold. Of particular importance for the pistol shooter is the fact that the sighting line lies closely over the hand clasping the pistol.

The sighting arrangement consists of a rigidly arranged triangular front sight and a lateral rear sight which is adjustable as to height, so that corrections in the grouping of hits are easily possible without the risk of losing any of the sights.

The pistol is furnished in an attractive pasteboard box, with 100 pellets, cleaning rod and cloth for cleaning.

Finish: all parts of the Tell are made in series and are therefore interchangeable precisely rifled barrel, for .177 caliber pellets; rigid front sight; adjustable trigger pull; all outside metallic parts are blued.

SPECIFICATIONS
BORE: .177 caliber
LENGTH OF BARREL: 5¼"
LENGTH OVERALL: 10"
WEIGHT: 35 oz.
SIGHTS: Adjustable
STOCK: Checkered walnut composition with matted thumb rest
BARREL: Rifled, 8 grooves
ACCURATE RANGE: 10 yards

HAENEL MODEL 28

Price $15.00

Model 28 is one of the finest pneumatic pistols ever designed. For extraordinary POWER and ACCURACY it is without equal. Sportsmen and hunters who desire a powerful weapon for small game shooting and target practice, without using powder ammunition, find Model 28 ideal for their purposes. In Model 28 is found that rare combination of qualities which marks the ideal small bore arm . . . balance, range, accuracy, power and ease of handling. Fine selected heavy gun steel is accurately gauged and burnished a deep black. The patented Haenel air valve and chamber assure absolute compression of equal force at all times.

SPECIFICATIONS
BORE: .177 and .22 calibers
LENGTH OF BARREL: 4¼"
LENGTH OVERALL: 10"
WEIGHT: 2½ lbs.
SIGHTS: Adjustable
STOCKS: Polished walnut
BARREL: Rifled, 12 grooves
SHOOTS: Ribbed pellets and darts
POWER: Penetrates ⅜" pine at 30 feet

STOEGER'S HORNET PELLETS

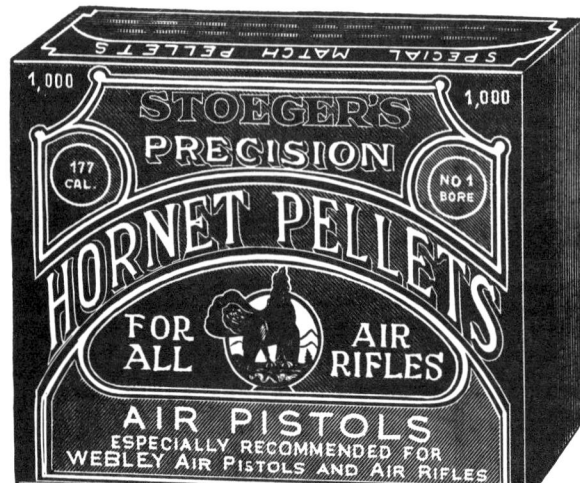

Stoeger's Hornet Pellets represent the best pellets available. They are English made, of the very finest quality pure virgin lead, perfectly shaped, pressed to correct size, and double checked for accuracy.

These pellets have been made up especially for the Haenel, Tell, Benjamin, and Webley Air Pistols, and the Webley, Stoeger, B. S. A., Benjamin, and Crosman Air Rifles. With any of these arms best results will be had through the use of Stoeger's Hornet Pellets, but these pellets may also be used in practically all other high power air guns of calibers .177 (4.25 m/m) or .22 (5.6 m/m).

CALIBER .177   **CALIBER .22**
Price per 1,000. $1.50   Price per 1,000. $2.25

As will be seen by the illustration of the pellets, they are spool-shaped, with the top rounded and closed, while the bottom is open and hollow. The head of the pellet guides it through the barrel, and the flange enters the rifling, thus giving it the proper spin necessary for accuracy and velocity. The sides of the pellets are ribbed.

Stoeger's Hornet Pellets are attractively packed in boxes of 500 in .22 caliber, and 1,000 in .177 caliber.

CAREFUL ATTENTION AND SAFE DELIVERY OF YOUR ORDER

WEBLEY AIR PISTOLS

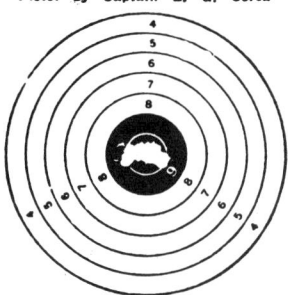

Shot Groupshot with Webley Air Pistol by Captain L. G. Corsa

THE NEW "SENIOR"
With Improved Grip and Design

You can engage in target practice right in your own home, with the Webley "Senior" Air Pistol, perfecting your aim, without smoke, dirt or expense of powder cartridges! Not a toy, and built to the high standards, both in materials and workmanship. Barrels rifled with precision.

Anyone may well be proud to own this fine arm, which is extensively used by banks, military bodies for training in revolver and pistol marksmanship. May be used out of doors and indoors.

IMPORTANT IMPROVEMENTS

1.—Adjustable Backsight, lateral and vertical regulation.
2.—The action of cocking, accomplished by means of the barrel, has been greatly facilitated by means of a patent double joint, multiplying the leverage to such an extent that any young man can easily operate it.
3.—Revolver stirrup, replacing top catch of the Mark I.
4.—Heavier barrel construction gives added strength.
5.—Increased muzzle velocity.

INTERCHANGEABLE BARRELS FOR SENIOR

Interchangeable spare barrels, permit the use of pellets of either caliber. Caliber .177 has greater distance and penetration while the .22, due to its weight has greater stopping power.

Spare Barrel, .177 or .22 caliber......................Each **$7.50**

STOEGER'S HORNET PELLETS

Cal. .177	Cal. .22
$1.50 per M.	$2.25 per M.

Every Webley "Senior" is mechanically tested for accuracy before leaving the factory. Packed in a substantial box with a sample supply of Special Pellets and cleaning rod.

Made in two calibers: .177 muzzle velocity about 400; .22 muzzle velocity about 310. Specifications, both models: Length over all 8½ inches. Length of barrel, 7 inches. Weight, 33 ounces.

No. 3002, "Senior" Webley Air Pistol, caliber .177............**$22.50**
No. 3003, "Senior" Webley Air Pistol, caliber .22.............. 22.50
Stoeger's Hornet Pellets, caliber .22....................Per M. 1.25
Stoeger's Hornet Pellets, caliber .177...................Per M. 1.75

THE NEW "MARK I"

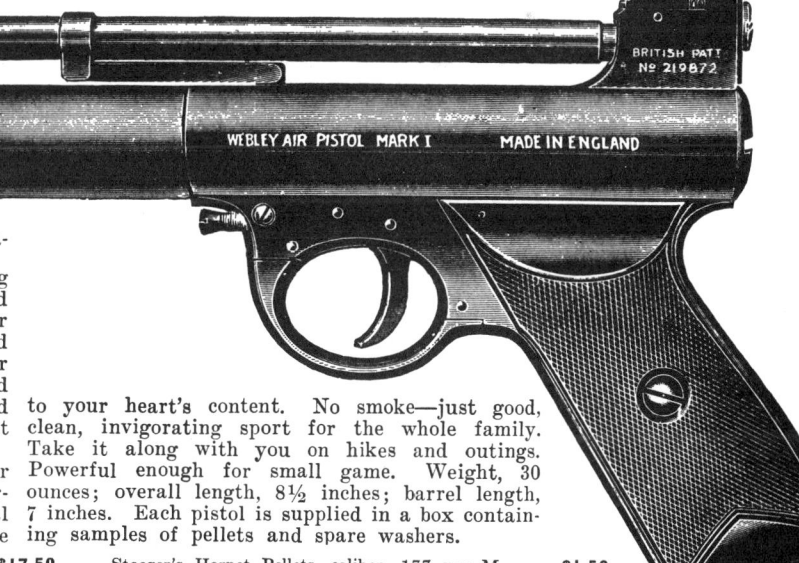

The new Mark I has been entirely redesigned and now has the same improved grip as the Senior.

The Webley Mark I is the original and standard grade air pistol produced by the factory. It has the appearance and feel of an automatic. It is the favorite practice air pistol of experts and preferred for its simplicity in handling. Manufactured throughout with the same mechanical perfection that features all the celebrated Webley & Scott firearms.

The muzzle velocity is unusually high, being about 370 foot seconds in the .177 caliber and about 280 in the .22 caliber. The larger caliber has greater stopping power due to the larger sized pellet, while the smaller caliber develops greater penetration. Barrels—are rifled, chambered and interchangeable. All barrels are carefully rifled with the same precision as in any fine target firearm.

Practice makes perfect, and the "Webley" Air Pistol keeps your shooting up to the mark. During the winter months it brings the days of real sport right into your home where you can practice to your heart's content. No smoke—just good, clean, invigorating sport for the whole family. Take it along with you on hikes and outings. Powerful enough for small game. Weight, 30 ounces; overall length, 8½ inches; barrel length, 7 inches. Each pistol is supplied in a box containing samples of pellets and spare washers.

No. 3000, Mark I, Webley Air Pistol, caliber .177......**$17.50**
No. 3001, Mark I, Webley Air Pistol caliber .22....... 17.50
Interchangeable Spare Barrels, .177 or .22 caliber, each.. 6.00
Stoeger's Hornet Pellets, caliber .177 per M......**$1.50**
Stoeger's Hornet Pellets, caliber .22 per M....... 2.25
No. 3900 Target Holder...................... 5.00

STOEGER'S HORNET DARTS
For All High Power Air Pistols and Rifles

.177 caliber per dozen....**$0.25**
.22 caliber per dozen...... .50

DART PULLER

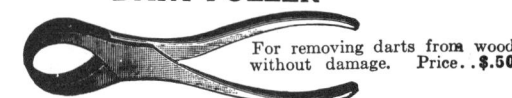

For removing darts from wood without damage. Price..**$.50**

TELL OTHERS ABOUT STOEGER'S CATALOG

DAISY AIR RIFLES AND RUBBER BAND PISTOLS

No. 25—PUMP ACTION DAISY

The fastest selling, high grade air rifle built, now further improved, and at a sensationally new low price. A 50 shot repeater, with forced feed, permitting easy firing from the shoulder. Cocks easily by simply pulling the slide toward the stock. Adjustable rear sight and hand-milled "non-slip" grooves on butt of its pistol

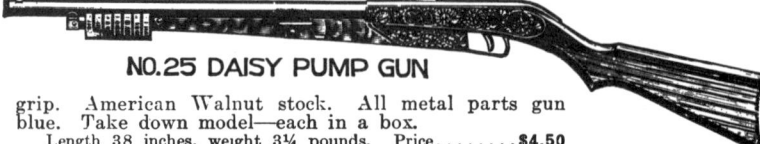

NO. 25 DAISY PUMP GUN

grip. American Walnut stock. All metal parts gun blue. Take down model—each in a box.
Length 38 inches, weight 3¼ pounds. Price........$4.50

No.107 DAISY BUCK JONES SPECIAL

No. 107—DAISY BUCK JONES SPECIAL

A gravity feed, 60 shot pump action repeater, sponsored by the boys' motion picture hero, Buck Jones. Has all the newest features. Jacket beautifully engraved with Buck Jones' name—needle type compass set in the natural finish hardwood stock beside sundial brand—safety bar prevents accidental discharge. Constructed of heavy blued gun steel with typical Daisy accuracy and care.
Length 35 inches, weight 2½ pounds. Packed 6 per shipping case, weight 20 pounds. Retail price, each..............$3.50

No. 50—GOLDEN EAGLE

Daisy's Golden Jubilee present to air rifle shooters. Positively the flashiest, most beautiful air rifle ever built. Absolutely new design, giving real streamlined appearance. ALL METAL PARTS HEAVILY COPPER PLATED, and beautifully polished; protected by heavy coat of clear lacquer. Stock is of genuine hardwood, finished a rich ebony. Superimposed on ebony stock is a golden eagle, backed by a red, white, and blue shield.

NO.50 - NEW DAISY "GOLDEN EAGLE"

It's a 1000 shot repeater, with improved telescopic type sights. Length 36 inches, weight 2¾ lbs. Packed EACH in a beautifully colored and varnished box, six per shipping case weight 22 lbs.
Price $2.75

BULLS EYE AND SHARPSHOOTER PISTOLS

It is the uncanny accuracy of this pistol that causes so many real shooters to fall for it and has made it a man's toy rather than a kid's toy, as one would expect before seeing it demonstrated.

Because of its lightness and lack of recoil, flinching (which is the direct cause of most poor shooting) is very noticeable. But the Bulls Eye tells them in a most convincing way and they are soon able to largely overcome the habit.

But above all else the Bulls Eye is a fun maker. The ordinary No. 6 chilled shot which it shoots is so light and the velocity given it by an ordinary small rubber band which propels it is so low, that there is hardly anything around the house or office that it will break except the light globes. And it takes a square center hit to do that, too. Therefore no particular precautions are necessary when one desires to do a little shooting, so you may pick it up and shoot whatever you please.

We also announce for the first time a new pistol known as the Sharpshooter. The latter is smaller than the Bulls Eye, made more rugged and is cheaper. Being shorter, it does not shoot quite so hard and is made more especially for the younger folk and for the ladies. It is also easier to operate, since it uses smaller rubber bands. The handle is too small for large hands. It is surprisingly accurate but since the sights are closer together than the Bulls Eye, it requires closer holding to make as good scores. Handle and barrel are made of one piece cold rolled or nickel steel. The latter is rust proof in any section of the country. The lower rail upon which the carrier rides is adjustable to take up the wear of the carrier so that they may be kept accurate for thousands of rounds. Trigger spring combination is of one piece spring steel.

The BULLS EYE PISTOL

We are offering the Sharpshooter in three different styles, so take your choice of them or the Bulls Eye. A lot of fun is in store and your marksmanship will be improved.

SHARPSHOOTER
Plain or Nickel Steel

Sharpshooter—Plain

The Sharpshooter. Made of cold rolled blued steel. Heavier and stronger than the Bulls Eye. Seven and one-quarter inches long. Does not shoot quite as hard as the Bulls Eye. Is surprisingly accurate.

Price with complete outfit as mentioned with with Bulls Eye $2.00
Price with tube of shot, loader and 6 rubber bands 1.60

Plain Nickel Steel Sharpshooter

Same as above, except made of rustless nickel steel.

Price with complete outfit..............$2.20
Price with shot, loader and rubber bands... 1.75

The Bulls Eye Pistol is nine inches long, and is built on the lines of a .22 automatic pistol. It is a repeater, shoots No. 6 chilled shot, the magazine holding 58 shot. It loads automatically one at a time when it is cocked. It shoots hard enough to penetrate light cardboard at 20 feet, but the light pellet does not break windows. Sights adjustable for elevation and windage.

Outfit includes full shaped hollow Celluloid birds, rubber stamp for printing targets, pistol and ammunition, packed in a very attractive box.
Each $2.50

SHARPSHOOTER
DE LUXE

Made of nickel steel with brilliant polish. Sights black. Handles made of very beautiful pearl-like resin. It is a beauty that you will have to see to appreciate. We cannot adequately describe it. The handles give it more weight and makes the grip larger so that it feels good in the hands of a man. However, it is not long enough that it can be gripped with all the fingers, but is fine for those who have adopted the modern method of shooting where pressure is exerted only between the trigger finger and the crotch of the thumb.

Price with complete outfit..............$2.75

Burred Slug **QUACKENBUSH AIR GUN SLUGS** Felted Slug

The slug with the improved burr produces sufficient friction to retain it in the barrel from sliding out, and accommodates itself without undue resistance to same. In the Felted Slug the Felt serves the same purpose as the burr; besides it prevents any air leakage, and is a little more desirable for accurate shooting.

Slugs are manufactured in the following sizes which diameters are given in fractions of an inch and in millimeters.

	Shipping weight per 1000	Price per 1000
.175-in. (4.44 m/m) Felted Slugs for No. 7 and No. 9 Air Gun, Daisy, King and others.....	1½ lbs.	$1.30
.175-in. (4.44 m/m) Burred Slugs............	1½ lbs.	1.08
.210-in. (5.33 m/m) Felted Slug for No. 1 and No. 2 Air Guns.....................	2½ lbs.	1.72
.210-in. (5.33 m/m) Burred Slugs for No. 1 and No. 2 Air Guns.....................	2¼ lbs.	1.30

BENJAMIN AIR PISTOLS AND RIFLES

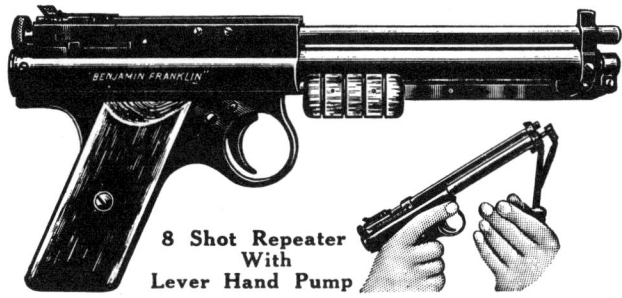
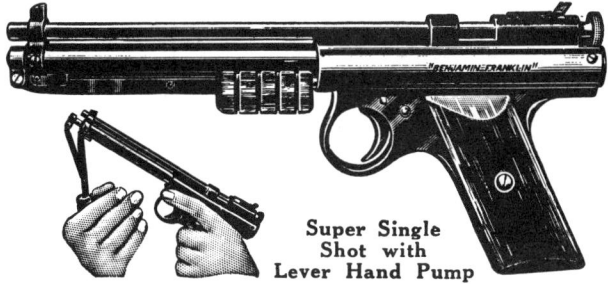

No. 150. Benjamin 8 Shot Air Pistol With Lever Hand Pump

Smooth bore—or shooting Steel Air Rifle BB Shot with Compressed Air. Magazine holds 8 shots. With a full charge of air which requires eight or ten strokes will penetrate up to ¼ inch in soft pine; will group 2 inches from rest at 10 yards. One shot advances from magazine and is placed in firing position each time the bolt is set, which also cocks the hammer. Length over all 10½ inches; shot barrel 6 inches long. Patridge type sight; distance between sights is 9 inches. Rear sight is adjustable for windage. Weight 2 pounds. Trigger pull 1½ to 3 pounds. Gun metal finish barrel and butt; genuine walnut stocks and handle.
Price $10.00

No. 110. Lever Hand Pump Super Single Shot

Smooth bore—for shooting Lead or Steel Air Rifle BB Shot with Compressed Air. Five or six strokes give ample power for ordinary use; eight or ten strokes will penetrate up to ¼ inch in soft pine; will group 2 inches from rest at 10 yards. Length over all 10½ inches; shot barrel 7½ inches long. Patridge type sights; distance between sights is 9 inches. Rear sight is adjustable for windage. Weight 1¾ pounds. Trigger pull 1½ to 3 pounds. Gun metal finish barrel and butt with genuine walnut stocks and handle.
Price $8.50

No. 112. Lever Hand Pump Super Single Shot

Rifled—for shooting caliber .22 Lead Pellets or Darts with maximum power and accuracy; will group 1 inch from rest at 10 yards.
Price $8.50

No. 117. Lever Hand Pump Super Single Shot

Rifled—for shooting caliber .177 Lead Pellets or Darts with maximum power and accuracy; will group 1 inch from rest at 10 yards.
Price $8.50

SUPER SINGLE SHOT AIR RIFLE

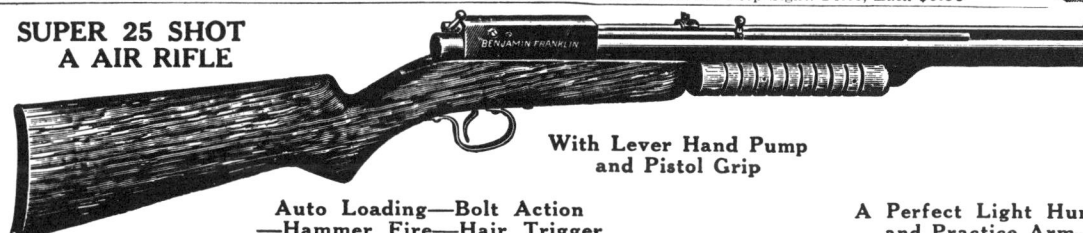

With Lever Hand Pump and Pistol Grip

Breech Loading—Bolt Action—Hammer Fire—Hair Trigger—Safety—Accurate—Economical—Reliable—Practical—Adjustable Shooting Force

—Ideal for Target Shooting Camping—Hunting—Small Game—Frogs—Etc.

No. 310. Benjamin Super Single Shot Air Rifle With Lever Hand Pump

Smooth bore—for shooting Lead or Steel Air Rifle (BB) Shot and caliber .177 Darts with Compressed Air. The air is compressed with a self contained lever hand pump quickly and easily without fatigue, and it can be used anywhere while standing erect or sitting. Four or five strokes give ample power for ordinary use; maximum shooting force is obtained with six or seven strokes which will penetrate up to ¾ inch soft pine, and will group 2 inches from rest at 15 to 20 yards. Length over all 36 inches; gun metal finish barrel is 24 inches long. Front blade sight. Rear V sight is adjustable for windage. Genuine walnut turned stock and pump handle. Fine trigger pull 2 to 3 lbs. Weight 4 pounds. Take down.
Price $7.50

No. 312. Benjamin Super Single Shot Air Rifle With Lever Hand Pump

Rifled—for shooting caliber .22 Lead Pellets which fit tight in grooves and seal themselves, thereby giving maximum power and accuracy. With six or seven strokes will penetrate ¾ inch in soft pine; will group 1 inch from rest at 15 to 20 yards.
Price $8.50
No. 317 Same as No. 312, But Caliber .77 .... $8.50

No. 273. Detachable Peep Sight

Adjustable for elevation and windage, with .040", .060" or .080" disc, for Benjamin Super Single Shot Air Rifles.
Price $1.00
Extra Discs for Peep Sight. Price, Each $0.35

SUPER 25 SHOT A AIR RIFLE

With Lever Hand Pump and Pistol Grip

Auto Loading—Bolt Action—Hammer Fire—Hair Trigger—Safety—

A Perfect Light Hunting and Practice Arm—Reserve Power for 7 or 8 Shots

No. 710. Benjamin Super 25 Shot Air Rifle With Lever Hand Pump

Smooth bore—for shooting Steel Air Rifle (BB) Shot with Compressed Air has been improved with lever action hand pump as shown. Magazine holds 25 shots. With a full charge of air which requires twenty strokes will penetrate up to ½ inch in soft pine, and will group 2 inches from rest at 15 to 20 yards. Shooting force decreases gradually due to a reduction in the air pressure, and after seven or eight shots a few additional pumps will restore the air pressure which was used or maximum shooting force can be maintained by pumping one or two strokes after each shot. Length 36 inches; barrel 24 inches. Front blade sight. Rear V sight is adjustable for windage. Walnut stock and pump handle. Fine trigger pull 2 to 3 lbs. Weight 4½ pounds. Take down.
Price $9.00

No. 277. Detachable Peep Sight

Adjustable for elevation and windage, with aperture .040", .060" or .080" disc, for Benjamin Super 25 Shot Air Rifles.
Price $1.00
Extra Discs for Peep Sight. Price, Each $0.35

Stoeger Arms Corporation, 507 Fifth Avenue, New York, N. Y.

STOEGER-HAENEL HIGH POWER AIR RIFLES

After years of experimentation with the leading high power air rifles we have succeeded in having made up especially for us by the oldest and most renowned maker our Stoeger-Haenel Air Rifle.

The Stoeger-Haenel Air Rifles are particularly noted for their excellent material, simplicity, rugged strength, finish, balance, perfect design, but most of all for their great accuracy, and consequently we offer the Stoeger-Haenel Air Rifle with the assurance that they will meet and surpass all reasonable requirements and expectations.

All Stoeger-Haenel Air Rifles except the model 2000 have finely bored rifling, the same as in any high grade target gun, and with the exception of the model 2000 they all have solid steel barrels exactly the same as on standard firearms. All Stoeger-Haenel Air Rifles are single shot. We have experimented with so-called repeating air rifles but these are never satisfactory, nor can they be because they depend upon an absolutely uniformly round pellet and because the pellets are made of soft lead many are frequently slightly irregular and cause jamming in repeating air rifles.

Furthermore, experience and testing has shown that Stoeger-Haenel Air Rifles may be fired much more rapidly than any number of so-called repeating models and even the best repeating air rifles can hardly be operated more quickly.

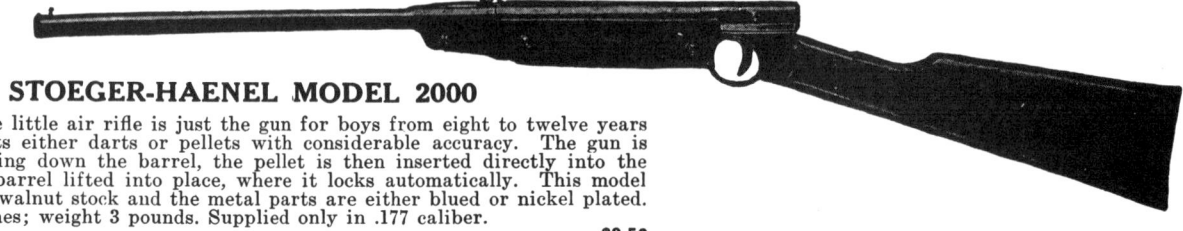

STOEGER-HAENEL MODEL 2000

This attractive little air rifle is just the gun for boys from eight to twelve years of age. It shoots either darts or pellets with considerable accuracy. The gun is cocked by breaking down the barrel, the pellet is then inserted directly into the breach and the barrel lifted into place, where it locks automatically. This model is supplied with walnut stock and the metal parts are either blued or nickel plated. Length 34½ inches; weight 3 pounds. Supplied only in .177 caliber.
Price **$8.50**

STOEGER-HAENEL MODEL 3100

This model is just the gun for growing boys. It has an adjustable rear sight, the barrel is carefully rifled and suitable for either pellets or darts and the accuracy is very good. This model has regulation walnut sporting stock and is particularly attractive. It operates in the same manner as the Model 2000. The gun weighs 3½ pounds; has an overall length of 36 inches and is supplied in caliber .177 only.
Price **$12.75**

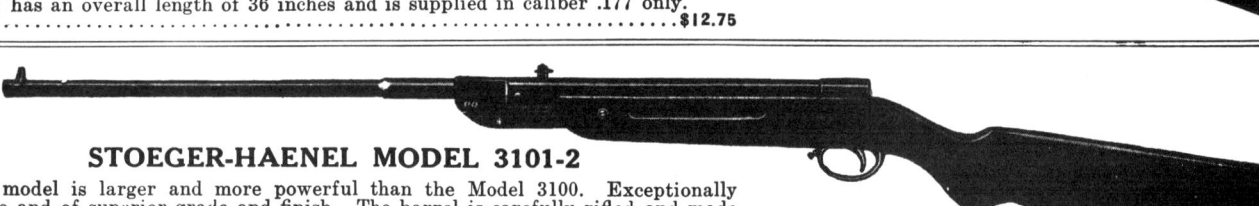

STOEGER-HAENEL MODEL 3101-2

This model is larger and more powerful than the Model 3100. Exceptionally accurate and of superior grade and finish. The barrel is carefully rifled and made of solid steel. The stock is of genuine walnut. This rifle represents by far the most popular of the Stoeger Air Rifles. Weight 4¾ pounds; length 38½ inches and is supplied in both .177 and .22 caliber.
Model 3101, caliber .177. Price **$17.50**
Model 3102, identical to 3101 but in .22 caliber. Price **17.50**

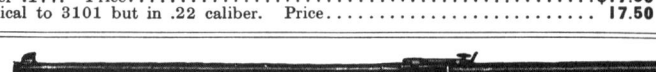

STOEGER-HAENEL MODEL 3102-3

This model is similar in construction to Model 3101 but has been built in response to the demand for a still larger and heavier air rifle suitable for small game and target work. The rear sight is of the adjustable screw type and is marked for distances of 25, 50 and 75 yards. The trigger guard is of forged steel carefully inletted into the stock. The stock itself is of genuine walnut with checkered pistol grip and steel butt plate. This gun will withstand very severe usage, and is perhaps the best value of all the Stoeger-Haenel Air Rifles. Weight 6¾ pounds; length 42½ inches; penetration in pine at 10 yards about ½ inch. Supplied in both .177 and .22 caliber.
Model 3102, caliber .177. Price **$24.50**
Model 3103 identical to 3102 but in .22 caliber. Price **24.50**

STOEGER'S HORNET PELLETS

Especially recommended for Stoeger-Haenel and Webley Air Rifles and Pistols.

Model 2000 Group

Model 3100 Group

Cal. .177
$1.50 per M.

Cal. .22
$2.25 per M.

Model 3101-2 Group

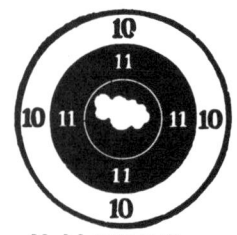
Model 3102-3 Group

FOR BEST RESULTS INSIST ON GENUINE HORNET PELLETS

STOEGER PRECISION SUPER-POWER AIR RIFLES

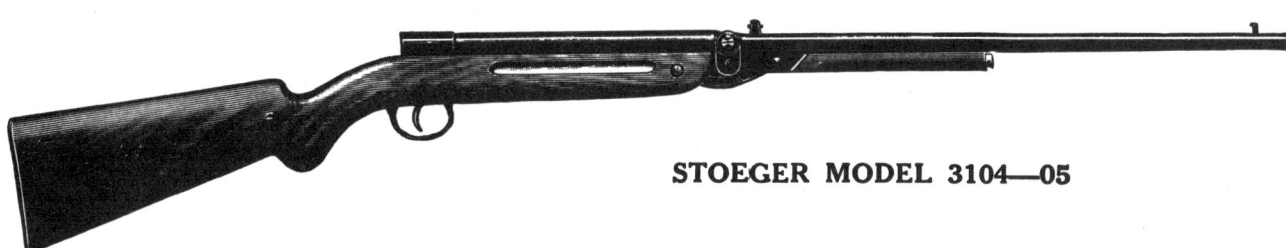

STOEGER MODEL 3104—05

Model 3104—Stoeger Precision Air Rifle, of particularly fine accuracy and penetration, fulfilling every requirement to which an air rifle may be put. In this model the barrel and cylinder are connected and cocking is effected by lowering of cocking lever which lies under the barrel. Only the very best material is used throughout in this gun, the stock is of well grained walnut; the rear sight is adjustable by means of a screw, with front ivory bead. The balance of this gun has been given especial consideration, in all, making this just the gun for the experienced shooter. Furnished with checkered pistol grip and forearm. Weight, 7 pounds; overall length, 46 inches.

Caliber .177 ....$48.00
Model 3105. Identical to 3104, but in .22 Caliber........... 48.00

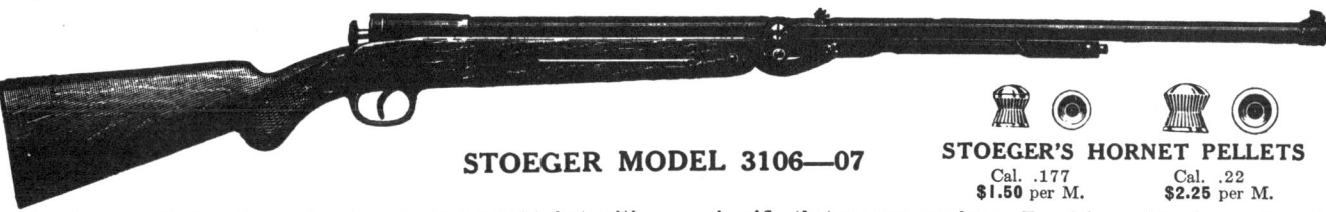

STOEGER MODEL 3106—07

STOEGER'S HORNET PELLETS
Cal. .177 — $1.50 per M.
Cal. .22 — $2.25 per M.

Model 3106—Similar in construction to Model 3104, but with special cocking bolt whereby the trigger functions independently of the main spring, and is cocked by pulling back the knurled bolt head. By this means the safety is not only increased but an exceptionally fine trigger pull may be obtained, not possible in any other model which aids greatly in obtaining the greatest degree of accuracy. This is the very finest air rifle that money can buy. Furnished with checkered pistol grip and forearm; weight, 8 pounds, 13 ounces; overall length, 48½ inches.

.22 Caliber $70.00
Model 3107. Identical to 3106 but in .177 Caliber. (This model will penetrate an inch of pine)......................... 70.00

CROSMAN PNEUMATIC .22 RIFLE
Power without Powder

Silent Powerful Economical

Price $12.45

Price $14.95

Crosman .22 Cal. Single Shot Air Rifle
(Illustrated at Left)

Crosman .22 Cal. Repeating Air Rifle
(Illustrated Below)

Similar to and identical in operation to the standard model but with magazine for twenty pellets, eliminating the necessity of inserting these singly into the breach.

The Crosman Silent Pneumatic is ideal for target or small game shooting. Its power, so great that the pells (bullets) can be driven out of sight in wood, is due to the explosive force of compressed air. The Crosman has a genuine pump and compression chamber. It is not actuated by a spring. Thus the power remains constant forever.

POWER IS ADJUSTABLE

Six to eight strokes of the forearm give maximum power for long distance target or small game shooting. A lesser number of strokes give lower power for indoor and short range work. The Crosman Rifle can be used in your living room with perfect safety—or it can be used outdoors to kill small game.

The Crosman Pneumatic has a spirally grooved or rifled barrel, with all the accuracy this word implies.

The Crosman shoots without the "crack" of the powder rifle, enabling the marksman to take a second shot at game. Recoil is zero—as a test, the butt of the gun can be placed on the bridge of the nose and fired without harm. Since there is no powder fouling or corrosive priming compounds, cleaning is never necessary and accuracy is maintained indefinitely. Ammunition cost is about 1/6 of a cent per shot. The Crosman is not classed as a firearm and no license is required for its use or possession in most states.

SPECIFICATIONS
Single Shot and Repeater

Length: 35 in.
Weight: 6 lbs. This is a man-sized gun.
Stock: Target-type oil finished walnut with semi-pistol grip.
Forearm: New "Clickless" Silent type.
Barrel: Rustless Super Bronze.
Action: Popular sliding bolt, rugged and fast.
Sights: Government-type blade front sight, rear peep adjustable for windage and elevation.
Type: Take-down.
Trigger-Pull: Light and smooth without take-up or creep.
No. of Shots: Single and 20-shot repeater models.

GUARANTEED

The Crosman Rifle is fully guaranteed for one year against defective materials and workmanship and any necessary replacement due to such defect will be made without charge.

KEEP IN PRACTICE WITH STOEGER TARGETS

Stoeger Standard

LITHOGRAPHED ON SPECIAL

The targets shown on these pages are all lithographed in accordance with N.R.A. or U.S.R.A. specifications, accepted and used by clubs and private shooters throughout the United States. Of primary importance in any target are three points: quality of paper; exact ring diameters; clear reproduction.

Stoeger targets are lithographed on the best non-glare tag board and leave clear cut holes. They are lithographed from exact drawings, in strict accordance with official N.R.A. specifi-

—No. 1— 100-YARD TELESCOPE TARGET

9 and 10 rings blacked to form aiming bull for use with telescopic sight. Ring diameters at foot of page.

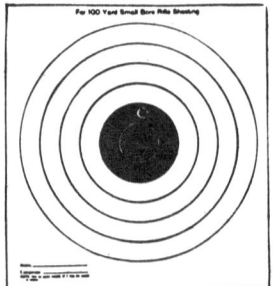

Size, about 13¾" x 13¾", shipping weight per 100 about 4 lbs.
Price per 100 (Minimum Order)........$1.20
Price per 1000....................$10.00

—No. 1B— 100-YARD PRACTICE TELESCOPE TARGET

This is a practice target consisting of five centers of target #1 using only 8, 9, and 10 rings. Rings 9 and 10 blacked to form aiming bull. Diameters at foot of page.

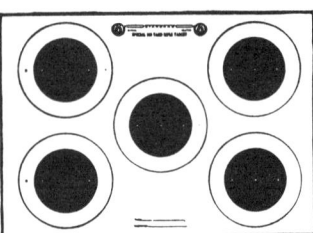

Size, about 14" x 20". Shipping weight, per 100 about 5 pounds.
Price per 100 (Minimum Order)........$1.25
Price per 1000....................$11.25

—No. 5B— 50-YARD TELESCOPE DOUBLE BULL

Target with 9, 10 rings blacked to form aiming bull. Ring dimensions at the foot of preceding page.

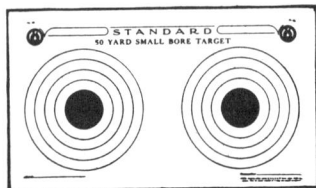

Size 8½" x 15". Shipping weight per 100, about 2¼ pounds.
Price per 100, Minimum Order.........$0.75
Price per 1000..................... 6.00

—No. 2— 200-YARD RIFLE TARGET

8, 9, and 10 rings blacked forming aiming bull. Ring diameters at foot of page.

Size, about 28" x 28", shipping weight per 100, about 13 lbs.
Price per 100 (Minimum Order)........$4.50
Price per 1000....................$37.50

No. 4A   GALLERY   No. 4B
50 FT.   TARGET   75 FT.

Indoor Gallery Practice Targets with 6, 7, 8, 9, and 10 rings blacked to form aiming bull. Ring diameters of 4B shown at foot of this page. Diameters of 4A, at foot of next page.

 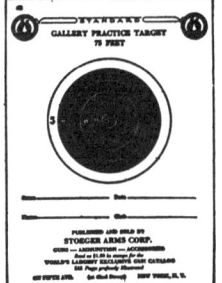

Size, about 5" x 6½", shipping weight per 100, ½ lb.
Price per 200 (Minimum Order)........$0.60
Price per 1000..................... $2.00

—No. 9— 50-YARD FIVE BULL

Same as #5 but with five bulls with 7, 8, 9, and 10. Ring diameter at foot of preceding page. With 8, 9, and 10 rings blacked to form aiming bull.

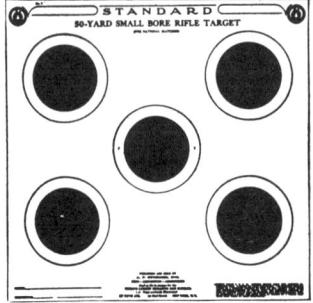

Size, about 13⅞" x 13⅞". Shipping weight per 100, about 4 pounds.
Price per 100, Minimum Order.........$1.00
Price per 1000..................... 9.00

—No. 3— 100-YARD RIFLE TARGET

Identical to #1 except that 8, 9 and 10 rings are blacked to form aiming bull. Diameters at foot of page.

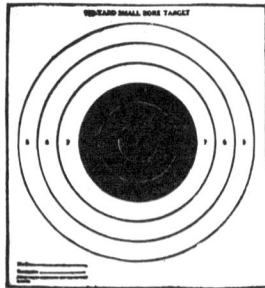

Size 13¾" x 13¾", shipping weight per 100 about 4 lbs.
Price per 100 (Minimum Order)........$1.20
Price per 1000....................$10.00

—No. 5— 50-YARD SMALL BORE TARGET

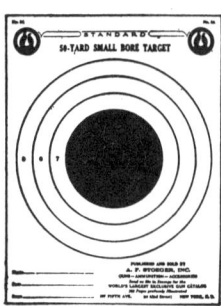

8, 9, 10 rings blacked to form aiming bull. Ring diameter at the foot of the page.

Size about 7" x 9". Shipping weight about 1 pound per 100.
Price per 100 (Minimum Order)........$0.70
Price per 1000.................... $5.00

—No. 10A— 75-FOOT FIVE BULL

Five 75' bull targets with 6, 7, 8, 9, and 10 rings blacked to form aiming bull. Two shots are fired at each bulls eye. Diameter at foot of preceding page.

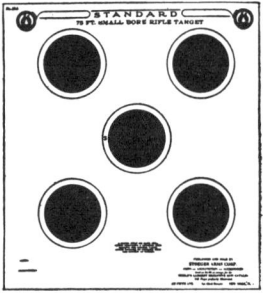

Size about 10⅜" x 12". Shipping weight per 100 about 2 pounds.
Price per 100, Minimum Order.........$0.60
Price per 1000..................... 5.00

PRACTICE MAKES PERFECT

AMERICA'S GREAT GUN HOUSE

Rifle Targets

TARGET TAG BOARD

cations and dimensions, which for the benefit of the shooter are shown in each instance.
We are constantly increasing and revising our line of targets in accordance with changes which occur from time to time in the official specifications. Paper targets are best shipped by express. Full prepayment must accompany target orders. When large quantities of targets are ordered, please order far enough in advance for targets to be shipped by freight, which is the cheapest method. All paper targets are wrapped in dustproof packages of 100.

—No. 11A—
50-FOOT FIVE BULL
Five bulls eye on card, 6, 7, 8, 9, and 10 rings blacked to form sighting bull. Two shots are fired at each bulls eye. Ring diameter at foot of page.

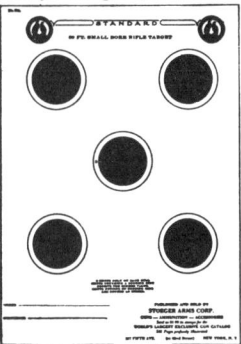

Size about 7¾" x 10½". Shipping weight per 100 about 1¼ pounds.
Price per 100, Minimum Order.........$0.60
Price per 1000......................5.00

—No. 11C—
50-FOOT TEN BULL
A new style 10 bull gallery target, same size bulls eye as the #11A. Ring diameters at the foot of the page.

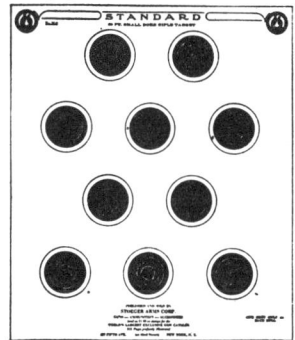

Size, about 10" x 12". Shipping weight per 100 about 2 lbs.
Price per 100, Minimum Order.........$0.60
Price per 1000......................5.00

—No. 16—
50-FOOT JUNIOR FIVE BULL
Five bulls, the same as 11A. Diameter of rings at the foot of the page.

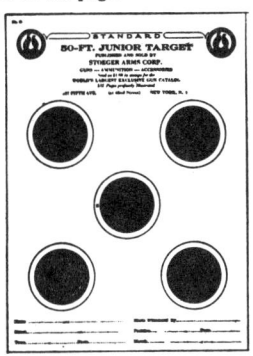

Size, about 6⅞" x 9⅛", shipping weight per 100 about 1¼ lbs.
Price per 100, Minimum Order.........$0.30
Price per 1000......................2.50

—No. 18—
50-METER INTERNATIONAL
50 Meters (164'5"). 4, 5, 6, 7, 8, 9, and 10 rings blacked to form the aiming bull. Ring diameter at the foot of page.

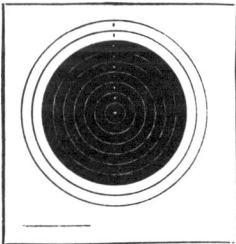

Size, about 11¼" x 13".
Shipping weight per 100 about 2¼ pounds.
Price per 100, Minimum Order.........$1.20
Price per 1000.....................10.00

—No. 19—
100-YARD INTERNATIONAL
Rings #5, 6, 7, 8, 9, and 10 blacked to form sighting bull. Ring Diameters at the foot of the page.

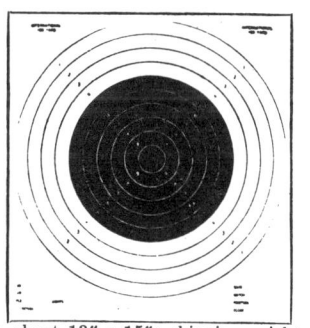

Size, about 13" x 15"; shipping weight about 3 pounds per 100.
Price per 100, Minimum Order.........$1.20
Price per 1000.....................10.00

—No. 20—
200 YARD INTERNATIONAL
Rings 5, 6, 7, 8, 9, and 10 blacked to form aiming bull. Diameters of ring at foot of the page.

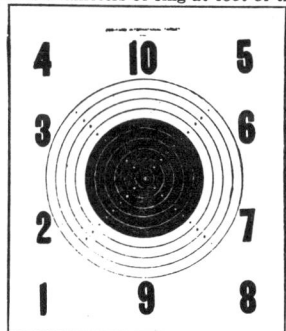

Size, about 28" x 36"; Shipping weight per 100 about 16½ pounds.
Price per 100, Minimum Order.........$4.50
Price per 1000.....................37.50

TARGETS ARE NUMBERED FOR YOUR CONVENIENCE WHEN ORDERING
PRICE PER 1,000 APPLIES TO LOTS OF NOT LESS THAN 1,000 TARGETS WHICH LIST AT $5.00 OR LESS PER 1,000.
PRICE PER 1,000 APPLIES TO LOTS OF NOT LESS THAN 500 TARGETS WHICH LIST AT $9.00 OR $10.00 PER 1,000.
PRICE PER 1,000 APPLIES TO LOTS OF NOT LESS THAN 300 TARGETS WHICH LIST AT $25.00 PER 1,000.

OFFICIAL N.R.A. DIMENSIONS

No. 1, 1B & No. 3—100-YARD	No. 2	No. 5, 5B, & 9	No. 4B, 10A
X ring............1 inch	X ring............2 inches	X ring.............39 inches	10 ring............335 inches
10 ring............2 inches	10 ring............4 inches	10 ring............89 inches	9 ring............8.35 inches
9 ring............4 inches	9 ring............8 inches	9 ring............1.89 inches	8 ring............1.335 inches
8 ring............6 inches	8 ring............12 inches	8 ring............2.89 inches	7 ring............1.835 inches
7 ring............8 inches	7 ring............16 inches	7 ring............3.89 inches	6 ring............2.335 inches
6 ring............10 inches	6 ring............20 inches	6 ring............4.89 inches	5 ring............2.835 inches
5 ring............12 inches	5 ring............24 inches	5 ring............5.89 inches	

No. 4A, 11A, 11C, 16	18, 50 METER	No. 19—100 METERS	No. 20—200 METERS
10 Ring............150"	10 Ring............787"	10 Ring............3 cm	10 Ring............6 cm
9 Ring............483"	9 Ring............1.574"	9 Ring............6 cm	9 Ring............12 cm
8 Ring............817"	8 Ring............2.361"	8 Ring............9 cm	8 Ring............18 cm
7 Ring............1.150"	7 Ring............3.148"	7 Ring............12 cm	7 Ring............24 cm
6 Ring............1.483"	6 Ring............3.936"	6 Ring............15 cm	6 Ring............30 cm
5 Ring............1.817"	2 Ring............7.084"	5 Ring............18 cm	5 Ring............36 cm
	5 Ring............4.723"	4 Ring............21 cm	
	4 Ring............5.510"	3 Ring............24 cm	
	3 Ring............6.297"		

APPROVED BY EXPERT SHOOTERS

STOEGER STANDARD PISTOL TARGETS

—No. 6—
50-YARD STANDARD AMERICAN
Used for slow fire with pistol at fifty yards: 8, 9 and 10 rings blacked to form aiming bull.

10 Ring......3.39"	7 Ring......11.00"
9 Ring......5.54"	6 Ring......14.80"
8 Ring......8.00"	5 Ring......19.68"
4 Ring......26.83"	

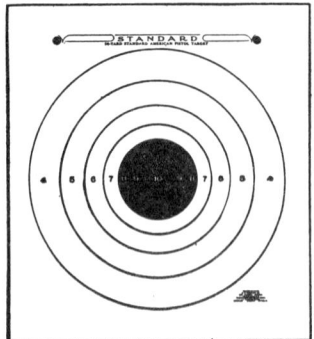

Size 28" x 28"; Shipping weight per 100 about 13 pounds.
Price per 100, Minimum Order.........$2.50
Price per 1000.....................$25.00

—No. 22—
50-FOOT STANDARD AMERICAN RAPID FIRE TARGET
Aiming bull 2.23" in diameter, used for rapid fire at 50 feet indoors.

10 Ring......1.80"	7 Ring......6.14"
9 Ring......3.06"	6 Ring......8.32"
8 Ring......4.46"	5 Ring......11.12"
4 Ring......14.66"	

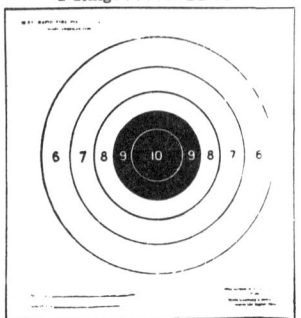

Size about 10⅜" x 12"; Shipping weight per 100 about 2 pounds.
Price per 100, Minimum Order.........$0.60
Price per 1000......................$5.00

—No. 27—
25-YARD RAPID FIRE
Used for slow, timed, and rapid fire at 25 yards. Exactly the same as No. 6 50 yard standard American, except that only the 9 and 10 rings are blacked to form aiming bull.

Size 28" x 28"; Shipping weight per 100 about 13 pounds.
Price per 100, Minimum Order........$2.50
Price per 1000....................$25.00

—No. 8—
20-YARD STANDARD AMERICAN SLOW FIRE TARGET
8, 9, and 10 rings blacked to form aiming bull.

10 Ring......1.12"	7 Ring......3.73"
9 Ring......1.88"	6 Ring......5.04"
8 Ring......2.72"	5 Ring......6.72"
4 Ring......8.84"	

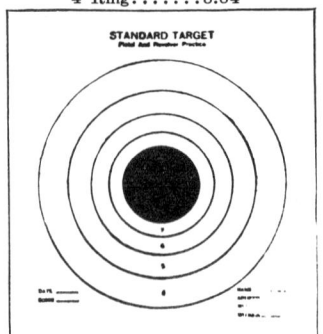

Size about 10½" x 11¾"; Shipping weight per 100 about 2 pounds, 6 oz.
Price per 100, Minimum Order.........$0.60
Price per 1000......................$5.00

—No. 23—
20-YARD STANDARD RAPID FIRE
Aiming bull 2.72" in diameter, part of 9 and all of ten blacked to form aiming bull.

10 Ring......2.24"	7 Ring......7.46"
9 Ring......3.76"	6 Ring......10.08"
8 Ring......5.44"	5 Ring......13.44"
4 Ring......17.68"	

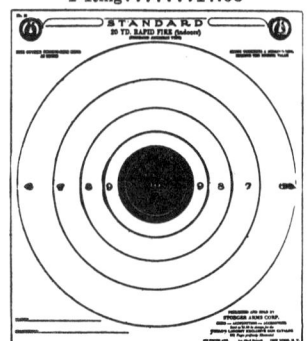

Size about 10½" x 11⅞"; Shipping weight per 100 about 2 pounds, 6 ounces.
Price per 100, Minimum Order.........$0.60
Price per 1000......................$5.00

—No. 28—
RESERVE AND NATIONAL GUARD
Bullseye and rings same as Army "L" Target, used for slow, timed, or rapid fire at 15, 25, and 50 yards. This target is used for army qualifications.

10 Ring......5.0"	6 Ring......19.0"
9 Ring......8.5"	5 Ring......22.5"
8 Ring......12.0"	4 Ring......26.0"
7 Ring......15.5"	3 Ring......46.0"

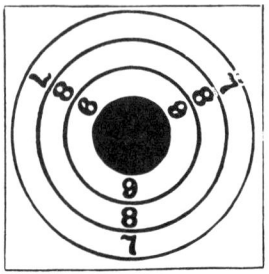

Size about 17⅜" x 20"; Shipping weight per 100, about 4¾ pounds.
Price per 100, Minimum Order.........$1.60
Price per 1000.....................$15.00

—No. 21—
50-FOOT STANDARD AMERICAN
Used for slow fire at 50', 8, 9, and 10 rings blacked to form aiming bull.

10 Ring.......90"	7 Ring......3.07"
9 Ring......1.53"	6 Ring......4.16"
8 Ring......2.23"	5 Ring......5.56"
4 Ring......7.33"	

Size about 10½" x 11¾"; Shipping weight per 100 about 2 pounds, 6 ounces.
Price per 100, Minimum Order.........$0.60
Price per 1000......................$5.00

—No. 24—
12-YARD STANDARD AMERICAN
Used for slow fire indoor and outdoor. 8, 9, and 10 rings blacked to form aiming bull.

10 Ring........½"	7 Ring......2 1/16"
9 Ring........1"	6 Ring......2 9/16"
8 Ring......1½"	5 Ring......3 5/16"
4 Ring......5 1/16"	

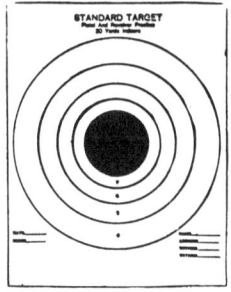

Size about 7" x 8¼"; Shipping weight per 100 about 1 pound.
Price per 100, Minimum Order.........$0.35
Price per 1000......................$3.00

—No. 37—
25-FOOT STANDARD AMERICAN TARGET
8, 9, and 10 rings blacked to form aiming bull.

10 Ring......34"	7 Ring......1.43"
9 Ring......66"	6 Ring......1.97"
8 Ring......1.01"	5 Ring......2.67"
4 Rings......3.56"	

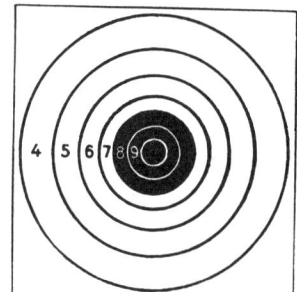

Size about 5" x 7½"; Shipping weight per 100 about ¾ pound.
Price per 200, Minimum Order.........$0.80
Price per 1000......................$3.50

TARGETS LITHOGRAPHED ON SPECIAL TAG BOARD

STOEGER'S NATURAL COLORED GAME TARGETS

The targets illustrated on this page represent a new idea in shooting. In introducing the following targets, we believe that we have fulfilled a long felt need. All Stoeger's Colored Game Targets are lithographed in full vivid natural colors and are approximately life size.

Stoeger's Colored Game Targets simulate actual hunting and field conditions and consequently are invaluable not only to the beginner but also the experienced hunter to keep in good shooting form. These targets will be of great interest and advantage to rifle and pistol clubs to relieve the dull monotony of shooting only at black bulls' eyes; they will create new enthusiasm amongst old and new members.

Most of the Stoeger Colored Game Targets represent running or flying game which will lend themselves most admirably as moving targets. Best results will be had by mounting targets on beaver-board or canvas frame, although any stiff backing will suffice. Moving targets may be easily rigged to an overhead trolley, permitting the shooter to have any desired range and speed of his favorite game target.

Colored pasters are available, which adds materially to the life and economy of these targets. Pasters are available in the following colors, black, white, buff, green, brown and gray, supplied in boxes of 500.
PRICE PER BOX..................................25c

ALL TARGETS APPROXIMATELY LIFE SIZE

No. 157—Large Running Deer (6 Parts). Size 44 x 69 inches. Running to left. Price.........$1.25
No. 306—Smaller deer running to right, one piece, size about 36" x 45". Price....................$.75

No. 100L—Standing Deer Target, facing left. Size 36 x 45 inches. Price....................$.75
No. 100R—Same, but facing right. Price....................$.75

No. 2908L—Running Elk (2 Parts), running left. Size 49½ x 71½ inches. Price....................$1.25
No. 2908R—Same, but running right. Price....$1.25

No. 145—Sitting Hawk. Size 15½ x 18½ inches. Price...$.20

LUCK TARGET
Size 6 x 10
Weight per 100..1 lb.
Price per 100...$.60
Price per 1000.$5.00

TARGET  **CENTERS**

SIZE "A" DIAMETER 4⅞"
Weight per 200, 12 oz.
Price per 200.................$.60
Price per 1000................$2.50
Especially for Target No. 28
SIZE "B" DIAMETER 5½"
Weight per 200, 1 lb.
Price per 200.................$.75
Price per 1000................$3.00
Especially for Target No. 26

No. 124—Flying Bevy of Quail (2 Parts). Size 22½ x 36 inches. Price............$.35

No. 103—Bandit Target. Life size man target, 25 x 34 inches for slow or rapid fire. In three colors, buff, black, and tan. Ideal for police and state troopers.
Price of 4.........$1.00
(Minimum Order)
Price per 100....$20.00

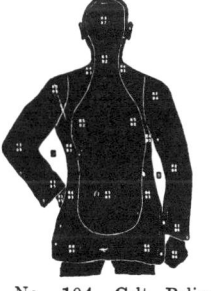

No. 104—Colt Police Silhouette Target. Target 34 x 44 inches, life size silhouette of man. This is the official target used by many police departments and state troopers.
Price for 10......$1.30
(Minimum Order)
Price per 100....$10.00

No. 159R—Duck flying to right. Size 18½ x 27 inches. Price.........$.30
No. 159L—Same but to left. Price........$.30

No. 143R—Pheasant running to right (2 Parts). Size 18½ x 35 inches. Price....$.35

No. 122L—Pheasant flying to left 2 Parts). Size 18½ x 35 inches. Price.........$.35
No. 122R—Same, but to right. Price.$.35

No. 137L—Fox running to left. Size 18½ x 49 inches..$.35
No. 137R—Same, but running to right. Price........$.35

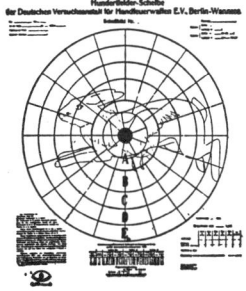

No. 102—Shotgun Pattern Size of circle 29¾ inches. Price..$.25

No. 153R—Rabbit running to right. Size 16 x 33 inches. Price.............$.30
No. 153L—Same but to left. Price........$.30

DUCK, GOOSE, OWL AND CROW DECOYS

VERI-GOOD DUCK DECOY

These decoys who move about with the slightest breeze are compact, light in weight, and can be opened or folded in a jiffy. They are perfectly colored and give a natural feathery effect made to resemble the Mallard. They are packed six drakes and six hens to the box. Shipping Weight 14 lbs.

Price per dozen $13.30
Price individually, drake or hen 1.25

FLAPPER DUCK DECOY

By simply pulling a cord from your blind this decoy flaps its wings and ripples the water around it giving unusual ability to coax shy old birds to within shooting range. Excellent for marsh, lake, pond, or river shooting. Can be opened or folded in a moment. Light weight and durable, made to resemble the drake mallard. Flapper Decoy complete.

Price $3.50

AUTO FOLDING DECOYS

These decoys, available in Mallards only, open and fold without adjustment, nothing necessary but the anchor cord. The decoy automatically expands by means of the spring when the anchor cord is unwound. Will float if punctured by stray shot. Packed six drakes and six hens per dozen complete with cords and anchors. Shipping weight about 14 lbs.

Price per dozen $12.70
Price individually, drake or hen 1.25

CANADA GOOSE DECOYS

Our profile Goose Decoys are used for field shooting, on sandbars and in shallow water. They are made of wood and fold up compactly as shown. The decoys represent full size geese in side view and may be set up with the head and neck in different positions to resemble a flock feeding. Packed in a strong fibre box. Weight about 14 lbs. per dozen.

Price per Dozen $14.50
Price per Half Dozen 7.50

FEATHERWEIGHT DECOYS

Price, Singly $1.25
Price, Full Dozen 13.50

M100—MALLARD DRAKE

Lightweight—average 8 to 9 ounces; Flatbottom—will ride upright in any weather; practically nondestructible; completely waterproofed; draws less than ¼" of water; and is constantly in motion; visibility—equal to live bird; full life size; anchor ring supplied; head, neck and bill integral with body; taxidermist eyes; body hand stitched—conformation and flat bottom guaranteed; stuffing—kapok and granulated cork.

M 100	Mallard Drake	
M 101	Mallard Hen	
S 105	Pintail or Sprig Drake	
S 106	Pintail or Sprig Hen	
B 109	Black Mallard or Black Duck	
L.S. 115	Lesser Scaup, Black Jack, or Bluebill	

FOLDING WOOD DECOYS

These fold up very compactly, light weight, easy to carry, painted in natural colors on both sides and attached to wooden floats in groups of three. Available in various species. Shipping weight per dozen, 10 lbs.

Price per dozen $7.60
Price per ½ dozen (Minimum Order) 4.00

STUFFED MECHANICAL OWL

Price $25.00

Large, perfect specimens, constructed to flap wings when cord is pulled.

COMBINATION PACKAGE

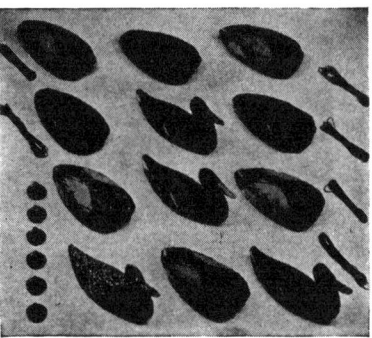

Exactly as illustrated 4 Featherweights and 8 Duck-In (headless) Decoys, complete with 6 Anchors, Anchor Cords and burlap carrying sack, ready to use. Weight of decoys only 6 pounds—Anchors, 1 pound, 6 ounces—Bag, 7 ounces. Total Weight 7 pounds, 13 ounces. Price Complete as Illustrated, Including Bag $10.00

MECHANICAL OWL

This is a life size stuffed canvas mechanical owl with three black stuffed crows. The owl is so constructed that a pull on the cord causes its wings to flap and its body to sway. Complete, as illustrated, with crow caller ... $6.65
Stuffed crows each .... .75

ALL SHIPMENTS ARE INSURED

X-RING CENTRIFUGAL BULLET TRAPS & TARGETS

X-Ring Centrifugal Bullet Traps have two exclusive safety features that are absolutely essential for the safe use of heavy calibers at short ranges. Namely a long slim funnel having a low impact angle of only 18° which practically eliminates the breaking up of the bullet at point of impact. This funnel guides the bullet in a more or less integral condition into the centrifugal trap casting where it travels "round and round" within the scroll shaped enclosure until friction on sides of the scroll created by centrifugal force absorbs its energy. It then falls by gravity into its receiver attached under the trap casting. Practically all bullet disintegration occurs within the scroll of the trap casting where a wall of solid metal is between the shooter and the bullet, preventing any possibility of dangerous back spatter.

Made of hi-carbon steel—will last indefinitely. Lighting system is scientifically designed to give proper illumination without shadows or glare. Handy spring clip holds target in position.

Recommended for .22 L. R.

This Pedestal Model is light and easy to handle and has the adjustable features. Fine for home or club ranges where distances are not too great. Has 12" funnel mouth—center adjustable 30" to 45" above floor. Weight 44 lbs. Price complete but without Lamp Bracket. **$16.50**

Handle and support pipe for converting 12" Pedestal Model into table type. Weight 2 lbs. Price.................**$1.10**

This table model is the ultimate in economy and portability—has a handle and carries like a suitcase. Ideal for home range, small clubs for use with rifle or with pistols, pistols at close range. Fine for carrying in the car to camp or country. Provisions are made for attaching one lamp bracket. Has 12" funnel mouth.

Weight 35 lbs. Price complete but without Lamp Bracket....................**$14.30**

48" Pedestal for converting 12" Table model into 12" Pedestal type.
Weight 10 lbs. Price................**$3.85**

For all pistol and revolver cartridges, also medium power rifles. 18" funnel mouth center adjusts 24" to 48" above floor.

Weight 82 lbs. Price complete but without Lamp Bracket **$30.80**
Shock Absorbing Lamp Bracket, which fits all traps, complete with spring mounted socket, 36" cord and connector. Weight 4 lbs. **3.00**

Nos. 9771 and 9772 Bird and Star Target
Made of cast iron finished in grey enamel. Each object falls out of sight when hit. Reset by means of rope attached to resetting rod. Birds measure 3½ inches.
No. 9771, 4 birds and 2 stars, weight 13½ lbs. . **$4.50**
No. 9772, 6 birds and 2 stars, weight 19 lbs. **6.50**

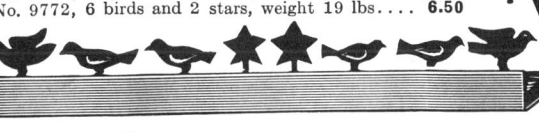

No. 9776 Rooster Target
Made of cast iron finished in black enamel, red comb and wattles, white target face. When bull's eye is hit, star appears. Reset by rope. Height 14 inches, width 11 inches. Diameter of target circle 4¼ inches. Bull's eye ½ inch. Weight each 10½ pounds.
Price **$7.50**

No. 9773 Bull's Eye Target

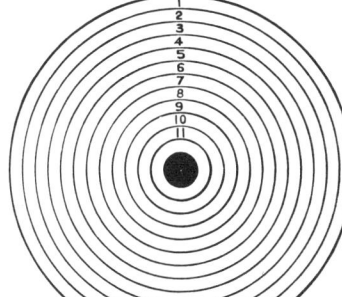

Made of cast iron finished in grey enamel. 12 inch diameter. A gong rings when bull's eye is hit. Specify size of bull's eye when ordering. Weight 14 lbs.
Price **$6.00**

No. 9744 Bull's Eye Target

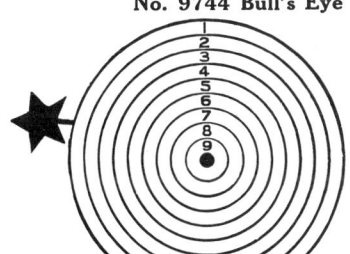

Made of cast iron finished in grey enamel. 12 inch diameter. Specify size of bull's eye when ordering. A gong rings and a star appears when bull's eye is hit. Weight 16 lbs. Price..... **$7.00**

SPINNING BIRD TARGET

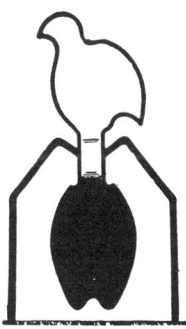

This very interesting target makes shooting a real pleasure. When hit, the birds spin and return to a vertical position. There is nothing to adjust or get out of order. A Spinning Bird Target gives good sport with all the trouble left out.

Length of target 10½ inches. Shipping weight 3 lbs.

Price **$2.00**

VAN-AU-MATIC TARGET

Breakable Disc Target

For 22 caliber cartridges only at 15 yards or more distance.

The TARGET automatically exposes in full view, one after the other, 10 breakable discs ("dusters") in highly contrasting colors.
Price
Targets **$5.00** Each

"BULL'S EYE DUSTERS" in Ten Colors

$.50 per box of 100

AMERICAN GAME CALLS

CROW CALL

Order by No. H-8

No. H-8 Shur-Lure Crow Call—all hard rubber, is the cheapest and finest call of its kind, small and plain, vest pocket size, 3½ inches in length. This call is guaranteed to stay in perfect tune if not tampered with. It is easy to operate, easy to blow and easy to imitate the crows "caw" perfectly.
Price .... $.60

MALLARD CALL

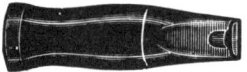

Order by No. C-3

No. C-3—the perfect Mallard Duck call. It is constructed throughout of genuine hard rubber, nicely polished, and is vestpocket size. This duck call is free from metallic sounds and is swell proof, shrink proof and weather proof. To operate, place it between the thumb and first finger of your hand closing the rest of the hand slightly to form a sound-ball or resonator and control. Place the small end to your mouth, with your lips partly covering same, and whisper the words, "TOOK TOOK TOOK."
Price $1.25

CROW CALL

Order by No. E-1

No. E-1 is made of fine polished hard rubber, only 3½ inches in length, swell proof, shrink proof, chip proof, dent proof, weather proof, and trouble free. It is easy to blow. To operate, blow into the small mouth piece tongueing the words, "TOOK TOOK TOOK." Learn to snarl through your call as the crow does when he is tormenting an owl or a hawk.
Price $1.00

HAWK CALL

Order by No. G-7

No. G-7. The perfect Hawk call made of finely polished brown hard rubber, vest pocket size, 3½ inches in length. It is easy to operate, easy to blow and easy to imitate the hawk's whistling call to perfection with. Simply blow into the small mouth piece and use your tongue to produce a sort of whistling scream, holding it between the thumb and first finger of your hand.
Price $1.00

GOOSE CALL

Order by No. A-5

No. A-5 Goose Call is hand made by experts and is so constructed so that nothing will be out of order and it will be ready for use whenever needed. It is perfect in workmanship, material and tone. The operation is simple; first blow a low note, and follow by a sharper high note of shorter duration produced by more breath pressure. This will bring out the wild goose "H-ONK, H-ONK" successfully.
Price $1.85

TURKEY CALL

Order by No. F-6

No. F-6. A two-tone turkey call made of the finest red cedar wood. It has the advantage of producing two distinct and different tone turkey "yelps." It is box type and has two lips or sides which produce a slight variation in tone, one from the other. Absolutely necessary to hunt wild turkeys as he has only one language.
Price $1.00

VARIABLE CALL

Order by No. B-4

No. B-4—an adjustable bird and game call. A convenient tone slide can be shifted in a second, giving an almost endless variety of realistic imitations to perfection. To operate, hold between the thumb and first finger of your hand and blow into the large end moving the adjustable tone slide until the desired effect is obtained—as for example, Mallard Duck, release slide from reed entirely. Crow—have slide touch reed slightly. Hawk—push slide forward to end.
Price $1.85

DUCK CALL

Order by No. D-2

No. D-2. The perfect regular duckcall will be found of effective clearness and trueness in tone eliminating the danger of the reed sticking due to its unique construction. Over 35 years of engineering skill and practical duck hunting knowledge were combined to make this exceptionally fine call. It operates the same way as No. C-3.
Price $1.00

TURKEY CALL

No. K-1. A simple and efficient type of Turkey Call, very easy to use. By pressing the lips tightly on the mouth piece and drawing in the air by suction the call of the wild turkey can be imitated easily. Mouthpiece made of cocobolo wood with horn tip.
Price .... $.85

DUCK CALL

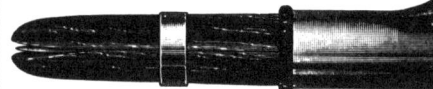

No. 760. This Duck Call is of very strong and almost indestructible construction. Made of cocobolo wood with nickel outlet. Will last indefinitely. The tune is very true and can be raised or lowered by blowing strongly or reducing the pressure.
Price .... $.60

SNIPE CALL

No. K-4. Made entirely of best quality selected horn, it represents one of the best Snipe Calls found anywhere. It blows very easily and simulates the call of the Snipe perfectly. An invaluable instrument for every lover of Snipe hunting.
Price .... $.90

CROW CALLER

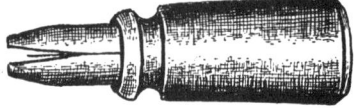

If you want a caller that is a real crow charmer give this one a trial, it can imitate the crows to perfection. It is a high quality call at a low cost and there is absolutely nothing to get out of order. It is made of the best materials, tuned and tested with utmost care; practical and inexpensive. This crow caller gives as nearly a lifelike imitation as is possible.
Price .... $.80

TRUETONE

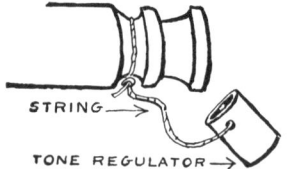

A special feature of the duck caller shown at the right is the removable tone regulator. When the caller is used without the regulator the little device hangs free, however for a louder variety of sound just slip the little device into the end of the caller, you will then have a louder properly tuned caller when you wish to use it on birds at a great distance from you $1.00

DUCK CALLER

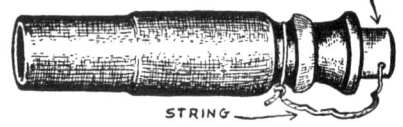

This duck caller gives as nearly a life like imitation as it is possible to devise. It is constructed to imitate the different calls of the various species of ducks and this necessitates a wide range of sound. It is made of high grade moisture proof material, easy to blow and very durable.
Price $1.00

DUCK CALL

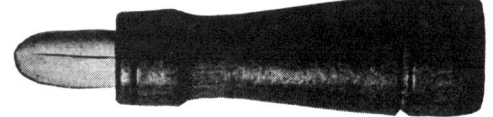

This call is made of black walnut upon which climatic changes will have no effect. It produces a natural duck call bringing ducks within shooting range. To operate, place hands around the small end to form a bell as on a horn with the larger end against the upper lip, and upper teeth and lower jaw free. Blow toot, toot, toot in repeated succession with a short pause between each breath.
Price .... $.60

CROW CALL

Made of durable black walnut. Operated by placing the mouth piece against the teeth and the hand around the end to form a bell. Blow a long blast, move the hands to vary the volume. Avoid regularity. This call produces the distress call most successfully. Never give three or four short quick calls as these are used as a warning by wise old birds who see danger.
Price .... $.60

A GOOD CALL INCREASES YOUR SPORT

ENGLISH GAME CALLS

PHEASANT

264. PHEASANT, also SCREECH OWL. Pheasant: Two strong blows—intermittently. Owl: Place finger over whistle, blow. Remove and replace finger quickly three times. Then finally remove finger, producing long wailing note.
Price .... $.90

QUAIL

281. QUAIL, short note of BLACKBIRD, also STOAT. Quail and Blackbird: Quick, sharp squeezes on rubber bulb.
Price .... $.80

GROUSE

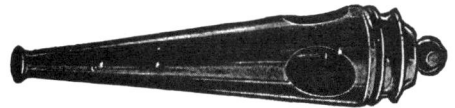

283. HEATH, MOOR OR WATER HEN AND GROUSE. Regular steady blows.
Price $1.50

OWL

266. OWL. Very short, sharp blows in quick succession.
Price .... $.90

STAG

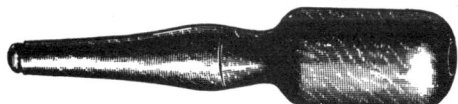

270. STAG. Hold call at end with half-clenched hand. Long blow increasing and then dying down. (Similar to a cow's "low".)
Price $1.75

HAWK

265. LAPWING, BIRD OF PREY, HAWK and BUZZARD OWL, also GULLS (Herring Gull, Common Gull, etc.). Bird of Prey, etc.: Two short blows (as "Vee-Vee"). Buzzard Owl: Several steady blows. Gulls: The familiar Gull is blown softly, producing mournful note, which rises quickly to a wail, occupying about three seconds. The other Gulls can only be imitated on hearing the actual note of the bird.
Price $1.20

RABBIT

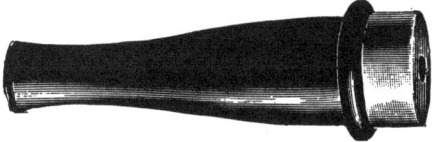

267. RABBIT. Very hard, sharp blows to produce a high pitched squeal. Close hand over end to muffle sound. With a little practice a life-like imitation of a rabbit can be obtained which acts as an excellent Fox decoy (as used extensively in Australia).
Price .... $.80

CROW

259. CROW. Long "caw" produced by steady blow, gripping flexible mouthpiece about ½ inch from end with teeth, and by holding base with half-closed hand. (Other positions will give various pitches.)
Price $1.20

WOODCOCK

254. BLACKBIRD, LARK, WILD FOWL, WOODCOCK. Short, sharp "in and out" breaths, also vary with buzzing noise in mouth at same time.
Price .... $.90

PARTRIDGE

251. PARTRIDGE. The fingers must be resined and dragged down cord as follows: Strong pull, immediately followed by a short one.
Price .... $.90

DUCK AND GOOSE

261. DUCK, TEAL and WIGEON, also GOOSE, DUCK, etc. Best results are obtained by holding the end of the call with clenched hand and opening same at the commencement of each blow. ("Kwa—Kwa—Kwa.")
GOOSE: Place finger over end of call. Blow. Remove finger for one second and replace it.
Price $1.20

SNIPE

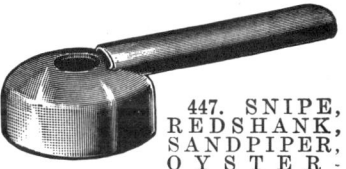

447. SNIPE, REDSHANK, SANDPIPER, OYSTERCATCHER (also Call of most of the Waders). Snipe: Short, hurried blows. Redshank: Render a series of plaintive whistling notes by placing the tongue against mouthpiece of whistle and giving five short, sharp blasts, terminating suddenly. Sandpiper: Note is similar to Redshank, only longer and more trilling interspersed by low, mournful notes. Oystercatcher: Sharp, strong note, made by removing tongue and quickly replacing it. Waders: The notes of most of the waders are similar to each other. The only way to imitate their cries is to hear the actual bird.
Price .... $.60

No. 236 DOG WHISTLE

No. 236. Dog Whistle. Made of black Acmeoid composition. Fine finish, penetrating tone; very attractive and realistic appearance. Makes an ideal gift for anyone.
Price .... $.90

SILENT DOG CALL

This whistle, which is not absolutely silent, is solely confined to use with dogs. The sound closely resembles the call of a grasshopper, highly pitched to produce high frequency notes which result in a perfect instrument for dog training at home without being a nuisance to the neighbors. It has adjustable sleeve for variety of pitch.
Price $1.50

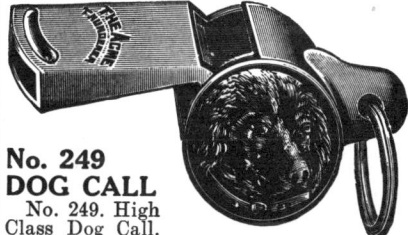

No. 249 DOG CALL
No. 249. High Class Dog Call. Rugged all-metal construction. Preferred by most fanciers. Nickel plated brass. Can be used for many other purposes. Efficient under most any conditions.
Price $1.00

RIFLE BARRELS FOR SHOTGUNS—AUXILIARIES

"SEMPER" AUXILIARY RIFLE BARRELS FOR SHOTGUNS

Above—.22 HORNET BARREL
Below—.22 L.R. BARREL

SPECIFICATIONS:
Length in .22 L.R. Cal., about 8″
Length in .22 Hornet Cal., about 12¾″
Weight in .22 L.R. Cal. (12 ga.) about 4 oz.
Weight in .22 Hornet (12 ga.) about 11 oz.

ADVANTAGES
1. High accuracy, 3/16″ groups at 50 yards
2. Repeated insertions and removals do not affect point of impact.
3. Light (120 gr.) handy, and compact (the .22 cal. may be fitted into the stock).
4. Easily and quickly fitted or removed.
5. Ejects empty case automatically in auto ejector guns and extracts in plain extractor guns.
6. May be adjusted to alter elevation and windage.
7. Low report, absence of recoil.

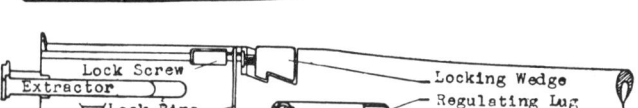

Makes possible the use as a rifle of any 12, 16, or 20 ga. shotgun even though the barrels may be entirely worn out. Suitable either for target work or for use against vermin, small game, predatory cats, birds, etc. It is also of considerable value to the skeet and trap shooter as well as the bird hunter, because it clearly shows the centre of the shot pattern, which is often rather difficult to ascertain.

Perhaps the chief advantage of the "Semper" Auxiliary barrel is the fact that because of its small size it may easily be carried in the pocket and is instantly ready for use as it may be inserted nearly as quickly as an ordinary shell. In this way the hunter has the benefits of two guns while carrying only one. In fact, by carrying both caliber barrels with him he has the advantage of three guns.

The auxiliary barrels are available in 12, 16, and 20 gauge, chambered for either the .22 Long Rifle or the .22 Hornet Cartridge. The .22 L. R. barrels are 8″ long and the stock may be fitted with a trap butt plate and hollowed out to accommodate this barrel. The auxiliary barrel has a regulating lug on either side which can be readily adjusted to give the proper head space. After the barrel has been inserted, it is locked in place by means of the lockscrew which pushes out the locking wedge. The lock screw is easily tightened or loosened by means of a combination cleaning rod and key supplied with each "Semper" Auxiliary Barrel.

The sub caliber barrel lies free in the shot barrel, just as a regular rifle barrel lies free at the muzzle and is not fastened at its muzzle, but only at the breech which is of the size of the corresponding shot shell, and it is due to this patented feature that the auxiliary barrel, in large degree, owes its accuracy.

When used on three barrel guns with automatic sight, a special sight holder to hold up the sight when the gun is adjusted to shoot the right shot barrel is available.

For accurate shooting with an ordinary double barrel shotgun a special folding leaf sight for fitting into the rib may be had, and is easily fitted by any gunsmith.

PRICES
"Semper" .22 L.R. Cal. Auxiliary Barrel for use in 12 or 16 ga. shotgun.................$15.00
"Semper" .22 L.R. Cal. Auxiliary Barrel for use in 20 ga. shotgun...................... 17.50
"Semper" .22 Cal. Hornet Auxiliary Barrel for use in 12 or 16 ga. shotgun................ 27.50
"Semper" .22 Cal. Hornet Auxiliary Barrel for use in 20 ga. shotgun...................... 30.00
Special Sight Holder for 3 barreled guns................... .75
Special folding leaf sight for standard guns................... 2.00

MARBLE'S AUXILIARY CARTRIDGES

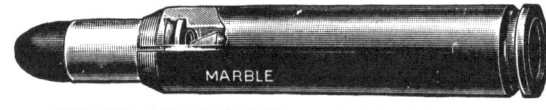

ORDER BY NUMBER—75 CENTS EACH

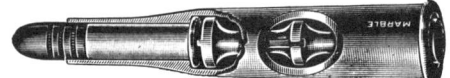

Places the pistol cartridge at the forward end of shell chamber for firing. Bullet takes rifling on being fired; does not strip and become deformed; does not lead the barrel. Gives thoroughly satisfactory results. It allows use of very cheap ammunition for small game or target shooting in a large high power rifle. The implement is simple, strong, and its use is perfectly harmless to any part of the rifle. Can be used through the magazine if desired. The States of Illinois and Michigan adopted Auxiliary Cartridges. This action was taken only after severe tests.

FURNISHED IN THE FOLLOWING SIZES

No. 150 Size .30 Rem., for use with .32 Short Colt cartridges.
No. 151 Size .30-30 for use with .32 Short Colt cartridges.
No. 152 Size .25-35 for use with .25 Colt Auto. cartridges.
No. 153 Size .303 for use with .32 S. & W. Smokeless.
No. 154 Size .303 Savage for use with .32 Colt Auto. cartridges.
No. 155 Size .30-40 for use with .32 S. & W. Smokeless.
No. 157 Size .30-40 for use with .32 Colt Automatic.
No. 158 Size .32 W. S. for use with .32 Colt Automatic.
No. 159 Size .30 Gov't. Rimless '03 and '06 for use with .32 Colt Automatic.
No. 159A. Size .30 Gov't. Rimless '06 for use with .32 Colt Automatic.
No. 161 Size .22 Savage H. P. for use with .22 L. R. Smokeless.
No. 162 Size .30 Gov't. Rimless '03 and '06 for use with .32 S. & W.

No. 163 Size .25 Rem., for use with .25 Colt Automatic.
No. 164 Size .32 Rem. for use with .32 Colt Automatic.
No. 165 Size .303 British for use with .32 S. & W.
No. 166 Size .303 British for use with .32 Colt Automatic.
No. 167 Size .35 Rem. for use with .380 Colt Automatic.
No. 168 Size .35 Win. Model '95 for use with .380 Colt Automatic.
No. 169 Size 8MM for use with .32 Colt Automatic.
No. 169A Size 8 MM for use with .32 S. & W. Automatic.
No. 170 Size .250-3000 Savage for use with .25 Colt Automatic.
No. 171 Size .250-3000 Savage for use with .25 Short Stevens R. F.
No. 172 Size .300 Savage for use with .32 Colt Automatic.
No. 173 Size 6.5 MM Mannlicher-Schoenauer, used with .25 Colt Auto.
No. 174 Size .220 Swift, for use with .22 L. R.

WINCHESTER SUPPLEMENTAL CHAMBERS
PRICE 50¢ EACH

For short range or indoor target practice it gives excellent results at minimum of expenditure for ammunition. Made for use with the .32 S. & W. cartridge with lead ball in the following rifles: 30 Gov't. Model 06; .30 caliber Win.; .30 caliber Army (Krag); .303 caliber Savage; .303 British. Made also for use with the .32 Short Colt or .32 Long Colt for .32 caliber W. S. and 32/40 rifles.
Price $0.50

SEE PAGE 8, "HOW TO ORDER"

THE TRI-PAK GUN KIT
A Practical Field Kit for All Shooters

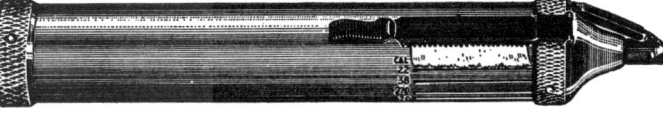

This Kit includes the following features:

Duralumin jointed cleaning rod for all calibers of rifles and pistols; also fits Tri-Pak Shotgun Cleaner. Length, 32 inches. Dowel and shoulder type joints for strength. Fits standard rifle brushes.

Multiple Cleaning Tip for all calibers. Dual bearing assures perfect swiveling in barrel.

Large angle type tool steel screw-driver with special ground bit for gun screws. Base reinforced for strength.

Replaceable roll of Gun Ribbon (special cloth) for use as patches, bandages, heavy cord, etc.

Calibrated scale covering popular calibers for measuring correct size cleaning patches as withdrawn for use.

Cutter for detaching cleaning patches, bandages, etc., as withdrawn.

Combination small screw-driver and oil applicator. Ideal for sight and set screws, etc.

Leakproof oil container constructed as integral part of Kit.

Actual Size: Length 7 in., Diameter 1 1/16 in., Weight 4½ oz. No. 100. **$2.50**

TRI-PAK SPECIAL CLEANING RODS FOR RIFLES AND PISTOLS

Made of duralumin for strength with lightness; are as soft as brass and will not mar or scratch the finest barrel. Equipped with special palm fitting bakelite handles with duralumin finger guards.

Swivels are connected to the rods in the handles. They are real radial and thrust ball bearing and withstand the severest strains. The complete rods revolve freely and the patch must always follow the rifling of the barrel.

The cleaning tips are detachable and are of a machined multiple jagged type. This gives an unusual cleaning surface and does not allow the patch to slip.

Constructed to fit standard brushes and cleaners.

Joints are accurately machined, dowel and shoulder type for sturdiness.

Heavy cloth bag furnished with all rods.

Tri-Pak rods are not only extremely attractive in appearance, but are built for practical service.

Jointed Rifle Rod..36 in.
No. 101—.22 to .27 Cal.
No. 102—.30 Cal. and up...........................$1.25
Average weight, per dozen, 4 lbs.
Including plug and slotted tips.

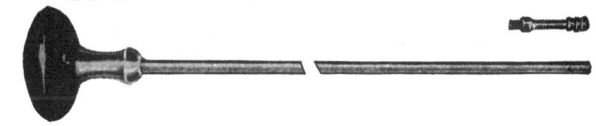

One Piece Rifle Rod....................................36 in.
No. 101-S—.22 to .27 Cal...........................$1.00
No. 102-S—.30 Cal. and up........................$1.00
Average weight, per dozen, 4 lbs.
Including plug and slotted tips.

COMBINATION PISTOL ROD

Cleans all calibers from .22 and up. Includes two interchangeable rods—one small and one large with three special jagged type cleaning tips for small, medium and large calibers.
No. 103...$1.25
Average weight, per dozen, 3 lbs.

ONE-PIECE PISTOL RODS

Same Swivel Handle construction as Combination Rod. Constructed in one piece for different calibers. One tip—removable to take standard brushes.
No. 109—.22-27 Cal. 14 in.........................$.75
No. 110—.30-32 Cal. 11½ in......................$.75
No. 111—.38-41 Cal. 10½ in......................$.75
No. 112—.45 Cal. 10½ in...........................$.75
Average weight, per dozen, 2¼ lbs.

TRI-PAK DURALUMIN SHOTGUN RODS WITH EXCLUSIVE FEATURES

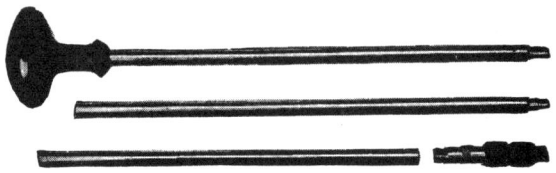

Made of solid Duralumin for strength with lightness . . . the joints are a sturdy machined shoulder type.

Has palm fitting Bakelite handle with rubber bumper to protect the fingers and barrel during cleaning process.

Equipped with exclusive cleaning tip with expandable ribbed NEOPRENE (not rubber) cloth patch or steel wool holders that actually improve with use of oil or solvent. Is adjustable to fit and tension, and is self contracting to compensate for choke in barrel. To adjust, simply screw up on rod while patch is in barrel, or turn adjustment nut before inserting rod.

"A twist of the wrist makes it form fitting."

Heavy cloth bag furnished with each rod.

No. 106—30 Inch—Services 20 to 10 Gauges...........$1.25
No. 107—32 Inch—Services 20 to 10 Gauges...........$1.25
No. 108—30 Inch—Services 410 to 20 Gauges.........$1.25
Average weight, per dozen, 6 lbs.

TRI-PAK ADJUSTABLE SHOTGUN CLEANER

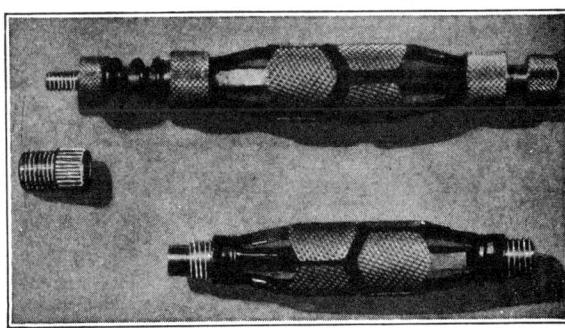

Adjustable to fit the bore perfectly in all shotguns from a 20 gauge to a 10 gauge. Special construction compels it to clean entire circumference of bore at each stroke of cleaning rod. Removes lead and fouling without scratching the bore.

Can be used on standard shotgun or rifle rods—is equipped with adapter for shotgun rods, which is removable for use on any Tri-Pak rifle rod.

Adjusts itself automatically to the various chokes through the action of the compensating coiled spring working in conjunction with the special type cleaner springs. Exerts even pressure at all times, which can be adjusted to any tension according to the amount of leading or fouling to be removed. Cleaner clips replaceable by complete new set when worn.

No. 104...$1.00
(Packed in handsome red, black and silver foil individual display box. Weight, per dozen, 18 ounces.)

No. 104-C...$ .25
(Complete assembly of six replacement clips.)

GOOD CLEANING RODS ARE ALWAYS SATISFACTORY

CLEANING RODS AND ACCESSORIES

STOEGER'S FLANNEL PATCHES FOR ALL GUNS

These Patches, made of the best material, are cut to the correct diameter suitable for the calibers indicated, and excellent results will be obtained. These Patches offer an efficient, convenient and easy method of cleaning the bore.

Stoeger's Flannel Patches are finished on both sides instead of one, as in ordinary patches, and are particularly adapted for use with Parker, Marble, Flexifold and Union Hardware Rods.

They are packed in convenient square cardboard cartons easy to open and close. Made in three sizes.

Packed 100 Per Box
No. 1 for .22 caliber-.25 caliber. Price......$0.25
No. 2 for .27 caliber-.35 caliber. Price....... .35
No. 3 for .38 caliber-.45 caliber. Price....... .40
We also supply Parker 12-gauge shotgun Patches.
Price .... .50

MARBLE'S JOINTED BRASS AND STEEL RIFLE RODS

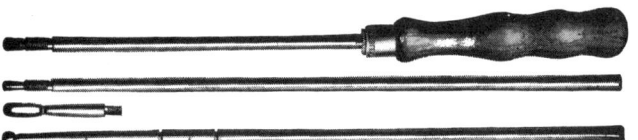

Cut below shows steel connection

Cut below shows roller bearing swivel

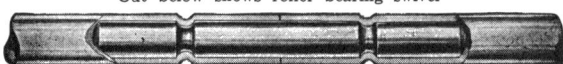

Will not "wobble," bend or break at the joint. When screwed together the rod is to all intents as solid as a one-piece rod, because the projection at end of the steel screw enters beyond the threads in the solid brass section and relieves the screw of all side strain. The end section has a steel swivel which prevents joints from unscrewing when in the barrel.

Furnished with jagged and slotted tips, bag and attachments which make rod fit any size and make of cleaner. Lengths, 30 and 36 inches.
No. 9622—Brass .22 and .25 caliber........................$1.25
No. 9628—Brass .28 caliber and up........................ 1.25
No. 9822—Steel .22 and .25 caliber........................ 1.25
No. 9828—Steel .28 caliber and up........................ 1.25

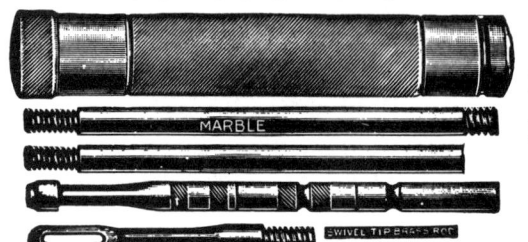

Marble's Revolver Rod

The screw capped, nickel-plated, brass handle accommodates the other parts, also any make or size of cleaner and an extra section if needed. It is ¾ by 5 inches in size. This makes a very complete, compact outfit which may be conveniently carried in the pocket. The sections are made of brass. One has a steel swivel. Will clean barrel up to 10 inches.
No. 99—State caliber.................................$1.00

MARBLE'S ONE-PIECE REVOLVER ROD

Brass rod, large and strong; large handle. The swivel is a steel roller-bearing in end of rod as shown in cut. Furnished with Jagged Tip.
No. 722—.22 and .25 caliber, .204 diameter, 7 and 11 inches....$0.50
No. 732—.32 caliber and up, .25 diameter, 7 and 9 inches.... .50

MARBLE'S RIFLE AND REVOLVER CLEANER

The sections are made of a number of discs cut from softest brass gauze. They are separated by small fiber discs and strung on a spirally-bent tempered steel wire.
Rifle Cleaner (order by number and caliber)...............Each $0.50

No. 100	.22 caliber	No. 108	.303 caliber	No. 114	.9 mm.
No. 102	.6 mm.	No. 108	.8 mm.	No. 116	.38 caliber
No. 104	.25 caliber	No. 108	.32 revolver	No. 118	.40 caliber
No. 106	.28 caliber	No. 110	.32 caliber	No. 118	.410 caliber
No. 106	.7 mm.	No. 112	.33 caliber	No. 120	.44 caliber
No. 108	.30 caliber	No. 114	.35 caliber	No. 122	.45 caliber
		No. 114	.38 revolver		

MARBLE'S FIELD CLEANER

The cleaner is the same as Marble's Rifle Cleaner. The loop can be put over some projection, the weight dropped through the barrel and held in one hand, while with the other the gun is moved back and forth. Made for all calibers, give caliber in ordering.................Price each $0.75

Brass or Steel (state which)

Made from solid brass or solid steel rod with wood handle.
The swivel is a steel roller-bearing—at the end of rod. This accurately fitted bearing withstands hard pulls and thrusts.
The wood handle projects beyond ferrule and prevents marring of muzzle.
Furnished with jagged and slotted tips and adaptor which make rod fit any size or make of cleaner.

SOLID BRASS
No. 522—.22 and .25 caliber. Lengths, 30 and 36 inch.........$1.00
No. 528—.28 caliber and up. Lengths, 30 and 36 inch........... 1.00
SOLID STEEL
No. 622—.22 and .25 caliber. Lengths, 30 and 36 inch.......... 1.00
No. 628—.28 caliber and up. Lengths, 30 and 36 inch.......... 1.00

U.H.CO. BRASS RIFLE CLEANING ROD

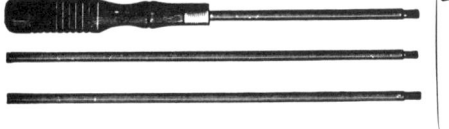

No. 141B—Brass Rod, slotted and jagged with revolving cocobolo handle and threaded tip, to take brass or bristle brushes .22 to .50 caliber. Packed one each in canvas bag for pocket, one dozen in a box. Made to take short brush.
Price, each $0.50
.22 Caliber Rod takes .22 Caliber Brush only. .25 to .33 Caliber Rod takes .25 to .33 Caliber Brushes; .35 to .50 Caliber Rod takes .35 to .50 Caliber Brushes. .22 Caliber Rod Joint 8½ inches long; .25 to .50 Caliber Rod Joint 9 inches long.

BRASS RIFLE CLEANING RODS

One Piece Rod
No. 139—Brass Rod, 32 inches long, with jagged and slotted tip, and revolving cocobolo handle, .22 and .50 caliber. Each.......$0.60

RIFLE CLEANING BRUSHES

Regularly Furnished for 141B Rod
No. 246—Bristle Brush with twisted brass core and shank, .22 to .50 caliber, each..$0.10
No. 246B—Brass Wire Brush with twisted core and shank, .22 to .50 caliber, each......$0.10
NOTE—.22 and .25 Caliber Rods and Brushes are not interchangeable with .30 to .50 Caliber

BRASS REVOLVER CLEANER

No. 400—Brass Rod, 11½ inches long, cocobolo revolving handle, slotted wiper, and No. 246B Brass Wire Brush. Especially adapted for cleaning target Revolvers, .22 to .50 caliber.
Price, each $0.50

U. S. GOVERNMENT CLEANER

Consists of a bristle brush with detachable cord and weight for dropping through barrel, and a separate slotted wiper for pulling through a dry cloth or for oiling purposes.
Brushes may be used with this cleaner.
No. 250 for all calibers, .22 to .50, each..$0.25

A NEW GUN CARRIES A FACTORY GUARANTEE

SHOTGUN CLEANING RODS AND ACCESSORIES

WOODEN SHOTGUN ROD

No. 95—Birch-wood, brass trimmings and implements; 10 to 28 and .410 gauge .... $.50
No. 121—Cocobolo wood, nickel trimmings and four implements; 10 to 28 gauge... $2.00

SHOTGUN ROD IMPLEMENTS

No. 232 Flannel Wiper

No. 212 Wire Brush

No. 232E Wiper

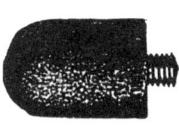
No. 202 Wool Swab

No. 202E—Red Wool Swab, 10 to 28 gauge, each............$ .10
No. 202E—44, 410 (12 M-M) and 32 gauge (14 M-M), each... .10
No. 212E—Steel Wire Brush, Short Shank, 10 to 28 gauge, each.. .10
No. 212E—44, 410 (12 M-M) and 32 gauge (14 M-M), each... .10
No. 232E—Wiper, 10 to 28 gauge, each...................... .15
No. 232E—44, 410 (12 M-M) and 32 gauge (14 M-M), each.... .15
No. 202—White Wool Swab, Brass Shank; 8 to 28 gauge, each... .15
No. 212—Wire Brush, Long Shank; 8 to 28 gauge, each........ .13
No. 232—Flannel Wipers, Double Slotted Brass; 8 to 28 gauge. Each .... .15

BRISTLE AND BRASS SHOTGUN BRUSHES

Adaptable to all Shotgun Cleaning Rods and Field Cleaners. These brushes are especially designed to remove rust, lead, caking, etc., and will not injure the finest shotgun barrel.

No. 248 Bristle Brush, with twisted steel core, brass shank and tip, 8 to 28 gauge..$.65

No. 248B Brass Wire Brush with twisted steel core, brass shank and tip, 8 to 28 gauge and 410 gauge...................................$.65

TOMLINSON SHOTGUN CLEANER

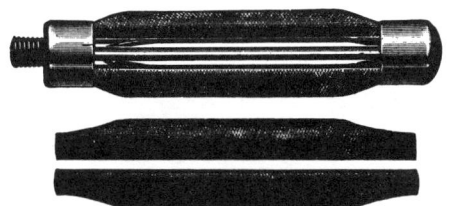

Guaranteed to remove all lead, rust, spots and foreign matter from breach to muzzle. 8 to 20 gauge and 410 gauge, each........$.40
Extra Brass Wire Sides, all gauges, per pair................. .20

ALUMINUM ALLOY SHOTGUN ROD

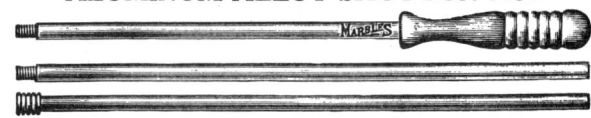

Made of solid, light metal—⅜ inch diameter—three sections. Light as wood and stronger. Joints heavily threaded. Knob holds rag for cleaning and oiling 10 to 20 gauge guns. Knob is threaded to take all standard makes of cleaners. Wooden handle that fits the hand. In cloth bag.
No. 400—10 to 20 gauge. Price....................$1.00
No. 410—.410 and 28 gauge, 5/16 inch diameter. Price....... 1.00

BRASS SHOTGUN ROD

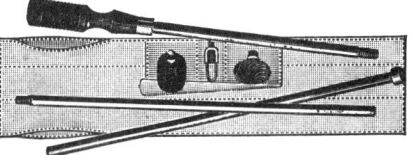
No. 9B

This set consists of a canvas partitioned case three Jointed Cleaning Rod, made of brass tubing, fitted with cocobolo handle. Eureka Implement composed of:
No. 232E Wiper
No. 202E Red Wool swab
No. 212E Steel Wire Brush
No. 9B Rods, 10 to 28 and 410 gauge..................Each $2.00

SHOTGUN CLEANER

Made to Fit All Standard Rods

The sections are made of a number of discs cut from softest brass gauge. They are separated by fiber discs and strung on a spirally-bent spring-tempered steel wire.
No. 136—10 gauge.........$.75 No. 139—28 gauge.........$.75
No. 136—12 gauge......... .75 No. 118—36 gauge (.410 or 12
No. 137—16 gauge......... .75   m/m Caliber) .... .50
No. 138—20 gauge......... .75

SHOTGUN PULL-THRU

The cleaner is made the same as the "Shotgun Cleaner." The loop can be put over any projection, the weight dropped through gun and held in one hand, while with the other the gun is moved back and forth. This cleaner can be attached to any shotgun rod.
No. 310—10 gauge........$1.00 No. 320—20 gauge........$1.00
No. 312—12 gauge........ 1.00 No. 328—28 gauge........ 1.00
No. 316—16 gauge........ 1.00 No. 119—36 gauge (410 or 12
                                 m/m) .... .75

ANTI-RUST ROPES FOR ALL GUNS

For Shotguns, Rifles and Revolvers

When saturated with oil these "ropes" exclude all air and moisture and make it impossible for the barrels to rust or become pitted. State length of barrel.
No. 140—For 10 Gauge Shotguns.........................$.60
No. 141—For 12 Gauge Shotguns.......................... .60
No. 142—For 16 Gauge Shotguns.......................... .60
No. 143—For 20 Gauge Shotguns.......................... .60
No. 146—For 28 Gauge Shotguns.......................... .60
No. 144—For Rifles (state caliber).......................... .60
No. 145—For Revolvers (state caliber).......................... .30

BELDING & MULL STAINLESS STEEL CLEANING RODS

BELDING & MULL CLEANING RODS are manufactured of Stainless Steel. They will not rust or become corroded. They have a highly polished, close grained surface. They will withstand the chemical action of all proper cleaning solutions, including ammonia preparations. They are straight and strong and will last indefinitely. They are furnished in two sizes—.203" for 25 and smaller calibers and .250" for 30 and larger calibers, with a set of Tips consisting of the Mull Tip, Brass Brush and Adaptor. There is also available as extra equipment, a Double Slotted Patch Tip and a Blank or Push Tip. Most shooters prefer the Mull Tip and this is furnished as standard equipment, but for those who prefer, the Double Slotted Tip may be had in place of it. When ordering, always state the caliber desired.

Type A Rod. This is a one piece Rod, 36" in length, designed primarily for home use. Every shooter should own a one piece Cleaning Rod. Complete with a set of Tips as described above. Shipping weight, 1 pound, 14 ounces.
Price 22 to 25 caliber................$2.25
30 caliber and larger............ 2.35

Type A-2 Rod is a two piece jointed Rod, 36" in length. It is more easily packed when traveling than the Type A. Complete with a set of Tips as described above, all in a convenient leatherette carrying case. Shipping Weight, 1 pound.
Price 22 to 25 caliber................$2.40
30 caliber and larger............ 2.50

Type B Rod is a three piece jointed Cleaning Rod consisting of two 12" and one 6" section. Complete with a set of Tips as described above, all in a convenient leatherette carrying case. Shipping Weight, 1 pound.
Price 22 to 25 caliber................$2.65
30 caliber and larger............ 2.75

Type C Rod is a six piece jointed Cleaning Rod consisting of six 6" sections and a small ⅜" Handle. It is designed for lightness and portability

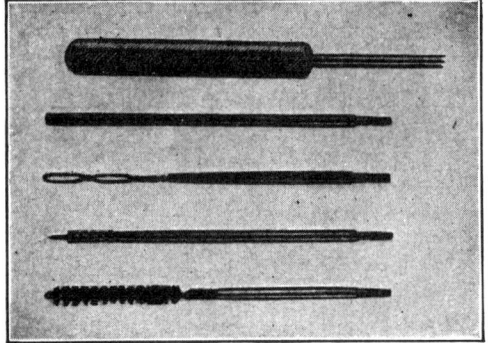

TYPE A CLEANING ROD

and can easily be carried in the pocket. Complete with a set of Tips as described above, all in a convenient leatherette carrying case. Shipping Weight, 1 pound.
Price 22 to 25 caliber................$2.90
30 caliber and larger............ 3.00

REVOLVER and PISTOL RODS. The Pistol or Revolver Rod consists of a small Type C Handle, 6" section and a set of Tips as described under Rifle Rods, all packed in a convenient zipper leatherette case. Shipping Weight, 12 ounces.
Price 22 to 25 caliber................$1.50
30 caliber and larger............ 1.65

B & M STAINLESS STEEL CLEANING RODS may be adapted to larger calibers than the one for which they were originally purchased by obtaining an Adaptor and extra Tips of the caliber desired. Adaptors may also be had for Parker, Marble and other popular makes of brushes. Prices of the component parts of B & M Cleaning Rods are as follows: Mull Tips, 50¢; Adaptors, 40¢; Brass Brushes, 10¢; Double Slotted Tips, 50¢ and extra 6" Sections, Blank or Push Tips, 25¢; 35¢. Shipping Weight of each of the above parts, 8 ounces.

HIGH GRADE ENGLISH CLEANING PREPARATIONS

B. S. A. CUNIRID

B. S. A. Cunirid is one of the B. S. A. scientific cleaners for the removal of firearm barrel fouling without abrading the steel. Cunirid should be applied to a clean patch with a slight twist motion, and run through the bore before any other cleaning. Cunirid will remove all solid fouling metallic and otherwise. After using Cunirid the barrel should be washed out with a first class good oil such as "Stoegerol" and finally if the gun is to be out of use for a considerable time B. S. A. Saftipaste shown elsewhere in this catalogue may be used with perfect results. Cunirid enjoys a well deserved world-wide reputation, and will be found satisfactory for all types of guns.
Price 3 oz. tube.........$0.75   Price per 10 oz. can..........$2.00

"MOTTY" RIFLE PASTE

This famous English Preparation is especially prepared for the removal of metallic fouling from firearms. It is guaranteed not to injure the barrel nor to contain emery. It is applied to a flannelet patch, preferably in connection with the Parker Trueform Jag. The paste is applied and the barrel rubbed until the nickel fouling has been removed. Also of use as a barrel preservative after firing, and for this purpose the barrel should be moistened from end to end with the paste, rubbed clean, and wiped out with "Stoegerol."
Price per ounce jar...75c

B. S. A. BORE POLISHING PASTE

B. S. A. Bore Polishing Paste is a scientific preparation for polishing the bores of barrels of all kinds of firearms. It should be used only after the bore has been freed from metallic fouling, either with "Motty" paste or Cunirid. Bores polished with B. S. A. paste will not pick up metallic fouling from bullet or shot as a roughened surface will invariably do. Applied either on a flannelet patch or on a buff barrel polisher. Of great value to those insisting on a bright spotless bore. Price per tube....$1.00

PARKER-HALE SHOTGUN CLEANING ACCESSORIES

The many owners of fine shotguns in the U.S.A. have always found it difficult if not impossible to obtain implements of first quality to safely maintain their guns in original condition.

The genuine Parker-Hale shotgun cleaning accessories are of such positively outstanding quality as to merit the patronage of those satisfied only with the best.

PARKER-HALE SHOTGUN CLEANING KITS

(Illustrated at left)

This Cleaning and Polishing Outfit consists of Rod, Jag, double twist phosphor bronze brush and bristle brush. Buff bore Polisher, Flannel patches, 3-oz. tin Young's .303 Cleaner equipped with "Valvespout," a 4-oz. Valvespout container of aqueous solvent. Motty Paste for polishing the bores. Maxwax for polishing the stocks, Clenveet Oiled Cloth for exterior wiping over. Selvyt polishing cloth for woodwork. All gauges. Price..$12.50

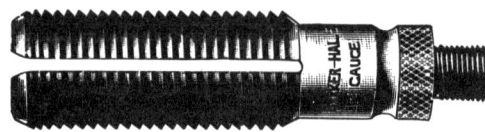

FLEXIBLE BRASS SHOTGUN JAG
Specially designed, the patch is slipped into the slot of the jag and wrapped around it. The implement being flexible causes the patch to press evenly on the bore thereby squeezing the oil into the pores of the steel. The slot allows the cleaner to be compressed by the choke. All gauges.
Price ....$.75

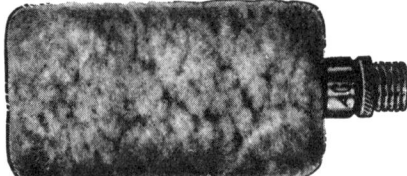

WOOL MOPS
Wool Mops of fine quality. Carefully made of best materials and of full size. Available in all gauges.
Price ....$.50

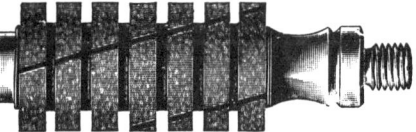

LEATHER SHOTGUN POLISHER
Built up of suitable buff leather discs that will absorb polishing materials such as Parker's Motty Paste or B.S.A. Cunirid that are necessary to restore a high polish to barrels which have been accidentally neglected. For 12 gauge only.
Price $1.50

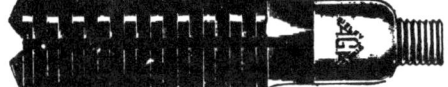

FLEXIBLE HORN SHOTGUN JAG
This is undoubtedly the nicest and best designed cleaning implement ever offered to shot gun users. The implement can be used with perfect safety in the most expensive shotgun because its metallic shank is well under the diameter of the jag even when uncovered by the flannel patch. All gauges.
Price $1.00

"DOUBLE TWIST" BRUSHES
An improved spiral brush for Shotguns combining quality and good service. Note the heavy mass of bristle scrubbing surface which assures not only thorough cleaning but also extra long wear. Available in all gauges.
Price ....$.75

WIRE SHOTGUN BRUSHES
Made of fine Brass Wire and ground perfectly circular to give a large wearing surface. Especially imported to fulfill the demand for a really first class wire brush. Available in all gauges.
Price $2.00

A GOOD GUN DESERVES A GOOD ROD

PARKER HALE CLEANING RODS AND ACCESSORIES

Parker's Celluloid Covered Cleaning Rods are world renowned for durability and service. The core is of hardened and tempered steel which does not buckle, and the celluloid is substantially laid on. The celluloid coating prevents rust and oxidation, and being soft and smooth cannot wear away the rifling. They stand a great amount of hard wear, do not absorb grease nor grit, and always retain a new clean appearance. Many of these rods made upward of 20 years ago are still in use.

The jags are round and grip the patch or gun tow perfectly. Each rod is supplied with one Diamond Trueform jag.

HARD BRISTLE BRUSHES FOR RIFLES

Best Bristle Brush with heavy crescent shaped stem.
For .22 Caliber Rifle, Price **$.40.** For .30 Caliber Rifle, Price **$.50.**

"DREADNAUGHT" EXTRA HARD BRISTLE BRUSH FOR RIFLES

The stem consists of two half round wires, into which a large body of bristles is twisted and then ground down to just over the size of the bore. A barrel brushed with a "Dreadnaught" is well scoured.
For .22 Caliber Rifle, Price **$.60.** For .30 Caliber Rifle, Price **$.80.**

PISTOL & REVOLVER BRONZE OR BRISTLE BRUSHES

Made of thin Phosphor Bronze Wire or best quality bristle. Will not harm the barrel. Cleans perfectly. When ordering state whether bronze or bristle is desired.
For .22 Caliber Revolver, Price **$.40** For .32 Caliber Revolver, Price **$.60**
For .38 Caliber Revolver, Price **.50** For .45 Caliber Revolver, Price **.60**

STRAIGHT WIRE BRUSH FOR RIFLES

If a barrel has been neglected, but not to a serious extent, it is possible to remove the hard fouling by means of a full bodied wire brush. Supplied in expanding tube covers and made of either iron wire or bronze.
For .22 Caliber Rifle, Price **$.55** For .30 Caliber Rifle, Price **$.60**

"DREADNAUGHT" DROOPED WIRE BRUSH FOR RIFLES

A heavily built brush for Armourer's and Gunsmith's use on barrels that have been neglected by the users. It will move hard fouling and rust with ease. Made of mild steel cleaning wire, or of bronze, supplied in tubular case.
For .22 Caliber Rifle, Price **$.70** For .30 Caliber Rifle, Price **$.90**

CLEANING ROD STOP

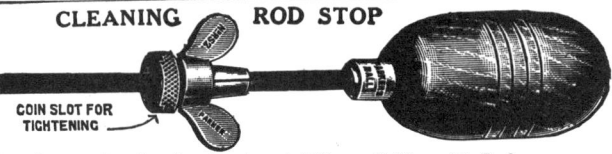

A real necessity for cleaning target Rifles. Caliber .22 Rod, Price .... **$.75**

STOEGER'S PARKER ADAPTORS

By means of these adaptors the Parker Brushes and Jags may be used on both Marbles and Union Hardware rods. Made in two sizes, "A" for use on .22 caliber rods with Parker .22 caliber brushes; "B" for use in larger caliber rods with larger caliber Parker brushes.
Size "A" .... **$.35**   Size "B" .... **$.45**

.22 CALIBER RIFLE ROD

.22 Caliber One Piece Rifle Rod Length 34½ inches with jag.
Price **$2.50**

.30 CALIBER RIFLE ROD

.30 Caliber One Piece Rifle Rod Length 34 inches with jag.
Price **$3.75**

DIAMOND TRUEFORM JAG FOR RIFLES

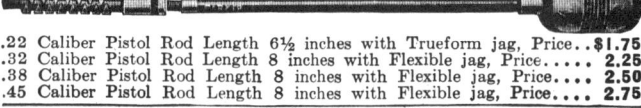

For cleaning rifles that have to be wiped out from the muzzle end it is far safer than the plug and disc system, because the flannelette or tow does not have to be dragged in, consequently the rifling is preserved instead of being worn away at a most vital spot.
For .22 Caliber Rifle, Price **$.35.** For .30 Caliber Rifle, Price **$.55.**

PISTOL AND REVOLVER RODS

.22 Caliber Pistol Rod Length 6½ inches with Trueform jag, Price.. **$1.75**
.32 Caliber Pistol Rod Length 8 inches with Flexible jag, Price..... **2.25**
.38 Caliber Pistol Rod Length 8 inches with Flexible jag, Price..... **2.50**
.45 Caliber Pistol Rod Length 8 inches with Flexible jag, Price..... **2.75**

FLEXIBLE BRASS JAG

Recommended for Pistols and Revolvers. Standard on Revolver Rods over .22 caliber.
For .38 Caliber Revolver, Price .... **$.65**
For .32 Caliber Revolver, Price .... **.70**
For .45 Caliber Revolver, Price .... **.75**

PLAIN CLEANING PLUG

For .22 Caliber Rods, Price .... **$.30**

WOOL MOP FOR OILING RIFLE OR REVOLVER

Caliber .22 Price .... **$.30**   Caliber .32, Price .... **$.35**
Caliber .38, Price .... **.40**   Caliber .45, Price .... **.45**

MOTTY RIFLE PASTE

This world famous English preparation was first sold in 1907 to meet the needs of riflemen requiring the removal of nickelling "on the spot" with a minimum of impediment and trouble.

It positively removes all traces of nickel. It polishes the bore without enlarging it. By removing the nickel it allows the Cordite neutralizing oil to get at the steel and preserve it.

It contains no emery or grit.
It can do no harm if left in the barrel.
It saves labor, one cleaning being sufficient.
Price per 1 ounce jar .... **$.75**

BUFF BARREL POLISHER

This consists of best buffing leather firmly held and exactly ground to a size that when used with Motty Paste will lay, both lands and grooves of the rifling. A ball bearing handle rod should be used to permit the lap to revolve in the barrel.
Price .... **$.75**

SHOTGUN CLEANING ROD SETS

   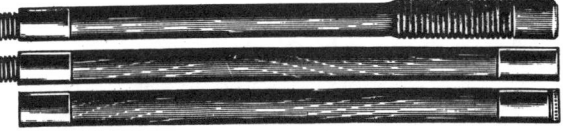

An unsurpassed ebony cleaning rod. Beautifully finished, polished brass fittings with jag, mop and turkshead wire brush. Complete. 12 and 16 gauge. Price **$3.75**

SEE PAGE 8, "HOW TO ORDER"

GUN CLEANING & LUBRICATING PREPARATIONS

HEAVY DUTY LEAD SOLVENT

A new preparation for stubborn cases of leading. Does a thorough job. A boon to every shooter.

Price .... $.50

B.S.A. SAFETIPASTE

The B.S.A. Safetipaste is used by small and large bore shooters in England. It is considered to be the finest barrel grease obtainable. It is particularly valuable and useful when guns are to be stored away. Insert in the barrel with or without cleaning. Will keep bore bright and in good condition for many months.

This preparation is rarely available elsewhere in the U.S.A. and has been especially imported by us in response to the steady demand by discriminating shooters.

Price per tube... $.50

THE STOEGER CLEANING KIT

Price Complete Only $1.00

Regular $1.50 Value

This handy kit is indispensable for the shooter, containing everything necessary to keep firearms in best condition. Contains full size can of Stoegerol, the combination gun oil and solvent, cleaning patches, Gunslick to smooth the action, and Noshine to darken the sights for accurate shooting. Supplied in compact, attractive, substantial carton. Supplied with a choice of .22, .30, or .38 to .45 cal. patches. Unless specified .22 cal. will be shipped.

Price, complete $1.00

NOSHINE

Noshine is a preparation for the instantaneous blackening of sights on target arms. It is applied with a brush which is attached to the stopper. It dries immediately imparting a lamp-black finish.

Price per bottle............... $.50

RIG

A popular scientific preparation for use both in the fore and exterior of firearms. A thin film of Rig after shooting prevents corrosion.

Price, ¼ lb. can... $.50

NEVAROST GUN GREASE

An absolutely pure and neutral petroleum product excellent for rust proofing and preserving the in- and outside of firearms of every description in perfect condition, especially during a time when these are not in use or during storage. Retains its properties during long periods of time under adverse conditions.

Price per 1 lb. can, $.50. Price per 5 lb. can, $2.00

GUNSLICK for Lasting Smoothness

GUNSLICK is different from any oil. The velvet smoothness it gives any action LASTS —and the trigger pull STAYS "sweet" and UNIFORM.

Prevents leading and metal fouling; protects against rust and corrosion.

Price .... $.25

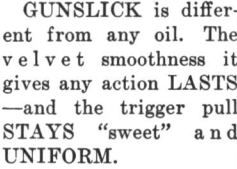 

Price 25c

  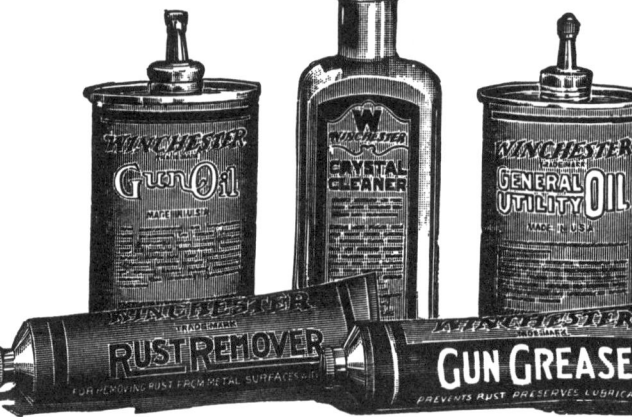

WINCHESTER
Cleaning and Lubricating Preparations

Each of these preparations has been specifically prepared according to formulas determined by chemists to do specific work. For the proper care of firearms these preparations are indispensable.

Gun Oil, in 3-ounce patent oil cans.......	$0.25
General Utility Oil, in 3-ounce patent oil cans	.25
Crystal Cleaner, in 3-ounce bottles.......	.25
Gun Grease, in collapsible tubes.........	.15
Rust Remover, in collapsible tubes.......	.25
Gun Grease, in 5-pound cans, per can....	3.50
Gun Oil, in gallon cans, per can.........	3.00
General Utility Oil, in gallon cans, per can..	3.00

REMINGTON
Cleaning and Lubricating Preparations

The Remington Powder Solvent, Oil, Rust Remover, and Gun Grease are scientifically prepared for the specific purpose of keeping firearms in first-class condition and prolonging their life and service.

Powder Solvent, per 3-ounce can........	$0.30
Rem Oil, per 3-ounce can..............	.25
Rem Oil, per quart....................	1.50
Gun Grease, per tube..................	.15
Rust Remover, per tube................	.25

HOPPE'S NO. 9 NITRO SOLVENT

A well known powder solvent for removal of primer and powder residue, leading and metal fowling.

Price per 2 oz. bottle.................. $.35

MARBLE'S NITRO-SOLVENT OIL

A solvent is combined with a fine oil and other ingredients. Stops corrosive action by neutralizing the acid of the residue before or after they have penetrated the steel. The solvent in the oil keeps it from gumming.

No. 244—Three-ounce can	$0.30
No. 544—Six-ounce can	.60
No. 644—One-quart can	1.50

SUPER NITRO POWDER SOLVENT

A modern solvent. Removes all metal and powder fouling and leading. Positively prevents electrolytic corrosion and pitting.

Prevents Rust. Not made with acids. Will not injure finest steel. Maintains bores in original factory new condition, bright and true.

Price per 2 oz. bottle.................. $.25

Stoegerol

THE 7 PURPOSE ECONOMICAL GUN OIL. A SHOOTER'S MUST!

- Unexcelled Nitro-Solvent
- Never Hardens or Gums
- Mixes with Water in Emulsion
- Loosens and Removes Rust
- Softens and Preserves Leather
- First Class Wound Sterilizer
- An Excellent Light Cleaning and Lubricating Oil

3 Ounce Can 50¢
Pint $1.75
Quart 3.00
Gallon 11.25

The chemical and physical action of "Stoegerol" is based on the peculiar properties which enable its gases to penetrate into the molecules of the steel during their expansion caused by the explosion of the nitro powder upon discharge of firearm and its power of neutralization of nitro-gases. All that is necessary to protect your gun is to have it well oiled with "Stoegerol"—the rest "Stoegerol" will do for you.

WORTH ITS WEIGHT IN GOLD TO EVERY LOVER OF A GUN!

Stoegerol IS RUST INSURANCE!

Stoegerol absorbs both water and dampness so that it will protect steel and iron even if kept under water or in a damp place for months. Only a single application after use is necessary to dissolve or prevent rust and corrosion. At Army tests, Stoegeroled rifles were submerged in water for several days, and then, without drying, were placed in a damp room for a month. These weapons remained rust free at the completion of the test.

Stoegerol kills bacteria and sterilizes wounds. Every sportsman should carry a can of Stoegerol in his pocket. It serves as a complete first aid kit. It is particularly effective when used to relieve chafing, frostbite, sores, dry-skin, sunburn, vermin affections, or colds. Physicians find it indispensable as a rust-protector for surgical instruments, and dentists state it never fails to separate positive plaster casts from the negative.

Stoegerol is invaluable to poultrymen, ranchmen and farmers. Beneficial results are obtained by daubing the feet, eyes or throat of poultry with Stoegerol. Application to check foot and mouth disease, or other inflammatory disorders of live stock, is found effective.

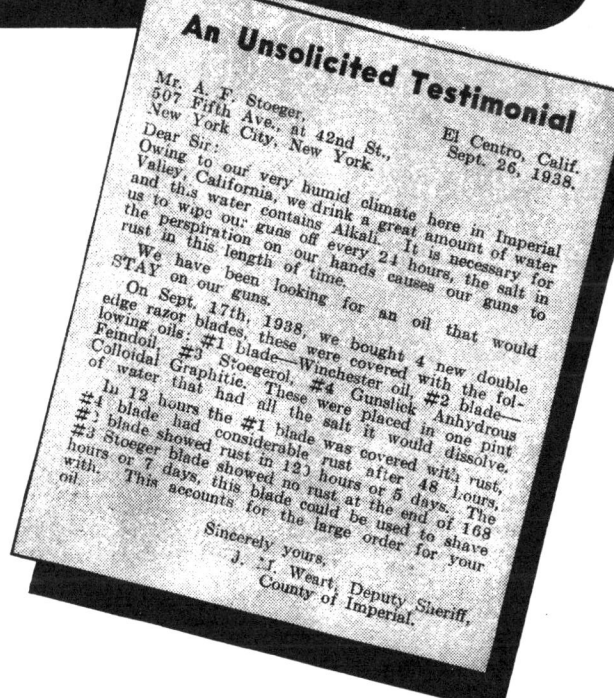

Stoegerol CLEANS, PROTECTS AND LUBRICATES

Stoegerol does not affect the bluing of arms, and in addition, it preserves both wood and leather. It destroys mold and ferment, and is absorbed into leather, making it both waterproof and durable. Stoegerol is recommended for protecting shoes, harnesses and saddles.

Stoegerol is an excellent lubricant for sewing machines, typewriters, ball bearings, motors, and other fine mechanisms. When dissolved two to five percent in water Stoegerol makes a fine cleanser and polisher for stocks or furniture.

ASK ANY LEADING DEALER FOR STOEGEROL

STOEGER ARMS CORPORATION, 507 FIFTH AVENUE, NEW YORK, N. Y.

Complete Your Library With These Gun-Books!

The following ten pages list a complete, comprehensive library of books pertaining to shooting, hunting, gunsmithing, wild life, and the history of firearms. Here is an authoritative bibliography of books that you will need to fill the shelves of your own library. Spend your idle hours enjoying the thrills of other gun-lovers, learning new techniques, or reviewing old procedure. Let Stoeger send the books that will help you understand and enjoy the thrills of hunting and shooting.

BOOKS
- A COMPREHENSIVE BIBLIOGRAPHY
- OF BOOKS PERTAINING TO THE
- ENTIRE FIELD OF GUNCRAFT

ART OF SHOOTING

The Woodchuck Hunter   By Paul C. Estey
This is the first book ever published on the highly popular and almost universally American Sport of "chucking." Most entertainingly written. All about the woodchuck—how he lives—and how to connect with him at long range with modern rifles. Plenty of hunting and stalking dope, reloading data. 136 illustrated pages........ **$1.50**

Game Bird Shooting   By Askins
The author well known as one of our foremost shooters, gives practical and valuable information. Even an experienced hunter will find many facts which have been a puzzle to him.................... **$4.00**

Wing and Trap Shooting   By Askins
The best and smallest investment you can make for all the expert and first hand news to be found in this edition. The writer in his element knows whereof he writes **$1.00**

Wild Fowl Decoys   By Joel Baker
The author has spent twenty years studying and collecting wild fowl decoys, from Nova Scotia to North Carolina. His book is the only one ever written on this subject. A textbook with 120 illustrations comprising the most complete pictorial record of decoys ever attempted. **$25.00**

Guns and Gunning   By Capt. Paul A. Curtis
A book that will be of absorbing interest to every sportsman, hunter and target shot. It exhaustively describes all types of guns—rifles, revolvers and shotguns for all uses—and their ammunitions... **$5.00**

Game Bird Shooting   By Chas. Askins
In this book are described the practical phases of bird shooting of every type. Each species of American and Canadian game bird is fully described together with its habits and the best method of hunting it. It also describes the various types of hunting dogs, their training, etc. **$4.00**

Upland Game Bird Shooting in America   By Eugene V. Vonnett
Thirteen of America's most prominent authorities have contributed to this comprehensive and up-to-date work on American Upland Shooting, treating its subject in a practical manner. Most profusely illustrated from photographs and a remarkable collection of American sporting artists etchings and paintings. **$35.00**

American Duck, Goose and Brant Shooting   By Dr. Wm. Bruette
An all-inclusive, authoritative, and beautifully illustrated work, highly praised by critics and sportsmen. It is the standard volume in its field. A book worth its weight in gold. **$4.00**

More Grouse Feathers   By Burton L. Spiller
It is an informal, reflective book on grouse and grouse shooting with reminiscences about places, people, dogs and guns in the woodland covers of Maine and New Hampshire. 7½x10 bound in maroon with gold decoration and a colored medallion of a grouse set in front cover. **$10.00**

Grouse Shooting   By Martin Stephens
The author the well known English shooting editor of The Field who knows his subject from scratch to finish gives you his best on this great sport. We all cannot go to Scotland, but it is fun just the same to read this book. **$2.00**

Grouse and Grouse Moors   By Maxwell & Malcolm
Shooting in Scotland the revelation of seeing thousands of these famous great game birds in a single shooting day, the care and keeping of same just to mention a few chapters of this book written by two well-known authors who are old hands in this field. **$3.00**

Rough Shooting   By G. K. Yeates & R. N. Winnall
For the novice this book will be an invaluable source of information taking care of all problems, from gun to the actual shooting. Profusely illustrated. **$2.00**

AN IDEAL GIFT FOR THE SHOOTER

AMERICA'S GREAT GUN HOUSE

Colonel Hawker's Shooting Diaries
By Eric Parker

Recently a number of letters, pictures and the diary of the author of "Instructions to Young Sportsmen" have come to light. These were entrusted to Eric Parker's careful editing and the result is a companion volume to Col. Hawker's work. Illustrated. **$7.50**

Sporting Firearms — By Kemphart

If you are a beginner and interested in Firearms the writer is well qualified. You will receive a thorough and easily understandable explanation on each weapon he selects for you. **$1.00**

Shotgun Psychology By Lawrence B. Smith

The Human Side of Shooting, its psychology, rather than the purely mechanical, is stressed throughout. The volume is designed pincipally for those who have had moderate experience, or are beginners, in the art of shooting. **$2.75**

Gun For Company — By E. C. Keith

A practical book, by an experienced English sportsman, on the shooting of partridge, pheasant, wildfowl and lesser game. With frontispiece in color and 12 pages of illustrations in half tones. **$5.00**

The Art of Shooting — By Chas Lancaster

From the pen of an English gunmaker who is well known as one of the best in his country. **$2.00**

Modern Shotgun Shooting
By Lawrence B. Smith

Lon Smith does not need introduction to the American shooter, his deeds and writings are too well known. He gives a wealth of information and advice on field, trap and skeet shooting. Fully illustrated from photographs and diagrams. **$2.50**

Better Trapshooting — By L. B. Smith

This is one of the most recent and comprehensive books written on the art of improving your score. It also goes fully into the game of skeet, and by careful reading and following of instructions, will enjoy better trapshooting and better scores. **$5.00**

Skeet and How to Shoot It
By Bob Nichols

Bob Nichols the well known gun editor of "Field and Stream" does not need introduction to the shooter. He explains this National Sport, how to hit " 'em" timing, the various stations, handicapping, just to mention a few of his interesting articles. **$3.50**

Partridge Shooting By Capt. J. B. Drought

A well known international authority on everything pertaining to this great game bird, tells you his life's experience from which even the most experienced will learn. The best book on Partridge ever written. **$2.00**

Pheasant Shooting — By Leslie Sprake

The author tells how to raise and keep this noble game birl, how to protect him from vermin. Anyone interested in pheasants will find his book interesting and authoritative. **$2.00**

Wildfowling — By C. T. Dalgerty

This book is probably the best treatise on practical wildfowling written; you cannot afford to miss reading it. **$2.00**

Pteryplegia, or the Art of Shooting Flying
By Mr. Markland, A.B. Fellow of St. John

This is the fourth edition since 1727 of this book on wing-shooting in the English language and with Col. Sheldon's remarkably fine introduction, is a book of great historical significance. Fine illustrations by Mr. Ball. **$35.00**

MILITARY AND TECHNICAL WORKS

The Pistol Atlas — By Dr. H. Walter Hess

This book is unique in the annals of crime detection. Several hundred fine photographs, covering every known make and model of automatic pistols, are clearly shown, together with type and depth of rifling, type or firing pin and breech block, as well as samples of identification marks on empty cases, and bullets. **$100.00**

The Identification of Firearms and Forensic Ballistics
By Major Gerald Burrard, D.S.O.

The only single book, written by a recognized expert, in which the salient facts of a subject important to lawyers and police officials are given. Fully illustrated. **$4.50**

Identification of Firearms
By Gunther & Gunther

An exhaustive guide for serious students of firearms. 342 well illustrated pages. **$4.00**

Textbook of Small Arms

An interesting, informative book upon war weapons. Exceedingly low priced at **$3.50**

A Rifleman Went to War
By McBride

Captain Herbert McBride, author of this intensely interesting book, tells of his thrilling experiences with the Canadian Expeditionary Force in the World War 1. He gives vivid examples to show importance of a modern rifle and telescope on the battlefield. 398 pages. **$3.50**

DICTIONARY FOR ARMS, AMMUNITION, AND EXPLOSIVES

This book makes it possible for sportsmen to study technical progress in foreign countries. It translates technical terms which are not found in most foreign dictionaries. The compilation gives more than 2000 technical terms, translated by American, German, French, Spanish, and Italian experts, to give absolute clarity. 446 pages. **$7.50**

Notes on German Ordnance
By Capt. E. J. Hicks

A complete compilation of German Ordnance equipment from 1841-1918. Excellently illustrated with reproductions of original, official drawings. Particularly interesting to collectors and military students. **75c**

Notes on French Ordnance
By Capt. E. J. Hicks

This book is invaluable to the student of military arms. It gives a wealth of information about small arms, pistols, revolvers, automatic weapons, artillery, ammunition, etc. (from 1717 to 1936). Profusely illustrated with original reproductions not found in other books of this type. Limited editions. **$3.50**

Notes on United States Ordnance
By Capt. E. J. Hicks

Here is a great new source of information. The author reveals original letters and data which answer questions which puzzle students of history, has been unable to find. It illustrates the weapons used by the U. S. Army from 1776 to the present day. Limited editions **$4.50**

United States Martial Pistols and Revolvers — By Major Arcadi Gluckman

Here is a long anticipated book for collectors, gun lovers, historians, and members of the armed services. It outlines the historical evolution of Marshall pistols and revolvers from 1776 to the present day. Limited editions **$4.50**

The Hodsock Ballistic Tables
By F. W. Jones

This book is the most complete work on ballistics ever attempted, and is invaluable to anyone who wishes to make a thorough study of the subect. H. Gerlich, inventor of the world famous super high velocity rifles praises the book. **$4.00**

IMPROVE YOUR KNOWLEDGE OF GUNCRAFT

HISTORICAL SHOOTING BOOKS

A GREAT SELECTION OF STORIES OF SPORT AND SHOOTING WHICH EVERY AMERICAN SHOULD KNOW AND WILL ENJOY

A History of Firearms By Hugh B. C. Pollard
An authoritative and lavishly illustrated study of American and European firearms, including about 2000 makers' names and dates as a guide to indentification. 284 pages, 400 photographs and line drawings, together with 175 reproductions of makers' marks and of typical specimens. **$12.50**

"Kentucky" Rifle By Dillin
The most authoritative book on the old Pennsylvania Flintlock gun, later called the Kentucky rifle. Profusely illustrated giving full data on the history, makers, old prints and handbills for the benefit of the collector and student of early American firearms. **$7.50**

Blood Lines By Nash Buckingham
A great selection of stories of Sport and shooting in the old South and today. 6x9¼, bound in maroon with gold decoration and a color plate medallion on the front cover. 1250 numbered copies. **$7.50**

Four Centuries of Sports in America, 1490-1890 By Herbert Manchester
Provides a history of the subject which every American gentleman and sportsman should be familiar with. The remarkable list of sources provides a totally new approach to sporting history, and represents years of research. Profusely and beautifully illustrated, bound in boards with brown cloth, gold stamping and a pasted label showing a charming old American print. **$30.00**

Early American Sporting Books, 1734-1844 By Ernest R. Gee
The only book on this interesting subject. Invaluable to collectors and of interest to all sportsmen. Bound in paper covered boards with cloth backstrip and pasted labels. **$7.50**

Some Early American Hunters
Three excerpts from the Cabinet of Natural History and American Rural Sports, 1830, with a hand-coloured plate. The Cabinet contained the first coloured plates of sporting subjects done in America. Stories of wolf and panther hunting. **$6.50**

The American Shooter's Manual By A Gentleman of Philadelphia County
Originally published in 1827. An important early American sporting book. This reprint is on Van Gelder paper with the original illustrations on Japan tissue. 375 numbered copies, Boards, Cloth Back. **$10.00**

The Sportsman's Portfolio of American Field Sports
Originally published in 1855. The finest American "picture book" of sport. 25 woodcuts with descriptive text. Printed on fine rag paper. 400 copies, Brown Boards, Cloth Back. **$10.00**

The Sportsman's Companion, or an Essay on Shooting
Originally published in 1873. This is the first American book on shooting. The present edition is the fourth, printed on Derrydale Press rag paper, in the style of the second edition. 200 copies, 150 for sale. **$10.00**

The Isle of Long Ago, Sporting Days By Edwin C. Kent
This book gives a complete picture of hunting and fishing in America, during the 70's and 80's The author's deep feeling and appreciation for the woods and wild life is evident on every page and his description of a vanished hunter's paradise will interest every sportsman. **$5.00**

Arms and Armour
A very rare and out of print book. Available only in good used condition. Weapons and Armour of all nations from the Stone Age to the sixteenth century. Absolutely indispensable to the curator and student of history. **$5.00**

Falconry By Gilbert Blaine
The old sport of noblemen and Kings through the ages and history of mankind perfected to an art, this book is a mine of information, instruction and advice to all who keep or contemplate keeping hawks. **$2.00**

Fire-Arms 1702., par le Sr. Surirey de Saint Remy Compiled by Capt. J. E. Hicks
The firearms section of the Memoires d'Artillerie by the Sr. Surirey de Saint Remy and published in 1702, has been faithfully reproduced from the original, including the interesting old illustrations. There is an English Translation accompanying. Covers weapons, accoutrements, and proof-firing from 1600-1700. **$2.25**

Blazing The Way West By Bliss Isely
This book puts into simple readable form the romantic story of French Exploration and colonization of North America. Much of the material has been hidden in archives of historical society. 30 illustrations, 9 maps. **$3.00**

THE ART OF GUNSMITHING

Elementary Gunsmithing By Perry D. Frazer
A concise yet complete manual intended solely for the beginner in gunsmithing. 210 pages of data and instructions on stocking, remodeling, finishing, bluing and necessary metal-working operations. 27 full page drawings of special gadgets, working kinks, templates, jigs and fixtures. **$2.00**

The Amateur Gun Craftsman By James V. Howe
Amateur gunsmiths and those interested in the remodeling of old or military rifles will find a wealth of practical pointers, the type of tools to equip your shop, the kind of wood you should choose, etc. **$4.00**

Modern Gunsmithing By Baker
The most useful book ever written for the average shooting man. Written for the ordinary gun-crank for use with the tools and facilities of the average home. Tells and illustrates how to do the hundred and one minor jobs. Over 525 pages and 200 illustrations. **$4.50**

THE MODERN GUNSMITH
By James V. Howe
This is the most authoritative work ever written on gunsmithing and gun-making.
Two handsome volumes of 800 pages contain over 300 artistic and scrupulously exact illustrations, including some of the handsomest guns ever made.
The Modern Gunsmith will be your advising friend and sympathetic counselor on every occasion when any question about guns arises.
2 Vols., 800 pages. **$15.00**

Advanced Gunsmithing By W. F. Vickery
A specialized manual, restricted to the various metal working operations involved in the production, repair and adjustment of modern, high-grade firearms. This book contains 432 pages of full instruction concerning barrel-making, chambering, reboring, remodeling, head-spacing, and action work. **$4.00**

Firearm Bluing and Browning By R. H. Angier
Is a qualified, practical and complete treatise covering the art of gun blueing. Here are formulae for various steels and processes; with complete working instructions clearly explaining how parts may be oxidized with solutions compounded at home. 155 pages. **$2.50**

Catalogue of United States Martial Short Arms
This booklet was published to meet a demand indicated in letters to the publishers and lists only the U. S. martial arms described in the United States Martial Pistols and Revolvers. The prices entered are the result of compilation of average prices **$1.95**

AUTHORITATIVE WORKS ON GUNSMITHING

AMERICA'S GREAT GUN HOUSE

RIFLES, PISTOLS AND REVOLVERS

THESE BOOKS GIVE YOU THE EXPERIENCES AND KNOWLEDGE OF THE OUTSTANDING HUNTING AND ORDNANCE AUTHORITIES

RIFLES

The American Rifle
By Lt. Col. Townsend Whelen
In this book the reader is given the benefit of the experience and knowledge of one of America's best known hunters and ordnance authorities. It is full of instruction and information. **$6.00**

Rifle and Target
By Capt. E. H. Robinson, G.M.
A book for the practical target shooter written by one of the greatest English Riflemen. It deals with every sort of weapon and ammunition and is packed with good advice. **$4.50**

Rifles and Rifle Shooting *By Askins*
A book worth much more than its small cost, for the novice with a wealth of first hand gun dope not found in any other book of its size. **$1.00**

Sportsman's Pocket Set
Consisting of three separate manuals, "Wing Shooting" by Askins, "Shooting Facts" by Askins, and "Big Game Hunting" by Whelen. All profusely illustrated. Per set .... **75¢**

Military and Sporting Rifle Shooting
By Crossman
A companion volume to "Book of the Springfield" and the most complete and applicable work on the actual shooting of the larger caliber rifles yet published. 500 pages. 100 illustrations. **$4.50**

.22 Caliber Rifle Shooting *By Landis*
The only book available on .22 rifles and .22 rifle shooting—both Small Bore and game shooting. It contains much helpful data of interest and value to the small game hunter and is a fine book for the boy with his first rifle. A chapter on what happens to the bullet in its flight is of especial interest and value to the student of ballistics. Especially helpful to the beginner. 400 pages. 100 illustrations. **$3.75**

Book of the Springfield *By Crossman*
A textbook devoted to all the details, facts and ballistics of the .30 Model 1906 Springfield. Contains full dope regarding the many different military, commercial and private models of rifles for this cartridge. 450 pages. 100 illustrations. **$4.00**

Big Game Rifles and Cartridges
By Elmer Keith
Keith takes up all our suitable modern big game rifles and cartridges and tells just what they are capable of. Here is the **real dope** on actual killing effect at all ranges. Its text is full of practical hunting notes. All about brush and timber rifles—long range, stalking rifles—double rifles—all-around rifles. **$1.50**

Telescopic Rifle Sights
By Townsend Whelen
The only complete manual ever published on this popular type sight. Herein are fully described all makes and types of scopes commonly used. Tells what rifles these scopes are adapted to and how they should be attached. All about the modern big-game hunting scope; varmint, small-game, junior and target scopes. 140 text. . **$1.50**

Mastering The Rifle *By Morris Fisher*
This book is intended for the beginner and the experienced shot who wants to improve his performance. By following the procedure outlined the beginner will be assured of good results, and by analysing his present practise in the light of the information given experienced shots can correct their faults. **$2.50**

THE RIFLE IN AMERICA
By Philip B. Sharpe

The author of this book, a well-known gun editor of today, spent months of research in assembling the greatest wealth of information from the beginning of the firearm to present day.

This book has illustrations on all important items invaluable to the collector and the student of firearms. The book is arranged in 6 sections and 33 chapters separately indexed, making it easy to find particular information wanted instantly. **$7.50**

HINTS ON THE CARE OF BOOKS

If books are to preserve their usefulness and appearance, they must be cared for the moment they are first opened. To avoid breaking the binding a book should be placed with its spine on a table, the leaves held upright and together, while the front and back covers are allowed to lie on the table. Beginning in the middle of the volume, the leaves may then be opened gently toward the covers, working toward the front and back at the same time.

All books should be stood upright on the shelf. Closed book cases with glass doors are preferable since they protect the books from dust, excessive heat and moisture.

Books should be so placed that strong sunlight will not fall on them. Direct light will dry out the bindings and fade the backstrips. The humidity in a room containing books should be between 50 and 65 degrees. When removing a book from its place on the shelf do not pull it out by the top of the backstrip, but push in the books on either side enough to permit grasping the book in the middle of the back.

PISTOLS AND REVOLVERS

Pistol and Revolver Shooting
By Himmelwright
The smaller edition is a practical guide to the novice of this great American game of Pistol and Revolver shooting, describing all the different types of arms, targets and ammunition used for this type of shooting. **$1.00**

The revised and enlarged edition with many illustrations covers its subject completely as written by Mr. Himmelwright one of our foremost pistol shots in his days. **$4.00**

English Pistols and Revolvers
By J. N. George
A complete history of the development and design of English Hand Firearms from the Seventh Century to present days with many rare illustrations, no collector or student can afford to be without this book. **$4.00**

Shooting *By J. H. Fitzgerald*
The latest and one of the best books on pistol and revolver shooting, with special chapters dealing on the subject in every branch, for police, bank, target, and defense work. For the expert or the tyro. **$4.00**

Automatic Pistol Marksmanship
By William Reichenbach
It coordinates with his first work, but does not in any manner duplicate. This manual concentrates upon automatic pistols and practical pistol shooting. The more suitable and popular American and European pistols are described in detail. ... **$1.50**

English Pistols and Revolvers
By J. N. George
An historical outline of the development and design of English hand firearms, from the seventeenth century to the present day. This book consists of 256 pages, and 28 special plates. **$4.00**

Fast & Fancy Revolver Shooting
By Ed McGivern
Advanced instruction in revolver shooting and speed shooting. Especially well adapted for police training. Outlines the latest scientific instruments for research and experimental work. **$3.00**

START BUILDING A GUN LIBRARY NOW!

BOOKS FOR EVERY MAN'S LIBRARY

LEARN MORE ABOUT YOUR HOBBY WITH THESE ENTERTAINING VOLUMES ON SUBJECTS WHICH EVERY HUNTER LOVES.

WOODWORKING

How To Build Cabins, Hunting and Fishing Lodges, Bungalows

Those interested in building their own cabins will find this book invaluable. 256 pages of diagrams, plans, and instructions which are extremely easy to follow. Build it yourself, have fun, and save money. **$2.00**

Woodcarving and Whittling

Every sort of wood carving explained in extreme detail. For those who love this old art, this book, written by experts, will be of great assistance. **$2.00**

Woodworkers Turning and Joining Manual

This book describes simple and practical ways to make gun racks, cabinets, and other shooter's equipment. Thoroughly illustrated. **$1.00**

Home Workshop Manual

The most complete reference book for the home workshop ever published, more than 500 pages, having 735 working drawings and diagrams which cover every conceivable subject. **$1.95**

COLLECTORS

Gun Collecting   By Charles E. Chapel

The love of guns is in our blood, and a number of questions about each gun come to mind. To answer these questions this book was written. Profusely illustrated with photographs. To be valued by anyone interested in arms. **$2.50**

The Old Gun Catalogs   By L. D. Satterlee

This book contains facsimile reproductions of the following old catalogs. Merrill (1864) Peabody (1865) (1866) Henry (1865) Spencer (1866) National (1865) Folsom (1869) Great Western (1871) James Bown (1876) Homer Fisher (1880). Of priceless interest to gun collectors, these old catalogs, seldom found in libraries, are now offered for sale in a bound volume. **$4.00**

What Price Arms?

If you collect, buy, sell or are at all interested in U. S. military or naval pistols or revolvers, you can hardly afford not to have a copy of the Catalog of U. S. Martial Short Arms. Illustrated. **$1.95**

History of Colt Revolvers   By Haven and Belden

Authentic and detailed description of every Colt from the first Paterson model. About 600 pages with more than 250 illustrations. Every Collector and lover of firearms will want this book. **$10.00**

SHOT GUNS

The Modern Shotgun   By Gerald Burrard

This great English Authority has written a book which is now recognized as the standard work of everlasting value. Gerald Burrard brings to you the study of the development of the modern shotgun from scratch to finish. Technical but easily understandable, three volumes.
Volume I   The Gun **$5.00**
Volume II   The Cartridge ... **$5.00**
Volume III The Gun and Cartridge **$5.00**

The Shotgun   By T. D. S. Purdey & Capt. J. A. Purdey

The name Purdey needs no introduction to the shooter's world. This book gives authoritative information on guns and gun handling and the care of the gun. **$2.00**

In the Gun Room   By Major G. Burrard

One hundred questions answered by gun experts. A unique book necessary to every man who owns a shotgun or rifle. It includes information that is impossible to find in any other source. **$2.00**

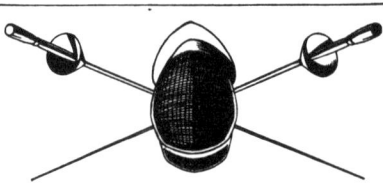

FENCING

Theory of Fencing   By J. Martinez Castello

This is a valuable volume and is written by a master in the art of fencing. The theory is divided into three parts, the theory of Foil, of Saber, and of Duelling Sword Fencing. Fundamental positions, preliminary actions, guards, and parries, and general technique are thoroughly up to date and written in English. Profusely illustrated. **$2.50**

Fencing Tactics   By Percy E. Nobbs

Here the art and tactics of fencing are described colorfully. The use of foil, sword and saber are interestingly described and illustrated with diagrams and useful appendices. **$2.00**

BOOKS MAKE FINE GIFTS

Modern Shotguns and Loads   By Capt. Chas. Askins

Written by America's outstanding shotgun expert. The first part contains technical and ballistical data on modern shotguns and their ammunition. There is an outstanding chapter covering the killing energy of various popular loads at different ranges with various degrees of choke—in all gauges. 436 pages, 100 illustrations. **$4.00**

GAME PRESERVATION

Rough Shooting for the Owner-Keeper   By Tennyson

If you are interested in wild birds, keeping or breeding, you will find this book filled with practically invaluable information told by a man whose experience qualifies him as an authority. **$4.75**

American Waterfowl   By John C. Phillips & Frederick C. Lincoln

A study of ducks, geese, and swans from the conservation point, 312 pages, 8 excellent illustrations. **$4.50**

The Gun Room Guide   By Hugh B. C. Pollard

A new kind of shooting book primarily concerned with preservation, shooting, and control of ground game, deer and game birds, 183 pages, 13 full colored illustrations and 11 line drawings illustrated. **$50.00**

Making a Shoot   By Major-General Sir John Goodwin

This book is written by a man who is well-known as an expert on game breeding. It reveals the methods of choosing the proper game for certain land, how to deal with vermin of all kinds, poachers, poaching methods and shooting arrangements. **$2.00**

Game Management   By Aldo Leopold

No conservationist, nor sportsman should fail to read this book. It is well written, humorous, and is unique in its field. **$5.00**

FORESTS

The Nation's Forests   By William Atherton Du Puy

A book written by a well known authority on this subect with an introduction by F. A. Silcox, Chief of the U. S. Forest Service. It contains chapters on forest wild life, recreation, forest fires, etc. **$3.00**

Ginseng and Other Medicinal Plants   By A. R. Harding

Tells how to grow Ginseng and Goldenseal, illustrates and describes these plants; also many other valuable roots and herbs; 367 pages, 35 chapters, 100 illustrations. **$1.25**

NATURAL HISTORY AND GAME PRINTS

SHARE THE AUTHOR'S ADVENTURES IN FAR OFF LANDS AND AT HOME WITH THRILLS, REMINISCENCES, ANECDOTES AND EXPERIENCES.

A Catalogue of Books on American Game Mammals and Birds
By John C. Phillips
1582-1925. This list of 6500 items, issued under the auspices of the Boone and Crockett Club, forms a comprehensive catalogue of work in this field, including trapping, woodcraft, firearms, etc. 639 pages. **$10.00**

A Sportsman's Scrapbook
By John C. Phillips
Reminiscences and anecdotes by one of America's best-known sportsmen and ornithologists. Author of "A Natural History of the Duck." 212 pages with 44 illustrations reproduced in gravure. Illustrated. **$5.00**

A Sportsman's Second Scrapbook
More good stories of a sportsman's experiences. 198 pages, with 39 pages of aquatone illustrations. Illustrated... **$4.50**

My Hunting Sketch Book
By Lionel Edwards
Ideal Hunting country landscapes done in the best manner by this famous artist, 15-full-page plates in color and many pencil sketches, every one a masterpiece. **$8.00**

The Bobwhite Quail
By Herbert L. Stoddard
One of our most sought game birds providing sport for thousands of hunters every year has found a real friend who is presenting the story from every conceivable angle with 4 color pages and 64 half tone illustrations. **$6.00**

The Ways of Birds By Thora Stowell
This book is by a well-known nature observer who takes the various attitudes of birds, peculiarities as to their life, ways of feeding, breeding, etc., and makes one see the shape and flight of birds as part of the general design of nature. It is profusely illustrated. **$2.00**

A. B. Frost—The American Sportsman's Artist By Henry W. Laine
To three generations of sportsmen the pictures of A. B. Frost have a definite meaning. They are a living history of a sport which is rapidly disappearing—the open shooting of wild game. The pictures are faithfully reproduced in collotype. The book is bound in cloth with gold stamping. **$17.50**

Woodcock and Snipe
By J. W. Seigne & E. C. Keith
A glorious story of these most sporting birds, a revelation of the habits, food, courtship and general life told in the simplest way, giving also practical advice how to hunt and how to assist these birds of migration for their proper care. **$2.00**

Wing Shots By Albert Dixon Simmons
The action photographs in this book are the finest collection of flight photographs ever published. From a pictorial standpoint they are outstanding examples of modern camera technique. **$15.00**

Game and Gun
Game and Gun is the leading British monthly magazine covering hunting and fishing throughout the British Empire. Sold only in an annual subscription basis. A copy will be mailed monthly from England. Price per twelve months subscription..... **$4.00**

BIG GAME AND ADVENTURE

Big Game of Africa
By Major H. C. Maydon
The writer will prove to you it is not the wealthy class privileged to hunt in Africa, you can do the same. He tells you what it costs, how to fit out your expedition, where to go for certain game. For the novice this book will be a real guide and friend. **$2.00**

CAMP AND GAME COOKING

The Derrydale Cook Book of Fish and Game By L. P. De Couy
The author who has been connected with the finest hotels is an authority and recognized for his world-wide and life-long experience in fine cooking. All the recipes are arranged for practical use in the home and the best and delicious ways of cooking all game are carefully explained. 1250 numbered sets, 2 Volumes, 6x9 boxed. **$15.00**

The Gun Club Cook Book
By Charles Browne
The preparation of game for the table is a very important matter. This book gives you receipes as used by the best known chefs, a well arranged and practicl handbook for those who like good cooking and good fun. **$3.00**

The Sportsman's Cookery Book
By H. Pollard
Pollard does not need any introduction as a sportsman and author. Here are some of his own experiences and those of others as picked up around campfires. Those who prefer to prepare their own game, this is your book you would not want to miss to read. **$2.75**

Green Hills of Africa
By Ernest Hemingway
The story which brings African scenery vividly to life, lovers of African game will revel in the flashing scenes bringing to you also a perceptive story of the contacts and conflicts of the hunters, making it supremely good reading. With many illustrations by Edward Shenton. **$2.75**

Big Game of India
By Major H. C. Maydon
Another book from the same author who knows his way around. It will save you many troubles and expense and will help you to avoid many difficulties on your first trip to the Orient. If you have the slightest interest in big game, buy it........ **$2.00**

Big Game Hunting and Adventure
By Daly
Real fascinating and interesting reading, from a writer who was on the trail for many good years, a book every shooter and hunter would not want to miss to read. **$3.50**

Hunting Countries By F. A. Stewart
This book contains 12 full color pictures and numerous black and white illustrations of individual hunts with descriptive text by leading English sporting writers. **$8.50**

Game in the Desert By Jack O'Connor
Mr. O'Connor who has lived and hunted and studied wild life in the Southwest since his boyhood, pictures the deserts as an area of indefinite variety, mule deer, whitetail deer, elk, antelope, bear, lion, jaguar, peccary, quail, doves, wild turkey and coyote. Thrilling experiences from cover to cover. An invitation to hit the trail as the author did. **$15.00**

Tales of a Big Game Guide
By Russell Annabel
The author is a professional guide in Alaska who has spent his entire life in this territory. He has written comprehensive chapters on hunting with much sound advice on packhorse travel. 6x9¼, bound in maroon with linen backstrip and corners with gold stamping. 950 numbered copies..... **$7.50**

In The Shadow of Mount McKinley
By William N. Beach
In this book the author describes what he found as a wilderness traveler, a big game hunter and an amateur photographer on one of the few remaining frontiers of our country. With over 60 illustrations and one in color, 750 copies only, 6¼x9¼. **$12.00**

North American Big Game
By Aldo Leopold
This is one of the finest books on the Scribner List. Big game hunters, conservation officials, wild life societies, and libraries will surely want a copy... **$7.50**

COMPLETE YOUR LIBRARY WITH THESE BOOKS

HUNTING STORIES BY FAMOUS WRITERS

HERE ARE PERFECT BOOKS FOR THOSE NIGHTS WHEN YOU HAVE THE URGE TO FONDLE A GUN AND HEAD FOR THE OUTDOORS

A Sportsman's Creed   By E. C. Keith
Shooting, Hunting, Farming, Nature are some of the subjects. The author is a landowner who spent his whole life close to nature. This book is beautifully illustrated. **$5.00**

The Moon is Waning   By Scott Hart
The background of the tale is rural Virginia, its characters almost without exception are 'possum-hunters. It is a charming story, with a most unusual sporting setting. To our knowledge it is the only book ever published about the typically American sport of 'possum-hunting. 950 numbered copies bound in blue linen stamped in gold. **$7.50**

Gee's Hunting Diary
An attractive book in which followers of foxhunting and harriers may conveniently record their sport. The design of the cover and pages is based on an old English diary. **$3.50**

The Happy End   By Ben Ames Williams
A Sportsman who is also the author of twenty-eight books of fiction is a rare combination. The author takes you behind the scenes of the upland coverts in Maine, the pinelands of Georgia, and the mountains of the Southwest, which led up to the stories of the book. You will like it. **$7.50**

Falling Leaves   By Philip H. Babcock
This is a grand collection of shooting stories, mostly placed in the hills of New England. Mr. Babcock has a long and interesting career as a hunter and has the fortunate ability to tell of his experiences in a most delightful and convincing manner. 6x9¼, bound in brown crushed levant pattern with collotype illustrations. .. **$7.50**

Just Hunting   By Harry T. Peters, M.F.H.
With a contribution by Harvey D. Gibson, Joint Master
For many years Mr. Peters has been Master of the Meadowbrook Hunt so that he is thoroughly familiar with the best practice in American foxhunting. He has also hunted with the finest packs in England and therefore is in a perfect position to interpret the difference between English and American hunting. This book promises to be a sporting classic not only because of its solid worth but also for its real flavor of the hunting field. Illustrated by Betty Babcock. **$7.50**

Firelight   By Burton L. Spiller
Stories of the woods and waters full of real wit and humor taken from real life which will give the reader many a good laugh and other pleasant moments from the author's personal experience. Illustrated by Lynn Bogue Hunt. Bound in maroon with gold decorations, a colored medallion of a woodcock is set in the front cover. **$10.00**

High Country   By Rutherford G. Montgomery
The stories and characters happen to be located in the Colorado Rockies, as wild and beautiful a setting as one can imagine. 6¼x9⅜, bound in terra-cotta linen with label stamped in gold. 95 numbered copies. **$7.50**

Tall Tales and Short   By Edmund Ware Smith
A recollection of stories by the author from northern Mine from the isolated backwoods regions. Uncle Jeff Coongate, the one eyed poacher of Mopang, is the hero of this book. 6x9¼, bound in forest green linen with gold decoration. 950 numbered copies. **$7.50**

A Tomato Can Chronicle and Other Stories of Fishing & Shooting   By Edmund Ware Smith
Mr. Smith expresses his love for and knowledge of wild places through the medium of a series of stories describing real persons and experiences, covering a number of localities in the north woods from the Atlantic to the Pacific. 6x9¼, illustrated, bound in brown cloth with gold decoration. 950 numbered copies. **$7.50**

Gunner's Dawn   By Roland Clark
The stories in this book are delightfully written recollections of a life crowded with experiences on the bays and marshes in the woods and fields, beautifully illustrated from original oil paintings and numerous pencil sketches by the author. 7½x10, printed on imported mould-made rag paper and bound in crimson with gold decoration and gilt top. **$25.00**

Hard Up on Pegasus   By Hugh B. C. Pollard
A very unorthodox book on hunting, written with gentle irony and lusty humor. With 208 pages, and ten full page illustrations in color and twenty in black and white by Gilbert Holliday. Illustrated. ... **$7.50**

Morning Flight: A Book of Wildfowling   By Peter Scott
The limited edition of this book which appeared in 1935 was immediately snapped up by collectors. Now the same text, all the famous color plates and half-tone reproductions of the rest are available in a lower priced edition. **$10.00**

Alec Maury: Sportsman   By Caroline Gordon
This American story is not only a vivid chronicle of shooting exploits, fox hunting and fishing, but is also a dramatic, emotional and brilliantly characterized novel with a background of the beautiful mountain and river country of Kentucky, Virginia and Tennessee. **$2.50**

The A B C of Fox Hunting   By D. W. E. Brock
In riding to hounds and in one's conduct in the field, there are thousand and one little things which though trivial in themselves, distinguish the beginner from the old hand. This admirable book is a guide of uniform excellence, precise and to the point. **$2.50**

Field Sports of Scotland   By Patrick R. Chalmers
Those who desire to get acquainted with the outdoors of England's most well known game section will find everything from trout to roedeer, grouse ptarmigan and mountain hares, delightfully written by this well known author. **$2.00**

Hunting England   By Sir William Beach Thomas
This book gives the most general picture yet attempted of the variety and local characteristics of foxhunting in England. Also included are sections on Stag Hunting, Otter Hunting, Beagling, etc. The narrative sections are spiced with delightful excerpts from the great hunting writers—Surtees, Peter Beckford and others. Illustrated. ... **$3.50**

Stray Shots   By Roland Clark
These are the personal reminiscences of a famous etcher of game birds and wild fowl, illustrated with thirteen original dry point etchings by the author. The thirteen plates will not be available in any other form. The book is printed on an unusual handmade paper imported from England. **$25.00**

Marsh and Mudflat   By Kenneth M. Dawson
For the hunter who likes to let his imagination follow the wild fowl the world over. Major Dawson's pages are pleasant and interesting reading. This book has also 16 illustrations. dry points and etchings by Miss Austen, admirably executed. **$6.00**

The Sporting Novels of Frank Forester   By Harry Worcester Smith
A set of four books: The Quorndon Hounds, The Deerstalkers, The Warwick Woodlands, My Shooting Box, representing the beginning of American sporting literature. We recommend them without reservation. Bound in cloth with gold stamping on dark blue panels with many original illustrations. **$35.00**

Classics of The American Shooting Field   By John C. Phillips in collaboration with Lewis Webb Hill
A collection of the best American hunting stories. 214 pages, 22 illustrations in aquatone and gravure, including reproductions of old prints and drawings by Frank W. Benson with a frontispiece by Benson in full color, and small head pieces for each story. Illustrated. **$7.50**

An Artist's Game Bag   By Lynn Bogue Hunt
America's leading bird painter made a special collection of paintings and drawings for this book. All species of wild fowl, upland game birds, predatory hawks and owls and many shore birds are included, superbly reproduced on fine rag paper in collotype and four plates in full color. Beautifully bound in brown crushed levant. **$15.00**

Feathered Game from a Sporting Journal   By Eugene V. Vonnett
A de Luxe edition of the highest order, with beautiful color plates of game birds painted by Dr. Burke, a masterful reproduction in color, an esthetic treat. 7½x10, with finest binding. **$25.00**

STORIES EVERY SPORTSMAN WILL ENJOY

THE HANDLING OF YOUR DOG

COMPLETE INFORMATION CONCERNING THE TRAINING, TREATMENT AND DEVELOPMENT OF MAN'S BEST FRIEND.

Your First Dog — By Lady Kitty Ritson
Lady Kitty Ritson, who is well known as a dog-show judge in this country as well as in England, sets down here full instructions for young dog owners. She advises them on how to select a satisfactory breed and from there on gives exact information on feeding, training and all aspects of general care. Illustrated. **$3.00**

Dog Training by Amateurs — By R. Sharpe
This is an invaluable and practical handbook for sportsmen. It conclusively shows that the task is not a formidable one, nor beyond the powers of the amateur. With many illustrations and photographs. **$3.00**

Thoroughbred — By Burton L. Spiller
A splendid group of stories on setters, pointers, field trials, and a group of human characters of unusual interest. With many fine illustrations by Lynn Bogue Hunt. Printed on deckle edge Andria paper and bound in blue crushed levant pattern with gold decorations and a white and gold central panel. **$10.00**

Sporting Dogs — By Croxton Smith
This book deals with the thirty-two breeds that are used in field sports, and with two or three exceptions all are also familiar at dog shows. The author is recognized as a leading authority on the subject. Profusely illustrated. **$5.00**

Thoughts on Beagling — By Peter Wood
By the author's own confession this is not a practical manual on the details of beagling, but it does contain many helpful hints on the subject and is designed to awaken interest in this revived sport. Beagling is ancient. Zenophon speaks of it. **$3.50**

The Art of Beagling — By Captain J. Otho Paget
Beagling is, in this country, a sport which is gaining rapidly in popularity, and about which there are few books available. This volume, therefore, fills a definite need for a practical handbook on the sport and on kennel management. Illustrated. .. **$3.50**

Just Dogs — By K. F. Barker
A book full of pictures, revealing the comedy, the drama, and the little tragedies of dogdom. For any dog lover this is the perfect gift book. Profusely illustrated by the author. **$3.50**

Hunting by Scent — By H. M. Budgett
The author is the E-Master of the Bicester and Warden Hounds. His conclusions are the result of wide study and of years of experience and observation in the field. His results are astounding, but they are accurate and demonstrable. **$7.50**

Hunting Dogs — By Hubert Hutton
This book contains chapters on the training methods used by many leading dog breeders and trainers of America embracing Setters, Pointers, Spaniels, Fox Hounds, Coon Hounds, Rabbit Hounds and Beagles. It also contains the timely advice of many experts on The Care of Dogs from the puppy stage to maturity. **$2.00**

Good Gun Dogs — By Capt. H. F. H. Hardy
Captain Hardy has spent twenty years in intimate contact with dogs, you have at your disposal all his own experience with all sorts of dogs and their training. Profusely illustrated. **$6.00**

The Dog's Medical Dictionary — By Alfred J. Sewell
This book which has been revised by Sir Frederick W. Cousens, canine surgeon to King George V is an encyclopedia of canine diseases, their diagnosis and treatment, poisons and their antidotes, and the physical development of the dog. Profusely illustrated. **$2.75**

Modern Gun Dogs — By Lawrence B. Smith
Every owner of bird dogs must read this book. It discusses in detail with numerous explanatory illustrations, kennels, feeding and conditioning, care and sanitation, training and home breaking, field trials of each breed. **$3.75**

Hounds of the World — By Sir John Buchanan-Jardine
A comprehensive study of all the various types of hounds employed for hunting in England, France and America, dealing with their history, their present and their future. **$10.00**

My Gun Dogs — By Ray P. Holland
All about the author's hunting dogs with many useful tips on hunting as well. 182 pages, with six illustrations in aquatone by A. L. Ripley. Illustrated. **$3.50**

The English Springer Spaniel in America — By Henry Lee Ferguson
Covers thoroughly every matter of interest to the breeder, handler, owner, or prospective owner of a Springer. It gives in full the "English Springer Spaniel Standard." It is beautifully and profusely illustrated with line drawings reproductions of old prints and photographs of noted Springers in action and repose **$7.50**

Dogs in the Field — By Margaret Kirmse
This book consists of fine collotype reproductions of Miss Kirmse's gun dog sketch book including appr. 300 dogs. All breeds of sporting dogs are pictured. Included with the book are six prints chosen from the book suitable for framing. 10x14, only a very limited number of copies available. **$25.00**

The Practical Dog Book — By Edward C. Ash
A comprehensive work dealing with the buying, selling, breeding, showing, care and feeding of the dog, with authentic histories of all varieties hitherto unpublished. Over 500 woodcuts, photographs and drawings. A remarkable reference book. **$7.50**

Hunting Dogs — By Oliver Hartley
Describes in a practical manner the training, handling, breeding, care and treatment, also types best adapted for Night Hunting as well as Gun dogs for Daylight Sport; 251 pages, 45 illustrations, 26 chapters. **$1.00**

The Coonhound — By Robert Legare
Written exclusively about Coonhounds. Proper breeding, training, right methods to meet various conditions. The care of puppies from birth to doghood. Crossbreeding and Inbreeding defined and results explained. Dog disease, their causes, cures and prevention. **$1.00**

THE BIRD, THE GUN AND THE DOG — By Ledyard Sands
Covers every type of American game bird shooting; Woodland Grouse, Prairie Grouse, Quail, Pheasant, Wild Turkey, Woodcock, Snipe, Rail, River and Pond Duck, Geese, Sea Fowl, and ideas on Conservation. **$7.50**

Cooning With Cooners — By O. Kuechler
Full of real stories of night hunting. A favorite book for every coon hunter. All the different states in the Union are represented in this volume. All the hunts described were actual happenings of dyed-in-the-wool coon hunters. **$1.00**

LEARN THE FUNDAMENTALS OF DOG CARE

TRAPPING—FURS—CAMPING—TAXIDERMY

FUR FARMING
by A. R. Harding
New completely revised edition giving up-to-date information on raising, feeding, breeding, housing and pelting the following animals: silver, cross and blue fox, mink, marten, fisher, fitch, weasel, muskrat, beaver, otter, nutria, raccoon, opossum, skunk and badger; 442 pages, 88 illus., 18 chapters. Price, $2.00.

SCIENCE OF TRAPPING
by E. Kreps
Describes habits and distribution of fur animals including skunk, mink, weasel, marten, fisher, otter, beaver, muskrat, fox, wolf, bear, raccoon, badger, opossum, lynx and wildcat, illustrates their tracks, and tells how to trap them; 245 pages, 24 chapters, 40 illus. Price, $1.00.

HOME TAXIDERMY for PLEASURE & PROFIT
by Albert S. Farnham
Cheapest, best, quickest way to learn Taxidermy — to prepare and mount animals, birds, fish, etc., for home, den or office—is to read this book; 246 pages, 31 chapters, 107 illustrations. Price, $1.50.

PRACTICAL MUSKRAT RAISING
by E. J. Dailey
Gives practical methods of raising, under natural conditions and in pens. Tells how to feed, ship stock and to make fences, dikes, ditches and dams; 136 pages, 22 illustrations, 11 chapters. Price $1.00.

DEADFALLS AND SNARES
by A. R. Harding
Splendid book on homemade traps, telling how and where to make, how to bait and where to set; 218 pages, 27 chapters, 84 drawings and illustrations. Save money by making your own traps and snares. Price, $1.00.

HOME TANNING and LEATHER MAKING GUIDE
by Albert S. Farnham
Information on how to tan and make leather from cattle, horse, calf, sheep, goat, deer and other hides; 176 pages, 40 illustrations, 20 chapters. Price, $1.00.

MINK RAISING
by L. H. Adams
A book of practical, detailed information, devoting 192 pages to raising mink with complete instructions on feeding, housing, care of mother and young, methods of trapping alive, etc. Also 30 pages on MARTEN and FISHER raising. Many illustrations. Price, $1.50.

WOLF & COYOTE TRAPPING
by A. R. Harding
Wolf and coyote are both cunning animals, but the methods given in this book "get 'em." Government recommended scent recipes explained, etc.; 252 pages, 21 chapters, 41 illustrations, Price, $1.00.

HOME MANUFACTURE OF FURS & SKINS
by Albert S. Farnham
Explains how to make more money out of your raw furs by tanning, dyeing and manufacturing; 285 pages, 34 chapters, 91 illustrations. Price, $1.50.

FERRET FACTS & FANCIES
by A. R. Harding
Tells how to raise, breed, handle and sell; also fur value. Fitch raisers will find this book valuable as fitch belong to the same family and are raised in the same manner. The book contains 214 pages, 21 chapters and 49 illus. Price, $1.00.

MINK TRAPPING
by A. R. Harding
Reliable information on where and how to set, including land, water and blind sets, baits and scent to use, methods in Northern and Southern states, size and care of skins, etc.; 188 pages, 20 chapters, 50 illustrations. Price, $1.00.

FOX TRAPPING
by A. R. Harding
Tells how to trap different kinds of fox, describing land, water and snow sets, making scent, and baiting traps, snaring, still hunting, etc. in such a way that the person with little or no experience can outwit them; 185 pages, 22 chapters, 50 illustrations. Price, $1.00.

LAND CRUISING & PROSPECTING
by A. F. Wallace
Practical information for Homesteaders, Prospectors, Trappers, Guides, etc. includes information on building cabins, what to take in your camp kit, how to sample ore, prospect for gold, furs, etc. 176 pages, 20 ch., 40 illus. Price, $1.00.

50 YEARS A HUNTER AND TRAPPER
by E. N. Woodcock
This book gives a vast store of knowledge of the outdoors in the interesting and thrilling experiences of a real old-time trapper and hunter, E. N. Woodcock, in the Allegheny Mts. and other parts of U. S. during 50 years of active outdoor life; 318 pages. Price, $1.00.

STEEL TRAPS
by A. R. Harding
This book describes the various makes of traps and illustrates how to set them, gives the correct size for different animals, etc.; 333 pages, 32 ch., 130 illus. A splendid book for the amateur as well as the professional trapper. Price, $1.00.

CAMP & TRAIL METHODS
by E. Kreps
Tells how to erect tents and shelters, how to build permanent log camps, how to make hunting boats, canoes, skis, toboggans, trail sleds, etc. along with valuable information about camping equipment, cooking, etc. Trappers, hunters and campers will want this 274 page book with 68 illus. and 19 ch. Price, $1.00.

CANADIAN WILDS
by Martin Hunter
The author was an employee of The Hudson Bay Co. for a number of years, beginning about the time of the Civil War. He tells about the history of the Hudson Bay Company, Northern Indians and their ways of hunting, trapping, etc.; 277 pages, 37 chapters. Price, $1.00.

TRAILS TO SUCCESSFUL TRAPPING
by V. E. Lynch
Latest and most up-to-date methods of preparing land, water and snow sets, tells how to make scents and trap mink, fox, coyote, wolf, opossum, 'coon, beaver, otter and bear; 172 pages, 20 chapters, 30 illustrations. Price, $1.00.

THE WILDERNESS TRAPPER
by Raymond Thompson
A book of master trapping methods. Tells of outfitting the wilderness trapper; the grub stake, fox trapping, war on wolves, how to trap, tracks and tracking, grading of furs. 226 pages, with many illustrations.
Price, $1.00

THE RIVER TRAPPER
by Walter Chandler
A book on the life of a house boat dweller and his river experiences, depicting the coves and bayous, lucky escapes and profitable pursuits in fishing, trapping, mussel shells, pearls, and root gathering. 214 pages, 28 illustrations. Price, $1.00

PRACTICAL FUR RANCHING
by O. Kuechler
Enclosures, kennels and dens, sites, breeding, feeding, diseases and remedies and other topics are dealt with. The contents are based on practice and experience. Fully illustrated. Price, $2.00

TRAPPING, TANNING, TAXIDERMY
For the man who wishes to realize a profit from the sale of furs, this inexpensive book will be valuable. It tells in plain language how to tan skins and mount heads. It is well illustrated with drawings. Price, $1.00

TRAPLINES AND TRAILS
by E. J. Dailey
A complete Manual on Trapping. Some of the latest methods on the handling of furbearers will be found therein. The author, E. J. Dailey, has made a life study of trapping and spent many years in the Adirondack Mountains. Price, $1.00

FUR BUYER'S GUIDE
by A. R. Harding
Contains complete, instructions about buying, handling, grading raw furs, including sizes, color, quality, how, when and where to sell, etc. Trappers as well as fur buyers need this book. It contains 370 pages, 160 illustrations, 35 chapters. Price, $2.00

A BOOK FOR EVERY SHOOTING NEED

SCIENTIFIC CRIME DETECTION EQUIPMENT

Combination Blood Test And Paraffine Gun Test

AMERICAN BLOOD TEST KIT is used to prove Existence of Blood on:

1st—Clothing of Criminal Suspect in attack and murder.

2nd—Weapons (Hammer, club, axe, etc.) used in crime.

3rd—Stains on Fenders, bumpers or springs of Suspected 'Hit and Run' Car.

4th—Premises of Suspected Scene of Crime.

The PARAFFINE GUN TEST is used to determine whether a Suspect has Fired a Gun within 24 hours prior to apprehension. Where several Suspects are Apprehended much time can be saved by applying test to all.

Chemicals necessary for BOTH Blood and Gun Tests are included in a HANDY CARRYING CASE (exactly as illustrated) complete with instructions enabling anyone to make tests in 2 minutes time. Complete......... **$20.00**

Sound and Voice Detector

1—Listen in on conversations of occupants of a room by using concealed microphone.

2—Listen through walls with wall contact microphone.

3—Listen in on telephone conversations using wire tapping unit.

Requires no batteries—just plug in to electric socket ... always ready to use and will operate indefinitely. Easy to operate, sturdy and easily carried.

The Sound and Voice Detector Set consists of the following: Detector Unit . . . 1 Concealment Microphone . . . 1 Contact Wall Microphone . . . 1 Telephone wire tapping unit . . . 2 sets Headphones . . . All necessary Wire . . . Handy Carrying Case . . . Nothing else to buy. Complete....... **$125.00**

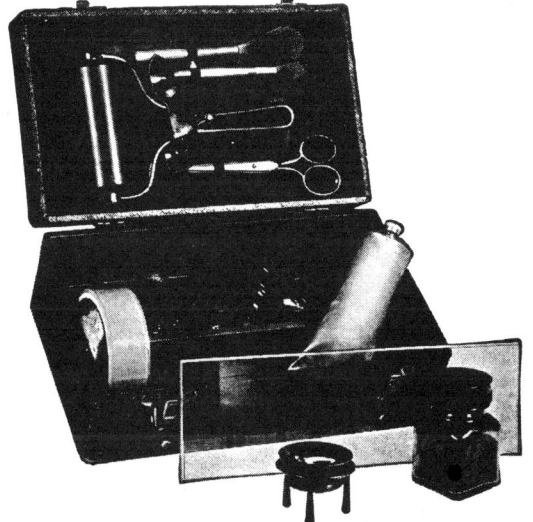

Official Fingerprint Outfit

The really COMPLETE SET which includes *everything* for Fingerprinting either in the office, or to carry out to the scene of a crime. IMPROVED ROLLER and ¼ pound of non-drying ink made especially for Fingerprinting. Four bottles of NEW POWDERS which may be used for locating prints on *any* surface.

Sold only as a complete set. Components will be sold only to those making original purchase of complete sets from us.

SET CONSISTS OF:

¼ lb. Tube of Ink
3 x 9 inch Plate Glass Slab
Ink Roller, 3 inches wide
8 Power Tri-pod Magnifying Glass
1 Pair Shears
2 Camel Hair Brushes

10 yards of Lifting Tape
2 oz. Bottle Black Powder
2 oz. Bottle Grey Powder
1 oz. Bottle White Powder
1 oz. Bottle Red Powder
Leather Carrying Case

Complete **$20.00**

NO SPECIAL TRAINING REQUIRED

CANVAS AND LEATHER GUN CASES

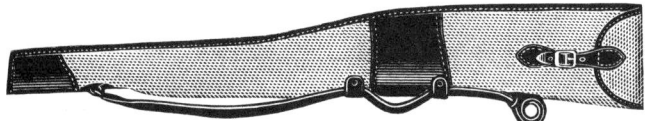

Grade B—Full Length Canvas Cover. Made of No. 6 O. D. Canvas, flannel lined, leather trimmed. State full length of gun.
No. 1417. Price, each.................................$3.50

Grade A—Full Length Canvas Cover; made of No. 1 unstarched O. D. colored duck; not lined; trimmed with cordovan colored leather.
No. 1420. Price, each*................................$5.00

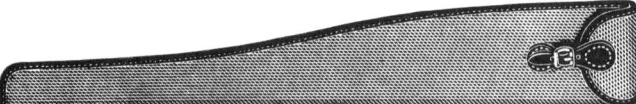

Plain brown canvas carrying case with buckle.
Price*..$1.75

Grade B—Take Down Canvas Cover—Made of No. 6 O. D. canvas, flannel lined, leather trimmed. No. 1409. Price, each†.........$3.50

Grade A—Take Down Canvas Cover—Made of No. 1 starched O. D. colored duck; not lined; trimmed with cordovan colored leather. Has gosset.
No. 1408. Price, each†.................................$5.00

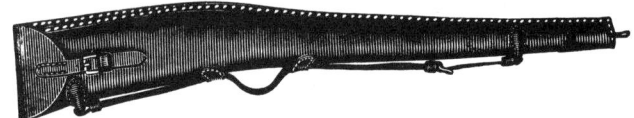

Leather Case—Especially designed for the Springfield Sporter, extra heavy brown leather and buck laced. Price................$22.50

Elliott Model—Made of top grain Steerhide over heavy trunk board, green felt linings. Caps at both ends removable. Space for cleaning rods and wiping cloths.
Elliott Model—Double Barrel or Pump Gun Case; length 28, 30 and 32 inches..$20.00

This is a first class genuine cowhide case for double barrel shotguns. It is carefully made of best leather and very serviceable. Price†....$14.00

Our very best cases. Heavy smooth steerhide of top grain, mahogany, over heavy trunkboard. Green felt lined, lockstitch sewed throughout, movable partition with cleaning rod pocket. Large raised handle. Brass finish hardware, heavy brass lock buckle. Sewed chapes. Heavy reinforced muzzle cap end. End and muzzle caps fit flush with case.
No. 830—Double Barrel Gun Case; length 28, 30 and 32 inches...$20.00

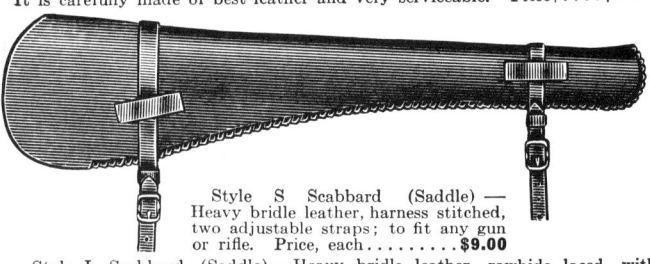

Style S Scabbard (Saddle)—Heavy bridle leather, harness stitched, two adjustable straps; to fit any gun or rifle. Price, each.........$9.00
Style L Scabbard (Saddle)—Heavy bridle leather, rawhide laced, with adjustable straps; to fit any gun or rifle. Price, each...........$12.00
Leather Case—Same as Style L, but of genuine sole leather, oil tanned; with cap (not illustrated). Price...........................$25.00

SHELL BAG

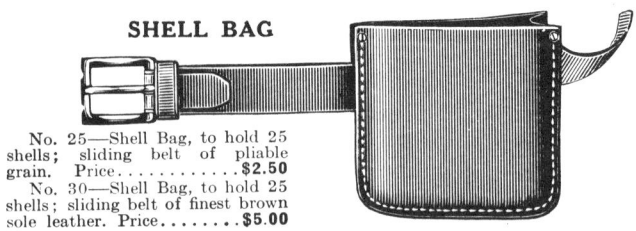

No. 25—Shell Bag, to hold 25 shells; sliding belt of pliable grain. Price.................$2.50
No. 30—Shell Bag, to hold 25 shells; sliding belt of finest brown sole leather. Price........$5.00

SHELL BAG No. 10

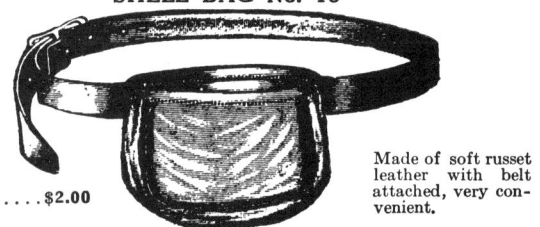

Price......$2.00

Made of soft russet leather with belt attached, very convenient.

GENUINE HEISER BELTS

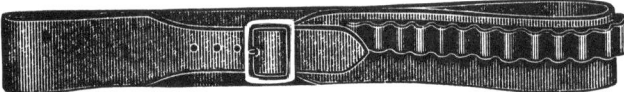

No. 136—2 inch leather and buckle, plain finish 30—¾ inch cartridge loops...$2.25

No. 40—2½ inch leather, plain finish, 30—⅞ inch cartridge loops. $5.25
No. 43—Same as No. 40, but Mexican Hand Carved........... 7.25

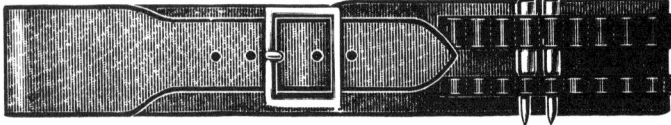

No. 34—3 inch leather, 2 inch buckle and 30 Rifle cartridge loops.
Price..$6.75
No. 82—Same as No. 34, except for Pistol; Mexican Hand Carved; 2 rows; 30 loops, each................................. 12.50
Note:—Our No. 82 Belt is made 4½ inches wide and 1½ inch buckle and billet.

SHEEPSKIN CASES AND ACCESSORIES

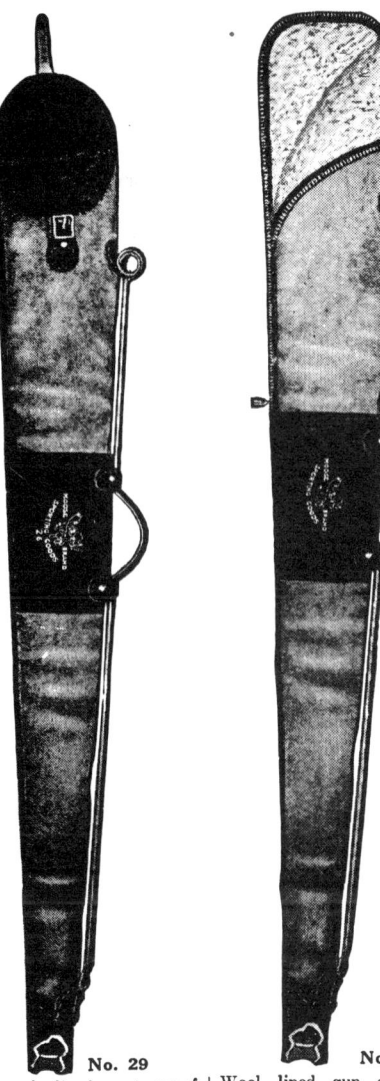
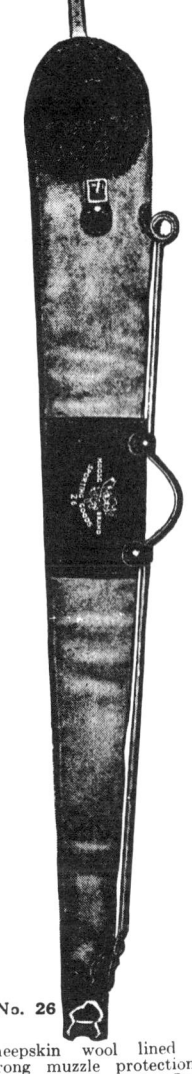

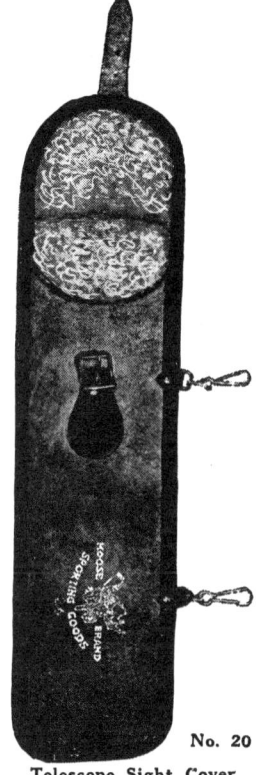

No. 27

This wool lined take-down leather gun cover is made for all types of take-down, pump and automatic shotguns with barrel as made for 26", 28", 30", and 32" barrel length.
Price $7.50

This case also available for extra barrel compartment, price..... $9.00

No. 20

Telescope Sight Cover

This sheepskin wool lined telescope cover is very well made and available for various types and styles of sights. It is made so that it may be attached to the gun cover with snaps. When ordering specify name and style of sight and overall length of scope.
Price $2.50

No. 29

New wool lined waterproof gun cover, covered with Forest Green waterproof Duck, heavy "Viscolized" leather sling and reinforcements. Thick wool lining protects gun from rusting. Heavy strap leather sling and handle is regular equipment. Will accommodate all pump style, lever and bolt action, automatic and double barrel guns.
Price $7.50
Also made to fit any rifle with telescope sight attached.
Price $9.00

No. 60

Wool lined gun cover with zipper opening. This case is of the same general description as No. 26 except that it has Talon zipper opening in place of buckle. This zipper opening assures the greatest protection for the gun, and not only lends a very pleasing appearance to the case, but also permits quick and easy opening and closing. Meets the requirements of discriminating sportsmen.
Price $8.00
For Rifles with telescope attached, Price..... $9.50

No. 26

Sheepskin wool lined with strong muzzle protection, of excellent quality. It has leather reinforcements over breech of gun, together with Sole Leather Cup End which protects the muzzle of gun from scratches or nicks. This cover is made in various sizes to accommodate pump style and automatic shotguns as well as slide action, bolt action, and carbine rifles.
Price $6.00
Also made to fit any rifle with telescope sight attached.
Price $7.50

Price $1.50

WOOL LINED HOLSTER

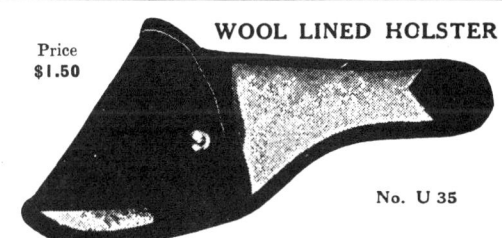

No. U 35

For those wishing to give their pistols and revolvers the very best possible protection, we recommend this genuine sheepskin wool lined holster which gives real protection to all parts of the gun. Available for practically all pistols and revolvers. When ordering state make, model, and barrel length.

WOOL LINED SHOOTERS' GLOVE
No. 22

Can be used on either hand. Reinforced Gun Rest. Very popular with Target shooters. Protects hand from barrels.
Price .... $.90

AUTOMATIC CLIP BOX
No. 7

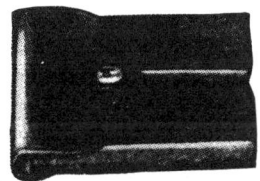

For two clips. Made of black Cowhide. Belt loop on back.
Price $1.80

CARTRIDGE BOX
No. 14

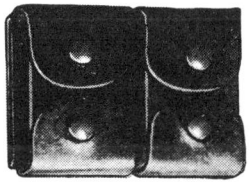

Double Carrier, black cowhide. Cartridges put in top come out bottom. Specify caliber.
Price $1.80

10-X ALL LEATHER GUN CASE

Made of No. 1 selected chrome tanned horsehide leather. A 36 inch Zipper fastener allows three-fourths of the cast to lie open. The Zipper is lapped—no rivets so no metal can touch your gun. Complete with Carrying Strap.

Price $5.50
Telescope attachment 6 00
Sheepskin lining 9.00

A GOOD GUN DESERVES A GOOD COVER

HIGHEST GRADE ENGLISH AND VIENNA GUN CASES

SHELL BAG

The shells are easily withdrawn from this Bag as the mouth is fitted with a patent flexible spiral spring and so is always kept open without being absolutely rigid. Absolutely waterproof and complete with stout web shoulder sling. This bag is of the finest workmanship and materials throughout.

	50	75	100
9A Best Pigskin lined texture	$13.50	$16.00	$20.00
9B Best Grained Cowhide lined texture	10.00	11.50	12.50
9C Best Waterproof Tan Mail Canvas	7.50	8.75	10.00

DE LUXE OAK AND LEATHER SHELL BOX

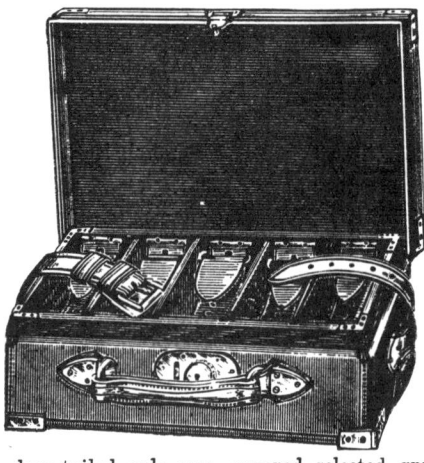

De-luxe dove-tailed oak case, covered selected grain hide, lid lined fine crimson cloth and inside French polished. Fitted with regulating straps inside to prevent rattling, and the partitions are removable so that the case can be used for other purposes. A pair of strong luggage straps are fitted except on 100/200 size leather, which have one wide strap only.

For 200 Shells .... $35.00 For 400 Shells $52.50
For 300 Shells .... 45.00 For 500 Shells 60.00

BEST ENGLISH SHELL BELTS

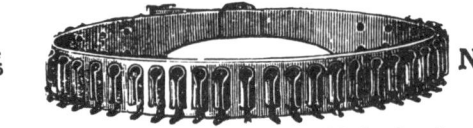

Price $2.75   No. 1

Made of finest coffee brown leather with leather bound buckle. Clips are made of special spring steel, securely riveted into place and into which cartridges are easily inserted and from which they are much more rapidly removed than from any other type of shell belt. Made in two sizes—one which takes 12 and 16 gauge interchangeable and the other for 20 gauge. In ordering give waist circumference and desired gauge.
Price $2.75

No. 2

English Shell Belt. This is the same quality as No. 1, but with the individual full leather loop for each shell and fully closed at the bottom. Made in 12, 16 and 20 gauge. In ordering be sure and specify gauge.
Price $3.50

FINEST VIENNA PLIABLE LEATHER CASES

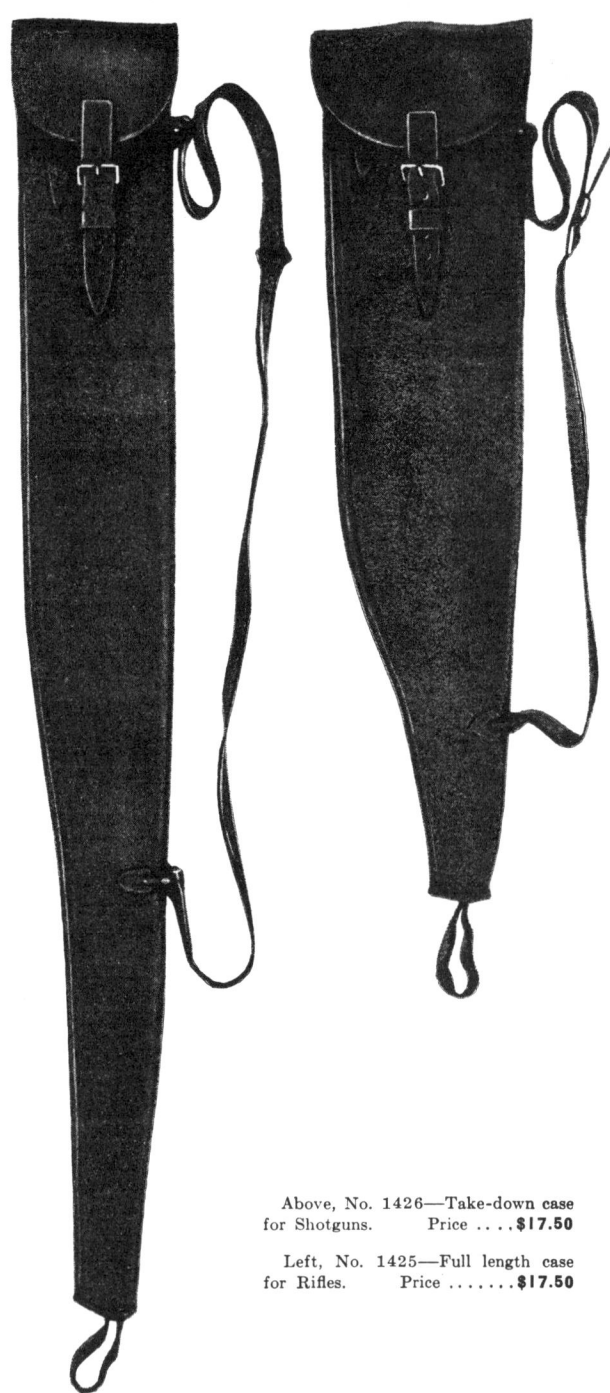

Above, No. 1426—Take-down case for Shotguns. Price $17.50

Left, No. 1425—Full length case for Rifles. Price $17.50

These cases are made of the finest 4-ounce soft cow hide leather with a special type of oil tanning which imparts an almost unbelieveable pliableness and protection against dampness. It has an extra flap at the mouth for added protection. Side pocket. Hand-made throughout of the highest grade workmanship and material. Made full length for rifle and take-down for shotguns. When ordering Model 1426 for shotgun, be sure to specify barrel length. When ordering Model 1425 for rifle, specify overall length of rifle.

HIGHEST GRADE ENGLISH GUN CASES
THE NEW PATTERN "LIGHTWEIGHT" GUN CASE

All cases shown except No. 1 are of the very popular English lightweight style. Weight 4½–6 lbs. according to size.
Very smart and neat in appearance. Built on strong yet light wood foundation with all corners and edges rounded off, these cases are the most compact made. With close and flush fitting lid they are dust and damp proof and suitable for any climate.

BEST QUALITY OAK & LEATHER CASE DE LUXE MODEL

Superfine whole-grain russet cowhide on stout oak dovetailed body. Cut-open case showing full polished oak rim inside lid, rim and wainscot inside body. Fully fitted and lined best wool cloth for Gun, all cleaning implements and space for a few shells. This case is fitted with special solid brass corners, handle plates, hinges, centre nameplate and push-in nozzle lock and is complete with handle and two luggage straps. De Luxe Model, hand made throughout and the finest case that is made in England.
Price $75.00

No. 1X
Superfine Waterproof tan mail canvas cover for the above case. Cover to open with lid and fitted with wide leather bands and strongly bound each end.
Price $18.50

No. 1B
Same as No. 1, but for two guns.
Price $100.00

BEST SOLID LEATHER "LIGHTWEIGHT" CASE. DE LUXE MODEL

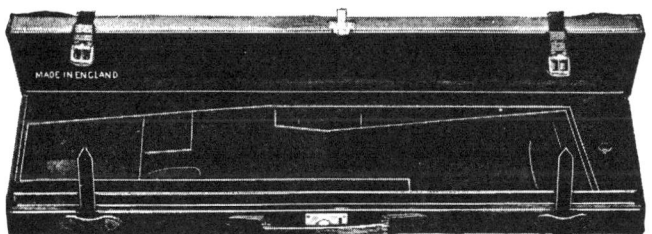

Superfine whole-grain russet cowhide, lined best cloth and fully fitted for cleaning implements, oil can and space for a few shells, etc. Very finely sewn and hand made throughout. Complete with handle, lock and two luggage straps.
The finest case of this type made.
Price $50.00
This case can be fitted with hand sewn solid block leather corners at an extra cost of $7.50.

SUPERIOR LEATHER "LIGHTWEIGHT" CASE

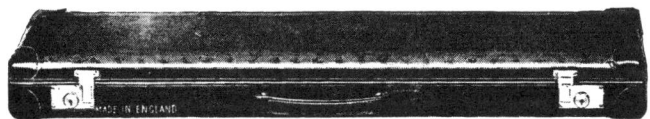

Superfine whole-grain russet cowhide on special strong yet light wood foundation, complete with handle and two locks and hand-sewn solid block leather corners. Lined best cloth and fully fitted for Gun and all cleaning implements and space for a few shells.
A superior case at a reasonable price.
Price $35.00

PLAIN LEATHER "LIGHTWEIGHT" CASE

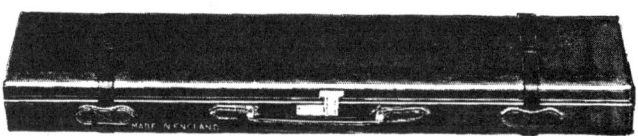

Best quality cowhide on strong yet light wood foundation complete with handle, lock and two luggage straps. Lined good cloth and fully fitted for Gun and all cleaning implements and space for a few shells.
A very pleasing case.
Price $27.50

"LIGHTWEIGHT" CASE
(De Luxe Model in Canvas)

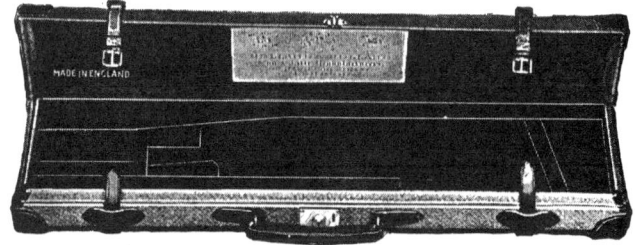

Covered superior green Willesden rot and damp proof canvas, made on strong yet light wood foundation and complete with handle, lock and two luggage straps and hand sewn solid block leather corners. Lined best cloth and fully fitted for Gun and all cleaning implements and space for a few shells.
A De Luxe Model for those who prefer a canvas covered case.
Price $22.50

BEST G.W.C. "LIGHTWEIGHT" CASE

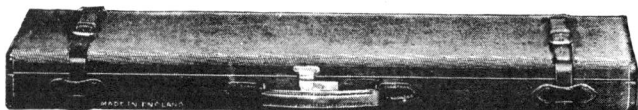

Best green Willesden rot and damp proof canvas on strong yet light wood foundation, fully fitted for Gun and all cleaning implements, space for a few shells and lined good cloth. Complete with handle, lock and two luggage straps.
A very pleasing case covered canvas.
Price $16.00

ENGLISH PATTERN BOX G.W.C. GUN CASE

Strong green Willesden rot and dust proof canvas on stout wood shell, lined good cloth and fitted for Gun and all cleaning implements and space for a few shells. Ends of case strongly leather bound and complete with handle, lock and two luggage straps.
Price $12.50

A GOOD GUN DESERVES A GOOD CASE

LAWRENCE STEER HIDE HOLSTERS AND CARTRIDGE BELTS

Since 1857, the name Lawrence on leather goods has meant the utmost in quality, service and value. Made in the West by expert craftsmen, Lawrence Holsters and Cartridge Belts are worn and used by outdoor men all over the world. Every item manufactured by Lawrence is unconditionally guaranteed for one year against flaws in material or workmanship.

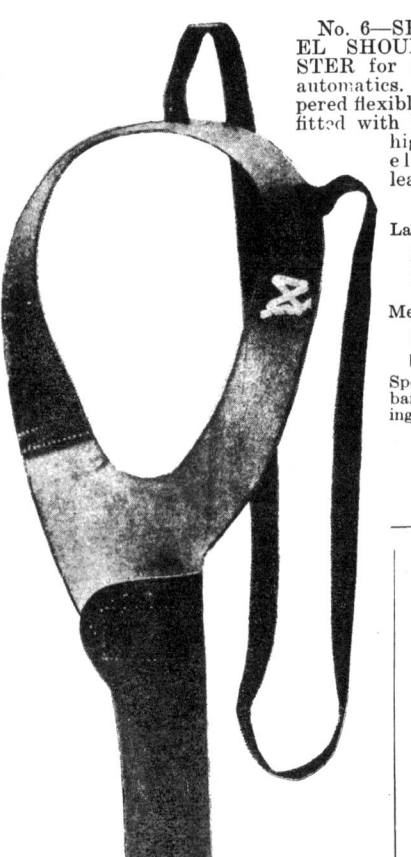

No. 6—SPRING MODEL SHOULDER HOLSTER
for revolvers and automatics. Finely tempered flexible steel spring; fitted with body strap of high grade live elastic. Tan leather only.

PRICES
Large size: (.32; .38; .45 caliber, with 6, 6½, 7½ inch barrels) **$4.75**
Medium size: (.32; .38; .45 caliber, with 4 and 5 inch barrels) ..**$4.75**
Specify length of barrel when ordering.

No. 122—QUICK DRAW HOLSTER
for revolvers and automatics.
Basket Stamped **$3.95**
Flower Stamped **$5.25**
Plain ... **$3.15**

For white laced edge add 75¢ to prices shown above. No extra charge for safety strap; specify if desired when ordering.

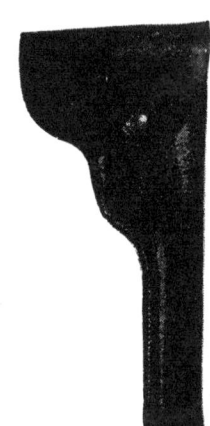

No. 14—FLAP HOLSTER.
A high quality flap top holster; hand made, molded, oiled and polished.
Hand Flower Stamped ... **$6.19**
Basket Stamped ... **$4.19**
Plain **$3.19**

No. 211—MEXICAN STYLE HOLSTER.
Hand flower stamped on selected clear leather. Oiled mahogany color. White leather laced edge. Blocked over form to guarantee a perfect fit.
A handsome and practical holster **$7.45**
No. 212—Same as No. 211 except Basket Stamped **$5.85**
No. 213—Same as No. 211 except Plain.. **$4.95**
Give caliber and length of barrel when ordering.

No. 18—POCKET HOLSTER
for revolvers and automatics. Seams lock-stitched; loop for belt; tan leather unless ordered otherwise.
Price **$2.45**

SEMI-MEXICAN STYLE HOLSTERS

High grade heavy steer hide holsters with blocked over forms. Safety strap for keeping gun secure. Open end prevents dirt from collecting. Closed end also available at no extra cost. White leather laced. Oiled to rich mahogany color and hand polished. A wide loop for belt or may be carried in pocket if desired. A favorite holster that will last a lifetime.

No. 25L—Hand Flower Stamped **$5.65**
Basket Stamped.. **$4.50**
Plain **$3.75**
No. 25—Plain. Sewed edge instead of lacing. **$2.95**

No. 27L—Hand Flower Stamped **$5.85**
Basket Stamped.. **$4.75**
Plain **$3.95**

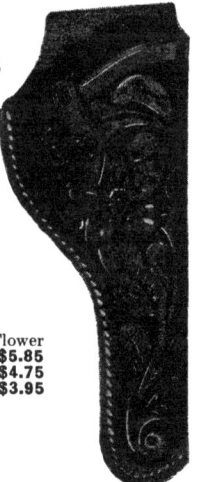

SAM BROWN BELT No. 1. Made of 8 oz. strap leather, lined under Dee end. Hook attachment makes it unnecessary to unbuckle belt. 2¼ inches wide, 1¼ shoulder strap, unlined, tapered to ⅞ inch buckle. Black or cordovan leather. Heavy Colonial hardware, nickel or brass.

Black leather with nickel hardware will be furnished unless ordered otherwise **$8.85**
Belt No. 2—Same as No. 1 but with full leather-lined shoulder strap and belt, **$10.25**

Give waist measure over uniform when ordering. We measure waist to center hole, allowing two holes on either side to take up or let out belt.

LAWRENCE STEER HIDE HOLSTERS AND CARTRIDGE BELTS

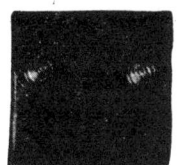

SAM BROWN CARTRIDGE POUCH. Holds 12 cartridges. **$3.65**

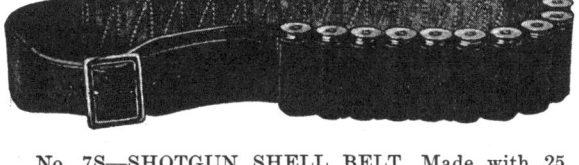

No. 40—BELT FOR RIMLESS SHELLS. Made of solid full grain leather, oil finish. Three inches wide with 1¾ inch brass buckle. Thirty loops lock-stitched with waxed linen thread. Lower loops smaller.

Lengths up to 44 inches.....................**$6.45**

Specify size of cartridge and waist measurement when ordering.

LEATHER CLIP POCKET FOR AUTOMATICS. Made of full grain tan leather. Snap button; flat loop on back for belt. Give caliber of shell when ordering.

No. 1 for one clip.........**$3.00**
No. 2 for two clips........ 4.25

No. 7S—SHOTGUN SHELL BELT. Made with 25 sewn loops. Nickel bar buckle. 2¼ inches wide. Tan only. Give gauge of shell and waist measurement when ordering.

Lengths up to 44 inches.....................**$3.65**

No. 25—CARTRIDGE CASE made of soft oil tanned leather. Wide loop for belt. Holds ten rifle cartridges in separate loops. Fits close to body.

Price **$2.75**

HANDCUFF POUCH with loop in back to slide on belt........**$3.20**

No. 11—CARTRIDGE BELT with 40 loops and quickly adjustable to fit any size cartridge. Specially adapted to .32 caliber and upward. Loop strap laced in and out to prevent the loop from slipping. Heavy wide nickel bar buckle. Border stamped. Tan only. Lengths up to 44 inches.

2 inches wide	**$3.95**
2½ inches wide	4.15
3 inches wide	4.45

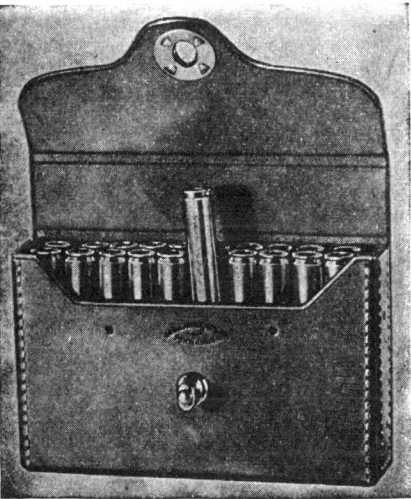

No. 20—CARTRIDGE CASE. Made of finest stiff saddle leather; seams lock-stitched; wide loop for belt; holds full box of 20 cartridges.

Price **$2.75**

Give caliber of shell when ordering.

Cartridge cases suitable for 30-30 caliber rifle or larger.

No. 15—PLAIN HOLSTER BELTS. Made of high quality steer-hide leather. Heavy bar buckle. Just the belt to use with your holster if you do not use a cartridge belt.

	1½ inch	1¾ inch	2-inch
No. 15F Hand Flower Stamped	$6.25	$6.45	$6.95
No. 15B Basket Stamped	2.65	2.95	3.25
No. 15 Plain	1.69	1.99	2.29

No. 35—SERIES CARTRIDGE BELT. Made of selected steer-hide. Cartridge loops lock-stitched with linen thread. Heavy bar buckle. Lengths up to 44 inches.

	3 inches wide	2½ inches wide
No. 35F Hand Flower Stamped	$10.45	$10.15
No. 35B Basket Stamped	6.45	6.15
No. 35 Plain	5.15	4.75

Give caliber of cartridge and waist measurement to center hole when ordering.

A GOOD HOLSTER is always a good Investment

GENUINE H. H. HEISER HOLSTERS

HEISER HOLSTERS are designed for those wanting the best it is possible to produce and who recognize real class and quality. Each holster is built individually with the best workmanship and finest material for the particular gun it is intended for, thus assuring that much desired "box fit." In ordering, give make, caliber and barrel length as well as catalog number. Unless especially requested, right hand holsters will be shipped; left hand holsters supplied at no additional cost, but delivery will be delayed about a week or ten days.

FOR REVOLVERS
LARGE SIZE................Barrel Length, 5½ inches to 7½ inches
MEDIUM SIZE..............Barrel Length, 4 inches to 5 inches
SMALL SIZE................Barrel Length, under 4 inches

FOR AUTOMATICS
LARGE SIZE................Colt .45 etc., and Luger
MEDIUM SIZE..............All .32 Automatics
SMALL SIZE................All .25 Automatics

No. 410.—Heiser Loop Style Holster for Revolvers

These extra heavy holsters are made of the finest Oak Tanned California skirting leather and have what is known as the "Quick Draw" belt loop, a design originated by one of the most expert men in the West. Waxed thread sewed, open end, riveted at end of stitches, not lined. Fine plain, smooth finish.

No. 410 Small $2.75
No. 410 Medium .. 3.25
No. 410 Large 3.75

No. 714.—Heiser Loop Style Belt Holster

Made of heavy California Oak Tanned skirting leather, waxed thread sewed, not lined, closed end. Gun sets high, exposing trigger and trigger guard. This holster is especially designed for single action guns, but can be had for any revolver. Not made for automatics. Full Mexican hand carved.

No. 714 Small $4.25
No. 714 Medium 4.75
No. 714 Large 5.25

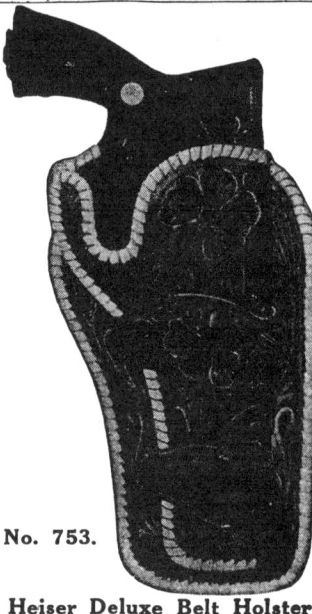

No. 753.

Heiser Deluxe Belt Holster

Made of the very best selected heavy California Oak Tanned skirting leather. Both pouch and back leather lined. Hand thong wrap stitched, back and bottom of pouch with white lacing. Belt loop has two snap button fasteners to permit removal from belt without taking off belt. Especially adapted for belts with extended loops, but can be used on any belt. Extra fine full Mexican hand carved.

No. 753 Medium............$9.50
No. 753 Large..............10.00

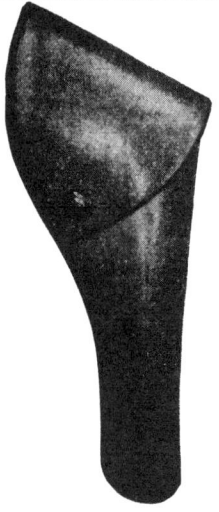

Automatic and Revolver Holsters with Flap

These holsters are made up unlined — of Heavy Oak Tanned, California skirting leather — durable snap button on flap, waxed thread stitched — loop on back for body belt; light in weight; very durable.
No. 434 for Revolvers.
No. 435 for Automatics.
No. 434 Large.... $2.75
No. 434 Medium.. 2.50
No. 434 Small.... 2.25

Heiser's Safety Strap Belt Holster

For Automatic. Made of Heavy Oak Tanned California skirting leather — safety strap with snap button to keep the gun from falling out; finest finish, not lined; closed end. Waxed Thread Stitched Edge.
No. 420 Large .$2.00
No. 420 Medium 1.75
No. 420 Small . 1.50

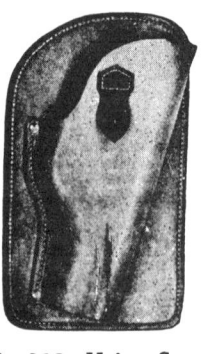

No. 903.—Heiser Sweat Proof Hip Pocket Holster

Made of medium weight Oak Tanned California skirting leather, the back is lined with patent leather to make this holster sweat proof. Button hole tab, heavy waxed thread stitched, open end, riveted at corners, plain finish only. Made for either revolver or pistol.
No. 903 Medium ..$2.30
No. 903 Small 2.15

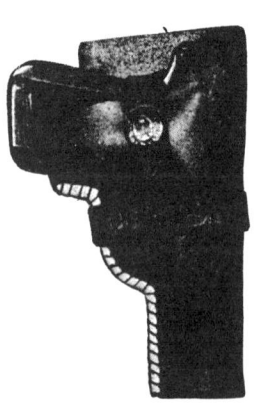

No. 422

These holsters made of Heavy Oak Tanned California skirting leather, thong stitched, reinforced ends, open end. Unlined pouch, durable snap button on flap. Belt loop sewed on back.
Large $2.75
Medium 2.50
Small 2.25

Half Breed Spring Shoulder Holster

Medium Weight California Oak Tanned Skirting. Spring on inside covered with chrome leather; stitched in with waxed thread; retaining cup at bottom. Entirely open on one side, permitting the wearer to gain instant possession of weapon. The shoulder strap is of soft chrome leather which never hardens. It has government bronze tongueless buckle to make it adjustable. Retaining strap does not entirely encircle, but crosses back and holds holster in place without interfering with any movement of body. Made to fit any revolver or automatic.
Price $4.50

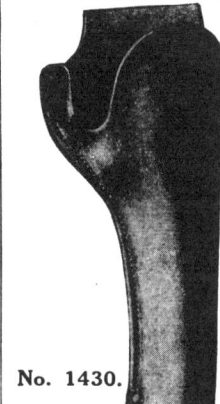

No. 1430.

Citizen's Favorite Belt Holster for Revolver

This holster is intended for those who want a holster of the lightest weight that will give the box fit and permit of a quick draw in a style that will not be cumbersome; it is especially recommended for "City Folks" who carry a gun for self protection. Plain smooth finish.
No. 1430 Small...$1.50
No. 1430 Medium. 1.75
No. 1430 Large... 2.00

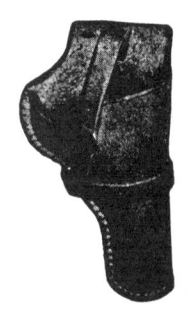

Heiser Loop Style Belt Holsters for Revolvers

Made of California skirting leather in original loop style of construction snap button safety strap to keep the gun from falling out; best finished, unlined, Thong Wrap Stitched Edge Closed End.
No. 419 Large $3.25
No. 419 Med.. 3.00
No. 419 Small. 2.75

EVERYTHING IN GUNS UNDER ONE COVER

AMERICA'S GREAT GUN HOUSE

GENUINE H. H. HEISER HOLSTERS

No. 7 Laced Loop Belt Holster for Automatics

An exclusive design of Heiser made of heavy Oak Tanned California skirting leather, leather lined, waxed thread stitched, made from one piece, loop laced together in front with thong. Open end and snap button safety strap.
No. 7 Small $4.75
No. 7 Medium 5.25
No. 7 Large 5.50

No. 772 Loop Style Belt Holster for Revolvers

The holster with a "box fit" made of extra heavy Oak Tanned California skirting leather of one solid piece, not lined, with closed end and thong wrap stitched, Mexican hand carved.
No. 712 Small ... $4.00
No. 712 Medium . 4.50
No. 712 Large .. 5.00

No. 705 Combination Hip Pocket and Belt Holster for Pistols and Revolvers

Made of one solid piece heavy Oak Tanned California skirting leather with belt loop at top, to take belt and keep holster from becoming over-balanced while in the pocket. Can also be used as a regular belt holster. Heavy waxed thread sewed, open end riveted at corners.
No. 705 Small $4.75
No. 705 Medium ... 5.00
No. 705 Large 5.25

No. 416 Loop Style Belt Holster for Revolvers
No. 916 the same but of Medium weight leather. See prices below.

These holsters are of the most popular type with snap button safety strap to keep gun from falling out, best finish, not lined with closed end.
No. 416 Small $1.75
No. 416 Medium .. 2.00
No. 416 Large 2.25
No. 916 Small 1.50
No. 916 Medium .. 1.75
No. 916 Large 2.00

No. 648 Automobile Holster

Made with straps to buckle around steering wheel of automobile. Medium weight Oak Tanned California skirting leather, wax thread sewed, not lined, open end.
No. 648 Small $2.00
No. 648 Medium 2.25
No. 648 Large 2.50

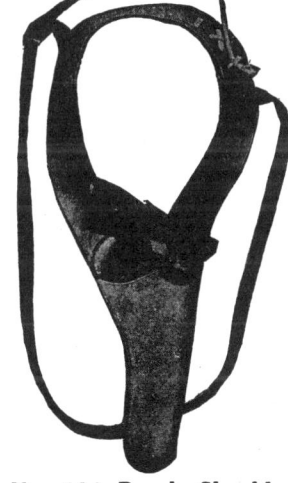
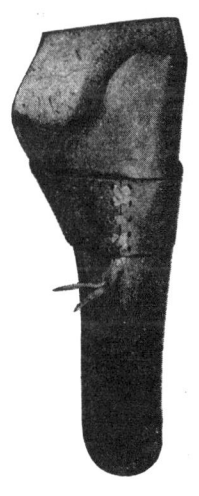

No. 724 Army Style Flexible Belt Holster

Made of heavy Oak Tanned California skirting leather. Lined, Hand thong wrap stitched edge. Belt loop is attached to the holster proper by means of a flexible pivot so that when the end of the holster is tied fast to the leg the pivot will permit the holster swinging with the movement of the leg. Open end, snap button safety strap. Mexican hand carved.
No. 724 Medium $5.25
No. 724 Large 5.50

No. 184 Pouch Shoulder Holster

Pouch of this holster is made of Oak Tanned California skirting leather. Medium weight, the back is double stitched and lined. The seam on the outer edge is waxed thread sewed and riveted. The shoulder strap is made of soft chrome tanned, sweat-proof leather. The flap as shown at the top of the pouch is intended as a protection to keep the hammer from injuring the wearer, as well as the gun from rusting because of perspiration under the arm. Made to fit any gun. When ordering state make, model and length of barrel.
Price $3.00

No. 426 New Laced Loop Belt Holster for Revolvers Only

Made of heavy Oak Tanned California skirting leather, waxed thread sewed, with a new pattern of thong laced belt loop, well finished, not lined, quick draw top, riveted corners.
No. 426 Small ...$2.50
No. 426 Medium . 2.75
No. 426 Large ... 3.00

No. 738 Army Style Flexible Belt Holster with Flap for Revolvers and Pistols

Made of heavy Oak Tanned California skirting leather, waxed thread sewed, reinforced at end of stitches, closed end, unlined. Durable metal stud button to fasten flap down. Mexican hand carved.

No. 738 Medium $5.50
No. 738 Large 5.75

NOTE: The same holster can also be had in plain smooth finish (No Mexican hand carving) but the same quality leather and workmanship.

No. 438 Medium $3.75
No. 438 Large 4.00

NOTE: Please do not fail to state make, model, calibre of gun as well as the length of barrel.

A GOOD GUN IS WORTH A GOOD HOLSTER

WALL GUN RACKS

For the sportsman possessing several guns, there is no more attractive way to store guns than on a handsome wall rack. In this way the guns cannot be mislaid, are out of harm, are readily accessible for use, examination or cleaning at any time, and in addition are extremely decorative.

These racks are particularly attractive when used in a club, hunting lodge or cabin over a fire-place. They are suitable for all types of shotguns as well as rifles in all shapes and size, and are of advantage in displaying antique guns with a decorative and pleasing effect.

No. 41—Walnut or Knotty Pine $15.00

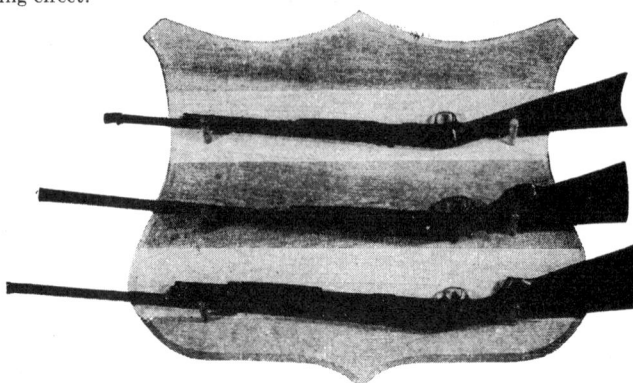

No. 11—Walnut or Knotty Pine $16.00

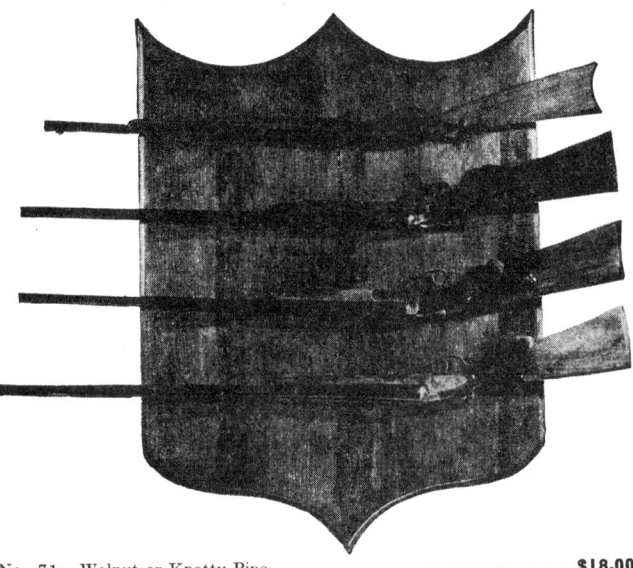

No. 71—Walnut or Knotty Pine $18.00

No. 21—Walnut or Knotty Pine $16.00

GENUINE STAG HORN GUN RACKS

These racks are made of solid oak with natural varnish finish. The prongs are of genuine stag horn, neatly polished and lacquered. Made in pairs of three sizes, for one, two or three guns.
Price per pair for one gun, $5.00; for two, $7.50; for three $10.00

OAK GUN RACKS FOR WALL AND CORNER

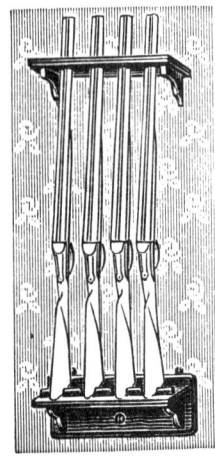

Oak wall rack for guns. This rack consists of two parts of quartered oak readily attached to any wall and assures safe and convenient storage for shotguns or rifles. Because of its attractive finish, it is not only useful but ornamental and is particularly adapted for the sportsman's den or cabin.
Price $10.00

Corner Gun Rack. As it quite often happens that a corner is the only available space, this rack has been especially designed to utilize this space in a practical and useful manner. It consists of two parts of quartered oak and is suitable for three rifles or shotguns.
Price $10.00

ENGLISH LEATHER GUN RACKS

This rack has solid, heavy leather base and leather covered steel hooks to hold four guns. It is particularly well made and attractive throughout and makes a handy and handsome rack to display or show guns.

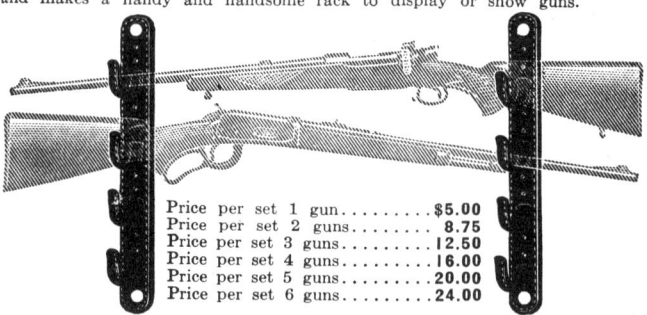

Price per set 1 gun $5.00
Price per set 2 guns 8.75
Price per set 3 guns 12.50
Price per set 4 guns 16.00
Price per set 5 guns 20.00
Price per set 6 guns 24.00

DISPLAY YOUR GUNS TO THEIR BEST ADVANTAGE

AMERICA'S GREAT GUN HOUSE

GUN ROOM REQUISITES

RIFLE VISE

For home, camp or target range use. A handy light weight vise for performing minor repairs to guns. Can easily be clamped on any bench. Reversible feature and felt lined jaws permits use for small parts or entire barrel.

Price $17.00

PRES-TO OILER

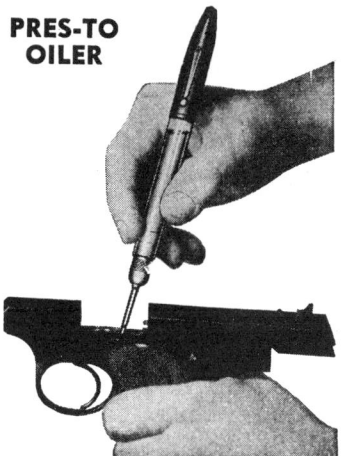

Built like a fountain pen with screwcap, clip, and transparent reservoir. May be carried in pocket without leakage. To use, merely depress point on part to be oiled. Each press ejects 1/10 drop of oil. Gets into out of the way places, prevents over oiling, easy to fill. Ideal for use on all guns.
Price $0.50

METAL OIL CANS

Best quality seamless, leakproof, metal oil containers, square, heavily nickled, with drop dipper attached to screw cap. A necessity for trunk cases.
Size 1½ x 1½ x 2", Price....$2.75
Size 1¾ x 1¾ x 2", Price.....2.75
Size 2 x 2 x 2¼", Price......3.50
Size 2¼ x 1⅝ x 2⅛", Price...3.50

HAND PROTECTOR

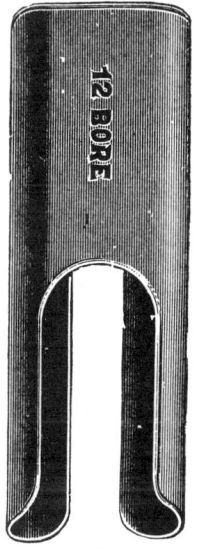

12, 16 or 20 ga.

This English made hand protector is finely made of spring steel covered with carefully sewn genuine blank leather. Available in 12, 16 and 20 gauge slips easily over barrel directly in front of the forend and prevents burning of fingers on the heated barrel.
Particularly recommended for those desiring to use their field gun at traps or skeet.
Price $4.50

ENGLISH TURNSCREWS
(Insets of 3)

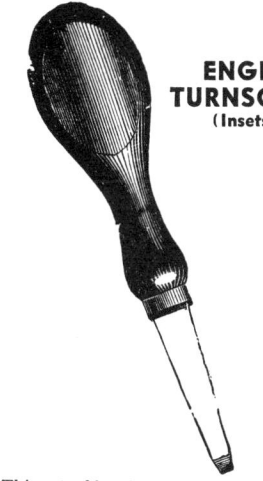

This set of hand made English turnscrews is intended for the sportsman who has the need to strip his gun.
Only the very best forged and tempered steel is used, the blade is highly polished, as is also the genuine ebony grip. The ferrule is polished brass.
Sold only in complete sets of three in assorted sizes.
Price per set of three $4.50

"FITEMAL" NIPPLE WRENCH SET

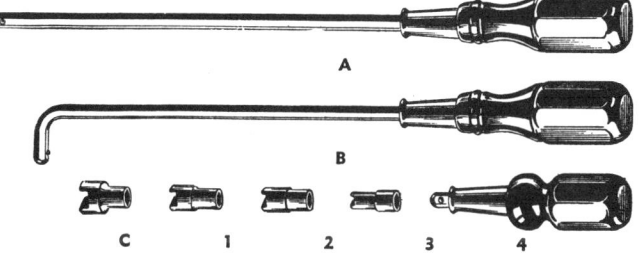

Scattered throughout the country there are still hundreds of thousands of breech loading percussion cap rifles, shotguns, revolvers and pistols. One of the commonest repairs required on these guns is replacement of the nipple. The removal of the old and refitting of the new is an extremely easy and rapid operation—provided the proper tool is available—but nine times out of ten it is not, and what should be easy becomes a "headache." Improper tools are used, and the result is usually bad disfigurement, if not actual ruination, not only of the old but of the new nipple as well, in addition to marring, gouging and general havoc to the area surrounding. While individual nipple wrenches have been available, these usually had wrong length or shape of handle, the wrong diameter of head, or wrong width of slot.
Illustrated above is our "Fitemal" set of nipple wrenches, it literally fits them all. It consists of a set of three hexagon shanks with handles. Two are straight, one ⅜" overall, the other 9⅝". The third is bent, measuring 9" overall. On the side near the base of the shank of each is a button. This button permits the use of any of the four heads interchangeably, giving twelve combinations.
The four heads have the following measurements—½" diameter with 9/32" slot—13/32" diameter with 9/32" slot—13/32" diameter with ¼" slot—11/32" diameter with 3/16" slot. All parts are hardened.
Before attempting to remove nipple, kerosene should be applied to loosen rust or dried grease.

"Fitemal" Nipple Wrench Set, complete as illustrated $2.75
"Fitemal" Single Shank with choice of one head 1.25
"Fitemal" Extra Heads, each.....................................50

SHOTGUN SNAP SHELL

Exceptionally well made light weight all metal snap caps, nickel plated with rebounding horn "primer." Should always be placed in chamber for dry snapping to prevent damage or breakage of the firing pins and hammers. Available in 12, 16 and 20 gauge. State gauge desired.
Price per pair $2.25
Price, each 1.25

"TRUWAIT" TRIGGER TESTER

This is a correctly designed instrument patterned after the official British Army model, and with it the trigger pull can be accurately measured by ¼ inch up to 16 pounds.
Price $7.50

SHOTGUN MUZZLE STOPS

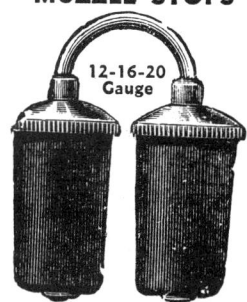

12-16-20 Gauge

These muzzle stops are invaluable in keeping the bore of a shotgun clean and free of dust and dirt. Nickel plated throughout with green felt stoppers. May be fitted or removed in a moment.
Price $2.50

EVERYTHING FOR GUNS UNDER ONE COVER

ATTRACTIVE ALL STEEL GUN CABINETS

Electrically welded all steel construction
for *lifetime* service

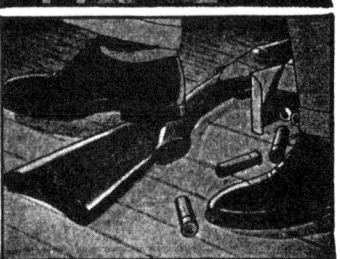

You'll find the cabinet you want in this wonderful assortment. Sportsmen told us what they preferred in cabinets—and we designed accordingly, to meet exact demands as expressed by hundreds of sportsmen customers. In the variety here shown you'll surely find the one you want.

All have chrome plated automotive type handle with built-in cylinder lock and two keys.

A new satin texture baked-on enamel gives these cabinets the most durable finish known.

ALL CABINETS WILL BE SHIPPED ONLY UPON FULL PREPAYMENT AND F.O.B. HORICON, WISCONSIN

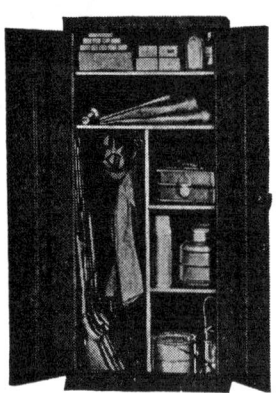

No. M-100 "Master Grade" Sportsman's Cabinet shown above. Adjustable shelves. Height of gun compartment 52 inches. Ample storage of six guns and other equipment. Three hooks for caps and coats. 72 in. high, 32 in. wide, 18 in. deep. Shipping weight 169 lbs.
Price **$22.00**

No. M-110 "Master Grade" double Gun and Storage Cabinet shown above. Upper cabinet 52 in. high, 32 in. wide, 10 in. deep, equipped with gun rack for eleven guns. Hook on each side for cartridge and pistol belts, etc. Roomy lower cabinet 42 in. high, 32 in. wide, 18 in. deep with adjustable shelves. Overall height, 92 inches. Shipping weight, 220 lbs.
Price **$27.10**
No. M-111 Top Gun Cabinet only. Shipping weight, 88 lbs.
Price **$11.65**
No. M-115 Bottom Storage Cabinet only. Shipping weight, 132 lbs.
Price **$15.45**

No. M-105 "Master Grade" Fisherman's Cabinet shown above. Designed particularly for the fisherman. Inside height of rod and gun compartment. 72 inches. Gun rack for six guns and hooks for six rods, also three coat hooks. All shelves adjustable. 72 in. high, 32 in. wide, 18 in. deep. Shipping weight, 171 lbs.
Price **$22.00**

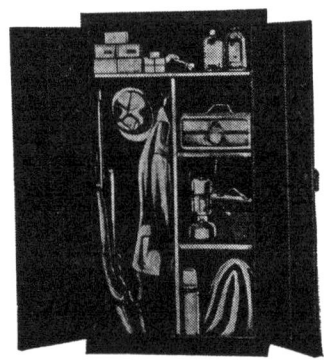

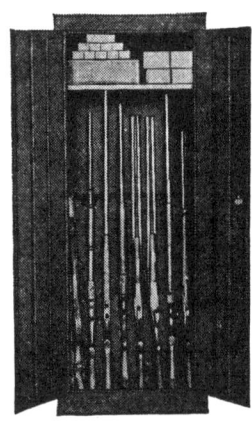

No. S-85 "Standard Grade" Sportsman's Cabinet shown above. All shelves welded in place. Gun compartment 52 inches high with rack for four guns. Two coat hooks. 63 in. high, 24 in. wide, 12 in. deep. Shipping weight, 84 lbs.
Price **$12.65**

No. S-80—Shown above— "Standard Grade" Sportsman's Cabinet. All shelves welded in place. Gun compartment 52 inches high with rack for four guns. Three coat hooks. 63 in. high, 32 in. wide, 12 in. deep. Shipping weight, 95 lbs.
Price **$14.60**

No. S-90 "Standard Grade" Gun Cabinet shown above. Single top shelf. Gun rack for eight guns or rods. Two coat hooks. 63 in. high, 24 in. wide, 12 in. deep. Shipping weight, 76 lbs.
Price **$12.15**

All Cabinets available in Green or Brown enamel

CUSTOM BUILT WALNUT GUN AND ROD CABINETS

Our Line of Gun and Rod Cabinets is the result of many years of improvement. They are practical nad complete in every respect. They are made of southern hardwoods and finished in a rich, dark, walnut, dull-rubbed finish. All hardware is of cast bronze in a statuary finish. All doors and all drawers can be locked securely so that your equipment may be admired but handled only at your invitation. In all cabinets there is room behind the shoulder guns for side arms and other smaller items.

Selected double strength glass is regularly furnished. Special prices on plate glass and extras are listed below.

Protect your investment in your hunting and fishing equipment by keeping it clean, dry, and safe in one of these beautiful cabinets. They are all real pieces of furniture made and finished in an up-to-date factory by men who appreciate and do fine work.

Should an especially fine deluxe finish be required, same may be had at an extra charge of 15% of the base price.

CABINETS SENT ONLY UPON FULL PREPAYMENT — ALL PRICES F.O.B. FACTORY IN IOWA

No. 67
Over all, 36" x 85" x 16".
Has two adjustable shelves.

No. 57 (open)

No. 57 COMBINATION GUN CABINET AND WARDROBE
51 x 70 x 16 inches over all.

No. 57 (closed)

No. 447
Measurements of base
30 x 18 x 16 inches.

Pattern Number	Gun Capacity	BASE PRICE Genuine Walnut Double Strength Glass	Blue Prints Only	EXTRAS—ADD TO BASE PRICE				Shipping Weight
				For Plate Glass Doors— Add	For Beveled Plate Glass Add	For Lighting Equipment Add	For Dust Proof Doors Add	
2250	8	$135.00	$3.00	$13.50	$22.50	$6.00	$7.50	250 lbs.
457*	8	126.00	3.00	7.50	12.00	6.00	4.50	225 lbs.
447*	9	84.00	3.00	7.50	12.00	6.00	4.50	175 lbs.
437*	8	75.00	3.00	7.50	12.00	6.00	4.50	140 lbs.
1031*	11	66.00	3.00	9.00	13.50	6.00	4.50	140 lbs.
1025	8	65.00	3.00	7.50	12.00	6.00	4.50	130 lbs.
67	13	111.00	3.00	9.00	13.50	6.00	4.50	250 lbs.
57	8	132.00	3.00	6.00	10.50	6.00	7.50	240 lbs.
47	8	89.00	3.00	7.50	12.00	6.00	4.50	140 lbs.
37	8	89.00	3.00	7.50	12.00	6.00	4.50	140 lbs.
0122	7	47.00	3.00					70 lbs.
17	5	60.00	3.00				4.50	85 lbs.

* Carried in stock—All other patterns require four weeks time.

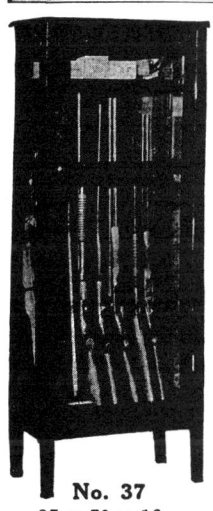

No. 37
27 x 70 x 16
inches over all.

No. 17
18 x 64 x 12
inches over all.

No. 457
Measurement of base, 48" x 12" x 16".
The two slender cabinets have removable, adjustable shelves.

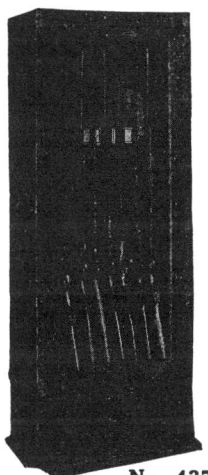

No. 437
25 x 66 x 16
inches over all.

No. 47
27 x 70 x 16
inches over all.

NO SHOOTER'S EQUIPMENT IS COMPLETE WITHOUT ONE OF THESE

ALL STEEL SHOOTER'S BOXES

No. B14 and BR14

Numbers B14 and BR14 are of the same design except that B14 has a ripple baked enamel finish and a full grip steel handle. BR14 has a smooth green finish and heavy wire handle. Are guaranteed water tight.

Dimensions
No.	Long	Wide	High	Net Wt.	Price
B14	14"	6⅛"	6¼"	4 Lbs.	$1.75
Br14	14"	6⅛"	6¼"	3½ Lbs.	1.50

No. CS16 and CS19

A quality product at exceedingly low price. The cantilever style shown above has smooth working tray which rests firmly when extended. Mar-proof green baked ripple enamel finish with fine white striping around lid. Nickel plated fittings, double seamed ends, full length piano (continuous) hinge, and corner irons feature this solidly constructed box.

Dimensions
No.	Long	Wide	High	Net Wt.	Price
SC16	16"	7"	7"	5¾ Lbs.	$3.00
CS19	19"	7"	7"	7 Lbs.	3.20

No. S19

Short tray permits ready access to lower part of box without removal and it slides easily from end to end. Continuous piano type full length hinge, leather handle, nickel plated fittings and mar-proof green baked ripple enamel finish with fine white striping around lid.

No.	Long	Wide	High	Net Wt.	Price
S19	19"	7"	7"	6¾ Lbs.	$2.80

Every Sportsman, target shooter, hunter, gunsmith, woodworker, and mechanic and hobbiest has undoubtedly experienced a definite need for some convenient compact and practical receptical, kit, case, or cabinet in which to store the many and diversified small and easily lost equipment.

On this, as well as the following page, we have assembled a very broad and extensive line of all-steel welded equipment which is diversified enough to include a kit for almost everyone. In the tool section of this catalog will be found another page devoted to regular shop equipment and gunsmiths cases and tool cabinets. Included in the description of every item will be found exact dimensions which will permit the proper selection of suitable box for the individual requirements of the purchaser.

In order to relieve our customers of paying double shipping expenses all prices quoted are f.o.b. factory, Van Wert, Ohio, from which point prompt shipment will be made direct to customer upon receipt of full prepayment. To arrive at shipping weight, from one to two pounds must be added to net weight.

No. S14 and R14

Number R14 is a well made convenient kit. Strong heavy wire handle. Finished in mar-proof green baked enamel and equipped with nickel plated lock and side catches. May be used as a shell box. By reversing the tray and placing it in the bottom it will hold 150 shells and lift the boxes flush to the top of the kit.

S14 has all-metal full sized "grip" handle and is finished in dark green ripple baked enamel with fine white striping around lid. Otherwise R14 is same as S14.

Dimensions
No.	Long	Wide	High	Net Wt.	Price
S14	14"	6¼"	6¼"	3¾ Lbs.	$1.50
R14	14"	6⅛"	6¼"	3¾ Lbs.	1.25

No. CS14 and CR14

Smooth working tray extends as lid is opened. Nickel plated fittings. SC14 has strong all-metal handle and is finished in green baked ripple enamel finish with fine white striping around lid. CR14 has heavy wire handle and smooth mar-proof green baked enamel finish.

Dimensions
No.	Long	Wide	High	Net Wt.	Price
CS14	14"	6⅛"	6¼"	4 Lbs.	$1.75
CR14	14"	6⅛"	6¼"	3¾ Lbs.	1.50

No. 319—321—324

Divided tray extends only part of the length of the Kit. Three skid rails are welded to bottom. Equipped with multiple change lock, side catches, and finished with seal brown ripple baked enamel outside and dark green smooth enamel interior. Nickel plated hardware.

Dimensions
No.	Long	Wide	High	Net Wt.	Price
319	19"	8"	9"	10¾	$5.50
321	21"	8"	9"	11¼	5.75
324	24½"	8"	9"	13¼	6.00

No. S16

Full length tray has two sections. Continuous piano type full length hinge, double seamed ends, comfortable leather handle and corner irons. Dark green baked ripple enamel finish will not easily scratch or rub off, and there is fine white striping around lid. Rugged, solid construction.

Dimensions
No.	Long	Wide	High	Net Wt.	Price
S16	16"	7"	7"	5½ Lbs.	$2.60

KEEP YOUR AMMUNITION AND ACCESSORIES IN ORDER

All Steel Tool Chests & Parts Cabinets

 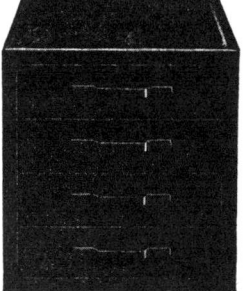  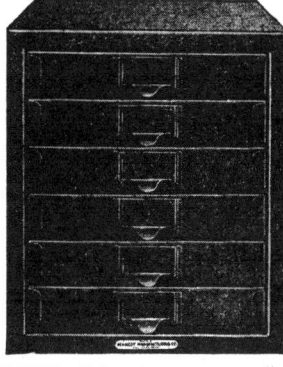

PARTS CABINET No. C

Number C cabinet, shown in the illustration above, is a companion number to 6D. Similar in design and construction this cabinet is finished in green ripple baked enamel on the outside, with a smooth green finish on the drawers.

There are six drawers, each measuring 5" x 8". Two drawers have ten compartments each, two have six, and two have three. Drawers are equipped with combination index card holders and drawer pulls and are removable.

No.	Long	Wide	High	Net Wt.	Price
C	8"	6"	9"	6 Lbs.	$3.00

UTILITY SMALL PARTS CABINET No. 4D (Above, 2nd from left)

This inexpensive little cabinet is practically indispensible for the gunsmith, the repair man, the gun enthusiast and many others for whom it can serve a thousand purposes. It is of steel finished with green lacquer and measures 5¾" in width, 6¼" in height, and 8¼" deep. Two of the drawers are divided into six compartments, one is divided into three compartments, and the other without any compartments at all.

No.	Long	Wide	High	Net Wt.	Price
4D	8¼"	5¾"	6¼"	4 Lbs.	$1.25

PARTS CABINET No. 6D

For general usage this cabinet is hard to beat. On the dealer's counter, shelf, or in the stockroom its countless uses make it invaluable. It provides a handy storage place for small parts and items that will prevent loss and save time and patience. It will also serve as a display cabinet. There are six drawers in all: one with fifteen compartments, one with twelve, two with six, two with four. Each drawer is 1½ inches deep inside. The card holders on each drawer are equipped with sturdy celluloid windows.

The shell is finished in a dark green ripple baked enamel, while the drawers are finished in a smooth green enamel presenting an attractive contrast. A few of the many uses for this cabinet are suggested below:

No.	Long	Wide	High	Net Wt.	Price
6D	13¼"	10⅛"	11⅜"	20 Lbs.	$6.00

COMBINATION CASE No. 716

The top tray is fitted with a folding handle. Lower tray is divided for small parts and tools, while the space under the tray is large enough to carry a complete assortment of tools. Three skid rails welded to bottom. Finished in seal brown ripple baked enamel outside and smooth dark green baked enamel interior. Multiple change lock and all hardware nickel plated.

No.	Long	Wide	High	Net Wt.	Price
716	16"	8"	9"	12	$6.50

DRILL BIT And TAP CABINET No. 12D (Above, 3rd from left)

A convenient and compact all steel cabinet designed with the cooperation of a large drill manufacturer to hold an ample supply of twist drills and taps up to and including 1" in size. Likewise suitable for countless other items.

Contains twelve drawers, each measuring 8" x 5" and divided as follows: three with six compartments each, one with four and eight with three, a total of forty-six separate compartments.

The drawers are easily removed and each draw-pull has an individual card holder to permit convenient indexing of contents kept in each compartment.

The shell of the cabinet is finished in dark green ripple baked enamel and the drawers in smooth baked enamel of the same color.

No.	Long	Wide	High	Net Wt.	Price
12D	8⅛"	11 9/16"	9⅝"	11½ Lbs.	$5.75

REPAIR KIT No. 1017-1018 1021

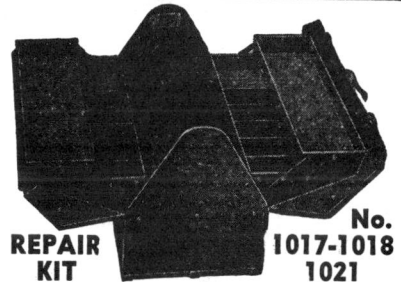

For the repairman, here is a general usage kit with four trays linked to the lids. The 1021 has compartments in the top trays. Equipped with leather handle, side catches, and multiple change lock. Three skid rails are welded to the bottom and reinforcing bars in ends insure great rigidity. Finished in seal brown riple baked enamel outside and dark green smooth baked enamel interior. Nickel plated hardware.

No.	Long	Wide	High	Net Wt.	Price
1017	17"	8"	10"	11¾	$7.50
1018	18"	10"	12½"	17½	8.00
1021	21"	10"	12½"	20¼	8.50

No. 20G — KIT BOX WITH TOTE TRAY

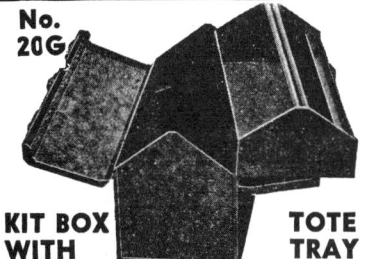

This style is designed for shop use. Heavy loads may be carried comfortably. Equipped with multiple change lock, side catches, and skid rail supports on bottom of box. Handle is leather, reinforced with steel core. Nickel plated hardware. Finished in brown baked ripple enamel outside with plain green interior.

No.	Long	Wide	High	Net Wt.	Price
20G	20"	10"	13"	16¼	$7.25

WOODWORKERS' TOTE BOX No. K32

Ample room for good assortment of tools including level, square, and three saws. Inside bottom of box is covered with ply wood. Slit at right end for end of square. Web shoulder strap.

No.	Long	Wide	High	Net Wt.	Price
K32	32"	8"	10"	13 Lbs.	$4.50

MECHANIC'S KIT No. 116-118-120-122

Tray has handy divisions for small parts. Three skid rails welded to bottom. Equipped with leather handle, side catches and multiple change lock. Nickel plated hardware. Seal brown ripple baked enamel outside finish with dark green smooth interior.

No.	Long	Wide	High	Net Wt.	Price
116	16"	9"	11"	9½	$5.50
118	18"	10"	13"	12	5.75
120	20"	11"	13"	15	6.00
122	22"	11"	13"	16	6.25

REVOLVER AND SHOOTER'S ACCESSORIES

SPUR GRIP ADAPTER

Price, each **$3.00**

Here are a few reasons why this Spur Grip adapter is replacing even $8.00 and $10.00 custom made grips:

1. The Spur between the first and second fingers makes even the amateur shooter take the correct high hold each time he shoots.
2. The Spur helps to keep the gun in correct position both in the timed- and rapid-fire stages; especially if the shooter uses the rolling method of cocking the gun.
3. The adapter has from two to three times the bearing surface for the middle finger.
4. The adapter comes down below the factory stocks thus giving the little finger, even on a large hand, a place to rest.

These adapters are available in a beautiful fiddle-black material or plain black.

No. 1 Fits Colt Official Police, Officers Model, Camp Perry, and Army Special.
No. 2 Fits Colt shooting Master, and Army.
No. 3 Fits S & W Military & Police, and K22 with regular stocks.
No. 4 Fits the same gun as No. 3 but with the Magna stocks.
No. 5 Fits S & W Military, Army, Mil & Target, 38-44 outdoorsman, and 357 Magnum with regular stocks.
No. 6 Fits the same as No. 5 but with Magna stocks.
No. 7 Fits New Service, New Service Target.

Price, each **$3.00**

COMBINATION CASE

Combination Pistol and Scope Case. A special designed case to carry two guns, spotting scope with additional room for ammunition, targets and cleaning accessories. Beautiful in appearance, covered with fine leather to give years of service and satisfaction. This case has been designed by one of the best known target shooters and its practical value can be readily seen. These cases are giving full protection to your guns at all times. Size 7½x11½x14½ inches.

Price **$22.50**

TRIGGER SHOE

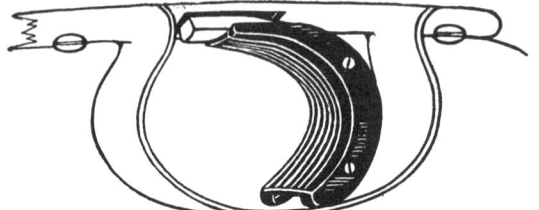

This Trigger shoe, which can be readily attached by means of two screws, is designed for use on almost any rifle or revolver trigger.

Its breadth, carefully corrigated, prevents slipping and allows a firm, steady, and comfortable pull. Its use assures not only a better "let off" but aids materially in improving your score.

Price **$1.25**

10 POINT GRIP
WITH ALL CUSTOM GRIP FEATURES

NO FITTING REQUIRED

Inside View

PRICE $3.75

Are made for the following Colt and S. & W. arms according to numbers given:

No. 1—Large and Small—Fits all Colt Police Positive Models, Detective Special and Bankers Special.
No. 6—Large and Small—Fits all Official Police, Officers Model, Army Special and Camp Perry.
No. 7—Large Only—Fits all Shooting Master, New Service, New Service Target and Army.
No. 9—Large and Small—Fits all Smith & Wesson Military and Police and K22.
No. 0—Large and Small—Fits all S. & W. Military, Army, Military & Target, Outdoorsman and Masterpiece and 1917 Army and Magnum.

Note: 1. No grips are made for S. W. Straightline and S. & W. Hammerless or any automatic.
Note: 2. Order according to model of gun as given on barrel, or by number and size as given above.

"10 Point" Custom Style Colt and S. & W. Pistol and Revolver Grips are the answer to the demand of all shooters and "gun cranks" for a grip with all custom advantages and built in accessories AT LOW COST. (Not made for any automatic.)

Tried and Proven by many of the best pistol shots.
Endorsed by Ness, Landis, Lee, Sharpe, Askins, Adams, etc.

"10 Point" Grips provide all Colt and S. & W. Guns with the same "feel" or "hold" on all guns. These are the only low cost commercial grips with custom features that can be used on all Colt and S. & W. pistols and revolvers. Can easily be cut or reshaped by the individual user so as to **FIT HIS HAND PERFECTLY**.

Installed or removed in a few seconds, same as regular factory grip stocks. No altering of gun necessary.

THE MICO IRIS EYE PIECE

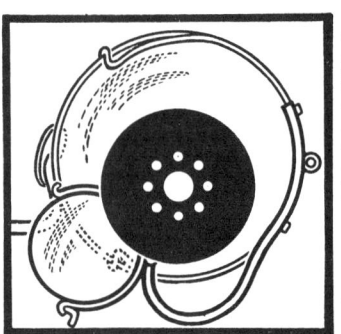

The Mico Iris Eye Piece snaps on the rim of eye glasses and will be found very convenient as one may instantly obtain a clear definition of the rear and front sights in any change of light or other conditions, simply by opening or closing the Iris diaphragm to the desired aperture which can be set making it suitable to the requirements of the shooter's eye. The Mico Iris Eye Piece is also equipped with a yellow filter which can be swung into place when shooting outdoors and the sunlight is found to be too strong. This is a novel feature and very desirable to the shooter. The Iris will stay in place at any desired point and the filter will also stay locked in or off position.

Price **$4.00**

PLEASE RECOMMEND US TO YOUR FRIENDS

TARGET SHOOTERS ACCESSORIES

STOEGER'S PISTOL SHOOTERS CASE

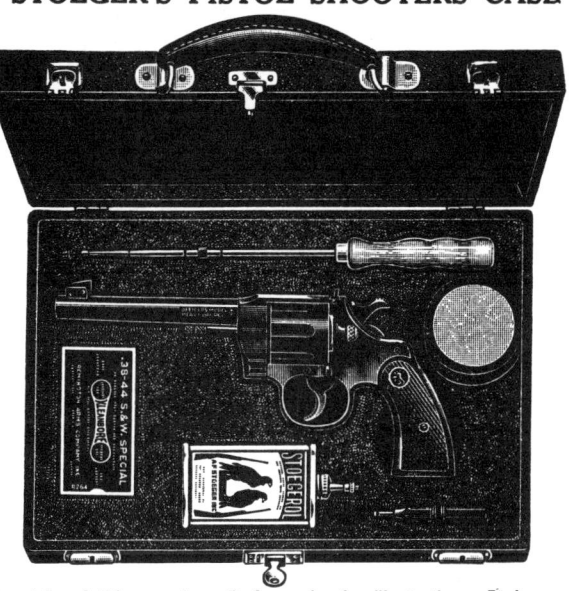

The style of this case is well shown in the illustration. It is compact but large enough to include beside the pistol or revolver an oil can, a box of cartridges, cleaning rod and patches. The case is of solid construction covered with imitation black leather and purple plush interior. It is supplied with brass fixtures including lock and key. These cases measure approximately 15½ x 8¼ x 2⅜" and weigh approximately 2½ lbs. They are made for the following guns and in ordering it is necessary to state for which gun the case is desired. Colt Officers' Model 6", Colt Official Police 6", S & W K22, S & W 38/44 Outdoorsman, S & W Military Police 6" square butt, Colt 45 auto., Colt Super 38, Colt Ace, Colt Woodsman and Luger 4" barrel. Price $7.50

PACHMAYR SURE GRIP ADAPTER

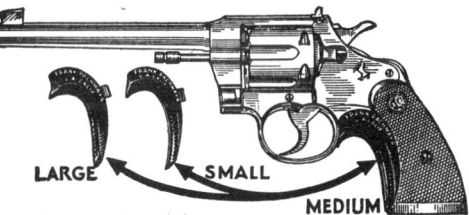

Three sizes—large, medium and small, for all Colt and S. & W. revolvers and single shot pistols except S. & W. hammerless and .22 S. & W. Single Shot "Straight Line." Generally, the large hand requires the small size; and a small hand the large size. Specify size of adaptor, caliber, and model of gun when ordering. Pachmayr's "Sure Grip" adaptors can be installed or removed in a few seconds' time by loosening the screw which holds the standard wooden or hard rubber grip stocks on gun handle frame. Your gun is not changed or marred in any way.
Price—each $1.50

SHOOTERS GLOVE

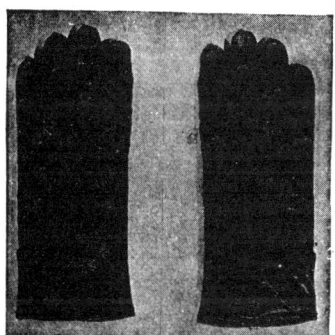

Best quality leather, padded for warmth and comfort. Stitched for flexibility. Sold singly; state whether for left or right hand. Price each.... $3.25

10-X GLOVE

Double leather, soft and pliable, with the correct amount of felt padding quilted between. It will not shrink or stiffen. Made in all sizes and for left-hand shooters.
Price $2.50
Index finger only separated 2.00

STOEGER'S OLYMPIC PISTOL GRIP

The grip you've been waiting for. For the first time a really full size walnut grip carved to completely fill the hand is offered to the shooter. The grip has finger grooves and thumb rest to steady the shooters' aim, eliminate muzzle heaviness, prevent slipping and absorb recoil. With the use of Stoeger's Olympic pistol grip accuracy is made easy. This grip is available for the Colt 45, the Colt Super 38, the Colt 22 Ace and the Colt Woodsman. It is made only of the best grade of Walnut. Circumference at point marked D on the illustration of the grip of the Woodsman is 7⅝" and the corresponding position for the other pistol is 8". This grip is suitable for any but very small hands and because of its full size can easily be filed down to meet the user's particular requirements.
Price including special screws $6.00

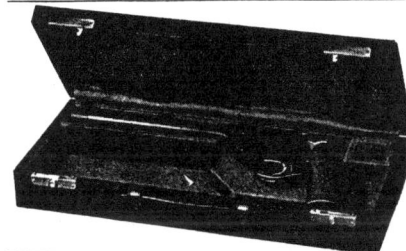

U. S. R. A. Pistol Shooters Case. Has room for pistol, ammunition, and accessories.
Price $5.00

* (State length of gun).
† (State barrel length).

TARGET SHOOTERS' CARTRIDGE BOXES

The illustration shows our No. 2 cartridge box. These cartridge boxes are made in various sizes and for various cartridges. They are made of best quality pine wood with brass fittings well fitted and cleanly made. Ideal for carrying match ammunition. Made in the following sizes: (The measurements are given in the following order, width, depth and length. Please order by number.)

No. 1. 1⅜ x 1⅜ x 4¾", cal. .22 L.R., 20 cart .... $ .50
No. 2. 3½ x 2 x 6", cal. .22 L.R., 50 cart 1.00
No. 3. ⅞ x 2 x 6", cal. .38 Spec., 10 cart .... .50
No. 4. 3⅜ x 2 x 6¼", cal. .38 Spec., 50 cart 1.00
No. 5. 3⅜ x 2 x 6¼", cal. .45 Colt Auto., 50 cart 1.00
No. 6. 1⅜ x 3⅞ x 6⅜", cal. .30/06, 20 cart 1.00

PLEASE RECOMMEND US TO YOUR FRIENDS

SHOOTERS' ACCESSORIES

BRILLIANT SEARCH LIGHT

INDISPENSABLE AND RELIABLE FOR HUNTING, TRAPPING, CAMPING

Will burn continuously at full flame for years at ½¢ an hour. Simply add water and carbide in the Generator. This is not a flashlight. Lights up like daylight. From penetrating beam to wide spreadlight instantly.

Head Piece: brass and steel 4 inch diameter, 3 inch deep, connects by rotary joint to leather head strap, fits any head or cap. Reflector: highly nickeled German silver 3½ inch diameter. Lenses: convex lens 2½ inch in hinged door for long distance beam. Hinged darkening door. Generator: all brass, automatic needle valve type, capacity 4½ ounce carbide, one filling burns 5 hours (the last hour just as bright as the first), hooks over belt, top of trousers, etc. Gas Hose: 5/16 inch rubber non-kinkable, 45 inches long, worn under the coat. Metal parts black hard baked enamel. Shipping weight 2½ pounds.

Style 3 Double Lens "Brilliant Search Light".............Price, $8.75

NO. 525 CARBIDE LAMP FOR BLACKENING GUNSIGHTS

This lamp is of solid brass, polished and lacquered. It has 2¾ inch chromium reflector and flat hook; can be used also as a camp light. Recommended for Range Officers and Gun Clubs. Has sturdy type burner assembly and is absolutely safe to use.

Price for above....................$1.25

IDEAL EAR STOPPERS

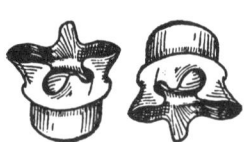

They are made of pure soft rubber, sanitary and necessary for every shooter. Used and endorsed by the Ordnance Department of the United States Army and Navy.

Price for above............Per pair $.50

"AUTO" GUN CLIP

This attachment makes it very convenient for carrying a revolver in an automobile safely and allows for a quick draw. The attachment fastens readily to the steering column of any automobile. Also, it can be used to hold a flashlight instead. Recommended for sheriffs and Police officers.

Price for above..................................$1.95

"NO SLIP" RIFLE BUTT PLATE

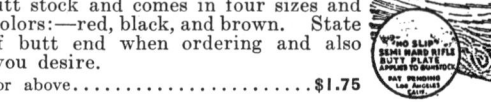

This butt plate has been especially designed for those who desire to obtain a butt plate with sharp checkered surface to allow for firm "No Slip" holding. It will not chip, crack, or break and will dress up any butt stock and comes in four sizes and three colors:—red, black, and brown. State size of butt end when ordering and also color you desire.

Price for above......................$1.75

"WHITELINE" SPACERS

Here is a simple way to enlarge the size of your revolver handle by attaching one of these white line spacers and also it greatly enhances the appearance of any standard factory pistol or revolver grip. They are made only for Colt and Smith & Wesson revolvers and come in 2 sizes.

Set No. 1 is made in thickness of 1/32 inch; therefore, one pair will widen a gun grip by 1/16 inch. Price for one pair set No. 1...... $.70
Set No. 2 is made in thickness of 1/16 inch; therefore, one pair will widen a gun grip by 1/8 inch. Price for one pair set No. 2........ $.90

"SURE SIGHT" GAUGE

For the Range Office of your Pistol Club

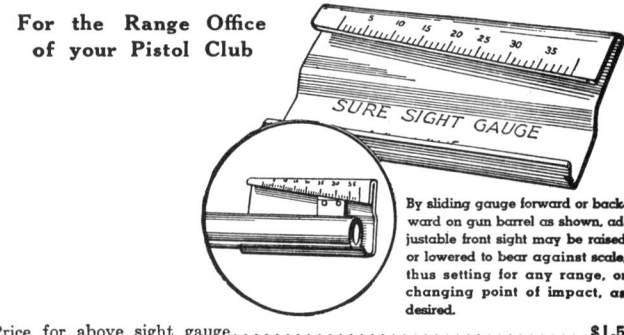

By sliding gauge forward or backward on gun barrel as shown, adjustable front sight may be raised or lowered to bear against scale, thus setting for any range, or changing point of impact, as desired.

Price for above sight gauge...............................$1.50

This handy instrument will save any shooter a great deal of trouble and time and does away with guess work in adjusting your sights, on your revolver for different ranges. By sliding the gauge forward or backward the adjustable front sight may be raised and lowered against the scale setting the sight automatically for any range instantly and accurately. Obtainable only for the following Colt revolvers and pistols only.

Woodsman .22
Shooting Master .38
New Service Target .45
Police Positive Target .22
Camp Perry .22
Officers Model .22 and .38

"FEATHERWEIGHT" TELESCOPE MOUNT

Here is a practical telescope mount made of Durall metal and weighs only 2 ounces. It will take any make of scope with a tube diameter of 22m/m (⅞") such as the Ajack, Zeiss, Hensoldt, etc. Installs on the side of the receiver and holds scope in correct central position. Recommended for all bolt action and lever action rifles in all calibres up to 30-06; state make and model of gun when ordering.

Price for above $6.50

SEND YOUR GUN TO STOEGER FOR EXPERT REPAIRING

TARGET SHOOTER'S ACCESSORIES

ANTI-FUDGE SHOT HOLE GAUGE

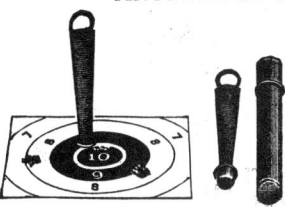

Anti-Fudge Shot Hole Gauges are generally used by Riflemen who want an absolutely accurate gauge. Obtainable in .22-.30-.38 and .45 calibers.

Cal. .22, Price.................. $.50
Cal. .30, Price.................. .75
Cal. .38, Price.................. .85
Cal. .45, Price.................. .85

COMBINATION CARTRIDGE BOX AND STAND

The Combination Cartridge Box and Stand will take 100 .22 Long Rifle Cartridges, without removing them from their original boxes. The lid, drilled with 10 holes, forms a very convenient Cartridge Stand.

Price $1.25

THE NEW SPRINGFIELD MICROMETER
(Trade Mark)

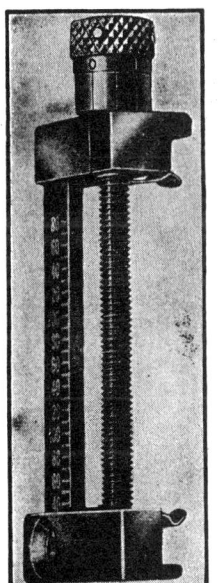

Indispensable to Springfield shooters. Its points of superiority are: Can be easily attached to Springfield Service Sight; can be left on sight during course of shooting; insures position accuracy, each click ½ inch at 100 yards; clicks make sight setting easy; can be worked with one hand, not necessary to change shooting position; blue-black finish, light weight, durable and strong.

Directions for Using the Springfield Micrometer Sight

Loosen Service Sight Leaf, first clip micrometer on top of leaf; next, clip it onto the sight leaf, then turn micrometer screw until sight leaf is at the desired range for shooting. Shoot a three shot group. The Micrometer screw may then be turned to raise or lower the elevation to bring the group into the bull's eye. Each click changes elevation one-half inch at 100 yards. Each two clicks (or one minute) changes group one inch at 200 yards, etc. Mark sight leaf for that particular range and take readings on the Micrometer and write data in range score-book.

The Springfield Service Rifle may be targeted in for any range using the instructions outlined above.

Springfield Micrometer, each $3.75

THE PARKER HALE "CUSHION RING" ELBOW PADS

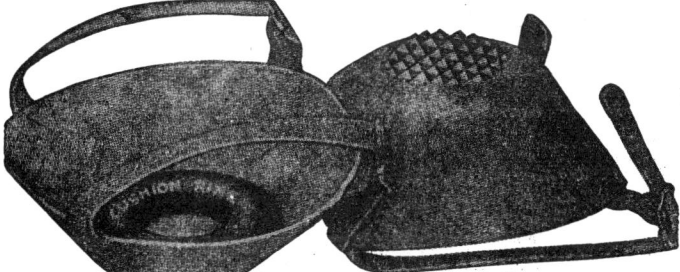

Prevents sore elbows and the nuisance of rolling or displacement of the pad when shooting. This pad is exceedingly comfortable and retains its position around the points of the elbow and prevents the latter being chafed by hard contact with the ground.
Price $5.00

PEEP SIGHT REAMER

A necessary part of every Rifleman's Kit is the "Peep" Reamers. A useful tool for many purposes. The left-hand end shown in illustration is used for enlarging the hole while the right-hand end is used for countersinking the back of it and sharpening the edge for clear definition. "Peep" Reamer furnished complete with nickel metal case. Each...$1.00

SIX HOLE EYE-PIECE WITH LENS HOLDER

 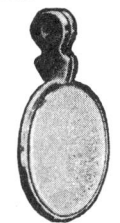

A much-needed accessory for shooters who require optical aid to get improved definition of sights or objects. The Six Hole Eye-piece with Lens Holder is similar to the Parker Hale No. 51-L "Dead Center" Six Hole Eye-piece. The Standard Eye-piece is supplied with fieuzal lens. Price, complete with Lens Holder and Fieuzal Tinted Lens, Medium Tinted $4.00
Price, Lens Frame only.......... .90
Price, Lens Frame with Fieuzal Tinted Lens, Medium Tint.... 1.75

"DEAD CENTER" SIX HOLE EYE-PIECE
FOR LYMAN & REDFIELD TARGET RECEIVER SIGHTS

For your Redfield Series 90, 100, and 102 as well as your Lyman No. 48 Receiver Sight. Recommended for use with Lyman 48 on Model 52 and other target rifles.
Price $2.50

Dead Black for Front Sights

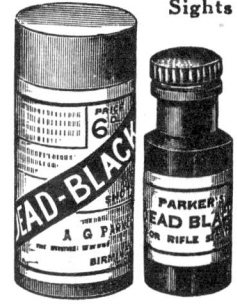

This famous preparation used for applying to front and rear sights to make them more distinct, is in constant demand by Target Riflemen.
Price ....$.75

RIFLE KIT METAL BOX

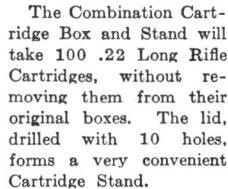

A light weight metal box. Size, 14 x 6 x 6½ inches. Price..................$2.00

ELASTIC FINGER GUARD

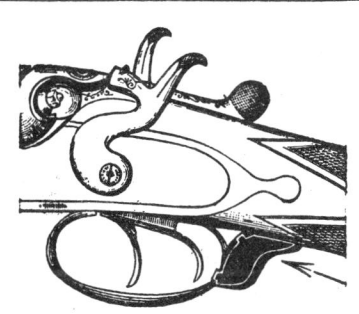

No. R 62 ....$1.00

VALVE SPOUT OIL CAN

A 4-ounce container, handy, well made and leakproof. Carry it with you in your shooting kit.

After shooting clean and oil your gun and it will always be serviceable.

Price, 4 oz. oil can......$1.00

LYMAN RECEIVER GUN SIGHTS

For Every Gun — *For Every Purpose*

No. 48Y—Receiver Sight for Savage Models 19 and 23

No. 48Y—Lyman Micrometer Sight—For Savage Model 19 N.R.A. and Savage Sporter 23A, 23B, 23C and 23D, Savage Model 1933. Sight mounted on the left side of receiver. Easily attached, needing no tapping and drilling of receiver. Use mounting screw holes provided in gun. No cutting of stock necessary. Windage and elevation knobs graduated to give ¼ minute of angle, with sharp distinct clicks. Sight closer to eye than factory rear sight. Base of sight forms rear base for Lyman 5A, No. 438, or Winchester A5 rear scope mounts.

Price 48Y complete with disc............$13.00

No. 56

No. 56—Lyman Receiver Sight with ¼ minute click adjustments for windage and elevation. Modern design for popular hunting rifles of lever action and slide action design as follows:
Winchester 03, 53, 55, 61, 63, 64, 65, 92, 94 models.
Remington 12, 14, 24, 25, 121, 141, 241. Savage 03, 14, 29. Marlin 32, 39, 92, 97.
Complete with disc............$7.00
Tap and drill if desired............ .50
Most guns require higher than regular front sight. Just the sight for hunters familiar with target shooting.

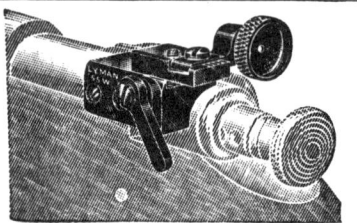

No. 55—Lyman Receiver Sight—Especially designed for Win.; Rem.; Sav.; Stevens; Springfield; Iver Johnson X, and Western Field. Marlin, Mossberg, late model .22 bolt action rifles.

Price............$2.00

Popular low-priced satisfactory sight for these guns. Tap and drill extra, if specified.. .50

No. 48—Lyman Micrometer Windgauge Receiver Sight—Especially designed for Springfield Model 1903, Newton and Ross .280 rifles. Graduations with corresponding clicks to ½ minute of angle, providing change of impact ½ inch at 100 yards, ¼ inch at 50 yards.
Price complete with disc............$11.50
Specify Tap and Drill if desired............ .50
Also available: No. 48M for Mausers; No. 48K for Krags; No. 48G for Savage 19 and 23.

No. 48WJS Receiver Sight — **For Winchester Models 54 and 70**

No. 48WJS — Lyman Receiver Sight for Winchester Model 54 and 70 Rifles. ¼ minute adjustment for windage and elevation. Attached by screw holes already in receiver. Moving parts handfitted; amply strong for hunting and has desirable adjustments for alignment or target shooting.
Price complete with disc and screws......$11.50

No. 57 With ¼" Micrometer Clicks — **For .22S**

Available as follows:
No. 57M for Mossberg Models 43, 46, complete with disc and mounting screws....$5.00
No. 57S for Stevens, complete with disc and mounting screws........................5.00
No. 57R for Remington 241 or 24, complete with disc and mounting screws....5.00
No. 57W for Winchester 54, 70, complete with disc and mounting screws.........6.00
No. 57F for Winchester 52, complete with disc and mounting screws..........6.00

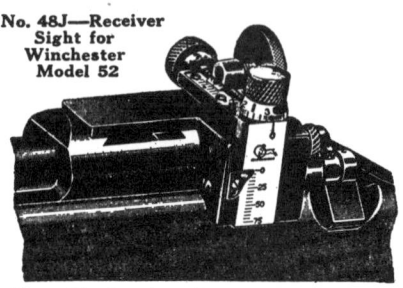

No. 48J—Receiver Sight for Winchester Model 52

No. 48J—Receiver Sight—For Winchester 52 Rifle. Has outstanding features, large adjustment knobs with clicks and graduated to ¼ minute, left side of receiver for convenience, close to eye, easily attached, no drilling of receiver necessary, increased distance between front and rear sight, large disc sand blasted. No. 48J with No. 17A give perfect metallic sight equipment for this gun.
Complete with disc............$13.00

No. 52 Extension Sight

No. 52—Lyman Extension Sight locates aperture closer to eye, adjustable for offhand, prone and intermediate positions; is self-aligning and rigid when locked. Provides extreme distance between sights. Windage and elevation click adjustments, ¼ minute, with ample elevation for 200 yards, and movement same direction as scope mounts. Close handfitted moving parts. Exclusive elevation screw adjustment to take up wear. Sight can be instantly removed when using scope and replaced without re-setting. Recommended for metallic sight matches with No. 17A or No. 77 front sights.
No. 52R for Remington 37, complete....$13.00
No. 52J for Win. 52 with factory rear sight slot on top of receiver...............13.00
No. 52F for Win. 52 for mounting on side of receiver...................13.00

No. 38—Lyman Windgauge Receiver Sight—Price **$6.50**, with disc if desired, price **$7.00**

No. 21—Similar to No. 38, without windgauge—Price **$5.00**. For Marlin 1893; Winchester 1886, 1894, and 1895. Used by shooters who prefer having the rear sight on the receiver rather than on the tang. Tap and drill for mounting, price.....................50c

---

LYMAN POLAROID TUBE SIGHT

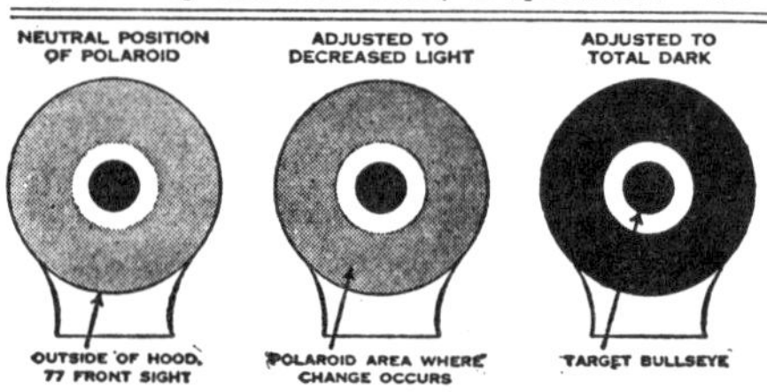

| NEUTRAL POSITION OF POLAROID | ADJUSTED TO DECREASED LIGHT | ADJUSTED TO TOTAL DARK |

OUTSIDE OF HOOD, 77 FRONT SIGHT — POLAROID AREA WHERE CHANGE OCCURS — TARGET BULLSEYE

Showing how action of the Polaroid Screens (in front sight and tube sight) control reflected light from target

1. Designed for target shooting only, and qualifies for iron sight matches. Contains no glass.
2. Approaches a scope sight in accuracy and is close to scope line of sight.
3. Reflected light from target can be quickly changed from clear bright to any decreasing amount of light down to total dark.
4. Eliminates light or glare around target bullseye. Pat. app'd for.

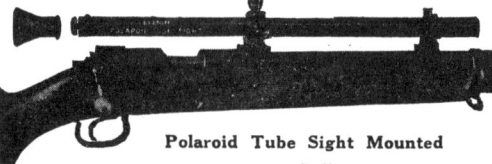
Polaroid Tube Sight Mounted

Ocular end showing adjusting knob, and sighting disc.

5. Relieves eye strain, permits the sharpest definition.
6. Eliminates reflected light inside of tube. Pat. app'd for.
7. Used in combination with Lyman 77 Target Front Sight.
8. Polaroid material in tube sight is adjustable through an arc of 90°.
9. Polaroid front sight insert is stationary. May be used with or without metal insert.
10. Tube rear mount is 3 point suspension, ¼ min. micrometer clicks.

Furnished with front and rear mounts, sighting disc, rubber eye cup, less bases; Price **$20.00**, With Bases, Price **$21.00**.

LYMAN REAR GUN SIGHTS

For Every Gun — **For Every Purpose**

 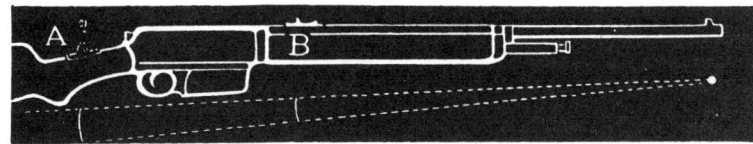 

Old eyes that can no longer use the crotch sights can use Lyman Sights and shoot better than they ever could with the common sight. Both eyes can be used as well as one eye; it is a hundred-fold easier to shoot moving objects, running or flying.

Distance A B shows added sight radius when rear aperture sights are used.

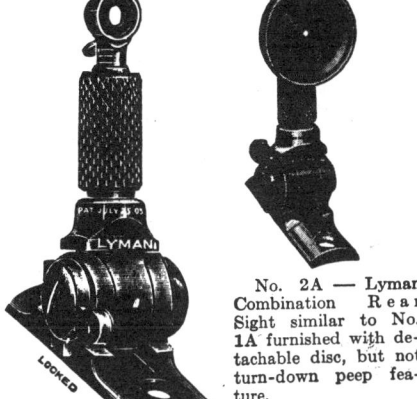

No. 2A — Lyman Combination Rear Sight similar to No. 1A furnished with detachable disc, but not turn-down peep feature.
Price **$5.00**

No. 1A—Lyman Combination Rear Sight with Locking Feature and Built-in turn-down peep. These are exclusive Lyman advantages. The smaller aperture built into the regular aperture prevents danger of losing it, and gives two sizes of aperture always instantly available.
Price **$4.50**

LYMAN DISC

All have sand-blasted face. Regularly furnished with aperture .052 inch. Special diameter of aperture can be supplied between No. 80 drill size (.0135 inch 1/64 inch (.146 inch) (9/64 inch). Various outside diameter discs available if desired. In ordering give aperture size and Lyman sight number.
Lyman Disc...................each **$.50**

Lyman 103
Complete With Disc
Price **$9.00**

No. 103—Lyman Micrometer Rear Sight has micrometer adjustments for windage and elevation. Made for following rifles—Winchester Model 90, 52, 61, 62, 64, 92, 94, 53 and 55, all calibers; Savage 19, 22 and 23A; Stevens Favorite and Ideal; Marlin 39.

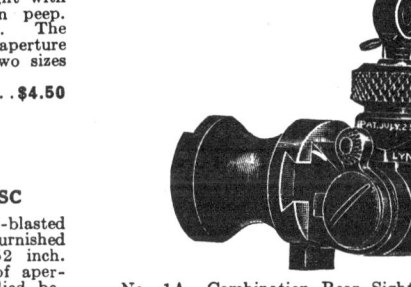

No. 1A—Combination Rear Sight for Springfield .30-'06, Krag, Mannlicher-Schoenauer, Mannlicher-Haenel and Mauser Rifles. Price of No. 1A sight........................**$4.50**
Special nut for Mauser, Mannlicher-Schoenauer, Mannlicher-Haenel **$1.50**
Tap and Drill for attaching nut to Mauser and Mannlicher-Schoenauer Rifles.........**$.50**

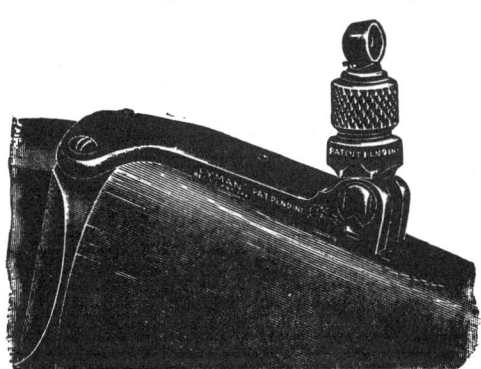

No. 1—Lyman Combination Rear Sight with turn-down peep feature designed especially for hunting purposes. Available for nearly all Sporting Rifles. Shown as mounted on Remington 12, 14, 24, 25, 121, 141 and 241.
Price **$4.00**
No. 2—Same as above but with detachable disc **$4.50**

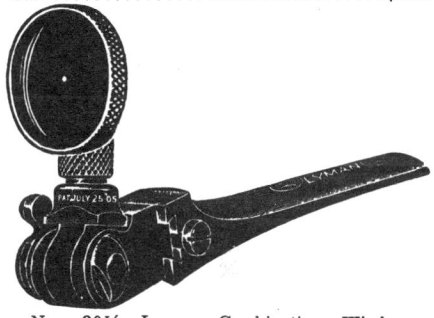

No. 30½—Lyman Combination Windgauge Rear Sight for all Lever Action Savage Rifles with windgauge in base, with disc........**$6.50**
No. 29½ similar to No. 30½, with built-in turn-down peep instead of detachable disc..**$6.00**

LYMAN RECEIVER GUN SIGHTS

For Every Gun — **For Every Purpose**

No. 34 Lyman Windgauge Receiver Sight—For Springfield 1903 and 1906. Krag-Jorgensen (Springfield 1896-1898) Lee Enfield.

Price, without disc.................**$6.50**
Price, with disc.....................7.00

No. 33—Similar to No. 34—Without windgauge. Price....................**$5.00**
Tap and drill......................**.50**

No. 35—Lyman Windgauge Receiver Sight with close adjustments for windage and elevation, turn down peep feature in aperture. Can be supplied with disc if desired. For Mauser rifles and to be attached to the left hand side of the receiver, base designed to fit over bolt stop. No extra mounting screw holes necesssary for fitting the sight **$10.00**
With disc..........................10.50

No. 36 — Lyman Receiver Sight — For Mannlicher-Schoenauer, Mannlicher-Haenel, and Russian 7.62 m/m rifles. Tap and Drill necessary for mounting No. 36 sight on Russian 7.62 m/m rifle.

No. 36 sight.......................**$10.00**
Tap and drill......................**.50**

CAREFUL ATTENTION AND SAFE DELIVERY OF YOUR ORDER

Lyman Front and Leaf Sights for Rifles, Carbines and Shotguns
For Hunting and Target Shooting

Lyman Front Sights for all Rifles and Carbines and Shotguns. These give the clear, sharp contrast against usual dark background presented by game and under dim light conditions permit best results. In ordering give make, model and caliber of rifle.

No. 3—Lyman ivory or gold bead front sight, $1/16$-inch bead. Price $1.00

No. 28—Lyman ivory or gold bead front sight, $3/32$-inch bead. Price $1.00

No. 20—Lyman ivory or gold bead front sight, $1/8$-inch bead. Price $1.00

No. 4—Lyman Special Hunting front sight. Ivory bead protected from injury by surrounding metal. Fit all rifles taking the regular rifle type of front sight. Price $1.50

No. 31—Lyman ivory or gold bead front sight, $1/16$-inch bead. Price $1.00

No. 37—Lyman ivory or gold bead front sight, $3/32$-inch bead. Price $1.00

No. 39—Lyman ivory or gold bead front sight, $1/8$-inch bead. Price $1.00

No. 5—Lyman Combination Front Sight, reversible globe and ivory post. Price $1.75

No. 5B—Lyman Combination Front Sight, reversible globe and ivory or gold bead. Price $1.75

No. 26—Lyman ivory or gold bead front sight, $1/16$-inch bead. Price $1.00

No. 32—Lyman ivory or gold bead front sight, $3/32$-inch bead. Price $1.00

No. 20—Lyman ivory or gold bead front sight, $1/4$-inch bead. Price $1.00

No. 26—Lyman ivory or gold bead front sight, for Springfield. Price $1.00

No. 26—Lyman ivory or gold bead front sight. Krag rifles and carbines. Price $1.00

No. 6—Lyman Folding Leaf Sight. For all American Sporting Rifles. Takes place of factory crotch rear, which should always be removed when Lyman Rear Sight is attached. A valuable auxiliary sight. Both leaves fold down close to barrel when not in use. Price $1.75

No. 6—Folding Leaf Sight for Remington Model 8 and Savage 1919. Price $2.50

No. 77 Detachable Sight
A special adaptation of #17A, furnished with nine interchangeable inserts. Designed for quick attachment or removal from gun where gun is provided with base similar to scope base. Clamping device locks the sight rigidly to base requiring that the base have a circular beveled mill cut. The removable feature is essential where the line of sight established by metallic sights and telescopic sights are close together. The quick removable feature of the slide is especially appreciated by shooters competing in matches allowing only metallic sights and in other matches permitting the use of "any sights."
Price complete with base is **$4.00**. No. 77 sight less base, **$3.50**. Taps and drill for making the mounting screw holes for the base, **$1.00**.

No. 12 — Slot Blank. Price..... 50c

No. 17A — Lyman Globe Target Front Sight with nine interchangeable inserts. For Springfield 1903 and 1922 MI, with special base. Price..... $2.50

No. 17A—Lyman Globe Target Front Sight with nine interchangeable inserts. A very popular front sight for target shooting. Furnished for guns having the rifle type of front sight slot and also Krag, Winchester 54, Remington 30 Express and 30S Special Rifles. Price.... $2.50

LYMAN IVORY SHOTGUN SIGHTS

With these sights on a gun the sportsman can tell at once whether the gun fits him or not. The large sale of these sights is not among the amateurs, as might be supposed, but among those who shoot a good deal and appreciate a help toward better work. They also show how very general is the fault of using a gun with too much drop in the stock.

There has always existed a serious difficulty in aiming shotguns, especially our modern choke-bored guns. The gun is seldom used twice from the same position, the shooter often having to take a sharp right or left position, which makes it more difficult to align the gun properly. By using a small and short ivory sight placed well forward on the rib, wonderfully good results are obtained. Not only is the vertical alignment readily obtained, but as the two sights are seen quite distinct and away from each other, the lateral alignment is made at the same time. This is a most important point, for one of the common mistakes is aiming too close to the gun rib, which results in under shooting. This system is sufficiently accurate for rifle shooting at short distances.

These sights are widely used both at the trap and in the field.

 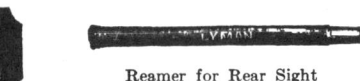

Reamer for Lyman Front Sight

Reamer for Rear Sight

No. 9—Set of two Lyman ivory shotgun sights with reamer. Price.................. $1.00
No. 10—Front, with reamer. Price..... .50
No. 11—Rear, with reamer. Price..... .50

Prevents Under Shooting and Cross Firing

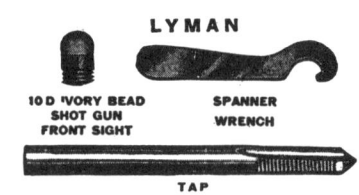

LYMAN

10 D IVORY BEAD SHOT GUN FRONT SIGHT — SPANNER WRENCH

TAP

No. 10D—Special Screw-in Type Front Sight for single barrel shotguns. Complete with tap and spanner wrench. Price.............. $1.00

PARKER AND MERIT SIGHTS

PARKER SKYLIGHT SIGHT

The Parker Skylight sight has been developed to give the best aiming and clearest vision under all shooting conditions. Its unique construction allows highest visibility for early morning or late evening shooting, it gives clear definition; it allows quickest alignment on running game and does not require rear sight adjustment for hunting range.

HIGH VISIBILITY is secured by cutting the face of the white metal bead perfectly flat at an angle of 45 degrees, so that all vertical light rays admitted by the sky-light are reflected straight back to the eye. In the back end of the revolving cylinder is an inlay of white, tarnish-proof metal also cut on an angle to pick up light. This provides, in effect, a white ring concentric with the bead at all times.

CLEAR DEFINITION against a light background such as snow or sky is obtained quickly by grasping the knurled portion of the inner cylinder and giving it a half turn. This closes the sky-light and at the same time shades the white inlay, causing the bead to appear black and the circle dark.

TARGET ACCURACY is secured at short range because the suspended bead is definitely smaller than those commonly used and also because at very short range, before the bullet has traveled upward to the line of sight, it is necessary to hold slightly over on a small target. Absence of a post or blade under the bead makes this compensation easy, since an unobstructed view is had under, as well as over, the bead.

QUICKEST ALIGNMENT on running game is assured by the high visibility which aids definitely in "catching" the front sight as it swings toward the center of vision without having to divide the attention of the eye between game and sight. In fact, at moderate ranges, all that is necessary in game shooting is to frame the vital area of the animal in the white circle—the bead itself may be disregarded.

NO REAR SIGHT ADJUSTMENT is necessary for the occasional shot at long range. All that is necessary in game shooting is to place the bead directly above the game, estimating hold-over by the apparent relative size of bead and target. Here again the absence of obstruction under the bead allows a clear view of the animal. The effective point blank of any rifle is more than doubled when it is equipped with the Skylight sight.

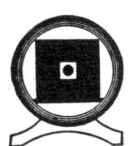 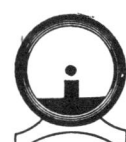

SUPER ACCURATE, DOUBLE-CHECK, SQUARE APERTURES as well as the conventional apertures and posts are available as optional equipment. This makes the Skylight sight the truly universal equipment. It may well save the price of an extra rifle.

PARKER SKYLIGHT SIGHT with standard medium fine white metal bead.
For all rifles having dovetail slot with or without ramp..........$4.75
For Springfield as issued..5.25
For rifles having carbine type slotted post (sight is mounted on short ramp which covers slotted post)......................5.75

EXTRA BEADS

Standard bead is approximately .045" in diameter. Extra beads will be supplied at the following prices: Standard .045"...........$.50
Coarse .060"; just under 1/16"...................................50
Fine .035"; just over 1/32"....................................1.00

If fine bead is desired in place of standard, add 50 cents to regular price. Coarse bead will be substituted for standard at no extra cost.
For set of three beads with order add.........................$1.25

TARGET INSERTS

Set consists of 3 Square Apertures, 3 Posts, 3 Round Apertures......$1.50
Individual inserts 25

Merit Iris Shutter Click Adjusted Peer Sight Discs for All Popular Sights

There are no extra discs to carry, change and lose. Eleven distinct clicks giving choice of twelve different apertures. The shooter can instantly meet any change of light conditions and range. The extremely thin sighting edge of the Iris Shutter gives the clearest definition obtainable. Zero remains unaffected, since the Iris Shutter opens from and closes towards the center, therefore, an absolute concentric aperture is maintained always.

  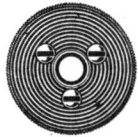

A (Closed)   A (Side)   A (Open)

MERIT No. 3 series disc showing minimum and maximum peep openings obtainable. Primarily used for target shooting.
MERIT No. 3A—Outside diameter of disc 11/16". Shank 7/16" long. Disc thickness 7/32". Price......................$2.75
MERIT No. 3SS—Outside diameter of disc 11/16". Shank 5/16" long. Disc thickness 7/32". Price......................$2.75
MERIT No. 3LS—Outside diameter of disc 11/16". Shank 11/32" long. Disc thickness 7/32". Price......................$2.75
MERIT No. 3S—Outside diameter of disc 11/16". Shank is the same as No. 3SS except that it has a shoulder and is for use on Winchester, Remington, Savage and Stevens receiver peep sights on the following rifles: Winchester 72, Remington 41P-341P, Savage 3S-4S-5S, Stevens Buckhorn 053-055-056-066-419.

MERIT MASTER TARGET DISC may be used on all sights having clearance for a disc 7/16" thick and 3/4" or larger in diameter. The 1½" high grade flexible rubber shield is permanently attached to the eye cup and is concentrically ribbed on its concave face for cutting to suitable size. This disc is particularly recommended for use on extension sights, telescope height sights and tang sights. Made in same shanks as No. 3A and No. 3LS. Price................$3.50

MERIT No. 4 series disc, the popular ½" (snap shooting) size especially recommended for all hunting purposes.
MERIT No. 4LS—Outside diameter of disc ½". Shank 11/32" long. Disc thickness ¼". Price......................$2.50
MERIT No. 4SS—Outside diameter of disc ½". Shank 5/16" long. Disc thickness ¼". Price......................$2.50
MERIT No. 4ELS—Outside diameter of disc ½". Shank ½" long. Disc thickness ¼". Price......................$2.50

Merit Click Adjusted Iris Shutter Front Sight

Adaptor for using the No. 4 disc in Lyman 17A-G front sight.
Price—Disc and adaptor......................$3.00

Adaptor for using the No. 4 disc in Redfield 65-66-67-68 front sights.
Price—Disc and adaptor......................$3.00

Discs and adaptors may also be had for the Lyman 77 and Redfield 63 and 64 front sights as well as a special MERIT disc for Wittek-Vaver front sights. Price......................$3.00
When Ordering, State Make and Model of Rifle

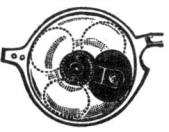

THE MERIT OPTICAL ATTACHMENT
For Use on All Regular and Shooting Glasses

solves the perplexing problem of fuzzy or blurred sights and target by cutting out objectionable side lights.
The IRIS SHUTTER is adjustable from .020 to .150. Instantly attached with a positive holding rubber suction cup on either lens of the average reading or shooting glasses. There are no springs, hooks or clamps to scratch the glass. Movable to practically any position on glasses having lenses 1¼" or over in diameter. Built of light weight metal, weight only 56 grains.
Optical Attachment $2.75
Extra Rubber Suction Cup..............................50

VAVER DIAL MICROMETER SIGHTS
FOR ALL POPULAR RIFLES

Vaver Dial Micrometer Sights are an outstanding development and advance in design. Engineered to meet the most exacting requirements, they offer the rifle shooter absolute, accurate and rapid adjustments in either direction for both windage and elevation without play or backlash. The micrometer action consists of a hardened cam with a "frusto conical spiral lead." Engaging this cam are the hardened pins in the staff. These two hardened parts, functioning in mesh, are capable of lifetime use without perceptible wear, they therefore maintain accuracy. Because these sights truly and consistently express the accuracy of modern guns and ammunition, they are—the choice of champions.

⅛ Inch Clicks—Correct Sighting Radii

Vaver Sights for target rifles are furnished with ⅛-inch clicks (¼ min. optional) to accurately move the impact of the bullet ⅛-inch per click on the target at 100 yards. The elevation dial is divided into eighty ⅛-inch clicks, the windage dial into forty ⅛-inch clicks. The lead on the cam, for each type sight, is generated to provide the correct movement of impact per click (1-inch at 100 yards) to coincide with the sighting radius of standard rifles.

All Readings Are From Zero

Vaver Sights are zeroed as follows: Adjust the sight on the rifle to fire central into a bullseye at 50 feet. With this setting, loosen set screws in elevation and windage dial—turn them to zero—retighten them firmly; also set the elevation and windage scale plates at zero. This zero once set remains permanent. All sight readings start from this zero and can be accurately predetermined for all other ranges.

Interchangeable Scale Plate

Vaver Sights are furnished with an interchangeable scale plate, the movement of which is synchronized with the elevation dial. The plate is held on the staff with a locked stud. After being zeroed to the rifle, it may be lifted off and its permanent zero retained. A plate zeroed to another ammunition can then be inserted in its place. The left side of the plate is blank and may be graduated in yards for a given ammunition.

Quick Removable Staff

To remove the staff—pull elevation dial outward against spring tension till clicker dog falls under cam. This disengages the cam from the staff, and the staff can then be pulled out. When replacing, push the finger tab on the clicker and the cam springs back into place.

Eye Cup and Adapters

Vaver Eye Cups with Adapters have been found to be a very decided improvement constructively and optically, for receiver sights. The thin apertures, mounted deep in the adapters, set out the target sharp and clear without halo or cobwebs. The adapters, made with seven different size apertures, screw into the eye-cup and can be readily interchanged to the required size for target and conditions. All Vaver Sights are furnished with an eye cup of suitable size and an .040 aperture. Additional apertures are available in Kits 7A and 7B.

Vaver Front Sights

These Front Sights are now recognized by target shooters as the peer of all Front Sights. The large globe provides a large field of vision to prevent cross fire. The shielded aperture admits only the required light to bring out the target sharply and clearly. The cross bars overcome cant and provide telescopic effect and accuracy. The apertures are readily interchangeable and are furnished in eight different sizes to meet requirements of various conditions, ranges, and targets. These sights are made in five different types to make up any sighting combination.

You will shoot better with VAVER Sights

VAVER DIAL MICROMETER SIGHTS
For "52" Winchester with Dovetail Receiver Slot

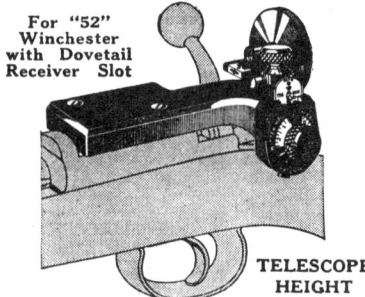

TELESCOPE HEIGHT

No. 35-MIELT (Illustrated) is an extension sight which brings the eye cup 2 inches closer to the eye than standard receiver sights. It mounts on the left side of the receiver by driving the mounting block into the dovetail receiver slot. The tang of the sight is channeled and is held onto the mounting block with two screws. This sight clears the bolt, which may be taken out without removing the sight.

The elevation dial is graduated into eighty ⅛ in. clicks—10 min. per revolution. The windage dial is divided into forty ⅛ in. clicks—5 min. per revolution. The leads in the cams are generated to provide the correct movement for the longer sighting radius, thus providing absolute sight adjustments.

For the Heavy Barrel "52," this sight is correct height in combination with Vaver Front Sight No. 36-FS and No. 35-EBB Barrel Band or, No. W-11-A Front Sight. For Standard Barrel (telescope height) use Front Sight No. 36-FWS or No. W-11-A.

No. 35-MIELT...................$15.00

WINCHESTER STANDARD HEIGHT
For "52" With Marksman Stock

No. W-52LT—No. W-52LT is a left hand extension sight, correct height (.200 in. lower than full telescope height) for Marksman Stock on the Heavy Barrel "52." Proper height in combination with Vaver No. W-11-A Front Sight or other scope block mount front sights. On the Standard Barrel this is correct height in combination with No. 36-FS Front Sight.

No. W52LT......................$15.00

FOR REMINGTON 37 "RANGEMASTER"

No. 37-RM—This is a telescope height sight with extension for mounting on the left side of the receiver using the screw holes drilled at the factory. Use telescope height front sights.

No. 37-RM......................$15.00

VAVER DIAL MICROMETER SIGHTS
For "52" Winchester with Round Receiver

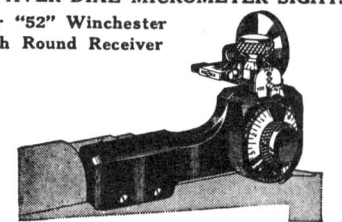

No. 5237 is a telescope height sight, with extension which brings the eye cup 2 inches closer to the eye than standard receiver sights. Mounts on the left side of the receiver with two screws, using screw holes drilled at the factory, no further drilling or cutting of the stock necessary. This sight clears the bolt, which may be taken out without removing the sight.

The dials for elevation and windage are graduated in ⅛ inch clicks, the leads on the cam being generated to provide the correct movement for the longer sighting radius, thus providing absolute, accurate sight adjustments. For proper front sight combinations use Vaver No. W-11-AT or No. 35-EBB with No. 36-FS or other Front Sights. For the Standard Barrel use Vaver No. W-11-A or No. 36-FWS.

No. 5237........................$15.00

No. 5238—This sight is Winchester Standard Height (.200 in. lower than full telescope height) for the "52" Heavy Barrel with round receiver and Marksman Stock. Correct height in combination with Vaver No. W-11-A Front Sight or other front sights of the scope block mounting type. For the Standard Barrel use Front Sight No. 36-FS.

No. 5238........................ 15.00

STANDARD SIGHTS FOR ROUND RECEIVER

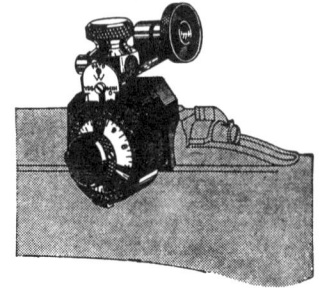

VAVER DIAL MICROMETER SIGHTS
For "52" Winchester with Dovetail Receiver Slot

This is a standard height sight for field or target use. The mounting block is driven into the dovetail slot in the receiver and locked in position with two set screws. The upper face of the mounting block is channeled to receive the tang of the sight which is held with a large coin-slotted screw making it quickly detachable without changing its zero. The dials in both elevation and windage are graduated in ⅛ in. clicks.

For use on Win. H.B. "52" with Marksman Stock it is necessary to raise the sight by inserting the illustrated block No. 187 under the sight tang. This is correct height in combination with No. W-11 or 36-FS scope block mount front sights.

To use No. 36-FS with Nos. 35-MIL and MIR on Standard Barrel Win. "52," raise the sight by inserting block No. 187 under sight tang. This provides the correct height with staff at nominal zero.

No. 35-MIL (For left side)..........$13.50
No. 35-MIR (For right side)......... 13.50
Block No. 187.......................   1.50

SEE ILLUSTRATION AT LEFT

No. 35-MW-522—This sight is Winchester Standard Height (.200 lower than full telescope height) for the H.B. Marksman Stock. Mounts on the left side of receiver using screw holes provided, no drilling or cutting of the stock necessary. Correct height in combination with Vaver No. W-11-A Front Sight or other scope block mount front sights.

No. 35-MW-522....................$12.50

No. MW-523—Same as No. 35-MW-522 except, it is Standard Height. Correct in combination with Vaver No. 36-FS or other Standard Height Globe Sights.

No. 35-MW-523....................$12.50

SEE PAGE 8, "HOW TO ORDER"

VAVER DIAL MICROMETER SIGHTS
FOR ALL POPULAR RIFLES

FOR STANDARD AND HEAVY BARREL "52"

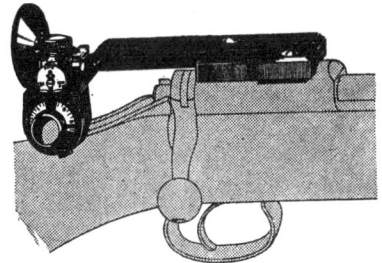

No. 35-MIE (Illustrated) Standard height extension sight for right side mounting. The tang is 1 7/8 in. longer than left hand extensions. It mounts on the right side of the receiver utilizing the dovetail slot. For front sight use No. 36-FS or other Globe Sight.
No. 35-MIE.....................$17.50

No. 35-MIERT—Telescope height sight for right side mounting. It mounts in the dovetail slot on the receiver of either Standard or Heavy Barrel "52". Proper height on the Heavy Barrel in combination with No. W-11-AT Front Sight, or No. 36-FS with No. 35-EBB. For Standard Barrel, telescope height, use front sight No. 36-FWS or No. W-11-A. These front sight combinations are quickly detachable.
No. 35-MIERT................$16.00

VAVER SIGHTS FOR SAVAGE RIFLES

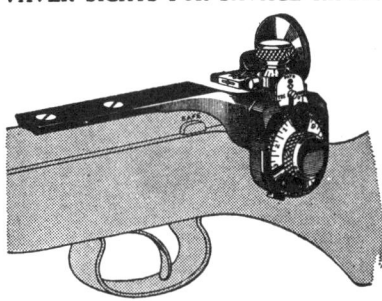

This sight is designed to fit Savage 1919, N.R.A., 1932 Sporter, and 1933 N.R.A. It mounts on the left side, using screw holes provided for same. The forepart of the tang is dovetailed to be utilized as a block for telescope mounting.
No. 35-M4A. 1919 N.R.A.-1923 Sporter. $13.50
No. 35-M4B. 1933 N.R.A.-Bolt Action.. 13.50

SIGHT FOR SEARS RANGER—MODEL 50 STEVENS 416

This is an extension sight that mounts on the left side of the receiver using screw holes provided, no cutting of the stock necessary. It is adjustable to match any height front sight from standard to telescope height. Telescope height position matches Vaver Front Sight W-11-AT or No. 36-FS with No. 35-EBB Barrel Band. (Quick detachable combinations.)
No. 37-SRR.....................$13.50

VAVER DIAL MICROMETER SIGHTS FOR HUNTING, SPORTING AND MILITARY RIFLES

These are precision sights which afford the Hunter and Shooter of Sporting or Military Rifles absolute accuracy on field or range. The micrometer action of both elevation and windage are the same as on our precision target sights with such additions as have been found practical in use for this type of rifle. The clicker mechanism is designed to give clear sharp clicks, however by means of a finger tab the clicks may be released so that the sight may be adjusted silently when noise is not permissible. The clicker further serves to positively lock the cam into position.

The rugged, sturdy construction and practical design, combined with the precision of target sights, makes this the outstanding sight for Hunting and field use under the most severe conditions.

VAVER DIAL MICROMETER SIGHTS FOR SPRINGFIELD 30-06 AND MAUSER

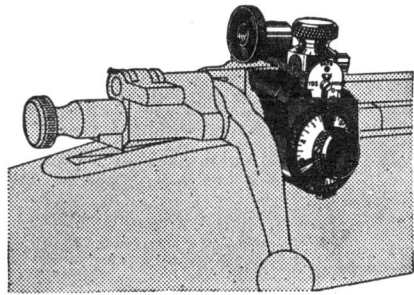

For Springfield 30-06. M1, M2, Target and Enfield

This sight mounts on the right side of the receiver no cutting of the stock is necessary. It is held in place with two screws, the screw holes matching those drilled in the receiver for standard sights.
No. 35-M6 ....$12.50

VAVER SIGHTS FOR WINCHESTER MODELS 54 AND 70

This sight mounts on the left side of the receiver using the screw holes provided—no further drilling or cutting of the stock necessary. The elevation dial is graduated into forty 1/4 min. clicks. Special dials and cams are available. Special windage slides as described are also available.
No. 35-M2.....................$12.50

REMINGTON SPECIAL AND EXPRESS

No. 35-M3 Mounts on the right side of the receiver using the screw holes provided.
Price $12.50

SIGHTS FOR STEVENS WALNUT HILL
417-417½-418-418½

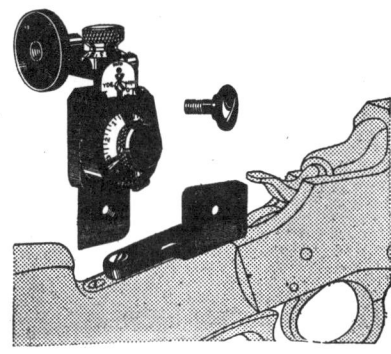

This sight mounts on the tang using the screw holes provided. The tang mounting block is a separate part to receive the sight adapter, thus being quickly detachable, always maintains its original zero. For telescope height use Vaver W-11-AT Front Sight, or No. 36-FS with No. 35-EBB Barrel Band.

No. 35-M5RT	Telescope Ht. Right	$15.00
No. 35-M5LT	Telescope Ht. Left	15.00
No. 35-M5SR	Std. Ht. Right	15.00
No. 35-M5SL	Std. Ht. Left	15.00

VAVER SIGHTS FOR B.S.A. RIFLES

This sight mounts on the left side and is held in place with two screws. Permits cleaning of rifle from breech. Screws furnished with sight, tap and drill loaned.

| No. 35-M10S | Standard Height | $12.50 |
| No. 35-M10T | Telescope Height | 12.50 |

VAVER FRONT SIGHTS

Vaver Front Sights are a decided improvement optically and in construction over conventional front sights. The field of vision afforded by the large globe reduces the hazard of cross fires. The cross bars instantly determine cant and provide telescopic effect and accuracy. Each sight assembly consists of globe body with dovetail mounting, two interchangeable light shades and eight apertures with a carrier plate. These features provide better definition and greater accuracy to the metallic sight shooter and lead to consistently higher scores.

No. 36-FS (Illustrated) Standard Height Front Sight mounts in the dovetail on the barrel.
Price $3.50

No. 36-FSS For Springfield.
Price $3.50

No. 36-FWS Quick detachable telescope height front sight for standard barrel Winchester only.
Price $4.50

SIGHTS FOR BALLARD

Left hand extension, mounts on the top of receiver with 2 screws. Tap and drill loaned.
No. 35-M12-SL Standard height left....$15.00
No. 35-M12-LT Telescope height left... 15.00

A GUN IS ONLY AS ACCURATE AS ITS SIGHTS

VAVER DIAL MICROMETER SIGHTS
FOR ALL POPULAR RIFLES

VAVER FRONT SIGHTS WITH SCOPE BLOCK MOUNT

These front sights, the W-11 series, are quickly detachable and mount on a telescope block permanently attached to the barrel. The blocks furnished are made to drive into the barrel dovetail or to mount with two screws on barrels without the dovetail slot. These blocks, and the sight base are hardened, therefore will not wear and are permanently accurate.

No. W-11-A (Illustrated) With dovetail mounting, is correct standard height for Winchester "52" H.B. with Marksman Stock. For the standard barrel with ramp it is telescope height.
Price $5.00

No. W-11-B is the same sight, scope block mounts with two screws.
Price $5.00

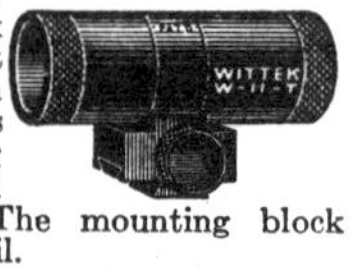

No. W-11-AT (Illustrated) is a telescope height quick detachable front sight. It locks on the barrel with a heavy screw which engages a wedge clamp collar making a very rigid mount that will not jar loose nor shift. The mounting block drives into the barrel dovetail.
Price (complete with 8 apertures and mounting block) $6.00

No. W-11-BT Same sight scope block mounts with two screws.
Price (complete with 8 apertures and mounting block) $6.00

VAVER EYE SHIELD AND TELECROPE APERTURE

This eye shield and telescope aperture has been found to be a practical necessity when shooting with a telescope. Will fit Target-spot, Fecker, and Unertl rifle telescope. Specify scope make.
No. 35-ETA $2.50

VAVER QUICK DETACHABLE BARREL BAND

This barrel band has a dovetail slot to receive front sight, bringing it up to telescope height. It is clamped on the barrel and held in fixed position with a locator driven into the dovetail slot of the barrel. (Specify size wanted.)
No. 35-EBB ⅞", 1⅛" or 1" $4.50
Larger or Special Sizes .... extra 1.50

VAVER QUICK DETACHABLE FRONT SIGHT BLOCK

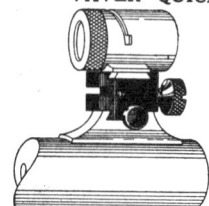

For "52" Winchester Standard Barrel. Brings the front sight up to telescope height for use with telescope height receiver sight. Has locator so it always comes to the same position.
No. 35-XB $2.00

VAVER EXTENSION TUBE FOR RECEIVER SIGHTS

Brings the eye-cup closer to the eye.
No. 37-RE .... $.75
No. 37-RE With eye-cup (½", ⅝", ¾", ⅞") and 7 apertures. $1.50
When ordering specify size eye-cup wanted.

VEVER EYE CUP WITH LENS ADAPTER

This eye-cup is made especially for shooters requiring optical aid. Will hold lens ¾" diameter. Can also be used as a regular eye-cup without the lens. Furnished with protection cap to protect lens when not in use.
No. 37-LA (Eye cup, 7 apertures, lens holder and protection cap).
Lens not furnished $2.50

VAVER MULTI-APERTURES SIGHTING DISCS

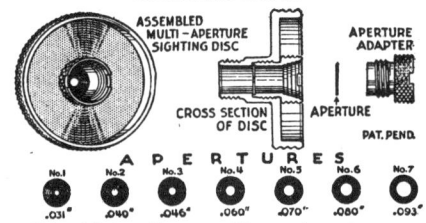

This sighting disc assembly consists of eye-cup, ½", ⅝", ¾", or ⅞", the adapter and seven apertures in different sizes as shown. The adapter is coin-slotted and removable for the changing of apertures. These sighting discs fit all standard receiver sights.
Vaver Multi-Aperture Sighting disc (eye-cup, one adapter and seven apertures) (9 pieces). Kit V.M.A $1.00
(Specify size eye-cup wanted, also make of receiver sight.)
1¼" Special $1.50

MULTI-APERTURES SIGHTING DISC IN KITS

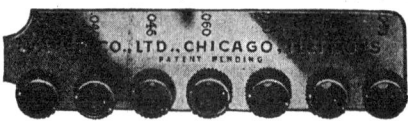

Kit 7B consists of seven adapters with apertures set in mounted on a holder plate marked with size of apertures. One end of the holder plate is a screw driver to fit the adapters which are slotted.
Kit 7B $1.75
Kit 7A consists of one Vaver eye-cup and seven adapters mounted on a holder plate. Each adapter has a different size aperture set in and will fit all Wittek eye-cups.
Kit 7A (½", ⅝", ¾", ⅞", or 1" eye cup) ... $2.50

VAVER EYE CUP ADAPTER FOR STANDARD WIN. REAR SIGHT

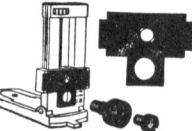

This adapter is a replacement for the sighting block on the Standard Winchester sight. Tapped with 7/32-40 thread to accommodate our Multi-Aperture Sighting.
No. 37-WB .... $ .75
No. 37-WB With eye-cup and 7 apertures 1.50

Light Shade for Front Sights—This Light Shade is 2¾" long with a ¾" hole knurled on one end, with the opposite end tapered and threaded, to screw into the front sight, replacing the front sight adapter.
No. 35-LS When ordering specify Lyman or Redfield $1.50

VAVER DIAL MICROMETER SIGHTS
Series No. "38"

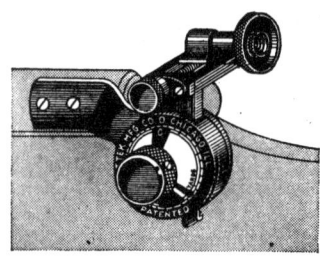

The Series "38" has been developed to meet the demand for a Dial Micrometer Sight for the lower priced, target, hunting and sporting rifles. This Series embodies the same mechanical principle for accurate adjustments, as our proven line of Precision Target Sights. Features found necessary and practical for field use have been added, making it the outstanding target and hunting Micrometer Sight in the low priced field.

The adjustments for both windage and elevation are divided into ¼ minute clicks. The elevation dial has 20 minutes per revolution and the windage dial 3 minutes. The elevation dial is graduated in minutes with a blank space for the shooter to scribe yardage readings for a given ammunition. These yardage readings are obtained by trial or by reference to a trajectory chart for the ammunition.

The advantage of this exclusive feature is of great importance to the shooter. It enables him to have a set zero for the ammunition used, and all readings then start from this zero. Elevation adjustments can be rapidly made by turning the dial to the proper yardage mark, doing away with minute of angle computations. The dials may be interchanged with others graduated for different ammunition or loads.

The clicker mechanism, consisting of a hardened pawl engaging notches on the rim of the cam, can be released by pressing the finger tab—therefore the adjustments can be made silently and rapidly, a necessity in many cases.

These sights are of rugged construction to withstand hard usage. The staff is readily removable and each sight is equipped with a Multi-Aperture Sighting Disc.

Sights of the "38" series are available for the guns and at the prices listed below.

No. 3861	For Winchester 61	$6.50
No. 3862	For Winchester 62	6.50
No. 3863	For Winchester 63	6.50
No. 3869	For Winchester 69	7.50
No. 3872	For Winchester 72	7.50
No. 3823	Savage 23 AA	7.50
No. 3841	For 341A Remington	7.50
No. 3821	For 121A Remington	6.50
No. 3839	For Marlin 39	6.50

For Rifles requiring special adapters $2.50 additional.

VAVER SERIES "38" SIGHT COMBINATION FOR MODEL 75 WINCHESTER RIFLE

No. 3875 Receiver Sight—Telescope Height—with extension Mounts on left side using screw holes provided—No further drilling or cutting of stock necessary. Complete with mounting screws, eye-cup and 7 interchangeable apertures $7.50

No. 1175 Quick Detachable Front Sight—Telescope Height—Complete with two interchangeable Light shades, 4 apertures mounted on a carrier plate and green and amber light filters $4.00

A GOOD GUN DESERVES GOOD SIGHTS

REDFIELD FRONT AND REAR SIGHTS

FRONT RAMP FOR HIGH POWER RIFLES
Ramp may be had with any series of blade sight

With Hood $6.50
Without Hood $5.50

Ramps are regularly supplied for the following:
- 22" Krag
- 24" Krag
- 24" Springfield
- 22", 24" and 26" Enfield 1917
- 23½" Russian
- M/54 Winchester
- M/30 Remington
- M/19 Savage
- M/23 Savage

PROTECTED GOLDFACE PATRIDGE SIGHTS
(SERIES "A")

The square gold bead is inset into the sight blade at an angle. In using this method of insetting the bead a protecting lip of steel is left across the top edge and corners of the comparatively soft bead, as may be seen in the above cuts, thereby preventing them from wearing off round, and also assuring a permanently square bead at all times with which to sight against. They are made for pratically all rifles, carbines, pistols and revolvers. Thickness of blade for use on rifles is made in 1/16 inch only. Thickness of blade for pistols and revolvers is made in 1/10 inch only.

Price each $1.50

IVORY AND GOLD TIP SIGHTS
(SERIES "C" AND "D")

Redfield ivory bead sights have been designed for those shooters who prefer an ivory or white bead front sight. They are made especially strong and have matted blade in front to prevent blur. Beads are made of pure elephant ivory and will show up clearly and distinctly on all colored objects.

Redfield gold tip front sights are of the same construction as our ivory bead sights except are furnished with gold tip. These sights show up well on any background, besides being extremely rugged and adaptable to rough usage.

Made for practically all rifles, carbines, pistols and revolvers. Made in two sized beads, 1/16-in. and 3/32-in.

Price (except No. 50-51-52, see lower right hand corner of page) $1.00

FULL GOLD BEAD SIGHTS
(SERIES "B")

This type of sight has been designed to show up well in the darkest timber, in early morning and late evening shooting, and can be seen after other types of bead sights have faded out. The gold bead extends the full length of the sight blade and is made from a solid steel block with the gold bead electrically welded onto the steel blade, so that the center of the bead is all steel.

It is especially designed and constructed for the hunter and will withstand the rough usage necessary for such a sight.

Made for practically all rifles, carbines, pistols and revolvers. Made in two size beads, 1/16-in. and 3/32-in.

Price (except No. 50-51-52, see bottom of column) $1.50

PISTOL AND REVOLVER SIGHTS

No. 30
- No. 30—For Smith & Wesson, Police Target and Military Revolvers.
- No. 31—For Smith & Wesson .22 Caliber Single Shot Target Pistols.
- No. 32—For Smith & Wesson .22 Caliber Revolvers.
- No. 33—For Smith & Wesson K-22 Revolvers.
- No. 36—For Colt New Service Target Revolvers and Officers' Model Target Revolvers .22 and .38.
- No. 37—For Colt Police Positive Target Revolvers, .22 and .32 Caliber, .22 Automatic Pistol and .22 Woodsman Model Automatic Target Pistol.
- No. 38—For Luger Automatic Pistols, Caliber .30 and 9mm. Stevens Diamond Model Pistols, all Calibers.

Price—Full Gold Bead or Protected Gold Face $1.50
Ivory Bead or Gold Tip 1.00

BLADE FRONT SIGHTS

No. 10
- No. 10—For Winchester Carbines. Model 1894, .25-35, .30-30 and .32 Special. Recommended for use with new high speed ammunition.
- No. 11—For Winchester Carbines. Model 1894, .25-35, .30-30 and .32 Special. Same as No. 10 except being 1/32 inch lower.
- No. 12—For Winchester Carbines, Model 1894, using black powder only, .32-40 and .38-55, Model 1892, all Calibers. Same as No. 11 except lower.
- No. 14—For Winchester Carbines, Model 1895, .30 Government '03, '06. Old Model 54 Bolt Action. All Calibers.
- No. 15—For Winchester Rifles. Model 1895, .30-40 and .303 British.
- No. 16—For Savage Rifles. Model 1899, .22 High Power and .250-3000. Featherweight, .25-35, .30-30 and .303.
- No. 17—For Savage, Model 1920 Bolt Action, .250-3000 and .300 H. P. Same as No. 16 except higher.
- No. 18—For all Savage Rifles having new and longer blade sight block.
- No. 20—For U. S. Springfield Rifles. For use with Military Rear Sight.
- No. 21—For U. S. Springfield Rifles. For use in combination with Redfield, Lyman, or other type of receiver or bolt sleeve sights.
- No. 22—For U. S. Krag Rifles.
- No. 23—For U. S. Krag Carbines. Same as No. 22 except lower.
- No. 24—For Remington Bolt Action .30 Express. For use in combination with Redfield 90-R, 100-R, and 102-R, or other Receiver Sights which require a high Front Sight.
- No. 25—For Remington Bolt Action .30 Express. For use in combination with open Rear Sight. Same as No. 24 except lower.
- No. 26—Remington Model 30-S only.

Price—Full Gold Bead or Protected Gold Face $1.50
Ivory Bead or Gold Tip 1.00

BUCKHORN SIGHTS

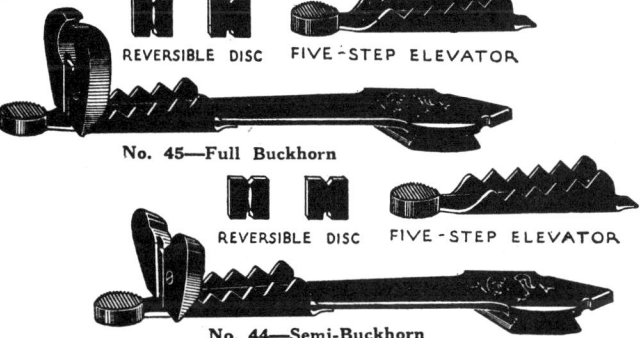

No. 45—Full Buckhorn

No. 44—Semi-Buckhorn

Note:—Nos. 40, 41, and 42, are for rifles. Nos. 43, 44, and 45 are for carbines and .22 caliber rifles.

No. 40—Flat Top	$1.75	No. 43—Flat Top	$1.75
No. 41—Semi-Buckhorn	1.75	No. 44—Semi-Buckhorn	1.75
No. 42—Full Buckhorn	1.75	No. 45—Full Buckhorn	1.75

In ordering, give Make, Model and Caliber of Rifle

DOVETAIL BASE SIGHTS

Supplied in varying heights from 9/32 inch to ½ inch with standard dovetail and 5/16 inch and 3/8 inch heights for the wide Stevens dovetail.

Price—Full Gold Bead and Protected Gold Face Patridge Sight $1.50
Ivory Bead or Gold Tip 1.00

FULL BLOCK SIGHTS

This sight has been designed to fit the Springfield fixed sight stud perfectly and should be considered for its neat appearance on the rifle. It is the strongest Springfield sight obtainable and is not liable to be broken during rough usage in the field as is the common type of knife blade sight.

- No. 50—For use in combination with ordinary military rear sight, Redfield folding leaf or Redfield sporting rear.
- No. 51—For use in combination with Redfield receiver sights or other receiver or bolt sleeve sights.
- No. 52—For use in U. S. Krag rifles when original Krag sight has been replaced by the Springfield fixed sight stud.

Price (in any of the four series) $2.00

In ordering, give Make, Model and Caliber of Rifle

SLOT BLANKS

For all rifles having a Standard Slot in barrel.
Price .... $.50

No. 1   No. 2

REDFIELD MICROMETER AND RECEIVER SIGHTS

SERIES No. 90 AND No. 100 MICROMETER RECEIVER SIGHTS

In presenting the numbers 90 and 100 Series Receiver Sights, we have endeavored to give the shooter a really accurate sight; one which will truly live up to the word "micrometer." Consequently the following sights are the result of many months of experiment, actual range firing and factory tests, and we do not hesitate to present them to the public as being accurate sights.

Special Features. Both elevation and windage are accurately adjustable to ¼ minutes. The elevation has been improved so that one may easily and readily set the sight at the desired range. No notching of rifle stock is necessary to fit the sight. All wearing parts have been hardened to prevent wear. The elevation may be locked and will not get out of place. Both elevation and windage adjustments have steel ball clickers which keep the adjustment knob from turning except when desired. The new type windage prevents all slack in the threads by means of a strong steel spring. This insures that the shooter will actually get a ¼ minute correction per click of elevation or windage. This sight is not only remarkable for target shooting but it is also very practicable for any game shooting; has lock for windage and elevation adjustment.

SERIES No. 102 RECEIVER SIGHTS

The new Redfield series No. 102 receiver sights have been especially designed for the sportsman who wants a sight that he can absolutely rely upon to stay in adjustment on his hunting trips. They are strong and reliable hunting receiver sights.

The new No. 102 series sight is furnished in two models. The illustration of the No. 102 A.M. for Remington Model 33 and 34 contains thumb screw adjustments, without clickers, for both elevation and windage. The No. 102 A.A. is identical except that it does not have screw adjustment for elevation. The other type (see illustration of No. 102-K for Krag) is without thumb screw adjustments for elevation. This model has however, wide slots for coin by which it may be quickly adjusted and then locked solidly into position.

The series No. 102 sights all have positive windage and elevation adjustment and will "stay fixed" when set at the desired range. Practically all of the Redfield sights can be easily installed without the aid of a gunsmith and without cutting or altering the stock.

In ordering, give make, model and caliber of rifle.

SERIES No. 90 AND No. 100 MICROMETER SIGHTS

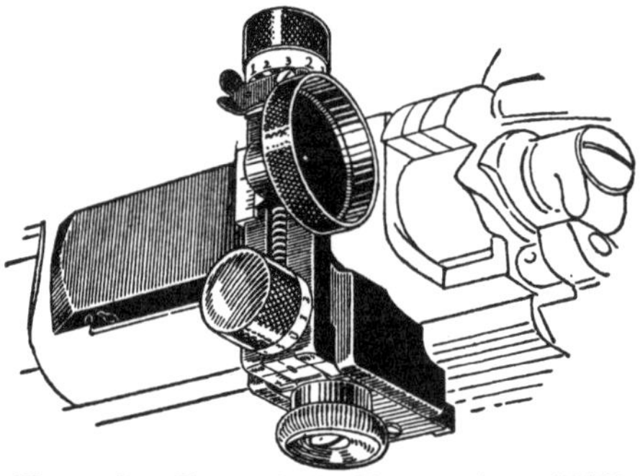

Illustration Shows Sight No. 100-A on M/52 Winchester With Quick Removable Staff.

Series No. 100, With Quick Removable Staff.

100-A—For Model 52, Winchester......	$12.00
100-AH—Same as above, telescope height.	12.00
100-F—For Model 52 Sporter..........	10.50
100-FH—Same as above, telescope height	10.50
100-G—For Models 19 and 23, Savage...	12.00
100-W—For Model 54, Winchester......	10.50
100-R—For Model 30, Express Remington	10.50
100-S—For Model '03, Springfield......	10.50
100-K—For Krag Rifles.............	10.50
100-M—For Mauser Rifles............	10.50
100-RW—For 1917 Enfield Rifles.......	10.50
Series No. 90, Without Quick Removable Staff	
90-A—For Model 52, Winchester.......	$9.50
90-G—For Models 19 and 23, Savage...	9.50
90-W—For Model 54, Winchester.......	8.00
90-R—For Model 30, Express Remington	8.00
90-S—For Models '03 and '06, Springfield	8.00
90-K—For Krag Rifles...............	8.00
90-M—For Mauser Rifles..............	8.00
90-RW—For 1917 Enfield Rifles........	8.00

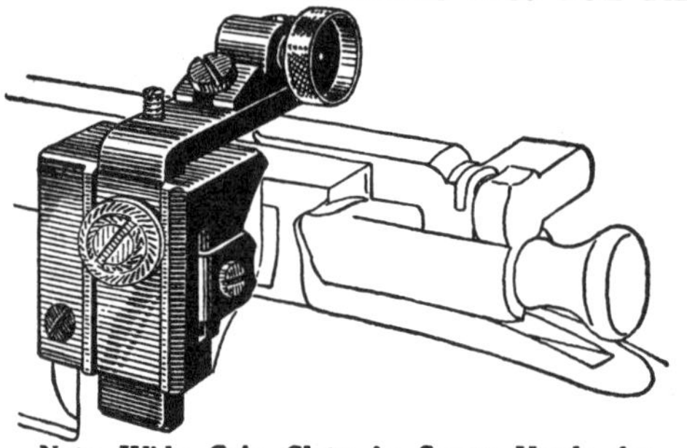

Note Wide Coin Slots in Screw Heads for Quick and Easy Adjustments. Illustration Shows Sight No. 102-K Mounted on Krag Rifle

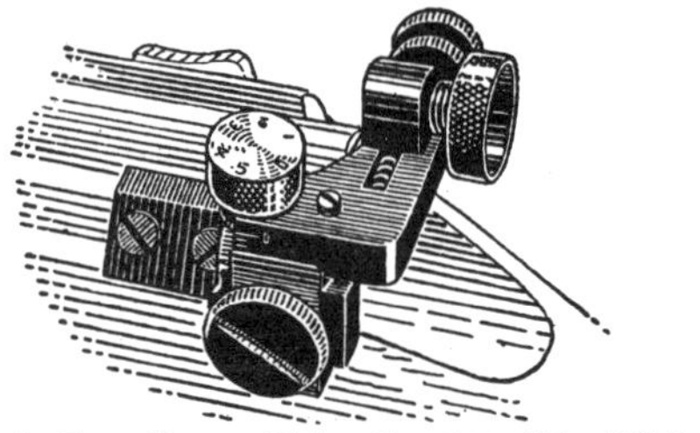

Illustration Shows Sight No. 102-AM (With Screw Type Elevation) on Remington 22 Cal. Bolt Action Models

Sight No. Make and Model of Rifle	Price Each
No. 102-B—For Remington Models 14, 141.	$4.00
No. 102-J—For Remington Model 24.....	4.00
No. 102-R—For Remington Model 30, Express	4.50
No. 102-T—For Remington Models 12, 25.	4.00
No. 102-D—For Winchester Model 1895..	3.75
No. 102-E—For Winchester Models 92, 94, 53, 55, 63, 64.....................	3.75
No. 102-F—For Winchester Model 1886 add Mod. 71.....................	3.75
No. 102-W—For Winchester Model 54, 70.	4.50
No. 102-L—For Savage Model 1899.....	3.75
No. 102-V—For Savage Models 40 and 45	4.00
No. 102-H—For Ross Model 1905......	4.50
No. 102-K—For U. S. Krag Rifles......	4.50
No. 102-M—For Mauser Rifles..........	4.50
No. 102-S—For Newton Rifles..........	4.50
No. 102-O—For Marlin Model 39.......	3.75
No. 102-S—For U. S. Springfield Rifles..	4.50
No. 102-RW—For Remodeled 1917 Enfield	4.50
No. 102-AA—For Remington Mod. 33 and 34 add Mods. 341, 41; Winchester Mod. 60 and 60-A; Savage Mod. 3; Stevens Mod. 65, 66 and 053; Springfield Jr. Mod. 53; Ranger No. 34 & Western Field Single Shot....................	$2.50
No. 102-AM—For Remington Mod. 33 & 34; add Mods. 341, 41; Winchester Mod. 60 and 60-A; Savage Mod. 3; Stevens Mod. 65, 66 and .053; Springfield Jr. Mod. 53; Ranger No. 34 & Western Field Single Shot............	3.75
No. 102-BB—For Savage Model 4; Springfield Model 56 and Western Field Box Magazine Repeater	2.50
No. 102-BM—For Savage Model 4; Springfield Model 56 and Western Field Box Magazine Repeater, Springfield 056....	3.75
No. 102-CC—For Winchester Models 56, 57 add Mod. 69; Model 50, Marlin...	3.50
No. 102-CM—For Winchester Models 56, 57 add Mod. 69; Model 50, Marlin...	4.50
No. 102-EE—Winchester Mod. 63, 03....	2.50
No. 102-EM—Winchester Mod. 63, 03...	3.75
No. 102-GG—For Sav. Mod. 19, 23 & 33	5.50
No. 102-GM—For Sav. Mod. 19, 23 & 33	6.50
No. 102-RR—For Sav. Mod. 3B Single Shot	2.50
No. 102-RM—For Sav. Mod. 3B Single Shot	3.75

Tap and drill furnished for any of the above sights at 50 cents extra.

SIGHTING DISCS

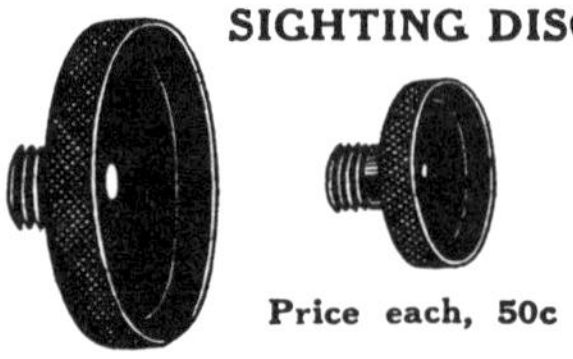

Price each, 50c

Discs are regularly supplied with apertures of .046 or .093 and available with outside disc diameter of ⅜ inch, ½ inch, ⅝ inch, 11/16 inch, and ⅞ inch.

PEEP SIGHT DISCS, EACH 35c

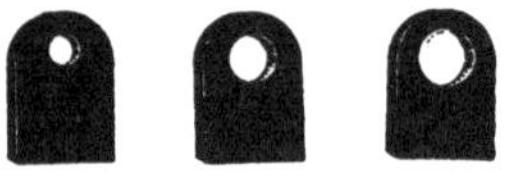

Adapted to all Redfield Sporting Rear or Folding Leaf Sights.

Sizes of apertures, 3/32 inch, 7/64 inch and ⅛ inch.

GLOBE FRONT SIGHTS

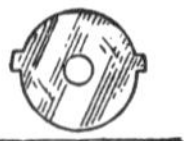

Price, Each $2.50

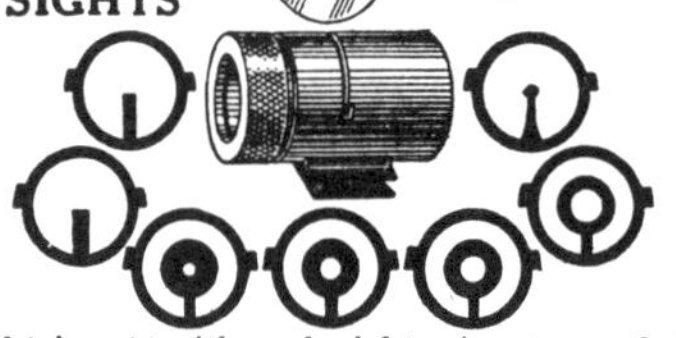

Eight inserts with each sight. Apertures of .070-inch, .095-inch, .110-inch, .125-inch, and a transparent insert having a .070-inch aperture. The widths of the posts are .063-inch and .100-inch.

No. 65—For rifles having standard dovetail slots and requiring a front sight ⅜-inch high, as M/52 Winchester, etc.

No. 66—For 1903 and 1906 Springfield.

No. 67—For Mark 1 Springfield.

No. 68—For heavy barrel M/52 Winchester, M/1919, 23 and 33 Savage.

No. 65-S—For all Stevens rifles having wide slot.

No. 63—Similar to above but for new Model 52 Winchester or Remington Model 37.

Price	$3.50
Extra for base and screws..............	.50

ADJUSTABLE FOLDING LEAF SIGHTS

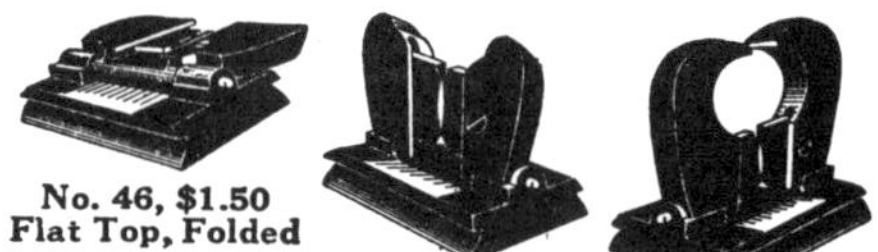

No. 46, $1.50 Flat Top, Folded

No. 47, $1.50 Semi-Buckhorn, Up

No. 48, $1.50 Full Buckhorn, Up

Nos. 46, 47, 48—Adapted to most rifles having standard barrel slots for rear sights....	$1.50
Nos. 46-S, 47-S, 48-S—For Savage rifles M/1899. Same as standard except higher.	1.50
Nos. 46-F, 47-F, 48-F—For U. S. Springfield rifles only...........................	1.50

This folding leaf sight is made to take the place of the elevator staff of the regulation military sight. With the Redfield folding leaf in place the windage features of the military sight are retained.

Nos. 46-R, 47-R, 48-R—Adapted to Remington M/8 only.....................	$2.00

Give make, model and caliber of rifle.

AMERICA'S GREAT GUN HOUSE

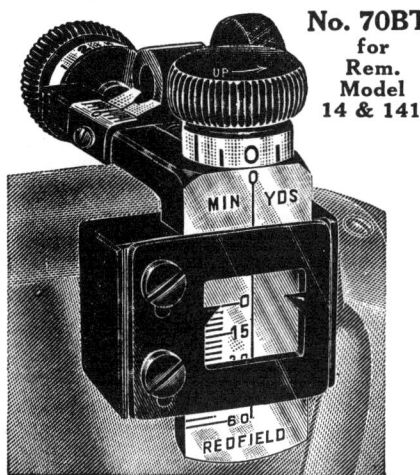

No. 70BT for Rem. Model 14 & 141

This sight can be used on any Remington model 14 or 141. On some early models 14 and 141 it will be necessary to install a higher front sight. Full attaching instructions and drilling template furnished with each sight.

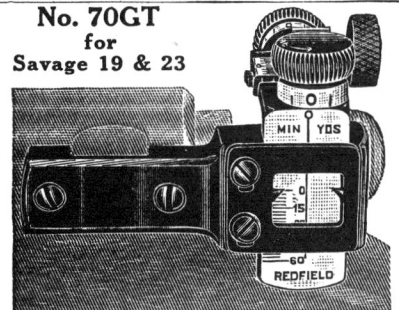

No. 70GT for Savage 19 & 23

Straddles safety on left side. Two holes to be drilled and tapped.

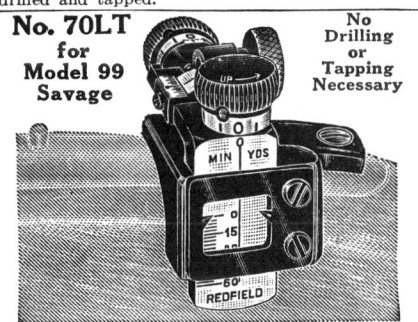

No. 70LT for Model 99 Savage — No Drilling or Tapping Necessary

This sight attaches by the screw holes provided in tang of rifle.

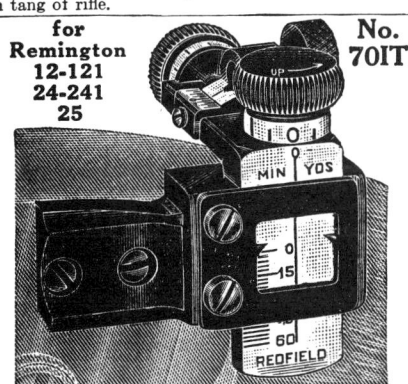

No. 70IT for Remington 12-121 24-241 25

Two holes must be drilled and tapped in left side of receiver, template furnished with sight. An identical sight is furnished for Winchester model 61. Nos. 70-ZT and 70-ZH attach to right side of receiver.

REDFIELD No. 70 and 75 MICROMETER SIGHTS

Entirely new design. Accurate and uniform adjustments. Positively no backlash or lost motion. Original Redfield steel ball clicker system, loud and positive clicks. Clearly marked adjustment graduations, easy to read. Adjustable zero scales for both windage and elevation. Newly designed Hunter adjusting knobs or knurled target knobs optional at no extra cost.

All Redfield 70 and 75 Micrometer Receiver Sights are sold subject to a 5 year guarantee.

Another original and exclusive Redfield feature —your choice of adjusting knobs that perfectly adapt the sight to your particular purpose. Redfield No. 70 receiver sights can be furnished with either knurled Target adjusting knobs or the new and exclusively Redfield Hunter adjusting knobs—at no extra charge.

HUNTER ADJUSTING KNOB

The answer to the hunter's prayer. Cannot be turned accidentally—scabbard-proof and foolproof —safe from the knob-turning friend—cannot be turned with the fingers—coin-slotted for easy operation with a penny, washer, knife blade, key, or screw driver. Clicks are loud and sharp.

TARGET ADJUSTING KNOB

This knob is designed for easy operation with the fingers and is marked for direction of adjustment. This is the most desirable adjusting knob for the target shooter. Unless otherwise specified, this target knob will be furnished on No. 70 sights.

IMPORTANT—When placing your order for Redfield receiver sights Nos. 70 or 75, please use the numbers shown on the list below. Be sure that you have the correct number to indicate your choice of Hunter or Target adjusting knobs—then to further eliminate any chance of error, mention the make, model and caliber of your rifle.

SERIES 70

With Target Knobs	With Hunter Knobs		Price
	70-AH	Remington 33, 34, 510, 511 Win. 60; Sav. 3; Stev. 65, 66, etc.	$6.50
70-BT	70-BH	Rem. 14, 141	6.50
70-CT	70-CH	Win. 56, 57, 69, 72, 75 Sporter	6.50
70-DT	70-DH	Win. M/95	6.50
70-ET	70-EH	Win. 92, 94, 53, 55, 64, 65	6.50
70-FT	70-FH	Win. 71, 86	6.50
70-GT	70-GH	Sav. 19, 23, 33	6.50
70-HT	70-HH	For Sav. 6, Stev. 76, Spgfld. 87	6.50
70-VT	70-VH	For Stevens 416, Ranger 50	6.50
70-JT	70-JH	Rem. 24, 241	6.50
70-LT	70-LH	Sav. 99	7.50
70-MT	70-MH	Mauser	6.50
70-RT	70-RH	Rem. 30	6.50
70-RWT	70-RWH	Remodeled Enfield	6.50
70-ST		Springfield Newton	6.50
70-TT	70-TH	Rem. 12, 121, 25, etc.	6.50
70-WT	70-WH	Win. 54 and 70	6.50
70-XT	70-XH	Win. M/03, 63	6.50
70-YT	70-YH	Right-hand Mossberg rifles on master action	6.50
70-ZT	70-ZH	Win. M/61	6.50
70-OT	70-OH	Marlin 39	6.50

Scope Height	Standard Height	SERIES 75	Price
75-HW		75 Winchester	$7.50
75-HG	75-SG	19 Savage	7.50
75-HV	75-SV	416 Stevens, Sears, Ranger, etc.	7.50
75-HM	75-SM	Mossberg, on master actions	7.50
75-HB	75-SB	Ballard	7.50
75-HR	75-SR	Win. SS—High Wall action only	7.50
75-HY	75-SY	Stevens Walnut Hill—417	7.50
75-HT	75-ST	Martini	7.50
		Tap and Drill, Extra	.50

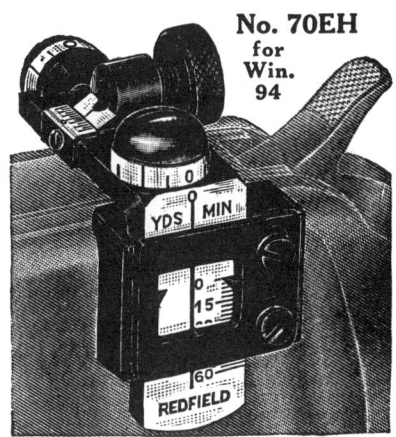

No. 70EH for Win. 94

Fits all Winchester models 92, 94, 53, 55, 64, 65 rifles and carbines; all but model 64 must be drilled and tapped. An identical sight is furnished for Winchester models 86, 71 and 95.

No. 70XT for Win. 03 & 63

Two holes to be drilled and tapped.

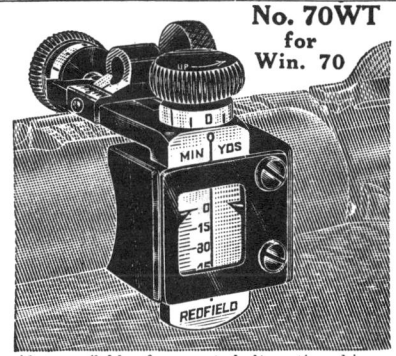

No. 70WT for Win. 70

Also available for most bolt action hi-power rifles. See list at right.

Easy to install, not necessary to cut stock. Service Springfield, Newton, Mauser and Enfield rifles must be drilled and tapped.

No. 75HW for Winchester 75 and Various Target Rifles

A special extension sight for Win. Mod. 75, Savage Mod. 19, Stevens Mod. 416 and Walnut Hill. Also Ballard, Martini, and other Falling Block Actions.

GOOD EQUIPMENT ALWAYS PAYS

MARBLE'S FLEXIBLE REAR SIGHTS

MARBLE'S REAR SIGHT DISCS

For Marble's Rear Rifle Sights

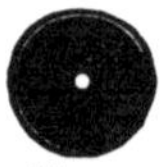

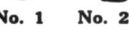

No. 9

No. 1

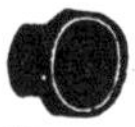

No. 2

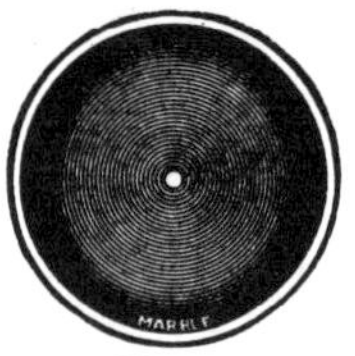

No. 5

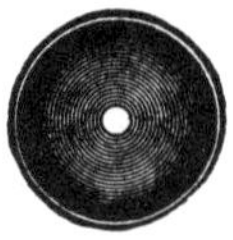

No. 7

(Cuts Are Actual Size)

Disc	Size	Aperture		Each
No. 1	—¼ inch	.052 inch		$0.25
No. 1s.	—¼ inch	.021 inch		.25
No. 2	—¼ inch	.081 inch		.25
No. 5	—⅞ inch	.052 inch	"Target Disc"	.50
No. 5s.	—⅞ inch	.021 inch		.50
No. 6	—⅞ inch	.081 inch		.50
No. 7	—9/16 inch	.081 inch	"Snapshooter Disc"	.50
No. 7a.	—9/16 inch	.052 inch		.50
No. 7s.	—9/16 inch	.021 inch		.50
No. 8	—9/16 inch	⅛ inch	"Snapshooter Disc"	.50
No. 9	—⅜ inch	.052 inch		.50
No. 9s.	—⅜ inch	.021 inch		.50
No. 10	—⅜ inch	.081 inch	"Hunter Disc"	.50

MARBLE'S FLEXIBLE REAR SIGHTS

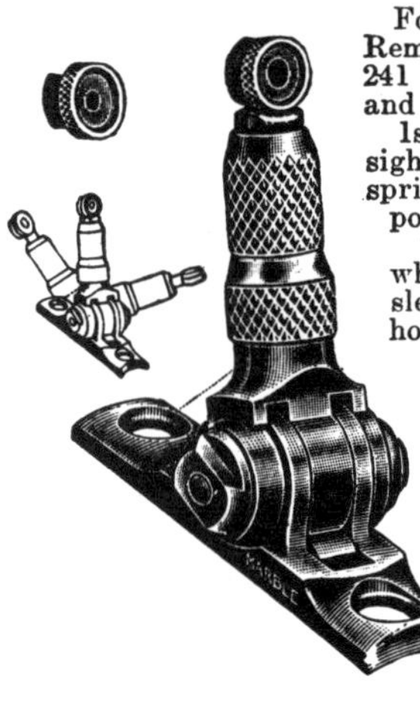

For all Standard American Rifles except Remington Model 12, 121, 14, 141, 16, 24, 241 and 25 Repeaters. Important features and advantages:

1st.—*Automatic Joint.* Whenever the sight is struck on front or back, the coiled spring in the hinge brings it instantly into position for shooting. Can be locked down.

2nd.—*Elevation Lock.* The lower sleeve, when turned up against the elevating sleeves prevents it from being turned and holds the disc stem true and rigid at any elevation.

3rd.—*Point Blank Adjustment.* A screw in the bottom of disc permits a quick change of point blank range without tools.

4th.—*Interchangeable Discs.* All Target, Hunter and Snapshooter Discs can be used.

State base number, make, model and caliber when ordering, and if rifle has pistol grip.

Flexible Rear Sight with Discs 1 and 2............Price **$4.00**

MARBLE'S RECEIVER SIGHTS

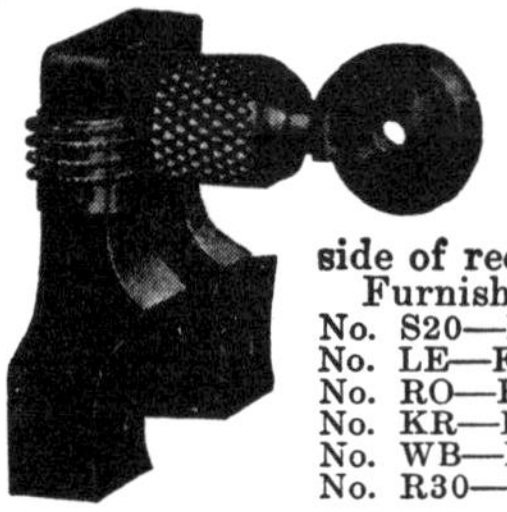

Adjustable for elevation and windage. Each quarter turn of elevation screw changes elevation .0125 inch and each quarter turn of wind gauge screw gives a variation of .0104 inch. Aperture in disc is 3-32 inch. Sight attaches to side of receiver, around ejector. Absolutely rigid. Furnished with drill, tap and screws.

No. S20—For Savage 1920 Bolt Action Rifles....**$6.50**
No. LE—For Lee-Enfield Military and Sptg. Rifles **6.50**
No. RO—For Ross Sporting and Military Rifles.. **6.50**
No. KR—For Krag Rifles and Carbines........ **6.50**
No. WB—For Winchester Model 54 Bolt Action.. **6.50**
No. R30—For Remington Model 30 Bolt Action.. **6.50**

MARBLE'S SIMPLEX REAR SIGHT

For .22 Caliber Rifles Only

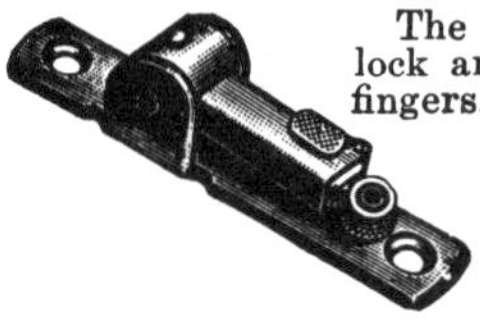

The elevation may be changed by raising the lock and moving the stem up or down with the fingers. The sight may be folded down.

Furnished with Discs No. 1 and No. 2. Mention make and model of .22 Cal. Rifle.

Not necessary to give base number.

Simplex Sight **$2.00**

MARBLE'S "SPECIAL" REAR SIGHT

It can be folded down to tang. It cannot be made with flexible joint on account of having to be low but it has all the other features of Marble's Flexible Rear Sights.

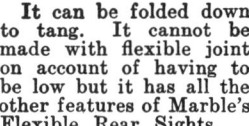

For Remington Rifles
(Not Flexible)

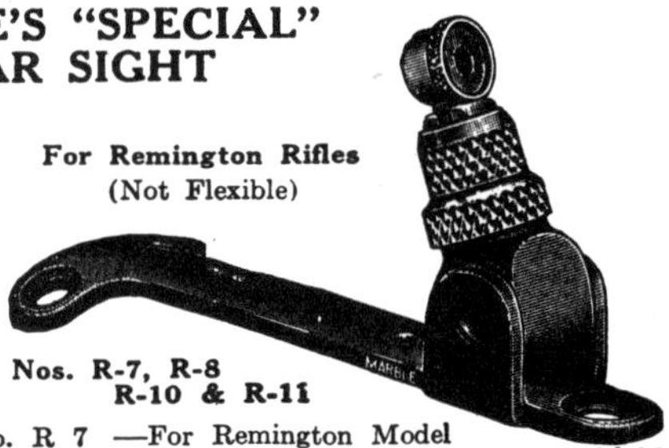

Nos. R-7, R-8 R-10 & R-11

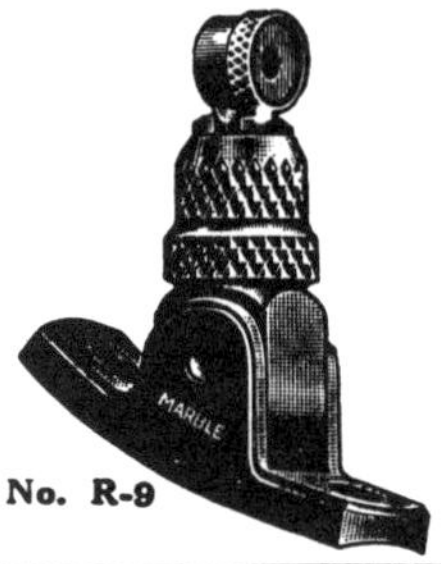

No. R-9

No. R 7 —For Remington Model 12, .22 Cal. Repeater **$4.00**
No. R 7 —For Remington Model 121, .22 Cal. Repeater **4.00**
No. R 7C—For Remington Model 12CS, .22 Cal. Repeater............... **4.00**
No. R 8 —For Remington Models 14 and 141, High Power............ **4.00**
No. R 9 —For Remington Model 16, .22 Auto. Loader **4.00**
No. R10 —For Remington Models 24 and 241, .22 Auto. Loader........ **4.00**
No. R11 —For Remington Mod. 25, .25-20 and .32-20 Cal.......... **4.00**

MARBLE'S REAR SIGHTS ARE MADE FOR NEARLY ALL STANDARD AMERICAN RIFLES

In ordering Marble Sights, give base number, make, model, caliber, and if rifle has pistol grip.

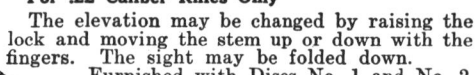

WINCHESTER RIFLES

No.	Model Caliber
W1	for 94—.25-35, .30-30 and .32 Special
W1	for 55—.30-30
W1PG	for 64—.30-30
W2	for 94—.32-40 and .38-55
W2	for 92—.25-20, .32, .38 and .44
W2	for 53—.25-20, .32 and .44
W2PG	for 65—.25-20, .32-20
W3	for 76—.40-60, .40-65, .45-75 and .45-90
W4	for 86—.45-70, .45-90 and .50-110
W4½	for 86—.33 caliber only
W4½PG	for 71—.348 cal.
W5	for Single Shot, all calibers except .22 and .30 Army (.30-40)
W6	for Single Shot, .22 C. F. and .30 Army
W7	for 73—.32, .38 and .44
W8	for 03—.22 Auto.
W8	for 63—.22 LR Auto.
W9	for 90—.22
W9	for 06—.22
W9	for 62—.22
W10	for 02—.22
W10	for 04—.22
W10	for 59, 60, 67, 68,—.22
W11	for 95—.37-72, .40-72 and .405
W12	for 95—.30 Army, .303, .35 and .30 Gov't, Rimless
W13	for 05—.32 and .35 Self Loader
W13	for 07—.351 Self Loader
W13	for 10—.401 Self Loader
W15	for 61—.22

MARLIN RIFLES

No.	Model Caliber
M1	for 92—.32
M2	for 94—.25-20, .32-20, .38-40 and .44-40
M3	for 92—.22
M3	for 97—.22 (Take-down)
M3	for No. 27—.25-20 and .32-20
M3	for No. 25—.22
M5	for 93—.25-36; .32 Special H.P.S., .30-30, .32-40, H.P.S., and .38-55 H.P.S. Only for guns stamped "Special Smokeless Steel"
	for 1936—.30 and .32 Special Rifle and Carbine
M4	for 93—.32-40 and .38-55, with or without "For Black Powder" stamped on the barrel
M6	for 95—.38-56, .40-65, .40-70-330, .40-82-260, .45-70, .40-85, .45-90 and .33 H.P.
M8	for No. 20—.22
M8	for No. 37—.22
M8	for No. 39—.22 Repeater
M8	for No. 47—.22 Repeater
M50	for No. 50—.22 Auto.

SAVAGE RIFLES

No.	Model Caliber
S1	for 99—.22 H.P., .25-35, .250-3000, .30-30, .300 and .303
S2	for 03—.22 (Take-down)
S2	for 12—.22 Auto.
S2	for 25—.22
S2	for 29—.22
S3	for 99—.32-40 and .38-55
S4	for 04—.22
S4	for 05—.22
S4	for 11—.22
S5S	for 19—.22 N.R.A.
S20	for 20—.250 Bolt Action (List $6.50)
S6S	for 22—Sporter, .22 Cal., or .23 Sporter, all calibers.
R12	for 3, 4 and 5—.22 Bolt Action

REMINGTON RIFLES

No.	Model Caliber
R1	for 3—.25, .32, .38, .40 and .45
R2	for 3—.22
R2	for 2—.22, .32, .38 and 44
R2	for 5—.30-30, 7 M-M, 30 U.S.A., .303, .32-40, .32 Special and .38-55
R3	for 4—.22, .25-10 and .32
R5	for 6—.22 and .32
R6	for 8—.25, .30, .32 and .35 Remington Auto. Loader
R6	for 81—Remington Auto. Loader
R7	for 12—.22 Repeater (not flexible)
R7	for 121—Remington .22 Repeater
R7C	for 12CS—Repeater (not flexible)
R8	for 14 and 141 H.P. Repeater (not flexible)
R9	for 16—.22 Auto. Loader (not flexible)
R10	for 24 and 241. Auto. Loader, .22 cal. (not flexible)
R11	for 25—.25-20 and .32-20 (not flexible)
R12	for 33 and 41—.22
R12	for 34—.22 Repeater
R13	for 341A

STEVENS RIFLES

No.	Model Caliber
V1	for Favorite—.22, .25 and .32 Rim-fire
V2	for Ideal—.22, .25, .28, .32, .38 and .44
V3	for Crack Shot—.22 and .32
V4	for Maynard, Jr.—.22
V6	for 70 and 71
V7	for 425—High Power
S2	for 75—Repeater .22
V8	for 65 and 66—.22 Bolt Action

MISCELLANEOUS

No.	Model Caliber
02S	for Ross Rifles
KS	for Krag Rifles and Carbines
S5S	for Savage 1919—.22 N.R.A.
S6S	for Savage 1932 Sporter

DRILLS—For all Rear Sight Tang Holes...**$0.30**
TAPS—For all Rear Sight Tang Holes..... **.30**

ALL SHIPMENTS ARE INSURED

AMERICA'S GREAT GUN HOUSE

MARBLE'S SPORTING LEAF & RECEIVER SIGHTS

When Nos. 63, 64 and 65 Sporting Rear Sight are used on Remington .22 caliber or Winchester .22 Self Loading, a front sight 1/16 inch higher than regular is required.

In Ordering Marble Sights Give Make, Model and Caliber of Rifle.

FLAT TOP

No. 63—For Winchester Carbines, all calibers; Savage .22 H. P., .250-3000 and .300 H. P. Rifles; and all makes of .22 caliber rifles having standard slots in barrel for rear sight.
Price $1.75
No. 63M—For Rem. Nos. 121, 241, 41A, 341A.
Price $1.75
No. 66 Similar to 63—Winchester; Savage; Marlin; Remington (except Autoloading H. P.); and other rifles having standard slot in barrel for rear sight.
Price $1.75
No. 66R—For Remington Nos. 8 and 81 H. P.
Price $2.50

SEMI BUCKHORN

No. 64—For Winchester Carbines, all calibers; Savage 22 H. P., .250-3000 and .300 H. P. Rifles; and all makes of .22 caliber rifles having standard slots in barrel for rear sight.
Price $1.75
No. 64M—For Remington Nos. 121, 241, 41A, 341A.
Price $1.75
No. 67 Similar to 64—Winchester; Savage; Marlin; Remington (except Autoloading H. P.) and other rifles having standard slots in barrel for rear sight.
Price $1.75
No. 67R—For Remington Nos. 8 and 81 H. P.
Price $2.50

FULL BUCKHORN

No. 65—For Winchester Carbines, all calibers; Savage .22 H. P., .250-3000 and .300 H. P. Rifles; and all makes of .22 caliber rifles having standard slots in barrel for rear sight.
Price $1.75
No. 65M—For Rem. Nos. 121, 241, 41A, 341A.
Price $1.75
No. 68 Similar to 65—Winchester; Savage; Marlin; Remington (except Autoloading H. P.); and, other rifles having standard slot in barrel for rear sight.
Price $1.75
No. 68R—For Remington Nos. 8 and 81 H. P.
Price $2.50

No. 69—Flat Top Leaf. For all Winchester; Marlin; Savage (except .22 H. P. .250-3000, and .300 H. P.); Remington (except Autoloading H. P.); and for all other rifles having standard slot in barrel for rear sight.
Price $1.50
No. 69H—Flat Top Leaf (extra high). For Savage .22 H.P., .250-3000 and .300 H. P.
Price $1.50
No. 70 — Semi - Buckhorn Leaf. For all guns listed under No. 69.
Price $1.50
No. 70H — Semi-Buckhorn Leaf (extra high). For all rifles listed under No. 69H.
Price $1.50
Nos. 69R, 70R and 71R Leaf for model 8 Rem. Auto Rifles, each.........$2.00
No. 71 — Full Buckhorn Leaf. For all guns listed under No. 69.
Price $1.50
No. 71H — Full Buckhorn Leaf (extra high). For all rifles listed under No. 69H.
Price $1.50

MARBLE-GOSS RECEIVER TANG SIGHT

1. Brings aperture nearest the eye.
2. Gives longest sighting radius (34" in intermediate position).
3. Gives sharper definition of front sight and target.
4. Has full 1½" adjustment forward or backward to suit your build, stock and shooting position.
5. Is the only sight with reversible disc carriage. Perfect fit with either high or low comb stocks.
6. Has positive, accurate micrometer adjustments with new type extra wide lapped-in thread.
7. Has true ¼ of minute of angle in long position adjustable tension clicks. (⅛ minute moves easily possible.)
8. Has clockwise movement for both windage and elevation. Eliminates confusion and wrong moves. Turn in the direction you want to move your shot.
9. Does not interfere witth bolt handling in any position.
10. Needs no locking device to insure holding elevation.
11. Has no metal corners or angles to interfere with holding disc close to eye. Disc rides 5/16" or more back of all other parts of sight.
12. Allows use of any standard thread disc. Permits use of larger discs and smaller apertures, reducing effect of bad side lights, etc. without loss of definition.
13. Is quickly and easily attached or dismounted, without disturbing adjustments. Coin slotted screw, no tool needed.
14. Has adjustable zeros and plainly marked minute of angle scales for both windage and elevation.
15. Has large diameter disc with recessed aperture diaphragm. Aperture sizes: .037, .041 and .045. Furnished regularly with .041 aperture. Extra discs with .037 or .045 apertures, 75c each. Spectacle lense can be inserted ahead of diaphragm with optical center in absolute alignment, on order.

No. MG52—For Winchester Model 52 Standard and Heavy Barrel Target Rifles with flat top, slotted receivers........$12.00
No. MG52MS—For Winchester Heavy Barrel Rifles with Marksman Stock, and flat top, slotted receivers............12.00
No. MG52B—For Winchester Standard Barrel Rifles with Round Receivers..12.00
No. MG52BH—For Winchester Heavy Barrel Rifles with Round Receivers..12.00
No. MG69—For Winchester Models 56, 57, and 69 Rifles.................12.00
No. MG19—For Savage Models 19, 22, 23, and 33 Rifles.................12.00
No. MG50—For Sears Ranger Model 50 Rifles; Stevens 416-1 Rifles......12.00
No. MG417—For Stevens Model 417 Rifles; Ballard Rifles...............12.00
No. MG37—For Remington Model 37 Rangemaster Rifles...............12.00
No. MG750—For Winchester M/75 Rifle 7.50
No. MG440—For Mossberg Target Rifle 7.50
No. MG500—For Sears Ranger M/50 Rifle and Stevens No. 416..........7.50
Also made for U. S. Enfield Rifles at $12.00; and for M1 and M2 Springfield, Model 34 Remington, and Winchester Single Shot Rifles, including B. S. A., at $13.50 each, list.

M-G EXTENDED RECEIVER SIGHT

For Remington 30S and Enfield Rifles. Easily attached. Brings eye disc 2 inches nearer the eye. Eliminates danger from recoil.
Price $12.00

M-G RECEIVER SIGHT
(Regular Type)

Made for Winchester Models 54 and 70, or any Rifle necessitating left hand mounting. No cutting away of stock to attach. Equipped with quick-detachable staff and reversible disc carriage. Fits high or low comb stocks, with either high or low front sights. Lapped-in threads insure positive movements.
Price $12.00

NEW M-G SLEEVE SIGHT

Built especially for the heavier calibre military, sporting, and "Bull" rifles, the new M-G Sleeve Sight puts the aperture where it belongs . . . closer to the eye! Equipped with quick-removable staff, reversible disc carriage, and left side precision micrometer adjustments, the new M-G Sleeve Sight gives a rigid-based, accurately adjustable sight with correct eye relief. Most models easily attached without drilling, tapping, or cutting away of stock.
For Springfield 30-06; Krag; Price complete, $15.00 each.

MARBLE'S ADJUSTABLE LEAF SIGHT No. 95L

The leaf for this leaf sight is firmly held in position by the spring of the long flat part when either up or down, and can be easily put in either position.
No. 95L. For Winchester Rifles; Marlin Rifles, all models and calibers except '93 and '95; Savage Rifles models '03, '04, '05, '22 and '23 Sporter; No. 40 and 45 Remington Rifles, models 4, 12, 14, 16, 24, 25, 33, and 34.$1.25
No. 95H. For Savage H. P. and Models 25 and 29, .22 caliber; for Martin H. P. Rifles..1.25
No. 95XH. For Savage 1920, Bolt Action Rifles.............................1.25
No. 95NRA. For Savage '19 and '33, and .22 N. R. A. Rifles.........................1.50
No. 95S. For Stevens Rifles............1.25
No. 95R. For Model 8 Remington Auto. Rifles.............................1.50
No. 95M. For. Remington Nos. 41, 341A, 121 and 241........................1.25

A NEW GUN CARRIES A FACTORY GUARANTEE

MARBLE'S FRONT SIGHTS
Made for Nearly All American Rifles; Gold or Ivory Bead; Choice of Bead Size

MARBLE'S REVERSIBLE SIGHT (Ivory and Gold Bead)

Both beads are the same size and are furnished in 1/16, 3/32 or 1/8 inch sizes. This sight can be instantly reversed. Simply pull up the bead carrier against the pressure of the spring until it clears the groove—then turn it around.

Reversible Sight, each.............................$1.50

MARBLE'S STANDARD (Ivory or Gold Bead)

They are made for all American rifles in 1/16, 3/32 and 1/8 inch Ivory or Gold beads.

Price $1.00

MARBLE'S V. M. FRONT SIGHT

As the eye quickly and surely finds the center of the peep sight, so it finds the center of the front sight. The advantage of the aperture over bead sights is that the object aimed at is not covered up by the front sight. The act of aiming is without effort and always accurate. Face and lining of aperture are made from our lustrous Popes Island Gold, visible in the dimmest light. The aperture is 5/32 inch inside diameter, 1/4 inch outside diameter, 1/8 inch deep.

V. M. Front Sight.............................$1.50

MARBLE'S IMPROVED (Ivory or Gold Bead)

This sight enables one to make accurate shots at any range without stopping to adjust the rear sight. On a range somewhat longer than the gun is sighted for, one can see the object aimed at, under the center of the bead as well as over. It is an exceptionally valuable sight for running shots and is used for shooting at objects in the air by the most famous professional riflemen. 1/16 and 3/32 inch ivory or gold beads.

Improved Sight, each.............................$1.00

Order Improved, Standard, V. M. and Reversible Front Sights by Sight Number Given in Table Below—State Size and Color of Bead Desired and Name of Sight—Each Sight Fits All Rifles Listed Under the Same Number

WINCHESTER RIFLES

Sight Size	Model	Caliber
No. 2	73 76 86 Single Shot. All except .30 Army 92 94—.32-40 and .38-55 90—.22 Repeater 95—.30 Government Model 1906, .38-72, .40-72 03—.22 Auto 04—.22 S. S. 05—.32 and .35 Self Loading 06—.22 Repeater 07—.351 Self Loading 10—.401 Self Loading 53—.25-20, .32-20, .44-40 55—.30-30 W. C. F.	
No. 57	92—Carbines with ramp 94—Carbines with ramp No. 54—Rifles with ramp No. 64—.30-.30 and .32 Spl No. 65—.25-.20 and .32-.20 No. 70 No. 71—.348	
No. 3	Single Shot. .30 Army 1894—.25-35, .30-30 and .32 Special. (When using regular smokeless ammunition.) 61—.22 Repeater	
No. 6	1895—.35 and .405 No. 56, .22 Bolt Action Repeater Nos. 59, 60 and 67, .22 Cal. Bolt Action No. 62—.22 Repeater 63—.22 L.R. auto.	
No. 52	M-52, .22 N. R. A. M-57, .22 Caliber 92—Rifles with ramp	
No. 5	1894—.25-35, .30-30 and .32 Special. (Using superspeed ammunition.) 1895—.30 Gov't .06, 150 and 180 gr. bullet Nos. 68 and 69—.22 cal.	

MARLIN RIFLES

Sight Size	Model	Caliber
No. 2	92—.32 only 93—.32-40 and .38-55 Black 94 95—All except .33 No. 20	No. 25 No. 27 No. 29 No. 37
No. 5	1893—.25-36 H.P.S., .30-30, .32 Special and .32-40 H.P.S. 1936—.30 and .32 Special	
No. 3	93—.38-55 H.P.S. 95—.33 H.P. No. 38 No. 39 Nos. 65, 80 and 100—.22. Nos. 50 and A-1—.22 Auto.	
No. 6	1892—.22 only 1897	

SAVAGE RIFLES

Sight Size	Model	Caliber
No. 5	99-A, B, C and D, .30-.30, .303 and .300 H.P. Caliber rifles up to serial number 297,000 99-H Carbines 1923—Sporter, all calibers No. 25—.22 No. 29—.22 Repeater	
No. 6	1922 Sporter, .22 Caliber 99T .30-.30 and .303	
No. 16B	99-A and B—.303 and .300 Caliber (serial numbers above 297,000) 99-E, F and G—.22 H. P., 250-3000 and .300 (serial numbers above 305,700)	
No. 3	99—.38-55 99 F and G, .22 H.P., 99 R.S. .250 99 F, G and K, .30-30 and .303; Carbines .250, .30-30 and .303 11—.22 Repeater 12—.22 Auto. Nos. 3, 4 and 5—.22 Bolt Action	
No. 2	03—.22 Repeater 04—.22 Single Shot 14—.22 Repeater	
No. 47	1919 and 1933—.22 N. R. A. (Standard Sheard and VM only)	

SAVAGE RIFLES (Continued)

Sight Size	Model	Caliber
No. 52	99-A and B—.30-30 caliber (serial numbers above 297,000) 99-F and G—.30-30 caliber (serial numbers above 305,000) No. 40 and No. 45 Super-Sporter	

REMINGTON RIFLES

Sight Size	Model	Caliber
No. 2	Nos. 2, 4 and 6 No. 12—.22 Repeater No. 16—.22 Auto Loader Nos. 33, 34, 41 and 341—.22	
No. 3	No. 121—.22 Repeater Nos. 24 and 241—.22 Auto Loader Nos. 14 and 141—Pump Action, all calibers No. 25—.25-20 and .32-20 Repeater	
No. 6	No. 8—Auto Loader, all calibers	
No. 50 No. 141	M-30 Rem. 30 Gov't Bolt Action All calibers	
No. 56	M-30 Express (using factory rear sight)	
No. 56H	M-30 Express (using Lyman No. 48-R receiver sight)	
No. 56S	M/30S Sporter	

STEVENS RIFLES

Sight Size	Model	Caliber
	Nos. 8 and 81 Favorite No. 70—.22 caliber Repeater Ideal	
No. 14	No. 35—Off Hand (Standard only) No. 16—Crack Shot (Standard only) No. 12—Marksman (Standard only)	
No. 510A	.22 S.S. Bolt Action	
No. 5	No. 75—Repeater .22	
No. 3	Nos. 50, 53 and 56 Springfield Jr. Nos. 65 and 66 Bolt Action No. 71—Visible Loader	
No. 5	No. 75—.22 Repeater	
No. 15	425, High Power (Standard and VM only)	
No. 48	No. 10 Pistol (Standard and Sheard only)	

Marble's Sheard "Gold" Hunting or Target Front Sights
MADE FOR NEARLY ALL SPORTING AND MILITARY RIFLES

No. 4   No. 6   No. 11

    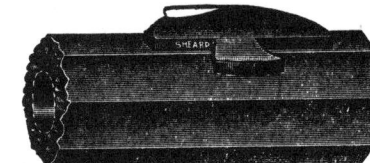

Made with Gold Bead Medium Size Only.

This sight is guaranteed to show up well in the darkest timber, under all circumstances, and not to "blur." Shows the same color on different colored objects; will stand rough work and improve the shooting greatly. Order by Number as Described Below..Price **$1.50**

WINCHESTER RIFLES
- **No. 2**—Winchester Rifles, Models 1892 and 1894, all calibers except 25-35, .30-30 and .32 Special High Power 1894 Model.
- **No. 4**—Winchester Model 95 Rifles, .30 Gov't. '06. 38-72 and .40-72, 35 W. C. F. and .405.
  Winchester Rifles, Models 1873, 1876 and 1886, all calibers, except .33, .45-70 and .45-90 H. P. S. and lightweights.
  Single shot rifles, all calibres, except .30-40 U. S. A.
  No. 56, 60 and 67, .22 caliber bolt action. Winchester No. 62, .22 Repeater. Winchester No. 63, .22 Auto. No. 72, with open rear sight.
- **No. 5**—Winchester Rifles, Model 1894, calibers .25-35, .30-30 and .32 Special using regular smokeless ammunition.
- **No. 6**—Winchester Carbines, 1894 Model, 25.35, .30-30 and .32 W. S.
- **No. 6L**—Winchester Carbine, Model 92, .25-20 H. V.
- **No. 7**—Winchester Carbines, Model 1894, calibers. 32-40 and .38-55.
  Winchester Carbines, Model 1892, all calibers. (Early models.)
- **No. 10**—Winchester M/95 Rifle .30 Army (30-40) and .303 British.
  Winchester M/95 Carbine .30 Gov't '06 220 gr. bullets.
  Winchester M/54 Bolt Action, .30 Gov't '03.
- **No. 13**—Winchester Model 94, .25-35, .30-30, .32 Special, using Super-speed ammunition.
  Winchester Nos. 68 and 69, .22 caliber.
- **No. 14**—Winchester Model 95 Carbine .30 Gov't '06 150 and 180 gr. bullets; Winchester Model 95 Carbine .30 Army (30-40) and .303 British; Winchester Model 54 Bolt Action 270 W. C. F.
- **No. 15**—Winchester Rifles, Model 1886, calibers .33, .45-70 and 45-90 High Power Smokeless.
  Winchester Self-Loading Rifles, Models 1905, 1907 and 1910, calibers .32, .35, .351 and .401.
- **No. 17**—Winchester Models 1890 and 1906, .22 caliber Repeating Rifles.
  Winchester Models 1903, .22 Auto.
  Winchester 1902 and 1904.
- **No. 19**—Winchester N. R. A. 1895 Model Musket .30 caliber.
- **No. 43**—Winchester Rifles, Models 53 and 55.
- **No. 52**—Winchester M/52, .22 cal. N. R. A.; Army S.S. Musket .22 and .30; M/57, .22 cal. Bolt Action; No. 61, .22 Repeater.
- **No. 57**—Winchester 92 and 94 Carbines with ramp.
  Winchester No. 54 Rifles with ramp.
  Winchester Nos. 64 and 65 Rifles, all calibers.
  Winchester No. 71, 348 caliber.
  Winchester No. 70.

SAVAGE RIFLES
- **No. 4**—Savage Model 1922 "Sporter," .22 caliber.
  Savage Models 99-T, in .30-30 and .303 calibers.
- **No. 5**—Savage 1909, 1911, 1912, No. 25, No. 29; 1923 Sporter, all calibers.
  Savage Model 99 T, 22 H. P., .250 and .300.
  Savage Model 99 E, F, G, K and R .250.
  Savage Model 99 G, K, R and RS, .300.
  Savage Rifles, Model '99, .38-55 caliber.
  Savage 1909, 1911, 1912, No. 25, No. 29, 1923 AA Sporter, .22 caliber.
- **No. 13**—Savage 1899 Model A, B, C, H and D Rifles and Carbines, calibers .25-35, .30, .300, .32-40 and .303, in serial numbers below 297,000.
- **No. 16**—Savage '99 E, F and G Fwt. Rifles, 22 H. P., .25-35 and 250-3000, up to serial number 705,700.
  Calibers .30-30 and .303 in serial numbers below 260,000.
- **No. 16NS**—Savage '99 E, F and G Fwt. Rifles in .30-30 .303 and .300 calibers in serial numbers 260,000 to 305,700.
- **No. 16A**—Savage M/20 Bolt Action, .250 and .300 in serial numbers below 9000.
  Savage '99 E, F and G Fwt. Rifles, .300 caliber in serial numbers below 260,000.
- **No. 16A-NS**—Savage M/20 .300 caliber in serial numbers above 9,000.
- **No. 47**—Savage Rifles, Models 1903, 1904 and 1914.
- **No. 47**—Savage Models 1919 and 1933, .22 N. R. A.
- **No. 52**—Savage M/99, F and G, .22 H. P., R.S. .250, F, G and K .30-30 and .303.
  Savage M/99 carbines, .250, .30-30 and .303.
  Savage Nos. 40 and 45 Super Sporter.
  Savage Nos. 3, 4, 5, 6 and 7, .22 caliber, Bolt Action.
  Savage M/99 A, E and F, .300.
  Savage M/23B, .25-20; M/23C, 32-20; M/23D, .22 Hornet.

MARLIN RIFLES
- **No. 4**—Marlin Rifles, Model 27, .25-20 and .32-20 caliber. Models 1886, 1892, 1893, 1894 and 1895, all calibers except .22, .25-36, 30-30 and .32 special; model 97, .22 caliber.
- **No. 5**—Marlin Rifles, Model '93, .38-55 H. P. S.
- **No. 8**—Marlin Carbines, Models 93, 94 and 95, all calibers except .25-36, .30-30 and .32 Special.
- **No. 9**—Marlin Carbines, calibers .25-36, .30-30 and .32 Special.
- **No. 9A**—Marlin Carbine Model 93, new model.
- **No. 13**—Marlin 1893 Model Rifles and Carbines (latest model) calibers .25-35, .30-30, .32 Special and .32-40 H. P. S.
  Marlin 1936, .30-30 and .32 Special.
- **No. 43**—Marlin Rifles, Models 18, 20, 25, 29 and 37, .22 caliber.
- **No. 52**—Marlin Rifles, Models 38, 39, 50, A1, 65, 80 and 100.

REMINGTON RIFLES
- **No. 4**—Remington, Autoloading Rifles, Nos. 8 and 81, all calibers.
- **No. 15**—Remington Single Shot Rifle, Nos. 2, 4 and 6, .22 caliber.
  Remington Model 12, Repeating Rifle, .22 caliber.
  Remington Model 16, .22 Autoloader.
  Remington Models 33, 34, 41 and 341, .22 caliber.
- **No. 50**—Remington M/30, .30 Govt. Cal. Bolt Action Rifle.
- **No. 52**—Remington Model 14 and 141, all calibers.
  Remington Model 121, .22 cal. Repeater.
  Remington Model 24 and 241, .22 R. F. Autoloading.
  Remington Model 25, .25-20 and .32-20 Repeater.
  Remington 510A, .22 S.S., Bolt Action.
- **No. 56**—Remington M/30 Express, using regular factory rear sight.
- **No. 56H**—Remington M/30 Express with Lyman No. 48R receiver sight.
- **No. 56S**—Remington M/30 S. Sporter.

STEVENS RIFLES
- **No. 4**—Stevens No. 50, No. 53, No. 56, Springfield Jr., Nos. 65 and 66, .22 Bolt Action.
- **No. 5**—Stevens No. 75, .22 caliber Repeater.
- **No. 28**—Stevens No. 12, Marksmen and No. 26 Crackshot Rifles, all calibers. No. 35, Off Hand Pistol.
- **No. 30**—Stevens Nos. 17, 18, 19, 20, 27, 44 and 70 Rifles, all calibers.
- **No. 31**—Stevens Nos. 44½, .044½, 45, 47, 49, 51, 52, 54, 55 Rifles, all calibers.
- **No. 45**—Stevens No. 425 High Power Rifles, all calibers.
- **No. 52**—Stevens No. 71—.22 caliber Repeater.

U. S. SPRINGFIELD RIFLES
- **No. 11**—U. S. Springfield, calibers .30, '03 and '06.
- **No. 11A**—U. S. Springfield, .22 caliber Armory Rifle.

KRAG RIFLES AND CARBINES
- **No. 46**—Krag Rifles and Carbines. Mention which.

MAUSER RIFLES
- **No. 26**—Sauer-Mauser Rifles and Carbines. (Send Samples.)
- **No. 49**—Mauser 7.9 caliber Carbines.

MANNLICHER-SCHOENAUER RIFLES
- **No. 51**—Mannlicher-Schoenauer Rifle 6.5 mm. cal.

HAENEL RIFLES
- **No. 12**—Haenel Model Mannlicher Carbines.

ROSS SPORTING OR MILITARY RIFLE
- **No. 44**—Ross Sporting or Military Rifles; in ordering state caliber.

LEE-ENFIELD RIFLE
- **No. 54**—Lee-Enfield Rifle, .303 British.

SHEARD "GOLD" SIGHTS FOR PISTOL AND REVOLVER

No. 27

Made in Gold Bead—Medium Size Only

- **No. 27**—Luger Automatic Pistols .30 or 9 mm. caliber.
- **No. 32A**—Smith & Wesson .22 caliber Straight Line.
- **No. 32**—Smith & Wesson .22 caliber Perfected S.S. Target Pistol.
- **No. 35**—Smith & Wesson Military and Police Target Revolvers. In ordering state caliber.
- **No. 28**—Stevens No. 35 Offhand Pistol.
- **No. 36**—Colt's .22 caliber Auto. Pistol, and Colt's Positive Target Revolvers, .22 and .32 calibers. In ordering state caliber. Colt's .22 caliber, old Officer's Model.

No. 35

Nos. 36 & 37

No. 40

Order by Number as described below—

Price $1.50

- **No. 37**—Colt's .38 Officer Model Target Revolver. Colt's New Service Target Revolver. Colt's Shooting Master, .38 caliber.
- **No. 40**—Colt's Single Action Army, Bisley Model, with plain sight or any other Colt's or S. & W. Revolver with stationary front sight, but the arm should be sent to have sight fitted correctly, although any gunsmith can do it.
- **No. 48**—Stevens Model 10 Pistol.

ALL SHIPMENTS INSURED

FOR CARBINES

MARBLE'S FRONT SIGHTS
IVORY BEAD, SIZE 1-16″ OR 3-32″, EXCEPT AS NOTED

FOR RIFLES

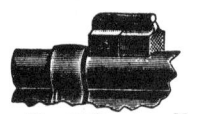
No. 94C

Nos. 94C and 93C

Order sights by number as described below and state size of bead, and if gold or ivory bead is desired.

No. 895

Nos. 894 and 94B

No. 94C—State color and size of bead............$1.00
 Made only for Winchester Carbine, Model 1894, having high pressure steel barrels. It is especially constructed to withstand the hard usage often given this rifle in the saddle and woods. A deservedly popular sight.
No. 9A—Marlin '93 Carbine, New Model, 1/16-inch bead........ 1.00
No. 93C—Marlin 1893 Model Carbine. Same as No. 94C, except smaller.................................... 1.00
No. 894—Winchester Carbine, Model 1894. For use only on high pressure steel barrels...................... 1.00
No. 894L—Winchester Model 92 Carbine, .25-20 H. V. 1/16 in. bead 1.00
No. 894—For Winchester 1894 and 1892 Model Carbines, using black powder only. Same as No. 894, except lower........ 1.00
No. 895R—Winchester Model 95 Carbine .30 Gov't. '06 150 and 180 gr. bullets; Win. M/95 Carbine .30 Army (30-40) and .303 British; Win. M-54 Bolt Action .270 W. C. F........ 1.00
No. 895C—Winchester Model 95 Rifle .30 Army (30-40) and .303 British; Win. M/95 Carbine .30 Gov't '06 220 gr. bullets; Win. M-54 Bolt Action .30 Gov't '06................. 1.00
No. 11—New Springfield Model '03 and '06................ 1.00
No. 11A—U. S. Springfield, .22 Armory Rifle, 1/16-inch bead only.. 1.00
No. 12—Haenel Model Mannlicher Carbines, 1/16-inch bead only.. 1.00

No. 16—Savage '99 E, F and G Featherweight rifles, calibers, 22 H. P. and .250-3000. Also calibers .30/30 and .303 below 260,000 ....$1.00
No. 16NS—Savage '99 E, F and G featherweight rifles, serial numbers 260,000 to 305,700 in .30, .303 and .300 calibers...... 1.00
No. 16A—Savage M-20 Bolt Action 250, and .300 (serial numbers below 9,000). Savage M-99 E, F and G Featherweight rifles. .300 calibers in serial numbers below 260,000................. 1.00
No. 16A-NS—Savage M-20 .300 caliber (serial numbers above 9,000). 1/16-inch bead........................... 1.00
No. 44—Ross Rifle, state caliber and if sporting or military, 1/16-inch bead only 1.00
No. 46—Krag Rifles and Carbines. Mention which, 1/16-inch bead only 1.00
No. 51—Mannlicher-Schoenauer Rifle 6.5 mm. 1/16-inch bead only. 1.00
No. 54—Lee-Enfield Rifle, .303 British. 1/16-inch bead......... 1.00
No. 56—Rem. M-30 Express using regular factory Rear Sight. 1/16-inch bead 1.00
No. 56H—Rem. M-30 Express with Lyman No. 48R Receiver Sight. 1/16-inch bead 1.00
No. 56S—Rem. M-30 S-Sporter, 1/16-inch bead.............. 1.00

No. 35

MARBLE'S PISTOL AND REVOLVER FRONT SIGHTS

Order sight, by number as described below and if gold or ivory bead is desired.

Nos. 36 & 37

No. 27—Luger Automatic Pistol, 1/16-inch bead only..............$1.00
No. 32—Smith & Wesson .22 S. S. Target Pistol, 1/16-inch bead only 1.00
No. 35—Smith & Wesson, Military and Police Target Revolvers. In ordering state caliber and length of barrel. 1/16-inch bead only. 1.00

No. 36—Colt's .22 Cal. Auto. Pistol; .22 and .32 Cal. Police Positive Target Revolvers, mention caliber; .22 Cal. Officers Model (Old Model), 1/16-inch bead only........................$1.00
No. 37—Colt's .38 Cal. Officers Model; New Service Target Revolvers; .38 Cal. Shootingmaster. 1/16-inch bead only....... 1.00
No. 40—Colt's Revolvers with stationary front sight, 1/16-inch bead only 1.00

MARBLE'S SHOT GUN SIGHTS
Sights for Double Guns

Bi-Color Front

Ivory Rear

GOLD
IVORY
STEEL
Bi-Color Front
Actual Size
5/32 in. dia.

Ivory Rear

Ivory Front

Bi-color Front is made with ivory body, gold cap and steel base. Construction eliminates danger of breakage. Can be seen in any light.
 Ivory Front, because of its whiteness and large size, is more easily seen than the ordinary metal front sights.
 The use of either sight greatly increases accuracy in shooting. Are easily attached by use of reamer.

Ivory Rear for Double Guns
 The Rear Sight should be placed at about the center of the barrels, or from 12 to 16 inches from the muzzle sight, according to length of gun and shooter's eyesight—never more than 18 inches.
 The rear sight keeps one from aiming too close to the gun rib, which prevents a clear view of the bird and causes undershooting. Good alignment cannot be secured without a rear sight.

Front Reamer

Rear Reamer

Sights for Single Guns

For Double Barrel Guns Only
No. 214—Ivory Front Sight, 11/64-inch diameter...............$0.40
No. 215—Ivory Front, Ivory Rear and Reamers............... 1.00
No. 220—Bi-Color Front, Ivory Rear and Reamers............ 1.20
No. 221—Bi-Color Front Sight, 5/32-inch diameter............. .60
No. 223—Ivory Rear Sight, 9/32-inch diameter................ .40
No. 224—Front Sight Reamer............................. .10
No. 226—Rear Sight Reamer............................. .10

Sights for Single Guns
No. 216—Ivory Front Sight, 11/64-inch, Tap and Wrench........ 1.00
No. 217—Ivory Front Sight, 11/64-inch diameter............... .75
No. 218—Bi-Color Front Sight only, 5/32-inch diameter......... .75
No. 219—Bi-Color Front Sight, 5/32-inch, Tap and Wrench...... 1.00

Bi-Color Front

Ivory Front

MARBLE'S SEMI-RIB FOR SHOTGUNS
 The optical effect in using this device is the same as when using a gun with the rib the full length of the barrel. If a person undershoots (a common fault) the Rib can be shimmed up with paper. The Rib prevents sighting over side of frame and assists in quick, accurate firing.
No. 227—For Model '97, and No. 12 Win. Repeaters, 12 gauge................$1.00

MARBLE'S SLOT BLANKS
No. 87. For Standard Slots.$ .25
No. 97S. Stevens Rifles with 9/32" Slots................. .25
No. 87A. For Models 8 and 81 Remington Auto Loader. .50

EVERYTHING IN GUNS UNDER ONE COVER

KING MODERN GUN SIGHTS

SUPER-POLICE SIGHTS FOR COLT, S. & W. REVOLVERS

The Super-Police sight combination has been designed especially for peace officers, cowboys and others requiring the extreme in strength and durability, and which can be seen under practically any light condition. The front sights are of full "Gold" with a steel center. The special bead material is very hard.

This sight combination "can be seen in the dark," as expressed by many officers. They show wonderfully under ordinary street lighting conditions and in moonlight.

The rear sight notch is outlined with a special white outline. The gun must be sent in for installation as this will only be done by the factory. This work takes about one to two weeks. Sights are tested and lined up. These sights can be installed on any standard Colt or Smith & Wesson revolver.

Price, complete job only................$5.00

PEEP SIGHTS FOR COLT TARGET MODEL REVOLVERS, .22 WOODSMAN AND .38 AND .45 AUTO. PISTOLS

 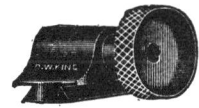
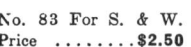

No. 83 For S. & W.   No. 81 For Colt. Adj.
Price ....$2.50   for windage.
                   Price $2.50

RAMP-RED-BEAD-REFLECTOR FOR LUGER PISTOLS

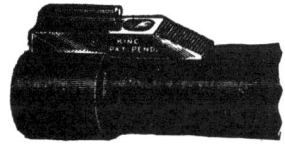 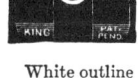

                                   White outline
                                   rear notch.
                                   Price ...$2.00

Price $5.00

Designed with white enamel outline under rear notch. This combination adds greatly to the efficiency and appearance of this pistol. Sights are fitted the same as to other models.

KING'S PAT. "SPARK POINT" GOLD BEAD

             For Luger Pistol and Stevens
                  Diamond Model Pistol
Gold Bead ......$1.50   Red or White..$1.00

RAMP-RED-BEAD-REFLECTOR TARGET SIGHTS, ADJUSTABLE FOR WINDAGE

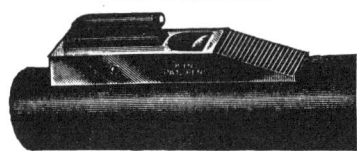
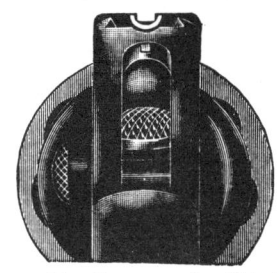

This combination can be fitted to any solid frame type Colt or S. & W. Revolver. The ramps are milled to fit perfectly over the original sight base after upper half of sight has been dressed off.

Front sight fitted.......................$5.00
S. & W. Target rear sight fitted........ 5.00

RAMP REFLECTOR SIGHTS FOR S. & W. MAGNUM REVOLVER

These ramp reflector sights can be had with luminous red, white, gold or dead black under-cut .080, 1/10 or 1/8" post, 1/16, 5/64 or 3/32" round bead in the ramp. State type wanted. These ramps are matted to correspond to the magnum rib.
Price $5.00

KING FRONT SIGHTS FOR COLT AND SMITH & WESSON REVOLVERS

No. 131   No. 135
Colt   Colt

No. 138   No. 139
S. & W.   S. & W.

Call or McGivern Red, Gold or Ivory Beads or Posts

In addition to the King Ramp-Red-Bead-Reflector Sights, we can supply the following front sights for target model pistols and revolvers:

Luminous Red Beads in 1/16, 5/64, and 3/32
  inch bead............................$1.50
Gold Beads in 1/16 and 3/32 inch beads.... 1.50
"Kingoid" White Beads in 1/16 and 3/32
  inch beads........................... 1.50
Luminous Red, Gold or White Post (Patridge) in .062, .080 and .100.......... 1.50
King "Call" or McGivern, with Red, Gold or White Bead................... 1.50

SUPER-POLICE SIGHTS FOR COLT ACE, SUPER .38, AND GVT. .45 AUTO. PISTOLS

         Price $2.50 Fitted
Also rear micrometered rear similar to Woodsman $3.50

For Colt .38 Super and .45 and .22 "Ace." The gold beads are of the same solid steel center as those adapted to rifles, but are riveted through the jacket by special equipment. Any other type front sight also supplied if desired. The rear sight is of special design to prevent catching in holster and is adjustable for micrometered windage and elevation. The sight notch slide, with or without white outline, is easily adjusted for elevation and rigidly locked by a set screw in side of sight. Luminous red beads can also be fitted to the Colt Automatics and a reflector set in the jacket of the .38 and .45. The jacket on the .22 Ace Pistol is too thin to receive the reflector, which must be fitted with special sight and base.

Front sight and reflector fitted on Ace....$4.00
Sight and Reflector set in .38, .45 Ace jackets 4.00

REVOLVER RAMP SIGHTS RED BEAD REFLECTOR

Colt .22 and .38 Officers Model, Shooting Master, and Woodsman .22 Caliber

Regularly supplied with 1/16" and 5/64" red beads or .080 and 1/10" red post (Patridge type). Ramp easily and quickly fitted by drilling one hole and driving in pin supplied. Original elevation of front sight not affected.
Price each........................$5.00

REAR SIGHTS FOR COLT OFFICERS MODEL, SHOOTING MASTER, AND WOODSMAN .22 AUTOMATIC

No. 122   No. 121

Rear sights with either "U" or square notch outlined with white enamel, frames the front sight perfectly. A wonderful combination.
Price $2.00

OUTLINE REAR SIGHTS FOR S. & W. REVOLVERS

No. 111   No. 112

Outline rear sights for Smith & Wesson target revolvers. Price each.................$1.00

SEE PAGE 8, "HOW TO ORDER"

KING'S MODERN GUNSIGHTS

RAMP-RED-BEAD-REFLECTOR RIFLE SIGHTS

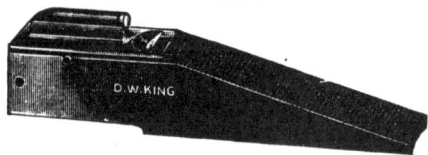

For rifles having the Springfield front sight, bases are easily and quickly fitted by removing the original sight and base only (not the collar). Ramps regularly supplied with 5/64 inch or 3/32 inch red beads. 1/16 inch beads or .062 or .080 red post sights optional. 1/16 inch or 3/32 inch Gold or White Beads also supplied on request.

No. 105S for Springfield and Krag rifles, with Springfield sight base, each $5.00
No. 105K requires the drilling of one hole, for Krags only, each $5.00
No. 105 for Winchester model 54 and 95 rifles, each $5.00
No. 105W for Winchester model 94 carbine. It is necessary to drill one hole through the old sight lug, each $5.00
No. 105WC short model for Winchester model 94 carbines, each $3.50
No. 105V for Savage Rifles having "blade" type front sights. Give model and Serial No. when ordering. Each $5.00

DETACHABLE HOODS FOR RAMP SIGHTS

Price of King Hoods fitted to Ramps at time of purchase $1.00

BLOCK SIGHTS WITH REFLECTORS
KING LUMINOUS RED, WHITE or GOLD
—Beads or Posts

No. 90E
Enfield and Remington 30

90K-90S-90W
Krag, Savage, Winchester

Price, Luminous Red, Gold or White Bead or Post $2.50
Price with detachable hood to any model 3.50
Enfield front sights remodeled, refinished and fitted with any of above sights 4.50
With detachable hood 5.50

No. 90S Springfield with Hood — All models of these sights are easily and quickly fitted to original sight bases (except Enfield).

KING REFLECTOR—POST OR BEAD SIGHTS
WITH DETACHABLE HOODS, STANDARD SLOT BASES AND ENFIELD

No. 64 with Bead   No. 64 with Bead and Hood   No. 58 with Post

Made in 5/64 inch or 1/16 inch Luminous Red, Gold or White Beads and 1/16 inch and .080 Luminous Red, Gold or White Posts. Special size beads or posts at extra price.

Price with Detachable Hood $3.00
Price without Hood 2.00

KING RED, GOLD OR KINGOID WHITE BEADS

With dove-tail base, supplied in the following heights:— 9/32, 5/16, 11/32, 3/8, 13/32, 7/16, 15/32, 1/2, and 17/32". Give model, make and caliber when ordering.

No. 17—1/16" bead, Price $1.00
No. 18—3/32" bead, Price 1.00

KING GOLD, RED OR WHITE BEAD SIGHTS

Adapted to Enfield Rifles

Gold Bead Sights 1/16" only $1.50
Luminous Red or White Bead 1/16" 1.00

KING "SPARK POINT" GOLD BEAD SIGHTS

Gold bead with a steel center, braced construction, protected bead, knurled steel extension. For all makes of rifles having slotted base front slot.

No. 15—1/16 inch beads $1.50
No. 16—3/32 inch beads 1.50

Give model, make and caliber when ordering.

KING BLADE TYPE FRONT SIGHTS

No. 20C   No. 24B   No. 48C

The Sights are "SPARK POINT" Full Gold, Steel Center Beads

No. 29B

No. 20B—For Winchester '94 Carbine $1.50
No. 21B—For Winchester '92 Carbine 1.50
No. 22B—For Winchester '95 Rifle 1.50
No. 24B—For Winchester '95 Carbine 1.50
No. 25B—For Savage High Power 1.50
No. 28B—For Springfield 1.50
No. 29B—For Krag Rifles 1.50
No. 47B—For Remington 30-S 1.50
No. 48B—For Remington 30 Exp 1.50
No. 54B—For Winchester 54 .... 1.50

King Blade Sights are now supplied with choice of Red, Gold Tip or "Kingoid" White Beads at $1.00. Specify bead desired R—Red; G—Gold; W—White.

No. 20C—For Winchester '94 Carbine $1.00
No. 21C—For Winchester '92 Carbine 1.00
No. 22C—For Winchester '95 Rifle 1.00
No. 24C—For Winchester '95 Carbine 1.00
No. 25C—For Savage High Power 1.00
No. 28C—For Springfield 1.00
No. 29C—For Krag Rifles 1.00
No. 47C—For Remington 30-S 1.00
No. 48C—For Remington 30 Exp 1.00
No. 54C—For Winchester 54 .... 1.00

KING "LITTLE GIANT" PEEP SIGHT
Price $3.50

Adapted to Enfield, Lebel, Russian, Winchester '95 and Other Model Rifles

The "Little Giant" Peep Sight is quickly adjusted for Windage and Elevation.

Can be fitted to any rifle which can be flattened on top of receiver.

EXTRA PEEP DISC

Adapted to all types King Sporting and Folding Leaf Rear Sights. Each ... $0.35

ADJUSTABLE REAR SIGHTS

No. 10—Flat Top $1.75
No. 11—Semi-Buckhorn 1.75
No. 49—Full Buckhorn 1.75
For Rem. Mod. 8 .... 2.50

SPORTING REAR SIGHTS

Adapted to Remington Models 121, 141, 241 rifles, (sight to be attached with two screws).

These sights have reversible white outlined notch discs.

No. 10-R Flat Top, Price $1.75
No. 11-R Semi-Buckhorn, Price 1.75
No. 49-R Full Buckhorn, Price 1.75

KING PATENT ADJUSTABLE REAR SIGHTS FOR SPRINGFIELD RIFLES

No. 8S

No. 8S—Flat Top $1.75
Extra Peep Disc .... .35
No. 9S—Semi-Buckhorn Sporting Rear ... 1.75
No. 51S—Full Buckhorn Sporting Rear .. 1.75

KING PAT. ADJUSTABLE FOLDING LEAF SIGHTS

No. 19   No. 7   No. 6

Price, any model $1.50

The New King Adjustable Folding Leaf Sight is without unsightly screws in the face of the leaf. They are adjustable to any reasonable shooting distance. Reversible notch disc with Four Notches gives Eight Combinations. A spring "snaps it up and snaps it down." Adapted to All Rifles and Carbines.

For Remington H. P. and Auto-Loading Rifles. Price $2.00

FOLDING LEAF SIGHTS FOR SPRINGFIELD AND KRAG

Flat Top (No. 6), Semi-Buckhorn (No. 7) and Full Buckhorn (No. 19) sights supplied for Springfield, Krag and Winchester Model '95 Carbines and fitting original factory bases.

No. 7S   Price $1.50

WHITE OUTLINE NOTCH DISCS

Adaptable to any King Rear Sight 50c

The above cuts illustrate the new King Notch Disc as fitted to Flat Top, Semi-Buckhorn and Full Buckhorn Sporting and Folding Leaf Sights. The white semi-circle outlined rear notch "frames" the front bead perfectly. These notch discs are supplied on King sights at no additional cost. Notch Disc only $0.50

KING'S MODERN SIGHTS AND ACCESSORIES

KING MICROMETERED AUTOLOCKING PEEP SIGHTS

No. 200
Price $4.50

Adapted to Winchester Model 61 only.

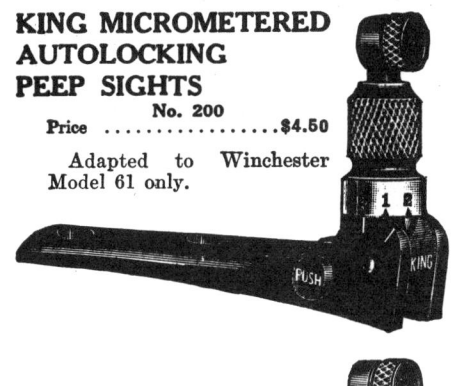

No. 200
Price $4.50
Adapted to Remington Models 12 and 25 only.

The new King Peep Sight has micrometered elevation adjustment of one-half minute of angle with "click." It is also automatically locked in upright or shooting position and also automatically locked against elevation adjustment. Press the button and the elevator stem is unlocked and elevation adjustment is automatically unlocked when in a semi-folded or "half-cocked" position only. Automatically locks itself again upon being raised or folded. No accidental change of elevation on this sight or guess work as to how much elevation is moved or what it means.

Sight has only ½-inch hinge which greatly reduces hand interference. Beautifully finished and blued.

Any peep sight equipped with non-glare target disc $5.00

KING "HANDFULL" GRIPS

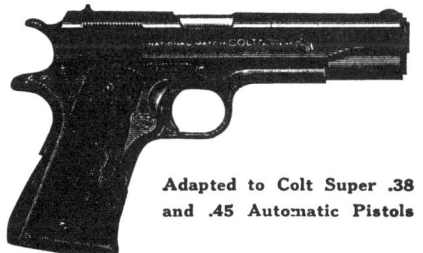

Adapted to Colt Super .38 and .45 Automatic Pistols

The New King "Handfull" Grips adapted to Colt Automatic pistols are just what that name implies, a "Handfull." They have been approved and adopted by a number of prominent pistol shooters. Extra material has been added at just the right places. The added material at bottom and lower front portion of the grips is of great assistance in keeping the pistol in just the proper position for steady holding and shooting. This is a very important point and of great assistance in "keeping the muzzle down" in rapid fire and timed fire shooting.

Plain grips $4.00
Grips with diamond checking............ 5.00
Fancy wood, beautiful full checking...... 6.50

FORMFIT REVOLVER GRIPS
For Colt and Smith & Wesson

Price $3.50

Furnished in right hand or left hand and without thumb guard. Each grip complete ready to fit revolver. Checkered aluminum or enamel finish.

Formfit Grips have four outstanding features: First, they fill up the space between frame and trigger guard which drops the hand ¼ inch lower than factory frame, thus allowing a "straight pull" on the trigger in place of the "lifting" pull with regular grips. Second, they also lengthen the grip ¼ inch, allowing the stock to be gripped by all four fingers. Third, they fill out the grip at the crotch of the hand where it receives the greatest recoil. This prevents bruising of the hand and "flinching." Fourth, they are supplied with right or left hand guards (also plain) which places the thumb in the proper position to equalize the pressure between the ball of thumb and forefinger, greatly reducing the horizontal movement of the gun.

Formfit Grips are available in six sizes, each size in righthand, lefthand, or neutral style as indicated below. Order by number and style.

FORMFIT PISTOL GRIPS

"A" Right Hand Guard
"B" Left Hand Guard
"AB" Neutral No Guard

Colt New Service Target and Reg. Colt Shooting Master	No. 3
Colt Officers Model .22 and .38 Colt Official Police .22 and .38 Colt Camp Perry .22 Target	No. 5
Colt Police Positive Special Colt Detective and Banker Spec. Colt Police Positive Reg. and Tgt.	No. 7
S. & W. .38-44 Super Police S. & W. .44 Target S. & W. .44 Military S. & W. 1917 U. S. A. .45 S. & W. .38-44 Heavy Duty S. & W. .38-44 Outdoorsman	No. 2
S. & W. Military and Police S. & W. K-22 Outdoorsman	No. 4
S. & W. .38 Military and Police Round Butt	No. 6

KING QUICK DETACHABLE FLUSH PLATE SLING SWIVELS

No. 301
1-inch loop.

No. 301
1¼-inch loop.

$2.00

Cut shows locking lugs and lock in position to be inserted in key-hole in plate which is set in flush with stock. Press lugs into key-hole and make one-eighth (⅛) turn to right and swivel is automatically locked securely in position. When locked

KING'S SHOTGUN SIGHTS
Red or White Bead Front or Middle Sights

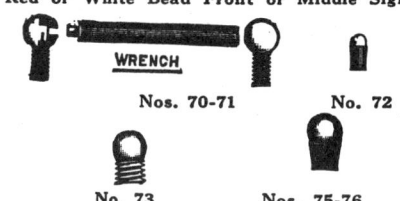

Nos. 70-71   No. 72

No. 73   Nos. 75-76

Nos. 70 and 71, Red or White Bead Sights are made of a round steel ball inset with a full round bead of special material. The stem of these sights is threaded with a 3⁄56 thread. They are especially designed to be fitted to Pump, Autoloading, Double or Single Barrel Guns—with or without rib—which have not been fitted with other large base sights. King sights are fitted by removing the original sights and tapping the hole in barrel or rib. If properly fitted they will stay permanently in pump or single barrel guns without ribs.

No. 70—Red or White Bead, .175 inch diameter—each $1.00
No. 71—Red or White Bead, .150 inch diameter—each 1.00
No. 45 Drill—each .... .20
No. 3-56 Tap—each .... .30

No. 72, White or Red "Middle" can be fitted to any double or single barrel gun with rib. Drill hole with No. 47 drill and ream with standard middle sight reamer. The bead is 1⁄16 inch in diameter.

White or Red Bead—each.............$0.50
No. 47 Drill—each .... .20

Nos. 73 and 74, Red or White Bead Sights, are designed to be fitted to double or single barrel guns with ribs, which have been reamed to receive a large base or "drive-in" collar sight. This type of King Sight has a threaded base (8-40) and is made from one piece of special material with a steel pin in center for added strength. To fit, remove old sight, thread old hole with 8-40 plug tap and screw in the King Sight. They will stay.

No. 73—Red or White Bead, .175 inch diameter—each $0.50
No. 74—Red or White Bead, .150 inch diameter—each .... .50
No. 8-40 Plug Tap—each............... .35

Nos. 75 and 76, Red and White Bead Sights are designed to be fitted to double or single barrel guns with ribs, without threading the sight holes. Just pull out the old sight and replace with a King Red or White Bead. They have steel collars and fit all standard size reamed holes perfectly.

No. 75—Red or White Bead, .175 inch diameter—each $0.50
No. 76—Red or White Bead, .150 inch diameter—each .... .50

the swivel barrel sits flush with stock plate. Small cut shows under side of plate with locking lugs in locked position. To remove swivels, press down on round pin in center of loop base with thumb or finger, make one-eighth turn to left and pull out. A few seconds will attach or remove sling strap and swivels.

By having extra plates fitted to any number of extra rifles one may attach sling strap to any rifle desired in a few seconds.

Price per pair, with 1 or 1¼ inch loops and screws $2.00
Extra plates with screws, per pair........ .75

No. 77—Red or White—especially designed for Remington, Browning and Savage Automatics and Cutts Compensator. Solid Steel Bead and base similar to No. 70 and 71. Has 8/40 thread, each...... 1.00

PACIFIC GUN SIGHTS

PLAIN ADJUSTABLE MODEL

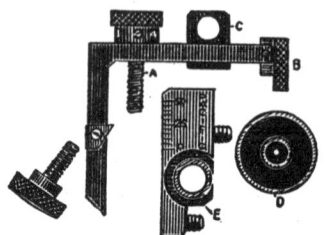

MICROMETER ADJUSTABLE MODEL

How Pacific Sights look when unassembled. All our receiver sights are built on these principles, the only difference being in the base, which is shaped correctly for the particular rifle the sight is intended for.

Many of the sights can be attached without boring holes or any machine work. To attach receiver and bolt sleeve sights all that you need is a screw driver and your hands. Open and tang sights fit in the slots on the rifle or use the existing holes on the rifle. Instructions for attaching sent with each sight.

The Plain Adjustable Model has the following important features:

(A) Guide Pin to make body of sight slide smooth when adjusting, also to hold more rigid. Screw on top makes fine adjustment possible.
(B) Lock Screw: to set windage adjustment tight. Disc holder has a groove which fits snug in the windage adjustment slot so it will not shift when carrying or firing.
(C) Elevation Lock Screw: Has a coin fitting slot to make locking more secure. Easy to get a grip on and built husky enough to make it impossible for your sightings to shift under any condition.
(D) Hunting Disc: Some prefer this disc; others prefer our target disc.
(E) Base: Which fastens on gun. Has same markings as the micrometer models. The base illustrated is for the Model K1 Krag sight. Each model has a different shaped base to fit the rifle it is intended for.

The Micrometer Adjustable Model has the following important features:

(A) Micrometer Elevation Adjustment Screw, 25 threads per inch, 5 clicks per turn, one minute of angle per click, or one inch per 100 yards. Models S2R and W2 have 10 clicks per turn, ½ inch per 100 yards.
(B) Micrometer Windage Adjustment Screw: Giving fine adjustment, 5 clicks per turn.
(C) Disc Holder: Has a scale in front, easy to see for adjusting.
(D) Improved Pacific Target Disc.
(E) Base: Which is fastened on gun. Has a scale with a movable indicator. The base illustrated is for the Model S2 Springfield sight. The shape of the base is different on each model.

EN2 FOR 1917 ENFIELD

Model EN2, for Enfield. This is a full micrometer sight having half-minute adjustments for windage and elevation, a very desirable sight for target work or hunting. The object of this model is to supply a practical, finely adjustable receiver sight for the Enfield that can be attached with the minimum of labor. By following directions, anyone can attach one of these sights.

All the tools needed are a file and screw driver. Price, including either hunting or target disc.......... **$7.00** Tap and drill......... **$.50**

EN4. Same as EN2 except that base is designed for use after original rear sight ears have been removed, and bridge rounded. Price..... **$7.00**

Model EN1, for Enfield, is the same sight as the EN2 except it is plain adjustable. A practical hunting sight. Has elevation guide pin and the dove tail, which fits snug and rigid in the dove tail slot on the rifle, taking the place of the military leaf spring. Price with choice of disc. **$4.50**

EN3. Same as EN1, except that base is designed for use after original rear sight ears have been removed and bridge rounded. Price..... **$4.50**

FOR WINCHESTER NOS. 54 AND 52

Model W2, for Winchester 54 or 52, has micrometer adjustments for windage and elevation. Ten clicks per turn, which changes point of impact ½ inch per 100 yards. No holes to bore. There are two tapped holes on the receiver of the rifle for attaching this sight, can be put on in a minute. The W2 model sets snug on the receiver and is built sturdy enough for hunting besides being a super accurate sight for target work. Price, including either style disc, **$7.00** post paid or C. O. D.

Model W1, for Winchester 54 or 52, is the same sight with plain adjustments for windage and elevation, very easy to adjust. This is a hunting model. Price, including either style disc................. **$4.50**

It is not necessary to mar the finish of your rifle or cut the stock when attaching one of these sights. Note how the base is machined to fit snug on the receiver and fit over the stock instead of cutting into it. Held in place with two strong screws; cannot shoot or knock loose.

FOR SAVAGE MODEL 19 N.R.A. AND MODELS 23

Without Micrometer

With Micrometer

Model SA1 is easily adjustable for windage and elevation. Built very rugged; made to stand hard usage. This is an ideal hunting sight. Easily attached by drilling and tapping two holes in the receiver. Price **$3.00** with the choice of any disc. Special tap and drill, **$.50**.

Model SA2 has micrometer adjustments for windage and elevation. Ten clicks per turn, each click changes the point of impact ½ inch per 100 yards. Price, including disc. **$7.00**. Special tap and drill.... **$.50**

FOR KRAG .30-40 AND SPRINGFIELDS CALIBER .30-06 AND .22 CALIBER

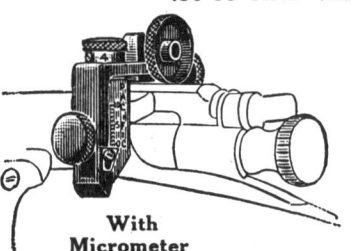

With Micrometer

Model K2, for KRAG, is a full micrometer sight. This sight will give you all the accuracy and fine adjustment that you could find in any sight, regardless of the price. Price, including one of either discs, and a screw driver for attaching.

$6.00

Model S2, for Springfield, though a target model is built substantial enough for hunting and is adjusted fine enough to suit the most exacting shooter. This sight is adaptable, by a slight alteration of the bore, for use on any Mauser action. Price, including one of either style disc, and a screw driver for attaching **$7.00**

FOR RUSSIAN RIFLES

Model R1, for Russians, adjustable for windage and elevation. Has micrometer clicks for elevation. It is the only practical sight for this type of rifle. Allows the full use of the safety, a very important item with any rifle, is close to the eye, making it especially good for quick follow shots and built strong enough to stand hard usage. Price, including one hunting or one target disc. **$4.00**

EN6. Similar to R1, but for use on bolt sleeve of Enfield Model 1917.

FOR KRAG .30-40 AND SPRINGFIELDS CALIBER .30-06 AND .22 CALIBER

Model KRAG 1 is easily adjustable for windage or elevation. Made to stand hard usage. It is in great favor with hunters. Price, including one aperture disc, and a screwdriver for attaching (state which disc is desired, hunting or target)..................... **$3.00**

Model S1, for Springfield, is easily adjustable to windage or elevation. This hunting model will stand rough handling. If desired body of sight can be taken off of rifle in an instant by unscrewing lock screw. This sight is adaptable, by a slight alteration of the bore, for use on any Mauser action. Price, including one of either discs, and a screw driver for attaching.............. **$4.50**

A new magazine cut-off (a bolt stop lever) as shown in Model S1 is supplied with each S1 or S2 sight.

PACIFIC & PARKER REAR SIGHTS

PARKER REAR SIGHTS

EN5 RECEIVER SIGHT

The EN5 Receiver sight is sturdy, compact, and practical for hunting, easily adjustable for windage and elevation. The receiver must be returned to us, as it takes a special machine set-up to shape the receiver and to assure perfect alignment.
Price of EN5 Receiver Sight.................................$3.00
Price of machining receiver and reblueing.................. 5.00

LB1 and LB2 RECEIVER SIGHTS

Are adapted for the Savage Models 29, 40 and 99 rifles and also for the Stevens Models 17, 20, 27, 44, 71, 75, and 414, for the Winchester Models 02, 06, 07, 10, 53, 55, 86, 92, 94, 95, and the Remington Models 12, 14, and 25.

Models LB1 has a special base with elevation slide attached. The base is fitted to the receiver by tapping and drilling two holes. Easily adjustable for windage and elevation.
Price $3.00
Tap and Drill, 50c extra.

MODEL LB2 RECEIVER SIGHT—has micrometer adjustments for windage and elevation, five clicks per turn. Each click changes the point of impact 1 inch per hundred yards. Attached the same as the Model LB1.
Price $6.00
Tap and Drill, 50c extra.

Parker Hale Sport Target Sight for Mannlicher Schoenauer

This sight has been especially designed for the Mannlicher Schoenauer rifle and comes with a special bolt nut ready to be installed without any tools. This sight is of rugged construction with knurled elevation screw with graduation allowing easy adjustment for the elevation and also has windage adjustment. The stem takes any standard size Lyman or Merit disc. The sight also folds down allowing use of the leaf sight. This sport target sight provides for greatest accuracy and has the great advantage that it is close as possible to the eye allowing easy and quicker sighting.
Price $15.00

Model EN6—Bolt Sleeve Sight

Adjustable for windage and elevation. It is close to the eye which makes it a very

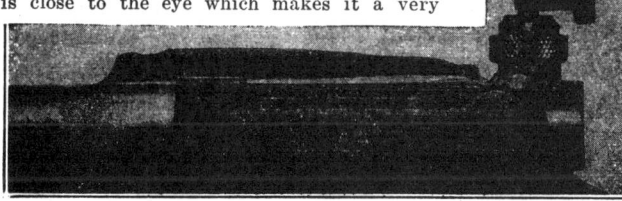

desirable hunting sight. Built strong and rigid.
Price $6.00
For installing, the bolt sleeve must be sent to us. A $3.00 labor charge will have to be made for installing same.

PARKER-HALE SPORTARGET SIGHTS

Sportarget Sight No. 1

Designed for Mauser bolt action rifles, it comes with special bolt nut which can be installed instantly without any extra labor and folds down and has special knurled screw adjustment for elevation with marked scale for setting. Has detachable disc with Lyman thread.

This sport target sight provides for greatest accuracy and has the great advantage that it is close as possible to the eye allowing easy and quicker sighting.
Price $15.00

AIM CORRECTOR FOR MILITARY RIFLES

Made Especially for the Springfield .30-06

The aim corrector clips on just in back of the rear or battle sight. The coach lies alongside of the rifle and can see just how the sights were when shot was fired. Does not interfere with Shooter. Invaluable for Rifle teams. Price $4.00

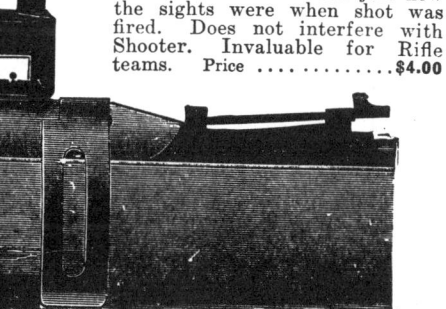

PARKER'S FLUID WHITE

Fluid White is a new preparation for the shooter to renew the white outline of open rear sights and the white of the front bead. This preparation is applied with a brush coming with each bottle. It can be applied very easily and will dry almost instantly. It will last indefinitely and give clear definition of the sights without glare. An absolute necessity to every shooter. Keep bottle always well closed and it will keep serviceable for a very long time.

Price $1

STOEGER'S SIDE MOUNTS—HENSOLDT & OIGEE 'SCOPES

For Bolt Action and Most High Power Rifles

THE FAMOUS STOEGER SIDE MOUNT

Illustration shows side mount on Mauser Rifle Cal. .30-06

THE STOEGER SIDE MOUNT is the finest of its type; it enables the sportsmen to use either the iron sight or the telescope sight at will, and when the scope and mount are removed from base, the rifle has an unusually clean appearance. The telescope is easily attached to the rifle by engaging the dove tail and sliding on until the stop catch engages the mount and telescope are locked securely to the base—detachment is equally easy. The base itself, as seen by the illustration, is fastened securely to the left side of the receiver by means of several special steel screws to insure ruggedness. Windage is taken care of by two large and strong windage screws sliding on dove tail, permitting accurate adjustment. The .22 m/m mount weighs about eight ounces. This mount we consider to be the finest side mount ever put on the market.

Price of 22 m/m mount together with tap drill, countersink and three screws.... $25.00
Price of mount with 26 m/m diameter ring together with tap drill, countersink and four screws 30.00
Charge for fitting mount and base to rifle including bore sighting............. 5.00

Illustration shows in detail workings of Stoeger Side Mount

GNOMET 2½X

One of the very finest all around hunting and target scopes. Personally recommended by us as the greatest value available. Has universal focus. Diameter, ½ inch; luminosity, 25; field of view at 100 yards, 10.7 yards; Diameter, 22 m/m; length, 8⅞ inches.
Price $25.00

OIGEE RIFLE TELESCOPES

Standard Graticule for Oigee

LUXOR-HELL 4X

This new and sensational Oigee "Luxor-Hell" is of unsurpassed brilliance, offering the tremendous luminosity of 81; field of view, 11 yards at 100 yards; 36 m/m objective; length, 12 inches; weight, 16 ounces. Recommended for medium and heavy hunting rifles.
Price $72.00

HENSOLDT ZIELKLEIN 2¾X

Ideal small caliber telescope. Objective aperture, 20 m/m; luminosity, 45; field of view at 100 yards, 9.5 yards; diameter, 22 m/m; length, 8⅝ inches; weight, 8 ounces.
Price $36.00

HENSOLDT WETZLAR

HENSOLDT ZIELYT 2¾X

A compact scope, suitable for all around hunting and target work. Luminosity, 45; field of view at 100 yards, 13.5 yards. Objective aperture, 18 m/m; length, 8⅝ inches; weight, 9 ounces; diameter, 22 m/m.
Price $45.00

HENSOLDT ZIELVIER 4X

This scope is particularly suited for large bore bolt action rifles and for use at long range. Magnification, 4 X; 26 m/m objective aperture; luminosity, 43; field of view at 100 yards, 10 yards; length, 9.3 inches; diameter, 22 m/m; weight, 11 ounces.
Price $54.00

Standard Graticule No. 5 Post Covers 3" at 110 Yards

HENSOLDT DIALYTAN 4X

Because of its exceptional light gathering power, this telescope is ideal for night shooting, or early morning. Magnification, 4 X; 36 m/m objective aperture; luminosity, 81; field of view at 100 yards, 10 yards; length, 10.9 inches; diameter, 26 m/m; weight, 14 ounces.
Price $75.00

SPECIAL FEATURE OF THE HENSOLDT 2¾X ZIELKLEIN

Whether the eye is 1 inch or 6 inches from eye-piece, the field of view diminishes little from normal. A remarkable Hensoldt optical achievement. This feature makes the "rim" obstruction of the tube so slight that the eye travels from "naked eye view" to the 2¾x magnification and aiming post and mark naturally, without effort, insuring quick and accurate shooting.

THE NEW FEATHERWEIGHT HENSOLDT RIFLE TELESCOPE

ZIELVIER 4 POWER

Same specifications as Zielvier illustrated above weight only 6 oz.
Price $70.00

DIALYTAN 4 POWER

Same specifications as Dialytan illustrated above but with 27, 5 mm diameter center tube. Weight only 10 oz.
Price $88.00

THE BEST MOUNTS FOR THE BEST RIFLES

HUNTING AND TARGET RIFLE TELESCOPES

Ajack — Trade Mark Registered U. S. Patent Office

The use of hunting scopes is constantly increasing in popularity particularly because of the interest aroused through the many cheap scopes on the market. These cheap scopes have pointed out to the average shooter the possibilities available to the possessor of a rifle with a really fine scope, and it is, therefore, with considerable pride that we offer herewith, for the first time since 1914 the world famous German made Ajack rifle scopes, of which we are sole U. S. Agents, and Distributors. These fine scopes are, moreover, offered at no higher price than those of comparable make.

All Ajack scopes have individual focusing just as on binoculars. Elevation adjustments are simple and positive by a mere turn of the disc, with locking screw, on top of scope. Windage is taken care of in the mounts, the best being the Stoeger Side Mount.

The Ajack rifle scopes represent the highest standard of optical achievement. They are distinguished by their extraordinarily great luminosity or light gathering capacity which assures a brilliant image. The field of view is perfectly clear all the way to the edge, and without any trace of color distortion. Ajack telescopes offer, by far, the largest field of view of any make of scope. Ajack scopes are of unusually rugged construction and will withstand any abuse which would wreck the average telescope. All Ajack scopes are supplied with leather lens protectors and connecting strap.

For target shooting, especially with small bore rifles, we particularly recommend our small bore telescope, the,

AJACK KLEIN

$36.00

Magnification, 2.4 X
Field of view, 9 yd. at 100 yd.
Luminosity—56
Length—10¼"
Tube Diameter, 22 mm.
Eye Relief, 3½"—6"
Weight, 180 Grams (6¼ oz.)

For off-hand shooting and shooting at running game we recommend the following models:

AJACK 1½ x 100

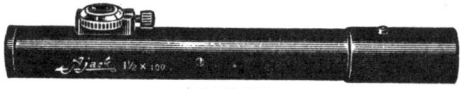

$45.00

Magnification, 1.5 X
Field of view, 24 yd. at 100 yd.
Luminosity—100
Length—9¾"
Tube Diameter, 26½ mm.
Eye Relief, 3"—6"
Weight, 300 Grams (10½ oz.)

AJACK 2.5 x 52

$45.00

Magnification, 2½ X
Field of view, 15 yd. at 100 yd.
Luminosity—52
Length—10¼"
Tube Diameter, 22 mm.
Eye Relief, 3"
Weight, 250 Grams (9 oz.)

AJACK 3 x 75

$55.00

Magnification, 3 X
Field of view, 15 yd. at 100 yd.
Luminosity—75
Length—10¼"
Tube Diameter, 26½ mm.
Eye Relief, 3"
Weight, 320 Grams (11¼ oz.)

AJACK 4 x 42

$55.00

Magnification, 4 X
Field of view, 10 yd. at 100 yd.
Luminosity—42
Length—10¼"
Tube Diameter, 22 mm.
Eye Relief, 3"
Weight, 240 Grams (8¾ oz.)

The following two types are general purpose telescopes that are equally suitable for still hunting or for running game; are likewise ideally suited for use in poor light and due to their large field of view adapted to use against driven game:

AJACK 4 x 90

$64.00

Magnification, 4 X
Field of view, 13 yd. at 100 yd.
Luminosity—90
Length—11"
Tube Diameter, 26½ mm.
Eye Relief—4½"
Weight, 13½ oz.

AJACK 6 x 50

$74.00

Magnification, 6 X
Field of view, 8 yd. at 100 yd.
Luminosity—50
Length—12½"
Tube Diameter, 26½ mm.
Eye Relief—3"
Weight, 400 Grams (14 oz.)

For night shooting and for use with heavy and large bore rifles we particularly recommend the following scopes:

AJACK 7.5 x 50

$84.00

Magnification, 7.5 X
Field of view, 6 yd. at 100 yd.
Luminosity—50
Length—14"
Tube Diameter, 26½ mm.
Eye Relief—3"
Weight, 500 Grams (18 oz.)

AJACK 10 x 50

$120.00

Magnification, 10 X
Field of view, 4.5 yd. at 100 yd.
Luminosity—50
Length—15¾"
Tube Diameter, 30 mm.
Eye Relief—3"
Weight, 880 Grams (31 oz.)

The telescopes of large magnification such as 6 X, 7.5 X, and 10 X, are also obtainable with flattened objective in order to permit the lowest possible mounting. The extra cost for this flattened objective is $17.50.

GRATICULES

All prices are understood to be for scopes with Standard Graticule which has been established as the most practical and popular. When any other but the standard graticule is specified the prices are increased as shown and scope must be procured on special order entailing a delay of about six weeks. Graticules built to special design, $7.50.

Standard Graticule | Graticule No. 1 NO EXTRA | Graticule No. 2 EXTRA $4.50 | Graticule No. 3 EXTRA $6. | Graticule No. 4 EXTRA $6. | Graticule No. 5 EXTRA $6.

ALL AJACK SCOPES AVAILABLE WITH INTERNAL WINDAGE

NOSKE FIELD TELESCOPES

NOSKE Telescopes have been recognized as the finest American make in Field Telescopes. Mr. Noske has been a pioneer in this field. His products are made to satisfy the most discriminate requirements expected of a high grade optical instrument of this type for strength, precision adjustment, clear vision and correct mounting. Mr. Noske was the first one using internal adjustments. The construction of these telescopes are throughout of the highest workmanship and recommended by the greatest authorities to those wanting a telescope to give service under any and all conditions.

TELESCOPE No. 1, TYPE A—2¼X

Price $52.00

With internal adjustments. Length 9¼ inches, diameter ⅞ inch, weight 9 ounces. Long eye relief. Field of view at 100 yards, 38 feet. Luminosity, 55. With all hand made precision adjustments for windage and elevation, positive self-locking. Same can be used on several rifles and will always give reliable service.

TELESCOPE No. 2, TYPE B—2¼X

Price $38.00

With machine made internal adjustments with spring locking device. Length, 9¼ inches, diameter, ⅞ inch, weight, 8 ounces. Long eye relief. Field of view, 38 feet at 100 yards. Luminosity, 55.

TELESCOPE No. 3, TYPE A—4X

Price $54.00

With all hand made internal high precision adjustments for windage and elevation. Positive locking device. Length 10¼ inches, Tube diameter, ⅞ inch, weight, 9½ ounces. Long eye relief. Field of view, 22 feet at 100 yards. Luminosity, 30.

TELESCOPE No. 4, TYPE B—4X

Price $40.00

Has machine made internal adjustments for windage and elevation with spring type locking device. Length 10¼ inches, Tube diameter, ⅞ inch, weight, 8 ounces. Long eye relief. Field of view, 22 feet at 100 yards.

UNERTL SCOPES

1½″ TARGET SCOPE

$70.00 less mounts.
$82.50, complete with Lyman ¼ minute click mounts, and bases.

The 1½″ target scope is designed with a 1½″ clear aperture objective. This scope was made to meet the demand for higher illuminosity and magnifications.

Focusing for ranges under 200 yards is accomplished by *moving the objective only*. This method is the most satisfactory way of focusing a target type telescope of moderate magnification.

The 1½″ scope is available in 10, 12, 14, 16, 18, and 20X equipped with ⅛″ Pope rib, clamp ring, recoil absorber and screw dust caps for both ends, priced.

This scope is 25″ long, can be mounted to any small-or big-bore rifle without danger to lenses or adjustments. The scope weighs 24 oz. with mounts.

The same reticules as supplied in our other telescopes are available, but medium cross wires will be furnished unless otherwise specified.

Present owners of 1¼″ Unertl scopes may have their scopes changed to the 1½″ scope by paying **$17.50**, which includes choice of any of above magnifications.

The 1½″ objective scope is shown mounted on a Vicker's Martini 22.-cal. match rifle.

Interchangeable eye pieces to raise or lower the original magnification of this scope 35% are available at **$6.50** each.

2″ TARGET SCOPE

$125.00, complete with oversize ¼ minute click mounts, and bases.

The 2″ target scope is designed with a 2″ clear aperture objective. This scope was made to meet the demand for extremely great light gathering and high magnifications, unobtainable with smaller objective sizes when a good size exit pupil is desired.

Like other target type telescopes, focusing for ranges under 200 yards is accomplished by moving the objective only.

The 2″ scope is available in 10, 15, 18, 20, 24, and 30x equipped with ⅛″ Pope rib, two clamp rings, screw dust caps for both ends, and oversize ¼ minute click mounts and bases.

The scope is 24″ long, can be mounted on any rifle by using 1/16″ higher bases than for our smaller scopes and has a **1″ main tube**.

The same reticules as supplied in other Unertl telescopes are available, but medium cross wires will be furnished unless otherwise specified.

An interchangeable eye-piece to raise the original magnification about 40% is available at **$12.00**.

A FINE SCOPE HELPS TO IMPROVE YOUR SCORE

ZEISS HUNTING RIFLE TELESCOPES

ZEISS ZIELKLEIN

ZIELVIER FEATHERWEIGHT

Small caliber sighting telescope for sporting guns, small bore and hunting rifles. Magnification 2¼ ×, field of view 11.5 yards per 100 yards, light-transmitting capacity 64, length 255 mm. (10 inches), weight 230 grm. (8 ounces).
Price $40.00
Zielklein with Internal Windage 52.00

ZEISS ZIELMAR

Small telescope useful for hunting moving game. Image field in telescope blends perfectly with the one seen with unaided eye. Magnification 1½ ×; field of view, 20 yards at 100 yards; light-transmitting capacity, 86.5; length, 260 mm. (10 inches); weight, 250 grm. (9 ounces).
Price $50.00

ZEISS ZIELVIER

Highest capacity sighting telescope. Available for use in twilight. Magnification 4 ×, field of view 10.8 yards at 100 yards, light-transmitting capacity 60, length 270 mm. (10⅝ inches); weight 390 grm. (13¾ ounces.)
Price $70.00
Zielvier with windage 99.00

ZEISS ZIELSECHS

Highest capacity sighting telescope for aiming in twilight and deep dusk. Magnification 6 ×, field of view 7 yards at 100 yards light-transmitting capacity 49, length 318 mm. (12½ inches), weight 490 grm. (17¼ ounces.)
Price $82.00
Zielsechs in featherweight execution, weight 12¾ oz. 101.00

Tube and objective end, as well as the bars for mounting, are made of but one piece light-weight metal. This insures an unsurpassed degree of rigidity, and makes the instrument absolutely dust and moisture proof. The possibilities afforded for mounting this scope eliminate the necessity of taking the instrument apart. The optical parts therefore remain undisturbed under all circumstances. This instrument weighs only 10 ounces. Yet, it is of sturdy construction. Optically it is the same as the standard model.
Price $85.00
With internal windage 112.00

ZEISS ZIELACHT

Highest capacity sighting telescope for night work. Magnification 8 ×, field of view 5.4 yards at 100 yards, light-transmitting capacity 42, length 370 mm. (14½ inches), weight 590 grm. (21 ounces.)
Price $93.00

ZEISS ZIELMULTI

Highest capacity sighting telescope with continuously variable magnification from 1 × to 4 ×. Field of view 6½ to 22.4 yards at 100 yards, light-transmitting capacity 36 to 100, length 264 mm. (10½ inches), weight 520 grm. (18½ ounces.)
Price $104.00

The prices include a standard graticule No. 1, or 2 or 6 or 7 and leather caps with strap. If desired, and at an increased price, the sighting telescopes can be supplied with other graticules.

ZEISS GRATICULES FOR ZEISS RIFLE TELESCOPES ONLY

Graticule No. 1
St'rd Graticule

Graticule No. 2

Graticule No. 3
Extra Cost $6.00

Graticule No. 4
Extra Cost $6.00

Graticule No. 5
Extra Cost $6.00

Graticule No. 6

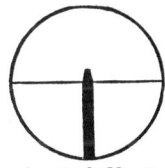
Graticule No. 7

Crosshair Graticule $6.00 extra

HOW TO JUDGE DISTANCES WITH ZEISS TELESCOPES

In the standard graticule and likewise the graticules Nos. 3, 4 and 5, the gap between the transverse bars conforms to a *width of 70 cm. at a distance of 100 metres* (or 38 inches at 150 yards), i. e. the overall length of an average small roebuck. These graticules provide accordingly an excellent means of estimating the distance of the animal, as shown in the illustrations. These relations are not affected by the magnifications and accordingly apply to all Zeiss sighting telescopes alike.

All Zeiss telescopes are adjusted to be free from parallax at the following distances:

ZIELEINS,	200 feet	ZIELVIER,	600 feet
ZIELMAR,	200 feet	ZIELACHT,	330 feet
ZIELKLEIN,	400 feet	ALL OTHERS,	260 feet

Those who more frequently shoot at ranges different from those given above, may have the graticule marks on the graticule disc set by the gunmaker for other distances according to the results of trial shots.

By way of a *graticule* we supply in the absence of directions to the contrary the Standard Graticule (No. 1). The sighting telescopes may be fitted with other graticules (such as Nos. 2 to 7), if so ordered.

Small buck deer, about 38 inches long, as seen at 150 yds.

Small buck deer, about 38 inches long, as seen at 300 yds.

A RIFLE IS ONLY AS ACCURATE AS ITS SIGHTS

UNERTL RIFLE TELESCOPES

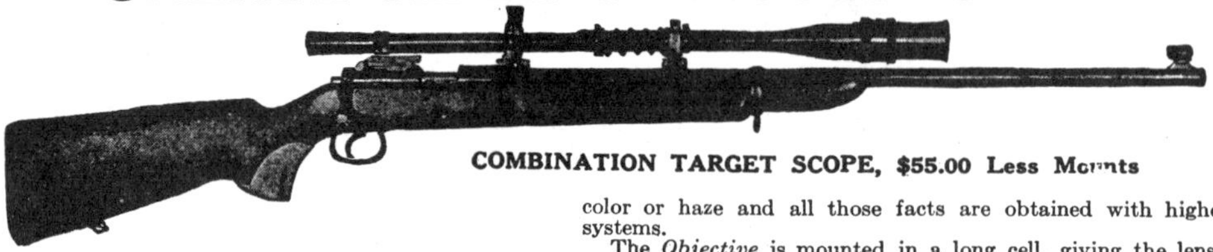

Special Powers 10% Additional

COMBINATION TARGET SCOPE, $55.00 Less Mounts

The latest developments in optical and mechanical design are embodied in the Unertl scope line.

Extreme care is taken in bedding and sealing the lenses into their cells, making the scope moisture and dust proof.

The inside surfaces of the lenses do not require any cleaning.

The Unertl scopes are so designed and constructed as to require little care and attention.

The scopes meet all the requirements of the high-class shooter as modern optical and mechanical principles are employed.

The sights are constructed to withstand the heaviest recoil of big bore rifles, without changing their adjustment.

The *Combination Target Scope* is designed with a 1¼ inch clear aperture Objective which enables the shooter to spot his group, thus eliminating a spotting scope. It will spot without difficulty at 100 yards and under reasonable light conditions spotting at 200 yards is not difficult.

Focusing with Objective lens for ranges under 200 yards is accomplished by moving the objective only.

This correct feature allows the shooter to focus and adjust for different ranges and eliminate parallax positively.

No focusing for ranges above 200 yards is required and the scope will focus down perfectly to 30 feet.

The entire field is clear and flat to the extreme edge, free from distortion, color or haze and all those facts are obtained with highest quality optical systems.

The *Objective* is mounted in a long cell, giving the lens a good mounting and eliminating any lost motion by applying a positive locking device which is graduated for different ranges.

The *inverter lens* is mounted rigid and requires no adjustment.

The *eye relief* is 2¼ inches, that is, view of full field is obtained when the scope is 2¼ inches from the eye.

The *eye piece* cell is cylindrical, ¾ inch clear aperture and has ⅞ inch outside diameter, just right so as not to interfere with the bolt handle, eliminating misalignment.

The standard length on all Target Scopes is 24 inches.

The Combination Target Scope can be furnished in 8-10-12-14 power, equipped with ⅛ inch Pope Rib, Clamp Ring, Recoil Absorber and Screw Dust Caps for both ends.

For the target rifle telescopes two *interchangeable eye pieces* are available, changing the original power of scope either way 35 per cent and are priced **$6.50** each.

Set of new Lyman ¼ min. click micrometer, mounts and bases...... **$12.50**
Less bases **11.50**

Small Game and Gallery Scopes

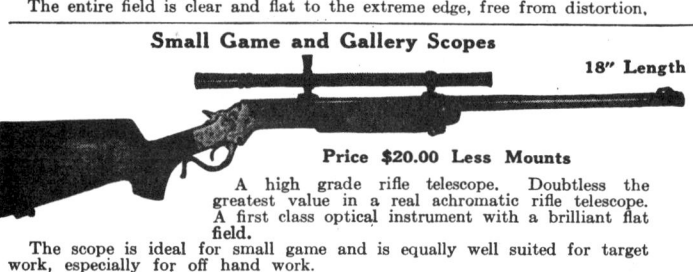

18" Length

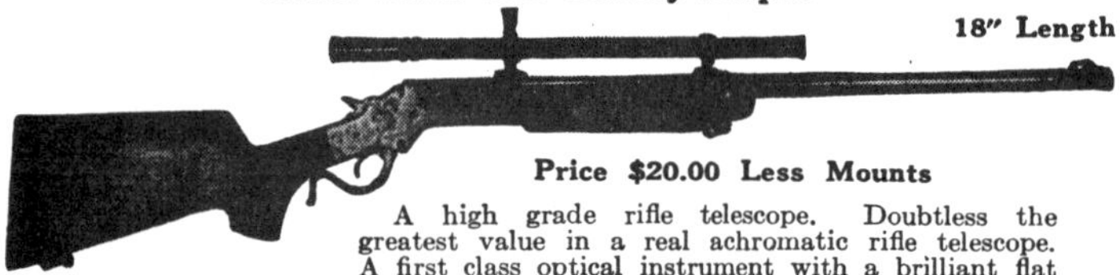

Price $20.00 Less Mounts

A high grade rifle telescope. Doubtless the greatest value in a real achromatic rifle telescope. A first class optical instrument with a brilliant flat field.

The scope is ideal for small game and is equally well suited for target work, especially for off hand work.

Adjustable for the individual eye and for parallax, although the lower powers hardly require any adjustment for parallax as they are practically universal focus. The same principles of seating the lenses is employed as in the high grade target scopes and those scopes will withstand the heaviest recoil from big bore rifles.

The entire field is clear and flat, free from distortion or haze, as will be expected from a good optical instrument.

It is made in 3, 4, or 6 power, 18 inches long, equipped with ⅛ inch Pope Rib, Clamp Ring, and Screw Dust Caps.

Diameter of tube is ¾ inch, diameter of objective is 11/16 inch, clear aperture diameter of eye piece is ¾ inch, eye relief 2¼ inches, field of view, depending on power, 28 feet in 3x, 25 feet in 4x and 17 feet in 6x at 100 yards.

Unless otherwise specified, the scope is furnished with medium cross-wires. Flat top, blunted or pointed post reticules are also available for this scope.

10" or 12" Length

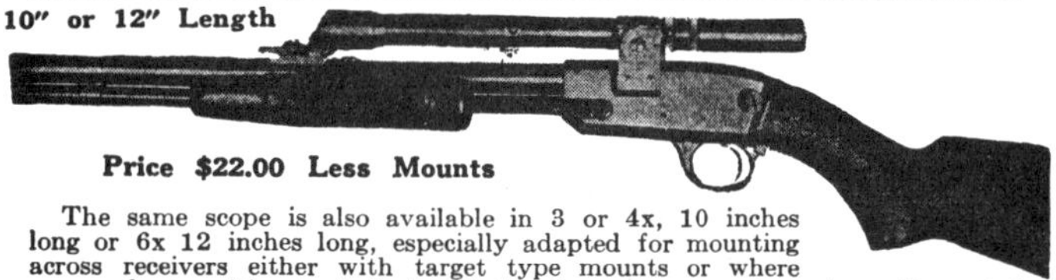

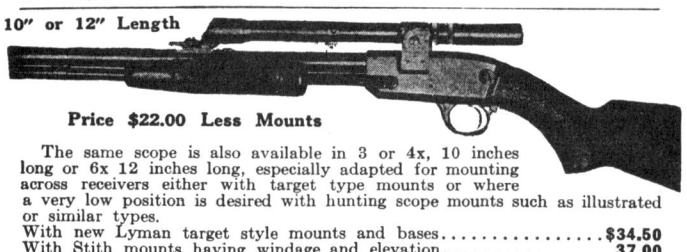

Price $22.00 Less Mounts

The same scope is also available in 3 or 4x, 10 inches long or 6x 12 inches long, especially adapted for mounting across receivers either with target type mounts or where a very low position is desired with hunting scope mounts such as illustrated or similar types.

With new Lyman target style mounts and bases................ **$34.50**
With Stith mounts having windage and elevation................ **37.00**

1" Clear Aperture Objective Target Scope

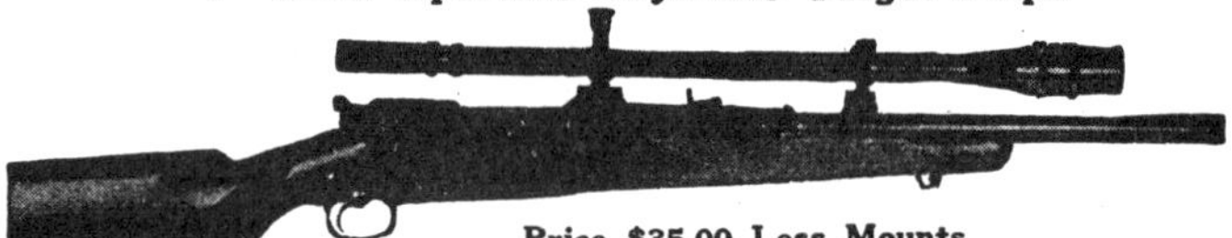

Price $35.00 Less Mounts

This scope was designed to meet the demand for a precision rifle telescope within a price range that could be afforded by every shooter.

This scope is of the same high quality as the rest of our optical instruments and rifle telescopes. It is primarily a target scope and due to its dimensions suited exceptionally well for fine accurate shooting of small game, pests, testing of ammunition, etc.

Focusing the scope for different ranges is accomplished by *moving the objective only,* which represents the correct way of focusing a target type telescope of moderate magnification most satisfactorily.

The scope is 21⅝ inches long overall, can be mounted on any small or big bore rifle without danger to lenses or adjustments. The same reticules as supplied in all Unertl rifle telescopes are available, medium cross wire will be furnished unless otherwise specified.

The 1 inch scope is furnished in 6, 8 or 10x equipped with ⅛ inch Pope rib, clamp ring and screw dust caps for both ends and is priced **$35.00** less mounts, or **$47.50** complete with the new Lyman 3 point suspension mounts and bases.

Interchangeable eye pieces to raise or lower the magnification of this scope 25 per cent are available at **$6.50** each.

2½ or 3X Big Game Hunting Scopes

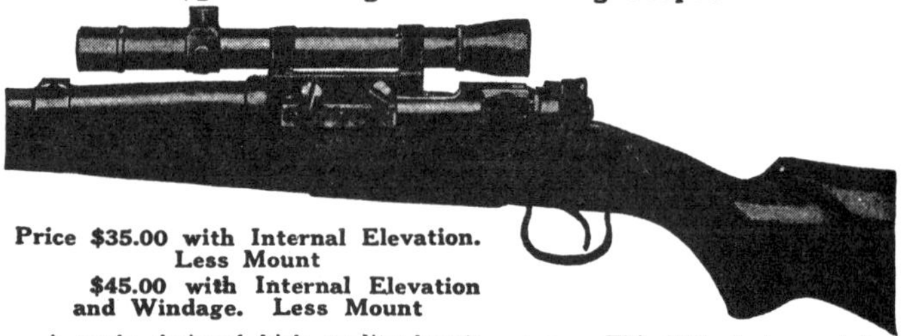

Price $35.00 with Internal Elevation. Less Mount
$45.00 with Internal Elevation and Windage. Less Mount

A newly designed high quality hunting scope. This little instrument is the latest development in an excellent sporting rifle telescope of the high quality type.

It has an overall length of 10½ inches with metal screw caps, diameter of tube ⅞ inch to fit the available various types of hunting scope mounts, screw adjustable eye piece with lock ring, internal elevation, eye relief is 3½ inches, field of view 36 feet in the 2½x, 34 feet in 3x at 100 yards, clear aperture of objective ¾ inch, clear aperture of eye lens ⅞ inch, weight 8 ounces.

This scope has an extremely bright, large undistorted field, very easy to focus and thoroughly adapted for all rifles.

Flat top, blunted and pointed posts with lateral wire and crosswire reticules in two sizes are available for this scope.

The elevation turret has been modified to prevent strangers from turning or disturbing the elevation.

Our opinion and advice to any hunting scope owner is to have the scope first of all correctly mounted and after having it sighted in for an intermediate range to leave the adjusting movements alone and forget about them, but learn to hold over or under if an unexpected long or short shot has to be made.

This telescope sight offers the shooter absolute accuracy, plus a more humane way of hunting.

Note: For a low and strong mount we recommend our side mount as found in this section of this catalog. The price of the mount must be added to the cost of the telescope plus **$5.00** labor charge to arrive at the total price of the equipment.

Styles of Reticules

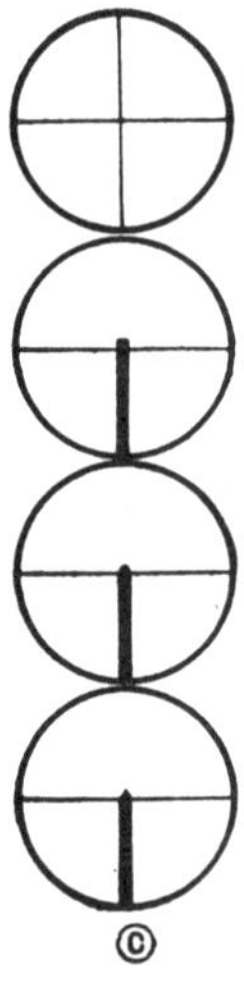

Cross Wires

Flat Top Post

Blunted Post

Pointed Post

Recoil Absorbers for Rifles

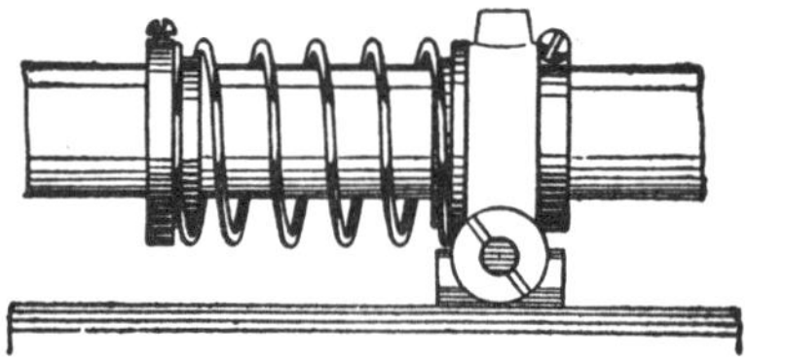

The rifle sight recoil absorber makes the action of the sight 100 per cent fool-proof and insures better success in shooting. The absorber will fit any rifle telescope with sliding mounts and where the tube has ¾ inch diameter.

Every shooter using a rifle knows that the sight is moved forward by the recoil and has to be pulled back by hand into its original position after each shot. An automatic return of the sight into the original position therefore is bound to improve the scores of a shooter considerably.

Price **$3.00**

THE BEST MOUNTS FOR THE BEST RIFLES

THE FECKER TELESCOPIC SIGHTS

For the rifleman, represent the highest standard and latest developments in optical design and construction. They are the result of many years' experience in the design and construction of optical ordnance material.

These sights are designed so that they can be used equally well on either low or high power rifles, and are of such length that they will fit ANY rifle. As a high powered rifle requires a sight of long eye relief, this feature has been made of primal importance, and size of field made a secondary consideration in the target scopes. The eye relief in all target scopes is a full 3 inches, that is, the full field is obtained when the eye is 3 inches from the end of the scope.

The sights are rigidly constructed so as to withstand the severest recoil without changing their adjustment. All lenses and moving parts are sealed in, making these scopes dust and moisture proof. The inside surfaces of the lenses will require no cleaning, so that it will never become necessary for the shooter to disassemble and clean the scope. All the Target Scopes are equipped with the Pope Rib and the micrometer focusing scale.

The correctness of the design and construction of these sights has been demonstrated daily on the various rifle ranges throughout the world. The fact that Fecker Scopes are used by the leading shooters, and that they have won an overwhelming majority of the matches wherever they have competed, is conclusive evidence of their quality and reliability.

One of the most important elements in a telescope sight is the objective. Upon the correctness of its construction depends to a large measure the brilliancy and clearness of the image. The objectives in these scopes give an image which is clear cut, brilliant, and equally clear throughout the entire field. The diameter of the objective is so proportioned to the magnification that proper illumination is obtained at any magnification. The objectives in the target scopes are made in three sizes, three-quarters of an inch clear aperture, one and one-eighth inches clear aperture, and one and one-half inches clear aperture.

With objectives of these sizes and Fecker quality, the shooter can see the bullet holes in the target up to 100 yards with average light conditions. In fact, many shooters have written that they could see .22 caliber bullet holes in the target at 200 yards with their Fecker Scopes.

In the Fecker Scope the objective which is the *most sensitive* lens in the optical train is held stationary. It is not necessary to move this lens to focus for various ranges. Focusing is effected by moving the erecting lens, the *least sensitive* element, thus making for increased stability of the optical system.

THE ¾ INCH TARGET TELESCOPIC SIGHT

The first Fecker telescopes were all made with ¾" objective. Their success was instantaneous and they were used by many shooters wherever shown. Their quality has been steadily improved, and today the ¾" scope is the choice of many shooters. The 4½ power scope with the high power eyepiece to give 8 power makes an ideal combination for offhand and prone shooting. The two eyepieces are instantly interchangeable without changing the zeroing of the scope, or the size of the field.

The scope can be supplied with either the plain or precision mounts, and at its price represents the greatest value in the scope market today.

Made in 4.5-6-8-10 powers. 20" length.

Price with ½ or ¼ minute click mounts, bases and caps............$45.00
Price with plain micrometer mounts, bases and caps.............. 52.50

THE 1⅛ INCH TARGET TELESCOPIC SIGHT

Many shooters asked for a scope with more light gathering power so that they could see their groups at longer ranges. The answer to this was the 1⅛" scope which takes in 2¼ times as much light as the ¾" scope. All improvements in the target scopes are so designed that they can be added to the older scopes. The ¾ inch scopes can be converted to the 1⅛ inch at a cost of $15.00 plus return postage. This change makes the older scope equal to the new 1⅛ inch scope.

An equally good score can be shot with any of the three types of the target scopes, only the larger objective makes it so much EASIER to shoot the same high scores.

Made in 6-8-10-12½ powers. 22" length.

Price with ½ or ¼ minute click mounts, bases and caps............$60.00
Price with plain micrometer mounts, bases and caps.............. 37.50

THE 1½ INCH CLEAR APERTURE OBJECTIVE COMBINATION TARGET AND SPOTTING SCOPE

This scope was designed to meet the demand of the shooter for a precision optical instrument which would serve the double purpose of a target scope and a spotting scope, eliminating the necessity for changing position from shot to shot in order to see his group.

The resolving power of a scope, or its ability to spot, is dependent upon the size of the objective, all other qualities being equal. The 1½" scope, with its high light gathering power, which is double that of the 1⅛", will spot with ease at 100 yards, and with good light conditions at 200 yards.

The scopes can be furnished in magnifications of 8, 10, 12.5 or 16; cross-wire reticules in five degrees of fineness, the finest of which will quarter a .22 caliber bullet hole at 50 yards. The scope is 25" long overall, and can be mounted on any target rifle. The scope weighs 19 oz. with mounts.

The scope is priced at $85.00, complete with precision micrometer mounts, hardened steel bases, threaded dust caps, and the new graduated focusing scale, which eliminates the necessity of counting the number of threads for setting at various ranges.

Present owners of Fecker Scopes may have their equipment rebuilt into the 1½" scope, by paying the difference between the price of their scope and the price of the 1½", which in the case of the ¾" is $40.00, and in the case of the 1⅛", $25.00.

The 1½-inch clear aperture objective combination target and spotting scope is supplied in 25-inch length.

Price with ½ or ¼ minute click mounts, bases and caps............$85.00
Price with plain micrometer mounts, bases and caps.............. 77.50

Conversion prices:*
    ¾" to 1⅛"..$15.00
    ¾" to 1½"... 40.00
    1⅛" to 1½".. 25.00

*These prices include complete rebluing of the scope.

High power eyepiece
  To fit any of the target scopes..........................$8.50

Extra reticules
  ....$2.50

Leather carrying case
  Specify objective size. If small game scope specify length......$5.00

Extra hardened steel bases and screws
  (Specify rifle)..$1.50

Mounts are not sold separately.

THE SMALL GAME SCOPE

The use of a scope on a sporting rifle gives the hunter a reliable means of sighting, which could not be attained by any other device. At the instant the rifle is brought to the shoulder, a clearly defined, well lighted picture of the game is presented to the eye. Holding off for sidelight and difficulty in focusing is eliminated. On dark days, in heavily wooded sections, during early morning or twilight hunting, game can easily be spotted which would not be visible with iron sights.

This scope is ideal for woodchucks, crows, hawks, squirrels, prairie dogs, and other small game.

There are new pleasures in store for the hunter who uses one of these scopes on his next trip into the field or woods.

The scope is made in 2¼, 3 and 4 power, is 16" or 18" long overall, diameter of objective 11/16", diameter of eyepiece ¾", eye relief 2", field of view 26 feet at 100 yards in the 3 power. The field is clear to the extreme edge, and is entirely free from any color or haze. The focus is universal and free from parallax from 25 yards on. The scope weighs 14 oz. It can be focused as short as 40 feet for offhand matches or shooting on a home range.

The scope with plain mounts, without clicks and straight edges, is priced at $30.00 complete with bases and caps; with our regular precision click micrometer mounts, with either ¼ or ½ minute of angle clicks, $37.50, complete with bases. Three grades of cross-wire, or flat top post reticule can be supplied. The Pope rib is standard equipment on this scope.

This scope is made with the same high standards of precision as our regular line of target scopes. All adjustments are sealed and locked, and the scope is waterproof and dustproof. It is rugged enough to use on any high power military or sporting rifle.

The small game scope in 10-12 or 14 in. lengths is priced at $42.00 with ½ or ¼ minute click mounts, caps and bases; $34.50 with plain micrometer mounts, caps and bases.

The small game scope being of an entirely different optical design *cannot* be converted to the larger objective.

Small game scope in lengths of 16 or 18 inches in powers of 2¼, 3 or 4.

Price with ½ or ¼ minute click mounts, bases and caps............$37.50
Price with plain micrometer mounts, bases and caps.............. 30.00

Small game scope in lengths of 10, 12 and 14 inches, in powers of 2¼, 3 or 4.

Price with ½ or ¼ minute click mounts, bases and caps............$42.00
Price with plain micrometer mounts, bases and caps.............. 34.50

A RIFLE IS ONLY AS GOOD AS ITS SIGHTS

LYMAN TELESCOPE SIGHTS
(IN ORDERING, GIVE MAKE, MODEL AND CALIBER OF RIFLE)

TARGETSPOT SCOPES

LYMAN JUNIOR TARGETSPOT. 6X and 8X. Combination hunting and target shooting. Objective lens diam. 19 mm. (¾ in.). Field of vision at 100 yds., 6X, 16 ft., 8X, 14 ft. Length, 21¾ in. Weight, 22 oz. State power desired, 6X or 8X. Price each..........$45.00

LYMAN TARGETSPOT. 8X and 10X. Target shooting. Spot shots up to 100 yds. Objective lens diam. 28 mm. (1⅛ in.). Field of vision at 100 yds., 8X, 14 ft., 10X, 12 ft. Eye relief appx. 2 in. Length 22 in. Wt., 24 oz. State power desired, 8X or 10X. Price each..........$60.00

LYMAN SUPER-TARGETSPOT. 10X, 12X and 15X. Target shooting. Spots shots up to 200 yds. Objective lens diam. 34 mm. Field at 100 yds., 10X, 12 ft., 12X, 9 ft. 3 in., 15X, 8 ft. 9 in. Length 24 in. Wt. 25 oz. State power desired, 10X, 12X or 15X. Price each..........$75.00

OUTSTANDING FEATURES OF ALL TARGETSPOT SCOPES

1. Graduated sleeve acting on non-rotating lens affords perfect method of focal adjustment.
2. Parallax completely eliminated with range focusing.
3. Front sleeve marked in clear white graduations for ranges of 50 ft., 25, 50, 100 and 200 yds.
4. Field of vision extra large, permits holding with less effort.
5. Finest quality Bausch & Lomb polaroid tested lenses, with remarkable light gathering power and clearest definition to extreme edge.
6. Ocular lens adjustment for individual eye.
7. Rear mounts 3 pt. suspension, ¼ min. micro-click. Front mount 3 pt. suspension. Clicks sharp and distinct.
8. Aluminum alloy parts save weight and retain strength. Workmanship and finish of best quality.
9. Objective and ocular lenses protected by metal lens caps.
10. Each complete with rubber eye-cup, mounts, bases, screws, taps, drills.

LYMAN "ALASKAN" HUNTING SCOPE 2½X

Designed for high power hunting rifles. The field of vision is 40 feet at 100 yards. Objective free aperture is 19mm. The optical system contains Bausch & Lomb polaroid tested lenses of highest brilliance. The scope has internal adjustment for windage and elevation. The adjusting screws are deep stamped and clearly marked in white, both screws with direction arrows. Adjustments are made by clicks, each click representing approximately 1 inch at 100 yards. After proper alignment, the adjustments can be securely locked and zeroed. Ocular lens adjustment. For mounting this scope we recommend our Stoeger side mount and also other types of mounts as found in this catalog. Weight without mounts 8 oz. Length of scope 10½ inches. Tube diameter 22 mm. Light transmitting power 81. Standard reticule is blunt picket post and cross wire. There are six other styles of reticule available.

Price Scope only without mount..............$45.00

Internal windage and elevation adjustment is patented. Clicks are sharp and distinct.

LYMAN "KNOWN-RANGER"

With gauges in position as when in use. Showing how 50 and 100 yd. gauges swing out to the side.

Lyman "Known-Ranger" (Pat. Pend.) easily attached to rear scope mount. Hinged gauges of definite thickness under elevating screw provide instant adjustments of scope for 50, 100 and 200 yd. distances. Saves time and wear on scope mount. Will fit any Lyman click target mount.
Price complete........$1.50

NO. 422 EXPERT SCOPE

The Lyman No. 422 Expert Scope for .22 caliber rifles including guns chambered for .22 Hornet cartridge; has Bausch & Lomb optics providing magnification of four power, with field of approximately 25 ft. at 100 yards and universal focus. The field is well illuminated and defined to extreme edges. Over all length of the scope is 13½" allowing ample adjustment to obtain the proper eye relief. The mount is provided with micrometer click adjustments for windage and elevation and holds the scope so that this need not be removed when using Metallic Sights. The points of contact between the mount and the gun are spaced 2¾" apart giving this installation rigidity which is obvious to the shooter. Scope and mount weigh only 14 ounces, a feature especially appreciated by field shooters.
Scope complete with mount, mounting screws, tap and drill........$10.00

LYMAN TELESCOPE SIGHT RETICULES

SINGLE CROSS WIRES | TAPER POST | APERTURE

At left:
Six styles of reticules available for all Targetspot Scopes, 438 and 422. (Single cross wires are regularly furnished). Reticules only, $1.80.

At right:
Seven reticules for Alaskan Scope only. (No. 1 is regularly furnished.) Reticules available only for factory installation. $10.00.

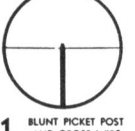   

1. BLUNT PICKET POST AND CROSS WIRE | 2. BLUNT PICKET POST | 3. SHARP PICKET POST AND CROSS WIRE | 4. SHARP PICKET POST

STRAIGHT POST | TAPER POST WITH LATERAL CROSS WIRE | POST WITH LATERAL CROSS WIRE

5. TAPERED POST AND CROSS WIRE | 6. TAPERED POST | 7. CROSS WIRES

IN ORDERING LYMAN SCOPES, GIVE MAKE AND MODEL OF RIFLE

REDFIELD TELESCOPE MOUNTS

Redfield mounts have been recognized as the correct link to install your telescope in the most convenient position on your rifle. They are constructed to hold the telescope rigid in the lowest place, allowing precise adjustment for windage. The scope will never change your point of impact in as much as the principle of the two point mount is the safest and most secure developed in the mounting of a telescope sight, adding only a minimum of weight to your equipment. The telescope can be detached instantly and put in position again without changing the sighting whatsoever.

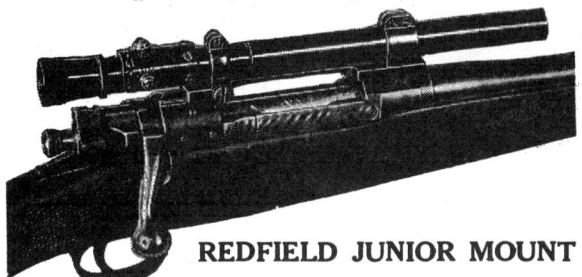

REDFIELD JUNIOR MOUNT

Here for the first time you can buy a mount correctly designed to hold your scope in lowest position at a price which allows you to obtain a high-class telescope the ideal of every sportsman and hunter. The Redfield Junior mount is made with one piece base and utilizes the same circular dovetail principle as all Redfield mounts. Windage adjustments are made with opposing screws. One screw remains permanently set so that the scope always returns to zero when put in position on the rifle. Only one screw must be released for removal or replacement of scope. The distance from center of front mount to center of rear mount is four inches making it impossible to knock the telescope out of alignment. The rear ring is held to the base by an opposing screw system working like a vise. The left hand screw is known as the point windage screw and should never be touched after the rifle has been sighted in. The right hand screw is the detaching and windage screw. These large headed screws are hardened and provided with coin slots and can be turned by using an ordinary iron washer, 25 cent piece or key ring. To remove the scope, remove the right hand screw, then push the scope off to the right until it can be lifted out of the front mount. The scope can be removed and replaced time after time without changing point of impact in the least. The weight of this mount is only 4½ ounces.

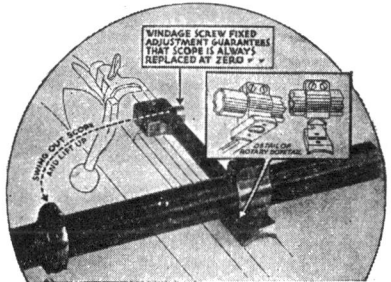

These new Redfield Junior mounts can be had for the following rifles:

Jr-52	Winchester 52 Sporter and 52 without dovetail cut in receiver
Jr-69	Winchester Models 56, 57, 69, and 72
Jr-63	Winchester Models 03 and 63
Jr-61-R	Winchester Model 61 with round barrel
Jr-61-O	Winchester Model 61 with octagon barrel
Jr-70	Winchester Models 70 and 54
Jr-75	Winchester Model 75
Jr-12-R	Remington Models 12 and 121 with round barrel
Jr-12-O	Remington Models 12 and 121 with octagon barrel
Jr-14	Remington Models 14 and 141
Jr-25	Remington Model 25
Jr-30	Remington Models 30S and 30Exp. remodeled Enfield
Jr-34	Remington Models 34 and 341, above bolt handle
Jr-40	Savage Models 40 and 45
xJr-23	Savage Models 19, 23, and 33
Jr-99	Savage Model 99, all styles
Jr-6	Savage Model 6, Stevens Model 76 and 076, Springfield 87 and 087
yJr-39	Marlin Models 37, 39, 93, 94
Jr-10	Mossberg Rifles and Master Action
Jr-S	Springfield 1906, M1, M2
Jr-M	Mauser

x Most lever action single shot rifles such as Ballard, Stevens, Winchester Musket, etc., with large round barrels can be fitted with this mount.
y Similar rifles with octagon barrels can be used with mount Jr-39

NOTE: Springfield, Mauser, Winchester Models 52 and 54 must have bolt altered for low scope mounting.

For any of the above mentioned Rifles:

	Price
Redfield Junior Mount for Weaver Telescopes	$8.00
Redfield Junior Mount for Ajack 2, 5X Telescopes	10.00
Redfield Junior Mount for Zeiss, Zielklein, Hensoldt, Lyman Alaskan and all other Telescopes of 22 mm Ring diameter	10.00

Full instructions for installing are included with each set of mounts. In case you prefer to have your scope mounted by us and bore sighted an extra labor charge of $2.50 will be made.

REDFIELD BRIDGE TYPE MOUNTS

Specially designed for those wanting a mount having micrometer adjustments. These mounts are made to take all sizes of telescopes using a larger ring diameter than 22mm, such as Ajack 4 and 6x Zeiss Zielvier and others.

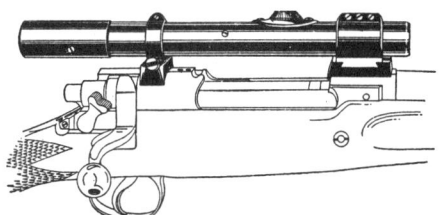

Redfield bridge mounts are specially made and recommended for the following rifles:

Springfield M/1903	M/56, 57 and 69 Winchesters
M/54 Winchester	M/61 Winchester
M/30 Remington	M/25 Remington
Mauser	Newton rifles
Remodeled Enfields	M/99 Savage
M/12, 14 and 24 Remingtons	M/40 and 45 Savages
M/03 and 63 Winchesters	M/19, 23 and 33 Savages
	M/52 Winchester

In ordering, be sure to specify for which rifle mount is intended.

Mounts for Scopes with 22M/M Tube Diameter	$20.00
Mounts for Hensoldt Zielyt 2¾X	23.00
Mounts for Scopes with 26M/M Tube Diameter	25.00
Extra Bases for Interchangeable Mounting	10.00
Mounting Charge	5.00
Bolt Handle Altered	5.00
Redfield Safety for Springfield, 54 Winchester and Mauser	4.50
Targeting High Power Rifles	5.00
Disc Block to Use on Rear Base	1.50

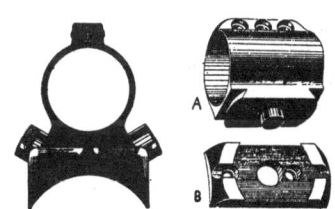
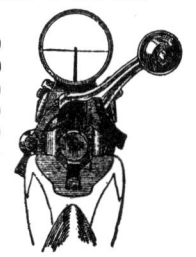

A FINE RIFLE DESERVES A FINE SCOPE

WEAVER RIFLE SCOPES
WITH INTERNAL WINDAGE AND ELEVATION

¼" click adjustments of the 330C and 440C Scopes.

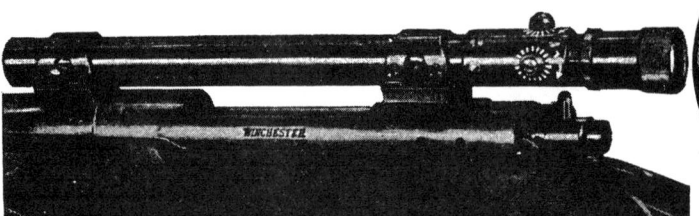

MODEL 330 SCOPE, TYPE B MOUNT

Click adjustment screws of the 333, 344, 355 and 29S Scopes.

The long eye relief of the 330 Scope permits attaching the scope forward of the safety or bolt handle. This long eye relief and the sturdy construction assures perfect results even on the very heaviest calibers.

LENS SYSTEM. Fully corrected, double cemented compound achromatic lenses are used. The field of vision is brilliant and sparkling showing true colors. The field of view is sharply defined at the edges as well as at the center.

RETICULES. Either cross hair or post is optional. The post is tapered with a narrow, flat top. It permits extreme accuracy but also allows great speed of aim and can be used in dim light when cross hairs would be difficult to see. The top of the post covers approximately 4 inches for each 100 yards of range and thus is a very convenient range finder.

THE 330 SCOPE is 2¾ power and is perfectly suited for offhand and game shooting allowing faster and more accurate aim than any other sight. Highly corrected lenses show as much detail as scopes of higher power. Illumination is surpassed by no other scope and is greater than the eye can absorb under all conditions. Aim can be taken in the poorest light and even in moonlight at night.

THE 440 SCOPE is similar to the 330 Scope except that it is about ¾ inch longer, is 4 power, and has 3¼ inch eye relief. When the greater proportion of shooting is done at still objects, such as small game and targets, the 440 Scope is often preferred.

330C and 330S with B Mount......$31.00, with T Mount......$27.50
440C and 440S with B Mount...... 36.00, with T Mount...... 32.50
Post reticule furnished unless ordered otherwise.

The 330C and 440C have ¼ minute click windage and elevation adjustments and are preferred usually for target and small game shooting and whenever frequent sight changes are required.

330S and 440S have adjustment screws equipped with knurled locking nuts and are often selected for big game shooting and when sight changes are seldom made.

FITTINGS AND EXTRAS

Narorw flat top tapered post reticule in Models 333, 344, 355, 29S, 329 .... $1.00
Rubber Dust Caps, pair.. .35
Rubber Eye Cup, each... .30
Leather lens caps for 330 and 440 Scopes, set.................. 1.00
Drill and Tap, set... .50
Attaching Scope to Rifle and Bore Sighting, T Mount............ 1.50
                               B Mount.....$3.00 to 5.00

(This includes all preliminary adjustments, bore sighting or alignment with metallic sights, etc. Final targetting or sighting in, if necessary, is easily done.)

Actual targetting at any specified range. Price on application.

Model 29S (3X)
(With T Mount)

The 29S Scope is the only low priced scope of its type and is adapted to high as well as low power rifles. It has gained world fame in the hunting field and has brought to bag numberless heads of game. The lens system is achromatic and produces a large and well defined field of view showing true colors. Vision is clear and bright. The 29S is a short, sturdy hunting type scope with ample strength for use in hunting and on high power rifles. Because of the click adjustments it is sighted in easily for any range on targets as well as game.

Model 29S Complete with T Mount......................... $11.70
Model 29S Complete with B Mount......................... 15.20

Model 329 (3X)
(With T Mount)

Model 329 is adapted to high power as well as low power rifles. It has a 3 inch eye relief and is constructed to withstand the roughest use in hunting. A special lens system was designed for this scope in order to secure the greatest economy consistent with good results. Windage and elevation adjustments are internal. They are not of the click type but permit very accurate sight changes. The adjusting screws are equipped with lock nuts so that they can be locked securely in any position.

Model 329 Complete with T Mount............................$4.75
Model 329 Complete with B Mount............................ 8.25

MODELS 333 (3X), 344 (4X) and 355 (5X) SCOPES

These three scopes are the most modern and advanced sights obtainable at very reasonable prices for use on rifles of light recoil. These scopes are constructed sturdily and would withstand the shock of high power rifles but they have a short eye relief identical to other makes of low priced scopes and so are not recommended on heavy recoil rifles. The positive and accurate micrometer click adjustments are perfect for target shooting and allow the critical sight alignment always desired for hunting woodchucks, squirrels, and other small game. Correctly matched and precision ground lenses are employed assuring excellent definition, sharpness, and good illumination.

Complete list of rifles and mounts on next page.

(With T Mount)

THE MODEL 333 is three power so is usually preferred for general shooting when many shots are taken offhand or standing.
Model 333 Complete with T Mount......$7.75
Model 333 Complete with B Mount...... 11.25

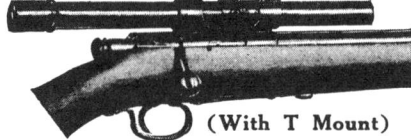

(With T Mount)

THE MODEL 344 is four power and is excellent as a combination target and small game scope.
Model 334 Complete with T Mount......$8.00
Model 334 Complete with B Mount...... 11.50

(With T Mount)

THE MODEL 355 is five power with ¼ minute click adjustments. It is well suited for both target and game shooting.
Model 355 Complete with T Mount......$10.00
Model 355 Complete with B Mount...... 12.25

ORDER BLANK IN MIDDLE AND INDEX IN BACK OF CATALOG

WEAVER MOUNTS AND LIST OF RIFLES

TYPE T-1—Low and central over bore.
Mounted extremely low being only about 1/16" to 1/8" above receiver. Must be removed when using metallic sights.

All guns listed under T-1 can be used with T-3 or T-03 which permits regular sights to be used in conjunction with the scope.
Winchester Models 56, 57, 69, 87, S.S.
Savage Models 6, 19, 19-33, 19-H, 19 N.R.A., Sporters. 23-A, 23AA, 23B, 23C, 23D, 40, 45.
Stevens Models 17, 26, 27, 44, 414, 417, 417½, 418, 418½, 76.
Marlin Models 50, A1; Ranger .22 Automatic.
Lee-Enfield, British—Mauser .22—Krag.
Mossberg Models 20, 21, 30, 34, 35, 40, 42, 44, 45, 46.

TYPE T-2—Low and central over bore.
Type T-2 holds the scope only about 1/16" above the receiver. It must be removed when using metallic sights. Permits attaching the 330 Scope ahead of the bolt handle on the Model 54 Winchester and Springfield rifles.

All guns listed under T-2 can be used with T-4 permitting use of regular sights in conjunction with the scope.
Enfield, U. S. Model 1917—Newton.
Remington Models 30, 308—Winchester Model 70.

TYPE T-3—High and central over bore.
Holds the scope in an elevated position and permits using the metallic sights without removing scope. The center or axis of the scope is about 1½" or less above the center of the barrel.

All guns listed under T-1 and T-03 can be used with T-3.
Savage Models 3, 3S, 4, 4S, 5, 5S, 04.
Stevens Models 53, 053, 55, 055, 56, 056, 66, 066, 419.
(Stevens Models 53, 053, 55, 055, 56, 056, 66, 066, 419 and Savage Models 3, 3S, 4, 4S produced prior to 1936 may require very slight bending of the bolt handle.)
Remington Models 33, 34, 41, 341—Marlin Model 80.
Mossberg Models 10, 14, 25—Western Field Bolt Action.
Ranger Bolt Action—Iver-Johnson Bolt Action.

TYPE T-03—Medium height, central over bore.
Type T-03 is intermediate in height between T-1 and T-3. It can be used on rifles having a medium high lift of the bolt handle. Open sights can be used with the scope in position. Center of scope is 1¼" or less above the center of the barrel.

All guns listed under S-1 can be used with S-03.
Winchester Models 52, 60, 60A, 67, 68.
Remington Models 33, 34, 41, 341, 37.

TYPE T-4—High and central over bore.
Type T-4 permits using the metallic sights without removing the Scope and does not necessitate altering the bolt handle. Center of the scope is only about 1 5/8" above the center of the barrel.

All guns listed under T-2 can be used with T-4.
(Above rifles can be used with T-2 when the bolt handle is altered.)
Winchester Model 54—Mauser—Springfield. Mannlicher—Savage Mod. 20.

TYPE T-5—Either high or low, central over bore.
Type T-5 can be attached either extremely low, so that it practically rests on the receiver, or in an elevated position to permit the regular sights to be used in conjunction with the scope.

Winchester Models 03, 07, 10, 61, 63—Savage Models 14, 29.
Remington Models 12, 12C, 12CS, 121, 14, 24, 25, 241, 141.
Stevens Model 75—Marlin Models 27, 39, 93, 94.
Ranger Slide Action—Western Field Slide Action.

TYPE T-6—Offset.
Type T-6 holds the scope in a slightly offset position, to the left of the receiver which permits top ejecting rifles to function properly. Metallic sights can be used with the scope in position.

Rifles listed under T-6 can also be used with T-5 mount. Due to the central position of T-5 these rifles must sometimes be tipped to allow the empty cartridge to fall clear of the gun, especially in the larger calibers, but .25-20 and .32-20 caliber rifles usually function perfectly without tipping the rifle. The offset position of T-6 permits a lower scope position than does T-5 when mounted on top ejecting rifles. T-6 does not interfere with the ejection of cartridges.

Winchester Models 53, 55, 64, 65, 71, 86, 92, 94, 95, 06, 62, 90.

TYPE T-7—Low and central over bore.
Type T-7 permits an extremely low position of the scope. The scope can be placed in actual contact with the receiver.
For Savage Model 99 only.

TYPE T-8—Offset.
Type T-8 is slightly offset to the left side, permitting use of the regular sights and the proper operation of the Remington Automatic. The base is not attached to the upper thin portion of the receiver but to the heavy lower part.

Remington Model 8, 81.

TYPE T SIDE BRACKET MOUNT

Made of tough alloy steel and with the exception of the upper scope clamps is of one piece construction. The base portion is reinforced, the clamps grip the scope as tightly as if they were welded to the tube. Mounting on the gun is not hard to do, no stock cutting is required.

This mount has been thoroughly proved under all conditions and on large caliber, high power rifles. It is quickly removable from the gun and is held securely by large hardened screws having knurled and coin slotted heads and tapered binding surfaces, which hold the base in accurate alignment.

Type T is made in several designs to fit different rifles and to hold the scope in either a high or low position. Please specify the make and model of your rifle and whether a high or low mount is wanted. The lowest mount is always recommended. Type T mount........................**$1.95**

TYPE B BRIDGE MOUNT

Type B is a bridge mount designed to hold the scope in a very low position and to make it practically an integral part of the gun. Because the mount gives results as good as though the bases were machined from the solid metal of the gun itself its reliability is unexcelled.

The scope and mounts can be easily detached and replaced in exact position. When removed no parts remain on the gun to detract from its appearance, the scope and mounts are detachable in one complete unit including the attaching screws which remain in the mount bases. These screws are heat treated, the heads are knurled and coin slotted, the bearing portion is tapered for best accuracy and greatest binding force.

Simple instructions for mounting, which is not difficult, are furnished. No cutting of a fine stock is necessary.

The simple design has eliminated all excess weight and the mount complete weighs but three ounces. The 330 Scope with Type B Mount weighs only 9½ ounces which deserves much consideration when the gun is to be carried for hours in the hunting field. Type B is well finished and gun blued.

Bases are numbered and designed for different rifles so be sure to mention make and model of rifle. Type B Mount, Complete..................**$5.50**

SPECIFICATIONS OF WEAVER SCOPES

When ordering be sure to mention make and model of rifle or the type of mount as shown in the chart.

Scope Model	330	440	333	344	355	29S	329
Lens System	Double cemented, compound achromatic, fully corrected.		Precision matched.			Achromatic...	Special single design.
Type of rifles	All rifles		.22, .22 Hornet, and all rifles of light recoil.			From .30/06 class to .22s.	
Reticule	Cross hair or flat top tapered post.		Cross hair standard — tapered flat top post on special order.				
Weight with mount	9½ ounces	10½ ounces	10 ounces	10½ ounces	11 ounces	9½ ounces	9 ounces
Length	10½ inches	11¼ inches	11 inches	12¼ inches	13½ inches	10⅛ inches	10 inches
Power	2¾X	4X	3X	4X	5X	3X	3X
Diameter of field of view	35 feet	27 feet	33 feet	28 feet	20 feet	31 feet	29 feet
Distance from eye	3½ inches (3"-6") (3–6 inches)	3¼ inches	2 inches	2 inches	2 inches	3¼ inches	3 inches
Type of adjustments	All Models — double internal adjustments for windage and elevation.						
Windage and elevation adjustment (Both adjustments internal)	330S, 440S — adjustment screws equipped with lock nuts. 330C, 440C—¼" click		½" click	½" click	¼" click	½" click	Screw and lock nut type.
Focus	All Models — Universal focus for distance. Micrometer eyesight adjustment.						
Finish	All Models — All steel, finely polished and gun blued. Not painted.						
Price with T Mount	$27.50	$32.50	$7.75	$8.00	$10.00	$11.70	$4.75
Price with B Mount	31.00	36.00	11.25	11.50	12.25	15.20	8.25

A CORRECT MOUNT FOR EVERY GUN

MOSSBERG RIFLE SCOPES

No. 5M4—4 POWER

FOR CALIBERS UP TO 25/20 AND .22 HORNET

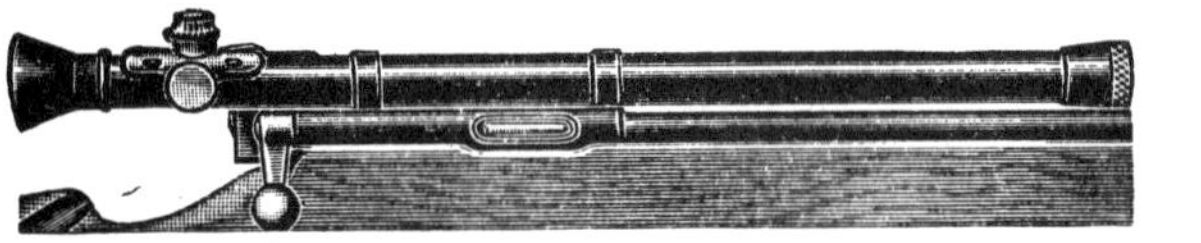

It sure has everything! Designed for use *low* on the rfle, it has a substantial mount which does just that, holds the tube *right down on top of the receiver* on the 1940 line of Mossberg rifles and many other makes.

Note what was done in order to *keep* the scope down, practically in line with the line of iron sights. The focus adjustment was made so as to move the objective lens by a simple twist of the cap on the front end. This construction eliminates all plates, screws, or other adjusting parts usually found on the *sides* of scope tubes, and allows the tube to be easily moved away from or toward the eye to get proper eye-relief (distance from eye to end of scope tube). The new type *internal* adjustments with patented "click" screws move the *cross hair* reticule instead of the whole scope tube, and have ¼ minute graduations. Furthermore, the entire reticule assembly, including adjusting screws, can be moved along the tube to bring the cross hairs into sharp focus *for your eyes.* The mount in itself has some adjujstment so that if a *perfect* job of mounting is not done, the scope tube can still be set correctly through the flexibility of the mounting itself. On the elevation screw is another new gadget—a little ring graduated from 25 yds. to 100 yds. Set the scope at 25 yds., move the ring to the point marked O, and from then on forget it. Shoot any range you wish from 25 to 100 yds. Simply turn the ring to the range you want to shoot, and shoot!

No. 5M4—4 power—Field of view at 100 yds., 20 ft. Weight, 1 lb.—Length, 16". See how snugly the 5M4 fits the Mossberg rifles. Price **$5.75**

No. 8M4—There are still some rifles which won't take a scope sight unless it is perched up in the air. For this type of rifle we offer No. 8M4, the above internal adjustment scope on a high base. Price **$5.75**

No. 9-2½—2½ POWER

WITH PATENTED "CLICK" ADJUSTMENT

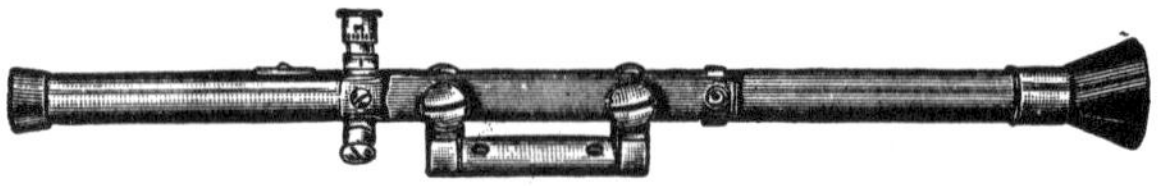

The "No. 9 series" of scope sights are built on the No. 9 scope mount. The steel base fastens securely to the action by two screws. The upper section, containing the adjustments, can be entirely removed at will, and can be attached to the base at two different heights. Patented "click" adjustments are graduated in half-minutes, equivalent to ½" change of bullet impact at 100 yds. This side-mounting principle has been developed in order to overcome the objection to top mounts. Side mounting will permit the use of the scope tube *as low as the design of the rifle will permit.* No. 9 mount will fit practically all small bore rifles by drilling and tapping two holes in the receiver. Side mounting, without any cuts in action, barrel or stock, allows clear vision under the scope tube (when the scope is in high position) for *combination use of scope and iron sight shooting.*

"No. 9 Series" telescope tubes are particularly fine optical instruments. They all have universal focus, medium fine reticules, and five lens systems and provisions for all necessary adjustments. *American Materials—American Made.*

No. 9-2½—No. 9 Mount fitted with 2½ power scope tube. This is the power recommended for hunting and general use. Medium fine cross hair reticule. Price **$4.95**

DOUBLE RETICULE

Some shooters want cross hairs, some want posts, but most would like *both!* Both reticules are contained in the scope tube at all times; either one brought into focus in a few seconds' time.

No. 9R—No. 9 Mount fitted with Mossberg's new four power *double reticule* scope tube. This is an *all-purpose* creation; use cross hair *or* post type for hunting, plinking target and short range spotting. Price **$6.50**

No. L9R—Same as above scope sight but *completely reversed* for use with Mossberg Left Hand Rifles, and at *no* extra cost. Price **$6.50**

SPECIFICATIONS

	No. 9—2½	No. 9R	No. L9R
Length	13"	15⅜"	15⅜"
Diameter of lenses	⅝"	⅝"	⅝"
Magnification	2½ power	4 power	4 power
Field of view at 100 yds...	36 ft.	27 ft.	27 ft.
Weight	16 oz.	18 oz.	18 oz.

AUTOMATIC RANGE FINDER SCOPE SIGHT

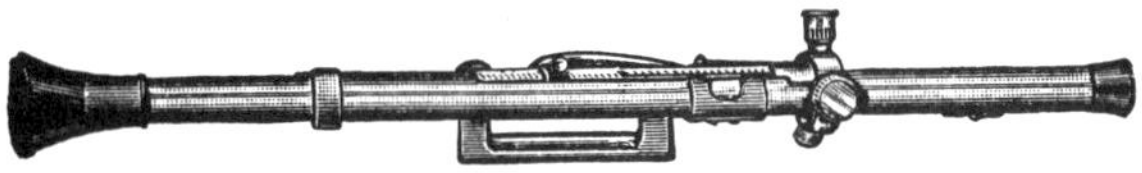

The most amazing and practical telescope sight you ever saw. Imagine—you sight through it, make an adjustment, and your elevation is set automatically whether your target or game is 25 yds. away or 200 yds. distant. You no longer have to guess the distance. If you *do* know the distance, set the instrument to the known yardage and you are automatically sighted in, ready to shoot.

How is it done? A fine wire lays just above the horizontal cross hair. As you move the cam plate on top of the scope, this wire or stadia hair moves up and down, and at the same tim the scope tube changes elevation. Regardless of the distance, when the cam is adjusted so that the two horizontal lines have about 6" of the object between them, *the scope is automatically set for elevation.* With a little practice *you'll shoot better than you ever did in your life.*

Model RFI is made for use with either .22 cal. high speed short or .22 cal. regular long rifle ammunition, as both these cartridges have approximately the same trajectory. Will fit all rifles which are drilled and tapped for Mossberg side-mounting scope sights, and can be attached to all other makes of rifles in the same manner as other Mossberg scope mounts. The micrometer click adjustments permit the use of this instrument as a regular scope sight.

Ranger Finder **RF1**—4 power—Field of view at 100 yds.—27 ft. Weight, 1¼" lbs.—Length, 15⅝". Price **$8.95**

No. 7M4—4 POWER

INTERNAL ADJUSTMENT

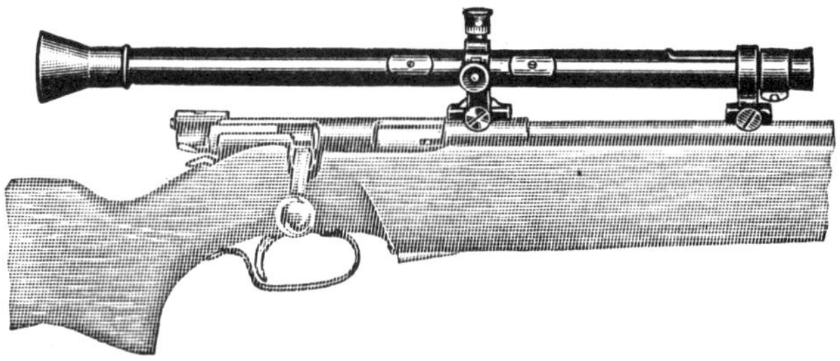

To make this the most complete line of telescope sights on the market, these top mounts are included so that Mossberg scope tubes can be fitted to rifles drilled for dove tail blocks on top of action. Complete with eyecup and drill and tap set for attaching to any make of rifle.

No. 7M4—Special mounts fitted with Mossberg 4 power scope tube with internal adjustments. Field of view at 100 yds., 20 ft. Weight 1 lb. Length 16". Price **$6.45**

No. 7R—Has No. 7 Mount fitted with Mossberg's new four power *double reticule* scope tube. This is an *all-purpose* creation; use cross hair *or* post type for hunting, plinking, target and short range spotting. Here you get micrometer click adjustments with ½ minute graduations at no extra cost, as usual. A complete set of shims with each scope, so that you don't have to order special bases for each particular rifle—complete with eyecup and drill and tap set. Price **$6.95**

A GOOD SCOPE IMPROVES YOUR AIM

Forecast: Fair Hunting Weather

No one is more interested in the weather than the hunter. Trips are often dependent upon the weather conditions—and advance information is essential in making hunting plans. With a good barometer it is possible to forecast weather conditions 12 to 48 hours in advance. These Airguide instruments are entirely American made and incorporate the latest in engineering advancements. The mechanism is sensitive and accurate. Weather information is simplified to make easy interpretation of weather changes by barometric pressure. Combined with the barometers in several models are accurate thermometer and relative humidity indicators. With these combinations the hunter may also check the air condition in his home. A wide range of models is available to fit nearly every purse.

SHIP'S WHEEL BAROMETER

Interest in this authentic ship's wheel barometer is not confined to mariners, but is attractive in any room or office. The ship's wheel case is solid walnut with polished brass spokes and studs. Dial is brass with black markings. Complete weather information furnished for easy weather forecasting. Case diameter, 5 inches. 1¼ inches deep. Can be used either as a desk piece and for wall mounting **$7.50**

PENDANT BAROMETER

A pendant barometer beautiful in design and workmanship. Essentially traditional in design yet it will harmonize perfectly with any surroundings. Two-tone walnut frame with burl walnut cap. Brass barometer dial and thermometer scale. Length 18 inches; width, 6½ inches **$15.00**

Similar to above model but not quite so elaborate and smaller in size. Combines barometer with thermometer in a walnut pendant case. Size, 11 inches long and 5 inches wide.

Price **$10.00**

INDOOR-OUTDOOR THERMOMETER

This remarkable instrument is located indoors but tells both indoor and outdoor temperatures. No longer is it necessary to raise a frosted window to tell the outdoor temperature. By means of a metal bulb and fine capillary tube the outside reading is accurately shown on the thermometer scale located inside the room. Case is of black bakelite with silver and black scales for both indoor and outdoor thermometers. Height, 9½ inches; width, 2¼ **$6.00**

No. 200

A precision barometer for home weather forecasting. In popular easel type case for use in home, office, or can be used for traveling. Sensitive and accurate barometer movement with well marked dial makes easy interpretation of pressure changes. Can be supplied with either gunmetal grey or brown bakelite case. Size, 4⅝ inches wide; 4¾ inches high.
Price **$5.00**

AIRGUIDE INSTRUMENT

Here is a magnificent new Airguide instrument which tells temperature, indicates relative humidity and forecasts weather changes. Three complete instruments in one attractive case! Forecast the weather for your hunting trips and check the air condition of your home or office at the same time. Large center dial emphasizes the fine American-made barometer. Black bakelite case with polished chrome fitting and silver colored dials. Truly a handsome instrument that you will be proud to own or use as a gift **$10.00**

No. 210

A popular ring model barometer with open center dial. Round wood case, bevelled glass crystal, and white enamel dial. Latest American-made barometer movement. Here is an instrument offering the utmost in dependability at low cost.
Price **$4.50**

WEATHER INFORMATION SIMPLIFIED

SPOTTING SCOPES

"Spotshot" $18.45
Folding Stand 5.95

MOSSBERG "SPOTSHOT"

A high grade optical instrument, 20 power, designed primarily for spotting targets on the firing line, but equally effective for camp, marine, and general observation. Materials of the first quality for light weight and adequate strength; erecting objective lens is achromatic, 38 mm. in diameter, ground to one hundred thousandth of an inch, equivalent to one-half the length of a light wave; eyepiece lens in 10 mm.; micrometer adjustment for focus; protective metal caps for both ends; black crinkle finish and chrome plated draw tube; length extended, 17 inches, closed 12⅛ inches; weight 1¾ lbs.; field approximately 7½ feet at 100 yards; American materials, American made. Has unqualified endorsement of every target shooter who has tested it. An outstanding value.

MOSSBERG FOLDING STAND

Unique in design, and decidedly practical; sturdily built of strong aluminum alloy and steel, finished in black crinkle and cadmium plate; screw adjustments for horizontal and vertical adjustments; can be used for all makes of spotting scopes; folds to 10" x 3¼" x 3" and weighs only 2¼ lbs.; stays firmly in position and yet allows adjustments to be made with one hand; adjusts from 9½" to 14½"; enthusiastic reception by riflemen already assured; American materials, American made.

Genuine Cowhide Leather Case; has 2 compartments to take both spotting scope and folded stand; a nice job comparable with its contents.

FECKER PRISMATIC SPOTTING SCOPE

In designing these spotting scopes for the rifleman's use, the points of greatest importance have been given first consideration, illumination and distinctness of image throughout the field.

To achieve these, the optical parts are computed, ground and assembled with extreme precision. The large objectives are hand figured to insure maximum definition.

Spotting can be done satisfactorily under adverse light and weather conditions; .22 caliber bullet holes can be seen in the black at 250 yards, .30 caliber holes at ranges of 400 yards.

PRICE $56.00 & UP

Other outstanding features of the Fecker spotting scopes are compactness, sturdiness and maintenance of adjustment at all times. Will be steady on the firing line even in the strongest wind.

The design of these instruments is based on years of experience in designing, manufacturing and testing under actual conditions of use, a long line of fire control instruments for the United States Army and Navy. Many of these spotting scopes are at present used by the Army and Navy teams on the firing line at Camp Perry and in various armories.

SPECIFICATIONS AND PRICES

No. 2 Clear Aperture Objective 2⅛"
Choice of eyepiece, power 12.5-18-21-25.
Field, 8 feet at 100 yards at 18 power.
Length 12 inches—Weight 2 pounds.
Price, with leather case and 1 eyepiece $56.00. Extra eyepieces $7.50

No. 1 Clear Aperture Objective 2⅛"
Choice of eyepieces, powers of 15-18-21-25-30 or 35.
Field, power 18, 7.5 feet at 100 yards.
Length 17 inches—Weight 2 pounds, 4 ounces.
Price with leather case and 2 eyepieces $62.50. Extra eyepieces $7.50

Where the shooter intends to do both .22 caliber and .30 caliber work, the eyepieces give a choice of magnifications that suits the observing conditions; higher power for favorable conditions; lower powers where it is desired to minimize haze and mirage.

No. 1 Special Spotting Scope with 2½" Clear Aperture Objective

For long range .22 and .30 caliber spotting under adverse lighting conditions the No. 1 Special Spotting Scope with 2½ inches objective, providing 56 per cent more illumination and proportionately greater spotting ability, than the regular No. 1 Spotting Scope, will give exceptional results. The No. 1 Special was designed to meet the demands of shooters for a spotting scope which would perform under the most trying atmospheric and range conditions.

Choice of eyepieces, powers of 15, 18, 21, 25, 30 or 35.
Field power 18, 7.5 feet at 100 yards.
Length 17 inches—Weight 2 pounds, 8 ounces.
Price with leather case and 2 eyepieces $100.00. Extra eyepiece $7.50

Price $96.00 and up

To meet the demand for extra high grade prismatic spotting and team scopes, we build to order 2½" and 3" objective prismaticscopes which will fulfill the most critical spotting and observation requirements under all conditions.

The 2½" prismatic scope has an over all length of 19", conical tube, olive drab crystallized finish.

The 3" prismatic scope has an over all length of 25", conical tube, olive drab crystallized finish.

These instruments are sturdily constructed. The optical components are highly corrected to obtain the best results.

UNERTL TEAM AND PRISMATIC SPOTTING SCOPES

Unertl 2½" prismatic spotting and team scope with one eyepiece **$96.00**.
Unertl 3" prismatic spotting and team scope with one eyepiece **$175.00**.
Choice of eye-pieces 16X, 24X, 32X.
Extra eye-pieces **$8.50**.
Both scopes will be equipped on special order at the price of **$45.00** additional with a *3 eye-piece revolving turret*, each eyepiece having individual focusing adjustment.

A GOOD SPOTTING SCOPE IS A TARGET NECESSITY

SPOTTING SCOPES

WOLLENSAK SCOPES

ADJUSTABLE TRIPOD
Made of Aluminum Alloy
Well Built, Sturdy,
Black Lacquer and
Nickel Finish. 16 Oz.
Price **$7.50**

STANDARD ACHROMATIC TELESCOPES

Wide field of view with crispy sharpness, free from objectionable color fringes and distortion usually found in cheaper telescopes. Chromium plated draw tubes, mounted in felt, assure permanently smooth action for quick and accurate focusing. Supplied with leather cases. The 20X glass is highly recommended as a spotting scope on the rifle range.

Small bore holes can be spotted with clarity and detail from 15 feet to 100 yards. For longer ranges the higher powered telescopes are recommended. Collapsed this telescope is very compact and will fit nicely in the shooting kit.

In addition, to range purposes the telescope is very handy to have while on a hunting trip for searching for and locating game.

VARI-POWER TELESCOPES

Each Vari-Power Telescope gives *several* magnifications—not ust one. For instance, the 15 x 40 gives *SIX* different magnifications—15X, 20X, 25X, 30X, 35X, 40X. Change magnifications merely by drawing power (smallest) tube in or out. Now you can have a whole battery of telescopes for the price of one. Spot your object with low power, magnify it greatly with high power.

In appearance, the Vari-Power is same as the standard Achromatic 20X illustrated, but has adjustable power tube with various powers marked.

All have knurled focusing ring, non-wobble joints, chrome plated tubes, uniformly sharp vision at every magnification. Body tubes Vulcanized Morocco grain. Leather cases.

STANDARD ACHROMATIC TELESCOPES

Power	Objective	Length Extended	Length Closed	Draw Tubes	Field at 1000 yds.	Weight	Price
10X	⅞"	14¾"	5⅝"	3	33 yds.	7 oz.	$3.75
15X	1¼"	18⅝"	6½"	3	25 yds.	12 oz.	11.00
20X	1⁷⁄₁₆"	24⅝"	8"	3	21 yds.	17 oz.	14.00
25X	1¹¹⁄₁₆"	30¾"	9"	4	17 yds.	26 oz.	20.00
35X	1¹⁵⁄₁₆"	38½"	10⅞"	4	15 yds.	40 oz.	35.00
*45X	2¼"	46⅜"	12½"	4	13 yds.	65 oz.	47.50

VARI-POWER TELESCOPES

Model	Range of Magnifications	Diam. Object	Lengths Ext.	Lengths Closed	Tubes Including Power Tubes	Field of View at 1000 yds. Max. Power	Min.	Weight	Price
5 x 20	5X to 20X	⅞"	19¼"	7½"	2	50'	180'	11 oz.	$10.00
10 x 30	10X to 30X	1¼"	20¼"	8¼"	2	44'	100'	16 oz.	13.50
15 x 40	15X to 40X	1⁷⁄₁₆"	26¾"	8½"	3	31'	79'	20 oz.	16.50
20 x 50	20X to 50X	1¹¹⁄₁₆"	31½"	9"	4	25'	66'	31 oz.	22.50

BAUSCH & LOMB SPOTTING SCOPES

N.R.A. Model

The Bausch & Lomb N.R.A. Spotting 'Scope for rifle and pistol shooting was designed after consulting scores of riflemen. Every popular make of 'scope was closely examined in the endeavor to make the B. & L. model the very best.

Several models were built and thoroughly tested under every conceivable condition. Thus the B. & L. Spotting 'Scope was designed by riflemen for riflemen.

The 'scope can be focused on objects as near as forty feet. This means that it can be used just as effectively on indoor pistol ranges as at the longer distances.

Regularly furnished with 19.5X Eyepiece as standard. Metal protective lens caps on both ends. Finished in olive drab baked enamel, length 13 inches, weight 2 pounds, 6 ounces; 2 inch objective lens equipped with 19.5X Eyepiece.

Price	$55.00
Extra Eyepieces: 36.5X (Orthoscopic)	7.50
12.8X	6.00
26.X	6.00
Leather Carrying Case and Strap	7.00
B. & L. Tripod with new Ball and Socket Clamp	10.50
Metal Lens Container for individual lens protection	1.50

This new Bausch & Lomb Spotting Scope is designed to answer the sportsman's need for a bigger scope than the N.R.A. Model. With a 65mm objective, greater light-gathering ability is supplied by this scope; a desirable range of magnifications is obtained by either 13X, 20X or 27X eyepieces.

No. 61-41-32 65mm Spotting Scope with 20X eyepiece	$78.00
No. 61-44-75 13X Eyepiece	7.50
No. 61-44-77 27X Eyepiece	7.50

B. & L. DRAW TUBE SPOTTING SCOPE

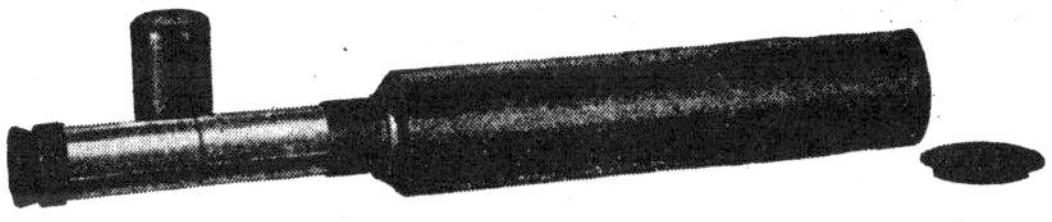

Riflemen everywhere are expressing enthusiasm over this new Bausch & Lomb Draw Tube erecting type Spotting 'Scope. Its power is 20X—ideal for all ranges used in small bore work. Therefore only one eyepiece (which is furnished) is necessary.

Its field of view of 7½ feet at 100 yards is ample for all ranges at which it will be used. Thus it is ideally suited to indoor as well as outdoor ranges.

A special micrometer focusing adjustment provides for push-pull coarse adjustment and screw fine adjustment. The body is made of aluminum alloy and has a durable, handsome black wrinkle finish with threaded metal caps.

SPECIFICATIONS—Size closed: 2¼ inches x 12⅝ inches over all. Extended: 17⅛ inches. Draw tube: 4⅞ inches. Weight: 2 pounds. Diameter of objective lens: 45 mm. Diameter of eyepiece lens: 10 mm.

Price $30.00

Binoctar 7X Magn.
Featherweight Model
Marine and night glass. This model is extensively used by the U. S. Navy. Price........$154.00

Binoctem
Featherweight Model
Same but with central focusing. Price $160.00

HUNTING BINOCULARS

The superiority of Zeiss Prism Binoculars lies in the material, the scientific construction and the workmanship. For hunting purposes a 6–8 times magnification is best recommended. A feature of the Zeiss Binoculars is their large field of view. It enables the eye to locate an object much more quickly and renders it easy to follow a swiftly moving object, such as a deer on the run or other rapidly moving game. For hunters the light transmitting power of the binocular, dependent on the diameter of the objective, is a deciding factor in failing light. The glasses pictured here are distinctive for this feature.

The new featherweight models are similar in every way to the regular models except that the weight has been reduced from 32% to 40%. Featherweight binoculars are preferred not only for the greater convenience with which they can be carried, but also for the greater steadiness and ease with which they can be held to the eyes for extended observation. Needless to say, the Featherweight models stand up optically and mechanically just as well as the standard weight models.

The SILVAMAR and SILVAREM are the most popular 6X all-purpose glasses for sports and general use. These glasses have a large field of view which is sharply defined up to the edge, and a high light transmitting power. They can, therefore, be used with success in advanced dusk, which is of importance to sportsmen and hunters. On the turf the SILVAREM is preferred, owing to its central focusing. The lightweight SILVAMAR weighs 12 ozs. and lists at $85.00, f.o.b. New York, and the SILVAREM, 13 ozs. at $90.00.

Deltar 8 X Magn.
Wide-Angle Featherweight Model
Price $209.00

The SPORTUR is a glass of 6 x magnification, available in Featherweight execution. It is a universal glass of typically fine Zeiss construction, at a price which will appeal to a large range of binocular users. Its large field of view, good light-transmitting power, and rapid adjustment by means of central focusing mechanism, make the Sportur an ideal glass for sports, traveling, hunting, etc. It weighs only 11¾ oz. and lists at $66.00.

The DELTRINTIS and DELTRINTEM have an 8X magnification and are wide-angle glasses eminently suitable for travel and all sports. The central focusing device provides easy and instantaneous adjustment for the DELTRINTEM, making it particularly suitable for sports. The DELTRINTIS weighs 13¾ ozs. and lists at $93.00, f.o.b. New York, and the DELTRINTEM, 14 ozs. at $99.00.

The TELAREM, 18X light weight models can be used as a view telescope. It is provided with central focusing, weighs 30 ozs. and lists at $202.00, f.o.b. New York.

Deltrintem 8 X Magn.
Featherweight Model
Price. $99.00

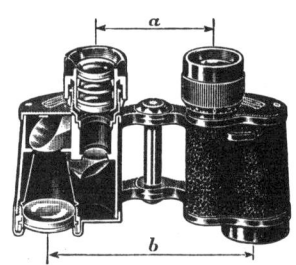

Path of Rays in Zeiss Binoculars

Sportur 6 X Magn.
Universal Glass
Featherweight Model
Price $66.00

Magnification	Diameter of objectives mm.	Weight of Binocular oz.	In tan or black leather case		Leather case only Price	In soft leather pouch		Soft leather pouch only
			Codeword	Price		Codeword	Price	
New Featherweight Models								
With Individual Focusing Eyepieces								
6X	30	12	Silvamar....	$85.00	$6.00	Silvamarwe...	$85.00	$6.00
7X	50	29½	Binoctar..	154.00	7.50			
8X	30	13¾	Deltrentis..	93.00	6.00	Deltrentiswe..	93.00	6.00
8X	40	34	Deltar...	209.00	7.50			
10X	50	30½	Dekaris....	171.00	7.50			
With Central Focusing Adjustment								
4X	20	10	*Turolem...	$85.00	$4.00	*Turolemwe...	$85.00	$4.00
6X	18	6	Telita.....	103.00	4.00	Telitawe.....	103.00	4.00
6X	24	11¾	Sportur....	66.00	6.00			
6X	30	13	Silvarem..	90.00	6.00	Silvaremwe...	90.00	6.00
7X	50	30½	Binoctem..	160.00	7.50			
7X	50	31¼	Septarem...	266.00	10.00			
8X	24	10¼	Turita.....	119.00	4.00	Turitawe.....	119.00	4.00
8X	30	14	Deltrintem..	99.00	6.00	Deltrintemwe..	99.00	6.00
8X	40	35½	Deltarem...	215.00	7.50			
10X	50	31½	Dekarem...	178.00	7.50			
15X	60	45	Delfortem..	228.00	15.00			
18X	50	30	Telarem...	202.00	7.50			

Deltrentis 8 X Magn.
Featherweight Model
Price $93.00

Silvamar 6 X Magn.
Hunting and Marine Glass
Featherweight Model
Price $85.00

A FINE FIELD GLASS IS A NECESSITY FOR THE HUNTER

AMERICA'S GREAT GUN HOUSE

BAUSCH & LOMB BINOCULARS AND FIELD GLASSES

Binoculars are scientific instruments and the best facilities and highest skill are required in their manufacture. Like other products of modern science binoculars are manufactured in various styles and types. The prism binocular has been developed to meet various uses: Highpower glasses for observation at great distances, medium power glasses for studying moderately distant objects and lower power for following moving objects. Bausch and Lomb Glasses besides having the proper and exact requirements for focusing, magnification, field of view, clarity of vision, alignment and brightness are as light and compact as it is practical to make them.

B. & L. BINOCULARS

Central Focusing

PRISMATIC
DESCRIPTION AND PRICES

Power	Focus	Diameter of Object in MM	Linear Field in Yds. at 1,000 Yds.	Weight in Oz.	Price with Case
6X	Individual	30mm	150	19½	$66.00
6X	Central	30mm	150	19½	72.00
7X	Individual	35mm	127	26	81.00
7X	Central	35mm	127	26	86.00
8X	Individual	30mm	150	22	76.00
8X	Central	30mm	150	22	82.00
8X	Central	40mm	112	30	98.00
8X	Individual	40mm	112	30	93.00
9X	Individual	35mm	127	26	88.50
9X	Central	35mm	127	26	93.50
7X	Individual	50mm	128	42	118.00
10X	Individual	50mm	93	41	132.00

B. & L. BINOCULARS

Individual Focusing

The Balar Field Glass

Here is an entirely new type of Field glass. It can be carried in the vest-pocket without bulging. It is made of black moulded plastic. Metal parts are of a special alloy for lightness. The size of the Balar is only 1³⁄₁₆″ thick, 4⁵⁄₃₂″ wide and 2¼″ high. Precision focusing is quick and easy by means of the conveniently located knurled button. The field of view at 1000 Yards is 453 feet. The images are crisp and brilliant. Weight only 6 ounces.
Price with genuine leather case **$19.50**

THE COMPANION GLASS

4x Magnification

A very fine field glass, weighing only 10½ ounces. Has a field of view 382 feet at 1000 yards. Ideal for hunting and observation. Supplied with an attractive durable leather case and shoulder strap.
Price **$19.50**

NIGHTHAWK

(Achromatic Oculars)

A small and compact but very powerful glass, 7X, weighs only 11 ounces with universal focus adjustment. The ideal glass for the hunter and sportsman. Comes with leather case.
Price $41.50

FIELD GLASS

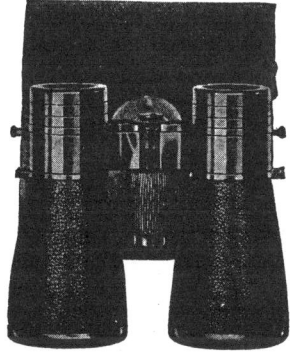

Sharp achromatic lenses, 4X, recommended for observation of moving game. With handsome leather case.
Price $17.50

HUNTER GLASS

A feather weight glass of the finest optical construction. Has very sharp definition and greatest brilliancy. A glass which is the favorite of hunters, trappers and shooters due to its compactness and light weight. Comes with fine strong leather case. To be had in two styles.
Hunter No. 1—8x30 Power Price......$56.00
Hunter No. 2—6x30 Power Price......54.00

ALL SHIPMENTS ARE INSURED

BINOCULARS *For Outdoor Life*

INEXPENSIVE, LIGHTWEIGHT, ALL-AMERICAN GLASSES

For the hunter with a limited budget and yet desiring the distinct advantage of glasses these American-made models are in a class by themselves. Designed for maximum quality of design, operation and construction the Trojan line offers amazing values. Lightweight construction, optically ground lenses and smooth operating adjustment mechanism are features of these low-priced glasses which are usually found only in more expensive lines.

Trojan No. 27 Binocular

An outstanding popular priced glass ideally suited for hunter, tourist or sports fan. Three power lenses are carefully ground and matched to assure a sharp, clear view. Hinger bridge adjusts the glass to the individual user's eyes. Black enamel finish. Grain leatherette body covering and soft leather case and carrying strap.

$1.85

Trojan No. 20 Junior Scope

An extremely handy glass to carry to all outdoor events. It provides 3 power magnification yet is only 2½ inches long when closed. For bird and wild life study this junior scope is an excellent choice. Sold only when included with orders amounting to five dollars or more.

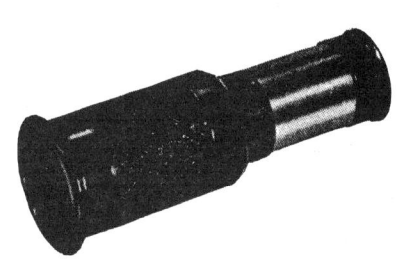

$0.35

Trojan No. 31 Binocular

A real sport glass that is lightweight, compact and easy to carry. Can easily be put in your pocket and used at sporting events, for bird study or for hunting. 2½ power 30 mm lenses are optically ground and polished. Black enamel finish and leatherette covering. Height when closed is 2 inches and width 4 inches. Weighs but 6 ounces. Supplied with convenient carrying case with snap fastener.

$1.50

Trojan No. 40 Field Glass

A new and extremely attractive low priced field glass. It is extensively used and recommended for hunting, fishing, sailing and every other type of outdoor sport. 3 power 40 mm lenses are scientifically matched. Black baked enamel finish and handsome leatherette barrel covering. Furnished with a smart heavy gauge sport carrying case.

$2.50

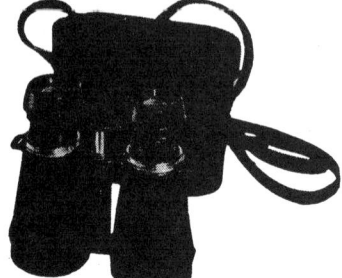

Trojan No. 34 Binocular

A real quality field glass at a price within every hunter's budget. Die cast frame assures long life and positive focus. Lenses can be taken off for easy cleaning. Full 3 power 40 mm objectives give a wide clear view that is so essential in a hunting glass. Furnished with a convenient neck strap and handy carrying case.

$3.50

Trojan No. 36 Field Glass

For spotting and observing game this quality field glass is excellent. 3½ power 40 mm objective lenses assure a clear close-up that means added usefulness. Rigid construction with many brass and aluminum parts provide a rugged glass that will stand up under the most severe outdoor conditions. A real glass within reach of every hunter.

$4.00

POPULAR PRICED GLASSES FOR THE HUNTER

ACHROMATIC GLASSES

A good field glass in many cases is not a luxury but actually a necessity. Better hunting, bird study, target shooting and exploring demands a clear close-up. The Achromatic glasses shown on this page are especially recommended for those who demand the finest in field and sport glasses. Each model is entirely American-made and has Achromatic lenses which mean no artificial color fringe just a clear, sharp view. A wide selection of models enables the hunter and sportsman to select the glass to best suit his purpose—and purse. The best in design from the mechanical point of view as well as appearance means complete satisfaction in every respect. American production methods enable these quality glasses to be brought to you at lower prices. Each glass is backed by an unconditional guarantee.

TROJAN No. 33A

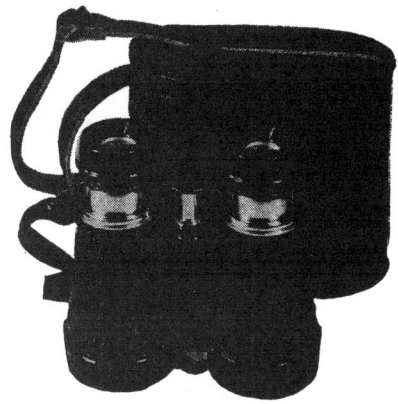

A good all around glass for sports use. It is compact, ruggedly constructed and beautifully finished. 3 power Achromatic 40 mm lenses give a wide clear field. Especially good for following moving game and picking out land marks. Size, 3¾" high when open, 5" when closed. Weight 14 ounces. Supplied with leather neck and case straps and heavy gauge leatherette carrying case. **$8.75**

AIRGUIDE No. 45A and No. 46A Field Glass

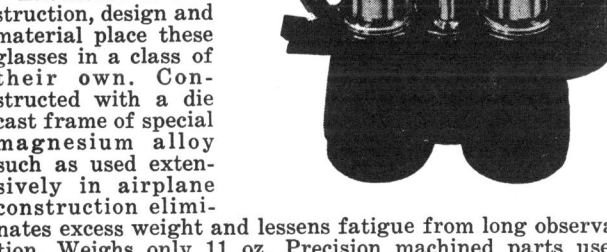

Excellence of construction, design and material place these glasses in a class of their own. Constructed with a die cast frame of special magnesium alloy such as used extensively in airplane construction eliminates excess weight and lessens fatigue from long observation. Weighs only 11 oz. Precision machined parts used throughout assure long and trouble-free life. Supplied with genuine leather carrying case and straps.
No. 45A—3X 40 mm Achromatic lenses **$12.00**
No. 46A—4X 40 mm Achromatic lenses **13.00**

AIRGUIDE No. 47A Field Glass

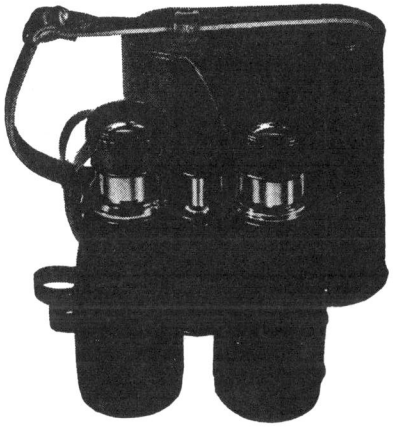

A powerful five power glass with the very finest of design and construction. Ideal for target work, observing game at a distance and wherever more power is desired. Magnesium die cast frame for extra light weight. 40 mm objectives allow brilliant illumination. This glass is especially recommended for night use. Supplied with leather carrying case and straps. Weight only 12 ounces. **$14.50**

No. 44A SPORT AND OPERA GLASS

Here is a precision built sport glass that weighs only 3½ ounces! No longer is it necessary to use a glass that tires your arm by its own weight. Extra wide field of 600 feet at 1,000 makes it easy to follow action whether you are hunting, watching a football game or at the races. 2½ power Achromatic lenses makes the object stand out in great detail and without any artificial coloring. Construction is of magnesium alloy, aluminum and brass. Bakelite eyepieces and adjusting knob. Attractively finished in soft grey lacquer. Supply with soft leather zipper carrying case.
Price **$14.00**

IT'S FUN TO HUNT WITH ONE OF THESE

WOLLENSAK BINOCULARS AND SPORT GLASSES

Watch him without making him run

A good field glass is an absolute necessity for the hunter. More than once you will hear the old story, "I saw something moving, too bad I did not have a pair of field glasses." Many steps can be saved and the valuable time lost could be used more successfully if you have a pair of these inexpensive but perfect optical field glasses with you. Now you can afford to buy a real fine American made product at a low price.

Find him before he sees you.

---

8 X 30 PRISM BINOCULAR

Unequalled for quality and beauty at anywhere near its popular price. In size and appearance, with its deep morocco grain it attracts instant favorable attention. Experience has shown that the most wanted power for widespread general use is 8 magnifications. The Wollensak is 8 power. Central focusing, with independently focused right eye-piece. Metal frame of castaluminum, for lightness, movable metal parts of stout brass, for durability. Complete with genuine leather case and two straps, as illustrated. Sharp color-free image, wide field, moisture-proof and dust-proof. The optical quality is surpassed only by glasses far, far higher in price, and is notably fine, even at first glance.

Magnification—8 diameters; Lenses—objectives, 30 mm diameter; eye-pieces, 17 mm; Exit pupil—3.5 mm; Relative brightness (light transmitting power)—12.3; Field of View at 1,000 yds.—135 yds.; Angular Field—7° 44'; Pupillary Distance—adjustable between 48 mm and 72 mm; Length—closed, 4¼ in.; extended, 4⅝ in.; Focusing—central; right ocular adjustable individually; Weight—18 oz.

Price $39.75

6X BIASCOPE

A light-weight six-power field glass for hunting, fishing, hiking, motoring, sailing or any place out of doors. It has an excellent achromatic optical system that gives a large, clear field of view, free from objectionable color fringes. It has the quickest one finger focusing device known and because of its compact size, it fits comfortably in the coat pocket. Made in six colors: Black, Oak, Mahogany, Green, Mottled Orange and Black, or Mottled Red and Black. Supplied with genuine leather case. Thousands are in satisfactory use everywhere by owners who are enthusiastic over this unusually fine glass at its popular price.

Magnification	6-power	Width	3¾"
Diameter of objective lens	1"	Thickness	1 9/32"
Height closed	3 11/32"	Weight	4½ oz.
Height extended	3 9/16"	Price	$5.00

ALLSCOPE

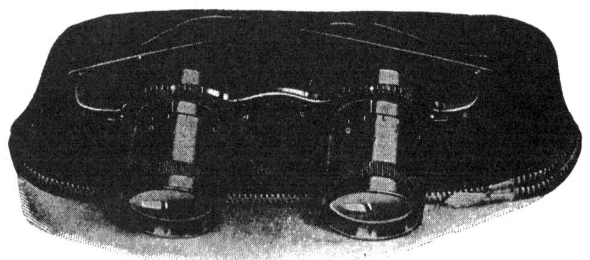

Really telescopic spectacles that fit the face as comfortably and securely as a pair of eyeglasses. Recommended for all sporting events. Give exceptionally wide vision and clear view. Supplied with leather case.
Model A, 2 power.. $14.00
Model B, 3¼ power... 16.00

4X COMMANDER

An excellent bird, sport and opera glass. Magnification four power, diameter objective lenses 1⅜", size 2⅝" high, 4⅛" wide. Weight seven ounces. Center screw focusing. Leather case and neck strap
$12.50

POCKESCOPE

A compact telescope designed for pocket use. Not much larger than a jackknife but a real telescope and a leader in its class. Precision lenses, black lacquered barrel and nickel-plated draw tubes. Furnished with genuine leather case.

	Power	Length Closed	Length Extended	Diameter	Price
Pockescope Jr.	3X	2⅝"	3 5/16"	¾"	$1.00
Pockescope Sr.	6X	3¼"	3 9/16"	1 3/16"	$2.00

BEST QUALITY SHOOTING GLASSES
B. & L. RAY BAN SUN GLASSES

To fill the demand of the shooter, hunter and sportsman for a real sun glass, Bausch and Lomb has developed a new orthogon Ray-Ban single vision lens outclassing all ordinary sun goggles. Objects seen through Ray-Ban's have the same comparative color relationship as when viewed with the naked eye. Ray-Bans are completely adjustable, at nose piece and temples, thus insuring perfect fit for every one. They are ideal for every purpose and indispensable for the hunter, target-trap and skeet shooter. Each pair is supplied with a sturdy leather case giving full protection.

 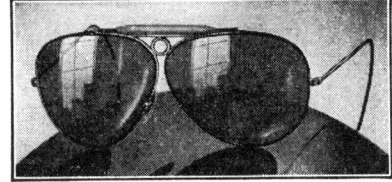 

Ray Ban Special Shooting Glass, America's Finest for maximum eye sight protection and efficiency. Size 62x54, 5 mm in metal case. Choice of Ray Ban or Kalichrome. Ray Ban has a greenish tint, the Kalichrome yellowish. The latter eliminates haze but is not glare reducing.
Price $12.50

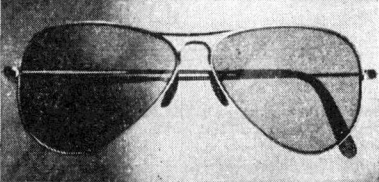  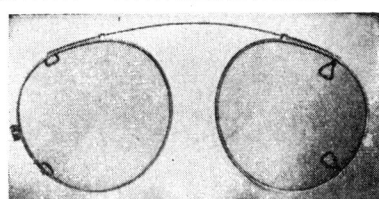

Ray Ban Sun Glass with Metal frame
size 58x51 mm. Price $7.75
Ray Ban Sun Glass with Metal frame
size 52x44.5 mm. Price 7.75
(State white or gold color frame desired)

Ray Ban Sun Glass with Zylonite frame
size 58x51 mm. Price $6.00
Ray Ban Sun Glass with Zylonite frame
size 52x44.5 mm. Price 6.00

Hook-over Ray Ban Sun Glass to fit
any eye glasses. Price $4.75
(State white or gold color frame desired)

POLAROID GLASSES
View Without Glare

  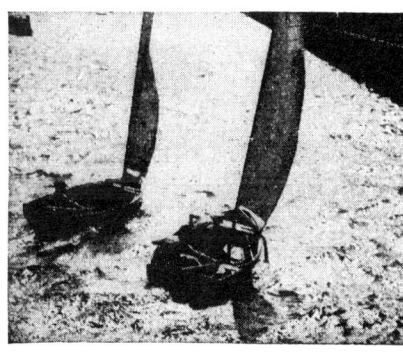

Your own eyes can see—*instantly*—the dramatic difference between Polaroid Glasses and any other sunglasses.
Even the finest of the usual sunglasses darken everything equally—the things you want to see and the glare don't.
Polaroid Glasses *greatly darken the glare* but darken the view only a little. *They give you the view without the glare.*
See a demonstration of this miraculous new scientific light control at:
Price $1.95

Through Polaroid Day Glasses

Through Ordinary Sun Glasses

UNIVERSAL APERTURE SHOOTING SPECTACLES

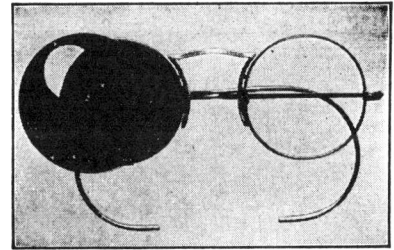

Makes Trap and Rifle Shooting a Pleasure

Interchangeable Right or Left. Various Apertures and Wide Open Center, Instantly. Totally shields eye from diagonal light rays, giving Maximum Definition. No "fussing" with slipping adjustments. Optometrist can insert lenses if imperatively needed. Don't shoot with your ordinary glasses.
Price $5.00

TUBASCOPE

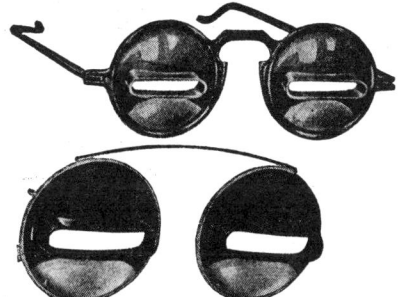

The National Vision Shooting Spectacles
See everything in natural colors without distortion of colored glasses. For hunting, shooting and all outdoor spectator sports.
Regular Tubascope $1.00
Slip Over Tubascope to fit over small eye-
glasses, 42 m/m 1.00
Slip Over Tubascope for large eye-glasses
m/m 1.00
Special Optical made Tubascope 3.00

STOEGER'S SHOOTING GLASSES

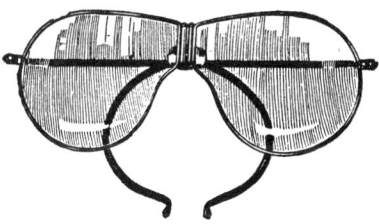

**Orthoptic Principle, No Lenses Are Required
Save Eyesight, Lay Aside Makeshifts
Secure Shooting Comfort**

DESCRIPTION—The frame is yellow gold filled —not plated. Temples covered with brown, moisture proof tubing. Brown case with brown lining to match, supplied with each one.

Price, each $5.00

LET A GOOD SHOOTING GLASS IMPROVE YOUR SCORE

.22 RIM FIRE CARTRIDGES
WESTERN — WINCHESTER

STANDARD VELOCITY

NON-CORROSIVE

Factory No.	Cartridge	Wt. of Bullet Grains	Style of Bullet	Price Per Box
K1201R	.22 BB	19	Lub. C'd	$0.37*
K1202R	.22 CB	29	Lub. C'd†	.41*
K1211R	.22 Short KANT-SPLASH	24	Synthetic†	.23
K1229R	.22 Extra Long	40	Lub. C'd†	.50
K1232R	.22 W. R. F. (22 Rem. Special)	45	Lub. C'd#	.56
K1236R	.22 Winchester Automatic	45	Lub. C'd#	.56
K1237R	.22 Winchester Auto. Hollow Point	45	Lub. C'd#	.59
K1238R	.22 Remington Autoloading	45	Lub. C'd#	.56

* Per Box of 100.

STAYNLESS

Factory No.	Cartridge	Wt. of Bullet Grains	Style of Bullet	Price Per Box
K2003R	B. B. caps	18	Lead	$0.37*
K2006R	C. B. caps	29	Lead Lub.*	.41*
K2361R	.22 Short Spotlight	26	Lead	.27
K2211R	Spatterproof .22 Short (1000 in carton)	26	Synthetic	4.44
K2311R	Spatterproof .22 Short (1000 in carton)	26	Wax C'd♦	4.44
K2213R	Spatterproof .22 Short (50 in carton)	26	Wax C'd♦	.23
K2212R	.22 Extra Long, lead lubricated	40	Lead Lub.†	.50
K2276R	.22 W. R. F. lead	45	Ins. Lub.*	.56
K2267R	.22 W. R. F. Kopperklad	45	Ins. Lub.*	.56
K2278R	.22 Automatic, lead	45	Ins. Lub.*	.56
K2205R	.22 Automatic, Kopperklad	45	Ins. Lub.*	.56
K2279R	.22 Automatic, H. P., Kopperklad	45	Ins. Lub.*	.59

INTERMEDIATE VELOCITY

XPERT

K1262R	.22 Short	29	Lead Gr.	$0.21
K1263R	.22 Long	29	Lead Gr.	.27
K1264R	.22 Long Rifle	40	Lead Gr	.34

LEADER

K2383R	.22 Short, lead lubricated	29	Lead Lub.†	$0.21
K2386R	.22 Long, lead lubricated	29	Lead Lub.†	.27
K2388R	.22 Long Rifle, lead lubricated	40	Lead Lub.†	.34

HIGH VELOCITY

SUPER-X

K1208R	.22 Short	29	Lub. C'd♦	$0.21
K1209R	.22 Short Hollow Point	27	Lub. C'd♦	.26
K1216R	.22 Long	29	Lub. C'd♦	.27
K1217R	.22 Long Hollow Point	27	Lub. C'd♦	.32
K1225R	.22 Long Rifle	40	Lub. C'd♦	.34
K1226R	.22 Long Rifle Hollow Point	37	Lub. C'd♦	.36
K1234R	.22 W. R. F. (22 Rem. Spec.)	45	Lub. C'd#	.56
K1235R	.22 W. R. F. Hollow Point	45	Lub. C'd#	.59

SUPER SPEED

K2214R	.22 Short, Kopperklad	29	Wax C'd♦	$0.21
K2215R	.22 Short, H. P. Kopperklad	27	Wax C'd♦	.26
K2216R	.22 Long, Kopperklad	29	Wax C'd♦	.27
K2217R	.22 Long, H. P. Kopperklad	27	Wax C'd♦	.32
K2208R	.22 Long Rifle, Kopperklad	40	Wax C'd♦	.34
K2207R	.22 Long Rifle H. P., Kopperklad	37	Wax C'd♦	.36
K2220R	.22 W. R. F., Kopperklad	45	Ins. Lub.* / Wax C'd♦	.56
K2221R	.22 W. R. F., H. P., Kopperklad	40	Ins. Lub.* / Wax C'd♦	.59

MATCH CARTRIDGES

K1228R	.22 Long Rifle SUPER-MATCH	40	Lead Gr.	$0.48
K1267R	.22 Long Rifle SUPER-MATCH, MK. 2	40	Lead Gr.	.48
K2238R	Precision EZXS .22 Long Rifle, Lesmok	40	Lead Lub.†	$0.48
K2340R	All-x Match, .22 Long Rifle, Staynless	40	Lead Lub.†	.48

Lub. C'd—Lubaloy Coated. Lead Gr.—Lead Greased.
† Greased. ♦ Wax Coated. # Inside Lubricated.

* Inside lubricated. ♦ Wax coated. † Lead lubricated.

ORDER BLANK IN MIDDLE AND INDEX IN BACK OF CATALOG

.22 RIM FIRE CARTRIDGES
REMINGTON   PETERS'

STANDARD VELOCITY

KLEANBORE

Factory No.	Packed 50 in a Box Except: B. B. and C. B. Packed 100 in a box; .22 Gallery 250 in a box	Wt. of Bullet Grains	Style of Bullet	Price Per Box
R2	.22 (B. B.) Bullet Breech Caps, K'BORE...	20	Lead	$0.37
R6	.22 (C. B.) Conical Bullet Caps, K'BORE..	29	Lead	.41
R32L	.22 Short, Gallery Special, Spatterless, KLEANBORE	30	Lead	1.11
R17	.22 Long Rifle, KLEANBORE.............	40	Lead	.34
R25	.22 Extra Long, KLEANBORE............	40	Lead	.50
R28	.22 W. R. F. (Rem. Spec.), Inside Lubricated, KLEANBORE...............	45	Lead	.56
R31B	.22 Remington, Autoloading, KLEANBORE	45	Lead	.56
R31	.22 Winchester, Automatic, KLEANBORE	45	Lead	.56
R31A	.22 Win., Automatic, Hollow Pt., K'BORE	45	Lead	.58

RUSTLESS

Factory No.	Packed 50 in a Box except: B. B. and C. B. Packed 100 in a box; Gallery Krumble Ball 250 in a box	Wt. of Bullet Grains	Style of Bullet	List Price Per Box
112	.22 B. B. Cap, Round Ball...............	20	Lead	$0.37
2241	.22 C. B. Cap, Conical Ball, Filmkote....	29	Lead	.41
2204	.22 Short Gallery, "Krumble Ball," Lub...	29	Lead	1.45
2295	.22 Short Gallery, "Krumble Ball," Fk....	29	Lead	.45
2298	.22 Extra Long, Filmkote................	40	Lead	.51
2281	.22 Winchester, Mod. 1890..............	45	Lead	.56
2237	.22 Winchester Automatic..............	45	Lead	.56
2238	.22 Winchester Automatic, Hollow Point..	45	Lead	.59
2239	.22 Remington Auto.-Loading...........	45	Lead	.56

INTERMEDIATE VELOCITY

NEW AND IMPROVED

R12	.22 Short, New and Improved, K'BORE...	29	Lead	$0.21
R15	.22 Long, New and Improved, K'BORE...	29	Lead	.27
*R19	.22 Long Rifle, New and Improved, K'BORE	40	Lead	.34

* Remington special formula of bullet lubricant supplied. Dry lubricant furnished only on special orders for case lots of 10M cartridges.

TARGET

2214	.22 "Target," Short Lub...............	29	Lead	$0.21
2218	.22 "Target," Long Lub................	29	Lead	.27
2224	.22 "Target," Long Rifle Lub...........	40	Lead	.34

HIGH VELOCITY

HI-SPEED

R11	.22 Short, Hi-Speed, KLEANBORE.......	29	Lead	$0.21
R13	.22 Short, Hi-Speed, Hollow Pt., K'BORE..	27	Lead	.26
R16	.22 Long, Hi-Speed, KLEANBORE........	29	Lead	.27
R18	.22 Long, Hi-Speed, Hollow Pt., K'BORE.	27	Lead	.32
R21	.22 Long Rifle, Hi-Speed, KLEANBORE...	40	Lead	.34
R23	.22 Long Rifle, Hi-Speed, Hollow Point....	36	Lead	.36
R28S	.22 W. R. F. (Rem. Spec.), Hi-Speed, Inside Lubricated, KLEANBORE...............	45	Lead	.56
R28AS	.22 W. R. F. (Rem. Spec.), Hi-Speed, Hollow Point, Inside Lubr., KLEANBORE.	40	Lead	.59

HIGH VELOCITY

2267	.22 Short, Filmkote, HIGH VELOCITY...	29	Lead	$0.21
2268	.22 Short, Hol. Pt., Filmkote, HIGH VELOCITY	27	Lead	.26
2269	.22 Long, Filmkote, HIGH VELOCITY...	29	Lead	.27
2270	.22 Long, Hol. Pt., Filmkote, HIGH VELOCITY	27	Lead	.32
2283	.22 Long Rifle, Filmkote, HIGH VELOCITY	40	Lead	.34
2284	.22 Long Rifle, H. P., F'mk't, HIGH VELOCITY	36	Lead	.36
2291	.22 Winchester, HIGH VELOCITY..... ¶	45	Lead	.56
2292	.22 Winchester, Hol. Pt., HIGH VELOCITY.............................. ¶	40	Lead	.59

MATCH CARTRIDGES

R54PM	.22 Long Rifle, Palma Match, Lead Lubricated, for fine target shooting, LESMOK..	40	Lead	$0.48
R54P	.22 Long Rifle, Palma, Lead Lubricated, for fine target shooting, KLEANBORE....	40	Lead	.48
R22T	.22 Long Rifle, Police Targetmaster, Lubricated, KLEANBORE................	40	Lead	.48

STANDARD VELOCITY

2226	.22 L. R. "Tackhole," Lesmok Lub........	40	Lead	$0.48
2296	.22 L. R. "Dewar" Lub.................	40	Lead	.48
2223	.22 L. R. "Police Match"...............	40	Lead	.48

PISTOL AND REVOLVER CARTRIDGES

REMINGTON		PETERS		CARTRIDGE	WINCHESTER		WESTERN	
STYLE OF BULLET	BULLET WEIGHT GR.	STYLE OF BULLET	BULLET WEIGHT GR.		STYLE OF BULLET	BULLET WEIGHT GR.	STYLE OF BULLET	BULLET WEIGHT GR.
M. C.	60	M. C.	50	**CAL. 25 AUTOMATIC (6.35 m/m)** — 50 Per Box — Price $1.50 For Colt, Browning, Mauser, Walther, H. R. and others.	F. P.	50	M. C.	50
Lead	88	Lead	88	**CAL. 32 S. & W.** — 50 Per Box — Price $1.08 For Smith & Wesson, Colt, Iver Johnson, H. R. and other Revolvers.	Lead	85	Lub. C'd	85
Lead Lead Lead	98 98 ⅜ 100	Lead Lead P.M. Lead	98 98 100	**CAL. 32 S. & W. LONG (32 New Police)** — 50 Per Box — Price $1.20 For Smith & Wesson, Colt, H. & R. and other Revolvers	Lead	98	Lub. C'd	98
Lead	80	Lead	80	**CAL. 32 SHORT COLT** — 50 Per Box — Price $1.08 For Colt, Webley, Marlin 1892 and others.	Lead	80	Lub. C'd	80
Lead	82	Lead	82	**CAL. 32 LONG COLT** — 50 Per Box — Price $1.20 For Colt, Webley and others.	Lead	82	Lub. C'd	82
M. C.	71	M. C.	71	**CAL. 32 AUTOMATIC (7.65 m/m)** — 50 Per Box — Price $1.63 For Colt, Browning, Mauser, Walther, Webley and other Pocket Auto. Pistols.	F. P.	74	M. C.	74
Lead M. C. S. P. Mush	100 100 100 80†	Lead S. P. M. C. M.C.H.P. S. P.	100 100 100 80† 100†	**CAL. 32 WINCHESTER (.32-20)** — 50 Per Box — Prices Lead $1.89, F.P.M.C.H.P. 1.97, S. P., Mush 1.97 For Winchester, Marlin, Remington, Savage, Colt and other guns.	Lead F. P. S. P. H. P. S. P.	100 115 115 80† 115†	Lub. C'd M. C. S. P. O. P. E.	115 115 115 80†
M. C.	85	...	...	**CAL. .30 MAUSER (7.63 m/m)** — 50 Per Box — Price $2.34 For Mauser Pistol Military Model. Mauser Military. (Pistol also made for 9 m/m Luger cartridge.)	F. P.	86	M. C.	86
M. C. S. P. H. P.	93 93 93	S. P. M. C. M.C.H.P.	93 93 93	**CAL. .30 LUGER (7.65 m/m)** — 50 Per Box — Price $2.34 For 7.65 m/m (Cal. .30) Luger Pistols. (Luger Pistols also made in 9 m/m.)	F. P. H. S. P.	93 93	M. C. S. P.	93 93
M. C. H. P.	124 124	M. C. M.C.H.P.	124 124	**CAL. 9 m/m LUGER PISTOL** — 50 Per Box — Price $2.43 The 9 m/m Luger cartridge is used by the German Army since 1908 and known as Model 08.	F. P. H. S. P.	125 125	M. C. H. S. P.	125 125
Lead Lead	146 150	Lead Lead Lead	146 200 150	**CAL. .38 S. & W. (.38 New Police)** — 50 Per Box — Price $1.40 For Colt, Smith & Wesson Revolvers and others.	Lead Lead Lead	145 200 150	Lub. C'd Lub. C'd Lub. C'd	145 200 150

FOR EXPLANATION OF REFERENCE MARKS AND ABBREVIATIONS SEE PAGE 234.

SEE INSIDE FRONT COVER "HOW TO ORDER"

PISTOL AND REVOLVER CARTRIDGES

REMINGTON		PETERS		CARTRIDGE	WINCHESTER		WESTERN	
STYLE OF BULLET	BULLET WEIGHT GR.	STYLE OF BULLET	BULLET WEIGHT GR.		STYLE OF BULLET	BULLET WEIGHT GR.	STYLE OF BULLET	BULLET WEIGHT GR.
Lead	125	Lead	125	**CAL. .38 SHORT COLT** — 50 Per Box — Price $1.40 — For Colt Revolvers and others, also Rifles.	Lead	130	Lub. C'd	130
Lead	150	Lead	150	**CAL. .38 LONG COLT** — 50 Per Box — Price $1.59 — For Colt D. A. Smith & Wesson, Colt Army Special, D. A. Pol. Pos. Special and others.	Lead	150	Lub. C'd	150
Lead	158	Lead	158	**CAL. .38 COLT SPECIAL** — 50 Per Box — Price $1.66 — For Colt and other revolvers.	Lead	158	...	...
Lead / Lead / Met. Pt.	158 / 200 / 158	Lead / Lead / M. P.	158 / 200 / 158	**CAL. .38 SMITH & WESSON SPECIAL** — 50 Per Box — Prices Lead $1.66, M. P. Met. Pt. 1.99 — For Colt and Smith & Wesson revolvers and others.	Lead / M. P. / Lead	158 / 158 / 200	Lub. C'd / M. P.	158 / 158
Lead / Lead T.G. / Lead R.N.	146 / 146 / 158	Lead P.M. / Lead W.C. / Lead P.M.	158 / 146 / 146	**CAL. .38 S. & W. SPECIAL SHARPSHOULDER** (Mid Range & Target Loads) — 50 Per Box — Prices Lead $1.44, F. C., T. G., R. N. 1.66 — For Colt, Smith & Wesson revolvers and others.	Lead / Lead F.C.	148 / 148	Lead W.C. / Lead F.C.	148 / 148
Lead / Met. Pt. / SP'L	158 / 158 / 110	SPCL. / Lead / M. P.	110 / 158 / 158	**CAL. .38 S. & W. SPECIAL (38-44)** (Special Loads) — 50 Per Box — Hi Velocity, Hi Speed, Super Speed — Prices Lub. C'd, Lead $1.87, SPCL., Met. Pt. 1.99, Met. Pt. 1.99 — For Colt and Smith & Wesson heavy frame revolvers.	Lead / M. P. / Met. Pt.	158 / 158 / 150	Lub. C'd / M. P.† / Lub. C'd	150 / 150 / 200
M. C.	95	M. C.	95	**CAL. .380 AUTOMATIC** — 50 Per Box — Price $2.02 — For Colt, Walther, Remington, Ortgies, and other .380 auto. pistols.	F. P.	95	M. C.	95
Met. Pt.	158	Lead	158	**CAL. .357 MAGNUM HIGH-SPEED** — 50 Per Box — Price M. P. $2.25, Lead 2.14 — For Colt and Smith & Wesson Magnum revolvers.	Lead	158	Lub. C'd / M. P.	158
M. C. / Mush	130† / 130†	M. C. / M.C.H.P. / M. C.	130 / 130† / 130†	**CAL. .38 SUPER AUTOMATIC** — 50 Per Box — Price $2.17 — For use in Colt Super Automatic pistols.	F. P. / H. S. P.	130† / 130†	M. C.	130†
S. P. / Mush	180 / 145†	S. P. / S. P.	180 / 180†	**CAL. .38 WINCHESTER (.38-40)** — 50 Per Box — Price $2.16 — For various Winchester, Marlin, Remington and Colt rifles, also S. & W. and Colt revolvers.	F. P. / S. P. / S. P.	180 / 180 / 180†	S. P.	180
Lead	195	Lead	195	**CAL. .41 LONG COLT** — 50 Per Box — Price $1.80 — For Colt D. A. and Single Action revolvers.	Lead	196	Lub. C'd	200

FOR EXPLANATION OF REFERENCE MARKS AND ABBREVIATIONS SEE PAGE 234.

PISTOL AND REVOLVER CARTRIDGES

REMINGTON		PETERS		CARTRIDGE	WINCHESTER		WESTERN	
STYLE OF BULLET	BULLET WEIGHT GR.	STYLE OF BULLET	BULLET WEIGHT GR.		STYLE OF BULLET	BULLET WEIGHT GR.	STYLE OF BULLET	BULLET WEIGHT GR.
Lead	246	Lead	246	**CAL. .44 S. & W. RUSSIAN** — 50 Per Box — Price $2.17. For S. & W. Russian and special models, Colt New Service revolvers also Remington single shot TARGET pistol and Colt S. A. Army.	Lead	246	Lub. C'd	246
Lead Met. Pt.	246 246	Lead M. P.	246 246	**CAL. .44 S. & W. SPECIAL** — 50 Per Box — Price Lead $2.27, M.P. 2.24. For use in S. & W. .44 cal. revolvers.	Lead	246	Lub. C'd	246
S. P. Mush	200 160†	S. P. S. P.	200 200†	**CAL. .44-40 WINCHESTER** — 50 Per Box — Price $2.20. For use in various Winchester, Marlin and Colt rifles also Colt, S. & W. and other revolvers.	S. P. S. P.	200 200†	S. P.	200
Lead	250	Lead	250	**CAL. .45 COLT** — Price $2.22. For Colt revolvers.	Lead	255	Lub. C'd	255
M. C. M. C. T. M. P. B.	230 230 173†	M.C.P.M. M. C. H.P.M.P.	230 230 173	**CAL. .45 AUTOMATIC** — 50 Per Box — Price M. C. $2.64, M. C. T. 2.64, M. P. B. 2.80. For Colt .45 automatic pistols.	F. P.	230	M. C. M.C.M.P.	230 230†
M. C. Lead	230 230	M. C. Lead	230 230	**CAL. .45 AUTO. RIM** — 50 Per Box — Price M. C. $2.64, Lead 2.63. For S. & W. Military and Colt New Service 1917 revolvers.	F. P. Lead	230 230	M. C.	280

EXPLANATION OF SYMBOLS USED

† Super Speed, Hi Velocity, Hi Speed, Super X.

* Lub. C'd—Lubaloy Coated.

Lead P. M.—Lead Police Match Wad Cutter.

Sharp Shoulder.

H. S. P.—Hollow Soft Point.

Lead P. M.—Police Match.

T. G.—TARGETMASTER Sharp Shoulder.

R. N.—Round Nose TARGETMASTER.

Sp'l—'Hiway' Master Metal Penetrating.

Met. Pt.—Metal Point.

Lead W. C.—Wadcutter.

Lead P. M.—Police Match Wad Cutter.

Spcl.—Highway PATROL Metal Penetrating.

Lead F. C.—Full Charge Wad Cutter

Metal Pc.—Metal Piercing.

M. P.†—Metal Piercing.

M. C. T.—Targetmaster Metal Case.

M. P. B.—Hi-Way Master Metal Penetrating.

M. C. P. M.—Metal Case 'Police Match.'

H. P. M. P.—'Highway-Patrol' Metal Penetrating.

M. C. M. P.—Metal Case Metal Piercing.

A NEW GUN CARRIES A FACTORY GUARANTEE

ELEMENTARY BALLISTICS

IN order that the shooter may thoroughly comprehend, choose, and enjoy his hobby, it is necessary that he have at least an elementary knowledge of ballistics.

Ballistics is a term used to describe the movement and property of the bullet from the time it leaves the shell case until it reaches its destination. Ballistics are divided into two groups, internal and external. Internal ballistics have to do with the bullet while still in the barrel; external ballistics have to do with the bullet after leaving the muzzle of the gun.

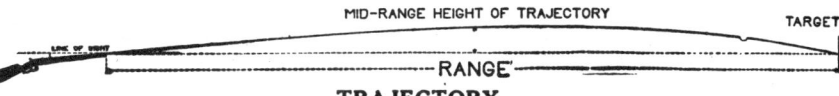
TRAJECTORY

The blow of the firing pin upon the primer ignites the priming mixture much in the manner that an ordinary match ignites when the tip is struck or scratched. The flash of the primer in turn ignites the powder which is instantaneously converted into gas, causing very high pressure in all directions. The base of the bullet, being the only surface offering little resistance, gets the full benefit of the gas pressure and is forced out of the shell case into the bore of the gun and driven at high speed out of the muzzle. The more progressive or slow burning the powder, the less jarringly the conversion from powder to gas takes place, and the more gradual and further from the chamber is the point of maximum pressure. The pressure exerted by the gas is expressed in atmospheres, or more commonly in pounds per square inch. Normal pressure in the 30/06 barrel is, for example, 45,000 pounds (15 tons) per square inch, and the Springfield Armory proof load for testing of the rifle is 68,000 pounds.

For different types of firearms different powders are necessary, for example, a powder suitable for a long barrel may be quite unsuited for use in a short barrel, as a portion of the powder would not be burned until after the bullet had left the muzzle, thereby causing great loss in velocity and energy. Consequently the shorter the barrel, the greater the muzzle pressure, the louder the report, and usually the muzzle blast.

When the bullet enters the barrel, it engages the rifling and is forced into rotation. Without this rotation, any cylindrical bullet would tumble and have no accuracy upon leaving the muzzle.

The rate of twist is usually expressed in the number of inches required for any single land or groove to make a complete turn. The U. S. Springfield, for example, has a 10-inch twist. The depth of the grooves and the rate of twist varies with the type of bullet and the velocity. In general, barrels for lead or light copper jacketed bullets have deeper grooves than for those with hard cupro nickel jackets such as used in all high velocity cartridges. In general also the faster the twist the faster the cartridge.

A minimum barrel, extra wide grooves, improper shape of the conical shoulder greatly increases the pressure, concentrate it near the chamber and cause disturbances in the barrel affecting the accuracy of the shot. External ballistics.

The muzzle velocity is given in foot seconds, representing the number of feet the projectile would travel in one second if it continued at the same rate as when leaving the muzzle. Since the bullet is subject to two forces, air resistance and gravity, the speed of flight begins to drop at once. The speed with which the bullet continues to travel is dependent upon the weight and form of the bullet, also upon the wind.

The flight of the bullet from muzzle to point of impact is in the form of a curve, with the highest point about 54 per cent of the way toward the target. The greater the distance of the target the more the muzzle must be elevated to provide against a drop short of the target. Point blank range is that range at which the bullet travels practically flat and before any perceptible drop due to air resistance or gravitation has taken place and coincides with the line from muzzle to target.

High velocity cartridges are those where the velocity is such that the height of the trajectory over a line drawn from muzzle to target is very low. High velocity increases accuracy and makes the altering of the rear sight for small differences in range unnecessary. It follows that the higher the velocity, the greater the point blank range.

At the moment of leaving the muzzle, the base of the bullet is subjected to an uneven push from the gas escaping directly behind it, and because the bullet is no longer guided by the barrel. This is detrimental to its balance and causes the base of the bullet to pendulate or "yaw." The degree of swing from the perpendicular is referred to as the "angle of yaw," and it is for this reason that a high velocity cartridge cutting a target at close range will keyhole, and its penetration be less than at a greater distance, because a well constructed bullet will rapidly lose its yaw and settle to a regular flight. The amount of yaw is directly influenced by the length of the bearing surface of the bullet against the barrel. The shorter this surface, the greater the angle of yaw. For this reason a long round nose bullet has more penetration at short range than a boat tail sharp pointed or Spitzer type. In general a full jacketed bullet has double the penetration of one of similar shape with soft nose.

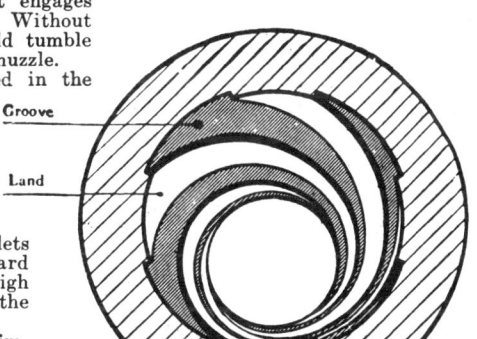
CROSS CUT VIEW OF BARREL

The muzzle report is caused by escaping gas striking the air. The bullet report is caused by the piling up of air in front of the bullet. At a distance, only the bullet report is heard, behind the gun the sound heard is a combination of both.

The muzzle flash is the dark reddish flash in front of the muzzle caused by powder not completely consumed in the barrel. A peculiar phenomenon familiar to all shooters, is the brilliant bluish ball of fire, usually known as the muzzle blast. When the highly heated gases strike the air they combine with it to create an explosive mixture which in turn explodes, intensifying the muzzle and bullet reports, all of which are heard as one by the shooter.

The amount of muzzle flash and blast varies according to bullet, powder, and barrel length.

DEVELOPMENT OF THE SPRINGFIELD SERVICE RIFLE

The Springfield Arsenal was opened shortly prior to 1799, when the first American army musket was built there. It was a copy of the French Charlesville rifle, caliber .69, shooting a one ounce ball with a muzzle velocity of 900 foot seconds. With a few changes, all arms built at Springfield were .69 caliber, until 1842 when the first rifling was introduced and a spherical bullet used. The caliber was next reduced to .58, doubling the effective range from 250 to 500 yards.

In 1866, the first .50 caliber metal cartridge was employed, but lasted only until 1873 when it was reduced to .45 caliber. This rifle stayed until 1893, when the Krag was introduced in the successive models of 1892, 1894, and 1898. The Krag, in turn was discontinued in 1905, when the present day model of 1903, built on the pattern of the Mauser Model 1898, of which it is partly a copy and partly a modification, was adopted.

In 1905, attention was given the Mauser Spitzer bullet, which was adopted in 1906, and one thread was removed from the barrel, reducing the original length from 24 to 23.79 inches. The Spitzer type 1906 cartridge has double the accuracy and about 30 per cent greater velocity, energy, and range than the original 1903 cartridge.

Since 1906 the development has not been in the mechanical features of the rifle, but in the quality of materials used and the ammunition. For this reason the purchaser of a Springfield rifle should see to it that his rifle, if made at Springfield, has a serial number over 800,000; at Rock Island, over 285,507.

We call attention to this because all actions under the respective numbers mentioned will be destroyed and replaced when returned to Springfield. On the latest actions nickel and chrome vanadium steels are used, together with new processes of heat treatment which assure the greatest degree of safety to the shooter; such rifles are numbered from 1,275,767.

The present trend in army rifles is the automatic type, and the time is close at hand when all armies will be so equipped. Such rifles have already been produced at Springfield, chambered for the 30/06 cartridge and experimentally issued to troops.

SEE PAGE 8, "HOW TO ORDER"

CORE-LOKT — SILVER-TIP — INNER-BELTED
HIGH SPEED HUNTING RIFLE AMMUNITION

SOFT NOSE
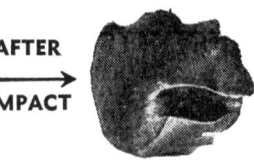
AFTER ↔ IMPACT
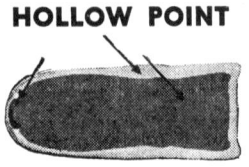
HOLLOW POINT
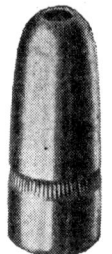

The latest and most important development in the line of American Ammunition is the introduction of a new type of bullet by all four leading makers. The new style bullet is made by Western and Winchester under the name "Silver Tip," by Peters as "Inner-Belted" and by Remington as "Core-Lokt".

The feature of this bullet is the unusual thickness of the base of the bullet casing, which however tapers very sharply toward the tip to a minimum thickness where, in the case of the mushroom or soft point bullet, this jacket is specially notched or serrated to permit symetrical expansion.

The result of this arrangement is that the thin casing quickly disintegrates giving the tip of the bullet maximum mushroom effect, whereas the base of the case is tightly locked in the reinforced casing of the base of the bullet insuring maximum penetration while preventing disintegration of the major part of the bullet and increases shocking power and proper bleeding of game.

An interesting feature is that this new type bullet, while designed primarily if not exclusively for game hunting, has improved accuracy over normal ammunition, although the ballistics remain the same.

It should be noted particularly that this ammunition is supplied exclusively in high speed loads which assures not only high accuracy and penetration, but also reduces to a minimum, the adjusting of sights to various distances.

Load No.	Caliber	Make	Weight of Bullet Grains	Style of Bullet	Price Per Box of 20
R84	.25 Rem. Express	Remington	117	Mush. C'KT	$1.41
R435	.25 Rem. Express	Remington	117	S. Pt. C'KT	1.41
2579	.25 Rem. HiVel.	Peters	117	I. B. S. Pt.	1.41
2569	.250 Savage HiVel.	Peters	100	Mush. I. B.	1.64
K2510C	.250-3000 Savage	Winchester	100	Exp. Si. Tip	1.64
K1700C	.250-3000 Savage	Western	100	Exp. Si. Tip	1.64
R472	.250 Savage	Remington	100	Mush. C'KT	1.64
R85	.257 Rem.-Roberts	Remington	100	Mush. C'KT	1.82
K1701C	.257 Roberts	Western	100	Exp. Si. Tip	1.82
K2511C	.257 Win.-Roberts	Winchester	100	Exp. Si. Tip	1.82
R72	.25-35 Win. & Sav.	Remington	100	Mush. C'KT	1.41
R439	.25-35 Win. & Sav.	Remington	117	S. Pt. C'KT	1.41
2582	.25-35 Win.	Peters	117	I. B. S. Pt.	1.41
R494	.270 Win.	Remington	130	Mush. C'KT	2.10
K1702C	.270 Win.	Western	130	Exp. Si. Tip	2.10
K2705C	.270 Win.	Winchester	170	Exp. Si. Tip	2.10
R130	.30-30 Win.	Remington	170	Mush. C'KT	1.46
R440	.30-30 Win.	Remington	170	S. Pt. C'KT	1.46
R450	.30-30 Win.	Remington	150	S. Pt. C'KT	1.46
3043	.30-30 Win.	Peters	170	I. B. H. P.	1.46
3044	.30-30 Win.	Peters	150	I. B. S. P.	1.46
3058	.30-30 Win.	Peters	170	I. B. S. P.	1.46
K1703C	.30-30 Win.	Western	170	Exp. Si. Tip	1.46
K3005C	.30-30 Win.	Winchester	130	Exp. Si. Tip	1.46
R127	.30 Rem.	Remington	170	Mush. C'KT	1.46
R436	.30 Rem.	Remington	170	S. P. C'KT	1.46
3048	.30 Rem.	Peters	170	I. B. H. P.	1.46
3054	.30 Rem.	Peters	170	I. B. S. P.	1.46
K1704C	.30 Rem.	Western	170	Exp. Si. Tip	1.46
K3090C	.30 Rem.	Winchester	170	Exp. Si. Tip	1.46
R100	.30-40 Krag	Remington	220	Mush. C'KT	1.93
R442	.30-40 Krag	Remington	220	S. P. C'KT	1.93
R101	.30-40 Krag	Remington	180	Mush. C'KT	1.93
R441	.30-40 Krag	Remington	180	S. P. C'KT	1.93
3045	.30-40 Krag	Peters	180	I. B. S. P.	1.93
3049	.30-40 Krag	Peters	220	I. B. H. P.	1.93
K1707C	.30-40 Krag	Western	180	Exp. Si. Tip	1.93
K1708C	.30-40 Krag	Western	220	Exp. Si. Tip	1.93
K3050C	.30-40 Krag	Winchester	180	Exp. Si. Tip	1.93
K3051C	.30-40 Krag	Winchester	220	Exp. Si. Tip	1.93
3046	.30-40 Krag	Peters	180	I. B. S. P.	1.93
3047	.30-40 Krag	Peters	220	I. B. S. P.	1.93
R135	.30-06 Springfield	Remington	180	Mush. C'KT	2.10
R443	.30-06 Springfield	Remington	180	S. P. C'KT	2.10
R138	.30-06 Springfield	Remington	220	Mush. C'KT	2.10
R144	.30-06 Springfield	Remington	220	S. P. C'KT	2.10
3037	.30-06 Springfield	Peters	180	I. B. H. P.	2.10
3036	.30-06 Springfield	Peters	220	I. B. H. P.	2.10
3056	.30-06 Springfield	Peters	180	I. B. S. P.	2.10
K1705C	.30-06 Springfield	Western	180	Exp. Si. Tip	2.10
K1706C	.30-06 Springfield	Western	220	Exp. Si. Tip	2.10
K3063C	.30-06 Springfield	Winchester	180	Exp. Si. Tip	2.10
K3064C	.30-06 Springfield	Winchester	220	Exp. Si. Tip	2.10
R445	.300 Savage	Remington	180	S. P. C'KT	1.85
R465	.300 Savage	Remington	180	Mush. C'KT	1.85
3022	.300 Savage	Peters	180	I. B. H. P.	1.85
3021	.300 Savage	Peters	180	I. B. S. P.	1.85
K1711C	.300 Savage	Western	180	Exp. Si. Tip	1.85
K3079C	.300 Savage	Winchester	180	Exp. Si. Tip	1.85
R466	.300 Magnum	Remington	220	Mush. C'KT	2.57
3027	.300 Magnum	Peters	220	I. B. H. P.	2.57
K1709C	.300 Magnum	Western	180	Exp. Si. Tip	2.57
K1710C	.300 Magnum	Western	220	Exp. Si. Tip	2.57
K3084C	.300 Magnum	Winchester	180	Exp. Si. Tip	2.57
K3085C	.300 Magnum	Winchester	220	Exp. Si. Tip	2.57
R475	.303 Savage	Remington	180	Mush. C'KT	1.46
R446	.303 Savage	Remington	180	S. P. C'KT	1.46
3032	.303 Savage	Peters	180	I. B. H. P.	1.46
3035	.303 Savage	Peters	180	I. B. S. P.	1.46
K1712C	.303 Savage	Western	190	Exp. Si. Tip	1.46
K3097C	.303 Savage	Winchester	190	Exp. Si. Tip	1.46
R191	.32 Special Win.	Remington	170	Mush. C'KT	1.46
R447	.32 Special Win.	Remington	170	S. P. C'KT.	1.46
3278	.32 Special Win.	Peters	170	I. B. H. P.	1.46
3279	.32 Special Win.	Peters	170	I. B. S. P.	1.46
K1713C	.32 Special Win.	Western	170	Ex. Si. Tip	1.46
K3226C	.32 Special Win.	Winchester	170	Exp. Si. Tip	1.46
R199	.32 Rem.	Remington	170	Mush. C'KT	1.46
R437	.32 Rem.	Remington	170	S. P. C'KT	1.46
3295	.32 Rem.	Peters	170	I. B, H. P.	1.46
3292	.32 Rem.	Peters	180	I. B. S. P.	1.46
K1714C	.32 Rem.	Western	170	Exp. Si. Tip	1.46
K3293C	.32 Rem.	Winchester	170	Exp. Si. Tip	1.46
R217	.348 Win.	Remington	200	Mush. C'KT	2.10
3483	.348 Win.	Peters	200	I. B. H. P.	2.10
K1715C	.348 Win.	Western	250	Exp. Si. Tip	2.10
K3423C	.348 Win.	Winchester	250	Exp. Si. Tip	2.10
R213	.35 Rem.	Remington	200	Mush. C'KT	1.64
R438	.35 Rem.	Remington	200	S. P. C'KT	1.64
3594	.35 Rem.	Peters	200	I. B. H. P.	1.64
3589	.35 Rem.	Peters	200	I. B. S. P.	1.64
K1716C	.35 Rem.	Western	200	Exp. Si. Tip	1.64
K3593C	.35 Rem.	Winchester	200	Exp. Si. Tip	1.64
K1717C	.375 H. & H. Mag.	Western	300	Exp. Si. Tip	2.83
K3755C	.375 H. & H. Mag.	Winchester	300	Exp. Si. Tip	2.83

FOR BEST RESULTS USE THE BEST CARTRIDGES

CENTER FIRE RIFLE CARTRIDGES

REMINGTON		PETERS		CARTRIDGE	WINCHESTER		WESTERN	
STYLE* OF BULLET	BULLET WEIGHT GR.	STYLE* OF BULLET	BULLET WEIGHT GR.		STYLE OF BULLET	BULLET WEIGHT GR.	STYLE OF BULLET	BULLET WEIGHT GR.
Mush.	46†	...	...	**CAL. .218 BEE** — Packed 50 Per Box — Price $1.80 — For use in Winchester Model 65	H. P.	46†	O. P. E.	46†
Mush.	46†	...	...	**CAL. .219 ZIPPER** — 20 Per Box — Price $1.31 — For use in Winchester Model 64, also others.	H. P. H. P.	46† 56†	O. P. E. O. P. E.	46† 56†
Mush. S. P.	45† 45†	M.C.H.P.	45†	**CAL. .22 HORNET** — 50 Per Box — Price $1.69 — For use in various bolt and single shot rifles.	S. P. H. P.	45† 46†	O. P. E. S. Pt.	46† 45†
Mush. S. P.	46† 48†	...	...	**CAL. .220 SWIFT** — 20 Per Box — Price $1.53 — For use in Winchester Model 70, also special rifles.	Ptd. S. P. H. P. H. P. F. P.	48† 46† 56† 46†	O. P. E. S. P.	46† 48†
Mush.	70†	S. P.	70†	**CAL. .22 HIGH POWER** — 20 Per Box — Price $1.37 — For use in Savage Model 99.	Ptd. S. P.	70†	S. P.	70†
M. C. S. P. Mush.	86 86 60†	S. P. M. C. M.C.H.P. S. P.	86 86 60† 86†	**CAL. .25-20** — 50 Per Box — Price $1.93 — For Winchester, Marlin, Remington, Savage and others.	F. P. S. P. H. P. S. P.	86 86 60† 86†	M. C. S. P. S. P. O.P.E.	86 86 86† 60†
S. P.	86	S. P.	86	**CAL. .25-20 SINGLE SHOT** — 50 Per Box — Price $1.99 — For Stevens and Winchester single shot rifles.	S. P.	86	...	...
M. C. C"kt. S. P. Mush. Mush.	117 117 117 87† 117	S. P. M. C.	117† 117	**CAL. .25-35** — 20 Per Box — Price $1.41 Except C"kt 1.41 — For Winchester Model 94, also Savage, and others.	F. P. S. P.	117† 117†	M. C. S.P.B.T. O.P.E.B.	117† 117† 117†
Mush. S. P. Mush. C"kt	87† 117† 117† 117†	S. P.	117	**CAL. .25 REMINGTON** — 20 Per Box — Price $1.41 Except C"kt 1.41 — For Remington auto loading or repeating and Remington Model 30 bolt action, standard automatic and Stevens repeating rifles.	S. P.	117	S.P.B.T. O.P.E.B.	117 117
Mush. Mush. C"kt	87† 100† 100†	P. P. Exp. S. P. M.C.H.P.	87 87† 100†	**CAL. .250 SAVAGE (.250-3000)** — 20 Per Box — Price $1.64 Except C"kt 1.64 — For Savage and Winchester rifles.	S. P. H. P.	87† 100†	S. P. O. P. E.	87† 100†
...	...	...	...	**CAL. .256 NEWTON** — 20 Per Box — Price $2.10 — For Newton high power and Meeker rifles.	...	...	O. P. E.	129

FOR EXPLANATION OF REFERENCE MARKS AND ABBREVIATIONS SEE PAGE 241.

© **ALL SHIPMENTS ARE INSURED**

CENTER FIRE RIFLE CARTRIDGES

REMINGTON		PETERS		CARTRIDGE	WINCHESTER		WESTERN	
STYLE OF BULLET	BULLET WEIGHT GR.	STYLE OF BULLET	BULLET WEIGHT GR.		STYLE OF BULLET	BULLET WEIGHT GR.	STYLE OF BULLET	BULLET WEIGHT GR.
				CAL. .257 ROBERTS — 20 Per Box — Price $1.82, Except C'kt 1.82 — For Winchester, Remington and special rifles.				
Mush.	87†	…	…		H. P.	87†	O. P. E.	87†
Mush.	100†	…	…		H. P.	100†	O. P. E.	100†
Mush.	117†	…	…		H. P.	117†	S. P.	117†
C'kt	100	…	…					
				CAL. 6.5 m/m MANNLICHER — 20 Per Box — Price $1.93 — For use in Model 1903 Mannlicher-Schoenauer rifles.				
S. P.	150	M.C.H.P.	123		S. P.	145	S. P.	160
		M.C.H.P.	160				O. P. E.	129
				CAL. .270 WINCHESTER — 20 Per Box — Price $2.10, Except C'kt 2.10 — For Winchester rifles Model 54 and 70.				
Mush.	130†	S. P.	150†		Ptd. Exp.	130†	S. P.	100†
S. P.	150†	P. P. Exp.	130†		S. P.	150†	O. P. E. B.	130†
C'kt	130†				Ptd. Exp.	100†	S. P.	150†
				CAL. 7 m/m MAUSER — 20 Per Box — Price $1.93 — For use in Mauser rifles.				
S. P.	175	S. P.	175		S. P.	175†	S. P. B. T.	175†
				CAL. 7.62 m/m RUSSIAN — 20 Per Box — Price $1.93 — For use in Russian military rifles.				
Exp.	150	…	…		H. C. P.	145	…	…
				CAL. .30 NEWTON — 20 Per Box — Price $2.32 — For Newton and Meeker rifles.				
…	…	…	…		…	…	O. P. E. B.	180
				CAL. .30 REMINGTON — 20 Per Box — Price $1.46, Except C'kt 1.46, Belted 1.46 — For Remington autoloading or repeating, Rem. Model 30 bolt action, standard automatic and Stevens' repeating rifles.				
M. C.	160†	Belted	180†		F. P.	160	S. P. B. T.	170
S. P.	170†	S. P.	170†		S. P.	170	O. P. E. B.	165
Mush.	110†	M. C.	160				O. P. E.	110†
Mush.	165†	M.C.H.P.	165†					
C'kt	170†	M.C.H.P.	125†					
				CAL. .30 WINCHESTER (.30-.30) — 20 Per Box — Price $1.46, Except C'kt 1.46, Belted 1.46 — For Winchester Model 1894, Marlin Model 1893, Remington-Lee, Savage Model repeating and Remington No. 5 rifle.				
Mush.	165†	Belted	180†		F. P.	170†	M.C.B.T.	170†
M. C.	160†	S. P.	170†		S. P.	170†	S. P. B. T.	170†
S. P.	170†	M. C.	160†		H. P.	150†	O. P. E.	150†
Mush.	110†	M.C.H.P.	165†		H. P.	110†	O. P. E.	110†
C'kt	170†	M.C.H.P.	135†					
				CAL. .30-06 SPRINGFIELD — 20 Per Box — Price $2.10, Except C'kt 2.10, Belted 2.10 — For Springfield and other Bolt Action Rifles.				
M. C.	172	P. P. Exp.	150		S. P.	220†	O. P. E.	150†
S. P.	220†	S. P.	180†		S. P.	180†	M.C.B.T.	180
Exp.	150†	M. C.	180		Ptd. Exp.	180†	S. P.	180
Exp.	180†	P. P. Exp.	180†		F. P.	180	O. P. E. B.	180†
S. P.	180†	Belted	180†		F. P.	180*	M. C.	220
Mush.	110†	M.C.B.T.	172		F. P.	172	M.C.B.N.	220†
C'kt	180†	Belted	225†		Ptd. Exp.	172	S. P. B. T.	220†
Mush.	220†				Ptd. Exp.	150†		
C'kt	220†				H. C. P.	145†		
M. C.	180*							

* Special Match Cartridge.

FOR EXPLANATION OF REFERENCE MARKS AND ABBREVIATIONS SEE PAGE 241.

SEND YOUR GUN TO STOEGER FOR EXPERT REPAIRING

CENTER FIRE RIFLE CARTRIDGES

REMINGTON		PETERS		CARTRIDGE		WINCHESTER		WESTERN	
STYLE OF BULLET	BULLET WEIGHT GR.	STYLE OF BULLET	BULLET WEIGHT GR.			STYLE OF BULLET	BULLET WEIGHT GR.	STYLE OF BULLET	BULLET WEIGHT GR.
S. P.	220†	S. P.	220	**CAL. .30-40 KRAG (.30 Army)** — Price $1.93, Except C"kt 1.93, Belted 1.93. 20 Per Box. For U. S. Krag, Remington-Lee and Winchester 1895 rifles; also Remington and Winchester single shot military and sporting rifles.		F. P.	220	O. P. E. B.	180†
Exp.	180†	M. C.	220			P. S.	220	M. C.	220
S. P.	180†	P. P. Exp.	150			Ptd. Exp.	180†	S. P. B. T.	220†
Mush.	220†	S. P.	180†			S. P.	180†	S. P.	180†
M. C.	220†	P. P. Exp.	180†			Ptd. Exp.	150†		
C"kt	220†	Belted	180†						
C"kt	180†	Belted	225†						
Exp.	150†	Belted	200†	**CAL. .300 SAVAGE** — Price $1.85, Except C"kt 1.85, Belted 1.85. 20 Per Box. For Savage cal. 300 repeating rifle.		S. P.	180†	O. P. E.	150†
S. P.	180	P. P. Exp.	150†			S. P.	150†	S. P.	180†
C"kt	180†	M.C.H.P	180						
C"kt	220†	Belted	225	**CAL. .300 H. & H. MAGNUM** — Price $2.57, Except C"kt 2.57, Belted 2.57. 20 Per Box. For bolt action rifles.		S. P.	220†	O. P. E. B.	180†
M. C.	180					H. P.	180†	S. P. B. T.	220†
						F. P.	180		
S. P.	195†	Belted	180†	**CAL. .303 SAVAGE** — Price $1.46, Except C"kt 1.46, Belted 1.46. 20 Per Box. For use in Savage Model 99 rifles.		S. P.	190	S. P.	190
C"kt	180†	S. P.	195						
M. C.	215	S. P.	215	**CAL. .303 BRITISH** — Price $1.93. 20 Per Box. For use in British Lee Enfield and Ross rifles.		S. P.	215†	S. P. B. T.	215†
S. P.	215†							O. P. E. B.	174†
...	...	S. P.	200	**CAL. 8 m/m MANNLICHER-SCHOENAUER** — Price $1.93. 20 Per Box. For use in Model 1908 Mannlicher-Schoenauer rifles.		...	...	...	...
S. P.	236†	S. P.	170	**CAL. 8MM MAUSER (8 x 57 m/m)** — Price $1.93. 20 Per Box. For use in Models '88 and '98 Mauser military rifles, also Mannlicher-Haenel and sporting rifles.		S. P.	236	...	...
S. P.	170†					S. P. B. T.	170†		
S. P.	170†	...	...	**CAL. 8 m/m LEBEL** — Price $1.93. 20 Per Box. For use in French Lebel military rifle.		...	...	...	...
S. P.	170†	Belted	180†	**CAL. .32 WINCHESTER SPECIAL** — Price $1.46, Except Belted 1.46, C"kt 1.46. 20 Per Box. For use in various Winchester, Marlin, and Remington rifles.		S. P.	170†	S. B. P. T.	170†
Mush.	110†	S. P.	170†			H. P.	110†	O. P. E. B.	165†
Mush.	165†								
C"kt	170†								
S. P.	165	S. P.	165	**CAL. .32-40 WINCHESTER** — Price $1.41. 20 Per Box. For use in Winchester, Marlin, and Savage repeating rifles, also Winchester, Remington and Ballard single shot.		S. P.	165	S. P. B. T.	165
								O. P. E. B.	165

FOR EXPLANATION OF REFERENCE MARKS AND ABBREVIATIONS SEE PAGE 241.

CENTER FIRE RIFLE CARTRIDGES

REMINGTON		PETERS		CARTRIDGE	WINCHESTER		WESTERN	
STYLE OF BULLET	BULLET WEIGHT GR.	STYLE OF BULLET	BULLET WEIGHT GR.		STYLE OF BULLET	BULLET WEIGHT GR.	STYLE OF BULLET	BULLET WEIGHT GR.
S. P.	165	S. P.	165	**CAL. .32 WINCHESTER SELF LOADING** — 50 Per Box — Price $2.63 — For use in Winchester Model 1905 self loader.	S. P.	165	S. P.	165
C"kt S. P. Mush. Mush.	170† 170† 110† 165†	Belted S. P.	180† 170†	**CAL. .32 REMINGTON AUTOMATIC** — 20 Per Box — Price $1.46, Except C"kt 1.46, Belted 1.46 — For Remington Autoloading and bolt action rifles also for standard automatic and Stevens rifles.	S. P.	165	S. P. B. T. O. P. E. B.	170 165
S. P.	200	S. P.	200	**CAL. .33 WINCHESTER** — 20 Per Box — Price $1.93 — For use in Winchester Model 86 rifles.	S. P.	200	S. P.	200
S. P. S. P. C"kt	150† 200† 200†	Belted S. P. S. P.	210† 150† 200†	**CAL. .348 WINCHESTER** — 20 Per Box — Price $2.10, Except C"kt 2.10, Belted 2.10 — **SOFT POINT** Used for the Model 71 Winchester.	S. P. S. P.	200† 150†	S. P. S. P.	150† 200†
S. P.	180	S. P.	180	**CAL. .35 WINCHESTER SELF LOADING** — 50 Per Box — Price $2.69 — For Winchester Model 1907 self loading rifle.	S. P.	180	S. P.	180
S. P. Mush. Mush. C"kt	200† 150† 200† 200†	Belted S. P. M.C.H.P.	210† 200† 200†	**CAL. .35 REMINGTON** — 20 Per Box — Price $1.64, Except C"kt 1.64, Belted 1.64 — For Remington auto loading or repeating and Remington Model 35 bolt action standard automatic and Stevens repeating rifle.	S. P.	200	S. P. O. P. E.	200 200
S. P.	250	S. P.	250	**CAL. .35 WINCHESTER** — 20 Per Box — Price $2.10 — For use in Winchester Model '95, Remington-Lee and Ross repeating rifles.	S. P.	250	S. P.	250
M. C. S. P.	177 180	S. P. M. C.	180 177	**CAL. .351 WINCHESTER** — 50 Per Box — Price $3.12 — For use in Winchester Model '07 self loading rifle.	F. P. S. P.	180 180	M. C. S. P.	180 180
...	...	...	...	**CAL. .375 MAGNUM** — 20 Per Box — Price $2.83 — For use in Mauser, Winchester and Special Magnum Rifles.	...	...	O. P. E. S. P. S. P. M.C.B.N.	235† 270† 300† 300†
S. P.	255	S. P.	255	**CAL. .38-55 WINCHESTER** — 20 Per Box — Price $1.57 — For Winchester, Marlin, Savage and Remington-Lee repeating rifles, also Remington high pressure single shot rifles.	S. P.	255	S. P.	255

FOR EXPLANATIONS OF REFERENCE MARKS AND ABBREVIATIONS SEE PAGE 241.

CENTER FIRE RIFLE CARTRIDGES

REMINGTON		PETERS		CARTRIDGE			WINCHESTER		WESTERN	
STYLE OF BULLET	BULLET WEIGHT GR.	STYLE OF BULLET	BULLET WEIGHT GR.				STYLE OF BULLET	BULLET WEIGHT GR.	STYLE OF BULLET	BULLET WEIGHT GR.
S. P.	255	S. P.	255	20 Per Box	**CAL. .38-56 WINCHESTER** For Winchester, Marlin and other repeating rifles, also Winchester single shot rifles.	Price $1.57	S. P.	255	...	...
...	...	...	...	20 Per Box	**CAL. .38-72 WINCHESTER** For Winchester Models 86 and 95.	Price $1.69	S. P.	275	...	...
S. P.	260	S. P.	260	20 Per Box	**CAL. .40-65 WINCHESTER** For Winchester Model 86 and Marlin repeating rifles, also Remington and Winchester single shot rifles.	Price $1.57	S. P.	260	...	...
S. P.	260	S. P.	260	20 Per Box	**CAL. .40-82 WINCHESTER** For Winchester Model 86, also Marlin and single shot.	Price $1.57	S. P.	260	...	...
S. P.	200	S. P.	200	20 Per Box	**CAL. .401 WINCHESTER** For Winchester Model 1910 self loader.	Price $1.57	S. P.	200	S. P.	200
S. P.	300	S. P.	300	20 Per Box	**CAL. .405 WINCHESTER** For Winchester Model 1895 repeating rifle.	Price $2.34	S. P.	300	S. P.	300
S.P. F.P.	405	S. P.	405	20 Per Box	**CAL. .45-70-405.** For Springfield and Hotchkiss repeating rifles, also single shot rifles.	Price $1.64	S. P.	405	S. P.	405
S. P.	300	S. P.	300	20 Per Box	**CAL. .45-90 WINCHESTER** For Winchester Model 1886, also Marlin repeating and Remington and Winchester single shot rifles.	Price $1.69	S. P.	300	...	...
...	...	...	...	20 Per Box	**CAL. .50-110 WINCHESTER** For Winchester Model 86 and Winchester single shot rifle	Price $2.10	S. P.	300	...	...

* STYLES OF BULLETS *
Explanation of Abbreviations Used

Mush.—Mushroom.
S. P.—Soft Point.
M. C. H. P.—Metal Case Hollow Point.
H. P.—Hollow Point.
O. P. E.—Open Point Expanding.
Ptd. S. P.—Pointed Soft Point.
F. P.—Full Patch.
M. C.—Metal Case.

C'kt—Core-Lokt.
S. P. B. T.—Soft Point Boat Tail.
O. P. E. B.—Open Point Expanding Boat Tail.
P. P. Exp.—Protected Point Expanding.
Ptd. Exp.—Pointed Expanding.
Exp.—Expanding.
H. C. P.—Hollow Copper Point.
Belted—Belted Bullet.

M. C. B. N.—Metal Case Blunt Nose.
S. P. F. P.—Soft Point Flat Point.
† Special High Speed Load indicating one of the following loads.
Remington   Hi-Speed.
Peters   Hi-Velocity.
Winchester   Super-Speed.
Western   Super X.

LEAD, SHOT, BLANK & RIM AND CENTER FIRE CTDGS.

RIM FIRE CARTRIDGES

CENTER FIRE SHOT CARTRIDGES

RIM FIRE SHOT CARTRIDGES

CENTER FIRE BLANK CARTRIDGES

RIM FIRE BLANK CARTRIDGES

CARTRIDGE	REMINGTON			WINCHESTER			WESTERN			PETERS		
	STYLE OF BULLET	BULLET WEIGHT GR.	PER BOX 50	STYLE OF BULLET	BULLET WEIGHT GR.	PER BOX 50	STYLE OF BULLET	BULLET WEIGHT GR.	PER BOX 50	STYLE OF BULLET	BULLET WEIGHT GR.	PER BOX 50
RIM FIRE LEAD CARTRIDGES												
.25 Stevens Short	Lead	67	$0.63	Lead	65	$0.63	Lubaloy	65	$0.63	Lead	67	$0.63
.25 Stevens	Lead	67	.85	Lead	65	.85	Lubaloy	65	.85	Lead	67	.85
.32 Short	Lead	80	.63	Lead	80	.63	Lubaloy	80	.63	Lead	80	.63
.32 Long	Lead	90	.72	Lead	89	.72	Lubaloy	90	.72	Lead	90	.72
.41 Short	Lead	129	.91	Lead	130	.91	Lubaloy	130	.91	Lead	129	.91
.41 Swiss	Lead	300	◆1.21	Lead	310	◆1.21				Lead	300	◆1.21
CENTER FIRE SHOT CARTRIDGES												
.44 Marble Game Getter	Shot		1.81	Shot▲	Size 8	1.81				Shot	Size 8	1.81
44 XL	Shot		2.12	Shot▲	Size 8	2.12	Shot	Size 8	2.12	Shot	Size 8	2.12
.45 Automatic Thompson Machine Gun										Shot▲	Size 7½	3.15
RIM FIRE SHOT CARTRIDGES												
.22 Long	Shot		.53	Shot	Size 12	.53				Shot	Size 11½	.53
.22 Long Rifle	Shot		.53	Shot	Size 12	.53						.53
.22 Klay Bird (For Miniature Trap and Skeet)										Shot		.53
.32 Long	Shot		1.05	Shot	Size 10	1.05				Shot	Size 10	1.05
9 m/m Long				Shot	Size 9	1.26						
CENTER FIRE BLANK CARTRIDGES												
.32 Smith & Wesson			.76			.76			.76			.76
.38 Smith & Wesson			.91			.91			.91			.91
.30 Army (.30-40 Krag)	Paper		◆1.93	Paper		◆1.93	Paper		1.93	Paper		◆1.93
.30—1906	Paper		◆2.10							Paper		◆2.10
RIM FIRE BLANK CARTRIDGES												
.22 Short			.17			.17			.17			.17
.32 Short			.32			.32			.32			.32

BOLD FACE LINES INDICATE BLACK POWDER ▲CHILLED SHOT ◆PRICE PER BOX OF 20

ALL SHIPMENTS ARE INSURED

POPULAR ENGLISH KYNOCH CARTRIDGES
(PRICES PER 100)

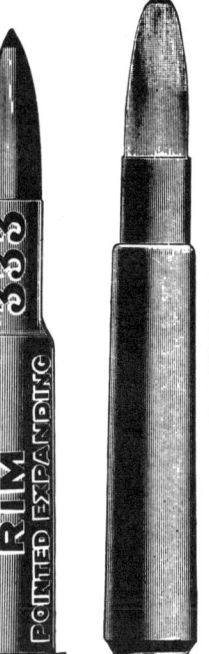

Cartridge		Bullet	Weight	Price
.275	Magnum, flanged	SP	160	$25.00
.275	Rimless Magnum Nitro Express	SP	160	25.00
.275	Mauser High Velocity	EX or S		25.00
.280	Jeffery Rimless Express, .333/.280	CP	140	27.50
300-.295	Rook Rifle Smokeless	S or HP	80	6.95
.30	Holland & Holland Super Rimless Nitro Express	HP	150, 180, 220	30.00
.318	Westley Richards Rimless Express	SN	180-250	25.00
.333	Jeffery Rimless Express	SN	300	27.50
.333	Jeffery Rimless Nitro Express	CP	250	30.00
.350	Rigby Magnum Rimless or Flanged	S	225	35.00
.360	No. 2 Lang Nitro Express	SN	320	35.00
.375	Holland & Holland 2½" Nitro Express	SN	300-270	25.00
.375	Holland & Holland Rimless Nitro Express	SN	300-400	25.00
.375	Magnum Flanged Nitro Express	CP	235	27.50

Cartridge		Bullet	Weight	Price
.375	Magnum Belted Rimless Nitro Express	CP	235	$27.50
.404	Jeffery Rimless Express	S or CP	300-400	27.50
.416	Rigby Magnum Rimless	HP	410	42.50
.425	Westley Richards Rimless Express	CP	410	42.50
.450	Westley Richards Nitro Express	SN & S	480	37.50
.450/400	Jeffery Nitro Express 3"	SN & S		35.00
.450/400	Magnum Nitro Express 3¼"	SN & S	400	35.00
.465	Holland & Holland Magnum Nitro Express	SN & S	480	37.50
.470	Nitro Express	SN	480	37.50
.475/No.2	Jeffery Nitro Express	SN & S		37.50
.500	Jeffery Magnum Nitro Express, 3¼"	S	570	37.50
.505	Gibbs Rimless Nitro Express	SN & S	525	37.50
.577	Nitro Express	SN & S	750	42.50
.600	Nitro Express	SN & S	900	45.00

SP—Soft Point. SN—Soft Nose. S—Solid.   EX—Expanding. HP—Hollow Point. CP—Copper Point.

WE SELL FRESH AMMUNITION ONLY

IMPORTED D. W. M. RIFLE CARTRIDGES WITH RIM
FOR DOUBLE BARRELED, OVER AND UNDER RIFLES AND THREE-BARRELED GUNS

We offer on these pages a list of the most commonly used cartridges of foreign manufacture. These are manufactured with but few exceptions, by the world famous D. W. M. factory at Karlsruhe, Baden, which factory, up to the time of the war, supplied the ammunition for a great number of European and Asiatic governments as well as practically all of the South American republics. The D. W. M. factory, for which we are the sole American agents is recognized the world over for the quality of its products, and it can truthfully be said that no factory in any country goes to greater pains and care to see that each cartridge is of proper specifications and perfect throughout.

Cartridges such as these combined with the high cost of transportation, expenses and duty, naturally cost somewhat more than domestic cartridges, but the consumer is assured of the very best that it is possible to produce.

NOTICE TO COLLECTORS

Most of the cartridges are sold in lots of 20 and we do not break boxes or sell single cartridges. Because of the incessant demand by Cartridge Collectors for single cartridges, we have decided to sell single cartridges when the order, at the prices quoted below, amounts to at least $5.00.

Cartridges priced up to $5.01 per box of 20 .... $0.40 each
Cartridges priced from $5.01 to $10 per box of 20 .... .60 each

THE NEW D. W. M. "STRONG JACKET" BULLETS

The new strong-jacket bullet is the most effective hunting bullet which overcomes in the best possible way the many and sometimes just diametrical requirements for hunting. The jacket is in its front part very thin and in the rear very thick and heavy. The front chief part of the bullet deforms easily, therefore it is of reliable retaining power. The rear massive jacket-part never bursts, but remains a solid and compact bulk, thus creating by itself with greatest certainty a perfect bleeding and passage through the animal hit. As only one part of the bullet bursts, the destroying of game is kept in moderate limits. "Strong Jacket" bullets are illustrated herewith.

Loaded cartridges with this new "Strong Jacket" bullet are supplied by us only in the 7x57 m/m and 9.3x62 m/m calibers at a 50 per cent increase in price.

For best results with imported rifles and pistols, these original imported D. W. M. Cartridges should be used. Individuals whose dealers do not supply D. W. M. Ammunition should remit in full when ordering, and on orders under $5.00, 50c packing charge must be included. Positively no ammunition will be sent C. O. D.

All Prices Per 20
Minimum order 20 cartridges

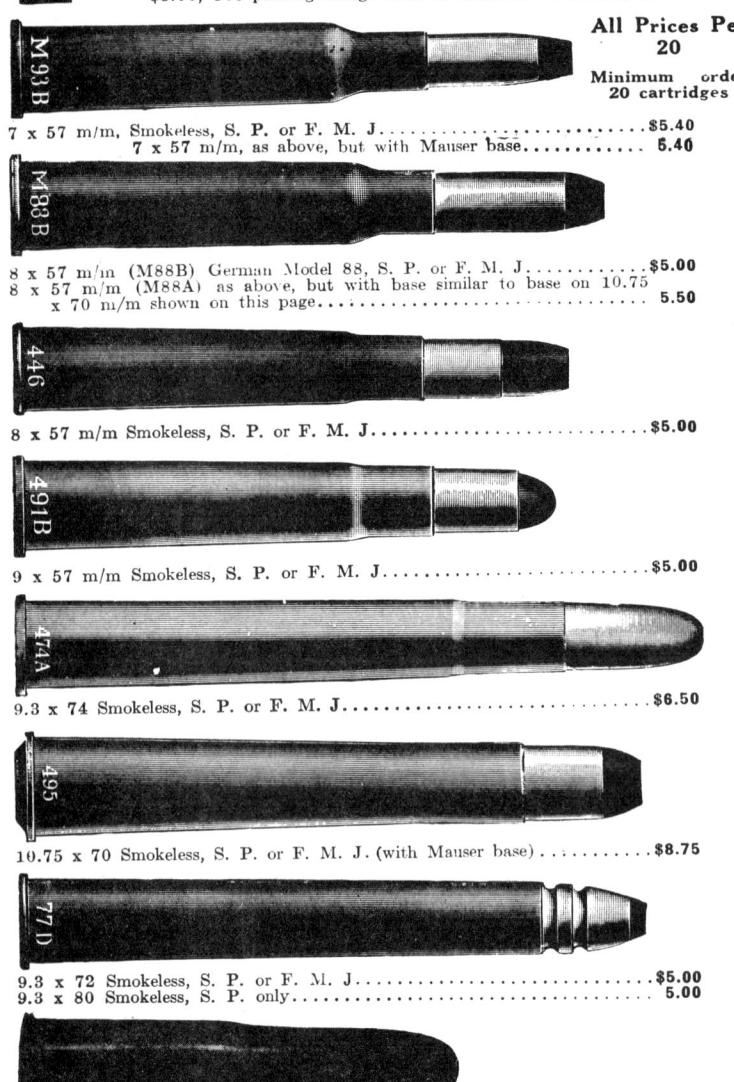

7 x 57 m/m, Smokeless, S. P. or F. M. J. $5.40
    7 x 57 m/m, as above, but with Mauser base 5.40

8 x 57 m/m (M88B) German Model 88, S. P. or F. M. J. $5.00
8 x 57 m/m (M88A) as above, but with base similar to base on 10.75 x 70 m/m shown on this page 5.50

8 x 57 m/m Smokeless, S. P. or F. M. J. $5.00

9 x 57 m/m Smokeless, S. P. or F. M. J. $5.00

9.3 x 74 Smokeless, S. P. or F. M. J. $6.50

10.75 x 70 Smokeless, S. P. or F. M. J. (with Mauser base) $8.75

9.3 x 72 Smokeless, S. P. or F. M. J. $5.00
9.3 x 80 Smokeless, S. P. only 5.00

Swiss Veterli, Model 78, 10.2 m/m, C. F. S. P. only $4.00

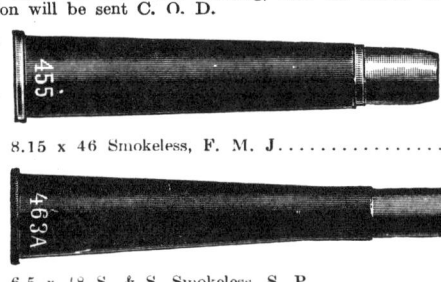

8.15 x 46 Smokeless, F. M. J. $5.00

6.5 x 48 S. & S. Smokeless, S. P. $5.00

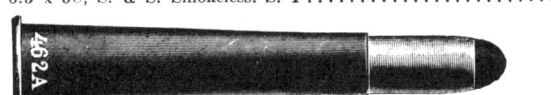

6.5 x 58, S. & S. Smokeless. S. P. $5.50

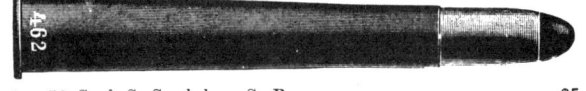

8 x 48 S. & S. Smokeless, S. P. $5.00

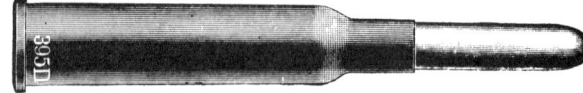

8 x 58 S. & S. Smokeless, S. P. $5.50

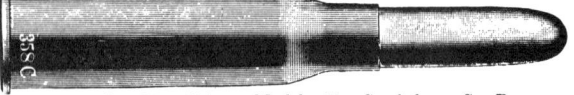

6.5 x 53 m/m Mannlicher, Model 93, Holland & Rumania, Smokeless, S. P. or F. M. J. $5.75

8 x 50 m/m Mannlicher, Model 95, Smokeless, S. P. or F. M. J. $6.50
This cartridge is suitable for the Mannlicher Model 1895 straight pull rifle used by Austria-Hungary during World War.

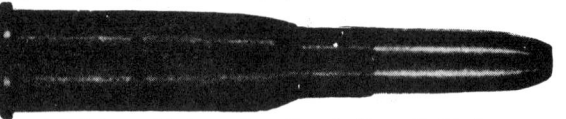

French Lebel 8 m/m Army Cartridge, S. P. or F. M. J. $5.00

IMPORTED D. W. M. RIFLE AND PISTOL CARTRIDGES
ORIGINAL MAUSER RIFLE CARTRIDGES
(ALL PRICES PER BOX OF 20)

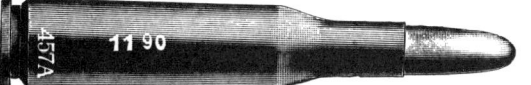

Mauser 6.5 x 54 m/m Short Smokeless, S. P. or F. M. J..........$5.00

Mauser 6.5 x 58 m/m Smokeless, S. P. or F. M. J.............. 5.50

Mauser 7 x 57 m/m Smokeless, S. P. or F. M. J............... 5.50

Mauser 8 x 51 m/m Short Smokeless, S. P. or F. M. J......... 5.00

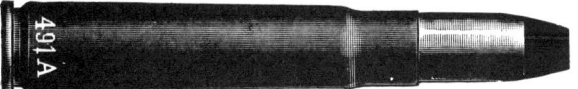

Mauser 9 x 57 m/m Smokeless, S. P. or F. M. J.............. $5.00

Price
Mauser 8 x 57 m/m—Model 88, Soft Nose or F. M. J..........$5.00
Mauser 8 x 57 m/m—Model 98, Spitzer Soft Point or F. M. J..... 5.00
These cartridges suitable for German Army Rifles used during the World War. Both models supplied only on Model 98 clips. Before ordering see note on page 291.

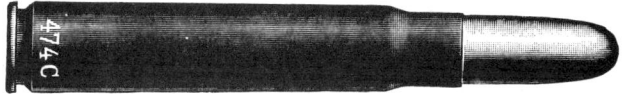

Mauser 9.3 x 62 m/m Smokeless, S. P. or F. M. J..............$6.00

Mauser 10.75 x 68 m/m Smokeless, S. P., F. M. J. or H. P......$7.00
Mauser 10.75 x 73 (.404 Jefferies).......................... 10.00

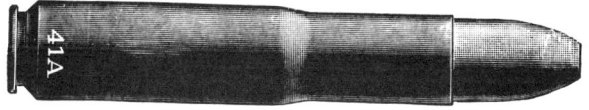

Mauser 11.2 x 60, Model 71/84 m/m Smokeless, S. P. only......$5.50

SPECIAL RIFLE CARTRIDGES

Caliber 6.5 Japanese Army Model, Ariska No. 481..............$6.00
Caliber 6.5 x 55 m/m Mauser, Krag Jorgensen, Sweden and Norway, Rimless, No. 431C.. 6.00
Caliber 6.5 Italian Model 1891, Rimless (Paravicino-Carcano) No. 473.. 6.00
Caliber 7.65 m/m Argentina, Bolivia and Turkey, Model 90/91, Rimless, No. 367.. 6.00

Caliber 7.62 m/m Mossin, Model 91, Russia (378).............$6.00
Caliber 8 x 60 m/m Mauser, Rimless, No. 542.................. 6.00
Caliber 7.7 m/m Lee Metford, Model 89, Great Britain (453).... 6.00
Caliber 8 m/m Krag Jorgensen, Model 29, Denmark (358A)...... 7.50
Caliber 8 m/m Schmidt-Rubin, Model 90, Switzerland (388).... 7.50
Caliber 11 m/m German Army Model 71, Rim. No. 11.15 x 60 Rim, German Army Model 71................................. 5.50

IMPORTED RIMLESS CARTRIDGES FOR MANNLICHER-SCHOENAUER RIFLES

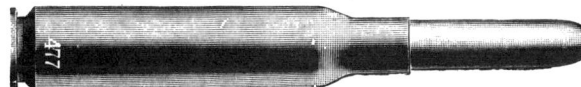

Mannlicher-Schoenauer 6.5 x 53 m/m Smokeless, S. P. or F. M. J..$5.00
(Mannlicher-Schoenauer 6.5 x 53 and 6.7 x 53 are one and the same cartridge.)

Mannlicher-Schoenauer 8 x 56 m/m Smokeless, S. P. or F. M. J....$5.00
(Formerly called 8.2 x 56.)

Mannlicher-Schoenauer 9 x 56 m/m Smokeless, S. P. or F. M. J....$5.75

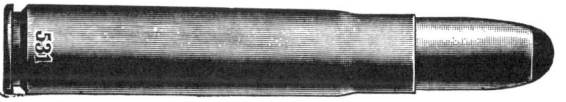

Mannlicher-Schoenauer, 9.5 x 57 m/m Smokeless, S. P. or F. M. J..$6.50

IMPORTED AUTOMATIC PISTOL CARTRIDGES

      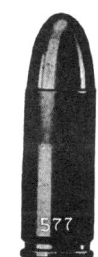   

Price Per Box of 50
.25 Cal. 6.35 m/m Mauser, Smokeless, F.M.J. (508A)..........$2.10
.32 Cal. 7.65 m/m Mauser, Smokeless, F.M.J. (497A)........... 2.50
.30 Cal. 7.65 m/m Luger, Smokeless, F.M.J. or H.P. (471)..... 4.00
.30 Cal. 7.65 m/m Luger Carbine Smkls, H.P. and F.M.J....... 5.00
9 m/m Cal. Luger, Smokeless, F.M.J. (480C)................. 4.25
9 m/m Cal. Luger Carbine, Smokeless, F.M.J. (480D)......... 5.25

Price Per Box of 50
7.63 m/m (30 Cal.) Mauser with Clips, Smokeless, F.M.J. (403)..$4.50
9 m/m Cal., Mauser, with Clips, Smokeless, F.M.J. (487)...... 6.00
9 m/m Short Browning, Orgies, Smokeless, F.M.J. (540)........ 3.75
7.65 m/m Mannlicher, Smokeless, F.M.J. (466)................ 5.60
7.65 m/m Mannlicher Carbine or Pistol, Smokeless, F.M.J. (497).. 5.70
9 m/m Steyr Pistol, with Clips, Smokeless, F.M.J. (577)...... 6.60

ODD SIZE SHOTGUN SHELLS
Price Per Box of 25, Size 7 Chilled Shot Only

14 Gauge $3.00
24 Gauge 2.75
32 Gauge 2.50

FRENCH AND ITALIAN CARTRIDGES

French Army Revolver, Mod. 1892, 8 mm., per box of 25......$2.40
French Army Revolver, Mod. 1873, 12 mm., per box of 25...... 1.75
French Army Aifle, Lebel, 8 mm., per box of 20............. 3.75
Italian Army Rifle, Mod. 1870-87, per box of 16............ 2.50

MISCELLANEOUS SPECIAL FOREIGN CARTRIDGE CLIPS

MAUSER MODEL '88 CARBINE
(Also Rifle)

The Model '88 rifle was the predecessor of the model '98 and was also made by various companies as a sporting rifle, for example, by Haenel and Schilling, and is often referred to as the Mannlicher Haenel. The cartridge has a round nose bullet of 236 grains and a powder charge lower than the model '98 since the model '88 action is not as strong as the model '98. This rifle uses a special clip containing five shells and after firing the last shell the empty magazine drops from the bottom of the magazine frame.

Model '88 cartridges per box of 20 without clips $5.00
Mauser Model '88 clip only .... .50

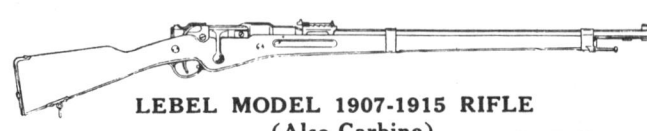

LEBEL MODEL 1907-1915 RIFLE
(Also Carbine)

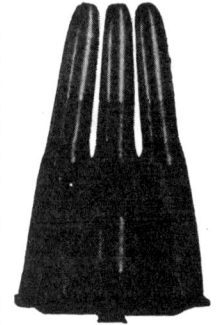

The Lebel rifle was the French army rifle during the World War and known as the Model 1907—15. The caliber is 8 m/m and the original bullet was a copper jacketed one showing exceptional ballistical properties. It is loaded with a special three shot clip. A later model 1916 with hand guard and a magazine capacity of five shots was introduced but no five shot clips are available in the U. S.

8 m/m Lebel cartridges (domestic) per box of 20 without clips $1.82
Three shot Lebel clip only .... .50

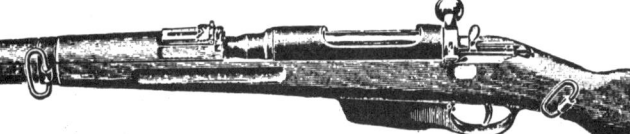

STEYR (BUDAPEST) MODEL '95 RIFLE

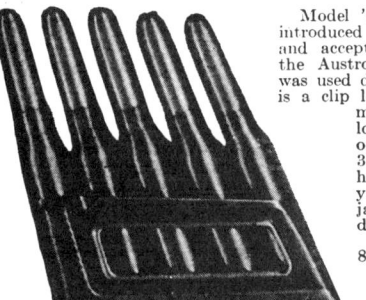

Model '95 Steyr is a straight pull rifle introduced in 1895 to the Austrian army and accepted as the Military weapon of the Austro-Hungarian army by whom it was used during the World War. This rifle is a clip loader with a special protruding magazine frame. Cartridges are loaded on clips of five. Capacity of the rifle is 17 aimed shots or 35 unaimed shots per minute and has a range up to five thousand yards. Penetration of the full metal jacketed bullet at 3300 yards in dry Pine is still approximately 3".

8x50 m/m cartridges with Spitzer soft point bullets, per box of 10 without clips $3.75
Model '95 Steyr clip only .. .50

RUMANIAN MODEL '93 RIFLE

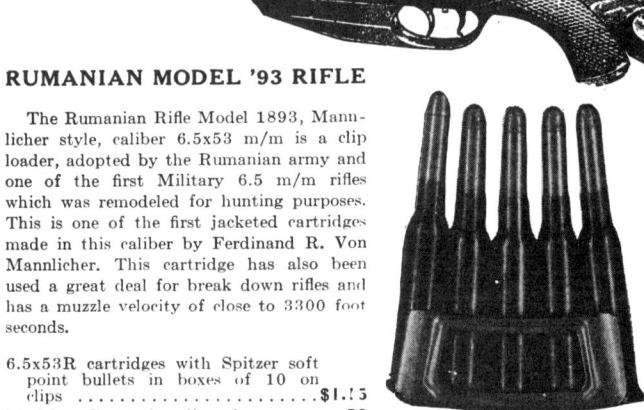

The Rumanian Rifle Model 1893, Mannlicher style, caliber 6.5x53 m/m is a clip loader, adopted by the Rumanian army and one of the first Military 6.5 m/m rifles which was remodeled for hunting purposes. This is one of the first jacketed cartridges made in this caliber by Ferdinand R. Von Mannlicher. This cartridge has also been used a great deal for break down rifles and has a muzzle velocity of close to 3300 foot seconds.

6.5x53R cartridges with Spitzer soft point bullets in boxes of 10 on clips $1.15
Model 93 Rumanian clip only .... .50

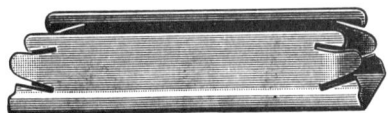

RUSSIAN MOSSIN MODEL '91 RIFLE

The Russian rifle, known as the Mossin Model '91 was built for Russia in the United States during the World War by various companies, particularly, however, by the Remington Arms Co. Very few of these rifles were ever delivered to Russia and consequently large quantities were disposed of at low prices in the U. S. The caliber is 7.62 m/m with rim and is equivalent to the .30 caliber. The cartridge has fine ballistical properties.

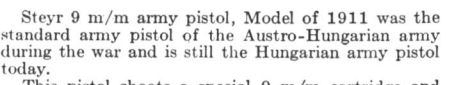

7.62x53 m/m cartridges with full patched bullets, per box of 10 without clips $3.00
Russian Mossin clip only .50

MAUSER MODEL '98 RIFLE
(Also Carbine)

The Model '98 rifle, is also finished as a carbine with shorter barrel and full stock to the muzzle. This was the standard German army rifle during the World War and is still used today without alteration except for a somewhat shorter barrel. The model 98 rifle is the most popular military rifle in the world and has been adapted by a number of countries as the regulation army rifle. The caliber is 7.92 but commonly referred to as 8 m/m.

Model '98 imported Spitzer soft point cartridges per box of 15 on clips $3.75
Mauser clip only .50

MAUSER MODEL 1896 AUTOMATIC PISTOL

The now discontinued Mauser 9 m/m military pistol, similar to 7.63 m/m Mauser illustrated, was originally chambered for the No. 487 Mauser 9 m/m cartridge. During the war, however, this model was chambered for the No. 480C 9 m/m Luger cartridge and such pistols are distinguished by the Figure "9" carved into the wooden grip. In ordering the ammunition for this pistol, it is essential to order by number—either 487 or 480C.
7.63 m/m cartridges per box of 20 on clips $1.80
9 m/m (487) per box of 20 on clips 2.40
9 m/m (480) per box of 50 on clips 1.90
7.63 or 9 m/m Mauser Pistol clip only .25

STEYR MODEL 1911 AUTOMATIC PISTOL

Steyr 9 m/m army pistol, Model of 1911 was the standard army pistol of the Austro-Hungarian army during the war and is still the Hungarian army pistol today.
This pistol shoots a special 9 m/m cartridge and is loaded on clips of 8 which is the capacity of the pistol. The pistol is rather unique in that the barrel rotates to unlock the breech.

9 m/m Steyr cartridges per box of 16 on clips. $2.64
Steyr 9 m/m clip only.. .25

See Pages 266 AND 267 FOR FOREIGN AMMUNITION

Original Brenneke Shotgun Slugs

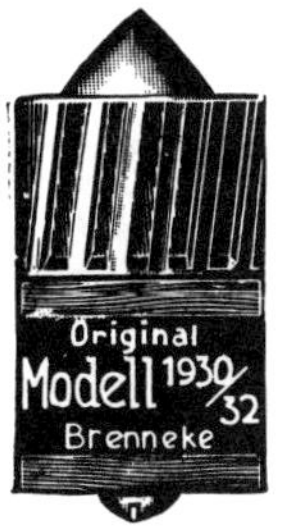

In response to the continued demand for a satisfactory shotgun slug, we now import in original Brenneke factory loaded shells with special powder, the world famous Brenneke Slugs—the finest made. Because of the excellent precision of these slugs, any shotgun, even those with heaviest choke bore, may be effectively used at ranges up to 100 yards against big game; up to 70 yards it is suitable for buffalo, bear, lion, tiger, etc. It may also be used in repeating and automatic shotguns. In use for over 40 years. Suitable for use in any Nitro tested shotgun barrel with or without choke boring. Capable of best results. Universally recognized in all countries as the best shotgun slug in the world.

Suitable for all large game, elk, bear and dangerous game of all sorts. The Brenneke bullet is the very best replacement for the unsatisfactory single ball and buckshot loads. Especially suited for the upland hunter who is principally dependent upon his shotgun, to whom it offers the possibility of using his gun as an accurate double barrel rifle through use of the Brenneke Slugs. Because of this the double barrel shotgun may be considered the general all purpose hand weapon.

Highest accuracy is combined with satisfactory effect at a distance of 60 to 75 yards. The muzzle velocity and energy of the Brenneke Slug in 12 gauge is as follows:

Velocity 1485 foot seconds.
Energy 2712 foot pounds.
Breech pressure about 420 atmospheres.

The penetration is surprisingly great, 6 to 7 inches, in pine. Large game weighing up to 330 pounds is ordinarily shot through with normal angle shots. For very large or dangerous game the bullet with steel tip is recommended. With steel tip the penetration is increased to 12 inches in pine at 50 yards, and is adapted for the heaviest and most dangerous game including elephants.

The accompanying illustration was originally shot at 25, 50 and 80 meters at the German Proof House in Berlin with a double barrel shotgun and shows excellent precision. The rise or drop of the slug from line of sight as tested at the Proof House in 12 and 16 gauge is as follows, ⊙ representing the point blank sight setting:—

	25 Meters (27½ yd.)	50 Meters (55 yd.)	75 Meters (82½ yd.)	80 Meters (88 yd.)
Distance	⊙	—1″	—3¾″	—4¾″
	+⅝″	⊙	—2½″	—3¼″
	+1¼″	+1⅝″	⊙	—1¼″
	+1⅜″	+2″	+⅝″	⊙

Opinions of actual shooters: Phenomenal unequalled sledge-hammer effect; Performance such as few rifle bullets offer; Astonishing precision. Many hundreds of bear, elk, leopard, crocodile, lion and other large game have been dropped immediately by its terrific lightning-like performance

Model 1935 Slug

Available for the first time in 1937. Replaces the Model 1932 being improved in details.

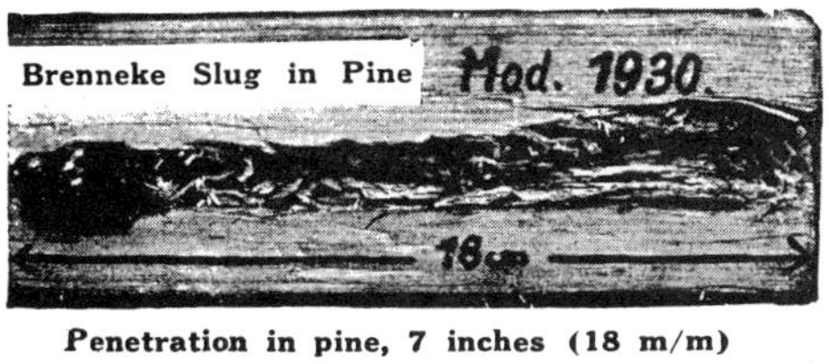

Penetration in pine, 7 inches (18 m/m)

ALL SHELLS

NON-CORROSIVE

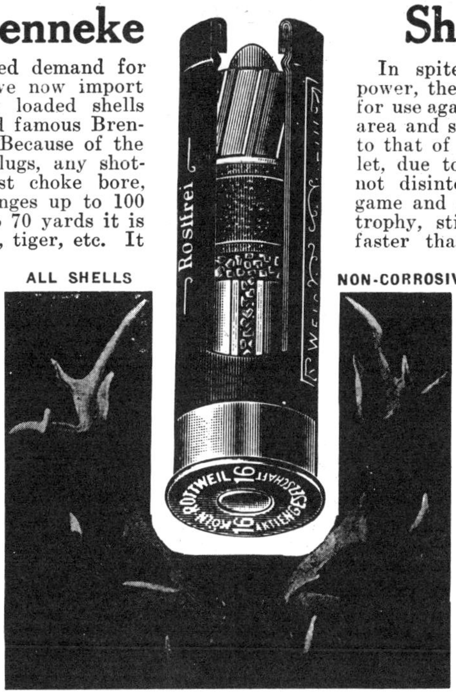

This 16 point elk was shot with Brenneke slug at a distance of 55 yards. The elk collapsed in its tracks without hearing the report of the gun

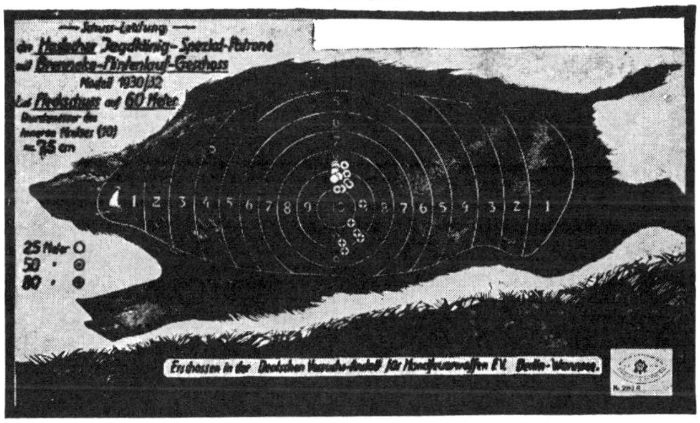

Official Proof House Target showing shots at 25 meters (27½ yards), 50 meters (55 yards), and 80 meters (88 yards)

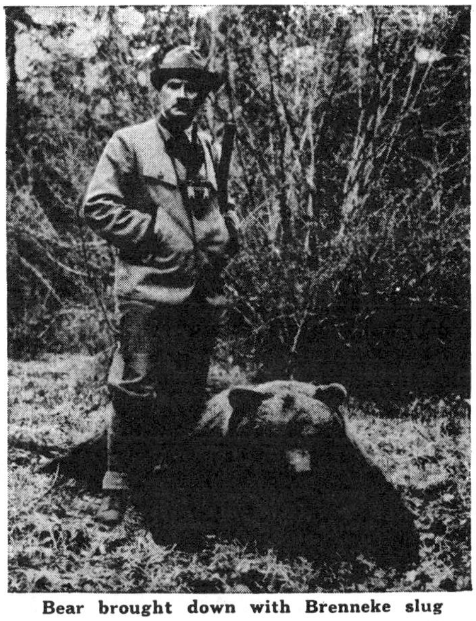

Bear brought down with Brenneke slug

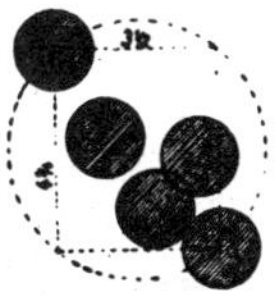

Official Proof House Group, 1⅜ x 1¾ inches (3½ x 4¼ Cm.) Shot at 66 yards

In spite of the tremendous shocking power, the Brenneke slug is ideally suited for use against deer because its tremendous area and shocking power is vastly superior to that of almost any other available bullet, due to the fact that the bullet does not disintegrate in passing through the game and consequently does not spoil the trophy, still the game is dropped much faster than would be thought possible. Many experienced hunters advise us that the use of the Brenneke slug in double barrel shotguns for running game is always better and more successful than the use of any rifle or double rifle. The Brenneke slug may be shot from barrels even with heaviest choke bore without danger because the slug is especially constructed for use in barrels having choke as high as .047″ at muzzle.

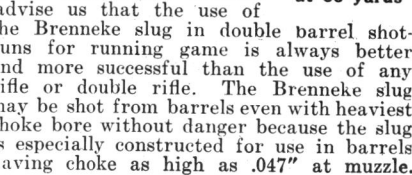

Attached Felt Wad

No slug without this highly important patented feature can possibly have the same stability, velocity, energy, and smashing effect. Slugs with loose wads are upset in flight.

The felt wad screwed onto the bullet prevents "key-holing" and with the point always forward, the accuracy is enhanced. The accuracy is about 3 inches at 50 yards and 6 inches at 100 yards. At 35 yards all shots can be placed in one irregular hole.

Special Powder

Two of the largest European powder factories have collaborated with Brenneke in the development of a special powder, the first of its kind, developed exclusively for maximum results with the Brenneke Slug. The success of this new powder, with which the shells are loaded in Europe, has been so startling, that we now import the factory loaded shells and can thus assure our customers of the very finest.

Hand Loading Brenneke Slugs

The usual powder load used in regular shot shells is employed; the gas pressure is, however, lower than in normal shot shells, consequently 10% increased charges may be used to increase penetration. As the heavy wad is permanently attached by a screw, no other wad should be used—to do so upsets the flight—and the slug is placed directly over the powder.

Police, Guard and State Troopers

Police Departments, Guards, State Troopers, and other organizations entrusted with law enforcement will find the Brenneke Slugs ideal. For use against automobile bandits the steel tip is recommended.

Prices Per Box of 10

Offered both as Brenneke factory loaded shells and also as slugs only, for reloading.

Brenneke Model 1935 with guide ribs, wad and hardened lead point.

	Slugs only	Loaded Shells
12 gauge	**$1.50**	**$2.50**
16 or 20 gauge	**1.25**	**2.25**

Brenneke Model 1935 with guide ribs attached wad and hardened steel point.

	Slugs only	Loaded Shells
12 gauge	**$2.25**	**$3.00**
16 or 20 gauge	**2.50**	**2.75**

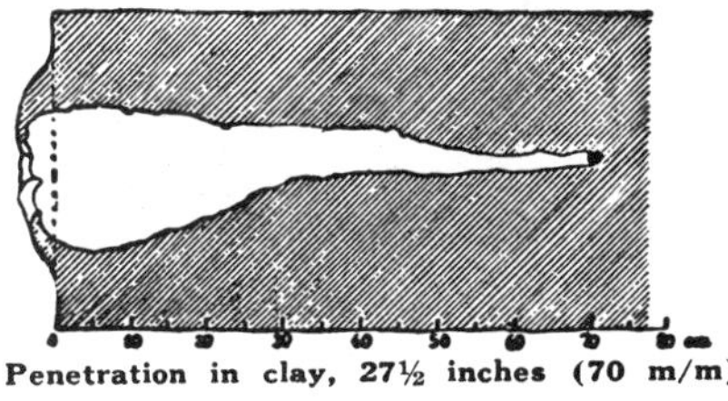

Penetration in clay, 27½ inches (70 m/m)

SEE PAGE 8, "HOW TO ORDER"

REMINGTON SHOTGUN SHELLS

KLEANBORE

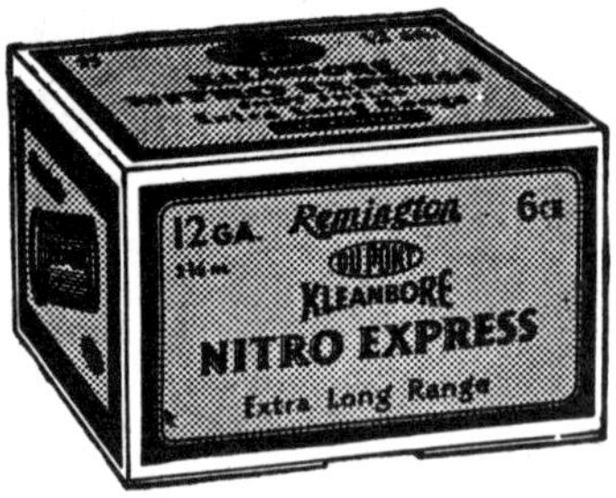

NITRO EXPRESS

LONG RANGE

Green Shells—Wetproof

Chilled Shot Only—Loaded only with Progressive Burning Powder

Load No.	Gauge and Brand	Length Shell Ins.	Powder Equiv. Drams	Ozs. Shot	Chilled Shot Only	Avg. Wgt. per Case	Price per Box of 25
10NE	10 Ga. Nitro Exp.....	2⅞	4¾	1⅝	2, 4, 5, 6............	80	$1.62
10NEBB	10 Ga. Nitro Exp.....	2⅞	4¾	1⅝	BB.................	78	1.62
10NE2	10 Ga. Nitro Exp.....	3½	5	2	2, 4, 5, 6 (Magnum)..	97	1.97
10NE2	10 Ga. Nitro Exp.....	3½	5	2	BB (Magnum).......	97	1.97
12NE	12 Ga. Nitro Exp.....	2¾	3¾	1¼	2, 4, 5, 6, 7, 7½......	65	1.32
12NEBB	12 Ga. Nitro Exp.....	2¾	3¾	1¼	BB.................	63	1.32
16NE	16 Ga. Nitro Exp.....	2 9/16	3	1⅛	2, 4, 5, 6, 7, 7½......	57	1.25
16NEBB	16 Ga. Nitro Exp.....	2 9/16	3	1⅛	BB.................	55	1.25
16ATX	16 Ga. Auto Exp......	2¾	3¼	1⅛	4, 5, 6, 7, 7½.........	58	1.32
20NE	20 Ga. Nitro Exp.....	2¾	2¾	1	2, 4, 5, 6, 7, 7½, 8....	52	1.25
28NE	28 Ga. Nitro Exp.....	2⅞	2¼	¾	4, 6, 7½, 9..........	37	1.20
410NE	410 Ga. Nitro Exp....	2½	....	½	4, 5, 6, 7½..........	25	.84
4103NE	410 Ga. Nitro Exp....	3	....	¾	4, 5, 6, 7½..........	33	.96

NITRO EXPRESS—BUCKSHOT SINGLE BALL AND RIFLED SLUG

Long Range Loads

*Load No.	Gauge and Brand	Length Shell Ins.	Powder Equiv. Drams	Ozs. Shot	Chilled Shot Only	Avg. Wgt. per Case	Price per Box of 25
10NEBK	10 Ga. Nitro Exp.....	2⅞	4¾	...	0 Buck—16 Pellets...	85	$1.69
12NEBK	12 Ga. Nitro Exp.....	2¾	3¾	...	0 Buck—12 Pellets...	68	1.39
12NEBK	12 Ga. Nitro Exp.....	2¾	3¾	...	00 Buck—9 Pellets...	65	1.39
12GRD	12 Ga. Nitro Exp.....	2¾	3¾	...	00 Buck—9 Pellets... (Protected Crimp Guard Work)	69	1.49
12GRD	12 Ga. Nitro Exp.....	2¾	3¾	...	0 Buck—12 Pellets.. (Protected Crimp Guard Work)	66	1.49
12NEBK	12 Ga. Nitro Exp.....	2¾	3¾	...	1 Buck—16 Pellets...	71	1.39
12NEBK	12 Ga. Nitro Exp.....	2¾	3¾	...	4 Buck—27 Pellets...	67	1.39
16NEBK	16 Ga. Nitro Exp.....	2 9/16	3	...	1 Buck—12 Pellets...	56	1.33
20NEBK	20 Ga. Nitro Exp.....	2¾	2¾	...	3 Buck—20 Pellets...	57	1.33
12NERS	12 Ga. Nitro Exp.....	2¾	3¾	1	Rifled Slug.........	55	2.11
16NERS	16 Ga. Nitro Exp.....	2 9/16	3	⅞	Rifled Slug.........	46	2.07
20NERS	20 Ga. Nitro Exp.....	2½	2¾	⅝	Rifled Slug.........	42	2.01
410NERS	410 Ga. Nitro Exp....	2½	....	⅕	Rifled Slug.........	53	1.77
12NESB	12 Ga. Nitro Exp.....	2¾	3¾	1	Single Ball..........	56	1.39
16NESB	16 Ga. Nitro Exp.....	2 9/16	3	⅞	Single Ball..........	47	1.33
20NESB	20 Ga. Nitro Exp.....	2¾	2¾	⅝	Single Ball..........	43	1.33
410NESB	410 Ga. Nitro Exp....	2½	....	⅕	Single Ball..........	16	.91
4103NESB	410 Ga. Nitro Exp....	3	...	⅕	Single Ball..........	18	1.04

KLEANBORE SHOTGUN SHELLS

Wetproof—Loaded with Smokeless Powder

*Load No.	Gauge and Brand	Length Shell Ins.	Powder Equiv. Drams	Ozs. Shot	Size Shot	Avg. Wgt. per Case	Price per Box of 25
					SHUR SHOT		
S17	10 Ga. Shur Shot.....	2⅞	4¼	1¼	4, 6 Soft............	65	$1.25
S17	10 Ga. Shur Shot.....	2 ⁄8	4¼	1¼	4, 5, 6 Chilled........	65	1.32
S6	12 Ga. Shur Shot.....	2⅝	3	1	4, 5, 6, 7, 8 Soft......	55	.91
S7	12 Ga. Shur Shot	2⅝	3	1⅛	4, 5, 6, 7, 8, 9, 10 Soft.	58	.96
S7	12 Ga. Shur Shot.....	2⅝	3	1⅛	4, 5, 6, 7½ Chilled....	58	1.02
S9	12 Ga. Shur Shot.....	2⅝	3¼	1⅛	2, 4, 5, 6, 7, 8 Soft....	58	1.02
S9	12 Ga. Shur Shot.....	2⅝	3¼	1⅛	BB................	56	1.08
S9	12 Ga. Shur Shot.....	2⅝	3¼	1⅛	4, 5, 6, 7½ Chilled....	58	1.08
S20	16 Ga. Shur Shot.....	2 9/16	2½	1	4, 5, 6, 7, 8, 9, 10 Soft.	51	.90
S20	16 Ga. Shur Shot.....	2 9/16	2½	1	4, 5, 6, 7½ Chilled...	51	.96
S20A	16 Ga. Shur Shot.....	2 9/16	2¾	1	4, 5, 6, 7½ Chilled....	51	.96
S23	20 Ga. Shur Shot.....	2½	2¼	⅞	4, 5, 6, 7, 8, 9, 10 Soft.	45	.90
S23	20 Ga. Shur Shot.....	2½	2¼	⅞	4, 5, 6, 7½ Chilled....	45	.96
S25	28 Ga. Shur Shot.....	2½	1¾	⅝	6, 7½ Chilled........	33	.88

SHUR SHOT SHELLS

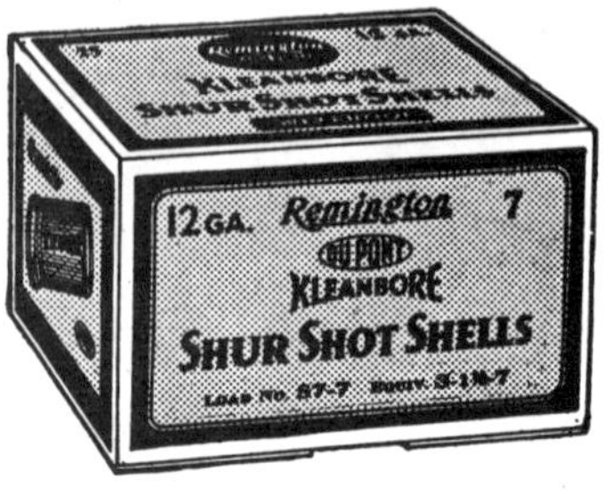

Green Shells—Wetproof

Loaded with Smokeless Powder

SHUR SHOT SCATTER LOADS

Load No.	Gauge and Brand	Length Shell Ins.	Powder Equiv. Drams	Ozs. Shot	Size Shot	Avg. Wgt. per Case	Price per Box of 25
SL7	12 Ga. Shur Shot.....	2¾	3	1⅛	6, 8 Soft............	60	$1.04
SL7	12 Ga. Shur Shot.....	2¾	3	1⅛	6, 7½ Chilled........	60	1.09
SL20	16 Ga. Shur Shot.....	2 9/16	2½	1	8 Soft..............	52	.97
SL20	16 Ga. Shur Shot.....	2 9/16	2½	1	6, 7½ Chilled........	52	1.02
SL23	20 Ga. Shur Shot.....	2½	2¼	⅞	8 Soft..............	46	.95
SL23	20 Ga. Shur Shot.....	2½	2¼	⅞	6, 7½ Chilled........	46	1.00

SHUR SHOT—BLANK LOADS

Loaded with Black Powder Only

S10B	10 Ga. Shur Shot Blks.	2⅞	8	...	....	40	$1.20
S12B	12 Ga. Shur Shot Blks.	2⅝	6	...	....	32	1.14

SHUR SHOT CRIMP SHELLS

Choice of M. X. or R. D. Powders

TRAP LOADS

CS4	12 Ga. Crimptrap....	2¾	2¾	1⅛	7½, 8 Chilled........	...	$1.02
CS7	12 Ga. Crimptrap....	2¾	3	1⅛	7½, 8 Chilled........	...	1.02
CS8	12 Ga. Crimptrap....	2¾	3	1¼	7½, 8 Chilled........	62	1.08
C12ST	12 Ga. Crimptrap....	2¾	3⅛	1¼	7½ Chilled...........	...	1.14
CS10	12 Ga. Crimptrap....	2¾	3¼	1¼	7, 7½ Chilled........	...	1.14
C12RTC	12 Ga. Crimptrap....	2¾	3	1¼	7½, 8 Coppered Shot.	...	1.27
C12HTC	12 Ga. Crimptrap....	2¾	3⅛	1¼	7½ Coppered Shot...	...	1.33
CS20F	16 Ga. Crimptrap....	2¾	2¾	1⅛	8 Chilled............	55	1.02
CS23G	20 Ga. Crimptrap....	2¾	2½	1	8 Chilled............	48	1.02
					SKEET LOADS		
C12SK	12 Ga. Crimpskeet....	2⅝	3⅛	1⅛	9 Chilled............	58	1.02
C16SK	16 Ga. Crimpskeet....	2¾	2½	1	9 Chilled............	51	.96
C20SK	20 Ga. Crimpskeet....	2¾	2¼	⅞	9 Chilled............	45	.96
S28	†28 Ga. Shur Shot....	2¾	2¼	¾	9 Chilled............	38	.96

ARROW EXPRESS—LACQUERED

12AE	12 Ga. Arrow Exp....	2¾	3¾	1¼	2, 4, 5, 6, 7 Chilled...	66	$1.49
12A34	12 Ga. Arrow Exp....	3	3¾	1¼	7, 7½ Chilled.......	66	1.62
12A33	12 Ga. Arrow Exp....	3	4	1⅜	2, 4, 5, 6 Chilled.....	71	1.62
12A33	12 Ga. Arrow Exp....	3	4	1⅜	BB................	71	1.62
12A35	12 Ga. Arrow Exp....	3	4¼	1⅝	2, 4, 5, 6 Chilled.....	75	1.7[illegible]
12A35	12 Ga. Arrow Exp....	3	4¼	1⅝	BB................	75	1.74
16AE	16 Ga. Arrow Exp....	2 9/16	3	1⅛	4, 5, 6, 7½ Chilled..	57	1.44
20AE	20 Ga. Arrow Exp....	2¾	2¾	1	4, 5, 6, 7½ Chilled.	52	1.38
					BUCKSHOT		
12A35	12 Ga. Arrow Express.	3	4¼	...	0 Buck—15 Pellets ..	78	1.81
12A35	12 Ga. Arrow Express.	3	4¼	...	00 Buck—12 Pellets..	78	1.81

ARROW

7	12 Ga. Arrow	2⅝	3	1⅛	6, 7, 8, 9 Soft........	60	$1.21
7	12 Ga. Arrow	2⅝	3	1⅛	6, 7½ Chilled........	60	1.26
9	12 Ga. Arrow.........	2⅝	3¼	1⅛	4, 5, 6, 7, 8 Soft......	61	1.25
9	12 Ga. Arrow.........	2⅝	3¼	1⅛	4, 5, 6, 7½ Chilled....	61	1.29
20A	16 Ga. Arrow.........	2 9/16	2¾	1	6, 7, 8, 9 Soft........	53	1.18
20A	16 Ga. Arrow.........	2 9/16	2¾	1	6, 7½ Chilled........	53	1.23
23	20 Ga. Arrow.........	2½	2¼	⅞	6, 7, 8, 9 Soft........	47	1.12
23	20 Ga. Arrow.........	2½	2¼	⅞	6, 7½ Chilled........	47	1.17

SEE PAGE 8, "HOW TO ORDER"

PETERS "RUSTLESS" SHOTGUN SHELLS

"HIGH VELOCITY"
Loaded with Smokeless Powder

Load No.	Gauge	Length Shell Inches	Powder Equiv. Drams	Ounces Shot	Size Shot Unlacquered	Price per Box 25
100CH	10	2⅞	4¾	1⅝	BB 2, 4, 5, 6 Chilled	$1.62
132	12	2¾	3¾	1¼	BB 2, 4, 5, 6, 7, 7½ Chilled	1.32
9150CH	*12	3	3¾	1¼	7, 7½ Chilled	1.62
9160CH	12	3	4	1⅜	BB 2, 4, 5, 6 Chilled	1.62
9170CH	12	3	4¼	1⅝	BB 2, 4, 5, 6 Chilled	1.74
160CH	16	2⅞	3	1⅛	BB 2, 4, 5, 6, 7, 7½ Chilled	1.25
170CH	16	2¾	3¼	1⅛	4, 5, 6, 7, 7½ Chilled	1.32
200CH	20	2¾	2¾	1	2, 4, 5, 6, 7, 7½, 8 Chilled	1.25
290CH	20	2½	2¾	1	4, 5, 6, 7½ Chilled	1.25
280CH	28	2⅞	2¼	¾	4, 6, 7½, 8 Chilled	1.20
4190CH	410	2½	...	½	4, 5, 6, 7½ Chilled	.84
4130CH	410	3	...	¾	4, 5, 6, 7½ Chilled	.96

SINGLE BALL LOADS

Load No.	Gauge	Length Shell Inches	Powder Equiv. Drams	Ounces Shot	Size Shot Unlacquered	Price per Box 25
HV12SB	12	2¾	3¾	1	Single Ball	$1.39
HV16SB	16	2⅞	3	⅞	Single Ball	1.33
HV20SB	20	2¾	2¾	⅝	Single Ball	1.35
HV410SB	410	2½	...	⅕	Single Ball	.91
HV413SB	410	3	...	⅕	Single Ball	1.04

BUCKSHOT LOADS

Load No.	Gauge	Length Shell Inches	Powder Equiv. Drams	Ounces Shot	Size Shot Unlacquered	Price per Box 25
X330	10	2⅞	4¾	...	No. 0-Buck 16 Pellets	$1.69
X3400	12	2¾	3¾	...	No. 00-Buck 9 Pellets	1.39
X341	12	2¾	3¾	...	No. 1-Buck 16 Pellets	1.39
X344	12	2¾	3¾	...	No. 4-Buck 27 Pellets	1.39
X340	12	2¾	3¾	...	No. 0-Buck 12 Pellets	1.39
XPC0	12	2¾	3¾	...	Prot. Crimp, No. 0 Buck	1.49
XPC00	12	2¾	3¾	...	Prot. Crimp, No. 00 Buck	1.49
X351	16	2⅞	3	...	No. 1-Buck 12 Pellets	1.33
X363	20	2¾	2¾	...	No. 3-Buck 20 Pellets	1.33

"DELUXE TARGET"
Loaded with Smokeless Powder

The new "DELUXE TARGET" made for the discriminating sportsman who wants a load of highest quality, superior in every detail. These shells have the easy loading "water-tite" bevel crimp, perfect shot, and reinforced long brass base.

Load No.	Gauge	Length Shell Inches	Powder Equiv. Drams	Ounces Shot	Size Shot Unlacquered	Price per Box 25
9120	12	2⅝	3	1⅛	6, 7, 8, 9 Soft	$1.21
9120CH	12	2⅝	3	1⅛	6, 7½ Chilled	1.26
9130	12	2⅝	3¼	1⅛	4, 5, 6, 7, 8 Soft	1.25
9130CH	12	2⅝	3¼	1⅛	4, 5, 6, 7½ Chilled	1.29
9230	16	2⅞	2¾	1	6, 7, 8, 9 Soft	1.18
9230CH	16	2⅞	2¾	1	6, 7½ Chilled	1.23
9350	20	2½	2¼	⅞	6, 7, 8, 9 Soft	1.12
9350CH	20	2½	2¼	⅞	6, 7½ Chilled	1.17

LACQUERED—"DELUXE TARGET"—LONG RANGE

Load No.	Gauge	Length Shell Inches	Powder Equiv. Drams	Ounces Shot	Size Shot Unlacquered	Price per Box 25
9140CH	12	2¾	3¾	1¼	2, 4, 5, 6, 7, 7½ Chilled	$1.49
9240CH	16	2⅞	3	1⅛	4, 5, 6, 7½ Chilled	1.44
9360CH	20	2½	2¾	1	4, 5, 6, 7½ Chilled	1.38
9370CH	20	2¾	2¾	1	4, 5, 6, 7½ Chilled	1.38

RIFLED SLUG LOADS

Load No.	Gauge	Length Shell Inches	Powder Equiv. Drams	Ounces Shot	Size Shot Unlacquered	Price per Box 25
120SG	12	2¾	3¾	1	Approx. Rifled Slug	$2.11
160SG	16	2⅞	3	⅞	Approx. Rifled Slug	2.07
200SG	20	2¾	2¾	⅝	Approx. Rifled Slug	2.01
410SG	410	2½	...	...	Approx. Rifled Slug	1.77

VICTOR SHELLS WITH CRIMP
Du Pont MX or Hercules Red Dot Powder

The mouth of this shell is tucked in and ironed out, eliminating use of any top wad to interfere with shot pattern. This new feature gives extra yardage, cleaner shooting, improved waterproofing, no more blown or "doughnut" patterns.

Load No.	Gauge	Length Shell Inches	Powder Equiv. Drams	Ounces Shot	Size Shot Unlacquered	Price per Box 25
TRAP LOADS						
PC-7120CH	12	2¾	3	1¼	7½, 8 Chilled Trap	$1.02
PC-7160CH	12	2¾	2¾	1¼	7½, 8 Chilled Trap	1.02
PC-7150CH	12	2¾	3	1⅛	7½, 8 Chilled Trap	1.08
PC-7170CH	12	2¾	3¼	1⅛	7, 7½ Chilled Trap	1.14
PC-7180CH	12	2¾	3⅛	1⅛	7½ Chilled Trap	1.14
PC-8150CP	12	2¾	3	1¼	7½, 8 Trap, Copper Plated	1.27
PC-8180CP	12	2¾	3⅛	1¼	7½ Trap, Copper Plated	1.33
PC-7560CH	16	2¾	2¾	1⅛	8 Chilled Trap	1.02
PC-7740CH	20	2¾	2¾	1	8 Chilled Trap	1.02
SKEET LOADS						
PC-7149CH	12	2¾	3	1⅛	9 Chilled Skeet	$1.02
PC-7539CH	16	2¾	2½	1	9 Chilled Skeet	.96
PC-7739CH	20	2¾	2¼	⅞	9 Chilled Skeet	.96

VICTOR—FIELD LOADS
Loaded with Smokeless Powder

Load No.	Gauge	Length Shell Inches	Powder Equiv. Drams	Ounces Shot	Size Shot Unlacquered	Price per Box 25
5370SOFT	10	2⅞	4¼	1¼	4, 6 Soft	$1.25
5370CH	10	2⅞	4¼	1¼	4, 5, 6 Chilled	1.32
5110SOFT	12	2⅝	3	1	4, 5, 6, 7, 8 Soft	.92
5140SOFT	12	2⅝	3	1⅛	4, 5, 6, 7, 8 Soft	.96
5140CH	12	2⅝	3	1⅛	4, 5, 6, 7½ Chilled	1.02
5160SOFT	12	2⅝	3¼	1⅛	2, 4, 5, 6, 7, 8 Soft	1.02
5160CH	12	2⅝	3¼	1⅛	BB 4, 5, 6, 7½ Chilled	1.08
5530SOFT	16	2⅞	2½	1	4, 5, 6, 7, 8, 9, 10 Soft	.90
5530CH	16	2⅞	2½	1	4, 5, 6, 7½ Chilled	.96
5540CH	16	2⅞	2¾	1	4, 5, 6, 7½ Chilled	.96
5730SOFT	20	2½	2¼	⅞	4, 5, 6, 7, 8, 9, 10 Soft	.90
5730CH	20	2½	2¼	⅞	4, 5, 6, 7½ Chilled	.96
5970CH	28	2⅞	1⅞	⅝	6, 7½ Chilled	.88

"VICTOR"—SPREADER LOADS
Loaded with Smokeless Powder

Load No.	Gauge	Length Shell Inches	Powder Equiv. Drams	Ounces Shot	Size Shot Unlacquered	Price per Box 25
6140SPR.	12	2⅝	3	1⅛	6, 8 Soft	$1.04
6140CH. SPR.	12	2⅝	3	1⅛	6, 7½ Chilled	1.09
6530SPR.	16	2⅞	2½	1	8 Soft	.97
6530CH. SPR.	16	2⅞	2½	1	6, 7½ Chilled	1.02
6730SPR.	20	2½	2¼	⅞	8 Soft	.95
6730CH. SPR.	20	2½	2¼	⅞	6, 7½ Chilled	1.00

"VICTOR"—BLANKS

	10	2⅞	8	...	Blanks, Black Powder	$1.20
	12	2⅝	6	...	Blanks, Black Powder	1.14

SEND YOUR GUN TO STOEGER FOR EXPERT REPAIRING

WESTERN SHOTGUN SHELLS

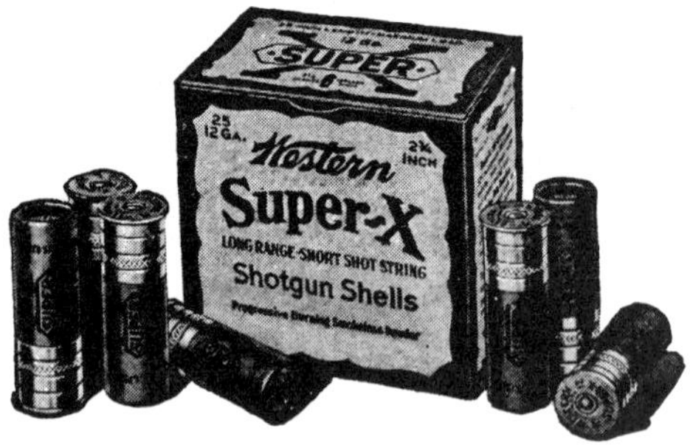

SUPER-X
The Original Long-Range Load

Supplied in a special Steel-Locked Shell with Progressive Burning Powder and Non-Corrosive Primers

Load No.	Gauge	Length Shell	Ounces Shot	Size, Chilled Shot	Wt. of Case	Price per Box–25
S14C	10	2⅞ in.	1⅝	BB, 2, 4, 5, 6 Chilled	76	$1.62
P15C	†*10	3½ Mag.	2	BB, 2, 4, 5, 6 Chilled	98	1.93
S36C	12	2¾ in.	1¼	BB, 2, 4, 5, 6, 7, 7½ Ch.	63	1.32
P37C	*12	3 in.	1⅜	BB, 2, 4, 5, 6 Chilled	71	1.62
P38C	*12	3 Mag.	1⅝	BB, 2, 4, 5, 6 Chilled	78	1.74
S61C	16	2 9/16	1⅛	BB, 2, 4, 5, 6, 7, 7½ Ch.	54	1.25
S66C	16	2¾ Mag.	1⅛	4, 5, 6, 7, 7½ Chilled	56	1.32
S05C	20	2¾	1	2, 4, 5, 6, 7, 7½, 8 Ch.	49	1.25
S82C	28	2⅞	¾	4, 6, 7½, 9 Chilled	39	1.20
S47C	410	2½	½	4, 5, 6, 7½ Chilled	24	.84
S48C	410	3	¾	4, 5, 6, 7½ Chilled	33	.96

*Loaded in Record high brass shell.
† Adapted only to guns weighing 10½ lbs. or more, with 3½ inch chambers and modern steel barrels. Specify Super-X Magnum.

SUPER X
Buckshot—Rifled Slugs—Single Ball

Load No.	Gauge	Length Shell	Size and Kind of Shot	Pellets in Layer	Wt. of Case	Price per Box–25
S140B	10	2⅞ in.	0 Buck–16 Pellets	4	83	$1.69
S5200B	12	3	00 Buck—12 Pellets		78	1.81
S520B	12	3	0 Buck—15 Pellets		79	1.81
S3500B	12	2¾ in.	00 Buck–9 Pellets	3	66	1.39
SR3500B	12	2¾ in.	00 Buck–9 Pellets (Riot)	3	66	1.49
S360B	12	2¾ in.	0 Buck–12 Pellets	3	66	1.39
SR360B	12	2¾ in.	0 Buck–12 Pellets (Riot)	3	66	1.49
S361B	12	2¾ in.	1 Buck–16 Pellets	4	66	1.39
S364B	12	2¾ in.	4 Buck–27 Pellets (*6 Pellets in top layer)	7*	66	1.39
S611B	16	2 9/16 in.	1 Buck–12 Pellets	3	54	1.33
S053B	20	2¾ in.	3 Buck–20 Pellets	4	49	1.33
S415	12	2¾ in.	Rifled Slugs		58	2.11
S350	16	2 9/16 in.	Rifled Slugs		50	2.07
S282	20	2¾ in.	Rifled Slugs		42	2.01
S93	410	2½	Rifled Slugs		19	1.77
S33S	12	2¾ in.	Single Ball		55	1.39
S60S	16	2 9/16 in.	Single Ball		45	1.33
S04S	20	2¾ in.	Single Ball		38	1.33
S41S	410	2½ in.	Single Ball		16	.91
S413S	410	3 in.	Single Ball		18	1.04

SUPER-X
With Lubaloy (Copperized) Shot

Supplied in the Record High Brass Shell with Progressive Burning Powder.

Load No.	Gauge	Length Shell	Ounces Shot	Size Shot	Wt. of Case	Price per Box–25
P15L	*10	3½ Mag.	2	BB, 2, 4, 5, 6	98	$2.52
P36L	12	2¾ in.	1¼	2, 4, 5, 6, 7, 7½	65	1.57
PP26L	12	3 in.	1¼	7, 7½	67	1.82
P37L	12	3 in.	1⅜	BB, 2, 4, 5, 6,	71	1.89
P38L	12	3 Mag.	1⅝	BB, 2, 4, 5, 6	78	2.07
P61L	16	2 9/16 in.	1⅛	4, 5, 6, 7½	56	1.48
P05L	20	2¾ in.	1	4, 5, 6, 7½	50	1.46

* Adapted only to guns weighing 10½ lbs. or more, with 3½ inch chambers and modern steel barrels. Specify Super-X Magnum Lubaloy.

XPERT

Loaded with Smokeless Powder and Non-Corrosive Primers.

Load No.	Gauge	Length Shell	Dram Equiv. Powder	Ounces Shot	Size and Kind of Shot	Wt. of Case	Price per Box–25
X11	10	2⅞ in.	4¼	1¼	4, 6 Soft	65	$1.26
X11C	10	2⅞ in.	4¼	1¼	4, 5, 6 Chilled	65	1.32
X24	12	2⅝ in.	3	1	4, 5, 6, 7, 8 Soft	54	.92
X34	12	2⅝ in.	3	1⅛	4, 5, 6, 7, 8, 9, 10 Soft	57	.96

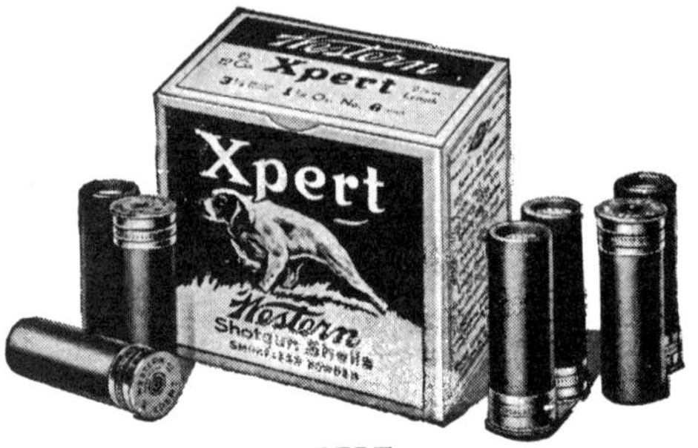

Continued **XPERT**

Load No.	Gauge	Length Shell	Dram Equiv. Powder	Ounces Shot	Size and Kind of Shot	Wt. of Case	Price per Box–25
X34C	12	2⅝ in.	3	1⅛	4, 5, 6, 7½ Chilled	57	$1.02
X42	12	2⅝ in.	3¼	1⅛	2, 4, 5, 6, 7, 8 Soft	57	1.02
X42C	12	2⅝ in.	3¼	1⅛	BB, 4, 5, 6, 7½ Ch.	57	1.08
X65	16	2 9/16 in.	2½	1	4, 5, 6, 7, 8, 9, 10 Soft	50	.90
X67C	16	2 9/16 in.	2½	1	4, 5, 6, 7½, 9 Chilled	50	.96
X01	16	2 9/16 in.	2¾	1	4, 5, 6, 7½ Chilled	50	.96
X01C	20	2½ in.	2¼	⅞	4, 5, 6, 7, 8, 9, 10 Soft	45	.90
X81C	20	2½ in.	2¼	⅞	4, 5, 6, 7½ Chilled	45	.96
	28	2½ in.	1¾	⅝	6, 7½ Chilled	34	.88

XPERT (Thicket Loads)

V34	12	2¾	3	1⅛	6, 8 Soft	57	$1.03
V34C	12	2¾	3	1⅛	6, 7½ Chilled	57	1.09
V65	16	2 9/16	2½	1	8 Soft	50	.97
V65C	16	2 9/16	2½	1	6, 7½ Chilled	50	1.02
V01	20	2½	2¼	⅞	8 Soft	45	.95
V01C	20	2½	2¼	⅞	6, 7½ Chilled	45	1.00

XPERT SUPER TRAP LOADS WITH CRIMP

Loaded with any standard smokeless powder listed herewith:—WESTERN MINIMAX (WM), DuPont MX (MX), Hercules Red Dot (HR).

XT22CS	12	2¾ in.	2¾	1⅛	7½, 8 Chilled	57	$1.02
XT34CS	12	2¾ in.	3	1⅛	7½, 8 Chilled	57	1.02
XT26CS	12	2¾ in.	3	1¼	7½, 8 Chilled	63	1.08
XT27CS	12	2¾ in.	3⅛	1¼	7½ Chilled	63	1.14
XT29CS	12	2¾ in.	3¼	1¼	7, 7½ Chilled	63	1.14
XT26LS	12	2¾ in.	3	1¼	7½, 8 Lubaloy	63	1.27
XT27LS	12	2¾ in.	3⅛	1¼	7½ Lubaloy	63	1.33
XT62CS	16	2 9/16 in.	2¾	1⅛	8 Chilled	53	1.02
XT03CS	20	2¾ in.	2½	1	8 Chilled	49	1.02

XPERT SUPER SKEET LOADS WITH CRIMP

Loaded with any standard smokeless powder listed herewith:—WESTERN MINIMAX (WM), DuPont MX (MX), Hercules Red Dot (HR).

XS34CS	12	2⅝ in.	3	1⅛	9 Chilled	57	$1.02
XS65CS	16	2 9/16 in.	2½	1	9 Chilled	50	.96
XS01CS	20	2½ in.	2¼	⅞	9 Chilled	45	.96
†XS83C	28	2¾ in.	2¼	¾	9 Chilled	40	.96
†S47C	*410	2½ in.		½	9 Chilled	24	.84
†S48C	*410	3 in.		¾	9 Chilled	33	.96

*Loaded with progressive burning powder. †Without crimp

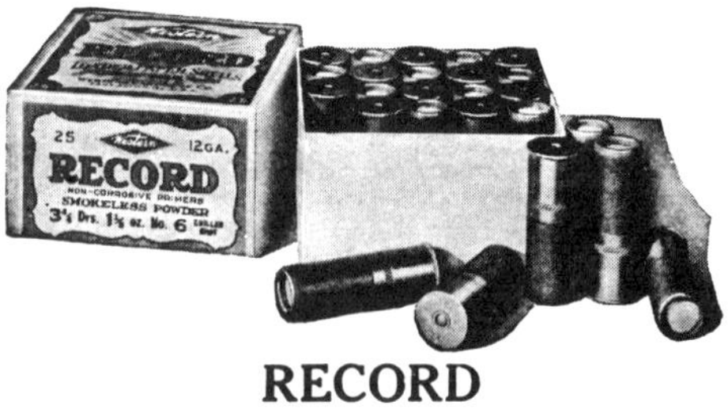

RECORD

High-Brass Steel-Locked Shells with Smokeless Powder and Non-Corrosive Primers.

Load No.	Gauge	Length Shell	Drams Equiv. Powder	Ounces Shot	Size and Kind of Shot	Wt. of Case	Price per Box–25
H34	12	2⅝ in.	3	1⅛	6, 7, 8, 9 Soft	60	$1.21
H34C	12	2⅝ in.	3	1⅛	6, 7½ Chilled	60	1.26
H42	12	2⅝ in.	3¼	1⅛	4, 5, 6, 7, 8 Soft	59	1.25
H42C	12	2⅝ in.	3¼	1⅛	4, 5, 6, 7½ Chilled	59	1.29
H67	16	2 9/16 in.	2¾	1	6, 7, 8, 9 Soft	52	1.18
H67C	16	2 9/16 in.	2¾	1	6, 7½ Chilled	52	1.23
H01	20	2½ in.	2¼	⅞	6, 7, 8, 9 Soft	46	1.12
H01C	20	2½ in.	2¼	⅞	6, 7½ Chilled	46	1.17

WINCHESTER SHOTGUN SHELLS

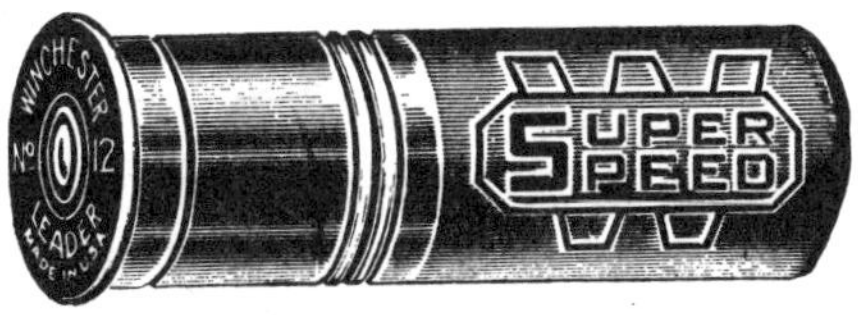

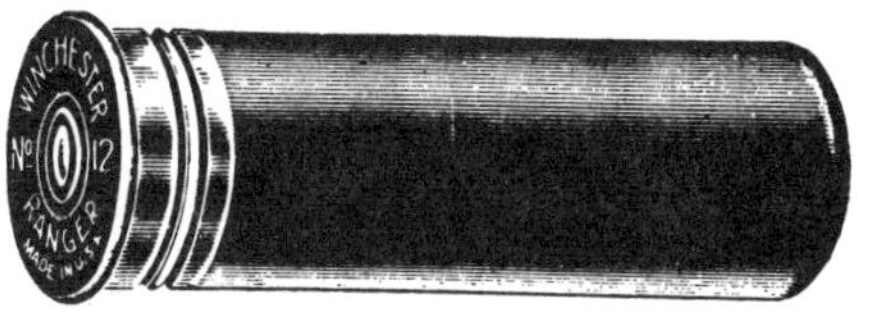

LEADER SUPER SPEED STAYNLESS

(Unlacquered)

Loaded with Progressive Burning Smokeless Powder

Load No.	Ga.	Powder Drams	Shot Oz.	Shell Length	Shot Sizes		Per Box of 25
46	12	3¾	1¼	2¾	2 4 5 6 7 7½	Ch.	$1.50
47	12	4	1⅜	3	BB 2 4 5 6	Ch.	1.62
48	12	4¼	1⅝	3	BB 2 4 5 6	Ch.	1.74
60	16	3	1⅛	2 9/16	4 5 6 7½	Ch.	1.44
57	20	2¾	1	2½	4 5 6 7½	Ch.	1.38
58	20	2¾	1	2¾	4 5 6 7½	Ch.	1.38

BUCKSHOT LOADS

K4900	12	...	...	3	00 Buck, 12 Pellets	...	$1.81
K490	12	...	...	3	0 Buck, 15 Pellets	...	1.81

SUPER SPEED STAYNLESS

Loaded with Progressive Burning Smokeless Powder

R92	10	4¾	1⅝	2⅞	BB 2 4 5 6	Ch.	$1.62
R46	12	3¾	1¼	2¾	BB 2 4 5 6 7 7½	Ch.	1.32
R60	16	3	1⅛	2 9/16	BB 2 4 5 6 7 7½	Ch.	1.25
R63	16	3¼	1⅛	2¾	4 5 6 7 7½	Ch.	1.32
R57	20	2¾	1	2½	4 5 6 7½	Ch.	1.25
R58	20	2¾	1	2¾	2 4 5 6 7 7½ 8	Ch.	1.25
R24	28	2¼	¾	2⅞	4 6 7½ 9	Ch.	1.20
R107	410	Max.	½	2½	4 5 6 7½	Ch.	.84
R109	410	Max.	¾	3	4 5 6 7½	Ch.	.96

Skeet Loads—410 Gauge

SR107		Max.	½	2½	9	Ch.	$0.84
SR109		Max.	¾	3	9	Ch.	.96

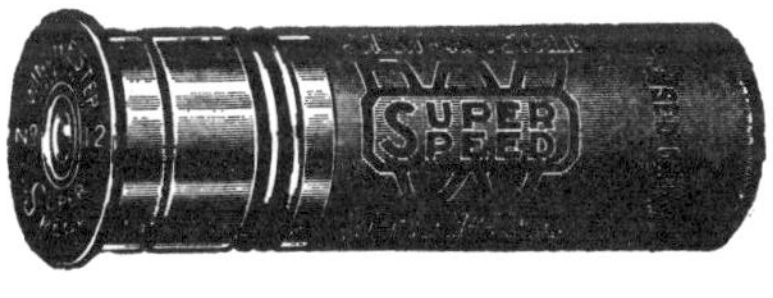

SUPER SPEED STAYNLESS

BUCKSHOT LOADS

Load No.	Ga.	Peliets	Size Eastern	Layers	Shell Length	Per Box of 25
RK91	10	16	0	4	2⅞	$1.69
RK43	12	9	00	3	2¾	1.39
RK46	12	12	0	4	2¾	1.39
RK42	12	16	1	4	2¾	1.39
RK42	12	27	4	4	2¾	1.39
RK60	16	12	1	4	2 9/16	1.33
RK57	20	20	3	5	2½	1.33

RIOT BUCKSHOT LOADS—(With Protected Crimp)

RK4300P	12	9	00	3	2¾	$1.50
RK460P	12	12	0	4	2¾	1.50

SINGLE BALL LOADS

Load No.	Ga.	Length Shell	Powder Charge	Weight of Ball	Per Box of 25
RS73	12	2¾	Max.	1 Oz.	$1.39
RS63	16	2 9/16	Max.	⅞ Oz.	1.33
RS58	20	2½	Max.	⅝ Oz.	1.33
RS107	410	2½	Max.	⅕ Oz.	.91
RS109	410	3	Max.	⅕ Oz.	1.04

RIFLED SLUG LOADS

RS415	12	2¾	Max.	415 Gr.	$2.11
RS350	16	2 9/16	Max.	350 Gr.	2.07
RS282	20	2½	Max.	282 Gr.	2.01
RS93	410	2½	Max.	93 Gr.	1.77

RANGER STAYNLESS—FIELD LOADS

Load No.	Ga.	Powder Drams	Shot Oz.	Shell Length	Shot Sizes		Per Box of 25
G86	10	4¼	1¼	2⅞	4 6		$1.25
G86	10	4¼	1¼	2⅞	4 5 6	Ch.	1.32
G70	12	3	1	2⅝	4 5 6 7 8		.92
G76	12	3	1⅛	2⅝	4 5 6 7 8 9 10		.96
G76	12	3	1⅛	2⅝	4 5 6 7½	Ch.	1.02
G78	12	3¼	1⅛	2⅝	2 4 5 6 7 8		1.02
G78	12	3¼	1⅛	2⅝	BB 4 5 6 7½	Ch.	1.08
G61	16	2½	1	2 9/16	4 5 6 7 8 9 10		.90
G61	16	2½	1	2 9/16	4 5 6 7½	Ch.	.96
G66	16	2¾	1	2 9/16	4 5 6 7½	Ch.	.96
G53	20	2¼	⅞	2½	4 5 6 7 8 9 10		.90
G53	20	2¼	⅞	2½	4 5 6 7½	Ch.	.96
G23	28	1¾	⅝	2½	6 7½	Ch.	.88

RANGER SKEET AND TRAP LOADS

SUPER SKEET LOADS WITH CRIMP

GS76CS	12	3	1⅛	2¾	9	Ch.	$1.02
GS61CS	16	2½	1	2¾	9	Ch.	.96
GS53CS	20	2¼	⅞	2¾	9	Ch.	.96
GS25	28	2¼	¾	2¾ (Not Crimped)	9	Ch.	.96

SUPER TRAP LOADS WITH CRIMP

GT74CS	12	2¾	1⅛	2¾	7½ 8	Ch.	$1.02
GT76CS	12	3	1⅛	2¾	7½ 8	Ch.	1.02
G77CS	12	3	1¼	2¾	7½ 8	Ch.	1.08
G38CS	12	3⅛	1¼	2¾	7½	Ch.	1.14
G79TS	12	3¼	1¼	2¾	7 7½	Ch.	1.14
G67CS	16	2¾	1⅛	2¾	8	Ch.	1.02
G56CS	20	2½	1	2¾	8	Ch.	1.02

HANDICAP LOADS WITH KOPPERKLAD SHOT & CRIMP

KG77KS	12	3	1¼	2¾	7½ 8	K	$1.27
KG38KS	12	3⅛	1¼	2¾	7½	K	1.33

BLANK LOADS—(Black Powder)

G108N	10	8	Blank	2⅞			$1.20
G126N	12	6	Blank	2⅝			1.14

RANGER BRUSH LOADS

GB76	12	3	1⅛	2¾	6 8		$1.04
GB76	12	3	1⅛	2¾	6 7½	Ch.	1.09
GB61	16	2½	1	2 9/16	8		.97
GB61	16	2½	1	2 9/16	6 7½	Ch.	1.02
GB53	20	2¼	⅞	2½	8		.95
GB53	20	2¼	⅞	2½	6 7½	Ch.	1.00

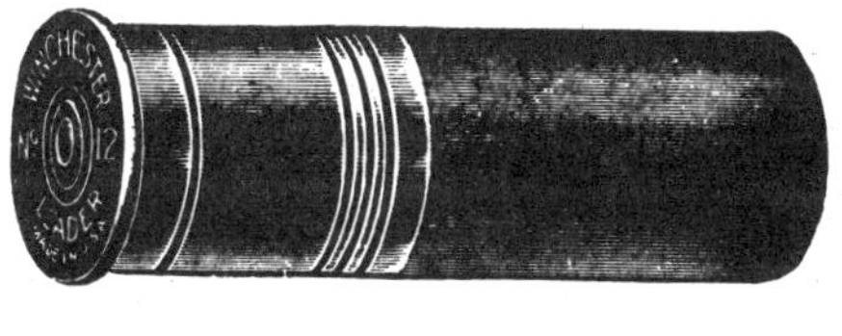

LEADER STAYNLESS

Load No.	Ga.	Powder Drams	Shot Oz.	Shell Length	Shot Sizes		Per Box of 25
76	12	3	1⅛	2⅝	6 7 8 9		$1.21
76	12	3	1⅛	2⅝	6 7½	Ch.	1.26
78	12	3¼	1⅛	2⅝	4 5 6 7 8		1.25
78	12	3¼	1⅛	2⅝	4 5 6 7½	Ch.	1.29
66	16	2¾	1	2 9/16	6 7 8 9		1.18
66	16	2¾	1	2 9/16	6 7½	Ch.	1.23
53	20	2¼	⅞	2½	6 7 8 9		1.12
53	20	2¼	⅞	2½	6 7½	Ch.	1.17

SEE PAGE 8, "HOW TO ORDER"

BORE, CHAMBER AND SHOT SIZES

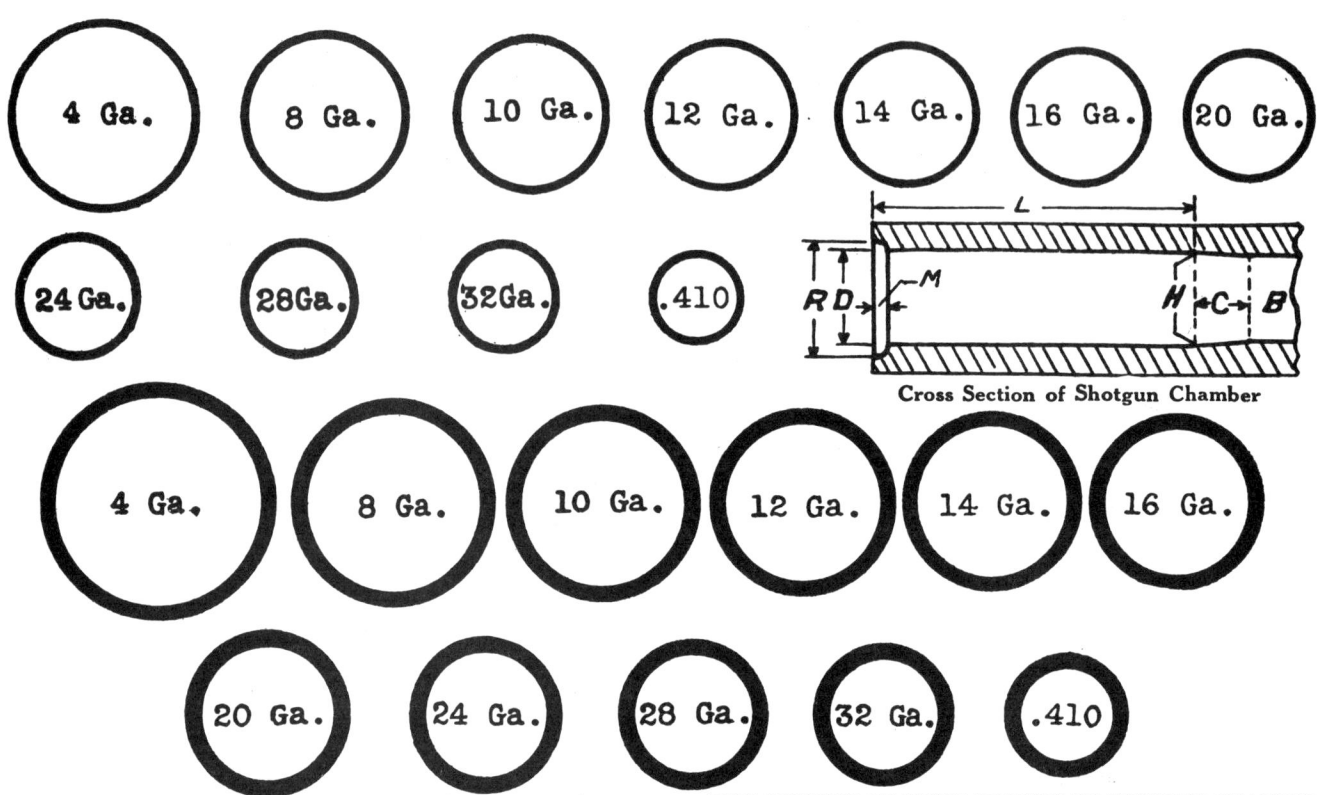

Cross Section of Shotgun Chamber

The upper two rows with light circles represent the exact natural true size of true cylinder bores of the gauges indicated. These true cylinder bore sizes represent the barrel diameter and wherever the barrel has any choke, the diameter at the muzzle will be somewhat smaller, depending on the amount and type of choke.

It will be interesting to many to know the origin of the gauge sizes. Originally the diameter of a one pound round ball of lead was accepted as one gauge; the diameter of a round ball of the same pound of lead equally divided into four round balls represented four gauge; the diameter of the balls formed by dividing the one pound of lead into eight, ten, twelve or more round balls produced the corresponding caliber. Due to variations, however, it has only been recently that the various manufacturers have standardized the various gauge dimensions. The inside diameters of the circles shown here are carefully drawn to about three thousandths of an inch. The gauges indicated in the heavy circles represent the chamber diameters and are equally accurate.

EXPLANATION OF CROSS SECTION OF SHOTGUN CHAMBER

"R" represents the circular milling cut at the breech, which is recessed to accommodate the rim of the shell case.

"M" represents the depth of the rim.

"D" represents the diameter of the shell chamber when measured directly in front of the rim. The accompanying illustrations with heavy circles represent this diameter in exact true size.

"L" represents the length of the unfired case.

"H" represents the diameter of the head of the chamber, and because the chamber is slightly tapered, this diameter is slightly less than the diameter "D".

"C" represents the cone of the chamber.

"B" represents the actual beginning of the barrel proper.

TATHAM'S STANDARD SHOT SIZES

STANDARD SIZES, SOFT AND CHILLED

No.	Chilled Shot No. in Oz.	Soft Shot No. in Oz.	Diameter in Inches	Diameter in Millimeters
Dust	4565		.04	1.02
12	2385	2326	.05	1.27
11	1380	1346	.06	1.52
10	868	848	.07	1.78
9	585	568	.08	2.03
8	409	399	.09	2.28
7½	345	338	.09½	2.41
7	299	291	.10	2.54
6	223	218	.11	2.79
5	172	168	.12	3.02

No.	Chilled Shot No. in Oz.	Soft Shot No. in Oz.	Diameter in Inches	Diameter in Millimeters
4	136	132	.13	3.30
3	109	106	.14	3.53
2	88	86	.15	3.78
1	73	71	.16	4.06
B		59	.17	4.32
Air Rifle		55	.17½	4.44
BB		50	.18	4.57
BBB		42	.19	4.83
T		36	.20	5.08
TT		31	.21	5.33
F		27	.22	5.59
FF		24	.23	5.84

BUCKSHOT

Eastern Size	Western Size	Diameter in Inches	Diameter in Millimeters	Balls in lbs. (About)
4	....	.24	6.09	341
3	8 or 9	.25	6.35	299
2	7	.27	6.86	232
1	5 or 6	.30	7.62	175
0	4	.32	8.13	144
00	3	.34	8.64	122
000	2	.36	9.14	103

EMPTY BRASS-SHOT SHELLS

	Per Box of 25
8 Gauge	*$1.00
10 Gauge—2⅝ inch	2.50
10 Gauge—2⅞ inch	2.65
12 Gauge—2⅝ inch	2.50
16 Gauge—2½ inch	2.50
20 Gauge—2½ inch	2.50
28 Gauge—2½ inch	2.50

* Per single shell.

LEAD BALLS

	Dia. in In.	Dia. in m/m	No. in Lb.
.44 Game Getter	.425	10.79	60
.44 S. & W. Russian Gallery	.428	10.87	58
.45-5 Armory Practice	.452	11.48	50
28 Gauge	.510	12.95	35
24 Gauge	.542	13.76	29½
20 Gauge	.545	13.84	28½
16 Gauge	.610	15.49	20½
12 Gauge	.645	16.38	17
10 Gauge	.710	18.03	13½

COMBINE YOUR RELOADING NEEDS IN ONE ORDER

CARTRIDGES IN GROUPS SHOWN BELOW WILL INTERCHANGE

NOTE: *High Velocity, High Power, Hi-Speed Cartridges must not be used in Revolvers. Exceptions: items marked (†) are designed especially for the .38-44 Smith & Wesson Revolver and the .38 Colt Shooting Master. Pressure of these two cartridges is safe for lighter guns, but the recoil is likely to be more unpleasant and the frame may be shaken loose in time.

RIM FIRE

.22 W. R. F.
.22 Remington Special
.22 Winchester M/1890

.25 Stevens Short
.25 Stevens

.32 Short
.32 Long

.38 Short
.38 Long

CENTER FIRE

.25-20 Winchester, Marlin, Remington
.25-20 Winchester and Marlin
.25-20 W. C. F.
.25-20 Winchester
.25-20 Marlin

.32 Short Colt
.32 Long Colt

.32 Smith & Wesson
.32 Smith & Wesson Gallery

.32 Winchester, Marlin, Remington*
.32 Winchester and Marlin*
.32 W. C. F.*
.32 Winchester*
.32-20 Marlin*
.32-20 Colt L. M. R.*

.32-20 W. C. F.*
.32-20 Winchester and Marlin*

.38 Smith & Wesson
.38 Colt's New Police

.38 Winchester, Marlin, Remington
.38 Winchester
.38 Remington
.38-40 Winchester
.38 W. C. F.

.30-30 Winchester, Marlin, Savage
.30-30 Winchester
.30-30 Marlin
.30 W. C. F.

8 m/m (7.9) Mauser
8 m/m (7.9) Mannlicher

.25 Colt Automatic
.25 Automatic Pistol
.25 (6.35 m/m) Automatic Pistol
6.35 Browning Automatic

.32 Colt Automatic
.32 Automatic Pistol
.32 (7.65 m/m) Automatic Pistol
7.65 m/m Automatic Pistol

.32 Smith & Wesson, Long
.32 Smith & Wesson, Long Gallery
.32 Colt's New Police
.32 Colt's Police Positive

.38 Short Colt
.38 Long Colt
.38 Colt Special
.38 Smith & Wesson Special
.38 Targetmaster

.38 Smith & Wesson Special Mid-Range
.38 Special Hi-Speed (†)
.38-44 Special (†)

.44 Winchester, Marlin, Remington
.44 Winchester
.44 Remington
.44-40 Winchester
.44 W. C. F.

.45-70 Government
.45-70 Government Flat
.45-70 Marlin
.45-70-405
.45-70-500
.45-70 High Velocity

8 m/m (7.9) German Mauser
8 m/m (7.9) Special—also many military rifles

RECOMMENDED SHOT SIZES

For Upland Shooting — Shot Sizes

Snipe, woodcock, rail, quail in early season and small shore birds .... 8 or 9
Dove, quail in late season, large shore birds, and small winged pests .... 7, 7½ or 8
Pheasant, prairie chicken, grouse, rabbit and squirrel ...... 5, 6 or 7
Turkey and large furred vermin .... 2, 4 or BB

For Skeet Shooting

For any Skeet shooting 9

For Wildfowl Shooting — Shot Sizes

Duck shooting over decoys .... 5 or 6
All other duck shooting 4
Goose shooting .... 2 or BB

For Trapshooting

16-yard singles and first barrel of doubles .... 7½ or 8
Second barrel of doubles and handicap targets 7½

Average Ballistics of Remington KLEANBORE and KLEANKOTE Rim Fire Cartridges
(KLEANKOTE Cartridges made in .22 Caliber only)

CALIBER	Style of Bullet	Weight of Bullet Grains	Muzzle Velocity Foot Seconds	Muzzle Energy Foot Pounds	TRAJECTORY 100 Yards Height at 50 Yards—Inches
.22 (BB) Bullet Breach Caps	Lead	20	780	27	
.22 (C.B.) Conical Bullet Caps‡	Lead	29	720	33	
.22 Short	Lead	29	970	65	5.8
.22 Long	Lead	29	1030	68	5.3
.22 Long Rifle	Lead	40	1100	108	4.2
.22 Long Rifle, Palma Match* LESMOK	Lead	40	1100	108	4.2
.22 Long Rifle, Palma	Lead	40	1080	124	3.7
.22 Extra Long‡	Lead	40	1030	94	5.0
.22 W. R. F. (Remington Special)†	Lead	45	1105	132	4.3
.22 Remington Autoloading†	Lead	45	920	85	5.5
.22 Remington Autoloading†	Hol. Pt.	40	940	79	6.0
.22 Automatic Rifle, Winchester M/1903†	Lead	45	1055	112	5.0
.22 Automatic Rifle, Winchester M/1903†	Hol. Pt.	45	1055	112	5.0
.25 Stevens Short†	Lead	67	945	133	
.25 Stevens†	Lead	67	1130	190	5.1
.32 Short†	Lead	80	945	159	
.32 Long†	Lead	90	945	179	
.41 Short†	Lead	129	520	78	
.41 Swiss†	Lead	300	1325	1170	3.0

* Not KLEANBORE   † KLEANBORE only   ‡ KLEANKOTE only

Average Ballistics of Remington HI-SKOR Rim Fire Cartridges

	Style of Bullet	Weight of Bullet Grains	Muzzle Velocity Foot Seconds	Muzzle Energy Foot Pounds	TRAJECTORY 100 Yards Height at 50 Yards—Inches
.22 Short, Hi-Skor	Lead	29	1030	68.3	5.0
.22 Long, Hi-Skor	Lead	29	1080	75	4.6
.22 Long Rifle, Hi-Skor	Lead	40	1180	23.6	3.7

Average Ballistics of Remington KLEANBORE and KLEANKOTE Rim Fire HI-SPEED Cartridges

	Style of Bullet	Weight of Bullet Grains	Muzzle Velocity Foot Seconds	Muzzle Energy Foot Pounds	TRAJECTORY 100 Yards Height at 50 Yards—Inches
.22 Short	Lead	29	1130	82	4.4
.22 Short	Hol. Pt.	27	1155	80	4.6
.22 Long	Lead	29	1375	122	3.7
.22 Long	Hol. Pt.	27	1395	117	3.3
.22 Long Rifle	Lead	40	1375	168	3.0
.22 Long Rifle	Hol. Pt.	36	1400	157	3.1
.22 W. R. F. (Rem. Special)‡	Lead	45	1450	210	2.5
.22 W. R. F. (Rem. Special)‡	Hol. Pt.	40	1475	195	2.5
.22 Long Rifle, Palma	Lead	40	1375	168	3.0

‡ Not supplied in KLEANKOTE

Average Ballistics of Remington Oil Proof Pistol and Revolver Cartridges

CALIBER	Type of Bullet	Weight of Bullet	Muzzle Velocity	Approx. Muzzle Energy	Barrel Length, Inches	Penetration 7/8" Pine Boards
.25 (6.35 m/m) Automatic Pistol	M. C.	50	820	75	2	3
.30 (7.63 m/m) Mauser Automatic Pistol	M. C.	85	1420	380	5½	11
.30 (7.63 m/m) Mauser Automatic Pistol	S. P.	90	1420	400	5½	11
.30 (7.65 m/m) Luger Automatic Pistol	M. C.	93	1250	325	4½	11
.30 (7.65 m/m) Luger Automatic Pistol	S. P.	93	1250	325	4½	11
.30 (7.65 m/m) Luger Automatic Pistol	H. Pt.	93	1250	325	4½	11
.32 Smith & Wesson*	Lead	88	720	100	3	3
.32 Smith & Wesson	Lead	88	720	100	3	3
.32 Smith & Wesson, Long*	Lead	98	820	146	4½	4
.32 Smith & Wesson, Long	Lead	98	820	146	4½	4
.32 Smith & Wesson, Long	M. Pt.	95	820	142	4½	4½
.32 Short Colt	Lead	80	800	114	4	3
.32 Long Colt	Lead	82	800	117	4	3
.32 Colt New Police (Police Positive)	Lead	100	795	139	4	3
.32 (7.65 m/m) Automatic Pistol	M. C.	71	980	152	4	5
9 m/m Luger Automatic Pistol	M. C.	124	1150	365	4	10
.357 Magnum	M. Pt.	158	1510	800	8¾	12½
9 m/m Luger Automatic Pistol	H. Pt.	124	1150	365	4	10
.380 (9 m/m) Automatic Pistol	M. C.	95	970	199	3¾	5½
.38 Super Automatic Colt Pistol	M. C.	130	1300	488	5	10
.38 Super Automatic Colt Pistol	H. Pt.	130	1300	488	5	10
.38 Colt Automatic Pistol	M. C.	130	1070	331	4½	9
.38 Smith & Wesson*	Lead	146	745	180	4	4
.38 Smith & Wesson	Lead	146	745	180	4	4
.38 Smith & Wesson	M. Pt.	143	745	177	4	4½
.38 Smith & Wesson—Special*	Lead	158	870	266	6	7
.38 Smith & Wesson—Special	Lead	158	870	266	6	7
.38 Smith & Wesson—Special	Lead	200	745	247	6	5
.38 Smith & Wesson—Special	M. Pt.	158	870	266	6	7½
.38 Smith & Wesson Special Sharp Shoulder Bullet	Lead	146	770	193	6	....
.38 Smith & Wesson Special Targetmaster	Lead	146	770	193	6	....
.38 Smith & Wesson Special Targetmaster	Lead	158	870	266	6	7
.38/44 Smith & Wesson—Special Hi-Speed	M. Pt.	158	1115	436	5	10
.38/44 Smith & Wesson—Special Hi-Speed	Lead	158	1115	436	5	7½
.38 Colt New Police (Police Positive)	Lead	150	695	161	4	4
.38 Short Colt	Lead	125	770	165	6	4
.38 Long Colt	Lead	150	785	205	6	6
.38 Colt Special	Lead	158	870	266	6	6½
.38 Colt Special Hi-Speed	M. Pt.	158	1125	445	6	10
.38 Colt Special Hi-Speed	Lead	158	1115	436	5	7½
.41 Short Colt	Lead	163	720	186	6	4
.41 Long Colt	Lead	195	745	241	6	5
.44 Smith & Wesson—American	Lead	218	695	235	6½	4
.44 Smith & Wesson—Russian	Lead	246	770	324	6½	4
.44 Smith & Wesson—Special	Lead	246	770	324	6½	....
.44 Smith & Wesson—Special	M. Pt.	246	770	324	6½	....
.45 Colt	Lead	250	870	421	5½	6
.45 Colt Automatic Pistol	M. C.	230	860	378	5	6
.45 Colt Automatic Targetmaster	M. C.	230	750	288	5	....
.45 Automatic Rim	M. C.	230	820	343	5½	6
.45 Automatic Rim	Lead	230	820	343	5½	6
.455 Webley Mark II	Lead	265	600	210	6½	....

*Not KLEANBORE

AVERAGE BALLISTICS OF REMINGTON CENTER FIRE RIFLE CARTRIDGES

CALIBER	BULLET		VELOCITY		ENERGY		MID RANGE TRAJECTORY			Penetration 7/8" Pine Boards
	Weight Grains	Type	Muzzle (Ft. per Sec.)	at 100 Yds	Muzzle (Ft. Lbs.)	at 100 Yds.	100	200	300	
.219 Zipper Hi-Speed	46	Mush.	3390	2720	1175	755	0.4	2.5	7.0	10⅞
.219 Zipper Hi-Speed	56	Mush.	3050	2530	1155	795	0.6	2.5	8.0	13½
.22 Hornet Hi-Speed	45	Mush.	2650	2080	700	430	0.8	4.0	12.5	12
.22 Hornet Hi-Speed	45	S. P. Ptd.	2600	2210	675	490	3.5	3.5	10.0	12
.22 Savage High Power	70	M. C. Ptd.	2780	2480	1200	955	0.6	3.0	7.0	52
.22 Savage High Power	70	Mush.	2810	2400	1230	900	0.7	3.0	8.0	12
.220 Swift	46	Mush.	4140	3370	1750	1160	0.3	1.5	4.5	8
.220 Swift	48	S. P. Ptd.	4140	3490	1825	1300	0.3	1.5	3.5	9
6.5 m/m Mann. Shoen.	150	S. Pt.	2260	2030	1700	1375	0.9	4.0	10.5	12
.25-20 Stevens & Win. SS	86	S. Pt.	1380	1150	365	255	2.6	13.0	33.5	9
.25-20 Win., Mar. and Rem.	86	M. C.	1450	1190	400	270	2.6	11.5	31.5	15
.25-20 Win., Mar. and Rem.	85	S. Pt.	1450	1190	400	270	2.6	11.5	31.5	8
.25-20 Win., Mar. and Rem.	86	Lead	1450	1190	400	270	2.6	11.5	31.5	9
.25-20 Win., Mar. Hi-Speed	60	Mush.	2210	1700	650	385	1.1	6.0	18.5	8
.25 Remington	117	S. Pt.	2300	2020	1375	1060	0.9	4.5	11.0	12
.25 Remington Hi-Speed	87	Mush.	2710	2300	1420	1020	0.7	3.5	9.0	11
.25 Remington Express	117	Mush.	2300	2020	1375	1060	0.9	4.5	11.0	12
.257 Remington Hi-Speed	87	Mush.	3220	2770	2005	1485	0.5	2.5	6.0	10
.257 Remington Hi-Speed	100	Mush.	2900	2530	1870	1420	0.6	2.5	7.0	10
.257 Remington Express	117	Mush.	2630	2330	1800	1410	0.7	3.0	8.0	12
.25-35 Win. and Sav.	117	M. C.	2280	1970	1350	1010	1.0	4.5	12.0	36
.25-35 Win. and Sav.	117	S. P.	2280	1970	1350	1010	1.0	4.5	12.0	12
.25-35 Win. and Sav. Hi-Speed	87	Mush.	2650	2250	1355	980	0.7	3.5	9.5	11
.25-35 Win. and Sav. Express	117	Mush.	2280	1970	1350	1010	1.0	4.5	12.0	11
.250 Savage	87	M. C. Ptd.	3000	2710	1740	1420	0.5	2.5	6.0	...
.250 Savage Express	100	Mush.	2810	2490	1755	1375	0.6	3.0	7.0	11
.250 Savage	87	Mush.	3040	2600	1785	1305	0.6	2.5	7.0	12
.270 Win. Hi-Speed	130	Mush.	3140	2820	2850	2295	0.5	2.0	5.5	13
.270 Winchester	150	S. P. B. T.	2770	2490	2560	2065	0.6	3.0	7.0	17½
7 m/m Mauser	175	S. Pt.	2460	2220	2350	1915	0.8	3.5	9.0	13
7 m/m Mauser Hi-Speed	139	Mush.	2900	2610	2600	2105	0.6	2.5	6.5	18
7 m/m Mauser	175	Mush.	2460	2220	2350	1915	0.8	3.5	9.0	16
.30-30 Win., Mar., and Rem.	160	M. C.	2200	1910	1720	1295	1.0	5.0	12.5	42
.30-30 Win., Mar., and Rem.	170	S. Pt.	2200	1930	1830	1405	1.0	4.5	12.0	12

ALL SHIPMENTS ARE INSURED

AVERAGE BALLISTICS OF REMINGTON CENTER FIRE RIFLE CARTRIDGES
(Continued From Preceding Page)

CALIBER	BULLET Weight Grains	BULLET Type	VELOCITY Muzzle (Ft. per Sec.)	VELOCITY at 100 Yds.	ENERGY Muzzle (Ft. Lbs.)	ENERGY at 100 Yds.	MID RANGE TRAJECTORY 100	MID RANGE TRAJECTORY 200	MID RANGE TRAJECTORY 300	Penetration 7/8" Pine Boards
.30-30 Win., Mar. and Rem. Hi-Speed	110	Mush.	2720	2260	1810	1250	0.7	3.5	10.0	14
.30-30 Win., Mar. and Rem. Express	165	Mush.	2200	1920	1770	1350	1.0	4.5	12.5	12
.30 Remington	160	M.C.	2170	1880	1675	2155	1.0	5.0	13.0	42
.30 Remington	170	S. Pt.	2170	1900	1780	1365	1.0	5.0	12.5	12
.30 Remington Hi-Speed	110	Mush.	2520	2080	1550	1060	0.8	4.0	11.5	14
.30 Remington Express	165	Mush.	2170	1890	1730	1310	1.0	5.0	12.5	12
.30-40 Krag and Win.	220	S. Pt.	2190	1980	2345	1915	1.0	4.5	11.0	16
.30-40 Krag and Win.	180	S. Pt.	2480	2210	2460	1955	0.8	3.5	9.0	16
.30-40 Krag and Win. Expdg. Hi-Speed	180	Br. Pt.	2460	2250	2420	2020	0.7	3.5	8.0	16
.30-40 Krag and Win. Express	220	Mush.	2190	1980	2345	1915	1.0	4.5	11.0	16
.30-40 Krag and Win. Express	220	M. C.	2190	1980	2345	1915	1.0	4.5	11.0	25
.30-06 Springfield	172	M.C.Ptd.T.H.	2700	2500	2785	2385	0.6	3.0	6.5	..
.30-06 Springfield	180	S. Pt.	2710	2420	2940	2340	0.7	3.0	7.5	11
.30-06 Springfield	220	S. Pt.	2410	2190	2840	2345	0.8	3.5	9.0	20
.30-06 Springfield Hi-Speed Expdg.	150	Br. Pt.	2960	2720	2920	2465	0.5	2.5	6.0	18
.30-06 Springfield Hi-Speed Expdg.	180	Br. Pt.	2690	2500	2895	2500	0.6	3.0	7.0	19
.30-06 Springfield Hi-Speed	110	Mush.	3380	2850	2790	1980	0.4	2.0	6.0	11
.30-06 Springfield Express	220	Mush.	2410	2190	2840	2345	0.8	3.5	9.0	20
.30-06 Springfield Express	220	M. C.	2410	2190	2840	2345	0.8	3.5	9.0	40

AVERAGE BALLISTICS OF REMINGTON CENTER FIRE RIFLE CARTRIDGES

CALIBER	BULLET Weight Grains	BULLET Type	VELOCITY Muzzle (Ft. per Sec.)	VELOCITY at 100 Yds.	ENERGY Muzzle (Ft. Lbs.)	ENERGY at 100 Yds.	MID RANGE TRAJECTORY 100	MID RANGE TRAJECTORY 200	MID RANGE TRAJECTORY 300	Penetration 7/8" Pine Boards
7.62 m/m Russian Expdg.	150	Br. Pt.	2810	2570	2635	2205	0.6	2.5	6.5	16
.300 Magnum	180	M. C. Pt.	3030	2820	3675	3180	0.5	2.0	5.5	....
.300 Savage Expanding	150	Br. Pt.	2660	2430	2360	1970	0.7	3.0	7.5	14
.300 Savage	180	S. Pt.	2380	2140	2265	1830	0.8	4.0	10.0	14
.303 Savage	195	S. Pt.	1960	1740	1665	1310	1.3	6.0	14.5	11
.303 British	215	M. C.	2160	1940	2230	1795	1.0	4.5	11.5	56
.303 British	215	S. Pt.	2160	1940	2230	1795	1.0	4.5	11.5	13
8 m/m (7.9 m/m) Mauser and Mann.	236	S. Pt.	2100	1890	2310	1875	1.1	5.0	12.0	12
8 m/m Special (7.9 m/m)	170	S. Pt.	2530	2210	2415	1845	0.8	3.5	9.0	13
8 m/m Lebel	170	S. Pt.	2610	2320	2575	2030	0.7	3.0	8.5	13
.32 Win., Mar. and Rem.	100	Lead	1280	1060	365	250	3.1	15.0	40.5	6½
.32 Win., Mar. and Rem.	100	M. C.	1280	1060	365	250	3.1	15.0	40.5	11
.32 Win., Mar. and Rem.	100	S. Pt.	1280	1060	365	250	3.1	15.0	40.5	6
.32 Win., Mar. and Rem. Hi-Speed	80	Mush.	2050	1520	745	410	1.4	7.5	23.0	9
.32 Special Winchester	170	S. Pt.	2260	1960	1930	1450	1.0	4.5	12.0	12
.32 Special Winchester Hi-Speed	110	Mush.	2630	2140	1690	1120	0.7	3.5	11.5	14
.32 Special Winchester Express	165	Mush.	2260	1950	1870	1395	1.0	4.5	12.0	15
.32 Win. Self Loading	165	S. Pt.	1390	1190	710	520	2.6	12.5	31.0	10
.32 Remington	170	S. Pt.	2200	1910	1830	1380	1.0	5.0	13.0	15
.32 Remington Hi-Speed	110	Mush.	2630	2140	1690	1120	0.8	4.0	11.0	14
.32 Remington Express	165	Mush.	2200	1900	1775	1325	1.0	4.5	12.5	15
.32-40 Win., Mar., Sav.	165	S. Pt.	1440	1230	760	555	2.6	12.0	28.0	10
.32-40 Win., Mar., Sav. Hi-Power	165	S. Pt.	1950	1650	1395	1000	1.4	6.5	17.5	10
.33 Winchester	200	S. Pt.	2180	1870	2110	1555	1.1	5.0	13.5	13
.348 Winchester Hi-Speed	150	S. Pt.	2880	2380	2765	1890	0.6	3.0	8.5	15
.348 Winchester Express	200	S. Pt.	2520	2160	2820	2075	0.8	4.0	10.0	17
.35 Win., S. L. Rifle	180	S. Pt.	1390	1170	775	545	2.5	13.0	31.0	9
.351 Win. S. L. Rifle	180	S. Pt.	1850	1560	1370	975	1.5	7.5	19.0	13
.351 Win. S. L. Rifle	177	M. C.	1850	1560	1345	960	1.5	7.5	19.0	26
.35 Winchester	250	S. Pt.	2160	1910	2590	2025	1.1	5.0	12.0	15
.35 Remington	200	S. Pt.	2180	1870	2110	1555	1.0	5.0	13.0	16
.35 Remington Hi-Speed	150	Mush.	2360	1930	1860	1240	1.0	5.0	13.5	15
.35 Remington Express	200	Mush.	2180	1870	2110	1555	1.0	5.0	13.0	16
.38 Win., Mar. and Rem.	180	S. Pt.	1310	1090	685	475	3.2	15.5	37.5	10
.38 Win., Mar. and Rem. Hi-Speed	145	Mush.	2060	1520	1365	745	1.3	8.0	22.0	11
.38-55 Win., Mar. and Savage	255	S. Pt.	1320	1150	985	750	3.0	13.5	32.5	14
.38-55 Win., Mar. and Sav. High Power	255	S. Pt.	1600	1370	1450	1065	1.9	9.0	24.5	12
.38-56 Winchester & Marlin	255	S. Pt.	1400	1210	1110	830	2.7	11.5	29.0	12
.40-65 Winchester & Marlin	260	S. Pt.	1360	1170	1070	790	2.9	12.0	30.5	12
.40-72 Winchester	330	S. Pt.	1380	1230	1400	1110	2.5	11.0	29.5	14
.40-82 Winchester & Marlin	260	S. Pt.	1500	1260	1300	915	2.3	11.0	27.0	11
.401 Win. S. L. R.	200	S. Pt.	2140	1750	2035	1360	1.1	5.5	16.5	14
.405 Winchester	300	S. Pt.	2220	1940	3285	2510	1.0	4.5	12.0	13
.44 Win., Mar. and Rem.	200	M. C.	1300	1070	750	510	3.3	17.5	38.0	13
.44 Win., Mar. and Rem.	200	S. Pt.	1300	1070	750	510	3.3	17.5	38.0	10
.44 Win., Mar. and Rem. Hi-Speed	160	Mush.	1980	1430	1395	730	1.6	8.0	25.5	11
.45-60 Winchester	300	Lead	1390	1170	1285	910	2.6	12.5	30.5	11
.45-70 Government	405	S. P. Flat Pt.	1310	1160	1545	1210	2.9	12.5	31.0	15
.45-90 Win. & Marlin	300	S. Pt.	1530	1270	1560	1075	2.2	11.0	26.5	15

Kleanbore, Hi-Speed, Express, Oil-Proof, Kleankote, Palma, Shur Shot, Arrow Express, Arrow, Wet-Proof, and Targetmaster are Reg. U. S. Pat. Off.; Hi-Skor is a trade-mark of Remington Arms Co., Inc., Bridgeport, Conn.

A NEW GUN CARRIES A FACTORY GUARANTEE

AVERAGE BALLISTICS OF PETERS "RUSTLESS" RIM FIRE CARTRIDGES

Cartridge	Weight of Bullet Grains	Type of Bullet	Muzzle Velocity Foot Seconds	Muzzle Energy Foot Pounds	Mid-Range Trajectory 100 Yards Inches
.22 BB Cap	20	Lead	780	27	...
.22 C. B. Cap, FILMKOTE	29	Lead	720	33	...
.22 Short Gallery, "Krumble Ball." FILMKOTE or lub	29	Lead	970	65	5.8
.22 Short, FILMKOTE	29	Lead	970	65	5.8
.22 Short TARGET	29	Lead	1030	68	5.0
.22 Long, FILMKOTE	29	Lead	1030	67	5.3
.22 Long TARGET	29	Lead	1080	75	4.6
.22 Long Rifle, FILMKOTE or lub	40	Lead	1100	108	4.2
.22 Long Rifle TARGET	40	Lead	1180	124	3.7
.22 L. R. TACKHOLE, lub. (Not Rustless)	40	Lead	1100	108	4.5
.22 L. R. DEWAR MATCH, lub	40	Lead	1100	108	4.5
.22 Extra Long, FILMKOTE	40	Lead	1030	94	5.0
.22 W. R. F.	45	Lead	1105	132	4.3
.22 Winchester Automatic	45	Lead	1055	112	5.5
.22 Winchester Automatic	40	Hol. Pt.	1055	99	5.5
.22 Remington Autoloading	45	Lead	920	85	5.5
.22 Remington Autoloading	40	Hol. Pt.	940	79	6.0
.25 Short Stevens, lub.	67	Lead	945	133	...
.25 Stevens, lub.	67	Lead	1130	190	5.1
.32 Short, lub.	80	Lead	945	159	...
.32 Long, lub.	90	Lead	945	179	...
.41 Short, lub.	129	Lead	520	78	...
.41 Swiss, lub.	300	Lead	1325	1170	3.0

PETERS "RUSTLESS" "HIGH VELOCITY" .22 RIM FIRE CARTRIDGES

Cartridge	Weight of Bullet Grains	Type of Bullet	Muzzle Velocity Foot Seconds	Muzzle Energy Foot Pounds	Mid-Range Trajectory 100 Yards Inches
.22 Short, FILMKOTE	29	Lead	1130	82	4.4
.22 Short, FILMKOTE	27	Hol. Pt.	1155	80	4.6
.22 Long, FILMKOTE	29	Lead	1375	122	3.7
.22 Long, FILMKOTE	27	Hol. Pt.	1395	117	3.3
.22 Long Rifle, FILMKOTE	40	Lead	1375	168	3.0
.22 Long Rifle, FILMKOTE	36	Hol. Pt.	1400	157	3.1
.22 L. R. WIMBLEDON MATCH, lub.	40	Lead	1375	168	3.3
.22 W. R. F.	45	Lead	1450	210	2.5
.22 W. R. F.	40	Hol. Pt.	1475	195	2.5

AVERAGE BALLISTICS OF PETERS "RUSTLESS" OIL-TITE PISTOL AND REVOLVER CARTRIDGES

CARTRIDGE	Bullet Weight Grains	Type of Bullet	Muzzle Velocity	Muzzle Energy	Barrel Length Inches	Penetration 7/8" Pine Boards
.25 Automatic Pistol (6.35 m/m)	50	M. C.	820	75	2	3
.30 Luger (7.65 m/m)	93	S. P.	1250	325	4½	11
.30 Luger (7.65 m/m)	93	M. C.	1250	325	4½	11
.30 Luger (7.65 m/m)	93	M. C. H. P.	1250	325	4½	11
.32 Short Colt	80	Lead	800	114	4	3
.32 Long Colt	82	Lead	800	117	4	3
.32 Colt New Police (Police Positive)	100	Lead	795	139	4	3
.32 Automatic Pistol (7.65 m/m)	71	M. C.	980	152	4	5
.32 Smith & Wesson (Not Rustless)	88	Lead	720	100	3	3
.32 Smith & Wesson	88	Lead	720	100	3	3
.32 Smith & Wesson Long (Not Rustless)	98	Lead	820	146	4¼	4
.32 Smith & Wesson Long	98	Lead	820	146	4¼	4
.32 Smith & Wesson Long	98	Met. Pt.	820	146	4¼	4½
.32 W. C. F. (32/20) (Not Rustless)	100	Lead	954	232	6	..
.32 W. C. F. (32/20)	100	Lead	954	232	6	..
.9 m/m Luger Auto Pistol	124	M. C.	1150	365	4	10
.9 m/m Luger Auto Pistol	124	M. C. H. P.	1150	365	4	10
.38 Smith & Wesson (Not Rustless)	146	Lead	745	180	4	4
.38 Smith & Wesson	146	Lead	745	180	4	4
.38 Smith & Wesson	143	Met. Pt.	745	177	4	4½
.38 Special*	158	Lead	870	266	6	7
.38 Special	158	Lead	870	266	6	7
.38 Special POLICE MATCH	158	Lead	870	266	6	7
.38 Special	200	Lead	745	247	6	5
.38 Special	158	Met. Pt.	870	266	6	7½
.38 Spec, Target Wad Cutter	146	Lead	770	193	6	..
.38 Special POLICE MATCH Wad Cutter	146	Lead	770	193	6	..
.38 Spec. HIGH VELOCITY	158	Lead	1115	436	5	7½
.38 Spec. HIGH VELOCITY	158	Met. Pt.	1115	436	6	10
.38 Colt New Police (Police Positive)	150	Lead	695	161	4	4
.357 Magnum	158	Lead	1510	800	8¾	12½
.38 Short Colt	125	Lead	770	165	6	4
.38 Long Colt	150	Lead	785	205	6	6
.38 Automatic	130	M. C.	1070	331	4½	9
.38 Super Automatic	130	M. C. H. P.	1300	488	5	10
.38 Super Automatic	130	M. C.	1300	488	5	10
.380 Automatic	95	M. C.	970	199	3¾	5½
.38 W. C. F. (38/40)	180	S. P.	985	388	5½	..
.41 Short Colt	163	Lead	720	186	6	4
.41 Long Colt	195	Lead	745	241	6	5
.44 S. & W. American	218	Lead	695	235	6½	4
.44 S. & W. Russian	246	Lead	770	324	6½	4
.44 S. & W. Special	246	Lead	770	324	6½	..
.44 S. & W. Special	246	Met. Pt.	770	324	6½	..
.44 W. C. F. (44/40)	200	S. P.	920	376	6	..
.44 W. C. F. (44/40)	200	M. C.	920	376	6	..
.45 Colt U. S. A.	250	Lead	870	421	5½	6
.45 Automatic	230	M. C.	860	378	5	6
.45 Automatic POLICE MATCH	230	M. C.	750	288	5	..
.45 Auto Rim	230	M. C.	820	343	5½	6
.45 Auto Rim	230	Lead	820	343	5½	6

AVERAGE BALLISTICS OF PETERS "RUSTLESS" CENTER FIRE CARTRIDGES

"RUSTLESS" Center Fire Sporting and Military Sizes	Bullet Weight Grains	Type of Bullet	Velocity Muzzle (Ft. per Sec.)	Velocity at 100 Yds.	Energy Muzzle (Ft. Lbs.)	Energy at 100 Yds.	Mid-Range Trajectory 100 Yds.	Mid-Range Trajectory 200 Yds.	Mid-Range Trajectory 300 Yds.	Penetration 7/8" Pine Boards
.22 Hornet	45	M. C. H. P.	2650	2080	700	430	0.8	4.0	12.5	12
.22 Savage High Power	70	S. P.	2810	2400	1230	900	0.7	3.0	8.0	12
.65 m/m Mannlicher-Schoenauer	123	M. C. H. P.	2450	2160	1640	1270	0.8	4.0	10.0	15
.65 m/m Mannlicher-Schoenauer	160	M. C. H. P.	2160	1950	1660	1350	1.0	4.5	11.5	17
.25/20 Repeater	86	Lead	1450	1190	400	270	2.6	11.5	31.5	9
.25/20 Repeater	86	S. P.	1450	1190	400	270	2.6	11.5	31.5	8
.25/20 Repeater	86	M. C.	1450	1190	400	270	2.6	11.5	31.5	15
.25/20 Repeater HIGH VELOCITY	60	M. C. H. P.	2210	1700	650	385	1.1	6.0	18.5	8
.25/20 Repeater HIGH VELOCITY	86	S. P.	1710	1380	560	365	1.8	9.0	25.0	8
.25/20 Single Shot	86	S. P.	1380	1150	365	255	2.6	13.0	33.5	8
.250 Savage	87	Prot. Pt.	3000	2710	1740	1420	0.5	2.5	6.0	12
.250 Savage	87	S. P.	3000	2710	1740	1420	0.5	2.5	6.0	12
.250 Savage	87	M. C.	3000	2710	1740	1420	0.5	2.5	6.0	50
.250 Savage	100	M. C. H. P.	2810	2480	1755	1375	0.6	3.0	7.0	11
.25/35 Winchester	117	S. P.	2280	1970	1350	1010	1.0	4.5	12.0	12
.25/35 Winchester	117	M. C.	2280	1970	1350	1010	1.0	4.5	12.0	36
.25 Remington	117	S. P.	2300	2020	1375	1060	0.9	4.5	11.0	12
.270 Winchester	130	Prot. Pt.	3120	2880	2810	2395	0.5	2.0	5.0	13
.270 Winchester	150	S. P.	2770	2490	2555	2065	0.6	3.0	7.0	15
7 m/m Mauser	175	S. P.	2460	2220	2350	1915	0.8	3.5	9.0	12
.30/30 Win. Mar. Sav.	180	BELTED	2120	1840	1800	1360	1.0	5.0	15.0	22
.30/30 Win. Mar. Sav.	170	S. P.	2200	1930	1825	1405	1.0	4.5	12.0	12
.30/30 Win. Mar. Sav.	160	M. C.	2200	1910	1720	1300	1.0	5.0	12.5	42
.30/30 Win. Mar. Sav.	165	M. C. H. P.	2200	1920	1770	1350	1.0	4.5	12.5	12
.30/30 Win. Mar. Sav.	125	M. C. H. P.	2560	2160	2110	1500	0.8	4.0	10.5	14
.30 Remington	180	BELTED	2070	1800	1720	1300	1.0	5.5	14.5	20
.30 Remington	170	S. P.	2170	1900	1780	1365	1.0	5.0	12.5	12
.30 Remington	160	M. C.	2170	1880	1675	1255	1.0	5.0	13.0	42
.30 Remington HIGH VELOCITY	165	M. C. H. P.	2170	1890	1730	1310	1.0	5.0	12.5	12
.30 Remington HIGH VELOCITY	125	M. C. H. P.	2450	2060	1670	1180	0.9	4.0	11.5	14
.30/40 Krag	220	S. P.	2190	1980	2345	1915	1.0	4.5	11.0	16
.30/40 Krag	220	M. C.	2190	1980	2345	1915	1.0	4.5	11.0	25
.30/40 Krag	150	Prot. Pt.	2660	2430	2360	1970	0.7	3.0	7.5	16
.30/40 Krag	180	S. P.	2480	2210	2460	1955	0.8	3.5	9.0	16
.30/40 Krag	180	Prot. Pt.	2460	2250	2420	2020	0.7	3.5	8.0	16
.30/40 Krag	180	BELTED	2380	2080	2260	1730	0.9	4.0	12.0	25
.30/40 Krag	225	BELTED	2110	1890	2230	1790	1.0	5.0	12.5	27
.30/06 Springfield	150	M. C.	2960	2720	2920	2465	0.5	2.5	6.0	75
.30/06 Springfield	150	Prot. Pt.	2960	2720	2930	2465	0.5	2.5	6.0	17
.30/06 Springfield	180	S. P.	2710	2420	2940	2340	0.7	3.0	7.5	11
.30/06 Springfield	180	M. C.	2690	2500	2890	2500	0.6	3.0	7.0	70
.30/06 Springfield	180	Prot. Pt.	2690	2500	2895	2500	0.6	3.0	7.0	19
.30/06 Springfield	180	BELTED	2720	2400	2960	2300	0.7	3.0	8.0	27
.30/06 Springfield	220	S. P.	2410	2190	2840	2345	0.8	3.5	9.0	20
.30/06 Springfield	172	Boat Tail	2700	2500	2785	2385	0.6	3.0	6.5	70
.30/06 Springfield	225	BELTED	2310	2070	2670	2150	0.9	4.0	10.5	33
.300 Magnum	225	BELTED	2560	2310	3270	2680	0.5	3.0	8.0	35
.300 Savage	200	BELTED	2220	1960	2190	1710	1.0	4.5	12.0	26
.300 Savage	150	Prot. Pt.	2660	2430	2360	1970	0.7	3.0	7.5	14
.300 Savage	180	M. C. H. P.	2380	2140	2265	1830	0.8	4.0	10.0	14
.303 British	215	S. P.	2160	1940	2230	1795	1.0	4.5	11.5	13
.303 Savage	180	BELTED	2120	1840	1800	1360	1.0	5.0	13.5	23
.303 Savage	195	S. P.	1960	1740	1665	1310	1.3	6.0	14.5	11
8 m/m Mauser (7.9 m/m)	170	S. P.	2530	2210	2425	1845	0.8	3.5	9.0	13
8 m/m Mannlicher-Schoenauer	200	S. P.	2105	1940	2055	1670	1.1	4.5	11.5	12
.32 W. C. F. (32/20) (Not Rustless)	100	Lead	1280	1060	365	250	3.1	15.0	40.5	6½
.32 W. C. F. (32/20)	100	Lead	1280	1060	365	250	3.1	15.0	40.5	6½
.32 W. C. F. (32/20)	100	S. P.	1280	1060	365	250	3.1	15.0	40.5	6
.32 W. C. F. (32/20)	100	M. C.	1280	1060	365	250	3.1	15.0	40.5	11
.32 W. C. F. (32/20) HIGH VELOCITY	80	M. C. H. P.	2050	1520	745	410	1.4	7.5	23.0	9
.32 W. C. F. (32/20) HIGH VELOCITY	100	S. P.	1670	1280	620	365	2.0	10.0	28.0	9
.32 Win. Special	180	BELTED	2200	1910	1940	1460	1.0	5.0	12.5	23
.32 Win. Special	170	S. P.	2260	1960	1930	1450	1.0	4.5	12.0	12
.32 Win. Self Loading	165	S. P.	1390	1190	710	520	2.6	12.5	31.0	9
.32 Remington	180	BELTED	2070	1800	1715	1295	1.2	5.5	14.0	26
.32 Remington	170	S. P.	2200	1910	1830	1380	1.0	5.0	13.0	16
.32/40 Win. Mar. Sav.	165	S. P.	1440	1230	760	555	2.6	12.0	28.0	10
.32/40 Win. Mar. Sav. HIGH VELOCITY	165	S. P.	1950	1650	1395	1000	1.4	6.5	17.5	10
.33 Winchester	200	S. P.	2180	1870	2110	1555	1.1	5.0	13.5	13
.348 Winchester	210	BELTED	2510	2180	2850	2220	0.8	3.5	10.0	20
.348 Win., HIGH VELOCITY	150	S. P.	2880	2380	2765	1890	0.6	3.0	8.5	15
.348 Win., HIGH VELOCITY	200	S. P.	2520	2160	2820	2075	0.8	4.0	10.0	17
.35 Win. Self Loading	180	S. P.	1390	1170	775	545	2.5	13.0	31.0	9
.35 Remington	210	BELTED	2080	1760	2020	1450	1.2	5.5	15.0	26
.35 Remington	200	S. P.	2180	1870	2110	1555	1.0	5.0	13.0	16
.35 Remington	200	M. C. H. P.	2180	1870	2110	1555	1.0	5.0	13.0	16
.351 Win., Self Loading	180	S. P.	1850	1560	1370	975	1.5	7.5	19.0	13
.351 Win., Self Loading	177	M. C.	1850	1560	1345	960	1.5	7.5	19.0	26
.35 Winchester	250	S. P.	2160	1910	2590	2025	1.1	5.0	12.0	15
.38 W. C. F. (38/40)	180	S. P.	1310	1090	685	475	3.2	15.5	37.5	10
.38 W. C. F. (38/40) HIGH VELOCITY	180	S. P.	1770	1380	1255	760	1.7	9.0	24.5	14
.38/55 Win. Mar. Sav.	255	S. P.	1320	1150	985	750	3.0	13.5	32.5	14
.38/55 Win. Mar. Sav. HIGH VELOCITY	255	S. P.	1600	1370	1450	1065	1.9	9.0	24.5	14
.38/56 Win. Mar.	255	S. P.	1400	1210	1110	830	2.7	11.5	29.0	12
.40/65 Win. Mar.	260	S. P.	1360	1170	1070	790	2.9	12.0	30.5	12
.40/82 Win. Mar.	260	S. P.	1500	1260	1300	915	2.3	11.0	27.0	11
.401 Win. Self Loading	200	S. P.	2140	1750	2035	1360	1.1	5.5	16.5	14
.405 Winchester	300	S. P.	2220	1940	3285	2510	1.0	4.5	12.0	13
.44 W. C. F. (44/40)	200	S. P.	1300	1070	755	510	3.3	17.5	38.0	10
.44 W. C. F. (44/40)	200	M. C.	1300	1070	755	510	3.3	17.5	38.0	13
.44 W. C. F. (44/40) HIGH VELOCITY	200	S. P.	1570	1220	1095	660	2.2	11.0	30.0	11
.45/60 Winchester (Not Rustless)	300	Lead	1390	1170	1285	910	2.6	12.5	30.5	11
.45/70 U. S. Government	405	S. P.	1310	1160	1545	1210	2.8	14.0	32.5	15
.45/90 Win. Mar.	300	S. P.	1530	1270	1560	1075	2.2	11.0	26.5	15

BALLISTICS OF WESTERN CARTRIDGES
WESTERN RIFLE CARTRIDGES—SPECIFICATIONS AND BALLISTICS
ALL CARTRIDGES LOADED WITH SMOKELESS POWDER

Load No.	Primer No.	CARTRIDGE	Bullet Wgt. Grs.	Bullet Type	Velocity Muzzle	Velocity 100 Yds.	Energy Muzzle	Energy 100 Yds.	Mid-Range Trajectory 100 Yds.	200 Yds.	300 Yds.
K1201R	...	22BB	19	Lubaloy C'd	780	570	24	13	...	...	...
K1202R	...	22CB Greased	29	Lubaloy C'd	720	605	33	24	...	...	...
K1211R	...	22 Short KANT-SPLASH Greased	27	Synthetic	970	...	...	...	...	...	...
K1208R	...	22 Short SUPER-X Wax Coated	29	Lubaloy C'd	1,130	925	82	55	4.1	...	...
K1209R	...	22 Short H. P. SUPER-X Wax Coated	27	Lubaloy C'd	1,155	925	80	51	4.1	...	...
K1262R	...	22 Short XPERT Greased	29	Lead	1,030	860	68	48	5.1	...	...
K1216R	...	22 Long SUPER-X Wax Coated	29	Lubaloy C'd	1,375	1,020	122	67	3.2	...	...
K1217R	...	22 Long H. P. SUPER-X Wax Coated	27	Lubaloy C'd	1,395	1,010	117	61	3.3	...	...
K1263R	...	22 Long XPERT Greased	29	Lead	1,080	900	75	52	4.3	...	...
K1218R	...	22 Long Shot	...	No. 12 Chilled	...	...	...	...	...	...	...
K1225R	...	22 Long Rifle SUPER-X Wax Coated	40	Lubaloy C'd	1,375	1,080	168	104	2.9	...	...
K1226R	...	22 Long Rifle H. P. SUPER-X Wax Coated	37	Lubaloy C'd	1,400	1,075	161	95	3.0	...	...
K1227R	...	22 Long Rifle Shot SUPER-X	...	No. 12 Chilled	...	...	...	...	...	...	...
K1264R	...	22 Long Rifle XPERT Greased	40	Lead	1,180	995	124	88	3.8	...	...
K1228R	...	22 Long Rifle SUPER-MATCH	40	Lead	1,180	995	124	88	3.8	...	...
K1229R	...	22 Extra Long Greased	40	Lubaloy C'd	1,030	900	94	72	4.9	...	...
K1234R	...	22 W. R. F. (22 Rem. Spec.) SUPER-X Inside Lub.	45	Lubaloy C'd	1,450	1,110	210	123	2.7	...	...
K1235R	...	22 W. R. F., H. P. SUPER-X Inside Lubricated	45	Lubaloy C'd	1,450	1,110	210	123	2.7	...	...
K1232R	...	22 W. R. F. (22 Rem. Spec.) Inside Lubricated	45	Lubaloy C'd	1,105	955	122	91	4.0	...	...
K1236R	...	22 Win. Auto. Inside Lubricated	45	Lubaloy C'd	1,055	930	111	86	4.6	...	...
K1237R	...	22 Win. Auto. H. P. Inside Lubricated	45	Lubaloy C'd	1,055	930	111	86	4.6	...	...
K1238R	...	22 Rem. Auto. Inside Lubricated	45	Lubaloy C'd	920	...	84	...	5.5	...	...
K1241R	...	25 Short Stevens Inside Lubricated	65	Lubaloy C'd	945	845	129	103	5.6	...	...
K1240R	...	25 Stevens Inside Lubricated	65	Lubaloy C'd	1,130	985	184	140	3.8	...	...
K1243R	...	32 Short Greased	80	Lubaloy C'd	945	840	159	125	5.5	...	...
K1244R	...	32 Long Greased	90	Lubaloy C'd	945	850	179	144	5.3	...	...
K1385T	6½	218 Bee SUPER-X	46	Op. Pt. Exp.	2,860	2,260	835	520	0.7	3.5	10.5
K1488C	8½	219 Zipper SUPER-X	46	Op. Pt. Exp.	3,390	2,720	1,175	755	0.4	2.5	7.0
K1489C	8½	219 Zipper SUPER-X	56	Op. Pt. Exp.	3,050	2,530	1,155	795	0.6	2.5	8.0
K1378T	6½	22 Hornet SUPER-X	46	Op. Pt. Exp.	2,650	2,090	715	445	0.8	4.0	12.5
K1386T	6½	22 Hornet SUPER-X	45	Soft Point	2,650	2,080	700	430	0.8	4.0	12.5
K1476C	8½	220 Swift SUPER-X	46	Op. Pt. Exp.	4,140	3,370	1,750	1,160	0.3	1.5	4.5
K1477C	8½	220 Swift SUPER-X	48	Soft Point	4,140	3,490	1,825	1,300	0.3	1.5	3.5
K1402C	8½	22 Savage High-Power SUPER-X	70	Soft Point	2,780	2,480	1,200	955	0.6	3.0	7.0
K1304T	6½	25-20 Winchester Inside Lubricated	86	Lubaloy C'd	1,450	1,190	400	270	2.6	11.5	31.5
K1305T	6½	25-20 Winchester	86	Metal Case	1,450	1,190	400	270	2.6	11.5	31.5
K1306T	6½	25-20 Winchester	86	Soft Point	1,450	1,190	400	270	2.6	11.5	31.5
K1308T	6½	25-20 Win. Hi-Velocity SUPER-X	86	Soft Point	1,710	1,380	560	365	1.8	9.0	25.0
K1309T	6½	25-20 Win. Hi-Velocity SUPER-X	60	Op. Pt. Exp.	2,210	1,700	650	385	1.1	6.0	18.5
K1403C	8½	25 Rem. Auto. Load	117	S.P. B.T.	2,300	2,020	1,375	1,060	0.9	4.5	11.0
K1404C	8½	25 Rem. Auto. Load	117	O.P.E. B.T.	2,300	2,020	1,375	1,060	0.9	4.5	11.0
K1405C	8½	25-35 Winchester SUPER-X	117	Metal Case	2,280	1,970	1,350	1,010	1.0	4.5	12.0
K1406C	8½	25-35 Winchester SUPER-X	117	Soft Point	2,280	1,970	1,350	1,010	1.0	4.5	12.0
K1407C	8½	25-35 Winchester SUPER-X	117	O.P.E. B. T.	2,280	1,970	1,350	1,010	1.0	4.5	12.0
K1490C	8½	250-3000 Savage High-Power SUPER-X	87	Soft Point	3,000	2,710	1,740	1,420	0.5	2.5	6.0
K1409C	8½	250-3000 Savage High-Power SUPER-X	100	Op. Pt. Exp.	2,810	2,490	1,755	1,375	0.6	3.0	7.0
K1410C	8½	6.5 Mannlicher-Schoenauer	160	Soft Point	2,160	1,950	1,660	1,350	1.0	4.5	11.5
K1411C	8½	6.5 Mannlicher-Schoenauer	129	Op. P. Exp.	2,370	2,090	1,610	1,255	0.9	4.0	10.0
K1412C	8½	256 Newton	129	Op. Pt. Exp.	2,770	2,500	2,200	1,790	0.6	3.0	7.0
K1481C	8½	257 Roberts SUPER-X	87	Op. Pt. Exp.	3,220	2,770	2,005	1,485	0.5	2.5	6.0
K1482C	8½	257 Roberts SUPER-X	100	Op. Pt. Exp.	2,900	2,530	1,870	1,420	0.6	2.5	6.0
K1483C	8½	257 Roberts SUPER-X	117	Soft Point	2,630	2,330	1,800	1,410	0.7	3.0	8.0
K1486C	8½	270 Winchester SUPER-X	100	Op. Pt. Exp.	3,540	3,210	2,785	2,290	0.4	1.5	4.5
K1413C	8½	270 Winchester SUPER-X	130	O.P.E. B.T.	3,120	2,880	2,810	2,395	0.5	2.0	5.0
K1414C	8½	270 Winchester SUPER-X	150	Soft Point	2,770	2,490	2,560	2,065	0.6	3.0	7.0
K1417C	8½	7 m/m Mauser SUPER-X	175	S.P. B.T.	2,460	2,220	2,350	1,915	0.8	3.5	9.0
K1420C	8½G	30 Newton	180	Op. Pt. Exp.	2,830	2,530	3,200	2,575	0.6	2.5	7.0
K1421C	8½	30-30 Winchester SUPER-X	170	M.C. B.T.	2,200	1,930	1,830	1,405	1.0	4.5	12.0
K1422C	8½	30-30 Winchester SUPER-X	170	S.P. B.T.	2,200	1,930	1,830	1,405	1.0	4.5	12.0
K1423C	8½	30-30 Win. Hi-Velocity SUPER-X	150	Op. Pt. Exp.	2,380	2,060	1,890	1,415	0.9	4.0	11.0
K1491C	8½	30-30 Win. Hi-Velocity SUPER-X	110	Op. Pt. Exp.	2,720	2,260	1,810	1,250	0.7	3.5	10.0
K1424C	8½	30 Rem. Auto. Load	170	S.P. B.T.	2,170	1,900	1,780	1,365	1.0	5.0	12.5
K1425C	8½	30 Rem. Auto. Load	165	O.P.E. B.T.	2,170	1,890	1,730	1,310	1.0	5.0	12.5
K1485C	8½	30 Rem. Auto. Load. SUPER-X	110	Op. Pt. Exp.	2,520	2,080	1,550	1,060	0.8	4.0	11.5
K1427C	8½	30 Springfield 1903 SUPER-X	150	Op. Pt. Exp.	2,960	2,720	2,920	2,465	0.5	2.5	6.0
K1428C	8½	30 Springfield 1903	180	M.C. B.T.	2,690	2,500	2,895	2,500	0.6	3.0	7.0
K1429C	8½	30 Springfield 1906 SUPER-X	180	Soft Point	2,710	2,420	2,940	2,340	0.7	3.0	7.5
K1430C	8½	30 Springfield 1906 SUPER-X	180	O.P.E. B.T.	2,690	2,500	2,895	2,500	0.6	3.0	7.0
K1433C	8½	30 Springfield 1906 SUPER-X	220	S.P. B.T.	2,410	2,190	2,840	2,345	0.8	3.5	9.0
K1493C	8½	30 Springfield 1906 SUPER-X	220	M. C. Rl. Nose	2,410	2,190	2,840	2,345	0.8	3.5	9.0
K1435C	8½	30-40 Krag (30 Army) SUPER-X	180	Soft Point	2,480	2,210	2,460	1,955	0.8	3.5	9.0
K1436C	8½	30-40 Krag (30 Army) SUPER-X	180	O.P.E. B.T.	2,460	2,250	2,420	2,020	0.7	3.5	8.0
K1437C	8½	30-40 Krag (30 Army)	220	Metal Case	2,190	1,980	2,345	1,915	1.0	4.5	11.0
K1438C	8½	30-40 Krag (30 Army)	220	S.P. B.T.	2,190	1,980	2,345	1,915	1.0	4.5	11.0
K1439C	8½	30-40 Krag (30 Army) Blank	...	No Bullet	...	...	...	...	...	...	...
K1494C	8½	30-40 Krag (30 Army) Blank	...	Paper Bullet	...	...	...	...	...	...	...
K1484C	8½	300 H. & H. Mag. (Rm'l B'td.) SUPER-X	180	O.P.E. B.T.	3,060	2,750	3,745	3,025	0.5	2.5	6.0
K1440C	8½	300 H. & H. Mag. (Rm'l B'td.) SUPER-X	220	S.P. B.T.	2,730	2,490	3,640	3,030	0.6	2.5	7.0
K1442C	8½	300 Savage SUPER-X	150	Op. Pt. Exp.	2,660	2,430	2,360	1,970	0.7	3.0	7.5
K1443C	8½	300 Savage SUPER-X	180	Soft Point	2,380	2,140	2,265	1,830	0.8	4.0	10.0
K1445C	8½	303 Savage	190	Soft Point	1,960	1,740	1,620	1,280	1.3	6.0	14.5
K1446C	8½	303 British SUPER-X	215	S.P. B.T.	2,160	1,940	2,230	1,795	1.0	4.5	11.5
K1447C	8½	303 British SUPER-X	174	O.P.E. B.T.	2,450	2,260	2,320	1,975	0.7	3.5	8.5
K1448C	8½	32 Winchester Special SUPER-X	170	S.P. B.T.	2,260	1,960	1,930	1,450	1.0	4.5	12.0
K1449C	8½	32 Winchester Special SUPER-X	165	O.P.E. B.T.	2,260	1,950	1,870	1,395	1.0	4.5	12.0
K1450C	8½	32 Win. Self-Loading Rifle (Oilproof)	165	Soft Point	1,390	1,190	710	520	2.6	12.5	31.0
K1451C	8½	32 Rem. Auto. Load	170	S.P. B.T.	2,200	1,910	1,830	1,380	1.0	5.0	13.0
K1452C	8½	32 Rem. Auto. Load	165	O.P.E. B.T.	2,200	1,900	1,775	1,325	1.0	4.5	12.5
K1329T	6½	32 Winchester (32-20) (Oilproof) Inside Lubricated	115	Lubaloy C'd	1,280	1,080	420	300	3.1	14.5	37.5
K1330T	6½	32 Win. (32-20) (Oilproof)	115	Metal Case	1,280	1,080	420	300	3.1	14.5	37.5
K1331T	6½	32 Win. (32-20) (Oilproof)	115	Soft Point	1,280	1,080	420	300	3.1	14.5	37.5
K1332T	6½	32 Win. Hi-Velocity (32-20) SUPER-X	80	Op. Pt. Exp.	2,050	1,520	745	410	1.4	7.5	23.0
K1454C	8½	32-40 Winchester	165	S.P. B.T.	1,440	1,230	760	555	2.6	12.0	28.0
K1455C	8½	32-40 Winchester	165	O.P.E. B.T.	1,950	1,650	1,395	1,000	1.4	6.5	17.5

KEEP UP TO DATE WITH STOEGER'S CATALOG

BALLISTICS OF WESTERN CARTRIDGES

Western Rifle Cartridges—Specifications and Ballistics—Continued

Load No.	Primer No.	CARTRIDGE	Bullet Wgt. Grs.	Bullet Type	Velocity Muzzle	Velocity 100 Yds.	Energy Muzzle	Energy 100 Yds.	Mid-Range Trajectory 100 Yds.	Mid-Range Trajectory 200 Yds.	Mid-Range Trajectory 300 Yds.
K1456C	8½	33 Winchester	200	Soft Point	2,180	1,870	2,110	1,555	1.1	5.0	13.5
K1457C	8½	8 m/m Mannlicher-Schoenauer	200	Soft Point	2,150	1,940	2,055	1,670	1.1	4.5	11.5
K1478C	8½	348 Winchester SUPER-X	150	Soft Point	2,880	2,380	2,765	1,890	0.6	3.0	8.5
K1479C	8½	348 Winchester SUPER-X	200	Soft Point	2,520	2,160	2,820	2,075	0.8	4.0	10.0
K1459C	8½	35 Winchester	250	Soft Point	2,160	1,910	2,590	2,025	1.1	5.0	12.0
K1460C	6½	35 Win. Self-Loading Rifle (Oilproof)	180	Soft Point	1,390	1,170	775	545	2.5	13.0	31.0
K1461C	8½	35 Rem. Auto. Load	200	Soft Point	2,180	1,870	2,110	1,555	1.0	5.0	13.0
K1462C	8½	35 Rem. Auto. Load	200	Op. Pt. Exp.	2,180	1,870	2,110	1,555	1.0	5.0	13.0
K1463C	6½	351 Win. Self-Loading Rifle (Oilproof)	180	Metal Case	1,850	1,560	1,370	975	1.5	7.5	19.0
K1464C	6½	351 Win. Self-Loading Rifle (Oilproof)	180	Soft Point	1,850	1,560	1,370	975	1.5	7.5	19.0
K1465C	8½	375 H. & H. Mag. (Rm'l B'td.) SUPER-X	235	Op. Pt. Exp.	2,860	2,520	4,270	3,315	0.6	2.5	7.0
K1466C	8½	375 H. & H. Mag. (Rm'l B'td.) SUPER-X	270	Soft Point	2,720	2,460	4,440	3,630	0.7	3.0	7.0
K1467C	8½	375 H. & H. Mag. (Rm'l B'td.) SUPER-X	300	Soft Point	2,540	2,290	4,300	3,495	0.7	3.5	8.5
K1492C	8½	375 H. & H. Mag. (Rm'l B'td.) SUPER-X	300	M. C. Bl. Nose	2,540	2,290	4,300	3,495	0.7	3.5	8.5
K1357T	7	38 Winchester (38-40) (Oilproof)	180	Soft Point	1,310	1,090	685	475	3.2	15.5	37.5
K1469C	8½	38-55 Winchester	255	Soft Point	1,320	1,150	985	750	3.0	13.5	32.5
K1471C	8½	401 Win. Self-Loading Rifle (Oilproof)	200	Soft Point	2,140	1,750	2,035	1,360	1.1	5.5	16.5
K1472C	8½	405 Winchester	300	Soft Point	2,220	1,940	3,285	2,510	1.0	4.5	12.0
K1363T	7	44 X. L. Shot	...	No. 8 Chilled	....	....	....	....	...	...	...
K1372T	7	44 Winchester (44-40) (Oilproof)	200	Soft Point	1,300	1,070	750	510	3.3	17.5	38.0
K1474C	8½	45-70 Government	405	Soft Point	1,310	1,160	1,545	1,210	2.8	14.0	32.5

WESTERN PISTOL AND REVOLVER CARTRIDGES—SPECIFICATIONS AND BALLISTICS

ALL CARTRIDGES LOADED WITH SMOKELESS POWDER

Load No.	Primer No.	CARTRIDGE	Wgt. Grs.	Bullet Type	Barrel Length	Muzzle Velocity Feet per Second	Muzzle Energy Foot Lbs.	Penetration ⅞" Soft Pine Boards at 15 Ft.
K1208R	...	22 Short SUPER-X Wax Coated	29	Lubaloy C'd	6"	1,035	69	....
K1262R	...	22 Short XPERT Greased	29	Lead	6"	925	55	....
K1216R	...	22 Long SUPER-X Wax Coated	29	Lubaloy C'd	6"	1,125	81	....
K1263R	...	22 Long XPERT Greased	29	Lead	6"	930	56	....
K1225R	...	22 Long Rifle SUPER-X Wax Coated	40	Lubaloy C'd	6"	1,160	120	....
K1264R	...	22 Long Rifle XPERT Greased	40	Lead	6"	980	85	....
K1228R	...	22 Long Rifle SUPER-MATCH Greased	40	Lead	6"	995	88	....
K1246R	...	41 Short Greased	130	Lubaloy C'd	3"	520	78	2
K1302T	1½	25 Auto. (6.35 m/m) (Oilproof)	50	Metal Case	2"	820	75	3
K1310T	1½	30 Mauser (7.63 m/m) (Oilproof)	86	Metal Case	5½"	1,420	385	11
K1312T	1½	30 Luger (7.65 m/m) (Oilproof)	93	Metal Case	4½"	1,250	323	11
K1313T	1½	30 Luger (7.65 m/m) (Oilproof)	93	Soft Point	4½"	1,250	323	11
K1314T	1½	32 Auto. (7.65 m/m) (Oilproof)	74	Metal Case	4"	980	158	5
K1317T	1½	32 S. & W. (Oilproof) Inside Lubricated	85	Lubaloy C'd	3"	720	98	3
K1320T	1½	32 S. & W. Long (Oilproof) Inside Lubricated	98	Lubaloy C'd	4¼"	820	146	4
K1384T	1½	32 S. & W. Long Clean Cutting Inside Lubricated	98	Lead	4¼"	770	129	....
K1323T	1½	32 Short Colt (Oilproof) Greased	80	Lubaloy C'd	4"	800	114	3
K1325T	1½	32 Long Colt (Oilproof) Inside Lubricated	82	Lubaloy C'd	4"	800	117	3
K1327T	1½	32 Colt New Police (Oilproof) Inside Lubricated	98	Lubaloy C'd	4"	795	138	3
K1329T	1½	32 Winchester (32-20) (Oilproof) Inside Lubricated	115	Lubaloy C'd	6"	1,030	271	6
K1330T	6½	32 Winchester (32-20) (Oilproof)	115	Metal Case	6"	1,030	271	6
K1331T	6½	32 Winchester (32-20) (Oilproof)	115	Soft Point	6"	1,030	271	6
K1381T	1½	357 Magnum (Oilproof) SUPER-X Inside Lubricated	158	Lubaloy C'd	8¾"	1,510	800	12.5
K1382T	1½	357 Magnum Met. Pier. (Oilproof) SUPER-X In. Lub. Lead Bear	158	Metal Point	8¾"	1,510	800	12.5
K1333T	1½	9 m/m Luger (Oilproof)	125	Metal Case	4"	1,150	365	10
K1334T	1½	9 m/m Luger (Oilproof)	125	Hol. S.P.	4"	1,150	365	10
K1337T	1½	38 S. & W. (Oilproof) Inside Lubricated	145	Lubaloy C'd	4"	745	179	....
K1339T	1½	38 Super Police (Oilproof) Inside Lubricated	200	Lubaloy C'd	4"	630	176	5
K1379T	1½	38 Spec. Met. Pier. (Oilproof) SUPER-X In. Lub. Lead Bearin	150	Metal Point	5"	1,175	460	11
K1380T	1½	38 Special (Oilproof) SUPER-X Inside Lubricated	150	Lubaloy C'd	5"	1,175	460	9
K1341T	1½	38 Special (Oilproof) Inside Lubricated	158	Lubaloy C'd	6"	870	266	7
K1346T	1½	38 Special Match (Oilproof) Inside Lubricated	158	Lead	6"	825	238	7
K1342T	1½	38 Special (Oilproof) Inside Lubricated, Lead Bearing	158	Metal Point	6"	870	266	7.5
K1343T	1½	38 Spec. Mid-Range (Oilproof) Inside Lubricated	148	Lead	6"	770	195	....
K1344T	1½	38 Spec. Full Charge (Oilproof) Inside Lubricated	148	Lead	6"	870	249	....
K1345T	1½	38 Spec. Super-Police (Oilproof) Inside Lubricated	200	Lubaloy C'd	6"	745	247	7.5
K1348T	1½	38 Short Colt (Oilproof) Greased	130	Lubaloy C'd	6"	770	171	4
K1350T	1½	38 Long Colt (Oilproof) Inside Lubricated	150	Lubaloy C'd	6"	785	205	6
K1352T	1½	38 Colt New Police (Oilproof) Inside Lubricated	150	Lubaloy C'd	4"	695	161	4
K1353T	1½	38 Auto. (Oilproof) SUPER-X	130	Metal Case	5"	1,300	488	10
K1354T	1½	380 Automatic (Oilproof)	95	Metal Case	3¾"	970	199	5.5
K1357T	7	38 Winchester (38-40) (Oilproof)	180	Soft Point	5"	975	380	6
K1361T	1½	41 Long Colt (Oilproof) Inside Lubricated	200	Lubaloy C'd	6"	745	247	3
K1366T	7	44 S. & W. Russian (Oilproof) Inside Lubricated	246	Lubaloy C'd	6½"	770	324	4
K1368T	7	44 S. & W. Special (Oilproof) Inside Lubricated	246	Lubaloy C'd	6½"	770	324	7.5
K1372T	7	44 Winchester (44-40)	200	Soft Point	7½"	975	422	6
K1374T	7	45 Colt (Oilproof) Inside Lubricated	255	Lubaloy C'd	5½"	870	429	6
K1375T	7	45 Automatic	230	Metal Case	5"	860	378	6
K1383T	7	45 Auto. Met. Pier. (Oilproof) SUPER-X	230	Metal Case	5"	940	450	11
K1377T	7	45 Automatic (Rim) (Oilproof)	230	Metal Case	5½"	820	343	6

WE SELL FRESH AMMUNITION ONLY

BALLISTICS OF WINCHESTER CARTRIDGES

RIFLE BALLISTICS OF WINCHESTER RIM FIRE CARTRIDGES

CARTRIDGE	Bullet Wt.-Grs.	VELOCITY Muzzle	VELOCITY 100 Yds.	Energy Muzzle	Energy 100 Yds.	Trajectories For 100 Yds. Hgt. at 50 Yds. Inches
B.B. Caps	18	780	570	24		
C.B. Caps	29	720	605	33		
.22 Short Spotlight	26	970				
Leader .22 Short Staynless	29	1,030	860	68		5.1
Spatterproof .22 Short	26	970				
Super Speed .22 Short	29	1,130	925	82		4.1
Super Speed .22 Short H.P.	27	1,155	925	80		4.1
Leader .22 Long, Staynless	29	1,080	900	75		4.3
Super Speed .22 Long	29	1,375	1,020	122		3.2
Super Speed .22 Long H.P.	27	1,395	1,010	117		3.3
Super Speed .22 Long	29	1,375	1,020	122		3.2
Leader .22 Long Rifle, Staynless	40	1,180	995	124		3.8
Precision EZXS .22 Long Rifle, Lesmok	40	1,100	950	108		4.3
Prec. Long Range EZXS 22 L.R., Lesmok	40	1,100	950	108		4.3
Staynless EZXS .22 Long Rifle, Match	40	1,180	995	124		3.8
Super Speed .22 Long Rifle, Wax-coated	40	1,375	1,080	168		2.9
Super Speed .22 L.R., Hollow Point	37	1,400	1,075	161		3.0
Super Speed .22 Long Rifle	40	1,375	1,080	168		2.9
Super Speed .22 Long Rifle, H.P.	37	1,400	1,075	161		3.0
.22 Extra Long	40	1,030	900	94		4.9
.22 W.R.F., Staynless	45	1,105	955	122		4.0
.22 W.R.F.	45	1,195	955	122		4.0
Super Speed .22 W.R.F.	45	1,450	1,110	210		2.7
Super Speed .22 W.R.F., K.K. H.P.	40	1,475	1,095	193		2.7
.22 Auto	45	1,055	930	111		4.6
.22 Auto, Kopperklad (inside lubricated)	45	1,055	930	111		4.6
.22 Auto, Kopperklad, H.P. (inside lubricated)	45	1,055	930	111		4.6
.25 Stevens, Staynless	65	1,130	985	184		3.8
.25 Short Stevens, Staynless	65	945	845	129		5.6
.32 Short, Staynless	80	945	840	159		5.3
.32 Long, Staynless	90	945	850	179		5.3
.41 Swiss, Staynless	310	1,325	1,165	1,210		2.9

K.K. = Lead, Kopperklad. H.P. = Hollow Point

REVOLVER BALLISTICS OF WINCHESTER RIM FIRE CARTRIDGES

When Fired in Revolver with 6-inch Barrel. All these Cartridges are Winchester Staynless (Smokeless powder)

CARTRIDGE	BULLET WT.	MUZ. VEL.	MUZ. ENERGY
Super Speed .22 Short	29	1,035	69
Leader .22 Short	29	925	55
Super Speed .22 Long	29	1,125	81
Leader .22 Long	29	930	56
Super Speed .22 Long Rifle	40	1,160	120
Leader .22 Long Rifle	40	980	85
Super Speed .22 W.R.F.	45	1,170	137
.22 W.R.F. Staynless	45	985	97
.41 Short Staynless	130	520	78

RIFLE BALLISTICS OF WINCHESTER CENTER FIRE CARTRIDGES

CARTRIDGE	Type	Wt.-Grs.	Muzzle	100 Yds.	Muzzle	100 Yds.	100 Yds. Hgt. at 50 Yds.	200 Yds. Hgt. at 100 Yds.	300 Yds. Hgt. at 150 Yds.
Super Speed .218 Winchester Bee	H.P.	46	2,860	2,260	835	520	0.7	3.5	10.5
Super Speed .219 Winchester Zipper	H.P.	46	3,390	2,720	1,175	755	0.4	2.5	7.0
Super Speed .219 Winchester Zipper	H.P.	56	3,050	2,530	1,155	795	0.6	2.5	8.0
Super Speed .22 Winchester Hornet	S.P.	45	2,650	2,080	700	430	0.8	4.0	12.5
Super Speed .22 Winchester Hornet	H.P.	46	2,650	2,090	715	445	0.8	4.0	12.5
Super Speed .22 High Power	P.S.P.	70	2,780	2,480	1,200	955	0.6	3.0	7.0
Super Speed .220 Winchester Swift	H.P.	46	4,140	3,370	1,750	1,160	0.3	1.5	4.5
Super Speed .220 Winchester Swift	P.S.P.	48	4,140	3,490	1,825	1,300	0.3	1.5	3.5
Super Speed .220 Winchester Swift	H.P.	56	3,690	3,090	1,695	1,190	0.4	2.0	4.5
.25/20 Winchester	Lead	86	1,450	1,190	400	270	2.6	11.5	31.5
.25/20 Winchester	F.P.	86	1,450	1,190	400	270	2.6	11.5	31.5
.25/20 Winchester	S.P.	86	1,450	1,190	400	270	2.6	11.5	31.5
Super Speed .25/20 W.H.V.	S.P.	86	1,710	1,380	560	365	1.8	9.0	25.0
Super Speed .25/20 Winchester	H.P.	60	2,210	1,700	650	385	1.1	6.0	18.5
.25/20 Single Shot	S.P.	86	1,380	1,150	365	255	2.6	13.0	33.5
.25 Remington Automatic	S.P.	117	2,300	2,020	1,375	1,060	0.9	4.5	11.0
6.5 m/m Mannlicher	S.P.	145	2,360	2,110	1,795	1,435	0.9	4.0	10.0
Super Speed .25/35 Winchester	F.P.	117	2,280	1,970	1,350	1,010	1.0	4.5	12.0
Super Speed .25/35 Winchester	S.P.	117	2,280	1,970	1,350	1,010	1.0	4.5	12.0
Super Speed .257 Winchester Roberts	H.P.	87	3,220	2,770	2,005	1,485	0.5	2.5	6.0
Super Speed .257 Winchester Roberts	S.P.	100	2,900	2,530	1,870	1,420	0.6	2.5	7.0
Super Speed .257 Winchester Roberts	H.P.	117	2,630	2,330	1,800	1,410	0.7	3.0	8.0
Super Speed .250/3000 Savage	F.P.	87	3,000	2,710	1,740	1,420	0.5	2.5	6.0
Super Speed .250/3000 Savage	S.P.	87	3,000	2,710	1,740	1,420	0.5	2.5	6.0
Super Speed .250/3000 Savage	H.P.	100	2,810	2,490	1,755	1,375	0.6	3.0	7.0
Super Speed .270 Winchester	P.E.	130	3,120	2,880	2,810	2,395	0.5	2.0	5.0
Super Speed .270 Winchester	S.P.	150	2,770	2,490	2,560	2,065	0.6	3.0	7.0
Super Speed .270 Winchester	P.E.	100	3,540	3,210	2,785	2,290	0.4	1.5	4.5
Super Speed 7 m/m Mauser	S.P.	175	2,460	2,220	2,350	1,915	0.8	3.5	9.0
7.62 m/m Russian	H.C.P.	145	2,810	2,570	2,545	2,130	0.6	2.5	6.5
Super Speed .30 Winchester	F.P.	170	2,200	1,930	1,830	1,405	1.0	4.5	12.0
Super Speed .30 Winchester	S.P.	170	2,200	1,930	1,830	1,405	1.0	4.5	12.0
Super Speed .30 Winchester	H.P.	110	2,720	2,260	1,810	1,250	0.7	3.5	10.0
Super Speed .30 Winchester	H.P.	150	2,380	2,060	1,890	1,415	0.9	4.0	11.0
.30 Remington Automatic	F.P.	160	2,170	1,880	1,675	1,255	1.0	5.0	13.0
.30 Remington Automatic	S.P.	170	2,170	1,900	1,780	1,365	1.0	5.0	12.5
Super Speed .300 Savage	S.P.	150	2,660	2,430	2,360	1,970	0.7	3.0	7.5
Super Speed .300 Savage	S.P.	180	2,380	2,140	2,265	1,830	0.8	4.0	10.0
.303 Savage	S.P.	190	1,960	1,740	1,620	1,280	1.3	6.0	14.5
Super Speed .303 British	S.P.	215	2,160	1,940	2,230	1,795	1.0	4.5	11.5
.30 Army (.30-40 Krag)	F.P.	220	2,190	1,980	2,345	1,915	1.0	4.5	11.0
.30 Army (.30-40 Krag)	S.P.	220	2,190	1,980	2,345	1,915	1.0	4.5	11.0
Super Speed .30 Army	P.E.	150	2,660	2,430	2,360	1,970	0.7	3.0	7.5
Super Speed .30 Army	S.P.	180	2,460	2,250	2,420	2,020	0.8	3.5	8.0
Super Speed .30 Army	S.P.	180	2,480	2,210	2,460	1,955	0.8	3.5	9.0
Super Speed .30 Government '06	H.C.P.	145	2,960	2,710	2,820	2,365	0.5	2.5	6.0
Super Speed .30 Government '06, Pointed	F.P.	150	2,960	2,720	2,920	2,465	0.5	2.5	6.0
Super Speed .30 Government '06, Pointed	P.E.	150	2,960	2,720	2,920	2,465	0.5	2.5	6.0
.30 Government '06, Pointed	F.P.	180	2,690	2,500	2,895	2,500	0.6	3.0	7.0
Super Speed .30 Government '06, Pointed	P.E.	180	2,690	2,500	2,895	2,500	0.6	3.0	7.0
Super Speed .30 Government '06	S.P.	180	2,710	2,420	2,340	2,340	0.7	3.0	7.5
.30 Government '06	S.P.	220	2,410	2,190	2,840	2,345	0.8	3.5	9.0
.30 Government '06 B.T. Precision	F.P.	172	2,700	2,500	2,785	2,385	0.6	3.0	6.5
.30 Government '06 B.T.	P.E.	172	2,700	2,500	2,785	2,385	0.6	3.0	6.5
.30 Government '06 Wimbledon Cup B.T.	F.P.	180	2,690	2,500	2,895	2,500	0.6	3.0	7.0
.300 H. & H. Magnum Match B.T.	F.P.	180	3,030	2,820	3,670	3,180	0.5	2.0	5.5
Super Speed .300 H. & H. Magnum B.T.	H.P.	180	3,060	2,750	3,745	3,025	0.5	2.0	6.0
Super Speed .300 H. & H. Magnum B.T.	S.P.	220	2,730	2,490	3,640	3,030	0.6	2.5	7.0

S.P. = Soft Point   H.P. = Hollow Point   F.P. = Full Patch   P.E. = Pointed Expanding   H.C.P. = Hollow Copper Point

SEND TO STOEGER FOR FRESH AMMUNITION

RIFLE BALLISTICS OF WINCHESTER CENTER FIRE CARTRIDGES

CARTRIDGE	BULLET Type	BULLET Wt.-Grs.	VELOCITY Muzzle	VELOCITY 100 Yds.	ENERGY Muzzle	ENERGY 100 Yds	TRAJECTORIES IN INCHES 100 Yds. Hgt. at 50 Yds.	200 Yds. Hgt. at 100 Yds.	300 Yds. Hgt. at 150 Yds.
8 m/m (7.9 m/m)	S.P.	236	2,100	1,890	2,310	1,875	1.1	5.0	12.0
Super Speed 8 m/m Mauser B.T.	S.P.	170	2,530	2,210	2,415	1,845	0.8	3.5	9.0
.32 Winchester	Lead	100	1,280	1,060	365	250	3.1	15.0	40.5
.32 Winchester	F.P.	115	1,280	1,080	420	300	3.1	14.5	37.5
.32 Winchester	S.P.	115	1,280	1,080	420	300	3.1	14.5	37.5
Super Speed .32 M/92 Special, W.H.V	S.P.	115	1,600	1,290	655	425	2.2	10.0	27.5
Super Speed .32 Winchester	H.P.	80	2,050	1,520	745	410	1.4	7.5	23.0
Super Speed .32 Winchester Special	S.P.	170	2,260	1,960	1,930	1,450	1.0	4.5	12.0
Super Speed .32 Winchester Special	H.P.	110	2,630	2,140	1,690	1,120	0.7	3.5	11.5
.32 Winchester Self Loading	S.P.	165	1,390	1,190	710	520	2.6	12.5	31.0
.32 Remington Automatic	S.P.	165	2,200	1,900	1,775	1,325	1.0	4.5	12.5
.32-40	S.P.	165	1,440	1,230	760	555	2.6	12.0	28.0
.32-40 W.H.V.	S.P.	165	1,950	1,650	1,395	1,000	1.4	6.5	17.5
.33 Winchester	S.P.	200	2,180	1,870	2,110	1,555	1.1	5.0	13.5
Super Speed .348 Winchester	S.P.	150	2,880	2,380	2,765	1,890	0.6	3.0	8.5
Super Speed .348 Winchester	S.P.	200	2,520	2,160	2,820	2,075	0.8	4.0	10.0
.35 Winchester	S.P.	250	2,160	1,910	2,590	2,025	1.1	5.0	12.0
.35 Winchester Self Loading	S.P.	180	1,390	1,170	775	545	2.5	13.0	31.0
.35 Remington Automatic	S.P.	200	2,180	1,870	2,110	1,555	1.0	5.0	13.0
.351 Winchester Self Loading	F.P.	180	1,850	1,560	1,370	975	1.5	7.5	19.0
.351 Winchester Self Loading	S.P.	180	1,850	1,560	1,370	975	1.5	7.5	19.0
Super Speed .375 H. & H. Magnum	H.P.	235	2,860	2,520	4,270	3,315	0.6	2.5	7.0
Super Speed .375 H. & H. Magnum	S.P.	270	2,720	2,460	4,440	3,630	0.7	3.0	7.0
Super Speed .375 H. & H. Magnum	S.P.	300	2,540	2,290	4,300	3,495	0.7	3.5	8.5
.38 Winchester	S.P.	180	1,310	1,090	685	475	3.2	15.5	37.5
.38 M/92 Spec., W.H.V.	S.P.	180	1,770	1,380	1,255	760	1.7	9.0	24.5
.38-55	S.P.	255	1,320	1,150	985	750	3.0	13.5	32.5
.38-55 Winchester H.V.	S.P.	255	1,600	1,370	1,450	1,065	1.9	9.0	24.5
.38-56 Winchester	S.P.	255	1,400	1,210	1,110	830	2.7	11.5	29.0
.38-72 Winchester	S.P.	275	1,480	1,300	1,340	1,030	2.4	10.0	26.5
.40-65 Winchester	S.P.	260	1,360	1,170	1,070	790	2.9	12.0	30.5
.40-72 Winchester	S.P.	300	1,420	1,240	1,345	1,025	2.3	11.0	27.5
.40-82 Winchester	S.P.	260	1,500	1,260	1,300	915	2.3	11.0	27.0
.401 Winchester Self Loading	S.P.	200	2,140	1,750	2,035	1,360	1.1	5.5	16.5
.405 Winchester	S.P.	300	2,220	1,940	3,285	2,510	1.0	4.5	12.0
.44 Winchester	F.P.	200	1,300	1,070	750	510	3.3	17.5	38.0
.44 Winchester	S.P.	200	1,300	1,070	750	510	3.3	17.5	38.0
.44 M/92 Special., W.H.V.	S.P.	200	1,570	1,220	1,095	660	2.2	11.0	30.0
.45-60 Winchester Black Powder	Lead	300	1,390	1,170	1,285	910	2.6	12.5	30.5
.45-70-405 Government	S.P.	405	1,310	1,160	1,545	1,210	2.8	14.0	32.5
.45-75 Winchester Black Powder	Lead	350	1,390	1,170	1,500	1,060	2.7	13.0	33.0
.45-90 Winchester	S.P.	300	1,530	1,270	1,560	1,075	2.2	11.0	26.5
.50-110 Winchester	S.P.	300	1,610	1,280	1,725	1,090	2.2	10.5	28.5

H.P.=Hollow Point F.P.=Full Patch P.E.=Pointed Expanding H.C.P.=Hollow Copper Point

PISTOL AND REVOLVER BALLISTICS OF WINCHESTER CENTER FIRE CARTRIDGES

CARTRIDGE	Bullet Type	Bullet Wt.-Grs.	Muzzle Velocity Feet Per Second	Muzzle Energy Foot Lbs.	Penetration 7/8" Soft Pine Boards at 15 ft.	Barrel Length Inches
.25 Auto Colt (6.35 m/m)	F.P.	50	820	75	3	2
.32 S. & W. black powder	Lead	85	720	98	3	3
.32 S. & W. Staynless	Lead	85	720	98	3	3
.32 S. & W. Long, black powder	Lead	98	820	146	4	4¼
.32 S. & W. Long, Staynless	Lead	98	820	146	4	4¼
.32 S. & W. Long, lead bearing	Metal Point	98	820	146	4.5	4¼
7.63 m/m Mauser (.30 Mauser)	F.P.	86	1,420	385	11	5½
7.63 m/m Mauser (.30 Mauser)	H.S.P.	86	1,420	385	11	5½
7.65 m/m Luger (.30 Luger)	F.P.	93	1,250	323	11	4½
7.65 m/m Luger (.30 Luger)	H.S.P.	93	1,250	323	11	4½
.32 Short Colt	Lead	80	800	114	3	4
.32 Long Colt	Lead	82	800	117	3	4
.32 Automatic Colt (7.65 m/m)	F.P.	74	980	158	5	4
.32 Winchester black powder	Lead	100	1,030	235	6	6
.32 Winchester Staynless	Lead	100	1,030	235	6	6
.32 Colt New Police	Lead	98	795	138	3	4
Super Speed S. & W. .357 Magnum	Lead	158	1,510	800	12.5	8¾
9 m/m Luger	F.P.	125	1,150	367	10	4
9 m/m Luger	H.S.P.	125	1,150	367	10	4
.38 Colt New Police	Lead	150	695	161	4	4
.38 Short Colt	Lead	130	770	171	4	6
.38 S. & W. black powder	Lead	145	745	179	4	4
.38 S. & W. Staynless	Lead	145	745	179	4	4
.38 S. & W. Staynless, lead bearing	Metal Point	145	745	179	4.5	4
.38 S. & W.	Lead	200	630	176	5	4
Super Speed .38 Special	Lead	158	1,115	436	7.5	5
Super Speed .38 Special, lead bearing	Metal Point	158	1,115	436	10	5
Super Speed .38 Special, metal piercing	Metal Piercing	150	1,175	460	11	5
.38 Colt Special	Lead	158	870	266	6.5	6
.38 S. & W. Special, black powder	Lead	158	870	266	7	6
.38 S. & W. Special, Staynless	Lead	158	870	266	7	6
.38 S. & W. Special, lead bearing	Metal Point	158	870	266	7.5	6
.38 S. & W. Special	Lead	200	745	247	7.5	6
.38 S. & W. Special, Mid Range Sharp Corner	Lead	148	770	195	..	6
.38 S. & W. Special, Full Charge, Sharp Corner	Lead	148	870	249	..	6
.38 Automatic Colt	F.P.	130	1,070	331	9	4½
Super Speed .38 Automatic Colt	F.P.	130	1,300	488	10	5
Super Speed .38 Automatic Colt	H.S.P.	130	1,300	488	10	5
.38 Long Colt	Lead	150	785	205	6	6
.380 Automatic Colt	F.P.	95	970	199	5.5	3¾
.41 Short Colt	Lead	160	720	184	4	6
.41 Long Colt	Lead	196	745	242	5	6
.44 S. & W. American	Lead	205	695	220	4	6
.44 S. & W. Russian	Lead	246	770	324	4	6½
.44 S. & W. Special	Lead	246	770	324	7.5	6½
.44 S. & W. Special, lead bearing	S.P.	246	770	324	8	6½
.45 Colt	Lead	255	870	429	6	5½
.45 Automatic Colt	F.P.	230	860	378	6	5
.45 Auto Rim	Lead	230	820	343	6	5½
.45 Auto Rim	F.P.	230	820	343	6	5½
.455 Colt Mark II	Lead	265	770	349	5	6½

S.P.=Soft Point H.P.=Hollow Point F.P.=Full Patch P.E.=Pointed Expanding H.C.P.=Hollow Copper Point

STANDARD BALLISTICS OF ENGLISH CARTRIDGES

DESCRIPTION	*Powder	†Bullet	Length of Barrel	Pressure at 60° F.	Muzzle Velocity	Muzzle Energy	50 Yards Velocity	50 Yards Energy	100 Yards Velocity	100 Yards Energy
			In.	Tons per sq. in.	Ft. per sec.	Ft.-lb.	Ft. per sec.	Ft.-lb.	Ft. per sec.	Ft.-lb.
.297/.230 (Morris) Short	3¼ grs. Black	37 gr. 1, 2, 3	26	—	875	63	789	51	715	42
.297/.230 (Morris) Short	1¾ grs. R. N.	37 gr. 1, 2, 3,	26	—	875	63	789	51	715	42
.297/.230 (Morris) Long	5½ grs. Black	37 gr. 1, 2, 3	27½	—	1,200	118	1,059	92	966	77
.297/.230 (Morris) Long	2¾ grs. C. N.	37 gr. 1, 2, 3	27½	—	1,200	118	1,059	92	966	77
.240 Flanged Nitro-Express (Holland)	38½ grs. N. C.	100 gr. 4, 5, 6	28	—	2,775	1,711	2,654	1,566	2,537	1,430
.240 Flanged Nitro-Express (Holland)	38½ grs. N. C.	100 gr. 4, 8	28	—	2,775	1,711	2,661	1,574	2,541	1,435
.240 Belted Rimless Nitro-Express (Holland)	40½ grs. N. C.	100 gr. 4, 5, 6	28	—	2,900	1,869	2,760	1,693	2,652	1,560
.240 Belted Rimless Nitro-Express (Holland)	40½ grs. N. C.	100 gr. 4, 8	28	—	2,900	1,869	2,760	1,693	2,652	1,560
.242 Rimless Nitro-Express (Vickers)	42 grs. N. C.	100 gr. 4, 5, 6, 8	28	19.0	3,000	2,000	2,867	1,827	2,738	1,665
.246 Purdey	40 grs. N. C.	100 gr. 4, 10	28	18.0	2,950	1,934	2,805	1,748	2,665	1,580
6.35 mm. (.25) Auto. Pistol	1½ grs. Rim N.	50 gr. 4, 2, 6	2	—	750	63	690	53	634	45
.297/.250 Rook Rifle	6½ grs. Black	56 gr. 1, 2, 3	27	—	1,150	165	1,046	136	972	117
.297/.250 Rook Rifle	3 grs. C. N.	56 gr. 1, 2, 3	27	—	1,150	165	1,046	136	972	117
.255 Rook Rifle	9 grs. Black	65 gr. 1, 2, 3	26	—	1,200	208	1,070	165	980	140
.255 Rook Rifle	4 grs. C. N.	65 gr. 1, 2, 3	26	—	1 200	208	1,070	165	980	140
6.5 mm. (.256) Mannlicher (Dutch)	36 grs. N. C.	160 gr. 4, 2, 6, 9	31	17.5	2,350	1,960	2,216	1,743	2,084	1,542
6.5 mm. (.256) Mannlicher (Dutch)	40 grs. N. C.	135 gr. 4, 2	31	17.5	2,650	2,104	2,546	1,942	2,442	1,786
6.5 mm. (.256) Mannlicher Schonauer	36 grs. N. C.	160 gr. 4, 2, 6, 9	28½	17.5	2,300	1,882	2,166	1,668	2,036	1,474
6.5 mm. (.256) Mannlicher Schonauer	40 grs. N. C.	135 gr. 4, 2	28½	17.5	2,600	2,028	2,494	1,866	2,392	1,716
6.5 mm. (.256) Mauser (Portuguese)	38 grs. N. C.	155 gr. 4, 2, 6	29	17.0	2,400	1,982	2,288	1,803	2,188	1,651
6.5 mm. (.256) Krag-Jorgensen	38 grs. N. C.	160 gr. 4, 2, 6, 9	30	18.5	2,400	2,050	2,265	1,825	2,135	1,620
6.5 mm. (.256) Krag-Jorgensen	40 grs. N. C.	135 gr. 4, 2	30	18.5	2,800	2,350	2,691	2,170	2,584	2,000
.256 Magnum (Gibbs)	35 grs. Cordite	145 gr. 4, 8	28	19.0	2,600	2,178	2,502	2,017	2,415	1,879
.26 Belted Rimless Nitro-Express (B.S.A.)	53 grs. N. C.	110 gr. 4, 2, 10	27	18.0	3,100	2,350	2,900	2,141	2,824	1,950
.275 Flanged Magnum Nitro-Express (Holland)	49 grs. N. C.	160 gr. 4, 5, 6, 8	28	—	2,575	2,357	2,454	2,141	2,342	1,950
.275 Belted Rimless Magnum Nitro-Express (Holland)	52 grs. N. C.	160 gr. 4, 5, 6, 8	28	—	2,675	2,550	2,554	2,320	2,439	2,120
.275 Rimless (Rigby)	43 grs. N. C.	140 gr. 4, 8, 5, 6	28	18.0	2,750	2,352	2,629	2,150	2,518	1,973
.275 Rimless (Rigby)	40 grs. N. C.	173 gr. 4, 2, 6	28	18.0	2,400	2,214	2,288	2,012	2,180	1,827
7 mm. (.276) Mauser (Spanish)	38 grs. N. C.	173 gr. 4, 2, 6, 11, 12	29	16.5	2,300	2,038	2,189	1,842	2,083	1,670
7 mm. (.276) Mauser (Spanish)	48 grs. N. C.	140 gr. 4, 2, 8	29	18.5	2,900	2,626	2,787	2,415	2,677	2,220
7 mm. Rigby Magnum	40 grs. N. C.	140 gr. 4, 8	29½	17.0	2,675	2,226	2,547	2,017	2,442	1,855
.280 Flanged Nitro-Express	52 grs. N. C.	160 gr. 4, 3	28	16.5	2,600	2,403	2,466	2,162	2,336	1,941
.280 Flanged Nitro-Express	52 grs. N. C.	140 gr. 4, 3, 8	28	16.5	2,800	2,440	2,640	2,160	2,485	1,920
.280 Flanged Nitro-Express	48 grs. N. C.	180 gr. 4, 2	28	16.5	2,425	2,383	2,319	2,160	2,215	1,970
.280 Flanged Nitro-Express	49½ grs. N. C.	150 gr. 4, 2	28	16.5	2,675	2,385	2,542	2,160	2,412	1,945
.280 Rimless Nitro-Express (Ross)	54 grs. N. C.	160 gr. 4, 3	28	18.0	2,700	2,592	2,563	2,335	2,430	2,100
.280 Rimless Nitro-Express (Ross)	54 grs. N. C.	140 gr. 4, 3, 8	28	18.0	2,900	2,617	2,736	2,330	2,578	2,065
.280 Rimless Nitro-Express (Ross)	50 grs. N. C.	180 gr. 4, 2	28	18.0	2,525	2,550	2,417	2,340	2,310	2,140
.280 Rimless Nitro-Express (Ross)	51½ grs. N. C.	150 gr. 4, 2	28	18.0	2,775	2,567	2,638	2,320	2,506	2,090
.280 Jeffery Nitro-Express Rimless	57 grs. N. C.	140 gr. 4, 8	28	18.5	3,000	2,800	2,846	2,520	2,697	2,268
Super .30 Magnum Flanged (Holland)	55 grs. Cordite	150 gr. 4, 5, 6	28	17.5	2,875	2,755	2,726	2,480	2,581	2,225
Super .30 Magnum Flanged (Holland)	50 grs. Cordite	180 gr. 4, 6	28	17.5	2,575	2,653	2,440	2,381	2,309	2,131
Super .30 Magnum Flanged (Holland)	46 grs. Cordite	220 gr. 4, 6	28	17 5	2,250	2,475	2,146	2,252	2,045	2,045
Super .30 Magnum Rimless (Holland)	58 grs. Cordite	150 gr. 4, 5, 6	28	18.5	3,000	3,000	2,846	2,700	2,698	2,425
Super .30 Magnum Rimless (Holland)	55 grs. Cordite	180 gr. 4, 6	28	18.5	2,700	2,915	2,561	2,624	2,426	2,355
Super .30 Magnum Rimless (Holland)	49 grs. Cordite	220 gr. 4, 6	28	18.5	2,350	2,700	2,244	2,464	2,141	2,242
.30 Mauser Auto. Pistol	9½ grs. C. N.	85 gr. 4, 2, 6	5½	—	1,400	370	1,216	280	1,090	224
.300 Revolver	6 grs. Black	80 gr. 1, 2, 3	4	—	600	64	572	58	546	53
.300 Revolver	2¼ grs. R. N.	80 gr. 1, 2, 3	4	—	600	64	572	58	546	53
.300 (or .295) Rook Rifle	10 grs. Black	80 gr. 1, 2, 3	27½	—	1,100	216	1,011	182	945	159
.300 (or .295) Rook Rifle	4½ grs. C. N.	80 gr. 1, 2, 3	27½	—	1,100	216	1,011	182	945	159
.300 Sherwood	8½ grs. C. N.	140 gr. 13, 2, 3, 14	27½	—	1,400	610	1,265	497	1,157	416
.300 Sherwood	8½ grs. C. N.	140 gr. 4, 2	27½	—	1,400	610	1,265	497	1,157	416
.300 Sherwood	8½ grs. C. N.	120 gr. 4, 12	27½	—	1,450	561	1,291	445	1,165	360
.30 Flanged (.30-40 Krag)	35 grs. N. C	220 gr. 4, 6	30	16.5	2,000	1,960	1,905	1,770	1,820	1,620
.30 Rimless (Springfield '06)	41 grs. N. C.	220 gr. 4, 6	26	18.0	2,200	2,360	2,100	2,160	2,010	1,980
.30 Rimless (Springfield '06)	47 grs. N. C.	150 gr. 4, 2, 8	26	18 0	2,700	2,425	2,565	2,189	2,435	1,973
.30 Rimless (Springfield '06)	52 grs. N. C.	180 gr. 4, 8	26	18.0	2,700	2,915	2,596	2,685	2,494	2,485
.30-30 Winchester	22 grs. Cordite	170 gr. 4, 2, 6	20	—	1,950	1,440	1,825	1,260	1,707	1,100
7.63 mm. Mannlicher Auto. Pistol	4 grs. R. N.	85 gr. 4, 2, 6	5	—	1,050	208	975	180	915	158
7.65 mm. (or .32) Auto. Pistol or .30 Browning Pistol	3 grs. R. N.	72 gr. 4, 2, 6	3½	—	900	129	818	107	743	88
7.65 mm. Parabellum Auto. Pistol	5 grs. R. N.	92 gr. 4, 2, 6	5	—	1,200	295	1,088	242	1,009	208
7.65 mm. (.301) Mauser (Belgian and Turkish)	35 grs. N. C.	219 gr. 4, 2, 6	29	16.0	2,025	1,996	1,926	1,805	1,830	1,630
7.65 mm. (.301) Mauser (Belgian and Turkish)	46½ grs. N. C.	154 gr. 4, 2	29	17.0	2,750	2,589	2,616	2,340	2,489	2,120
.303 British (Mark VI)	31 grs. Cordite	215 gr. 4, 2	25	17.5	2,050	2,007	1,950	1,817	1,853	1,641
.303 British	31 grs. Cordite	215 gr. 4, 6, 11, 3	25	17.5	2,050	2,007	1,950	1,817	1,853	1,641
.303 British	31½ grs. Cordite	192 gr 4, 14	25	17.0	2,200	2,065	2,037	1,770	1,885	1,515
.303 British (Mark VII)	37 grs. Cordite	174 gr. 4, 2	25	18.5	2,450	2,330	2,342	2,130	2,236	1,940
.303 British	41 grs. N. C.	174 gr. 4, 10	25	18.5	2,450	2,330	2,356	2,160	2,260	1,985
.303 British	38 grs. Cordite	150 gr. 4, 8	25	18.5	2,700	2,430	2,581	2,220	2,464	2,025
.303 Savage	29 grs. N. C.	180 gr. 4, 2, 6	22	—	1,975	1,558	1,853	1,372	1,739	1,211
.310 Cadet (Greener)	6 grs. C. N.	120 gr. 1, 2, 3	26	—	1,200	384	1,146	350	1,100	322
7.9 mm. (.311) Mauser (German)	38 grs. N. C.	227 gr. 4, 2, 6, 11	29	15.5	2,075	2,168	1,934	1,884	1,798	1,628
7.9 mm. (.311) Mauser (German)	52 grs. N. C.	154 gr. 4, 2	29	18.0	2,875	2,824	2,730	2,545	2,590	2,290
8 mm. (.315) Mannlicher (Austrian, Bulgarian and Greek)	41 grs. N. C.	244 gr. 4, 2, 6, 11	30	14.0	2,025	2,223	1,893	1,943	1,767	1,693
8 mm. (.315) Mannlicher-Schonauer	42 grs. N. C.	200 gr. 4, 2, 6, 11	20	—	2,200	2,147	2,047	1,860	1,900	1,605
.318 Rimless Nitro-Express	52 grs N. C.	250 gr. 4, 2, 6, 11, 12	28	18.5	2,400	3,194	2,295	2,922	2,191	2,670
.318 Rimless Nitro-Express	55 grs. N. C.	180 gr. 4, 2, 12	28	18.5	2,700	2,920	2,540	2,580	2,390	2,290
.32 S. & W. Revolver	4½ grs. Black	85 gr. 1, 2	3	—	600	68	551	57	504	48
.32 S. & W. Revolver	2 grs. R. N.	85 gr. 1, 2	3	3.0	600	68	551	57	504	48
.32 S. & W. Long Revolver	10 grs. Black	98 gr. 1, 2	3¼	—	700	106	653	93	608	81
.32 S. & W. Long Revolver	3 grs. R. N.	98 gr. 1, 2	3¼	3.0	700	106	653	93	608	81
.320 Revolver	6 grs. Black	80 gr. 1, 2, 3	3	—	550	54	513	47	478	41
.320 Revolver	2 grs. R. N.	80 gr. 1, 2, 3	3	—	550	54	513	47	478	41

Abbreviations are to read as follows:

* Powder: Black — B. Revolver Neonite — R. N. Cadet Neonite — C. N. Revolver Cordite — R. C. Rim Neonite — Rim N. Nitro Cellulose — N. C.

† Bullets: Lead — No. 1, Solid Point — 2, Hollow Point — 3, Metal Covered — 4, Semi Pointed — 5, Soft Nosed — 6, Semi Pointed Soft Nosed — 7, Copper Pointed — 8, Improved Split — 9, Soft Nosed Pointed — 10, Split Cap — 11, W. R. Cap — 12, Metal Based — 13, Copper Tubed — 14.

SEE PAGE 8, "HOW TO ORDER"

STANDARD BALLISTICS OF ENGLISH CARTRIDGES

DESCRIPTION	*Powder	†Bullet	Length of Barrel	Pressure at 60° F.	Muzzle Velocity	Muzzle Energy	50 Yards Velocity	50 Yards Energy	100 Yards Velocity	100 Yards Energy
			In.	Tons per sq. in.	Ft. per sec.	Ft.-lb.	Ft. per sec.	Ft.-lb.	Ft. per sec.	Ft.-lb.
.320 Long (Rifle)	8 grs. Black	80 gr. 1, 2, 3	26½	—	1,100	215	990	174	910	147
.320 Long (Rifle)	4 grs. C. N.	80 gr. 1, 2, 3	26½	—	1,100	215	990	174	910	147
.32 Colt New Police Revolver	11 grs. Black	100 gr. 1, 2	6	—	725	117	685	104	648	93
.32 Colt New Police Revolver	2½ grs. R. N.	100 gr. 1, 2	6	—	725	117	694	107	664	98
.32 (.32-20) Winchester	19 grs. Black	115 gr. 1, 2	28	—	1,225	384	1,113	317	1,033	273
.32 (.32-20) Winchester	8 grs. C. N.	115 gr. 13, 2	28	—	1,400	501	1,244	396	1,128	325
.32 (.32-20) Winchester	8 grs. C. N.	115 gr. 4, 2, 6	28	—	1,400	501	1,244	396	1,128	325
.32 Winchester "Special"	23 grs. Cordite	170 gr. 4, 2, 6	26	—	2,000	1,510	1,861	1,308	1,733	1,135
.32-40 Marlin and Winchester	18 grs. Cordite	165 gr. 13, 2, 14	26	—	1,600	998	1,520	847	1,400	720
.32-40 Marlin and Winchester	18 grs. Cordite	165 gr. 4, 2, 6	26	—	1,600	998	1,520	847	1,400	720
.33 Belted Rimless Nitro-Express (B.S.A.)	60 grs. N. C.	165 gr. 10, 2	28	18.0	3,000	3,300	2,837	2,951	2,680	2,640
.333 Flanged Nitro-Express	63 grs. N. C.	300 gr. 4, 2, 6, 11	28	—	2,100	3,090	2,069	2,857	1,930	2,640
.333 Flanged Nitro-Express	67 grs. N. C.	250 gr. 4, 2, 6	28	—	2,400	3,200	2,306	2,950	2,215	2,730
.333 Rimless Nitro-Express	65 grs. N. C.	300 gr. 4, 2, 6, 11	28	18.5	2,200	3,230	2,119	2,997	2,039	2,777
.333 Rimless Nitro-Express	70 grs. N. C.	250 gr. 4, 2, 6	28	18.0	2,500	3,480	2,404	3,210	2,310	2,960
.35 Winchester	48½ grs. N. C.	250 gr. 4, 2, 6	24	—	2,200	2,690	2,090	2,430	1,981	2,180
.400/.350 Flanged Nitro-Express	43 grs. N. C.	310 gr. 4, 2, 6, 11	28	16.0	2,000	2,752	1,920	2,537	1,842	2,335
.350 Magnum (Rigby)	65 grs. N. C.	225 gr. 4, 2, 5, 7, 8	24	17.5	2,625	3,440	2,465	3,033	2,307	2,657
.351 Winchester Self-loading	20 grs. Cordite	180 gr. 4, 2, 6	20	—	1,800	1,297	1,644	1,081	1,495	894
9 mm. Auto. Pistol	5 grs. R. N.	110 gr. 4, 2, 6	5	—	1,000	244	904	200	832	169
9 mm. Parabellum Auto. Pistol	5½ grs. R. N.	124 gr. 4, 2, 6	4	—	1,100	333	1,033	294	978	264
9 mm. Mannlicher-Schonauer	45 grs. N. C.	245 gr. 4, 2, 6, 11	22½	17.0	2,100	2,397	1,989	2,150	1,880	1,921
9 mm. Mauser	47 grs. N. C.	245 gr. 4, 2, 6, 11	24	—	2,150	2,515	2,035	2,255	1,926	2,015
.360 No. 5 Rook Rifle	14 grs. Black	134 gr. 1, 2, 3	26	—	1,025	312	935	252	860	220
.360 No. 5 Rook Rifle	5 grs. R. N.	145 gr. 1, 2, 3	26	—	1,075					
.360 Nitro-Express	30 grs. Cordite	300 gr. 4, 2, 6, 11	29	14.0	1,650	1,820	1,562	1,630	1,478	1,460
.360 Nitro for Black Powder Express	22 grs. Cordite	190 gr. 13, 14	29	—	1,650	1,148	1,495	942	1,354	773
.360 Black Powder Express	50 grs. Black	155 gr. 1, 3	29	10.0	1,700	1,000	1,520	800	1,360	640
.360 Black Powder Express	50 grs. Black	190 gr. 1, 14	29	—	1,550	1,015	1,406	834	1,281	693
.360 Black Powder Express	50 grs. Black	215 gr. 1, 2	29	—	1,450	1,005	1,317	828	1,205	694
.400/.360 Nitro-Express (Purdey)	40 grs. Cordite	300 gr. 4, 2, 6, 11	28	15.5	1,950	2,537	1,862	2,312	1,776	2,102
.400/.360 Nitro-Express (Westley Richards)	41 grs. Cordite	314 gr. 4, 2, 6, 11, 12	28	15.5	1,900	2,520	1,811	2,290	1,724	2,072
.360 No. 2 Nitro-Express	55 grs. Cordite	320 gr. 4, 2, 6	28	14.5	2,200	3,442	2,098	3,130	1,999	2,845
9.3 mm. Mauser	54 grs. N. C.	285 gr. 4, 2, 6, 11	24	17.5	2,250	3,200	2,107	2,807	2,009	2,551
.369 Purdey	64½ grs. N. C.	270 gr. 4, 5, 6	31	17.0	2,525	3,815	2,407	3,465	2,292	3,145
9.5 mm. Mannlicher-Schonauer	45 grs. N. C.	270 gr. 4, 2, 6, 11	25	—	2,150	2,768	2,031	2,470	1,916	2,195
.375 Rimless Nitro-Express	43 grs. Cordite	270 gr. 4, 2, 6, 11	25	—	2,100	2,640	1,980	2,350	1,870	2,100
.375 Flanged Nitro-Express	40 grs. Cordite	270 gr. 4, 2, 6, 11	25	14.5	1,975	2,340	1,860	2,080	1,760	1,860
.400/.375 Nitro-Express (Holland)	43 grs. Cordite	270 gr. 4, 2, 6, 7	28	—	2,175	2,840	2,050	2,522	1,930	2,235
.375 Flanged Magnum Nitro-Express (Holland)	56 grs. Cordite	300 gr. 4, 2, 6, 12	28	—	2,425	3,930	2,300	3,526	2,183	3,180
.375 Flanged Magnum Nitro-Express (Holland)	59 grs. Cordite	270 gr. 4, 5, 6	28	—	2,600	4,060	2,482	3,700	2,367	3,362
.375 Flanged Magnum Nitro-Express (Holland)	60 grs. Cordite	235 gr. 4, 8	28	—	2,750	3,950	2,615	3,571	2,489	3,240
.375 Belted Rimless Magnum Nitro-Express (Holland)	58 grs. Cordite	300 gr. 4, 2, 6, 12	28	—	2,500	4,070	2,370	3,744	2,253	3,390
.375 Belted Rimless Magnum Nitro-Express (Holland)	61 grs. Cordite	270 gr. 4, 5, 6	28	—	2,650	4,210	2,531	3,837	2,415	3,496
.375 Belted Rimless Magnum Nitro-Express (Holland)	62 grs. Cordite	235 gr. 4, 8	28	—	2,800	4,090	2,660	3,695	2,535	3,360
.38 S. & W. Revolver	10 grs. Black	145 gr. 1, 2, 3	4	—	625	126	584	110	545	96
.38 S. & W. Revolver	3 grs. R. N.	145 gr. 1, 2, 3	4	—	625	126	584	110	545	96
.38-200 or .380 Mk. 1 (for Mark IV Revolver)	3½ grs. R. C.	200 gr. 1, 2	5	4.0	600	160	574	147	548	134
.38 Colt Police Positive Revolver	10 grs. Black	150 gr. 1, 2	4	—	650	141	610	124	571	109
.38 Colt Police Positive Revolver	3 grs. R. N.	150 gr. 1, 2	4	—	650	141	610	124	571	109
.38 S. & W. "Special" Revolver	18 grs. Black	158 gr. 1, 2	6½	—	925	300	867	263	814	232
.38 S. & W. "Special" Revolver	5 grs. R. N.	158 gr. 1, 2	6½	4.0	925	300	867	263	814	232
.380 Revolver	10 grs. Black	124 gr. 1, 2, 3	4	—	625	108	576	92	530	78
.380 Revolver	3 grs. R. N.	124 gr. 1, 2, 3	4	4.0	625	108	576	92	530	78
.380 Long (Rifle)	15 grs. Black	124 gr. 1, 2, 3	26½	—	1,050	304	970	259	910	228
.380 Long (Rifle)	4 grs. R. N.	124 gr. 1, 2, 3	26½	—	1,050	304	970	259	910	228
.380 Auto. Hammerless Pistol, or .380 Auto. Webley or 9 mm. Short Auto. Pistol	3¼ grs. R. N.	95 gr. 4, 2, 6	4½	—	850	152	762	122	690	101
.38 Auto. Pistol	5¼ grs. R. N.	130 gr. 4, 2, 6	6	6.5	1,100	349	981	278	880	223
.38-40 Winchester	31 grs. Black	180 gr. 1, 2	24	—	1,325	702	1,196	570	1,101	484
.400 Purdey, 3"	47 grs. Cordite	230 gr. 13, 2, 3, 14	20½	—	2,050	2,148	1,855	1,759	1,687	1,455
.450/.400 Nitro for Black Powder Express, 2⅜"	32 grs. Cordite	270 gr. 13, 2, 14	27	—	1,650	1,640	1,520	1,390	1,400	1,180
.450/.400 Black Powder Express, 2⅜"	80 grs. Black	230 gr. 1, 14	27	10.0	1,750	1,563	1,597	1,302	1,454	1,079
.450/.400 Black Powder Express, 2⅜"	80 grs. Black	210 gr. 1, 2	27	—	1,750	1,740	1,610	1,470	1,480	1,240
.450/.400 Nitro-Express, 3"	60 grs. Cordite	400 gr. 4, 2, 6, 11	30	16.0	2,125	4,010	2,033	3,668	1,946	3,361
.450/.400 Magnum Nitro-Express, 3¼"	60 grs. Cordite	400 gr. 4, 2, 6, 11	26	16.5	2,150	4,110	2,060	3,780	1,980	3,490
.450/.400 Magnum Nitro for Black Powder Express, 3¼"	40 grs. Cordite	270 gr. 13, 14	26	—	1,850	2,050	1,705	1,743	1,572	1,480
.450/.400 Magnum Black Powder Express, 3¼"	110 grs. Black	230 gr. 1, 14	26	11.0	2,000	2,045	1,821	1,690	1,662	1,410
.450/.400 Magnum Black Powder Express, 3¼"	110 grs. Black	210 gr. 1, 2	26	—	1,900	2,045	1,749	1,735	1,609	1,465
.401 Winchester Self-loading	32 grs. Cordite	200 gr. 4, 2, 6	20	16.5	2,125	2,010	1,907	1,620	1,705	1,290
.404 Rimless Nitro-Express	60 grs. Cordite	400 gr. 4, 2, 6, 11	28	16.0	2,125	4,010	1,996	3,540	1,872	3,115
.404 Rimless Nitro-Express	70 grs. Cordite	300 gr. 4, 2, 8	28	16.0	2,625	4,595	2,500	4,166	2,390	3,808
.405 Winchester	57½ grs. N. C.	300 gr. 4, 2, 6	24	—	2,200	3,230	2,080	2,880	1,960	2,560
.416 Rigby	70 grs. Cordite	400 gr. 4, 2, 6	26	17.0	2,300	4,702	2,200	4,302	2,110	3,957
.416 Rigby	71 grs. Cordite	410 gr. 4, 6	26	18.0	2,300	4,702	2,200	4,302	2,110	3,957
10.75 mm. (.423) Mauser	66 grs. N. C.	347 gr. 4, 2, 6, 11	24	16.0	2,175	3,641	2,058	3,260	1,943	2,906
.433 (11 mm.) Gras	81 grs. Black	386 gr. 1, 2	30½	—	1,500	1,930	1,410	1,710	1,330	1,520
.433 (11 mm.) Mauser	77 grs. Black	386 gr. 1, 2	31½	—	1,425	1,740	1,240	1,540	1,260	1,360
.44 S. & W. Revolver (American)	18 grs. Black	220 gr. 1, 2	6½	—	700	239	663	215	627	192
.44 S. & W. Revolver (American)	5¼ grs. R. N.	220 gr. 1, 2	6½	4.0	700	239	663	215	627	192
.44 S. & W. Revolver (Russian)	18 grs. Black	246 gr. 1, 2	6½	—	700	268	666	243	633	220
.44 S. & W. Revolver (Russian)	5½ grs. R. N.	246 gr. 1, 2	6½	4.0	700	268	666	243	633	220
.44-40 Winchester	33 grs. Black	200 gr. 1, 2, 8	24	—	1,300	750	1,130	568	1,020	462
.44-40 Winchester	10½ grs. R. N.	200 gr. 13, 2, 14	24	—	1,300	750	1,130	568	1,020	462

Abbreviations are to read as follows:

* Powder: Black — B. Revolver Neonite — R. N. Cadet Neonite — C. N. Revolver Cordite — R. C. Rim Neonite — Rim N. Nitro Cellulose — N. C.
† Bullets: Lead — No. 1, Solid Point — 2, Hollow Point — 3, Metal Covered — 4, Semi Pointed — 5, Soft Nosed — 6, Semi Pointed Soft Nosed — 7, Copper Pointed — 8, Improved Split — 9, Soft Nosed Pointed — 10, Split Cap — 11, W. R. Cap — 12, Metal Based — 13, Copper Tubed — 14.

STANDARD BALLISTICS OF ENGLISH CARTRIDGES

DESCRIPTION	*Powder	†Bullet	Length of Barrel	Pressure at 60° F.	Muzzle Velocity	Muzzle Energy	50 Yards Velocity	50 Yards Energy	100 Yards Velocity	100 Yards Energy
			In.	Tons per sq. in	Ft. per sec.	Ft.-lb.	Ft. per sec.	Ft.-lb.	Ft. per sec.	Ft.-lb.
.44-40 Winchester	10½ grs. R. N.	200 gr. 4, 2, 6	24	—	1,300	750	1,130	568	1,020	462
.442 Revolver	13 grs. Black	220 gr. 1, 2	4½	—	700	239	660	213	620	188
.442 Revolver	5¼ grs. R. N.	220 gr. 1, 2	4½	—	700	239	660	213	620	188
.45 Colt Auto. Pistol	6½ grs. R. N.	200 gr. 4, 2	5	5.0	870	337	808	290	753	252
.45 Colt Auto. Pistol (U. S. A.)	5½ grs. R. N.	230 gr. 4, 2	5	—	800	327	750	288	710	258
.450 Revolver	13 grs. Black	225 gr. 1, 2	6	—	650	211	610	186	591	175
.450 Revolver	5 grs. R. N.	225 gr. 1, 2	6	—	700	245	656	215	615	189
.45-70-405 Marlin and Winchester	57 grs. Black	405 gr. 1, 2	26	—	1,300	1,520	1,190	1,270	1,108	1,105
.450 Nitro-Express	70 grs. Cordite	480 gr. 4, 2, 6, 11, 12	28	17.0	2,150	4,930	2,050	4,490	1,960	4,100
.450 Nitro for Black Powder Express	52 grs. Cordite	365 gr. 13, 2, 14	28	—	2,100	3,578	1,950	3,084	1,809	2,655
.450 Black Powder Express	120 grs. Black	270 gr. 1, 14	28	11.0	1,975	2,340	1,875	2,110	1,780	1,900
.450 Black Powder Express	120 grs. Black	310 gr. 1, 2	28	—	1,800	2,240	1,650	1,880	1,510	1,570
.450 Black Powder Express	120 grs. Black	325 gr. 1, 14	28	—	1,775	2,280	1,630	1,920	1,490	1,600
.450 Black Powder Express	120 grs. Black	365 gr. 1, 2	28	—	1,700	2,340	1,540	1,920	1,415	1,620
.500/.450 No. 1 Black Powder Express, 2¾″	110 grs. Black	270 gr. 1, 14	27	10.0	1,900	2,170	1,691	1,720	1,500	1,350
.500/.450 No. 1 Black Powder Express, 2¾″	110 grs. Black	310 gr. 1, 2	27	—	1,825	2,300	1,645	1,870	1,480	1,510
.500/.450 Magnum Nitro-Express, 3¼″	75 grs. Cordite	480 gr. 4, 2, 6, 11, 12	28	15.5	2,175	5,050	2,078	4,610	1,987	4,220
.500/.450 Magnum Black Powder Express, 3¼″	140 grs. Black	325 gr. 1, 14	28	11.0	1,950	2,745	1,795	2,325	1,656	1,980
.500/.450 Magnum Black Powder Express, 3¼″	140 grs. Black	365 gr. 1, 2	28	11.0	1,875	2,850	1,715	2,380	1,568	2,000
.450 No. 2 Nitro-Express	80 grs. Cordite	480 gr. 4, 2, 6, 11, 12	28	13.0	2,175	5,050	2,038	4,430	1,904	3,700
.500/.450 No. 2 Musket	76 grs. Black	450 gr. 1, 2	26	—	1,300	1,805	1,225	1,600	1,155	1,420
.577/.450 Solid Martini-Henry	85 grs. Black	480 gr. 1, 2	33	—	1,350	1,945	1,273	1,730	1,201	1,535
.577/.450 Solid Martini-Henry	90 grs. Black	325 gr. 1, 14	33	—	1,600	1,850	1,465	1,550	1,345	1,310
.577/.450 Solid Martini-Henry	38½ grs. Cordite	480 gr. 1, 2	33	—	1,350	1,945	1,273	1,730	1,201	1,535
.577/.450 Solid Martini-Henry	44 grs. Cordite	365 gr. 13, 2, 14	33	—	1,425	1,650	1,302	1,370	1,200	1,165
.577/.450 Solid Martini-Henry Carbine	34 grs. Cordite	410 gr. 1, 2	21½	—	1,150	1,200	1,091	1,080	1,041	980
.577/.450 Coiled Martini-Henry	85 grs. Black	480 gr. 1, 2	33	—	1,325	1,873	1,245	1,654	1,175	1,473
.577/.450 Coiled Martini-Henry	90 grs. Black	320 gr. 1, 14	33	—	1,575	1,790	1,434	1,485	1,300	1,220
.577/.450 Coiled Martini-Henry Carbine	70 grs. Black	410 gr. 1, 2	21½	—	1,150	1,200	1,091	1,080	1,041	980
.455 Revolver	18 grs. Black	265 gr. 1, 2	6	—	700	289	669	264	639	241
.455 Revolver	4 grs. R. N.	265 gr. 1, 2	6	—	600	212	572	193	545	175
.455 Webley Self-loading Pistol	6 grs. R. N.	224 gr. 4, 2	5	—	700	244	655	214	613	187
.500/.465 Nitro-Express	73 grs. Cordite	480 gr. 4, 2, 6, 11	28	14.0	2,150	4,930	2,054	4,490	1,962	4,100
.470 Nitro-Express	75 grs. Cordite	500 gr. 4, 2, 6, 11	31	14.0	2,125	5,030	2,023	4,660	1,923	4,120
.475 Nitro-Express	75 grs. Cordite	480 gr. 4, 2, 6, 11	28	15.0	2,175	5,050	2,065	4,550	1,959	4,090
.475 No. 2 Nitro-Express	85 grs. Cordite	480 gr. 4, 2, 6, 11	28	15.5	2,200	5,170	2,084	4,640	1,974	4,160
.475 No. 2 Nitro-Express (For Jeffery rifles)	85 grs. Cordite	500 gr. 4, 2, 6, 11	28	—	2,120	5,000	2,023	4,550	1,930	4,130
.476 Nitro-Express	75 grs. Cordite	520 gr. 4, 2, 6, 11, 12	28	16.0	2,100	5,090	2,000	4,620	1,903	4,180
.500 Nitro-Express, 3″	80 grs. Cordite	570 gr. 4, 2, 6, 11, 12	28	16.0	2,150	5,850	2,048	5,300	1,948	4,800
.500 Nitro for Black Powder Express, 3″	55 grs. Cordite	440 gr. 13, 2, 14	28	—	1,900	3,530	1,747	2,990	1,617	2,560
.500 Black Powder Express, 3″	136 grs. Black	340 gr. 1, 14	28	—	1,925	2,800	1,747	2,310	1,585	1,900
.500 Black Powder Express, 3″	136 grs. Black	380 gr. 1, 2	28	—	1,850	2,890	1,691	2,410	1,546	2,020
.500 Nitro-Express, 3¼″	80 grs. Cordite	570 gr. 4, 2, 6, 11, 12	28	15.5	2,125	5,720	2,022	5,180	1,923	4,690
.500 Nitro for Black Powder Express, 3¼″	55 grs. Cordite	440 gr. 13, 2, 14	28	—	1,900	3,530	1,747	2,984	1,617	2,555
.500 Black Powder Express, 3¼″	142 grs. Black	440 gr. 1, 14	28	11.0	1,775	3,080	1,651	2,660	1,533	2,300
.500 Black Powder Express, 3¼″	142 grs. Black	480 gr. 1, 2	28	—	1,700	3,080	1,586	2,680	1,478	2,330
.577/.500 No. 2 Nitro for Black Powder Express, 2 13/16″	53 grs. Cordite	440 gr. 13, 2, 14	28	—	1,675	2,743	1,547	2,340	1,427	1,991
.577/.500 No. 2 Black Powder Express, 2 13/16″	130 grs. Black	340 gr. 1, 14	28	10.0	1,850	2,590	1,676	2,120	1,520	1,750
.577/.500 No. 2 Black Powder Express, 2 13/16″	130 grs. Black	380 gr. 1, 2	28	—	1,775	2,660	1,627	2,235	1,490	1,875
.577/.500 Magnum Nitro for Black Powder Express, 3⅛″	60 grs. Cordite	440 gr. 13, 2, 14	28	—	1,725	2,910	1,594	2,485	1,471	2,116
.577/.500 Magnum Black Powder Express, 3⅛″	164 grs. Black	440 gr. 1, 14	28	11.0	1,875	3,440	1,739	2,960	1,615	2,550
.577/.500 Magnum Black Powder Express, 3⅛″	164 grs. Black	480 gr. 1, 2	28	—	1,800	3,460	1,677	3,000	1,563	2,605
.577 Solid Snider	70 grs. Black	480 gr. 1, 2	36	—	1,250	1,660	1,124	1,350	1,034	1,140
.577 Coiled Snider	70 grs. Black	480 gr. 1, 2	36	—	1,200	1,535	1,087	1,260	1,008	1,083
.577 Nitro-Express, 2¾″	90 grs. Cordite	650 gr. 4, 1, 6, 11	28	—	1,950	5,500	1,840	4,890	1,736	4,350
.577 Nitro-Express, 2¾″	90 grs. Cordite	750 gr. 4, 2, 6, 11, 12	28	12.5	1,800	5,400	1,711	4,880	1,626	4,410
.577 Black Powder Express, 2¾″	160 grs. Black	520 gr. 1, 14	28	10.0	1,725	3,440	1,587	2,910	1,452	2,440
.577 Black Powder Express, 2¾″	160 grs. Black	560 gr. 1, 2	28	—	1,650	3,380	1,522	2,880	1,400	2,440
.577 Nitro-Express, 3″	90 grs. Cordite	650 gr. 4, 2, 6, 11	28	—	1,950	5,500	1,840	4,890	1,736	4,350
.577 Nitro-Express, 3″	100 grs. Cordite	750 gr. 4, 2, 6, 11, 12	28	14.0	2,050	7,010	1,960	6,400	1,874	5,860
.577 Black Powder Express, 3″	167 grs. Black	570 gr. 1, 14	28	10.0	1,725	3,770	1,574	3,140	1,426	2,570
.577 Black Powder Express, 3″	167 grs. Black	610 gr. 1, 2	28	—	1,650	3,690	1,529	3,170	1,413	2,700
.600 Nitro-Express	100 grs. Cordite	900 gr. 4, 2, 6	28	11.0	1,850	6,840	1,711	5,860	1,582	5,010
.600 Nitro-Express	110 grs. Cordite	900 gr. 4, 2, 6	28	14.0	1,950	7,600	1,807	6,530	1,676	5,620

STANDARD BALLISTICS OF RIM-FIRE CARTRIDGES

DESCRIPTION	*Powder	†Bullet	Muzzle Velocity	Muzzle Energy	50 Yards Velocity	50 Yards Energy	100 Yards Velocity	100 Yards Energy
			Ft. per sec.	Ft.-lb.	Ft. per sec.	Ft.-lb.	Ft. per sec.	Ft.-lb.
.22 Short Smokeless I. C. I. Non-rusting	0.8 gr. Rim Neonite	30 gr. 1, 2, 3	975	51	787	41	711	34
.22 Short Indoor Smokeless	0.5 gr. Rim Neonite	30 gr. 1, 2	700	33	633	27	571	22
.22 Short High Velocity I. C. I. Non-rusting	1.1 grs. Acurim	30 gr. 1, 2, 3	1,150	88	979	64	870	51
.22 Long Smokeless I. C. I. Non-rusting	1.1 grs. Rim Neonite	30 gr. 1, 2, 3	1,100	81	954	61	850	48
.22 Long High Velocity I. C. I. Non-rusting	1.7 grs. Acurim	30 gr. 1, 3	1,300	113	1,052	74	926	57
.22 Long Rifle Smokeless I. C. I. Non-rusting	1.2 grs. Rim Neonite	40 gr. 1, 2, 3	1,060	100	960	82	880	69
.22 Long Rifle Semi-Smokeless "Nobel"	2.7 grs. Semi-Smokeless	40 gr. 1, 2	1,060	100	960	82	880	69
.22 Long Rifle High Velocity I. C. I. Non-rusting	2.7 grs. Acurim	40 gr. 1, 2, 3	1,400	174	1,174	122	1,024	93
.22 Long Rifle "All-range" I. C. I. Non-rusting	1.75 grs. Acurim	40 gr. 1, 2	1,200	128	1,037	96	943	79

Abbreviations are to read as follows:

* Powder: Black — B. Revolver Neonite — R. I. Cadet Neonite — C. N. Revolver Cordite — R. C. Rim Neonite — Rim N. Nitro Cellulose — N. C.

† Bullets: Lead — No. 1, Solid Point — 2, Hollow Point — 3, Metal Covered — 4, Semi Pointed — 5, Soft Nosed — 6, Semi Pointed Soft Nosed — 7, Copper Pointed — 8, Improved Split -- 9, Soft Nosed Pointed — 10, Split Cap — 11, W. R. Cap — 12, Metal Based — 13, Copper Tubed — 14.

©

WE SELL FRESH AMMUNITION ONLY

CONVERSION TABLE

On the two following pages we have listed as nearly complete a set of German D. W. M. rifle cartridges as possible. Due to their unusual completeness, we have found it impractical to convert the units, which are all given in the metric system, to the American equivalents. On the other hand, we give herewith complete conversion tables which will readily enable one to determine the exact figures in terms of inches, foot seconds, foot pounds, or grains as the case may be.

German rifle cartridges are designated by two figures, first the caliber of the bullet, then the length of the brass case without bullet. When a cartridge has a rim, it has "R" added. Hence, 5.6 x 35R means a cartridge with rim, caliber 5.6 m/m and case 35 m/m long; 7 x 57 means a rimless cartridge, caliber 7 m/m with a case 57 m/m long. In the case of the 8 x 57IR, Infantry cartridge with rim is meant—the 8 x 57 m/m which is the regulation German Army cartridge, has about the same ballistics but is rimless.

The second column gives the factory number of the shell; the third column gives the powder used; the fourth, powder weight in grammes; the fifth, the jacket material, if any, which is of cupro-nickel plated ingot iron unless otherwise stated; the sixth, the length of the jacket; the seventh, bullet length; eighth, factory number of bullet; ninth, bullet weight in grammes. The remaining columns are self-explanatory.

COMPARATIVE TABLE OF DIMENSIONS
In "Millimetres" and "Inches," with their respective parts.

Millimetres (mm)	Inches (″)	Millimetres (mm)	Inches (″)	Millimetres (mm)	Inches (″)
1	.039	.1	.004	.01	.00039
2	.079	.2	.008	.02	.00079
3	.118	.3	.012	.03	.00118
4	.157	.4	.016	.04	.00157
5	.197	.5	.020	.05	.00197
6	.236	.6	.024	.06	.00236
7	.276	.7	.028	.07	.00276
8	.315	.8	.031	.08	.00315
9	.354	.9	.035	.09	.00354
10	.394	1.0	.039	.10	.00394
11	.433	1.1	.043	.11	.00433
12	.472	1.2	.047	.12	.00472
13	.512	1.3	.051	.13	.00512
14	.551	1.4	.055	.14	.00551
15	.591	1.5	.059	.15	.00591
16	.630	1.6	.063	.16	.00630
17	.669	1.7	.067	.17	.00669
18	.709	1.8	.071	.18	.00709
19	.748	1.9	.075	.19	.00748
20	.787	2.0	.079	.20	.00787

COMPARISON OF AMERICAN and METRIC UNITS

LENGTH
1 inch = 25.4 millimetres.   1 millimetre = 0.0394 inch.
1 foot = 0.3048 metre.   1 metre = 3.2808 feet.
1 mile = 1.6093 kilometre.   1 kilometre = 0.6214 mile.

WEIGHT
1 grain = 0.0648 gramme.   1 gramme = 15.432 grains.
1 oz. (avdp.) = 28.35 grammes.   1 gramme = 0.0353 oz. (avdp.)
1 lb. = 0.4536 kilogramme.   1 kilogramme = 2.2046 lbs.
1 ton = 1016 kilogrammes.   1000 kilogrammes = 0.9842 ton.

VARIOUS
1 square inch = 6.4516 square centimetres.   1 cubic centimetre = 0.061024 cubic inch.
1 cubic inch = 16.387 cubic centimetres.   1 litre = 1.76 pints.
1 pint = 0.5682 litre.
1 foot per second = 0.3048 metre per second.   1 metre per second = 3.2808 feet per second.
1 ton per square inch = 157.49 kilo. per square centimetre.   1 kilo. per square centimetre = 0.00635 ton per square inch.
1 foot-pound = 0.1382 kilogrammetre.   1 kilogrammetre = 7.233 foot-pounds.
1 square centimetre = 0.155 square inch.
1 dram = 27.34 grains.
1 dram = 1.771 grammes.
1 drachm = 60 grains.
16 drams = 1 ounce.

COMPARATIVE TABLE OF WEIGHTS
in "Grammes" (g) and "Grains" (gr) with their respective parts.

Grammes = g	.00	.10	.20	.30	.40	.50	.60	.70	.80	.90
1	15.4	16.9	18.5	20.1	21.6	23.1	24.7	26.2	27.8	29.3
2	30.9	32.4	34.0	35.5	37.0	38.6	40.1	41.7	43.2	44.8
3	46.3	47.8	49.4	50.9	52.5	54.0	55.6	57.1	58.6	60.2
4	61.7	63.3	64.8	66.4	67.9	69.4	71.0	72.5	74.1	75.6
5	72.2	78.7	80.2	81.8	83.3	84.9	86.4	88.0	89.5	91.0
6	92.6	94.1	95.7	97.2	98.8	100.3	101.9	103.4	104.9	106.5
7	108.0	109.6	111.1	112.7	114.2	115.7	117.3	118.8	120.4	121.9
8	123.5	125.0	126.5	128.1	129.6	131.2	132.7	134.3	135.8	137.3
9	138.9	140.4	142.0	143.5	145.1	146.6	148.1	149.7	151.2	152.8
10	154.3	155.9	157.4	159.0	160.5	162.0	163.6	165.1	166.7	168.2
11	169.8	171.3	172.8	174.4	175.9	177.5	179.0	180.6	182.1	183.6
12	185.2	186.7	188.3	189.8	191.4	192.9	194.4	196.0	197.5	199.1
13	200.6	202.2	203.7	205.2	206.8	208.3	209.9	211.4	213.0	214.5
14	216.0	217.6	219.1	220.7	222.2	223.8	225.3	226.9	228.4	229.9
15	231.5	233.0	234.6	236.1	237.7	239.2	240.7	242.3	243.8	245.4
16	246.9	248.5	250.0	251.5	253.1	254.6	256.2	257.7	259.3	260.8
17	262.3	263.9	265.4	267.0	268.5	270.1	271.6	273.1	274.7	276.2
18	277.8	279.3	280.9	282.4	283.9	285.5	287.0	288.6	290.1	291.7
19	293.2	294.8	296.3	297.8	299.4	300.9	302.5	304.0	305.6	307.1
20	308.6	310.2	311.7	313.3	314.8	316.4	317.9	319.4	321.0	322.5
21	324.1	325.6	327.2	328.7	330.2	331.8	333.3	334.9	336.4	338.0
22	339.5	341.0	342.6	344.1	345.7	347.2	348.8	350.3	351.9	353.4
23	354.9	355.5	358.0	359.6	361.1	362.7	364.2	365.7	367.3	368.8
24	370.4	371.9	373.5	375.0	376.5	378.1	379.6	381.2	382.7	384.3
25	385.8	387.3	388.9	390.4	392.0	393.5	395.1	396.6	398.1	399.7
26	401.2	402.8	404.3	405.9	407.4	408.9	410.5	412.0	413.6	415.0
27	416.7	418.2	419.8	421.3	422.8	424.4	425.9	427.5	429.0	430.6
28	432.1	433.6	435.2	436.7	438.3	439.8	441.4	442.9	444.4	446.0
29	447.5	449.1	450.6	452.2	453.7	455.2	456.8	458.3	459.9	461.4
30	463.0	464.5	466.0	467.6	469.1	470.7	472.2	473.8	475.3	476.8

EXPLANATION OF POWDER TYPE

T12 — Troisdorfer Smokeless Target Powder 1912.
WL — Walsroder Semi-Smokeless Lesmok Powder.
HO — Hirsch Brand Black Powder Grain No. 0.
R1 — Rottweil Smokeless Rifle Leaf Powder No. 1.
R2 — Rottweil Smokeless Rifle Leaf Powder No. 2.
R5 — Rottweil Smokeless Rifle Leaf Powder No. 5.
W19 — Walsroder Smokeless Rifle Leaf Powder No. 1919.
W20 — Walsroder Smokeless Rifle Leaf Powder No. 1920.
NK6 — Nassbrand Black Powder Grain No. 6.
RP — Rottweil Smokeless Target Powder "P."

EXPLANATION OF BULLET JACKET

K — Copper.
B — Lead (no jacket).
R — Round Nose.
T — Soft Point.
S — Spitzer (Pointed).
P — Boat Tail.
V — Full Metal.
L — Hollow Point.
F — Flat Nose.
N — Nickel.

REGARDING THE 8 M/M CARTRIDGE

Probably the most misunderstood cartridge in America today is the 8 m/m, and this perhaps not without adequate reason, when it is considered that most gun experts are confused on the subject with seeming good cause. For these reasons, we believe a few words of explanation on this subject would be of genuine interest to all. The German Army cartridge is, and has been since 1888 the 8 x 57 rimless. Until 1898 the bullet was round nose, when the Model 1888 rifle was discontinued and the Model 1898 accepted. The cartridge case remained practically the same, but the Spitzer bullet was adopted. The so-called Mannlicher Haenels, Schilling Mannlichers, etc., are mostly the Model 1888 rifle. The actual caliber is 7.85 m/m, usually called 7.9 m/m, and generally known as the 8 m/m—they are all the same. The Model 1888 uses the box magazine and cannot be used as a repeater without it. The Model 1898 uses a flat clip, similar to the Springfield but can be fully loaded without clip.

Particular attention should be called to the fact that while the Model 1888 cartridge and the Model 1898 will interchange and the Model 1888 cartridge may be safely used in the Model 1898 rifle, the Model 1898 cartridge should, under no circumstances, be used in the Model 1888 rifle. The reason for the foregoing is that the Model 1898 rifle is considerably stronger than the Model 1888 and the Model 1898 cartridge has 47.8 grains of leaf powder and a 154.3 grain Spitzer bullet which develops a considerably higher breech pressure than the Model 1888 cartridge which is loaded with 38.6 grains of leaf powder and with a 226.9 grain round nose bullet. In ordering ammunition be sure and state whether the Model 1898 or the Model 1888 is desired.

THE MANNLICHER SCHOENAUER, 8 M/M (8.2 x 56 M/M), MODEL 1908, TAKES A SPECIAL SHELL WHICH IS POSITIVELY NOT INTERCHANGEABLE WITH THE MAUSER 8 M/M, INASMUCH AS THE MAUSER CASE IS 1 M/M LONGER AND THE NECK IS SLIGHTLY DIFFERENTLY PLACED. Cartridges are made which are supposed to be interchangeable—and sometimes are interchangeable—but their use is dangerous due to incorrect chambering and faulty head space.

The misunderstandings are, however, due to the fact that tens of thousands of converted military rifles were made up and sold in Germany for as low as $2 apiece. Where chamber and barrel were rusty they were merely reamed open until bright or any untried poorly made barrel substituted. These rifles flooded America and were sold as genuine 8 m/m rifles, and as each one was different, the impression created was that the 8 m/m was very poor. Actually, the original 8 m/m is a very fine and accurate rifle, ideally suited for big game such as bear and moose, and is very popular in Africa. See Remington and Peters ballistics on the 8m/m cartridge.

SEND YOUR GUN TO STOEGER FOR EXPERT REPAIRING

BALLISTICS OF GERMAN D. W. M. CARTRIDGES

Designation	Cart. case No.	Bullet No.	Bullet Kind	Bullet L. mm	Bullet Wgt. g	Powder Wgt. g	Powder Kind	V 25 m/s	E 25 kgm	Pressure kg/cm²	Barrel length cm
5.6 x 35R	539	425	Solid round head (Copper jacket)	12	2.5	0.4	Tr. T. P. 1912	531	36	1600	60
		426	Lead	12.5	2.7	0.4	Tr. T. P. 1912	535	40	1600	
		425	Solid round head (Copper jacket)	12	2.5	0.6	Spec.	700	68	2750	
5.6 x 35R	578	496	Solid round head (Copper jacket)	14	3	0.6					67
.22 H.O. Hornet		496A	Soft-nosed round head (Tombac jacket)	14	3			650	66	2800	
5.6 x 52R	545	461	Solid pointed	21	4.6	1.9	R. 2	820	158	3500	60
		441	Soft-nosed pointed (Nick. tombac jacket)	20							
6 x 58	489	294K	Soft-nosed holl. pointed	30	8.2	3	R. 1	810	274	3500	65
6.5 x 27P	476	458E	Soft-nosed flat head	17	5.3	0.5	Tr. T. P. 1912	447	54		58
6.5 x 48R	463A	267A	Soft-nosed round head	26	8.2	1.5	R. 5	632	161		65
6.5 x 52	519A	444H	Soft-nosed round head (Nick. tombac jacket)	26	7.7	1.75	W. 1919	540	131	3100	62
6.5 x 52	519A			26	7.7	1.9	W. 1919	690	186	3200	
6.5 x 52R	519			26	7.7	1.4	R. 5	570	127	1900	
6.5 x 53R	395C	210A	Soft-nosed round head	31	10.3	2.75	P. 1	640	215	2700	45
6.5 x 53 M.-Sch.	477	430H	Soft-nosed round head	25	7.7	2.9	R. 2	680	242	3000	
		3050	Soft-nosed pointed	29	8	2.75	R. 2	740	259	2000	
					6	2.8	R. 2	750	229	2800	
6.5 x 54	457	267A	Soft-nosed round head	26	8.2	2.75	R. 2	791	262	2700	60
		218A	Soft-nosed round head	32	10	3	R. 2	713	262	3100	
		430H	Soft-nosed round head	25	7.7	3	R. 2	822	264	3200	
6.5 x 55	431C	3050	Soft-nosed pointed	29	8	3	R. 2	789	253	2700	60
6.5 x 57	404A	498B	Soft-nosed pointed	22	6	2.9	39	980	294	3400	65
6.5 x 58R	463	267A	Soft-nosed round head	26	8.2	1.8	W. 1919	620	160		60
6.5 x 58	457	218A	Soft-nosed round head	32	10	3	P. 1	751	290	3100	65
		430H	Soft-nosed round head	25	7.7	3	R. 2	348	282	2900	
		3050	Soft-nosed pointed	29	8	3	R. 2	325	297	2800	
		498B	Soft-nosed pointed	22	6	2.9	39	980	294	3400	
6.5 x 61	431LL	218A	Soft-nosed round head	32	10	3.5	R. 5	796	327	3250	65
		3050	Soft-nosed round head	29	8	3.2	W. 1919	875	311	3350	
		430H	Soft-nosed round head	25	7.7	3.2	W. 1919	898	316	3450	
		409J	Solid Torpedo	33	9	3.45		849	330	3450	
7 x 57	380L	143A	Soft-nosed round head	30	11.2	2.4	P. 1	676	260	2900	
	380H	253S	Soft-nosed pointed	29	10	3.2	R. 5	714	274	2800	65
7 x 57R	380J						W. 1919	734	255	2600	
						3.25	Spec.	788	339	2900	
		488A	Strong jacket	29	10	2.6	W. 1919	731	272	28	
		488K	Strong jacket	32.5		3.2	Spec.	813	339	3300	
		488HS	Strong jacket		10	3.05	R. 2	792	320	3000	
		253R	Soft-nosed Torpedo	33	9	2.9	R. 5	790	287	2450	
		429H	Soft-nosed round head	26	7	2.5	W. 1919	782	218	2550	
		491P	Soft-nosed flat head	18	10	2.9	R. 1	848	255	2800	
		479	Torpedo hollow pointed (Copper jacket)	29		3.2		708	301		
	557	143A	Soft-nosed round head	30	11.2	3.3	R. 2	745	316	2700	
7 x 64	557A	253S	Soft-nosed pointed	31	10	3.7	R. 2	805	369	3100	68
		253P	Soft-nosed Torpe-lo	33	10	3.8	Spec.	857	373	3230	
		488A	Strong jacket	29	10	3.9	R. 3	916	428	4000	
		488K	Strong jacket	29	10	3.65	R. 2	835	355	3300	
		488HS	Strong jacket	32.5	9	3.75	Spec.	830	351	3500	
		429H	Soft-nosed round head	26	9	3.7	W. 1919	872	349	3000	
		479	Torpedo hollow pointed (Copper jacket)	29	10	3.5	R. 2	835	355	3300	
		491?	Soft-nosed flat head	18	7	3.3	R. 3	795	225	2400	
7 x 65R		469	Soft-nosed Torpedo (Hollow alum.-point)	35	10.5	3.3	W. 1919	884	278	3030	
						3.5	R. 2	854	390	3300	

Designation	Cart. case No.	Bullet No.	Bullet Kind	Bullet L. mm	Bullet Wgt. g	Powder Wgt. g	Powder Kind	V 25 m/s	E 25 kgm	Pressure kg/cm²	Barrel length cm
7 x 72R	573	429H	Soft-nosed round head	26	9	2.85	R. 2	735	248	2600	62
		488A	Strong jacket	29	10	2.75	R. 2	655	218	2700	
		488K	Strong jacket	29	10	2.65	R. 2	670	229	2150	
		479	Torpedo hollow pointed (Copper jacket)	29		2.5	W. 1919	701	177	2100	
		491P	Soft-nosed flat head	18	7	2.6	W. 1919	704	208	2500	
7.62 x 51R M/94 Cal. 30/30	543	433A	Soft-nosed round head (Nick. tombac jacket)	25	11	1.9	W. 1920	637	228	2600	66
7.62 x 63 Cal. 30	379E	130M	Soft-nosed pointed	27	9.7	3.85	R. 2	857	303	3000	60
		277S	Soft-nosed Torpedo	33	11.1	3.7	Spec.	795	338	3350	
		480	Soft-nosed Torpedo	30	10.8	3.5	Spec.	774	330	2700	
						3.5	Spec.	824	374	3100	
8 x 48R	462A	299A	Soft-nosed round head	26	12.7	1.6	W. 1920	530	181		65
8 x 50Z	358C	113A	Soft-nosed pointed	32	15.8	2.7	R. 5	505	231	3100	65
		3543	Soft-nosed pointed	27	10	3.15	R. 5	782	311	3200	
8 x 51	366L	117Y	Soft-nosed Torpedo	22	10	2.5	R. 5	630	207	2800	51
8 x 56 M.-Sch.	528	398A	Soft-nosed Torpedo	26	13	2.65	W. 1920	635	266	2800	51
		463A	Strong jacket Torpedo	29	12	2.9	R. 5	695	295	2500	
8 x 57R .330	446	299A	Soft-nosed round head	26	12.7	2.3	R. 5	637	262	2800	68
		117Y	Soft-nosed round head	22	10	2.4	R. 5	668	232	2400	
8 x 57JR M/88R	366D	299A	Soft-nosed round head	30	14.7	2.5	R. 5	633	300	2400	68
8-57R M/88A	366B					3.25	Spec.	677	344	2750	
8 x 57J	560	473A	Strong jacket flat head	28	12.7	3.5	Tr. 1910	633	362	2750	
		343C	Strong jacket flat head	29	12.8	3.5	Spec.	748	304	2800	
						2.6	Spec.	742	336	2500	
						3.4	W. 1920	685	328	2750	
						2.7	Spec.	710	358	2700	
						3.5	R. 5	790	324	3200	
8 x 57JS	56L	117XL	Soft-nosed hollow point	22	10	2.7	R. 5	738	276	2800	
		342F	Soft-nosed flat head	22	11.6	2.5	R. 5	652	251	1900	
8 x 58R	462	3543	Soft-nosed pointed	27	10	3.1	R. 5	856	372	3600	68
		463A	(Nick. copper jacket)	30	12	3	W. 1919	775	366	3200	72
		463K		29		2.1	L. 5	530	203	1600	
		463HS					W. 1920	624	202	2000	
8 x 60	542	299A	Soft-nosed pointed	26	12.7	3.1	W. 1919	695	362	3100	68
8 x 60R	542A	117Y		22	10	3	W. 1919	745	358	3100	
		117A	Soft-nosed round head	30	14.7	3	P. 4	889	405	3600	
		299A	Soft-nosed round head	26	12.7	3	W. 1919	748	364	3100	
		3513	Soft-nosed round head	27	10		P. 5				
		343C	Soft-nosed flat head	29	12.8						
8 x 60 Magnum Bozabe	342	473A	Strong jacket rd. head	28	12.7	3.5	Spec.	737	351	3200	65
		433A	Strong jacket Torpedo	30	12	3.15	W. 1919	755	358	3100	
		433K	Strong jacket Torpedo	29		3.5		789	380	3300	
		463HS	Strong jacket Torpedo	34		3.5					
		117A	Soft-nosed round head	30	14.7	3.7	Spec.	860	454	3900	65
8 x 64	558	229A	Soft-nosed pointed	23	12.7	4	Spec.	748	416	3100	
8 x 65R	538A	334A	Soft-nosed pointed	27	10	4	Spec.	773	355	2700	65
		343C	Soft-nosed flat head	29	12.8	3.6	Spec.	871	395	3500	
							Spec.	782			
		473A	Strong jacket rd. head	28	12.7	4	Spec.	758	371	2800	
		463A	Strong jacket Torpedo	30	12	4	Spec.	856	447	3500	
		463K	Strong jacket Torpedo	29							
		463HS*	Strong jacket Torpedo	34							

* For loading in magazines of at least 88 mm length.

BALLISTICS OF GERMAN D. W. M. CARTRIDGES

Designation	Cartr. case No.	Bullet No.	Bullet Kind	L. mm	Wgt. g	Powder Wgt. g	Powder Kind	V 25 m/s	E 25 kgm	Pressure kg/cm²	Barrel length cm
8 x 72R	574	117A	Soft-nosed round head	30	14.7	2.4	R. 5	585	256	2500	
		299A	Soft-nosed round head	26	12.7	2.65	R. 5	660	281	2600	
		343C	Soft-nosed flat head	29	12.8	2.65	R. 5	660	285	2800	62
		342F	Soft-nosed flat head (Nick. copper jacket)	23	11.6	2.75	R. 5	680	274	2750	
		473A	Strong jacket rd. head (Nick. copper jacket)	28	12.7	2.65	R. 5	660	281	2700	
		117A	Soft-nosed round head	30	14.7	4.6	R. 1	791	468	2800	
						3.2	R. 5	705	321	3000	
		299A	Soft-nosed round head	26	12.7	{4.6, 3.2}	R. 5	{781, 781}	{394, 312}	{3100, 3200}	
		354B	Soft-nosed pointed	27	10	4.2	W. 1919	878	392	3200	65
		343C	Soft-nosed flat head (Nick. copper jacket)	29	12.8	4.4	R. 2	784	398	3000	
8 x 75	514A	473A	Strong jacket rd. head	28	12.7	{4.6, 3.2}	R. 2 / R. 5	{786, 704}	{400, 321}	{3200, 3100}	
9 x 75R	514	463A	Strong jacket Torpedo	30	12	4	W. 1919	863	454	3900	
		463K	Strong jacket Torpedo	29				833	424	3350	
		463HS†	Strong jacket Torpedo	34		3.9	R. 3				
8.15 x 46R	455	343	Soft-nosed flat head (Nick. copper jacket)	19	9	1.8	R. 5	546	136	1400	68
		16H	Lead	19	9	0.75	R. "P"			1050	
9 x 56 M.-Sch.	491E	381A	Soft-nosed round head	28	16	2.9	R. 5	617	310	2300	50
		373A	Soft-nosed pointed (Nick. copper jacket)	25	13.3	2.9	W. 1920	658	294	2400	
9 x 57	491A	303A	Soft-nosed round head	28	16.5	3	R. 5	667	363	2500	
9 x 57R	491B	330A	Soft-nosed round head	25	14.5	3	R. 5	684	356	2100	72
		373A	Soft-nosed pointed (Nick. copper jacket)	25	13.3	3	R. 5	696	329	2200	
9 x 70R	474B	332A	Soft-nosed round head	25	14.6	3.75	W. 1919	725	403	3100	58
9.3 x 62	474C	298A	Soft-nosed round head	30	18.5	3.5	R. 5	685	442	3000	
		472A	Soft-nosed rd. head	29	18.5	3.5	R. 5	700	463	3500	
		489K	Strong jacket Torpedo	29	17	3.7	W. 1912	740	474	3300	72
		489HS	Strong jacket Torpedo	33		3.8	R. 4	755	491	3800	
		372A	Soft-nosed pointed	28	15	3.7	R. 5	755	436	3000	
9.3 x 72R	77D	400	Lead	22	14.5	1.3	R. "P"	465	160	1200	72
		341A	Solid flat head (Nick. copper jacket)	20	11.8	2.6	R. 5	555	185	1500	
		341T	Soft-nosed flat head (Nick. copper jacket)	20.5	12	1.4	Tr. 1912	485	144	2100	68
9.3 x 74R	474A	298A	Soft nosed round head	30	18.5	3.5	R. 5	675	430	3000	
		472A	Strong jacket rd. head	31	18.5	3.5	W. 1912	697	459	3300	
		489K	Strong jacket Torpedo	29	17	3.9	R. 3	720	490	3300	72
		489HS	Strong jacket Torpedo	33		4		755	491	3200	
		372A	Soft nosed pointed	28	15	3.75	R. 5	773	458	3000	
9.5 x 57 M.-Sch.	531	407A	Soft nosed round head	28	17.6	3.25	R. 5	627	354	2600	60

Designation	Cartr. case No.	Bullet No.	Bullet Kind	L. mm	Wgt. g	Powder Wgt. g	Powder Kind	V 25 m/s	E 25 kgm	Pressure kg/cm²	Barrel length cm
10.75 x 68	515A	320A	Soft nosed round head	27	22.5	{4.2, 3.8}	R. 5 / R. 5	{645, 590}	{478, 400}	{3800, 3200}	60
10.75 x 73 Cal. 404	555	449L	Sort nosed round head	30	26	{4.4, 5.2}	R. 5 / W. 1919	{625, 675}	{519, 608}	{2600, 3150}	69
11.15 x 60R	41	11A	Lead	27.5	25	5	Black P. 71/84	428	234		72
11.2 x 60	41A	324A	Soft nosed round head	25	21.5	4	R. 5	645	453	2500	72

† For loading in magazines of at least 99 mm. length.

Cartridges for use during closed season

Designation	Cartr. case No.	Bullet No.	Bullet Kind	L. mm	Wgt. g	Powder Wgt. g	Powder Kind	V 25 m/s	E 25 kgm	Barrel length cm
6.5 x 53 M.-Sch.	477	492P	Soft-nosed flat head	12	3.3	1.05	Tr. target P. 1912	648	70	60
6.5 x 54	457A	492P	Soft-nosed flat head	12	3.3	1.0	Tr. target P. 1912	648	70	60
6.5 x 57	404A	492P	Soft-nosed flat head	12	3.3	1.0	Tr. target P. 1912	648	70	60
6.5 x 58	457	492P	Soft-nosed flat head	12	3.3	1.0	Tr. target P. 1912	648	70	60
6.5 x 58R	463, 380L, 380H, 380J	492P	Soft-nosed flat head	12	3.3	0.85	Tr. target P. 1912	648	70	60
7 x 57	557, 557A	493P	Soft-nosed flat head	14.5	5.0	1.1	Tr. target P. 1912	600	92	60
7 x 57R		493P	Soft-nosed flat head	14.5	5.0	1.2	Tr. target P. 1912	600	92	60
7 x 64	573	493P	Soft-nosed flat head	14.5	5.5	1.1	Tr. target P. 1912	600	92	60
7 x 65R	366D1, 366B	494P	Soft-nosed flat head	12.5	5.5	1.1	Tr. target P. 1912	560	87	60
7 x 72R	560	494P	Soft-nosed flat head	12.5	5.5	1.05	Tr. target P. 1912	560	87	60
8 x 57J	446	494P	Soft-nosed flat head	12.5	5.5	1.2	Tr. target P. 1912	500	87	60
8 x 57JR360	542, 542A	494P	Soft-nosed flat head	12.5	5.5	1.2	Tr. target P. 1912	560	87	60
8 x 60		494P	Soft-nosed flat head	12.5	5.5	1.05	Tr. target P. 1912	560	87	60
8 x 60R										
8 x 64	558, 558A	494P	Soft-nosed flat head	12.5	5.5	1.2	Tr. target P. 1912	560	87	60
8 x 65R	574	494P	Soft-nosed flat head	12.5	5.5	1.05	Tr. target P. 1912	560	87	60
8 x 72R										

The ballistics shown on this page are those of the most popular D. W. M. cartridges.

A comprehensive 136 page, bound book of complete ballistics of all D. W. M. cartridges together with a treatise on ballistics as well as many diagrams, formulas, and illustrations can be supplied. This book is available only in German.

Price, Postpaid... $1.50

MARBLE'S KNIVES AND SAFETY AXES
MARBLE'S IDEAL KNIVES

The thick forged blade is relieved by hollow grinding which provides proper balance for weight and size. Strength of back is necessary for splitting kindling or digging holes in hard ground or ice. The hollows aid quick sharpening and allow the original strength of back to remain. Blade is adapted to sticking and skinning. Back of point is beveled for breaking small bones.

The *Ideal* is an every-purpose knife.

OUTER'S KNIFE

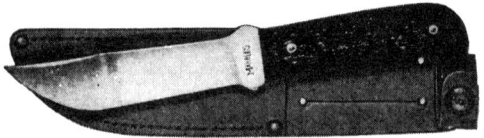

The 4-inch blade, tempered, polished and sharpened, is made from high grade cutlery steel, as used in all Marble Knives. Blade extends clear thru the bone stag handle. Just the knife for hunting, fishing and camping trips.

No. 40—Blade 4 inches; Bone Stag Handle. Weight with sheath, 4 ounces $1.00

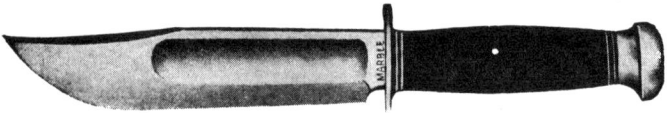

IDEAL KNIFE

Handle is made of washers of sole leather, red and black fibre and brass. Brass Hilt. Aluminum Tip. Blade and tang forged from one piece of high grade cutlery steel, expertly tempered, polished and sharpened to a keen edge.

No. 45, Leather Handle Ideal. Has Hilt. Sheath Furnished
No. 45—With Sheath.
4¼" blade........ 6 oz. $2.50   7" blade........10 oz. $3.25
5" blade......... 7 oz. 2.75   8" blade........14 oz. 3.50
6" blade......... 8 oz. 3.00

No. 46, Stag Handle Ideal. Has Hilt. Sheath Furnished
No. 46—With Sheath.
4¼" blade........ 6 oz. $3.25   7" blade........10 oz. $4.00
5" blade......... 7 oz. 3.50   8" blade........14 oz. 4.25
6" blade......... 8 oz. 3.75

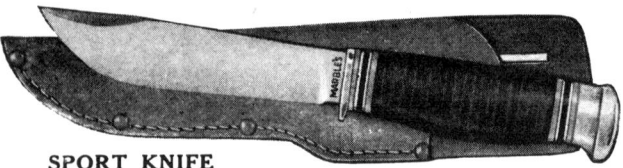

SPORT KNIFE

For outdoor or indoor use by the camper, canoeist, hiker, hunter, or fisherman.

Leather handle, 3½ inches, is of same construction as Marble's Ideal Knife. Blade forged from high grade cutlery steel, polished and sharpened to a keen edge.

No. 60—Leather handle, blade 4 inches, weight with sheath, 4 oz... $1.50

GIRL SCOUT KNIFE

Leather handle, 3½ inches, is of same construction as Marble's Ideal Knife. Blade forged from high grade cutlery steel, polished and sharpened to a keen edge.

No. 251—Blade 4 inches, weight, with sheath, 4 ounces........ $1.35

BOY SCOUT KNIFE

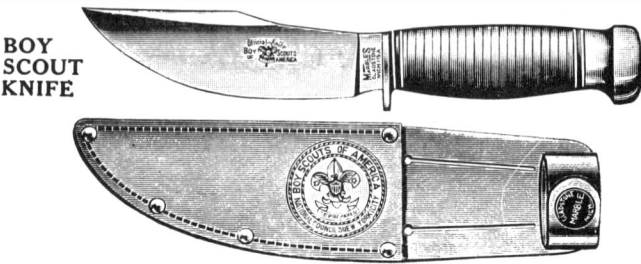

Beautiful handle, made of washers of sole leather, colored fibre and brass, waterproofed and polished—aluminum tip. Blade and tang forged from one piece of high grade cutlery steel; carefully tempered, polished and sharpened to a keen edge.

No. 1560—Blade 4½ inches, with sheath.................. $1.75
No. 1562—Blade 4 inches, with sheath.................. 1.35

SAFETY HUNTING KNIFE

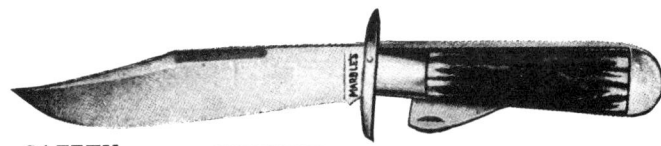

The extension guard acts as a safety lock when the knife is open, and makes it rigid as a one-piece knife. When either open or closed, the blade is held in position by a spring. The hilts, bolsters and linings are of nickel silver. Side plates are genuine staghorn. Sheath furnished.

No. 83—Blade 4¼ inches, weight 4 ounces.................. $3.50
No. 85—Blade 5 inches, weight 6 ounces................... 4.00

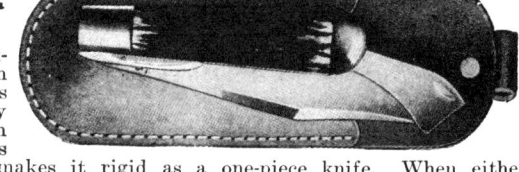

WOODCRAFT KNIFE

The thick back with tapering bevel blade carries the strength from handle to point, so that it serves as well as a thin blade, yet has the surplus of strength found usually in heavier knives. It's an all-purpose knife for hunting, fishing, or canoeing. Thousands of Boy Scouts own these knives. Blade 4¼ inches. Aluminum tip. Blade forged from high grade cutlery steel, polished and sharpened to a keen edge.

No. 49—Leather handle, weight with sheath 7 ounces.......... $2.00
No. 50—Staghorn handle, weight with sheath 7 ounces......... 3.00

TRAILMAKER KNIFE

There is not one cutting tool that will serve as many purposes as the "Trailmaker." Tent poles, light firewood and trees up to several inches in diameter can be cut as quickly as with an axe.

No. 56—Blade 10 inches; leather handle 5 inches, with leather sheath, weight, 1 pound.. $5.50

The handiest tool a Sportsman ever carried. The nickel-plated spring-hinged guard is lined with lead and folds into the handle. The blade is made of tool steel, carefully tempered and sharpened. The nickel-plated metal handles are drop-forged and never break. The side plates are hard rubber. Carried in pocket or belt, a snap of the guard makes it ready for action.

No. 2—Weight 22 ounces; length 11 inches; solid steel blade, 2⅜x4 in..... $3.25
No. 3—Weight 27 ounces; length 11½ inches; solid steel blade, 2½x4⅜ in.... 3.50
No. 2½—Axe No. 2 with Claw.......... 3.50
No. 2P—Axe No. 2 with pick.......... 4.50
No. 5—Hickory handle, weight 16 oz.; length 10½" solid steel blade, 2⅜x4¾".... 2.00
No. 6—Hickory handle, weight 22 oz.; length 11½"; solid steel blade, 2¾x4¾".... 2.25

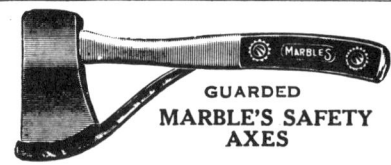

GUARDED
MARBLE'S SAFETY AXES

HUNTING KNIVES AND COMPASSES

J. A. HENCKEL'S HUNTING KNIVES

It is an undisputed fact that the name Henckel stands as the leader among cutlery manufacturers of the world. Realizing the great importance of a good knife in every hunter's equipment we have listed the most popular models of these famous Henckel hunting knives—A good knife is second only in importance to the hunter's gun. Where you see the well known twin trade mark you see the best in cutlery.

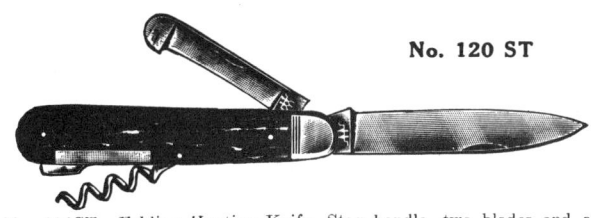

No. 120 ST

No. 120ST—Folding Hunting Knife, Stag handle, two blades and corkscrew. Sturdy main blade which locks when open to insure safety. Small blade fitted with metal knob and ground to very keen edge. Used for ripping open carcass. Knob prevents punching through intestines. **$7.65** ea.

No. 633/5

No. 633/5—Ellery Hunter. A light blade hunting and skinning knife. Black wood handle with two tubular rivets. 5 inch blade. Black fitted leather sheath. **$3.25** ea.

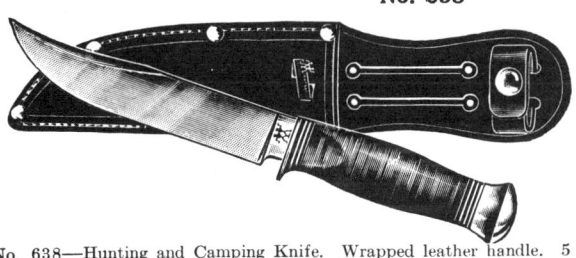

No. 638

No. 638—Hunting and Camping Knife. Wrapped leather handle. 5 inch blade. Fitted dark brown leather sheath. **$3.25** ea.

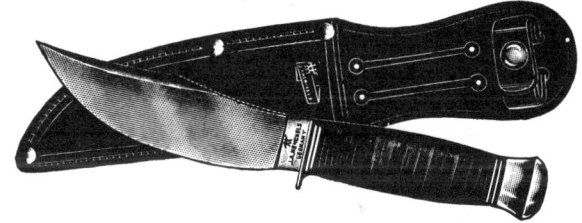

No. 639

No. 639—Hunting and Camping Knife. Genuine stag handle. 5 inch blade. Fitted dark brown leather sheath. **$3.75** ea.

No. 640

No. 640—Same as above, but with composition pearl handle. Very durable, will not crack. 5 inch blade mirror finished. **$5.00** ea.

No. 641

No. 641—Hunting and Camping Knife. Wrapped leather handle. 5 inch blade. Curved edge excellent for skinning. Fitted dark brown leather sheath. **$3.25** ea.

MARBLE COMPASSES

COAT COMPASS

No. 182   No. 082

Boxes are 1⅛-in. in diameter. Bearings are agate.
No. 182—Coat Style. Stationary Dial. Weight, 2 oz............ **$1.25**
No. 082—Coat Style. Revolving Dial. Weight, 2 oz............ **1.50**
No. 082L—Coat Style. Luminous Dial. Weight, 2 oz............ **2.00**

Made with waterproof screw case. Fastens securely to front of coat, on sleeve or vest. It is in plain view at all times, and you can't lose it or leave it in camp. It is especially convenient in stormy weather.

POCKET COMPASS

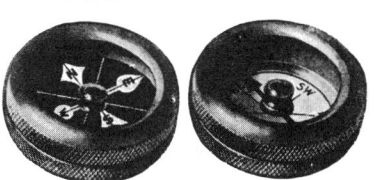

No. 186   No. 184

Boxes are 1⅛-in. diameter. Agate Bearings. Waterproof Case.
No. 184—Pocket Style. Stationary Dial. Weight, 1 oz..... **$1.00**
No. 186—Pocket Style. Revolving Dial. Weight, 1 oz..... **1.25**
No. 186L—Pocket Style. Luminous Dial. Weight, 1 oz..... **1.75**

Luminous Dial

In the darkness the luminous arrow on the revolving dial of the No. 082L and 186L compasses glows like a bar of light, and points the way nearly as plainly as in broad daylight. During the day it is used as an ordinary compass.

WRIST COMPASS

No. 187—Wrist Style. Revolving Dial. Weight, 1 oz............ **$1.50**
No. 187L—Wrist Style. Revolving Luminous Dial. Weight, 1 oz.... **2.00**

Case of polished brass, 1 3/16 inch in diameter. Unbreakable domed crystal. Agate bearing. Extremely accurate. High grade leather wrist strap. For the hunter, fisherman, camper, tourist, scout, and woodsman.

Waterproof Match Box

It can be quickly opened and closed and is absolutely waterproof. There is a rubber gasket in the cover. Made of seamless drawn brass, heavily nickeled, ¾ inch inside diameter. They are always a comfort and sometimes they save lives by assuring dry matches under every condition. No. 181................... **$0.60**

America's Great Gun House
REMINGTON POCKET KNIVES

R-6873

Stag Handle; Nickel Silver Lining and Trim; Mirror Finished Blades. Length, closed, 3 inches. Weight, 5/6 oz. Price.................$1.00

R-7543

Stag Handle; Nickel Silver Lining and Trim; Mirror Finished Blades. Length, closed, 3¼ inches. Weight, 1 1/6 oz. Price........$1.00

R-203

Stag Handle; Brass Lining; Mirror Finished Blades; Nickel Silver Trim. Length, closed, 3⅝ inches. Weight, 3 1/3 oz. Price........$1.00

R-153

Stag Handle; Brass Lining; Mirror Finished Blades; Nickel Silver Trim. Length, closed, 3½ inches. Weight, 2¾ oz. Price...........75¢

R-363

Stag Handle; Brass Lining; Mirror Finished Blades; Nickel Silver Trim. Length, closed, 3¾ inches. Weight, 3 oz. Price...........$1.00

R-4633

Stag Handle; Brass Lining; Mirror Finished Blades; Nickel Silver Trim. Length, closed, 3⅜ inches. Weight, 2 oz. Price...........$1.00

R3843

Stag Handle; Six Blades. 1 Large Spear, Etched, 1 Screw Driver-Cap Lifter, 1 Clip, 1 Can Opener, All Mirror Finished; 1 Corkscrew, Blue Glazed; 1 Punch Blued Inside and Polished Back. Nickel Silver Bolsters, Shackle, Shield and Rivets; Brass Lining. Length, closed, 3½ inches. Weight, 3 2/3 oz. Price....................$3.50

OFFICIAL KNIFE, BOY SCOUTS OF AMERICA REGULATION SIZE

RS3333

Stag Handle; Four Blades, 1 Large Spear, Etched with Scout Insignia; 1 Combination Bottle Opener and Screw Driver, 1 Can Opener, All Mirror Finished; 1 Punch Blued Inside and Polished Back. Nickel Silver Bolsters, Shackle and Emblem Shield; Brass Lining. Milled Center Scale. Length, closed, 3¾ inches. Weight, 4 2/3 oz. Price.$1.50

R-100-A

Stag Handle; Brass Lining; Mirror Finished Blades; Nickel Silver Trim. Length, closed, 3¼ inches. Weight, 2 1/3 oz. Price........$1.00

R-6424

Genuine Pearl Handle; Nickel Silver Lining; Mirror Finished Blades. Length, closed, 2¾ inches. Weight, 1 oz. Price...................$3.75

R-6785

White Pyremite Handle; Brass Lining; Mirror Finished Blades. Length, closed, 3⅜ inches. Weight, 1 1/3 oz. Price................75¢

R-8059

Solid Nickel Silver Handle; Stainless Steel Blade. Length, closed, 3 inches. Weight, 1 oz. Price.$1.50

R-3535

Pyremite Handle; Brass Lining; Mirror Finished Blades; Nickel Silver Trim. Length, closed, 3⅜ inches. Weight, 1 1/3 oz. Price........$1.00

R-675

Pyremite Handles; Brass Lining; Mirror Finished Blades; Nickel Silver Trim. Length, closed, 3 inches. Weight, 1½ oz. Price...........75¢

R-165

Pyremite Handle; Brass Lining; Mirror Finished Blades; Nickel Silver Trim. Length, closed, 3½ inches. Weight, 2 5/6 oz. Price.........75¢

RB-43

Brown Bone Handle; Steel Lining and Trim; Mirror Finished Blade. Length, closed, 3⅜ inches. Weight, 2 2/3 oz. Price.................50¢

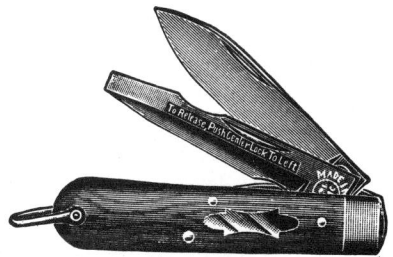

R-2111

Rosewood Handle. Spear Blade and Screwdriver—Wire Scraper with Lock, both fine blue glazed. N. S. Bolsters and Shackle Brass Lining. Length, closed, 3⅜ inches. Weight, 3½ oz. Price..$1.25

PLEASE RECOMMEND US TO YOUR FRIENDS

STOEGER ARMS CORPORATION, 507 FIFTH AVENUE, NEW YORK, N. Y.

WINCHESTER
TRADE MARK

FLASHLIGHTS FOR THE SPORTSMAN AND CAMPER

Designed for convenience, full service and supreme satisfaction, Winchester flashlights are admirably adapted to the requirements of sportsmen and campers for use under rough conditions where dependability and convenience are paramount. They are made of sturdy materials, have positive operating switches and most of the numbers are equipped with shock absorber to protect the bulb in case the flashlight is dropped or hits against something. All tubular style lights are equipped with octagon non-rolling lens ring to prevent rolling when they are laid down. Several special designs, such as the Winchester designed headlight-lanterns, are particularly adapted to special service in the out of doors because of their features of design or construction. In the list shown below is a wide range of styles of lights for various uses and also a varied price selection to meet all requirements.

HEADLIGHT LANTERN
No. 79124

Price without batteries ... $4.50

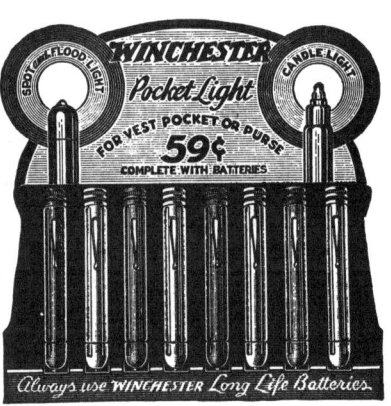

Winchester Fixt-Focus Spotlight—Here is a light that hits a new high in both efficiency and attractive appearance. Through the use of a new fixt-focus Mazda lamp and a new special type Winchester mechanism this light projects a powerful long range and uniform spot beam of great effectiveness. It is also so designed as to furnish an indirect floodlight at close range which makes this number a supremely serviceable flashlight. Produces 70% more light power than the ordinary spotlight of the same cell capacity. 2 cell beautiful Sunset Finish solid 22k copper case. Positive 3-position safety lock switch. Shock absorber. Ring hanger. Spare bulb carrier.

No. 0818

This type light is also furnished in 3 cell size with the same Sunset finish and in both 2 and 3 cell sizes in chromium plate finish.

Price, each with batteries............$1.35

Winchester Twin Service Headlight Lantern—The Winchester Twin-Service headlight lantern combines four lights of genuine service and convenience in one. Fitting easily over the head it can be used as a long range focusing headlight or for a spreadlight that places a broad field of light just where it is wanted,—light that moves with every turn of the head to give illumination wherever it is desired and yet leaves both hands free. Or it can be carried by a convenient bail handle as an electric lantern—again either as a focusing light or a spreadlight. Furnished in two styles.

No. 7924

No. 79124—5-cell.
No. 7924—3-cell.
Each style is equipped with silver mirror reflector for long range focusing use and with matted finish reflector for spreadlight service.

Price without batteries ... $2.95

No. D-6610—A streamlined Winchester pocket light in the new Penlight case style. Has simple fool-proof switch which will never wear out. The switch is arranged that it cannot accidently short circuit. It has a removable lamp cap for floodlight or candle-light use. Constructed of seamless brass tube with heavy chromium plating.

Price with battery .... $.59

No. 1714—A Winchester two cell fixed focus spotlight with black tube and chrome fittings. It has new bullet type base cap and carries a spare bulb holder.

Price with battery $1.20

No. 8326—3-cell Tri-color Signal light. An especially useful and convenient flashlight for signaling purposes and especially in camping and on sporting adventures. Equipped with 3 separate bulbs of different colors—white, red and green, each operated by its own separate switch. Sturdy fibre case with chrome plated fittings. Winchester positive 3-position safety lock switch—easy and simple in operation. Octagon, non-rolling lens ring. Folding ring hanger.

Price without batteries $2.95

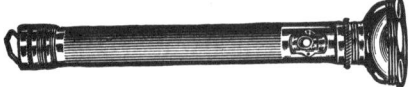

No. 69121—A 5-cell extra heavy gauge solid brass focusing searchlight designed for use where a powerful long range beam is required. Exclusive Winchester rotating band focusing device. Easily operated positive lock and flash contact switch. Shock absorber to protect bulb. Folding ring hanger. Octagon non-rolling lens ring. Handsome full chrome finish.

Price without batteries $1.95

No. 59121—A 5-cell solid brass, nickel plated long range focusing searchlight. Positive 3-position safety lock switch. Octagon, non-rolling recessed lens ring. Efficient shock absorber to protect bulb. Folding hanger. Designed also to be used as a candle-light.

Price without batteries $1.35

A FLASHLIGHT IS A NECESSITY

AMERICA'S GREAT GUN HOUSE 273

WINCHESTER
TRADE MARK

FLASHLIGHTS FOR THE SPORTSMAN AND CAMPER

No. 998—A Winchester two cell streamlined fixed focus spotlight in beautiful two-tone and solid 22 K copper design—represents an extraordinary achievement. It is the most serviceable all around scientifically-built flashlight offered to sell at such a low price.

Price each with batteries .... $.98

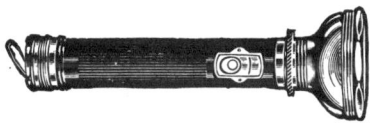

No. 6924—A 3-cell, solid brass case with black finish, focusing searchlight. Handsome chrome fittings. Exclusive Winchester rotating band focusing device. Positive lock and flash contact switch. Integral stock absorber. Folding hanger. Octagon non-rolling lens ring. Extra heavy gauge brass stock in case.

Price without batteries $1.65

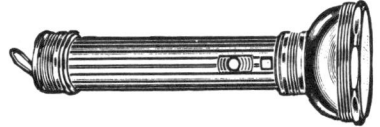

No. 5921—3-cell brass focusing searchlight, nickel plated finish. Positive 3-position safety lock switch insuring excellent service. Octagon, non-rolling recessed lens ring to protect lens. Shock absorber. Folding ring hanger. Candle-light feature. Mirror finish reflector.

Price without batteries $1.09

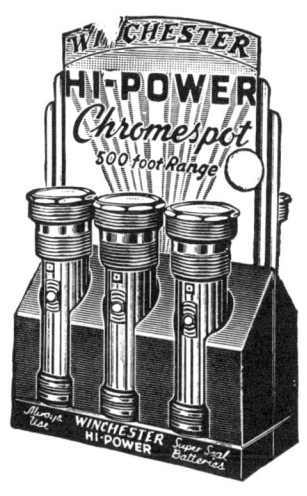

No. 5810—Winchester Hi-power 2-cell all Chrome finished spotlight. Another handsome design focusing light with 500 foot range. New type 3-position safety lock switch. Shock absorber for bulb. Folding hanger. Octagon, non-rolling recessed lens ring. Candle-light feature.

Price, each without batteries .... $.65

No. 6814—2-cell black metal focusing spotlight with chrome fittings. Exclusive Winchester rotating band focusing device for setting focus. Easily operated positive lock and flash contact switch. Shock absorber to protect bulb. Octagon, non-rolling lens ring. Highest quality silvered reflector. Extra heavy gauge brass case.

Price without batteries .... $.95
No. 6824—3 all 1.30

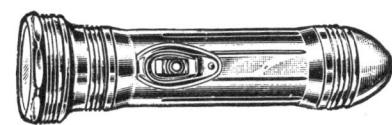

No. 9810—A Winchester two cell streamline fixed focus spotlight in beautiful two-tone and solid 22 K copper design—represents and is an extraordinary achievement. It is the most serviceable all around scientifically-built flashlight offered to sell at such a low price.

Price each with battery .... $.98

No. K-59—This two cell focusing spotlight "has everything" in appeal galore. Heavy durable construction made from seamless copper, new positive two way guard rail switch—recessed octagon non-rolling ring—Candle-lite feature—brilliant reflector—Mazda Bulb (available space in end cap for spare bulb)—Bullet Speed Lines.

Price without batteries .... $.59

WINCHESTER HI-POWER SUPER SEAL BATTERIES

Winchester Hi-power Super Seal flashlight batteries give high illuminating output and longer brilliant light. The moulded Super Seal prevents power loss—insures supreme and long lasting service. Batteries always fresh—dated for your protection. Made in both standard unit cell size and in junior size. Insist on Winchester batteries for supreme satisfaction.

		Price
No. 1311	Junior Unit Cell	$.10
No. 1511	Standard Unit Cell	.10
No. 2311	2 Cell Junior Tubular	.20
No. 2511	2 Cell Regular Tubular	.20
No. 3511	3 Cell Regular Tubular	.30
No. 4812	Lantern Battery, 6 Volt	.50

Minimum order on batteries 6 pieces, single pieces only when ordered with flashlight.

EVERYTHING FOR THE SHOOTER

Stoeger's Superbly Grained
WALNUT STOCK BLANKS
Like the Briar of a Fine Pipe!

Because of an increasing demand we have combed the entire world for highest quality walnut stock blanks, and now, from the rocky regions of southern France, we bring you the finest, most varied line ever offered.

Color variations, curl and unusal figurings make this French walnut extremely beautiful. And because of its great strength, splintering is avoided. It is quite understandable that most fine grade English shotguns are made with this wood, which dealers and stockmakers often call "Circassian" or "English" walnut.

These French walnut stock blanks are available in nine qualities, as listed below. The "Unique" (illustrated) and the "De Luxe" have the same appearance and fine quality as genuine Circassian walnut stocks.

In addition to these stocks we offer the highest quality western American walnut stock blanks. These have fine texture and color, are thoroughly dried, and are completely free from checks and defects.

FRENCH WALNUT
Rifle Stock Blanks
(full length)

(Approximate dimensions: Length, 36 inches; Width 2 3/8 inches; Width at pistol grip, 5¾ inches; Depth at butt, 7 inches). Any blank may be turned to Peerless specifications for rifles listed, at an additional charge of $3.00 (rough), or $10.50 (finished).

"Standard" grade—A plain blank of sound quality, closely grained, of good appearance. Price.................................. $4.50
"Utility" grade—A high quality blank with straight grain with good contrasts. Price....................................... 7.50
"Select" grade—A blank especially selected for good coloring and figure. Price....................................... 10.00
"Figure" grade—This blank is chosen for its fine figure and grain. Price.. 12.50
"Fancy" grade—A handsome well figured blank, suitable for better restocking. Price.................................... 15.00

"Premier" grade—A high quality blank showing contrasting figures. $17.50
"De Luxe" grade—An excellent, curley figured blank, suitable for highest quality guns. Price............................ 20.00
"Super De Luxe" grade—Our highest grade blank, most carefully selected for beauty and general perfection. Price........... 22.50
"Unique"—This blank represents our experts' choice of our entire stock and is the finest of the fine, defying description. Supply limited, as such pieces are extraordinarily scarce. Price...... 25.00

AMERICAN WALNUT
Rifle Stock Blanks
(full length)

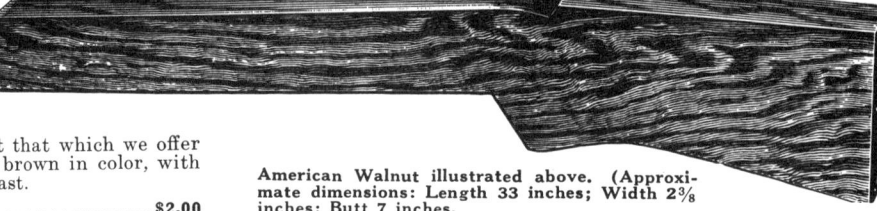

American walnut varies considerably, but that which we offer is of specially selected quality, usally dark brown in color, with lighter grain which forms a pleasant contrast.
American walnut $2.00

American Walnut illustrated above. (Approximate dimensions: Length 33 inches; Width 2⅜ inches; Butt 7 inches.)

French Shotgun Blanks

"Plain" Grade, good quality..... $3.75
"Selected" Grade, a well figured straight grain stock........... 5.00
"Excel" Grade, a fancy, dark piece of wood 7.50
"Premier" Grade, a fine selected curly fancy blank........... 10.00 and up
"De Luxe" Grade, a Superlatively fine curly dark grain, especially selected for its unusual contrasts. The best obtainable........... 15.00 and up
Fore end, regular size........... 1.50
Fore end, beaver tail size........ 2.50

SHOTGUN BLANKS

Any French or American Shotgun Blank may be rough turned to duplicate any broken stock sent in at an additional charge of $5.00.

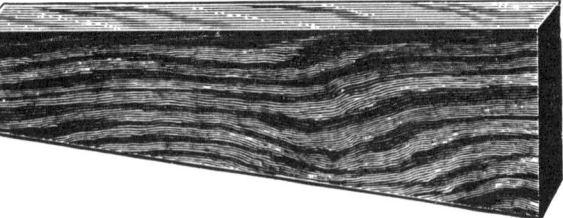

American Shotgun Stock Blanks

"Crotch". This is a feather crotch showing feather on both sides.. $13.50
"Semi Crotch". This shows the feather on one side only....... 9.00
"Full Stump". This shows good stump figure on both sides..... 7.50
"Semi Stump". A good stump figure on one side of the stock....... 4.50
"Grain". A slightly figured better quality stock blank........... 2.25
"Plain". A plain, straight grain stock, good quality........... 1.50
Fore end blanks standard size.... .75
Fore end blanks, beaver tail size... 1.25

UNFINISHED INLETTED STOCK BLANKS

Since no variations can be made from standard specifications either in the unfinished or finished Peerless Stocks, we offer these unfinished inletted stock blanks. These offer the professional or amateur an opportunity to finish the stock of individual requirements, permitting more or less drop, wide forend, special cheek piece, etc.
American Walnut inletted stock blank for rifles mentioned above.................. $5.00

Extra for French Walnut.................. $2.50
If desired we will fit customer's barrel and action to inletted stock blank at an additional charge of 3.00

EXTRA WIDTH STOCKS

Unfinished Inletted Stocks of extra width (2¾") for making special stocks with heavy tail forearm, available only in French Walnut 8.00

Inletted Stock Blanks Are Available For These Rifles

Enfield ....Model 1917
Springfield, (Sporter or Service Rifle) Model .30-06 and M-1 Model 1922.
Krag ....Model 1898
Mauser..Models 98, 8m/m Military Rifle
Winchester..Models 52, 54 and 70
Remington....Models 30 and 34
Russian......Model 7.62 Mossin
Newton French Lebel and Lee Enfield
No work is executed on the outside of the stock blank.

MODERNIZE THAT FINE OLD GUN
Yourself
WITH A PEERLESS GUN STOCK

Is your favorite gun outmoded? Stoeger's have embodied fifty years remodeling experience into making the sensational Peerless gunstock, with which your old-fashioned musket can be transformed into a well-balanced, handsome hunting or target rifle. This solid walnut gun stock, while offered at a price lower than any other stock on the market, has the quality and appearance which rivals the finest.

Because this remarkable stock, complete with accessories, sells for only $5.00, it is economically possible for all to have a de luxe, masterbilt gun. Stoeger's Peerless stocks are made of carefully selected, properly seasoned American or French walnut, accurately inletted for the well known rifles listed below.

UNFINISHED INLETTED PEERLESS STOCKS

PEERLESS STOCKS Are Made for These Rifles

Enfield	Remington, 30 and 34
Springfield .30-06	Krag
Mauser Model 98	French Lebel
Winchester 52, 54 and 70	
Russian 7.62 mm	Newton

WHY PEERLESS STOCKS?

1. The original popular priced sporting stock and made by Stoeger.
2. Perfected dimensions and best balance.
3. Closest tolerances and most machining of any similar stock on the market.
4. Well seasoned and perfect walnut, etc., highest quality used exclusively.
5. Years of restocking experience, put at your service, ensures the best work at minimum cost.
6. Every stock guaranteed to give satisfaction or may be returned within three days for refund.
7. The only stock offered complete with all necessary accessories at no extra charge.

In fitting our Peerless stocks the outside surface should be finished only after gun has been entirely let into stock. For inletting we recommend a ¼" medium course round file, a barrel grove inletting rasp or large round file, a ½" flat chisel, ½" round chisel and ½" round file.

For fitting screws of pistol grip and butt plate we recommend ⅛" drill and for fitting swivels 3/16" drill. For finishing the outside we recommend a course 12" wood rasp about 1½" wide, a medium 12", and a fine file. For finishing the stock we recommend 1st #8, then #150 and then #320 emery cloth, although lacking this, course, medium and fine sand paper may be used.

PEERLESS STOCK, rough turned only, with accessories as illustrated, American Walnut............$5.00
Extra for French Walnut............2.50

PEERLESS $5.00 Complete With Accessories Shown Below

So simple to assemble and finish that the amateur can complete the work in 6 hours.

Detailed instructions for attaching and finishing accompany each stock.

ALL THIS EXTRA ABSOLUTELY *Free*
- Genuine Ebony Forend Cap
- Steel Pistol Grip Cap & Screw
- Steel Butt Plate and 2 Screws

STOCKS
Completely Masterbuilt

STOEGER PEERLESS FINISHED GUN STOCKS

These Peerless gun stocks are completely finished and ready to attach to the barrel or action. Each stock is individually fitted to a sample gun before leaving our shop, so that very little fitting is required. The accessories include a fine forend tip, a full sized pistol grip cap, a slightly curved butt plate which fits snugly into the shoulder, and detachable swivels. The stock is oil-finished to make it impervious to moisture and serviceable.

Peerless Springfield Stock of checkered French Walnut

Peerless Stock, for rifles as described above................$12.50
Additional for selected French Walnut.....................2.50
Additional for checkering pistol grip......................2.50
Additional for checkering forend..........................3.00

Peerless REMODELING of SPRINGFIELD Makes the "All American" Gun

Approximate Dimensions
Drop: 1⅞ x 2¾
Length: 13¾ inches
Weight: 8½ (N. M.)

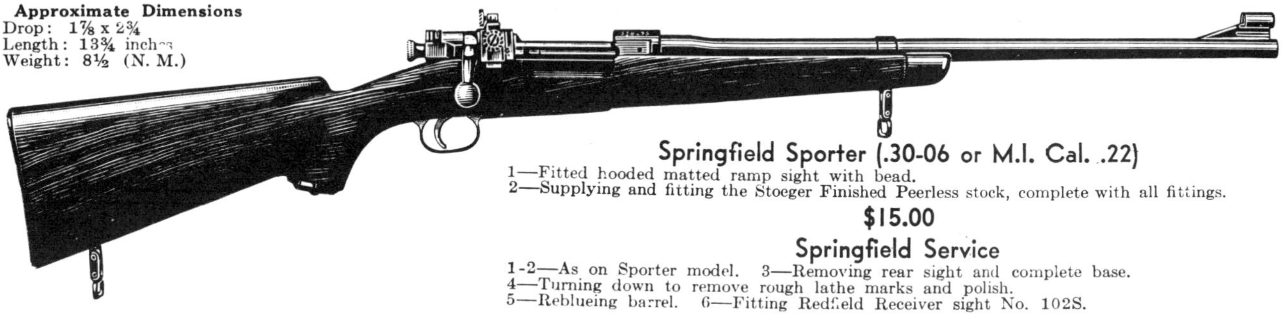

Springfield Sporter (.30-06 or M.I. Cal. .22)
1—Fitted hooded matted ramp sight with bead.
2—Supplying and fitting the Stoeger Finished Peerless stock, complete with all fittings.

$15.00

Springfield Service
1-2—As on Sporter model. 3—Removing rear sight and complete base.
4—Turning down to remove rough lathe marks and polish.
5—Reblueing barrel. 6—Fitting Redfield Receiver sight No. 102S.

$27.50

The Springfield Model 30-06, Sporter, illustrated above, as well as the regular Service and National Match Rifles, are the most popular high power rifles in America today. Their tremendous popularity is justified because of their fine construction, great accuracy, and adaptability to the large range of loads and bullet weights available. This makes these rifles suitable for all American game from woodchuck to grizzly. Of particular importance is the fact that the caliber 30-06 ammunition is to be found in practically every country store. The National Match rifle is identical in appearance to the Service rifle, except that it has a headless cocking piece, specially finished action, and a barrel selected for superior accuracy.

Peerless Springfield Stock

This stock is completely finished, as illustrated, with steel butt-plate, black forend tip, pistol grip cap, cheekpiece, and detachable swivels.

Ready to attach to rifle	$12.50
Extra for checkered forend	3.00
Extra for checkered pistol grip	2.50
Extra for French Walnut	2.50
Unfinished (with accessories)	5.00

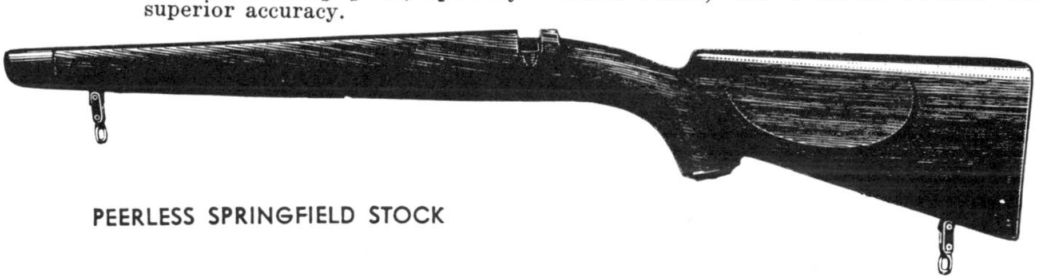

PEERLESS SPRINGFIELD STOCK

PEERLESS DELUXE REMODELING

While the regular Peerless restocking jobs shown on these pages represent a maximum value we do have, however, so many inquiries for Deluxe remodeling that we have decided to undertake this as a regular extra for those wishing a restocking job which when finished will rival the best high priced custom work. We suggest the following complete set of alterations or additions to our normal remodeling:—1, "Fancy" grade, French walnut; 2, checkering of forearm and pistol grip; 3, special hand fitting of barrel and action; 4, hand rub English oil finish; 5, Redfield #70, ¼ minute click micrometer rear sight; 6, Redfield ramp front sight with protector; 7, barrel ring encircling barrel and extending through forend to form forend swivel base; 8, special care throughout.

Extra cost on any regular Peerless remodeling job, in addition to cost of regular Peerless remodeling **$36.50**

REAR CONNECTING SCREW REAMER

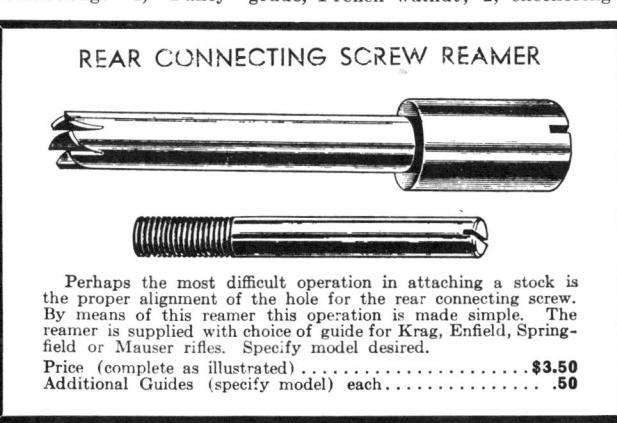

Perhaps the most difficult operation in attaching a stock is the proper alignment of the hole for the rear connecting screw. By means of this reamer this operation is made simple. The reamer is supplied with choice of guide for Krag, Enfield, Springfield or Mauser rifles. Specify model desired.
Price (complete as illustrated) **$3.50**
Additional Guides (specify model) each .... **.50**

STOEGER LONDON OIL FINISH
For Finishing New Stocks and Refinishing Old
Preserves—Darkens—Excludes Moisture

Factory new or perfect stocks need only be rubbed with old London Finish to preserve them. Roughened, spotted, or new unfinished stocks should be sandpapered, then dampened with water or preferably vinegar, then resandpapered and this operation repeated until no more grain is raised. After final sandpapering apply with wool rag or rub in with ball of hand.

If the very finest dull English finish is desired, the stock should then be rubbed with rottenstone, and fully rubbed with Stoeger London Oil Finish. The longer and more often applied the smoother, darker, and more beautiful the finish.

Available in three shades as follows:
#1 Regular—For fine stocks where only natural color is desired.
#2 Medium—For average stocks where it is desired to darken.
#3 Special—For hard to darken stocks and those with sapwood.

(4 oz. bottle) Price **$1.00**

YOUR OLD GUN NEEDS *STREAMLINING!*

KRAG
PEERLESS REMODELING

The Krag Rifle was the arm used by the American forces, in the Spanish-American War, and although an excellent weapon, was superseded in 1905 as the official U. S. Army Rifle by the present Model 1903 Rifle. To close out its enormous stock and to aid civilian marksmanship, the War Department disposed of these through the Director of Civilian Marksmanship to members of the National Rifle Association.

This rifle shoots the popular 30-40 Krag cartridge which is available in practically every sporting goods store throughout the land. It is suitable for all American game, and with Peerless Remodeling makes up into an attractive sporting rifle.

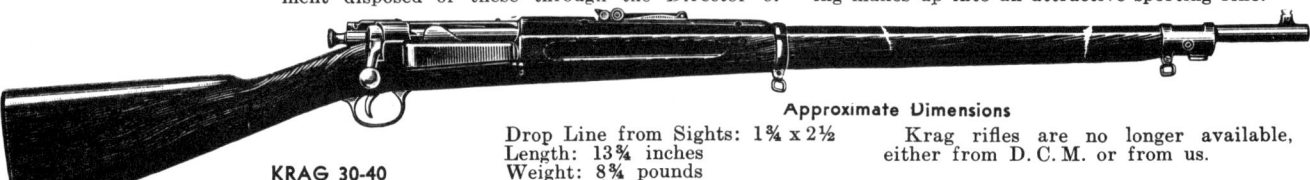

KRAG 30-40

Approximate Dimensions
Drop Line from Sights: 1¾ x 2½
Length: 13¾ inches
Weight: 8¾ pounds

Krag rifles are no longer available, either from D.C.M. or from us.

1. Cutting barrel to 24 inches, round, refinish and polish muzzle.
2. Fitting hooded matted ramp sight with bead.
3. Removing military rear sight and complete base.
4. First class rebluing of barrel and receiver.
5. Supplying and fitting Redfield Receiver Sight No. 102K.
6. Supplying and fitting Stoeger's Finished Peerless Stock or sporting rear sight, complete with all fittings..........................$24.00

PEERLESS KRAG STOCK

This stock is completely finished, as illustrated, with steel butt plate, black forend tip, pistol grip cap, cheekpiece, and detachable swivels.

Ready to attach to rifle..............$12.50
Extra for checkered forend...........3.00
Extra for checkered pistol grip......2.50
Extra for French Walnut..............2.50

Unfinished Peerless Krag Stock
This stock is rough turned and accessories are included.
Price $5.00
Extra for French Walnut..............2.50

MAUSER
Peerless Remodeling

The Mauser 8 m/m German Service rifle was used by Germany during the World War. This rifle was manufactured by arsenals and by the Mauser factory in Oberndorf, with the year of manufacture stamped on top of the receiver. The Mauser action with its light tapered, polished barrel is famous and the 8 m/m cartridge is one of the finest big game cartridges, and is available in domestic brands.

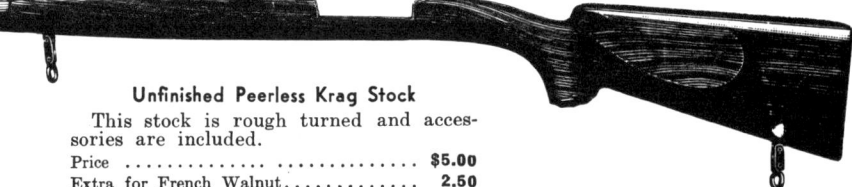

MAUSER 8 m/m Model '98 (as issued)

Approximate Dimensions
Drop line from sights: 1⅛ x 2½ inches
Length: 13¾ inches
Weight: 8 pounds

Altering to caliber .30/06. If desired, we will supply special new .30/06 barrel and alter magazine accordingly.
Extra charge........$25.00

MAUSER 8 m/m With Peerless Remodeling

1. Cutting barrel to 24 inches, round, refinish and polish muzzle.
2. Fitting hooded matted ramp sight with bead.
3. Removing military rear sight and complete base.
4. First class rebluing of barrel and receiver.
5. Bending bolt down same as on sporting rifles, re-shaping and polishing.
6. Supplying and fitting Redfield No. 102M Receiver Sight.
7. Supplying and fitting Stoeger's Finished Peerless Stock or sporting rear sight, complete with all fittings..........................$27.50
8. Supplying and fitting firing pin, if necessary.....................2.50

MAUSER PEERLESS STOCK

This stock is complete finished, as illustrated, with steel butt plate, black forend tip, pistol grip cap, cheekpiece, and detachable swivels.

Ready to attach to rifle..............$12.50
Extra for checkered forearm..........3.00
Extra for checkered pistol grip......2.50
Extra for French Walnut..............2.50

Unfinished Mauser Peerless Stock
This stock is rough turned and includes accessories.
Price $5.00
Extra for French Walnut..............2.50

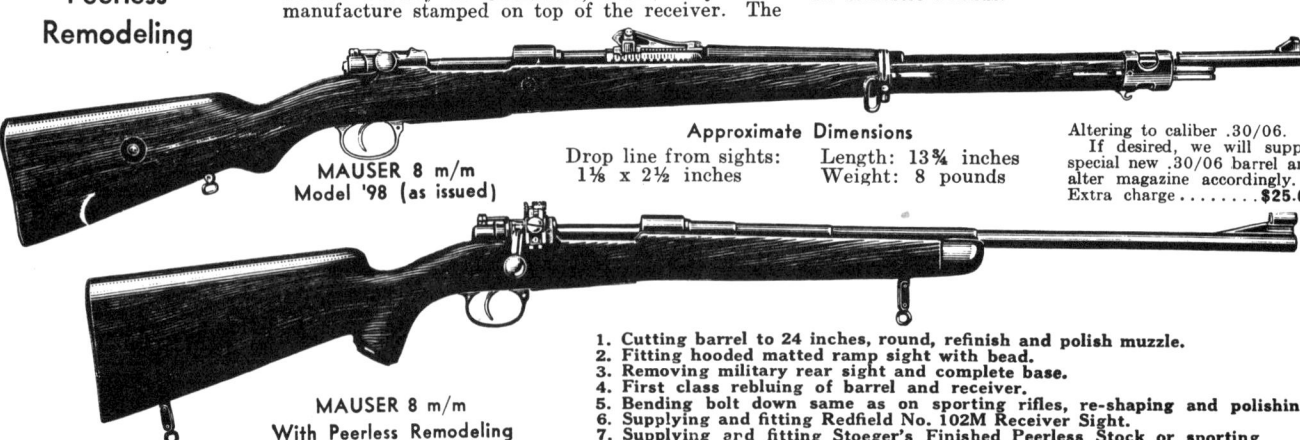

OLYMPIC RESTOCKING

ALL OLYMPIC STOCKS MADE EXCLUSIVELY OF GENUINE FRENCH WALNUT

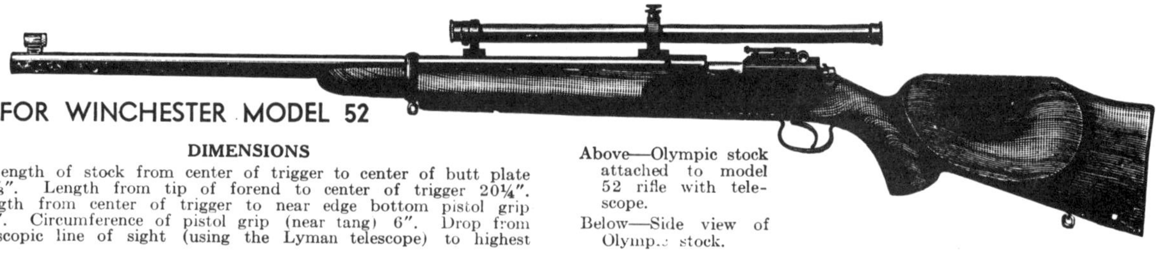

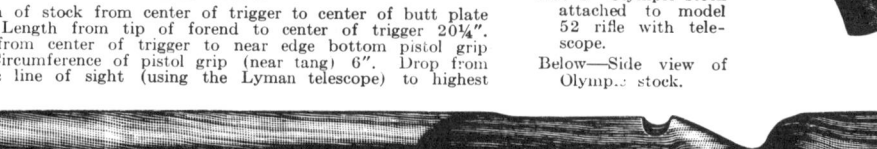

FOR WINCHESTER MODEL 52

DIMENSIONS

Length of stock from center of trigger to center of butt plate 13⅜". Length from tip of forend to center of trigger 20¼". Length from center of trigger to near edge bottom pistol grip 3⅝". Circumference of pistol grip (near tang) 6". Drop from telescopic line of sight (using the Lyman telescope) to highest point on comb 1⅜". Drop from line of Iron sights (using the aperture front sight and the standard Winchester rear sight) to highest point of comb 1 3/16". Drop at heel to top of butt plate 2⅜". Length of beaver tail from center of trigger 16". Width of beaver tail 2½". Drop at heel 2½". Pitch on butt plate 2¾". Depth 1¾" (measured from bore axis).

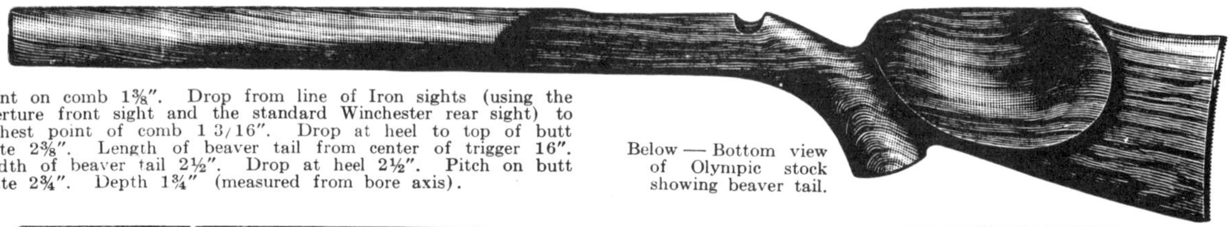

Above—Olympic stock attached to model 52 rifle with telescope.

Below—Side view of Olympic stock.

Below — Bottom view of Olympic stock showing beaver tail.

After years of experience in making special stocks for the Winchester model 52 we have designed this stock primarily for the Winchester model 52 rifle using the telescope. The illustration shows the elaborate cheek piece hollowed out which conforms to the shooter's face and gives him a perfect rest. The comb has been made high enough so that it will enable the shooter's eye, when in shooting position, to look straight down the line of telescopic sight without any strain whatsoever. The pistol grip has been made longer, fuller and with a very sharp curve. The forend has been made of ample size for any prone or off-hand shooting. Throughout the designing of this stock we have borne it in mind that certain shooters wish to adapt the stock slightly more to their individual requirements. For this reason we have left an excess of wood all over the stock so that alterations can be made to this stock to fit practically any target shooter.

The barrel groove is inletted for the standard model 52 barrel, but the forend is of such size that it can be widened easily to accommodate the heavy barrel.

In case a shooter wishes to use Iron sights it is only necessary to raise up both the front and rear sights so that the line of Iron sights conforms with the line of sight through the telescopic sights.

Price, unfinished **$8.00**
Price, finished, including special checkered steel butt plate **15.00**
Special checkered steel butt plate with screws........... **1.00**
Extra for checking forend **$3.50** Extra for checking pistol grip **3.00**

Olympic Stocks for Enfield and Springfield 1903

The pattern for these new Olympic stocks is that of the popular model 52 Olympic, with slight modifications. The stock for the Enfield and Springfield was designed primarily for prone shooting, but is one of the most comfortable, well-handling stocks ever produced. The unfinished stocks require about a day's work for the average amateur to finish. The stock has an oil finish and checkered steel butt plate.

STOCK SPECIFICATIONS

Drop at cone 1½"; drop at highest part of comb, 1⅛"; drop at heel, 2⅞" These specifications are taken from the line of sight. Length, 13⅝"; other dimensions about the same as for Win. Mod. 52 Olympic Stock.

SPECIAL OLYMPIC DELUX REMODELING OF SPRINGFIELD RIFLE

This work consists of converting the Military rifle as issued into the De Luxe Match Rifle illustrated above, increasing the weight to about 9 lbs. and comprises the following work:

1—Removal of Military Sights.
2—Repolishing and Bluing of the entire receiver, action and magazine.
3—Supplying and fitting of either Lyman No. 48 or Redfield No. 100-S.
4—Supplying and fitting of Redfield De Luxe Hooded Ramp.
5—Supplying and fitting of Olympic Stock of finished French Walnut.
6—Supplying and fitting of special barrel band including swivel.
7—Supplying and fitting of detachable rear swivel with base.
8—Special care to all details.

PRICE FOR WORK OUTLINED ABOVE............. **$48.00**
OLYMPIC UNFINISHED STOCK ONLY............. **8.00**
OLYMPIC FINISHED STOCK ONLY................ **15.00**
OLYMPIC BARREL BAND WITH SWIVEL AS ILLUSTRATED **2.00**

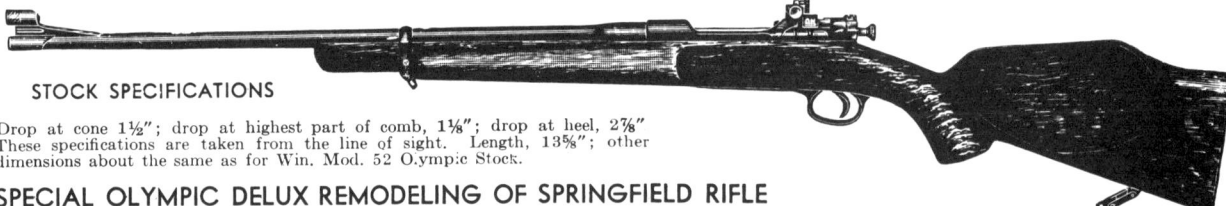

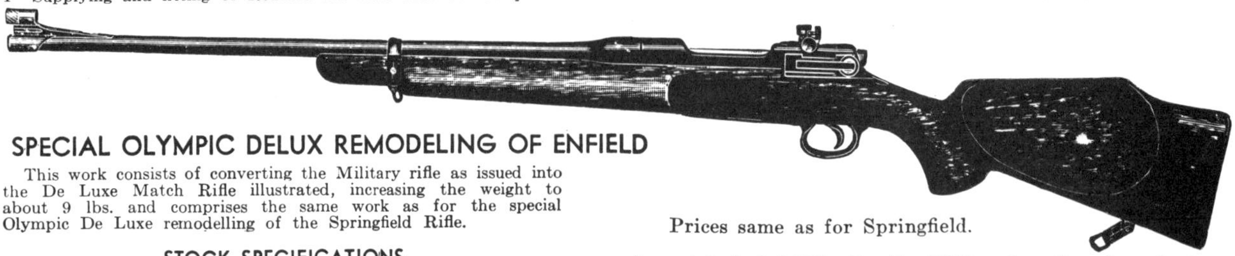

SPECIAL OLYMPIC DELUX REMODELING OF ENFIELD

This work consists of converting the Military rifle as issued into the De Luxe Match Rifle illustrated, increasing the weight to about 9 lbs. and comprises the same work as for the special Olympic De Luxe remodelling of the Springfield Rifle.

STOCK SPECIFICATIONS

Drop at cone, 1-9/16"; drop at highest part of comb, 1-3/16"; drop at heel, 2-3/16"; Length, 13½"; other dimensions about the same as for Win. Model 52 Olympic Stock.

Prices same as for Springfield.

Carbine
The Aristocrat of Remodelings
NOW MADE BY STOEGER FOR ONLY $48.00

Stoeger has pioneered in the manufacture of Peerless gun stocks. The success of these is attested by the presence of numerous imitations. Each succeeding season we have improved the workmanship so that Peerless stocks are maintaining their reputation as the best.

This reputation has resulted in a flood of requests for CARBINE stocks. Because of the technical difficulties of manufacture, Carbine stocks were available only as hand made, individual stocks. Our vast experience, gained turning out thousands of Peerless stocks, has made possible a method of producing Carbine stocks on a production basis, at a price within reach of all. We therefore, proudly present our Peerless Carbine stock.

We caution our customers against the imitations which will undoubtedly appear on the market, because the manufacture of a properly fitted Carbine stock is a matter of utmost technical difficulty. It requires experience and costly machinery, and unless skill and extreme care are devoted to the job, the resulting product will be useless.

Only superior wood lends itself to the manufacture of Carbine stocks. Stocks of this length must be well-seasoned, free of defects, and not susceptive to warping. We therefore, use only the highest quality French Walnut. This assures strength and beauty.

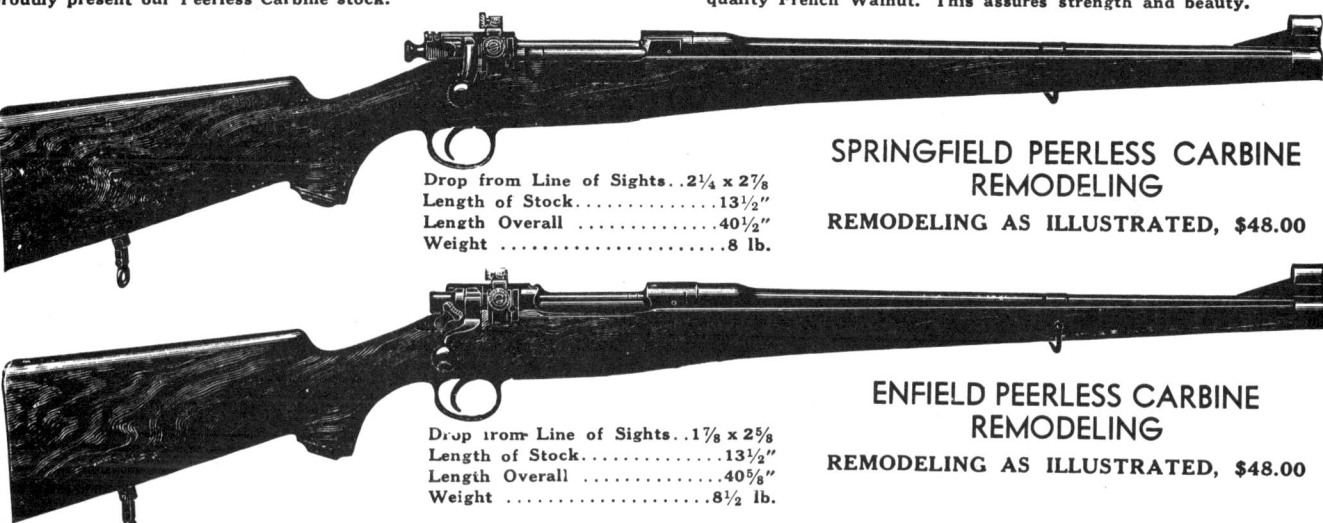

SPRINGFIELD PEERLESS CARBINE REMODELING

Drop from Line of Sights..$2\frac{1}{4}$ x $2\frac{7}{8}$
Length of Stock............$13\frac{1}{2}$"
Length Overall ....$40\frac{1}{2}$"
Weight ....8 lb.

REMODELING AS ILLUSTRATED, $48.00

ENFIELD PEERLESS CARBINE REMODELING

Drop from Line of Sights..$1\frac{7}{8}$ x $2\frac{5}{8}$
Length of Stock............$13\frac{1}{2}$"
Length Overall ....$40\frac{5}{8}$"
Weight ....$8\frac{1}{2}$ lb.

REMODELING AS ILLUSTRATED, $48.00

The Springfield and Enfield rifles lend themselves particularly well to remodeling into Carbines as illustrated herewith. Our complete Peerless Carbine remodeling job consists of cutting the barrel to 20", repolishing and rebluing barrels, fitting Stoeger Peerless Ramp, Redfield No. 102 receiver sight and Carbine stock with steel pistol grip cap and butt plate as well as detachable rear swivel and front loop swivel attached to a special barrel band and at the muzzle with a special steel muzzle cap.

PEERLESS CARBINE STOCK
FOR
SPRINGFIELD, ENFIELD, KRAG & MAUSER '98
UNFINISHED PEERLESS CARBINE STOCKS

These stocks are as illustrated above, without any metal accessories but carefully turned of French Walnut and can be finished and fitted by the average amateur in about one day's work. The inletting is held very slightly under-size to assure perfect hand fitting.
Available for Springfield, Enfield, Mauser Model 98, and Krag..**$12.50**

FINISHED PEERLESS CARBINE STOCKS

This stock is as illustrated above but includes steel butt plate, steel pistol grip cap and detachable rear swivel. This stock has been fitted to a Master action. The outside of the stock is hand oiled.
Available for Springfield, Enfield, Mauser Model 98, and Krag....**$20.00**

PEERLESS CARBINE STOCK ACCESSORIES

In the assembling of a Carbine certain parts are required which are not readily available. These are somewhat expensive because they are for the most part, hand made. Many of our customers will be able to make these themselves but should they not all the parts listed below are available at the prices shown.

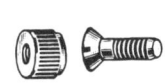 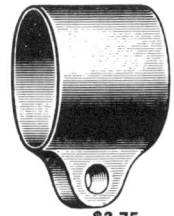   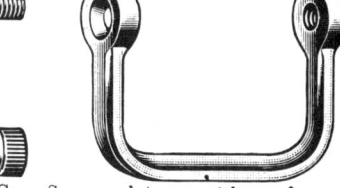

Peerless Muzzle Cap with Screw and Escutcheon. Price.........$3.75
Peerless Barrel Band for use with swivel at right. Price......$2.00

Peerless Swivel Bow including Cross Screw and two escutcheons for use with Peerless Barrel Band illustrated at left. Price.........$2.50

IS YOUR GUNSTOCK DAMAGED?

REPLACE ECONOMICALLY WITH STOEGER'S REPLACEMENT STOCKS

The stocks shown on this page are all made by ourselves, and are offered with the intention of enabling the gunsmith or individual to replace at low cost a broken or damaged original factory stock. They are carefully turned and inletted, but require individual fitting, finishing, and attachment of original butt plates, pistol grip cap, and other accessories with which the original stock is fitted.

Since these stock are made solely for economical replacement and are not offered as "custom built" the original standard specifications have been followed, and we positively cannot supply variations of any kind as to drop, length, type of wood, etc. Please do not ask for same.

All stocks are of carefully, seasoned American walnut.

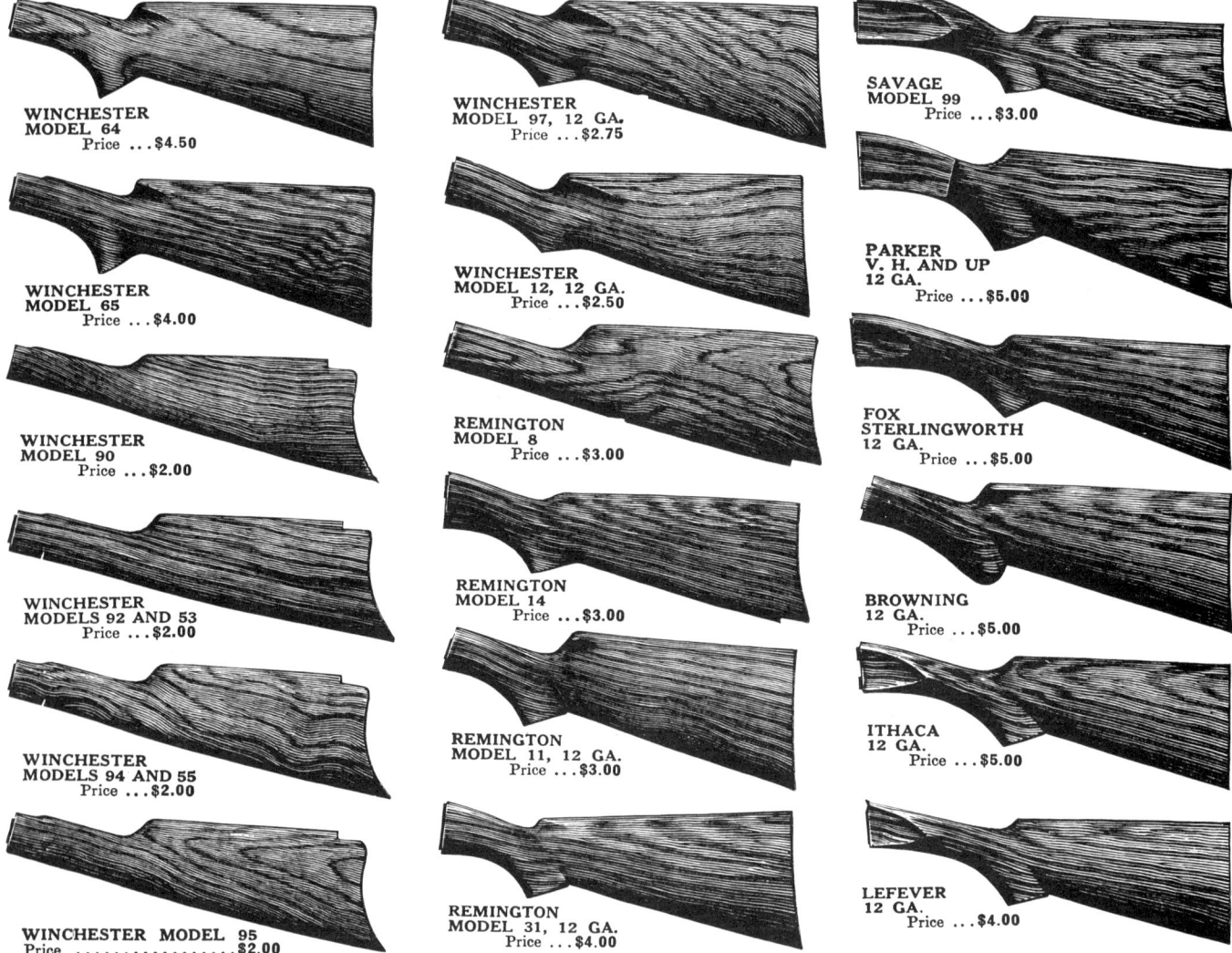

Stock	Price
WINCHESTER MODEL 64	$4.50
WINCHESTER MODEL 65	$4.00
WINCHESTER MODEL 90	$2.00
WINCHESTER MODELS 92 AND 53	$2.00
WINCHESTER MODELS 94 AND 55	$2.00
WINCHESTER MODEL 95	$2.00
WINCHESTER MODEL 97, 12 GA.	$2.75
WINCHESTER MODEL 12, 12 GA.	$2.50
REMINGTON MODEL 8	$3.00
REMINGTON MODEL 14	$3.00
REMINGTON MODEL 11, 12 GA.	$3.00
REMINGTON MODEL 31, 12 GA.	$4.00
SAVAGE MODEL 99	$3.00
PARKER V. H. AND UP 12 GA.	$5.00
FOX STERLINGWORTH 12 GA.	$5.00
BROWNING 12 GA.	$5.00
ITHACA 12 GA.	$5.00
LEFEVER 12 GA.	$4.00

In addition to the stocks illustrated above, we also supply the following at $5.00 each:

Savage Mod. 40 or 45 (cal. 30/30, 250/3000, and .300). Savage Mod. 40 or 45 (cal. 30/06). Savage Mod. 20 (old style). Savage Mod. 20 (new style). L. C. Smith 12 Ga. (State Grade and Serial Number). Remington Model 10 Repeater.

DUPLICATION OF BROKEN STOCKS

Upon special order we can duplicate almost any stock sent in to us. Such stocks will be carefully turned and inletted, though they will require the same fitting and finishing as described for Standard stocks at top of this page. Since the customer's original stock must be specially prepared for use as a model, its further possible use on the gun is out of question, and for this reason we do not assume any liability for damage to customer's sample stock.

The price of this work varies, depending on the individual details of the stock, and the amount of work we have in preparing the sample for use as a model. Ordinarily the prices are as follows:

Shotgun or Short Rifle Stocks, turning only..............$5.00
Sporting Rifle Stocks (up to 32 inches) turning only......10.00
(Above prices are for American Walnut)

To the above prices, which represent only labor charges, must be added price of whichever stock blank may be selected.

If customer insists upon use of own wood, the turning charges will be double, as this work is usually only an accommodation for purchasers of our stock blanks.

HAND MADE SHOTGUN STOCKS

In addition to the standard Peerless and factory stocks listed herein, we make a specialty of building any stock by hand to order. Our shop personnel includes several of the finest and most experienced stockers of high grade guns. Our work will be found satisfactory to the most fastidious.

Since there is an endless variety of actions and they vary even in the same make and model, it is impossible to quote definite prices for this work until we have had an opportunity to examine the particular gun. In general the following will serve as a guide:

First quality side lock guns such as Purdey, Woodward, Scott, etc. Best Circassian Walnut and checkering........$100.00

First quality box lock guns such as Greener, Daly, Francotte, etc. Fine French or Circassian Walnut and best checkering.. 65.00

Ordinary box lock guns, such as obsolete American and Foreign. Good American Walnut. Without checkering..$20.00—$30.00

SEND YOUR GUN TO STOEGER'S FOR EXPERT REPAIRING

INDIVIDUAL REMODELING OPERATIONS

Because of the low prices of our Peerless stocks and remodeling, based upon quantity production, no allowance of any kind can be made for the omission of any operations or accessories. The exceptions made will be on the sights in cases where we are to furnish more expensive receiver sight or front ramp. In such cases, the allowance on the front sight will be $1.75 and on the receiver sight, the catalog value.

For the benefit of those who do not care to take advantage of our specially priced Complete Peerless remodeling jobs, we quote below prices for each of those operations most frequently in demand.

Note: As will be seen from the rebluing methods described below, partial rebluing as of the receiver bridge is impractical as it requires approximately the same work as to reblue entire barrel and receiver. If specially requested, we will use New Method Bluer without extra charge on refinished receiver bridge. This bluer is a lacquer and applied with a brush.

1. Removing military rear sight on Enfield, milling off ears, finishing to approximate appearance of Remington Model 30, polishing but not rebluing $3.75
2. Removing ears from front sight: Since this work entails more labor than the value of a Peerless ramp, we do not undertake this work.
3. Bluing Enfield or Krag barrel and receiver only............... 4.00
4. Bluing Springfield or Mauser barrel and receiver only.......... 5.00
5. Cutting any rifle barrel to any length over 18 inches including crowning and polishing... 1.25
6. Fitting recoil pad to rifle, including pad...................... 5.50
7. Supplying fitting barrel ring and swivel base through forearm... 3.00
8. Furnishing and fitting Peerless hooded ramp................... 3.75
9. Checking under side bolt knob................................. 3.00
10. Bending Bolt knob on Mauser.................................. 2.00
11. Checking pistol grip.. 2.50
12. Checking forearm... 3.00

On all guns sent in for remodeling operations where the total work to be done amounts to less than $5.00, a service charge of $1.00 must be added to cover unpacking, bookkeeping, repacking and handling for return shipment.

SPECIAL WORK ON OLYMPIC AND PEERLESS STOCKS AND REMODELING

FACTORY FITTING OF GUNS TO STOCKS

When gun is sent to us to have finished Peerless or Olympic stocks attached a service charge of $2.50 will be made. We positively do not undertake any special work or fitting on unfinished stocks. Fitting finished Olympic stock to heavy barrel model 52, $3.50.

RECEIVER SIGHTS

Peerless remodeling jobs are regularly carried out with the Redfield 102 receiver sight. This sight has all the benefits of the more expensive receiver sights except that it does not have click adjustments nor detachable staff. If a better grade of receiver sight is desired this may be had by paying the difference between the cost of the desired sight and the price of the Redfield 102 (value of Redfield 102 is $4.50).

FRONT SIGHT RAMPS

Peerless remodeling jobs are regularly carried out with our special Peerless ramp which is very carefully soldered to the barrel and will not come off. It is available only with silver bead sight and sight protector; the ramp itself is matted. If barrel ramp with ring is desired we recommend the Redfield ramp which is available with either ivory or gold bead or Patridge style gold sight at an additional charge of $4.00; this ramp also includes hood.

BARREL LENGTH

Upon request barrel may be shortened to any desired length not under 20" at no extra cost. Barrel may also be left at its original length but no reduction can be allowed.

ALTERATIONS FROM STANDARD STOCK MEASUREMENTS

The only alteration that can be made in our Peerless stock is to shorten it. This we undertake to the customer's length at an additional cost of $1.50. A stock may be lengthened by the addition of a recoil pad.

RECOIL PADS

If recoil pad is required we recommend the Hawkins pad and the extra cost on our remodeling is $4.00. If any other pad is desired the cost is that of the pad selected plus $2.00 for fitting. These prices include allowance for steel butt plate which is otherwise regular equipment.

SPECIAL BARRELS

Since in many cases special barrels which have a different diameter from standard are attached to actions such as Springfield, Enfield or Mauser and our regular Peerless will not fit we undertake to hand fit a specially finished Peerless stock at an additional cost of $6.00. This also assures extra care in the selection of a close fitting stock.

BARREL RINGS

Except in the case of the Krag where the forend can easily warp because of the very thin connection with the rear of the stock and where we consequently fit a forend screw base into the bottom of the barrel by means of a small dovetail, we use the floating type of barrel which is advocated by many of the best rifle makers.

Where a customer insists upon a barrel ring as a front swivel screw base in order to hold the forend tightly against the barrel we can fit our regular barrel forend swivel ring and screw at an additional cost of $2.00 provided that this be specified when the order for the complete remodeling job is given. The barrel ring cannot be slid onto the barrel over any sight or ramp and must therefore be fitted before the ramp is attached.

STRAIGHTENING TANG AND ALTERING BOLT

While we have many inquiries relative to straightening the magazine tang and cutting down the magazine on the Enfield model we do not recommend this because our Peerless stocks are of such a design that the awkward shape of this model directly in front of the magazine has been eliminated and in addition the operation entails a reduction of the cartridge capacity. Consequently we do not undertake this work. We also do not undertake to make the bolt cock on opening.

UNOILED STOCKS

Because of repeated requests by many who desire to do their own wood finishing we will upon special order and full prepayment but at no extra cost supply any finished Peerless or Olympic stock carefully sandpapered but unoiled.

USE OF CUSTOMER'S OWN WOOD

Where a customer has his own walnut blank or a blank of any other kind of wood we are glad to turn same to any of our Peerless or Olympic specifications at the regular price of either the unfinished or finished stock. In view of the special handling and attention necessary on such orders we cannot make any allowance for the small saving we affect by not using our own walnut. When blanks are sent into us they must have a minimum thickness of 2⅝" thickness and length of 35" and butt end must measure 6" in width for the Peerless stock. For the Olympic stock the length must be 35" the thickness 3" and the butt end 7". An examination of the illustrations will serve to give the general size necessary although all dimensions should be left as full as possible.

CARBINE AND FULL LENGTH STOCKS

While we receive many inquiries for full length carbine or Mannlicher style stocks we are unable to fill these orders because of mechanical difficulties. A stock of this type must be entirely handmade and the cost runs about $75.00.

ORIGINAL STOCK NOT REQUIRED

In sending in guns for Peerless or Olympic remodeling we do not require the original stock, in fact we prefer the gun be sent without stock.

PRICES ARE FOR REMODELING ONLY

All prices of Peerless and Olympic remodeling and all prices shown herein apply only to the actual remodeling work and do not include the rifle in any case nor are we able to supply the rifles for remodeling as these are mostly government issue and not commercial items.

PARTS FOR MILITARY RIFLES

We carry in stock parts for Mauser Military rifles (except barrels) but for all other military rifles we refer our customers to the National Rifle Association, Barr Bldg., Washington, D. C., since parts for U. S. Government rifles are not commercial items and can only be obtained by N. R. A. members through the Director of Civilian Marksmanship.

REMEMBER, ONLY STOEGER DOES PEERLESS REMODELING

Accessories and Butt Stock Swivels

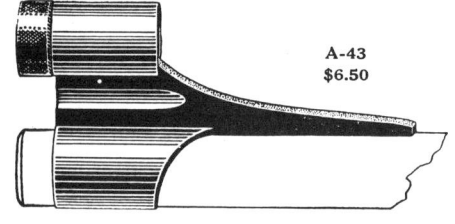

A-43 $6.50

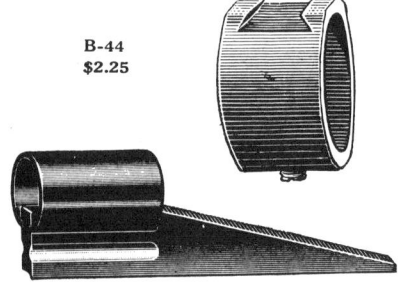

B-44 $2.25

C-45 $2.75

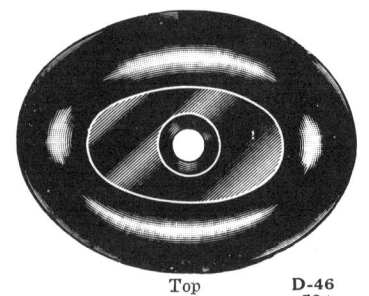

Top D-46 50¢
Side E-46 $1.25

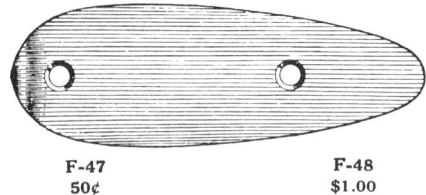

F-47 50¢   F-48 $1.00

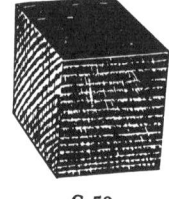

G-50 $1.00

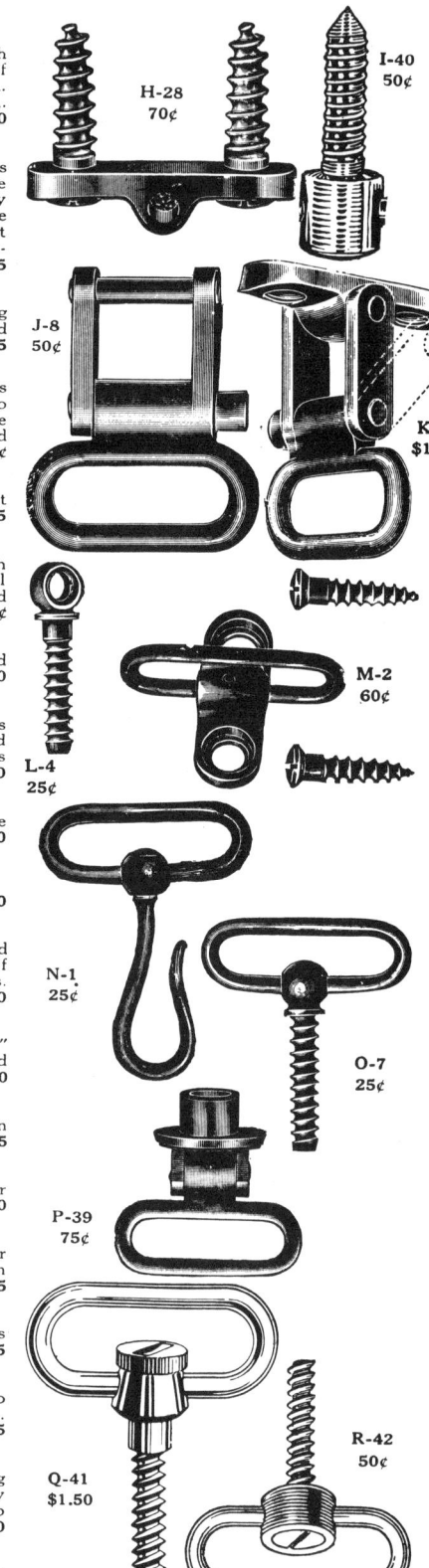

A-43—REDFIELD RAMP for all popular high powered rifles, available with choice of ivory, gold or protected gold face sight. In ordering specify rifle and barrel length. With hood $6.50

B-44—REAR SIGHT SLEEVE This sleeve has been especially designed for use on the Enfield rifle to serve as a base for any standard open rear sight, but may be altered to fit the same purpose on almost any military rifle barrel solving the problem of open sights $2.25

C-45—PEERLESS HOODED RAMP for soldering to barrel available in two heights .38" and .46". Height of sight above ramp .2" $2.75

D-46—STEEL PISTOL GRIP CAP This cap is especially well shaped and adds finish to any gun. Leigth 1.24/32" width 11/32". These are unpolished and unblued and is supplied with screw .... 50¢

E-46—This is the same as D-46 except that it is polished and blued $1.25

F-47—STEEL BUTT PLATE unfinished, length 5¼" with closest width of 1¾" and full toe. Supplied with screws, unpolished and unblued .... 50¢

F-48—The same as F-47 except it is polished and bluer. Price $1.00

G-50—GENUINE EBONY FOREND BLOCK This is supplied in a size of about 2" square and is suitable for forend tips on rifles. Permits of a lustrous black finish $1.00

H-28—DETACHABLE SWIVEL BASE complete with 2 screws .... $.70

I-40—DETACHABLE SWIVEL SCREW BASE .... $.50

J-8—DETACHABLE SWIVEL may be released by pressure on button shown on right of illustration. Made in 1" and 1¼" widths. .... $.50

K-9—DETACHABLE SWIVEL, 1" or 1¼" widths, complete with base and two wood screws $1.20

L-4—STOCK SCREW EYE suitable for any gun in connection with snap hook swivel .. $.25

M-2—STOCK SWIVEL BASE complete for 1" or 1¼" strap. Will work with any gun. $.60

N-1—SWIVEL SNAP HOOK made for 1" or 1¼" strap. Will fit any gun equipped with eyes .... $.25

O-7—STOCK SCREWEYE SWIVEL for all guns available for 1" or 1¼" strap .... $.25

P-39—REVOLVER SWIVEL for attaching to revolver butt. Available only ⅝" width. $.75

Q-41—DETACHABLE SWIVEL for 1¼" sling strap. Swivel can be instantly removed by unlocking nut. Swivel can be locked so that it will not turn $1.50

R-42—STOCK SWIVEL for 1¼" strap .... $.50

SEND YOUR GUN TO STOEGER

BARREL AND FOREARM SWIVELS

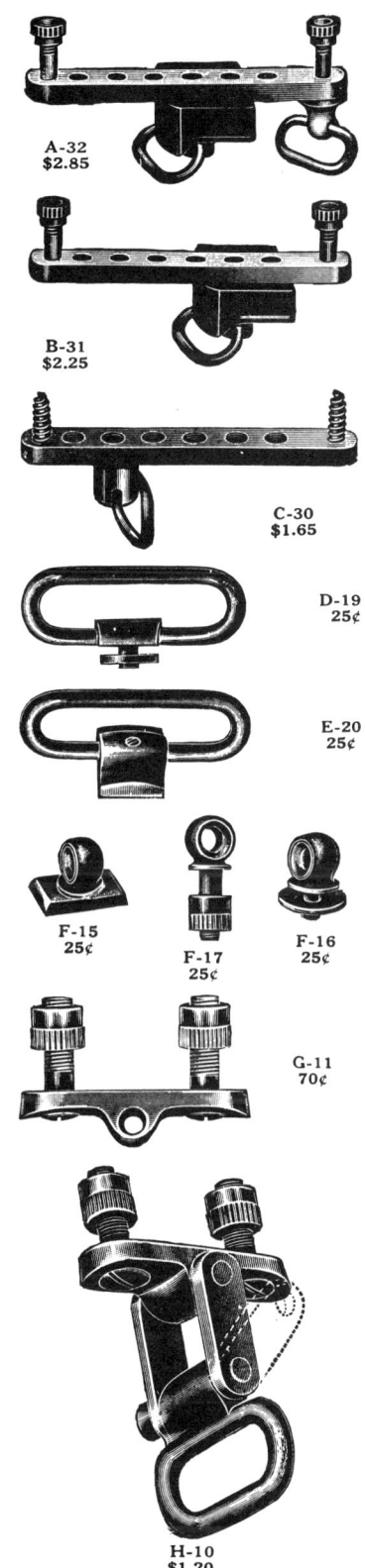

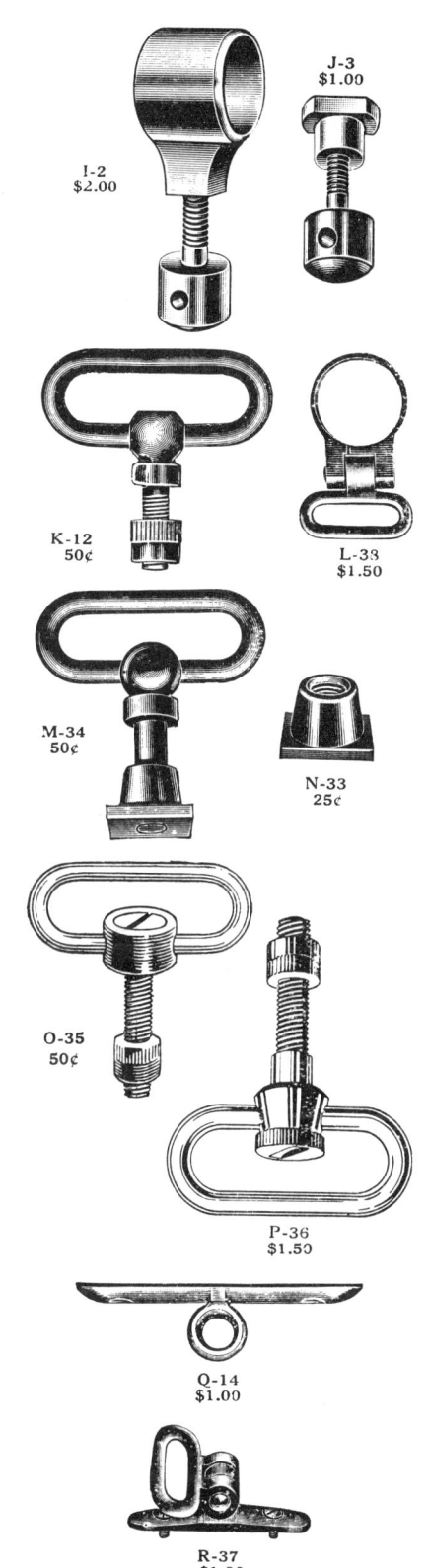

All Swivels Polished and Blued, Ready to Install

A-32—FOREARM ADJUSTABLE BASE complete with one permanent fixed swivel and adjustable swivel 1¼" mounted on elevated block for the shooter's comfort......$2.85

B-31—FOREARM ADJUSTABLE BASE complete with 1¼" swivel for heavy weight target rifles with Beavertail forearm.$2.25

C-30—FOREARM ADJUSTABLE BASE complete with 1¼" swivel designed for use on forearms of target rifles, such as Winchester Model 75, Savage Model 19, etc...$1.65

D-19—FOREARM TIP SWIVEL BOW complete. For riveting to rifle forearm tip or carbine rear band, also to magazine bands or magazine plugs of shotguns. Specify 1" or 1¼" size when ordering............$0.25

E-20—FOREARM TIP SWIVEL BOW complete. It is necessary to cut a seat in the underside of barrel dovetail shape to take the base of the swivel bow.........$0.25

F-15—BARREL SWIVEL EYE complete with base. A dovetail slot must be cut in the underside of the barrel to take the base of the swivel eye..................$0.25

F-16—FOREARM TIP SWIVEL EYE complete for riveting to rifle forearm tip or carbine rear band, also can be used the same way on magazine bands or magazine plugs of shotguns $0.25

F-17—FOREARM SCREW EYE with escutcheon for light weight cal. .22 rifles and others of similar weight $0.25

G-11—DETACHABLE SWIVEL BASE complete for forearm with two screws and two escutcheons to take Fig. 1 or Fig. 8 detachable swivels $0.70

H-10—SLING STRAP SWIVEL complete for 1" or 1¼" strap for sporting rifles and remodeling jobs $1.20

I-2—PEERLESS BARREL BAND with screw to take Fig. 8 detachable swivel, for use through the forearm. Available in three sizes inside ring diam. .85 inch, .78 inch and .74 inch..................$2.00
Screw only 0.50

J-3—FOREARM SWIVEL BASE with screw complete. Nut to be countersunk in foreend, can also be dovetailed into underside of barrel $1.00

K-12—FOREARM SCREW EYE SWIVEL complete with escutcheon. Escutcheon to be countersunk into forend, available in sizes 1" or 1¼"...................$0.50

L-38—DETACHABLE BARREL BAND with swivel complete. Comes with inside ring diameters of 9/16", 5/8", 45/64", 25/32" and 55/64". Swivels for ¾", ⅞" and 1¼" strap. Specify desired combination when ordering $1.50

M-34—FOREARM SCREW EYE SWIVEL complete with forearm screw eye stud. Stud to be countersunk into forend. Size of swivel 1¼" only.................$0.50

N-33—FOREARM SCREW EYE STUD (base of swivel M-34) for use in forearm or dovetailed into barrel.............$0.25

O-35—UPPER SWIVEL 1¼" with threaded screw and escutcheon type stud. Stud to be countersunk into forend........$0.50

P-36—UPPER DETACHABLE SWIVEL 1¼" with threaded shank and stud. Stud to be countersunk into forend. Swivel can be instantly removed by unlocking nut. Swivel also can be locked so it will not turn.$1.50

Q-14—BARREL SWIVEL EYE complete for double barrel shotguns, comes with two screws. For use with Fig. 1 snap hooks $1.00
Extra tap for screws to attach......0.35
Extra drill size No. 41............0.35

R-37—UPPER SWIVEL BASE with bow and 2 screws for double barrel shotguns. Size of bow ⅞" only...................$1.00

FOR COMPLETE EXPERT REPAIRING

BLUING PROCESSES ARE MADE
with Stoeger's Unexcelled

STOEGER GUNSMITH BLUER

This is the bluer that we have always used in our own shop on our very finest guns including the most expensive shotguns and rifles and have for the last ten years offered to our gunsmiths trade with never a failing of success. It is without doubt the finest bluing solution on the market regardless of price and makes it possible for the average gunsmith to produce a job unsurpassed by even the best original factory job. It is in no sense a quick bluer but the slower process procures evenness of results with a permanence and lack of corrosion absolutely impossible with the usual quick method acid bluer. The process ordinarily takes from three to four days. For bluing a pair of barrels only about 25 drops of Stoeger's Gunsmith Blue are necessary. Complete instructions accompany each bottle.

#1700A 4 oz. bottle $1.50
#1700B Utility pint size bottle 5.00

STOEGER DAMASCUS BROWNER

This solution is especially prepared according to a very old formula for the purpose of rebrowning genuine damascus, twist or laminated steel barrels where a reddish brown is desired. With each bottle detailed instructions for the successful use of this browner is given and if these are carefully followed, a beautiful effect can be achieved. With little experience, it is even possible to vary the tone. To our very best knowledge our Damascus browner is the only one of its kind available in America.

Price per 4 oz. bottle.................$2.50
Shipping rate 1 lb.

STOEGER BLUING OIL

Stoeger's bluing oil is recommended for the rapid bluing of small parts such as screws, sights, etc. While air results may be attained with ordinary oils by dipping the heated item, this particular oil has been specially selected for this particular purpose and gives superior results. Instructions accompany each bottle.

Price .... $.50
Shipping rate 1 lb.

STOEGER CIRCULAR BRUSHES

No. 1716. This brush is the ideal type for use in bluing wherever a buffing machine or power wheel of any type is available. The wire is of hardened steel and yet nearly as soft to the touch as hair.

This brush may also be used for buffing and cleaning rusty parts. However, a brush which is used for bluing should never be used for any other purpose, and above all should never be contaminated with grease or oil, because such a brush on account of the oil on it spoils the bluing. Many failures in bluing are due to just this. Available in three sizes.

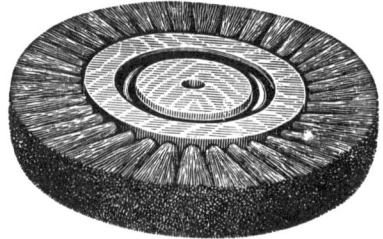

Price
4 inch diameter $2.00
6 inch diameter 3.00
8 inch diameter 5.00

STOEGER BLUING BASIN

These basins are especially made of extra heavy black iron with reinforced rim and separate cover. They are suitable for several barrels and will hold 5 gallons. This basin is a necessity to any gunsmith doing a considerable amount of bluing. Two basins are required, one for boiling in order to degrease and a second for boiling after oxidation.

Size 38 x 6 x 6. Weight without cover 12 lbs. Cover 1½ lbs.
Basin only $7.50
Cover only 2.50

BLACK DIAMOND LIGHTNING BLUER

Our astonishing new Black Diamond Lightning Bluer is by far the most efficient and speediest genuine oxidation blue on the market. It ushers in a new era of bluing. With this bluer a finished job of finest quality is assured with lustrous deep, but not shiny black, or satiny sheen. The actual bluing process requires but ten to fifteen minutes, recommended for all parts and firearms except soldered shotgun barrels. It may even be used on worn barrels without the removal of old bluing with fair results, and will blue damascus steel.

For pistols, revolver parts, etc., the 5 lb. size is ideal; for rifle barrels the 20 lb. size is recommended; for gunsmiths the 40 lb. size is recommended.

The salts may be used repeatedly and when the strength lessens may be revived by the addition of our special rejuvenation salts.

Prices are the same for Black Diamond Bluer or Black Diamond Rejuvenating salts.
5 lb. container.................... $3.75
20 lb. container 12.00
40 lb. container 20.00

Black Diamond Finishing Oil
1 pint $1.00
1 quart 1.75
1 gallon 6.00

Bluing Thermometer
For best results. Made of nickel silver, resistant to acids, magnifying lens thermometer. Spring clip for attaching to bluing tank. Modern design, wood handle of natural maple finish. Range 50° to 350° F. Size 11½"x1⅝".
Each $1.50

SUPERIOR, SIMPLER, SPEEDIER!

Bluing Equipment

OLD CONNECTICUT BLUER

Old Connecticut Bluer is a real boon to the average gunsmith or private party who has occasion to undertake reblueing. It is particularly valuable for the gunsmith who is desirous of giving a first-class factory-like finish, but who for reasons of time or economy cannot afford to take the time that our regular Gunsmiths Bluer requires, Old Connecticut Bluer has proven itself over many years to the most practical rapid bluer on the market and the process which in brief consists of cleaning, applying solution, rusting and brushing, is almost identical to that of our Gunsmiths Bluer except that the rust occurs in a few minutes instead of many hours and permits a high class blueing job in little more than an hour. Old Connecticut is unique amongst rapid bluers because of its great permanency and richness of color and has the advantage that this solution will not easily burn the hands and is therefore very easy to work with. Complete instructions included with each bottle.

Price, per 4 oz. bottle $1.00
Utility pint size bottle 3.00

PEERLESS BLUEING KIT

For gunsmiths and others who have occasional reblueing jobs we recommend our Peerless blueing Kit which only is complete with all the necessary accessories required in the normal course of blueing, but in addition is one of the most rapid genuine chemical bluers on the market. Full directions accompany each kit and permit blueing of the average shotgun or rifle in about one hours time. This kit includes not only two Peerless blueing solutions, but in addition 4 tapered dowels for use as combination barrel plugs and handles, 1 pair of acid resisting rubber gloves, 1 package of steel wool, and a generous supply of emery and crocus cloth and one package of selected oilfree cotton and a bottle of finishing oil.

Price $3.00
Shipping rate 2 lbs.

STOEGER SPRAYBLUE

Sprayblue offers an entirely new and extremely simple and rapid method of blueing, particularly recommended for nickel, and stainless steel barrels on which regular rust bluers have no effect. Sprayblue is a special type of metal lacquer particularly adapted for use through a sprayer by means of which a thin and uniform blue-black coating may be applied. By means of our Sprayblue outfit an entire gun can be nicely reblued in a few minutes. Complete instructions with each outfit. Complete outfit includes sprayer, and 2 oz. can of Sprayblue.

Syrayblue, Price $1.00
4 oz. can of Sprayblue alone 1.00

STOEGER METAL CLEANING WOOL

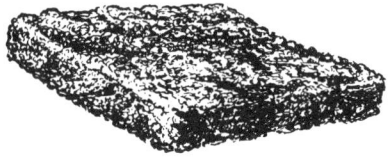

This especially selected high grade metal cleaning wool indispensable in blueing where a circular brush is not available. This metal wool is supplied in 16 square pads weighing 1 oz. each.

Price $1.00
Shipping rate 2 lb.

STOEGER METAL HAND BRUSH

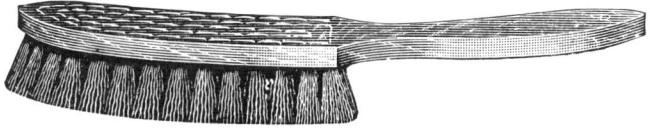

This brush has been especially designed for amateur gunsmiths who do not have a power wheel. It is made of extra fine hardened steel wire. Gunsmiths will find this brush valuable for use in corners and crevices where the circular machine brush cannot extend. The surface size of the brush measures 1⅜ by 6 inches.

No. 1718, price $1.25

CUSTOM BUILD YOUR OWN GUN

STOEGER PEERLESS ACTION

This Peerless action is built for us with a long magazine designed for the .30-06, 7m/m, .220 Swift and other rimless high power cartridges. The action is made entirely of high grade steel, properly hardened, well polished and blued. All parts are held to closest tolerances and are interchangeable. Trigger is of the regulation double-pull style; detachable magazine floor plate; pear-shaped bent bolt handle to permit low mounting of telescope.

As described.......$18.00

LOCK, STOCK AND BARREL With These STOEGER PEERLESS PARTS for only $42.50

For the benefit of the ever increasing number of professional and amateur gunsmiths who are desirous of building an entire gun "from the ground up" we offer a really fine bolt action of Mauser design, especially adapted for the .30-06 cartridge, but suitable for almost any American high power cartridge. This style of action is regularly used in England in the building of .375 and other magnum cartridges.

The action we offer is built by the world famous Belgium arms company, the Fabrique National, which was founded for the purpose of supplying the Belgian government with Mauser rifles. The model produced today is the '98 model, which is practically identical to the original Mauser rifle, manufactured in Germany. Because it is standard quality, it is made in large quantities and is available at a low price.

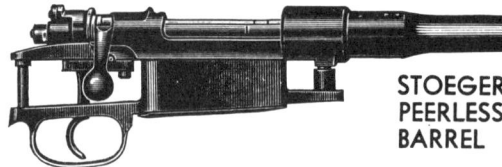

STOEGER PEERLESS BARREL

Because the fitting, threading and chambering of a barrel to an action represents an almost insurmountable obstacle to the amateur, we have decided to offer the Stoeger Peerless action, as described above, fitted with 24" round tapered barrel, polished but unblued, without sights, chambered for the .30-06 cartridge. Other calibers only on special order at an extra charge.

The barrel has a V thread with a pitch of 12 threads to the inch. The major diameter is 1.104 and the root diameter is .960. The actions are threaded to receive this thread which is identical to that of the original Mauser Model 98 Military rifle. For this reason it is possible to fit this barrel to an original Model 98 action and by filing the front and rear of the magazine to approximately ½ the original thickness, the .30-06 cartridge may be used.

The barrels are all officially government proof tested. They are of manganese steel, perfectly straightened and bored with a tolerance of less than .00118 inches.

Action and Barrel...$36.00

Barrel only, (chambered and threaded).......................$18.00
Additional for installing in standard Model 98 Mauser Military action... 5.00

PEERLESS STOCK

For use with the Stoeger Peerless barrel and action, as illustrated above, we have made up a special Peerless stock along the lines of our regular Mauser Peerless stock, available both rough turned and finished.

Price, Rough turned but including accessories................................. $6.50
Price Finished 14.00
Extra for checkering forearm.. 3.00
Extra for French Walnut.. 2.50
Extra for checkering pistol grip... 2.50

STOEGER PEERLESS SPORTER

As Illustrated.......$75.00

For those not interested in undertaking the building or finishing of a rifle as described on this page, we undertake this work in our own shop using the assembled barrel and action together with our finished Peerless stock. Our standard F.N. rifle, as illustrated, is fitted with Redfield #70 Micrometer receiver sight, Mauser ramp front sight encircling barrel with gold bead and removable sight protector, oil finished French walnut stock checkered pistol grip, Mauser swivels, steel pistol grip and pistol grip cap, weight about 7¾ lb. This is an extremely beautiful well balanced hunting rifle comparable with the best custom built jobs.

EVERYTHING IN GUNS UNDER ONE COVER

PEERLESS GUNSMITH'S STEEL AND ACCESSORIES

PEERLESS SPECIAL TOOL STEEL

Peerless Special Water Hardening Tool Steel is of the highest quality and particularly recommended for the manufacture of precision instruments, dies, gauges, reamers, punches, gun parts, subject to unusual wear such as sears and all general shop requirements. It is a 1.00–1.09 straight carbon steel. It may be forged at 1600°–1750°, annealed at 1400°–1425° hardened at 1400–1440 degrees in water and drawn at 350°–500°.

Peerless Tool Steel comes in varying lengths of six to ten feet. When less than a full bar is ordered, a cutting charge of 50 cents is made. Minimum order, one foot.

Size	Weight per foot	Price per foot
1/8" Round	.261	$.24
1/8" Square	.332	.33
3/8" Round	.376	.36
3/8" Square	.478	.48
1/2" Round	.668	.60
1/2" Square	.850	1.05
1" Square	2.67	2.25
1" Round	3.40	3.00

Add 50 cents for cutting charge when less than full bar (6-10 ft.) is ordered. Minimum order is for one foot.

PEERLESS COLD DRAWN STEEL

Peerless Cold Drawn Steel also known as Cold Rolled Steel, is an easily workable steel for all general use, when the steel is not subjected to particular strain; it may be used for most gun parts except firing pin, sears, etc. Peerless Cold Drawn Steel can only be case hardened, which is done by heating it to a cherry red, holding it one minute in cyanide, reheating to cherry red, then plunging it in water.

Peerless Cold Drawn Steel is supplied in varying lengths of from ten to twelve. Where less than a full bar is ordered, a cutting charge of 50 cents will be added.

Size	Weight per foot	Price per foot
1/4" Round	.167	$.03
1/4" Square	.213	.06
1/8" Round	.261	.06
1/8" Square	.332	.09
3/8" Round	.376	.11
3/8" Square	.478	.14
7/8" Round	.511	.12
7/8" Square	.651	.18
1/2" Round	.668	.15
1/2" Square	.850	.21
5/8" Round	1.043	.21
5/8" Square	1.328	.33
3/4" Round	1.502	.33
3/4" Square	1.913	.45
1" Round	2.670	.54
1" Square	3.400	.72

Add 50 cents for cutting charge when less than full bar (10-12 ft.) is ordered. Minimum order is for one foot.

PEERLESS SPRING STEEL

An exceptionally fine grade of spring steel, especially selected for gunsmithing, in the manufacture of all types of flat and "V" springs. Available in sizes indicated.

The 1/32 inch thickness is available only as cold rolled annealed spring steel, and is sold in coil form. To harden it is heated to 1450°, quenched in oil, polished off, then drawn in salt bath to about 600°.

All other thicknesses are round edge hot rolled raw annealed spring steel made up in lengths of from ten to twenty feet. To harden, it is heated to 1450°, quenched in oil or water, and drawn to about 600°.

Peerless Spring Steel is supplied in varying lengths of about fifteen feet. Where less than a full bar is ordered, a cutting charge of 50 cents will be added.

Size	Weight in pounds per foot	Price per foot
1/32" x 1/8"	.0104	$.03
1/32" x 1/4"	.0208	.03
1/32" x 3/8"	.0312	.06
1/32" x 1/2"	.0416	.06
1/16" x 5/16"	.066	.06
1/16" x 3/8"	.080	.06
1/16" x 1/2"	.106	.06
3/32" x 1/1"	.080	.06
3/32" x 5/16"	.100	.09
3/32" x 3/8"	.120	.09
3/32" x 1/2"	.159	.09
1/8" x 1/8"	.053	.06
1/8" x 1/4"	.106	.09
1/8" x 3/8"	.159	.09
1/8" x 1/2"	.213	.09
3/16" x 5/16"	.199	.09
3/16" x 3/8"	.239	.12
3/16" x 1/2"	.319	.09
1/4" x 1/4"	.213	.06
1/4" x 3/8"	.319	.15
1/4" x 1/2"	.425	.09

Where less than a full bar is ordered, a cutting charge of 50 cents will be added.

PEERLESS STEEL DRILL ROD

Peerless Steel Drill Rod is especially selected for gunsmiths. It is a water hardening .09–.10 carbon tool steel, suitable for most small parts. To harden, it should be heated to between 1375° and 1450°, Fahrenheit, then quenched in water; size of 1/8 inch or less should be quenched in oil. In rounds, it is available in practically all 1/64 inch sizes and in squares in 1/16 inch sizes. Prices of sizes not listed are available on request. The manufacturing tolerances are held to plus or minus .0015 on sizes from 3/4 inch to 1 inch, .001 on sizes from 1/4 to 11/16, and .0005 on sizes less than 1/4 inch.

All Peerless Steel Drill Rod is sold only in three foot lengths, and both prices and weights shown herewith are for units of this size. Drill rod will positively not be sold in lesser units.

ROUND STEEL DRILL ROD

Size in inches	Decimal equivalent	Weight per 3 foot rod	Price per 3 foot rod
1/16	.0625	.03	$.12
5/64	.0781	.05	.15
3/32	.0937	.07	.21
7/64	.1093	.10	.24
1/8	.125	.13	.27
9/64	.1406	.16	.30
5/32	.1562	.20	.36
11/64	.1718	.24	.42
3/16	.1875	.29	.39
13/64	.2031	.33	.45
7/32	.2187	.39	.51
15/64	.2343	.44	.54
1/4	.250	.50	.54
17/64	.2656	.57	.60
9/32	.2812	.64	.72
19/64	.2968	.71	.81
5/16	.3125	.79	.81
21/64	.3281	.87	.90
11/32	.3437	.95	.96
23/64	.3593	1.04	1.05
3/8	.375	1.13	1.20
25/64	.3906	1.23	1.26
13/32	.4062	1.33	1.35
27/64	.4218	1.43	1.44
7/16	.4375	1.54	1.59
29/64	.4531	1.65	1.68
15/32	.4687	1.76	1.83
31/64	.4843	1.88	1.95
1/2	.500	2.00	1.86
33/64	.5162	2.2	1.95
17/32	.531	2.3	2.10
35/64	.5469	2.4	2.25
9/16	.562	2.6	2.34
37/64	.5781	2.7	2.52
19/32	.594	2.8	2.61
39/64	.6094	3.0	2.79
5/8	.625	3.2	2.94
41/64	.6406	3.3	3.00
21/32	.656	3.5	3.27
43/64	.6719	3.6	3.36
11/16	.687	3.8	3.54
45/64	.7081	4.0	3.72
23/32	.719	4.2	3.90
47/64	.7344	4.4	4.05
3/4	.750	4.5	4.20
25/32	.781	5.0	4.65
13/16	.821	5.3	4.95
27/32	.844	5.7	5.31
7/8	.875	1.9	5.76
29/32	.906	2.1	6.15
15/16	.937	2.2	6.51
31/32	.969	2.4	7.08
1	....	2.5	7.44

SQUARE STEEL DRILL ROD

Size in inches	Decimal equivalent	Weight per 3 foot rod	Price per 3 foot rod
1/16	.0625	.04	$.30
1/8	.125	.16	.63
3/16	.1875	.40	1.02
1/4	.250	.70	1.38
5/16	.3125	1.00	1.80
3/8	.375	1.5	2.49
7/16	.4375	2.0	3.30
1/2	.500	2.6	4.29
9/16	.562	3.3	5.46
5/8	.625	4.	6.60
11/16	.687	4.8	7.92
3/4	.750	6.	9.90
13/16	.821	6.8	11.22
7/8	.875	7.8	12.87
15/16	.937	9.	14.85
1	1.00	10.2	16.83

PEERLESS SILVER STEEL SPRING WIRE

(Specifications and Prices Shown on Right)

A superior domestic wire of high quality, made with greatest care, true to gauge, and regular in temper throughout.

This wire is suitable for springs of all descriptions wherever extra high-tempered wire of great tensile strength and toughness is required.

The wire can be formed into any type of coil spring without tempering, in other words, a spring can be wound, instantly from the natural wire.

IMPORTANT NOTICE

In ordering tool, cold drawn, or spring steel by the bar, remittance should be made for the minimum length mentioned, and the steel will be shipped C.O.D. for the balance. It is impossible to quote in advance exact lengths available because these continually vary with each shipment from the steel mills.

No.	Diam.	Feet Per Lb.	Price	No.	Diam.	Feet Per Lb.	Price
00	.0085	5180	$7.28	23	.051	145	$1.00
0	.009	4625	5.22	24	.055	124	.98
1	.010	3740	4.36	25	.059	107	.98
2	.011	3090	3.82	26	.063	94	.96
3	.012	2600	3.42	27	.067	83	.96
4	.013	2215	3.15	28	.017	74	.94
5	.014	1910	2.90	29	.074	68	.94
6	.016	1460	2.30	30	.078	61	.94
7	.018	1155	2.00	31	.082	55	.92
8	.020	935	1.90	32	.086	51	.92
9	.022	770	1.80	33	.090	44	.92
10	.024	650	1.74	34	.095	41	.90
11	.026	555	1.68	35	.100	37	.90
12	.028	475	1.64	36	.105	34	.90
13	.030	415	1.22	37	.110	31	.90
14	.032	365	1.16	38	.115	28	.90
15	.034	322	1.12	39	.120	26	.90
16	.036	288	1.10	40	.125	24	.90
17	.038	200	1.08	41	.130	22	.90
18	.040	236	1.06	42	.140	20	.90
19	.042	212	1.04	43	.150	18	.90
20	.044	193	1.02	44	.160	16	.90
21	.046	177	1.02	45	.170	14	.90
22	.048	162	1.02	46	.180	12	.90

Note: Add 25¢ per 1/4 lb. coil for packing and cutting.

ALL SHIPMENTS ARE INSURED

STANDARD FACTORY BARRELS

Ely Whitney at his First Rifling Machine. By Courtesy of Scribner Magazine

The following barrels can be supplied by us. These barrels are completely finished in and outside, rifled, chambered, blued, threaded and polished, ready to be attached to the receiver.

REMINGTON:
Model 24, Cal. .22 Autoloading rifle
Cal. .22 short..........$6.00   Cal. .22 long rifle.........$6.00
Model 33, Cal. .22 Single shot................................ 3.00
Cal. .22 taking Cal. .22 short, long and long rifle........... 3.00
Model 24 slide action repeating rifle Cal. .25-20. Cal. .32-20. State caliber when ordering. Barrel......................... 8.00
Model 12, Cal. .22 slide action repeating rifle
W5A Barrel Grade A......$5.00   W5D Barrel Grade D..... 12.00
W5B Barrel Grade B......$6.00   W5E Barrel Grade E..... 16.00

Barrels for all other Remington models 30S, 8 and 14 will only be supplied if the rifle is sent for installation as special fixtures and tools are required to adjust and insure proper function of same. Prices on request.

WINCHESTER:
Model 62—Cal. .22 Hammer Repeating Rifle
No. 1462 Barrel Standard Grade Cal. .22 short, long and long rifle 23 inches 4.00
No. 1462A Barrel Cal. .22 short only 23 inches................ 4.00
Model 61 Cal. .22 Hammerless Repeating Rifle
No. 961 barrel round Cal. .22 short, long and long rifle..... 4.00
No. 1061 barrel octagon Cal. .22 short only................... 5.00
No. 1161 barrel octagon Cal. .22 long rifle................... 5.00
No. 1261 barrel octagon Cal. .22 W. R. F...................... 5.00
Model 63 Cal. .22 Automatic Rifle
No. 163 barrel, round tapered 20 inches...................... 6.50
Model 90 and 06 Cal. .22 Repeating Rifle
No. 1090 barrel Model 90 Cal. .22 short 24 inches............. 5.00
No. 1190 barrel Model 90 Cal. .22 long 24 inches.............. 5.00
No. 1290 barrel Model 90 Cal. .22 long rifle 24 inches........ 5.00
No. 1390 barrel Model 90 Cal. .22 W. R. F. 24 inches.......... 5.00
No. 1406 barrel Model 06 Cal. .22 short, long and L. R., 20 inches 3.60
Model 52 Cal. .22 Bolt Action Rifle
No. 152 barrel, Standard..$15.00   No. 352 barrel heavy model
No. 152A barrel, sporting   28"............... 25.00
   model 24" with ramp..$17.50
Model 56 and 57 Bolt Action Rifle
No. 156 Model 56 .22 short.$8.00   No. 357 Model 57 .22 short. 8.00
No. 256 Model 56 .22 L. R.$8.00   No. 457 Model 57 .22 L R. 8.00
Model 94 and 55 Lever Action Cal. 25/35, 30/30, 32 Win. Special.
194 barrel round, full magazine, solid frame 26 inches....... 9.00
394 barrel round, ¾ magazine, solid frame 26 inches.......... 9.00
594 barrel round, 2-3 magazine, solid frame 26 inches........ 9.00
794 barrel round, ½ magazine, solid frame 26 inches.......... 9.00
994 barrel octagon, full magazine, solid frame 26 inches.....12.00
1194 barrel octagon, ¾ magazine, solid frame 26 inches........12.00
1394 barrel octagon, 2-3 magazine, solid frame 26 inches......12.00
1594 barrel octagon, ½ magazine, solid frame 26 inches........12.00
1794 barrel carbine, full magazine, 20 inches................. 9.00
1794A barrel carbine, full magazine, 20 inches with ramp base. 9.00
1894 barrel carbine, ¾ magazine, 20 inches.................... 9.00
1894A barrel carbine, ¾ magazine, 20 inches with ramp base.... 9.00
1994 barrel carbine, 2-3 magazine, 20 inches.................. 9.00
1994A barrel carbine, 2-3 magazine, 20 inches with ramp base.. 9.00
2094 barrel carbine, ½ magazine, 20 inches.................... 9.00
2094C barrel carbine, ½ magazine, 20 inches with ramp base.... 9.00
2355A barrel 30 W. C. F. lightweight, round ½ mag., Model 55, 24" 9.00
2355B barrel 25/35 light wgt. round ½ mag. Model 55, 24 inches. 9.00
2355C barrel 32 W. Spec. light wght., round ½ mag. Model 55, 24". 9.00
Winchester Model 92, and 53, Cal. 25-20, 32-20, 38/40, 44-40
192 barrel round, full magazine, solid frame 24 inches....... 7.00
392 barrel round, ¾ magazine, solid frame 24 inches.......... 7.00
592 barrel round, 2-3 magazine, solid frame 24 inches........ 7.00
792 barrel round, ½ magazine, solid frame 24 inches.......... 7.00
1192 barrel octagon, full magazine, solid frame 24 inches..... 9.00
1392 barrel octagon, ¾ magazine, solid frame 24 inches........ 9.00
1592 barrel octagon, 2-3 magazine, solid frame 24 inches...... 9.00
1792 barrel octagon, ½ magazine, solid frame 24 inches........ 9.00
1992 barrel carbine, full magazine, solid frame 20 inches..... 7.00
1992A barrel carbine, full magazine, with ramp base 20 inches. 7.00
2092 barrel carbine, ¾ magazine, solid frame 20 inches........ 7.00
2092A barrel carbine, ¾ magazine, with ramp base 20 inches.... 7.00
2192 barrel carbine, 2-3 magazine, solid frame 20 inches...... 7.00
2292A barrel carbine, ½ magazine, with ramp base, 20 inches... 7.00
2292 barrel carbine, ½ magazine, solid frame 20 inches........ 7.00
Model 86 solid frame, Cal. .33 Winchester, 47/70. In ordering barrels, give length, round or octagon, full, ¾, 2-3 or ½ magazine, solid frame, rifle or carbine
186 barrel, Cal. .33 round   686 barrel, octagon 26
   light weight 24 inches..$14.25   inches 10.75
486 barrel, round 26 inches 9.00
Model 95 Rifle, Cal. .30/40, .303 British, 35 Win. 405 Win.
195A barrel, round, rifle solid frame......................... 12.00
295 barrel, round, carbine 22-inch solid frame............... 12.00
Model 65 Winchester Lever Action Repeating Rifle
165 barrel Cal. .25/20 round 22 inches tapered with ramp...... 9.00
265 barrel Cal. .32 W. C. F. round 22 inches tapered with ramp. 9.00
Model 64 and 64 Deer Lever Action Rifles
164 barrel Cal. .25/35 round 24 inches tapered with ramp..... 9.00
164A barrel Cal. .25/35 round 20 inches....................... 9.00
264 barrel Cal. .30 W. C. F. round 24 inches ramp tapered.... 9.00
264A barrel Cal. .30 W. C. F. round 20 inches with ramp....... 9.00
364 barrel Cal. .32 Win. Spec. 24 inches round, tapered with ramp 9.00
364A barrel Cal. .32 Win. Spec. 20 inches round, with ramp.... 9.00
All above models in the take down type must be sent in for special fitting and adjusting. Model 54, Barrels will only be supplied on the condition that rifle is sent in for fitting. Prices will be quoted on request.
Model 60 Take-down and Model 60A Target Bolt Action Rifle
160 Bbl. T. D. 27" round tapered—specify if letter "A" on barrel.. 3.00
160B barrel (target) 27 inches round tapered.................. 3.50
Model 03 self-loading rifle, Cal. .22 Winch. Auto—103 barrel 20". 6.50
Model 67 and 68 Bolt Action Cal. .22 Rifle
167 Model 67—barrel round 27 inches tapered................. 3.00
167A Model 67 barrel round 27 inches tapered smooth bore..... 4.00
268 Model 68 barrel round 27 inches tapered................. 3.00
Model 69—Cal. .22 Bolt Action Repeating Rifle
169 barrel 25 inches round with rear sight dovetail........... 6.00
269 barrel 25 inches round without rear sight dovetail........ 5.65

SAVAGE:
Model 99. Rifles must be sent in for fitting new barrel
2B 44 barrel 20 inches, 22 inches or 26 inches round, all calibers, plus fitting, labor charge from $2.50 to $3.50................12.00
Model 40 and 45 Super Sporter Rifles—3-S23 barrel. Rifle has to be sent in for fitting of barrels, labor charge extra..........12.00
Model 4—.22 Cal. Single Shot Rifle—3C1 barrel................. 4.00
Model 05—.22 Cal. Rifle—Barrel no longer obtainable. Barrel for Model 4 adaptable.. 4.00
Model 29 Slide Action Cal. .22 Repeater—29-58 barrel.......... 8.00
Barrels for Model 19 Rifle and Model M/22 Sporter with serial number below 25,000 are no longer obtainable.
Model 19NRA Serial Number 25,000 to 45,000
Model 23A Sporter Serial Number 25,000 to 127,000
3N89 Barrel Model 19NRA   3N64 Barrel Model 23A 23
  25 inches...........$10.00   inches 9.00
Model 23AA Model 1933 NRA and Model 19 Hornet
Model 23AA barrel 23 inches................................... 9.00
Model 19 barrel .22 Cal. 25 inches............................11.00
Model 19 barrel 22 Hornet.....................................12.00
Model 23B 25-20 Cal. .23c 32-20 Cal. Sporting Rifle
3N67 Cal. 25-20........$10.00   3N100 Cal. 32-20.......10.00
Model 23D Hornet Rifle—3N67 barrel 25 inches..................11.50
Model 3, Model 3-A and Model 3-B Cal. .22 Single Shot Rifle—
Part No. 1 barrel only.. 3.50
Model 4, Cal. .22 Bolt Action Rifle—Part No. 1 barrel......... 4.50

SEE PARTS SECTION FOR BARRELS NOT SHOWN HERE

PEERLESS HIGH PRESSURE STEEL BARRELS
STOEGER'S PEERLESS RIFLE BARREL BLANKS

A rifle is no better than the performance of the barrel. The barrel, being subjected to erosion upon every shot and still more frequently to corrosion, due to faulty care, must often be replaced to restore the original accuracy of the rifle. This is where our barrel service will be found to be of the greatest assistance, offering you really first quality barrels for practically every type of rifle at moderate prices.

Peerless Rifle Barrels are made from the best material, carefully selected and tested by the most modern scientific methods in its metallic composition to stand the high pressures of the modern smokeless powder as used from the smallest to the largest caliber.

Peerless Super High Pressure Steel Barrels are machined carefully to insure a perfect balance and rifled most carefully for the highest accuracy. Every barrel is gauged under the most severe test similar to the famous star gauge test as used at the Springfield Armory to assure that seconds not coming up to the standard, will not be sold. Peerless Barrels have a tolerance of plus .001, minus 0.

Barrels are only supplied to the customer on the condition that we are not responsible for the fitting, chambering, head spacing and other consequences. Therefore full responsibility must be assumed by the purchaser of the barrel. For the present we do not fit barrels to action or chamber them. We only supply barrels and barrel blanks.

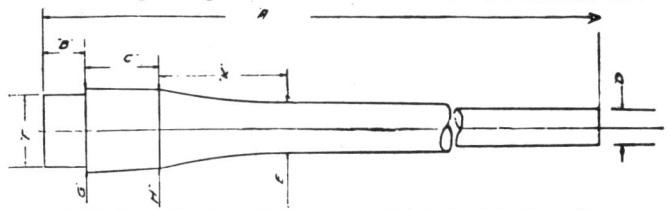

Barrel blanks of the above design are supplied in the following calibers:— .25, .30, .32, .35, .25 Roberts, 7 m/m and .30/06. Weight, about four pounds and seven ounces.
A—Length .... 24"
B—Shoulder Length ..... .765"
C—Cylindrical Length ... 1.110"
D—Diameter at muzzle .. .700"
E—Diameter at barrel ... .895"
F—Diameter at chamber.. 1.125"
G—Diameter at barrel shoulder .... 1.125"
H—Diameter at start of chamber .... 1.125"
K—Length of sharp taper.. 2.500"
Price $12.50

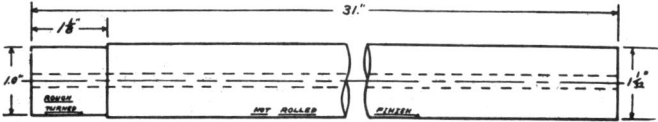

Barrel blanks of the above design and dimensions are supplied for Cal. .30/30, .300 Savage, .303 Savage, Cal. .30/06. Barrel of best grade smokeless steel; bore diameter .300 inch; depth of rifling .004 inch; six grooves; one turn in 12 inches; right hand twist; weight about 5½ pounds.
Price $14.50

Barrel blanks of the above design and dimensions are supplied for experimental purposes in caliber .32/20. Barrel of best smokeless steel; bore diameter .3045 inch; depth of rifling .003 inch; 6 grooves; one turn in 20 inches; right hand twist; weight about 6½ pounds.
Price $13.50

Same specifications as above, but in caliber .25/20; bore diameter .250 inch; depth of rifling .003 inch; 6 grooves; one turn in 14 inches; right hand twist; approximate weight 6½ pounds.
Price $13.50

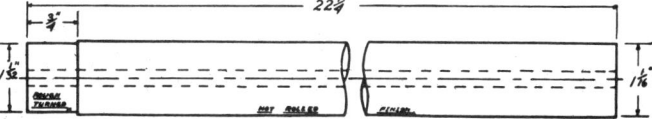

Barrel blanks of the above design and dimensions are supplied for experimental purposes in caliber .250-3000. Barrel of best smokeless steel; bore diameter .250 inch; depth of rifling .0035 inch; 6 grooves; one turn in 14 inches; right hand twist; approximate weight 5¼ pounds.
Price $14.50

SMALL BORE STANDARD AND MATCH BARRELS

SUPER ACCURATE MATCH GRADE BARREL BLANK

This barrel we recommend for the shooter who desires really a barrel giving the utmost accuracy regardless of money. Delivery takes about two to three weeks, as these barrels are only made up on special order. We recommend them specially for single shot rifles—Luna, Martini, and Ballard actions, etc.

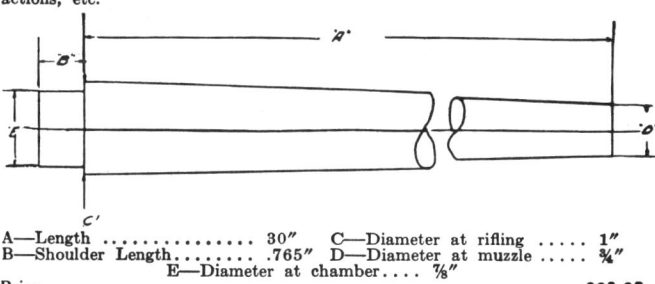

A—Length .... 30"   C—Diameter at rifling ..... 1"
B—Shoulder Length ..... .765"   D—Diameter at muzzle .... ¾"
E—Diameter at chamber .... ⅞"
Price $30.00

STANDARD FIRST QUALITY BARREL BLANK

Barrel blanks of the above design and dimensions are supplied for experimental purposes in caliber .22 Long rifle. Barrel of low carbon barrel steel; bore diameter .217 inch; depth of rifling .0025 inch; 4 grooves; one turn in 16 inches; right hand twist; weight about 6½ pounds.

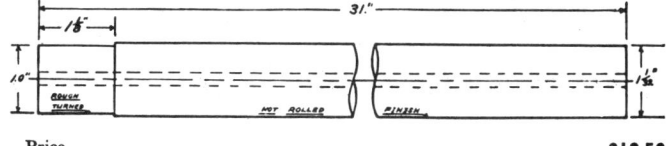

Price $10.50

Same as above, but for .22 Cal. Hornet, barrel of best smokeless steel.
Price $13.50

WINCHESTER BARREL BLANKS

No. 406080, Diameter at breech 1.16 inch, cylindrical length 3 inches, straight taper from there on to muzzle .010 inch per inch, finish ground, total length 28⅜ inches, diameter at muzzle .906 inch.

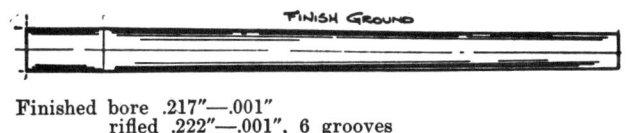

Finished bore .217"—.001"
rifled .222"—.001", 6 grooves
Obtainable for caliber .22 Long Rifle, .22 Hornet, .22-3000 Lovell
Barrel Blank, Price $20.00

No. 42816, Diameter at breech 1.250 inch, cylindrical length 3 inches, straight taper .014 inch per inch from there on to muzzle, finish ground, total length 30 inches, diameter at muzzle .875 inch.

Obtainable for caliber 220 Swift, 257 Roberts, 270 Winchester, 250-3000 Savage, 30-06 Winchester 7 m/m.

Barrel Blank, Price $25.00

RECOIL PADS

JOSTAM ANTI-FLINCH RECOIL PAD

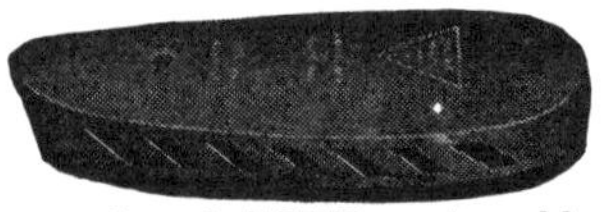

Best grade of LIVE red rubber vulcanized on black hard rubber base plate. Oblong holes through soft rubber, slanting at an angle of 45 degrees in line with stock, eliminates upward whip of muzzle and takes up the recoil. Maintains balance of gun for following shots. Leading trap, skeet and game shooters everywhere use them.

Our No.	Size	Weight	Lght.	Wdth.	Thk.	Price
No. 1.	Rifle	...4 oz.	4½	x 1 9/16	x 1"	$3.25
No. 2.	Small	...5 oz.	4⅞	x 1 11/16	x 1"	3.25
No. 3.	Medium	..6 oz.	5 5/16	x 1 13/16	x 1"	3.25
No. 4.	Large	...7 oz.	5 9/16	x 2	x 1"	3.25

JOSTAM HY-GUN RECOIL PAD

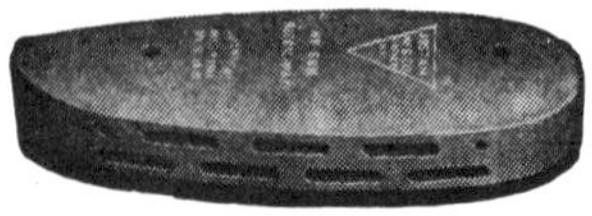

Live red rubber, vulcanized to black, hard rubber base. Attached permanently by two wood screws. Alternative holes through red rubber increases resiliency and takes up recoil when pressure is brought to bear from discharge of gun or rifle.

Our No.	Size	Weight	Lght.	Wdth.	Thk.	Price
No. 2.	Small	...4 oz.	5	x 1⅝	x 1"	$2.75
No. 3.	Medium	..5 oz.	5 5/16	x 1 13/16	x 1"	2.75
No. 4.	Large	...7 oz.	5 9/16	x 2	x 1"	2.75

JOSTAM NO-KICK RECOIL PAD

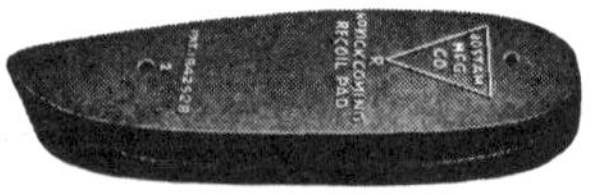

High grade moulded red rubber imbedded with metal base. A newly constructed cushion base insures no breakage.

All shooters will appreciate the resiliency of this new Jostam pad.

Our No.	Size	Weight	Lght.	Wdth.	Thk.	Price
No. 2.	Small...	2¾ oz.	5	x 1¾	x ¾"	$1.75
No. 3.	Medium.	3½ oz.	5½	x 1⅞	x ¾"	1.75

JOSTAM "SPONGE RUBBER" RECOIL PAD

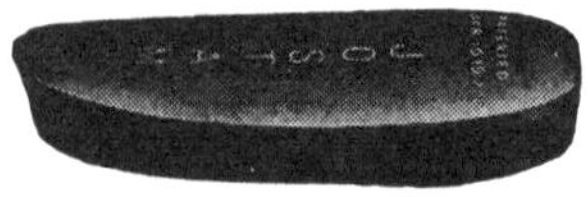

Softest pads on the market. Made of high grade black sponge rubber, 1, 2, or 3 ply. At the base there is a removable strip of red sheet rubber, which is taken off of pad, tacked and cemented to the stock, and the pad in turn is cemented to the red strip. These pads are faced with soft, red moulded rubber. Special tacks furnished with each pad, also instructions for attaching.

Black gasket rubber strip and moulded face used with Red Sponge Pads.

ONE PLY BLACK and RED SPONGE PADS

Our No.	Size	Weight	Lght.	Wdth.	Thk.
No. 2.	Small	.......4 oz.	5¼	x 1¾	x ⅞"
No. 3.	Medium	.....5 oz.	5½	x 1¾	x ⅞"

All sizes, Black **$1.50**; Red **$2.00**

TWO PLY BLACK and RED SPONGE PADS

Our No.	Size	Weight	Lght.	Wdth.	Thk.
No. 2.	Small	......5 oz.	5¼	x 1¾	x 1¼"
No. 3.	Medium	....6 oz.	5½	x 1¾	x 1¼"

All sizes, Black **$2.00**; Red **$2.50**

THREE PLY BLACK and RED SPONGE PADS

Our No.	Size	Weight	Lght.	Wdth.	Thk.
No. 2.	Small	......6 oz.	5	x 1¾	x 1⅝"
No. 3.	Medium	....8 oz.	5¼	x 1¾	x 1⅝"

All sizes, Black **$2.50**; Red **$3.00**

JOSTAM "AIR CUSHION" RECOIL PAD

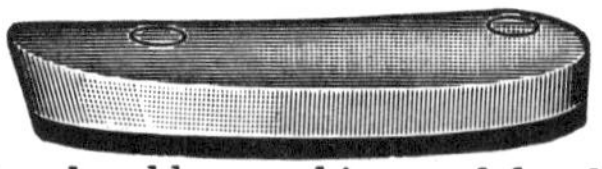

Soft red rubber cushion and hard black base plate. Hollow cushion. Chamber extending from toe to heel. High grade of rubber used. Best pad of this type on the market. Screws to stock and can be buffed to fit any gun.

Our No.	Size	Weight	Lght.	Wdth.	Thk.	Price
No. 2.	Small....	3½ oz.	5	x 1⅝	x ⅞"	$3.00
No. 3.	Medium..	4½ oz.	5½	x 1¾	x ⅞"	3.00
No. 4.	Large....	5 oz.	5 11/16	x 1⅞	x ⅞"	3.00

JOSTAM ALL-RUBBER SLIP-ON BOOT RECOIL PAD

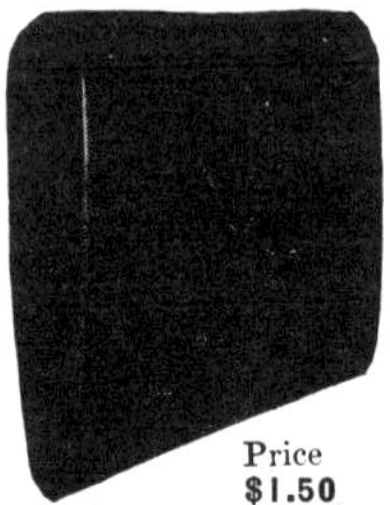

Made in one piece, of live RED RUBBER. Slips on over gunstock. No screws or laces. Base is soft, moulded RED RUBBER. Fits stock snugly. Slips on easily.

Price **$1.50**

Size No. 2—Butt, 4¾"x1 11/16" Wt. 2 oz. Thk. ⅜"
Size No. 3—Butt, 5 "x1¾" Wt. 2½ oz. Thk. ⅜"
Size No. 4—Butt, 5¼"x1¾" Wt. 3 oz. Thk. ⅜"

MONTE CARLO CHEEK PAD

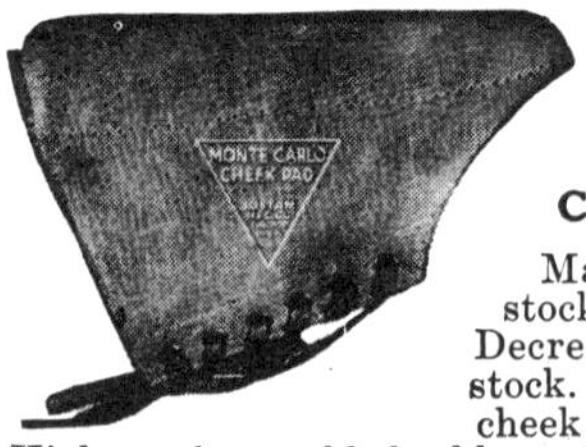

Makes your gunstock straighter. Decreases drop of stock. Protects your cheek from recoil.

High grade moulded rubber cheek pad enclosed in top quality leather. It has the Jostam high standard of quality.

Our No.	Size	Weight	High.	Long	Price
No. 2.	Low	2 oz.	⅛	x 7"	$3.00
No. 3.	Medium	2½ oz.	¼	x 7"	3.00
No. 4.	High	3 oz.	½	x 7"	3.00

COMBINATION LEATHER LACE-ON AND RECOIL PAD

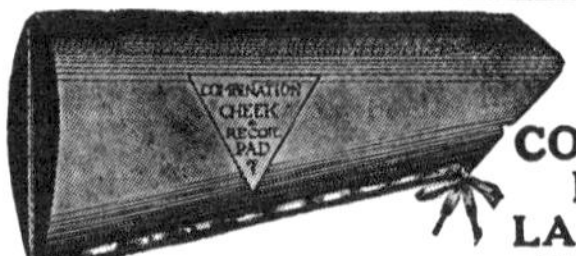

A good pad for use in the field to protect the stock from scratches and other effects of rough field hunting, besides taking up recoil of gun and protecting the cheek when shooting.

Made of brown sheepskin glove leather, extended from heel to comb—full length of stock. Sponge rubber base inserted for recoil and felt pad for cheek. Laces on stock and protects finish of stock. Takes up recoil at butt of stock and at comb.

Our No.	Size	Weight	Lght.	Wdth.	Thk.	Price
No. 2.	Small....	2 oz.	4⅞	x 1⅝	x ⅜"	$2.00
No. 3	Medium..	3 oz.	5¼	x 1¾	x ⅜"	2.00
No. 4	Large....	3½ oz.	5½	x 1¾	x ⅜"	2.00

THE HAWKINS RECOIL PAD

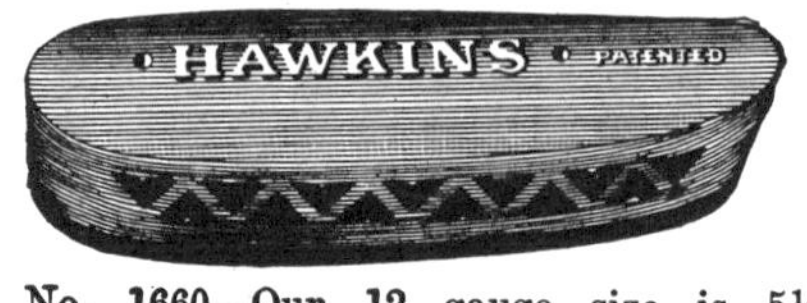

No. 1660—Our 12 gauge size is 5½ inches long, and will trim down to 4¾ inches, while the 16-20 size is 5 inches long and will trim to 4¼ inches long.

Price **$3.25**

AKRON RECOIL PAD

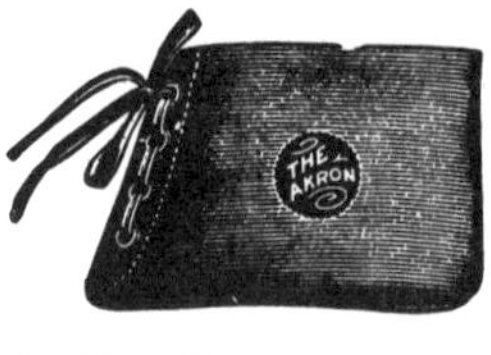

Made of high quality tan leather with high grade moulded sponge rubber firmly cemented in the boot. Laces tightly to the stock.

Our No.	Size	Weight	Lght.	Wdth.	Thk.	Price
No. 2.	Small....	2 oz.	4¾	x 1⅝	x ½"	$2.00
No. 3.	Medium..	2½ oz.	5¼	x 1 11/16	x ½"	2.00
No. 4.	Large....	3 oz.	5½	x 1 13/16	x ½"	2.00

THE "NORKA"

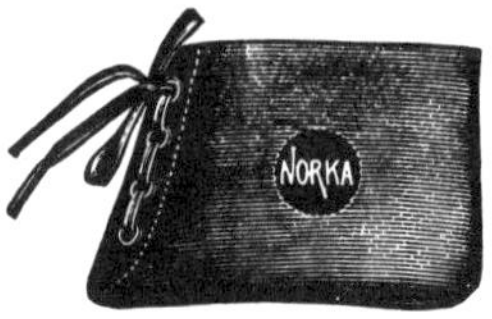

Constructed the same as the Akron, of tan leather, cut sponge rubber base. This pad is very serviceable—an excellent article where lace-on pad is desired.

Our No.	Size	Weight	Lght.	Wdth.	Thk.	Price
No. 3.	Medium..	2 oz.	5⅛	x 1⅝	x ½"	$1.50
No. 4.	Large....	2½ oz.	5¼	x 1 13/16	x ½"	1.50

THE "BROADWAY"

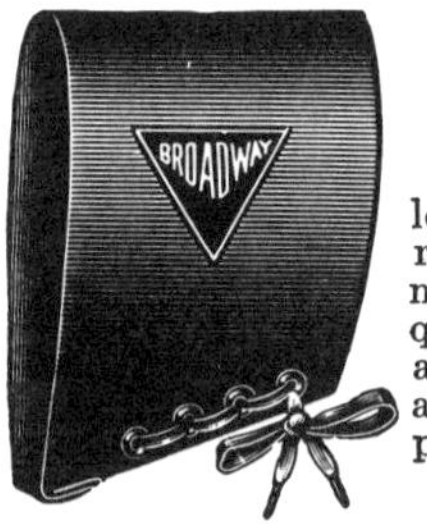

Made of high grade leather, with cut sponge rubber base firmly cemented together. High quality workmanship and material. A durable pad at a low price.

Our No.	Size	Weight	Lght.	Wdth.	Thk.	Price
No. 2.	Small....	2 oz.	4⅞	x 1 11/16	x ⅜"	$1.25
No. 3	Medium..	2½ oz.	5¼	x 1¾	x ⅜"	1.25
No. 4.	Large....	3 oz.	5½	x 1¾	x ⅜"	1.25

MILITARY LEATHER RECOIL PAD FOR RIFLES

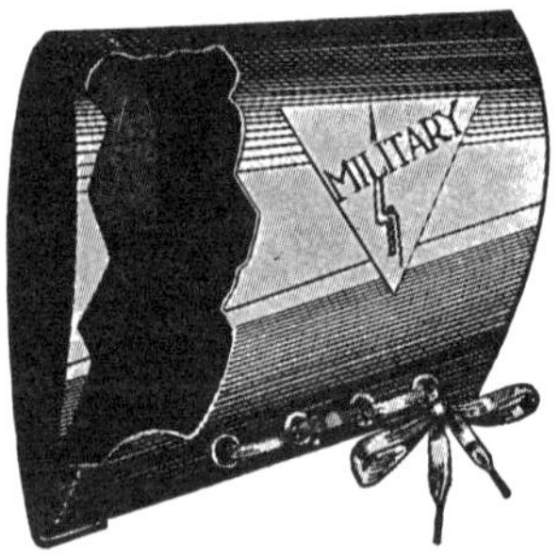

Made In 4 Sizes

Price **$3.00**

Made of high quality calf mahogany leather, with moulded sponge rubber base. Front face of sponge is concaved and curved to mesh with rifle curved butt stock. Rear face of pad is straight, same as shotgun butt. It changes rifle butt to shotgun butt.

No. 2. For Winchester Models 86, 92, 94, and 95, rifle butt stocks.

No. 3. For Remington Models 8, 14 and 30, and Savage Models 1921, 99.

No. 4. For Winchester Models 53, 54, 55, 92 and 94 shotgun butts and Savage Model 1920 and X shotgun butts.

No. 5. For regular Government Springfield and Krag rifles.

Our No.	Size	Weight	Wt. doz.	Lght.	Wdth.	Thk.
No. 2.	Winchester.	1½ oz.	2 lbs. 2 oz.	4 5/16	x1 7/16	x⅝"
No. 3.	Rem. & Savage....	2 oz.	2 lbs. 4 oz.	4¾	x1½	x⅝"
No. 4.	Win. & Savage....	2½ oz.	2 lbs. 7 oz.	5	x1 9/16	x⅝"
No. 5.	Government	3 oz.	2 lbs. 10 oz.	5 3/16	x1⅞	x½"

A PAD FOR EVERY GUN

RECOIL AND CHEEK PADS

WESTERN PNEUMATIC SLIP-ON RECOIL PAD
Cheek Pads Unnecessary

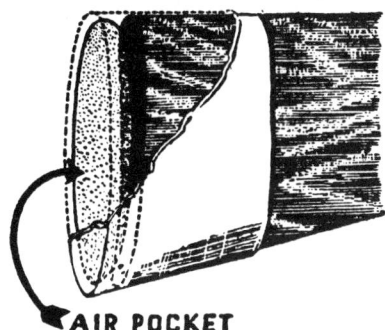

Shooting with the Western Pneumatic Recoil Cushion completely eliminates the use of cheek pads, as the gun comes straight back into the air pocket. All the recoil from the hardest kicking gun is entirely absorbed.

The air pressure within the pad is easily and quickly regulated, enabling the adjustment of the length of your stock to meet your own particular requirements.

The Western Pneumatic Recoil Cushion is constructed of the best rubber it is possible to obtain.
Price $1.50

Also to be had for permanent mounting with two screws.
Price $3.00

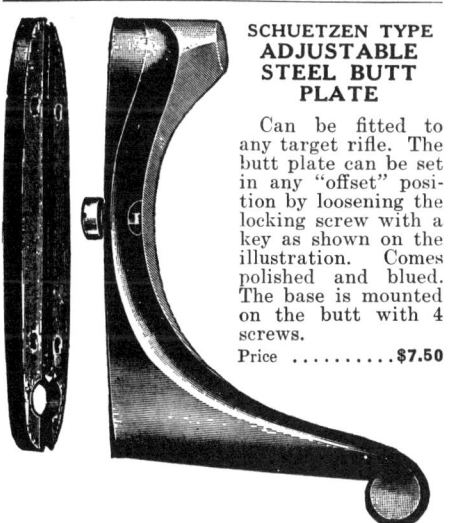

SCHUETZEN TYPE ADJUSTABLE STEEL BUTT PLATE

Can be fitted to any target rifle. The butt plate can be set in any "offset" position by loosening the locking screw with a key as shown on the illustration. Comes polished and blued. The base is mounted on the butt with 4 screws.
Price $7.50

DETACHABLE RUBBER CHEEK PAD

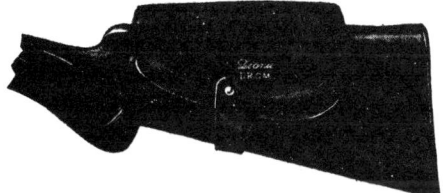

Detachable Rubber Cheek Pad will fit any rifle stock. Very desirable to raise the comb for telescope shooting.
Price $4.25

"WHITE LINE" RECOIL PAD

Regular Style   Skeet Style

The "White Line" Recoil is one of the finest made and best appearing recoil pad ever put on the market.

Made in two styles, two sizes and three colors—brown, black and red. Made of finest quality and longest lived rubber for its purpose, thereby insuring permanent flexibility and perfect cushioning of recoil.

The "REGULAR" Style has a saw-tooth, no-slip back, similar to some rifle butt plates. The "SKEET" Style is the only recoil absorber made especially for Skeet shooting and has a longitudinal anti-friction ribbed back.
Price, Each $2.50

STEEL BUTT PLATE WITH TRAP

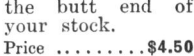

Steel Butt Plate with trap for rifle sporter stocks. Comes ready to be installed. Very desirable to carry your field-cleaner, or two extra cartridges in the butt end of your stock.
Price $4.50

Also to be had with engraving and checkering.
Price $10.00

STOEGER'S WALNUT CHEEK PIECE

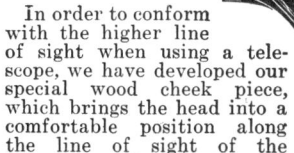

In order to conform with the higher line of sight when using a telescope, we have developed our special wood cheek piece, which brings the head into a comfortable position along the line of sight of the telescope. Thus assuring steady, comfortable aim and ease in firing.

The wood itself is always comfortable to the cheek and there are no cold, metal parts to make the shooter uncomfortable when shooting in cold weather. This cheek piece will fit almost any stock satisfactorily.

The Stoeger Walnut Cheek Piece is about 6½ inches long and the further dimensions are shown quite clearly in the illustration. To attach: drill holes and counter-sink wood screw.
Price $1.75

For Use With Rifle Scopes

"NOSHOC" RECOIL PAD

The "NOSHOC" Recoil Pad takes up shock from heel to toe and has an outer shell of rubber remaining soft and resilient indefinitely. Takes up shock, vibration and thrust most efficiently in its large inner cushion. Trapped in the live rubber of the outer shell, this cushion of spongy jell DEADENS recoil as nothing else can. Has a thick, tough base-plate of semi-rigid black hard rubber that conforms to the butt of your gun.
Price $1.50

PISTOL GRIP ATTACHMENTS
For Winchester Model 52

This device was made for shooters who want an improved pistol grip on their Winchester 52. It is very simple to attach and no altering of the stock is required.

When ordering state model of stock as two different attachments are made, one for the latest target stock and one for the model before. It is made of aluminum, the surface covered with insulating enamel, but it is available in bright finish also. The lip of the bottom covers the original Winchester grip similar to a cap.

The price is $1.25 with brass woodscrew or $1.50 with threaded brass bushing and machine screw.

ITHACA

ITHACA GUN CO. RECOIL PAD

This red rubber pad is built like a bridge. Perfectly designed. Absolutely shockless.
Medium size only. Each $2.25

H. & R.

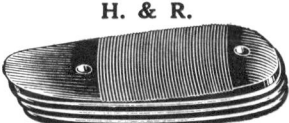

No. 75. Red Rubber Pad is easily attached. No fitting, no cementing. Size 5 inches by 1⅝ inches.
Each $0.75

FIRST QUALITY BRIDLE LEATHER SLING STRAPS

THE "WHALEN" SLING STRAP

Considered by many the best and most easily adjustable sling strap for target and long range hunting shots. It is finely adjustable with a minimum of light reflecting claw hooks and buckles. Rawhide thongs for lacing make up this feature. This sling is made of first quality russet or oil tanned cowhide and in three widths—⅞", 1", and 1¼". For the target or military shooter we recommend the 1¼" width in either finish; for the hunter, we recommend either the ⅞" or 1" in oil tanned finish since this darker color blends better with the background.

Price ⅞", oiled or unoiled $1.80
Price 1", oiled or unoiled 2.10
Price 1¼", oiled or unoiled 2.40

THE "MILITARY" SLING STRAP

Regulation! Strong, sturdy, and dependable. Keeps the military rifle in conformity with regulations. Its two sets of claw hooks permit very fine and speedy adjustments in length. This type of sling is particularly adapted for use with the heavier target rifles and is a great favorite with men accustomed to the regular U. S. service rifle. It is recommended to riflemen wishing a particularly sturdy, reliable and foolproof strap. This strap is available either in oil tanned finish or light russet and may be had in a choice of three widths.

Oiled	PRICES	Unoiled
⅞" $1.50		⅞" $1.65
1" 1.65		1" 1.80
1¼" 1.95		1¼" 2.10

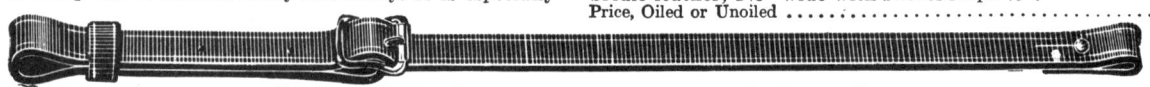

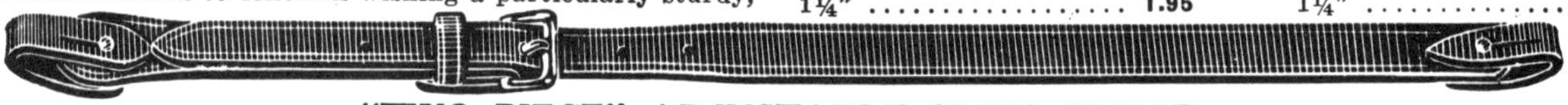

"TWO PIECE" ADJUSTABLE SLING STRAP

The simplest and best carrying strap. Is easily detachable being fastened at both ends with brass sling buttons. A sturdy brass buckle permits of a reasonable amount of adjustment. A rifle fitted with this type of strap can be carried easily and safely. It is especially recommended for deer hunters who have the problem of transporting their guns to and from the stands with due regard for the safety of all members of the party. Available in heavy russet, or oil tanned bridle leather, 1⅜" wide with swivel loops ⅞".

Price, Oiled or Unoiled $1.75

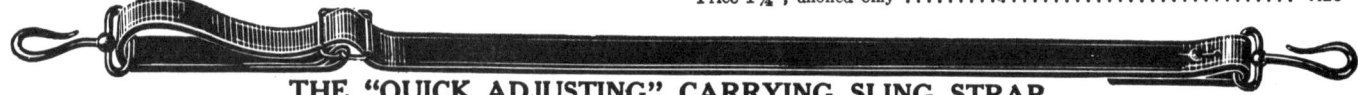

"ONE PIECE" ADJUSTABLE SLING STRAP

A very serviceable and inexpensively priced item for the man who wants a combination carrying strap and adjustable sling yet who does not feel the need of its being very speedily detachable. This strap fastens at its forend with a strong brass sling button. A removable brass buckle permits length adjustment. Furnished in top-grain unoiled russet cowhide in ¾", ⅞", 1", and 1¼" widths.

Price ¾", unoiled only $0.75
Price 1", unoiled only 1.00
Price 1¼", unoiled only 1.25

THE "QUICK ADJUSTING" CARRYING SLING STRAP

The "Quick Adjusting" carrying strap is supplied with two hooks which permit instantaneous attaching or detaching, thus being ideally suited to the hunter and wilderness traveler who does not regularly use a sling strap, but who must be able to carry his gun with minimum encumberance and have his hands free though the gun must be ready for instant use. This strap is suitable equally well for either rifle or shotgun. The strap itself is adjustable and available only in 1" widths and oil tanned finish.

PROPERT'S LEATHER AND SADDLE SOAP

Unsurpassed preparation for cleaning leather straps, gun cases, etc. Restores life, making it soft and pliable.

Price, ½ pound can.....50c

LEATHER CLEANING SOLUTION

This is very good for softening and restoring life to leather. It will improve the looks and bring life to leather slings, gun cases, etc.

Price per 8 ounce can........$1.00

SLING STRAP BUTTON

Suitable for most slings. Made of steel, dull black finish. Outside width, ⅜"; diameter, 7/16".

Price, per pair 25c

SLING STRAP KEEPER

Wedged shaped, 1½" long, 1¼" wide. Maximum thickness 7/16". Made of best rubber. Prevents slipping.

Price 25c

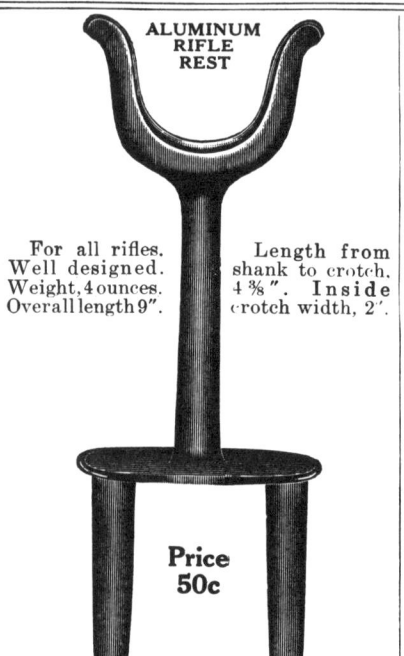

ALUMINUM RIFLE REST

For all rifles. Well designed. Weight, 4 ounces. Overall length 9". Length from shank to crotch, 4⅜". Inside crotch width, 2".

Price 50c

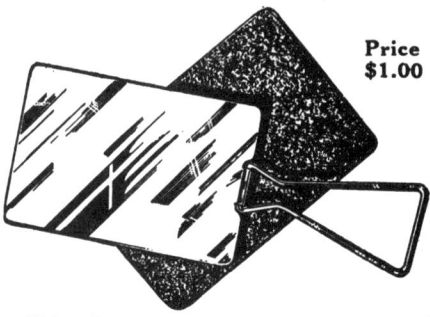

STAINLESS STEEL MIRROR

Price $1.00

This mirror has been especially designed for outdoor use and hard knocks which would quickly ruin any ordinary mirror. It is made of thin chromium plated steel, polished to a mirror surface on *both* sides, giving the same sharpness, and thinness without distortion as a fine glass mirror.

This mirror measures 3⅝" x 5¼", and is fitted with a hinged rest, permitting it to be stood either upright or sideways or to be hung on a nail, a branch or in fact almost anywhere.

Each mirror is supplied with an imitation alligator leather case, and being extremely compact and practically indestructible, can be carried in the pocket, or baggage without fear of damage.

MINIMUM SHIPPING ORDER $1.00

AMERICA'S GREAT GUN HOUSE

STOEGER'S FIRST AID KITS

POCKET KIT

This compact, convenient equipment is also ideal for Sportsmen, Campers, Boy Scouts and Travellers.

LIST OF CONTENTS
- 2—"Vaporole" Aromatic Ammonia
- 2—"Vaporole" Iodine, min. 10
- 1—"Tabloid" Bandage Boric Compress, 2 in. x 2 in.
- 2—"Tabloid" Adhesive Boric Compresses, Waterproof, 1 in. x 1 in.
- 1—Tube of "Borofax" Boric Acid Ointment, 5 gm., with eye-tip
- 1—Adhesive Plaster, ½ in. x 1 yd.
- 1—"Tabloid" Pleated Compressed Bandage, 2½ in. x 3 yds.
- 1—Tube of "Tannafax" Tannic Acid Jelly
- 1—Direction Card

Measurements: 4 x 2½ x ⅞ in.
Weight, complete, 3 oz.

Price $1.00

WOOD'S EMERGENCY CASE

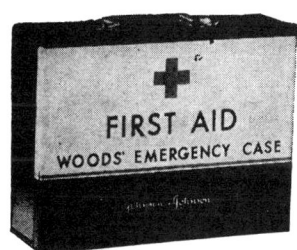

Especially designed for camps, shooting clubs, gunsmiths shops. Size 9x7½x3. Contains an adequate quantity of the most essential First Aid Products.

- 1—Red Cross Bandage 1 inch x 10 yards
- 3—Red Cross Bandages 2 inch x 10 yards
- 2—Cotton Roller Bandages 2 inch x 6 yards
- 2—Pkgs. Red Cross Gauze 1 yard
- 1—Pkg. Red Cross Cotton 1 ounce
- 1—Waterproof Adhesive ½ inch x 5 yards
- 1—Bottle Iodine 1 ounce
- 1—Bottle Aromatic Ammonia 1 ounce
- 1—Pair Scissors
- 1—Pair Tweezers
- 2—Envs. Cotton Wound Applicators 6's
- 1—Handbook of First Aid
- 1—Tube Joncolia 1½ ounce
- 1—Burn Dressing Packet
- 1—Buckle Tourniquet
- 1—First Aid for Wounds Packet
- 1—Box Waterproof Band Aid 25¢ size

Price $5.25

SNAKE BITE KIT
(SUCTION TYPE)

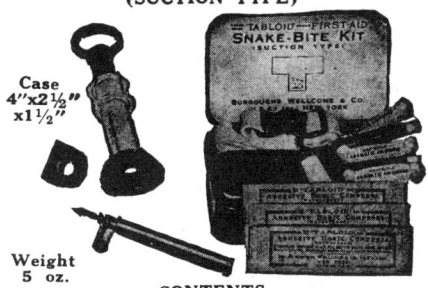

Case 4"x2½"x1½"
Weight 5 oz.

CONTENTS
- 1—Plunger Type Glass Suction Syringe
- 1—Large Rubber Suction Cup (Will cover two fang holes up to 1" apart)
- 1—Small Curved Rubber Suction Cup (For bites on fingers or toes)
- 1—"Tabloid" Tourniquet
- 1—Lancet with all metal handle
- 3—"Vaporole" Iodine, min. 10
- 3—"Vaporole" Aromatic Ammonia
- 3—"Tabloid" Adhesive Boric Compresses

Price $4.25

SUPER POCKET KIT

WELDED STEEL CASE

Size 5¼"x3½"x1½"

Weight 14 oz.

This compact kit will stand rough handling and provides an excellent assortment of standard first aid products.

CONTENTS
- 2—"Tabloid" Bandage Boric Compresses, 2 in.
- 16—"Tabloid" Adhesive Boric Compresses
- 6—"Vaporole" Iodine, min. 10
- 3—"Vaporole" Aromatic Ammonia
- 1—Tube "Tannafax" Tannic Acid Jelly
- 1—Tube "Borofax" (Borated Ointment) 5 gram, (with eye tip)
- 1—Tourniquet

Price $2.50

"PAC-KIT"

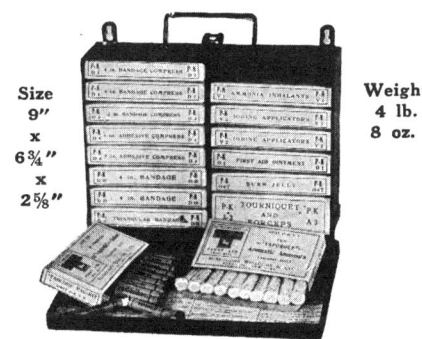

Size 9" x 6¾" x 2⅝"

Weight 4 lb. 8 oz.

FOR THE SMALL SHOP
- 2—4 in. Bandage Compress
- 1—2 in. Bandage Compress
- 2—1 in. Adhesive Compress, Waterproof
- 2—4 in. Bandage (with two Safety-Pins)
- 1—Triangular Bandage, 40 in. (with two Safety-Pins)

- 1—"Borofax" Boric Acid Ointment (with eye-tip), 5 gm.
- 1—"Vaporole" Ammonia Inhalants
- 2—"Vaporole" Iodine Applicators
- 1—Tourniquet and Forceps
- 1—Wire Splint
- 1—"Tannafax" Tannic Acid Jelly

Price $9.10

AUTO KIT

Ideal for campers, motorists, hunters, etc.

Electrically-welded steel case with baked enamel finish and fitted with khaki canvas cover.

LIST OF CONTENTS
- 1—Splinter Forceps
- 1—First-Aid Snake-Bite Outfit (B. W. & Co.)
- 1—Pair of Scissors
- 1—Box of "Vaporole" Iodine, min. 10
- 1—Box of "Vaporole" Aromatic Ammonia
- 2—"Tabloid" Pleated Compressed Bandages, 1 in. x 6 yds.
- 2—"Tabloid" Pleated Compressed Bandages, 2½ in. x 6 yds.
- 1—"Tabloid" Absorbent Gauze, 1 yd.
- 1—"Tabloid" Adhesive Boric Compresses, 1 in. x 3 in. (Box of 12)
- 1—"Tabloid" Bandage Boric Compresses, 4 in. x 4 in.
- 2—"Tabloid" Bandage Boric Compresses, 2 in. x 2 in.
- 1—Adhesive Plaster, 1 in. x 1 yd.
- 1—Tube of "Tannafax" Tannic Acid Jelly, ¾ oz.
- 1—Tube of "Borofax" Boric Acid Ointment (with eye-tip), ½ oz.
- 1—"Tabloid" "Empirin" (Acetylsalicylic Acid) Compound
- 1—Tourniquet

Measurements: 7⅝x4¼x2 in.
Weight (approx.), 1½ lb.

Price $9.00

FIRST AID KIT

Indispensable to hunters and sportsmen. Comes in a small container of 7¼x5¼x1¼ size. Convenient to carry in the pocket and contains the following items:

- 3—Red Cross Bandages 1 inch x 10 yards
- 1—Pkg. Red Cross Gauze ½ yard
- 1—Pkg. Red Cross Cotton ¼ ounce
- 1—Waterproof Adhesive ½ inch x 2½ yards
- 1—Bottle Mercurochrome ⅛ ounce
- 1—Bottle Aromatic Ammonia ⅛ ounce
- 1—Pair Scissors
- 1—Env. Cotton Wound Applicators 6's
- 1—First Steps to First Aid Folder
- 1—Tube of Joncolia ¼ ounce
- 6—Waterproof Band-Aid
- 2—Paper Drinking Cups.

Price $1.00

BE PREPARED FOR ANY EVENTUALITY

ALL WOOL HUNTING SHIRTS

Stoeger all-wool flannel shirts are made in weights to suit a hunter's requirements in all seasons of the year. He has a choice of colors, and a selection of patterns; plaid, plain and checked. These shirts are all made roomy and comfortable, and both wear and color are guaranteed to give complete satisfaction. Order your shirts from Stoeger today!

STYLE C-244
Price $6.50

STYLE H-283
Price $5.50

STYLE E-231
Price $5.50

STYLE S-364
Price $6.00

STYLE Z-274
Price $5.50

HEAVYWEIGHT OR LIGHTWEIGHT SHIRTS FOR COMFORTABLE OUTDOOR WEARING

STOEGER SHIRTS IN THESE FIVE STYLES

Style Z-274—All Wool Medium weight Flannel Shirt. Zipper pullover model. Red and Black. Price $5.50

Style E-231—All Wool Heavy weight Flannel Shirt. Gray Diagonal Cloth. Button Pullover Model. Price $5.50

Style C-244—Medium weight Wool Red and Black Hunting Shirt. Button coat style with double back forming game pocket. Price ...$6.50

Style H-283—Medium weight All Wool Black and White and Red and Black Hunting Shirt. Button Coat Model. Price $5.50

Style S-364—Fine All Wool Red and Black Flannel Sport Shirt. Button Coat Style. May also be had in Black and White and Green and Black. Price $6.00

CORRECT SIZES FOR MEN AND BOYS

Real COLD WEATHER FRIENDS

VIRGIN WOOL HUNTING COATS

Style 296-35—Women's all wool hunting coat. Red and Black double breasted model, with belt, two side pockets and two breast pockets. A fine, warm, comfortable coat for general outdoor wear. Please state size when ordering. Price. $14.00

ALL WOOL MACKINAW COAT

Style 293-38—All Wool Rainproofed 32-ounce Mackinaw Coat. Full-Lined with Suedecloth. Concealed buttons on front. Hand warmer pockets and large side pockets. Price...........$14.00

RAINPROOFED COAT

Style 291-55—All Wool Rainproofed 26-ounce Mackinaw Coat. Full-lined with Suedecloth. Large pockets including hand-warmers. Price....$12.50

LONG MODEL HUNTING COAT

Style 293-31—Long Model Red and Black Hunting Coat. Made of 32-ounce All Wool Mackinaw. Back lined with Suedecloth making game pocket. Hand warmer pockets. Price....$10.00

WOMEN'S LACED BREECHES

Style 296-77 — Women's laced-leg hunting breeches. All wool. Red and black. Made to match Style 296 Women's hunting coat. Have suspender buttons and belt loops, roomy front and hip pockets. Price......$9.50

PANT WITH WORSTED CUFF

Style 95—Pant with Worsted Cuff. All Wool Rainproofed. Zipper Fly. Large strong pockets.
Price 293-95 32-ounce cloth......$7.50
Price 291-95 26-ounce cloth......$7.00

LACED LEG BREECHES

Style 79—Laced Leg Breeches. All Wool Rainproofed. Zipper Fly.
Price 293-79 32ounce cloth......$7.50
Price 291-79 26-ounce cloth......$7.00

YOU WON'T MIND THE RAIN....

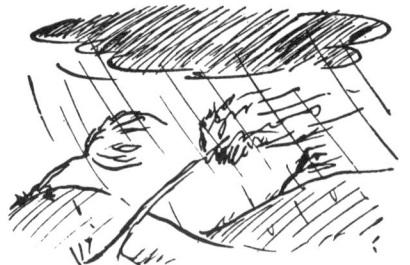

IN THESE WATERPROOFED HUNTING COATS AND TROUSERS

First in the line-up for sportwear comes this waterproofed cloth developed to combat the sportsman's greatest enemy to comfort . . . rain. As nearly waterproof as cloth can be without being rubberized. This cloth comes in olive brown and roseberry green shades, repels rain, sleet and snow and maintains healthful ventilated body warmth.

WOOL LINED PARKA

Style 9-01—Wool lined Parka made of Duxbak cloth with all-wool lining, and zipper front; has three roomy pockets and hood which can be dropped back when not in use. Price $12.50

WOMEN'S HUNTING COAT

Style 2-16—Women's Duxbak hunting coat. Made of rainproofed Duxbak cloth. Double, except under sleeve. Three button front. Large side pockets. Price..................$8.50

DUCKSHOOTER'S PARKA

Style 41-19—Duckshooter's Parka. Made of Rainproofed Duck and lined with Wool Flannel. Knee Length. Zipper front. Price..................$13.50

BIRDSHOOTER'S HUNTING PANTS

Style 72 and 73—Birdshooter's Pant with Worsted Cuff at ankle. Double front and seat.
Price Duxbak style
2-72 ....$5.50
Price Utica Duck style
41-73 ....$3.25

Style 2-69—Women's Birdshooter's Model Hunting Pants of Rainproof Duxbak Cloth. Zipper Closure.
Price $5.50

Style 2-68—Women's Hunting Trouser. Made of Rainproofed Duxbak Cloth. Zipper Closure. Price......$5.00

Style 95—Worsted Cuff Pant. Made in a number of Woolen cloths. Very comfortable style.
Price (252-95 20-ounce
Forestry) $12.00
Price (268-95 16-ounce
Forestry) $9.50

UP-TO-DATE STYLES

STOEGER HUNTING CLOTHES

WEAR LONGER AND FEEL MORE COMFORTABLE

These hunting togs give more than the fundamental requirements of serviceability and lasting quality. They give fitting comfort and up-to-date styles. Stoeger's wide selection of modern sportswear is the answer to every question of what is best in outdoor clothing.

SKEET SHOOTER'S COAT

Style 09—Skeet Shooter's Coat. Made in Navy, Light Blue, and Army Drab fine mercerized Twill. Worsted insert in back for comfort. Price..................$7.50

RIFLE SHOOTER'S COAT

Rifle Shooter's Coat—Style 06 as shown has worsted inserts in back. Style 26 does not have these inserts. Bi-swing back on both coats.
Price 3-06.................$8.50   Price 15-26.................$7.00

COAT WITH BLOODPROOF POCKETS

Style 41-21—Hunting Coat with Bloodproof Pocket and all regular Hunting Coat pockets. Roomy pockets. Freedom of action. Rainproofed. Price..................$6.50

HUNTING COAT

Style 2-10—Duxbak Hunting Coat. The Standard Model Duxbak Coat. Made of Rainproofed Duxbak Cloth with all the regular pockets. Cut full and roomy. Double throughout except under sleeve. Price..................$8.50

FINEST QUALITY HUNTING COATS

COMFORTABLE HUNTING CLOTHES

CRUISER COAT

Style 29—Cruiser Coat. Made of 16-ounce and 20-ounce Forestry Cloth. Double back forming game pocket.
Price 252-29 20-ounce cloth....$19.50
Price 268-29 16-ounce cloth.... 17.00

PRACTICAL CAPS TO MATCH YOUR HUNTING CLOTHES

Style 41-H — Reversible Red Top Cap. Made of Rainproofed Duck with inside band. Price......$.75

Style 2-D—Duxbak Deerstalker's Cap. Made with red reversible crown and inside band for cold weather wear.
Price $1.50

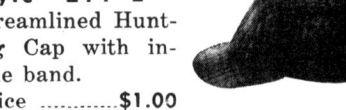

Style 271-L—Streamlined Hunting Cap with inside band.
Price $1.00

Style Stag. Red Leather Hunting cap. Made with inside band.
Price $1.75

Style 271-D—Reversible Red Top Hunting Cap with inside band for cold weather. Rainproofed.
Price $1.25

THESE SOLVE THE GAME BAG PROBLEM

Style 40-R-27—Game Bag made of Rainproofed Duck with Bloodproof Pocket. Price $3.25

Style 2-07 — Duxbak Bloodproof Pocket Coat. Pocket may be dropped down to sit on leaving a full sized pocket for carrying. Detachable hood is $1.50 extra. Price....................$9.00

ALL WOOL SOCKS

Half Hose. Wool Core yarn socks- Alaska-Fleece-lined gray or white.
Price $1.00
Rib Legged Hunting Socks. Wool Core yarn.
Price Otter, Gray, White or Tan $1.25
Price Ranger, Gray or Camel.... .65
Price Quail, Gray or Camel........ .65

STYLED FOR APPEARANCE AND COMFORT

IMPROVE YOUR SHOOTING
RUGGED GARMENTS FOR ROUGH OUTDOOR WEAR

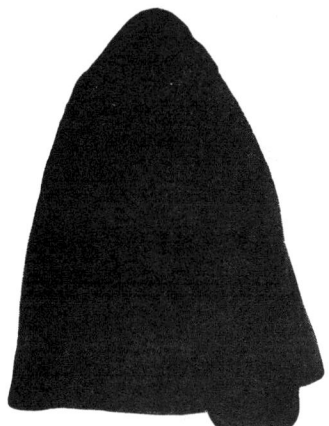

WOOL COAT

Woolly Coat. Made of patented cloth. Cotton back with wool face knitted into the backing. Two patch pockets. A practical coat for general outdoor wear.

Made of a special Knitted Fabric with long pile. Light weight but warm and comfortable.
Price $12.00

HUNTING TROUSERS

Style 41-98 Hunting Trousers made with Double Front and Seat with large strong pockets. Just the trousers for rough wear for both hunting and general outdoor use.

Price $3.50

DUXBAK LACED BREECHES

Style 2-70 Duxbak Laced Leg Breeches. Cut full and roomy of Rainproofed Duxbak Cloth with double seat and knees. Large strong pockets. These breeches are adapted for wear with high boots or stockings and are ideal for hunting where freedom of leg action is necessary. Price $5.50

DUXBAK TROUSERS

Style 2-71 Duxbak Trousers. Made of Rainproofed Duxbak cloth with double seat and knees. Large strong pockets. These trousers are light weight and practical for rainy weather hunting. Price $5.00

LACED LEG BREECHES

Style 79 Laced Leg Breeches. All Wool Rainproofed. Zipper Fly. Because these breeches are the finest quality available for the price they will give long, comfortable wear. Price 281-79, 24-ounce Diagonal $6.75
Price 294-79 32-ounce Double & Twist $8.50

SEE STOEGER FOR FINE HUNTING CLOTHES

CANVAS HUNTING CLOTHES

SLEEVELESS JACKET

A sportsman's jacket demanded by the Hunter and Fisherman for its many qualities. Made of closely woven pliable Army Duck. All-around rubberized game pocket as well as four additional patch pockets. Two-needle, lap-felled seams. Bar tacked at all points of strain.

No. K-2246 made exactly like above except of heavier Army Duck and equipped with sixteen elastic shell loops for 12, 16, and 20 gauge shells.

No. K-2245 $3.06
No. K-2246   3.69

Regular sizes 34 to 46. 10% extra, sizes 48 & 50

ZIPPER HUNTING COAT

A quality coat of many features for the duck hunter. Genuine Army Duck, **guaranteed waterproof or your money back.** Four cut-in shell pockets. All-around game pocket with front and rear openings. Rubber recoil pad. Shell loops. Corduroy storm collar. Two-button sleeves. Two-needle, lap-felled seams. A roomy coat throughout. A special treated fabric that is soft and pliable.

No. K-2225 Regular sizes 34 to 46 **$10.74**
10% extra, sizes 48 & 50

LIGHTWEIGHT COAT

A mighty good coat where light weight is essential and quality a necessity. Low in price—high in workmanship. Closely woven waterproofed Duck. Rubberized all-around game pocket. Two large shell pockets, hand warming pockets and corduroy collar. 16 shell loops.

No. K-2222

Regular sizes 34 to 46

$4.88

10% extra, sizes 48 and 50

DOUBLE DUTY COAT

An excellent value made of hard twisted water-repellent Army Duck. Brush Brown Color. All-around washable game pocket. Leather shoulder pads. Corduroy lined collar. Two large shell pockets and shell loops. Free-swing action back. Two-needle, lap-felled seams.

No. K-2233

Regular sizes 36 to 46

$7.86

10% extra, sizes 48 & 50

FOR AMERICAN SPORTSMEN

GAME CARRIER
No. K-2210

No. K-2210 Game Carrier made in two qualities for the Hunter and Fisherman. Rubberized waterproof Duck. All-around game pocket. Three large outside pockets and four pockets in flaps. Adjustable web strap shoulder braces.

No. K-2209—Exactly like No. K-2210 but of slightly lighter weight waterproofed Army Duck with fewer pockets.

No. K-2210 Small, Medium, Large $2.96
No. K-2209 Small, Medium, Large 2.40

WOOL BOTTOM PANTS
No. K-2219

An All Wool Anklet or Bottom. Made of heavy Brush Brown Army Duck, thoroughly waterproof treated, rubberized seat and knee, two back, two swing and one watch pocket. Seven loops for belt. Long front and back rise. Five buttonfly. Inside pant curtain. Cut full to measure. 31-in. inseam. 10% extra, sizes 46 to 50.

No. K-2219   Sizes 30 to 44 $4.84

HUNTING JACKET

The Southern Hunter appreciates this quality jacket for field and stream. A fine, closely woven Duck with soft pliable Cotton Moleskin sleeves. Wool wristlets. Three-button model without collar. Nicely tailored, close fitting and snappy looking. All-around rubberized game pocket with two large bellows pockets and two small pockets, all with flaps. Two-needle, lap-felled seams.

No. K-2244   Regular sizes 34 to 46 $5.00
10% extra, sizes 48 & 50

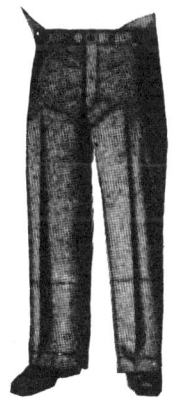

HUNTER'S PANTS
No. K-2216

Waterproofed Army Duck Pants. Marsh Grass Color. Rubberized double seat and knee. Standard full cut patterns. Closely double-stitched seams. Five-button fly. Extra full seat. Long front and back riser. 32-in. inseam with 1½-in. cuff. Five pockets. Loops for belt. Cuff turned up and fully bar tacked.

No. K-2216 Regular sizes
  30 to 44 ....$3.92
10% extra, sizes 46 to 50

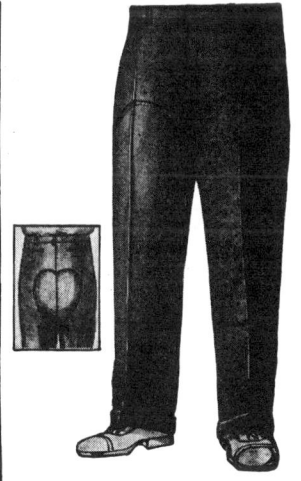

ELASTIC BREECHES
No. K-2229

Roomy, peg top, waterproofed Breeches. Brush Brown Army Duck. Rubberized double seat and knee. Long front and back riser. 26-in. inseam. Five-button fly. Five pockets. Belt loops. Elastic web bottom.

No. K-2229 Regular sizes 29
  to 44 ....$3.92
10% extra, sizes 46 to 50

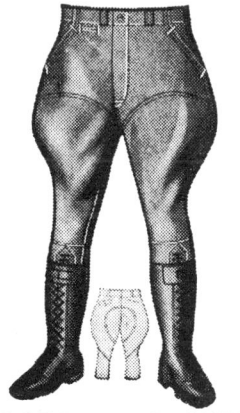

LACE-LEG BREECHES
No. K-2217

A full cut, waterproofed Breeches of Brush Brown Army Duck. Rubberized double seat and knee. Long riser in front and rear. Five-button fly. Two front pockets, 2 rear pockets and one watch pocket. 26-in. inseam. Loops for belt.

No. K-2217 Regular sizes
  30 to 44 ....$3.92
10% extra, sizes 46 to 50

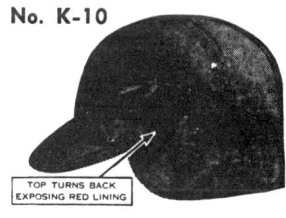

No. K-10

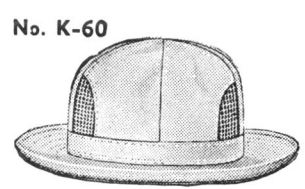

No. K-60

CAPS AND HATS

Made of light weight Brown waterproofed Twill. Finely tailored. Six quarter crown.. Two ventilated openings. Taped seams. Full 2½ in. closely stitched brim.
No. K-10 Sizes 6⅞ to 7⅝ $1.10

Waterproofed Duck in Brush Brown color. Six quarter crown. Reinforced stitched visor. Fully lined throughout. Fur lined ear flaps with red inner lining for the deer hunter.
No. K-60 Sizes 6¾ to 7⅝ $.92

WATERPROOFED SHOOTING COATS

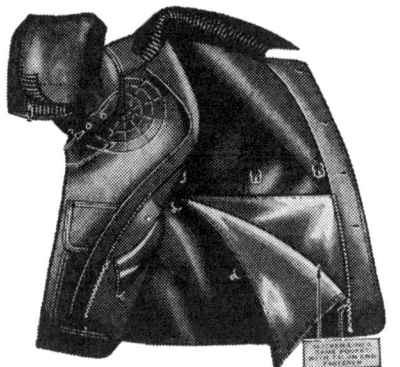

SANITARY GUN COAT
No. K-2247

A double coat made of the best quality waterproof treated Army Duck. Brush Brown Color. Patented slicker-lined washable game pocket with Talon fastener. Sponge rubber recoil pad. Quick action, free-swing back. Horsehide leather, padded shoulders. Two-button corduroy cuffs. Large storm collar. Two large shell pockets, two breast pockets with flaps. Lap-felled, double-stitched seams. Strain points bar tacked.

No. K-2247 Regular sizes 34 to 46 **$9.44**
10% extra, sizes 48 & 50

FEATHERWEIGHT COAT
No. K-5105

Combed Poplin is the new cloth that makes a fine garment better. Zelan finish, a finish that is water-repellent. Will launder or dry clean. Sand Tan color.

Fully lined with light weight, aeroplane cloth. All-around Talon fastened, slicker-lined game pocket.

No. K-5105 Sports Coat **$9.44**
Regular sizes 36 to 46—10% extra, 48 & 50
No. K-5107 Breech to match **$5.82**
Regular sizes 30 to 44—10% extra, 46 to 50

SKEET JACKET
No. K-2224

The celebrated "Grand American" light tan whipcord Trap or Skeet Coat. Finely tailored and expertly made to please the most discriminating shooter. Sanforized pre-shrunk diagonal fabric. Double front. Free-swing back. Padded recoil shoulder. Two cut-in pockets. Removable buttons to permit laundering. Reinforced, full length shoulder straps. Lap-felled, two needle stitched seams. A quality garment in every respect.

No. K-2224 Regular sizes 34 to 46 **$5.96**
10% extra, sizes 48 & 50

REVERSIBLE COAT
No. K-2251

Two complete coats in one at one low price. Red dyed Duck on one side—Brush Brown Army Duck, the other. Guaranteed fast colors. Large all-around game pocket with front and rear entrances. Four shell pockets, breast pockets and full corduroy collar. Double-stitched, lap-felled seams. A combination coat for the hunter who goes into the woods.

No. K-2251 Regular sizes 36 to 46 **$8.88**
10% extra, sizes 48 & 50

ALL WEATHER COAT
No. K-2254

Genuine Army Duck outside with Brown Moleskin lining. All-around slicker-lined game pocket with front and rear entrances. Two hand-warming pockets, two shell pockets and corduroy storm collar.

No. K-2254 Regular sizes 36 to 46 **$8.88**
10% extra, sizes 48 & 50

SPORTSMAN'S COAT
No. K-2259

Made of a closely woven, hard twisted Army Duck, every fibre of which has been thoroughly saturated with a weather-resisting, water-repellent compound. Free-swing action back. Double cloth over sleeves and shoulders. Two large pockets, two small pockets and corduroy storm collar. Ventilated gussets. Two-button sleeves. All-around sanitary game pocket.

No. K-2259 Regular sizes 34 to 46 **$6.84**
10% extra, sizes 48 & 50

ENJOY YOUR TRIP WITH THE PROPER OUTFIT

10-X SHOOTING COATS AND JACKETS

10-X Shooting Coats are especially designed, tailored and manufactured by expert shooters who know what shooters want and need. They have everything that the ideal shooting coat should have . . . correct padding, cool, durable cloth, and plenty of room where you want it. They have made a definite hit with shooters from the first day they were worn. Moderately priced.

10-X ARISTOCRAT SHOOTING COAT

Made of sanforized light weight, fine wearing khaki cloth, olive drab shade. Heavily padded with wool felt and covered with soft chrome tanned hide leather; patch pockets with small micrometer pocket on the breast.

Price $6.50
With talon front on special order only 7.00

10-X ARISTOCRAT SKEET JACKET

Popular because of its superior quality and low price. It is made of light weight khaki cloth, olive drab shade. Fitted and belted back. Set in expanding shoulder, suspended pockets with corners leather reinforced. Very fine for either Skeet or Trap shooting.

Price $5.50

10-X IMPERIAL SKEET JACKET

Made of light weight, cool sanforized fast color government cloth, caribou shade. The butt pad is three thicknesses of quilted cloth. It will not wrinkle. Fitted for free arm movement, belted back, set in tailored shoulder, suspended pockets. For Sheet or Trap.

Price $10.00

10-X IMPERIAL SHOOTING COAT

Made of light weight, cool durable sanforized vat dyed fast color government cloth, caribou shade. Adequately padded and covered with selected soft horsehide leather. Belted back with handy back pocket. Pockets reinforced at corners with leather. Button flap micrometer pocket on left breast. Talon fastener front at no extra cost if so ordered.

Price $9.00

WINDPROOF VEST

Reindeer
Light Brown
Dark Brown

Even Sizes
34-46

Model No. 1049

Price
$1.75

Made of Weatherproof Suede material with bear fleece lining. Comfortable fitting, with four ball and socket fasteners down the front. Two patch pockets of contrasting shade.

Made in Light or Dark Brown and Reindeer shades.

ADIRONDACK HUNTING COAT

Made with Heavy Bear Fleece Lining

Even Sizes
34-36

Model No. 377

Price
$4.95

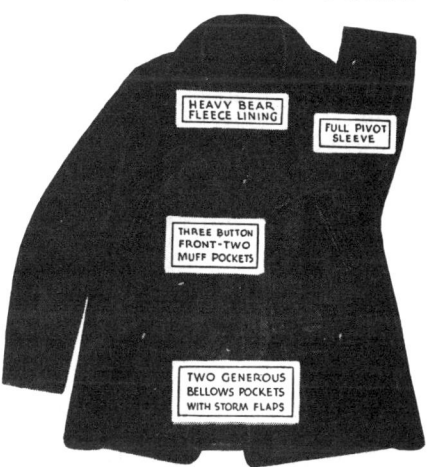

Coat is made with full pivot sleeve—three buttons front—two muff pockets—two generous bellows pockets with storm flaps—wide open, clear vision, waterproof, bloodproof, game pocket with rubber lining.

Made in Reindeer or Red Material.

HUNTING BOOTS AND MOCCASINS

OLIVE DRAB ROB ROY

Flex-Weave Shock-Proof Insole. Extremely Popular Lightweight 15" High Hunting Shoe. Blue Ribbon quality compounds throughout—plain vamp — toe cap — strong reinforcements—back stay of special Tire Cord—"Strong-Grip" eyelets—heater finish—crepe sole. Made in one width only.

	Sizes	Price
ML730 Men's Crepe Sole	5–12	$6.25

O. D. DUCK HUNTERS' BOOT

For wear over Leather Shoes or Sheep Lined Shoes. The O. D. color in which this boot is made blends perfectly with marsh grass. A flexible instep strap and top strap are provided for fastening. Made in Hip height only, with a straight top. Net lined—no half sizes.

	Sizes	Price
MB575 Men's	6–12	$7.75

LEGGIN BOOT

Used by many sportsmen. Giving knee high protection, and eliminates the necessity of changing footwear when an emergency or quick change in weather demands waterproof protection.

All black with Patrol foot. Net lined. Plain edge. Heater finish. Red sole. British last. Whole sizes.

	Sizes	Price
MB956 Men's Short	6–13	$4.55

O. D. FLYWEIGHT BOOT

Flex-Weave Shock-Proof Insole. An extra lightweight, smart looking boot for sports wear. Inside laced harness fastens below the knee. Hard toe tip prevents injury to wearer's toes when worn in rocky streams.

Sporting height only. Net lined. Heater finish. Olive Drab.

	Sizes	Price
MB521 Cleated Sole	5–13	$7.75
MB527 Felt Sole	5–13	9.75

YUGO HUNTING SHOE—LEATHER TOP

New Flex-Weave Shock-Proof Insole. This leather top Hunting Shoe carries an L. L. Bean patented Tan Elk Top which will not become hard even after constant wetting and drying. Super-quality, rubber bottom with knurled, non-slipping crepe outsole, so light that it floats. Pressure cured. Ribbed vamp construction. Special back construction carefully shaped and reinforced to prevent heel chafing. Chrome leather lacing. Pull-on loop for ease in putting on. One width, heater finish. No Half Sizes.

	Sizes	Price
ML510 12 Men's—12"	5–12	$7.25
ML510 16 Men's—16"	5–12	8.50
WL510 12 Women's—12"	3–9	7.00

HUNTER'S MOCCASIN

This Moccasin represents a new high in shoes of this type for use in camp and country. It is made with raw cord soles which grip even on slippery surfaces. It is entirely hand sewn giving exceptionally great durability. The leather is of best quality mellow pebble grain, easy and soft on the foot. For added comfort this moccasin is made with built in arch support so that your feet are comfortable after an all day hike.

Price $3.95

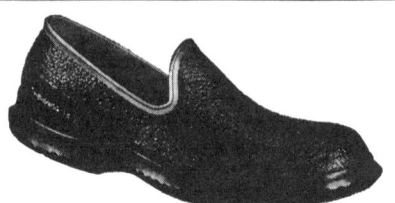

ROYAL PATROL

Tempered Rubber quality all-black work rubbers. Pigskin finish. Tire tread outsole. Heater finish. Made Storm and Hi-Cut. One width, no letter.

	Sizes	Price
MS171 Men's Storm	6–12	$1.95

O. D. SNUGLACE

Flex-Weave Shock-Proof Insole. A Blue Ribbon quality laced boot made in 12" and 16" heights. Snugleg is provided with a Shock-Proof insole and has the new "Flex-Weave" covering which lessens slipping of the foot back and forth in the boot as a result of better adherence to the sock. Carries lacing closure in front at top. Plain edge—heater finish—made F or FF width—net lining.

Made with plain edge sole.

	Sizes	Price
ML952 Men's O. D. 16" Plain Edge	6–12	$5.00

BE SURE TO SPECIFY SIZE WHEN ORDERING BOOTS OR MOCCASINS

AMERICA'S GREAT GUN HOUSE

STOEGER BOOTS

10 BIG FEATURES BUILT INTO EACH PAIR OF STOEGER BOOTS

Built-in Steel Arch Support
Oak Leather middle soles
Velvet leather insoles
Ventilated insoles
Barbour Stormtight
Hooks and Eyelets
Triple Stitched
Cork Cushioned
Goodyear Welt
Form Fitting

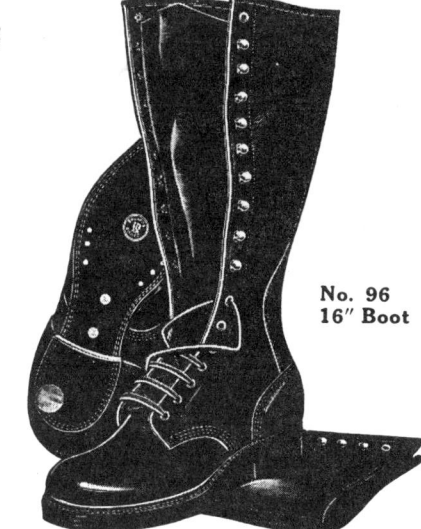

No. 96
16" Boot

No. 56 16" Boot

No. 56 and 66 BOOTS

Rugged long-wearing all-purpose boots. For real battleship durability and complete comfort at a moderate price these fine boots can't be beat. You can't buy a better boot for hunting, hiking or general all round every day wear. Both styles No. 56 (16") and No. 66 (18"), shown here are made with full length bellows tongue and soft mellow upper leather, triple stitched for added strength. They are as rugged as the Rockies and will wear like iron.

No. 56, 16", Price $6.95
No. 66, 18", Price 7.95

SIZES
All boots available in sizes 5 to 12 and width D, E, and EE. Specify size and width.
IMPORTANT

No. 106—10" LIGHTWEIGHT UPLAND GAME BOOT

This popular moccasin type boot was designed for those who want an extremely lightweight, all purpose boot. For bird hunting, squirrel shooting, rabbit hunting this Upland Game Boot is the leader. They are real "Featherweights" and as comfortable as a pair of bedroom slippers. No matter what price you have paid for a boot of this kind the fact is they could not give you more satisfaction or comfort than a pair of Stoegers Upland Game Boots. Made of dark brown mellow chrome waterproof leather, patented non-slip Raw Cord soles and heels.

Price $8.95

No. 96—16" BOOT

Made of the finest No. 1 grade dark brown chrome Veal leather. Only the choicest "Hand Sorted" leather soles are selected for the 16 inch boot. A newly patented "Waterproof" toe lining will keep your feet dry and comfortable. It is used exclusively and only in the 16 inch boot. Has double leather soles and leather heels. "Tops" in quality throughout.

Price $10.85

No. 36—12" BOOT

We are proud of this beautiful 12 inch boot. We know, too, that any man who wears them will be proud of them. For a genuine water-resisting boot they can't be beat. They are extremely rugged and as comfortable as an old pair of shoes. These quality boots are built like No. 66 shown on this page, except all eyelets. They are low priced and will give you extra long wear.

Price $6.75

BOOTS OF SHORTER HEIGHT

For those requiring a lower boot, we offer a boot identical to No. 36, except that it may be had in 10", 8", or 6".
No. 46, 10". Price .. $6.45
No. 86, 8". Price .. 5.95
No. 522, 6". Price .. 4.95

No. 63
18" Boot

No. 36
12" Boot

BE SURE TO SPECIFY SIZE WHEN ORDERING BOOTS OR CLOTHES

STOEGER'S CAMP EQUIPMENT

No. 367 LUNCH BAG

This bag is made of brown waterproof canvas and has an extra bag on front and comes with adjustable shoulder strap and loop for belt. It is an excellent carry-all for ammunition, fishing tackle, lunch, etc. Weight, 10 oz. Size, 12" x 10" x 2".

Price $2.50

No. 357 RUCK SACK

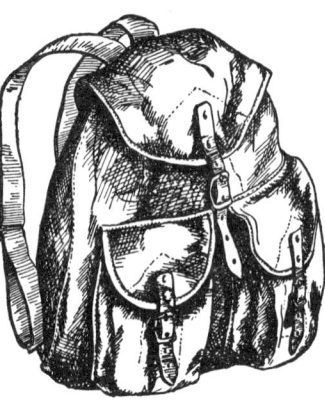

A necessity for mountain climbers and hikers. Made of forest green waterproof shelter duck. Top is closed by a cord through grommets and a flap covers the very small opening left. It is adjustable with leather shoulder straps and fastened to corner buckles of brass. Weight, 1¼ lbs.

Price $4.75

No. 362 CRUISER TOTE BAG

This bag is specially designed to be a combination Duffle bag and pack. It is supplied with an extra large pocket on the outside with flap. The bag is of oblong shape with double reinforced bottom. It comes with adjustable Indian tanned shoulder straps and inner drawstring throughout. Made of waterproof canvas measuring 27" high and 46" circumference.

No.	Wgt.	Price
362	2¾ lb.	$8.00
362A		$1.50

Tump line for above.

No. 362J JUNIOR CRUISER TOTE BAG

Smaller in size to the regular tote bag but of the same fine construction as the Cruiser Tote Bag. Size, 24" x 40" in circumference. Weight, 2¼ lbs.
Price $7.00

No. 358 ALPINE RUCK SACK

Made of same material and style as No. 357 Ruck Sack, but equipped with strong, adjustable web shoulder straps. A light and practical pack for week-end hikes. Weighs 1 lb. No. 358, 16½"x19", double pockets $3.50

No. 361 CROSS COUNTRY PACK

This bag is our most popular number. It is very roomy and has two pockets outside. It is made of 8 oz. waterproof khaki with adjustable Indian hand tanned shoulder straps. Weight is 2 lbs. Size, 18" x 22".

Price $6.00

No. 364 NORTHWESTERN PACK

A pack which is a favorite in the North Woods and is also called Poirer or Duluth pack made of heavy brown waterproof duck with shoulder straps of heavy Indian tanned leather. Weight, 3 lbs. Size, 28" x 28".

Price $8.50

No. 366 SCOUT PACK

Very popular with growing Girl Scouts made of forest green waterproof cloth with webbed straps. Very neat in appearance and adapted for a light load. Especially suitable for day hiking. Weight, 10 oz. Size, 14" x 14" x 3".

Price $2.00

No. 334 HOOKLESS HAVERSACK

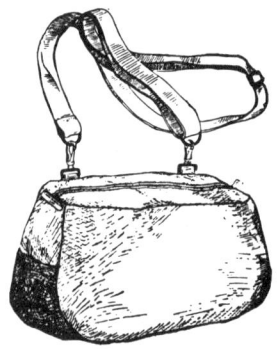

Especially recommended for the hunter fisherman or hiker. It is made of forest green shelter duck and has one outside bag pocket and one inside pocket besides the main body pack. It has Hookless Fastener across the top and reinforced leather bottom. Size 10" x 16" x 4½". It is furnished with detachable adjustable web shoulder straps. Weight, ½ lb.

Price $3.50

TELL YOUR FRIENDS ABOUT STOEGER'S CATALOG

STOEGER'S CAMP EQUIPMENT

SLEEPING ROBE

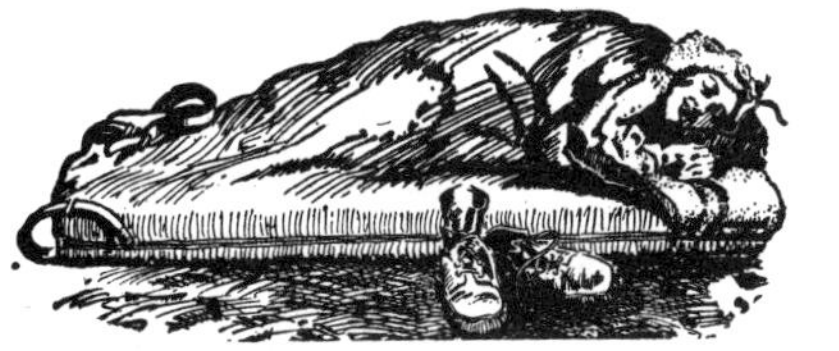

Here is a sleeping bag giving real comfort in freezing weather and weight is only 8½ lbs. It is Pure lambs wool interlined, tufted, with camel and wool blanket and forest green jeans cover. It rolls up to a minimum of space and has drawstring bag. Full size opened is 66x80" with Talon Fastener, full length and across the bottom.

Price for above........................**$26.00**

No. 202 same as above but with Pure Down Robe with wool flannel lining, size 36x84", weight 10 lbs.............. **55.00**

No. 200 the same sleeping bag particularly built with Hudson's Bay Down Robe good in sub-zero to 40° below zero. Weight 14½ lbs. Size 36x84". Price for same........................ **62.00**

OFFICER'S BED ROLL

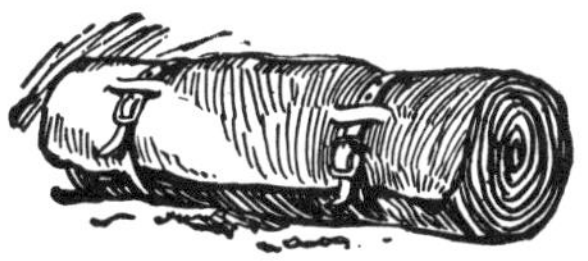

A very neat outfit made of heavy waterproof canvas on the bottom and lighter waterproof flaps on the ends. In one end are a series of wall pockets and at the other end a flap to hold in the blankets **and mattress or for use as a pillow holder.** Made of proper size to hold full length Kapoc Pad or Air Mattress and when rolled up the side ends are protected and have a frame with handle to carry and two webbing straps to fasten.

No.	Space	Weight	Price
219	30"x78"	7½ lbs.	**$14.50**

WATER BAGS

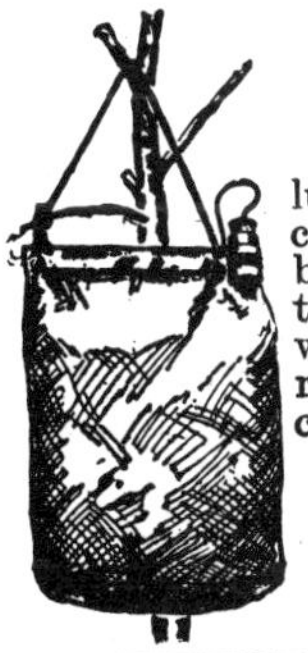

An item which is absolutely necessary for the **camper. It is light and can** be folded up very easily and takes a sufficient quantity of water according to the size required. It keeps the water cool and palatable.

No.	Size	Price
291	1 Gal.	**$1.35**
292	2½ Gal.	**1.70**
293	5 Gal.	**2.50**

MONEY BELT

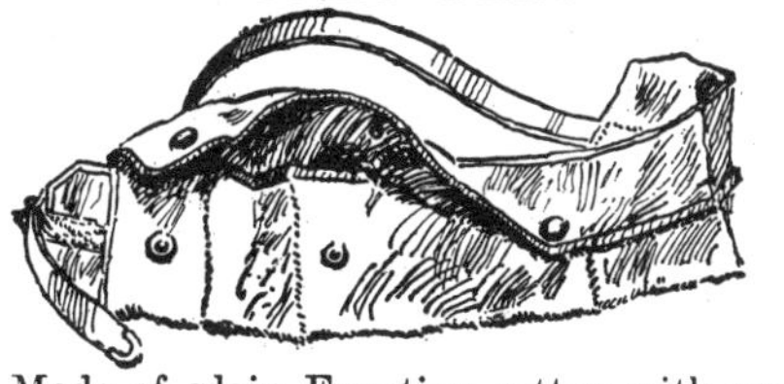

Made of plain Egyptian cotton with our extra light waterproof lining. Divisions for coin and separate pocket for bills. **Snap button flaps with webbing strap** and buckle adjustable to any waist measurement. For passport use we can add additional snap buttons.

No. 567, weight 4 ozs.................**$1.25**

BASINS

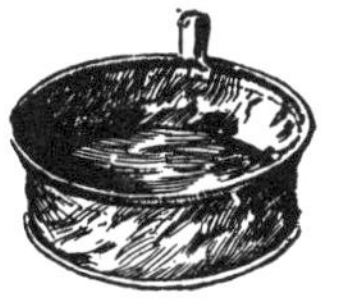

Always appreciated as it is extremely light, weighing only 7 oz. and holds sufficient water to clean vegetables and also can be used for many other purposes.

No.	Size	Price
296	7 Oz.	**$.85**

SPORTOTE UTILITY BAGS

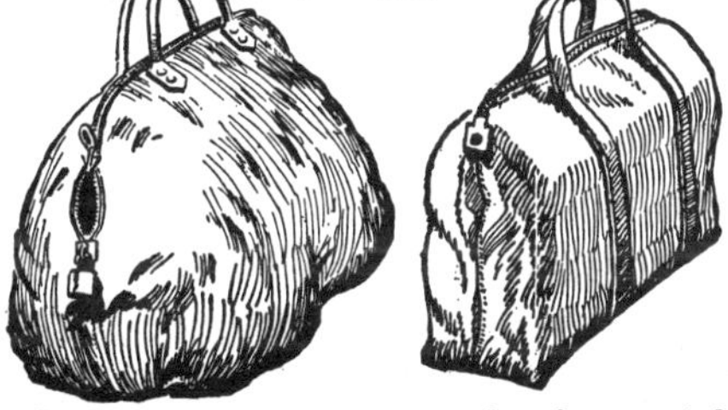

This convenient bag is made of a special waterproof duck, and closed by two Hookless Fasteners meeting at the top and locking. Equipped with leather handles. Four small pockets are stitched inside to hold the little things that are usually lost in the bottom. Excellent for the few extras needed by the fisherman, hunter or golfer.

No. 322 10" x 18" x 14" high. Weight, 1 lb. $3.75

Very convenient to carry shotgun shells or any small articles for the hunter or fisherman. Made of waterproof canvas, drab **color, with Talon Fastener.** Web handles extend under the bag giving extra strength. When half full, top can be folded down and package placed in bag.

No.	Size	Wgt.	Price
561	5"x8½"	7 Oz.	**$1.50**

TALON HOOKLESS FASTENER DUFFLE BAG

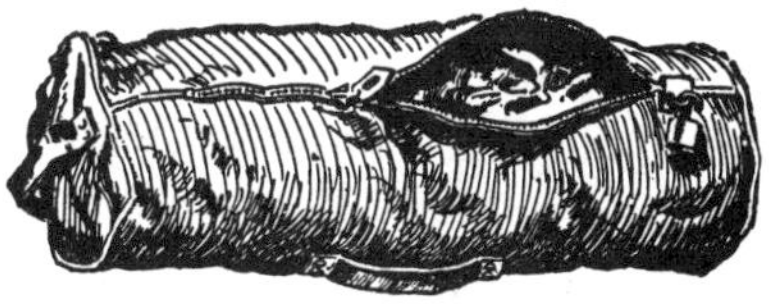

This is a great improvement having the patent Hookless Fastener device making it possible to open the bag the entire length. it is absolutely waterproof and with padlock which insures protection from tampering. It has two handles on both ends and side and made of the same material and workmanship as the regular Duffle Bag.

No.	Dia.		Length	Wgt.	Price
318A	9"	x	24"	1 lb.	**$2.90**
800	12"	x	24"	1½ lb.	**3.50**
318	12"	x	36"	1⅝ lb.	**3.85**
319	15"	x	36"	2 lb.	**4.50**
320	18"	x	36"	2⅝ lb.	**5.00**

NOTE: Padlock included on all of above bags.

DUFFLE BAGS

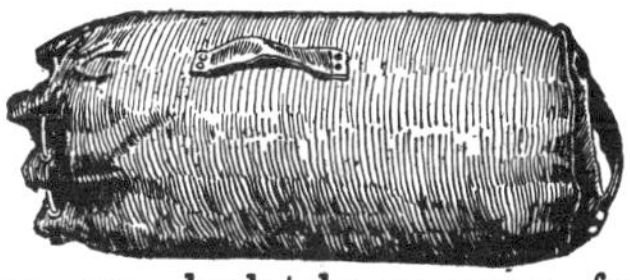

These are absolutely necessary for the camper to pack laundry and other items safely. These bags are made of brown waterproof duck, double seamed with handle provided on the bottom and side with extra patches inside of bag reinforced when strain comes. The handles are riveted on with copper rivets and burrs reinforced at riveting points by leather patches. An inside top or throat piece is tied up, preventing dust, dirt, and water entering. Top closed by rope drawn through grommets.

No.	Dia.		Length	Wgt.	Price
300	9"	x	24"	1 lb.	**$1.85**
301	12"	x	36"	1½ lb.	**2.70**
302	15"	x	36"	2⅛ lb.	**3.10**
303	18"	x	36"	2½ lb.	**3.75**
304	21"	x	36"	3 lb.	**4.50**
305	12"	x	42"	2 lb.	**2.90**
306	15"	x	42"	2⅜ lb.	**3.50**
307	18"	x	42"	3 lb.	**4.30**
308	21"	x	42"	3½ lb.	**5.00**

BUCKETS

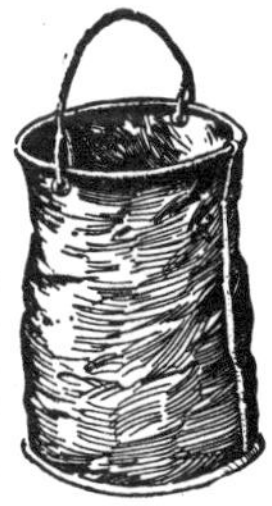

Specially designed for the hunter and camper to take two gallons of water. Made of best grade material and workmanship. Has galvanized iron ring inserted in top and spliced rope handle. Size 9½x11" folds down to ¾".

Price, as Illustrated......**$1.00**
Price, with Spout........ **1.50**

CHAIN LOCK

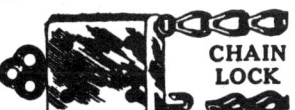

For closing and locking a duffle bag. It consists of a chain 20 inches long with padlock on the end, a hook on padlock engages a link on the chain. The chain is put through the grommets of the bag and drawn until the mouth of bag is closed, and then locked. Two keys are furnished.

No. 321, weight 5 ozs..........**$1.00**

PACK CLOTH

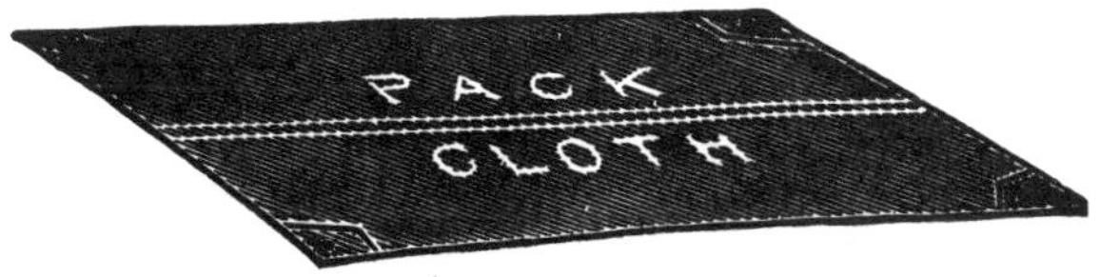

There are so many uses for a rectangular piece of waterproof cloth that at least one or many should be in every outfit. These pack cloths are made to be used with a tump line and are made of brown waterproof canvas for this purpose.

No.	Size	Wgt.	Price
348	5'6"x6'	1¾	**$2.85**
349	5'6"x7'	2½	**3.75**
349A	7' x8'	3½	**5.00**

Dynamo Pocket Lamp

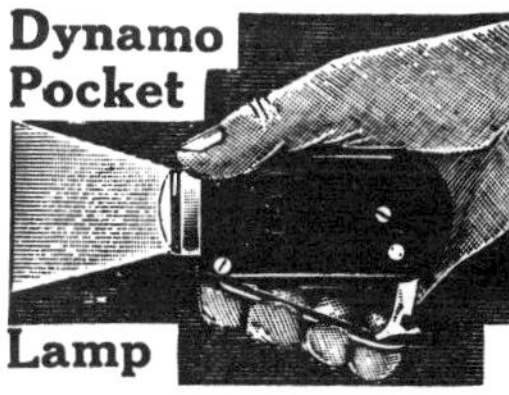

$5.50

Operates without batteries. While holding this flashlight in the hand a side lever is alternately pressed and released. This simple motion operates a small dynamo which supplies an electric current to the bulb. No batteries to wear out.

SEE PAGE 8, "HOW TO ORDER"

STOEGER'S CAMP EQUIPMENT

TARP TENT

BAKER OR SHELTER TENT

Here is a tent which appeals particularly to the hunter. The cloth of rectangular shape comes in handy in many other ways—not only as a tent but as dining fly, pack, cache cover, and ground sheet. The illustration shows three ways a paulin can be used. The dining fly covers 10'x12' on the ground, as a tent 6½' high, 7' wide, 7' deep, as a shelter 7'x13'.

No.	Space	Wgt.	Price	No.	Space	Wgt.	Price
45	13'x10'	9 lbs.	$33.00	107	13'x10'	10½ lbs.	$16.00
46	13'x10'	5 lbs.	28.00	108	13'x10'	5½ lbs.	14.00

This Baker or Shelter Tent is one of our most popular numbers. It can be arranged to give comfort in all kinds of weather. Extended fly gives room for working, eating and sitting. Tying the fly down makes the tent absolutely tight. A fire under the fly warms the whole tent amply on a cool evening.

No.	Width-Depth	Front Hgt.	Back Hgt.	Wgt.	Talon Hookless Bobbinet	Price
47	7⅓x7⅓	7	2½	10½	$9.25	$65.00
48	9¾x7⅓	7	2½	12½	12.00	75.00
49	6½x6½	5	1½	7	8.50	42.00
50	8x6½	6	2	9	8.50	58.00
51	7½x7½	7	2½	13½	9.25	38.00
52	10x7½	7	2½	16	12.00	42.00
49A	6½x6½	5	2½	7½	6.00	23.00
50A	8x8	7	2½	11½	10.00	32.00

MINER'S TENT

HIKER'S TENT

A very simple and strongly constructed tent. Only one single center pole is required. This tent will stand up well in any storm. This is very light in weight for the amount of ground which it will cover and for this reason it is preferred by the plainsman or miner still today.

No.	Width-Depth	Hgt.	Wgt.	Price
91	7⅓x7⅓	7	7¼	$48.00
92	9¾x9¾	8½	9¾	62.00
93	8x8	7½	6¾	42.00
94	9½x9½	8½	8¾	52.00
95	7½x7½	7	10¾	24.00
96	10x10	8½	14¾	32.00
96A	6½x6½	7	6½	17.00
96B	8x8	7½	8¾	22.00

This tent is to the advantage of those taking in nature by hiking as it can be carried in two parts. It is light in weight for those walking and carrying their shelter. It is especially recommended for Boy Scouts as their staffs can be used as poles. No ridge pole is required.

No.	Width-Depth	Hgt.	Wgt.	Price
112	5x7	3½	3½	$10.50
113	6x8	4½	4¾	14.50

NOTE: All tents are supplied in neat bag. Poles and Stakes extra.

GOOD EQUIPMENT MAKES CAMP LIFE ENJOYABLE

STOEGER'S CAMP EQUIPMENT

You will enjoy your outdoor life only if you have the right equipment. More than once we have heard people say "We had to give up, the weather was too bad; after we left the next day, the best weather set in again." Do not let such things happen to you. Be prepared with good tents, outdoor clothes and shoes and take in all the fun nature is giving us in all seasons. You will find tents, sleeping bags, blankets and all other necessary outdoor equipment we are offering of the most practical design, tested by trappers, explorers and hunters from the tropics to the arctic. They are priced moderately and built to give long and satisfactory service.

WALL TENT

These tents are most practical for permanent camping. They have ample head room which comfortably permits the use of furniture inside and allows for pitch in case of heavy rain and wind. The green coppercloth used for all our tents is treated by an exclusive process making it waterproof, also protects them against damage by Termites, Ants, Crickets, and other vermin. The weight of these tents is very light and when folded, they take up very little room due to their neat and unique construction. They are to be had in the following sizes:

No.	Space	Hgt.	Wgt.	Price	Front Flap Extra
12	7½ x 7½	6½	16 lbs.	$32.00	$6.00
13	7½ x 10	7	20 lbs.	40.00	6.50
15	9 x 11	7½	29 lbs.	46.00	8.75
16	10 x 12½	8	32 lbs.	58.00	10.00
17	12½ x 13½	9	36 lbs.	70.00	14.00
18	6½ x 6½	6	8 lbs.	24.00	4.75
19	6½ x 8	6	9½ lbs.	27.00	4.75
20	8 x 8	7	11 lbs.	31.00	7.00

NOMAD TENT

Same is designed in the style of the well known Lean-To or Baker tent. The front sides taper closer to the ridge. It has a three foot ridge with panel door lined with Marquisette and fastened with Hookless Fastener from top to bottom. It also has a ground cloth sewed in to keep vermin and insects out. The front fly can be put up as an awning (See illustration) and also can be completely closed in stormy weather. The straight roof with reinforced parrel 18" high to guy out enlarges same in a triangular wall in the rear. This tent is absolutely waterproof, light in weight and can be easily packed and folded to the size of 6"x24". The tent measures 6' wide, 7' deep and 6' high with 2' door and weighs only 9½ lbs.

No. 120 Nomad tent, illustrated $25.00

SIDE CURTAINS FOR CRUISER TENTS

No.	Price	No.	Price
36	$4.65 Each	38	$2.75 Each
37	3.75 Each	39	2.70 Each

NOTE: All tents supplied in neat bag. Poles and Stakes Extra.

EXPLORER'S TENT

This tent is preferred by explorers, hunters and trappers and has stood the test of expeditions in all parts of the world. It is absolutely insect proof and has bobbinet lined front and ventilator. A special ground cloth to keep vermin and insects out is sewed in making this tent a real comfortable and clean place. Furnished with hookless fastener front and hooded canopy which prevents rain from blowing in and running down the front. These tents have 7½' height and 2½' back, with 28" ridges, except 6½' sizes which have 7' height with 18" ridge.

No.	Space	Weight	Price	No.	Space	Weight	Price
30	7½ x 7½	15 lbs.	$70.00	31	9¾ x 7½	17½ lbs.	$82.00
32	6½ x 6½	9 lbs.	55.00	33	8 x 8	13 lbs.	65.00
34	7½ x 7½	21 lbs.	40.00	21	6½ x 6½	10½ lbs.	30.00
35	9 x 7½	21 lbs.	45.00	25	8 x 8	13⅞ lbs.	38.00

NOTE: Special Steel Pole and Ridge for any of above tents, $2.75.
NOTE: All tents supplied in neat bag, Poles and Stakes are extra.

IDEAL CRUISER AND ONE MAN TENTS

These tents are specially designed for fishermen, explorers, canoeists, hunters and trappers where a light outfit is required. It is water, snake, and bug proof and has a special ventilator in the roof which even in stormy weather may be left open, and the ridge gives added head room. The bobbinet door, well protected by a fly, may be either oval or Hookless Fastener style. The ground cloth is sewed in and made of waterproof material. It is roomy enough so that two persons can use it in a "pinch". The Ideal Cruiser tent measures 5'x7' on the ground, 5' high with 1½' triangular wall in rear. It can be rolled into a package 15" long and 5" in diameter. An extra side curtain may be used with the tent giving greater protection in the awning. It has a Hookless Fastener door the same as the Explorers tents.

No.	Wgt.	Oval Door Type	Hookless Fastener Type	No.	Wgt.	Oval Door Type	Hookless Fastener Type
36	8¾ lb.	$33.00	$35.00	38	9½ lb.	$21.00	$23.00
37	7¼ lb.	30.00	32.00	39	7¼ lb.	21.00	21.75

No-Wate Pole and Ridge $2.75

A TENT FOR EVERY HUNTING NEED

The Vista — Air-Cooled

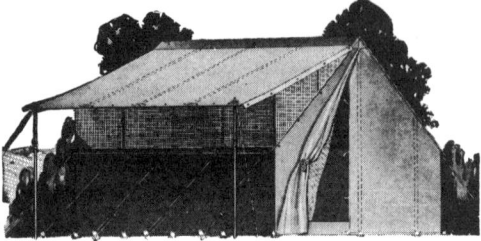

Selected for its Practical Utility and Convenience by Scientists, Explorers and Doctors

PATENTED "HOLD-TITE" CLAMP
Adjustable Steel Ridge and Corner Poles
Equipped with our Automatic Lock

Men with years of experience, who fully know tent requirements, claim the "Vista" to give more pleasure and protection than any other tent used.

The "Vista" not only protects the camper from insects and bugs, but is a refuge against rain and sun. Its clear vision, its awning extension and air circulation, provide the comforts of home when inclement weather is at hand. "Vista" tents are exceptionally well made of finest quality Khaki color tent materials thoroughly "Arctic Bay" waterproofed treated.

Patented adjustable telescopic steel frame with automatic lock-tight clamp. Two rustproofed steel upright poles and two for eave extension. Larger tents have extra strong tubular steel ridge poles. In stormy weather the entire top can be lowered and fastened down with snaps attached to tent.

No. K-2310	Size—Floor, 9'4"x 7' —Walls, 3' —Center, 7'	Sh. Wt. 62 lbs.	$34.44
No. K-2311	Size—Floor, 9'4"x11'8"—Walls, 3' —Center, 7'	Sh. Wt. 83 lbs.	47.22
No. K-2312	Size—Floor, 14' x11'8"—Walls, 3'6"—Center, 8'	Sh. Wt. 106 lbs.	60.56

The Camper

No. K-1829. A very popular size recently added that has proven a volume seller. Full size 5 ft. x 6 ft. 4 in. x 4 ft. 8 in. high with 1 ft. 6 in. wall. Skillfully tailored of genuine "Arctic Bay" Oil-Tempered light weight waterproofed Khaki tent material. Lap-felled double "Hickory" stitched seams.

No. K-1834 and **K-1835.** Both standard sizes with the same fine construction of a slightly heavier "Arctic Bay" waterproofed material in larger sizes. Khaki color. Packed complete with two upright poles, wood ridge pole, heavy Manila guy ropes and steel stakes.

No.	Size	Center	Walls	Sh. Wt.	Price
K-1829	5' x 6'4"	4'8"	1'6"	16 lbs.	$ 7.12
K-1834	5' x 7'	4'8"	1'6"	17 lbs.	8.00
K-1835	7' x 7'	5'6"	2'6"	23 lbs.	10.56

The "Lite-Pak"

An ideal tent for fishermen and hikers out on one night stands. Constructed of strong light-weight Green tent cloth with special mildew and water resisting finish. The "Lite-Pak" Tent is equipped with a bobbinette front, 6 ft. zipper opening, canvas flaps, with tie-tapes on front, and sewed-in floor.

Ease of erection, compactness and portability make this tent the last word in light-weight camping equipment. Packed complete with one center pole, steel stakes and ropes.

No. K-1303 Size 5'10" x 7' x 6' x 1'6" **$19.88** ea.

Sportsmen's
Wall Tent

"Arctic-Bay" Waterproofed
Bobbinet Door and Rear Window
Seams Lap-Felled and Double-Stitched
All Strain Points Reinforced
Door-riser—Storm Flap—Sod Cloth

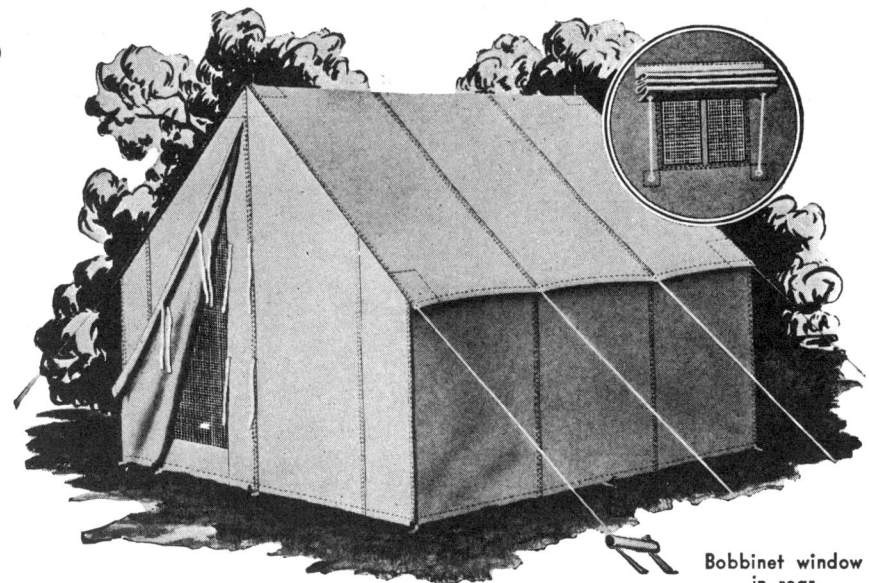

Bobbinet window in rear

Stoeger continues to lead the field in offering the latest developments in wall tents that meet all the requirements for real camping comfort.

Incorporating expert workmanship with the finest closely woven Special Tent Drill, thoroughly waterproofed by our exclusive "Arctic Bay" Oil-Tempered process, which does not harden the material, crack or peel off.

A roomier Wall Tent, with a full center height and 3 ft. side walls. Lap-felled, double "Hickory" stitched seams. Sewed-in 6" Sod Cloth so that floor cloth can be used. Reinforced throughout with double goods. Well ventilated with bobbinet door curtain and 24 in. rear window (inset). Both door and curtain have protecting storm flaps. Fully equipped with mahogany stained poles, steel stakes, and adjustable ropes.

Actual Size	Walls	Center	Sh. Wt.	Lot No.	Price
7' x 7'	3'	6'	30 lbs.	K-1520	$17.34
7' x 9'	3'	6'	35 lbs.	K-1521	20.34
8' x 10'	3'	6'	45 lbs.	K-1522	22.78
9'4" x 11'8"	3'	6'6"	58 lbs.	K-1524	27.44
11'8" x 14'	3'	7'	76 lbs.	K-1525	35.00

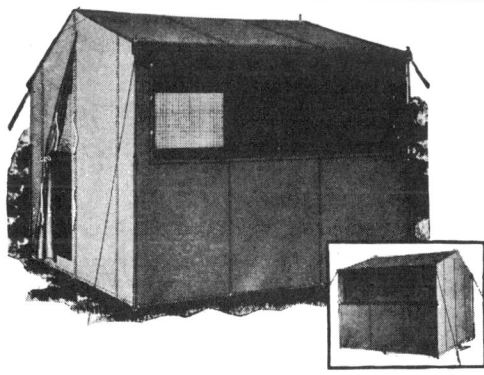

More Air With
Cottageaire

Adjustable Cross Ventilation
Protecting Storm Curtain & Door
"Arctic-Bay" Waterproofed

SHELTER TENT

The tent that withstood the 1938 eastern seaboard "Hurricane"—proving that this tent offers maximum **storm protection**, along with the features of cross-ventilation and roominess.

This genuine Khaki color "Arctic Bay" treated fabric is meeting the requirements of the most exacting sportsmen and campers. Excellent for convalescents.

Guaranteed full size—9 ft. x 7 ft. and 9 ft. x 11 ft. 8 in. with 5 ft. 6 in. walls. Adjustable steel ridge poles, four lock-tight adjustable steel corner poles and two center poles.

Sewed-in bobbinet sides 22 in. high. Equipped with storm curtains that can be adjusted or closed from the inside by means of turn fasteners and circingle snaps. This low price also includes the waterproofed sewed-in canvas floor and bobbinet door with storm flaps.

Equipped with sewed-in waterproofed canvas floor and riser. Sewed-in two-piece bobbinet door curtain along with storm flaps made of same material as tent. Heavy Manila rope ridge sewed in. Size 7 ft. x 7 ft. x 6 ft. high. Only one 6 ft. jointed pole necessary. Complete with pole, 1/4 in. Manila guy lines and steel stakes.

Lot No.	Floor	Center	Wall	Sh. Wt.	Price
K-2315	9' x 7'	7'	5'6"	72 lbs.	$41.44
K-2316	9' x 11'8"	7'	5'6"	103 lbs.	55.44

$41.44 ea.
No. K-2315

No. K-1300 .... $16.56

ORDER YOUR TENT FROM STOEGER

A PRACTICAL TENT MADE FOR
Discriminating Sportsmen
MAUMEE BRAND

Two grades of genuine "Arctic Bay" waterproofed tent materials.

Grade A—High quality closely woven tent duck waterproofed with our genuine "Arctic Bay" process. Khaki or Green color. Laboratory tested—rated "extra shower-proof."

Grade B—A special light weight construction similar to our Grade A and treated by the exact same "Arctic Bay" process. Khaki color only. Laboratory tested—rated "shower-proof."

Lap-felled seams double stitched with "Hickory" cord. Strain points reinforced with double goods. Extra wide extension with wide weather lap and tie straps for storm protection. Packed complete in heavy carton for quick, easy erection. Poles, ropes and steel stakes included.

DEFIANCE TENTS

Meeting the demands of the experienced camper for a tent of the utmost dependability. Two weights of the highest grade closely woven duck, thoroughly waterproofed by "Arctic Bay" process.

Heavy grade weighing 9.93 oz. per square yard before treating. Guaranteed to withstand any ordinary rainfall.

Extra heavy grade weighing 12.41 oz. per square yard before treating, insures the utmost safety in the most severe storms.

Lap-felled and double-stitched seams with genuine "Hickory" cord, known for its lasting qualities. Peak, corners and all other strain points reinforced with double goods. Wide weather lap at door.

Fully equipped with sewed-in rustproofed iron rings for guy lines and ropes, steel stakes and mahogany-stained hardwood poles.

Weights are Per Sq. Yd. Before Treating			Heavy 9.93 Oz.		Extra Heavy 12.41 Oz.	
Size	Center	Walls	Lot No.	Price	Lot No.	Price
7' x 7'	6'6"	3'	*K-1731	$15.44	*K-1931	$17.56
7' x 9'	6'6"	3'	*K-1732	18.66	*K-1932	21.12
8' x 10'	6'6"	3'	*K-1733	21.44	*K-1933	24.12
9' x 9'	7'	3'	*K-1734	21.78	*K-1934	24.88
9'4"x11'8"	7'	3'	*K-1735	26.12	*K-1935	29.66
11'8"x14'	8'	3'6"	*K-1737	36.12	*K-1937	40.56
14' x 16'	9'	4'	*K-1740	48.12	*K-1940	54.44
14' x20'6"	9'	4'	K-1741	58.10	K-1941	65.56

Walls Actual Size	3' Center	Khaki Grade "A"		Green Grade "A"		Khaki Grade "B"	
7' x 7'	6'	K-1499	$13.88	K-1505	$13.88	K-1580	$12.56
7' x 9'	6'	K-1500	16.66	K-1506	16.66	K-1581	15.22
8' x 10'	6'	K-1501	19.12	K-1507	19.12	K-1582	17.44
9' x 9'	6'6"	K-1504	19.54			K-1583	17.66
9'4"x11'8"	6'6"	K-1502	23.66	K-1508	23.66	K-1584	21.44
11'8"x14'	7'	K-1503	30.78	K-1509	30.78	K-1585	28.12

RUSTPROOFED STEEL TENT STAKES

Durable rustproofed (black painted) steel tent stakes. Three required sizes —9 in., 12 in., and 15 in. Specify lot number and size when ordering.

No. K-1209	2½ lbs. doz.	$ .80
No. K-1212	5 lbs. doz.	1.20
No. K-1215	7 lbs. doz.	1.44

ADJUSTABLE "LOCK-TITE" METAL POLES

Green lacquered metal pole with patented automatic "Hold-tite" clamp. Instant draw-tight erection. Remain rigidly in place. 6 ft. collapses to 44 in. 7 ft. to 50 in.

| No. K-77 | 6 ft. 3½ lbs. | $1.00 |
| No. K-79 | 7 ft. 4¼ lbs. | 1.20 |

"Arctic Bay" Waterproofing Compound
MAKES LEAKY TENTS AND CANVAS WATERPROOF AND LOOK LIKE NEW

Our Oil-Tempered Waterproofing compound is recognized as the finest obtainable. Thoroughly waterproofs by penetrating and saturating every pore and fibre. Prolongs the life of materials by keeping them soft and pliable.

Used extensively for waterproofing leaky tents, paulins and all kinds of canvas goods. One quart, when mixed with two quarts of gasoline, will cover approximately 75 sq. ft. Anyone can apply with satisfactory results.

No. K-142	Quart	Weight 2½ lbs.	$0.90
No. K-143	Half-Gallon	Weight 4½ lbs.	1.50
No. K-144	Gallon	Weight 8 lbs.	2.50

EVERYTHING FOR THE CAMPER

MINIATURE ANIMAL HEADS
An Ideal Decoration For Home Or Office

The deer, elk and moose heads illustrated below are ideal decorations for your home or office. The actual size of the heads is approximately six times larger than shown in the picture and they are exact reproductions of actual mounted heads. They are hand carved, finished with a natural gloss blend and are mounted on a brilliantly grained and highly finished walnut panel, shaped in shield form. The horns and ears are made of metallic alloy, so that they may be bent to proper shape without fear of breaking. The standing deer and the elk are made entirely of metal. The name of your club, town, state, park, business or resort can be lettered in gold on the panel at very little additional cost. This makes the miniature head an ideal souvenir. The heads make excellent gifts to any lover of the outdoors. The panels are supplied with eyelets so that they may be hung on the wall just like a real trophy of the hunt. The standing models make fine desk decorations and the wall models are supplied with feet brackets on which a pipe, pencil, ribbons or medals may be hung. Regardless the type of shooting that interests you, these miniature heads make a utilitarian, attractive decoration. They are available in sixteen different varieties, as shown in the price list below, and are extremely inexpensive. Why not make note of this on the order blank, so that when you make your next purchase from Stoeger, this will be included?

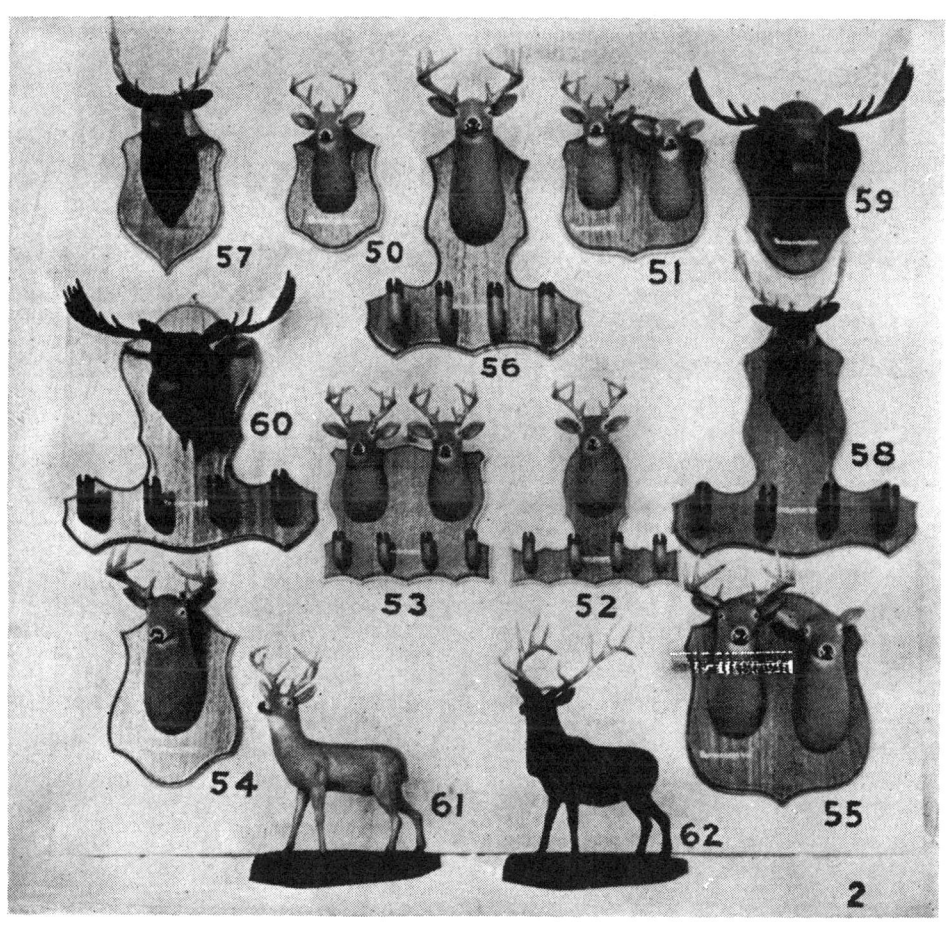

PRICES

Number		
50	Small Buck Deer	$1.00
51	Small Buck Deer and Doe set	2.00
52	Small Buck Head with 4 Feet	1.50
	Small Buck Head with 2 Feet	1.30
53	Double Small Buck Head with 4 Feet	2.40
	Double Small Buck Head with 2 Feet	2.20
54	Large Buck Head	1.50
55	Large Buck Head and Doe Set	2.70
56	Large Buck Head with 4 Feet	2.20
	Large Buck Head with 2 Feet	2.00
57	Elk Head	1.60
58	Elk Head with 4 Feet	2.30
	Elk Head with 2 Feet	2.10
59	Moose Head	1.60
60	Moose Head with 4 Feet	2.30
	Moose Head with 2 Feet	2.10
61	Standing Buck on Base	2.80
62	Standing Elk on Base	3.00
63	Double Large Buck Head with 4 Feet	3.20
	Double Large Buck Head with 2 Feet	3.00
	Six Geese attached to Hand-Painted Oil Picture, beautifully framed	7.00
	Six Ducks attached to Hand-Painted Oil Picture, beautifully framed	7.00
	Gold Lettering printed on each panel. Town or state free. Additional lettering, 2c per word	

A WELCOME GIFT TO EVERY SPORTSMAN

CAMP RADIUS STOVES

Generates its own gas by forcing kerosene vapor through the burner, which has been preheated. RADIUS Stoves and Burners are flattered by many imitations, but the peculiar construction of the ORIGINAL Radius burner insures perfect combustion with a hot intense blue flame, which does not soot the cooking utensils.

RADIUS HUNTER'S STOVE No. 43

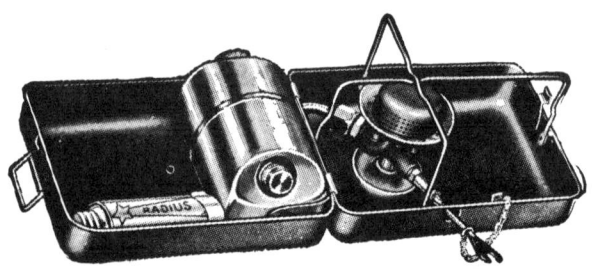

A very convenient and practical outfit for hunters. Occupies a minimum of space. This outfit consists of a stove in a flat practical carrying case. The tank is of heavy gauge polished brass, and the Silent Burner has a built-in cleaning device and regulating valve. Complete size of stove when packed is 7" x 5½" x 3¼" high, and will boil one quart of water in 3 to 4 minutes. Complete weight with case 2 lbs.

Price: No. 43 .... $6.35

RADIUS HUNTER'S STOVE No. 20

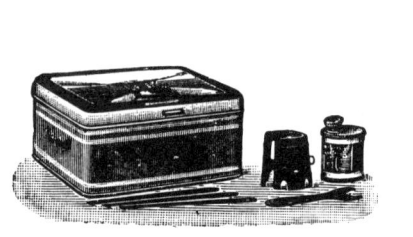 

This stove is especially designed for hunters and hikers, etc. Very compact, camera size, pressure kerosene stove. Tank of heavy gauge solid polished brass. Packed in light metal box, containing alcohol can, windshield and cleaning needles. Dimensions of metal box. 5¾" x 4½" x 2½". Capacity of tank ½ pint, sufficient to burn for two hours. Boils one quart of water in 6 to 7 minutes. No. 20 Radius Stove: 1⅝ lb.

Price: No. 20 .... $4.50

RADIUS CABIN RANGE No. 12-F

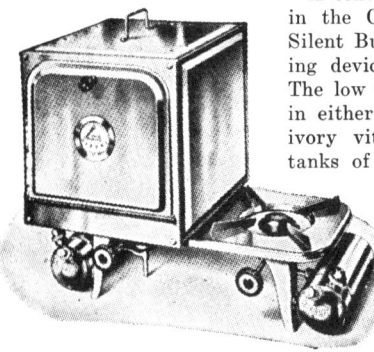

A convenient safe Range for use in the Cabin. Supplied with two Silent Burners, with built-in cleaning devices and regulating valves. The low sturdy frame may be had in either nickel finish or green or ivory vitreous enamel. Kerosene tanks of heavy gauge solid brass, nickel plated. Very economical to operate, as fuel consumption is only 2 quarts in five hours using both burners. Capacity of each tank 1¾ pint. Weight 8 lbs.

Price: No. 12-F Nickel Plated Frame $17.65
" No. 12-AF Green Vitreous Enamel 19.10
" No. 12-AF Ivory Vitreous Enamel 19.10
" 190 Radius Oven 11.00

RADIUS COOKER-HEATER No. 31

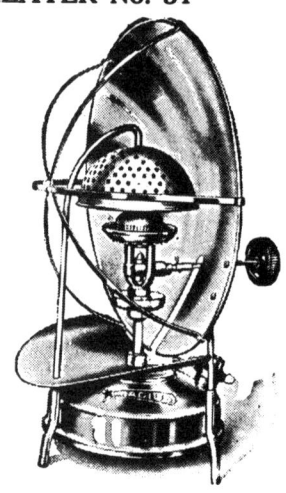

This outfit is very practical for heating cabins, tents, etc. Burns kerosene without wick. Consists of a regular single burner stove with detachable brass reflector and heating cone with holder. Easily and quickly detached to make a cooker or vice versa. Supplied with Silent Burner with built-in cleaning device and regulating valve.

No. 31 Cooker-Heater: Capacity of tank 2 pints. Weight 4½ lbs.

Price: No. 31 Complete $10.25

RADIUS STORM LANTERN No. 119

RADIUS Incandescent Storm Lantern burns kerosene without a wick, using a silk mantle. Tank of chromium plated brass, supplied with patented generator, with automatic cleaning device. No need of buying new generator. Fuel capacity 2 pints. RADIUS Lanterns are supplied with a removable green enamel top, and heat resisting glass that cannot crack.

No. 119. Capacity of oil tank, 2 pints, sufficient for about 12 hours burning; full height 14¼", 300 candle power; weight 4½ lbs.

Price: No. 119 .... $12.00

No. 17 RADIUS STOVE

This Stove comes packed in a plain cardboard box, without carrying case and accessories, but with wrench and cleaning needles. Stove of heavy gauge bright polished brass. A very practical stove for use in the camp when a two-burner stove is not needed. Weight 2⅜ lb. Capacity of tank 2 pints. Height of stove 8 inches.

Price: No. 17 .... $4.50

CAMP STOVES AND ACCESSORIES

In response to the call for a high quality, yet low priced line of camp stoves, we present the models shown on this page as being everything that the average hunter, camper, or outdoorsman might require. The stoves are sturdily built and all surfaces coming into contact with food are finished with pure tin which assures you of freedom from rust and tarnish.

Several of these models, notably No. 110, No. 100 and No. 190 are supplied in extremely neat durable "airplane luggage" carrying cases. This facilitates handling and packing, at the same time preventing soot, grease, etc., from soiling other items of equipment.

These stoves are intended for use with charcoal, and it is a common fact that a charcoal fire gives the best cooking results and the finest flavor to steaks, and many other foods.

Select your equipment from this complete line and enjoy the thrill of outdoor cooking at its best.

> To save our customers the unnecessary shipping expenses on the heavier models 110, 100 and 90, these items will be shipped f.o.b. factory, Niles, Michigan, but only upon full prepayment.

No. 110 GRIDIRON CHEF

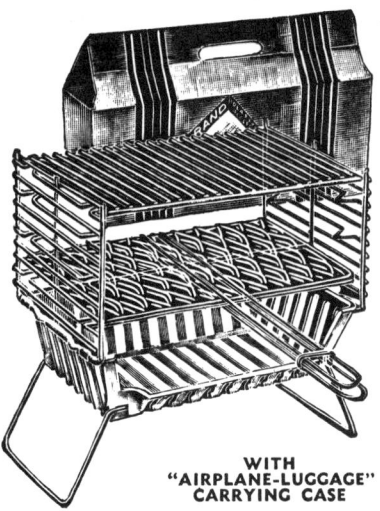

WITH "AIRPLANE-LUGGAGE" CARRYING CASE

Buy the Gridiron Chef and enjoy the advantages of controlled heat for charcoal cookery. Hinged, divided top provides five different cooking levels. Adjustable Shelf-X broiler. Sturdy wire warming shelf. Pure tin finish on all parts coming in contact with food. Cast iron grid basket 15" wide x 9" deep x 14¾" high with top raised. 7" from fire to highest cooking level. Sides fold down to form top grate for use in the regulation manner.

Packed in airplane-luggage-type carrying case. Shipping weight 16 lbs.

Price—F. O. B. Niles, Mich. ...$4.30

No. 4893 CAMP GRID

Strong, substantial grid for campfire picnics. High, pointed steel legs, when pushed into ground, give rigid support to grid. Dipped in varnish to prevent rusting. Electro-welded throughout.

No. 4893—Size 11" x 17". Legs 11" high. Frame and legs No. 4 wire; bars No. 11. Shipping weight 4 lbs.

Price ...$1.00

No. 100 DELUXE GRIDIRON

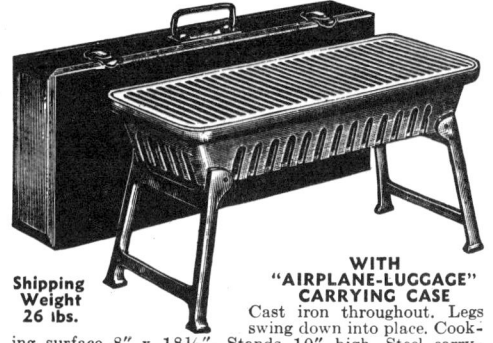

Shipping Weight 26 lbs.

WITH "AIRPLANE-LUGGAGE" CARRYING CASE

Cast iron throughout. Legs swing down into place. Cooking surface 8" x 18½". Stands 10" high. Steel carrying case has three hinges, two sturdy clasps and handles, and measures 21" x 9" x 4". Packed one in a carton.
Price F. O. B. Niles, Mich. ...$5.90

No. 66 LONG HANDLE BROILER

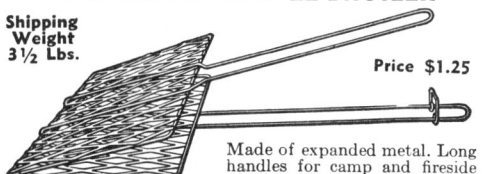

Shipping Weight 3½ Lbs.

Price $1.25

Made of expanded metal. Long handles for camp and fireside cookery. Can be used on No. 90 or 100 DeLuxe Gridirons with room for coffee pot. Size—8½" x 14". Length overall 27. Frame and handle of No. 6 wire. 16 gauge Shelf-X with 2¾" x 1¼" diamond shaped mesh. Finished in pure tin.

No. 62 DOUBLE CUBE STEAK BROILER

Price 75c

For broiling cube steaks, cooking the new "flat-hots" and many other foods. Size 8" x 5". Long handle. 24" overall. Shipping weight 1 lb.

No. 24 RED HOT ROASTER

Price 25c

Just the thing to roast weiners to perfection—also useful as a small broiler for picnickers and tourists. Easy to use for campfire or fireplace roasting in homes and club houses, at picnics, weiner roasts and parties. Long handle for comfort and safety. Length, 24", shipping weight 1 lb.

No. 25 HAMBURGRILL

Cook hamburgers "just right". Can also be used to fry bacon, eggs and many other foods. 22" long. Welded and strongly reinforced. Dipped in varnish to prevent rusting. Shipping weight 1 lb.
Price ...25c

No. 432 EXTENSION FORK

The handiest extension fork ever made for cooking food over an open fire. Interlocking steel wire parts will not come apart or weaken when extended. No ferrules. Rigid joint, absolutely foolproof. Handle is enameled. Overall length 19½". Extends to 30". Shipping weight 1 lb.
Price ...25c

No. 90 GRIDIRON

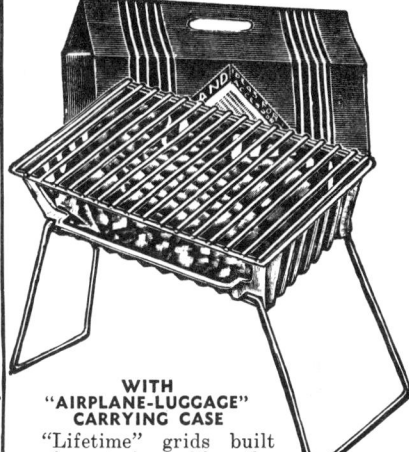

WITH "AIRPLANE-LUGGAGE" CARRYING CASE

"Lifetime" grids built of cast iron like the grates of your furnace. Can't warp, rust or wear out. Husky, practical and attractively priced.
Open front and projecting hopper make it unnecessary to remove cooking utensils when refueling. Cast iron grid basket has removable steel wire grating top. Steel legs fold flat. Individually packed in new airplane-luggage-type carrying case.
Safe and handy for campers, picnickers, hunters, and tourists. Charcoal burns without smoke, flame or odor and gives an intense, concentrated heat.

No. 90—Size 19" x 9½". Grating top made with No. 1 wire frame and No. 8 cross-bars. Legs of No. 1 wire. Weight 16½ lbs.

Price—F. O. B. Niles, Mich. ...$3.90

No. 120 PICNIC STOVE

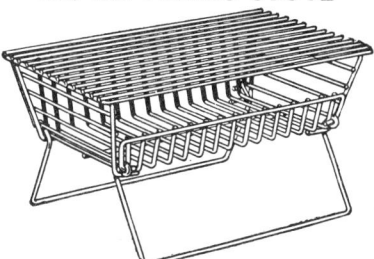

A new type wire stove patterned after our cast gridirons. Removable top grate. Strong steel wire electro-welded throughout. Light weight but sturdy. Legs fold flat for nesting. Cannot warp or break. Varnished to prevent rusting. Cooking surface 13" x 8". Height 7". Size folded flat 4" x 13" x 8". Top grate and body made of No. 6 and No. 8 wire; legs of No. 6 wire.
Shipping weight, 4 lbs. per carton.
Price ...$1.25

THE DISCOVERY AND HISTORY OF GUNPOWDER

The origin of gunpowder, the only explosive known until the middle of the nineteenth century, is uncertain. There is a theory that it was known in China many centuries before its first appearance in Europe, and that knowledge of it gradually worked westward. Legend goes back to the time of Alexander the Great, who, it is asserted, refused to attack the Oxydracae, a race occupying the country between the Hyphasis and the Ganges, because they "lived under the protection of the gods and overthrew their enemies with thunder and lightning, which they shot forth from their walls."

SCHWARTZ EXPERIMENTING

Some authorities regard Greek Fire, rather extensively used in the defense of Constantinople in the seventh century, as a form of gunpowder, but it may have been merely an incendiary mixture, to which crude nitre was added to make it burn more fiercely. On the strength of passages in the works of Roger Bacon, an English monk who lived in the thirteenth century, he is spoken of as the inventor of gunpowder. In his later works, "Opus Tertium," "De Secretis," and "Opus Magnus," published about 1270, there is no doubt that he was acquainted with explosive mixtures of sulphur, charcoal, and nitre, the ingredients of gunpowder.

Berthold Schwartz, a monk of Freiburg, in Germany, studied the writings of Bacon regarding explosives, and manufactured gunpowder whilst experimenting. He has commonly been credited as the inventor, and at any rate the honour is due to him for making known some properties of gunpowder; its adoption in Central Europe quickly followed his announcement, which is supposed to have taken place about 1320. It is probable that gunpowder was well known in Spain and Greece many years prior to its being used in Central and Northern Europe.

The early uses of gunpowder, however, were confined to warfare, no use being made of it for sporting purposes for several hundred years. In the later years of the fourteenth century, frequent references to gunpowder are made in literature, often in a way which makes it evident that the properties of gunpowder as a propellant were well known to the majority of people. From Chaucer's reference in "The House of Fame," it is apparent that the "pillet" which was fired out of the "gonne" by the explosion of the "pouder" was a single projectile.

The manufacture of gunpowder was carried out originally by the very crude method of pounding the ingredients together by hand in mortars, but edge runners were introduced toward the end of the sixteenth century, which greatly facilitated the incorporating or milling process. During this century, the process of "corning" or "granulating" was introduced, whereby grains of standard size are assured.

In manufacturing gunpowder, care is required in the selection of material. The potassium nitrate, or nitre, should be chemically pure. The sulphur must contain no non-volatile matter, and must be free from sulphuric acid. The quality of the powder depends considerably on the quality of the charcoal, so that it is customary for powder mills to prepare their own.

The composition of gunpowder varies widely with the different grades manufactured. Coarse grains are used for blasting, and fine grains for gunpowder. The composition of French military powders remained the same from 1598 until the adoption of modern smokeless powders, which developed from Schoenbein's discovery of guncotton in 1846. From this, Vielle, a French chemist, invented smokeless powder, in 1886, which possesses the ability to burn without creating much smoke.

Almost all sporting powder propellants today are smokeless powders. These can be divided into two classes, the dense powders and the bulk powders, both being used in rifle shooting and in shotguns. Though smokelessness is the characteristic of these powders, their superior power is a factor of prime importance, for, while black gunpowder imparts to the projectile an initial velocity of 1,700 feet a second, initial velocities of over 3,000 foot seconds have been attained with smokeless powders.

Another division of smokeless powders into types, is the nitroglycerin smokeless powders and the nitrocellulose. Both nitroglycerin and nitrocellulose powders consist of colloidal masses of gelatined nitrocellulose which have been pressed into ribbons, cords, tubes, or sheet, these being frequently cut into flakes, when intended for use with small arms.

Nitroglycerin was the discovery of Sobrero, an Italian chemist, in 1846, but nothing was done about it until Alfred Nobel recognized its possibilities for blasting. Later, he found it was possible to so mix and treat nitrocellulose dissolved in nitroglycerin, so that a hard colloid substance could be produced, and that this substance had all the properties which would make it desirable as a rifle propellant. This led to the production, in 1888, of ballistite, the first propellant of this class.

Today, nitroglycerin powders are manufactured for use in both shotguns and rifles. They usually are referred to as double-base powders, possessing the advantages of regular ballistics, and are less liable to produce back-flash than nitrocellulose powders. They have excellent keeping qualities.

THIS RELOADING GAME
By Courtesy of PHIL SHARPE

Perhaps the most ardent gun bug in the entire clan is the handloading expert. Some call him a handloader; some call him a re-loader and still others—just a pest. Nevertheless, this type of individual has probably done more for the development of the modern American rifle than any other single class of individual.

Handloading is a hobby and one inclined to give practical results. The handloader makes possible the development of a flexible gun. He assembles individual components into either super-accurate loads—or junk; depending entirely upon the seriousness of his work.

In my talking with handloaders I find a surprisingly small number of them who handload purely for economy's sake. If you do huge quantities of shooting, handloading will save a great deal of money. If you do a small amount of shooting, handloading will not save enough to pay for the cost of the tools—but it produces results in other ways.

Despite modern American machine methods, no two guns are alike. Pick two Model 70 Winchester rifles out of individual cartons, both the same caliber. Try these in a machine rest with standard factory ammunition and you will note some difference in accuracy.

Then experiment further. Try a few handloads. Use the same bullet but raise or lower velocities. Use different kinds of powder. Soon you will find a way to produce a handload to fit the individual gun which may practically cut the factory group-size in half. Try this in the other gun and accuracy may be slightly better than the factory load but not as good as in the first gun. This does not mean that the second gun is not "as accurate." You just haven't properly fitted your load to that barrel.

This merely shows the possibilities of handloads. That is the major aim of the serious handloader—accuracy. He may seek power but power without accuracy is usually more or less useless except for hunting purposes at extremely short range.

A handloader is not limited in his selection of components as is the man who confines himself to factory ammunition. A good example of this is the man who handloads for the .257 Roberts. He can use in this gun the .25 Remington bullets of the same diameter as the .257 Roberts. The difference is that the Roberts bullets cost 3¢ each and the Remington bullets 1¢, the Remington bullets having a slightly lighter weight jacket and will not stand the full Roberts speed but that 87-grain load can be stepped up to around 3100 f.s. and is certain to fly to pieces upon contact with any form of game.

The man who handloads must abide by certain basic ideas. He can spend a great deal of money buying tools. The skillful handloader with the finest tools made can produce excellent ammunition. By the same token, the skillful handloader with the poorest tools on the market could also produce good ammunition. Regardless of the type of tools some individuals cannot assemble a respectable load. Loading tool makers cannot build the human element into the equipment.

Advising hundreds of individuals on the selection of loading tools, the writer always recommends that the beginner spend a minimum amount of money for his equipment. The economically priced tools may be unsatisfactory but they will give him the basic training. As soon as he expands in skill he will acquire definite ideas. He can then better understand the various features of all loading tools and make a wiser choice in his final selection.

There is no perfect tool on the market today. In the better class of more expensive equipment each make and style has certain features, advantages, and disadvantages over those of other makes. It is up to the user to make his selection considering just what he wants to assemble.

Another basic problem in handloading is that of safety. You can smoke while loading but this is unwise—and unhealthy.

The manufacturer of ammunition welcomes a handloading expert contrary to the opinion of a few individuals who believe that this man is taking business from the ammunition makers. He must buy his components and the man who handloads invariably shoots many times the amount of ammunition of the average non-reloader. He also quickly branches out so that he does not fall in the class of the "one-gun" shooter.

Early in 1938 manufacturers of powders discontinued the release of handloading information. This involved the element of safety and it does not mean that they consider it dangerous to handload. The true story of this has never been published.

For many long years firearms editors have been warning handloaders against the use of mercuric primers. They gradually faded out of the picture but are today actually fading back in again. The answer is the non-corrosive primer.

Non-corrosive primers are excellent but still far from being 100% developed. Changes in priming composition is constantly being made by all our ammunition manufacturers. No announcement of this is being made to the public. Whenever they can improve they will improve.

In their standard factory loads there are a great many mercuric primer numbers. *All components sold to reloaders for handloading purposes are positively non-mercuric primed.* No mercuric primers are sold. Nevertheless, the man who salvages miscellaneous shells may get into extreme difficulty with numbers previously fired with mercuric primers. It is well to bear this in mind.

If you want to play safe order your components to start with primed shells having non-mercuric primers. Then stick to the non-mercuric variety of primer. High pressures, shells previously fired with a mercuric primer combine to produce but one result—a blown up gun. The writer has handled several such rifles shipped him for inspection during the past few years and in every case has traced it to mercuric primers, despite the fact that during reloading the man did not use mercuric primers himself.

Not one manufacturer of metallic cartridges today is 100% non-mercuric. The nearest is Winchester. Again I should like to repeat that components sold to reloaders by all makers are not only non-corrosive but non-mercuric.

Another safety recommendation is to never exceed recommended loading data. One of our prominent authorities in developing special loads blew up several very good Colt revolvers. Finally, he had his loads tested. He discovered a breech pressure in excess of 38,000 pounds per square inch. Only one revolver is specifically designed and engineered to handle the pressure in this class—the .357 Magnum as turned out by Smith & Wesson. Accordingly this experimenter realized after considerable damage had been done that his loads were a bit too "hot" for his guns to handle.

Before you begin to load you should study available printed data on various types of powders and components. You should learn how to handle a pair of micrometers and thus be in a position to know exactly the size of the bullets you are using and the barrel in which they are being shot. To determine the size of the barrel it is necessary to merely push a soft, lead slug through the barrel with a cleaning rod. Make sure it is properly expanded as you can readily determine by briefly viewing the slug as it comes out of the bore. Then measure it. Do not attempt to shoot a bullet through the barrel into some container and then measure it. It might upset and give a false reading.

Powders have certain peculiar qualities. Use the powder designed for your particular type of cartridges and for given loads.

For target purposes never attempt to load maximum velocity numbers. They rarely are equal in accuracy to those loaded slightly under that level.

This low velocity loading is used for several purposes. It is economical, the charge of powder is very low, pressure is in the 30,000 pound class, thus meaning much longer barrel life. What is far more important, it can be shot all day long without tiring the shooter, as recoil is practically negligible compared with the regular Mark I load with the same bullet at about 500 f.s. higher velocity. For a number of reasons, it is entirely satisfactory.

In loading for varmint cartridges, use bullets which will explode readily. Load for the highest practical velocity in keeping with the normal pressure level. Develop your loads for accuracy and by all means shoot them in your barrel to determine the best load. Once you find it, chart all data and stay with that load. Sight you rifle in and you are ready to take care of all kinds of vermin.

Ultra high velocity bullets are inclined to blow up upon impact. This means a clean kill but what is far more important it eliminates ricochets.

A few final notes in closing. Develop practical loads. Until you have had plenty of experience do not attempt to load full charge numbers. Do not experiment with powder not recommended. Select bullets carefully. Popular bullets are more widely approved than freaks, for practical reasons.

And above all, keep a detailed record of your loading experiences. If you develop an inaccurate load, do not dismiss it but record it in as much detail as possible. It may save you making the same mistake at a later date.

Handload your own ammunition and the smell of burning powder will be sweeter.

SMOKELESS RIFLE POWDERS

To meet the ever growing demand of our hand-loading customers, we have greatly increased our Powder Department and have for the first time re-arranged and classified the various types of powder in such a way that the beginner will have no trouble in locating easily the proper type of powder. While it is obviously impossible to go into great detail as to the exact use of these various powders, still a summary of the general type is given, which should be sufficient guide. With each canister, can or keg of powder, a complete list of proper loads for every popular type of cartridge is given.

All powders will be shipped either direct from our own New York office or from the manufacturing plant at our discretion. Smokeless, and semi-smokeless may be sent by express, whereas black powder may be sent only by freight.

Because of the bulk and shipping expenses connected therewith, the powder will positively be sent out only upon pre-payment, and no exchange, refund, or credit will be allowed. No order of less than $2.30 can be accepted.

We positively guarantee all powders sold by us to be as fresh and perfect as the factory can offer.

DU PONT No. 4759

Sporting Rifle Powder No. 80 is especially suitable for use in reduced loads in large capacity cartridges, such as the .30/06 Springfield and similar cartridges, and is suitable for both reduced and full service loads in the small capacity rifle cartridges, pistol and revolvers.

While Sporting Rifle Powder No. 80 is termed a "bulk" smokeless powder, it cannot be measured "bulk for bulk" with black powder. The weight of charge, therefore, must be accurately weighed for the best result.

1 Canister (8 oz.) ....$1.10   25 Canisters $22.00

DU PONT No. 4227
This powder replaces DU PONT-No. 1204.
As Improved Military Rifle Powder No. 4227 is designed for relatively small capacity cartridges as it is obviously too quick in burning characteristic to function to the best advantage in relatively large capacity cartridges.
1 Canister (1 lb.)...$1.70
25 Canisters 35.00

DU PONT No. 3031
This powder replaces Du Pont No. 17½ and is particularly recommended for medium capacity and mid-range loads. For the purpose indicated the re-loader will find this one of the most satisfactory powders on the market.
1 Canister (1 lb.)....$1.70
25 Canisters 35.00

DU PONT No. 4198
This powder replaces No. 25½. It has been developed for use in medium capacity cartridges and for reduced loads. An extremely popular powder with handloaders.
1 Canister (1 lb.)....$1.70
25 Canisters 35.00

DU PONT No. 4064
This powder replaces Du Pont No. 15½ and is designed primarily for Magnum capacity cartridges. When properly loaded this powder will give uniform results and accuracy.
1 Canister (1 lb.)....$1.70
25 Canisters 35.00

DU PONT No. 4320
This powder replaced Du Pont No. 1147. It has been particularly developed for use in Military cartridges, but is equally satisfactory in all ordinary high-power cartridges. This powder will give satisfaction under all conditions.
1 Canister (1 lb.)....$1.70
25 Canisters 35.00

HERCULES
Lightning smokeless Rifle Powder, very accurate for Target work. Chosen by many experts throughout the country for its satisfactory performance.
Keg (5 lbs.) $7.50
Keg (20 lb. Net)....27.00

HERCULES
Sharpshooter, smokeless, specially recommended for Autoloading Rifles. Burns very easy. Also recommended for long tapered cases, as caliber 45-90, 32-20, 38-40, 44-40, etc.
Keg (5 lbs.) $7.50
Keg (20 lb. Net)....27.00

HERCULES
Unique smokeless Rifle Powder. For short range work or for reduced loads in caliber 30/06, 7 mm, 30/40, 250/3000, etc. specially recommended.
Keg (4 lbs.) $7.50
Keg (15 lbs.) 26.00

HERCULES
"2400" Smokeless Rifle Powder. Specially recommended for caliber .22 Hornet, .25-20, and other small capacity cartridges. Very accurate.
Keg (5 lbs.) $7.50
Keg (20 lb.) 27.00

HiVel No. 3 Discontinued
HERCULES
Hercules HiVel No. 2. One of the best known smokeless progressive burning powders, giving Hi Velocity at low pressure. Specially recommended for caliber 30/06, etc.
Keg (5 lbs.) $7.50
Keg (20 lb. Net)....27.00

(Hercules rifle powders must be shipped by freight)

SMOKELESS, SEMI-SMOKELESS, AND BLACK POWDERS
PISTOL AND REVOLVER POWDERS

This well-known dense powder has been a favorite for many years with reloaders for all pistol and revolver cartridges.
1 Canister (8 oz.) $1.10
25 Canisters (8 oz. each) ...$24.50

Bullseye Revolver and Pistol Powder. The Standard, the old reliable known for its quality by reloaders.
Canister (8 oz. Net) $1.00
Case (25 Can.) ...22.00
Keg (15 lb. Net) 26.00

This is a newly developed powder, similar to No. 5, and especially recommended for .38 Special reloading and target work.
1 Canister (8 oz.) $1.10
25 Canisters (8 oz.) $24.50

HERCULES
SMOKELESS SHOTGUN POWDERS
Sold only in 3 and 23 pound Kegs

Hercules E. C. Bulk Smokeless Powder for Shotgun Shells, specially recommended for Trap and Skeet Shooting.
3 pound Keg......$6.00
23 pound Keg......41.40

RED DOT

Readily distinguished by its uniform red grains. A progressive burning powder, giving consistent results. Virtually non-hygroscopic and therefor practically unaffected by climatic or weather changes.
1 Keg (3 lbs.)....$6.00
23 pound Keg......41.40

Due to the new sales policy all Hercules Powder must be shipped by freight

Hercules Infallible Dense Smokeless Shotgun Powder Immune against moisture. The Ideal Powder for the Tropics.
3 pound Keg......$6.00
23 pound Keg......41.40

BLACK POWDERS

Hercules L. & R. Orange Extra, Black Powder. Recommended for Shotguns, Rifles and Revolvers. Comes in 3 sizes: FG—coarse, FFG—medium, FFFG—fine.
6¼ pound Keg......$2.50
25 pound Keg.......9.25

The Standard DuPont black powder. The various firearms require, for the best work, that the size of grain be carefully selected. For that reason, this Company manufactures its Sporting Powders in three standard granulations, viz.: Fg, FFg and FFFg, from coarse to fine, respectively—the greatest care being taken to have the grains uniform in size.
1 lb. can $1.00
¼ Keg (6¼ lb.)....2.80
1 Keg (25 lb.).....10.00

DUPONT
SMOKELESS SHOTGUN POWDERS

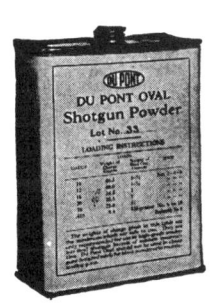

A progressive burning dense powder, particularly recommended for heavy loads. Develops high velocity combined with uniform patterns.
½ lb. Canister $1.15

This powder is of the bulk type, and has been a favorite for many years. Is suitable for all around use.
½ lb. Canister......$1.15
1 Keg (3 lbs.).... 6.25
1 Keg (5 lbs.)....10.20

A relatively non-hygroscopic bulk powder, stable, uniform in loading and igniting, clean burning, non-corrosive and non-erosive. Will give consistently excellent results.
½ lb. Canister......$1.15
1 Keg (4 lbs.).... 8.00
1 Keg (8 lbs.)....16.00

KING'S SEMI-SMOKELESS POWDER

King's semi-smokeless powder is an ideal powder for reloading rifle and revolver ammunition due to the fact that it will give velocities practically equal to those obtained with smokeless powder, while maintaining the low breech pressures experienced with the use of ordinary black powder. It is just as safe to handload as black powder as the volume is just as bulky as that of black powder whereas the weight is much less. In rifle and revolver ammunition it gives only slightly more smoke than that obtained with high priced smokeless powder, whereas it does not deteriorate nor is it affected by climatic influences as are most smokeless powders.

Comes in 4 sizes; FG—coarse, FFG—medium, FFFG—fine. FFFFG—very fine. Be sure to state granulation when ordering.
1 Canister, (13 oz. net) $1.00
Case of 5 Canisters, 13 oz. net weight, one grain or assorted 4.25
Case of 10 Canisters, 13 oz. net weight, one grain or assorted ..$7.00
Keg (20 lbs. net) ...11.50

Note: This powder at prices quoted above will be shipped only FOB, Cincinnati, Ohio.

COMBINE YOUR RELOADING NEEDS IN ONE ORDER

PRIMED SHELLS, BULLETS AND PRIMERS
AVAILABLE IN ALL STANDARD BRANDS. NAME BRAND, WHEN ORDERING

Primer	Caliber	Style of Bullet	Weight of Bullet	Primed Shells Per 100	Bullets Per 100
6½	.218 Bee	H. P.	46	$2.52	$0.99
8½	.219 Zipper	H. P.	46	3.78	1.68
8½	.219 Zipper	H. P.	56	3.78	1.68
6½	.22 Hornet Hi-Speed, K'bore	S. P.	45	2.52	.99
6½	.22 Hornet	H. P.	45	2.52	.99
8½	.22 Savage, High Power Ptd.	Mush.	70	3.78	1.68
8½	.220 Swift Hi-Speed	Mush.	46	4.73	1.68
8½	.220 Swift Hi-Speed	S. P.	48	4.73	1.68
8½	6.5 m/m Mannlicher-Schoenauer	S. P.	150	4.73	2.60
6½	.25-20 Stevens and Winchester Single Shot Kleanbore	S. P.	86	2.52	1.53
6½	.25/20 Win. Mar. & Rem.	M. C.	86	2.52	1.53
6½	.25/20 Win. Mar. & Rem.	S. P.	86	2.52	1.53
6½	.25/20 Win. Mar. & Rem. Hi-Speed	Mush.	60	2.52	1.53
8½	.25 Remington	S. P.	117	3.78	2.31
8½	.25 Remington Hi-Speed	Mush.	87	3.78	2.31
8½	.25 Remington Express	Mush.	117	3.78	2.31
8½	.25 Rem. Corelokt	C'kt	117	3.78	2.31
8½	.25/35 Win. & Sav. Corelokt	C'kt	117	3.78	2.31
8½	.25/35 Winchester & Savage	S. P.	117	3.78	2.31
8½	.25/35 Winchester & Savage Hi-Speed	Mush.	87	3.78	2.31
8½	.25/35 Winchester & Savage Express	Mush.	117	3.78	2.31
9½	.250 Sav. Exp. Mush. K'bore	Mush.	100	4.73	2.31
8½	.250 Savage Corelokt	C'kt	100	4.73	2.31
8½	.250 Savage Mushroom	Mush.	87	4.73	2.10
9½	.257 Rem Roberts Hi-Sp. Mush. Kleanbore	Mush.	87	4.90	2.10
9½	.257 Rem Roberts Hi-Sp. Mush. Kleanbore	Mush.	100	4.90	2.10
9½	.257 Rem Roberts Hi-Sp. Exp. Mush. Kleanbore	Mush.	117	4.90	2.10
9½	.257 Roberts Corelokt	C'kt	100	4.90	2.10
8½	.270 Winchester Hi-Speed	Mush.	130	5.04	2.52
8½	.270 Win. Express	S. P.	150	5.04	2.52
8½	.270 Win. Corelokt	C'kt	100	5.04	2.52
8½	7 m/m Mauser	S. P.	175	4.90	2.73
8½	.30/30 Win. Mar. & Savage	M. C.	160	4.41	2.73
8½	.30/30 Win. Mar. & Savage	S. P.	170	4.41	2.73
8½	.30/30 Win. Mar. & Savage Hi-Speed	Mush.	110	4.41	2.73
8½	.30/30 Win. Mar. & Savage Express	Mush.	165	4.41	2.73
8½	.30/30 Win. Mar. & Savage Corelokt	C'kt	170	4.41	2.73
8½	.30 Remington	M. C.	160	4.41	2.73
8½	.30 Remington	S. P.	170	4.41	2.73
8½	.30 Remington Hi-Speed	Mush.	110	4.41	2.73
8½	.30 Remington Express	Mush.	165	4.41	2.73
8½	.30 Rem. Exp. Corelokt	C'kt	170	4.41	2.73
8½	.30/40 Krag & Winch.	S. P.	220	4.90	3.57
8½	.30/40 Krag & Winch. Hi-Speed Brz. Pt.	Exp'g	180	4.90	2.98
8½	.30/40 Krag & Winch. Express	Mush.	220	4.90	3.57
8½	.30/40 Krag & Win. Exp.	M. C.	220	4.90	3.57
9½	.30-46 Krag & Win. K'bore	S. P.	180	4.90	2.98
8½	.30/40 Krag Exp. Corelokt	C'kt	180	4.90	3.57
8½	.30/40 Krag Exp. Corelokt	C'kt	220	4.90	3.57
8½	.30 Springfield '06 Taper Heel	M. C.	172	5.04	3.57
8½	.30 Springfield '06	S. P.	220	5.04	3.57
8½	.30 Springfield '06 Hi-Speed Brz. Pt.	Exp'g	150	5.04	2.52
8½	.30 Springfield '06 Hi-Speed Brz. Pt.	Exp'g	180	5.04	3.57
8½	.30 Springfield '06 Hi-Speed	Mush.	110	5.04	3.57
9½	.30 Springfield '06 K'bore	S. P.	180	5.04	3.57
8½	.30 Springfield '06 Express	Mush.	220	5.04	3.57
9½	.30 Springfield '06 Corelokt	C'kt	180	5.04	3.57
9½	.30 Springfield '06 Corelokt	C'kt	220	5.04	3.57
8½	7.62 m/m Russian Bronze Point	Exp'g	150	4.90	2.98
6½	.300 Savage Bronze Pointed	S. P.	150	4.73	2.52
9½	.300 Savage Kleanbore	S. P.	180	4.73	2.73
9½	.300 Savage Corelokt	C'kt	180	4.73	2.98
8½	.303 British	S. P.	215	4.90	2.98
8½	.303 Savage	S. P.	195	4.41	2.73
8½	.303 Savage Corelokt	C'kt	180	4.41	2.98
8½	8 m/m Mauser & Mannlicher	S. P.	236	5.04	2.98
8½	8 m/m Special	S. P.	170	5.04	2.98
8½	8 m/m Lebel	S. P.	170	5.04	2.98
1½	.32 Smith & Wesson	Lead	88	1.77	.95
1½	.32 Smith & Wesson Long	Lead	98	1.89	1.68
1½	.32 S & W Long Sharp Shoulder	Lead	98	1.35	.69
6½	.32 Short Colt	Lead	80	1.77	.95
1½	.32 Long Colt	Lead	82	1.89	.95
1½	.32 Colt New Police (Police Pos.)	Lead	100	1.89	1.68
6½	.32 Win. Mar. & Rem.	M. C.	100	2.52	2.31
6½	.32 Win. Mar. & Rem.	Mush.	80	2.52	2.10
8½	.32 Special Win. & Mar.	S. P.	170		
8½	.32 Special Win. & Mar. Hi-Speed	Mush.	110	4.41	2.73
8½	.32 Special Win. & Mar. Express	Mush.	165	4.41	2.73
8½	.32 Special Win. & Marlin	C'kt	170	4.41	2.73
8½	.32 Remington	S. P.	170	4.41	2.73
8½	.32 Remington Hi-Speed	Mush.	110	4.41	2.73
8½	.32 Remington Express	Mush.	165	4.41	2.73
8½	.32 Rem.	C'kt	170	4.41	2.73
8½	.32/40 Win. Mar. & Savage	S. P.	165	4.20	2.73
8½	.33 Winchester	S. P.	200	4.90	2.98
8½	.348 Win. Express	S. P.	200	5.04	2.98
8½	.348 Win. Hi-Speed	S. P.	150	5.04	2.73
8½	.348 Win. Corelokt	C'kt	200	5.04	2.98
8½	.35 Remington	S. P.	200	4.73	2.98
8½	.35 Remington Hi-Sp. Mush.	Mush.	150	4.73	2.98
8½	.35 Remington Express Mush.	Mush.	200	4.73	2.98
8½	.35 Rem. Exp. Corelokt	C'kt	200	4.73	2.98
6½	.38 Smith & Wesson	Lead	146	2.10	2.00
1½	.38 S & W Special Oil-Proof Kleanbore	Lead	200	2.52	2.00
1½	.38 Smith & Wesson Special	Lead	158	2.52	1.80
1½	.38 Smith & Wesson Special	M. P.	158	2.52	2.31
2½	.38-44 Spec. Hi-Sp. K'bore	Lead	158	2.52	2.00
1½	.38/44 Smith & Wesson Spl.	M. P.	158	2.52	2.20
8½	.38 S. W. Spl., Mid. Range	Lead	146	1.79	.94
8½	.38 Colt New Police	Lead	150	2.10	2.00
1½	.38 Short Colt	Lead	125	1.89	1.90
6½	.38 Long Colt	Lead	150	2.10	2.00
1½	.38 Colt Special	Lead	158	2.52	1.90
2½	.38 Win. Mar. & Rem.	S. P.	180	3.36	2.73
2½	.38 Win. Mar. & Rem. Hi-Speed	Mush.	145	3.36	2.73
8½	.38/55 Win. Mar. & Savage	S. P.	255	4.20	3.57
8½	.38/56 Win. & Marlin.	S. P.	255	4.17	3.57
8½	.40/65 Winchester & Marlin	S. P.	260	3.58	2.50
8½	.40/82 Winchester & Marlin	S. P.	260	4.77	2.50
8½	.405 Winchester	S. P.	300	5.04	4.20
1½	.41 Long Colt	Lead	195	2.52	2.20
2½	.44 S&W Russian	Lead	246	2.73	2.40
2½	.44 S&W Special	Lead	246	3.36	2.40
2½	.44 Win. Mar. & Rem.	S. P.	200	3.36	2.98
2½	.44 Win. Mar. & Rem. Hi-Speed	Mush.	160	3.36	2.98
2½	.45 Colt	Lead	250	3.36	2.40
8½	.45/90 Winchester & Marlin	S. P.	300	4.77	2.50

EMPTY PAPER SHOT SHELLS

Packed 100 in a box; 5,000 in a case.

Gauge	Length Shell	Shur Shot Per 100	Arrow Per 100
8	3¼"	....	$4.94
10	2⅞"	$2.37	2.54
12	2⅝"	2.15	2.54
12	2¾"	2.37	2.74
12	3"	....	2.74
16	2 9/16"	2.03	2.54
20	2½"	2.03	2.54
20	2¾"	2.26	2.74
20	3"	....	2.74
28	2½"	2.03	....
410	2½"	1.92	....

SHOTGUN WADS

Wads are packed 250 in a box: 1,000 in a package and 50,000 in a case, except ⅜" wads, which are packed 125 in a box, 500 in a package and 10,000 in a case.

Gauge	Cardboard A or B Thickness List 1,000	Cardboard Printed B Thickness List 1,000	Black Edge List Per M
10 Regular	$1.25	$1.25	$3.05
¼"	....	....	4.30
⅜"	....	....	7.10
12 to 410 Regular	1.20	1.20	2.50
¼"	....	....	3.65
⅜"	....	....	6.60

A NEW GUN CARRIES A FACTORY GUARANTEE

POWDER SCALES, PRIMERS AND PERCUSSION CAPS

STOEGER'S SPECIAL POWDER SCALE

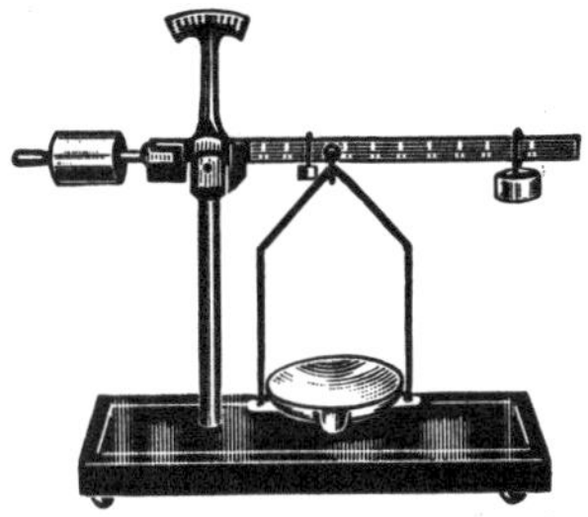

An extremely accurate scale with a sensitivity of 1/10 grain. Has the advantage of having weights permanently attached thus avoiding the possibility of mislaying or losing loose weights.

Beam of Nickel Silver is graduated with two sets of graduations and is supplied with two different size poises. To operate the poises should be set each on its own zero point, as shown in the illustration. The beam will then be in balance. The powder to be weighed is then placed in the pan and the poises moved to the left until the beam balances. The weight reading is then taken from the beam, the heavier graduations at the right side reading from 5 grains to 300 grains and the light graduations reading from 1/10 grain to 5 grains. Capacity 305 grains. Nickel Silver Pan, 3 inch diameter Upright pointer and indicator, Iron Base and Column.

Price **$13.50**

RELOADERS HAND SCALE

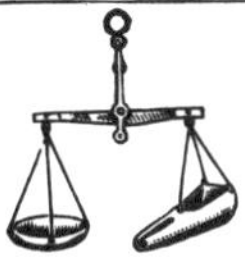

An accurate low priced special powder scale. May be held in the hand or hung from a hook. Excellently made with all metal parts beautifully nickle plated. Capacity about 75 grains. Beam, 4¾ inches wide. Price **$3.75**

RELOADERS' POWDER SCALE

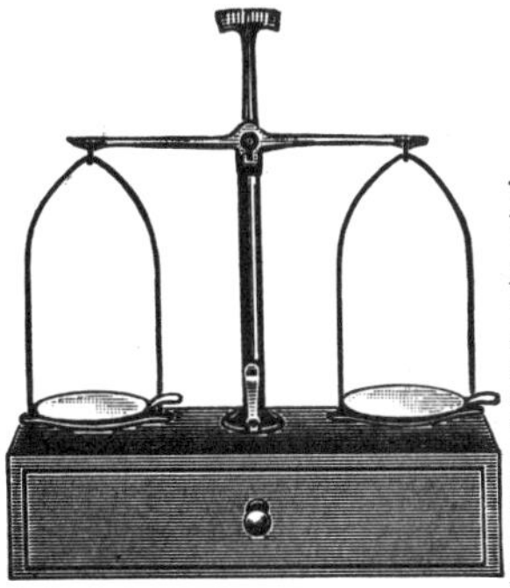

This balance is of a type approved by hand loaders throughout the United States, and many years of experience have proven its success. It has a sensibility up to ¼ of a grain, and has a capacity of 225 grains. The beam is 5¾ inches and the pans have a diameter of 2 inches. The balance is fitted onto a finished wood box, and may be taken apart and packed away in box drawer.

Price **$6.75**

SPECIAL POWDER GRAIN WEIGHTS

Grain weights, octagon, made of pure sheet aluminum, concave, so they can be picked up readily. Set, 6 pieces, ½ grain to 10 grains, in paper box. Price **$1.20**

PRICES SINGLE, SEPARATE FROM FULL SETS

½, 1, 2, 5, or 10 grain weights, each 25c

Brass Pincets 3 inch for handling weights 50c

AMERICAN PRIMERS FOR MODERN RELOADING

MAKE	30/06 and up (.210 diameter)	Large Rifle (.210 diameter)	Small Rifle (.175 diameter)	Large Revolver (.210 diameter)	Small Revolver (.175 diameter)
REMINGTON:	9½	8½	6½	2½	1½
WINCHESTER:	120	115	116	111	108
WESTERN:	8½ G (Corrosive)	8½	6½	7	1½
PETERS:		12	65	20X	15

(All Primers Shown Are Non-Corrosive and Non-Mercuric)

While desirable to use the same make of primer and case, this is not necessary, as primers shown in each column are interchangeable. The foregoing list covers almost all the requirements of the modern reloader. If any particular primer, not listed but not yet obsolete is specifically required, we can procure same in lots of not less than 1,000 at **$3.80.**

Primers packed in boxes of 100. Price per 100, **50c.** Price per 500, **$2.00**

SHOTGUN SHELL PRIMERS

For brass or black powder shells........Per 100, **50c.** Per 1,000, **$3.80**

For all other shotgun shells............Per 100, **75c.** Per 1,000, **6.75**

Note:—Make, brand, and gauge of shell in which primer is to be used must be given.

NOTES ON RELOADING FOREIGN CARTRIDGES

For the removal of the fired primer and insertion of the new one, a special combination decaper and caper is supplied by us. This is an adjustable tool, suitable for nearly all foreign cartridges. The price is $6.00.

Regarding proper powder loads using standard American powder, this must be arrived at by experimentation, starting with the lowest load of the nearest corresponding American cartridge. For further information see the Ideal Handbook (price 50c).

Bullets of practically all calibers are available, and we suggest that the Ideal Handbook be consulted wherein will also be found the various bullet moulds.

Bullet seaters, while not absolutely necessary, may be procured on special order from abroad. Cartridge case resizers are not necessary where the cartridge case is to be used successively in the same chamber, but may also be had on special order if required.

Scattered throughout the U.S.A. are tens of thousands of excellent foreign rifles and combination guns chambered for cartridges not manufactured in America. While we have always made it a point to stock the necessary foreign cartridges (which will be found illustrated and priced in this catalog), the present high foreign costs, transportation, customs duty, and excise taxes have made the price so high that the majority of these guns are either disposed of at a fraction of their value or are seldom used.

The only solution to the problem of obtaining proper ammunition at low cost is hand-loading which, however, has been impossible until now. It has been impossible because the European cartridge cases are, almost without exception, designed with a built in anvil, requiring the Berdan type of primer which has never been commercially available in the U.S.A.

For the first time we are now importing the genuine D.W.M. primers in the three sizes which cover all the principal foreign calibers. These primers are all non-corrosive and non-mercuric, and with the exception of No. 71C are lacquered over the tinfoil, thus assuring unlimited stability under all conditions.

BERDAN PRIMERS

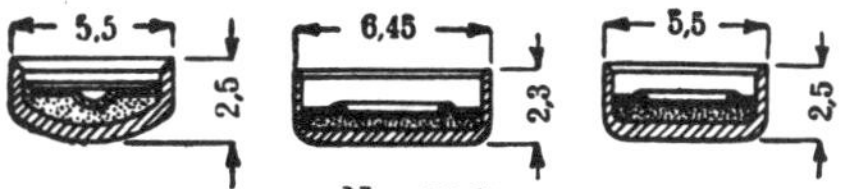

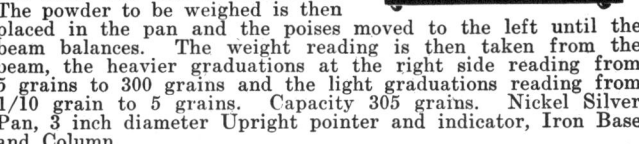

No. 5.5A No. 71C No. 5.5E

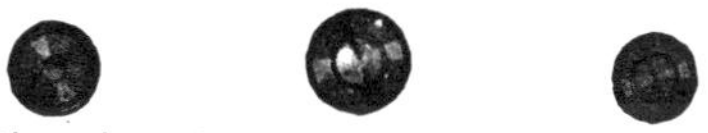

Dimensions shown are in millimeters.

All primers have Nicorro priming, which is non-mercuric and non-corrosive.

All primers sold only in boxes of 250.
Price per box.......................$3.00

No. 5.5A is of copper, a highly sensitive primer for cartridges with rim. It has a round bottom and is lacquered. Suitable for the following D. W. M. Cartridges:

Cal. 6.5x53R (No. 395C)	Cal. 8x571R (No. 366D)
Cal. 6.5x58R (No. 463)	Cal. 8x57R (No. 366B)
Cal. 6.5x61R (No. 431M)	Cal. 8x58R (No. 462)
Cal. 7x57R (No. 380J)	Cal. 8x60R (No. 542A)
Cal. 7x57R (No. 380H)	Cal. 8x60R (No. 542AMB)
Cal. 7x65R (No. 557A)	Cal. 8x65R (No. 574)
Cal. 7x72R (No. 573)	Cal. 8x72R (No. 574)
Cal. 7.62x51R oNo. 543)	Cal. 9x57R (No. 491B)
Cal. 8x48R (No(. 462A)	Cal. 9x70R (No. 474B)
Cal. 8x50R (No. 358C)	Cal. 9.3x74R (No. 474A)

No. 71C is copper plated brass, unlacquered and flat bottom. Suitable for the following D. W. M. Cartridges:

Cal. 8.15x46R (No. 455)	Cal. 11.15x60R (No. 41)
Cal. 9.3x72R (No. 77D)	Cal. 11.2x60 (No. 41A)

No. 5.5E is of brass, with flat bottom and lacquered. Suitable for the following D. W. M. Cartridges:

Cal. 6.5x52 (No. 519E)	Cal. 8x57 (No. 560)
Cal. 6.5x53 (No. 477)	Cal. 8x60 (No. 452)
Cal. 6.5x54 (No. 457A)	Cal. 8x60 (No. 542MB)
Cal. 6.5x55 (No. 431C)	Cal. 8x64 (No. 558)
Cal. 6.5x57 (No. 404A)	Cal. 8x75 (No. 514A)
Cal. 6.5x58 (No. 457)	Cal. 9x56 (No. 491E)
Cal. 6.5x61 (No. 431L)	Cal. 9x57 (No. 491A)
Cal. 7x57 (No. 380L)	Cal. 9.3x62 (No. 474C)
Cal. 7x64 (No. 557)	Cal. 9.5x57 (No. 531)
Cal. 7.62x63 (No. 379E)	Cal. 10.75x68 (No. 515A)
Cal. 8x51 (No. 366L)	Cal. 10.75x73 (No. 555)
Cal. 8x56 (No. 528)	

PERCUSSION CAPS

Goldmark Brand

F. 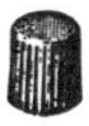 L.

F. L., Foil Lined	Inside Diameter	Length	Price: Per 100	Per 1000
Size 9................	.163-.152	.200-.210	**$0.20**	**$1.50**
Size 10................	.170-.159	.205-.215	**.20**	**1.50**
Size 11................	.175-.165	.205-.215	**.20**	**1.50**
Size 12................	.178-.168	.205-.215	**.20**	**1.50**
Size 13................	.184-.174	.205-.215	**.20**	**1.50**

MUS 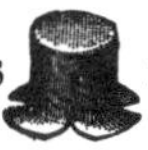 KET

Musket Caps	Inside Diameter	Length	Price: Per 100	Per 1000
No. 4 Split, U. S. Army	.228-.220	.215-.225	**$0.30**	**$2.30**
No. 6 Split, Varnished..	.228-.220	.215-.225	**.30**	**2.30**
No. 6 Split, Foil Lined.	.228-.220	.215-.225	**.30**	**2.30**
Spanish Rib, Musket Caps	.238-.220	.250-.260	**.30**	**2.30**

STOEGER'S RELOADING
"IT PAYS TO RELOAD"

Stoeger's enlarged and up to date department for reloading rifle, revolver and pistol cartridges and shotgun shells is complete.

The growing demand of shooters for reloading their own ammunition has been recognized by us for some time and after searching the whole field and under the cooperation of the best known manufacturers in this line we are pleased to present for the first time in a comprehensible way, the simplest and most economical tools and accessories best suited for this purpose.

IDEAL RELOADING TOOLS

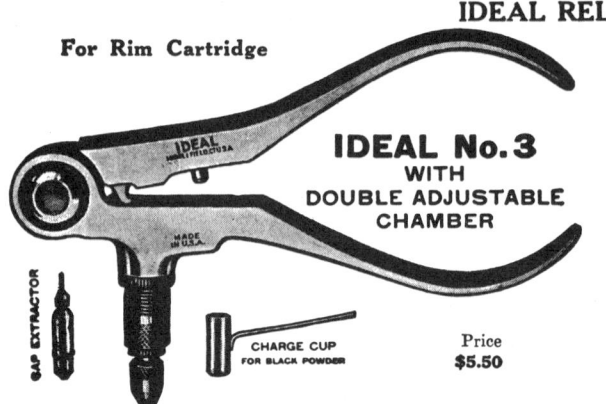

For Rim Cartridge

IDEAL No. 3 WITH DOUBLE ADJUSTABLE CHAMBER

Price $5.50

For Rimless Cartridges

IDEAL No. 10 WITH DOUBLE ADJUSTABLE CHAMBER

Price $5.50

The number 3 Ideal Tool is specially adapted for rim cartridges. The double adjustable chamber allows quick adjustment to seat different style bullets. Seating screw must be changed to conform to shape of bullet nose.

The number 10 Ideal Tool is handled the same as the number 3 and the number 10 tool is designed for reloading rimless cartridges. A special hook is provided for holding the case in the recapping hole.

The operation of both tools is simple, the old primer is extracted and a new one inserted, the muzzle of the shell may be reduced or expanded to fit the bullet, the end of the shell may be crimped on the bullet or left uncrimped, the bullet may be sized to fit the gun and can be seated in the shell any depth desired. These tools can be used for the following most popular calibers and also for many other calibers not listed.

.22 Hornet, .218 Bee, .219 Zipper, .220 Swift.

Rim Cartridges for Rifles

.22 Sav. H. P.	.30-30 W.C.F.	.32 Win. Spc.	.38-40 Rem.
.25-20 S. S.	.30-40 Krag.	7.62 M/M Russ.	.38-55
.25-20 Rept'r.	.303 Sav.	8 M/M Lebel.	.405 Win.
.25-35 W.C.F.	.303 British.	.348 Win.	.44-40
.32-20 W.C.F.	.32-40 Win.	.35 Win.	.45-70

RIMLESS CARTRIDGES FOR PISTOL AND REVOLVER

.32 Auto.	.38 Auto.	.380 Auto.	.45 Auto.

RIMLESS CARTRIDGES FOR RIFLES

250-3000 Sav.	.270 Win.	.30 Gov. '06	7 M/M Mauser.
.25 Rem. Auto	.30 Rem.	.300 Magnum	8 M/M Mauser.
.257 Rem.	.300 Sav.	.35 Rem. Auto	

RIM CARTRIDGES FOR PISTOLS AND REVOLVERS

.32 S. & W.	.38 Sp. Colt or S. & W.	.44 S. & W. Spec.
.32 Colt N. P.	.38 Long Colt.	.45 Colt Revolver.
.357 S. & W. Magnum	.38 S. & W.	

ACCESSORIES FOR NO. 3 AND NO. 10 RELOADING TOOLS

Shell Expander Chamber
Price $1.75

Muzzle Resizer
Price $1.00

Bullet Sizing Chamber
Price $1.75

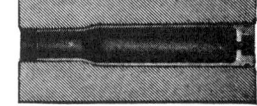

Full Length Resizing Die
Price $3.00

Fired shells are over expanded by gas pressures, the neck must be reduced by using the muzzle resizer, then the shell expanding chamber is used with plug to bring them back to the correct size for the particular bullet used. If the entire length of shell needs resizing it is necessary to use the shell resizing tool.

IDEAL BULLET MOULDS

Ideal Improved Single Mould

The Ideal Improved Single Bullet Mould is especially constructed to mould your own bullets and is very easy to handle. This mould consists of two sections, handles and block. Blocks will fit handles interchangeably. The prices of complete moulds are regular style bullet, $5.00; Express and Hollow Nose Bullet, $6.50. If blocks only are required, deduct $1.00. Moulds for special list bullets, 50c extra.

No. 5 Universal Powder Measure

The No. 5 Universal Powder Measure is adjustable to measure any desired charge of any kind of powder whether black or smokeless for rifles, pistols or shotguns. It is almost a necessity for reloading with smokeless powders.

Price $7.50

No. 5 Micrometer Powder Measure

The No. 5 Ideal Micrometer Measure (not illustrated) is of the same size and shape as the No. 5 Universal Powder Measure but has micrometer adjustment that permits it to be set with a little greater accuracy. It is made primarily for reloading rifle cartridges and is not recommended for use with pistol powders.

Price $10.00

THE IDEAL HANDBOOK

The 160-page Ideal Handbook cover subject of reloading metallic cartridges and shotgun shells and contains tables of powder charges, bullets, etc. This book is essential to shooters who wish to obtain best and most accurate results. The information is the result of half a century of reloading. Price 50c per copy.

BULLET MOULDING ACCESSORIES

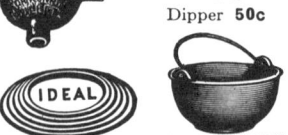

Dipper 50c

Lead Pot Holder Price 75c

Lead Pot Price $1.00

The Ideal lead pot is large enough for melting about 10 pounds of material. Fill dipper from melting pot, connect mould with nozzle, turn dipper with mould to vertical position and let lead run into mould until full. The Ideal lead pot holder is a very simple device to keep the metal at an even temperature and can be used on any old kitchen stove, fitting any size hole, as the pot fits perfectly and reaches down into the fire.

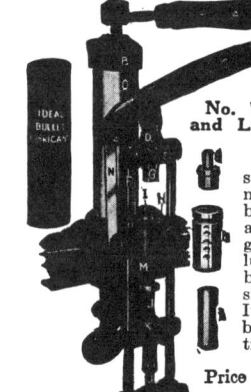

No. 1 Sizer and Lubricator

A great time saver and this machine sizes the bullet correctly and affixes the gas check and lubricates the bullet in one single operation. It leaves the bullet perfectly true and clean.

Price ... $10.00

IDEAL LUBRICANT

Good for from 500 to 2500 Bullets.. 25c

MODERN BOND RELOADING TOOL

MODEL C STRAIGHTLINE LOADING TOOL

The Bond Straightline reloading tool Model C is the result of years of experience and our constant endeavor to give the pistol and rifle shooters a tool that will perform all of the operations necessary for reloading metallic cartridges in the simplest and most accurate manner.

The Model C reloading tool can be set up for the five following operations.

No. 1—Inserting the decapping shank in the shaft and decapping bushing in frame and the tool is ready for decapping.

No. 2—Remove pin from the capping shank and replace nut also reverse the capping bushing and adjust so that it clears shell 3/32 inch. Place primer in pocket and seat in vertical position and seat by operating handle.

No. 3—Remove bushing in shank, insert anvil, guide bushing and neck die adjust so that when anvil is touching the guide bushing, the neck of the shell is sized to the bottom length.

No. 4—Remove neck die and insert double adjustable chamber and expander, hold die by the adjusting screw, set the chamber so that when the anvil touches the guide bushing the shell is in the proper length. Work the tool the same as when reducing.

No. 5—Remove expander and replace with bullet seater if you wish to crimp the shell on the bullet. Set the chamber so that the anvil will be about 1/32 inch from the bushing when operating with shell in position. Lock chamber with locknut. If you have a loaded cartridge it is an easy matter to adjust the bullet seater by placing it in the tool and turning the adjusting screw until you can feel the seater pressing on the anvil. If you do not want to crimp, set the chamber so that shell does not come in contact with the crimp anvil.

The Model C tool can also be used to size alloy bullets. In case you do not own a sizer and lubricator by forcing them through the die using the bullet seater as a plunger after the tool is set in the reverse position from the other operations. Bullets should be lubricated after they are sized by dipping in the lubricant and remove the excess grease with a cake cutter. This tool can also be used to remove bullets from any 30 calibre or 7.62 Russian cartridges with an extra attachment which must be equipped with the corresponding anvil and guide bushing.

Please do not forget to state the calibre of cartridges you shall reload and also style of bullet to be used. This tool can be set up for other cartridges by obtaining additional parts which you will find listed herewith.

PRICES

Item	Shipping Weight	Price
Model C. Tool Complete	5 lb.	$9.00
EXTRAS		
No. J Guide bushing	4 oz.	.60
No. K Anvil	1 lb.	1.15
No. L Decapping shank	8 oz.	.30
No. E Expander	3 oz.	.80
No. F Neck Die	2 oz.	1.00
No. G Bullet Seater	2 oz.	.60
No. H Double Adj. Chamber	5 oz.	1.40
Bullet Die	4 oz.	1.00
Thrust Bar	8 oz.	.30
Large Lock Nut	2 oz.	.25
Small Lock Nut	2 oz.	.20
Adjusting Screw	8 oz.	1.10
Re and Decapping Bushing	4 oz.	.80
Clamp and Screw	1 lb.	1.00
Lever	1 lb.	2.00
Lever Pin	2 oz.	.15
Shaft	8 oz.	1.50
Shaft Pin	2 oz.	.30
Decapping Shank Block	4 oz.	.30
Bullet Extractor Complete	4 oz.	8.85
Bullet Extractor	1 oz.	3.50

BOND POWDER MEASURE

In reloading it is necessary that the powder be quickly and accurately measured and this can only be accomplished by using a device where the movements are uniform as a slight knock or jar at certain times will pack the powder and add several grains to the charge.

The Bond Powder Measure will throw charges that will not vary one-half of a grain providing instructions are followed.

It is entirely different from any Measure that has been on the market, the measuring device being a combination of two cylinders and revolving wheel. The small cylinder measuring to fifteen grains and the large to one hundred and five grains, both can be easily and quickly adjusted.

The measure is equipped with two short tubes taking a wide range of shells. Special tubes can be furnished as an extra. When ordering state powder to be used and table of weights will be furnished.

Shipping weight 6 lbs.   Price................$7.50

BOND DOUBLE CAVITY BULLET MOULD

Bond moulds are made of carefully selected metal and accurately cut by specially trained mechanics. After cutting they are heat treated so that it is not necessary to break them in, as perfect bullets can be made as soon as the moulds are up to the proper heat for casting.

When working up our line we found that a mould casting two bullets, cut with the same cherry, could be made at practically the same cost as a single, so all our stock moulds are made in this manner in quantities.

Specify calibre and also weight of bullet mould is wanted for.

	Wgt.	Price
Shipping weight (mould block only)	1 lb.	$4.50
Shipping weight (mould handle only)	2 lb.	1.25
Shipping weight (Double Cavity mould with handle)	3 lb.	5.50

BOND BULLET SIZER AND LUBRICATOR

All Bond moulds are cut a few thousandths of an inch larger than standard so that the bullets are cast over size in order that they may be put through a sizing die to make them perfectly round and remove imperfections.

A very satisfactory sizing dies is furnished with out tools, but the method is slow and laborious and it is also necessary to lubricate by another operation.

A bullet sizer and lubricator should be used when the bullets are made in quantities, as by the use of this tool the lubricant is forced into the grooves under the pressure while the bullet is in the die and surplus grease is removed when the bullet is ejected. All the work is accomplished with ease and dispatch.

The Bond Lubricator and Sizer comes to you with a stick of lubricant in the cylinder and dies in place ready for use.

	Wgt.	Price
FULL LENGTH RESIZER	1½ lb.	$3.50
Straight Shell	2 lb.	6.00
Taper Shell	2 lb.	6.00
BULLET SIZER AND LUBRICATOR	6 lb.	10.00
Set of Dies and Plungers (Lub.)	1 lb.	3.50
Lubricant per stick	1 lb.	.30

B. & M. RELOADING TOOLS

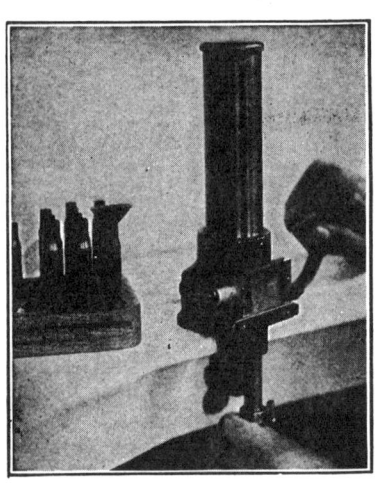

B. & M. Visible Powder Measure

Powder measure is absolutely dependable and very simple to operate due to its unique construction. The charge tube or measuring chamber is graduated in numbers from one to thirty-five and is easily adjusted by means of a thumb screw.

With each powder measure a table is supplied, which lists all powders for the weight of each kind of powder and how to set the measure for the correct amount of grains for each kind, weight 3½ lbs.
Price $8.00

B. & M. BULLET SIZER

The B. & M. bullet sizer is designed to be attached to a work bench, having a hole bored underneath to allow the resized bullets to drop through into a padded box. It is a fine, very accurate straightline tool consisting of four parts—the base casting, guide sleeve, driving plunger and sizing die. These are furnished for all standard calibers to resize bullets to the standard diameters. These standard diameters will in most cases be three thousandths larger than the groove diameter of your arm and thus conform to the accepted over size qualifications for cast bullets. The bullet is started base first in the guide sleeve and is forced down and through the die. This operation sizes the bullet exactly. Shipping weight 1 lb. 13 ozs. B. & M. bullet sizers may be adapted to any caliber.

Bullet sizer complete............ $3.00

Extra Parts

Plungers .... .75
Guide sleeves 1.00
Sizing dies 1.00

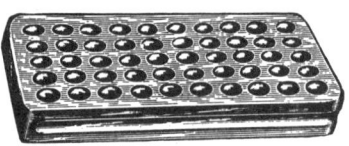

LOADING BLOCKS, 50c EACH

Loading Blocks to hold cartridge cases during the reloading process are a necessary part of every reloader's equipment. They may be purchased from Stoeger or made by the reloader if material is available. They consist of hardwood boards, 8 x 4 x 1 inches, in which have been bored holes of the correct diameter to accept the base of the cartridge case. B. & M. furnish Loading Blocks of planed oak, varnished, containing fifty holes of any caliber desired. The corners have been rounded and the blocks grooved along their length to facilitate handling. They are usually sold in pairs. When ordering state caliber desired.
Shipping weight 12 ounces each.

B. & M. GAS CHECK CUPS

B. & M. gas check cups are made from copper and are to be used on the bases of cast bullets designed to receive same. They permit the use of heavier charges in connection with bullets made of one part of tin to ten parts of lead. The bullet without gas check will be deformed by the excessive heat of the smokeless powder in heavier loads destroying the accuracy of same. Energy sufficient up to ranges of 600 yards can be imparted without danger of fusing or deforming their bases or sides. B. & M. gas checks are available in any caliber up to and including 35 caliber. The care in their manufacture results in increased shooting accuracy. State caliber of bullet when ordering.
Price per 1000 gas check cups (Shipping weight per 1000, 13 oz.) .. $2.00

THE B. & M. HANDBOOK

Full information regarding all phases of hand-loading together with a detailed description of all B. & M. reloading tools and accessories and their use. Price...................... 50c

B. & M. MODEL 28 RELOADING TOOL

Price, with Bullet Seating Attachments..$14.00
Price, less Bullet Seating Attachments..$12.00

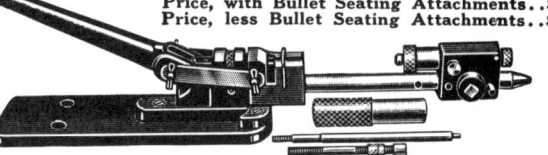

The Model 28 Tool represents the most recent development in B & M Reloading Tools. It decaps, reprimes, resizes case necks and can be had with attachments for seating bullets, accurately performing all necessary reloading operations except powder charging. As furnished with standard bullet seating attachments, it is recommended for use in reloading any cartridge used in single shot or bolt action rifles when no crimp is necessary or desired. For reloading cartridges which must be crimped, it is furnished less the standard bullet seating attachments but with the Model 26 Bullet Seater shown below.

The Model 28 Reloading Tool may be adapted to calibers in addition to the one for which it was originally obtained by the purchase of additional parts.

Extra Bullet Seating Die....$1.25   Extra Neck Die..........$1.00
Extra Bullet Seating Plunger...75   Extra Decapper 1.25
Extra Expanding Plug........75   Extra Decapping Pin......10

When ordering parts for additional calibers, write us for a list of those necessary.
Shipping Weight Model 28 Tool 5 lbs.

B. & M. BULLET SEATER MOD. 26

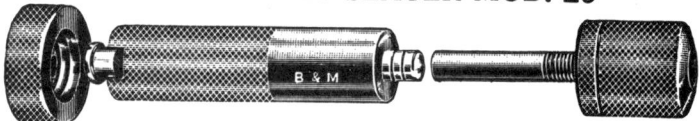

The model 26 bullet seater is a special tool for seating bullets. It consists of a die to hold the cartridge case, a base and an adjustable bullet seating plunger. The bullet is guided straight into the case, which is a fundamental ballistic requirement. The bullet seating plunger is threaded for adjusting bullet seating depth and the adjustment is maintained by a split washer and heavy knurled nut under the head. It is designed to crimp or not to crimp as desired.
Price for model 26 Bullet seater........................ $2.50
Shipping weight, 1 lb. 14 oz.

B. & M. BULLET MOULD

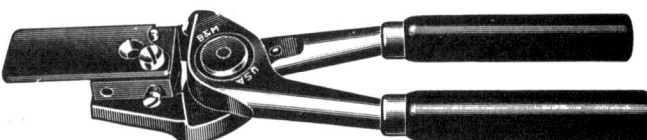

The B. & M. fine bullet mould is of the latest design. These moulds are of the highest precision and will cast bullets correctly. The large blocks with good thickness of metal at every side of the bullet cavity are important in securing uniformly full bullets. The blocks hold an even casting temperature at base, sides and point of the bullet cavity. They come together with the utmost precision, whether cool or hot and they maintain this true fit under long and continued hard service.
Price $5.25
For hollow point bullets add............................. 2.50

LUBRICATION OF BULLETS

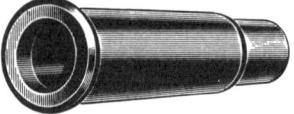

Materials required: 1 cake cutter—1 stick lubricant. If the number 1 lubricator and sizer are not used, the best method is to dip the bullets in the melted lubricant. After lubricant has hardened pass the cake cutter over the bullet cutting off the surplus lubricant. State caliber when ordering.

Cake cutter, price.......... 50c

Price for lubricant, 8 sticks to a pound..................... $1.00

B. & M. LOADING FUNNELS—50c EACH

The Powder Charge must be funnelled into the cartridge case. Funnels are therefore a necessary part of every reloader's equipment. B. & M. furnish aluminum funnels with mouths large enough to accept charges from scale pans, and tapered to various sizes to fit case muzzles. Shipping weight 8 ounces.

SEE PAGE 8, "HOW TO ORDER"

JORDAN MULTIPLE RELOADING PRESS

Shipping weight about 20 pounds.

This reloading press is so constructed that all tools necessary for reloading two different cartridges may be set up on the press at one time. This enables the reloader to have ready for immediate use two calibers of dies in perfect adjustment. The dies are all equipped with special lock nuts which permits the removal and replacement of the die without losing the adjustment in case the press is used with more than two sets of dies. Any number of dies can be used with the press as they are interchangeable. Each set of dies includes resizing die, decapper, expander, recapper, bullet seater, one extra primer punch and one primer pocket cleaner. In addition, the Jordan Neck Trimmer is included with every set of high power rifle dies. This is very powerful, accurate and speedy reloading tool.

Crimped primers are readily removed with the regular primer punch with the die. A primer pocket sizing plug which is operated by the press is furnished at additional cost. This plug re-forms the primer pocket after removal of these crimped primers.

In ordering be sure to state caliber or calibers desired, also the bullet or bullets which will be used. If cast bullets are used include three resized samples. In ordering rifle dies include three fired cases from the rifle for which it is desired to reload. In ordering bullet resizing die include four cast bullets.

*Magnum Press, no dies included	$20.00
*Pistol Dies, per set, for 1 caliber	7.50
*Rifle Dies, per set for one caliber, including Neck Trimmer	7.50
Custom built rifle dies, per set for one caliber, including trimmer	12.00
*Bullet Sizing Die	3.00
*Lubricator for Sizing Die	2.00
Case neck trimmer	4.75

IMPORTANT NOTICE

In ordering be sure to state caliber or calibers desired, also the bullet or bullets which will be used. If cast bullets are used include three resized samples. In case of rifle dies include three fired cases from the rifle for which it is desired to reload. In ordering resizing die include four cast bullets.

We ship each press complete with a wrench for the special screws, one extra primer punch for each set of dies, four screws for attaching the base to the table, a Jordan Neck Trimmer with each set of high-power rifle dies and 1 primer pocket cleaner for each set of dies.

EXTRA PARTS FOR MULTIPLE REL. PRESS

*Bullet Puller	$0.50
*Primer Pocket Sizing Plug	1.00
*Primer Punches, package of 5	.50
Bullet Seating Plug, No. 64-A	1.00
Neck Expanding Plug, No. 45	1.00
Lock Nut, No. 19	.25
Header, Rifle, No. 30	1.00
Header, Pistol No. 32	1.00
Header, Pistol, Seating, No. 32-S	1.00
Primer Seating Die	1.00
Base	2.50
Bullet Seating Sleeve Assembly, 64-A-65-10	1.75
Bullet Seating Die, Rifle, 47-A	1.50
Bullet Seating Die, Pistol, 62	1.50
Bullet Seating Plug Nut, No. 18	.25
Extra Necking Die, Special Size Rifle. Necessary to return lower half sizing die No. 40 for fitting	2.00
Do. Ordered as extra with set of dies	1.50
Cutter and Sleeve Assembly for Neck Trimmer, No. L-2 and No. L-3	3.00
*Loading Strips—20 Holes	.30
*Primer Pocket Cleaner	.10

JORDAN CASE NECK TRIMMER

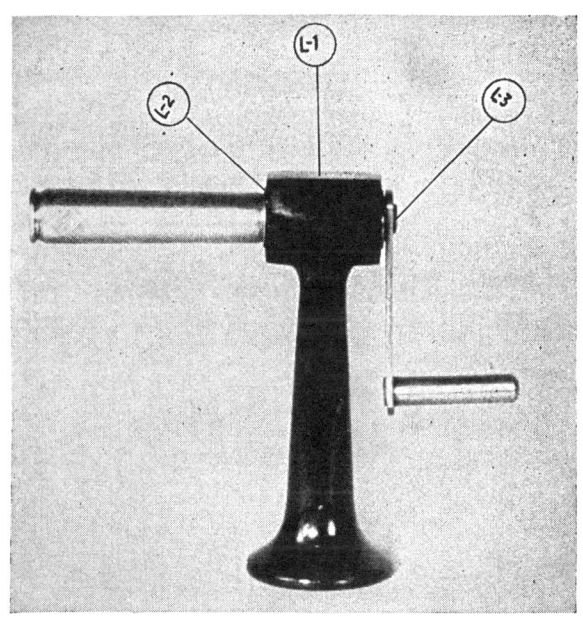

*Case Neck Trimmer $4.75

This case neck trimmer, like the Jordan dies, is built to close limits. It trims the case neck to standard length and chamfers the inside of the neck at one operation. It operates by placing the neck of the case in the revolving guide sleeve L-2 which contains the cutter assembly L-3 and turning the handle as the case is held in the hand and pressed against the cutter. Due to the entire assembly of the guide sleeve and cutter turning the case necks will be trimmed uniformly square. If the case necks are already the proper length the tool will only chamfer the inside to facilitate bullet seating. This trimmer is made in all popular calibers and is set for standard length of neck. The sleeve and cutter assembly, (L-2 and L-3) is interchangeable in the bearing and support L-1 and any number of different calibers of sleeve and cutter assembly may be used. The change can be made in a few seconds. Several hundred case necks can be trimmed in one hour with this tool. Cutters are removable and may be ground without changing their form. This tool is included with every set of dies for reloading high power rifle cartridges as it is extremely important to trim cases after resizing.

PACIFIC — RELOADING TOOLS — SCHMITT

SCHMITT MODEL 12

Automatic Priming Feed

For those who must have extra speed. With this device it is possible to recap and prepare the shell for the powder and bullet as fast as the operator can feed the shells in the die. This is the only operation in reloading that can be speeded up without sacrificing accuracy. When ordering state size of primers.

Price of feed (with one tube) . $3.00
Price of extra tubes (each) ... 1.50

The Pacific tool is a real time saver and very simple to operate. With one throw of the handle, up and down, the fired primer is removed, a new primer inserted, neck and full length of the shell resized and inside expanded. The entire operation takes only a few seconds. Bullet seating is done the same easy and speedy way. By exchanging the dies you can reload any kind of cartridge of all the different calibers you desire. This is really the most practical and inexpensive tool you can buy for reloading in mass production. Some features of this tool:

Note: Shell holder grips the shell easily but firmly so that the case will enter the die without guiding it with the fingers. Decapping discs are quickly and easily replaced. A new supply is furnished with each tool. The dies are adjusted for head space. All bullet seating dies for pistol and revolver cases are made with crimpers as standard equipment. Bullet seating dies for rifle cases can be equipped with crimpers at a slight additional cost. Bullet seating and crimping is done in one operation.

Shipping weight 10 lbs.

PRICE LIST

Pacific tool complete with high speed tool steel resizing die	$22.50
Pacific tool complete with carbon steel dies (weight 11 lbs.)	20.50
Full length or neck resizing die (does not include expander) made from high speed tool steel—all calibers	5.50
Full length or neck resizing die (does not include expander) made from carbon steel all calibers	3.50
Expanders all sizes, including decapping pin and holding nut	1.75
Seating dies including seater, for any bullet, not including crimper	3.00
Crimper complete for rifle cases, including seater for any shape bullet	2.50
Bullet seater for rifle, any shape bullet	1.00
Bullet seater to be used with crimper	1.00
Seating dies for pistol or revolver including crimper and seater for any shape bullet	4.00
Bullet seater for pistol or revolver, any shape bullet	1.00
Priming cups, cup and arm are included, for either large or small size primer (primers are made in two sizes, state size or number of primer used)	1.50
Shell holder (any caliber shell)	2.00
Bullet puller (all calibers)	5.00
Automatic Priming device (with one tube)	3.00
Extra tubes (each)	1.50
Bullet sizers (any caliber)	3.75
Graphite compound (large size)	.50

PACIFIC BULLET MOULDS

Regular base single mould	$3.50	Hollow point single mould	$4.50
Hollow base single mould	4.50	Gas checks for bullets—per M	1.75

The Pacific moulds are made of bronze, are perfectly machined and have long cool handles. Bronze moulds are easy to break in and cast clean bullets. Moulds are sold complete with handles. When ordering send sample bullet or full description and dimensions.

Description: The Model 12 Schmitt Reloading Tool is the best designed tool of its type and has the distinction of simplicity, speed and accuracy combined. The manufacturer of this tool claims it is three times faster than any other tool on the market. With this tool one can comfortably resize, expand and recap 500 or more cases per hour. The construction of the tool allows an uninterrupted combination operation. Some of the finest features are the automatic primer feed, the straight line operation of the tool itself, the "set case" type bullet seater, the low cost of extra parts for additional calibers.

Instructions for ordering: To assure a perfect fit of dies, send several fired cases (full load to be used only) for which dies are to be made. This applies for rifle cartridges specially. Otherwise standard dies will be sent. For pistol cartridges, kindly specify if for Peters cases or other makes as Peters cases are about .002 inch smaller. This applies specially to caliber 38 S. & W. Special.

Price: Tool complete with resizing die, seating tool extractor (shell holder), primer slide, recapping pin, seating block crosshead, primer tubes and tray.

For rifle cartridges	$26.50
For pistol cartridges	25.50

Shipping weight for each tool complete 12 lbs.

Prices for additional parts for popular cartridges.
Prices for special, foreign and obsolete cartridges, will be furnished on request.

Extra rifle seating tool	$4.00
Extra pistol seating tool	3.00
Extra resizing dies, rifle or pistol (this includes expanding plug for rifle or expanding cone for pistol)	3.00
Extra crossheads	.80
Extra extractors (shell holders)	.60
Extra expanding plugs	.40
Extra recapping pins	.25

PACIFIC POWDER AND BULLET SCALE

A scale accurate to $\frac{1}{10}$ grain at a new low price. Capacity to 242 grains.

Price complete with weights	$7.00
Price without weights	6.50
Weights, separately, consisting of four $\frac{1}{10}$, one each ½, 1, 2, 3, 4, 5, and 6, also two 20 grain weights	2.00

PACIFIC POWDER MEASURE

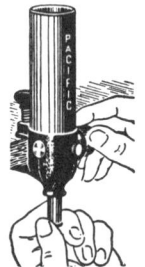

It is made for the pistol and Hornet reloader only. With this measure, you get speed and accuracy, one charge or 10,000 charges will all be the same. Does not stock and the moving parts work freely. Regularly supplied with cylinders to throw 2½, 3, and 3½ grains. Shipping weight 1¾ lbs.

Price for measure	$4.50
Extra charge cylinders	each .75
Milling the charge cylinder to any specified charge	1.00

SCHMITT & LYMAN RELOADING PRESSES

SCHMITT MODEL 24 RELOADING TOOL

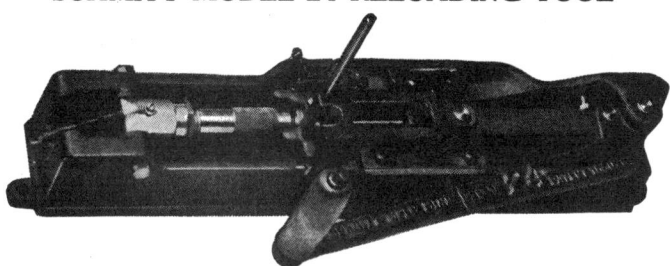

The Model 24 Schmitt tool has been designed for heavy duty and long service for quantity reloading. It does the following operations with one uninterrupted forward and backward movement of the operating lever;—full length resizing, expanding, re and decapping any rifle or pistol cases. Has micrometer head spacing adjustment.

Due to the arrangement of the operating lever and side rod this tool has by far the best leverage of any tool yet produced. The primer slide is wider and thicker and the decapping operation has been changed so it supports the entire head of case. The depth of seating the primer is controlled by a screw at the end of the base. All model 12 dies and seater can be used on the Model 24 tool by using Model 24 cross heads. Weight of complete tool is 27 pounds. Total length 20 inches.

Price of the Model 24 tool complete with full length resizing die and seater for rifle	$36.50
Extra rifle resizing die, full length	4.00
Extra die holder	1.50
Extra rifle bullet seater	4.00
Extra rifle bullet seater choke	.50
Price of the Model 24 tool complete with seater for pistol is	34.80
Extra resizing die for pistol, full length or neck	3.00
Extra pistol bullet seater	3.00
Extra pistol bullet seater choke	.50
Extra cross head	.80
Extra extractor	1.10
Extra primer slide for large or small primers	1.50
Extra expanding plug for rifle	.40
Extra recapping pin	.25
Extra decapping pins, per dozen	.40

LYMAN IDEAL TRU-LINE LOADING PRESS

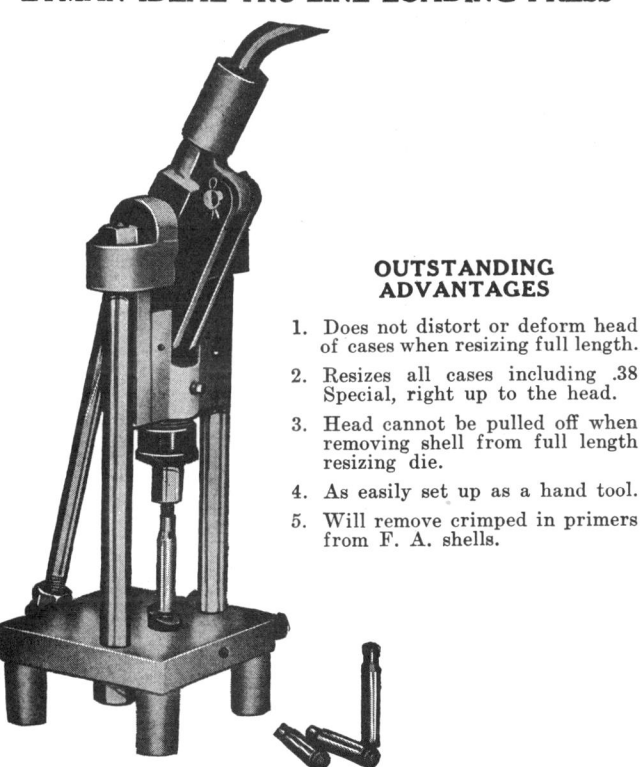

LYMAN-IDEAL TRU-LINE LOADING PRESS

OUTSTANDING ADVANTAGES

1. Does not distort or deform head of cases when resizing full length.
2. Resizes all cases including .38 Special, right up to the head.
3. Head cannot be pulled off when removing shell from full length resizing die.
4. As easily set up as a hand tool.
5. Will remove crimped in primers from F. A. shells.

In presenting the Ideal Tru-Line loading press we bring to individual handloaders a first-class bench outfit at a price within their reach. Practical features of improved design will be appreciated by reloaders because each advantage offered simplifies the work and insures uniform, high quality ammunition.

The Tru-Line press is constructed with the slide traveling on steel rods instead of in a casting. More finger room is thus provided all around the press and a great deal more light admitted which was heretofore shut off by the casting. Sockets in the base and slide are in perfect line, eliminating all necessity for adjustment of the dies for alignment.

Full length case resizing and decapping are now combined in a single operation. This is accomplished by placing the decapping pin in the end of a fixed ejector rod inside the sizing die. The decapping pin does not travel with the die. The operation consists of setting the case in the sizing shell holder and bringing the die clear down to the shell holder. On the up-stroke the case is lifted out of the shell holder by the die, and on reaching the primer punch the primer is forced out. As the die continues upward, the ejector rod forces the case out of the die. By this improved design, no strain is put upon the rim or extractor groove of the case.

Another advantage of this press is that this design permits a rim case to be sized clear to the head and a rimless or semi-rimless one to the solid portion of the head. As there is no lifting strain on the shell holder, it is located and held in place by a knurled head pilot screw. There are no belts or clamps required for the shell holder.

The Tru-Line press reduces priming and muzzle expanding to a single operation. The priming lever is quickly and easily attached to the base which stands 1½ inches high above the bench. With the shell holder and case set in position, the muzzle expanding plug is brought down into the neck of the case and held while the priming lever inserts primer.

The bullet is seated by the loading chamber at the desired depth, the depth being controlled by the adjustment of the bullet seating screw. The amount of crimp is controlled by the adjustable stop.

The four 1½-inch legs supporting the press are threaded inside for ⅜-inch 16 cap screws which will securely hold the press to the bench. No cuts in the bench are necessary for the priming lever.

All dies and expanding punches are made of special alloy steel, machined to close tolerances and specially heat treated and polished to a smooth, glass hard surface. In every detail the Tru-Line Press is sturdily constructed for easy, positive action and designed for long service.

Ideal Tru-Line Loading Press complete for .38 special and 30/06. Price	$35.00
Ideal Tru-Line Loading Press complete for .22 Hornet, .220 Swift, .257 Roberts, .270 Winchester, .250-3000, .30-40, .45 A.C.P. and .44 Special. Price	37.00

EXTRAS

Resizing shell holder	1.00
Loading shell holder	1.75
Shell Resizer for 38 Special and 30/06	3.00
Shell Resizer for other calibres	3.50
Loading chamber No. 5 only	2.00
Expanding plug standard size	2.00
Seating screw	1.00
Recapping punch	.50
Recapping punch spring	.25
Decapping rod, complete	1.00
Decapping pin (5)	.25

Prices on accessories necessary to load additional calibres subject to special quotation to avoid duplication of items.

POTTER DUPLEX & GEM RELOADING MACHINES

POTTER DUPLEX STANDARD MODEL

Price $35.00

(Complete with Powder Measure)

POTTER AUTOMATIC DUPLEX WITH POWDER MEASURE

PRICE $40.00

DESIGN

The POTTER reloading machine is so arranged that all operations required to reload fired shells may be set-up simultaneously. With this tool the necessity of re-handling the shells several times and storing them in containers between operations has been eliminated. From the time that a fired shell is picked up for the first operation, it is not laid aside until it is completely loaded and may be placed directly into a cartridge box as a finished product. However, if desired any of the separate operations may be performed on a quantity of shells without any change in the set-up or adjustments of the machine.

This machine is furnished with or without the attached powder measure shown in the cut. With the measure attached greater speed of reloading is possible, since this separate operation is eliminated, and no difficulty should be experienced in loading over 300 shells an hour.

Seating die may be adjusted to crimp or not as desired.

Easily adjustable for various calibers by interchanging dies.

CHANGING CALIBERS

A set of dies and parts to change the set-up to any other standard caliber, except .22 caliber cartridges, and using the same primers will cost $10.50. If both size primers are to be used, an extra magazine and feed slide would be required at a cost of $3.00.

PRICES

Loading Machine, complete	$35.00
Loading Machine, without Measure	31.50
Powder Measure Cylinders	2.00
Sizing and De-capping Die complete	5.00
Sizing Die	1.50
De-capping Screw and Pin	1.50
De-capping Pins, Revolver 6 for	.25
Bullet Seater Complete, Rifle or Revolver	4.00
Bullet Seating Screw	1.25
Shell Holding Plate	1.50
Primer Feed Slide	1.25
Primer Punch (flat or concave)	.50
Primer Punch Wrench	.25
Primer Punch Guide Plate	.25
Primer Magazine	1.75
Cartridge Box Holder	.50

This model is practically the same as our Standard Duplex, except that the priming lever at the left side of the base has been eliminated, since the priming devise is operated automatically.

Automatic Duplex with Powder Measure	27 lbs.	$40.00
Sub-base for Duplex	8 lbs.	2.25

POTTER GEM RELOADING TOOL

The GEM TOOL is equipped with the same bullet seating and sizing die assemblies as are furnished with the Duplex Loading Machine.

To operate, place a fired shell in the shell holding plate and lower the sliding head. This will re-size the case and remove the old primer, which drops through a hole in the base. The decapping screw is fitted with a shoulder, to remove the crimp, which leaves the shell slightly bell-mouthed, so as to facilitate the bullet entering without shaving. The shell is then put into the priming holder and a primer placed in position. By again lowering the head of the tool, the primer will be seated. The priming screw is adjustable, so that the depth to which the primer is seated may be regulated. The re-priming device is so designed that it is always set up and ready for use, since it does not in any way interfere with the sizing and seating operations.

The bullet seating set-up is quickly made by unscrewing the sizing die assembly and replacing it with the seating die. This die is adjustable, so that the amount of crimp may be regulated on revolver cases. Die to crimp rifle shells are furnished only on special order, at an extra cost of $1.00. The bullet seating screw is also adjustable to regulate the seating depth of the bullets for both rifle and revolver shells.

Gem Loading Tool .... 12 lbs. **$16.50**

POTTER RELOADING EQUIPMENT

ELECTRIC FURNACE
MODEL A
Price $10.00

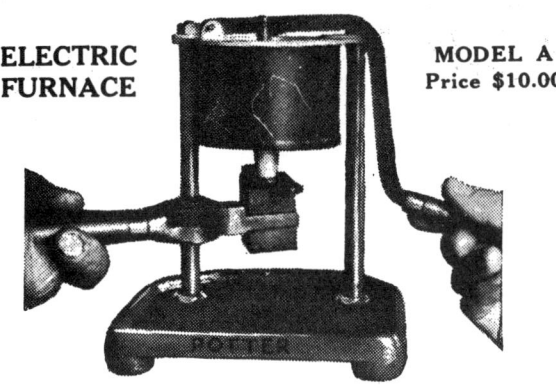

This method of casting bullets has several distinct advantages over previous methods. The electric furnace may be operated wherever current is available. The weight of the metal above the mould will force all of the air out and so cast more perfect bullets. With the electric furnace the handles of the mould do not become nearly as warm as with the old fashioned method, and no gloves are required for comfort.

The bullets may be cast more rapidly, and about 250 to 350 an hour may be produced with a single mould, depending upon the ability of the operator.

Model A Electric Furnace............................9 lbs. **$10.00**
(For 1 and 2 Cavity Moulds)

ELECTRIC FURNACE
MODEL B
Price $15.00

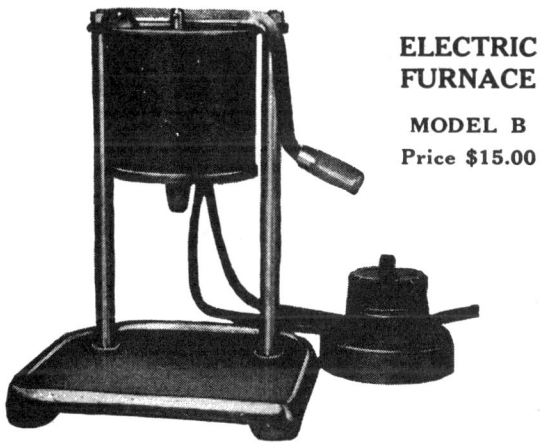

This furnace is of practically the same design as our smaller model but has a larger capacity, is equipped with a double heating element and a special switch so that it may be operated at two different temperatures, making it suitable for use with both mutiple and single cavity moulds.

Model B Electric Furnace............................12 lbs. **$15.00**
(For 1 to 6 Cavity Moulds)

THE MERIT MELTING POT

Makes casting perfectly uniform bullets extremely easy and fast—(from 400 to 500 bullets per hour with a single cavity mold). No bother with slag or dirt as it is gravity fed and the molten metal drawn from beneath the surface. Flow of metal controlled by simple, efficient valve. Shipping weight about 6 lbs.
Price **$6.50**

LEAD TESTER
Price $8.00

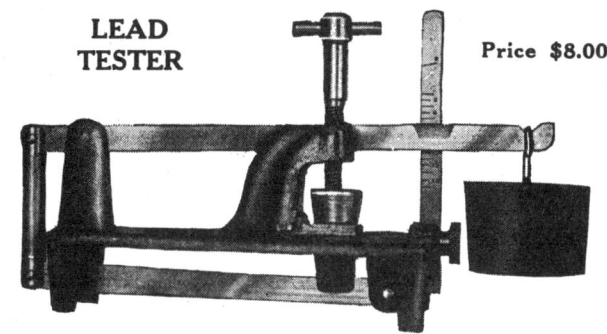

In order to produce bullets of uniform hardness, when both new lead and scrap lead are used in making the bullet alloy, we would recommend our Bullet Lead Tester. This instrument measures the hardness of bullet alloy by forcing a small steel ball into the metal. The depth to which the ball pierces the metal is indicated on a scale which is used as a measure for the hardness.
Lead Tester..8 lbs. **$8.00**

LEAD MIXING KETTLE
Price $2.00

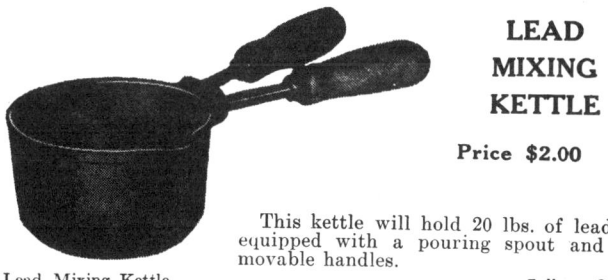

This kettle will hold 20 lbs. of lead, is equipped with a pouring spout and removable handles.
Lead Mixing Kettle..................................7 lbs. **$2.00**

CARTRIDGE BOX HOLDER
Price $.65

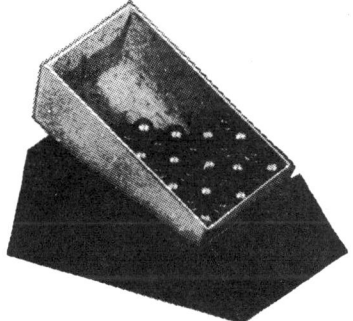

This is a very handy accessory, made of cast iron and so shaped that it will hold a cartridge box at just the right angle to allow the shells to be easily stacked with one hand.

Cartridge Box Holder................................2 lbs. **$.65**

INGOT MOULD
Price $.65

One ingot mould is supplied with each Potter Electric Furnace. It is convenient, however, to have extra moulds in order to speed up the casting of these ingots.
Ingot Mould...3 lbs. **$.65**

PRIMER TRAYS
Price $.85

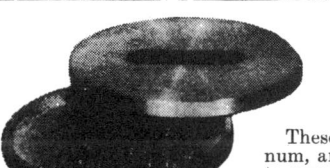

These trays, which are made of aluminum, are a very handy device in which to spread out the primers, so that they may be readily picked up by the primer magazine.
Primer Trays.. **$.85**

RELOAD FOR PLEASURE AND PROFIT

PEERLESS BULLET MOULDS

SINGLE CAVITY MOULD $4.00
Weight 2 lb.

TWO CAVITY MOULD $6.00
Weight 2 lb.

FOUR CAVITY MOULD
Weight 3 lb.

SIX CAVITY MOULD
(.32 or .38 cal. only)
Weight 5 lb.

Peerless Moulds are made as single cavity, 2 cavity, 4 cavity, and 6 cavity for a very large variety of bullets, the principal ones being shown on the opposite page. Except for the 6 cavity mould which is available only in .32 and .38 caliber, any of the three other moulds may be had for any of the bullets referred to on the opposite page.

The single cavity moulds are for the occasional hand loader where time and quantity are of little importance. Where these factors do enter, and larger quantities and economies are desired, the larger capacity moulds will be found more suitable.

All Peerless moulds are cut by machinery and the cavities are properly centered, of the same length and square with the cutoff side. The material is a mixture of iron, steel, and nickel, made in an electric furnace and is dense, tough and less subject to distortion than iron or steel alone. The handles are steel and can be bent slightly to suit the user. The whole mould is light in weight and the handles long, making it convenient to use.

Bullet weights are based on the proper lead and tin mixture and are guaranteed only within two to five grains.

All moulds are guaranteed to be of good material and workmanship and to eject the bullet easily. Any mould that does not meet these requirements will be replaced if it is returned promptly in good order.

PRICES

Single cavity, shipping weight 2 lbs. $4.00

Two cavity, shipping weight 2 lbs. 6.00

Four cavity, shipping weight 3 lbs. 12.00

Six cavity, (.32 or .38 cal. only), weight 5 lbs. 18.00
(.32 or .38 cal. only)

Any mould for a flat pointed bullet can be made to cast hollow pointed bullets, at a cost of $2.00 per each cavity so fitted.

Moulds cut for two different bullets $1.00 extra.

Most moulds can be furnished to cast bullets slightly over or under standard—specify sizing diameter.

TERMS

Since bullet moulds are individually made up to order and are therefore not returnable except where defective, we require full prepayment or 50% with order and balance c.o.d. upon delivery.

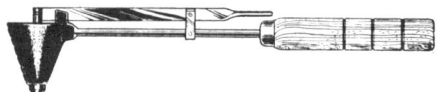

PRESSURE LEAD DIPPER

This dipper was designed for moulds with individual sprue holes—the nozzle machined to make a ground joint between the mould and dipper. In this manner the full weight of lead in dipper will be directly in the cavity of mould, which insures good, full base bullets, thereby eliminating practically all culls.
Price $2.50

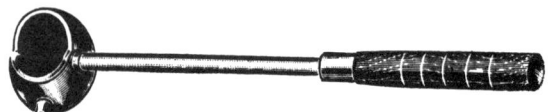

THE BIG DIPPER

The Big Dipper was designed to fill the need for a large, heavier dipper for gang mould work. It will be found a great convenience and time saver in quantity casting. Ample capacity is provided for the ten cavity mould, and the construction is heavy enough to prevent cooling of the metal prematurely.
Price $1.00

HINTS ON CASTING BULLETS

To harden lead and prevent lead deposits, tin should be added to the lead in the proportion of one to thirty for revolver bullets and black powder loads. For general use, fifteen parts lead to one part tin will be found satisfactory, whereas for maximum velocities the alloy should be one to ten.

The metals may be melted in any one of the various pots or furnaces shown in this section and to this mixture should be added a small amount of bees wax or tallow to flux the mixture of impurities, after which the latter may be skimmed off.

To cast perfect bullets, it is necessary that the mould be neither too cool nor too hot—the former condition causing incomplete bullets, the latter a burned or frosted appearance. After the bullets have been properly cast, the gas checks are attached if required, whereupon they should be greased and the excess removed by a cake cutter. For high accuracy, all bullets should be sized with a bullet sizer of which various ones will be found in this section.

BE SURE TO SPECIFY FOR WHICH BULLET MOULD IS REQUIRED
SEE PAGE 8, "HOW TO ORDER"

TYPES OF PEERLESS BULLETS

The proper selection of the bullet for the shooter is most important. We are listing, herewith, a large variety of bullets that have been in use for some time and are the product of shooters famous for their success in creating them. The shape and weight are thoroughly tested and can be relied upon to give you complete satisfaction.

On the left side of this page you will find the most popular standard sizes for revolver and rifle target shooting in caliber .25, .30, .38, .44, and .45. On the right we list special sizes of different calibers used for hunting and target shooting.

In case you do not find the type of bullet you require, we are prepared to have a mould made almost for any other size not listed here. A sample bullet should be sent in, in such cases. Please note the first number is the bullet number, the second the nominal diameter it will size to, and the third the approximate weight in grains.

Illustrations are only for the purpose of showing the different types of bullets which may be cast with the Peerless Moulds shown on the opposite page, and thus to facilitate the proper selection. We positively do not sell any of the bullets on this page.

Top or seating punches, cut with the bullet cherry, can be furnished at regular prices, insuring proper fit and avoiding mutilation of the bullet point.

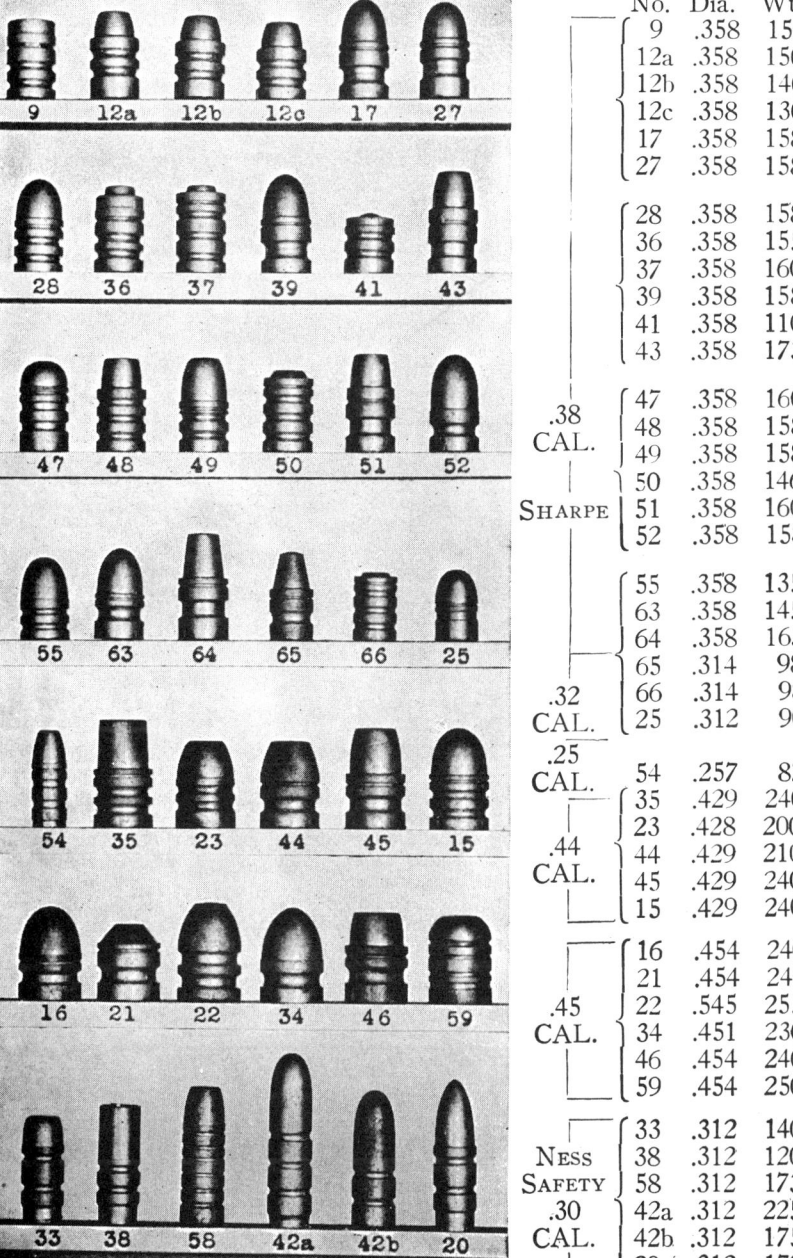

	No.	Dia.	Wt.
	9	.358	150
	12a	.358	150
	12b	.358	140
	12c	.358	130
	17	.358	158
	27	.358	158
	28	.358	158
	36	.358	155
	37	.358	160
	39	.358	158
	41	.358	110
	43	.358	173
.38 CAL.	47	.358	160
	48	.358	158
	49	.358	158
SHARPE	50	.358	146
	51	.358	160
	52	.358	158
	55	.358	135
	63	.358	145
	64	.358	163
	65	.314	98
.32 CAL.	66	.314	98
	25	.312	90
.25 CAL.	54	.257	87
	35	.429	240
	23	.428	200
.44 CAL.	44	.429	210
	45	.429	240
	15	.429	240
	16	.454	240
	21	.454	240
.45 CAL.	22	.545	255
	34	.451	230
	46	.454	240
	59	.454	250
NESS SAFETY	33	.312	140
	38	.312	120
	58	.312	173
.30 CAL.	42a	.312	225
	42b	.312	175
	20	.312	170

1—Round Ball in various Calibers.
2—Picket Type in various Calibers.
11—22 Cal. 45 Grs. G. C.
14—22 Cal. Gas Check 47 Grs.
4—22 Cal. designed by Perry D. Frazer, 47 Grs.
5—25 Cal. Frazer bullet, 87 Grs.
69—270 Winchester Gas Check, 140 Grs.

24—7 M M Gas Check, 140 Grs.
67—Made in 30 and 32 Calibers. 115 Grs.
26—32 S & W Round Nose. 98 Grs.
10—Made for 32-40 or 33-40, 190 Grs.
8—35 W. C. F. Gas Check, 250 Grs.
19—38-55 Gas Check, Weighs to 300 Grs.

7—9 M. M. 125 Grs.
56—358-165, 38 S. & W. Spec.
31—358-130, 38 S. & W. Spec.
57—358-175 and 200 "Manstopper"
61—358-148, 38 S. & W. Spec.
6—38-40 W. C. F. Also made for 40 Cal.

18—40 Caliber, 240 to 300 Grs.
68—45 Colts Auto, 200 Grs. wadcutter*.
71—45 Colts Auto. Standard Ogive, 200 Grs.
72—45 Colts Auto, 200 Grs.
70—45 Caliber, 300 to 500 Grs.
3—50 Caliber, 400 Grs.

* Note—Number 68 is the new Crawford 45 Colt Auto. 200 grain bullet that improves 25 yard timed and rapid scores. Exceptionally pleasant to shoot when loaded with 3 (three) grains Bull's Eye, or equivalent. Cuts clean hole in target. Reduces recoil. Functions positively.

A BULLET FOR EVERY NEED

CRAMER BULLET MOULDS

Cramer Bullet Moulds are designed to give maximum precision in reload bullet castings. The cavities in these moulds are cut in a machine that was designed and built especially for this purpose.

The larger five and eight cavity moulds, and especially the ten cavity model are especially useful for Police Ranges and Clubs where a great quantity of bullets must be made. The enthusiastic recommendations of police departments throughout the country are a guarantee of the quality, practicalness and efficiency of these moulds.

PRECISION

Cramer Bullet Moulds are made to an extremely high degree of precision, the manufacturing tolerance being unusually close. The result is that even in a large-capacity mould like the ten cavity, the variation in bullet weights will be within one grain.

The importance of this can hardly be over-estimated in target practice, and is in considerable degree responsible for the fine target records made by many users of Cramer Bullet Moulds.

DEEP POURING GROOVES

Extra deep pouring grooves are a feature of Cramer Moulds. The grooves are wide and deep, providing a sufficient weight of metal above the bullet to insure the metal flowing to every part of the cavities, and resulting in perfect, full-base bullets.

LONG LIFE

Cramer Bullet Moulds will give years of service and satisfaction even in the hardest types of service. From Mexico City to Vancouver, British Columbia as well as throughout the United States, Cramer Bullet Moulds in the hands of Police Departments and pistol and rifle clubs are giving satisfactory service.

TWO-THREE-FIVE-EIGHT CAVITY MOULDS

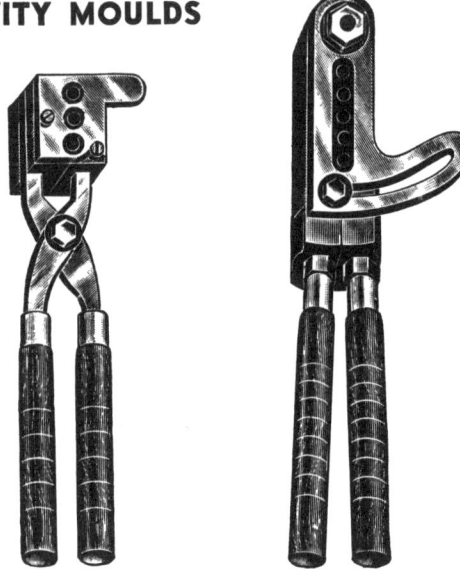

TEN CAVITY MOULD

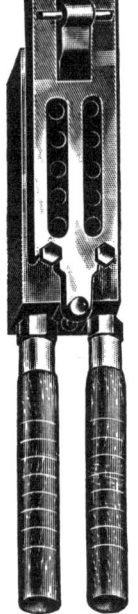

Particularly Recommended for Police Departments and Clubs

Ten Cavity Mould Open

Made of virgin iron, accurately machined. The mould blocks are set loose in the handles to insure perfect alignment. Long comfortable handles, permit casting of many bullets without tiring.

Price: 2 Cavity Mould $6.00
       3 Cavity Mould 7.50

Hollow point or hollow base moulds can only be had in 2-cavity blocks. Either one or both cavities hollow point or hollow base. **$1.00 Extra Per cavity**

Price: 5 Cavity Mould $15.00
       8 Cavity Mould 20.00

SPECIAL CHERRIES

The bullets illustrated and described on opposite page cover nearly every requirement of the pistol or rifle range, Police Department, or hunter. However, from time to time we have requests for moulds for bullets of special design. If you require a bullet not shown in the illustration we can make a mould for you to fit your specifications exactly. The mould price remains the same, but a charge of $8.50 is made for the special cherry required in machining the cavities. Cherry remains manufacturer's property.

The CRAMER Ten-Cavity Mould is the only mould of its size on the market. For Police Ranges and clubs where large quantities of bullets are cast, the ten-cavity mould will be found a great time saver.

Due to the patented construction of this ten-cavity mould, the ejection of bullets is automatic, resulting in greatly increased production and efficiency.

Construction is entirely of cast iron. The handles are large and comfortable permitting casting for long periods without fatigue.

As with all Cramer Moulds, the pouring grooves are wide and deep, giving a sufficient weight of metal above the bullets to insure perfect, full-base bullets.

Price: Ten Cavity Mould $30.00

A RECOMMENDATION

During the years I have supervised the reloading operations for the Los Angeles Police Department, I have used Cramer Moulds exclusively. A ten-cavity mould was in constant use for twelve months during which time eighteen tons of lead was moulded. At the end of this time it was still moulding perfect bullets.— J. J. (Jake) Engbrecht, 1936 Calif. State Pistol Champion National All-around Pistol Champion.

ALL MOULDS AVAILABLE FOR ANY BULLET ON OPPOSITE PAGE

CRAMER BULLETS

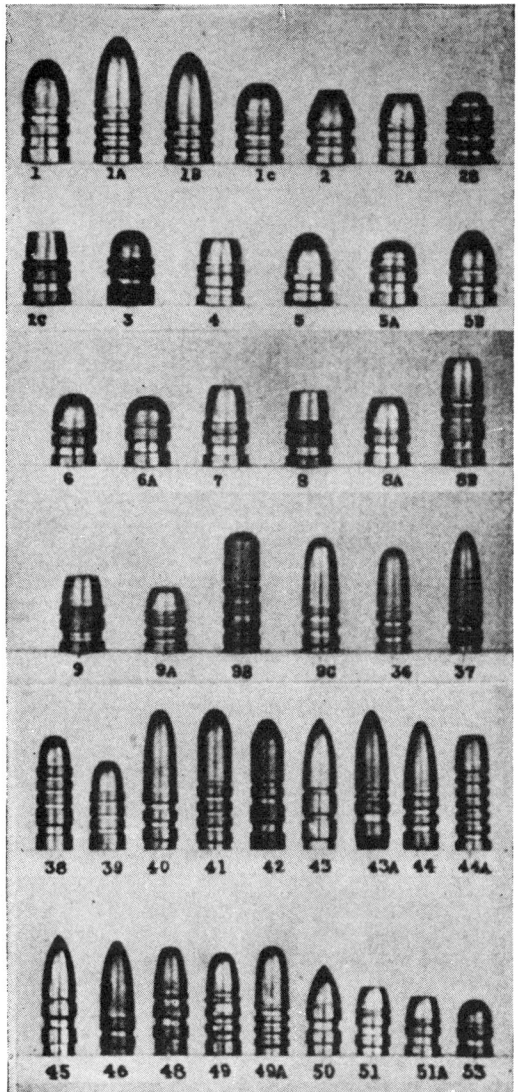

THE bullets illustrated and numbered are those for which any Cramer Mould may be had. The bullets themselves are not offered for sale.

The selection is varied, and each bullet has been designed, tested, perfected and used extensively over a long period of time.

In selecting the proper type of bullet it is always advisable for the beginner to take into consideration one of the standard reloading tables such as are to be found in either the Lyman or Belding & Mull Handbooks. Either book is available from us at a cost of 50c.

A special group of bullets is shown for the great fraternity of .38 Special and .357 Magnum enthusiasts.

Remember that a well cast bullet is absolutely necessary for accurate shooting, and that such bullets can only be had with such high quality moulds as are shown on the opposite page.

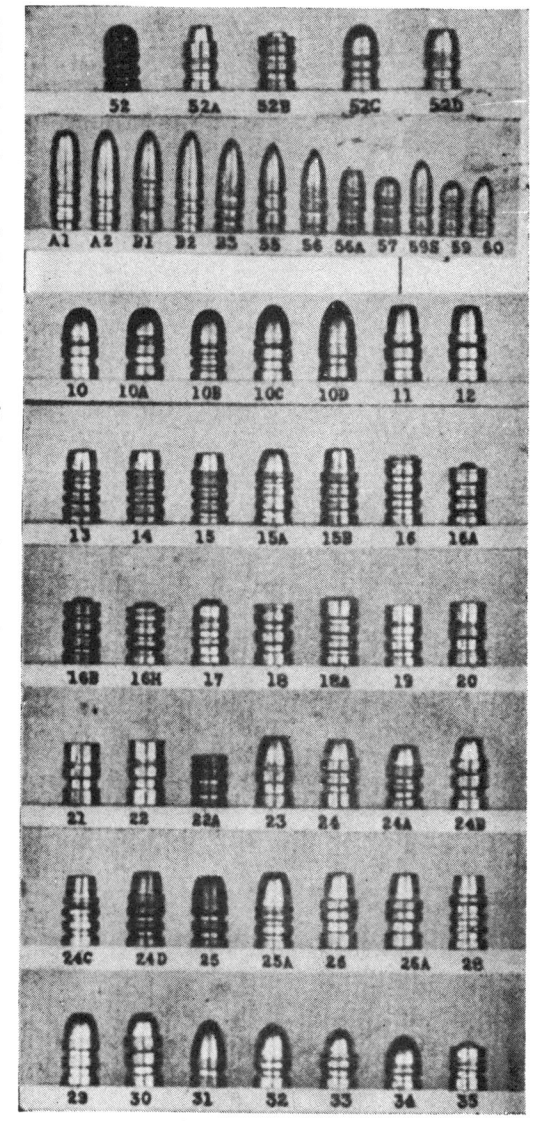

STANDARD BULLETS

No.	Spec	Description
1	457—387—45—70	Springfield
1A	458—425—45—70	Springfield
1B	458—360—45—70	Springfield
1C	458—290—45—70	Springfield
2	454—255—45	Colt Frontier
2A	454—250—45	Colt Frontier
2B	454—250W—45	Colts
2C	454—240 H. B.—45	Colts
3	454—255A—45	Colts Frontier
4	452—240—45	Auto Rim
5	452—230—45	Colts Automatic
5A	452—225—45	Auto Rim
5B	452—235—45	Colts Automatic
6	431—248—44	S & W Special
6A	431—244—44	S & W Special
7	431—250—44	S & W Special
8	431—240 H. B.—44	Special
8A	429—220—44	Colts
8B	413—335—.405	Winchester
9	401—180 H. B.—38—40	Colts
9A	401—175—38—40	Colts
9B	359—280—.35	Winchester
9C	358—245—.35	Winchester
36	326—190—8MM	
37	326—185—8MM	
38	323—180—32—40	Schuetzen
39	323—146—32—40	Schuetzen
40	311—200S—30	Cal. gas check
41	311—208—30	Cal. gas check
42	311—200—30	Cal.
43	311—191—30	Cal. gas check
43A	311—195—30	Cal.
44	311—180—30	Cal.
44A	311—175—Pope	
45	311—169—Squib gas check	
46	311—158—300	Savage gas check
48	311—160—30-30	Winchtr. gas check
49	311—150—30-30	Winchester
49A	311—170—30	Cal. gas check
50	311—122—30	Cal. gas check
51	311—122—30	Cal. gas check
51A	311— 95—30	Cal.
53	311— 84—30	Cal. Indoor
52	313—100—32	Cal. S & W
52A	313— 95—32	Cal.
52B	313— 95W—32	Cal.
52C	313—100R—32	Cal.
52D	313— 95A—32	Cal.
A1	287—140—7MM	
A2	287—130—7MM	
B1	280—123—270	Winchester
B2	280—125—270	Winchester
B3	280—115—270	Winchester
55	257— 93—250	Savage
56	257— 85—250	Savage
56A	257— 75—25—20	Winchester
57	257— 75—250	Savage
59S	228— 62—22	High Power
59	225— 48	Hornet
60	225—48H	Hornet

.38 SPECIAL & MAGNUM

No.	Spec	Description
10	358—158	S. T. D. round nose
10A	358—158B	Round nose Bullet with bevel Base for easy loading
10B	358A—158	Round nose two grease rings
10C	358—158	I. D.
10D	358—160S	
11	358—160	H. P. Hollow Point Kieth type
12	358—173	Solid Point Kieth type
13	357—158	S. A.
14	357—169	Same as No. 13 except solid point
15	357—158	Magnum
15A	357—160	Magnum
15B	358M—158	Magnum
16	358—155	H. B. Deep seating hollow base w. c.
16A	358P—148	Wadcutter
16B	358P—158	Wadcutter
16H	358B—146	Wadcutter
17	358—155	T. G. Wadcutter
18	358—149	Wadcutter
18A	358—158M	Hollow Base Miller Special
19	358—152X	Wadcutter
20	358—158	W. C.
21	358—147	Wadcutter
22	358—150	H. B. Wadcutter
22A	358B—130	
23	358—158Y	This is a very satisfactory all-round bullet
24	358—150	F. N. Semi Wadcutter
24A	358—130	F. N. Semi Wadcutter
24B	358D—150	Semi Wadcutter
24C	358E—158	Semi Wadcutter
24D	358O—158	Semi Wadcutter
25	358—160	Flat Nose hunting bullet
25A	358—158H	Hunting bullet
26	358—158	K. H. B. Hollow point Kieth
26A	358C—160	Kieth type
28	358—158	M. H. B. Hollow Base Magnum
29	358—158B	An accurate bullet with no crimping groove
30	358—158F	Semi wadcutter
31	358—136—9MM	Luger
32	358—127—.38	Super
33	358—115	Indoor Semi Wadcutter
34	358—100—.380	Colts Auto.
35	358—106	Indoor wadcutter

HOME CAST BULLETS CUT SHOOTING COSTS

MEEPOS RELOADING TOOLS

RELOADING TOOL

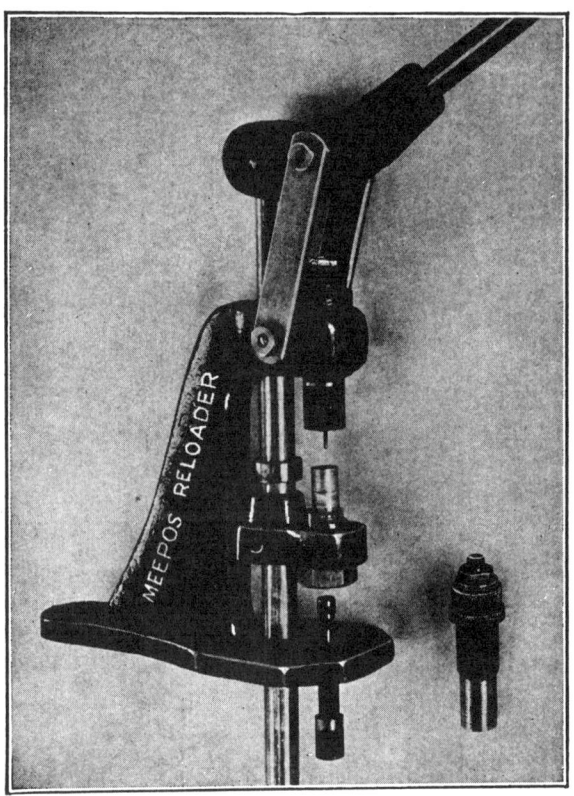

Upright Position—No Powder Spilling

Furnished complete with dies to resize, decapp, recapp, expand case, and seat bullet

Price Complete (For One Caliber) **$18.00**

(Shipping weight approximately 10 lbs.)

The Meepos Reloader is a straight line vertical Tool that combines decapping, resizing, expanding of neck and recapping of case in one up and down stroke of the lever, when reloading either Rifle or pistol cases.

The dies are interchangeable for any caliber in the same tool. They can be easily and quickly removed or adjusted as there are no pins to remove or get loose.

Shell holder is held by a lock nut, and the dies screw in their respective holders. All dies have lock nuts with set screws that are locked in position so that the die may be removed without affecting its adjustments.

Full length dies are standard for Pistols and neck sizing dies are standard for Rifles. Full length dies for Rifle are $2.00 additional. Bullet seating is quickly accomplished and the bullets are seated absolutely straight as the bullet and case are held in line by the seating die before and while the bullet is seated to the proper depth. Adjustable to any length bullet.

AN AUTOMATIC PRIMER FEED

An Automatic primer feed that holds a hundred primers can be purchased for $2.50. The primers are filled in the tubes by inverting the tube and pressing over primer one at a time. The entire tube can be filled in less than two minutes. Small or large primer size must be specified when ordering.

The decapping pins will punch out a 30-06 government crimped Primers without breaking. Cases are crimped at the same time as bullets are seated, or may be left straight as desired. The Primer cup is on a screw adjustment. The Primers are seated at the end of the stroke to the proper depth and does not depend on the pressure exerted on lever. This is an important feature in Reloading as a protruding primer may cause a Gun to jam or give other difficulties while a Primer that is mashed by seating too deep will give uneven ignition, or cause misfire.

To size bullets in this reloader you can buy a bullet sizing die pin and holder priced at $2.75 complete.

Extra dies $2.00, bullet pin 50c for any shaped bullet.

All dies are made of carbon tool steel and are hardened by liquid carborising.

BULLET SIZER AND LUBRICATOR

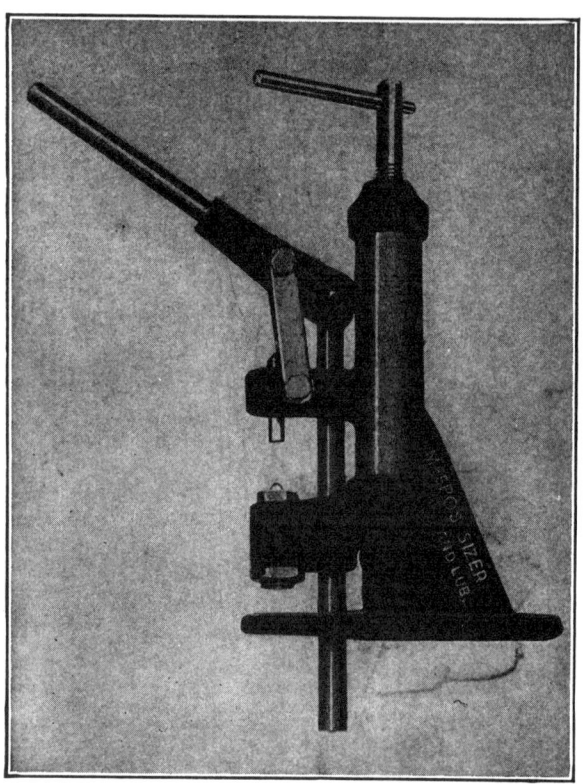

The Meepos Bullet Sizer and Lubricator is a speedy easy working tool, a real time saver. The bullets are sized and lubricated in one operation. The Lubrication of your bullets is done in the most efficient and cleanest manner and does away with the slow and messy job of hand dipping. One stock of lubricator takes care of 500 to 2500 bullets depending on the caliber and size.

(Shipping weight approximately 10 lbs.)
Price complete with one set of dies...........................$12.00
Extras dies.. 2.00
Bullet pins... .50

PRICES FOR RELOADER PARTS

Full length Sizing die for straight cases..............$2.50
Neck sizing die for bottle neck cases 2.00
Full length sizing dies for bottle neck cases 4.00
Pistol or rifle expanders and decappers 1.50
Shell holders (all calibres) 1.50
Small or large primer seaters 1.25
Seating dies (straight cases) 3.00
Seating dies (bottle neck cases) 3.50
Bullet seating pins .... .50
Decapping pins ....6 for 15c

A LOAD FOR EVERY PURPOSE

WILSON TOOLS AND GAGES

UNIVERSAL CASE TRIMMER

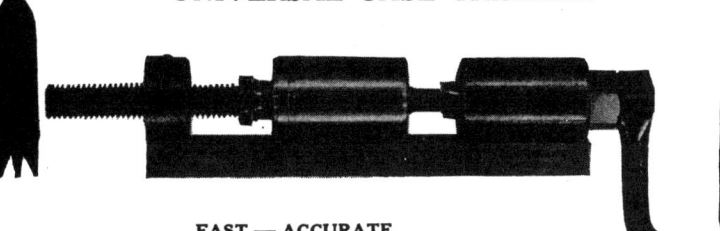

FAST — ACCURATE

The one cutter trims all cases from .22 to .437 neck diameter. Trimmer will handle the short Hornet case or the long .300 Magnum with equal facility. The case head stop, as shown in the illustration, has screw adjustment. In changing from one caliber to another it is necessary only to substitute shell holders and adjust the stop.

With each trimmer, without extra cost, is included a hardened tool steel burring tool of our own design which is used by hand to remove the sharp edge left after trimming. This tool, shown in cut on the left, is a double-ended affair, one end being used on the outside edge and the other side on the inside edge of the case mouth. Cuts in both directions and the sharp edge is removed in a jiffy. One burring tool handles all calibers within the range of the trimmer. Price, when sold separate from trimmer, 90c.

Price, with one shell holder (in any of above calibers) $7.50. Extra shell holders in above calibers, $1.00, each.

Carried in stock in the following calibers: .22 Hornet, .22-3000 Lovell, .22 Savage High Power, .22 Niedner Magnum, .219 Zipper, .220 Swift, .25-20 Single Shot, .25-.35, .250-3000 Savage, .257 Roberts, 6.5 MM, 7 MM, .270 Winchester, .30-30, .30 Remington Auto, .30-40 Krag, .30-'06, .300 Savage, .300 H. & H. Magnum, .303 Savage, .32 Winchester Special and .375 H. & H. Magnum.

By the use of a special type shell holder, the trimmer is now available in .38 S. & W. Spl. caliber. Price with soft steel shell holder, $7.50 (not recommended in this caliber). Price with hardened tool steel shell holder, $8.50. Shell holders alone, soft, $1.00, hardened, $2.00.

We will make up special shell holders for odd calibers at a special price. Customers should submit one or two sample fired cases for quotation. Usually these special holders can be made up for $2.00, each.

INSIDE NECK REAMER
(Illustration on Left Side)

ILLUSTRATION BELOW shows INSIDE NECK REAMER used in conjunction with SHELL TRIMMER

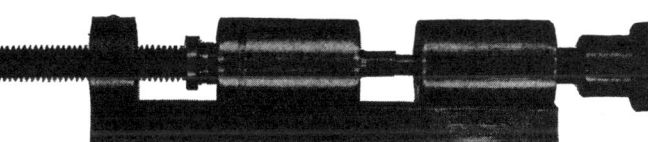

Left illustration shows the Wilson inside neck reamer for the .220 Swift case. Right illustration shows how this reamer is used in conjunction with the shell trimmer. If you have a Wilson shell trimmer with a shell holder for the Swift case all you need to buy to ream the inside of your case necks is this new reamer. IMPORTANT: This reamer is designed for use on the cases just as they come from the rifle chamber and NOT after resizing. If they need reaming, the reamer will cut. Otherwise it will not. The reamer is made from .0025 to .003 inches larger than the Swift bullet and if the case neck has thickened so as to reduce the clearance below that figure, the reamer will remove the excess metal. The short bearing portion of the reamer shank is ground slightly undersize purposely so as to "float" the reamer for better cutting effect. Like the rest of our tools and gages, this reamer is guaranteed satisfactory. Price, $4.50, postpaid.

CAL. .30-'06 HEAD SPACE GAGES

These Head Space Gages are made of high grade tool steel hardened and ground. They are absolutely necessary to check the head space on new chambering jobs, or on used rifles from time to time. Indispensable to gunsmiths, rifle clubs and service organizations. They come in sets of three: Minimum 1.940 size, Maximum 1.946, Field gage, 1.950. Each gage can also be had separately. Price, $5.00, each.

CARTRIDGE CASE GAGE
Made in .30-'06 only
FOR CHECKING RESIZED CASES

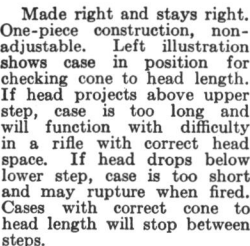

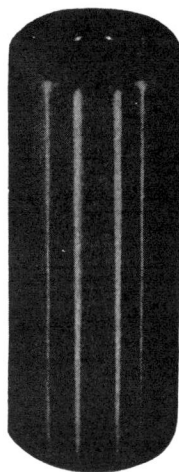

Made right and stays right. One-piece construction, non-adjustable. Left illustration shows case in position for checking cone to head length. If head projects above upper step, case is too long and will function with difficulty in a rifle with correct head space. If head drops below lower step, case is too short and may rupture when fired. Cases with correct cone to head length will stop between steps.

Opposite end of gage checks over-all length as shown in right illustration. If mouth of case projects above upper step, case is too long and may bottom in chamber. Such cases should be trimmed or discarded. Few cases will be found under minimum over-all length but many will be found over maximum, especially if they have been full-length resized a number of times.

Price $3.50   Price $3.50

In nearly every case involving a broken cartridge case in .30-'06 rifles the trouble is caused by excess head space, either due to a faulty rifle or improperly resized cases—and equally as dangerous from the one cause as the other. Why take chances?

In addition to the illustrated and listed tools and gauges the following items produced by the same maker can be had. They are a necessity to the handloader and shooter.

Cartridge case trimmers complete in .38 Spec. with hardened holder.. $8.50
Shell holders, all calibers listed except .38 Spec. 1.00
.38 Spec. hardened holders 2.00
Straight line full length resizing die, .22 Hornet, 22-3000, 220 Swift,
  257 Roberts, .30-'06 and 300 Magnum............................ 6.00
Cartridge case micrometer, .30-'06 only............................ 7.50
Throat gage, .30-'06 .... 7.50

Club Set of Four .22 Cal. Barrel Gauges

It cannot be too well known among riflemen how great is the danger of a worn muzzle. Not only the lands but the grooves are worn away without its being discernible to the eye on account of its being overshadowed. In order that rifles can be periodically checked we recommend the following gauges.

.2165 inch—the average bore diameter of the .22 caliber rifle; it will either pass through or it will gauge to what depth the muzzle end is worn.

.218 inch—may sometimes pass through a good barrel.

.2185 inch—over bore size, it indicates the extent to which wear has taken place by the depth it will pass in at the muzzle.

.221 inch—is nearly the average groove diameter of a .22 inch barrel. If it enters at all it shows that the groove diameter is also worn.

Price $20.00

RELOADING BRINGS PLEASURE AND PROFIT

IDEAL SHOTSHELL RELOADING TOOLS

The reloading of shotshells is safe, economical, and simple, enabling the reloader to load shells which will give better results than the factory product in his particular gun. The skeet shooter, trap shooter or hunter will find that he can save enough in a short time in reloading his fired cases to pay for a good set of reloading tools, besides providing himself with a most fascinating pastime or hobby.

STRAIGHTLINE RE- and DE-CAPPER
Furnished for All Gauges from 10 to .410

Expels plain or battery cup primers but will be furnished for battery cup primers unless otherwise specified. For plain primers, a different Stud "A" and Crosshead "D" is required. It can be adapted to any gauge by purchasing extra Guide Bushings "H."

This tool combines the operations of re- and decapping in a highly satisfactory manner. In priming shotgun cartridges, it is of the utmost importance to seat primers to a uniform depth. The IDEAL Straight Line Re- and De-Capper is the *only* tool that will seat plain primers to an absolutely uniform depth.

Price $3.00
Weight 1¼ lb.

Extra Guide Bushing..........50c.   Extra Crosshead..........50c.

LOADING MACHINE FOR SHOT SHELLS
Made for 10, 12, 16 and 20 Gauges Only

This machine is designed to perform the operations of charging shells with powder, ramming the over-powder and filler wads, and measure the shot charge with only one handling of the shell. It is the only machine that will handle fired cases and measure all kinds of powders in either drams or grains. It can be set to throw charges of many powders by the graduations alone but, in common with all mechanical measures, the setting should be checked with a scale when dense powders are used.

The shot measure is graduated in ounces and is easily and accurately adjustable.

The powder measure can be used for charging rifle and pistol cases as it can be swung to one side and used independently of the charging tube. For this purpose the funnel "R" will be required which can be supplied at small additional cost.

The method of adjusting the measuring slide is the same as for the IDEAL No. 5 Powder Measure except that the slide takes the place of the "D" and "E" slides of the No. 5 Measure.

The arrangement of the charging cavities is such that one is in the charging position when the other is in the discharging position. There is a stop so located that the charging handle can be left in a half-way position with the cavities cut off from the powder and shot reservoirs, eliminating any possibility of irregular charges settling in the cavities from the jarring due to ramming the wads.

The operation of the machine is simple and convenient.

Ideal Loading Machine No. 1 price........................$17.00
Ideal Loading Machine No. 2........................18.00
Attachments (10-20 ga.) No. 1........................3.00
Attachments (10-20 ga.) No. 2........................4.00
Rammer Tube 10-20 ga. No. 1........................85
Rammer Guide Bushing 10-20 ga. No. 1........................75
Shell Receiver 10-20 ga. No. 1........................2.00
Shell Receiver 10-20 ga. No. 2........................3.00
Funnel "R"........................85
Reservoir (powder or shot)........................50

IDEAL Pocket and Shot Measure $.50
IDEAL Pocket Closer $1.00

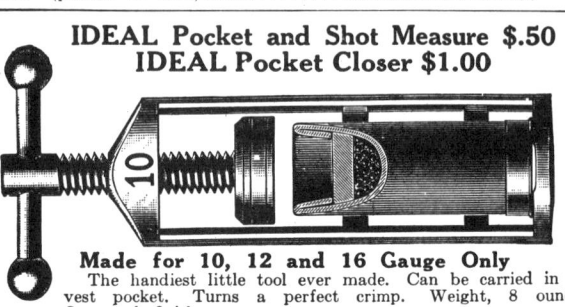

Made for 10, 12 and 16 Gauge Only

The handiest little tool ever made. Can be carried in the vest pocket. Turns a perfect crimp. Weight, 8 ounces. Japanned finish.

IDEAL SHELL TRIMMER

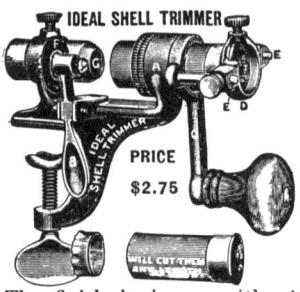

PRICE $2.75

No outfit for reloading paper shot shells is complete without this implement. With it the soft and frayed ends of shells that have been fired a number of times, may be ironed at the mouth or cut off to any length.

These implements will be made for 10, 12, 16, 20, 24 and 28 gauge only. They will cut shells any length from 3½ to 2 inches. They are light and strong, made of malleable iron.

The finish is japan, with nickel trimmings. The cutter of the best quality of tool steel, hardened properly, tempered and ground. Will last a lifetime. The plug G and the Shell Holder D may be purchased for different gauges so that one Shell Trimmer may be used for all or any of the gauges listed. Weight about 1½ lb.

Extra shell Holder.............50c.   Extra Plug.............50c.

STRAIGHTLINE HAND LOADER

Those who do not load in sufficient quantities to warrant the purchase of a complete loading machine, will find this implement all that they desire. The illustration shows it is a handy portable hand loader that may be used by being fastened to a bench or not, as desired. The "Straightline" Hand Loader will be made for 10, 12, 16, 20, 28 gauge only. Parts "A" and "B" are different for each gauge; the part "C" is the same for all gauges. Those having an Ideal Loading Machine, desiring a portable hand implement to take with them on a trip, may purchase only the parts "A", "C" and "D" and use the chamber that is with the loading machine, for the part "B" in the "Straightline" Hand Loader is the same as chamber No. 2 in the Loading Machine.

Shipping weight about 1¼ lbs.

10-28 gauge $4.00

IDEAL Pocket Loader $1.50

Weight 6 oz.

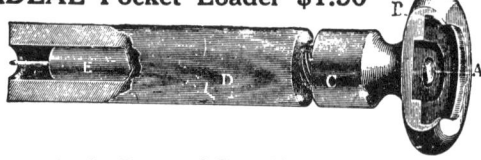

Loader for Paper and Brass Shot Shells.
Capper, De-Capper, Rammer and Extractor.

EUREKA SHOTGUN SHELL LOADING SET

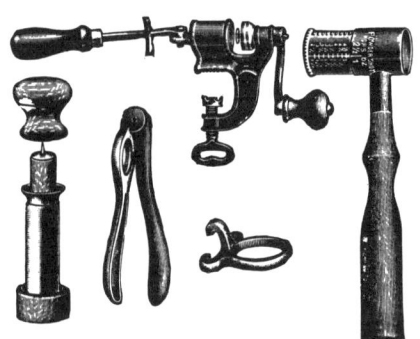

No. 160—Brass and Paper Shell Set in partitioned box—comprising No. 189 Loader, No. 0 Closer, No. 1180B Recapper, No. 20R Powder and Shot Measure and No. X Extractor—10 to 28 gauge.
Price, each........$1.75
410 (12 M-M) and 32 gauge (14 M-M), each......2.25
Loading Block No. 75, 10 to 28 gauge, each......1.10
Wad Cutter No. 199, 8 to 28 gauge, each......60

SHOT SHELL RELOADING MACHINES AND ACCESSORIES

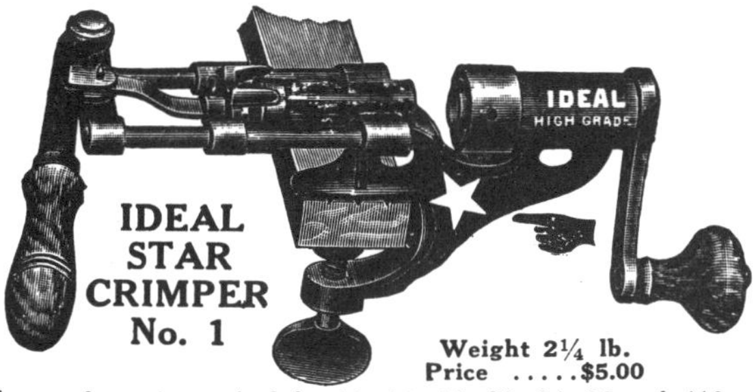

IDEAL STAR CRIMPER No. 1

Weight 2¼ lb.
Price $5.00

Only one frame is required for 10, 12, 16, 20, 24, 28 and 410 gauges. We are now using a new Solid Steel Crimping Head that turns a perfect Round Crimp equal to that found on factory ammunition. These Crimping Heads are made of carefully heat treated steel and will give long service. Ideal Crimping Machines are the only ones that operate in a perfectly straight line that will turn a perfect crimp and will permit of interchangeable Heads and Followers for all popular gauges.

The IDEAL Star Crimper No. 2

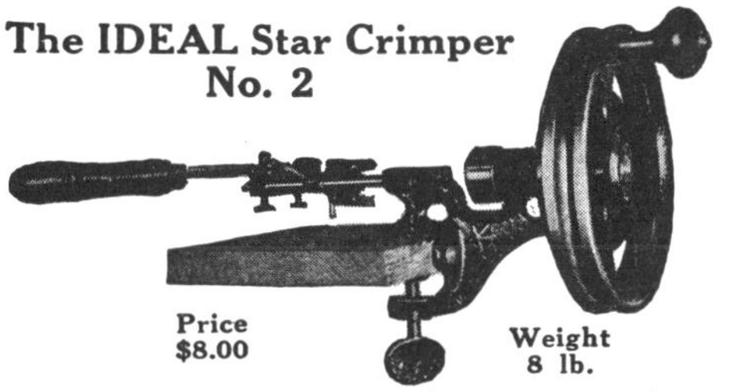

Price $8.00
Weight 8 lb.

Made especially for the application of power. The frames, crimping heads and grips are the same as for the No. 1 Star Crimper. Heavy balance wheel and two speed diameters, 6 inches and 3 inches. Bearing or journal is long, insuring greater length of service and steady running. Balance wheel also equipped with handle for hand operation if desired. The No. 2 Star Crimper is satisfactory when driven by electric motor, but is recommended for intermittent use, that is, for the use of the individual reloader. There is an advantage in a power driven Crimper as it can be driven steadily at a higher speed than by hand. Friction thus generated between Crimping Head and paper shell softens water proofing compound in the paper which rehardens on cooling, making a firm crimp. The No. 2 Star Crimper is used and recommended by one of the large powder companies. Made for 10, 12, 16, 20, 24, 28 and 410 gauges. For Crimping Shot Shells in large quantities and where the crimper is to be driven for long periods, we recommend our No. 5 Star Crimper.

IDEAL Star Crimper No. 5
Heavy Duty Power Machine

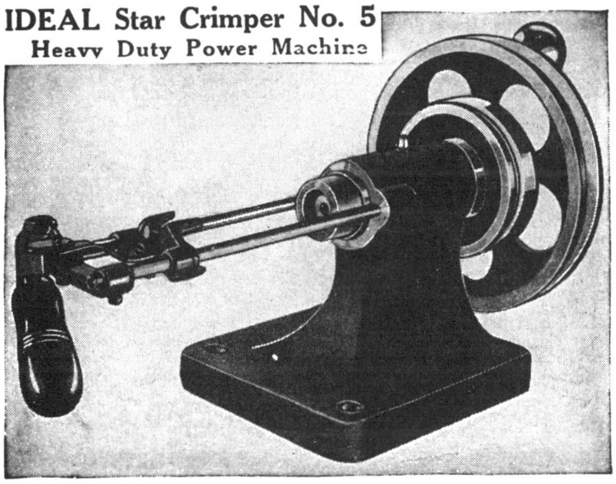

The No. 5 Star Crimper is an improvement of our No. 4 Star Crimper. The design has been modified to permit the Shell to be held by the fingers conveniently while being crimped, thereby preventing the possibility of the shell being rotated by friction between the Crimp and the Crimping Head which sometimes happened with the No. 4, causing the head of the case to be scraped and scored at the rim. While equipped with a handle for hand operation in an emergency, the No. 5 is primarily designed as a power machine. Materials and workmanship are the best. Equipped with oil cups and bronze bearings. Recommended to dealers and gun clubs who load or reload shot shells in quantities. The No. 5 will be made to special order only, necessitating a slight delay in filling orders. Furnished for 10, 12, 16, 20, 24, 28 and 410 gauges and uses the regular Star Crimping Heads.

Price	**$30.00**
Extra Crimping Heads	**1.80**

GUN WADS AND CARDBOARDS

Wads Will Be Supplied in One-Half Gauges, Cut to Order

WHITE FELT, ⅜ INCH THICK

An ungreased cushion wad, for heavy loads. To be fitted over grease proof wad or cardboard.

	Price Per Box of 125
10 Gauge	**$1.90**
21, 16, 20, 24, and 28 Gauge	**1.85**

BLACK EDGE, 3/16, ¼ and ⅜ INCH THICK

A filler wad, may be used instead of white felt wad, for lighter, cheaper loads.

	Price Per Box of 125 3/16"	Price Per Box of 125 ¼"	Price Per Box of 125 ⅜"
10 Gauge	**$.40**	**$.50**	**$.85**
12, 16, 20, 24, 28, and .410 Ga.	**.35**	**.45**	**.80**

PINK EDGE, 3/16 and ¼ INCH THICK

Similar to black ledge, but softer.

	Price Per Box of 125 3/16"	Price Per Box of 125 ¼"
10 Gauge	**$.65**	**$.85**
12, 16, 20, 24, and 28 Gauge	**.55**	**.75**
Packed in boxes, number of wads per box	**.35**	**.20**

NITRO FELT, ⅛, ¼ and ⅜ INCH THICK

A very soft filler wad for fitting between cardboard or greasy roof and shot wad.

	Price Per Box of 125 ⅛"	Price Per Box of 125 ¼"	Price Per Box of 125 ⅜"
10 Gauge	**$.40**	**$.60**	**$1.00**
12, 16, 20, 24, and 28 Ga.	**.35**	**.50**	**.85**

GREASE PROOF

A wad with glazed finish bottom for use immediately over powder to seal powder against moisture.

	List Per Box of 250
10 Gauge	**$.20**
12, 16, 20, 24, and 28 Gauge	**.20**

SEAL-TITE COMPOSITION WADS

A modern filler wad designed to hold gases and improve pattern.

Thickness	Price Per Box 10 Gauge	12 Gauge	16 Gauge	20 Gauge
*¼ inch	**$.50**	**$.45**	**$.45**	**$.45**
**⅜ inch	**.85**	**.80**	**.80**	**.80**

* Price per box of 250. ** Price per box of 125.

CARDBOARD

	For Over Powder List Box of 250	For Over Shot List Box of 250	Extra Thin List Box of 250
10 Gauge	**$.30**	**$.30**	**$.30**
10 Gauge Printed	**.30**	**.30**	**.30**
12, 16, 20, 24, 28 and .410 Ga.	**.30**	**.30**	**.30**
12, 16, 20, 24, 28 and .410 Ga. Printed	**.30**	**.30**	**.30**

NITRO CARD

A heavy cardboard for use over powder.

	List Per Box of 250
10 Gauge	**$.35**
12, 16, 20, 24, 28, and .410 Gauge	**.35**

EMPTY PAPER SHOT SHELLS

Brands	Size	Per 100
Winchester-Ranger, Western Expert, Remington Shur Shot, Peters Victor	10 ga., 2⅞"	**$2.20**
	12 ga., 2⅜"	**2.20**
	12 ga., 2⅝"*	**2.00**
	16 ga., 2 9/16"	**1.90**
	20 ga., 2½"	**1.90**
	28 ga., 2½"	**1.90**
Winchester-Leader, Western Super X, Remington Nitro Express, Peters Hi-Velocity	12 ga., 2⅝"	**$2.40**
	12 ga., 2¾", 2⅞", 3"	**2.55**
	16 ga., 2 9/16"	**2.40**
	20 ga., 2½"*	**2.40**
	20 ga., 2¾"	**2.55**

LEAD SHOT IN 5 AND 25 LB. BAGS

(For Sizes See Page 188)

	Per 25-lb. Bag	Per 5-lb. Bag
DROP, Nos. 2 to 10 inc.	**$4.40**	**$ .95**
CHILLED, Nos. 2 to 10 inc.	**4.90**	**1.00**
BUCK	**4.90**	**1.00**
B.B. (AIR RIFLE SHOT)	**4.90**	**1.00**
DUST	**5.20**	**1.15**

SPRATT'S MEAT FIBRINE BISCUIT FOODS
FOR GUN DOGS

THE DOG'S CONSTITUTION NEEDS A DOG'S DIET: What you feed your dog predetermines in a large measure his health, appearance, disposition and length of life. The primitive dog was accustomed to hunt his own food and subsisted principally on a raw meat diet. The dog of today is thoroughly domesticated and exists under totally different conditions, for he no longer gets the strenuous exercise of his roaming ancestors. Moreover, his dietary requirements have also changed definitely, consequently the dog of the twentieth century needs a "domesticated" diet in preference to the natural food of his canine ancestor.

Meat is still a necessary part of his daily fare, but it should be in a form best suited to the requirements of his present existence. A generous meat diet without the necessary exercise can easily become a potent cause of digestive disorders, skin troubles, etc. Another important addition consists of cereals which the dog's primitive forebear found in the crops and paunches of his kill. These semi-predigested carbohydrates helped in a small measure to counteract the effect of an entirely meat diet. In the baking process, Spratt's biscuits pass through sufficient heat to break down the starch granules into digestible and assimilative dextro glucose. Bread, compressed cereal foods and other combinations of a like nature improperly baked are unsuited to the present day dog's digestive system.

FIBO . . . Granulated food (about the size of peas). Highly nourishing and appetizing. Can be fed dry or mixed with vegetables, soup, broth, etc.

5 lbs.—**90c**; 10 lbs.—**$1.70**; 25 lbs.—**$3.35**; 50 lbs.—**$6.35**; 100 lbs.—**$12.50**

OVALS . . . Oval Biscuits. Contain plenty of meat; crunchy and satisfying. Suitable for all breeds.

5 lbs.—**80c**; 10 lbs.—**$1.50**; 25 lbs.—**$3.00**; 50 lbs.—**$5.70**; 100 lbs.—**$11.25**

CHARCOAL OVALS . . . Same as Ovals with pure charcoal added. Black in color. Aid in absorbing intestinal and stomach gases. All dogs eat them with avidity. A safeguard against canine ills.

5 lbs.—**85c**; 10 lbs.—**$1.55**; 25 lbs.—**$3.05**; 50 lbs.—**$5.95**; 100 lbs.—**$11.75**

CHALLENGE . . . A Granulated food. Fine or Coarse. Excellent for Gun Dogs. Lower in price but of full nutritional value. Can be fed dry or mixed with vegetables, etc.

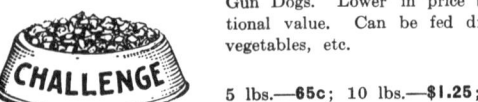

5 lbs.—**65c**; 10 lbs.—**$1.25**; 25 lbs.—**$2.65**; 50 lbs.—**$4.75**; 100 lbs.—**$9.00**

DOG CAKES . . . (Large Square) . . . For 75 years the standard dog food. Staple diet for the larger breeds. Should be fed dry.

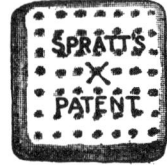

5 lbs.—**70c**; 10 lbs.—**$1.35**; 25 lbs.—**$2.85**; 50 lbs.—**$5.45**; 100 lbs.—**$10.75**

HOUND CAKES . . . Same size as Dog Cakes. High meat content. For hounds in training and all hard working dogs.

5 lbs.—**80c**; 10 lbs.—**$1.50**; 25 lbs.—**$3.00**; 50 lbs.—**$5.70**; 100 lbs.—**$11.25**

HOUND MEAL . . . Regular Hound Cakes, machine broken for convenience in mixing.

5 lbs.—**80c**; 10 lbs.—**$1.50**; 25 lbs.—**$3.00**; 50 lbs.—**$5.70**; 100 lbs.—**$11.25**

RODNIM . . . A kibbled food for hunting and working dogs. A special meat biscuit, broken up, is mixed into this food. Excellent as a change for Gun Dogs.

5 lbs.—**85c**; 10 lbs.—**$1.60**; 25 lbs.—**$3.25**; 50 lbs.—**$6.05**; 100 lbs.—**$11.90**

SPRATT'S DOG MEDICINES

Spratt's Medicines are made from the purest ingredients obtainable and are always kept up to the highest level of modern veterinary science. Dosage and directions appear on all packages and should be followed closely.

TONIC AND CONDITION TABLETS FOR DOGS and PUPPIES (a general tonic) **60c** pkg.

WORM CAPSULES FOR DOGS and PUPPIES (for large round worms or ascarids) **60c** pkg.

THE BEST FOODS FOR HUNTING DOGS

APPLIANCES FOR GUN DOGS

BRUSHES

		Price Each
No. 40	Whalebone Brush, with handle	$1.75
No. 62	Whalebone Brush, with handle	2.00
No. 25	Small Wire and Fibre Spaniel Brush, with strap	1.25
No. 27	Large Wire and Fibre Setter Brush, with strap	1.45

LEADS—Best quality Bridle Leather

No. 4862	Round Russet Leads	$2.25
No. 104	½" Flat Scissor Leads	1.35
No. 104	¾" Flat Scissor Leads	1.90
No. 65	½" Flat Billet Leads	1.00
No. 65	¾" Flat Billet Leads	1.50

COMBS—Heavily nickel-plated steel

No. 3	Steel Combs, 7" long (Medium and Coarse)	$1.75
No. 9X	Steel Combs, with handle (Coarse)	1.35

CHAINS—Heavily nickel-plated steel

No. 1—Light	$1.25
No. 2—Medium	1.25
No. 3—Heavy	1.75

No. 202	Dog Couples—Nickel-plated	
Size 1—For Spaniels		1.00
Size 2—For Setters and Pointers		1.00

WHISTLES

No. 33	Stag Horn Whistles, Mellow Tone	$0.75
No. 32	Silent Whistles	3.50

COLLARS
Best quality Bridle Leather

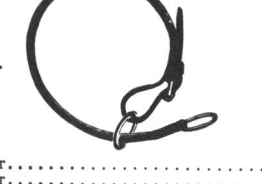

		Price Each
No. 570	½" Round Russet Leather	$1.00
No. 570	¾" Round Russet Leather	1.50
No. 570	⅞" Round Russet Leather	1.75
No. 921	¾" Round Russet Leather Gag Collars	2.00
No. 921	⅞" Round Russet Leather Gag Collars	2.50

No. 922 CHAIN CHOKE COLLARS
(Heavily nickel-plated steel)

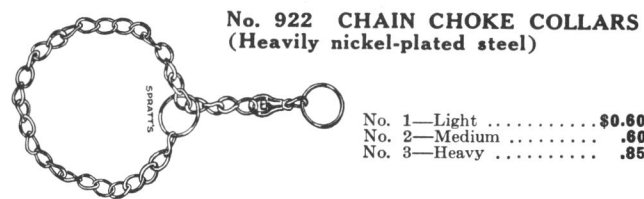

No. 1—Light	$0.60
No. 2—Medium	.60
No. 3—Heavy	.85

DISHES (Non-Upsettable)

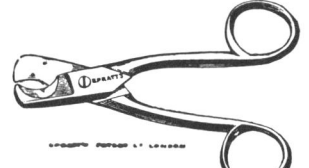

No. 34	Enamel Spaniel Dishes	$2.25
No. 35	Galvanized Spaniel Dishes	1.50
No. 35	8" Galvanized Dishes	.75
No. 36	8" Enamel Dishes	1.60
No. 23	Round Earthenware Dishes	
	4½" Diameter	1.00
	5½" Diameter	1.25
	6½" Diameter	1.75
No. 20	Solid one-piece Galvanized Pans, shaped to hang on wire fences, etc.	
	1 Quart Size	.50
	2 Quart Size	.90

NAIL NIPPERS
(Heavily nickel-plated steel)

No. 4—4½" long	$2.00
Resco Nail Nipper	2.25
Duplex Nail Nipper	2.00

FOODS FOR PHEASANTS AND QUAIL

FOR PHEASANTS

PHEASANT FOOD No. 3 (Split Pea Size). A cooked food for grown pheasants. Used regularly, it will insure healthy stock and vigorous poults.

PHEASANT MEALS Nos. 12 & 5 . . . A cooked food for poults. This should be fed from the time they are 36 hours old.

MAXCO . . . A granulated biscuit food containing Cod Liver Oil. It is rich in protein and carbohydrates, both of which are essential for rapid growth, strong framework and quick feathering.

CRISSEL . . . A substitute for insect life. This preparation is very rich in protein.

FOR QUAIL

QUAIL MEAL No. 12 . . . An easily digested granulated biscuit food of great merit.

SPECIAL QUAIL MASH . . . A starting food for quail chicks up to three months.

LAYING MASH . . . Is rich in protein and other albumenoids or egg-producing elements, therefore it should be fed before and during the laying season.

QUAIL GRAIN . . . A perfectly blended mixture of grain, meat, seeds, etc. of the highest quality.

The above foods are packed in 5, 10, 25, 50 and 100 pound bags. Prices Obtainable on Application. Due to Constantly Fluctuating Prices.

PRIZE TROPHIES

No. 4277	No. 4276	No. 4275	No. 4274	No. 4273	No. 4272	No. 4271	No. 4270
18¾" high	17" high	14¼" high	12¼" high	16¾" high	15" high	13" high	11" high
Price $34.00	$27.00	$24.00	$18.00	$24.00	$19.50	$15.75	$12.00

TROPHIES

No effort has been spared to make each Trophy found on these pages an outstanding example of originality, fine design and craftsmanship in sizes and prizes to meet every requirement and for every event. These Cups are made of High Britannia Metal very nicely finished in Silver Plate. All bases are Ebony colored.

ENGRAVING

We are equipped to execute all orders for engraving by expert engravers at standard trade prices. Always print names and specifications to avoid errors and loss.

Price, per block letter.....**.05**
Script or other fancy type will cost from 7 to 10 cents per letter.

No. 4150	No. 4251	No. 4252—7⅞" high—**$9.00**	No. 4228	No. 4011	No. 4149
Loving Cup	Loving Cup	No. 4253—9½" high—**$10.50**	Loving Cup	Loving Cup	Loving Cup
3⅝" high	6½" high	No. 4254—11½" high—**$15.75**	8" high	6" high	3⅝" high
Price **$3.00**	**$6.75**	No. 4255—14⅛" high—**$20.25**	**$7.50**	**$5.25**	**$3.00**

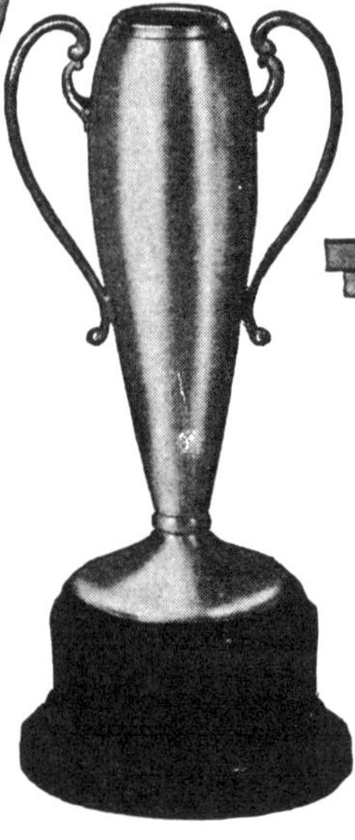

ALL TROPHIES AVAILABLE IN LUXURIOUS GOLDEN BRONZE, BRIGHT SPARKLING AND ENDURING FINISH AT NO EXTRA CHARGE

CAREFUL ATTENTION AND SAFE DELIVERY OF YOUR ORDER

AMERICA'S GREAT GUN HOUSE

SHOOTING PRIZES AND TROPHIES

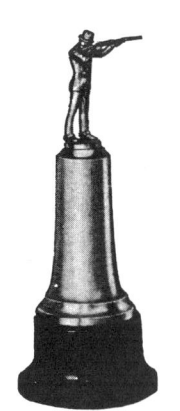

T793—Trophy column with shooter mounted on pedestal in grey finish. Height 15¾"....$18.00
With pedestal band. 21.00

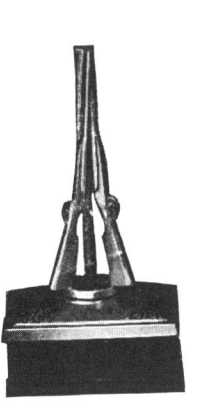

T661—Cigarette desk case with 3 guns mounted on lid. Black Bakelite box holds 40 cigarettes. Height 8"............$12.00

T872—Modern Mantle clock with shooting figure on top. Figure to be had in any style illustrated on this page. When ordering state figure desired. Has mounted shield to take engraving. Mahogany color Bakelite case; General Electric Co. movement; for A.C., 110-125 volts. Height 9¼"...$33.00

T801—Ornamental stand provided with plaque for engraving. Height 8¾"; solid Walnut.
Price $15.00

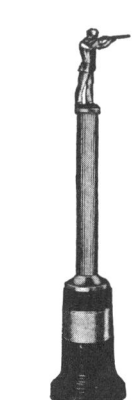

T811—Shooter mounted on high pedestal with silver band circling pedestal, grey finish. Height 22¾" (black bakelite pedestal).$22.50

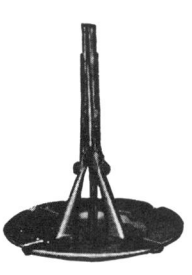

T637—Ashtray in silver grey finish with center mounting of 3 guns which is very attractive. Height 5½".
Price $8.00

T861—Ornamental stand with 3 figures and silver plaque provided for special engraving. Any type of figures as found on these pages. Please do not fail to specify same when ordering. Height 10", solid Walnut......................$30.00

T865—Ashtray mounted in solid walnut base with removable glass lining and silver plaque for engraving. Figure in any style desired as listed on this page. Height 5¼".........$12.00

V714—Very attractive shield of solid walnut equipped with chain. Size 10¼x8¼". Metal shield 7¼x5½". Recommended for club honor listing and other functions.......$15.00

MOUNTS

T728—Trophy shield of solid walnut equipped with chain which does not show when hung on wall; is very attractive. Walnut; size 13¾x18". Silver metal plate 9¼x10". Especially recommended for honor group listings....................$45.00

Mounts as illustrated on this page can be installed on any of the prizes, cups, trophies, or trophy shields as found on the preceding pages. Please be sure to state number as listed. Whereas these mounts can be had separately we believe it will be best to let us apply all mounts at the factory.

Silver plated, grey finish, not applied..............................Each $1.20
Silver plated, applied..Each 2.25
Gold plated, not applied..Each 1.80
Gold plated, applied...Each 3.00
Numbers illustrated are No. 28, No. 95 and No. 112.

PRIZE CUPS AND TROPHIES

We are presenting herewith a selected line of shooting trophies and prizes of distinctive design, finest workmanship and beautiful finish. These trophies are made of the finest white metal and heavy silver plate to give a lifetime of service. They are also to be had in bronze or copper finish, or either grey or bright finish. In case 24 Karat gold plate for special occasions would be desired same can be applied over the silver plate at an additional charge of about 75 per cent of the cost of the prizes. We cannot give a definite figure as the cost of the gold depends on the current gold market quotations and also on the amount of the gold required. Pedestals are furnished regularly in ebony or red mahogany color. If not specified, black color will be furnished.

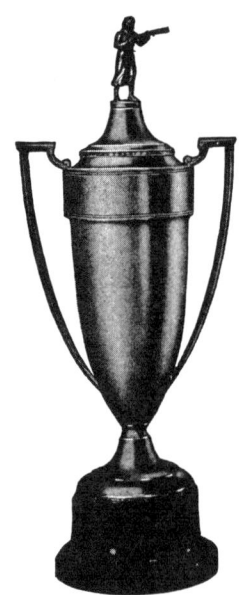

Silver Lined—Grey Finish
T313/24—Height 30" $69.00
    With pedestal band 74.00
T313/22—Height 27" 54.00
    With pedestal band 58.20
T313/20—Height 24" 45.00
    With pedestal band 48.30
T313/18—Height 22" 37.50
    With pedestal band 40.50

Silver Lined—Grey Finish
T356/14—Height 21¼" $36.00
    With pedestal band 39.00
T356/11—Height 19½" 30.00
    With pedestal band 32.70
T356/ 9—Height 16¼" 24.00
    With pedestal band 26.25
T356/ 7—Height 12¾" 18.00
    With pedestal band 19.50

Silver Lined—Bright Finish
T353/14—Height 22¼" $45.00
    With pedestal band 48.30
T353/12—Height 19¾" 36.00
    With pedestal band 38.70
T353/10—Height 17¼" 30.00
    With pedestal band 32.25

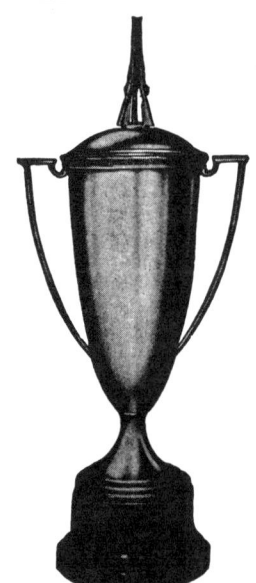
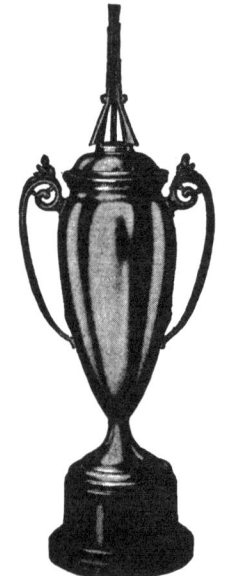

Silver Lined—Grey Finish
T324/18—Height 28" $72.00
    With pedestal band 77.00
T324/15—Height 24" 54.00
    With pedestal band 58.20
T324/12—Height 20¼" 37.50
    With pedestal band 40.50
T324/19—Height 16½" 27.00
    With pedestal band 29.25

Silver Lined—Grey Finish
T341/14—Height 21" $37.50
    With pedestal band 40.50
T341/11—Height 18" 30.00
    With pedestal band 32.70
T341/ 9—Height 15" 24.00
    With pedestal band 25.80
T341/ 7—Height 13" 21.00
    With pedestal band 22.50

Silver Lined—Grey Finish
T349/13—Height 20" $36.00
    With pedestal band 38.70
T349/11—Height 17½" 30.00
    With pedestal band 32.25
T349/ 9—Height 16¼" 24.00
    With pedestal band 25.80
T349/ 7—Height 14¼" 18.00
    With pedestal band 19.50

A FINE TROPHY INCREASES SHOOTING INTEREST

AMERICA'S GREAT GUN HOUSE

PRIZE CUPS AND TROPHIES

Gold Lined—Grey Finish
T358/13—Height 16¾"...$24.00
　　With pedestal band 27.00
T358/11—Height 14¼"... 19.50
　　With pedestal band 22.20
T358/ 9—Height 12"..... 15.00
　　With pedestal band 17.25
T358/ 7—Height 9½"... 10.50
　　With pedestal band 12.30
T358/ 5—Height 6½"..... 8.25
　　With pedestal band 9.45

Gold Lined—Grey Finish
T352/13—Height 16¼".....$24.00
　　With pedestal band 27.00
T352/11—Height 14½".... 19.50
　　With pedestal band 22.20
T352/ 9—Height 11½"..... 15.00
　　With pedestal band 17.50
T352/ 7—Height 9⅝"..... 10.50
　　With pedestal band 12.30
T352/ 5—Height 6½"...... 8.25
　　With pedestal band 9.45

Gold Lined—Grey Finish
T355/10—Height 12"......$13.20
　　With pedestal band 15.00
T355/ 8—Height 10"...... 10.50
　　With pedestal band 12.00
T355/ 6—Height 8"....... 7.50
　　With pedestal band 8.70
T355/ 5—Height 6"....... 6.00
　　With pedestal band 6.75

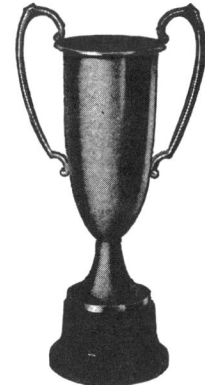

Gold Lined—Grey Finish
T31/13—Height 16".......$21.00
　　With pedestal band 24.00
T31/10—Height 13"...... 15.00
　　With pedestal band 17.70
T31/ 8—Height 10"...... 11.25
　　With pedestal band 13.05
T31/ 6—Height 7"........ 7.50
　　With pedestal band 8.70
T31/ 4—Height 5"........ 5.00
　　With pedestal band 5.74

Gold Lined—Grey Finish
With high pedestal as illustrated. Ebony color only.
T41/11H—Height 17½"....$20.25
　　Without pedestal band 18.00
T41/ 9H—Height 15"...... 14.55
　　Without pedestal band 12.75
T41/ 7H—Height 12"...... 12.00
　　Without pedestal band 10.50
T41/ 6H—Height 9½".... 9.00
　　Without pedestal band 7.80

Gold Lined—Grey Finish
T42/11H—Height 17½"....$20.00
　　Without pedestal band 18.00
T42/ 9H—Height 15"...... 14.55
　　Without pedestal band 12.75
T42/ 7H—Height 12"..... 12.00
　　Without pedestal band 10.50
T42/ 6H—Height 9½"..... 9.00
　　Without pedestal band 7.80

Gold Lined—Grey Finish
T42/11—Height 12½".....$17.10
　　With pedestal band 18.90
T42/ 9—Height 10¾"..... 12.00
　　With pedestal band 13.50
T42/ 6—Height 7"........ 7.50
　　With pedestal band 8.25
T42/ 7—Height 8¾"...... 9.90
　　With pedestal band 11.10

Gold Lined—Bright Finish
T12/13—Height 16¼".....$24.00
　　With pedestal band 27.00
T12/11—Height 13⅞"..... 19.50
　　With pedestal band 22.20
T12/ 9—Height 11½"..... 15.00
　　With pedestal band 17.25
T12/ 7—Height 9⅛"...... 10.50
　　With pedestal band 12.30
T12/ 5—Height 6½"....... 8.25
　　With pedestal band 9.45

Gold Lined　　**Grey Finish**

T21/13—Height 15⅞".....$22.50
　　With pedestal band 25.20

Gold Lined 　　**Grey Finish**

E129
Height 6"
$6.75
　　With pedestal band **$7.95**

Gold Lined 　　**Grey Finish**

E127
Height 4½"
$3.90
　　With pedestal band **$4.65**

NOTICE: All trophies, prize cups, medals, shields and plaques can be engraved with an inscription at an additional charge of 5c per block letter. Be sure to typewrite or print out the wording exactly as you desire it. The greatest care will be taken to execute this additional work in the best possible manner from the standpoint of workmanship and pleasing arrangement. As the engraving of all inscriptions is hand work, orders for same should allow extra and sufficient time for this engraving. All figures illustrated are interchangeable. Please state the type wanted. All dimensions stated with each cup include figure and pedestal.

Gold Lined　　**Bright Finish**

E9384—Height 7½", bright
　finish $8.25
　　With pedestal band. 9.75

PLEASE RECOMMEND US TO YOUR FRIENDS

TROPHIES WITH MOUNTED FIGURES

No. 36 Rifle Shooter Height 6½ in.

No. 37 Civilian Pistol Height 6¾ in.

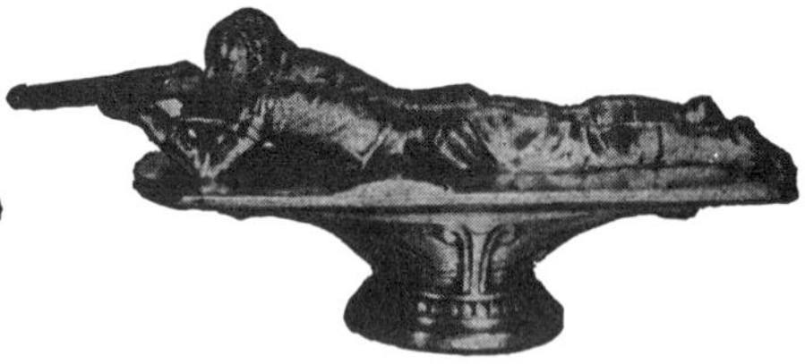

No. 49 Prone Rifle Height 3½ in. ($2.25 Extra)

No. 34 Trap Shooter Height 6½ in.

No. 35 Skeet Shooter Height 6½ in.

No. 45 Police Pistol Height 7¼ in.

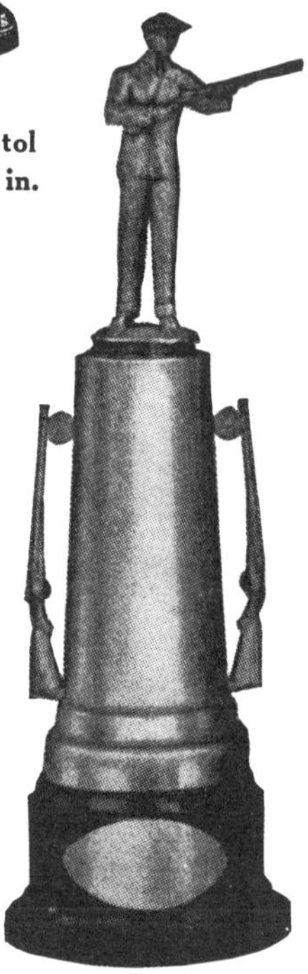

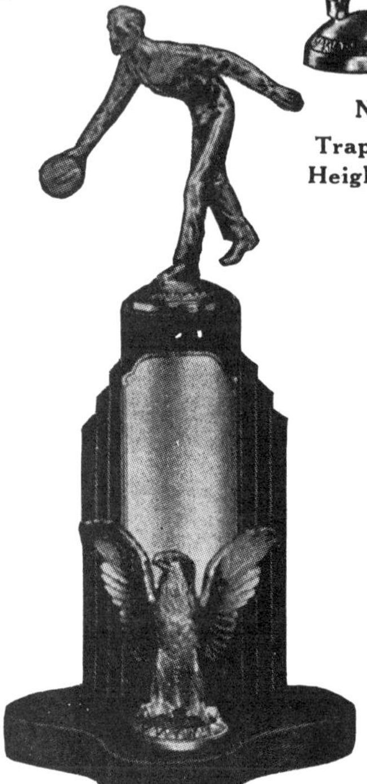

No. 44 Police Pistol Height 7¼ in.

The two cups shown in the center of this page are amongst the most modern, up-to-date and popular types now being offered.

Cup No. 1213G stands 17½" high without the figure on top. It may be had in a variety of finishes such as sunglow, silver oxidize or Modern Bond's. The price with any figure is **$28.50**.

Fig. 1269 is of walnut with metal eagle and shield. The height of the trophy is 9½" without figure. The trophy may be had with any of the figures shown at a price of **$19.50**.

No. 168, National Guard Rifle

The Figures, 34, 35, 36, 37, 44, and 45 represent the choice of figures available on either of the cups. Fig. 49 may be had at an extra charge of **$2.25**.

The six illustrations at the foot of the page are scenes and designs which may be sketched on to the surface of the cup or the shield at an extra charge of **$2.00**.

The choice of figures and scenes makes possible almost any desired trophy for any event in the two price classes **$19.50** or **$28.50** complete.

Scenes and designs that may be sketched on the surface of the cup or shield trophy at an extra charge of **$2.00**.

No. 165, Skeet Shoot   No. 164, Women's Trap Shooting   No. 163, Men's Trap Shooting

No. 167, Rifle Shooter   No. 166 Military Pistol

ALL SHIPMENTS ARE INSURED

TROPHIES FOR ALL SPORTS

Cocktail Shaker. Capacity 6 pints. Silver Plated only No. 4298C—20" high.
Price $28.50

"FAME" Silver plated engraving band ornamental ebony colored base, 12½" high—No. 4260.
Price $10.50

All American Trophy. 11¼" high—No. 4058. A striking new trophy. Can be supplied in Golden Spray or Antique Bronze finish with Silver plated or Golden Bronze plate.
Price $10.50

Skeet Shooter. Very smart in design with ebony base and removable silver plated engraving plate. 10½" high—No. 4230.
Price $9.00

Skeet or Trap Shooter with silver plated shield and ebony colored base. 9" high—No. 4234.
Price $6.75

CHOICE OF ARTISTIC FIGURES FOR VARIOUS SPORTS

The above illustrated figures of the same artistic design and highest workmanship can be had instead of the shooting figure at no increase in price. We are listing these figures for the convenience of our customers. As you will notice these figures cover almost any sport and are very desirable for such events. They can also be had for cups with lids as found on other pages of this section. A charge of 5 cents per letter (block style) will be made for engraving of shields as mounted on above bases. Script engraving and other styles desired are 7 to 10 cents per letter. Kindly print descriptions desired clearly.

A TROPHY FOR EVERY SPORT

PISTOL, REVOLVER, AND RIFLE MEDALS

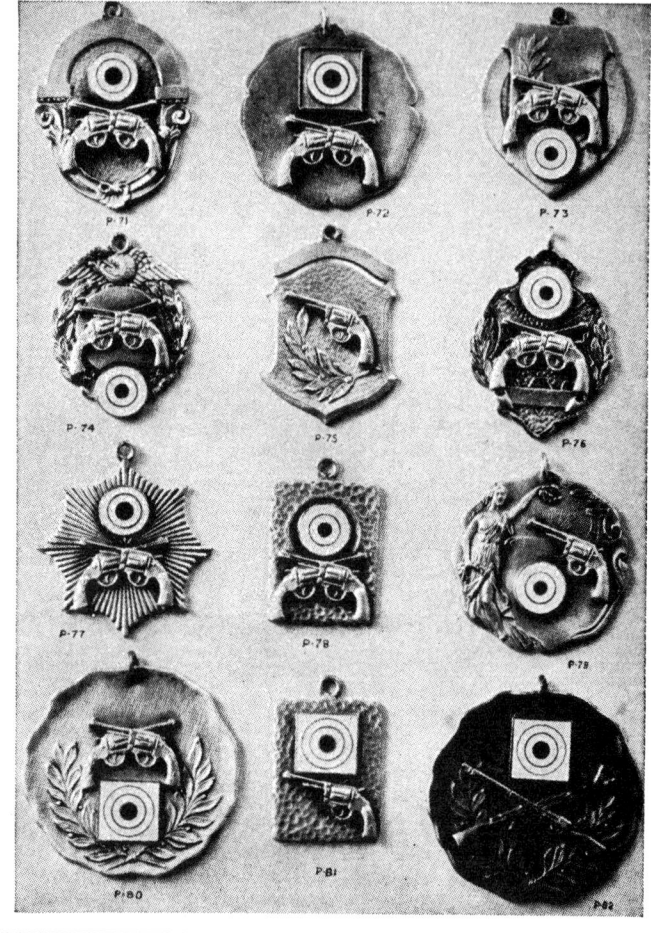

PRICES

No.	14K	10K	Sterling Silver	Rolled Gold	Bronze	No.	14K	10K	Gold Filled	Sterling Silver	Bronze
P.71	$20.00	$16.00	$4.50	$7.00	$2.00	P.77	$20.00	$16.00	$7.00	$4.50	$2.00
P.72	20.00	16.00	4.50	7.00	2.00	P.78	18.00	15.00	6.50	4.20	2.00
P.73	20.00	16.00	4.50	7.00	2.00	P.79	20.00	16.00	7.00	4.50	2.00
P.74	20.00	16.00	4.50	7.00	2.00	P.80	24.00	18.00	8.00	4.80	2.50
P.75	18.00	15.00	4.20	6.50	2.00	P.81	18.00	15.00	6.50	4.20	2.00
P.76	20.00	16.00	4.50	7.00	2.00	P.82	24.00	18.00	8.00	4.80	2.50

	No. 842-843-844	No. 851	No. 848-849	No. 850	No. 475-044	No. 042	No. 845-846-847
Solid Gold	$14.00	$14.00	$14.00	$20.00	$18.00	$8.00	$6.00	$2.50
Rolled Gold	8.00	8.00	8.00	10.00	9.00	4.00	3.00	1.50
Sterling Silver	1.65	3.00	3.00	7.00	2.50	2.50	1.30	1.00
Nickel	.85	1.30	1.30	2.00	1.10	.60	.60	.50
Bronze	.35	1.50	1.50	3.00	1.50	.60	.60	

No.	14K	10K	Rolled Gold	Sterling Silver	Bronze	No.	14K	10K	Rolled Gold	Sterling Silver	Bronze
S.401	$20.00	$16.00	$7.00	$4.50	$2.00	S.405	$22.00	$18.00	$8.00	$4.50	$2.50
S.402	20.00	16.00	7.00	4.50	2.00	S.406	20.00	16.00	7.00	4.50	2.50
S.403	20.00	16.00	7.00	4.50	2.00	S.407	18.00	15.00	6.50	4.00	2.20
S.404	18.00	15.00	6.50	4.00	2.00	S.408	18.00	15.00	6.50	4.00	2.20

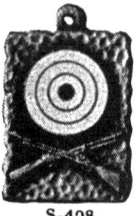
S-408

S-407

S-405

S-403

EB 600 RIFLE   **EB 600 PISTOL**

EB 600, Gold, Silver, or Bronze Plated..$0.50
EB 600, Sterling Silver.................2.00
EB 600, 1/20, 10K Gold Filled..........2.25

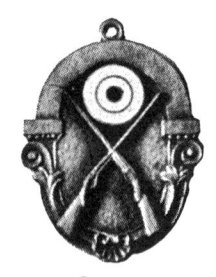
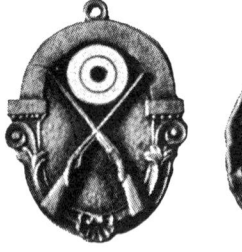
S-406

S-401

S-402

S-404

KEEP IN BEST FORM WITH STOEGER TARGETS

AMERICA'S GREAT GUN HOUSE

SHOOTING MEDALS

No. 2566 (Large)

No. 36 (Small)

No. 32 (Small)

No. 2550 (Large)

No. 49 (Small)

No. 2517 (Medium)

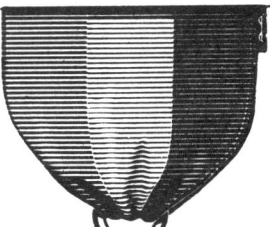

No. 2597 (Large)

The Medals shown on this page and the opposite page are of exceptionally fine quality and of sufficient variety to meet the requirements of almost any club or organization. Each medal is carefully designed and well executed and is an article which the wearer will esteem and be proud to display. Each medal on this page is available only in the size shown next to the number. All medals on this page fall into three price groups: Large, Small, and Medium.

PRICES

	Large	Medium	Small
Gold filled	$4.50	$3.80	$2.80
Sterling silver	3.20	2.80	1.80
Golden bronze	2.00	1.80	1.00
Bronze	1.80	1.60	.90

PRESENTATION BOXES

For special occasions and when specially so desired medals can be supplied in attractive hinged covered presentation boxes with velvet pads. The outside of the box has imitation hammered gold finish.

Price .... 30¢

No. 2594 (Large)

Bar with Ribbon

No. 2470 (Large)   No. 2478 (Large)   No. 2479 (Large)

No. 2564 (Large)

Ribbon with Concealed Pin

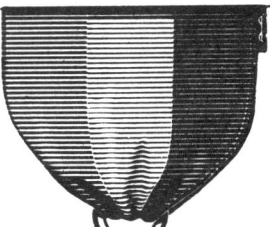

STOCK BARS

These bars are designed for attaching ribbons and medals. They may be had furnished with the words, First Place, Second Place, Third Place or 1st Place, 2nd Place, and 3rd Place. These so-called "stock" bars are carefully die stamped with the letters and border raised. The word "place" may be substituted by "prize."

Bronze	$1.00
Sterling Silver	2.50
1/10" 10 K. Rolled Gold	4.00
10 K. Solid Gold	8.00

Note: Price of bar includes fine ribbon, solid red, white or blue, or combination red, white and blue. Ring may be bronze, silver, or gold plated.

Ribbon with Concealed Pin

For those requiring only a ribbon and no bar, we offer the ribbon illustrated which has a concealed pin in the rear. Available in solid red, white, or blue or in combination. Ring of bronze, silver, or gold plate.

Price .... 30¢

SPECIAL BARS

These bars are regularly supplied with no engraving whatsoever and are intended for those who wish to engrave them to their own taste. If desired, we shall be glad to engrave bar as required.

Bronze	$1.20
Sterling Silver	2.80
1/10 10 K. Rolled Gold	4.00
10 K. Solid Gold	8.00
Lettering, in script, Gothic, or Bold, per letter	6¢

Prices include ribbon as for stock bar.

No. 2559 (Medium)

No. 2572 (Medium)   No. 2574 (Medium)

No. 2496 (Large)

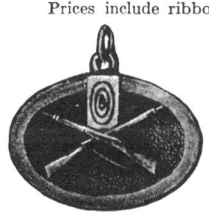

No. 251033 (Medium)

No. 2449 (Medium)

No. 2473 (Medium)

SEE PAGE 8, "HOW TO ORDER"

KEYSTONE MOVIE CAMERAS

The Keystone Camera is the last word at a reasonable price to "shot" those salient events which you have enjoyed in the woods, in the field and on your hunting trip and so keep a permanent record of them. To reexperience these memories by reproducing them in your time of leisure will always be a welcome and interesting pastime to be enjoyed by your friends and yourself. These cameras are of the latest design and allow you now to take pictures not only in black and white but also in natural colors; in fast, normal or slow motion; indoors and outdoors. You are prepared to record all scenes of your hunting trip and give undisputable proof of your achievements as an outdoorsman or Sportsman.

The Keystone Camera will use 50 or 100 ft. films in color or black and white, purchased in any first class camera goods or drug store and developed free of charge. The cost of black and white film is no more than 10¢ per average shot and in color about 15¢. Use your Keystone Camera out of season for those Wildlifeshots, enjoy making your own movie.

KEYSTONE
16 MILLIMETER
MODEL A-3
THREE SPEEDS
HALF SPEED
NORMAL
SLOW MOTION

PRICE WITH F.3.5 LENS
$35.00

PRICE WITH F.1.5 LENS
$67.50

KEYSTONE
MODEL K-"8"
WITH F.3.5 LENS
8 MILLIMETER

FOR COLOR PICTURES
OR
BLACK AND WHITE

PRICE
$27.95

CONVENIENT SIZE—2¾" thick x 9" long x 4" wide, with 1" lens extension.
HIGH POWER LENS—f.3.5 LENS—universal focus with adjustable mechanical iris.
MONOCULAR VIEWFINDER—Built right into Camera.
TRIPOD CONNECTION provided for, but tripod is not necessary to obtain steady pictures.
SPRING MOTOR—Designed to withstand severe use.
3 SPEEDS—Half speed (8 frames) normal and s-l-o-w motion.
EASY WINDING—Winds very easily. Similar to winding a clock.
CAPACITY—100-foot or 50-foot 16 millimeter film.
LOCKING KNOB can be locked into place permitting operator to step into scene and take own picture.
DAYLIGHT LOADING—Camera may be loaded in broad daylight.
FILM REGISTER—Automatically indicates the amount of film used after taking each scene.
AUDIBLE FOOTAGE SIGNAL to determine footage as taken (patented).
DISTINCTIVE FINISH—Attractive wrinkle enamel with highly polished chrome trimmings.

MODEL A-7
7 SPEED CAMERA

SAME AS THREE SPEED CAMERA WITH S-L-O-W MOTION, NORMAL AND INTERMEDIATE SPEEDS

PRICE WITH F.2.7 LENS..................$44.50
PRICE WITH F.1.5 LENS.................. 71.00

EXCLUSIVE ECONOMY FEATURE

If you do not have enough subject matter to use up a full 25-ft. double "8" film you can economically use the single width 30-ft. Agfa film for shorter subjects and promptly mail for developing. The Keystone K-8 Camera has the exclusive feature of using both these reels purchased at any first class camera and drug store.

MODEL K-8 WITH F.3.5 LENS..........................$29.95
ALSO MODELS K-8 WITH F.2.7 LENS.................... 36.00
ALSO MODELS K-8 WITH F.1.9 LENS.................... 60.00

10c A SHOT

One foot of 8mm film records as many photo-images as **Four Feet** of standard 16 mm film. The cost is about one-third. Film for the Keystone "8" may be purchased at any Camera Goods store, and at many Drug Stores. When film is completed, simply mail to nearest developing station (noted on film carton). It will be developed **Free of Charge** and returned to you.

OTHER MODEL K-8 FEATURES

Pocket Size fits in overcoat pocket. **Finish**—Bronzed grain—smart, durable. **Size**—6 5/16" high, 2¾" deep, 1¾" wide. **Weight**—Only 1 lb., 12 oz. **Universal Lens** for taking close or distant shots—f.3.5 with iris diaphragm. **Interchangeability of Lens Equipment**—High Speed f.1.9 and 1½ inch f.3.5. Telephoto lenses can also be used with the Keystone "8." The change can be made in a jiffy. **Three Speeds**—Normal, low and s-l-o-w motion. **Direct Vision View Finder**—Shows the picture just as it will appear on the film. **Auxiliary View Finder**—A special view finder for centering difficult or distance shots is also provided. **Visual Mechanical Footage Indicator** shows number of feet of film used. **Exposure Chart**—Shows exactly how to adjust lens for bright, cloudy or rainy days. **Tripod Socket**—Enables you to use tripod when you wish. **Silent Winding Key**—Folds flat against camera when not in use. **Camera Strap Handle**—For convenient carrying.

KEEP A MOTION PICTURE RECORD OF YOUR TRIP

KEYSTONE MOVING PICTURE PROJECTORS
4-MINUTE — 8-MINUTE AND 16-MINUTE SHOWS

Keystone Machines are guaranteed to show clear pictures. Connect with ordinary house current. All ready to run complete with special bulb, two spools, cord and plug. These machines operate in principle the same as the large Keystone Projectors that are used in schools, auditoriums and churches. Any 16mm film can be used on any of these projectors. Keystone Projectors are known throughout the world as one of the leading makes on the market. You can't go wrong with a Keystone. Ask any user of a Keystone!

500 WATTS PLUS THESE FEATURES

- Perfect for Color Pictures.
- Fully Achromatic f.1.85 Projection Lens, 1" Focus.
- Cast Lamp Housing.
- Cast Heavy Base.
- Strong Draft directly on lamp.
- Adjustable Tilt.
- Separate Switch for Lamp.
- Pilot Light.
- Electric Rewind.
- Manual Framer.
- Fixed Roller Guides.
- Polished Reflector.
- Speed Control.
- Carrying Handle.
- Fully Guaranteed.
- Universal Motor, 115 Volts A.C. and D.C.

KEYSTONE MODEL L-"8"
THEATER BRILLIANCY
DETAIL—STEADINESS
THE OUTSTANDING PROJECTOR VALUE

PRICE **$55.00**

Keystone engineers have designed in the economy price field a projector equal in performance to projectors for 8mm film at about twice the price. The illumination power, the cooling system, the ease of threading and the central control of operation leave nothing to be desired.

KEYSTONE MODEL A-75
WITH F.2.5 LENS
500 WATT
16 MILLIMETER
PRICE **$55.00**

KEYSTONE MODEL A-81
WITH F.1.65 LENS
750 WATT
16 MILLIMETER
PRICE **$69.50**

Equipped with 500 watt special concentrated filament pre-focus projection lamp. A 750 watt lamp can be used. A ventilating fan is connected to motor which forces cool air through lamphouse, thereby cooling lamphouse and mechanism. **UNIVERSAL MOTOR DRIVE:**—For Direct Current or Alternating Current (special rheostat for controlling speed). **LENS:**—f.2.5, finely ground and polished, 2" achromatic. **CONSTRUCTION:**—Die Cast. Baked brown wrinkle enamel finish **MANUAL FRAMER.** **CAPACITY:**—400-foot, one empty aluminum spool furnished. **SIMPLE THREADING:**—Special aperture plate and lever controlled by one finger. **PRECISION MOTION MOVEMENT:**—By two claw movement with grip on two sprocket holes. **ANGLE PROJECTION:**—By turning a knob on the base any angle can be obtained. **SIZE OF PICTURE:**—Up to 40" x 52" at a distance of about 24 feet. **REWIND MECHANISM:**—High-speed re-wind with motor. **OILING SYSTEM:**—At all important friction points.

The Keystone Projector will give you a precision performance in film motion, in brilliancy and in film protection. The simplicity in threading a Keystone and the availability of all moving parts can quickly be appreciated. Will satisfy the wants of family use or the requirements of schools, churches, lodges and average size indoor gatherings.

- 750 Watt Pre-focus Lamp
- Auditorium Projection Lens f.1.65
- Lens 2" fully achromatic
- Forward and Reverse
- Rapid Motor Rewind
- New Cooling System
- Pilot Light
- Picture Size — up to 14 feet wide at distance of **75 feet**
- Quiet Operation
- Framer
- Device for Tilting
- Die Cast Construction
- Central Control of Electrical Operations

A GOOD PROJECTOR ASSURES PERFECT PICTURES

AN INTRODUCTION TO GUNSMITHING TOOLS

Gunsmithing was a highly developed art in the early days of this country when the only weapons available were those brought over from Europe and which could not very well be sent back to the maker for repair. In addition, and of still greater importance, was the influx of numerous German gunsmiths to Pennsylvania to whom main credit for the Kentucky rifle is due and the manufacture of these rifles constitutes the beginning of actual gun building in the United States. Thus old time gunsmiths were forced to make every single part of the gun by hand and often from the crudest materials and with the plainest tools. Such work naturally entailed ingenuity, skill and pains, and the reputation of these gunsmiths was high.

With the advent of the large arms factories in the United States after the Civil War, and the consequent mass production and standardization of firearms, the capable old gunsmiths gradually died out. As a consequence of the mode of manufacture there was very little opportunity for replacement since the possibility of acquiring a general knowledge of the complete field was practically eliminated. Thus it came to pass that the average "gunsmith" confined his efforts to fitting factory replacement parts and only the very simplest type of adjustments. The few really expert gunsmiths were mostly without exception from Europe, where the art of individual gun building has to this day never died out and where gunsmithing is a very definite profession requiring years of apprenticeship and instruction.

Of late years, but particularly since the World War which revived the interest in firearms, there has been a steadily increasing demand for specialized improvements and specific alterations suited to the personal requirements of the individual shooter. This movement has been sponsored by the National Rifle Association, which has created a strong upswing in the demand for good gunsmiths and the specialized tools which they require.

Our many years of experience in dealing in and repairing firearms has given us the conviction that in no country in the world is there such a great loss of even the finest guns due entirely to neglect or the absence of proper facilities to repair and recondition them, as in America.

In view of all the foregoing and the fact that even a thoroughly intelligent workman, be he a gunsmith or of any other profession, can accomplish but little without the proper tools at his disposal. The old time gunsmiths were given time and opportunity to acquaint themselves with the proper use of those tools peculiarly adapted to gunsmithing, but the problem is far more difficult for the present generation as there is almost no one to whom a young gunsmith can turn to for advice. For this reason we have taken the trouble to list below a number of the most important tools which are absolutely indispensable to the successful gunsmith.

For the most part, gunsmithing consists today of the remodeling of Military rifles, the fitting of new stocks to both shotguns and rifles as well as the refinishing of old stocks, the fitting of special sighting equipment, reblueing, the removal of obstructions from the barrels of rifles, the removal of dents from shotgun barrels, tightening up of actions, adjustment of trigger pull, the alteration of special pistol stocks and for the more advanced gunsmith, the fitting of new barrels, rechambering, rebushing, and relining.

All of this work and a great deal more can be accomplished with the tools listed below and for excellent working instructions and information we would strongly urge everyone interested in gunsmithing to procure one of the several excellent books now available on the subject and which will be found listed under "Gunsmithing" in the book section of this catalog.

Gunsmithing not only furnishes a pastime and hobby offering an opportunity to develop one's own ideas, but also is a great time saver. In view of the fact that ordinarily guns must be sent away to the larger cities or factories who themselves are quite busy, and because a month is consumed usually before the gun is returned, it becomes apparent that many a hunting trip will be saved if the shooter is in a position to take care of at least the elementary repairs by himself. For the man who wishes to go into the matter more fully and is able to devote all or part of his time to this work, it will not be difficult—after he has obtained a certain efficiency—to make his hobby into a worthwhile and paying business. For those, however, who are interested in gunsmithing in a professional way, we recommend the addition of a power drill and lathe, which, while somewhat expensive, will quickly repay themselves.

It is with all of the foregoing in mind and because of the fact that these special tools, many of which are imported, are extremely difficult to obtain even in the larger cities, that we, as exponents of shooting and due to our close contact with the shooting fraternity, have been making a steady and increasing effort to develop and improve our presentation of all such tools as may tend to increase the efficiency of both amateur and professional gunsmiths throughout this country.

RECOMMENDED TOOLS

Block Plane	Files	Screw Chest
Breast Drill	File Cleaners	Screw Pitch Gage
Bunsen Gas Burner	Hack Saw	Scribers
Caliper, Vernier	Hammers	Sight Spanner
Center Gages	Hand Vises	Spring Spanner
Center Punches	Inletting Chisels	Square
Chisels	Micrometer	Steel Clamps
Combination Squares	Oilstone	Steel Parallels
Dent Remover	Pencil Divider	Steel Rules
Depth Gages	Pin Vises	Stock Bending Apparatus
Drills	Pliers	Straight Edge
Drill Blocks & Clamps	Quick Opening Vise	Taps
Drill Sets	Rasps	Tap Wrenches
Drop Measurer	Ratchet Brace	Trigger Pull Tester
Engraving Tools	Screw Drivers	Vise Jaws

KNOW YOUR HOBBY AND MAKE IT PAY

BURKE MILLING MACHINE

Years of experience in manufacturing Milling Machines has enabled the Burke Machine Tool Co. to build a machine in which are combined convenience, power, rigidity, accuracy and the ability to rapidly handle any work within the range of the machine.

"BURKE" Milling Machines are built with a degree of accuracy that is seldom found in tools selling for much higher prices. The spindle is made of high carbon steel running on Ball or Timken Roller bearings. Spindle and cone is carefully balanced to run at high speed. Knee is very rigid and of solid top construction. This prevents the dirt and chips from getting into the working parts. All bearing surfaces are hand scraped to alignment. Knee, saddle and table are held in place by adjustable gibs. This Milling Machine has power longitudinal feed, graduated dials on both the traverse and vertical feeds, and is equipped with heavy overhanging arm. The Spindle of this machine is mounted on anti-friction bearings, either ball or Timken roller.

At an extra charge we can furnish Stationary or Tilting Head Index Centers, Vertical Milling Attachments, Slotting Attachment (not illustrated), Draw-In Collet Attachment, Plain, Swivel Base, or Quick Opening Vise. Arbors ½, ⅝, ¾, ⅞ or 1 inch in diameter, and Column or Pedestal, 23 or 28 inches high. All prices are F.O.B. Factory.

"Burke" No. 4 Milling Machine, furnished complete with motor driven drum type switch, necessary belting and wrenches.

Price, F.O.B. Factory....................$355.00

"Burke" No. 4 Milling Machine may also be had without motor for use by those who prefer to install their own motor or have overhead power drive.

Price for this model, F.O.B. Factory........$245.00

Illustration shows machine mounted on special cabinet column. Weight of column 217 lbs., height 28", price $24.00

SPECIFICATIONS FOR No. 4 MILLING MACHINE

Longitudinal feed of table................8 inches
Traverse Feed ....3 inches
Vertical Motion to Knee...................8 inches
Maximum distance between center of spindle and table........................8 inches
Working Surface of Table..........3½ x 16 inches
Taper Hole in spindle.............B. & S. No. 9
Hole through spindle....................¾ inches
Height over all......................25½ inches
Weight Boxed ....350 pounds

INDEX CENTER
(Stationary Head)
Weight 15 lb.
Price $30.00

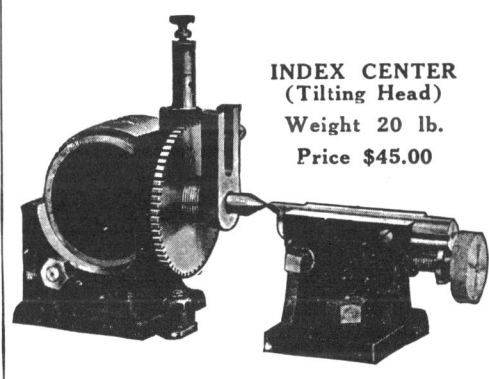

INDEX CENTER
(Tilting Head)
Weight 20 lb.
Price $45.00

VERTICAL MILLING ATTACHMENT
Weight 20 lb.
Price $65.00

These Index Centers are especially designed for the rapid production and indexing of light work of any kind. (Will swing six inches.) The Spindle is threaded for face plate or chuck, inside Taper No. 7, B. and S. One Dial Plate of 48 Divisions furnished with each head unless otherwise ordered. Additional plates can be furnished. Also furnished with draw-in collet attachments.

ARBORS—½ to 1 Inch—Price $6.00

Ball-Bearing Spindle equipped with draw-in Collet, having maximum capacity of one-half-inch. One collet is supplied with attachment.

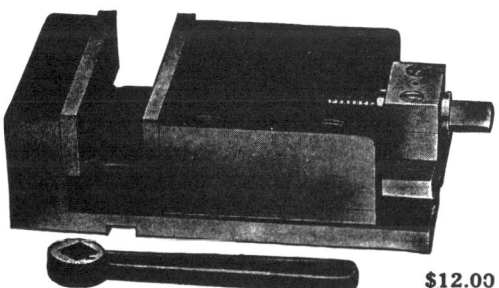

$12.00

PLAIN VISE

Price $12.00

QUICK OPENING VISE

$15.00

SWIVEL BASE VISE

Vise Jaws ....3½x1⅛ inch..............3½x1⅛ inches.............3½x1⅛ inches
Maximum Opening...........2 inches................1½ inches................2 inches
Weight ....11 pounds................11 pounds................16 pounds

Atlas 10-INCH BENCH LATHES

$98.50 COMPLETE AS SHOWN (less motor)

10-Inch Swing—16 Speeds—4 Bed Lengths

Automatic, Reversible Power Feed

Cuts Standard Threads Between 4 and 96 Per Inch

EQUIPMENT FURNISHED

Graduated Compound Rest; Tool Post, Ring and Rocker; L. H. Tool Holder, Tool Bit; Complete Set of Change Gears to cut standard threads from 4 to 96 per inch; Threading Chart and Dial; Ready-mounted Countershaft; All Belts and Pulleys; Motor pulley furnished is for ½-inch diameter motor shaft—prices for other size motor shafts on request; 10 Amp. Switch and Cord—switch is for single-phase current only, prices for 3-phase on request; Motor Mounting Bracket; 6-inch Face Plate; Two 60 degree Lathe Centers; Reducing Sleeve for Headstock Center; Combination Tool Post and Compound Wrench; 1-inch Lathe Dog; Instruction Book—Atlas "Manual of Lathe Operation."

THE ATLAS back-geared screw-cutting lathes have the power, strength, versatility, and accuracy required in every up-to-date shop. The outline below and specifications at the right describe features of design and construction which have made the Atlas preferred by modern shop men.

Whenever the spindle speed must be exceptionally high for long intervals, select an Atlas Lathe with Timken Bearings for the headstock spindle. On the 10-inch lathes the additional cost of these bearings is $15.00—they must be installed before the lathe is shipped from the factory.

CONSTRUCTION FEATURES

The Atlas Lathe bed is a heavy, semi-steel iron casting—scientifically ribbed and cross-braced for maximum rigidity; ways are rough-milled, seasoned, finish-milled, and precision-machined, trued and polished for extreme accuracy. The heavy grey-iron headstock is ribbed and reinforced for permanent rigidity and strength. Heavy duty headstock spindle machined from solid bar of steel, accurately ground and polished. Ball bearing absorbs spindle end thrust. High-speed babbitt headstock bearings are 2-piece splitcap type similar to those used in automobile motors and large industrial machine tools. Bearings of each lathe are accurately bored after headstock has been fitted to bed, insuring positive alignment of spindle with ways. Laminated shims on each side of bearings provide means for simple take-up if ever necessary. Pulleys, gears, handwheels, and other small parts are made of a rugged metal alloy, Zamak, permitting a compact modern design, eliminating idle weight and providing greater strength and longer lathe life. Legs have total bearing surface of 48 inches on bed, keeping vibration at a minimum. Standard equipment includes countershaft assembly and motor mounting bracket attached directly to headstock. Countershaft spindle runs on Hyatt roller bearings. Belt tension lever has 3 steps: Forward to release belts for speed changes, upright for normal work, and a third step for extra heavy cuts. Complete V-belt drive from motor to countershaft to spindle is standard equipment. Oversized back gears engaged quickly by eccentric lever and removal of lock-pin from spindle pulley. Face of front spindle back gear has 60 indexing holes. Carriage has 6 bearing surfaces on bed, each 8½" long, assuring smooth carriage action and minimizing wear. Compound rest base casting is machine-graduated through 180° and can be swiveled and locked at any angle for taper turning and boring. Direction of feed changed instantly by lever on gear box. On-off switch built into headstock casting. Heavy, accurately machined tailstock provides rigid work support—has gib adjustment, graduated ram, and ¾" setover.

SPECIFICATIONS

Swing over Bed...10¼"
Swing over Carriage..6⅝"
Number of Spindle Speeds......................................16
Speed Range...........28, 45, 70, 83, 112, 134, 164, 211, 266, 345, 418, 500, 685, 805, 1270 and 2072 RPM
Thread Cutting Range.........4 to 96 Right or Left Hand (Standard)
Feeds per Spindle Revolution.........0087", .006", .0043" or .0033"
Lead Screw..................................8 Acme Threads per inch
Headstock Spindle.........1½" diameter, 8 pitch National Form threads, 25/32" hole through entire length, nose bored for No. 3 Morse Taper with reducing sleeve to take No. 2 Morse Taper.
Spindle Bearings...........High-speed Babbitt with full-split cap and laminated shims with five .002" laminations on each side. Spindle has thrust take-up nut and collar—ball bearing for end thrust.
Countershaft Spindle.................................Hyatt Roller Bearings
Hole through Motor Pulley.............................½" diameter
Back Gears..............................12 Pitch, ⅞" Width
Backgear Shaft Bearings..........................Oilless Bronze
Cross Feed Travel..6⅝"
Cross Feed Screw.................½" Diameter, Acme Threads
Tool Post Slide Travel..2¼"
Tool Post..⅜"x⅞" slot to take ⅜" Tool Bits or Tool Holder for ¼" Tool Bits
Tool Post Swivel...............Graduated 0 to 90° right and left
Tailstock Ram Travel...2¾"
Tailstock Ram Graduated.....................0 to 3" by 1/16ths
Tailstock Set-Over ....¾"
Tailstock Ram..............................No. 2 Morse Taper
Automatic, Reversible Power Feeds, Integral Countershaft, V-Belt Drive, 60-Hole Indexing Mechanism, Chrome Plated Control Handles. Finish, Special Atlas Gray.

No.	Bed Length	Between Centers	Length Overall	Weight	Less Motor
1036	36"	18"	40"	242 lb.	$98.50
1042	42"	24"	46"	254 lb.	105.50
1048	48"	30"	52"	262 lb.	113.50
1054	54"	36"	58"	267 lb.	122.50

Timken Bearings for Headstock Spindle, extra.................$15.00

All Models: Overall Depth 21", Height 24"

Designed to be run from 1/3 or ½ HP 1740 RPM Motor

A GOOD LATHE IS A GUNSMITH'S FIRST REQUIREMENT

NEW *Atlas* 6-INCH LATHES

16 Speeds—Back-Geared Screw-Cutting—Reversible Power Feed—Two Bed Lengths

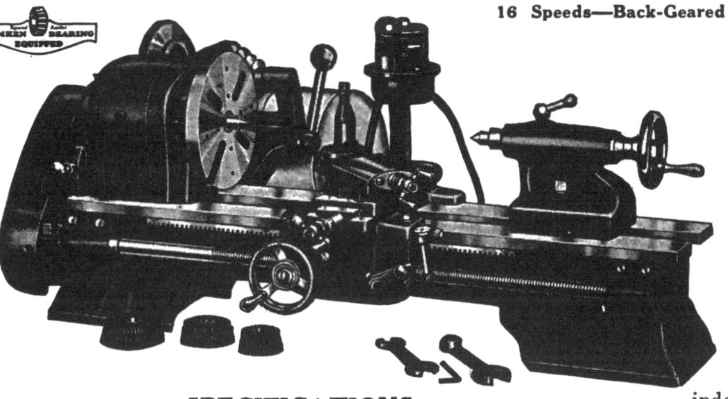

In this new machine tool Atlas presents the first precision-built small lathe at a popular price. It has the strength, power, versatility, accuracy, and performance which have placed the Atlas Lathe in the front rank of modern machine tools.

The new Small Atlas Lathes are built of the same fine materials as all Atlas Lathes, machined on the same precision equipment, and before shipment must pass the same strict working tests for alignment and accuracy.

The 6-inch Lathes include the distinctive construction features which identify the modern Atlas Lathe: Built-in Adjustable Countershaft Attached Directly to Lathe; Complete V-Belt Drive from Motor to Countershaft to Spindle; Bed Ways Precision Machined to .001" of Perfect. The following features add to versatility and ease of operation: Reversible power feeds to control carriage travel; 16 speeds between 54 and 3225 RPM; threading dial, gears, and chart to cut standard threads from 8 to 96 per inch; tumbler-type reversing lever for quick feed-direction changes; 60-hole indexing mechanism, graduated tailstock ram, conveniently located reversing switch, handy belt tension lever, micrometer graduated feed screw collars. Headstock spindle is machined from a solid bar of special fine-grained steel, accurately ground and polished. Timken Tapered Roller Bearings for the headstock spindle carry both radial and thrust loads with a minimum of friction. Carriage bearings, tailstock bearing, and cross slide and tool post slide dovetails have gibs or laminated shims for take-up adjustment to maintain permanent accuracy. Full provision is made to permit thorough lubrication.

Headstock, bed, legs, carriage, compound rest, tailstock, gear guards, countershaft support, and switch bracket are heavy grey iron castings. Pulleys, gears, handwheels, handles, and other small parts are made of Zamak, a rugged, durable metal alloy.

EQUIPMENT FURNISHED: Compound Rest; Tool Post, Ring and Rocker; ⅜" Tool Bit; Complete Set of Change Gears; Threading Chart and Dial; Ready-mounted Countershaft; All Belts and Pulleys; Motor Pulley furnished is for ½" diameter motor shaft—prices for other size motor shafts on request; Reversing Switch and Cords; 5¼" Face Plate; Two 60° Lathe Centers—No. 2 Morse Taper for headstock, No. 1 Morse Taper for tailstock; 3 Wrenches; Instruction Folder.

SPECIFICATIONS

Swing over Bed	6"
Swing over Carriage	4⅛"
16 Speeds	54, 82, 122, 140, 187, 287, 317, 365, 481, 550, 820, 940, 1250, 1925, 2125, 3225 RPM
Feed per Spindle Revolution	.0026", .0042", .0052", or .0083"
Headstock Spindle	1" diameter, 10 pitch National Form threads, 17/32" hole through entire length, nose bored for No. 2 Morse Taper
Tool Post	⅜" x ¾" slot to take ⅜" tool bits or tool holder for 3/16" bits
Tailstock Ram Travel	1¼"
Tailstock Setover	9/16"

Reversible Power Feeds, Integral Countershaft, V-Belt Drive, 60-Hole Indexing Mechanism.

THE NEW ATLAS 6-INCH LATHES

No.	Bed Length	Between Centers	Length Overall	Weight	Less Motor
612	24"	12"	26½"	90 lb.	**$59.50**
618	30"	18"	32½"	98 lb.	**64.50**

Both Models: Overall Depth less motor 18", Height 11". Designed to be run from a ¼-Hp. motor

LATHE ATTACHMENTS

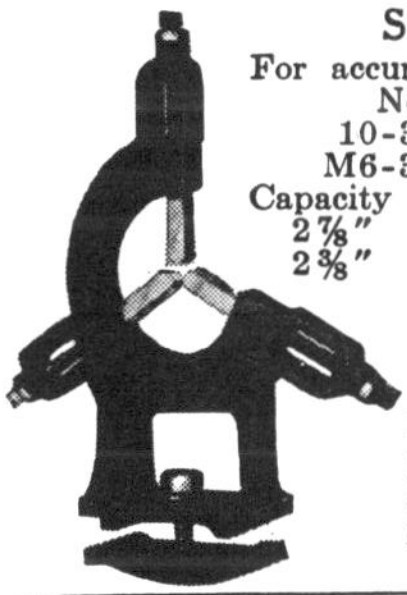

STEADY REST

For accurate work on long pieces.

No.	For
10-325	10" lathes
M6-325	6" lathes

Capacity	Wt.	Price
2⅞"	5 lb.	**$5.25**
2⅜"	3 lb.	**3.75**

FOLLOWER REST

For long slender work.

No.	For	Price
425	10" lathes	**$3.75**
M6-395	6" lathes	**2.75**

LATHE DOGS

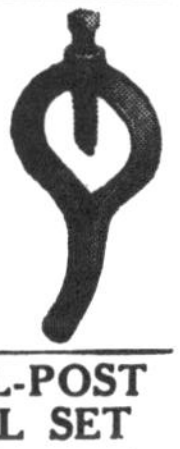

For 10" and 6" lathes—wt. 2 lb. (set)

No.	Opening	Weight	Price
142	½"	4 oz.	**$.50**
143	¾"	5 oz.	**.60**
144	1"	7 oz.	**.70**
145	1½"	10 oz.	**.80**
142A Set of Above 4		2 lb.	**2.60**

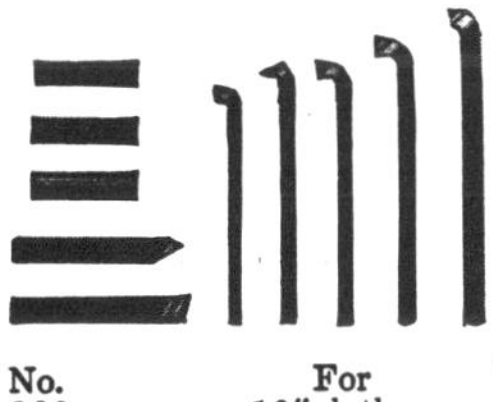

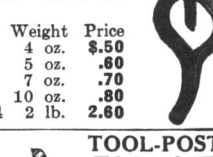

TOOL-POST TOOL SET

Hi-speed ready-ground. Set includes 5 internal tools, 2 heavy-duty external tools V-block, spacers. Used directly in lathe tool post.

No.	For	Weight (set)	Price
380	10" lathes	2 lb.	**$5.25**
M6-380	6" lathes	2 lb.	**5.25**

HIGH SPEED CUTTER BITS

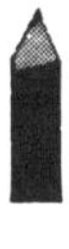

Ready-ground for turning, facing, and threading.

No.	Size	For	Weight	Price
386	¼"x¼"	10" lathes	12 oz.	**$1.60**
M6-386	3/16"x3/16"	6" lathes	12 oz.	**1.25**
385S	⅜"	Set of 6 Unground	1 lb.	**2.10**

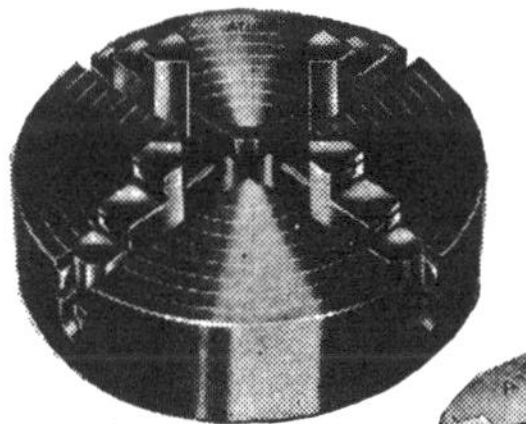

INDEPENDENT CHUCKS

Rugged and accurately built for holding work of all shapes. Sizes below.

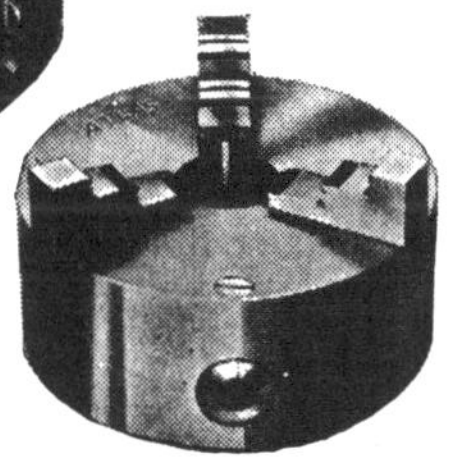

UNIVERSAL CHUCKS

Self-centering jaws for round and hexagonal work. 2 sets of jaws furnished.

Atlas Independent and Universal Chucks

Threaded to Fit Spindle Nose

No.	Description	For	Weight	Price
370	6" Independent	10" lathes	9 lb.	**$12.75**
M6-370-4B	4" Independent	6" lathes	8 lb.	**12.75**
M6-439	4" Indep. Utility	6" lathes	3 lb.	**7.50**
M6-438	3" Indep. Utility	6" lathes	2 lb.	**5.50**
435	5" Universal	10" lathes	11 lb.	**18.95**
M6-437	4" Universal	6" lathes	9 lb.	**15.50**
M6-436	3" Universal	6" lathes	6 lb.	**13.50**

Jacobs Headstock Chucks

Threaded to Fit Spindle Nose

No.	Capacity	For	Weight	Price
375B	¼" to ¾"	10" lathes	5 lb.	**$14.00**
377	⅛" to ⅝"	10" lathes	4 lb.	**11.75**
M6-375	0 to 17/32"	6" lathes	5 lb.	**9.50**

Jacobs Drill Chucks

Arbors Required as Listed

No.	Capacity	Weight	Price
BD1-60	1/16" to ½"	2 lb.	**$5.75**
40-60	0 to ½"	2 lb.	**6.75**

MILLING ATTACHMENT

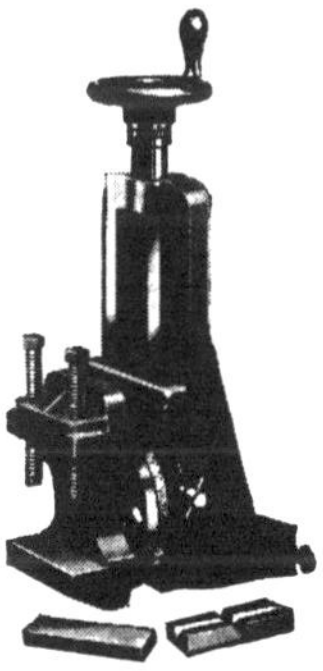

Clamps in place of compound rest. Handles face-milling and routing, keyways and slots, dovetails, squaring shafts, dies and molds. A versatile accessory.

No.	500A	M6-500
For	10" lathe	6" lathes
Vise Cap'y	2⅜"	2"
Jaw Depth	⅞"	¾"
Jaw Width	2½"	2"
Vertical Feed	3¾"	1⅞"
Cross Feed	5"	3⅝"
Weight	13 lb.	9 lb.
Price	**$16.75**	**$14.75**

For milling cutters, holding collet set, etc., consult complete Atlas catalog.

TOOL HOLDERS

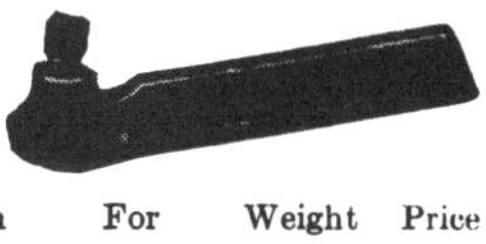

Drop-forged steel with heat-treated alloy set screw.

No.	Description	For	Weight	Price
139L	LH Offset	10" lathes	1 lb.	**$1.25**
139R	RH Offset	10" lathes	1 lb.	**1.25**
139	Straight	10" lathes	1 lb.	**1.25**
M6-139L	LH Offset	6" lathes	8 oz.	**1.10**
M6-139R	RH Offset	6" lathes	8 oz.	**1.10**
M6-139S	Straight	6" lathes	8 oz.	**1.10**

ARBORS

378	Arbor for 10" lathe	8 oz.	**$1.00**
L2-378	Arbor for 6" lathe tailstock	8 oz.	**1.00**
378	Arbor for 6" lathe headstock	8 oz.	**1.00**

Jacobs Center Rest Chuck

Arbors Required as Listed

No.	Capacity	Weight	Price
445	¼" to ¾"	3 lb.	**$9.50**
377	Arbor required for 10" lathe	8 oz.	**1.00**
M6-377	Arbor required for 6" lathe	8 oz.	**1.00**

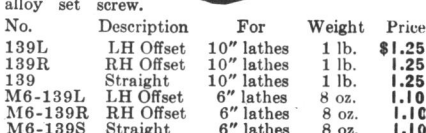

LATHES AT PRICES YOU CAN AFFORD

DRIVER BAND AND JIG SAWS, GRINDERS AND SANDERS

SERIES 700 12 INCH BAND SAW

The band saw cuts curves quickly and accurately. It is used for shortening gun stocks, cutting stocks roughly to shape from rough blanks and all similar operations where curves and contours are to be cut.

This is the most completely equipped 12" band saw built. It includes all guards and ripping fence. Wheels are carefully balanced to minimize vibration. Bearings are all ball bearing, dust-sealed for long life. The frame is a hollow casting for rigidity and strength.

Besides its work on guns, this band saw has numerous other applications to warrant its investment. Lawn furniture, boats, indoor furniture and games ... in fact practically every item having curved edges or contours, is made or repaired easily and quickly with a 12" band saw. Compare the DRIVER 12" Band Saw to any other on the market. You will be impressed by the comparison. For then you will realize how superior the DRIVER band saw really is,—how much *extra value* has been built into it.

BN730 Ball bearing 12" Band Saw **$34.95**

SPECIFICATIONS

Wheels balanced and rubber faced.

6 SKF ball bearings.

Cast iron frame, tubular construction.

Diameter of disc wheels, 12".

Maximum distance upper guide to table 6".

Improved cushion type spring tensioner.

Table tilts to 45° (geared control mechanism).

Table size 12½" x 12" (with wood extension 18" x 12").

Ball bearing guide rollers (upper and lower). Flexo lamp available.

Removing small guard between upper and lower guards increases capacity above 12".

New guide pins of oil-impregnated bronze relieve friction and add to life of blade.

Height over all 33½".

Motor recommended ⅛ H.P. 1740 R.P.M.

Shipping weight 103 lbs.

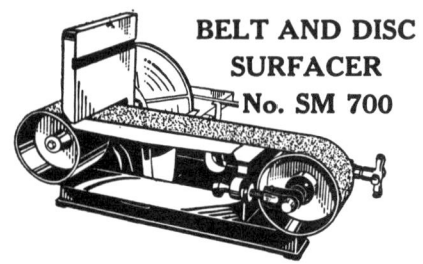

BELT AND DISC SURFACER No. SM 700

SM700 Belt and Disc Surfacer, as shown above including motor pulley, belt and mitre gauge............. **$29.95**

A surfacer or sander as shown in the above illustration is an extremely handy, efficient and above all a time saving tool which should be included among the equipment of every professional and amateur gunsmith. This surfacer will do a great many of the jobs that were ordinarily done on the grinder and in addition permits the polishing of flat surfaces, is a great time saver in the fitting of recoil pads, which in itself would be sufficient reason for its inclusion. This tool includes motor pully, belt and mitre gauge.

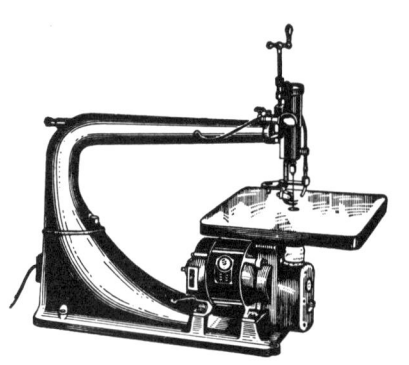

There's many a job in the gun shop for a 24" Jig Saw. It cuts metal up to ¼" thick and wood 2¾" thick. It is used for cutting out butt-plates, targets and silhouette designs of all kinds. It is also used for cutting out shot gun fore ends and for rough shaping special grips.

NEW DIRECT-DRIVE JIG SAW

This new 24" model with direct-drive motor, finger-tip control of speeds, adjustable blade tensioner and other superior features has set an entirely new standard of jig saw performance. Its simplicity provides greater safety, efficiency and economy of operation than have been available heretofore.

A wide variety of blades is available for cutting solid wood, veneers, plywood, celluloid, moulded plastics, metal, fibre, bone, hard rubber and numerous other materials.

MJ917 24" Jig Saw (two speeds) **$47.50**

MJ744 24" Jig Saw (one speed) **38.50**

⅓ H.P. MOTOR GRINDER

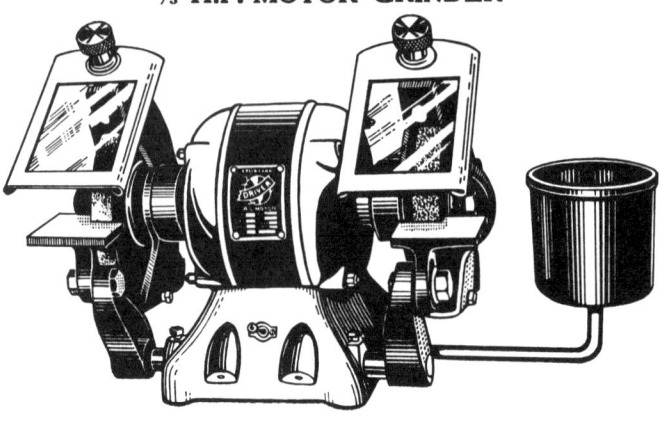

A good grinder is absolutely necessary to the gunsmith not only for sharpening tools, and for working down rough metal and fitting of recoil pads of all sorts, but it can also be used as a buffer and polisher and is a real necessity in reblueing.

This new grinder uses the DeLuxe type motor of 1/3 hp. 3450 r.p.m. 110 volts, a.c. 60 cycles. It is highly efficient, economical to operate, and dependable. Wheels are 6" in diamter, ¾" wide. Guards are designed in accordance with latest safety code requirements.

Large safety glass shields, and cooling cup standard equipment. Wheel guards and tool rests are fully adjustable.

Bearings are large, grease-sealed SKF's. Motor and bearings are fully protected from dust and dirt. Equipment includes rubber-covered cord, plug and snap switch in base. Shipping weight 60 lbs.

GR30 ⅓ H.P. Grinder (110 volts, 60 cycle, A.C.) **$29.95**

A TOOL FOR EVERY PURPOSE

DRIVER DRILL PRESSES FOR WOOD AND METAL WORKING

SERIES 900 DRILL PRESS

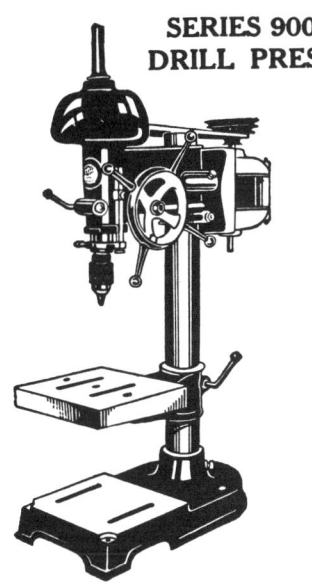

SERIES 700 DRILL PRESS

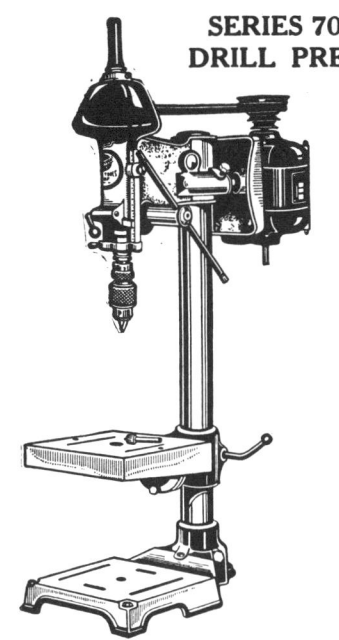

SERIES 500 DRILL PRESS

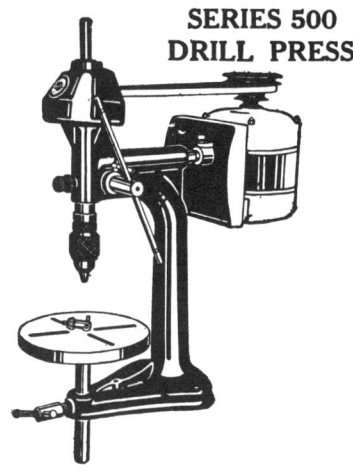

Probably the most valuable of all power tools for the gunsmith. This drill press can be used for drilling or sanding wood, metal, bone, plastics or hard rubber. It will save hours of tedious hand work ordinarily spent in inletting rifle and shot gun stocks. It can be used for boring horn, dowelling buffalo fore-end tips, mounting telescopic sights, routing and mortising wood, and drilling receivers for micrometer sights.

SPECIFICATIONS

6-spline spindle reduces vibration to the lowest possible minimum. Spindle is 5/8" diameter, tapered at lower end for Jacobs Chuck.
4 SKF Precision ball bearings, one directly above the pulley, another below it and two in the quill.
Jacobs (0 to 1/2") Key Chuck standard equipment.
Pilot wheel feed with calibrated depth stop.
Maximum distance chuck to table 12".
Maximum distance chuck to base (bench models) 17 1/2".
Distance chuck to base on floor model 46".
Center of chuck to column 7 1/2".
Table size 10" x 9" adjustable to tilt at any angle. Base 10" x 9". Round base 22" in diameter.
Diameter of steel column 2 3/4".
Spindle travel 4". Unusually soft, yet positive, return spring action.
Steel quill 1 1/8" diameter with teeth to match feed pinion milled into it.
Head close-grained gray iron, extremely rigid and machined to close tolerances. Belt guard is an integral part of the head. A cap over the exposed top end of spindle prevents any possibility of oil being thrown out and acts as a safety feature.
Improved locking device for holding spindle in any position. Slow speed pulley available.
Speeds with standard pulley 600-1250-2440-5000 R.P.M. (with 1740 R.P.M. motor).
Speed with slow speed pulley 480-940-1300-2900 R.P.M. (with 1740 R.P.M. motor). For still lower speeds use 1150 R.P.M. motor.
Height over all—Bench Model 39 1/2". Floor Model 69".
Collet chuck available for holding mortising, carving, routing, and dovetail cutters. For shaping use 9D5 Adapter. May be operated in either direction, for shaping with RX10 Reversing Switch.
Motor recommended for ordinary use 1/4 or 1/3 H.P. 1740 R.P.M. For shaping and other high speed operations use 1/3 H.P. or 1/2 H.P. 3450 R.P.M.
Shipping weight without motors—Bench Model 125 lbs. Floor Model 185 lbs.

D925 Drill Press as shown at right, less motor **$39.95**

D926 Drill Press, same as D925 but with slow speed pulley 40.95

This model, illustrated above, is somewhat lighter in weight and has slightly less capacity than the 900 model. Yet it handles practically all of the operations the 900 model does and has the same distinctive 6-spine spindle and 4 ball bearing construction of the 900.

SPECIFICATIONS

Jacobs Key Chuck regular equipment.
Chuck capacity 1/16" to 1/2" drills.
4 SKF ball bearings mounted one above and one below the pulley, other two in quill.
Maximum distance chuck to table 11 1/2".
Maximum distance chuck to base 17".
Distance center of chuck to column 6 1/2".
Table 9" x 8", base 9" x 8".
Diameter of steel column 2".
Spindle travel 3 1/2".
Spindle 5/8" diameter, tapered at end for Jacobs Chuck.
Idler for countershaft drive available extra.
1/3 H.P. 1740 R.P.M. motor recommended.
Height over all 38".
Speeds 765, 1350, 2270, 4000 R.P.M.
Shipping weight (without motor) 95 lbs.

D710 Drill Press, as shown less motor **$29.95**

ACCESSORIES

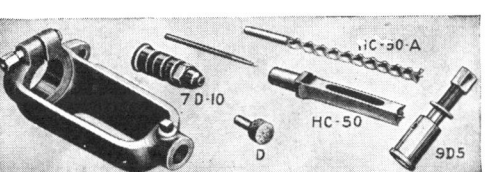

7D10 Mortising attachment (including 7D11)	$3.00
7D11 Collet chuck (for holding bits)	1.05
HC25 1/4" Hollow chisel	1.65
HC25A 1/4" Bit	1.35
HC37 3/8" Hollow chisel	1.65
HC37A 3/8" Bit	1.35
HC50 1/2" Hollow chisel	1.65
HC50A 1/2" Bit	1.35
HC21 Hold down and guide complete	1.90
9D5 Threaded adapter (for shaping cutters)	1.05
D Grinding stone for sharpening chisel	1.05
MD18 Jackshaft complete SKF ball bearing (for mounting on bench)	4.65

Strength and stability are apparent in every line of this drill press. The same strict standards of accuracy are maintained in this model as in the more expensive models. While it is not intended for routing or shaping on a production basis, it is perfectly satisfactory for the occasional job of either type. Mortising cannot be done on this model.

SPECIFICATIONS

Four-speed cone pulleys on motor and spindle provide four speeds without shifting position of motor.

Available with Jacobs Key Chuck or 1/2" Driver Chuck.

Capacity Jacobs Chuck (1/16" to 1/2" straight shank drills).

Rigid cast iron frame.

Height over all 24".

Distance from table to chuck 7".

Distance from frame to center of chuck 5 1/2".

Cast iron table, diameter 8".

Table adjustable up and down.

Spindle travel 2 7/8". Diameter of spindle 5/8".

Bronze bearings, and ball thrust bearing.

Quill is made from solid steel bar with teeth milled into it.

Quill may be locked in any position.

Motor base slides in and out to regulate belt adjustment.

Speeds 765, 1350, 2275, 4000 R.P.M.

Motor recommended 1/4 or 1/3 H.P. 1740 R.P.M.

Shipping weight 32 lbs.

D570 Drill Press, as shown above, less motor, with Jacobs Key Chuck **$19.25**

D573 Same as D570 but with DRIVER 1/2" screw chuck instead of Jacobs **$13.15**

DRILL PRESSES FOR EVERY PURPOSE

"HAND-EE" TOOLS

HAND-EE "HI-POWER"

You have always wanted a tool such as the Hand-ee to complete your difficult projects. You can grind, drill, rout, carve, saw, polish, sand, cut and engrave. Your materials are not restricted . . . for the Hand-ee works equally well in wood, metals, glass, in fact anything that can be machined. The many accessories can be changed quickly and with little effort. You have never dreamed a tool could be so convenient as the Hand-ee . . . whether it's grinding, drilling, reconstructing fossils or sharpening a pair of scissors . . . you need a Hand-ee. The Hand-ee is as essential to the craftsman with a complete workshop as it is to one cramped for room who uses the kitchen table for his work-bench. Anyone from the novice to the most expert craftsmen will get a real thrill from the Hand-ee's universal adaptability.

The Hi-Power Grinder is a heavy powerful tool . . . designed for jobs obviously beyond the capacity of either of the two other models.

The utmost in grinding efficiency plus the last word in ease and convenience. Designed to save extra time and effort. The grinder body is shaped to fit the hands. Total length is 10 inches, weight 3 pounds, with ample power to drive a wheel 2 inches in diameter.

A complete array of "CHICAGO" Mounted Wheels and Steel Cutters have been designed for use with this many purpose tool. All the accessories available for use with the Hand-ees can be used with the Hi-Power.

Based on tests conducted in many shops the Hi-Power had the lowest operating cost for any tool of its character. The speed is ideal for full efficient operation. The universal type motor embodies the most advanced design. A sturdy cast aluminum housing stands up under the hardest daily use. Full dynamic and statically balanced armatures insures smooth vibrationless performance with utmost efficiency. The Hi-Power is packed complete in a wood carrying case with three "CHICAGO" Mounted Wheels, 1x1" Drum Sander and three sanding bands, necessary wrenches, dressing stone and ¼" capacity Interchangeable Spring Collet Chuck.

Price $35.00
Extra for 32 or 220 Volts 3.50

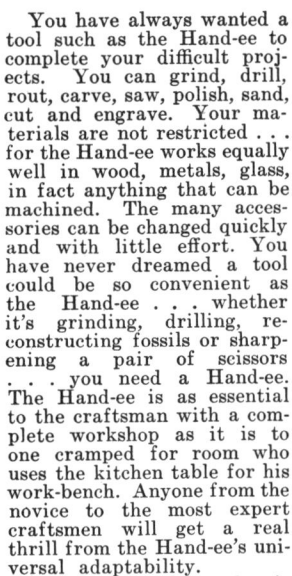

STANDARD HAND-EE

The most advanced design in electric motors is incorporated in the Standard Model Hand-ee which operates from any 110 volt, AC or DC, 25 to 60 cycle current. The speed, 13,000 r.p.m., coupled with the light weight, one pound, is ideal for all operations. Ball bearing construction and an ingenious arrangement automatically taking up all end play assure long and uninterrupted service.

The grip sleeve illustrated on the tool at the left acts as a steady rest when working at close quarters and provides a grip for the fingers. This accessory fits any Standard Model Hand-ee. We recommend that you specify a model with a Grip Sleeve for all delicate or precise work.

Illustration shows grip sleeve model

Collet for Shank diam.	Mounted Wheels Furnished	Standard Finish		With Grip Sleeve	
		No.	Price	No.	Price
⅛"	3	2 AB	$10.75	7 AB	$12.25
⅛"	15*	2a AB	14.75	7a AB	16.25
3/32"	3	3 AB	10.75	8 AB	12.25
3/32"	15*	3a AB	14.75	8a AB	16.25

Chuck collets are interchangeable.
For accessories having a smaller diameter than 3/32" shank we suggest our No. 38 spindle chuck.
* With 15-Wheel Assortment.

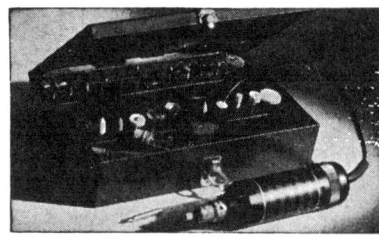

ULTRA DE LUXE HAND-EE SET

Only the most popular accessories from the complete list are included in the Ultra DeLuxe Assortment. Everything that you need for grinding, drilling, polishing, sanding, sawing, carving and engraving. Packed complete in a substantial steel carrying case, perfect for storing and carrying. The contents are conveniently arranged for accessibility. You will find daily uses for this complete assortment on hundreds of different applications. Discriminating craftsmen prefer the Ultra DeLuxe Assortment for its meets any demand made upon the tool.

Price $25.00
Extra for 32 or 220 volts 1.85

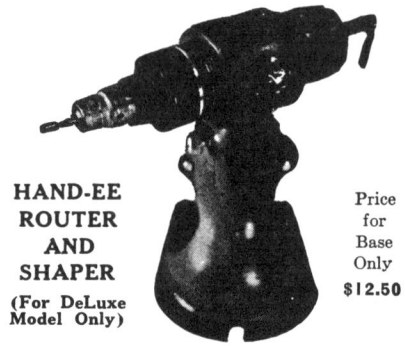

HAND-EE ROUTER AND SHAPER
(For DeLuxe Model Only)

Price for Base Only
$12.50

Converts the DeLuxe Hand-ee into a router, shaper, high speed spindle carver or polisher with this easy-to-handle accurately made fixture.

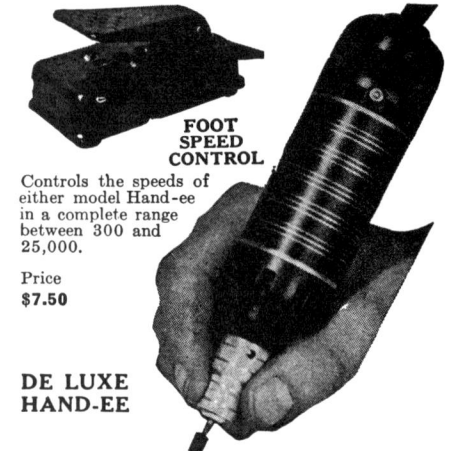

FOOT SPEED CONTROL

Controls the speeds of either model Hand-ee in a complete range between 300 and 25,000.

Price $7.50

DE LUXE HAND-EE

The complete tool weighs but twelve ounces, turns up 25,000 r.p.m. and has by far more power than any unit of its weight or type ever developed. You can quickly change accessories with the improved, easy acting interchangeable spring collet chuck. The new convenient rotary type switch gives you full one hand control of the DeLuxe Hand-ee. In the hidden details of construction you will find the stamina that enables it to perform day in and day out. Built to the most precise and exacting standards it is in every respect a constant duty tool.

SPECIFICATIONS

Length overall including chuck 6". Extreme diameter, 1⅝". Weight, 12 ozs. Speed, 25,000 r.p.m. Ample for all ordinary requirements. Motor*, Universal type operating on AC (25 to 60 cycles) or DC, 110 volts. Available for special voltages. Brushes—special carbon graphite composition. Easily replaceable. Bearings—Special selected precision ground . . . grease-sealed ball type bearing construction. Cord—6 ft. Underwriters' approved, reinforced rubber covered cable, with special soft rubber attachment plug. Equipment—6 "Chicago" Mounted Wheels or six craftsman's accessories. Power Consumption—Lowest operating cost.

Price, complete $18.50
Extra for 32 or 220 volts 1.85

A HANDY TOOL FOR EVERY PURPOSE

HAND-EE TOOL ACCESSORIES

SANDING DISCS

Sanding discs for use with Mandrel No. 18, 525 assorted coarse, medium and fine, in various sizes, packed complete in a box. These discs work equally well on wood and metal. Leave a fine finish and saves much hand work.

Catalog No. 22. 525 assorted sandpaper discs (box complete)..$1.50
Catalog No. 46. 100 cloth - back 7/8" discs, coarse, stiff back, boxed complete........ $ .60
Catalog No. 47. 100 cloth - back 7/8" discs, medium, stiff back, boxed complete........ $ .60
Catalog No. 48. 100 cloth - back 7/8" discs, fine, stiff back, boxed complete........ $ .60

DRUM SANDERS AND BANDS

"CHICAGO" Abrasive Bands are ideal for giving a smooth, fine finish to either wood or metal. The bands are of lapless construction and can be run in either direction. The edges will not ravel.

Nos. 23   44   34   36

Catalog No. 23. 3/4 x 1/2" Drum mounted 3/32" shank only, ea........$1.00
Catalog No. 44. 1/2 x 1/2" Drum mounted 1/8" shank only, ea........ .75
Catalog No. 34. 3/8 x 1/2" Drum mounted 3/32" shank only, ea........ .75
Catalog No. 36. 1/4 x 1/2" Drum mounted 3/32" shank only, ea........ .75

EXTRA BANDS

Catalog No. 24. Extra 3/4" bands for No. 23, dozen.............$0.30
Catalog No. 45. Extra 1/2" bands for No. 44, dozen............. .30
Catalog No. 35. Extra 3/8" bands for No. 34, dozen............. .30
Catalog No. 37. Extra 1/4" bands for No. 36, dozen............. .30
In ordering state whether coarse, medium or fine.

SAWS

A wide variety of saws for undercutting, slitting, purfling will work with any model Hand-ee on wood, Bakelite, Calinin, Trafford and soft metals.

Nos. 19   27   28   26   20   25

Catalog No. 19. Slitting or undercutting saw, permanently mounted 3/32" shank only, ea............................$0.75
Catalog No. 20. 3/8" dia. slitting saw, permanently mounted 3/32" shank only, ea............................. .75
Catalog No. 26. 1/2" dia. saw .023" thick, 1/8" hole, saw only, (use mandrel No. 16), ea................................. .60
Catalog No. 27. 3/4" dia. saw .023" thick, 1/8" hole, saw only (use mandrel No. 16) ea................................ .75
Catalog No. 28. 3/4" dia. saw .032" thick, 1/8" hole, saw only (use mandrel No. 16) ea................................ .75
Catalog No. 3016. 1 1/2" dia. .023" thick (use mandrel No. 3014) saw only (not illustrated)........................... 1.25
Catalog No. 3017. 2" dia. .032" thick (use mandrel No. 3014) saw only (not illustrated)........................... 1.50
Catalog No. 3018. Extremely thin saw .005" thick, 7/8" dia. (use mandrel No. 17) saw only, ea....................... .50
Catalog No. 25. Rubber cutting disc 7/8" dia. 3/64" thick (use mandrel No. 17) dozen.............................. .35

BRUSHES

These brushes work equally well with all model Hand-ees, reaching hard to get at places, cleaning out cavities, removing rust and for a host of other applications. Each is specially designed for use on Hand-ee equipment.

Nos. 11   12   14   14-B   14-S   15   49

Catalog No. 11. Disc cleaning brush, 3/32" shank only, ea..........$0.20
Catalog No. 12. Cup cleaning brush, 3/32" shank only, ea.......... .20
Catalog No. 14. Bristle-type brush for deep cavity work, 3/32" shank only, ea...................................... .20
Catalog No. 14-B. Bronze wire cavity brush also for ferreling, 3/32" shank only, ea................................... .40
Catalog No. 14-S. Steel wire cavity brush, 3/32" shank, ea........ .40
Catalog No. 15. 1" dia. wire scratch brush, 3/32" shank, ea........ .50
Catalog No. 49. Extra stiff wire brush only. Use mandrel No. 39, ea. 1.00
Catalog No. 3012. 2" brush complete with special 1/4" mandrel for use only on Hi-Power.................................. 1.25

MANDRELS

These mandrels are made to the most precise limits of the highest quality steel. They are ideal for correctly mounting the various accessories designed for use with the Hand-ees.

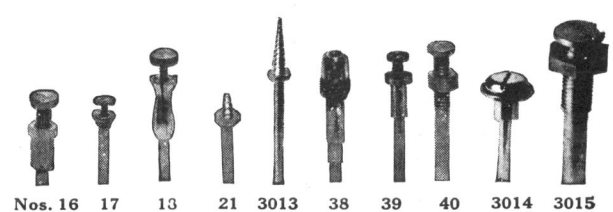

Nos. 16   17   18   21   3013   38   39   40   3014   3015

Catalog No. 16. Mandrel 1/8" hole for mounting Nos. 26, 33, 27, 28 and 29, 3/32" shank only, ea......................$0.40
Catalog No. 17. Screw mandrel 8/x" hole for mounting Nos. 25, 3018, 3/32" shank only, ea............................ .15
Catalog No. 18. Push pin mandrel for sanding discs Nos. 22, 46, 47 and 48, 3/32" shank only, ea....................... .75
Catalog No. 21. Special screw shoulder mandrel for mounting points Nos. 30 and 31, 3/32" shank only, ea............... .45
Catalog No. 3013. Long screw shoulder mandrel for mounting point No. 41, 3/32" shank only, ea........................ .60
Catalog No. 38. Spindle chuck, fits either 1/8" or 3/32" Hand-ee chuck, will grip even the finest hair line drills. Maximum capacity No. 52 Drill, ea.. 1.50
Catalog No. 39. 1/8" dia. heavy screw mandrel for Nos. 29, 33 and 49, 1/8" shank only, ea........................... .40
Catalog No. 40. 1/8" dia. nut mandrel, 1/8" shank only, ea......... .40
Catalog No. 3014. Special saw mandrel, screw top 1/8" shank for saws Nos. 3016 and 3017, ea........................ 1.00
Catalog No. 3015. 1/4" wheel adapter mandrel for Hi-Power only, ea. .60

SPECIAL SET CHICAGO MOUNTED WHEELS

Set No. 3 Containing 15 Wheels

You will find all the necessary practical shapes and sizes of Mounted Wheels in the correct grade and grains in this set.
Net price, complete set...................................$4.65

HAND-EE TOOL ACCESSORIES

POLISHING

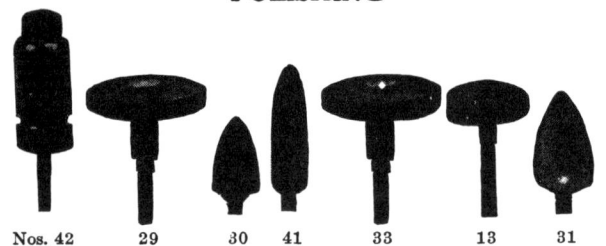

Nos. 42 29 30 41 33 13 31

Soft rubber polishing wheels and points are especially adapted for working with metals of all kinds. They have sufficient grinding action to remove marks and scratches and are impregnated with a special type of polishing compound which leaves a brilliant finish. Felt polishing wheels can be used with regular compounds such as Tripoli, Rouge, etc.

Catalog No. 42. Special eraser and rubber polishing tip holder with one eraser, $\frac{3}{32}''$ shank only, each..........$1.50
Extra rubber erasers No. 43, dozen.......... .40

Catalog No. 29. Soft Rubber Polishing Wheel $\frac{7}{8} \times \frac{1}{8}''$, gives exceptional finish to all types of metal. Wheel only. (Use mandrel No. 16, 39 or 40).......... .20

Catalog No. 30. Rubber polishing tip (use mandrel No. 21), each.. .15

Catalog No. 41. Long soft rubber polishing tip, 1" (use mandrel No. 3013), Tip only.......... .15

For complete catalog of "CHICAGO" Soft Rubber Polishing Wheels ask for F.860.

FELT POLISHING WHEELS

Catalog No. 33. Felt wheel $1 \times \frac{1}{8}''$ (Use mandrel No. 16, 39 or 40) wheel only..........$ .20

Catalog No. 13. $\frac{1}{2}''$ diameter polishing wheel permanently mounted, $\frac{3}{32}''$ mandrel, each.......... .20

Catalog No. 31. Small polishing tip (use mandrel No. 21, each.... .20

MASTER CRAFTSMAN SET

This set of especially selected accessories make it possible for you to perform countless operations impossible with any tool except the Hand-ee. Included are accessories for grinding, drilling, polishing, sawing, cutting, carving, sanding and engraving. They work equally well with any model Hand-ee.

The set consists of seventeen (17) accessories catalog numbers as follows: No. 27 Saw with No. 16 Mandrel. No. 23 Drum Sander. No. 5W211 "CHICAGO" Mounted Wheel. No. 4936 Steel Cutter. No. 31 Point with No. 21 mandrel. No. 14 Bristle Brush. No. 30 Point with No. 21 mandrel. No. 4925 Steel Cutter. No. 1 Drill. No. 10 Drill. No. 11 Disc cleaning brush. No. 12 Cup cleaning brush. No. 25 Rubber disc with No. 17 mandrel. No. 18 Push pin mandrel. No. 29 Rubber polishing wheel with No. 16 mandrel. No. 13 Felt polishing wheel No. 15 Wire scratch brush. Dozen assorted discs.

Craftsmen throughout the world, based on their purchases of accessories, are responsible for the selection. Each is a valuable adjunct for any Hand-ee Owner.

This set is an exceptional value.

Price Complete..........$5.00

All accessories in the Master Craftsman's Set are mounted on $\frac{3}{32}''$ mandrel. Included with every set is a reducing collet for using the tools with Hand-ees having $\frac{1}{8}''$ chuck.

SPECIAL SELECTION OF CUTTERS WITH $\frac{1}{4}''$ SHANK

DESIGNED FOR OPERATION ON THE HI-POWER GRINDER AND OTHER EQUIPMENT LARGER THAN EITHER THE STANDARD OR DELUXE MODEL HAND-EE. Cutters are made from the finest quality steel carefully machined and ground to precise limits, they are in every way precision cutting tools. The group shown below is available only on $\frac{1}{4}''$ steel shank.

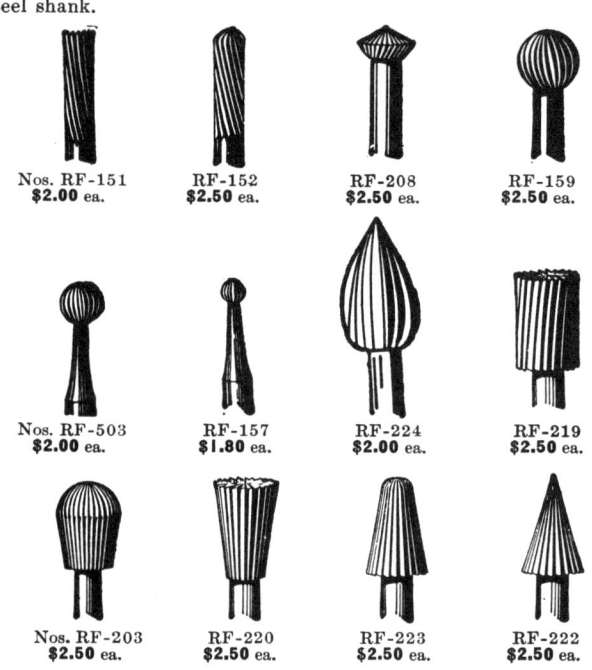

| Nos. RF-151 | RF-152 | RF-208 | RF-159 |
| $2.00 ea. | $2.50 ea. | $2.50 ea. | $2.50 ea. |

| Nos. RF-503 | RF-157 | RF-224 | RF-219 |
| $2.00 ea. | $1.80 ea. | $2.00 ea. | $2.50 ea. |

| Nos. RF-203 | RF-220 | RF-223 | RF-222 |
| $2.50 ea. | $2.50 ea. | $2.50 ea. | $2.50 ea. |

SPECIAL SET OF $\frac{1}{4}''$ SHANK STEEL CUTTERS

Complete set of $\frac{1}{4}''$ shank "CHICAGO" Steel Cutters that every die shop, pattern shop and craftsmen have everyday use for.

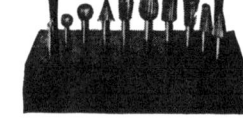

Catalog No. 3042. Special value net price at..........$27.00

CUTTERS SHOWN $\frac{1}{2}$ ACTUAL SIZE

"CHICAGO" ROUTER BITS

STRAIGHT ROUTER BITS
S-93—$\frac{1}{8}''$ Lip
S-94—$\frac{3}{16}''$ Lip
S-95—$\frac{1}{4}''$ Lip
$1.75 ea.

VEINING BITS
V-90—$\frac{1}{16}''$ Lip
V-91—$\frac{3}{32}''$ Lip
V-92—$\frac{1}{8}''$ Lip
$1.35 ea.

FISH TAIL BITS
F-96—$\frac{1}{8}''$ Lip
F-97—$\frac{3}{16}''$ Lip
$2.50 ea.

Each of these bits have been designed for working with the Hand-ee, either Standard or DeLuxe Model. With them you can rout, inlay, mortise, make molding cuts on all wood and soft metals. These special bits are available only on $\frac{1}{8}''$ shank.

SPECIAL PURFLING TOOL

Ideal for purfling, inlaying, undercutting. Works equally well with either model Hand-ee.

Catalog No. 5922. Net price each..........$2.50

No. 5922

HAND-EE TOOL ACCESSORIES

"CHICAGO" Steel Cutters provide craftsmen, mechanics and tool makers a new, rapid and efficient method for working soft metals such as brass, magnesium, aluminum, lead, bronze, babbit and tin. They are perfect cooperative instruments in executing the most delicate designs in hard or soft wood. Sculptors, pattern-makers and carvers, find that they can make, shape, engrave and finish, in minutes what formerly took them hours and days.

CUTTERS SHOWN IN THIS GROUP AVAILABLE ON SHANKS 3/32"x1½"

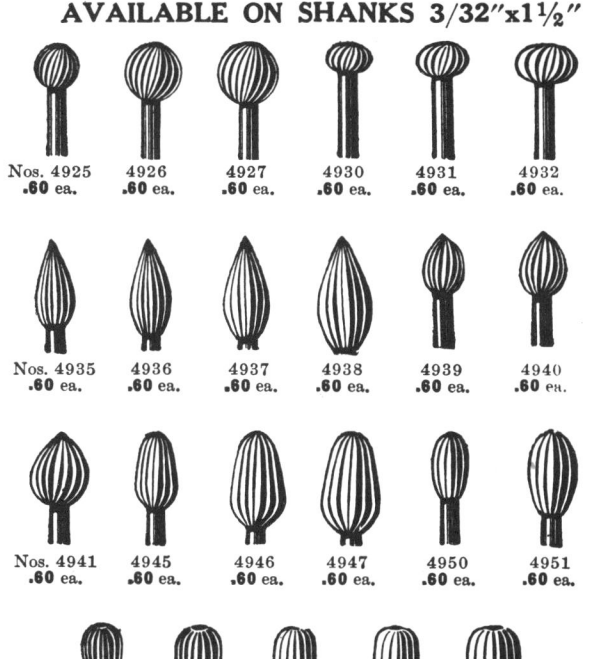

Nos. 4925, 4926, 4927, 4930, 4931, 4932 — .60 ea.
Nos. 4935, 4936, 4937, 4938, 4939, 4940 — .60 ea.
Nos. 4941, 4945, 4946, 4947, 4950, 4951 — .60 ea.
Nos. 4955, 4956, 4960, 4962, 4961 — .60 ea.

SPECIAL SET OF 3/32" SHANK CUTTERS

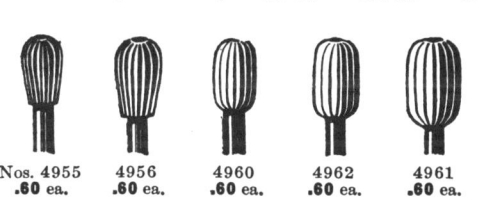

Popular group of the above shapes are the choice of many craftsmen. Includes Nos. 4925, 4927, 4932, 4935, 4938, 4939, 4941, 4945, 4947, 4951, 4955 and 4961 all mounted on 3/32" steel shank.
Catalog No. 3040. Special value net price $7.00

CUTTERS SHOWN ACTUAL SIZE

HAND-EE SPEED DRILLS

Drill with lightning speed in wood, soft metals, Bakelite, in fact everything but hardened surfaces. Ideal with any model Hand-ee for shallow drilling. These drills are indispensable to any model-maker, available only on 3/32" shanks.

No.	1	2	3	4	5
Dia.	.035	.037	.040	.045	.050
No.	6	7	8	9	10
Dia.	.055	.065	.070	.080	.090

Net price .... .30 ea.

SHANKS ⅛x1½

Chicago Steel Cutters should not be used on hard steel, or other materials of high-tensile strength. Use Chicago Mounted Wheels shown on Page 371 for hard metals. Cutters shown below are mounted on ⅛" shanks only.

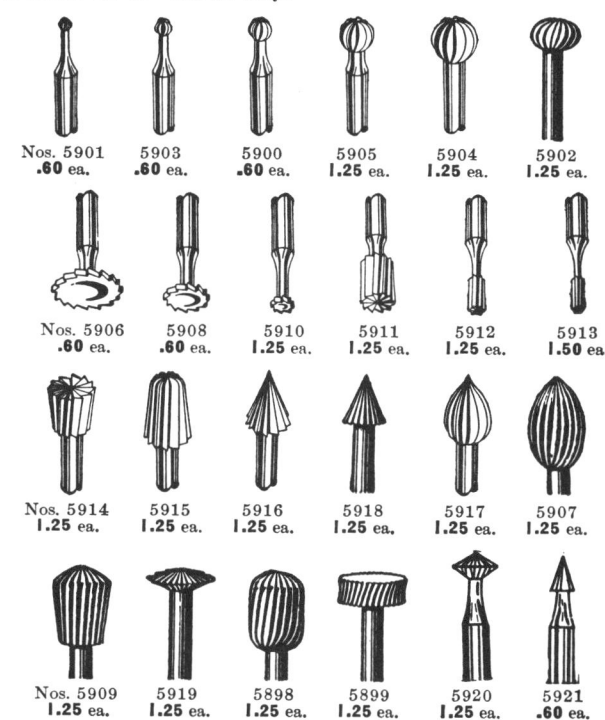

Nos. 5901 .60 ea., 5903 .60 ea., 5900 .60 ea., 5905 1.25 ea., 5904 1.25 ea., 5902 1.25 ea.
Nos. 5906 .60 ea., 5908 .60 ea., 5910 1.25 ea., 5911 1.25 ea., 5912 1.25 ea., 5913 1.50 ea.
Nos. 5914 1.25 ea., 5915 1.25 ea., 5916 1.25 ea., 5918 1.25 ea., 5917 1.25 ea., 5907 1.25 ea.
Nos. 5909 1.25 ea., 5919 1.25 ea., 5898 1.25 ea., 5899 1.25 ea., 5920 1.25 ea., 5921 .60 ea.

SPECIAL SET OF ⅛" SHANK CUTTERS

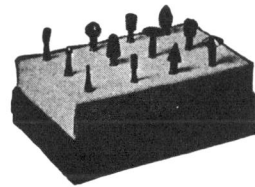

A group of the most popular "CHICAGO" Steel Cutters on ⅛" steel shank includes Nos. 5901, 5900, 5904, 5906, 5908, 5910, 5913, 5914, 5915, 5916, 5917 and 5919.
Catalog No. 3041. Special value net price $12.00

SPECIAL CUTTER SETS

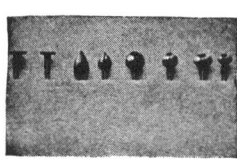

A set of eight "CHICAGO" Steel Cutters mounted on 3/32" shanks consisting of: Nos. 4925, 4927, 4930, 4932, 4937, 4939, 4919 and 4920.
Catalog No. 3043. Illustrated. Special value net price $5.00

A set of seven "CHICAGO" Steel Cutters mounted on ⅛" shanks consisting of: 5901, 5903, 5900, 5906, 5908, 5913 and 5921.
Catalog No. 3044. Not Illustrated. Special value net price $5.00

SPECIAL HIGH SPEED DRILLS

These drills are of a special design, made from the finest quality of high speed steel with polished flutes for drilling depths not exceeding ¾" in all but hardened materials.
High speed Steel Drill ⅛" diameter $1.00
High speed Steel Drill 3/32" diameter 1.00

FLEXIBLE SHAFT UTILITY TOOL AND ROTARY FILES

This Flexible Shaft Utility Tool was designed especially for use in gun shops, die shops, pattern shops, machine shops, tool rooms, engraving and printing establishments. The tool is particularly adapted to the finishing of small openings, radii and irregular shapes in all types and kinds of patterns. It is also a practical tool for use in building of models.

This tool, carefully tested and tried in our own shop will, when once used, become indispensable to the gunsmith. In this one tool, when used for small items, will be found all the combined advantages of a drill press, a lathe, a milling machine, a grinder, and a polisher with the great added convenience of easy portability. The tool is especially well adapted to fine inletting of gun stocks, particularly shot gun actions. It will be found invaluable in working on sears, triggers, etc., and will grind surfaces a file will not touch.

The tool is designed so that the flexible shaft can quickly be attached directly to the armature at one end of the motor or to the shaft of the gear reduction unit at the opposite end. This makes it possible to secure either high or low speeds at the handpiece. Maximum idling speed—approximately 12,000 RPM., direct from armature.

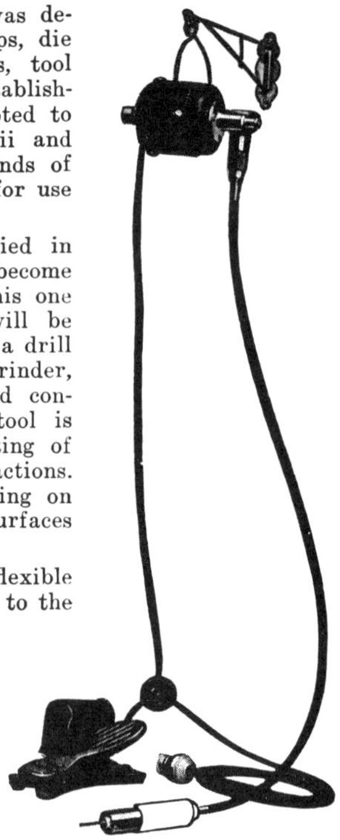

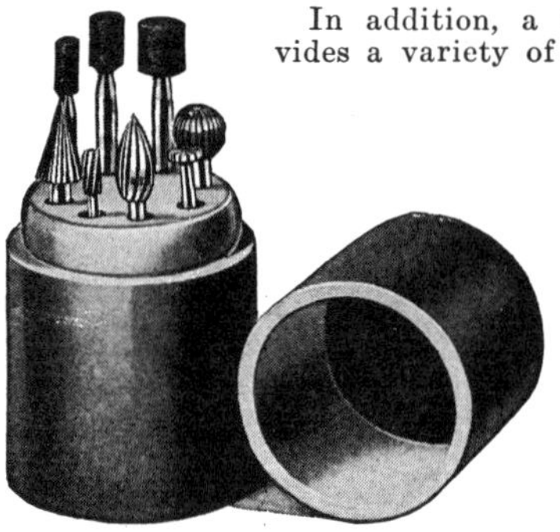

In addition, a foot controlled rheostat provides a variety of speeds to suit the operator's need. The handpiece is equipped with two ball bearings, and it is designed so that it will not heat even under continuous operation. Shaft and sheath are of ample strength to transmit the load required.

A set of five diesinker's burs and three pencil wheels are regularly furnished with this tool. The burs consist of one No. 7 round shape, one No. 10 size cone shape, one No. 18 wheel shape, one No. 8 square cylinder and one No. 1 flame. Shank is approximately 3/32". The pencil wheels are ⅛" x ¼", 3/16" x ¼", ¼" x ¼" in size. Size of shank is ⅛" x 1⅞".

In experimenting with this tool we have found that the diesinker's burs perform very efficiently using high speed on brass, copper, aluminum and soft substances; low speeds for toolsteel and hardened metals.

SPECIFICATIONS

Motor—1/16 H.P. Universal type.
Finish—Black.
Speed of motor—12,000 RPM idling, direct from armature shaft.
36½" flexible shaft from end of motor coupling to ball bearing handpiece.
Special ball bearing handpiece.
No. 0 balanced Jacobs chuck, ⅛" capacity.
Net weight—8 lbs.
Shipping weight—12 lbs.
Price complete **$45.00**

HAND CUT ROTARY FILES

Made of High Speed Steel

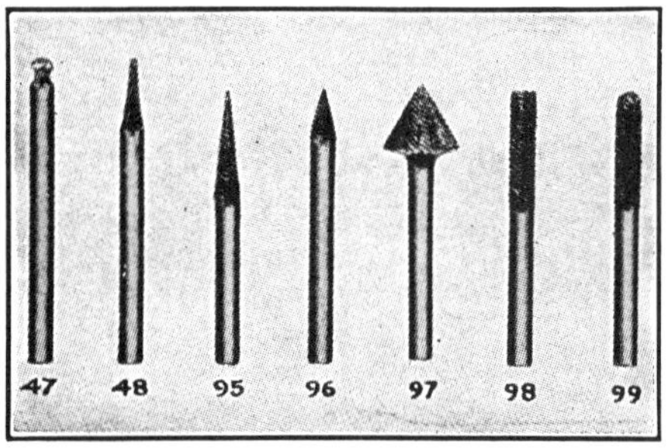

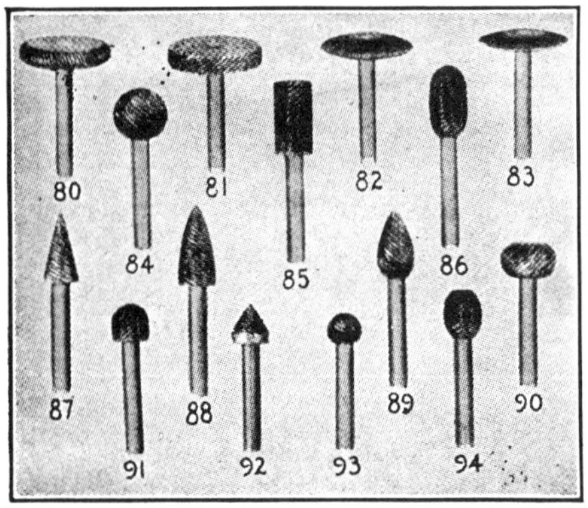

File No.	Dia. of File Inches	Length of Body Inches	Dia. of Shank Inches	Length Over-all Inches	Price Cut Coarse
47....	⅛	3/64" Radius	⅛	1¾	$1.00
48....	⅛	⅜	⅛	1½	1.00
80....	⅝	⅛	⅛	1⅛	$1.50
81....	⅝	⅛	⅛	1⅛	1.50
82....	⅝	⅛	⅛	1⅛	1.50
83....	⅝	⅛	⅛	1⅛	1.50
84....	⅜	⅜	⅛	1⅛	1.25
85....	¼	½	⅛	1¼	1.25
86....	¼	½	⅛	1¼	1.25
87....	¼	½	⅛	1¼	1.25
88....	¼	½	⅛	1¼	1.25
89....	¼	½	⅛	1¼	1.25
90....	⅜	7/32	⅛	1	1.25
91....	¼	¼	⅛	1	1.25
92....	¼	¼	⅛	1	1.25
93....	¼	¼	⅛	1	1.25
94....	¼	5/16	⅛	1⅛	1.25
95....	⅛	9/16	⅛	1 5/16	1.00
96....	⅛	¼	⅛	1 5/16	1.00
97....	⅜	⅜	⅛	1 1/16	1.25
98....	⅛	⅝	⅛	1⅜	1.00
99....	⅛	⅝	⅛	1⅜	1.00

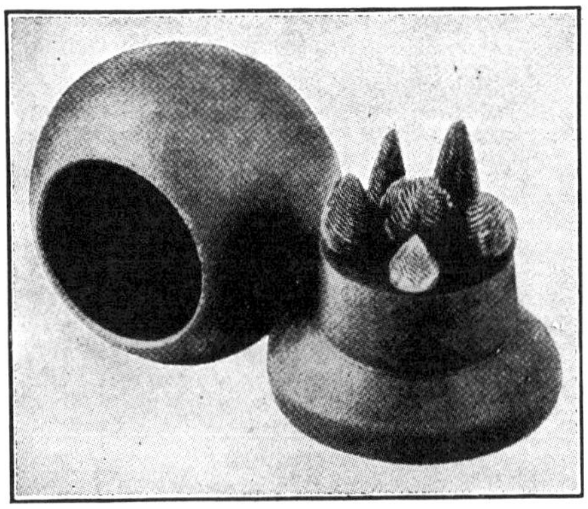

FILES FURNISHED IN SETS

The set illustrated herewith consists of files Nos. 84, 87, 88, 89, 92, and 94; coarse cut.—Per set—**$7.50.** If finished in wooden case, as illustrated, price is **$7.75 (25c extra).**

HAND CUT ROTARY FILES AND CABINET RASPS

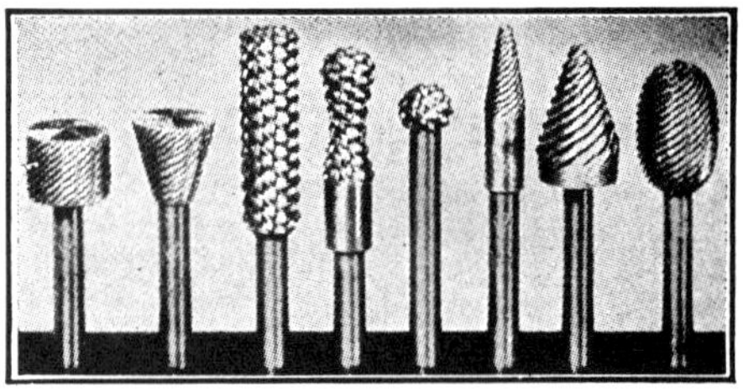

They are furnished in a high grade of Tool Steel and are heat treated.

These Files and Rasps may be used on cast iron mild stel, bronze, brass at a speed of 600 to 800 R.P.M., also, on aluminum, magnesium, bakelite, celluloid, horn, bone and wood at a speed up to 10,000 R.P.M.

Our standard set, as shown above, is a combination of cuts which will fill every need. However, any of the shapes can be furnished in the following cuts—Extra Coarse, Coarse, Fine, Smooth or Cabinet Rasp. Unless otherwise specified, the standard set will be furnished. There is an extra charge for other than coarse cut.

DESCRIPTION

No.	Dia. of File Inches	Length of Body Inches	Length Over-all Inches	Price
301........	⅝	½	2½	$.90
302........	⅝	⅝	2¼	.90
A303........	⅜	1½	2¾	.85
A304........	⅜	1½	2½	.85
A305........	⅜	⅜	2¼	.85
306........	5/16	1¼	2¾	.85
307........	⅝	1	2¾	.90
308........	⅝	1	2⅝	.90
Wooden Case..........................				.25
Set No. 501-C, (8 files as illustrated and described) Complete in Wooden Case......				**6.75**

WHEN ORDERING PLEASE SPECIFY CUT OR COARSE FILE WILL BE FURNISHED

Extra coarse cut has about..12 teeth per inch
Coarse cut has about.......18 teeth per inch
Fine cut has about.........30 teeth per inch
Smooth cut has about.......50 teeth per inch

Extra Coarse Cut Files are the same list as Coarse Cut, Fine Cut Files 25% additional, Smooth Cut Files are 50% additional.

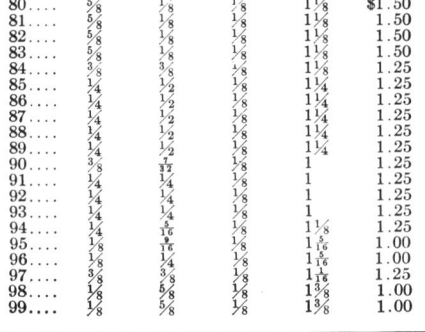

GAS EQUIPMENT

You find herewith a line of gas burners absolutely necessary for every gunsmith shop. They are well made, being machined from heavy brass tubing, with orifices machined from brass rod. Requiring a small flame with an intense heat, these burners are unexcelled for such purposes as blueing small parts, sights, soldering, tempering of springs, etc.

No. 416 TORCH

No. 416 Torch is very suitable where a portable flame is desired. Length 11¾ inches, weight ¾ lbs. burns 6 cubic feet gas per hour.

Price $3.00

GAS BURNERS

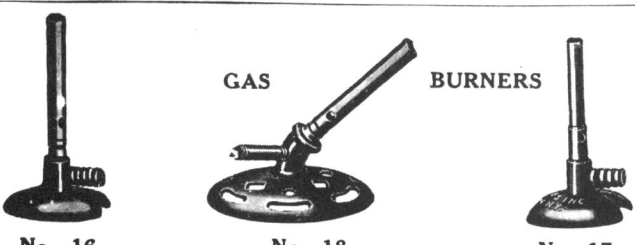

No. 16   No. 18   No. 17

No. 16 Gas Burner with cast iron base, height 5¾ inches. Diameter of base 3 inches, uses 6 cubic feet of gas per hour, weight ½ lb., recommended for bench use.
Price $1.00

No. 18 is the same as No. 16 but on 45 degree angle. Price.... $1.25

Note: Each of these burners has a gas adjustment by simply turning the burner tube, giving a short hot blast flame or long soft blue flame according to the setting.

No. 17 has a fixed orifice with air shutter adjustment only. Price.... $.50

No. 43 GAS SOLDERING FURNACE

No. 43 Gas Soldering Furnace is of similar construction as the No. 1 and has two burners, larger in size, heating width is 5¾ inches, chamber depth 7 inches, opening 3¼ inches. The upper section of hood takes a melting pot 10 inches long, 5¼ inches and 1½ inches deep. The pot can be removed and lid is supplied to cover hole. Weight 27½ pounds.

No. 43 Gas Soldering Furnace complete with melting pot.
Price $20.00
No. 43 Gas Soldering Furnace complete without Melting Pot.
Price $17.50

No. 1 GAS SOLDERING FURNACE

No. 1 Gas Soldering Furnace designed for heating soldering coppers, to melt soft metals, for hardening parts or springs, to anneal receivers and heat treating same. No blower or power is required and the gas consumption is very economical with the Venturi high powered gas burners used in connection of same. Each furnace is equipped with pilot light. The abrasive rest in the bottom of the heating chamber not only protects the soldering coppers and prevents the tinning from being burned off, but retains the heat. No lining to break or disintegrate, is used in the hoods. Built to last a lifetime. Weight 14 lbs. Opening 2¼ inches, Depth 5¼ inches, Heating width 3½ inches, Gas connection ⅜ inch. Price $8.00

No. 53 GAS BENCH FURNACE

No. 53 Gas Bench Furnace recommended for tempering small carbon steel tools and parts, annealing, forging, etc. It is equipped with three high powered Venturi together with pilot light and is lined throughout with heavy refractory. Included with the No. 53 is a heavy refractory piece to partially close off front opening, together with plugs for side openings when not used for heating long rods or materials. Weighs 40 lbs. Heating chamber is 7 inches deep, 6¼ inches wide, 4½ inches high and uses ½ inch connection.
Price $25.00

No.	Length	Weight	Gas per hour	Price
06	13"	12 oz.	6 c.f.	$3.50
07	12"	12 oz.	6 c.f.	3.50
08	16"	26 oz.	22 c.f.	5.00
09	15"	26 oz.	22 c.f.	5.00

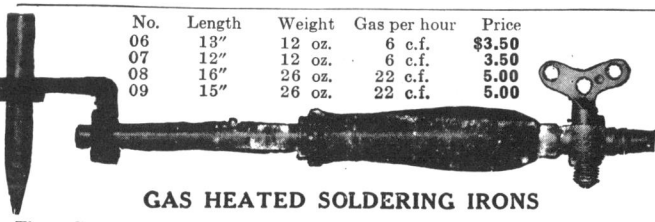

GAS HEATED SOLDERING IRONS

These Gas Heated Soldering Irons do not take more than 1½ minutes for heating. They also can be used as a torch by detaching the copper. No. 06 and No. 07 are equipped with ½-inch diameter coppers or if desired, with ¼-inch or ⅜-inch coppers. No. 08 and No. 09 have ¾-inch coppers. Also, No. 08 and No. 09 are equipped with high powered automatic blast burners.

PLAIN DRILLED PIPE BURNERS—(Mounted on legs)

These pipe burners are complete with plain air mixers and are ideal for heating blueing tanks to blue gun barrels. Will be supplied in the following sizes. Can also be made up on special order to requirements.

Pipe size	Flame length	Total length	Gas per hour	Burner Mounted
1 inch	24 inches	34 inches	30 cu. ft.	$6.00
1¼ inch	30 inches	42 inches	60 cu. ft.	7.90
1¼ inch	36 inches	48 inches	72 cu. ft.	8.15

PROJECTING PORT PIPE BURNERS—(Mounted and baffled)

The advantage of the projecting Port Pipe Burner is not being likely to clog very readily; they are equipped with the Venturi air mixer and the burners are ⅛-inch pipe nipples screwed into burner head. Especially recommended to applications where there is dirt or grease. Supplied in the following sizes; also can be had on special order according to requirements.

Pipe size	Flame length	Total length	Gas conn.	Gas per hr.	Mounted with baffle legs less with brackets	Mounted on legs, adjustable
1 inch	24 inches	38 inches	¼ inch	68 cu. ft.	$11.10	$13.15
1¼ inch	30 inches	47 inches	⅜ inch	95 cu. ft.	13.50	15.50
1¼ inch	35 inches	53 inches	⅜ inch	110 cu. ft.	14.25	16.25

KEILPART PRECISION VERNIER CALIPERS

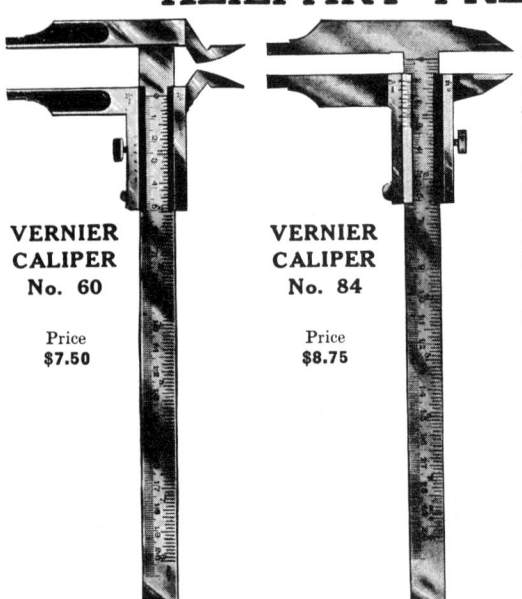

VERNIER CALIPER No. 60
Price $7.50

VERNIER CALIPER No. 84
Price $8.75

The firm of Fr. Keilpart & Co. has been known for generations as one of the world's finest manufactories of highest grade precision measuring instruments. It has kept step with technical developments and the constantly increasing requirements of accuracy. The factory has the most modern equipment and only the most highly skilled workmen and it is their constant endeavor to produce only the best to maintain their world wide reputation.

CALIBRATIONS OF VERNIER CALIPERS No. 60, 84, and 107

These calipers are supplied with divisions of measurements as follows: Below—inches with Vernier for reading in 1000″. Above—inches with Vernier for reading in 128″. On the rear side it is equipped with depth measurement for 16″ without Vernier.

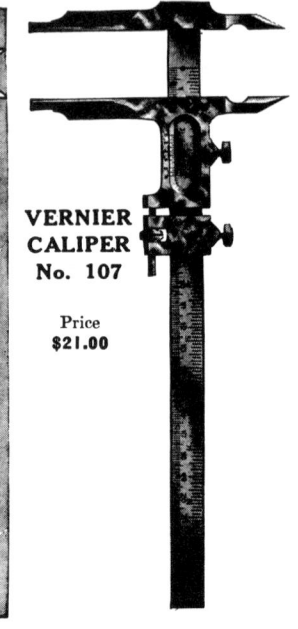

VERNIER CALIPER No. 100
Price $7.00

VERNIER CALIPER No. 107
Price $21.00

Made of rolled steel, durably and carefully executed. The general finish is considerably better than ordinary. The divisions and numerals are engraved according to a special process and chemically blackened. The caliper is equipped with points for direct reading of internal measurements. The capacity of this caliper is 8″ and the inside length of anvils is about 2¼″. Supplied with three styles of marking.

In this caliper the anvil and main body as well as the slide are each of one piece construction. This caliper is especially carefully and ruggedly built of rolled steel. Divisions and numerals are engraved according to a special system and chemically blackened. This caliper is equipped with knife point for marking. Its capacity is 8″ with anvil length of 2¼″. Supplied with three styles of markings.

Made entirely of forged steel, with special lapping and glass hardening of the ways and equipped with inside measurements with measuring capacity of 5¼″ and anvil about 1½″. With two sets of markings as follows: Below—inches with Vernier for thousandths of an inch—reading above—inches with Vernier for 128″ reading. This is a caliper of exceptionally high accuracy.

Made entirely of special steel in most exact execution with closed movable slide. Tips as well as full length of measuring surface are glass hardened. The lapped measuring surfaces, clean cut workmanship of slide and the highly exact divisions and engraved numerals distinguish it as a measuring tool of highest quality. Capacity 8″ with 2¼″ anvil length with three sets of markings.

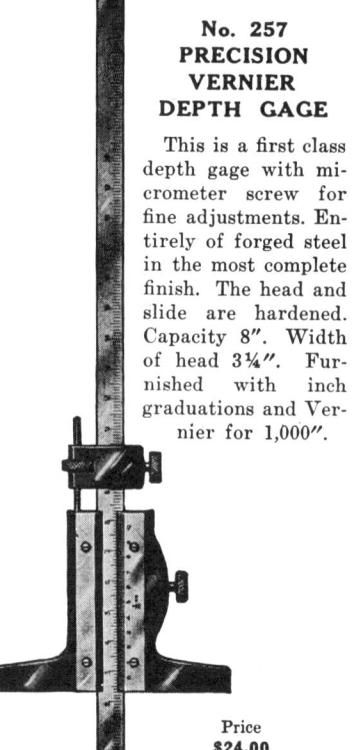

No. 114 VERTICAL BENCH TYPE VERNIER CALIPER

This is a precision tool of the first order. The bent scribing point permits measuring from the surface plate and transferring measurements to the work. All surfaces used for measuring are lapped and glass hardened to prevent wear. In the case of worn measuring surfaces, the apparatus may be re-ground without trouble. For this purpose, in the base a plate is fitted with a wedge tightened with a screw which holds the plate in a steady position making any play impossible. The apparatus is equipped with a micrometer screw for fine adjustments. The capacity is 12″. The inside length of the large anvil is about 2¼″ equipped with measurements divisions in inches and the Vernier for 1/1000″.

Price $65.00

No. 257 PRECISION VERNIER DEPTH GAGE

This is a first class depth gage with micrometer screw for fine adjustments. Entirely of forged steel in the most complete finish. The head and slide are hardened. Capacity 8″. Width of head 3¼″. Furnished with inch graduations and Vernier for 1,000″.

Price $24.00

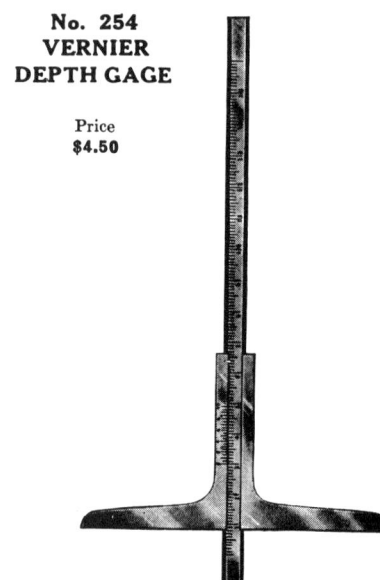

No. 254 VERNIER DEPTH GAGE

Price $4.50

This depth gage is made of forged steel of very light design. Has a bevelled slide measuring only 8 x 3 mm. The measuring tip is of hardened steel removable pin—capacity 6″, length of cross arm, 3¼″—furnished with 1″ graduations and Vernier for 128″.

THE BEST WORK REQUIRES THE BEST TOOLS

America's Great Gun House — 365

KEILPART PRECISION MICROMETERS, SURFACE PLATES, ETC.

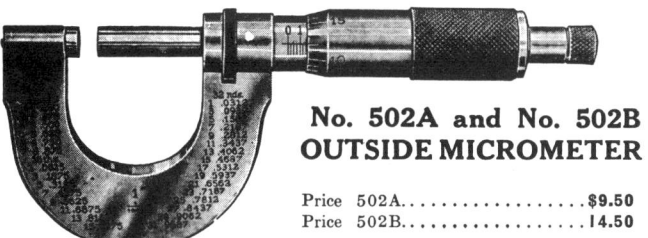

No. 502A and No. 502B OUTSIDE MICROMETER

Price 502A.................$9.50
Price 502B.................14.50

No. 502A. Dull Chromium finish. Capacity to 1″ with divisions for reading in thousandths. Spindle thread, accurately ground, spindle equipped both with ratchet and lock.

No. 502B. Made of stainless steel. Otherwise same as above. Special bright finish.

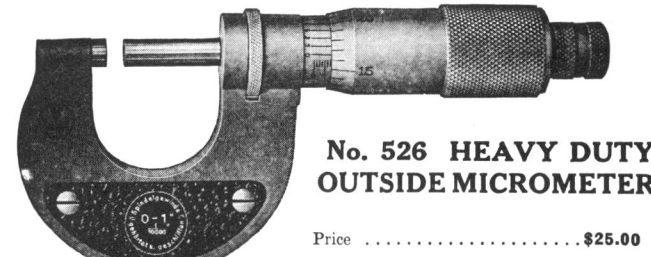

No. 526 HEAVY DUTY OUTSIDE MICROMETER

Price $25.00

This is a first class Precision Micrometer of extra heavy construction. The Spindle is entirely hardened and the thread is ground after hardening. This micrometer is equipped with ratchet and lock and the anvil is fitted with insulating-cheeks to prevent the effects of hand temperature on the reading of the micrometer. Capacity 1″ with Vernier graduations reading in 1/10,000″.

No. 1705 Surface Plate

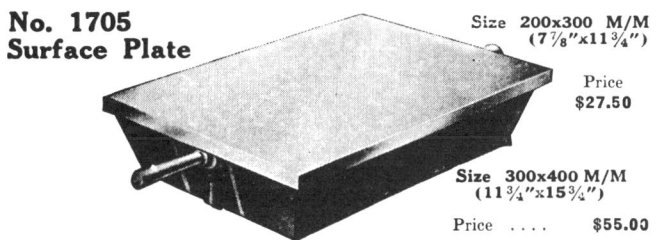

Size 200x300 M/M (7⅞″x11¾″)
Price $27.50

Size 300x400 M/M (11¾″x15¾″)
Price $55.00

This surface plate is made of an especially close grained special grade cast iron. It has a thoroughly tested rib construction which offers utmost resistance against any tendency to warp. Supplied in sizes 200 x 300 and 300 x 400. The price includes a wooden cover and grips.

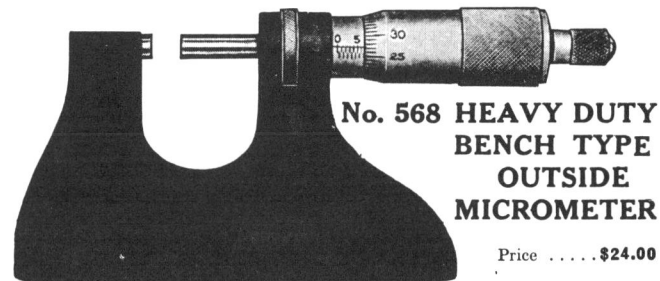

No. 568 HEAVY DUTY BENCH TYPE OUTSIDE MICROMETER

Price $24.00

This is a first class micrometer with the same general advantages of No. 526, especially recommended for convenient measuring in the shop and particularly for small parts. It has the further advantage that the warmth of the hand is kept from the instrument. Measuring capacity 1″ with Vernier readings of 1/10,000″.

No. 1750 Long Type Surface Plate

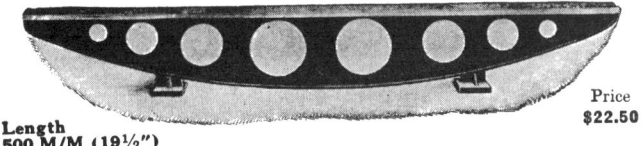

Length 500 M/M (19½″)
Price $22.50

This surface plate is made of a close grained special type of cast iron with bridge type reinforcements which prevent warpage. These plates are therefore, of especial use in testing and straightening long piece precision instruments, etc. The upper surface is scrapped absolutely flat, length 500 m/m (19½″).

No. 2380 and 2385 TOOLMAKERS SQUARES

No. 2380—This square is made of a good grade of steel for exact work. Carefully assembled and adjusted.

PRICES
50x40 M/M (2″x1⅝″).........$2.25
100x70 M/M (4″x2¾″)........ 3.75
150x100 M/M (6″x4″)........ 5.00

No. 2385—Same as above but not so accurately adjusted.

PRICES
50x40 M/M (2″x1⅝″).........$1.50
100x70 M/M (4″x2¾″)........ 2.50
150x100 M/M (6″x4″)........ 3.75

No. 1780 PRECISION KNIFE EDGED PARALLEL BAR

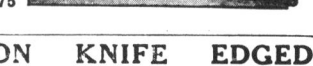

This Parallel Bar is entirely hardened and is intended for exact testing of flat surfaces. They have a wedge shaped cross section. The holes along the sides make possible easy and safe handling. Length 4″. Price $4.50

No. 1740 V BLOCKS

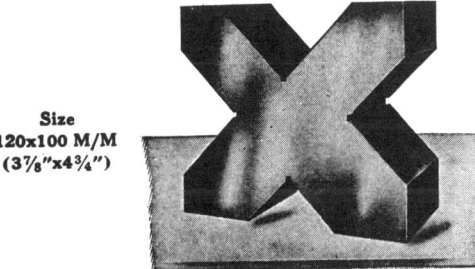

Size 120x100 M/M (3⅞″x4¾″)
Price Per Pair $35.00

With four different cuts and supplied in pairs. Size 120 x 100.

No. 1770 PARALLEL BAR

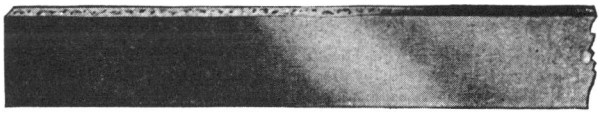

Made of high grade steel—Length 500 m/m (19½″). Cross section 50 x 10 m/m (2″ x ⅜″). Price $11.00

TOOLS YOU CAN USE WITH CONFIDENCE

BROWN & SHARPE TOOLS
"World's Standard of Accuracy"

The selection of tools is important and much depends upon having the proper tool for the job and upon having that tool reliable.

For over 100 years Brown & Sharpe Products have been leaders in their fields. The man who uses Brown & Sharpe Tools can have confidence that his measurements will be accurate.

A few of over 2300 different tools are shown here—there is a Brown & Sharpe Tool for every mechanical need.

NO. 12 MICROMETER CALIPER
Patented

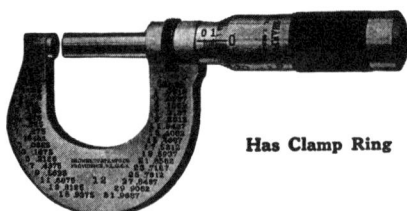

Has Clamp Ring

Range, 0 to 1"

by thousandths of an inch

Combines the utility of the "C" type frame with the advantages of frame with narrow anvil end for measuring deep in slots. Scientifically designed frame is proportioned for strength and rigidity.

Price.................$9.50   Case.................$1.25

NO. 12RS MICROMETER CALIPER
Patented

Has Clamp Ring and Ratchet Stop

Range, 0 to 1"

by thousandths of an inch

Combines the utility of the "C" type frame with the advantages of frame with narrow anvil end for measuring deep in slots. Scientifically designed frame is proportioned for strength and rigidity.

Price.................$10.00   Case.................$1.25

NO. 13 MICROMETER CALIPER
Patented

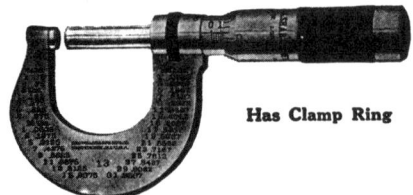

Has Clamp Ring

Range, 0 to 1"

by ten-thousandths as well as thousandths of an inch

Combines the utility of the "C" type frame with the advantages of frame with narrow anvil end for measuring deep in slots. Scientifically designed frame is proportioned for strength and rigidity.

Price.................$11.25   Case.................$1.25

NO. 13RS MICROMETER CALIPER
Patented

Has Clamp Ring and Ratchet Stop

Range, 0 to 1"

by ten-thousandths as well as thousandths of an inch

Combines the utility of the "C" type frame with the advantages of frame with narrow anvil end for measuring deep in slots. Scientifically designed frame is proportioned for strength and rigidity.

Price.................$11.75   Case.................$1.25

NO. 47 MICROMETER CALIPER
Patented

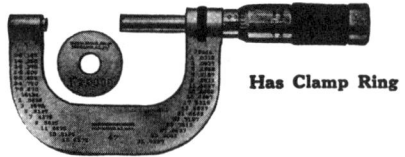

Has Clamp Ring

Range, 1" to 2"

by thousandths of an inch

A Standard is furnished for adjusting the Micrometer.

Price.................$10.50   Case.................$1.60

NO. 47RS MICROMETER CALIPER
Patented

Has Clamp Ring and Ratchet Stop

Range, 1" to 2"

by thousandths of an inch

A Standard is furnished for adjusting the Micrometer.

Price.................$11.00   Case.................$1.60

A MICROMETER FOR EVERY USE

BROWN & SHARPE TOOLS

NO. 48 MICROMETER CALIPER
Patented

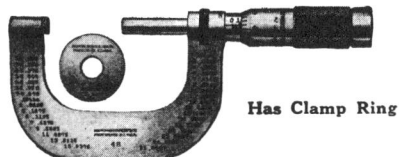

Has Clamp Ring

Range, 1" to 2"
by ten-thousandths as well as thousandths of an inch
A Standard is furnished for adjusting the Micrometer.

Price.............$12.25   Case.............$1.60

NO. 48RS MICROMETER CALIPER
Patented

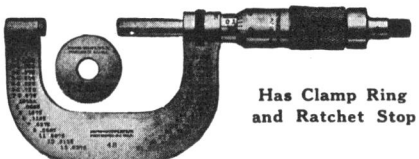

Has Clamp Ring and Ratchet Stop

Range, 1" to 2"
by ten-thousandths as well as thousandths of an inch
A Standard is furnished for adjusting the Micrometer.

Price.............$12.75   Case.............$1.60

NO. 226 BALL ANVIL ATTACHMENT

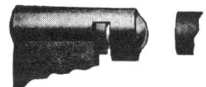

Easily applied. Equips a micrometer to measure tubing. The ball is .250 inch in diameter, and this dimension is subtracted from the actual caliper reading. Fits the following micrometers: Nos. 8, 8RS, 8S, 8SRS, 10, 10RS, 10S, 10SRS, 12, 12RS, 12B, 12BRS, 13, 13RS, 13B, 13BRS, 19, 19RS, 20, 20RS, 24, 24RS, 38, 38RS, 47, 47RS, 48, 48RS, 50, 50RS, 52, 52RS, 53 and 53RS.

Price ....$.50

NO. 250 INSIDE MICROMETER CALIPER

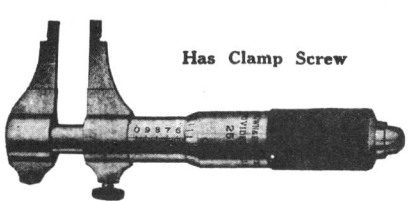

Has Clamp Screw

Range, .200" to 1"
by thousandths of an inch

Measures small internal dimensions. Measuring surfaces are hardened and ground on a radius to insure accurate measurements and prevent cramping.

Price.............$15.00   Case.............$1.25

NO. 252 INSIDE MICROMETER CALIPER

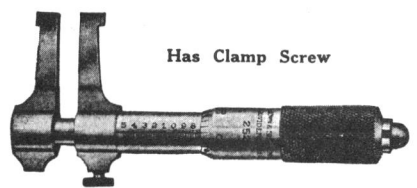

Has Clamp Screw

Range, ½" to 1½"
by thousandths of an inch

The nibs of this Inside Micrometer are hardened and ground on a radius. The shape of the jaws, also, enables measurements to be taken over a flange or shoulder.

Price.............$15.00   Case.............$1.50

NO. 300 TEMPERED STEEL RULES

These rules are about 1-20th of an inch thick excepting the 48 inch which is about 1-10th of an inch thick.

Length, Inches	Approx. Width, In.	Number of Graduation	Price	Length, Inches	Approx. Width, In.	Number of Graduation	Price
1	9/32	4	$0.30	12	1 1/8	1, 2 or 4	$1.65
2	1/2	4	.45	18	1 1/4	4	2.60
3	35/64	4	.60	24	1 1/4	4	3.25
4	5/8	4	.75	36	1 3/8	4	7.00
6	3/4	1, 2, 4 or 7	.90	*48	1½	4	10.00
9	13/16	4	1.35				

*Not tempered. For Graduation Numbers, see next page.

BROWN & SHARPE TOOLS

NO. 306 FLEXIBLE STEEL RULES

These rules are tempered and very springy. 4 inch to 12 inch sizes are about 1-64th of an inch thick. 18 inch and 24 inch sizes are about 1-32 inch thick. Graduated on both corners of one side only.

Length, Inches	Approx. Width, In.	Number of Graduation	Price	Length, Inches	Approx. Width, In.	Number of Graduation	Price
4	½	10	$0.75	12	½	10, 11 or 12	$1.65
6	½	10, 11 or 12	.90	18	¾	10	2.60
9	½	10	1.35	24	¾	10	3.25

For Graduation Numbers, see below. Leather Case for 6 inch Rule $0.15 extra.

NO. 306A FLEXIBLE STEEL RULE
WITH FIGURED GRADUATIONS

6″ length only, with No. 10 graduation, 32nds and 64ths. Has figured graduations. The 32nds are numbered every 4th graduation and the 64ths every 8th graduation as shown at left. Rule is approximately 1-2 inch wide, and 1-64 inch thick. Leather case, 15 cents extra.

Price .... $.90

GRADUATIONS

Rules are divided into parts of an inch, as follows:

	No. 1 Grad.	No. 2 Grad.	No. 3 Grad.	No. 4 Grad.	No. 7 Grad.
1st corner,	10, 20, 50, 100	8	10	8	16
2nd corner,	12, 24, 48	10, 20, 50, 100	50	16	32
3rd corner,	14, 28	12, 24, 48	32	32	64
4th corner,	16, 32, 64	16, 32, 64	64	64	100

	No. 10 Graduation	No. 11 Graduation	No. 12 Graduation
1st corner,	32	64	50
2nd corner,	64	100	100

NO. 388 POCKET SLIDE CALIPER RULE

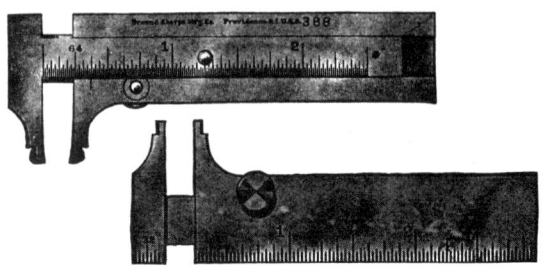

This rule accurately measures inside and outside diameters. The nibs of the jaws can be inserted in holes as small as ⅛ inch.
The clamp nut locks the slide and holds it set for any particular measurement. The button on the slide aids in opening and closing the jaws.
Rule is 3 inches long, 11/16 inch wide and about ⅛ inch thick. One corner is graduated in 32nds and the slide in 64ths for 2½ inches. The jaws are ⅝ inch long, and when open, measure up to 2 inches.
Price $4.00

NOS. 400 AND 402 COMBINATION SQUARES
Patented

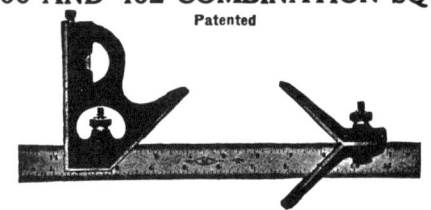

Blades are tempered

	With Heads Hardened			With Heads not Hardened	
No.	Size	Price	No.	Size	Price
400	6 inch	$4.60	402	6 inch	$2.40
	9 inch	5.30		9 inch	3.00
	12 inch	6.20		12 inch	3.60
	18 inch	7.30		18 inch	4.50
	24 inch	8.20		24 inch	5.40

GRADUATIONS
Nos. 400 and 402 — No. 4 or No. 7*

1st Corner	8	16	3rd Corner	32	64
2nd Corner	16	32	4th Corner	64	100

* No. 7 Graduation not furnished on 18″ and 24″ Squares.

NOS. 401 AND 403 COMBINATION SQUARES
WITHOUT CENTER HEADS
Patented

Blades are tempered

	With Heads Hardened			With Heads not Hardened	
No.	Size	Price	No.	Size	Price
401	4 inch	$2.30	403	4 inch	$1.50
	6 inch	3.10		6 inch	1.80
	9 inch	3.40		9 inch	2.40
	12 inch	4.30		12 inch	3.00
	18 inch	5.40		18 inch	3.90
	24 inch	6.30		24 inch	4.80

GRADUATIONS
Nos. 401 and 403 — No. 4 or No. 7*

1st Corner	8	16	3rd Corner	32	64
2nd Corner	16	32	4th Corner	64	100

* No. 7 Graduation not furnished on 4″, 18″ and 24″ Squares.

BROWN & SHARPE TOOLS

NO. 585 VERNIER HEIGHT GAGE 10″

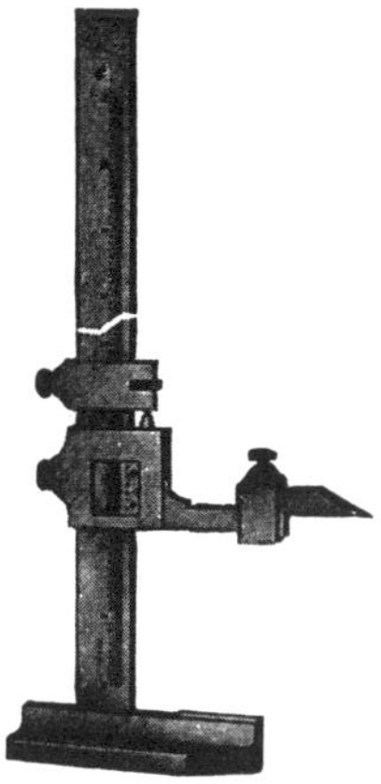

Designed to measure and mark off vertical distances from a plane surface, this Vernier Height Gage is an essential tool for jig and fixture making, and brings a high degree of accuracy to any work for which it is used.

A combination marker and extension is furnished for the movable jaw and is very handy for scribing lines on work.

Base is approximately 3¾″ long, 1½″ wide and ¾″ high. It is ground and lapped on the top and bottom. Measurements may be taken on both inside and outside of the jaws.

One side of vernier is for use as a height gage from 1⅛″ to 10″, and the other side as an outside caliper from 0 to 10″. Both measurements are read directly in thousandths of an inch.

This tool can also be used as an outside caliper. Measurements between the jaws are determined by deducting from the reading the thickness of the jaw and base. This thickness can be ascertained by bringing jaw and base to closed position and noting reading of tool at that point.

Price, in Case........$45.00 Price, without Case........$40.00

Furnished in Case unless otherwise ordered.

NO. 590 TELESCOPING GAGES

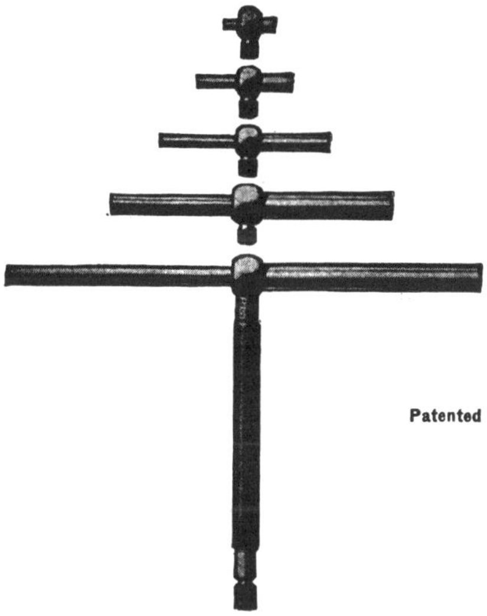

Patented

These gages are compact, simple and durable, and are intended for use with a micrometer caliper to determine quickly internal measurements which are otherwise hard to obtain. The Brown & Sharpe design incorporates two important features. 1. Only the small leg telescopes. This brings handle near to point of contact in the most sensitive position for accurate measurement. (See illustration above.) 2. When handle is removed, heads will not fly apart and become lost. Ends of each head are hardened and faces are ground on radius of smallest hole gage will enter, thus adapting tool, especially for accurate use on curved surfaces. The five heads are interchangeable.

In use, head expands to exact size of hole and is then locked by turn of knurled screw in end of handle. Gage is withdrawn and measured with micrometer.

	Price
No. 590—Complete Set, Range ½″ to 6″ (including handle)	$12.00
No. 590A—Handle	.50
No. 590B—Range, ½″ to ¾″ (without handle)	2.00
No. 590C—Range, ¾″ to 1¼″ (without handle)	2.00
No. 590D—Range, 1¼″ to 2⅛″ (without handle)	2.50
No. 590E—Range, 2⅛″ to 3½″ (without handle)	2.50
No. 590F—Range, 3½″ to 6″ (without handle)	3.00

Unless otherwise ordered, complete set will be furnished.

NO. 600 VERNIER DEPTH GAGE

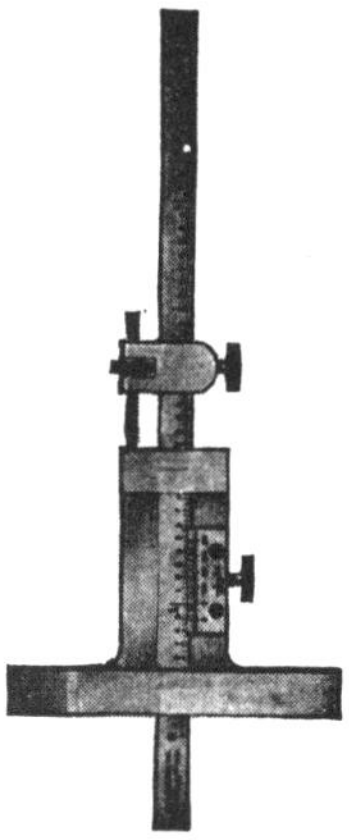

GAGE WITH 6″ BLADE

	Price
In Case	$16.25
Without Case	14.50

GAGE WITH 6″ AND 12″ BLADES

In case	$24.55
Without Case	22.30

Furnished in case unless otherwise ordered.

For obtaining the depth of holes, recesses in dies, distance from a plane surface to a projection, etc. Base is 2⅝″ wide and .3″ in thickness. The blades are ¼″ or 7 mm wide. The six-inch blade allows measurements to be made 3½″ or 88 mm deep and the 12″ blade 9½″ or 238 mm deep.

Graduated on the front to read, by means of a Vernier, in thousandths of an inch.

NOS. 607 AND 607R MICROMETER DEPTH GAGES

With or Without Ratchet Stop

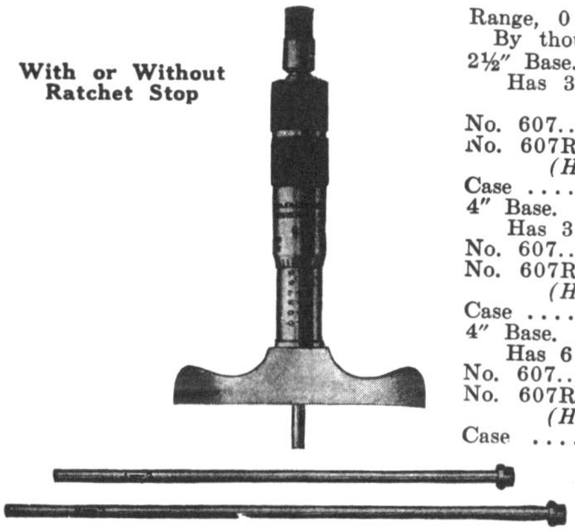

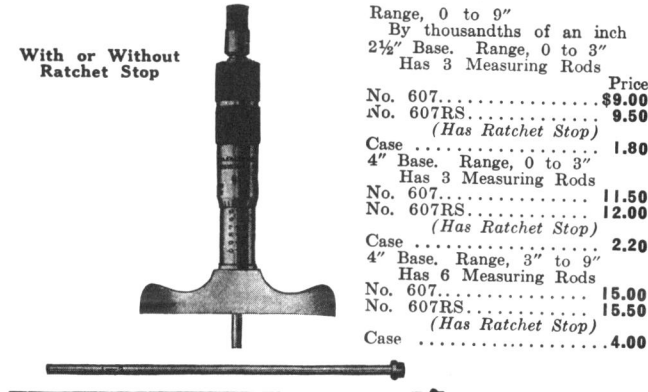

Range, 0 to 9″
By thousandths of an inch

2½″ Base. Range, 0 to 3″
Has 3 Measuring Rods

	Price
No. 607	$9.00
No. 607RS *(Has Ratchet Stop)*	9.50
Case	1.80

4″ Base. Range, 0 to 3″
Has 3 Measuring Rods

No. 607	11.50
No. 607RS *(Has Ratchet Stop)*	12.00
Case	2.20

4″ Base. Range, 3″ to 9″
Has 6 Measuring Rods

No. 607	15.00
No. 607RS *(Has Ratchet Stop)*	15.50
Case	4.00

The Micrometer Screw has a movement of 1″ and the range from 0 to 3″ or 3″ to 9″ is obtained by the use of the measuring rods furnished. Rods of Gages measuring 0 to 3″ are ⅛″ in diameter, those measuring 3″ to 9″ are 3/16″ diameter. End of all rods are hardened. The rod desired is easily and quickly inserted in the Gage through a hole in the Micrometer Screw. Bases are about 3/16″ wide and are hardened.

NO. 616 DEPTH GAGE

Range, 0 to 5″

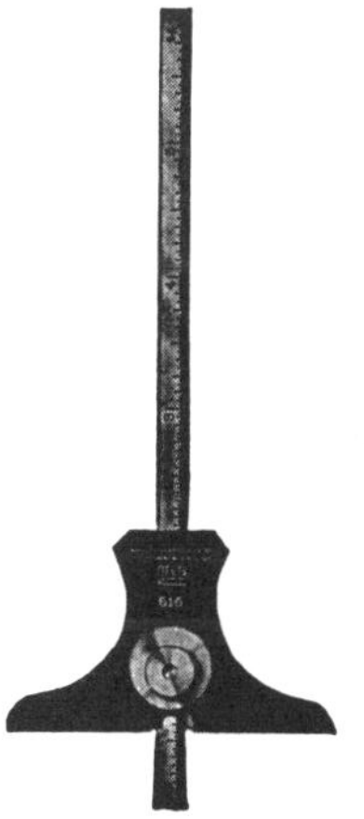

The blade of this Rule Depth Gage may be adjusted easily to any angle in relation to the head. The turret is graduated to 10°, 20°, 30°, 40°, 45°, 50°, 60°, 70°, 80° and 90°. The blade is locked at the proper angle by the larger of the two clamp nuts on the front side of the head and is locked for any depth by the smaller clamp nut.

The head of this Rule Depth Gage is made of hardened steel, 2½″ wide and ⅛″ thick, and is of a form especially designed for convenience in measuring. The blade is a 6″ Narrow Tempered Steel Rule with No. 10 Graduations, 32nds and 64ths.

Price $2.25

BROWN & SHARPE TOOLS

NO. 620 UNIVERSAL SURFACE GAGES

Adjustments of this Universal Surface Gage are made readily by means of the knurled adjusting screw. The spindle and the bolt and bushing through which it passes are locked in the position of approximate adjustment by the knurled nut at the boss on the base. The fine adjustment can then be used to obtain the exact setting.

A distinct advantage of the Brown & Sharpe design is the location of the fine adjustment, which permits the gage to be held and adjusted with one hand.

The base is of a form most convenient to handle. A V-shaped groove in the bottom especially adapts it for cylindrical work. It has two gage pins in the rear end that can be pushed down and used against the edge of a surface plate or the side of a T slot.

The spindle swivels and can be securely clamped in any position from horizontal to vertical either above or below the base. The scriber may be used below the base as a depth gage. For small work the spindle may be removed and the scriber inserted in the spindle swiveling bolt where it is readily adjusted.

Universal Surface Gages for obtaining larger measurements are also available.

Price
No. 620A With 4" Spindle, Base not hardened................$3.50
No. 620B With 4" Spindle, Base hardened....................4.10

Size of Base, approximately 2¼" x 1½"

NO. 633 SCREW PITCH GAGE

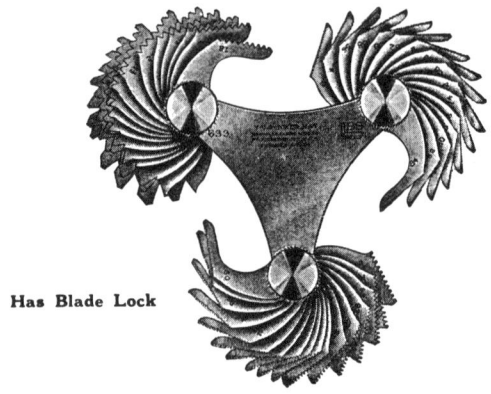

Has Blade Lock

For the mechanic who has use for a gage with a great variety of pitches, this gage is just the tool. The triangular shape of the frame permits the compact housing of 51 blades.

All pitches of V threads including pipe threads, threads per inch, 11½ and 27, and American National and U. S. Threads are covered.

This gage contains 51 blades for the following threads per inch: 4, 4½, 5, 5½, 6, 7, 8, 9, 10, 11, 11½, 12, 13, 14, 15, 16, 18, 20, 22, 24, 26, 27, 28, 30, 32, 34, 36, 38, 40, 42, 44, 46, 48, 50, 52, 54, 56, 58, 60, 62, 64, 66, 68, 70, 72, 74, 76, 78, 80, 82 and 84.

V, American, National or United States Standard Threads
Price
51 Pitches, 4 to 84..$2.75

NO. 645 THICKNESS GAGE

Blades, 3" Long
Price, $1.50
Has Blade Lock

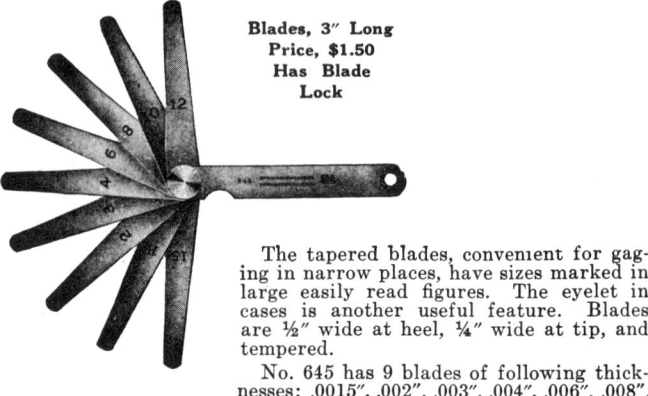

The tapered blades, convenient for gaging in narrow places, have sizes marked in large easily read figures. The eyelet in cases is another useful feature. Blades are ½" wide at heel, ¼" wide at tip, and tempered.

No. 645 has 9 blades of following thicknesses: .0015", .002", .003", .004", .006", .008", .010", .012" and .015".

NOS. 650 AND 651 CENTER GAGES

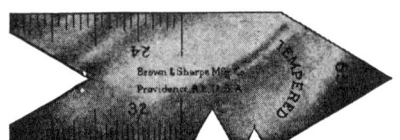

Front Side

Back Side

With table on the gage for determining the size of tap drills for American National or U. S. Standard threads, shows in thousandths of an inch the double depth of thread of tap and screw of the pitches most commonly used.

The angles used on these gages are 60° for the American National or U. S. Standard and 55° for the Whitworth or English Standard. The four graduations, 14, 20, 24 and 32 parts to the inch, are useful in measuring the number of threads to the inch.

No. 650—American, National or United States Standard
Price.................$.40   Tempered, Price.........$.50
No. 651—Whitworth or English Standard
Price.................$.40   Tempered, Price.........$.50

NO. 707 TWIST DRILL AND MACHINE SCREW TAP GAGE

Price, $2.40

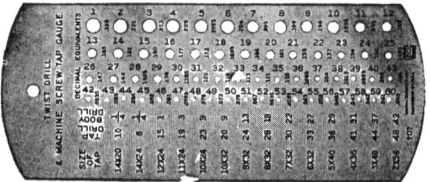

Hardened

Tells at a glance correct drill for any common size machine screw tap. Carefully tested after hardening.

Gage is about 1/16" thick, 2⅝" wide, 6⅛" long and is polished. Table gives size of tap, pitch of thread and size of drill required and size of drill for making hole through which outside diameter of tap will pass.

BROWN & SHARPE TOOLS

NO. 740 UNIVERSAL DIAL INDICATOR SET

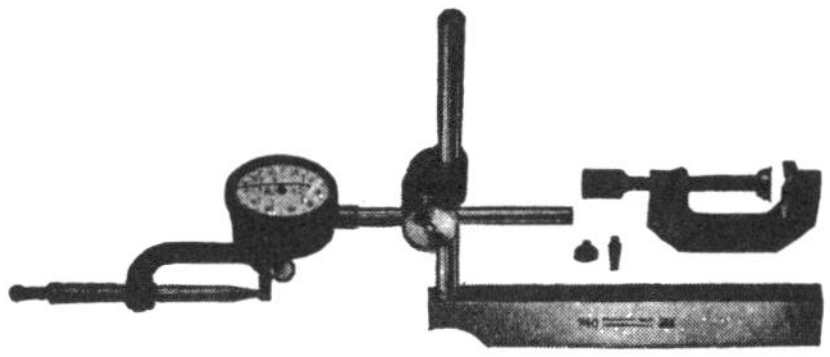

Spindle Movement .2″ by thousandths of an inch

Price, Complete............$16.00
Finished Wooden Case, extra. 2.50

Diameter of Dial, 1¾″
Dial Holding Rod, ¼″ Dia., 3 3/16″ Long
Upright 5/16″ Dia., 5″ Long

Complete set includes Dial Gage with Hole Attachment, Bar with upright Rod, Clamp, Sliding Swivel, Dial Holding Rod and three chromium plated contact points.

Can be adjusted to almost any position and used in places inaccessible to ordinary indicators. Hole attachment will enter approximately 1½″ in hole as small as ¼″ diameter. Clamp has brass swivel to prevent marring work. Bar is case hardened steel 6″ long, ⅜″ thick and ⅞″ wide. Swivel, also, fits Surface Gages No. 621, a particularly convenient combination, (see opposite page).

Dial Gage is extremely durable and has simple adjustment for wear. Measures by thousandths of an inch. By bringing contact point against work with enough pressure to give hand complete revolution, readings may be taken 1-10″ either side of zero. Knurled rim turns to bring zero under hand.

Packed one in a box.

SEPARATE PARTS

	Price
Dial Gauge only, with 3 Contact Points	$12.00
Hole Attachment	1.75
Clamp	.90
Bar with Upright	.90
Dial Holding Rod	.50
Sliding Swivel	.90
Contact Points, each	.20

NO. 750A V BLOCKS AND CLAMPS

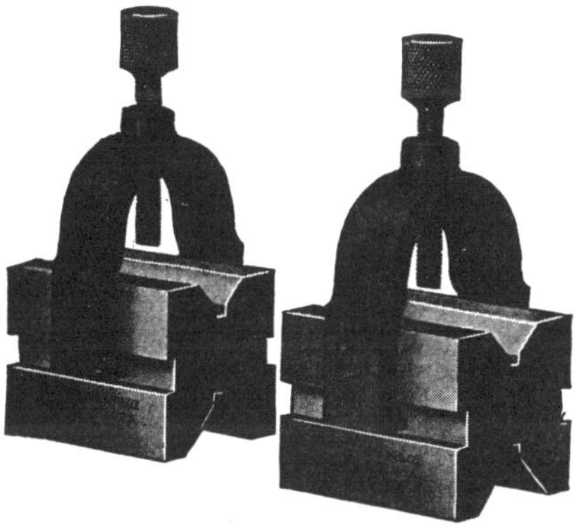

These blocks are hardened tool steel and very accurate. The sides are ground parallel and the V grooves carefully ground central and parallel to the bottom and sides. Finish ground on all four sides. They are made and sold in numbered pairs, so that the V grooves in blocks of the same numbers are always in alignment. (We cannot agree to furnish a mating block at a later date.) Especially useful for accurately laying out work in connection with a surface plate, angle iron or knee.

Each block is approximately 1¼″ x 1¼″ x 1⅝″ and will take work to 1″ in diameter.

Price, per Pair.. $6.75

NO. 754 TOOLMAKERS' CLAMPS

Designed to insure greatest strength and rigidity. Made of steel, case hardened. Ends of jaws are rounded to facilitate clamping under shoulder or in recess. Clip holds "loose" jaw in position when clamping screw is released, a very convenient and an original Brown & Sharpe feature.

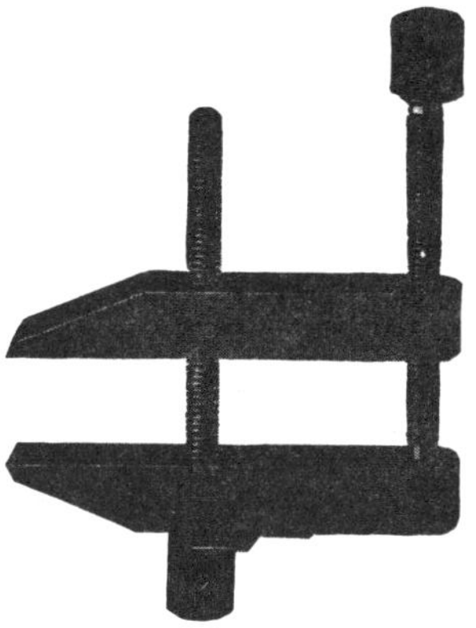

No.	Opening of Jaws, Inches	Length of Jaws, Inches	Price, Each
754 A	⅝	1½	$0.70
754 B	1	2⅛	.85
754 C	1½	2¾	1.00
754 D	2	3⅜	1.20
754 E	2½	4	1.50
754 F	3½	5	2.30

NO. 765 MACHINISTS' CENTER PUNCHES

These punches are of convenient sizes and knurled on the body to afford a good finger grip. Both ends are tempered, and the points carefully ground to an angle. They are about 4″ in length.

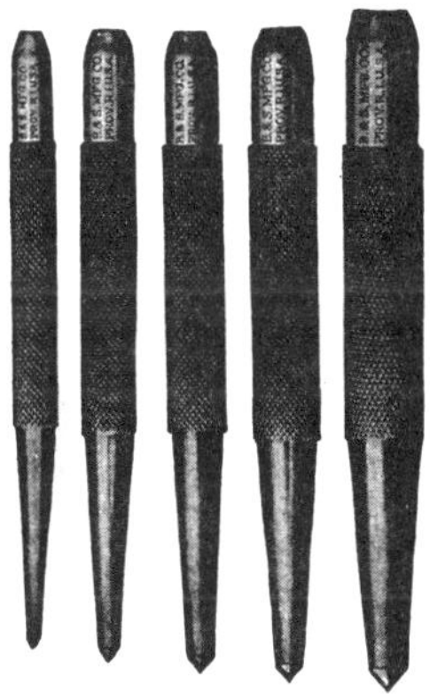

No.	Diameter at Top of Tapered Point, Inches	Price
765 A	1/16	$0.25
765 B	3/32	.25
765 C	⅛	.25
765 D	5/32	.25
765 E	7/32	.30

Set of five sizes in case, Price, $1.55

NO. 770 AUTOMATIC CENTER PUNCHES

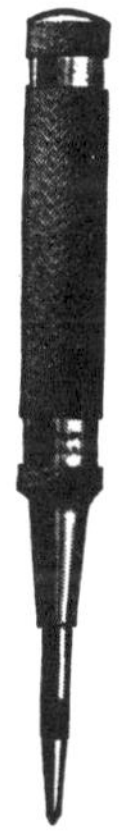

	Price
Style 1, 4⅛″ long, ⅜″ diameter	$2.00
Style 2, 5¼″ long, 9/16″ diameter	3.00
Style 3, 6″ long, ¾″ diameter	4.00

The striking mechanism of this Automatic Center Punch is enclosed in the knurled handle, which is of such a size and form as to be held conveniently in the hand. A downward pressure releases the striking block and makes the impression. The punch marks are of uniform depth.

The points on Styles 2 and 3 can be taken out for grinding and are easily replaced if broken.

Style 1 is adapted for carrying in the pocket, and is a small, light tool suitable for the more delicate work required in tool making.

Style 3 differs from the Style 2 in being slightly heavier in construction and capable of striking a much heavier blow.

	Price
Extra Points for Style 1 Punch......each	$.60
Extra Points for either Style 2 or 3 Punch......each	.20

© PRICES ON OTHER BROWN AND SHARPE TOOLS ON APPLICATION

REAMERS AND COUNTERBORES

Hand Reamers

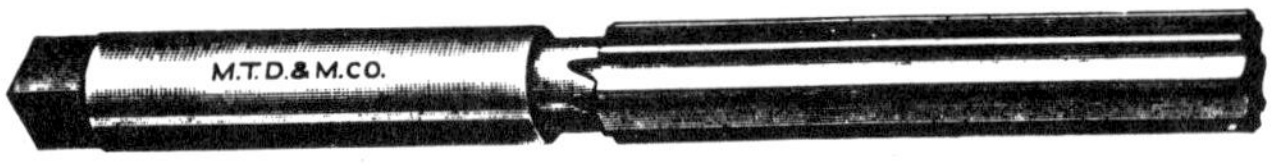

No. 601
Carbon Steel

No. 1601
High Speed Steel

64th sizes, ⅛ to ¾ inch inclusive, of carbon steel furnished at price of next larger size. All other 64th sizes at special prices.

Hand Reamers with threaded ends and all sizes and dimensions not listed are special and subject to special prices.

Reamers for Brass or Bronze require special clearance and are so furnished on request.

Diam., Inches	Price Each: Carbon Steel	Price Each: High Speed Steel	Whole Length, Inches	Length of Flutes, Inches	Diam., Inches	Price Each: Carbon Steel	Price Each: High Speed Steel	Whole Length, Inches	Length of Flutes, Inches
⅛	$1.00	**$3.00**	3	1½	19/32	$2.20	**$6.25**	6¾	3⅜
5/32	1.20	**3.25**	3¼	1⅝	⅝	2.20	**6.25**	7	3½
3/16	1.20	**3.25**	3½	1¾	21/32	2.40	**6.75**	7⅜	3 11/16
7/32	1.40	**3.50**	3¾	1⅞	11/16	2.40	**6.75**	7¾	3⅞
¼	1.40	**3.50**	4	2	23/32	2.60	**7.25**	8⅛	4 1/16
9/32	1.50	**3.75**	4¼	2⅛	¾	2.60	**7.25**	8⅜	4 3/16
5/16	1.50	**3.75**	4½	2¼	25/32	2.80	**7.75**	8¾	4⅜
11/32	1.60	**4.25**	4¾	2⅜	13/16	2.80	**7.75**	9⅛	4 9/16
⅜	1.60	**4.25**	5	2½	27/32	3.10	**8 50**	9⅜	4 11/16
13/32	1.75	**4.75**	5¼	2⅝	⅞	3.10	**8.50**	9¾	4⅞
7/16	1.75	**4.75**	5½	2¾	29/32	3.40	**9.50**	10	5
15/32	1.90	**5.25**	5¾	2⅞	15/16	3.40	**9.50**	10¼	5⅛
½	1.90	**5.25**	6	3	31/32	3.70	**10.50**	10⅝	5 5/16
17/32	2.00	**5.75**	6¼	3⅛	1	3.70	**10.50**	10⅞	5 7/16
9/16	2.00	**5.75**	6½	3¼					

Taper-Pin Reamers

No. 680
Carbon Steel

With Straight Flutes

No. 1680
High Speed Steel

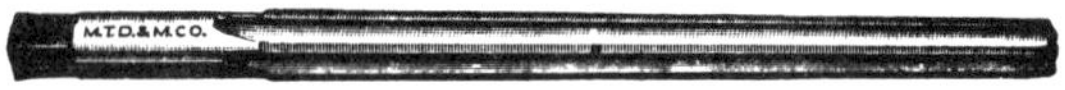

Taper-Pin Reamers

No. 684
Carbon Steel

With Spiral Flutes

No. 1684
High Speed Steel

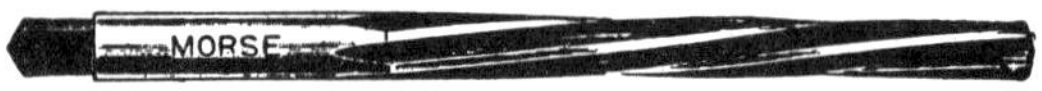

These Reamers have the same taper, and each will overlay in convenient measure the next size smaller. Taper ¼ inch per foot.

Sizes, dimensions and styles not listed are special and subject to special prices.

Size Number	Price Each: No. 680 Carbon Steel	Price Each: No. 1680 High Speed Steel	Price Each: No. 684 Carbon Steel	Price Each: No. 1684 High Speed Steel	Diameter at Small End, Inches	Whole Length, Inches	Length of Flutes, Inches
7/0	$1.75	**$3.50**	$2.10	**$3.85**	.0497	1 13/16	13/16
6/0	1.60	**3.50**	1.95	**3.85**	.0611	1 15/16	15/16
5/0	1.50	**3 25**	1.80	**3.60**	.0719	2 3/16	1 3/16
4/0	1.50	**3.25**	1.80	**3.60**	.0869	2 5/16	1 5/16
3/0	1.50	**3.25**	1.80	**3.60**	.1029	2 5/16	1 5/16
2/0	1.35	**3.00**	1.65	**3.30**	.1137	2 9/16	1 9/16
0	1.00	**2.80**	1.20	**3.10**	.1287	2 15/16	1 11/16
1	1.00	**2.90**	1.20	**3.20**	.1447	2 15/16	1 11/16
2	1.25	**3.00**	1.50	**3.30**	.1605	3 3/16	1 15/16
3	1.50	**3.00**	1.80	**3.30**	.1813	3 11/16	2 5/16
4	1.75	**3.25**	2.10	**3.60**	.2071	4 1/16	2 9/16
5	2.00	**3.50**	2.40	**3.85**	.2409	4 5/16	2 13/16
6	2.25	**4.25**	2.70	**4.70**	.2773	5 7/16	3 11/16
7	2.50	**5.25**	3.00	**5.80**	.3297	6 5/16	4 7/16
8	3.00	**6.75**	3.60	**7.45**	.3971	7 3/16	5 3/16
9	3.50	**8.25**	4.20	**9.10**	.4805	8 5/16	6 1/16
10	4.50	**9.00**	5.40	**9.90**	.5799	9 5/16	6 13/16

Center Reamers

No. 750
Carbon Steel

No. 1750
High Speed Steel

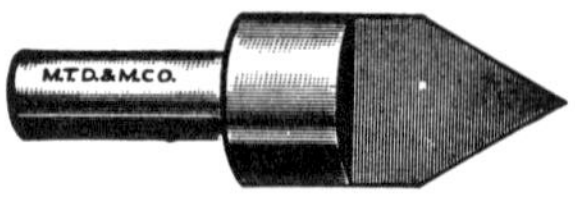

STYLE NO. 1
60°, Carbon Steel only.

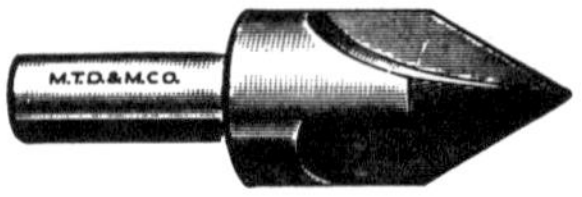

STYLE NO. 2
60°, 82°, Carbon Steel.
60°, 82°, High Speed Steel.

Sizes, dimensions and styles not listed are special and subject to special prices.

Size Cut, Inches	Style No. 1 Price Each Carbon Steel	Style No. 2 Price Each: Carbon Steel	Style No. 2 Price Each: High Speed	Whole Length, Inches	Diam. Shank, Inches	Length Shank, Inches
¼	$0.25	$0.40	**$1.00**	1½	3/16	¾
⅜	.30	.45	**1.15**	1¾	¼	⅞
½	.35	.55	**1.40**	2	⅜	1
⅝	.60	.70	**1.75**	2¼	⅜	1
¾	.80	.85	**2 15**	2⅝	½	1¼

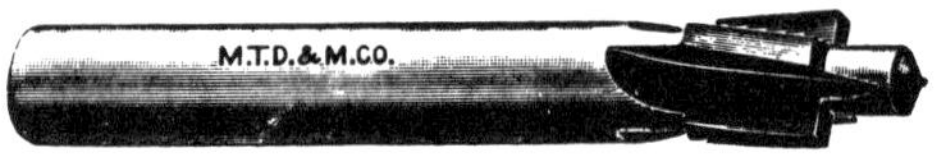

Machine Screw Counterbores

No. 757—Straight Shanks

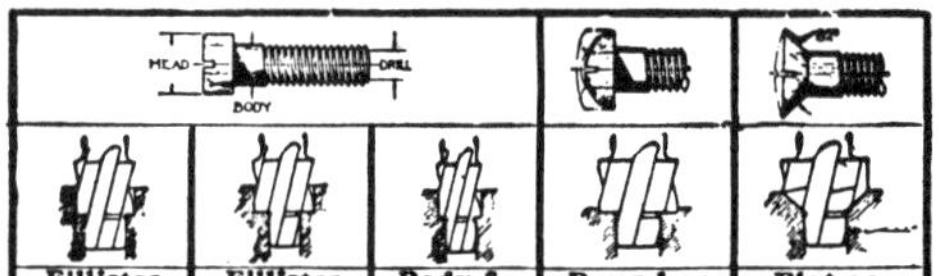

A: Fillister Head Mach. Screw. Head & Body
B: Fillister Head Mach. Screw. Head & Tap Drill
C: Body & Tap Drill for any Screw.
D: Round or Hex. Head Mach. Screw. Head & Body
E: Flat or Oval Head Mach. Screw. Head & Body

Screw Sizes	Pitch	Price Each	Fillister Head Screws (A): Bore for Head	(A): Pilot for Body	(B): Bore for Head	(B): Pilot for Tap Hole	(C): Bore for Body	(C): Pilot for Tap Hole	Round or Hex. Head (D): Bore for Head	(D): Pilot for Body	Flat or Oval Head (E): Bore for Head	(E): Pilot for Body	Tap Drills	Whole Length, In.
0	80	$1.00	.096	.060	.096	.046	.062	.046	.125	.060	.125	.060	3/64	2
1	72 64	1.00	.118	.073	.118	.059	.075	.059	.156	.073	.156	.073	53 53	2
2	64 56	1.00	.140	.086	.140	.070	.088	.070	.187	.086	.187	.086	50 50	2
3	56 48	1.00	.161	.099	.161	.082 .078	.101	.082 .078	.203	.099	.218	.099	45 47	2
4	48 40	1.00	.183	.112	.183	.093 .089	.114	.093 .089	.234	.112	.250	.112	42 43	2
5	44 40	1.00	.205	.125	.205	.104 .101	.127	.104 .101	.250	.125	.281	.125	37 38	2¼
6	40 32	1.00	.227	.138	.227	.113 .106	.140	.113 .106	.281	.138	.312	.138	33 36	2¼
8	36 32	1.10	.270	.164	.270	.136 .136	.166	.136 .136	.328	.164	.375	.164	29 29	2¼
10	32 30 24	1.10	.313	.190	.313	.159 .157 .149	.192	.159 .157 .149	.375	.190	.437	.190	21 22 25	2½
12	28 24	1.10	.357	.216	.357	.182 .177	.218	.182 .177	.437	.216	.500	.216	14 16	2½
¼	20 28	1.20	.414	.250	.414	.201 .213	.252	.201 .213	.500	.250	.562	250	7 3	3.
5/16	18 24	1.35	.519	.312	.519	.257 .272	.314	.257 .272	.625	.312	.656	.312	F I	3¼
⅜	16 24	1.50	.622	.375	.622	.312 .332	.377	.312 .332	.750	.375	.781	.375	5/16 Q	3½
7/16	14 20	1.65	.719	.437	.719	.368 .390	.439	.368 .390	.875	.437	.937	.437	U 25/64	3¾
½	13 20	1.80	.820	.500	.820	.421 .453	.502	.421 .453	1.000	.500	1.062	.500	27/64 29/64	4

DIE STOCKS, TAPS, COMBINED DRILLS AND COUNTERSINKS

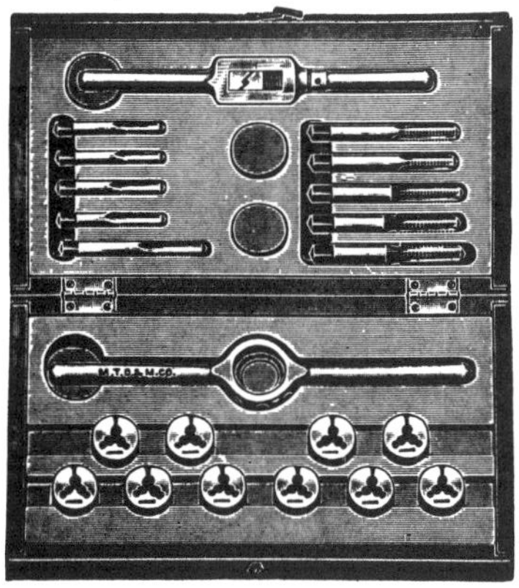

NO. 1265 SETS OF ROUND ADJUSTABLE DIES, TAPS, DIE STOCKS AND WRENCHES

MACHINE SCREW AND FRACTIONAL SIZES

Each Set includes one Tap and one Die of each listed size, one Die Stock and one Tap Wrench.

Other Sets besides those listed below can be assembled. Prices on application.

Set No.	35	36	37	39	51	52	54	59
Cutting Sizes and Threads per Inch				2-56			1/16-64	2-64
				3-48			3/32-48	3-56
	4-36	4-36		4-36	1/8-40	1/8-40	1/8-40	4-48
				5-36	5/32-36	5/32-36	5/32-36	
	6-32	6-32	6-32	6-32	3/16-24	3/16-24	3/16-24	6-40
	8-32	8-32	8-32	8-32	7/32-24	7/32-24	7/32-24	8-36
				10-32	1/4-20	1/4-20	1/4-20	
	10-24	10-24	10-24	10-24		5/16-18	5/16-18	10-32
	12-24	12-24	12-24	12-24				12-28
	14-20			14-20				14-24
Diameter of Dies, In.	5/8	5/8	5/8	5/8	13/16	13/16	13/16	13/16
Die Stock No.	21	21	21	21	22	22	22	22
& Length, In.	5	5	5	5	7 3/8	7 3/8	7 3/8	7 3/8
TapWrenchNo.	0	0	0	0	0	1	1	0
& Length, In.	5 1/8	5 1/8	5 1/8	5 1/8	5 1/8	6	6	5 1/8
Price, per Set	$9.00	$8.00	$7.25	$12.75	$9.50	$11.00	$12.50	$10.75

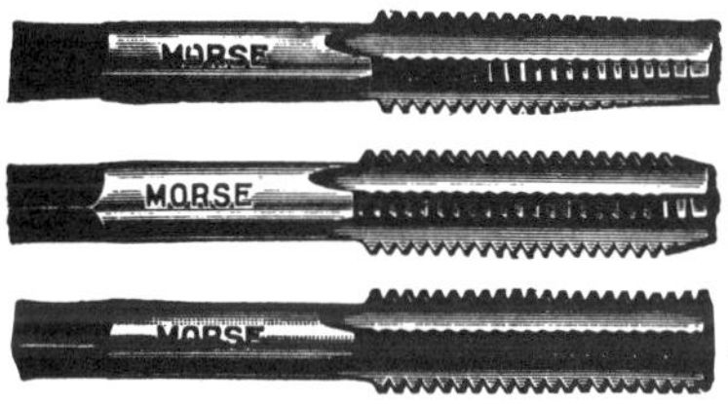

Carbon Steel Hand Taps (No. 1040)

A (A Taper)

B (B Plug)

C (C Bottoming)

Diam. of Tap, Inches	Price: Carbon Steel Each	Price: Carbon Steel Per Set	Number of Threads to the Inch: N.C. (U.S.S.)	N.F. (S.A.E.)	N.S. (U.S.F.)	Whit-worth Std.	British Std. Fine	Whole Length, Inches
1/16	$0.50	$1.50	....	....	64	60	....	1 5/8
3/32	.40	1.20	....	....	48	48	....	1 3/4
1/8	.35	1.05	....	....	40	40	....	1 15/16
5/32	.35	1.05	....	....	32, 36	32	....	2 1/16
3/16	.40	1.20	....	....	24, 32	24	....	2 3/8
7/32	.45	1.35	....	....	24, 32	24	....	2 3/8
1/4	.45	1.35	20	28	24, 27, 32	20	26	2 1/2
5/16	.50	1.50	18	24	20, 27, 32	18	22	2 23/32
3/8	.55	1.65	16	24	20, 27	16	20	2 15/16
7/16	.60	1.80	14	20	24, 27	14	18	3 5/32
1/2	.70	2.10	13	20	12, 24, 27	12	16	3 3/8
9/16	.80	2.40	12	18	27	12	16	3 19/32
5/8	.90	2.70	11	18	12, 27	11	14	3 13/16

NO. 1066 CARBON STEEL MACHINE SCREW TAPS

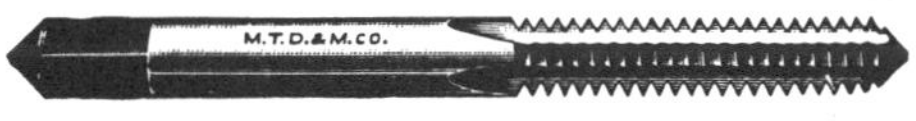

Screw Gauge No.	Basic Major Diam., Inches	Price Each	Price Per Dozen	Threads Per Inch: N.C.	N.F.	N.S.	Length of Thread, Inches	Whole Length, Inches
0	.060	$0.50	$6.00	....	80	....	5/16	1 5/8
1	.073	.50	6.00	64	72	56	3/8	1 11/16
2	.086	.45	5.40	56	64	....	7/16	1 3/4
3	.099	.40	4.80	48	56	....	1/2	1 13/16
4	.112	.40	4.80	40	48	32, 36	9/16	1 7/8
5	.125	.35	4.20	40	44	36	5/8	1 15/16
6	.138	.35	4.20	32	40	36	11/16	2
8	.164	.35	4.20	32	36	30, 40	3/4	2 1/8
10	.190	.40	4.80	24	32	28, 30	7/8	2 3/8
12	.216	.45	5.40	24	28	32	15/16	2 3/8
14	.242	.45	5.40	....	....	20, 24	1	2 1/2

NO. 1145 TAP WRENCHES

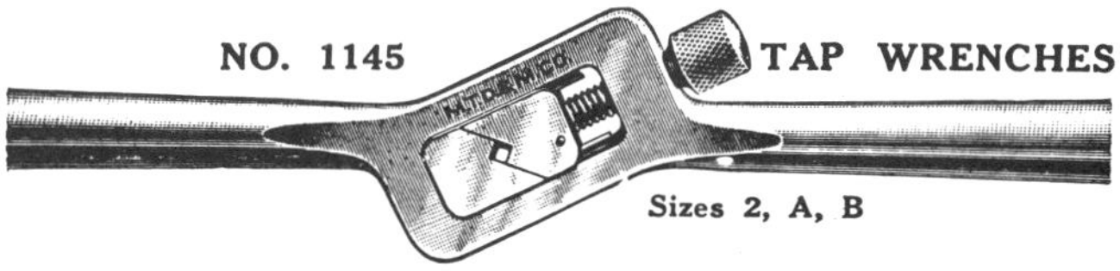

Sizes 2, A, B

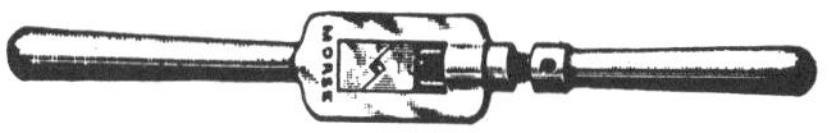

Sizes 0, 1

Size	Price Each	Whole Length, Inches	Fitting Taps	Fitting Reamers	Fitting Squares
0	$1.60	5 1/8	1/16 to 1/4	1/8 to 11/32	1/16 to 3/16
1	2.00	6	1/16 to 5/16	1/8 to 15/32	1/16 to 1/4
2	2.50	8 1/2	3/16 to 9/16	3/16 to 15/32	1/8 to 5/16
A	3.00	12 3/4	1/4 to 13/16	1/4 to 11/16	3/16 to 7/16
B	4.00	17 1/8	1/2 to 1 1/8	3/8 to 1 11/32	1/4 to 3/4

Die Stocks for Round Adjustable Dies

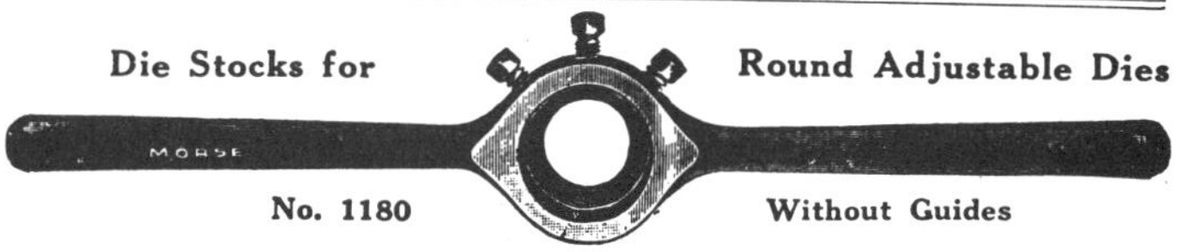

No. 1180 Without Guides

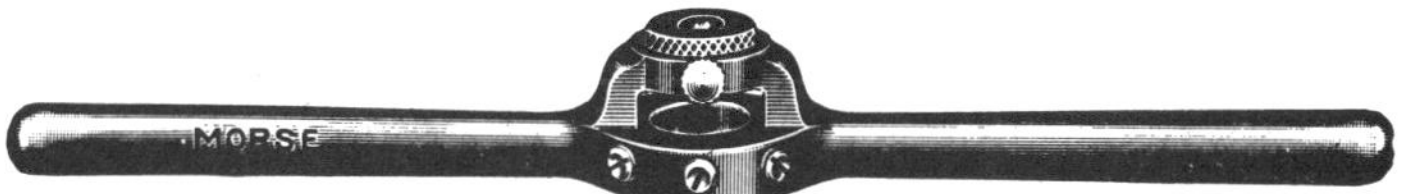

No. 1182 With Guides

Guides for No 42 Stock $0.15 each. No. 43 and No. 45 $0.30 each.
Guides for No. 48 Stock $0.40 each. No. 50 $0.50 each.

For Dies fitting these Stocks, see pages 255–262.

The Handles on Die Stocks Nos. 28, 29, 30, 31 and 32 screw into the body instead of being made solid.

No. 1180: Size of Die Stock, No.	No. 1180: Price Each Without Dies	No. 1182: Size of Die Stock, No.	No. 1182: Price Each Without Dies or Guides	Whole Length of Die Stock, Inches	Holding Round Dies: Outside Diam.	Holding Round Dies: Thickness	Limits of Cutting Size: Fractional	Limits of Cutting Size: Machine Screw Gauge
21	$0.40	....	....	5	5/8	1/4	1/16 to 1/4	0 to 14
22	.50	42	$1.50	7 3/8	13/16	1/4	1/16 to 5/16	0 to 18
23	1.00	43	2.00	10 1/4	1	3/8	1/8 to 7/16	4 to 18
25	1.25	45	3.00	12 1/8	1 5/16	7/16	1/4 to 1/2	....
26	1.25	....	....	14 1/8	1 1/2	1/2	1/4 to 5/8	....
27	1.50	....	....	14 1/8	1 9/16	9/16	1/4 to 5/8	....
28	1.50	48	3.50	18	1 3/4	9/16	1/4 to 3/4	....
29	1.50	....	....	22	2	5/8	1/4 to 7/8	....
30	1.75	50	4.50	26	2 1/4	3/4	1/4 to 1	....
31	1.75	....	....	30	2 1/2	3/4	1/2 to 1	....
32	2.25	....	....	42	3	1	7/8 to 1 1/2	....

COMBINED DRILLS AND COUNTERSINKS

No. 495 Carbon

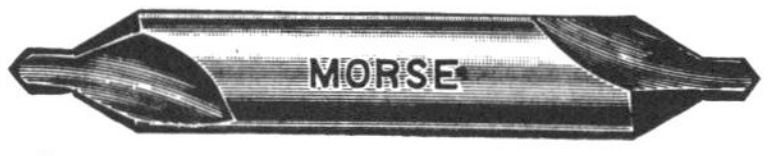

No. 1495 High Speed

Included Angle, 60°. Other angles made to order at special.
Sizes and dimensions not listed are special.

Always specify Style Number and Size Number

Size	Diameter Drill	Price Per Dozen: Carbon Steel	Price Per Dozen: High Speed Steel	Diameter of Body	Decimal Equivalent of Drill
A1	3/64	$2.50	**$8.00**	1/8	.0468
C2	1/16	3.00	**8.00**	13/64	.0625
D1	5/64	3.25	**8.00**	15/64	.078
E1	3/32	3.50	**8.00**	3/10	.0938
E2	1/8	3.50	**8.00**	3/10	.125
F1	5/32	4.50	**12.00**	7/16	.1563
F2	3/16	4.50	**12.00**	7/16	.1875

SETS OF COMBINED DRILLS AND COUNTERSINKS

Combined drills and countersinks are also offered in complete sets, neatly packed in a well made, practical and durable wooden container with lid.

1 Combined Drill and Countersink each. A1, C2, D1, E1, E2, F1, F2.

No. 50. Carbon Steel.......................... Per Set $2.80
No. 50 H. High Speed Steel.......................... Per Set $5.45

ADJUSTABLE ROUND SPLIT DIES AND DRILL SETS

ADJUSTABLE ROUND SPLIT DIES

FRACTIONAL SIZES

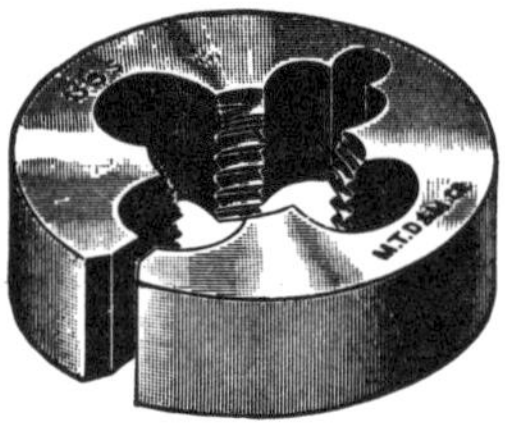

No. 1183

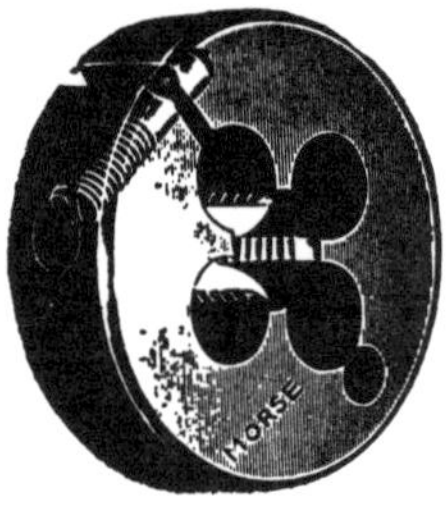

No. 1184
SCREW ADJUSTING

*5/8 Inch Outside Diameter, 1/4 Inch Thick
13/16 Inch Outside Diameter, 1/4 Inch Thick
1 Inch Outside Diameter, 3/8 Inch Thick
1 5/16 Inch Outside Diameter, 7/16 Inch Thick
1 1/2 Inch Outside Diameter, 1/2 Inch Thick

American National form of thread furnished unless otherwise specified.
Sizes and dimensions not listed are special.
High Speed Steel Dies are special.
Left Hand Dies are special
*Style 1183 only.

Cutting Size, Ins.	Number of Threads to the Inch					Outside Diameter Price Each				
	N.C. (U.S.S.)	N.F. (S.A.E.)	N.S. (U.S.F.)	Whitworth Std.	Brit. Std. Fine	5/8 Inch Fitting Stock No. 21	13/16 Inch Fitting Stocks No. 22 No. 42	1 Inch Fitting Stocks No. 23 No. 43	1 5/16 In. Fitting Stocks No. 25 No. 45	1 1/2 In. Fitting Stock No. 26
1/16	....	....	64	60	......	$0.80	$0.90	....	....	....
3/32	....	....	48	48	......	.60	.70	....	....	....
1/8	....	....	40	40	......	.50	.60	$0.75	....	....
5/32	....	....	32, 36	32	......	.50	.60	.75	....	....
3/16	....	....	24, 32	24	......	.50	.60	.75	....	....
7/32	....	....	24, 32	24	......	.50	.60	.75	....	....
1/4	20	28	24, 27, 32	20	26	.50	.60	.75	$1.25	$1.25
5/16	18	24	20, 27, 32	18	22	....	.60	.75	1.25	1.25
3/8	16	24	20, 27	16	20	....	....	.75	1.25	1.25
7/16	14	20	24, 27	14	18	....	....	.75	1.25	1.25
1/2	13	20	12, 24, 27	12	16	....	....	....	1.25	1.25
9/16	12	18	27	12	16	....	....	....	....	1.25
5/8	11	18	12, 27	11	14	....	....	....	....	1.25

ADJUSTABLE ROUND SPLIT DIES

MACHINE SCREW SIZES

*5/8 Inch Outside Diameter, 1/4 Inch Thick
13/16 Inch Outside Diameter, 1/4 Inch Thick
1 Inch Outside Diameter, 3/8 Inch Thick

Sizes and dimensions not listed are special.
High Speed Steel Dies are special.
Left Hand Dies are special.
*Style 1183 only.

Size of Screw Gauge	Number of Threads Per Inch			Outside Diameter Price Each		
	N.C.	N.F.	N.S.	*5/8 Inch Diameter Fitting Stock No. 21	13/16 Inch Diameter Fitting Stocks Nos. 22 & 42	1 Inch Diameter Fitting Stocks Nos. 23 & 43
0	....	80	....	$0.80	$0.90	....
1	64	72	56	.80	.90	....
2	56	64	....	.70	.80	....
3	48	56	....	.60	.70	....
4	40	48	32, 36	.50	.60	....
5	40	44	36	.50	.60	....
6	32	40	36	.50	.60	$0.75
7	....	....	32	.50	.60	.75
8	32	36	30, 40	.50	.60	.75
9	....	....	32	.50	.60	.75
10	24	32	28, 30	.50	.60	.75
12	24	28	32	.50	.60	.75
14	....	....	20, 24	.50	.60	.75

Sets of Straight Shank Drills

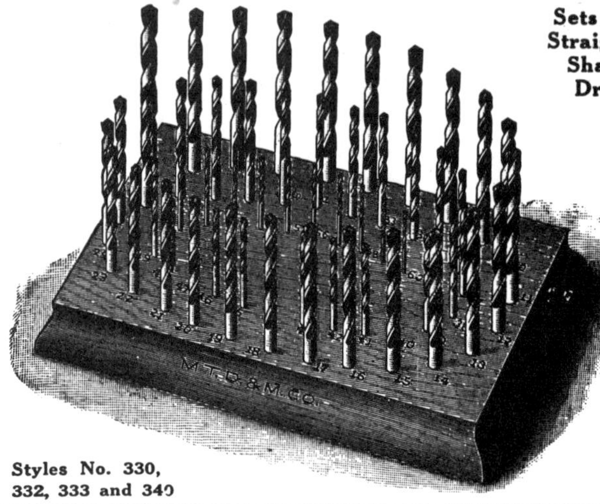

Styles No. 330, 332, 333 and 340

Set No.	Sizes Included	Style No.	Price Per Set	
			With Block as Above	Without Block
5	1/16 to 1/2 inch by 64ths	330	$15.00	$12.50
5H	**1/16 to 1/2 inch by 64ths, High Speed**	**1330**	....	***24.75**
6	1/16 to 1/2 inch by 32nds	330	9.50	7.00
7	Nos. 1 to 60 and 1/4 to 3/8 inch by 32nds	340 330	15.75	13.25
8	Nos. 1 to 60	340	13.35	10.85
8H	**Nos. 1 to 60, High Speed**	**1340**	....	***18.85**
9	Nos. 1 to 59, alternate numbers	340	8.50	6.00
15	A to Z	332	13.50	11.00
15H	**A to Z, Letter Sizes, High Speed**	**1332**	....	***22.50**
16	Nos. 1 to 70	340	15.25	12.50
17	Nos. 1 to 80	340	16.50	13.75
18	.5 M. M. to 6 M. M. by 1/10 M. M	333	13.35	10.00
19	1 M. M. to 13 M. M. by 1/2 M. M	333	13.40	11.00
20	1 M. M. to 6 M. M. by 1/4 M. M	333	6.75	4.50
21	6 1/4 M. M. to 10 M. M. by 1/4 M. M	333	9.75	7.50

Block without Drills, for above sets, each **$2.50**

Nos. 330, 332 333 and 340

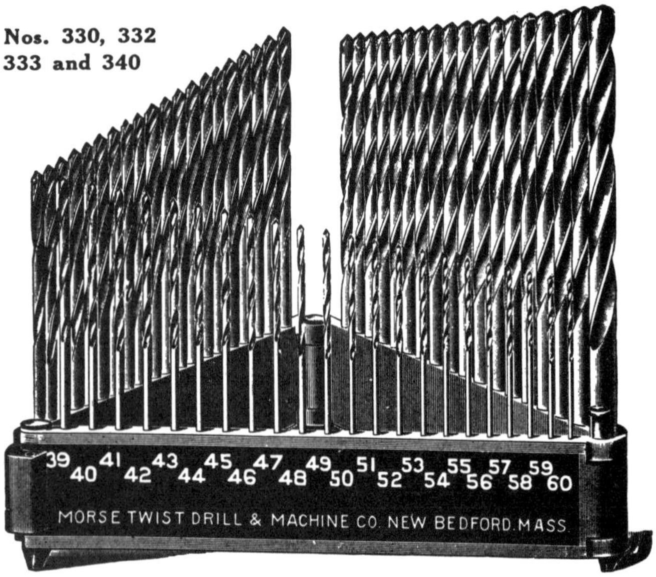

FOLDING DRILL HOLDER
FOR STRAIGHT SHANK DRILLS

Set No.	Sizes Included	Style No.	Price Per Set
5B	1/16 to 1/2 inch by 64ths	330	$16.00
7B	Nos. 1 to 60 and 1/4 to 3/8 by 32nds	340 330	16.75
8B	Nos. 1 to 60	340	14.35
15B	A to Z	332	14.50

Holders without Drills, for above sets, each **$3.50**

MORSE HIGH SPEED AND CARBON DRILLS

STRAIGHT SHANK DRILLS

No. 330 — CARBON STEEL, JOBBERS' LENGTHS
No. 1330 — HIGH SPEED STEEL, JOBBERS' SIZES

Diameter, Inches	Price per Dozen Carbon Steel	Price per Dozen High Speed Steel	Whole Length, Inches	Twist Cut, Inches	Decimal Equivalent	Diameter, Inches	Price per Dozen Carbon Steel	Price per Dozen High Speed Steel	Whole Length, Inches	Twist Cut, Inches	Decimal Equivalent
1/64	$1.50	$4.25	7/8	7/32	.0156	17/64	$3.50	$7.50	4 1/8	2 7/8	.2656
1/32	1.50	3.50	1 1/2	9/16	.0312	9/32	3.80	8.25	4 1/4	2 23/32	.2812
3/64	1.55	2.40	1 3/4	13/16	.0468	19/64	4.00	9.00	4 3/8	3 3/32	.2968
1/16	1.60	3.00	2 1/2	1 1/4	.0625	5/16	4.35	9.75	4 1/2	3 3/16	.3125
5/64	1.65	3.10	2 5/8	1 3/8	.0781	21/64	4.70	10.75	4 5/8	3 5/16	.3281
3/32	1.70	3.20	2 3/4	1 1/2	.0937	11/32	5.05	11.75	4 3/4	3 13/32	.3437
7/64	1.75	3.40	2 7/8	1 11/16	.1093	23/64	5.50	12.75	4 7/8	3 17/32	.3593
1/8	1.80	3.60	3	1 13/16	.125	3/8	6.00	13.75	5	3 5/8	.375
9/64	1.85	3.90	3 1/8	1 15/16	.1406	25/64	6.50	15.00	5 1/8	3 3/4	.3906
5/32	1.90	4.20	3 1/4	2 3/32	.1562	13/32	7.00	16.25	5 1/4	3 27/32	.4062
11/64	2.00	4.50	3 3/8	2 7/32	.1718	27/64	7.75	17.50	5 3/8	3 31/32	.4218
3/16	2.25	4.85	3 1/2	2 5/16	.1875	7/16	8.50	13.75	5 1/2	4 1/16	.4375
13/64	2.50	5.25	3 5/8	2 7/16	.2031	29/64	9.25	20.00	5 5/8	4 3/16	.4531
7/32	2.75	5.75	3 3/4	2 17/32	.2187	15/32	10.00	21.25	5 3/4	4 9/32	.4687
15/64	3.00	6.25	3 7/8	2 21/32	.2343	31/64	11.00	22.75	5 7/8	4 13/32	.4843
1/4	3.25	6.75	4	2 3/4	.25	1/2	12.00	24.25	6	4 1/2	.5

STRAIGHT SHANK WIRE DRILLS

No. 340 — CARBON STEEL, WIRE GAUGE SIZES
No. 1340 — HIGH SPEED STEEL, WIRE GAUGE SIZES

Number by Gauge	Price per Dozen Carbon Steel	Price per Dozen High Speed Steel	Decimals of 1 Inch	Approximate Length, Inches	Twist Cut, Inches	Number by Gauge	Price per Dozen Carbon Steel	Price per Dozen High Speed Steel	Decimals of 1 Inch	Approximate Length, Inches	Twist Cut, Inches
1	$2.75	$6.45	.2280	4	2 21/32	41	$1.70	$2.80	.0960	2 5/16	1 5/16
2	2.75	6.45	.2210	3 15/16	2 5/8	42	1.70	2.75	.0935	2 5/16	1 1/4
3	2.75	6.15	.2130	3 15/16	2 5/8	43	1.70	2.60	.0890	2 1/4	1 7/32
4	2.75	5.95	.2090	3 7/8	2 19/32	44	1.70	2.60	.0860	2 3/16	1 3/16
5	2.75	5.95	.2055	3 13/16	2 9/16	45	1.70	2.60	.0820	2 3/16	1 1/8
6	2.50	5.95	.2040	3 13/16	2 17/32	46	1.65	2.50	.0810	2 1/8	1 1/8
7	2.50	5.45	.2010	3 3/4	2 1/2	47	1.65	2.50	.0785	2 1/8	1 13/32
8	2.50	5.45	.1990	3 11/16	2 15/32	48	1.65	2.50	.0760	2 1/8	1 1/16
9	2.50	5.45	.1960	3 11/16	2 7/16	49	1.65	2.50	.0730	2	1
10	2.50	5.25	.1935	3 5/8	2 3/8	50	1.65	2.40	.0700	1 15/16	31/32
11	2.25	5.25	.1910	3 9/16	2 11/32	51	1.60	2.40	.0670	1 15/16	15/16
12	2.25	5.25	.1890	3 9/16	2 5/16	52	1.60	2.40	.0635	1 7/8	7/8
13	2.25	4.85	.1850	3 1/2	2 9/32	53	1.60	2.40	.0595	1 13/16	27/32
14	2.25	4.85	.1820	3 7/16	2 1/4	54	1.60	2.40	.0550	1 13/16	27/32
15	2.25	4.85	.1800	3 7/16	2 7/32	55	1.60	2.40	.0520	1 3/4	13/16
16	2.00	4.65	.1770	3 3/8	2 3/16	56	1.55	2.40	.0465	1 11/16	25/32
17	2.00	4.65	.1730	3 5/16	2 5/32	57	1.55	2.40	.0430	1 11/16	23/32
18	2.00	4.50	.1695	3 5/16	2 1/8	58	1.55	2.40	.0420	1 5/8	23/32
19	2.00	4.35	.1660	3 1/4	2 3/32	59	1.55	2.40	.0410	1 9/16	1 1/16
20	2.00	4.35	.1610	3 3/16	2 1/16	60*	1.55	2.40	.0400	1 9/16	1 1/16
21	1.90	4.35	.1590	3 3/16	2 1/16	61	1.50	3.50	.0390	1 1/2	5/8
22	1.90	4.15	.1570	3 1/8	2	62	1.50	3.50	.0380	1 1/2	5/8
23	1.90	4.05	.1540	3 1/8	1 31/32	63	1.50	3.50	.0370	1 1/2	5/8
24	1.90	4.05	.1520	3 1/16	1 15/16	64	1.50	3.50	.0360	1 1/2	5/8
25	1.90	3.90	.1495	3	1 29/32	65	1.50	3.50	.0350	1 1/2	5/8
26	1.80	3.90	.1470	2 15/16	1 7/8	66	1.50	3.50	.0330	1 1/2	9/16
27	1.80	3.90	.1440	2 15/16	1 27/32	67	1.50	3.50	.0320	1 7/16	9/16
28	1.80	3.60	.1405	2 7/8	1 13/16	68	1.50	3.50	.0310	1 7/16	9/16
29	1.80	3.60	.1360	2 13/16	1 3/4	69	1.50	3.50	.0292	1 3/8	9/16
30	1.80	3.60	.1285	2 13/16	1 23/32	70†	1.50	3.50	.0280	1 5/16	9/16
31	1.75	3.30	.1200	2 3/4	1 11/16	71	1.50	4.25	.0260	1 5/16	1/2
32	1.75	3.30	.1160	2 11/16	1 5/8	72	1.50	4.25	.0250	1 1/4	7/16
33	1.75	3.30	.1130	2 11/16	1 5/8	73	1.50	4.25	.0240	1 3/16	3/8
34	1.75	3.15	.1110	2 5/8	1 9/16	74	1.50	4.25	.0225	1 1/8	5/16
35	1.75	3.15	.1100	2 9/16	1 1/2	75	1.50	4.25	.0210	1 1/16	1/4
36	1.75	3.10	.1065	2 9/16	1 1/2	76	1.50	4.25	.0200	1	1/4
37	1.75	2.95	.1040	2 1/2	1 7/16	77	1.50	4.25	.0180	15/16	7/32
38	1.75	2.95	.1015	2 7/16	1 3/8	78	1.50	4.25	.0160	7/8	7/32
39	1.75	2.95	.0995	2 7/16	1 11/32	79	1.50	4.25	.0145	13/16	3/16
40	1.75	2.80	.0980	2 3/8	1 11/32	80	1.50	4.25	.0135	3/4	3/16

* Sizes above 60 in High Speed sold in not less than full dozen lots.
† Sizes above 70 in Carbon sold in not less than full dozen lots.

STARRETT PRECISION TOOLS

STEEL SQUARES

No. 20

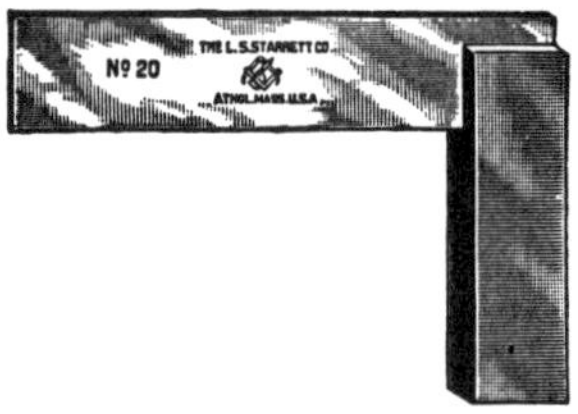

Specially recommended as a standard square. The 15, 18 and 24-inch squares have a stock support.

Squares larger than listed can be furnished. Prices upon application.

Cases furnished at prices shown in list below.

Packed 1 in a box.

Length Blade Inches	Length Beam Inches	Price Each	Price Case Each
1	1	**$3.00**	....
1½	1½	**3.60**	**$2.00**
2	1⅞	**3.90**	**2.15**
3	2⅜	**4.50**	**2.25**
4½	3½	**6.90**	**2.50**
6	4 5/16	**9.00**	**3.00**
9	5 9/16	**13.50**	**3.25**
12	7	**18.00**	**3.75**
15	8⅝	**30.00**	**5.00**
18	10½	**38.00**	**5.50**
24	12 5/16	**54.00**	**7.00**

DOUBLE SQUARES

No. 13

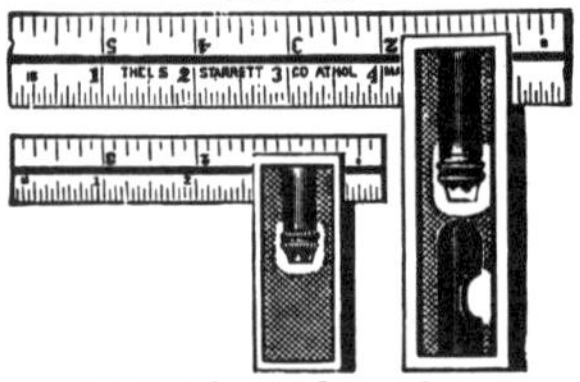

For machinists', tool makers' and pattern makers' use. The sliding blade, shortened or extended full length makes it more valuable than a full set of the common kind, while with the extra bevel blade both the hexagon and octagon angles can be made; a great convenience. The seat against which the blade is clamped being convex the accuracy of the square is not affected should corners of the blade get injured. Furnished in No. 4 graduation. A level is contained in the 6, 9 and 12-inch sizes. Packed 1 in a box.

Size.......inches	4	6	*4	*6	9	12
Price, No. 13 each	**$1.85**	**2.85**	**2.35**	**3.45**	**3.60**	**4.75**

* With both blades, and always sent unless otherwise specified. Bevel blades for 4 and 6-inch only.

COMBINATION SETS

No. 434

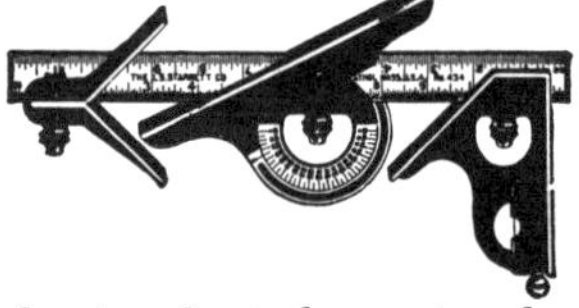

Has hardened stock, center head and blade, also reversible protractor.

Furnished with No. 4 and No. 7 graduation. Sent with blades of No. 4 graduation unless otherwise ordered.

Length Inches	Price Each	Length Inches	Price Each
9	**$9.50**	18	**$11.50**
12	**10.40**	24	**12.40**

MICROMETER DEPTH GAGE

No. 440

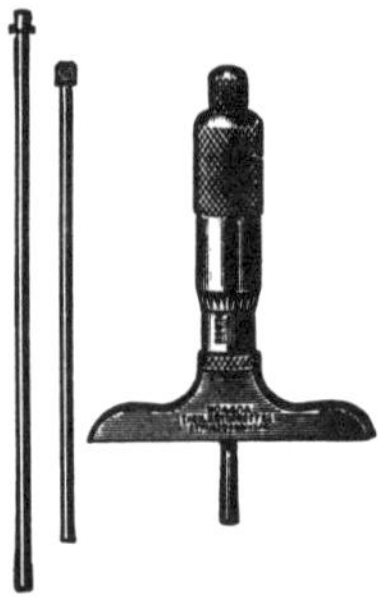

This gauge provides measurements of the depths of holes, projections, etc., from 0 to 3 inches by thousandths of an inch.

Each gauge has three measuring rods which are inserted through a hole in the screw and brought to a positive seat by a small knurled nut.

Base is about 4/10 inch thick and is hardened, ground and lapped. Sent with case unless otherwise ordered.

	Price
No. 440A, with 2½-inch Base......each	**$9.00**
No. 440A, with Case..............each	**10.80**
No. 440B, with 4-inch Base........each	**11.50**
No. 440B, with Case..............each	**13.70**

Above furnished with Ratchet @ **.50** extra.

DEPTH GAGE AND HOOK RULE

No. 236H

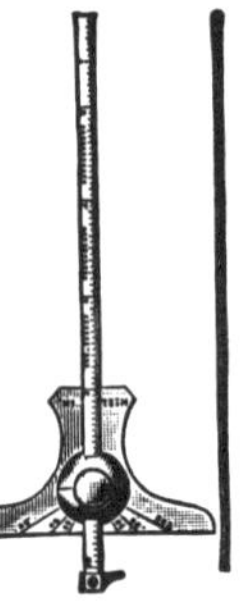

Hook used with base as a Depth Gauge or independently as a Hook Rule. Rod used for measuring in small holes where rule will not enter.

No. 236 H.A. Gauge with Hook Rule....	**$2.75**
No. 236 H.B. Same with Rod extra.....	**2.95**
No. 236 H.C. Hook Rule only..........	**1.50**
No. 236 H.D. Rod only...............	**.20**

No. 236 H.B. complete as shown in cut sent unless otherwise ordered.

MICROMETER CALIPERS

Nos. 230-231

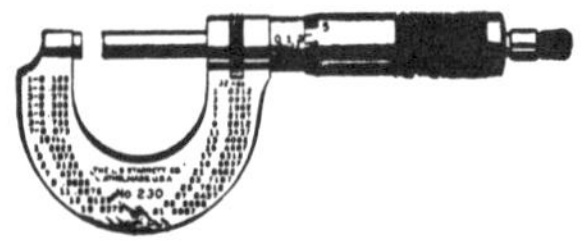

Capacity 0 to 1 inch. Has ratchet stop, lock nut and short anvil.

	Price
No. 230, Graduated to 1000ths....each	**$10.00**
No. 231, Graduated to 1000ths....each	**11.75**
Leather Case ....each	**1.25**

DIE MAKERS' SQUARE

No. 453

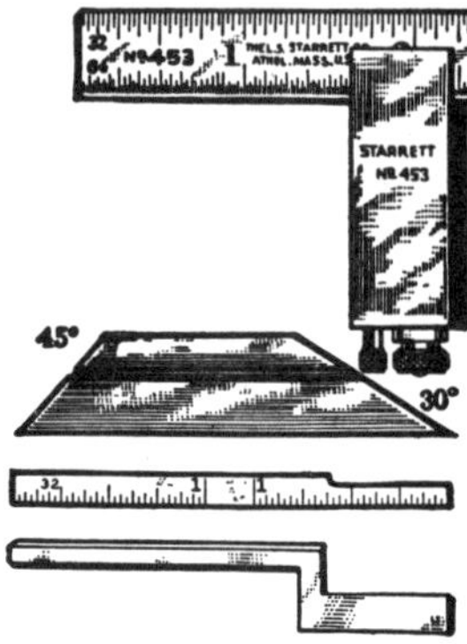

The purpose in designing this tool was to provide simple means whereby the blade could be adjusted at an angle with the beam. This makes an excellent gage for filing the clearance in dies, etc., as shown by the sectional view.

By releasing the smaller screw (see sectional view) the blade can be clamped firmly to its seat and then used as a regular square. Fitted to take the standard, bevel, narrow graduated and offset blades.

These dimensions may be of interest. STANDARD BLADE—approximately ½ inch wide by 2½ inches long with 64ths and 32nds graduations. BEVEL BLADE—½ inch wide and to determine 30 degrees and 45 degree angles. NARROW BLADE (graduated)—approximately 5/32 inch wide and 2¼ inches long with 64ths and 32nds graduations. Cut away at one end ⅝ inch back to 3/32 inch width. OFFSET BLADE—protrudes from square 1½ inch, is ⅛ inch wide and beveled on each edge to give a line contact.

No. 453A—Square, with standard blade...	**$4.00**
No. 453B—Square, with standard and bevel blades	**4.30**
No. 453C—Square, with standard and narrow graduated blades.........	**4.50**
No. 453D—Square, with standard, bevel and narrow graduated blades......	**4.80**
No. 453E—Square, complete, with standard bevel, narrow graduated and offset blades..................	**5.80**

No. 453E complete sent unless otherwise ordered.

PROTRACTOR AND DEPTH GAGE

No. 493

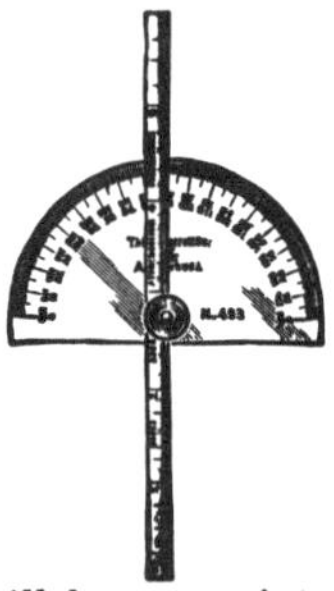

This tool will be appreciated by machinists, draftsmen and shop foremen. Any angle in one-half circle (180°) may be obtained and the back is finished to permit its being laid flat upon paper or work. Blade being adjustable permits its being set at any length within its capacity, permitting its use as a depth gauge. Scale, clamped by a conveniently knurled nut, is graduated to 32nds and 64ths.

Price, No. 493..................each **$3.00**

PRICES ON OTHER STARRETT TOOLS WILL BE QUOTED ON APPLICATION

STARRETT PRECISION TOOLS

DRILL BLOCKS AND CLAMPS

No. 278

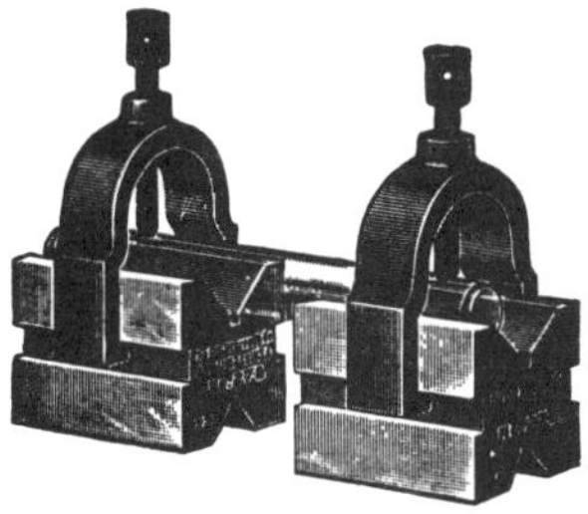

Milling or grinding work clamped in the V's of this tool will be held fast and true.

Made of tool steel, hardened and ground throughout. The V's are ground central, parallel and square with the ends and sides. The blocks are numbered in pairs so that the V's in each block are always in alignment.

Each block is about 1¼ inches square, 1⅝ inches long, and has a clamping capacity of 1 inch in diameter. Sold only in pairs.

No. 278, Comprising Two Drill Blocks and Two Clamps............per pair Price **$6.75**

DRILL BLOCKS AND CLAMPS

No. 271

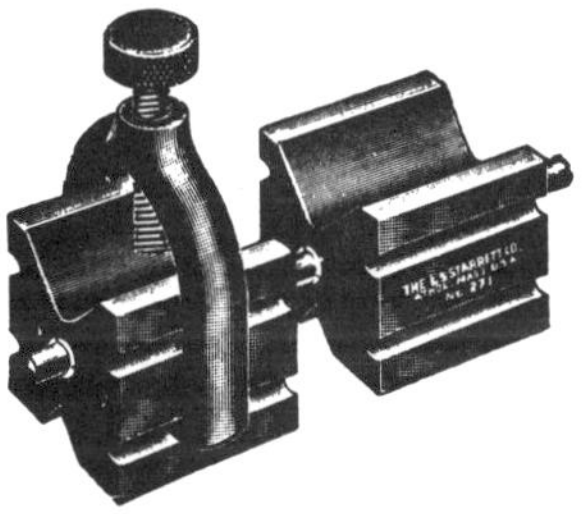

These blocks are designed to be used singly or in pairs in connection with drill presses and for laying out work. They may be used close together or separated, and are kept in line by a spindle 6 inches long passing through friction bushings.

The blocks are 1¼ inches square and will hold round pieces to 1¼ inch diameter. The clamp is a steel forging finished all over and case hardened.

	Price
No. 271A, Two Drill Blocks............	$2.40
No. 271B, Clamp......................	.90
No. 271C, Set Complete...............	3.30

NO. 132 LEVELS

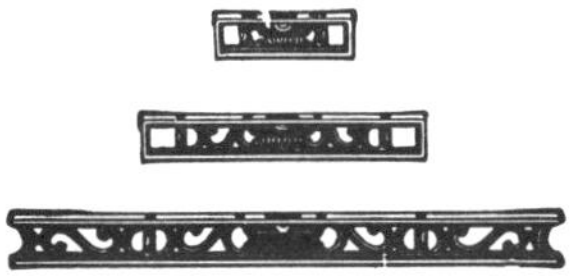

With double plumb; this level has a concave groove the length of base for shafting, etc. Sizes 4 to 12-inch have square ends, 18 to 24-inch, concave ends.

Length Inches	Price Each	Length Inches	Price Each	Length Inches	Price Each
4	$1.80	9	$2.40	18	$3.75
6	2.10	12	2.70	24	4.50

T HANDLE TAP WRENCH

No. 93

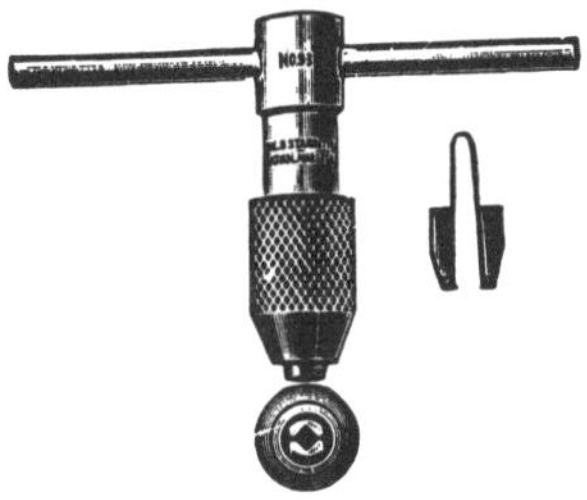

Useful for holding taps, drills, reamers and other small tools, and the body is centered for use against lathe centers, etc. Size C is made with a sliding handle. It will be found a very convenient all-round wrench in garages and motor service shops as its capacity permits holding the sizes of taps most commonly used.

		Price
No. 93A	Length 1¾ in., Capacity 1/16 in. to 5/32 in. sq..................	$1.00
No. 93B	Length 2 1/16 in., Capacity 5/32 in. to ¼ in. sq..................	1.25
No. 93C	Length 3 1/16 in., Capacity 3/16 in. to 5/16 in sq..................	2.25
No. 93D	Length 6 in., Capacity 1/16 in. to 5/32 in. sq..................	1.75
No. 93E	Length 9⅜ in., Capacity 5/32 in. to ¼ in. sq..................	2.00
No. 93F	Length 12⅞ in., Capacity 3/16 in. to 5/16 in. sq..................	3.00

No. 91 TAP WRENCH

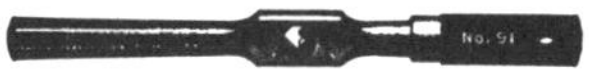

This wrench is of new design—strong, neat and efficient. It will hold firmly a tap with square or round shank. Inside the knurled adjusting screw a spring connected with the plunger holds it back and causes instant movement with the screw.

No. 91A. 5¾ inches long, holding 5/64 inch to ¼ inch .... **$.90**
No. 91B. 9 inches long, holding 3/16 inch to ½ inch **1.80**

BENCH BLOCK

NO. 129

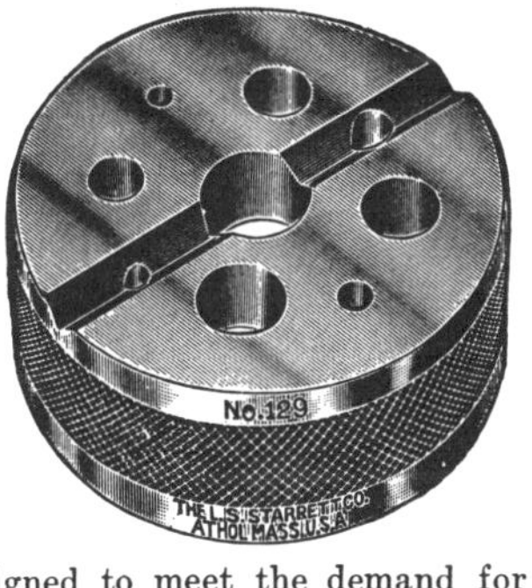

Designed to meet the demand for something better to drive pins in round or flat work. Made from a forging and is hardened and ground. The knurling makes it easy to handle. Recess in base decreases weight, but it is strong enough to withstand hard usage. The V in center needs no explanation. Holes vary in size from ⅛ to ⅝ inch. The block is about 1½ inches high and 3 inches in diameter. Appeals to mechanics particular in preserving a finished piece of work where fitting of dowel pins is necessary.

Price, No. 129 ....each **$2.50**

TOOL STEEL PARALLELS

No. 384

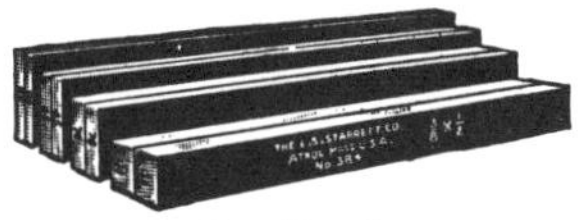

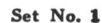

Set No. 1

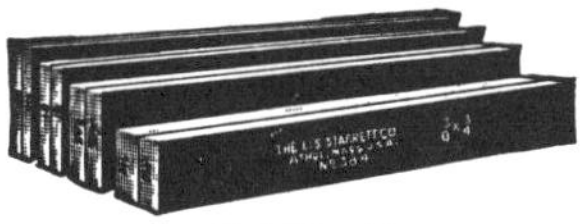

Set No. 2

Useful in milling, grinding and shaper vises, on machine platens and face plate set-ups and in checking and laying out work. These parallels are made from a special grade of tool steel, hardened and nicely ground on the four sides.

They should be purchased only in pairs. Eight pairs have been standardized, making possible many combinations.

Numbered on the ends in pairs and their relative accuracy is held to extremely close limits. Made in 6-inch length only.

Each size one pair in a box. One set in a box.

No.	Thickness In.	Width In.	Pair per Pair	No.	Thickness In.	Width In.	Pair per Pair
384A	⅛	1	$6.00	384E	¼	¾	$7.00
384B	⅛	1 3/16	6.00	384F	¼	1	7.00
384C	3/16	⅞	6.00	384G	⅜	½	7.00
384D	3/16	1⅛	6.00	384H	⅜	¾	7.00

	Price
Set No. 1, 4 pairs, consisting of sizes A, C, E and G...................per set	$26.00
Set No. 2, 4 pairs, consisting of sizes B, D, F and H...................per set	26.00

TOOLMAKER'S PARALLEL CLAMPS

No. 161

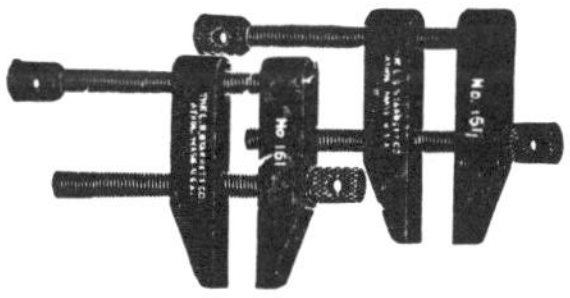

Made of steel, case hardened, useful for holding small work together in tapping, drilling, etc. When ordering jaw only, state length desired.

No.	161AA	161A	161B	161C	161D
Opening Jaw, inches	¾	1¼	1¾	2¼	2¾
Length Jaw, inches	1⅝	2	2½	3	4
Price, per pair	$1.40	1.70	2.00	2.40	3.00

TOOLMAKER'S STEEL CLAMPS

No. 160

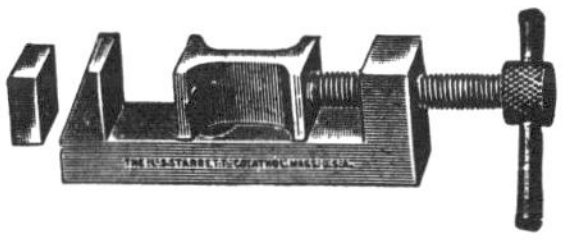

These clamps are made from drop forgings, nicely finished, case hardened, and have take-up blocks to slip on or off end of screw, and are held to same in a novel manner. They will hold work square and parallel for laying out on surface plates, fitting or drilling. A round piece may be rigidly held in two of the clamps and drilled on an upright, central and parallel. Put up and sold in pairs.

1 inch, per pair..........................**$2.50**
2 inch, per pair.......................... **3.00**

STARRETT PRECISION TOOLS

NAIL SETS

NO. 265

Square with Knurled Grip

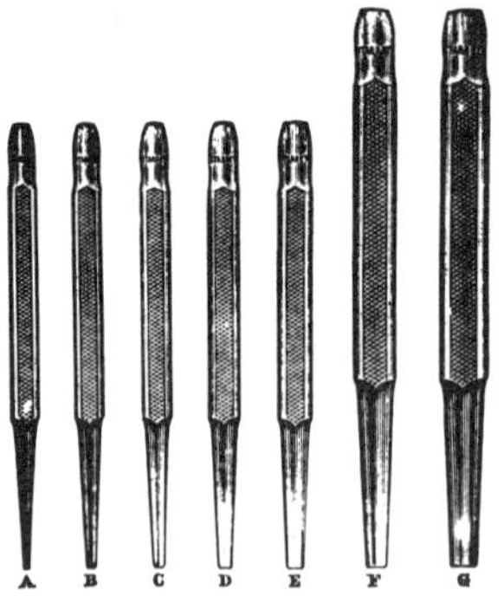

CENTER PUNCHES

NO. 264

Square with Knurled Grip

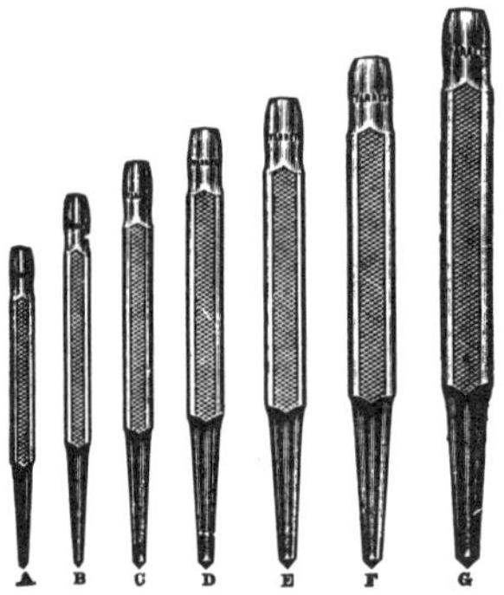

Made in seven sizes ranging in length from 2⅞ to 5 inches. All sizes 12 in a box, except G, six in a box.

Size No.	Diam. at Points, In.	Price Each	Price per Doz.
A	1/16	$.25	$3.00
B	5/64	.25	3.00
C	3/32	.25	3.00
D	1/8	.25	3.00
E	5/32	.35	4.20
F	3/16	.35	4.20
G	1/4	.40	4.80
Assort. A, B, C, D..........			3.00

DRIVE PIN PUNCHES

No. 565

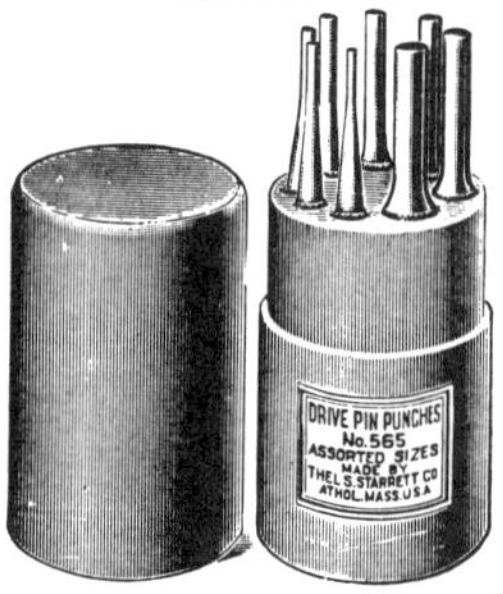

Made of good quality steel, neatly shaped, hardened and polished, with knurled centers.

Length of each size, 4 inches. Diameter of points: A, 1/16 inch; B, 3/32 inch; C, 1/8 inch; D, 5/32 inch; E, 3/16 inch; F, 7/32 inch; G, 1/4 inch; H, 5/16 inch.

Price, No. 565 ....per dozen	$2.40
Price, No. 565 ....each	.25
Price, No. 565, Set of Eight (One of each Size) in Round Wooden Box, as shown per set	1.80

PIN VISES

No. 162

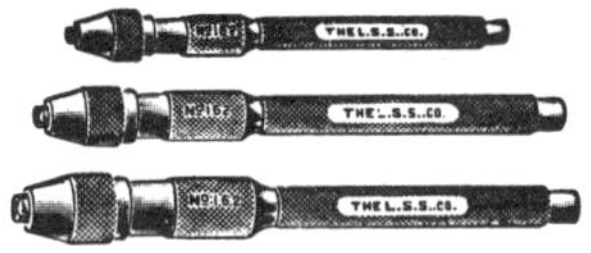

Hardened jaws with chucks made to hold firm. Convenient for holding scribers, small files, taps and extensions for small drills.

		Price
No. 162A	0 to .040 inch.............	$0.65
No. 162B	.030 inch to .062 inch.......	.65
No. 162C	.050 inch to .125 inch.......	.65
No. 162D	.115 inch to .187 inch.......	.80
Set complete (one of each size)..........		2.75

COMBINATION HAND VISES

No. 86

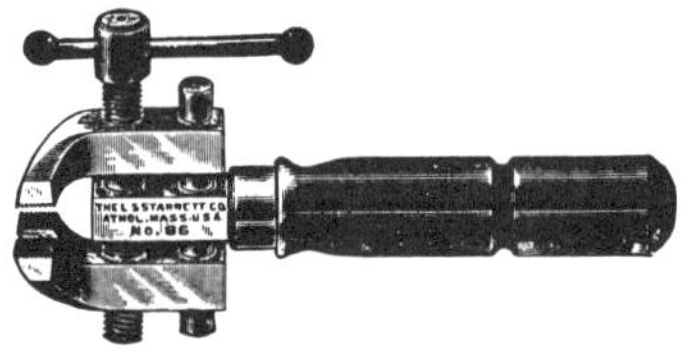

By removing the handle and substituting the clamp which is furnished, the tool may be fastened to benches, shelves, etc., having a thickness of ½ to 2⅛ inches. Can be adjusted to different positions. When used as a hand vise the leverage obtainable with the ball-end handle will be appreciated.

The jaws are made from forgings and are properly tempered. Width of jaws 1½ inches. Capacity, 1½ inches. Length, 7 inches.

	Price
No. 86A, with Clamp.............each	$5.00
No. 86B, without Clamp..........each	4.00

SCREW DRIVERS

No. 555

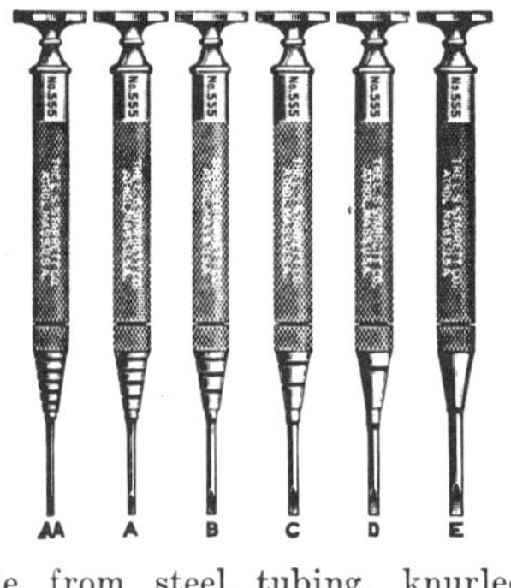

Made from steel tubing, knurled and nickel-plated. Blades vary from .025 to .100 inch in width.

Top is finished with a swivel knob, concaved to fit the finger.

Each size packed 6 in box.

No.	Diam.,In. Handle	Blade	Price Each
555AA	1/4	.025	$.45
555A	1/4	.040	.45
555B	1/4	.055	.45
555C	1/4	.070	.45
555D	1/4	.080	.45
555E	1/4	.100	.45
No. 555, Set of 6 ....per set			$2.70
Extra Blades ....each			.15

TAP AND DRILL GAGE

No. 185

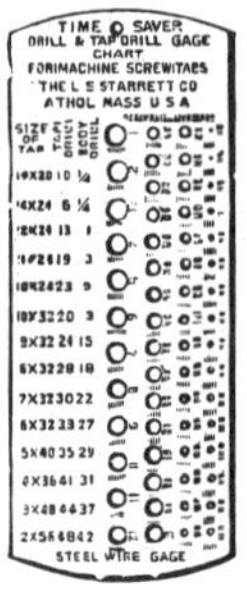

Approximately 5/64 inch thick, 2 1/16 inches wide and 6¼ inches long. Enables one to select at once right sized drill to suit machine screw taps most commonly used.

Price, No. 185..........**$2.40**

DRILL AND WIRE GAGE

No. 286

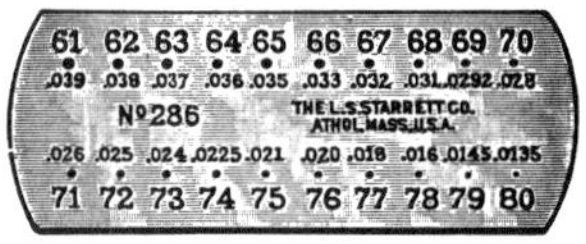

Gives number and decimal equivalents of standard sizes from 61 to 80 inclusive. Adapted to gauge small twist drills and fine drill rods. Is 1/16 inch thick, ¾ inch wide and 2 inches long.

Price, No. 286......................**$2.40**

WIRE GAGES

Nos. 281 and 282

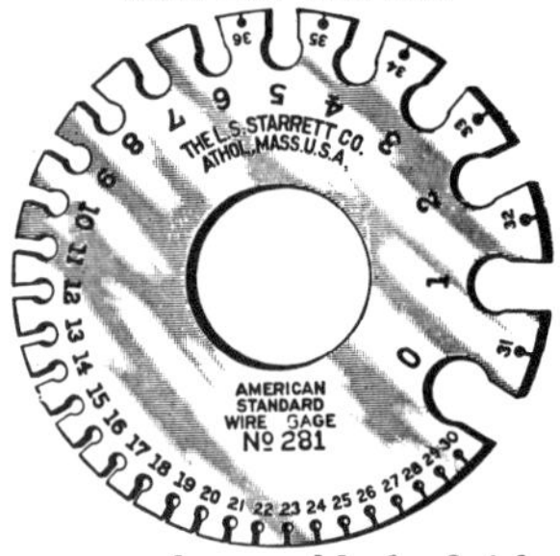

Each gauge has a black finish and is carefully tested after hardening.

American standard gauge.

Decimal equivalents of numbers are stamped on back.

	Price.
281—0 to 36	$3.00
282—5 to 36	2.50

SCREW AND WIRE GAGE

No. 227

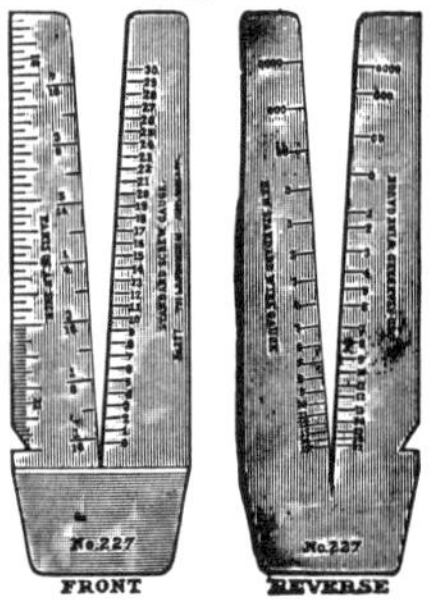

A pocket gauge made of spring tempered steel for use in stock rooms, hardware stores, etc., for measuring screws and wire.

One side is marked on the right to show all sizes of American Standard Screw Gauge from 0 to 30 and can be used for wire as well as wood and machine screws. Also measures A.S.M.E. standard screws. On left, is shown fractions of an inch from 1/16 to 7/16 and divisions for 32nd readings.

The 3½-in scale, 2½ inches graduated by 16ths and 1 inch by 32nds is ordinarily enough to take length of screw.

Reverse side is marked with old and new wire gauge.

Price, Packed 3 in a Box.........each **$3.00**

SEE PAGE 8, "HOW TO ORDER"

STARRETT PRECISION TOOLS

TEMPERED STEEL RULES

Nos. 600 and 603

Front

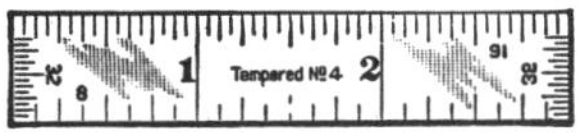

Reverse

No. 600. 1 inch to 24 inch lengths, has No. 4 graduation, with 8ths and 16ths on one side and 32ds and 64ths on the other.

No. 603. 2 inch to 24 inch lengths, has No. 4 graduation, graduated in 32ds on both ends of one side.

Thickness, 3/64 inch, or No. 18 gauge.

Width, Inches...	½	½	9/16	⅝	¾	⅞	1	1⅛	1¼
Length..	1	2	3	4	6	9	12	18	24
Price Each...	$.30	.45	.60	.75	.90	1.35	1.65	2.60	3.25

FLEXIBLE RULES

Nos. 320-321-322

These are very thin spring tempered rules, nicely graduated on one side only. Those from 1 inch to 12 inches are ½ inch wide, and will easily conform to a 2-inch circle. Those from 18 to 48 inches are ¾ inch wide, and are made from a trifle heavier stock.

2	3	4	6	9	12	18	24	36	48
.30	.45	.60	.75	.90	1.35	1.65	2.60	3.25	7.00	10.00

No. 320. No. 10 Grad. (32 and 64)

No. 321. No. 11 Grad. (64–100)—6 and 12 in. only.

No. 322. No. 12 Grad. (50–100)—6 and 12 in. only.

METRIC & ENGLISH RULES

Nos. 350-351-355

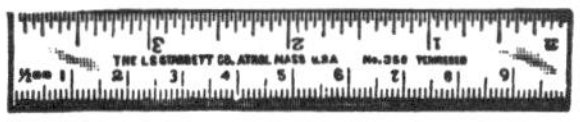

No. 350. Graduated one corner each in millimeters, ½ millimeters, 32nds and 64ths of an inch, all lengths.

No. 351. Made in 15 and 30-cm. lengths. The 15-cm. length is graduated as follows: First corner in ½ mm., second corner in 1 mm., third corner in 1/64 inch, fourth corner in 1/100 inch. The 30-cm. length is graduated as follows: Two inches of third corner in 64ths, the rest of that corner in 16ths of an inch. Two inches of fourth corner in 100ths, the rest of that corner in 50ths of an inch.

Length Cm.	Length In.	Price Each	Length Cm.	Length In.	Price Each
5	1.9685	$.55	30	11.8110	$1.65
10	3.9370	.75	50	19.6850	2.65
15	5.9055	.90	*1	39.3700	10.00
20	7.8740	1.20			

* Length in meters.

No. 355, Flexible

Graduated one edge in millimeters, the other in 64ths.

Made in the following lengths: 10, 15, 20 and 30 cm. Prices the same as for corresponding lengths listed above. Graduated on one side only.

CENTER GAGES

For use in grinding and setting screw cutting tools.

No. 390	Not tempered, graduated one corner each in 32ds, 24ths, 20ths and 14ths.	$0.40
No. 391	Spring-tempered	.50
No. 395	Whitworth, not tempered	.40
No. 396	Whitworth, spring-tempered	.50
No. 397	Metric, not tempered	.40
No. 398	Metric, spring-tempered	.50

The angles are 60°, except in No. 395, in which they are 55°.

No. 588 STARRETT HANDY READY REFERENCE TABLES

WITH RULE

Spring Steel, Quick Reading

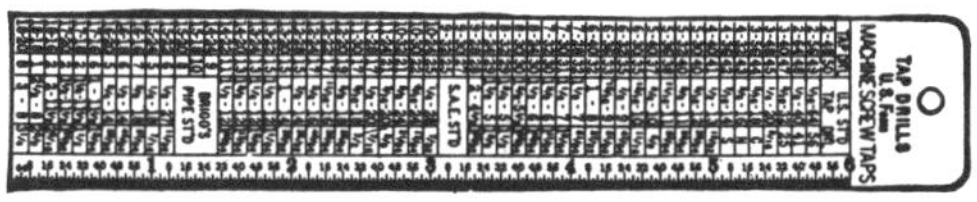

Handy for toolmakers and machinists.

Size, 6¾ inches long, 1¼ inches wide and 2/100ths inch thick.

Has decimals, fractions and 6-inch rule with 32nds divisions on one side and tap and drill data and 6-inch rule with 64ths divisions on the other.

The 32nds divisions marked every 4, 8, 12, etc., lines; the 64ths divisions marked every 8, 16, 24, etc., lines.

Quick reading feature on both sides.

The rule is incorporated so that no turning end for end is necessary—32nds or 64ths always in the natural position.

Price, each.......................... $.90

POCKET STEEL TAPES

No. 501

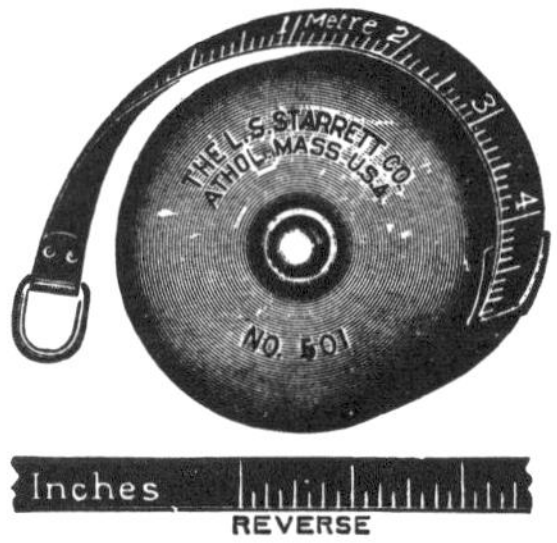

REVERSE

This tape is ¼ inch wide, in well finished nickel-plated case, with rounded edges. Spring wind with center stop.

Graduated in inches and sixteenths of an inch on one side, millimeters on the other side.

Packed 1 in a box; 6 boxes in a carton.

Length Inches	Length Meters	Weight Ounces	Price Each
36	1	1½	$1.00
60	1½	2	1.35
72	2	2¼	1.55
96	2½	2½	2.15
120	3	3	2.70

POSITIVE STOP SCREW PITCH GAGE

No. 476

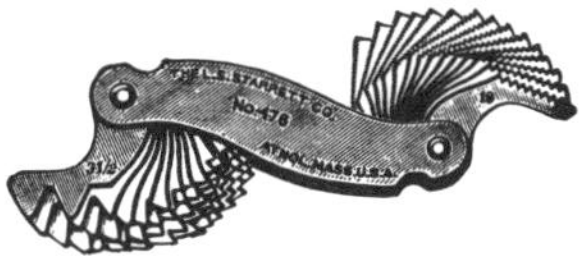

Contains 30 pitches, Whitworth Standard: 3½, 4, 4½, 5, 6, 7, 8, 9, 10, 11, 12, 13, 14, 16 and 18 in one end of case; 19, 20, 22, 24, 25, 26, 28, 30, 31, 32, 36, 40, 44, 48, 50, 60 in other.

Price, No. 476.................. each $1.80

THICKNESS GAGE

No. 172

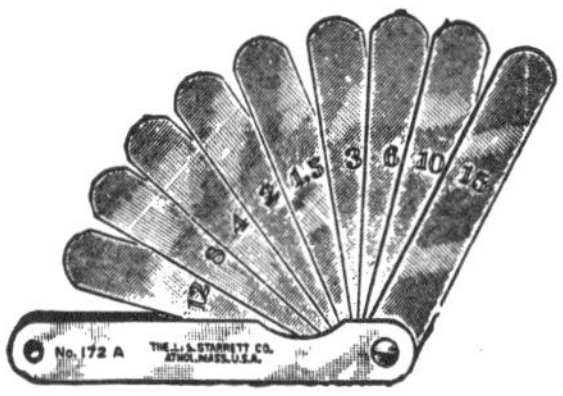

For gaging slots, fitting pistons, setting valve tappets, spark plugs, breaker points, etc. The leaves fold neatly in a metal case which protects them from kinks and is a convenient size to carry in the pocket.

No. 172A contains nine leaves as follows: .0015, .002, .003, .004, .006, .008, .010, .012, and .015.

Sizes B and C have eight leaves the same as A with the omission of .0015. Sizes D and E have eight leaves viz: .002, .003, .004, .005, .006, .008, .010, and .015.

		Price
No. 172A	Leaves 3 1/16 inches long by ½ inch wide	2.50
No. 172B	Leaves 4½ inches long by ½ inch wide	2.50
No. 172C	Leaves 6 inches long by ½ inch wide	3.00
No. 172D	Leaves 9 inches long by ½ inch wide	3.25
No. 172E	Leaves 12 inches long by ½ inch wide	4.25

TAPER GAGES

No. 269

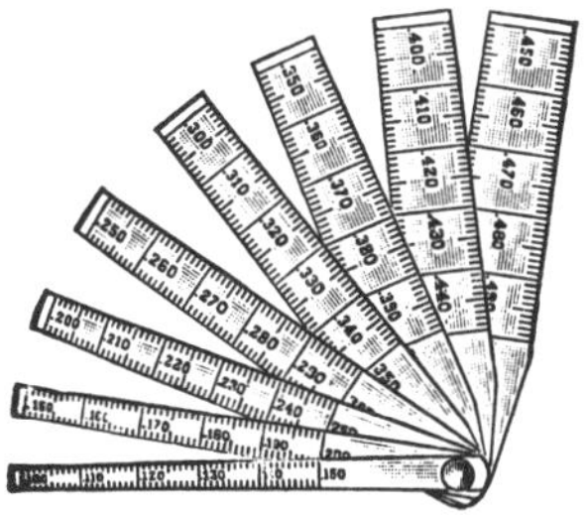

For determining the size of holes in dies, etc. Made from spring-tempered stock .012 inch thick. No. 269A is 2½ inches long, graduated to read from 1/10 to ½ inch in thousandths of an inch. No. 269B is 2¾ inches long, graduated to read from ½ to 1 inch in thousandths of an inch.

	Price
No. 269A, with 8 Leaves.......... each	$5.50
No. 269B, with 10 Leaves........ each	6.75

STARRETT PRECISION TOOLS

SURFACE GAGES
No. 257
Case Hardened Steel Base

This gauge has a heavy base, grooved through the bottom and end, adapting it for use on or against circular work as well as flat surfaces. The spindle may be set upright or at any angle, or turned so as to work under the base, and can be sensitively adjusted to any position.

In the base are 4 pins which may be pushed to bear against the edge of a surface plate, or in the slot of a planer bed for linear work also adapting the gauge to be used as a locomotive guide liner.

No.	Size Base Inches	Size Spindles Inches	Price Each
257A	3	9	$4.75
257B	3	9 and 12	5.25
257C	3½	12	5.85
257D	3½	12 and 18	6.50

PENCIL DIVIDER
No. 596

An excellent tool for layout work. Points open from 7/8 inch to 3 inches. Chucks hold steel points or pencil leads, nickel plated.

Price, each.......... $2.00

HERMAPHRODITE CALIPERS
No. 563

With firm joint and adjustable round point. For laying off centers and lines from an edge.

	Price
4 inch	$0.80
6 inch	1.00

DRILL POINT GAGE
No. 22C

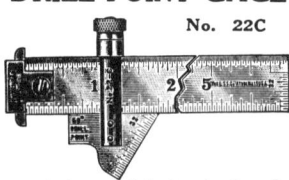

This tool is useful to tool-makers and machinists. It is a combination tool made with No. 303 rule, with adjustable hook and No. 22D small drill point gauge, depth **gauge**, try square and slide caliper.

Graduations are 8ths, 16ths, 32nds, and 64ths of an inch.

No. 22D, head only, fits spring tempered rules of the same width and thickness as Nos. 300, 303, 600 and 603.

Price, No. 22C, Complete........each $2.50
Price, No. 22D, Sliding Head only..each 1.25

SCRIBERS
No. 67

All parts are interchangeable. The knurled sleeve is nickeled. Packed 6 in a box.

	Price
No. 67, Complete ....each	$.60
No. 67, without Long Point........each	.45
No. 67, Long Bent Point...........each	.20
No. 67, Straight Point or Short Bent Point each	.15

POCKET SCRIBERS
No. 70

Scriber is reversible, telescoping into the stock and is held by a slight turn of chuck.

No.	70A	70B
Diameter Handle........inches	¼	3/8
Length of Blade........inches	2 3/8	2 7/8
Price, No. 70...........each	$.35	.50

AUTOMATIC CENTER PUNCH
No. 18

No hammer is needed. Point can be removed for regrinding.

No.	Length Inches	Diameter Inches	Price
18AA	3¾	3/8	$1.80
18A	5	½	2.40
18B	6	5/8	3.00

SPACING ATTACHMENT FOL AUTOMATIC CENTER PUNCH
NO. 185

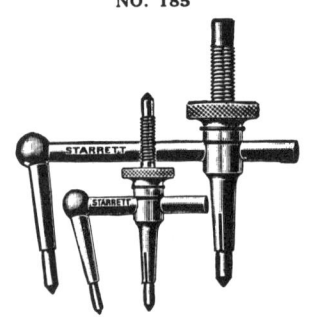

For use with automatic center punches No. 18. A tool for the rapid and accurate spacing of any center distances within its range. The locating point is on the principle of a spring plunger, held in its lowest position by a light spiral spring. Made in two sizes: Size A has a capacity from 1/8 to ¾-inch and fits either center punch No. 18AA or 18A. Size B has a capacity from 1/8 to 1¾-inch and fits No. 18B.

Price, No. 18S, Size A or B.......each $1.50
Price, Extra Points ....each .20

TOOLMAKERS' CALIPERS
Nos. 275 and 274

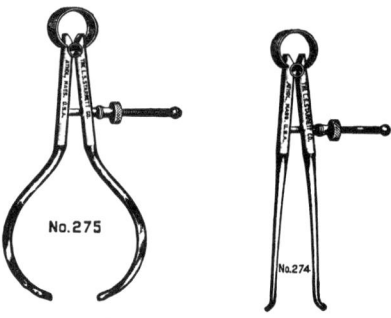

No. 275, Outside   No. 274, Inside

These calipers and dividers are made from round stock with legs drawn down, making them tough and rigid.

The fulcrum is hardened, bows extra strong, screw and nut nicely fitted, all highly finished.

They are made with solid nut only.

No. 277, Dividers

Size .....inches	2	3	4	5	6
Price .....each	$1.20	1.50	1.80	1.80	2.10

DUPLICATE PARTS

	Price Each		Price Each
Screw and Ball..	$.20	Spring	$.30
*Thumb Attachment	.20	Jam Washer....	.15
Nut	.15	Fulcrum Stud....	.15
Leg	.40	* For No. 277 Dividers only.	

TRAMMEL POINTS
No. 50

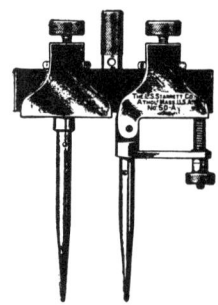

These trammels are made of bronze metal, with forged steel points, hardened. Either point can be removed, and the pencil socket accompanying each pair put in its place.

The bar shown in illustration, holding pencil socket in center with frames at each end, is similar to what would be used as a beam in using this tool, but is only long enough to permit easy packing in the tool chest, as well as in shipping.

No. 50A sent unless otherwise ordered.

Nickel-plated

No. 50A with 3-inch Points, Adjustable each $3.50
No. 50B with 3-inch Points, Not Adjustable ....each 2.25
No. 50C Extra Long Points, 5 Inches per set .50

STARRETT PRECISION TOOLS

STARRETT GROUND FLAT STOCK

No. 495

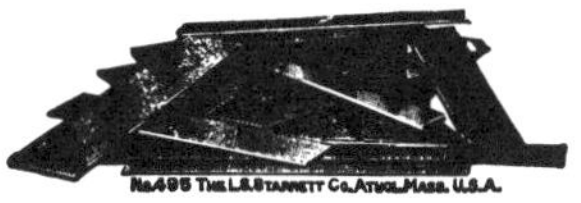

Made of First Quality Tool Steel ground to one thousandth of an inch in thickness. Annealed so that it is easily machined. Very necessary for making flat gauges, test tools, jig work, etc. Each piece of stock packed in properly labeled envelope, showing size at a glance.

Size, Inches	Price Per Piece
1-64	
1 x 18 x 1/64	$0.85
1½ x 18 x 1/64	1.05
2 x 18 x 1/64	1.25
2½ x 18 x 1/64	1.55
3 x 18 x 1/64	1.85
4 x 18 x 1/64	2.50
1-32	
¾ x 18 x 1/32	.60
1 x 18 x 1/32	.60
1½ x 18 x 1/32	.80
2 x 18 x 1/32	1.00
2½ x 18 x 1/32	1.25
3 x 18 x 1/32	1.50
3½ x 18 x 1/32	1.75
4 x 18 x 1/32	2.00
5 x 18 x 1/32	3.00
6 x 18 x 1/32	4.00
3-64	
1 x 18 x 3/64	.55
1½ x 18 x 3/64	.75
2 x 18 x 3/64	.95
2½ x 18 x 3/64	1.15
3 x 18 x 3/64	1.40
4 x 18 x 3/64	1.90
5 x 18 x 3/64	2.75
6 x 18 x 3/64	3.75
1-16	
½ x 18 x 1/16	.40
¾ x 18 x 1/16	.45
1 x 18 x 1/16	.50
1¼ x 18 x 1/16	.65
1½ x 18 x 1/16	.70
2 x 18 x 1/16	.90
2½ x 18 x 1/16	1.10
3 x 18 x 1/16	1.35
3½ x 18 x 1/16	1.60
4 x 18 x 1/16	1.85
5 x 18 x 1/16	2.50
6 x 18 x 1/16	3.50
3-32	
½ x 18 x 3/32	.55
¾ x 18 x 3/32	.65
1 x 18 x 3/32	.70
1½ x 18 x 3/32	.85
2 x 18 x 3/32	1.00
2½ x 18 x 3/32	1.20
3 x 18 x 3/32	1.40
3½ x 18 x 3/32	1.65
4 x 18 x 3/32	1.90
5 x 18 x 3/32	2.75
6 x 18 x 3/32	3.75
1-8	
½ x 18 x ⅛	.60
¾ x 18 x ⅛	.70
1 x 18 x ⅛	.75
1¼ x 18 x ⅛	.85
1½ x 18 x ⅛	.90
2 x 18 x ⅛	1.05
2½ x 18 x ⅛	1.30
3 x 18 x ⅛	1.50
3½ x 18 x ⅛	1.75
4 x 18 x ⅛	2.00
5 x 18 x ⅛	2.85
6 x 18 x ⅛	4.00
5-32	
¾ x 18 x 5/32	75
1 x 18 x 5/32	.85
1½ x 18 x 5/32	1.10
2 x 18 x 5/32	1.40
2½ x 18 x 5/32	1.60
3 x 18 x 5/32	1.80
4 x 18 x 5/32	2.30
3-16	
½ x 18 x 3/16	.75
¾ x 18 x 3/16	.90
1 x 18 x 3/16	.95
1¼ x 18 x 3/16	1.15
1½ x 18 x 3/16	1.20
2 x 18 x 3/16	1.50
2½ x 18 x 3/16	1.70
3 x 18 x 3/16	2.00
3½ x 18 x 3/16	2.30
4 x 18 x 3/16	2.60
5 x 18 x 3/16	3.50
6 x 18 x 3/16	4.50
7-32	
1 x 18 x 7/32	1.05
1½ x 18 x 7/32	1.35
2 x 18 x 7/32	1.60
2½ x 18 x 7/32	1.90
3 x 18 x 7/32	2.20
4 x 18 x 7/32	3.00
1-4	
¼ x 18 x ¼	1.00
½ x 18 x ¼	.95
1 x 18 x ¼	1.15
1½ x 18 x ¼	1.45
2 x 18 x ¼	1.80
2½ x 18 x ¼	2.20
3 x 18 x ¼	2.60
3½ x 18 x ¼	3.05
4 x 18 x ¼	3.50
5 x 18 x ¼	4.50
6 x 18 x ¼	5.50
5-16	
5/16 x 18 x 5/16	1.25
½ x 18 x 5/16	1.20
1 x 18 x 5/16	1.50
1½ x 18 x 5/16	1.80
2 x 18 x 5/16	2 15
2½ x 18 x 5/16	2.60
3 x 18 x 5/16	3.05
4 x 18 x 5/16	4.00
3-8	
⅜ x 18 x ⅜	1.50
½ x 18 x ⅜	1.50
¾ x 18 x ⅜	1.65
1 x 18 x ⅜	1.75
1½ x 18 x ⅜	2.05
2 x 18 x ⅜	2.40
2½ x 18 x ⅜	2.95
3 x 18 x ⅜	3.50
4 x 18 x ⅜	4.50
1-2	
½ x 18 x ½	1.75
¾ x 18 x ½	2.15
1 x 18 x ½	2.65
2 x 18 x ½	3.30
3 x 18 x ½	4.40
4 x 18 x ½	5.40
3-4	
¾ x 18 x ¾	2.50
1	
1 x 18 x 1	3.25

Other sizes furnished to order
Prices upon Application

CUTTING NIPPERS

No. 1

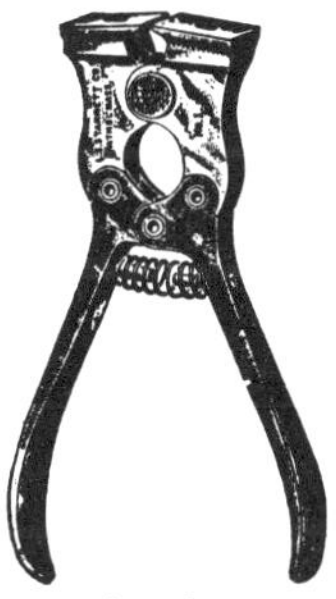

Jaws for Bicycle Use — Jaws for Music Wire — Jaws for Common Use

Has adjustable jaws. Packed 1 in a box.

Size .... inches	5½	7
Price, No. 1	$3.50	$4.50
Price, Extra Jaws .... per pr.	.60	.60
Price, Screws .... per doz.	.30	.30
Price, Splines .... per doz.	.30	.30

HIGH SPEED HACK SAWS

No. 840

For Hand Frames

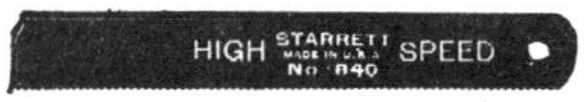

Cuts Quicker—Lasts Longer

Made from high speed steel and is steadily meeting favor for cutting the hardest alloys and materials. Will cut faster and show much more endurance over tungsten-alloy saws and will show a material saving when cutting the tougher metals such as nickel, chromium, high speed and certain tool steels. Can be run as high as 140 strokes per minute.
Furnished 18 teeth to the inch.

No.	Dimensions, Inches Length	Width	Thickness	Teeth per in.	Price per Gross
840	10	9/16	.025	18	$40.32
840	12	9/16	.025	18	48.96

NARROW HOOK SAW FRAME

No. 150

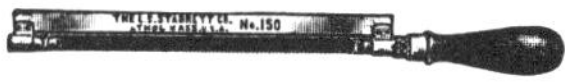

Holds 8 inch saw. Gets into places no other frame can. 4-way blade adjustment, nickel plated.

Price, each .... $.90

HACKSAW FRAME

No. 144

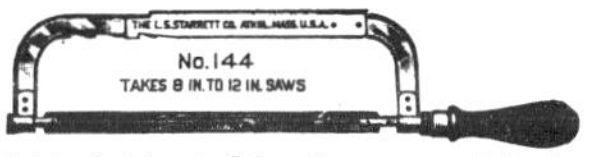

No. 144 Adjustable frame, nickel plated, dull finish.

Price, with one blade $1.00

FLEXIBLE BACK HACK SAWS

No. 250

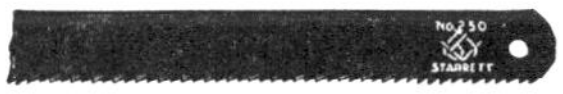

These saws are hardened and tempered on the cutting edge only with flexible or soft back. The user gets the full efficiency from each blade until the teeth are worn dull, without the saw breaking.

No. 250—18 Teeth to Inch

Length Inches	Width Inches	Thickness Inches	Price per Gross
8	7/16	.025	$8.00
10	½	.025	10.00
12	½	.025	12.00

NARROW HOOK RULES

No. 422

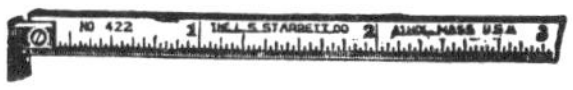

Graduated one side in 32ds and the other in 64ths of an inch.
No. 422. No. 330 rule, with hook.

Length, inches	4	6	9	12
Price, each	$1.00	1.20	1.65	2.00

© PRICES ON OTHER STARRETT TOOLS WILL BE QUOTED ON APPLICATION

ABRASIVES AND POLISHING PREPARATIONS

ALUNDUM and CRYSTOLON GRAIN

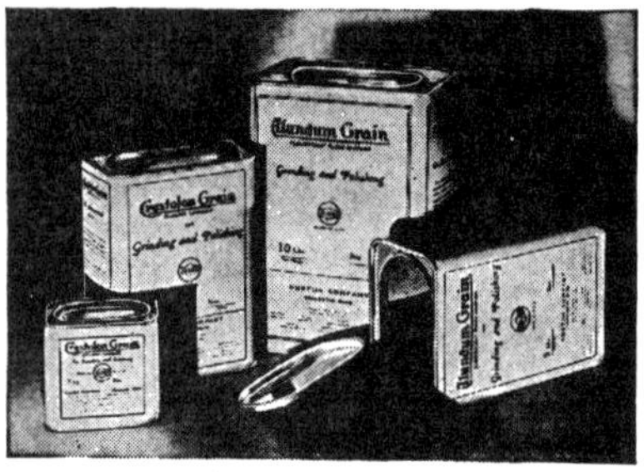

These Norton electric furnace abrasives when mixed with oil, vaseline or water are ideal for grinding. When coated on polishing wheels they will far out-cut and out-last emery.

ALUNDUM GRAIN (Aluminum Oxide)
Unclassified Flours—F, 2F, 3F, 4F, XF.
Classified Flours—280, 320, 400, 500, 600.

	Sizes F, 2F, 3F 4F, XF	Sizes 280, 320 400, 500	Size 600
1 lb. Cans, Per Can......	$0.45	$0.50	$0.80
5 lb. Cans, Per Can......	1.50	2.00	3.25
10 lb. Cans, Per Can......	2.00	3.10	4.80

CRYSTOLON GRAIN (Silicon Carbide)
Unclassified Flours—F, 2F, 3F, 4F, XF.
Classified Flours—280, 320, 400, 500, 600.

Quantity	Sizes F, 2F, 3F 4F, XF	Sizes 280, 320 400, 500	Size 600
1 lb. Cans, Per Can......	$0.50	$0.60	$0.90
5 lb. Cans, Per Can......	1.75	2.50	4.00
10 lb. Cans, Per Can......	2.50	3.50	5.50

GARNET PAPERS

Sheet Size 9" x 11"

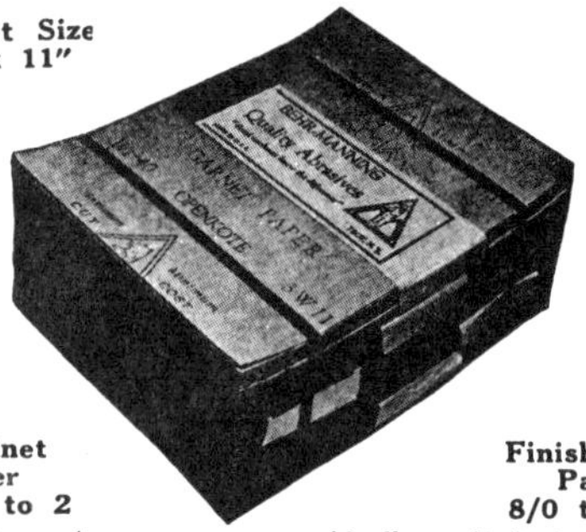

Cabinet Paper 4/0 to 2

Finishing Paper 8/0 to 0

These two papers are ideally suited to the hand sanding of fine gun stocks. Both papers are coated with first quality Adirondack garnet on a strong pliable backing.

Cabinet Paper is on a heavier weight backing than the light flexible finishing paper.

PRICES

Grit Nos.	Per Ream	Per ½ Ream	Per Quire
8/0 to 2/0	$22.50	$11.25	$1.13
0	25.00	12.50	1.25
½	29.00	14.50	1.45
1	33.00	16.50	1.65
1½	37.50	18.75	1.88
2	42.00	21.00	2.10

Sheets 9" x 11"

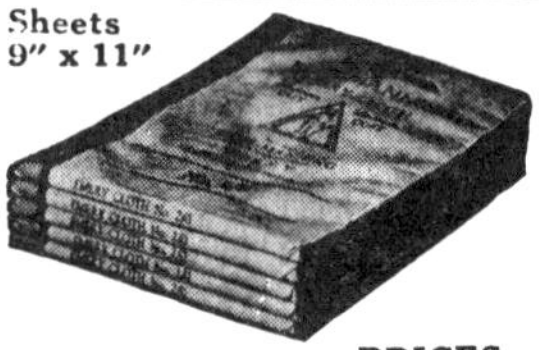

EMERY CLOTH

On blue jeans cloth backing. This is the standard gunsmiths' smoothing and polishing cloth.

PRICES

Grit Nos.	Per Ream	Per ½ Ream	Per Quire
3/0 to 0	$30.00	$15.00	$1.50
½	31.20	15.60	1.56
1	32.75	16.38	1.64
1½	34.30	17.15	1.72
2	36.50	18.25	1.83
2½	39.40	19.70	1.97
3	42.50	21.25	2.13
Assorted Ream	33.25	.....	....
Crocus Cloth	30.00	15.00	1.50

GRINDING WHEELS

For Hand or Power Grinders

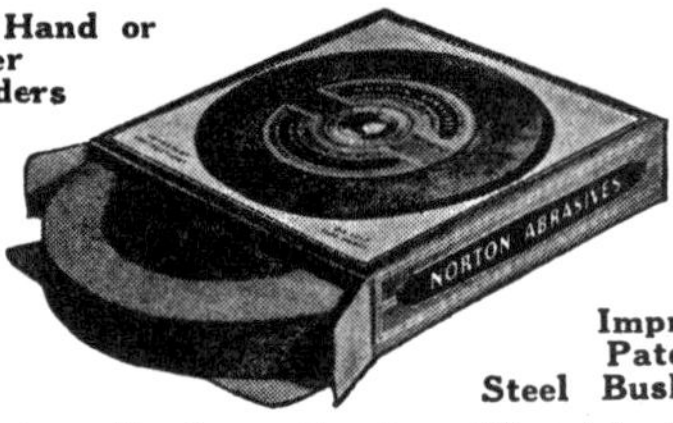

Improved Patented Steel Bushings

Norton Alundum Abrasive (Electric)—Vitrified Bond—Uniform Quality—Cut Cool, Fast and Free—Unaffected by Oil or Water—Long Wearing—True Running—Lead Bushed Holes—Wheels over 4 inches are Blottered.

Wheels are equipped with standard 1" lead bushings but are instantly converted to ¼, 5/16, ⅜, ½, ⅝, ¾ and ⅞" arbors by inserting the correct size steel bushing (furnished free). Bushings are made slightly larger than the wheel hole and have straight sides which give them a full seat. They have a "tight press" fit and remain firmly in place after being seated. They are easily pressed into the arbor hole with the fingers.

PRICES

Size in Inches	Price Each	No.	Grain and Grade
2 x ¼	$0.60	A-37-C	150P Fine
	0.60	A-33-C	100P Medium
	0.60	A-36-C	60P Coarse
2 x ½	0.70	A-22-C	100N Fine
	0.70	A-35-V	80P Medium
	0.70	A-38-C	60P Coarse
2½ x ¼	0.75	A-41-C	100P Fine
	0.75	A-40-C	80P Medium
	0.75	A-39-C	60P Coarse
3 x ¼	0.90	A-77	120N Fine
	0.90	A-80	80N Medium
	0.90	A-76	60N Coarse
3 x ½	1.05	A-67-C	120P Fine
	1.05	A-52	60P Medium
	1.05	A-51	46P Coarse
4 x ¼	1.55	A-187	120N Fine
	1.55	A-186	80N Medium
	1.55	A-101-C	60N Coarse
4 x ⅜	1.65	A-188	120N Fine
	1.65	A-139	100N Medium
	1.65	A-184	60N Coarse
4 x ½	1.75	A-190	120P Fine
	1.75	A-189	80P Medium
	1.75	A-103	46P Coarse
4 x ¾	2.05	A-152-M	100M Fine
	2.05	A-135	60P Medium
	2.05	A-113	46P Coarse
4 x 1	2.35	A-192	100M Fine
	2.35	A-191	60P Medium
	2.35	A-152-V	46P Coarse
5 x ¾	2.90	A-254	80O Fine
	2.90	A-212	60P Medium
	2.90	A-203	46P Coarse
5 x 1	3.30	A-233-P	80M Fine
	3.30	A-217	60O Medium
	3.30	A-218	46P Coarse
6 x ¼	2.50	A-325-C	100M Fine
	2.50	A-319-M	60M Medium
	2.50	A-303-C	46M Coarse
6 x ½	3.00	A-332	100M Fine
	3.00	A-345	60M Medium
	3.00	A-376	46M Coarse
6 x ¾	3.50	A-329-M	100M Fine
	3.50	A-308	60P Medium
	3.50	A-307	46P Coarse
6 x 1	4.00	A-326-C	100M Fine
	4.00	A-318	60P Medium
	4.00	A-313-M	46M Coarse
7 x ¾	4.30	A-405-M	80M Fine
	4.30	A-405	60P Medium
	4.30	A-404	46P Coarse
7 x 1	4.90	A-412	60P Fine
	4.90	A-409	46P Medium
	4.90	A-410	30Q Coarse
8 x ½	4.30	A-592	80P Fine
	4.30	A-502	60P Medium
	4.30	A-501	46P Coarse
8 x ¾	5.15	A-593	80P Fine
	5.15	A-506	60P Medium
	5.15	A-504	30Q Coarse
8 x 1	6.00	A-514	60P Fine
	6.00	A-506-P	46P Medium
	6.00	A-512	36Q Coarse
8 x 1¼	7.00	A-526-M	60M Fine
	7.00	A-519-M	46M Medium
	7.00	A-520-M	30P Coarse
8 x 1½	8.00	A-502-P	60M Fine
	8.00	A-511-M	46M Medium
	8.00	A-568	30P Coarse

Prices for larger sizes on application

LAPOWDERS

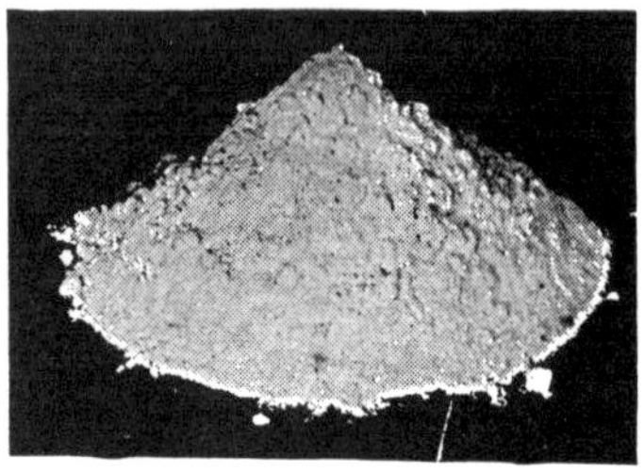

Crushed natural oilstone rock for use where high polish or finish without scratching is required. Can be used without danger of charging or loading the work. Used by gun factories, gunsmiths and in the making of all gun parts.

Supplied in two qualities: Silkite for lapping softer metals like gold, silver, brass, copper and bronze; and Velvite for harder metals like nickel and high carbon steel.

Silkite Lapowder

Size	Price Per Lb.	No.
0	$0.35	XS10
1	0.30	XS1

Velvite Lapowder

Size	Price Per Lb.	No.
00	$0.35	XV20
0	0.30	XV10
1	0.25	XV1

LIGHTNING METALITE CLOTH
(Aluminum Oxide)

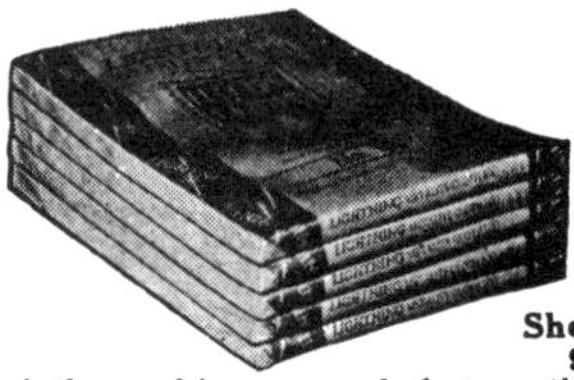

Sheet Size 9" x 11"

This cloth combines several factors that have never before been completely present in any one cloth.

The result of this is a cloth of extraordinary efficiency, remarkable cutting speed, and extremely long life. Sufficiently rugged for flat work, it is still flexible enough to wrap around a file or block. It is the ideal metal sanding cloth.

PRICES

Grit Nos.	Per Ream	Per ½ Ream	Per Quire
320-240-180 150-120-100	$54.70	$27.35	$2.74
80	58.10	29.05	2.91
60	63.10	31.55	3.16
50	67.60	33.80	3.38
40	72.70	36.35	3.64
36	78.40	39.20	3.92

LIGHTNING METALITE CLOTH
(Aluminum Oxide)

In Handy Rolls

50 Yards Long

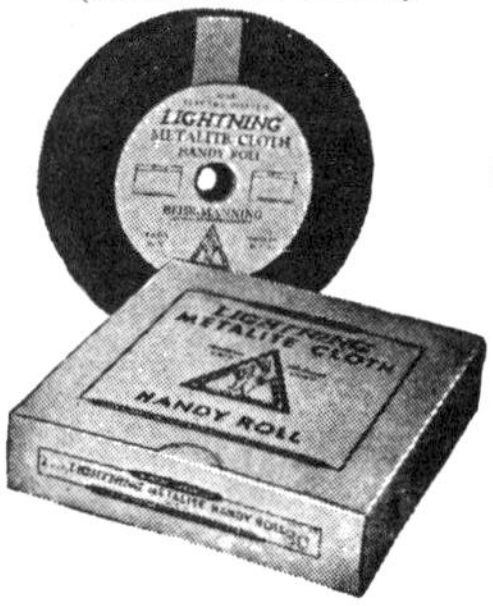

Handy Rolls are cut with smooth, sharp edges of proper widths and may be torn to any required length.

Simply reach over and rip off just enough for the job. Time is saved—material is saved—money is saved—to say nothing of temper.

PRICE PER 50-YARD ROLL

GRIT NUMBERS

Width	320 to 100	80	60	50	40	36	30	24
1"	$2.90	$3.00	$3.25	$3.40	$3.60	$3.85	$4.05	$4.30
1½"	4.05	4.20	4.50	4.80	5.10	5.45	5.75	6.10
2"	5.15	5.40	5.80	6.15	6.55	7.00	7.45	7.95

24 Sheets = 1 Quire 24 Quires = 1 Ream

STOEGER'S GUNSMITH'S OILSTONES

We have listed below, an assortment of gunsmith's oil stones, which are absolutely indispensable to the amateur and professional gunsmith. The reader will find in the descriptions set forth, the particular use which each oil stone has.

Oil stones are positively necessary in certain barrel, action, sight fitting, adjusting and sharpening the various gunsmith's tools. These stones are the same as are used in our own repair division and we consider them the finest available.

HARD ARKANSAS SQUARE FILE
HF 43—½" x 3¼" Long

This square stone is very handy for the sharpening of gun stock chisels, polishing revolver, rifle and shotgun hammers. It comes in very handy to fit parts to actions and in obtaining a fine adjustment of head space. This should not be used on sears.
Price .... $.70

HARD ARKANSAS SQUARE FILE
HF 13—¼" x 3½" Long

This file is particularly useful in sharpening engraver's tools and any other gunsmith's tools made of hard, highly tempered tools. It may be used for all gunsmithing purposes except on sears.
Price .... $.50

HARD ARKANSAS TRIANGULAR FILE
HF 143—½" x 3½" Long

This file is well adapted to the straightening out of V notches of rear sights (iron sights). It is also recommended for the correcting of ejectors on shotguns and for the smoothing up of any sear.
Price .... $.70

HARD ARKANSAS DIAMOND FILE
HF 843—½" x 3¾" Long

Especially for sears and ejectors on high grade shotguns, rifles, revolvers and pistols, in order to give a clean smooth and crisp trigger pull.
Price .... $.60

HARD ARKANSAS PENKNIFE PIECE
HB 13—¼" x 3½" Long

This stone is primarily intended to use in correcting the sears of all bolt action guns including the well known Springfield, Mauser, Winchester and Remington rifles.
Price .... $.50

MEDIUM 32 INDIA
MF 56—¾" x ¾" x 6" Long

For rough grinding on rifles, shotgun, pistol and revolver actions and parts. Removes rust spots, pits and does rough polishing, preparatory to the finishing polish for blueing.
Price .... $.65

MEDIUM 14 INDIA
MS 34—⅜" x 4" Long

This stone is used to sharpen chisels and other tools with a V cross section. It can also be used for half round and flat chisels.
Price .... $.65

COMBINATION 29 INDIA
IB 6—1" x 2" x 6" Long

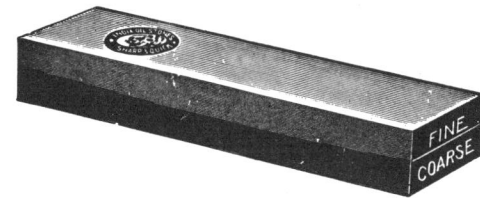

A fine stone for sharpening tools, with two surfaces, hard and soft. It is sturdy, strong and a utility stone for the gunsmith.
Price $1.25

MEDIUM 6 INDIA
MF 14—¼" Square x 4"

A first finish for rifle sears, before the finishing work. Very useful for any smoothing and cleaning up of parts before using a stone to make the final polish.
Price .... $.40

MEDIUM 8 INDIA
MF 134—⅜" Triangular x 4" Long

A particularly useful stone for the first cut in adjusting sears and ejectors on shotguns.
Price .... $.55

MEDIUM 12 INDIA
MF 214—¼" Round x 4" Long

For sharpening small round stocker's chisels and smoothing out the inside of rifle bolts. Very useful for smoothing out the inside of any bushings such as front ramp bushing and barrel bands.
Price .... $.60

MEDIUM 39 INDIA
MS 42—¼" x 1" x 2" Long

This stone is very handy to use on cocking levers and ejectors of fine shotguns.
Price .... $.50

SPORTSMAN STONE IN CASE
WIP 13—½" x 1¼" x 3" Long

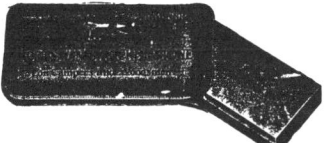

A general utility stone for the sportsman's use. Will sharpen knives, axes, tools and in an emergency can be used to straighten sights and for any repair work on a firearm where a cutting surface is needed. Can also be used to sharpen fish hook barbs. Regularly furnished with neat leather case.
Price .... $.50

SPECIAL OFFER: A complete set of gunsmiths' oil stones consisting of one each of the above (13 pieces) may be had for the special price of... $7.25

SEE PAGE 8, "HOW TO ORDER"

UTICA GUNSMITHS' PLIERS

NO. 50 • UTICA STANDARD SIDE CUTTING PLIER

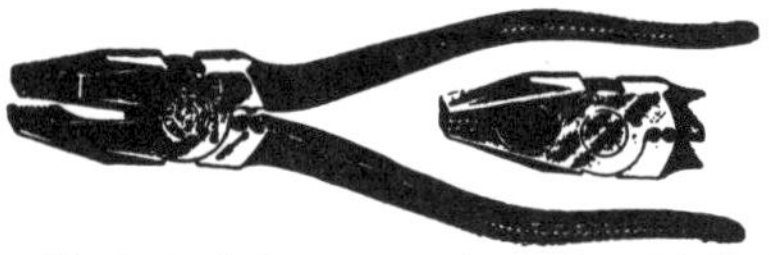

An ideal tool for general work. Light in weight, forged from Alloy Steel and skillfully tempered. Its cutting qualities are unsurpassed by any side cutting plier.

Utica Finish Size	4"	5"	6"	7"	8"
Price	$1.05	1.15	1.25	1.40	1.50

NO. 1033 • UTICA LONG CHAIN NEEDLE NOSE PLIER

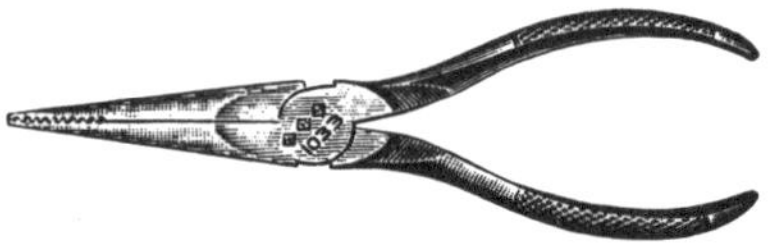

This is a long needle nose type of plier without a side cutter. It has a spring-tempered needle nose with a fine balance for delicate work.

Utica Finish Size	5½"	6"	7"
Price	$1.25	1.30	1.45

NO. 3400 • UTICA EXTRA LONG CHAIN NOSE ALLOY STEEL PLIER

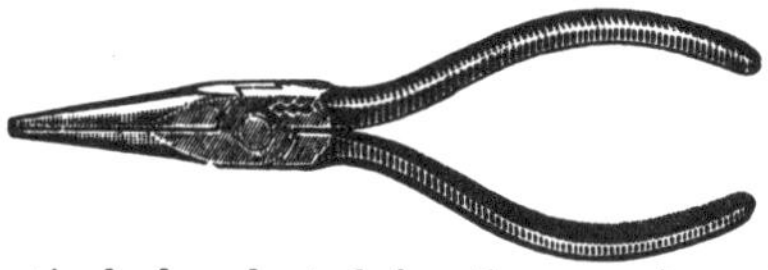

Particularly adapted for the use of repair men. It has a long spring-tempered nose with "Perfect Fit" handles.

Utica Finish Size............6½"
Price $1.90

NO. 60 • UTICA BULL DOG END CUTTING NIPPER

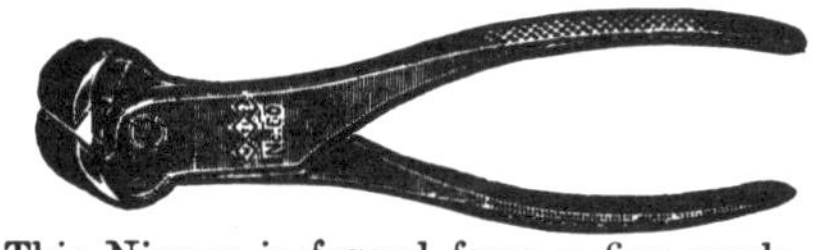

This Nipper is forged from a fine grade of Alloy Steel, carefully tempered, and is a strong, easy cutting tool. Used by repairmen and other mechanics who require a high quality End Cutting Nipper that will hold its edge.

Utica Finish Size	5"	6"	7"	8"
Price	$1.05	1.15	1.30	1.75

NO. 141 • UTICA WOODWORKER'S PINCER

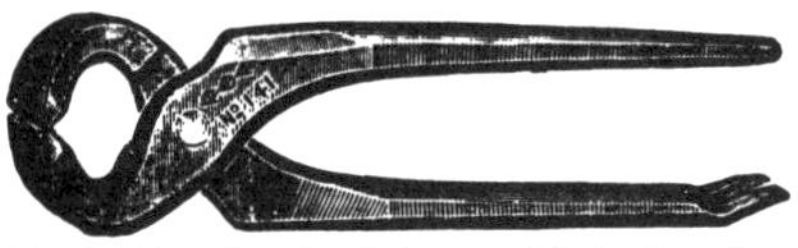

This is the standard type of Woodworker's Pincers of the claw type, with strong sharp-cutting edges "that will cut."

Utica Finish Size	6"	7"	8"	10"
Price	$.70	.75	.80	.95

In presenting the "Utica" line of pliers we feel that we are offering the gunsmith and repair man the very best in this line. In general repairs and in gunsmithing work in particular, an assortment of proper pliers is a fundamental necessity. As in files, one single tool is not sufficient to take care of the multitude of operations peculiar to this work and for this reason we have assembled here a line of those pliers which we feel will cover every practical requirement in the gunsmithing field.

NO. 622 • UTICA SHORT CHAIN NOSE MECHANIC'S PLIER

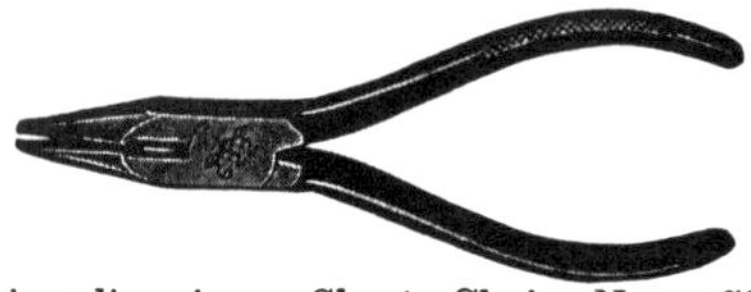

This plier is a Short Chain Nose Side Cutting Plier, hand-honed cutting knives. It makes an all round Mechanic's plier.

Utica Finish Size..............5"
Price $1.15

NO. 888 • UTICA CURVED NEEDLE NOSE PLIER

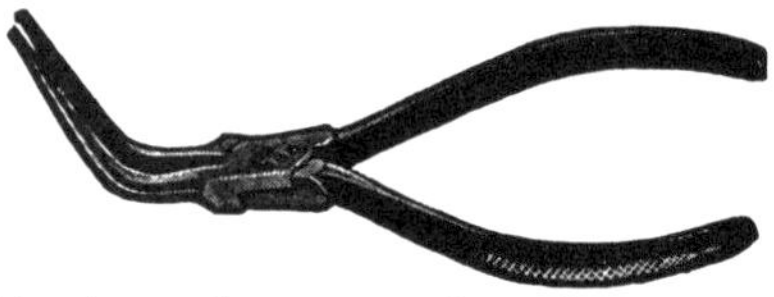

This is a long curved spring-tempered Needle Nose Plier and used in deep and narrow places. It may be used without turning or twisting the hand in the assembling of small parts, etc.

Utica Finish Size	5½"	6"
Price	$1.75	1.90

NO. 1300 • UTICA BARREL AND TUBE PLIER

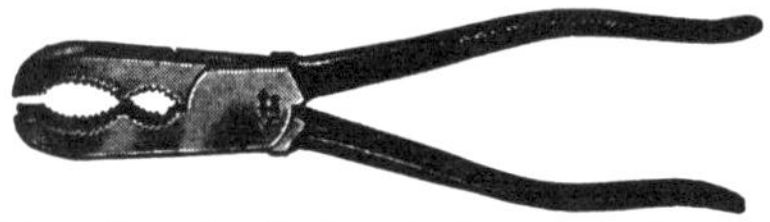

This plier is designed to meet the ever increasing demand for a quality Tube and Barrel Plier, with full fashioned handles. This plier has a larger capacity than the ordinary plier of this type.

Utica Finish Size	5"	6"	7"	8"	10"
Price	$.80	.90	1.00	1.20	1.40

NO. 91 • UTICA THIN ALLOY STEEL WRENCH

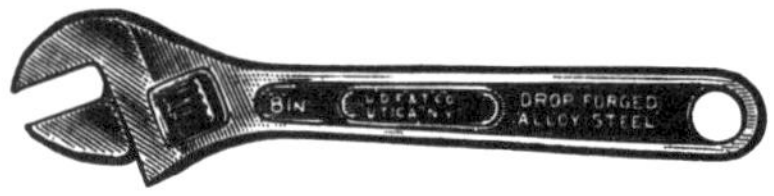

Size	Capacity	Price
4"	⅝"	$.85
6"	¾"	.85
8"	15/16"	1.05
10"	1⅛"	1.30
12"	1 5/16"	1.90

This new Utica Thin Pattern Full Alloy Steel Wrench is not just another wrench! It's different in that the jaws are designed to get at places inaccessible with the ordinary wrench of this type . Thinner and stronger.

NO. 41 • UTICA ALLOY STEEL DIAGONAL CUTTING PLIER

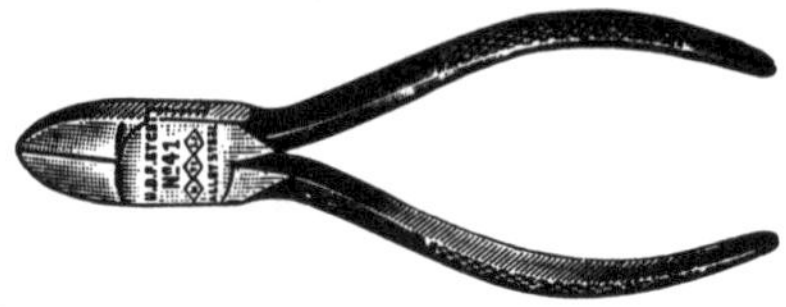

Properly designed all round Diagonal Cutting Plier with hand-honed cutting knives.

Utica Finish Size	4"	5"	5½"	6"
Price	$1.35	1.50	1.65	1.80

NO. 650 • UTICA LONG REACH FLAT NOSE SIDE CUTTING PLIER

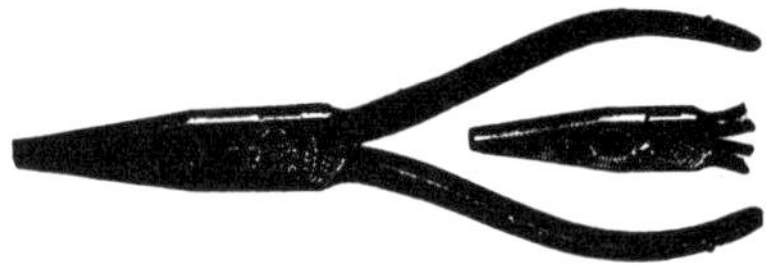

This is drop forged from Alloy Steel. Long Flat Nose Side Cutting plier, spring-tempered nose, hand-honed cutting knives.

Utica Finish Size	5½"	6"
Price	$1.50	1.65

NO. 777 • UTICA LONG NEEDLE NOSE PLIER

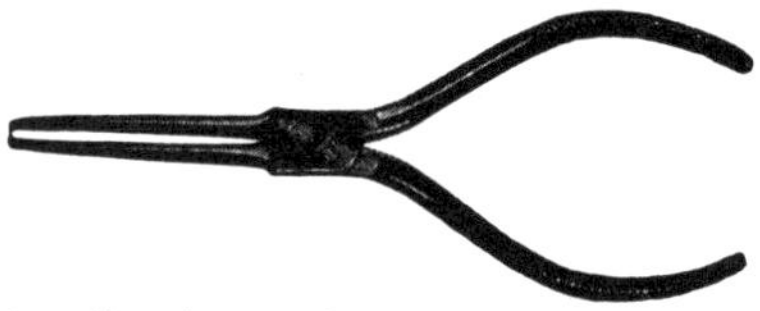

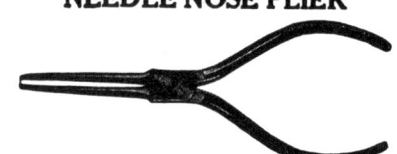

This plier has a long, half-round, spring-tempered nose for very fine work in assembling small apparatus, and removing small parts.

Utica Finish Size	5½"	6"
Price	$1.60	1.65

NO. 511 • UTICA HEAVY DUTY SLIP JOINT COMBINATION PLIER

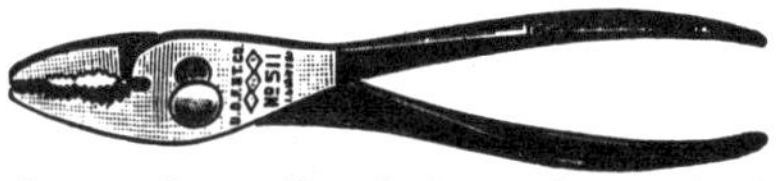

A heavy duty plier designed for work that the ordinary plier will not stand. The cutting knives pass at an angle and will give a clean cut. Made in Utica Finish.

Size	6"	8"	10"
Price	$1.00	1.15	1.50

NO. 518 • UTICA MECHANIC'S LONG THIN NOSE SLIP JOINT PLIER

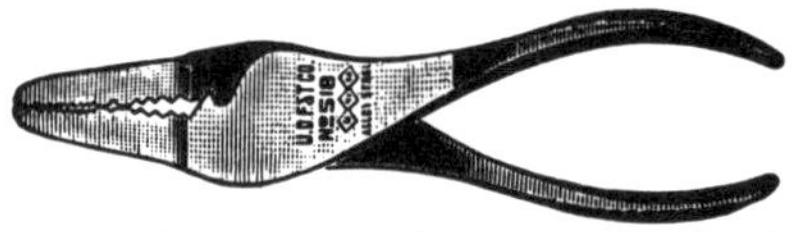

A special extra long thin nose Mechanic's Plier for the hard-to-get-at places. Drop forged from Alloy Steel, heat treated and tempered in oil.

Size ....7"
Price $1.35

GOOD TOOLS ARE SAFE AND RELIABLE

GENUINE SWEDISH GUNSMITHS' PLIERS

In the manufacture of BERG Pliers and Nippers only the best Swedish Charcoal Steel is used. The material is subjected to careful examinations at our factory, both before and in the course of the manufacturing.

The principal factor for obtaining the greatest benefit from the superior properties of Swedish

Eskilstuna   Sweden

Charcoal Steel is proper heat treatment. BERG Pliers are annealed, hardened and tempered in automatically temperature-controlled electric furnaces fitted with the most up-to-date appliances. These processes being simultaneously controlled metallographically in our Steel Laboratory enable us to guarantee the highest obtainable quality.

No. 526 BERG DIAGONAL CUTTING PLIER

Accurately fitted jaws. Will cut fine insulated copper wire and hard steel wire. This is the famous "Swedish" Plier. Box Joint.
Black Finish, length . 5"   5½"   6"   7"   8"
Price, each $2.37 2.56 2.76 3.21 3.67

No. 1525 BERG DIAGONAL CUTTING PLIER

Same type as No. 526 but with BERG patented single joint.
Black Finish, length ..... 5"   5½"   6"   7"
Price, each $2.15 2.28 2.43 2.77

No. 1528 BERG DIAGONAL PIANO WIRE CUTTER

Especially designed for cutting piano wire and used in gunsmith shops, where very hard wire is used. BERG Single Joint.
Black Finish, length .... 4½" 5½" 6½"
Price, each $1.72 1.87 1.98

No. 2528 BERG SPOON-SHAPED DIAGONAL CUTTING PLIER

This Plier provides ample space for the hand, owing to the spoon shape of the cutting edges. The line of the cutting edges is slightly curved, which further enables close cutting. Will cut hardened steel wire.
Black Finish, length .... 6½" 7½"
Price, each $2.07 2.50

No. 1529 BERG OFFSET DIAGONAL COTTER KEY PLIER

Especially designed with cutting edges spread out to reach inaccessible places, narrow curves, etc. BERG Single Joint.
Black Finish, length .... 6½"
Price, each $2.53

No. 515 BERG DOUBLE ACTION JOINT END CUTTING NIPPER

This powerfully constructed Nipper will cut piano wire. Between the shanks is an adjustable stop screw for preventing the cutting edges from coming together and damaging each other.
Black Finish, length .... 6"
Price, each $3.71

No. 527 BERG PIANO WIRE END CUTTING NIPPER

A powerful Nipper fitted with BERG Single Joint. Wide jaws extending beyond each side of the joint.
Black Finish, length .... 6"   7"
Price, each $2.03 2.25

No. 1518 BERG POWER-LEVERAGE PIANO WIRE CUTTER

A most powerful cutting tool for heavy piano wire and rivets. Interchangeable cutting jaws which are easily replaced.
Black Finish, length .... 9"   10"
Price, each $3.63 4.29
Extra Cutters .... 9"   Price per pair $0.80
Extra Cutters ....10" Price per pair .... .80

No. 1519 BERG POWER-LEVERAGE END CUTTER

This Nipper will cut heavy gauge piano wire and rivets. Same as No. 1518 but with end cutters.
Black Finish, length .... 9"
Price, each $4.29
Price, extra cutters 9" $1.00

No. 590 BERG LONG NOSE PLIER WITH SIDE CUTTER

A very practical Plier which will cut hard steel wire. The long tapered half round jaws provide free sight and possess good gripping power. Box Joint.
Black Finish, length .... 5"   6"
Price, each $2.37 2.87

No. 1590 BERG LONG NOSE PLIER WITH SIDE CUTTER

Same as No. 590 but with BERG Single Joint.
Black Finish, length ..... 4"   5"   6"   7"
Price, each $1.92 2.03 2.37 2.70

No. 2533 BERG EXTRA LONG NEEDLE NOSE PLIER

The extra long jaws of this Plier make it invaluable for all kinds of work requiring a slender, yet strong and durable Plier. Supplied with BERG Single Joint.
Black Finish, length .... 6"   7"   8"
Price, each $1.92 2.25 2.58

No. 541 BERG WOODWORKER'S PINCER

A very strong and well made Pincer. Hardened and tempered to meet the highest strains to which these tools are subjected to in actual work.
Black Finish, length .... 5"   6"   8"   10"
Price, each $1.02 1.36 1.63 2.03

No. 616 BERG SLIP JOINT PLIER WITH SIDE CUTTER

An all-around Combination Plier. Thin nose with milled teeth and with side cutter, which is tempered to cut hard steel wire.
Black Finish, length .... 5½" 7½"
Price, each $1.73 1.99

A TOOL FOR EVERY PURPOSE

WOOD CHISELS AND CARVING TOOL SETS

#1188 WOOD CHISELS

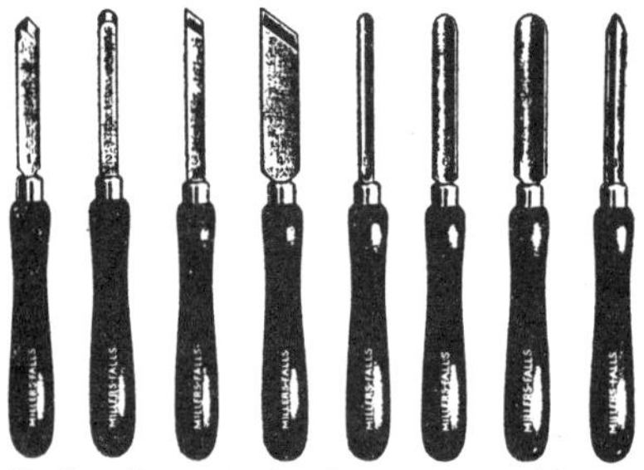

Full size, heavy tools that are essential to the best results, especially for work on gun stocks. Blades are 4½ inches long, forged from a fine quality of tool steel. The heavy tangs are solidly seated in long, smooth, finely finished handles, and allow two-hand control. The blades are heat-treated to take and hold a keen edge. The edges are ground and honed ready for use and the rest of the blade is nicely polished. Handles are hardwood with a mahogany lacquer finish. Length overall, 13 inches.

No.	Type	Price	No.	Type	Price
1	Spear point	$.70	5	¼" Gouge	$.70
2	Round Nose chisel	.70	6	½" Gouge	.70
3	½" Skew chisel	.70	7	¾" Gouge	.90
4	1" Skew chisel	.90	8	Parting Tool	.75

No. 1188 Set of one each of Nos. 1 to 8 . **$6.05**

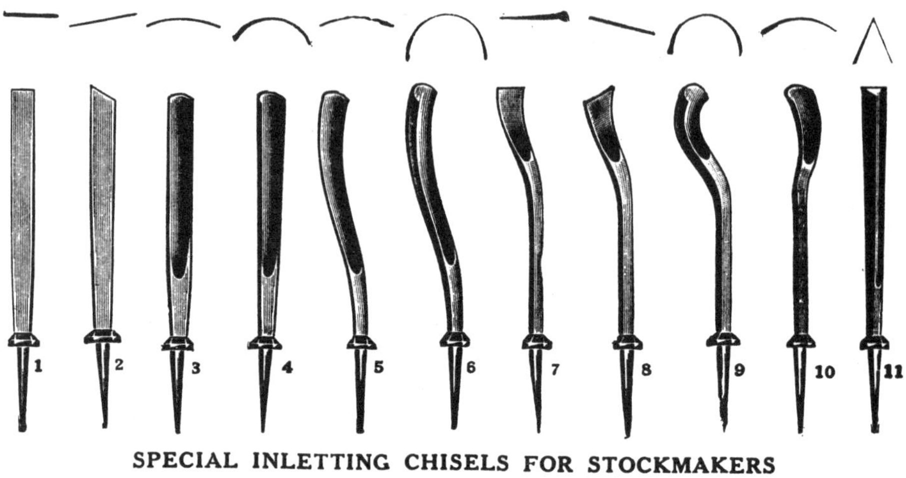

SPECIAL INLETTING CHISELS FOR STOCKMAKERS

The eleven chisels illustrated are those necessary for first class stock work. With a complete set of these chisels, any work can be done. While it is advisable to purchase the entire set, they are offered individually.

No. 1, .394" wide **$0.90**	No. 5, .157" wide **$1.35**	No. 9, .236" wide **$1.35**
No. 2, .394" wide .... **.90**	No. 6, .157" wide **1.35**	No. 10, .236" wide **1.35**
No. 3, .236" wide **1.00**	No. 7, .315" wide **1.15**	No. 11, .236" wide **1.75**
No. 4, .315" wide **1.00**	No. 8, .394" wide **1.15**	

#109 CARVING TOOL SET

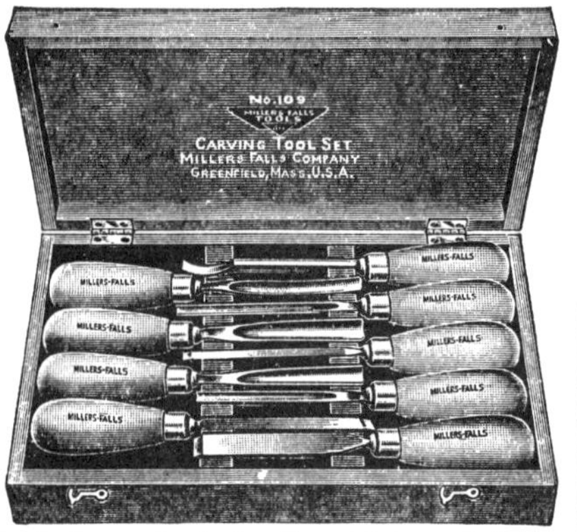

A de luxe set of nine fine chisels packed in a substantial, beautifully finished lock corner box with hinged cover that serves as a permanent container. The blades, hammer forged from the finest tool steel, are 8 inches long and are fitted with a forged bolster that protects the handle when a mallet is used. The blades are beautifully polished and the cutting edges carefully honed. The following tools make up the set:

½" Str. Chisel	⅜" Bent Chisel
¼" Curved Gouge	7/16" Gouge
¼" V Tool	½" Gouge
¼" Skew Chisel	¼" Str. Chisel
¼" Gouge	

The handles protected with nickeled ferrules, are natural lacquered maple.

#109	Length of Tools	Weight Set	Price per set
	8 inches	2¾ lbs.	**$8.00**

#108 CARVING TOOL SET

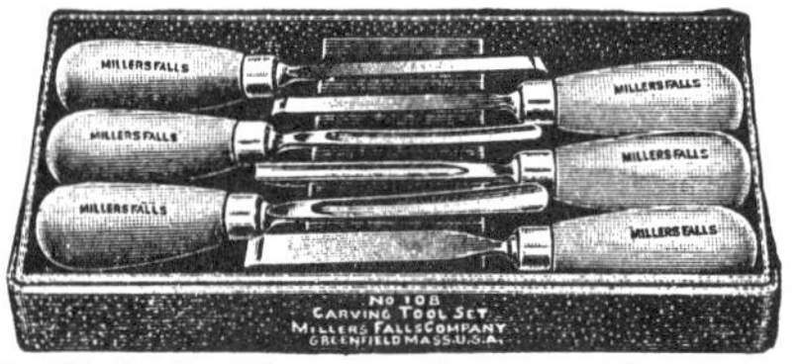

The blades in this set are longer and heavier and are equipped with a forged bolster that protects the handles when a mallet is used. They consist of the following:

½" Straight Chisel	¼" Gouge
V Tool	7/16" Gouge
¼" Skew Chisel	¼" Straight Chisel

#108	Length of Tools	Weight	Price per set.
	8 inches	¾ lb.	**$4.40**

No. WH8N WOOD TURNING CHISEL AND GOUGE SET

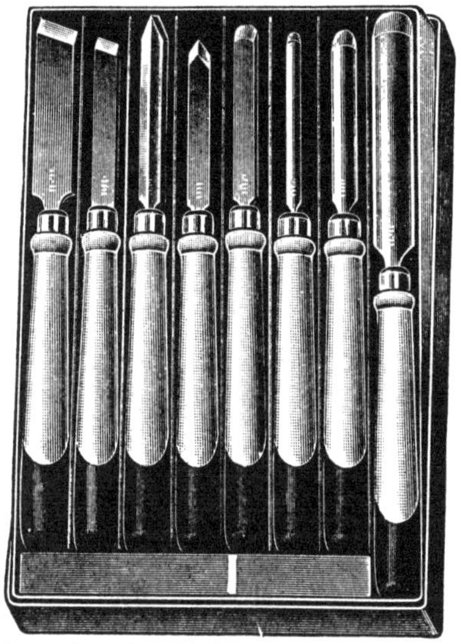

This wood turning chisel and gouge set is the most complete and will solve almost any need you will find yourself up against in wood working or re-stocking. This set is made by one of the foremost manufacturers in this country and designed according to specifications found the most useful and practical for this type of work. They are made throughout of forged tool steel and are correctly heat treated. Blades are 4 inches long except the ¾-inch gouge which is 5½ inches. All tools are of polished mirror finish, sharpened for uses. They are equipped with extra long 9½" handles, finished in attractive Ivory with black ends. Ferrules are brass. A compact and cardboard box with compartments for each individual tool affords protection. A genuine Washita Oil Stone for honing, size 3¼"x2"x1", furnished with each set. Complete set packed weighs 4 lbs.

SPECIFICATIONS:

No.	Size	Blade	Item	Price each
208	¼"	4"	Turning Gouge ...	**$.65**
208	½"	4"	Turning Gouge ...	**.65**
208	¾"	5½"	Turning Gouge ...	**.90**
209	½"	4"	Round Nose Chisel	**.65**
210	½"	4"	Skew Chisel	**.65**
210	1"	4"	Skew Chisel	**.90**
212	⅛"	4"	Parting Chisel	**.65**
214	½"	4"	Spear Point Chisel	**.65**

For set **$5.60**

#106 CARVING TOOL SET

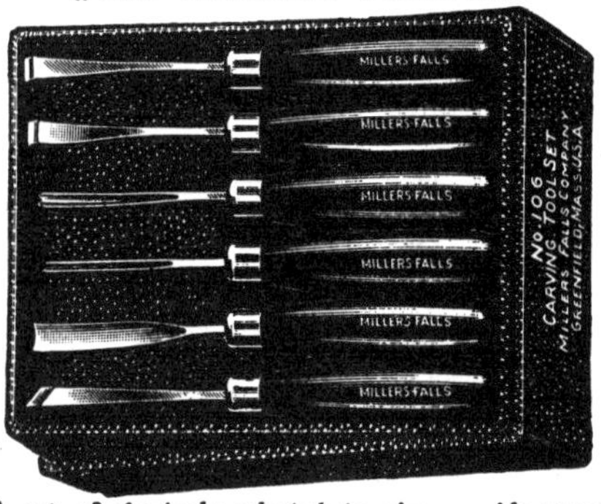

A set of six tools selected to give a wide range of operation and effects. The blades are forged from high quality steel, carefully heat-treated, nicely polished and edged. The handles, protected with nickeled ferrules, are hardwood, with a fine mahogany lacquer finish. Tools consist of:

⅜" Bent Gouge	5/16" Str. Chisel
⅜" Bent Chisel	3/32" U Tool
¼" Skew Bevel Chisel	3/32" Veining Tool

#106	Length of Tools	Weight	Price per set
	6¼ inches	¾ lb.	**$3.00**

#107 CARVING TOOL SET

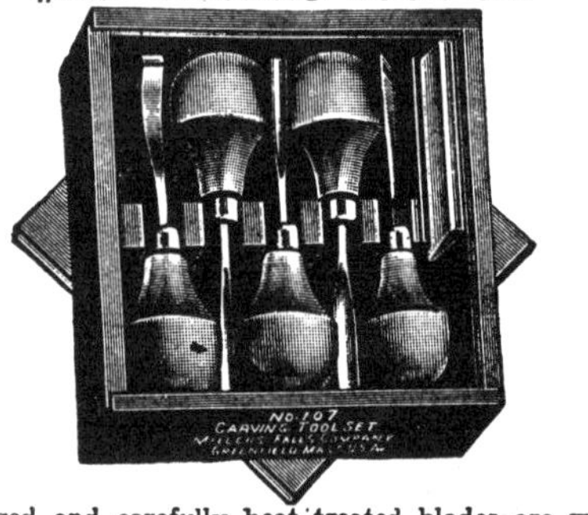

Forged and carefully **heat-treated blades are well** edged and nicely polished. The lacquered maple handles are of a special shape that fits snugly into the palm of the and. They are flatted on one side so that they are in the proper working position when picked up off the bench. Set consists of six tools as follows:

Carborundum Stone	⅜" Bent Gouge
⅜" Bent Chisel	3/32" U Tool
¼" Skew Bevel Chisel	3/32" Veining Tool

#107	Length of Tools	Weight	Price Each
	5 inches	¾ lb.	**$2.50**

GENUINE SWEDISH CHISELS AND GOUGES

SHARK BRAND — THE UTMOST IN QUALITY

The Shark Brand Chisels are forged in Sweden from best quality Swedish Charcoal Tool Steel. Scientifically heat-treated and tempered. Durable cutting edges. Sharpened, ready for use. Fitted with smooth, highly polished spotted birch handles; full turned, polished blue steel rings at ends. Manufacturing carried out under strictest control. Every chisel fully guaranteed, thereby ensuring lasting satisfaction.

CHISELS

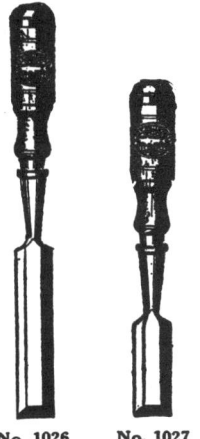
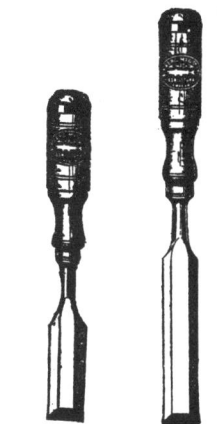

SOCKET PATTERN FIRMER CHISELS

No. 1026—Width, inches	1/8	1/4	3/8	1/2	5/8	3/4	7/8	1	1 1/4	1 1/2	1 3/4	2
Length of blade, inches	3 11/16	3 3/4	4	4 1/8	4 3/16	4 3/16	4 3/8	4 1/2	4 5/8	4 5/8	4 5/8	4 5/8
Weight a dozen, lbs.	2 1/8	2 1/4	2 1/2	2 3/4	3 1/4	3 3/4	4	4 1/2	6	6 3/4	8 3/4	9 1/2
Price $	1.40	1.40	1.50	1.60	1.75	1.75	1.95	2.00	2.30	2.65	3.15	3.90

SOCKET PATTERN BUTT CHISELS

No. 1027—Width, inches	1/8	1/4	3/8	1/2	5/8	3/4	7/8	1	1 1/4	1 1/2	1 3/4	2
Length of blade, inches	2 1/2	2 1/2	2 1/2	2 1/2	2 1/2	2 1/2	2 1/2	2 1/2	2 1/2	2 1/2	2 1/2	2 1/2
Weight a dozen, lbs.	2	2	2 1/4	2 1/4	2 1/2	3	3 1/4	3 1/2	4 1/4	4 3/4	5 1/2	6 1/4
Price $	1.40	1.40	1.50	1.60	1.75	1.75	1.95	2.00	2.30	2.65	3.15	3.90

TANGED PATTERN BUTT CHISELS

No. 1030—Width, inches	1/8	1/4	3/8	1/2	5/8	3/4	7/8	1	1 1/4	1 1/2	1 3/4	2
Length of blade, inches	2 1/2	2 1/2	2 1/2	2 1/2	2 1/2	2 1/2	2 1/2	2 1/2	2 1/2	2 1/2	2 1/2	2 1/2
Weight a dozen, lbs.	2	2	2 1/8	2 1/4	2 1/4	2 1/2	3	3 1/2	4 1/2	5	5 1/2	7 1/2
Price $	1.40	1.40	1.50	1.55	1.60	1.75	1.75	1.85	2.15	2.45	2.95	3.40

TANGED PATTERN FIRMER CHISELS

No. 1031—Width, inches	1/8	1/4	3/8	1/2	5/8	3/4	7/8	1	1 1/4	1 1/2	1 3/4	2
Length of blade, inches	3 11/16	3 3/4	4	4 1/8	4 3/16	4 3/16	4 3/8	4 1/2	4 5/8	4 5/8	4 5/8	4 5/8
Weight, a dozen lbs.	1 1/2	1 3/4	2 1/4	3	3 1/2	3 3/4	4	5	6	6 3/4	8	9 1/2
Price $	1.40	1.40	1.50	1.55	1.60	1.75	1.75	1.85	2.15	2.45	2.95	3.40

No. 1026 No. 1027 — No. 1030 No. 1031

GOUGES

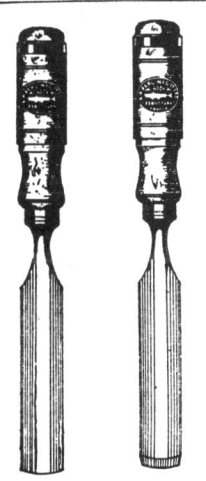
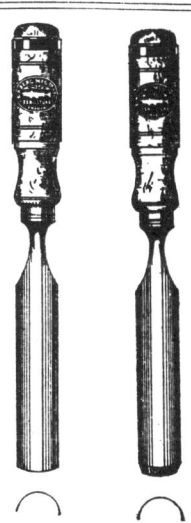

"SHARK" Brand Gouges are made from the same high quality Swedish Steel as our "SHARK" Brand Chisels. Tempered two-thirds of the length of the blade, fitted with Birch Root handles. Ground and polished. Length of blade 4 3/4". Packed one-half dozen in a box.

Half Hollow with Spotted Birch Handles.
9270 Outside Cut (Inside bevel)
9271 Inside Cut (Outside bevel)

1/8 in.	$1.80
3/16 in.	1.80
1/4 in.	1.80
3/8 in.	1.85
1/2 in.	1.95
5/8 in.	2.00
3/4 in.	2.05
7/8 in.	2.20
1 in.	2.30
1 1/4 in.	2.55
1 1/2 in.	3.30
1 3/4 in.	3.75

Full Hollow with Spotted Birch Handles.
9280 Outside Cut (Inside bevel)
9281 Inside Cut (Outside bevel)

1/8 in.	$1.85
1/4 in.	1.85
3/8 in.	2.15
1/2 in.	2.25
5/8 in.	2.35
3/4 in.	2.45
7/8 in.	2.60
1 in.	2.70
1 1/4 in.	3.15
1 1/2 in.	4.00
1 3/4 in.	4.50
2 in.	5.00

No. 9270 No. 9271 — No. 9280 No. 9281

No. 275 • UTICA CIRCULAR UTILITY SNIP

Dropped forged from Alloy Steel hardened and tempered to cut. Designed specially for cutting out intricate patterns and curves.

Size	7 1/4"	12"
Price	$5.20	$2.55

HAND FORGED ALLOY STEEL COLD CHISELS

Made of the very highest grade special formula steel, insuring excellent service and longer life. They are tempered the full length of the long flat taper, thus permitting many resharpenings without causing tool to become too blunt or to lose its original temper.

No.	Stock	Length	Cutting Edge	Price
105	1/4"	4"	3/8"	$0.30
106	5/16"	5"	7/16"	.35
107	3/8"	6"	1/2"	.40
108	7/16"	6"	5/8"	.45
109	1/2"	6"	5/8"	.50
110	5/8"	7"	3/4"	.75
111	3/4"	8"	7/8"	.90
112	7/8"	8"	1"	1.25
113	1"	9"	1 1/8"	1.50

DROP FORGED LAID BLADE REGULAR TINNER'S SNIPS

Bar tool steel laid blades. Gun metal blue finish handles.

Number	Full Length	Length of Cut	Price
6 1/2	15 1/2"	4"	$4.35
7	14"	4"	3.60
8	13"	3 1/2"	2.95
9	12"	3"	2.55
10	11"	2 1/2"	2.35
11	9"	2 1/4"	1.75
12	8"	2"	1.50

The length of cut is the standard cutting edge of blade.

GOOD TOOLS SAVE TIME AND EXASPERATION

IMPORTED SWEDISH WOOD CARVING KNIVES

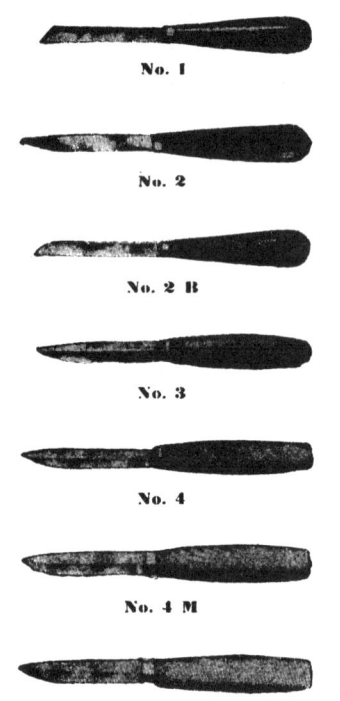
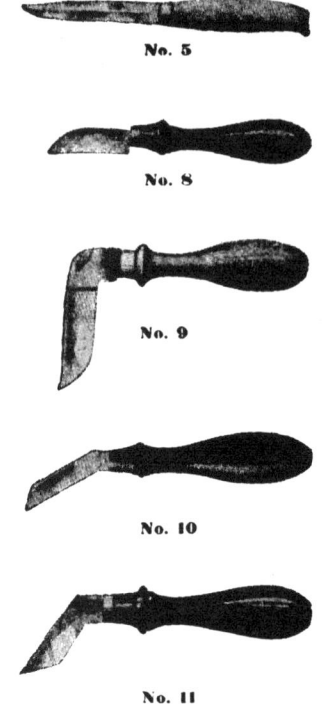

No. 1. "Berg's," black lacquered oval birch handle, oxidized steel ferrule. Highly polished blade. Tang extends through handle and is riveted. Length of blade 3½ in.
Price $1.50

No. 2. "Berg's," black lacquered oval birch handle, oxidized steel ferrule. Highly polished blade. Tang extends through handle and is riveted. Length of blade 3½ in.
Price $1.50

No. 2 B. "Berg's," black lacquered oval birch handle, oxidized steel ferrule. Highly polished blade. Tang extends through handle and is riveted. Length of blade 3½ in.
Price $1.50

No. 3. "Berg's," polished and varnished oval curly birch root handle. Ornamented nickelplated bolster of German silver. Highly polished blade. Tang extends through handle and is riveted. Length of blade 3½ in.
Price $1.35

No. 4. "Berg's," same as No. 3 but has a polished and varnished oval birch handle. Ornamented brass bolster. Polished blade. Tang extends through handle and is riveted Length of blade 3½ in.
Price $1.25

No. 4 M. "Berg's," polished and varnished oval birch handle. Nickelplated steel bolster, polished blade. Tang extends through handle and is riveted. Length of blade 3 in.
Price $1.45

No. 4 L. Polished and varnished oval birch handle. Nickelplated steel bolster. Polished blade. Tang extends through handle and is riveted. Length of blade 2¾ in.
Price $1.35

No. 5. Polished and varnished oval curly birch root handle. Nickelplated brass bolster. Highly polished blade. Tang extends through handle and is riveted. Length of blade 4 in.
Price $2.00

No. 8. Black lacquered round birch handle, oxidized steel ferrule. Polished blade. Used for stencil cutting. Length of blade 2 in.
Price $1.20

No. 9. Polished and varnished round birch handle, oxidized steel ferrule. Polished blade. Used for wood carving. Length of blade 1½ in.
Price $1.35

No. 10. Black lacquered round birch handle, oxidized steel ferrule. Polished blade. Used for wood carving. Length of blade 1¾ in.
Price $1.25

No. 11. Black lacquered round birch handle, oxidized steel ferrule. Polished blade. Used for wood carving. Length of blade 1⅝ in.
Price $1.25

No. 12. Spoon Knife polished and varnished round birch handle, oxidized steel ferrule. Polished blade. Used for grooving and hollowing. Blade is ground and sharpened on both edges and rounded end, therefore has cutting edge all around. Tang extends through handle and is riveted. Length of blade 2½ in.
Price $1.35

No. 513. Round birch handle. Polished blade. Used for grooving and hollowing. Length of blade 1½ in.
Price $1.30

No. 13. Black lacquered, rectangular birch handle. Polished blade. Used for wood carving. Length of blade 2 in.
Price $1.25

No. 14. Polished and varnished round birch handle, oxidized steel ferrule. Polished blade. Used for wood carving. Length of blade 1⅝ in.
Price $1.35

No. 15. Polished and varnished oval birch handle, brass bolster. Polished blade. Length of blade 4¾ in.
Price $2.00

No. 27. Polished and varnished oval birch handle. Brass bolster or ferrule. Polished blade. Length of blade 4½ in.
Price $1.90

No. 402. Polished round birch handle, oxidized steel ferrule. Polished blade. These knives are made with long and short points, and should be ordered as follows:
No. 402 Long Point.
No. 402 Short Point.
Used for wood carving and stencil cutting. Length of blade 2½ in.
Price $0.75

STOEGER SPECIAL CHECKERING AND ENGRAVING TOOLS

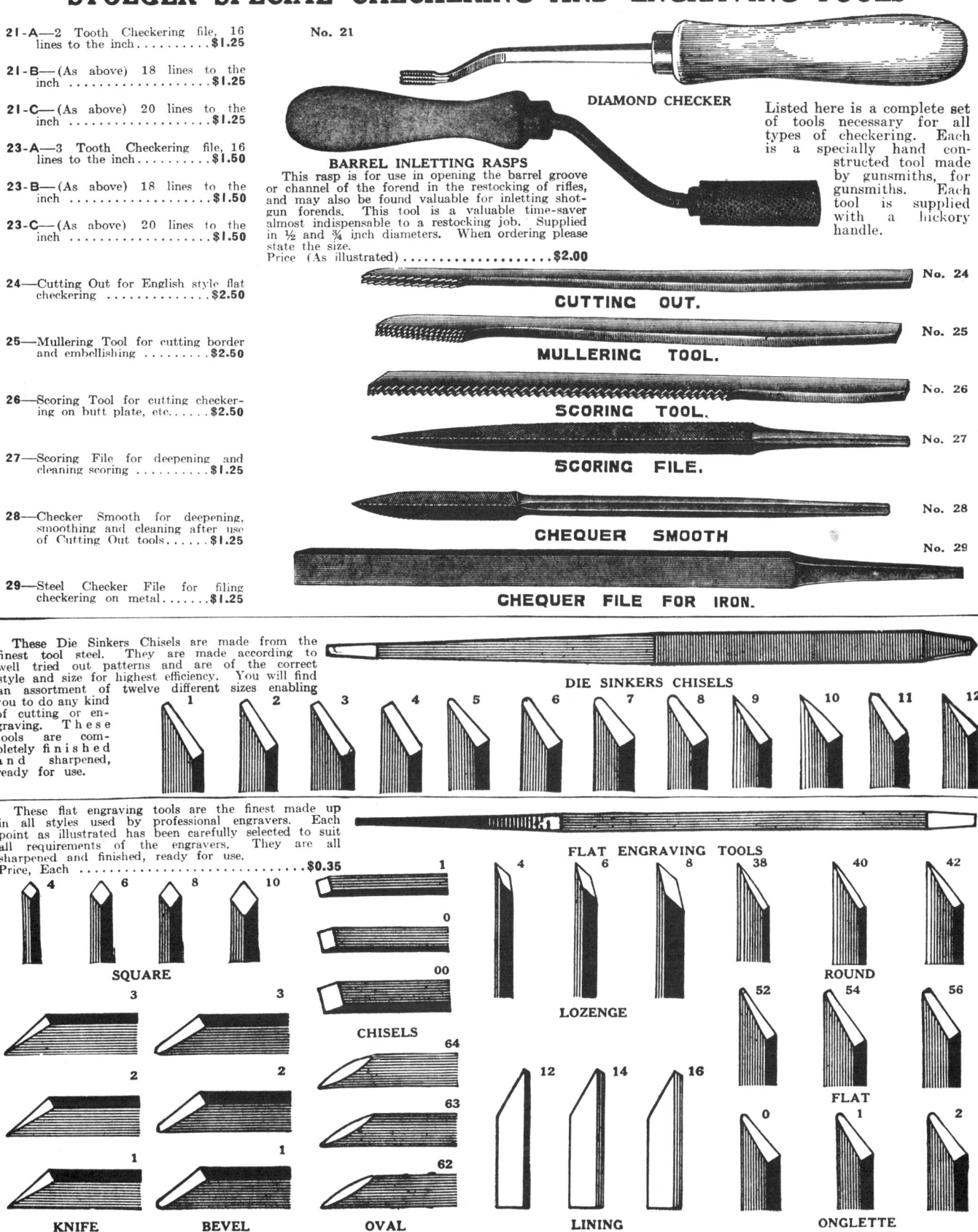

21-A—2 Tooth Checkering file, 16 lines to the inch $1.25

21-B—(As above) 18 lines to the inch $1.25

21-C—(As above) 20 lines to the inch $1.25

23-A—3 Tooth Checkering file, 16 lines to the inch $1.50

23-B—(As above) 18 lines to the inch $1.50

23-C—(As above) 20 lines to the inch $1.50

24—Cutting Out for English style flat checkering $2.50

25—Mullering Tool for cutting border and embellishing $2.50

26—Scoring Tool for cutting checkering on butt plate, etc. $2.50

27—Scoring File for deepening and cleaning scoring $1.25

28—Checker Smooth for deepening, smoothing and cleaning after use of Cutting Out tools $1.25

29—Steel Checker File for filing checkering on metal $1.25

No. 21

DIAMOND CHECKER

BARREL INLETTING RASPS
This rasp is for use in opening the barrel groove or channel of the forend in the restocking of rifles, and may also be found valuable for inletting shotgun forends. This tool is a valuable time-saver almost indispensable to a restocking job. Supplied in ½ and ¾ inch diameters. When ordering please state the size.
Price (As illustrated) $2.00

Listed here is a complete set of tools necessary for all types of checkering. Each is a specially hand constructed tool made by gunsmiths, for gunsmiths. Each tool is supplied with a hickory handle.

No. 24 — CUTTING OUT.
No. 25 — MULLERING TOOL.
No. 26 — SCORING TOOL.
No. 27 — SCORING FILE.
No. 28 — CHEQUER SMOOTH
No. 29 — CHEQUER FILE FOR IRON.

These Die Sinkers Chisels are made from the finest tool steel. They are made according to well tried out patterns and are of the correct style and size for highest efficiency. You will find an assortment of twelve different sizes enabling you to do any kind of cutting or engraving. These tools are completely finished and sharpened, ready for use.

DIE SINKERS CHISELS
1 2 3 4 5 6 7 8 9 10 11 12

These flat engraving tools are the finest made up in all styles used by professional engravers. Each point as illustrated has been carefully selected to suit all requirements of the engravers. They are all sharpened and finished, ready for use.
Price, Each $0.35

FLAT ENGRAVING TOOLS

SQUARE — 4, 6, 8, 10
CHISELS — 1, 0, 00
LOZENGE — 4, 6, 8
ROUND — 38, 40, 42
KNIFE — 3, 2, 1
BEVEL — 3, 2, 1
OVAL — 64, 63, 62
LINING — 12, 14, 16
FLAT — 52, 54, 56
ONGLETTE — 0, 1, 2

SPECIAL TOOLS A SPECIALTY

PROFESSIONAL GUNSMITH'S NECESSITIES
SPECIAL VISE JAWS

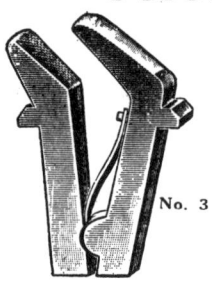  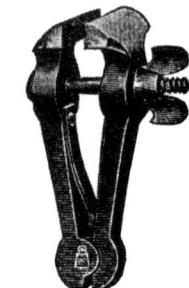

Steel Angle Jaw
Model 1 is made of iron with spring and aluminum jaws. 3⅛ inches wide. Specially recommended for holding shotgun barrels and other gun parts.
Price $4.25

Wood Jaws
Model 2 is a wooden Vise Jaw made of the best quality hardened wood with spring 3⅛ inches wide. Particularly recommended for holding polished parts, etc.
Price $1.75

Aluminum Jaws
SPANNER WITH ANGLE JAW ... made of forged steel, black with head carefully polished. Length about 5 inches. Weight about 2¼ pounds.
Price $3.75

Special Hand Vise
This excellently made little tool is of great assistance for working on small parts, springs, etc., and is practically indispensable. Length, 4¾ inches.
Price $1.75

SPRING SPANNER

This Spring Spanner is well-made, hardened and polished. It is nearly indispensable in fitting main springs in any sidelock gun.
Price $2.50

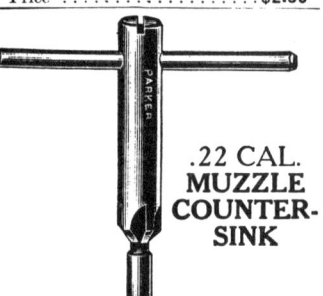

.22 CAL. MUZZLE COUNTERSINK

A well made tool, with a guide peg or pilot and a correctly angled cutting edge for refinishing the muzzle end of a .22 caliber rifle to improve or restore its accuracy.
Price $5.00

ADJUSTABLE SPRING SPANNER

This Adjustable Spring Spanner is made of the finest Styrian Spring Steel very carefully hardened and tempered and finely polished. With this one spanner it is possible to clamp the very smallest pistol springs as well as the

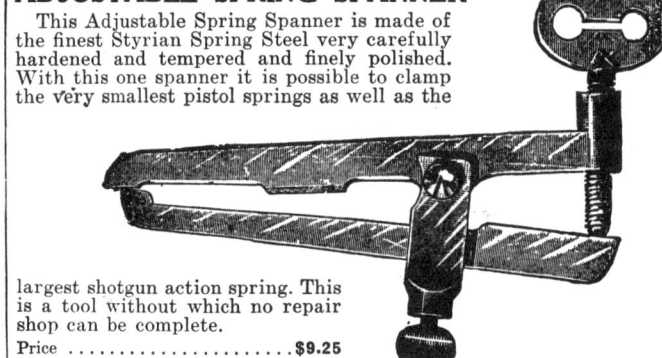

largest shotgun action spring. This is a tool without which no repair shop can be complete.
Price $9.25

REVOLVER SPRING PLIER

This special imported plier is especially made for the easy compressing and fitting of springs. It is particularly useful in revolver repair work.
Price $1.25

Gunsmith Hammers

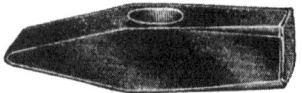

The ordinary type of hammer is absolutely unfitted for gunsmithing, and yet a well made hammer of the correct shape and proportions is a necessity. Such hammers are not easily available, so we offer the most approved style in various weights. Price without handle.
Hammer, 3½ oz., Price $0.50
Hammer, 7 oz., Price 0.60
Hammer, 9 oz., Price 0.75
Hammer, 18 oz., Price 1.00

SIGHT SPANNER

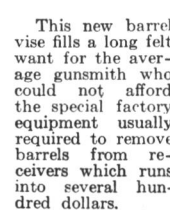

This Spanner is fastened into the vise and is intended for holding the smallest part such as front sight, small pins, etc.
Price $2.25

MARBLES BROKEN SHELL EXTRACTOR

Every sportsman should carry one of these for his rifle, absolutely necessary to remove broken cases from chamber of rifle. The best and easiest way without harming rifle chamber. State caliber when ordering.
Price $0.75

BARREL VISE

This new barrel vise fills a long felt want for the average gunsmith who could not afford the special factory equipment usually required to remove barrels from receivers which runs into several hundred dollars.

No matter how hard the barrel is stuck in the receiver, you can remove it with this vise. Weight, 33 lbs., has a 1⅝" screw with a ¾" hole through the head. Place the barrel between two pieces of grooved hardwood (comes with vise), put an iron bar through the screw head and tighten. The tremendous pressure is evenly distributed around the barrel making it impossible to move or mar. We have never found a barrel that we could not easily remove and install. No gunsmith shop is complete without a Barrel Vise. A few jobs and it pays for itself.
Price $12.00

ANSON HAMMER KEY

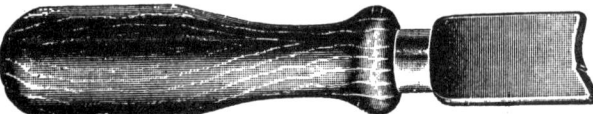

This key is a tremendous time and temper saver in the removal of hammers from box lock guns of the Anson & Deeley type, and should be part of every gunsmith's equipment.
Price $1.50

EVERYTHING FOR THE GUNSMITH

GUNSMITH'S AND GUNSTOCKER'S VISES

These vises are made of the finest material and are of the latest design to give a life time of service. They are guaranteed not to chip, crack or break. The jaw vises are made of tool steel, accurately machined and heat treated. They are dowelled into the jaws for instant exchange when worn or damaged. Gripping surfaces are machine knurled. The handles with the ball ends are made of one piece from cold rolled steel and therefore, cannot come off. A hardened steel washer under the screw head prevents wear and eliminates end-play. The swivel base models lock positively in any position and the forged steel lock bolt is equipped with teeth which mash into the gear-like corrugations in the malleable iron bench plate. The bases of all vises are flat and no cutting into bench tops is required for fastening same.

Malleable Iron Vises

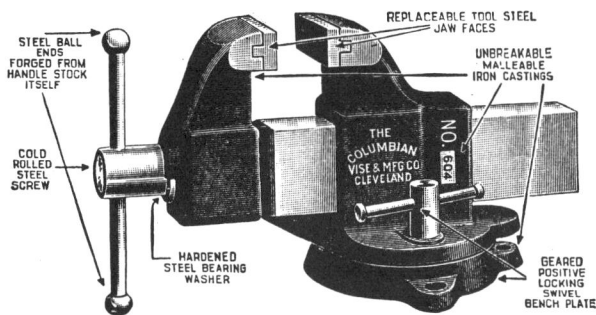

SWIVEL BASES—600 SERIES

These vises are built for heavy duty with swivel base to allow setting in any desired angle. The greatest value for the money.

Vise	Jaw Width	Jaws Open	Weight Lbs.	Price
602½	2½	3½	15	$12.00
603	3	4½	25	13.00
603½	3½	5½	34	15.00
604	4	6	42	17.00

ADJUSTABLE JAW SWIVEL BASE —400 SERIES

Recommended for general purpose use in all shops having a wide variety of work. When removing pin the back jaw swivels for gripping tapered or irregular pieces.

Vise	Jaw Width	Jaws Open	Weight Lbs.	Price
403	3	4½	26	$17.50
403½	3½	5	35	20.00
404	4	5½	45	24.00

COMBINATION PIPE VISES —200 SERIES

This vise serves a double purpose. It has an extra set of jaws to allow for clamping round objects which is sometimes very desirable. The round jaws can be removed if not wanted and are also interchangeable or reversible.

Vise	Jaw Width	Jaws Open	Holds Pipes	Weight Lb.	Price
203½	3½	4	⅛-2½	36	$17.50
204½	4½	5	⅛-3½	60	24.00

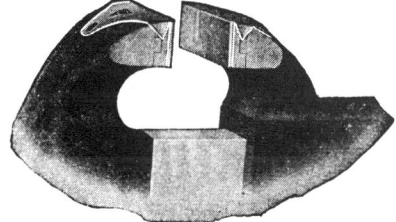

COPPER JAW CAPS

Carefully designed to fit snugly over the jaw and cover the knurled steel vise faces. They can be slipped on the vise readily and removed whenever regular gripping vise faces are required.

Jaw Width, Inches	3	3½	4	4½	5	5½	6
Price Per Pair	$1.50	$1.80	$2.10	$2.50	$3.10	$4.00	$5.00

Cast Iron Vises

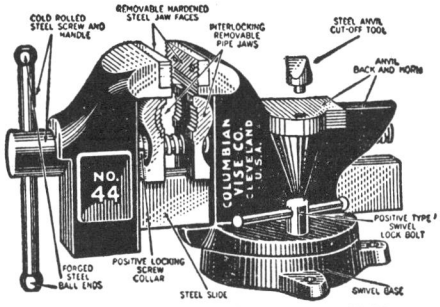

UTILITY VISES

Low priced but very serviceable group of vises to provide a selection for the home workshop and other general uses. They are made out of close grained grey iron castings and the heavy steel slide will provide the necessary strength.

Vise	Width Jaws	Jaws Open	Holds Pipe	Weight Lbs.	Price
43	3	3½	1½	14	$3.00
43½	3½	4	1½	17	4.50
44	4	4½	2	28	7.50

HOMESHOP VISES

The homeshop vises are of very sturdy construction. No. 30 comes with stationary base. Nos. 31, 32, 33 have swivel base. Nos. 30 and 31 are equipped with steel jaw faces. Has also special Concave jaws for holding barrels or tubing.

STATIONARY BASE — **SWIVEL BASE**

Vise	Width Jaws	Jaws Open	Weight Lbs.	Price	Vise	Width Jaws	Jaws Open	Weight Lbs.	Price
30	3	3½	11	$2.00	31	3	3½	13	$2.75
					32	3½	4	15	4.00
					33	4	4¼	21	5.00

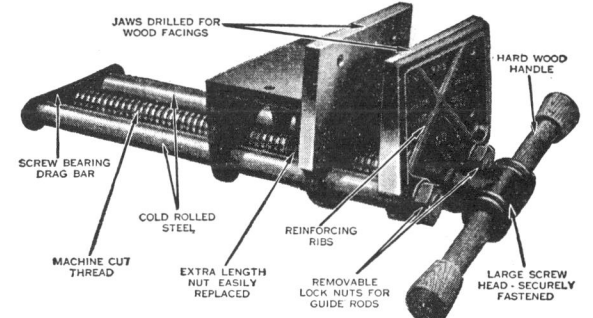

GUNSTOCKER'S VISES

These vises are designed for general use in wood working. Construction of same is simple, durable and reliable with fewest possible number of parts. Heavy steel screw with double fast round thread provides positive action.

PLAIN FRONT JAW

Vise	Jaw Size	Jaws Open	Weight Lbs.	Price
5C	4x7	9	22	$8.00
3C	4x10	12	30	10.00

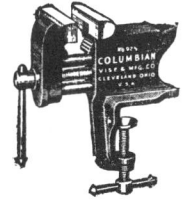

CLAMP BASE VISES

A handy compact outfit can be set up instantly on a bench table or other handy support.

Vise	Width Jaws	Jaws Open	Weight Lbs.	Price
92	2	2	2¼	$1.00
92½	2½	2¾	3½	1.40
93	3	3½	7	2.00

A NECESSITY NO GUNSMITH CAN BE WITHOUT

HIGH QUALITY PLANES, DRILLS AND AUGURS

#56 LOW ANGLE BLOCK PLANE

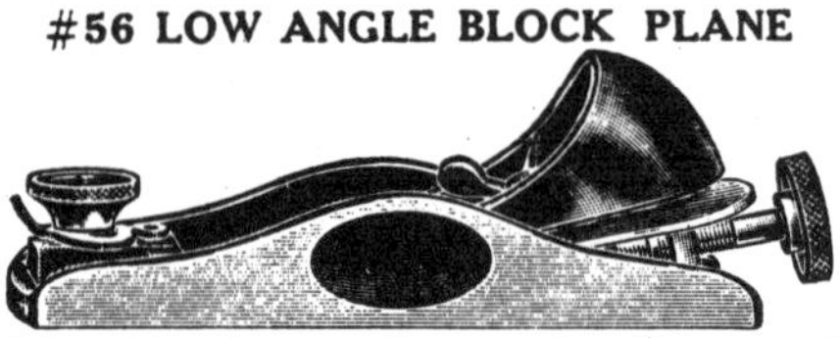

Adjustable throat. Screw end adjustment of cutter. Cutters made of one solid piece of fine, high carbon steel set at an angle of 12 degrees, with the bottom making it particularly well suited for cutting across the grain of hard woods.

No.	Length	Cutter	Weight	Trimming	Price Each
56	6″	1⅜″	1¼ lb.	Black Enamel	**$2.10**

#141 PLAIN BRACE

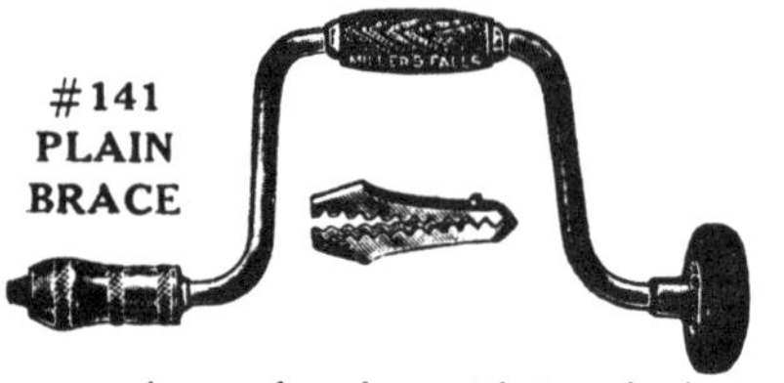

On many classes of work a ratchet mechanism on a brace is unnecessary and a plain or sleeve brace fills the requirements. Has Barber chuck with alligator jaws. Head has a plain bearing and is screwed securely to the quill. Head and handle mahogany stained hardwood. Exposed metal parts polished.

No.	Sweep	Weight	Price Each
141	12″	1⅞ lb.	**$1.10**

AUGUR BIT SETS

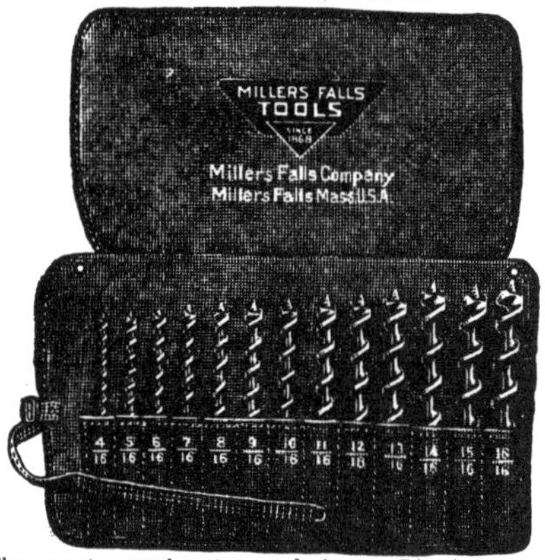

The most popular type of Auger Bit for general all-round use, distinguished by a solid stem or core running the entire length of the twist, making a very rigid, powerful tool throughout and putting plenty of strength in the head where it is needed most. The head has two extension lips and spurs and two cutting edges. The deep, clean thread on the screw is pitched to pull the bit through hard or soft wood and make a smooth, straight hole. Sizes below are in sixteenths of an inch.

Beautifully finished with a high polish. Length of twist, 4 inches to 5½ inches; length overall, 7½ inches to 9½ inches. Supplied in heavy water-proof fabricoid roll case as illustrated.

Set No.	Assortment by Sixteenths of an Inch	Price
32½	4, 5, 6, 7, 8, 9, 10, 11, 12, 13, 14, 15, and 16, one each	**$8.05**
25½	4, 5, 6, 7, 8, 9, 10, 11, 12, 14, and 16, one each	**6.65**
24	4, 5, 7, 9, 11 and 12, one each and 6, 8 and 10, two each	**6.45**
22½	5, 7, 9, 10, 11, and 12 one each and 4, 6, and 8, two each	**6.30**
21	5, 6, 7, 9, 10, 11, and 12, one each and 4 and 8, two each	**5.95**
20½	4, 5, 6, 7, 8, 10, 12, 14, and 16, one each	**5.25**
18¾	4, 5, 6, 8, 10, 12, 14, and 16, one each	**4.70**
18	4, 5, 6, 7, 8, 9, 10, 11, and 12, one each	**4.85**
17½	4, 6, 8, 10, 12, 14, and 16, one each	**4.35**
15¼	4, 5, 6, 8, 10, 12, and 16, one each	**4.00**
14	4, 6, 8, 10, 12, and 16, one each	**3.50**
11¼	4, 5, 6, 8, 10, and 12, one each	**3.10**

#29A BREAST DRILL

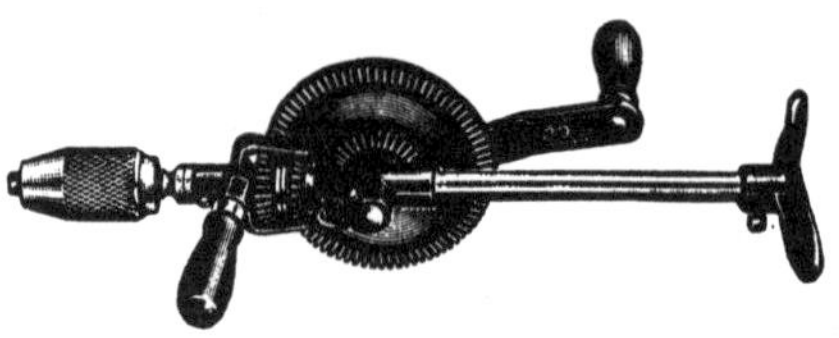

Strong black enameled frame and breastplate connected by a polished steel shank. Two speeds with ratios of 3 to 1 and 1 to 1. Large gear red enameled. Steel pinions. Ball thrust bearing on spindle. Chuck has three jaws with protected springs and holds 0 to ½″ round shank drills. Side and crank handle mahogany finished hardwood.

No.	Capacity	Length	Weight	Price Each
#29A	½″	16½″	4⅝ lb.	**$4.95**

FORGED COUNTERSINK

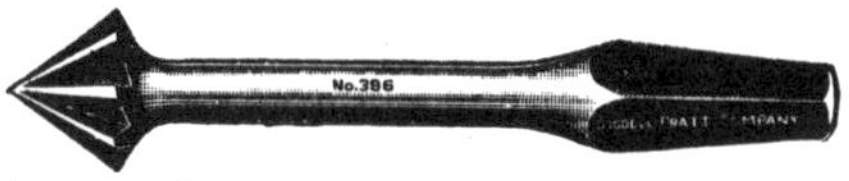

An unusually fine countersink forged from the very best quality tool steel, correctly hardened and well polished, then carefully tempered to straw color to stand the gruelling work expected of it. The cutting edges are clean and sharp. This tool has an enormous variety of uses and is a necessity to every gunsmith.

No.	Extreme Diameter	Price
396	¾″	**$ .50**
691	1¼″	**.75**

STOCKMAKER'S 18″ BIT

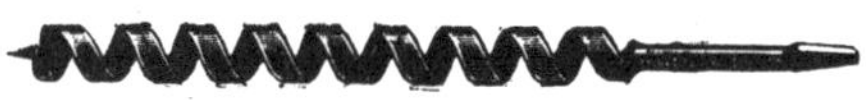

A long single twist bit without spur which is specially efficient for boring holes through length of stock for shank and stock bolt. Cuts easily and freely to the full length of the twist and makes an exceptionally smooth hole. Length of twist 12″, overall length 18″. High overall polish.

No.	Size	Price
4	¼″	**$1.00**
6	⅜″	**1.00**
8	½″	**1.00**
10	⅝″	**1.00**
12	¾″	**1.10**
14	⅞″	**1.25**
16	1″	**1.50**

STOCKMAKER'S 18″ QUICK CUTTING BIT

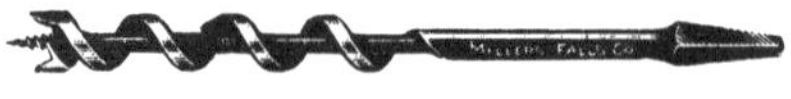

A long bit with solid stem or core, very rigid and fast cutting, for use in boring stocks for stock bolt.

No.	Size	Price
4	¼″	**$ .80**
6	⅜″	**.80**
8	½″	**1.00**
10	⅝″	**1.25**
12	¾″	**1.50**
14	⅞″	**1.75**
16	1″	**2.00**

#55 ADJUSTABLE BLOCK PLANE

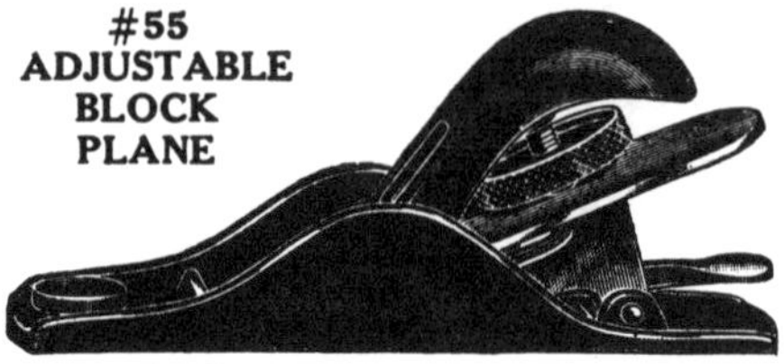

Lever end adjustment. Screw operated cap clamp. Bottoms polished. Sides black enameled.

No.	Length	Cutter	Weight	Trimming	Price Each
55	5½″	1⅜″	⅞ lb.	Black Enamel	**$1.00**

#30 RATCHET BRACE

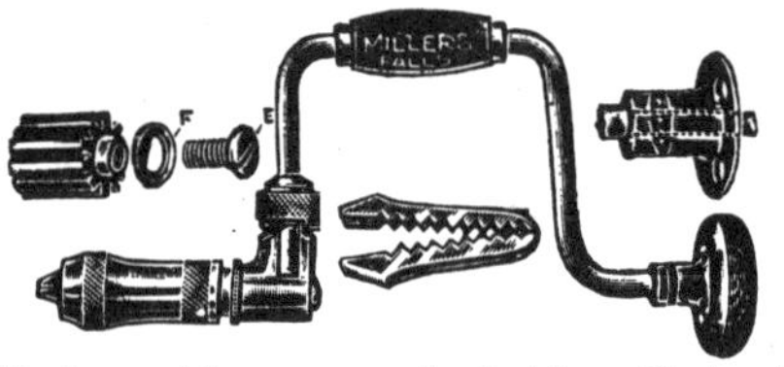

This brace takes square shank bits. Equipped with Barber chuck with self-opening, forged steel alligator jaws. Steel clad, ball bearing head. Handle has inserted metal rings. Boxed ratchet with ring shift. Head and handle finely finished tropical hardwood. All exposed metal parts nicely polished, nickel plated and buffed.

No.	Sweep	Weight	Price Each
30	14″	3⅜ lbs.	**$5.40**

BENCH DRILLS

Capacity 0 to ⅜ Inch

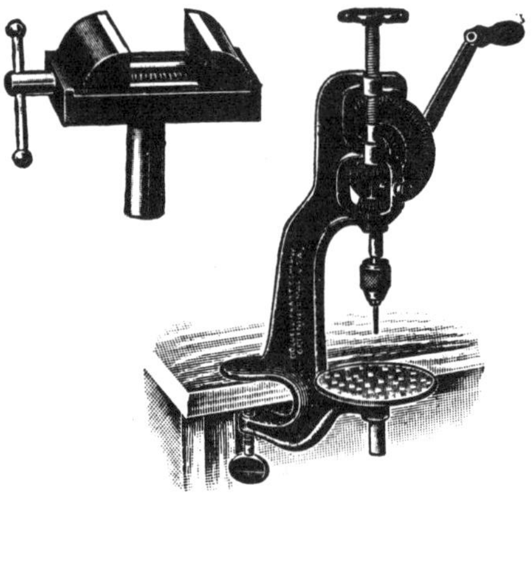

These drills are larger and heavier than the above and are equipped with a three-jawed chuck holding 0 to ⅜ inch round shanks. Also equipped with two speeds changed by means of the shifter knob on the front of the frame. Hand operated screw feed. Height above bench, 18 inches.

A vise which fts the table bracket with 2½-inch jaws that open 2 inches can be supplied when specified.

Eight drill points, 1⁄16 to 11⁄64 inch in diameter, furnished with each machine.

Iron parts finished in red and black enamel, steel parts polished.

			Price Each
No. 9	Without vise	WYIBD	**$14.00**
No. 9½	With vise	WYIJL	**17.50**
No. 217	Vise only	WYILN	**3.50**

No. 1 GUNSTOCKER'S SAW

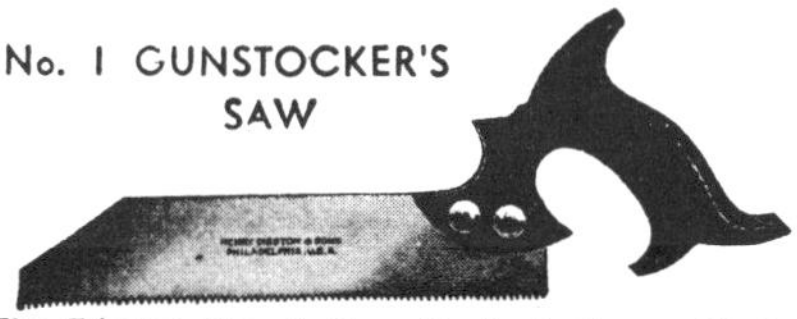

The Disston No. 1 Gun Stocker's Saw. Blade is extremely thin. Designed for small accurate work. The teeth are shaped to make a fine, exact cut; 15 points to the inch. Blade of Saw of Disston steel with Disston temper. Open handle, applewood; brass screws.

Length	Width	Weight	Price
7½ inches	1¼ inches	6 ounces	**$1.10**

No. 71 DOVETAIL SAW

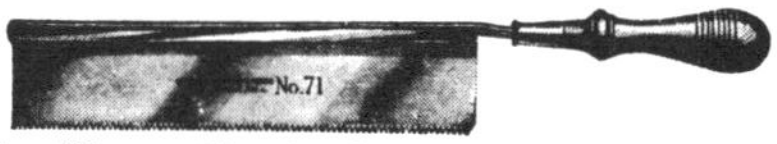

The Disston No. 71 Dovetail Saw has an offset handle and blade, to permit cutting with blade flush. Blade of Disston steel, 26 gauge; 17 points to inch. Brass-plated back supports the blade, and extends into the handle. Hardwood handle, comfortable grip; brass-plated ferrule with rivet through ferrule, tang and handle.

Length	Width	Weight	Price
10 Inches	1½ Inches	½ Pound	**$2.00**

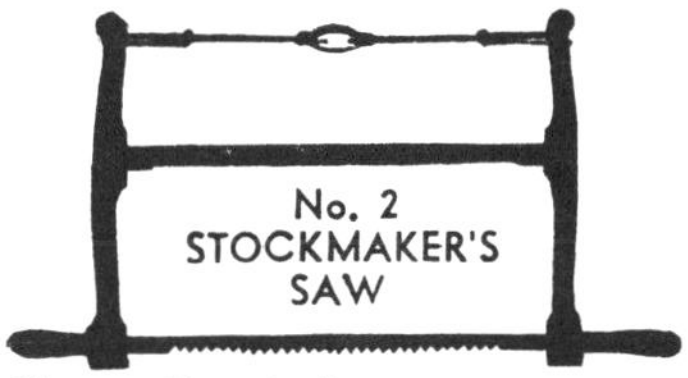

No. 2 STOCKMAKER'S SAW

The Disston No. 2 Stockmaker Saw is very popular amongst gunsmiths and stock makers. It allows very correct trimming and cuts speedily inasmuch as it has a longer saw blade than the conventional type of saw. Blade 10 points.

Length	Width	Weight	Price
14 Inches	3/16 Inch	27 Ounces	**$1.70**
18 Inches	3/16 Inch	2 Pounds	**1.75**

No. 2 TURNING SAW BLADES ONLY

14 Inches	3/16 Inch	1/16 Pound	**$.27**
18 Inches	3/16 Inch	9/16 Pound	**$.35**

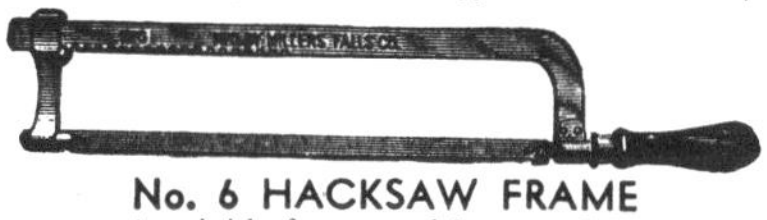

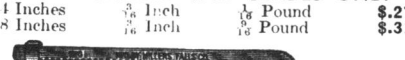

No. 6 HACKSAW FRAME

A compact, rigid frame with a solid back and adjustable for 8 to 12-inch blades by moving the sliding end post. Tension on blade secured by turning handle. Blade can be traced in four directions. One 10-inch blade furnished with each frame. Entire tool well polished and nickel plated. Attractive tropical hardwood handle.

No.	Capacity	Depth	Stock	Weight	Price Each
6	28–12″	¾″	3/16 x 13/16	1½ lb.	**$2.35**

No. 6 STOCK SHAPER SAW

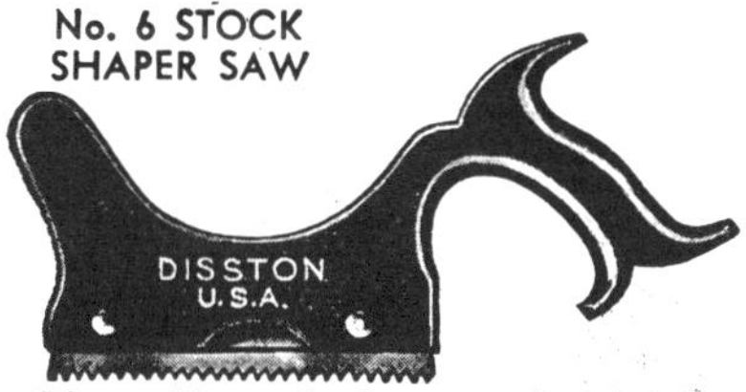

The Disston No. 6 Stock Shaper Saw is adjustable to cut various depths up to ¾ inch; concave curve in frame to receive hand when extra pressure is desired. Blade of Disston steel; 8 points to inch. Handle and frame of one piece of hardwood; frame slotted to receive blade which is fastened by two saw screws.

Length	Width	Weight	Price
6 Inches	1⅝ Inches	12 Ounces	**$1.05**

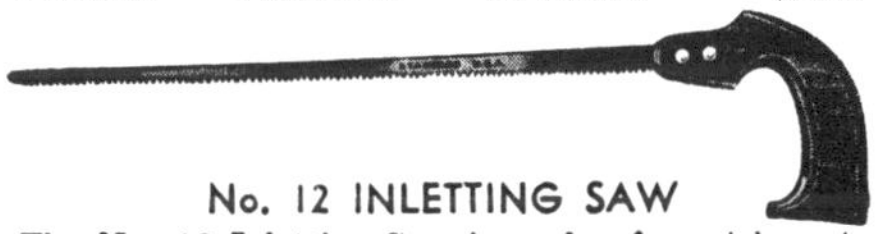

No. 12 INLETTING SAW

The No. 12 Inletting Saw is made of special steel, 10 points to the inch. Open-grip handle.

Length of Blade	Weight Each	Price Each
10 Inches	5 Ounces	**$.35**
12 Inches	5 Ounces	**.35**
14 Inches	6 Ounces	**.35**

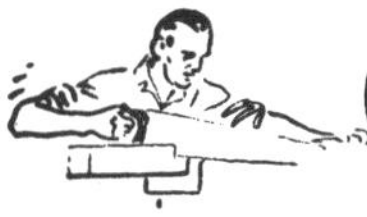

GUNSTOCKER'S HAND SAWS and DRAW KNIVES

Genuine Swedish "Sandvik" Hand Saws

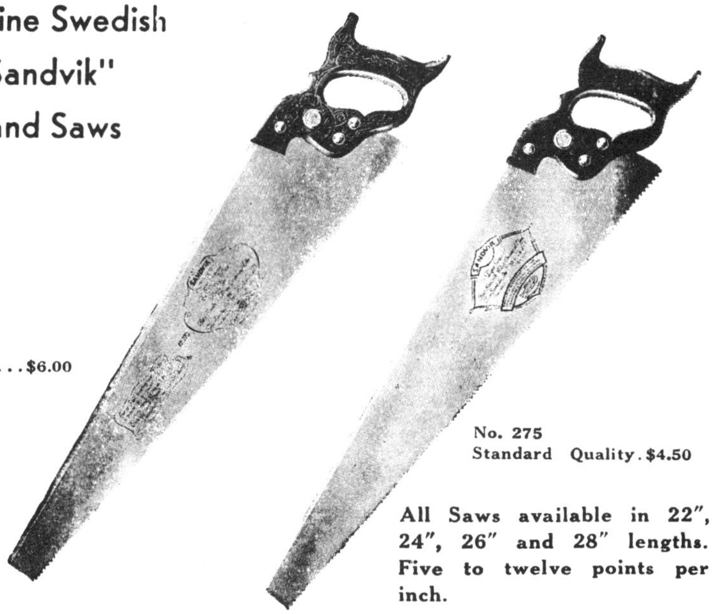

No. 270
Extra Quality...$6.00

No. 275
Standard Quality.$4.50

All Saws available in 22″, 24″, 26″ and 28″ lengths. Five to twelve points per inch.

THE MATERIAL in these Saws is SANDVIK charcoal alloy steel, long known and esteemed in all parts of the World. The composition of the Sandvik Saw Steel gives the saws a degree of sharpness and elasticity never attained before. HARDENING: The special method of hardening ensures an exceptional flexibility of the blade combined with the greatest cutting power, without making the teeth unduly hard. DESIGN AND FINISH: The blades are well balanced and highly polished. The weight is distributed in such a way as to make the sawing light and convenient. HANDLES: Are of Pear Wood and polished, fitted to the blade so as to transmit the power to the row of the teeth in the most efficient way.

GUNSTOCKER'S DRAW KNIVES

No. 5 DRAW KNIFE

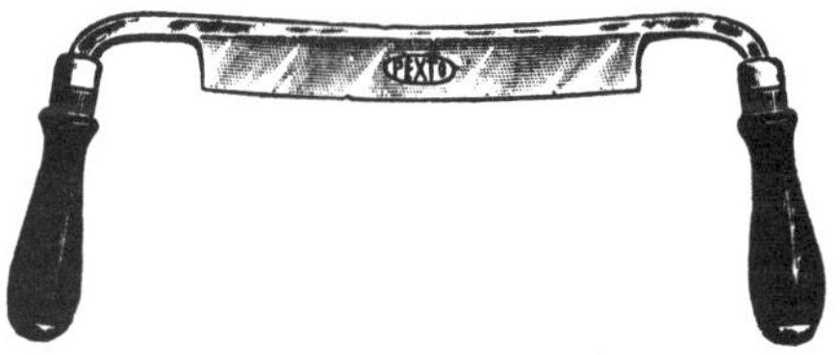

Forged from special steel and fitted with heavy ferrules and metal capped handles. The knives are highly polished.

Length	8″	9″	10″	12″
Price	**$1.25**	**$1.35**	**$1.45**	**$1.55**

Nos. 3 and 4 DRAW KNIVES

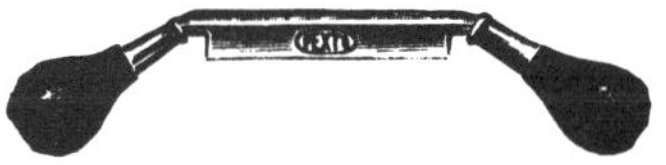

Forged from special steel with fully polished blade and round ebonized handles. The handles are set at an angle of 45° with the blade.

No. 3	6″ Blade	Price **$.90**
No. 4	4″ Blade	Price **$.75**

No. 15 DRAW KNIFE

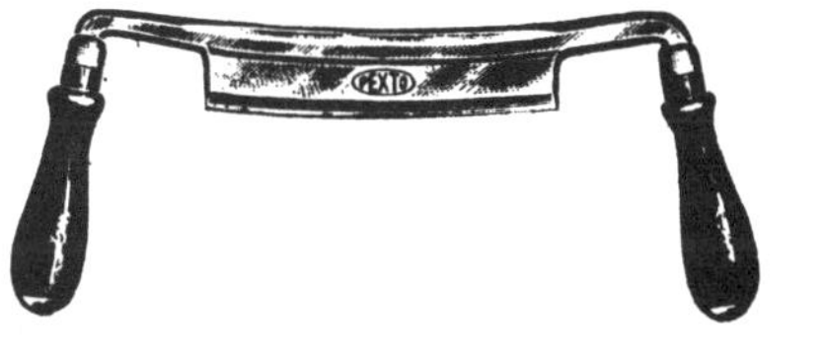

Of heavier metal especially recommended for heavy duty with a razor blade style.

Length	6″	7″	8″	9″	10″	12″	14″
Price	**$1.15**	**$1.25**	**$1.35**	**$1.45**	**$1.55**	**$1.65**	**$1.75**

No. 17 EXTRA HEAVY DRAW KNIFE

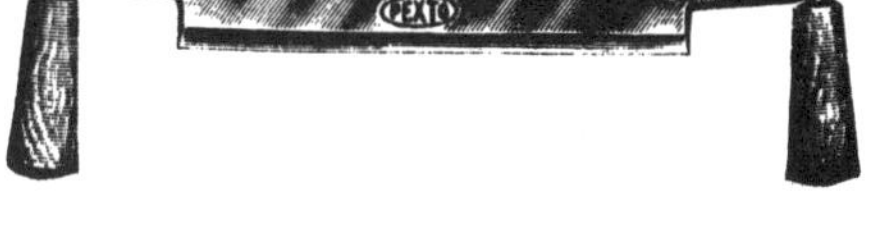

A simply constructed knife with an extra heavy forged blade to stand rough usage.

Length	12″	14″
Price	**$2.60**	**$2.95**

UTICA SCREW DRIVERS, METAL SHEARS AND CHISELS

SHORT HEAVY DUTY SCREW DRIVER

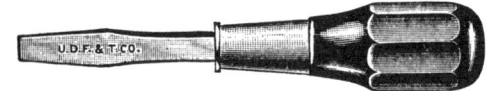

HAND FORGED

Utica Short Heavy Duty Screw Driver, forged from special Alloy Steel, heat treated. Handle shaped to fit the hand in its natural, most powerful gripping position. These Screw Drivers are guaranteed to break any screw which they fit without any injury to the Screw Driver. Blades are hardened the full length. Made of square steel, permitting use of wrench for starting or tightening stubborn screws.

No.	Stock	Blade	Price
912	3/8"	3 1/8"	$.85

MIDGET KNOB SCREW DRIVER

HAND FORGED

A convenient short Screw Driver for close work.
The Midget Knob Screw Driver is one which will be found of particular use to gunsmiths. Its small size and great strength, adapt it very well for the loosening of screws which are sometimes nearly impossible to move. Made of special forged steel, carefully heat treated and carefully finished to allow maximum strength combined with necessary elasticity to prevent breakage.

No.	Stock	Blade	Price
920	1/4"	2"	$.50

LONG SERVICE SCREW DRIVERS

HAND FORGED BITS

Utica Screw Drivers are strongly made from specially treated stock. Handles are of good size and carefully fitted and will not turn on blade. These Screw Drivers are guaranteed to break any screw which they fit without any injury to the Screw Driver. Blades are hardened the full length—Made of square steel, permitting use of wrench for starting or tightening stubborn screws.

Tool No.	Stock	Blade Length	Price	Tool No.	Stock	Blade Length	Price
900	1/8"	1 1/2"	$.30	906	5/16"	7"	$.90
901	3/16"	3"	.45	907	5/16"	12"	1.00
902	3/16"	8"	.70	908	3/8"	8"	1.15
903	1/4"	4"	.70	909	3/8"	12"	1.25
904	1/4"	6"	.75	910	3/8"	18"	1.35
905	1/4"	9"	.80				

6" and shorter packed 12 in box; other sizes packed 6 in box

THE NEW UTICA AMBERGRIP SCREW DRIVER

HAND FORGED BITS

Just the right size to fit snugly into the palm of the hand, and the special fluting prevents slipping.
The blades are forged of a Chrome Tungsten Alloy Tool Steel with tips accurately ground, insuring a positive non-slip fit in screw slots.
The blade extends far into the handles to prevent any possibility of turning. The blades are heat-treated to give maximum service.

Tool No.	Stock	Blade Length	Price	Tool No.	Stock	Blade Length	Price
1210	3/8"	16"	$1.75	1205	1/4"	1 1/4"	$.65
1209	3/8"	12"	1.60	1204	3/16"	9"	.85
1208	5/16"	12"	1.10	1203	3/16"	6"	.75
1207	5/16"	7"	1.00	1202	3/16"	3"	.65
1206	1/4"	10"	.90	1201	1/8"	3"	.35
1212	1/4"	6"	.85	1200	1/8"	2"	.30
1211	1/4"	4"	.75				

GUNSMITHS' HEAVY DUTY SCREWDRIVERS

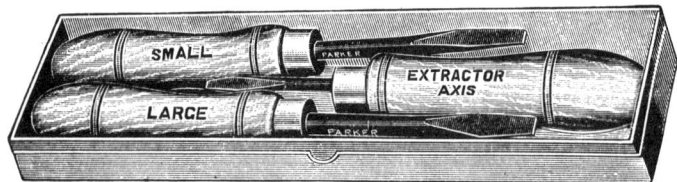

The want of a screw driver which will move rifle and shotgun screws without breaking or bending has long been acute. We have solved this by offering herewith a set of three tools of the same shape and material as used by the best English gunmakers.
Price, per set of three.................................$4.00

HAND FORGED ALLOY STEEL OFFSET SCREW DRIVERS

A very handy tool for use in places where ordinary Screw Drivers cannot possibly reach. The length of tool gives sufficient leverage to move the most stubborn screw. Points are at right angles, and thus by reversing the user is enabled to catch screw in any position. Blades are of same shape and strength as found in our standard Screw Drivers.

No.	Stock	Length	Bit	Price
1151	1/4"	6"	1/16"	$.45
1152	5/16"	6"	3/8"	.50
1153	3/8"	6"	1/2"	.55
1154	1/2"	8"	5/8"	.85

STEEL NUMBERING AND LETTERING STAMPS

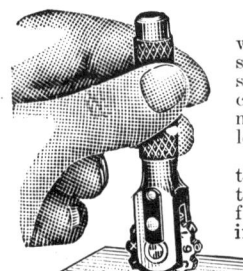
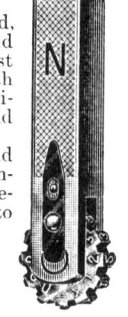

This strongly constructed, well-balanced handy hand stamp is made of the finest steel for the purpose, with characters engraved for maximum stamping service and legibility.
Scientifically hardened and tempered in thermostatic controlled electric furnaces, carefully inspected and tested to insure long stamping life.

This stamp now supplied with square grip as shown in illustration to right.
Price, with 1/16" numbers.................................$3.00
Also available as letter rotary stamp with all letters of the alphabet.
Price, with 1/16" letters.................................$7.00
Available in larger sizes also at an extra charge.

NUMERICAL AND ALPHABETICAL HAND DIES

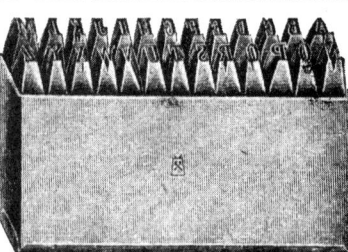

SET OF NUMERICAL STEEL DIES
These dies consist of a set of ten from 1 to 0, and will be found useful in the numbering of guns, parts, etc. The numerals are .1 inch high.
Price, per set.................................$2.50

SET OF ALPHABETICAL STEEL DIES
These dies consist of a set of 27 from A to Z. Suitable for stamping iron or steel. The letters are .1 inch high.
Price.................................$7.50

A TOOL FOR EVERY JOB

PROFESSIONAL GUNSMITH'S NECESSITIES

STOCK BENDING APPARATUS

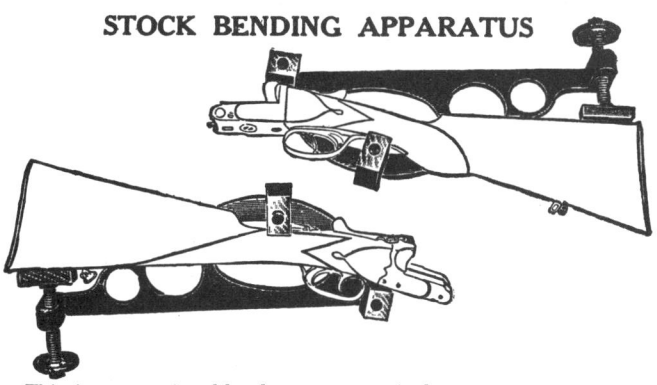

This is unquestionably the most practical apparatus yet put on the market for the simple and practical bending of stocks. The apparatus is built so that with it, it is possible to,
1. increase the drop,
2. lessen the drop,
3. put cast-off into the stock,
4. put cast-in on to the stock.

This tool is made of aluminum with steel screws, three wooden blocks and is supplied with an oil container and cup; directions with each apparatus. Price $23.50

GUNSMITH'S FIELD KIT

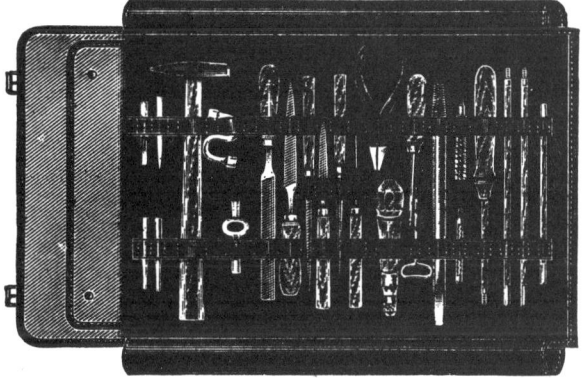

Consists of 18 high grade special gunsmith's tools, sufficient for amateur repairing. Indispensable for minor adjustments, particularly handy for travelling, useful in field, while camping or hunting. Supplied in durable leather bound waterproof canvas case with extra pocket, as illustrated. Price $17.50

DROP MEASURER

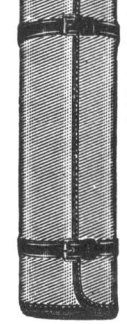

The tube is laid flush upon the barrel and the drop both at comb and heel may be read off the scale.

Very necessary to every gunsmith and sporting goods store. Price $10.25

MAUSER CALIPER MODEL 1-S

This is a combination caliper for outside, inside, and depth, the three measurements are obtained simultaneously in one setting without deducting from the reading.

Due to its fine Vernier reading in 1/1000 inch, it is recommended for mechanics, toolmakers, inspectors, students in technical schools, etc.

This tool is made by the Mauser Werke, which in itself is a guarantee that both workmanship and accuracy are of the very highest order.

Total length, 8 inches; measuring capacity, 5 1/16 inches; weight, 4¼ ounces; graduation, 1/16 inch; with Vernier, 1/128 inches, with Vernier, 1/1000 inch. Price $6.50

SHOTGUN DENT RAISER

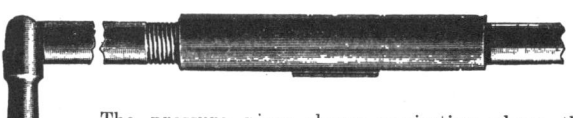

The pressure piece shown projecting above the left hand diameter is raised to meet the dent by the right hand screw "leed," operating against an angle piece supporting it.

Price 12, 16 or 20 gauge $20.00

.22 CALIBER DRIVING ROD
(NOT ILLUSTRATED)

Made for cleaning obstructions from barrels. The driving rod is inserted, a smart tap with a good sized hammer will be found sufficient to move any ordinary obstruction.
Price $3.00

SHOTGUN RECTIFYING CYLINDERS

These cylinders are sold in sets of five and are invaluable for the removal of dents from shotgun barrels. No gunsmith can afford to be without them. The diameter of the first cylinder is .006 less than the true barrel size; the second is .004 inch less; the third, .002 inch less; the fourth is true caliber size; the fifth is .002 inch oversize. Available in 12, 16, 20, 28, and 32 Gauge. Made of finest grade hardened steel.
Price per set of five cylinders in any gauge $10.00

GUNSMITH'S SCREW CHEST

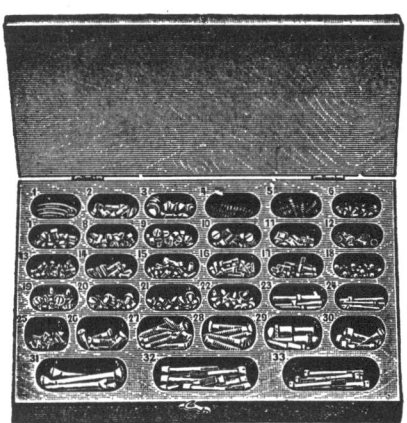

This Screw Chest is neatly made of wood with thirty-three milled compartments for the most popular screws, firing pins, small springs, sights, etc. Supplied complete with three hundred pieces of the most popular screws, springs, etc.
Price $17.75

CARTRIDGE MAGAZINES

The magazines illustrated above are intended to be fitted into the lower section of the stock of any rifle, and thus form a cartridge reserve which will often be found exceedingly valuable to the hunter. Made in two types as illustrated.
Model 1 .... $4.50
Model 2 .... $3.80

A GOOD TOOL SOON PAYS FOR ITSELF

GENUINE FRIEDERICH DICK SELECTED GUNSMITH'S FILES

F.D.

While the file is undoubtedly the most ancient of tools it still remains today the most important of all hand tools being an absolutely indispensable item, without which it would be quite impossible to carry on any kind of metal work and to a great extent, wood work as well. For this reason, the file is by far the most important implement that a gunsmith can possess. The file alone is the only single implement with which it would be possible to build an entire gun as practically all other tools and machines are merely aids in accomplishing the same work at a faster rate where large quantities of metal must be removed.

When one considers the foregoing one is not surprised to learn that in the European Arms factories an apprentice spends his entire first year exclusively learning how to file. He must first be able to file a perfectly flat surface and then to file a perfect cube. This test, while apparently simple is one which only comparatively few mechanics are able to accomplish.

Another apparently simple test of filing consists in taking a bar of iron perhaps $\frac{1}{4}''$ thick and 1" wide, cutting it in half and rejoining it by means of dovetail which will fit from either side without showing light.

In view of the endless uses for a file it is understandable that a multitude of shapes, lengths and cuts are made by various factories in every civilized country in the world, and because of the tremendous demand for files it is also quite clear that these are often made just as cheaply as possible to meet competitive prices. Such files, however, are either so soft that they lose their sharpness almost immediately, or are so hard that they break under the least strain, and moreover, the teeth are so cheaply and improperly constructed that it is impossible to acquire a satisfactory cut.

The firm of Friedr. Dick is probably the largest file company in Europe. Founded in 1778, the reputation of the trade mark, based on 150 years of experience, is a guarantee for first class quality and has set a World's standard for thoroughness and care of manufacture. The firm of Friedr. Dick is also the only concern which has devoted special research and care to the development of files practically adapted to gunsmithing requirements, and every file listed on this and the following page has been carefully thought out and manufactured. Every individual Dick file is made not only of the very finest material possible but of the very best design and cut and each individual file is subjected to a most rigid examination and test for hardness, finish and workmanship before leaving the factory.

The purchase of files is a matter of confidence, and it is poor policy to buy files out of consideration of cheap initial cost, because the best files will prove to be the cheapest in the long run.

Long experience with gunsmiths has proven that three cuts are usually sufficient, and we, therefore, list most Dick files merely as course, medium and fine. The "Fine" files correspond to the 00 Swiss cut, the "Medium" to the No. 1 and the "Course" cut is mid-way between the Swiss cuts 3 and 4.

It is, therefore, with special pleasure that we announce that we have been selected sole U. S. Agents for the Friedr. Dick line of gunsmith's files which we are sure gunsmiths everywhere will learn to appreciate.

ALL PRICES OF DICK FILES ARE FOR SINGLE PIECES

HAND FILES

This file is a very practical all-around file for all purposes when a flat surface is desired. Due to its exceptionally fine cutting qualities, it reduces work to a minimum and is a great time saver.

Lengths:	12"	10"	8"	6"	4"
Coarse Cut	$1.25	$1.10	$.90	$.75	$.50
Medium Cut	1.75	1.25	1.00	.85	.60
Fine Cut	....	.....	....	....	.70

PILLAR FILES

This file is a general purpose file for all flat work and is of a particularly convenient size. Every gunsmith should have several of these files in various cuts and will find them unusually handy and durable.

Lengths:	8"	6"	5"	4"
	$\frac{1}{2}$ x $\frac{3}{16}$	$\frac{7}{16}$ x $\frac{5}{32}$	$\frac{15}{64}$ x $\frac{1}{8}$	$\frac{13}{64}$ x $\frac{5}{64}$
Coarse Cut	$.90	$.70	$.60	$.50
Medium Cut	1.00	.75	.75	.60
Fine Cut	....	....	....	....

HALF ROUND FILES

This file as its name indicates is for filing grooves and concave surfaces. It is a file of exceptional quality and one for which every gunsmith will be sure to find hundreds of occasions to use.

Lengths:	12"	10"	8"	6"	4"
Coarse Cut	$1.25	$1.10	$.90	$.75	$.50
Medium Cut	1.75	1.10	1.00	.85	.60
Fine Cut	....	.....	....	....	.70

THREE SQUARE FILES

This file is suitable for filing notches or cleaning up square holes. It is also suitable for opening up "V" notch sights. Due to the many styles of work requiring a file of this type, it will be found quite indispensable.

Lengths:	6"	5"	4"
Coarse Cut	$.70	$.60	$.50
Medium Cut	.85	.75	.60
Fine Cut	....	....	.70

SQUARE FILE

This file is particularly suitable for opening circular holes in outside shotgun hammers which must be squared before fitting. It may also be used for filing new sight slots as well as useful on many other occasions.

Lengths:	6"	$4\frac{1}{2}''$
Coarse Cut	$.75	$.60
Medium Cut	.85	.70
Fine Cut	....	....

ROUND FILE

With this file any opening may be enlarged to any desired diameter. It may also be used for deepening "U" notch sights. The uses of a round file are so varied that no gunsmith can afford to be without several.

Lengths:	8"	6"	5"	4"
Coarse Cut	$.90	$.70	$.60	$.50
Medium Cut	1.00	.75	.70	.60
Fine Cut	....	....	....	....

GENUINE FRIEDERICH DICK SELECTED GUNSMITH'S FILES

KNIFE FILE

This file is particularly designed for reducing the tension of "V" springs as well as filing of sear notches. As one of the most common gunsmith's jobs is reducing and correcting trigger pulls, we cannot recommend this file too highly.

Length: 4½"
Coarse Cut.................................. $.75
Medium Cut................................. .90

V SPRING FILE

This file is particularly designed for reducing the pressure of flat "V" springs by filing the inside of the "V". It is made with only one cutting surface and may be had either left or right. For the average gunsmith either right or left is satisfactory and both right and left are only recommended where a large quantity of springs must be filed, whereby considerable time can be saved by having both.

Length: 4"
Coarse Cut.................................. $.70
Medium Cut................................. .85
(Left or Right)

CROSSING FILE

This file may be used to replace the half ground with the advantage that it may be suited to any radius. This file will be found suitable for work on surfaces and in odd places where conventional style files cannot be used.

Length: 5"
Medium Coarse Cut 2........................ $.90

SIGHT SLOT FILE

This file is particularly designed for cutting "V" shaped slots and sight notches although hundreds of other purposes can be found therefor. This file has two cutting surfaces, the third side being smooth.

Length: 4"
Coarse Cut.................................. $.70
Medium Cut................................. .85

SQUARE TESTING FILE

This file may be used the same as any other square file but has the added feature and purpose due to its extraordinary hardness enabling it to cut where the ordinary file fails and thus permits hardness testing, since any surface that it will not touch may be considered hard.

Length: 6"
Medium Coarse Cut........................... $1.00

SEAR NOTCH FILE

This file is perhaps the only one on the market which has been especially built and designed for the sole purpose of cutting perfect sear notches. It is so built that only one surface cuts and thus avoids injury to adjacent parts. No gunsmith can well afford to be without one of these excellent files.

Length: 4"
Fine Cut................................... $.85

SLOTTING FILE

This file, while not in common use will be found most helpful in enlarging slots, filing grooves, etc., without injuring adjacent sights. The sides of this file are smooth and only the two edges have cutting surfaces.

Lengths: 7" 6"
Extra Coarse Cut................ $.85 ....
Coarse Cut...................... .... $.80

HEART SHAPED FILES

This file is used for filing oval shaped notches or grooves. This is a general utility file which not only can be used in the place of a round, half round, or triangular file to cut oval notches or slots. Because of its unusual contour it will often be found to fill the bill where nothing else will do.

Length: 5"
Fine Cut................................... $.85

CHECKERING FILE

This file may be used for checkering or knurling steel and may be used on bolt handles, butt plates, ramps, etc. The work which can be done with this file is a revelation to the uninitiated. Soon pays for itself.

Lengths: 5½"   6"
              ½ x ¼   ⁹⁄₁₆ x ¼
Extra Coarse Cut...... $1.10   ....
Medium Coarse Cut..... .... $1.35

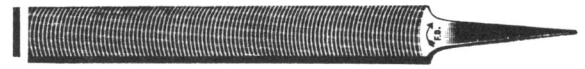

CIRCULAR CUT SOFT METAL FILE

This file is particularly designed for filing off the metals, such as copper, lead, aluminum and because of special cut, designed not to clog up on these soft metals and will consequently cut very fast and clean. Don't ruin your other files on work requiring a special soft metal file.

Length: 5"   4"
Medium Cut.... $1.85 $.85

HARD NEEDLE FILES

Hard Needle Files, with round handles, of which the three square is shown here, are also available in round, barrette, square, half round and three square. Files of this nature are an absolute necessity for all kinds of gun work where only slight retouching or refinishing is required. Sold in sets of six, styles as mentioned.

Price per set of six assorted styles................ $1.75
Price individually .... .35

SCREW HEAD FILE

This file is designed for recutting and deepening old or damaged screw heads and for cutting new ones where necessary. Almost every old gun brought in for repair requires one or more screws to be refinished and recut.

Length: 4½"
Fine Cut.................................. $.80

CABINET RASPS

This rasp is one which has been particularly evolved for the stock maker. It not only cuts fast and clean but will give many years of service under the hardest use. It is particularly recommended by us for use in finishing our Peerless Rough Turned Stocks.

Lengths: 10"   6"
Cut No. 16 (Halfsmooth)......... $1.50 $1.25

SAVE TIME WITH GENUINE DICK FILES

STOEGER'S GUNSMITHS FILES

The gunsmith's file is the most important tool in his workshop. With sufficient time and a complete assortment of files, the master gunsmith can accomplish practically any operation necessary in the repair of firearms and the fitting in of new parts. The files on this page are the finest that can be had for repairing, making new parts and alteration on firearms.

These files are fast and accurate in their cuts and are the correct size and cut for the purposes outlined in the various descriptions. It is much the better practice to have a file for each purpose. Files that are used for wood should not be used for metal and vice versa.

The files we have listed below are used in our Repair Division and we recommend them to the amateur and professional gunsmith wishing to do accurate and expert gunsmithing. These files in the hands of the expert gunsmith should last three or four years.

HAND FILE 12" NO. 2

For smoothing and finishing gun stocks preparatory to oil finishing. This file finishes wood very nicely and leaves the surface smooth. Price .... ea. **$1.20**

HALF-ROUND FILE 12" NO. 2

For finishing pistol grips, cheek piece, for ends and the inside of stocks, to let in the action. Price.................... ea. **$1.55**

HALF-ROUND FILE BASTARD 12"

For roughing out the inside and outside of stocks, to shape and let in the action. Price .... ea. **$.65**

ROUND FILE 12" BASTARD

For inletting barrel into stock. For inside stock cuts. Price .... ea. **$.40**

ROUND FILE 16" SECOND CUT

For stock work, widening holes, rounding out cheek piece, rounding corners and inletting stock for the barrel. Price................ ea. **$1.65**

CABINET RASP 10" OR 8" DEAD SMOOTH

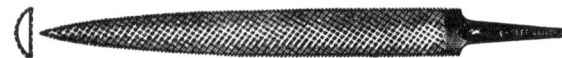

For outside work on stock of hard wood. Cuts very fast and leaves surface smooth. Price .... ea. **$1.15**

CIRCULAR CUT HAND UTILITY 10"

Special for smooth and quick work on stock. This file can also be used on brass, copper, aluminum, lead, solder and iron. It has two cuts, rough on one side, smooth on other side. Either side will cut quickly, easily and leave a smooth surface. This is one of the best files ever manufactured. Price................. ea. **$1.15**

CROSSING FILE 8" NO. 4

For fine finish work on gun parts, hammers and any action work. Can be used on parts set up on the lathe. Price................. ea. **$1.20**

ROUND FILE 8" NO. 3

For action and parts work, correcting holes to center, etc. Price .... ea. **$.60**

HALF ROUND RING 7" NO. 2

To smooth and correct cheek piece, comb, and for inside work on stocks to let in action and barrel. Price....................... ea. **$.80**

THREE-SQUARE FILE 6" NO. 2

For utility work on metal parts of firearms. Price.......... ea. **$.55**

SQUARE FILE 5" NO. 4

For fitting hammers to tumblers and making square holes. Can be used on cross bolts and locks. Price.................... ea. **$.90**

KNIFE FILE 6" NO. 3

To cut springs, to file out and fit to action also for the finishing cut of screw slots. Price.. ea. **$.55**

PARALLEL ROUND FILE 6" NO. 4—7/64"

To round out holes, to straighten and enlarge holes which have not been correctly bored. Price................................. ea. **$.45**

SCREW HEAD FILE WITH TANG 3" NO. 4

To make slots in the heads of fine, small screws. Price........ ea. **$.40**

PILLAR CHECKING FILE 6"

No. 2. Sixty lines to the inch. For checking small adjusting screws and engraving. Price................................. ea. **$.90**
No. 1. Thirty-eight lines to the inch. For checking small adjusting screws and engraving. Price................................. ea. **$.90**
No. 0. Thirty lines to the inch. For checking knobs, screws, etc. Price .... ea. **$.90**
No. 00. Twenty-two lines to the inch. For course checking bolt knobs, plates, screws, etc. Price................................. ea. **$.90**

PILLAR TESTING FILE 6" NO. 1

For testing the hardness of steel. Take file in hand and file on steel and listen to sound to determine degree of hardness. Cannot be used on case hardened steel but can be used on all other steel. Price...... ea. **$.80**

EXTRA NARROW PILLAR FILE 6" NO. 4

For square cuts, action work, shotgun, rifle, pistol or revolver. Price .... ea. **$.55**

NEEDLE HALF ROUND FILE 5¾" NO. 3

For use on small gun parts and gun sights. Price............ ea. **$.25**

NEEDLE THREE SQUARE FILE 5¾" NO. 3

For Sears, ejectors and fine action work. Price............. ea. **$.25**

NEEDLE ROUND FILE 5¾" NO. 3

For peep sight apertures, to open round open sights, for hammers, firing pin holes. Price...................................... ea. **$.25**

NEEDLE EQUALLING FILE 5¾" NO. 3

For small cuts in action work, sights, etc. Price............ ea. **$.25**

NEEDLE SQUARE FILE 5¾" NO. 3

For small square holes, for Patridge rear sights and to widen sears. Price .... ea. **$.25**

NEEDLE BARRETTE 5¾" NO. 3

Special for shotgun sears only   Price..................... ea. **$.25**

SPECIAL OFFER   One set 27 Master Gunsmiths' files listed on this page, complete in neat can, canvas case............. **$15.00**
NOTE: This represents a saving of $4.65 when files are purchased in a set instead of individual purchases.

EVERYTHING IN GUNS UNDER ONE COVER

NICHOLSON X.F. SWISS PATTERN FILES
(ALL PRICES PER DOZEN)

HAND FILES

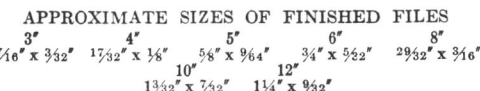

Hand Files are parallel in width and tapered in thickness. The flat sides are double cut. Hand Files in cuts Nos. 00, 0 and 2 are single cut on one edge, the other edge being safe. Hand Files in cuts Nos. 3, 4 and 6 have two safe edges. Made in lengths of 3, 4, 5, 6, 8, 10 and 12 inches and in cuts Nos. 00, 0, 1, 2, 3, 4 and 6. Sizes 6 and shorter, packed 12 to the box. All over that length packed 6 in a box.

APPROXIMATE SIZES OF FINISHED FILES

3"	4"	5"	6"	8"
7/16" x 3/32"	17/32" x 1/8"	5/8" x 9/64"	3/4" x 5/32"	29/32" x 3/16"

10"	12"
1 3/32" x 7/32"	1 1/4" x 9/32"

	HAND						PILLAR				
Length	Approx. Size	00&0	1&2	3&4	6	Length	Approx. Size	00&0	1&2	3&4	6
3	7/16 x 3/32	3.70	3.90	4.30	5.20	3	9/32 x 3/32	3.00	3.10	3.40	4.30
4	17/32 x 7/64	3.70	3.90	4.30	5.20	4	11/32 x 7/64	3.00	3.10	3.40	4.80
5	5/8 x 1/8	4.20	4.60	5.20	6.30	5	27/64 x 9/64	3.20	3.40	3.80	4.80
6	23/32 x 5/32	4.90	5.40	6.30	7.60	6	31/64 x 5/32	3.40	3.70	4.30	5.30
8	29/32 x 3/16	7.00	7.70	8.60	9.90	8	39/64 x 13/64	4.80	5.20	6.00	7.20
10	1 3/32 x 15/64	9.30	10.40	11.50	13.40	10	47/64 x 1/4	6.60	7.00	8.40	10.00
12	1 9/32 x 17/64	12.30	13.80	15.40	17.60	12	27/32 x 1/4	9.00	9.80	11.20	13.00

PILLAR FILES

Pillar Files are similar in shape to Hand Files but about two-thirds as wide. Double cut on the two flat sides only, the edges being left safe. Made in lengths of 3, 4, 5, 6, 8, 10 and 12 inches and in cuts Nos. 00, 0, 1, 2, 3, 4 and 6. Sizes 6 and shorter, packed 12 to the box. All over that length packed six in a box.

APPROXIMATE SIZES OF FINISHED FILES

3"	4"	5"	6"	8"
9/32" x 3/32"	3/8" x 7/64"	7/16" x 9/64"	1/2" x 5/32"	5/8" x 13/64"

10"	12"
3/4" x 7/32"	7/8" x 1/4"

NOTE—Other widths of Pillar Narrow and Pillar Extra Narrow can be furnished when required, at special prices.

PILLAR NARROW FILES

Pillar Narrow Files are similar to Pillar Files, but narrower for the same length. Double cut on the two flat sides only, the edges being safe. Made in lengths of 3, 4, 5, 6, 8, 10 and 12 inches and in cuts Nos. 00, 0, 1, 2, 3, 4 and 6. Sizes 6 and shorter, packed 12 to the box. All over that length packed six in a box.

APPROXIMATE SIZES OF FINISHED FILES

3"	4"	5"	6"	8"
3/16" x 5/64"	7/32" x 7/64"	5/16" x 1/8"	23/64" x 5/32"	29/64" x 7/32"

10"	12"
35/64" x 9/32"	5/8" x 5/16"

	PILLAR NARROW						PILLAR EXTRA NARROW				
Length	Approx. Size	00&0	1&2	3&4	6	Length	Approx. Size	00&0	1&2	3&4	6
3	7/32 x 3/32	3.00	3.10	3.40	4.30	3	9/64 x 3/32	3.00	3.10	3.40	4.30
4	17/64 x 1/8	3.00	3.10	3.40	4.30	4	11/64 x 7/64	3.00	3.10	3.40	4.30
5	5/16 x 9/64	3.20	3.40	3.80	4.80	5	13/64 x 9/64	3.20	3.40	3.80	4.80
6	23/64 x 5/32	3.40	3.70	4.30	5.30	6	15/64 x 5/32	3.40	3.70	4.30	5.30
8	29/64 x 7/32	4.80	5.20	6.00	7.20	8	19/64 x 7/32	4.80	5.20	6.00	7.20
10	35/64 x 9/32	6.60	7.00	8.40	10.00	10	23/64 x 1/4	6.60	7.00	8.40	10.00
12	41/64 x 5/16	9.00	9.80	11.20	13.00	12	27/64 x 11/32	9.00	9.80	11.20	13.00

PILLAR EXTRA NARROW FILES

Pillar Extra Narrow Files similar to Pillar and Pillar Narrow Files but narrower than the Pillar Narrow for their length. Cut on the two flat sides only, the edges being safe. Made in lengths of 3, 4, 5, 6, 8, 10 and 12 inches and in cuts Nos. 00, 0, 1, 2, 3, 4 and 6. Packed 12 to the box.

APPROXIMATE SIZES OF FINISHED FILES

3"	4"	5"	6"	8"
1/8" x 3/32"	5/32" x 7/64"	3/16" x 1/8"	7/32" x 5/32"	5/16" x 7/32"

10"	12"
3/8" x 1/4"	7/16" x 11/32"

WARDING FILES

Warding Files are rectangular in section with thickness approximately one-eighth of their width, tapering to a point in width and tapering slightly in thickness. Double cut on the two flat sides and single cut on both edges. Made in lengths of 3, 4, 5, 6, 8 and 10 inches and in cuts Nos. 00, 0, 1, 2, 3, 4 and 6. Packed 12 to the box.

APPROXIMATE SIZES OF FINISHED FILES

3"	4"	5"	6"	8"	10"
3/8" x 3/64"	7/16" x 3/64"	33/64" x 1/16"	19/32" x 5/64"	3/4" x 9/32"	15/16" x 7/64"

	WARDING						CROCHET			
Length	Approx. Size	00&0	1&2	3&4	6	Length	Approx. Size	00&0	1&2	3&4
3	23/64 x 3/64	2.80	3.00	3.30	3.80	3	1/4 x 5/64	4.50	4.80	5.40
4	7/16 x 3/64	3.20	3.60	4.10	4.80	4	23/64 x 7/64	5.00	5.40	6.00
5	33/64 x 1/16	3.80	4.40	5.10	6.00	5	7/16 x 7/64	5.80	6.30	7.00
6	19/32 x 5/64	4.60	5.30	6.10	7.00	6	1/2 x 1/8	6.80	7.40	8.20
8	3/4 x 3/32	6.20	6.90	8.10	9.60	8	21/32 x 5/32	9.60	10.40	11.20
10	59/64 x 7/64	8.20	9.50	11.50	13.50	10	49/64 x 3/16	12.80	13.80	14.80

CROCHET FILES

Crochet Files taper to a point in both width and thickness and are made with both edges well rounded. Double cut on the flat sides and on both edges. Made in lengths of 3, 4, 5, 6, 8 and 10 inches and cuts Nos. 00, 0, 1, 2, 3 and 4. Sizes 6 and shorter, packed 12 to the box. All over that length packed six in a box.

APPROXIMATE SIZES OF FINISHED FILES

3"	4"	5"	6"	8"	10"
1/4" x 5/64"	3/8" x 3/32"	13/32" x 7/64"	1/2" x 1/8"	5/8" x 5/32"	3/4" x 3/16"

KNIFE FILES

Knife Files are made from steel that is knife shaped, the included angle of the sharp edge being 10 degrees. They taper in width and thickness to the point. Double cut on both flat sides and single cut on both edges. Made in lengths of 3, 4, 5, 6 and 8 inches and in cuts Nos. 00, 0, 1, 2, 3, 4 and 6. Packed 12 to the box.

APPROXIMATE WIDTH OF FINISHED FILES

3"	4"	5"	6"	8"
3/8"	29/64"	9/16"	5/8"	7/8"

	KNIFE						BARRETTE				
Length	Approx. Width	00&0	1&2	3&4	6	Length	Approx. width	00&0	1&2	3&4	6
3	11/32	4.00	4.40	4.80	5.40	3	21/64	5.00	5.10	5.30	5.50
4	29/64	4.40	5.00	5.60	6.60	4	1/2	5.50	5.60	5.80	6.00
5	35/64	5.00	5.60	6.60	8.40	5	9/16	6.00	6.20	6.60	7.10
6	41/64	6.00	7.00	8.00	10.50	6	21/32	6.60	7.00	7.60	8.40
8	27/32	8.60	9.80	11.40	15.00	8	7/8	8.60	9.20	10.00	11.00

BARRETTE FILES

Barrette Files are flat on one side, the back being beveled at both edges as indicated by the cross section, the included angle being 33 degrees. Double cut on the wide flat side only, the back and the beveled edges being left safe. Made in lengths of 3, 4, 5, 6 and 8 inches and in cuts Nos. 00, 0, 1, 2, 3, 4 and 6. Sizes 6 and shorter, packed 12 to the box. All over that length packed six in a box.

APPROXIMATE WIDTH OF FINISHED FILES

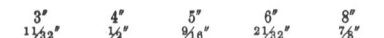

3"	4"	5"	6"	8"
11/32"	1/2"	9/16"	21/32"	7/8"

10% EXTRA CHARGE ON LESS THAN FULL BOXES

NICHOLSON X. F. SWISS PATTERN FILES
(ALL PRICES PER DOZEN)

EQUALING FILES

Equaling Files are parallel in both width and thickness throughout their length. Double cut on the two flat sides and single cut on both edges. Made in lengths of 3, 4, 5, 6 and 8 inches and in cuts Nos. 00, 0, 1, 2, 3, 4 and 6. Sizes 6 and shorter, packed 12 to the box. All over that length packed six in a box.

APPROXIMATE SIZES OF FINISHED FILES

3″	4″	5″	6″	8″
5/16″ x 1/16″	13/32″ x 5/64″	1/2″ x 3/32″	19/32″ x 7/64″	3/4″ x 9/64″

	EQUALING					SQUARE			
Length	Approx. Size	00&0	1&2	3&4	6	Length	Approx. Width	00&0	1&2	3&4	6
3	21/64 x 1/16	3.20	3.50	3.90	4.40	3	5/64	3.40	3.50	3.60	3.80
4	27/64 x 5/64	3.60	4.00	4.40	5.40	4	1/8	3.80	4.00	4.40	4.80
5	1/2 x 3/32	4.00	4.40	5.00	6.20	5	5/32	4.20	4.50	5.20	6.00
6	19/32 x 7/64	4.40	4.90	5.60	7.00	6	3/16	5.00	5.40	6.20	7.40
8	3/4 x 9/64	6.00	6.60	7.60	9.00	8	1/4	6.00	6.80	8.40	10.20
						10	21/64	7.40	9.00	10.80	13.20
						12	27/64	8.80	11.20	14.00	17.00

SQUARE FILES

Square Files are square in section and taper on all four sides to a fine point. Double cut on all four sides. Made in lengths of 3, 4, 5, 6, 8, 10 and 12 inches and in cuts Nos. 00, 0, 1, 2, 3, 4 and 6. Packed 12 in a box.

APPROXIMATE WIDTH OF FINISHED FILES

3″	4″	5″	6″	8″	10″	12″
5/64″	1/8″	5/32″	3/16″	1/4″	11/32″	7/16″

ROUND FILES

Round Files taper throughout their length to a fine point. Double cut. Made in lengths of 2½, 3, 3½, 4, 5, 6, 8, 10 and 12 inches and in cuts Nos. 00, 0, 1, 2, 3, 4 and 6. Packed 12 to the box.

APPROXIMATE WIDTH OF FINISHED FILES

2½″	3″	3½″	4″	5″	6″	8″	10″	12″
1/16″	5/64″	7/64″	1/8″	5/32″	3/16″	1/4″	21/64″	27/64″

	ROUND					PIPPIN			
Length	Approx. Width	00&0	1&2	3&4	6	Length	Approx. Size	00&0	1&2	4
2½	1/16	2.50	2.70	2.90	3.20	3	7/32 x 3/32	4.60	5.00	5.60
3	5/64	2.50	2.70	2.90	3.20	4	9/32 x 1/8	5.40	5.80	6.40
3½	7/64	2.80	3.00	3.20	3.60	6	23/64 x 3/16	7.40	8.00	8.80
4	1/8	2.80	3.00	3.20	3.60	8	15/32 x 7/32	10.00	10.60	11.40
5	5/32	3.40	3.70	4.00	4.40					
6	3/16	4.00	4.40	4.80	5.20					
8	1/4	5.80	6.20	6.60	7.30					
10	21/64	7.80	8.60	9.60	11.20					
12	27/64	10.00	11.30	13.70	16.80					

PIPPIN FILES

Pippin Files have rounded backs tapering to a sharp edge and they taper in both width and thickness to a point. Double Cut. These files are sometimes called "Apple Seed" files.

Made in lengths of 3, 4, 6 and 8 inches and in Cuts Nos. 00, 0, 1, 2 and 4.
Packed 12 to the box.

APPROXIMATE SIZES OF FINISHED FILES

3″	4″	6″	8″
7/32″ x 3/32″	9/32″ x 1/8″	3/8″ x 5/32″	1/2″ x 3/16″

THREE SQUARE FILES

Three Square Files are triangular in section with angles of 60 degrees, taper to a point and have sharp corners. Double cut on the three sides and single cut on the edges. Made in lengths of 3, 3½, 4, 5, 6, 8 and 10 inches and in cuts Nos. 00, 0, 1, 2, 3, 4 and 6. Sizes 6 and shorter, packed 12 to the box. All over that length, packed six in a box.

APPROXIMATE WIDTH OF FINISHED FILES

3″	3½″	4″	5″	6″	8″	10″
5/32″	7/32″	1/4″	5/16″	3/8″	1/2″	5/8″

	THREE SQUARE					METAL SAW			
Length	Approx. Width	00&0	1&2	3&4	6	Length	Approx. Width	0	1&2	3&4
3	11/64	3.90	4.20	4.50	5.00	3	5/32	3.90	4.20	4.50
3½	7/32	3.90	4.20	4.50	5.00	3½	7/32	3.90	4.20	4.50
4	15/64	3.90	4.20	4.50	5.00	4	1/4	3.90	4.20	4.50
5	19/64	4.30	4.70	5.20	5.80	5	19/64	4.30	4.70	5.20
6	11/32	4.80	5.20	5.90	6.60	6	11/32	4.80	5.20	5.90
8	15/32	6.20	6.80	7.60	9.00	8	15/32	6.20	6.80	7.60
10	39/64	8.40	9.10	10.40	12.20					

METAL SAW FILES

Metal Saw Files are the same in section as Three Square Files but are parallel throughout their length. Double cut on the three sides and single cut on the edges. Made in lengths of 3, 3½, 4, 5, 6 and 8 inches and in cuts Nos. 0, 1, 2, 3 and 4. Sizes 6 and shorter, packed 12 to the box. All over that length packed six in a box.

APPROXIMATE WIDTH OF FINISHED FILES

3″	3½″	4″	5″	6″	8″
5/32″	3/16″	7/32″	5/16″	3/8″	1/2″

ACTUAL COARSENESS OF 6-INCH HAND FILES

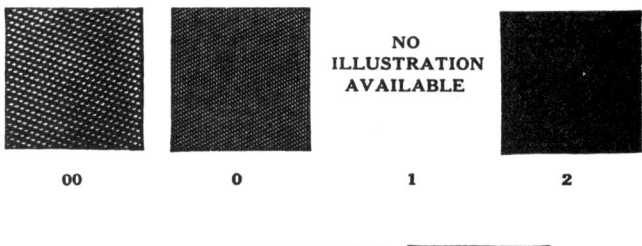

00   0   1   2

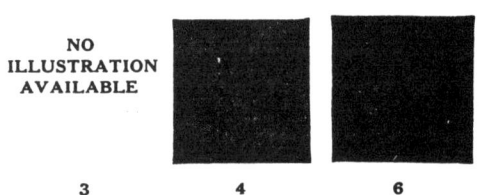

3   4   6

The Nicholson File Company manufactures a very complete line of files, in accordance with original Swiss designs or patterns, called Nicholson X. F. Swiss Pattern Files.

While for many kinds of work the ordinary Files are all that are required, for more particular purposes, particularly gunsmithing, these files, made to exacting measurements and generally in much finer cuts, are necessary. These files were first manufactured for jewelers, watch and fine tool makers but there is a large demand for them for gun making and similar fine work requiring superior workmanship and extra fine tools. The coarseness of these files is designated by numbers ranging from No. 00 the coarsest to No. 6 the finest. The illustrations show the various degrees of coarseness. They are made in a separate part of the Providence factory designed and built especially for the manufacture of these Extra Fine Files.

10% EXTRA CHARGE ON LESS THAN FULL BOXES

NICHOLSON X. F. SWISS PATTERN FILES

(ALL PRICES PER DOZEN)

CANT FILES

Cant Files are triangular as shown by the cross section and taper to the point in both width and thickness. Double cut on three sides and single cut on the two sharp edges. Made in lengths of 3, 4, 5, 6 and 8 inches and in cuts Nos. 00, 0, 2 and 4. Sizes 6 and shorter, packed 12 to the box. All over that length packed six in a box.

APPROXIMATE WIDTH OF FINISHED FILES

3″	4″	5″	6″	8″
11/32″	13/32″	15/32″	1/2″	23/32″

	CANT				SLITTING		
Length	Approx. Width	00&0	2	4	Length	Approx. Width	00&0	2	4
3	11/32	$6.70	$7.50	$8.80					
4	13/32	6.70	7.50	8.80	4	7/16	$5.60	$6.60	$7.60
5	15/32	7.70	8.60	10.00	5	1/2	7.40	8.40	9.60
6	1/2	7.70	8.60	10.00	6	37/64	8.80	10.00	11.20
8	23/32	9.70	10.60	12.00	8	49/64	10.60	11.80	13.20

SLITTING FILES

Slitting Files are made of double angular section, the included angle between the sides being approximately 15 degrees. Double cut on the four sides and single cut on the two sharp edges. Made in lengths of 4, 5, 6 and 8 inches and in cuts Nos. 00, 0, 2 and 4. Sizes 6 and shorter, packed 12 to the box. All over that length packed six in a box.

APPROXIMATE WIDTH OF FINISHED FILES

4″	5″	6″	8″
7/16″	1/2″	19/32″	3/4″

HALF ROUND FILES

Half Round Files taper in width and thickness to the point. Double cut on both flat and half round sides. Made in lengths of 3, 3½, 4, 4½, 5, 6, 7, 8, 10 and 12 inches and in cuts Nos. 00, 0, 1, 2, 3, 4 and 6. Sizes 6 and shorter, packed 12 to the box. All over that length packed six in a box.

APPROXIMATE SIZES OF FINISHED FILES

3″	3½″	4″	4½″	5″	6″
15/64″ x 3/32″	21/64″ x 7/64″	11/32″ x 1/8″	27/64″ x 1/8″	7/16″ x 1/8″	17/32″ x 9/64″
7″	8″	10″	12″		
43/64″ x 11/64″	23/32″ x 13/64″	29/32″ x 1/4″	17/64″ x 19/64″		

	HALF ROUND					CROSSING			
Length	Approx. Size	00&0	1&2	3&4	6	Length	Approx. Size	00&0	1&2	3&4	6
3	15/64 x 3/32	$4.50	$5.00	$5.90	$7.40	3	19/64 x 3/32	$5.20	$5.60	$6.40	$7.80
3½	21/64 x 7/64	5.10	6.00	6.90	8.40	4	13/32 x 7/64	5.60	6.20	7.20	9.00
4	11/32 x 1/8	5.10	6.00	6.90	8.40	5	1/2 x 9/64	6.30	7.20	8.40	10.40
4½	27/64 x 1/8	5.90	7.00	8.10	10.40	6	5/8 x 3/16	7.60	8.60	9.80	12.00
5	7/16 x 1/8	5.90	7.00	8.10	10.40	8	25/32 x 1/4	11.30	12.40	13.80	16.20
6	17/32 x 9/64	6.80	8.00	9.20	11.60	10	61/64 x 5/16	15.00	16.40	19.00	23.00
7	43/64 x 11/64	8.00	9.30	10.60	13.00	12	19/64 x 3/8	19.00	21.10	23.80	28.20
8	23/32 x 13/64	10.00	11.30	12.70	15.20						
10	29/32 x 1/4	13.30	14.60	16.80	19.60						
12	17/64 x 19/64	17.20	18.40	20.90	24.00						

CROSSING FILES

Crossing Files are made of double circular section, one side having the same radius as the Half Round File and the other side having a flatter curve or larger radius. They taper to a point in both width and thickness. Double cut on both sides. Made in lengths of 3, 4, 5, 6, 8, 10 and 12 inches and in cuts Nos. 00, 0, 1, 2, 3, 4 and 6. Sizes 6 and shorter, packed 12 to the box. All over that length packed six in a box.

APPROXIMATE SIZES OF FINISHED FILES

3″	4″	5″	6″	8″
5/16″ x 3/32″	7/16″ x 7/64″	17/32″ x 5/32″	5/8″ x 3/16″	13/16″ x 15/64″
		10″	12″	
		61/64″ x 5/16″	19/64″ x 3/8″	

JOINT FILES

ROUND EDGE JOINT THICK NO. 0

ROUND EDGE JOINT THIN NO. 2

SQUARE EDGE JOINT THICK NO. 2

SQUARE EDGE JOINT THIN NO. 0

Joint Files are parallel in width and thickness, with round or square edges, thick or thin. Double cut on the edges only, the sides being left safe. Made in lengths of 3, 4, 5, 6 and 8 inches and in cuts Nos. 0 and 2. Packed 12 to the box.

APPROXIMATE SIZES OF FINISHED FILES

	Thick	Thin
3-inch	5/16″ x 1/16″	5/16″ x 1/32″
4-inch	13/32″ x 7/64″	13/32″ x 3/64″
5-inch	1/2″ x 3/32″	1/2″ x 1/16″
6-inch	19/32″ x 7/64″	19/32″ x 5/64″
8-inch	3/4″ x 9/64″	3/4″ x 7/64″

Length	Rd. Edge 0&2	Sq. Edge 0&2	Approx. Dimensions	
			Thick	Thin
3	$3.00	$2.80	5/16 x 1/16	5/16 x 1/32
4	3.40	3.20	13/32 x 7/64	27/64 x 3/64
5	4.20	4.00	1/2 x 3/32	1/2 x 1/16
6	5.20	5.00	19/32 x 7/64	19/32 x 5/64
8	7.00	6.80	25/32 x 9/64	25/32 x 7/64

SPUN FERRULED HANDLES

These handles have very strong spun brass ferrules. They are made from seasoned White Birch, shaped to fit the hand and coated with shellac.

2.25	No. 00, for 16″ files	$2.25	per doz.
2.00	No. 0, for 14″ files	2.00	per doz.
1.75	No. 1, for 12″ files	1.75	per doz.
1.50	No. 2, for 10″ files	1.50	per doz.
1.25	No. 3, for 8″ files	1.25	per doz.
1.00	No. 4, for 6″ and under	1.00	per doz.

FILE CLEANERS

Price, Each.........$1.00

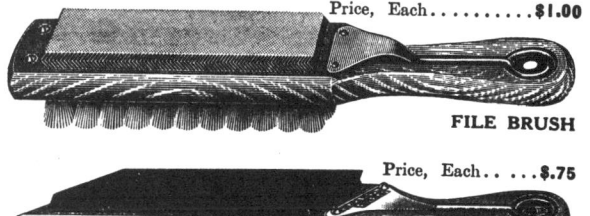

FILE BRUSH

Price, Each.....$.75

FILE CARD

These File Cleaners are made in two styles as illustrated. The File Card with Scorer for more general use and the File Brush (combining the Brush, Card and Scorer) for use especially on the finer cut files. The Scorer is made of soft iron and is used to remove the pins which fill up and clog the teeth of files causing scratches in the work if not removed. The over-all length of these Cleaners is 10 inches.

File Card with Scorer.........................$ .75
File Brush with Card and Scorer..............1.00

10% EXTRA CHARGE ON LESS THAN FULL BOXES

WOOD RASPS AND X. F. FILES

CABINET FILES AND RASP

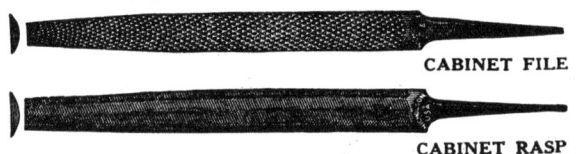

CABINET FILE

CABINET RASP

Used by gunsmiths and woodworkers. The curved side of these files and rasps is similar to that of Half Round Files and Rasps, but of larger radius. Made in lengths of 6, 8, 10, 12 and 14 inches. Cabinet Files are made in one coarseness of cut only, and Cabinet Rasps are made in both Second cut and Smooth cuts. Sizes 8 and shorter, packed 12 to the box. All over that length packed 6 in box.

Inch	Cabinet Files	Cabinet Rasps		Half Rd. Wood Rasps		Flat Wood Rasps	
		2d Cut	Smooth	Bast.	Smooth	Bast.	Smooth
6	8.10	10.10	11.70	8.10	10.10	......	......
8	10.10	12.80	15.50	10.10	13.70	9.40	12.80
10	13.70	17.50	20.70	13.70	18.70	12.80	17.50
12	18.70	22.80	26.80	18.70	24.80	17.50	23.20
14	24.80	29.60	33.90	24.80	32.90	23.20	30.80
16				32.90	43.60	30.80	40.90

WOOD RASPS
FLAT AND HALF ROUND SECTIONS

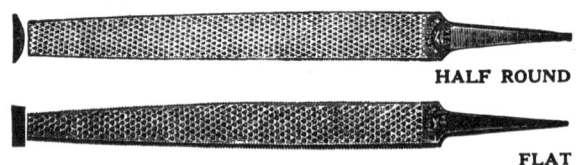

HALF ROUND

FLAT

Are used by gunsmiths, woodworkers, mechanics, repairmen, etc. Made in Bastard and Smooth cuts and of the same sections of steel as Flat and Half Round Files. Made in Flat sections in lengths of 6, 8, 10, 12, 14 and 16 inches and in Half Round sections in lengths of 6, 8, 10, 12, 14 and 16 inches. Coarseness of teeth is the same for Flat and Half Round Rasps of the same size. Sizes 8 and shorter, packed 12 to the box. All over that length are packed six in a box.

DIE SINKERS FILES

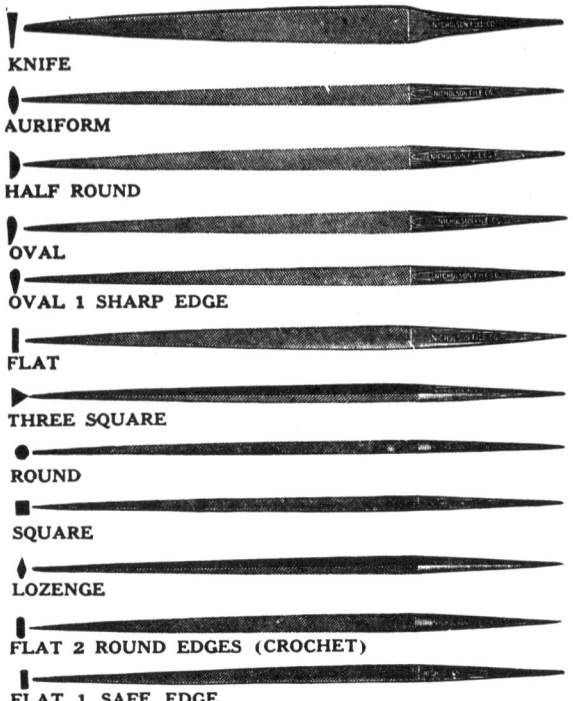

KNIFE

AURIFORM

HALF ROUND

OVAL

OVAL 1 SHARP EDGE

FLAT

THREE SQUARE

ROUND

SQUARE

LOZENGE

FLAT 2 ROUND EDGES (CROCHET)

FLAT 1 SAFE EDGE

Die Sinker Files are designed for die sinkers for dressing and finishing dies of all kinds, and are especially useful for gunsmiths. They are made in twelve shapes as illustrated, 3½ inches long, and in cuts Nos. 0, 1 and 2. In assorted sets they are supplied in wooden boxes.
Price $4.40

ROUND HANDLE NEEDLE FILES
WITH KNURLED HANDLES

BARRETTE

SLITTING

EQUALING

JOINT

THREE SQUARE

FLAT

KNIFE

SQUARE

ROUND

HALF ROUND

MARKING

CROSSING

Round Handle Needle Files are used principally by gunsmiths, die makers and fine toolmakers. They are made in twelve different shapes as illustrated, in over-all lengths of 4", 4¾", 5½" and 6¼" and in cuts Nos. 0, 2, 4 and 6. In 4" and 4¾" lengths Oval are furnished instead of Crossing. These files have Knurled Handles as illustrated and when purchased in assorted sets are supplied in wooden boxes.
4 Inch .... $2.50   5½ Inch $3.20
4¾ Inch .... 2.80   6¼ Inch 3.50

5½" SQUARE HANDLE NEEDLE FILES

SLITTING

FLAT

CROSSING

KNIFE

SQUARE

ROUND

EQUALING

JOINT

HALF ROUND BLUNT

HALF ROUND

BARRETTE

THREE SQUARE

Square Handle Needle or Escapement Files are made especially for very fine gun work. They are made in twelve different shapes as illustrated, in one size only, 5½ inches over-all, and in cuts Nos. 0, 2, 4 and 6. May be had in boxes of assorted shapes.
Price $3.30

10% EXTRA CHARGE ON LESS THAN FULL BOXES OR SETS

NICHOLSON "SWISS PATTERN" RIFFLERS & SCRAPERS
(ALL PRICES PER DOZEN)

RIFFLERS MADE IN CUTS 0 AND 2, LENGTH 7½"

RIFFLERS MADE IN 6, 6½ AND 7" LENGTH

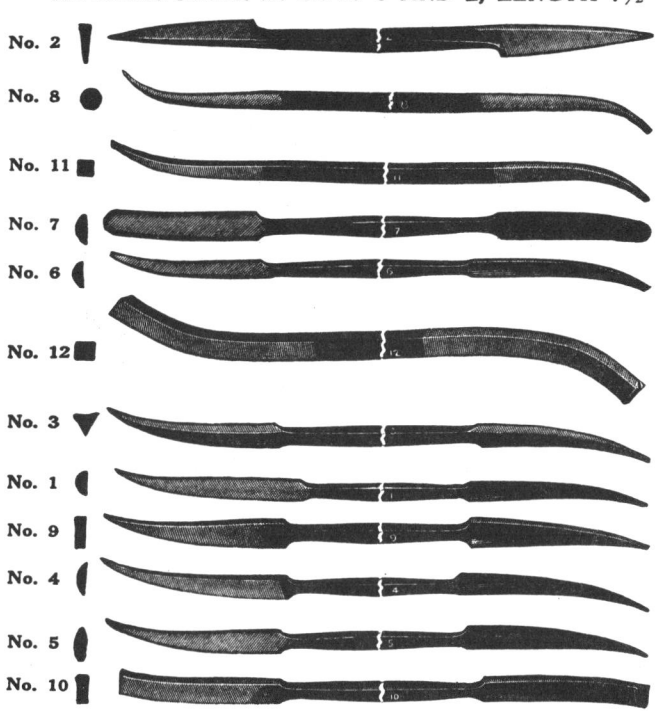

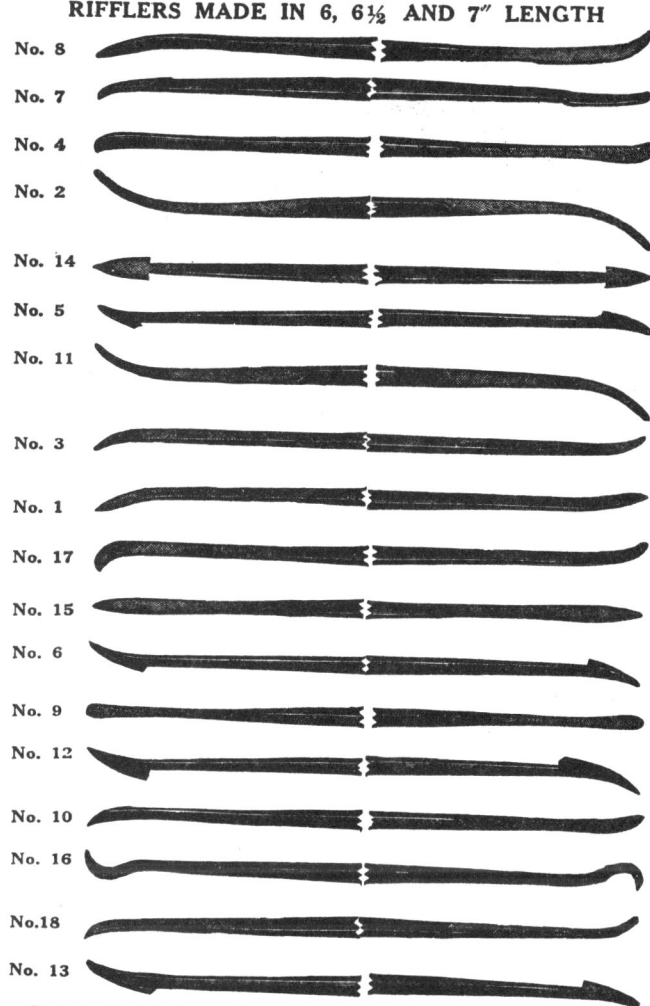

These Rifflers are made in 7½" length only, in twelve shapes as illustrated, and in cuts Nos. 0 and 2. May be purchased in assortments or in any quantity of each shape.

Price $10.80

Packed either in boxes of one dozen or in boxes of a complete assortment of eighteen.

Price, per doz. 6" .... $7.50   Price per assorted set of 18, 6" ... $11.25
Price, per doz. 6½" .. 8.00   Price per assorted set of 18, 6½" . 12.00
Price, per doz. 7" .... 8.50   Price per assorted set of 18, 7" ... 12.75

BENT RIFFLERS HANDLED

THREE SQUARE BASTARD

HAND BASTARD

FLAT FLOAT SAFE SIDES

HALF ROUND BASTARD

THREE SQUARE RASP

ROUND RASP

Bent Rifflers are used principally by stock makers, wood carvers, and metal workers for shaping and finishing in and about the many irregular places of pattern work.

They are made in six different shapes and styles of cuts as illustrated. The over-all length of these tools, including the handle, is approximately 7¾ inches.

Price per set of six $3.75

SCRAPERS HANDLED

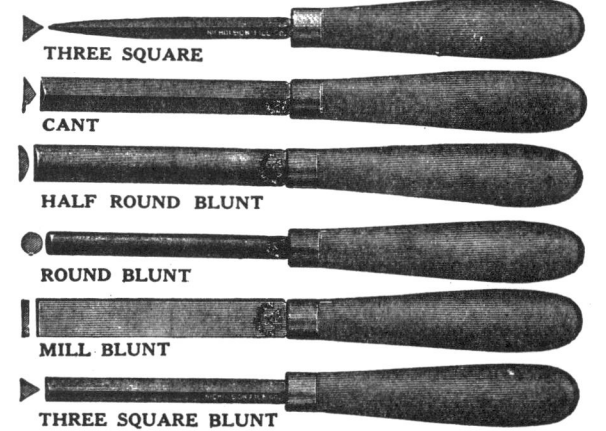

THREE SQUARE

CANT

HALF ROUND BLUNT

ROUND BLUNT

MILL BLUNT

THREE SQUARE BLUNT

Gunsmiths Scrapers are adaptable to a wide range of work. They are furnished "dead hard." The over-all length of these tools including the handle is approximately 9¼ inches.

Price per set of six $3.50

10% EXTRA CHARGE ON LESS THAN FULL SETS

ALL STEEL TOOL CHESTS AND CABINETS

MACHINIST'S CHEST
No. 620

Drawers slide easily on super-compound slides that stop only after they are extended giving a clear view of the contents. Front panel, which slides under drawers when box is open, fits against drawers locking them with lid lock. Nickel fittings; dark green ripple baked enamel finish; soft felt-like finish inside of drawers.

	Dimensions				
No.	Long	Wide	High	Net Wt.	Price
620	20"	8½"	13"	26 Lbs.	$12.00

ROLLER DOLLY
For No. 27 Chest

The roller dolly provides a stand for the number 27 tool chest that may be rolled to the job. It is wider than the chest so as to hold it firmly when the drawers are open and heavily loaded. The legs are enclosed to provide space for a tool box or other equipment you may wish to lock up when not on the job. Finished in brown or dark red ripple baked enamel.

	Dimensions			
No.	Long	Wide	High	Price
28-D	27½"	17¼"	24"	$10.75

MACHINIST'S CASE
Nos. 516 and 520

Neither heat nor moisture will affect case. The drawers slide easily on super-compound drawer slides that stop only after they are extended out of the case. Drawers lined with felt.
Case is strongly reinforced with boxed ends. Front panel slides under drawers when box is open, fits against drawers, locking them with lid lock. Sixty-change lock. Nickeled fittings. Seal brown ripple baked enamel finish.
An adjustable partition is placed in each drawer except the bottom.

	Dimensions				
No.	Long	Wide	High	Net Wt.	Price
516	16"	8½"	13"	24 Lbs.	$16.50
520	20"	8½"	13"	27¾ Lbs.	17.50

ROLLER TOOL CABINET
Nos. 34RC, 100RC, 134RC

No. 34RC is a handy cabinet to have in the shop. A till in the top provides for heavy tools, and there are two strong drawers that slide easily on positive double drawer slides. Angle iron legs and the casters permit easy moving.
No. 100 RC is an enclosure for the legs that provides space for tools or parts which you wish to lock up.
No. 134RC is the cabinet with the enclosure as illustrated. All three are finished in either red or brown ripple baked enamel.

No.		Net Wt.	Price
34RC	Without Enclosure	68 Lbs.	$19.50
100RC	Enclosure Alone	18 Lbs.	4.50
134RC	Cabinet with Enclosure	86 Lbs.	24.00

SHOP CHEST
No. 27

This large heavy duty tool chest has a 14" tote tray in which to carry tools to the job. The top drawer, for precision tools, lined with felt, is equipped with adjustable divisions. The middle drawer has a space for socket wrenches, and the lower deep (3¼") drawer is reinforced for heavy tools. The spill proof drawers move easily on strong compound drawer slides. The drawers and lid lock with one padlock. Finished in brown or dark red ripple baked enamel.

	Dimensions			
No.	Long	Wide	High	Price
27	27"	12½"	15¼"	$20.00

TOOL CHEST AND
ROLLER DOLLY
Nos. 27 and 25D (Combined)

This heavy duty tool chest is ideal for the gunsmith. The top drawer, for precision tools, is lined with felt and has adjustable divisions. The middle drawer has a division for socket wrenches, and the lower drawer is reinforced for heavy tools. The spill-proof drawers move easily.
The roller dolly provides a stand for No. 27 that may be rolled to the job. Both are finished in either brown or dark red ripple enamel.

No.	Shipping Wt.	Net Wt.	Price
27	68 Lbs.	56 Lbs.	$20.00
28D	45 Lbs.	42 Lbs.	10.75

A NECESSITY IN EVERY SHOP

REPAIRS

PARTS AVAILABLE

This large section of our catalog contains a listing with illustrations of all parts for the most popular guns in present day use. We realize that there are many discontinued makes and models still in use and, although some parts may still be available for them, most are obsolete and no longer obtainable from the manufacturers as production of such parts has been discontinued and fixtures for making same disposed of. It is useless to try to call on the factories for further supply, and we ourselves do not have obsolete parts; to make these by hand is not practical, as cost would be prohibitive.

DELIVERY

We know how important it is to our customers to obtain repairs for their guns, and for this reason we have specially trained men for this type of service. A large section of our stock room is devoted entirely to storing thousands of parts of the different makes to give prompt service. It is an impossibility, however, to keep on hand a complete line of all parts for all guns at all times. All orders received for parts on hand are shipped within 24 hours. If not on hand, they are immediately ordered from the factory, and any resulting delay is that of the manufacturer and not ourselves.

For these reasons we must urge you to order replacement parts not at the last moment when you are ready to go on your hunting trip, but as soon as you find you are in need of such parts.

IDENTIFICATION OF PARTS

To simplify this service and to save our customers time and unnecessary correspondence it is necessary to order all parts by number, stating make, model and caliber of gun also serial number of gun. In case you cannot determine the part from the parts list, send in the broken part and state the make, model and caliber of the arm to the best of your ability.

PAYMENTS—POSTAGE—INSURANCE

Since many parts must be specially procured, we can only make shipment upon full prepayment. No parts will be sent c.o.d., nor can parts be returned for credit. For the ordinary small part or parts, weighing not over 3 ounces including shipping envelope, there is 7¢ charge for mailing, including postage and insurance. For this reason 7¢ should be added to all small orders to cover this item.

SENDING IN BROKEN PARTS

When sending in guns, or sample parts, each item should be clearly tagged with customers name, address, and requirements. A letter should be written advising us of shipment, or may be attached to parcel post shipment. Letters attached to parcel post shipments require a 3¢ stamp in addition to regular parcel post rate.

SERVICE CHARGE

Certain items, particularly barrels, are sometimes not supplied except when the entire gun is sent in. Such parts are usually particularly marked. The reason for this is that special tools, headspacing, and experience are required, and to attempt the fitting locally would more than likely create not only an unsatisfactory but downright dangerous job, thus endangering the user and injuring the reputation of the maker. On this type of replacement, the entire gun should be sent in and a $2.00 service charge to cover handling, transportation to factory, fitting, etc., will be made in addition to the cost of the barrel or part.

The $2.00 service charge will also be made on guns sent in for estimate as the estimating involves considerable work and handling.

WHEN ADDITIONAL PARTS ARE REQUIRED

When a gun is sent in for fitting of a specific part or repair, it is frequently found upon examination that other parts are broken or so badly worn as to necessitate replacement. In such cases, the necessary parts will be fitted, *unless the contrary is specifically stated* when gun is sent in. Such parts will be charged at the regular prices but *no* additional service charge will be made.

MINIMUM ORDER $1.00

Because of the large amount of clerical and detail work connected with the handling and filling of each mail order, regardless of the value of the order we have found it impossible to continue filling mail orders for less than $1.00 because each such order represents a direct loss, and since the enormous quantity of such orders, mostly for small parts, over-burdens all normal facilities, thereby slowing down the general efficiency and service on all orders. Surely a perusal of this catalog will show some additional item or items sufficient to bring the total value of the order to $1.00.

ORDER BLANK IN MIDDLE AND INDEX IN BACK OF CATALOG

GENUINE MAUSER REPAIR PARTS

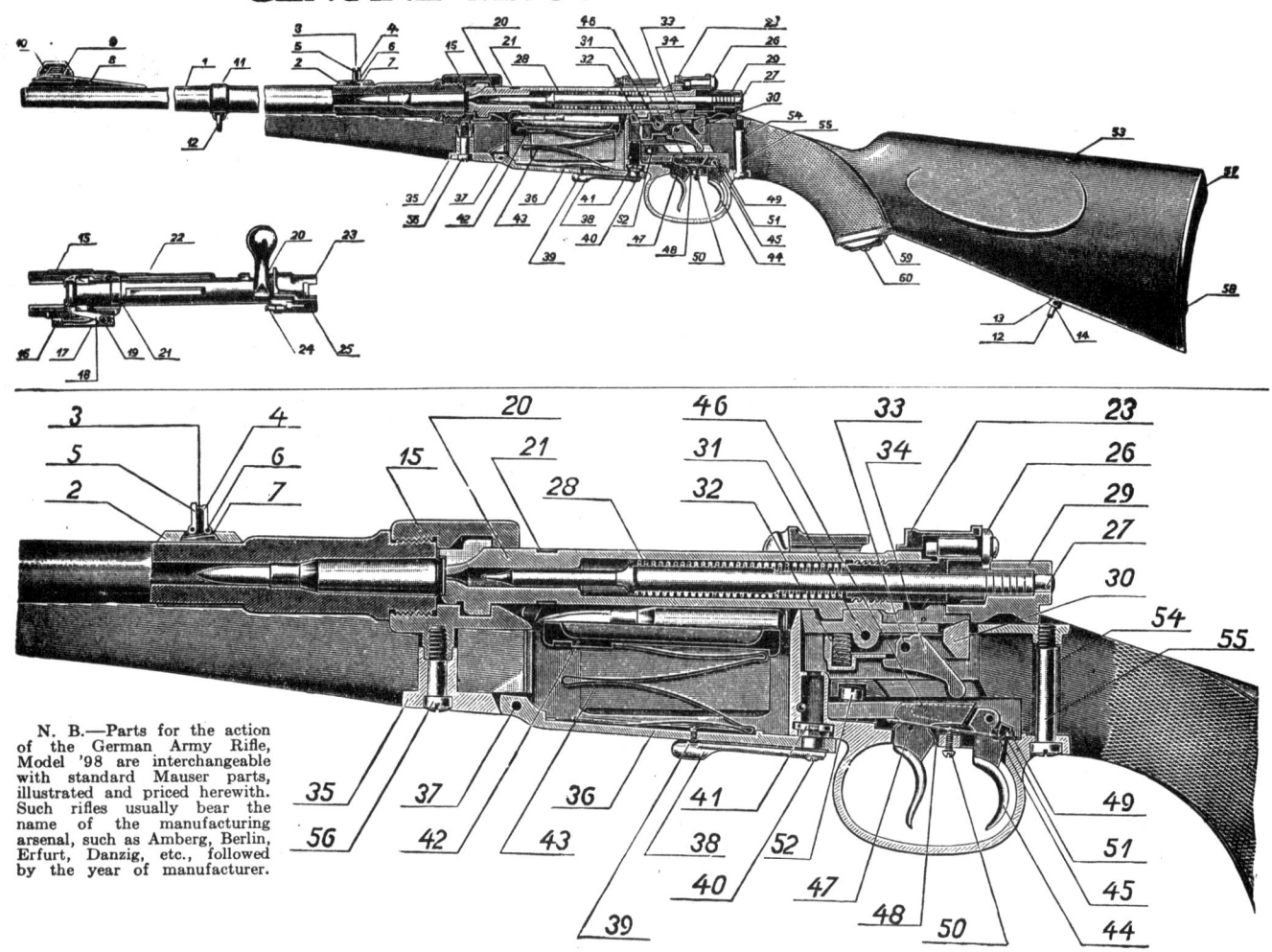

N. B.—Parts for the action of the German Army Rifle, Model '98 are interchangeable with standard Mauser parts, illustrated and priced herewith. Such rifles usually bear the name of the manufacturing arsenal, such as Amberg, Berlin, Erfurt, Danzig, etc., followed by the year of manufacturer.

INDEX OF REPAIR PARTS FOR MAUSER SPORTING RIFLE
ILLUSTRATED ABOVE AND ON OPPOSITE PAGE

No.	Part	Price
1	Barrel	$25.00 to $40.00
2	Rear sight base	1.75
3	Standard sight for 100 m.	1.75
4	Sight leaf for 200 m.	1.00
5	Sight leaf for 300 m.	1.00
6	Sight leaf pin	.25
7	Sight leaf spring	.25
8	Front sight block	1.75
9	Bead sight	1.75
10	Sight protector	1.00
11	Swivel ring	1.00
12, 13, 14a	Lower swivel with pin and screw	1.25
12, 14a	Upper swivel and screw	1.25
15a	Receiver	18.50
15b	Receiver with telescope fitting	20.00
16	Bolt stop	2.50
17	Bolt stop spring	1.75
18	Ejector	1.25
19	Bolt stop screw	.25
20a	Round bolt	11.50
20b	Flat bolt	12.50
21	Extractor ring	1.75
22	Extractor	4.00
23	Bolt plug	6.00
24	Bolt plug stop	1.00
25	Bolt plug stop spring	.25
26	Safety	3.00
27	Firing pin	4.00
28	Firing pin spring	1.25
29	Firing pin nut	3.00
30a	Sear	3.00
30b	Sear for trigger	3.00
31	Sear pin	.50
32	Sear spring	.50
33	Trigger pin	$0.50
34	Sear lever	.80
35	Magazine	10.00
35a	Magazine for set trigger	10.00
36	Magazine bottom plate	5.00
37	Hinge pin	.50
38	Magazine lever	1.25
39	Locking screw for mag. lever	.25
40	Magazine lever screw	.25
41	Locking plate	.75
42	Feeder	3.50
43	Feeder spring	1.25
44	Set trigger	1.25
45	Set trigger screw	.50
46	Pull trigger	1.25
47	Pull trigger pin	.50
48	Pull trigger spring	.50
49	Pull trigger spring screw	.50
50	Regulating screw	.50
51	Set trigger spring	.75
52	Set trigger spring	2.00
53	Stock	$40.00 and up
54	Tube	.50
55	Rear connecting screw	.50
56	Front connecting screw	.50
57a	Hard rubber or horn heel plate	2.00
57b	Metal heel plate	2.50
57c	Metal heel plate with trap (99-102 complete)	4.00
58	Heel plate screw	.25
59a	Horn grip cap	.50
59b	Metal grip cap	.50
60	Grip cap screw	.25
61	Regulation trigger	2.00
62	Bottom plate release	1.25
63	Bottom plate release screw	.50
64	Bottom plate release spring	$0.50
75	Tangent curve sight base	2.25
76	Tangent sight leaf	1.75
77	Sight slide	1.50
78	Push button	1.75
79	Slide tooth spring	.50
80	Tangent sight leaf spring	.50
81	Tangent curve sight base for octagon barrel	2.25
81a	Tangent sight complete without base	6.00
82	Barrel swivel ring	1.50
83	Wire swivel	.35
84	Swivel pin	.10
85	Stock swivel screw	.50
86	Front swivel base with eyelet for octagon barrel	1.50
87	Front swivel base with stud	1.50
88	Barrel ring with stud	2.50
89	Front swivel base retaining screw	.75
90	Washer	.50
91	Front sight ramp	3.00
91c	Front sight ramp complete with silver bead sight and sight protector (made in various sizes, see page 19)	5.00
92	Barrel swivel ring with ear	2.00
93	Front swivel for carbine	1.60
94	Stock rosettes, per pair	.50
95	Forend swivel screw	.25
96	Steel forend cap for carbine	2.50
97	Forend cap nut	.25
98	Forend cap screw	.25
99-102	Steel trap buttplate complete (1 21/32 x 5 1/16)	6.00
110	Special take-down cleaning rod	4.50

AMERICA'S GREAT GUN HOUSE 407

REPAIR PARTS FOR MAUSER SPORTING RIFLE

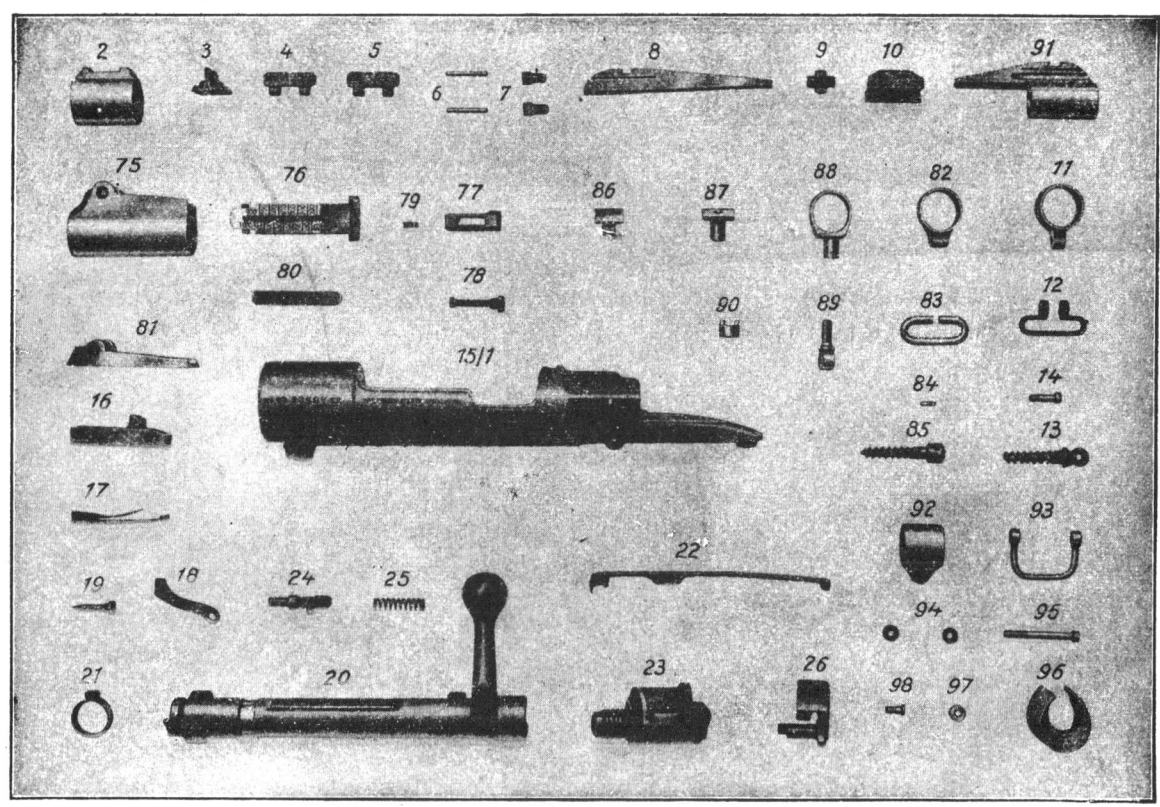

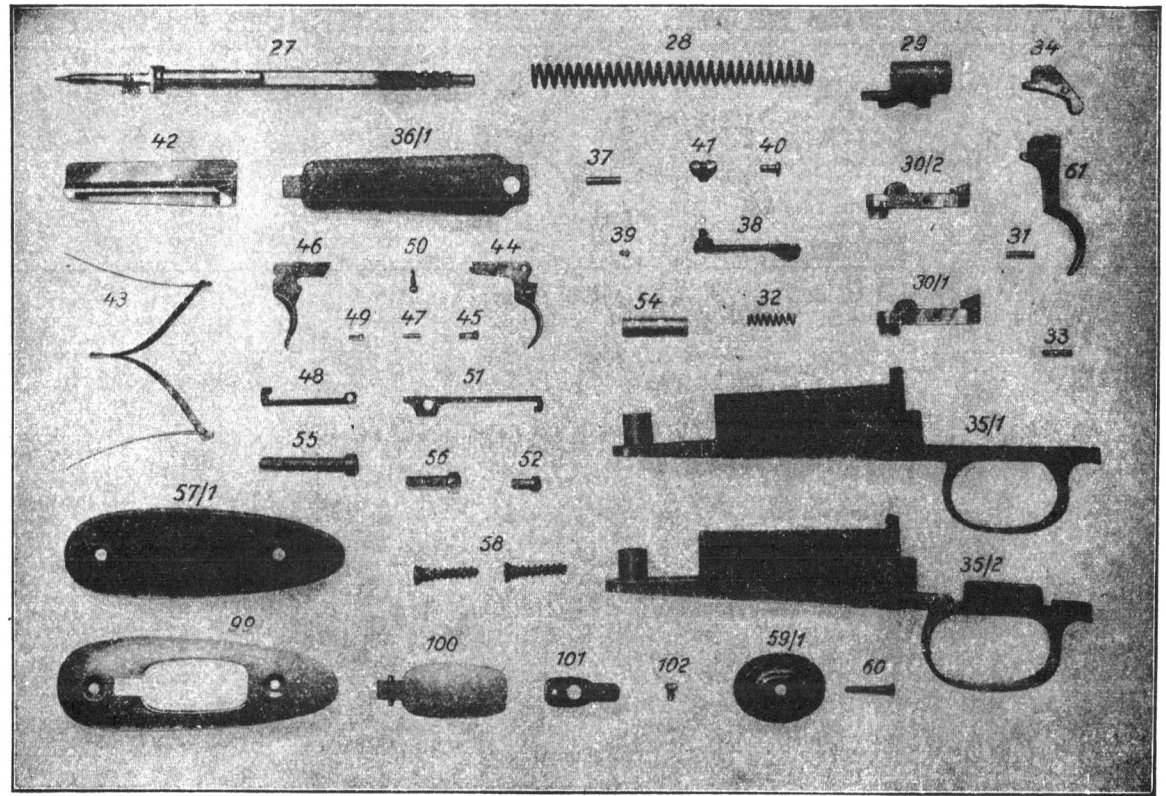

FIRING PINS FOR GERMAN ARMY RIFLES (MODEL 1898) $4.00

Tell Others About Stoeger's Catalog

DETAILS OF MANNLICHER-SCHOENAUER RIFLES

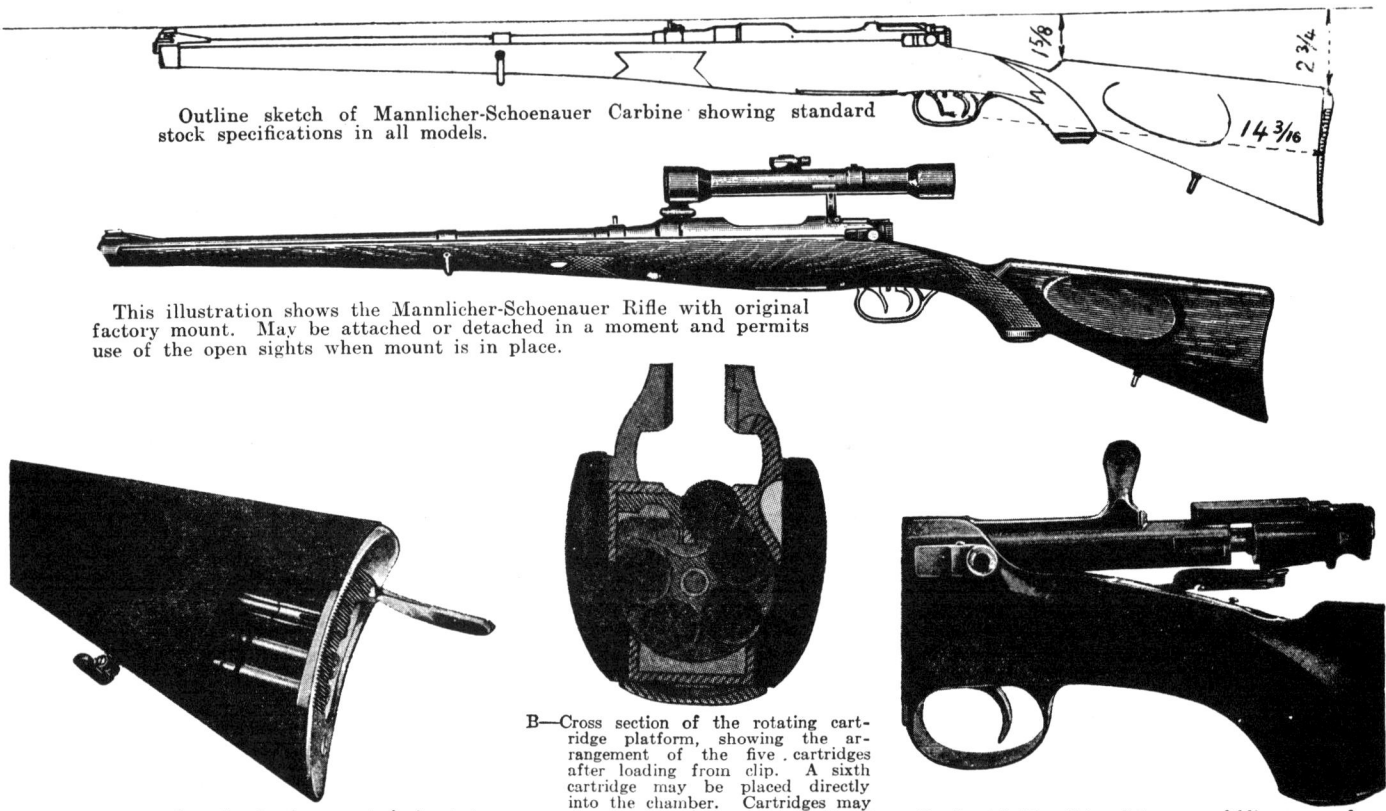

Outline sketch of Mannlicher-Schoenauer Carbine showing standard stock specifications in all models.

This illustration shows the Mannlicher-Schoenauer Rifle with original factory mount. May be attached or detached in a moment and permits use of the open sights when mount is in place.

A—Cross section of stock, showing receptacle in stock for cleaning rod and two spare cartridges.

B—Cross section of the rotating cartridge platform, showing the arrangement of the five cartridges after loading from clip. A sixth cartridge may be placed directly into the chamber. Cartridges may also be loaded separately without the use of a clip.

C—Special Mannlicher-Schoenauer folding peep, showing how bolt slides over on opening.

CONSTRUCTIVE BALLISTICS OF THE MANNLICHER-SCHOENAUER SPORTING RIFLES

Caliber	Cartridge	Powder Wt. Grains	Style of Bullet	Bullet Wt. Grains	Bullet length inches	Muzzle velocity ft. sec.	Muzzle energy ft. lbs.	Trajectory, Inches Height at Mid-Range		
								100 yds.	200 yds.	300 yds.
6.7		37	Soft-Nose ogival	157.5	1.2	2395	1990	.6"	3.2"	9"
6.7		38.5	S-Soft-Nose	123.5	1.24	2690	1980	.44"	2.45"	7"
8.2	Mannlicher-Schoenauer	43	Soft-Nose ogival	200.6	1.05	2225	2150	.79"	4"	11"
8.2		48	S-Soft-Nose	170	1.1	2515	2418	.63"	2.9"	8.2"
9.0		48.5	Soft-Nose ogival	247	1.07	2160	2564	.85"	4.2"	11.5"
9.5		52.5	Soft-Nose ogival	271.6	1.04	2225	2980	.85"	4.2"	12.6"
30–06	Springfield	53	Brass-Point	180.5	1.24	2760	3000	.5"	2.3"	6.3"
7.0	7 x 64	51	Hollow-Point	173	1.25	2650	2700	.6"	2.6"	6.5"
8.0	8 x 60	54	Copper-Point-Torpedo	185	1.3	2775	3285	.4"	2.5"	6.07"

Original Mannlicher-Schoenauer Rifle Parts

Part No.	Name	Price
*1	Barrel	$25.00
2	Foresight	1.50
*3	Foresight block	1.75
*5	Backsight base	2.00
*6	Stand. sgt. for 1 leaf	1.25
*7	Sight leaf	1.00
8	Sight leaf pin	.25
14	Body	27.50
15	Bolt catch	1.50
16	Bolt catch spring	.25
17	Bolt catch pin	.25
*18	Bolt	7.50
18/1	Spring catch for firing pin nut	1.00
19	Cocking piece	4.50
20	Safety catch	3.00
21	Safety catch spring	.25
22	Firing pin spring	1.00
23	Firing pin	3.50
24	Firing pin nut	1.75
25	Bolt head	3.50
*26	Ejector	1.50
27	Ejector screw	.25
*28	Extractor	2.00
*29	Mag. cartridge stop	2.50
30	Spg. for mag. cart. stp.	.25
31	Scw. for mag. cart. stp.	.25
32/1	Hairtrigger plate	3.00
32/2	Set trigger	1.50
32/3	Set trigger spring	1.50
32/4	Set trig. spg. screw	.35
32/5	Set trig. reg. screw	.35
32/6	Set trigger pin	.25
32/7	Hair trigger	1.50
32/8	Hair trigger spring	.35
32/9	Hair trigger pin	.25
32/10	Hair trigger catch	.25
34	Sear lever	2.00
35	Pivot pin for sear lever	.25
36	Sear	1.50
37	Sear pivot	.25
37/1	Trigger lever	2.00
37/2	Trigger lever pivot	.25
37/3	Roller for trig. lever	.35
37/4	Roller pin	.25
38	Trigger spring	.50
*39	Cartridge carrier	4.00
*40	Cartridge carrier frame	4.00
*41	Cart. car. cover plate	2.50
42	Cover plate catch	1.25
43	Fast. spg. for cov. plate	.25
45	Cartridge carrier spg.	.50
*46	Front pivot for car.	1.25
48	Back pivot for car.	.75
49	Trigger guard	3.00
50	Trigger guard screw	.35
51	Upper sling ring	1.00
52	Upper sling band	1.00
53	Upper sling ring scrw.	.35
54	Up. slng. rng. scrw. nut	.25
55	Lowel sling swivel	1.25
56	Low. sling swiv. screw	.50
57	Lower sling swivel connecting screw	.25
58	Butt plate	
59	Butt plate trap	
60	Butt plate trap spg.	3.50
61	Butt plate trap spring screw	
63	Rub. lin. for butt plate	1.25
64	Screw	.35
*65	Stock	40.00
66	Fore-end cap	1.75
67	Fore-end cap screw	.25
68	Fore-end cap nut	.75
69	Fore-end cap nut scrw.	.25
70	Screw sleeve	.25
71	Rear connect. screw	.50
72	Front connect. screw	.50
73	Frnt. con. scrw. washer	.25
74	Horn end for grip end	1.00
75	Horn cap scrw.	.25
76	Horn cap pin	.25
	Various Parts for the Sporter Half Stock	
6a	Stand. sight for 1 leaf with wide notch	1.75
7a	Sgt. lf. with wide ntch.	1.00
14/1	Grooved tang	1.75
32	Single trigger	1.50
49/1	Trig. grd. for sing. trig.	5.00
49/2	Trigger guard catch	.75
49/3	Trig. guard ctch. lev.	.75
49/4	Trig. grd. catch. spg.	.25
49/5	Trig. guard catch. pin	.25
49/6	Trig. guard lever pin	.25
69	Scrw. for spg. pin plate	.25
71a	Rear connect. screw	.35
80a	Upper sling eye	2.50
81a	Up. sling eye. scrw.	.50
85	Spring pin	1.00
86	Spring pin spring	1.25
87	Spring pin plate	.50
88	Fore sight protector	1.00

* Complete bolt assmb. 17.50
* Complete bolt head. 6.00
* Complete blued barrel with sgts. & swivel 30.00
* Complete stock 37.50
* Four piece collap. clng. rod for stock 3.50

Note: All Mannlicher-Schoenauer parts are interchangeable, but in ordering those parts marked with an asterick*, it is essential to state caliber.

ALL SHIPMENTS ARE INSURED

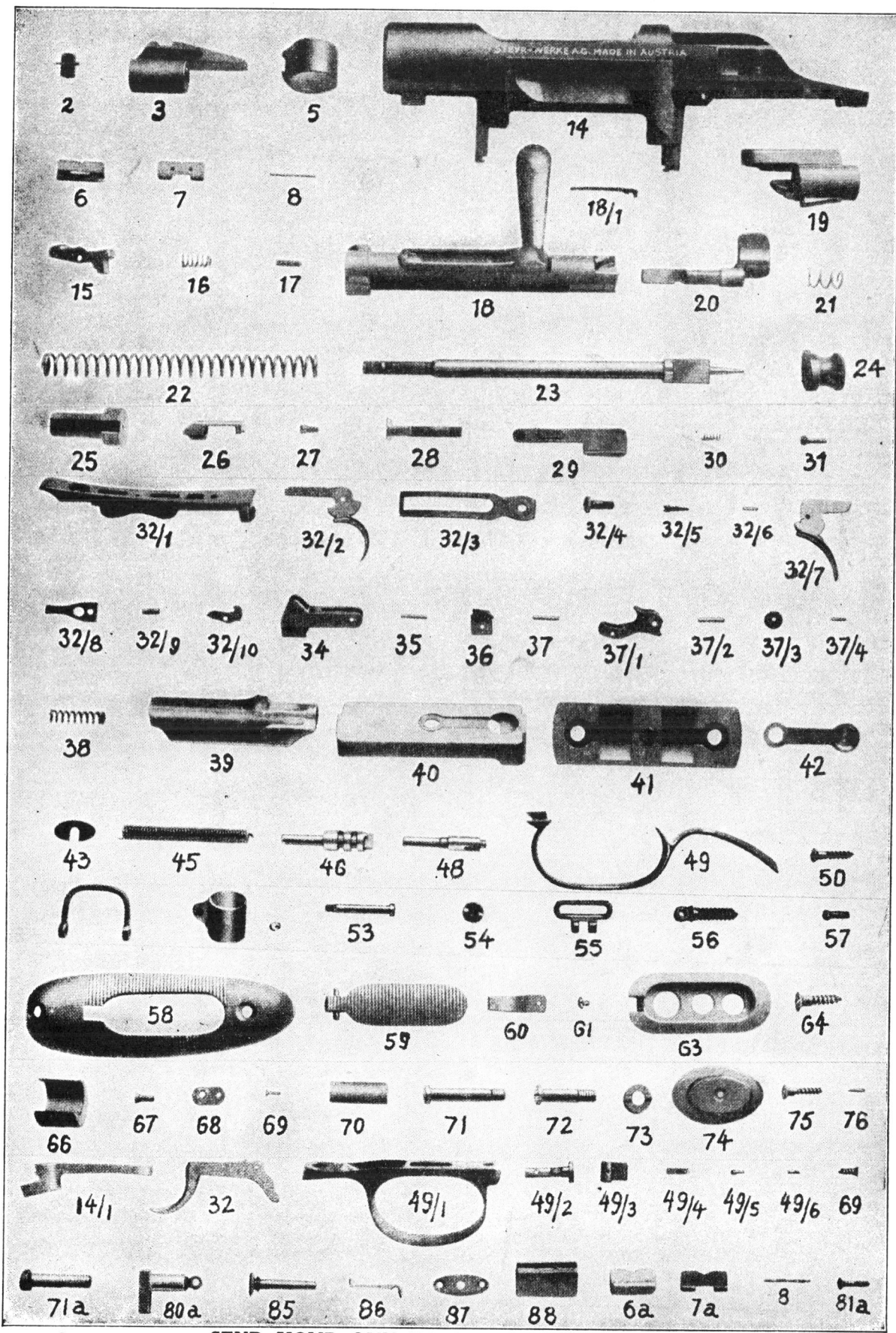

HAENEL AIR PISTOL AND RIFLE PARTS

MODEL 28 AIR PISTOL

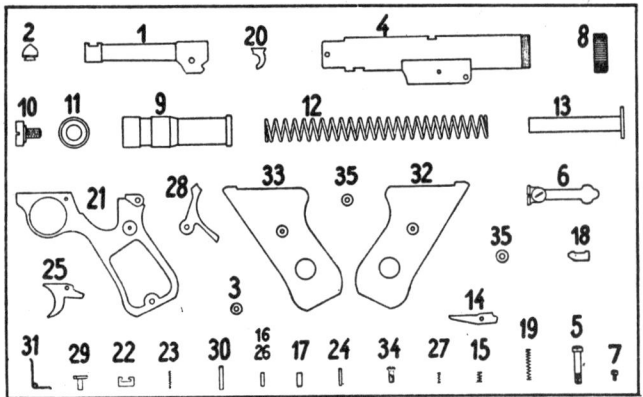

Part No.		Price	Part No.		Price
1	Barrel	$5.00	19	Locking Bolt Spring	$ .25
2	Front Sight	.50	20	Catch	.75
3	Barrel Joint Washer	.25	21	Grip Frame	3.00
4	Housing	2.50	22	Bolt	.60
5	Joint Screw	.50	23	Bolt Spring	.25
6	Rear Sight	.60	24	Bolt Pin	.25
7	Joint Lock Screw	.25	25	Trigger	1.25
8	Base Cap	.60	26	Trigger Pin	1.25
9	Piston	1.50	27	Trigger Spring	.25
10	Piston Screw	.25	28	Cocking Lever	1.75
11	Piston Washer	.25	29	Cocking Lever Hinge Pin	.35
12	Piston Spring	.75	30	Pin for cocking Lever Spring	.25
13	Piston Spring Guide	.50	31	Cocking Lever Spring	.25
14	Sear	.75	32	Right Grip Plate	1.25
15	Sear Spring	.25	33	Left Grip Plate	1.25
16	Sear Pin	.25	34	Grip Plate Screw	.25
17	Grip Hinge Pin	.25	35	Grip Escutcheons	.25
18	Locking Bolt	.50			

MODEL 3100 AIR RIFLE (HAENEL MOD. 40)

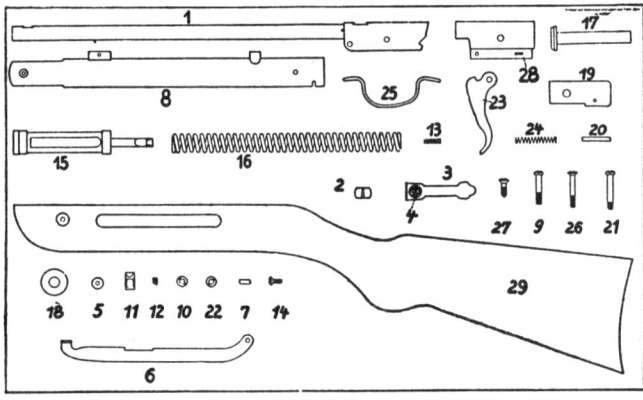

Part No.		Price	Part No.		Price
1	Barrel with base	$2.50	17	Piston Spring Guide	$.75
2	Front Sight	1.00	18	Large Washer for Housing	.35
3	Rear Sight, Complete	1.25	19	Base	.35
4	Rear Sight Screw	.25	20	Base Pin	.25
5	Washer	.25	21	Trigger Screw with nut	.40
6	Cocking Lever	1.50	23	Trigger	1.00
7	Pin for Cocking Lever	.30	24	Trigger Spring	.25
8	Housing	3.00	25	Trigger Guard	.65
9	Joint Screw and Washer	.35	26	Front Trigger Guard Screw	.25
11	Bolt	.25	27	Rear Trigger Guard Screw	.25
12	Bolt Screw	.25	28	Housing	1.75
13	Bolt Spring	.25	29	Stock	7.50
14	Lock Screw	.25			
15	Piston, Complete	2.25			
16	Piston Spring	1.50			

MODEL 3101-2 AIR RIFLE (HAENEL MOD. 1)

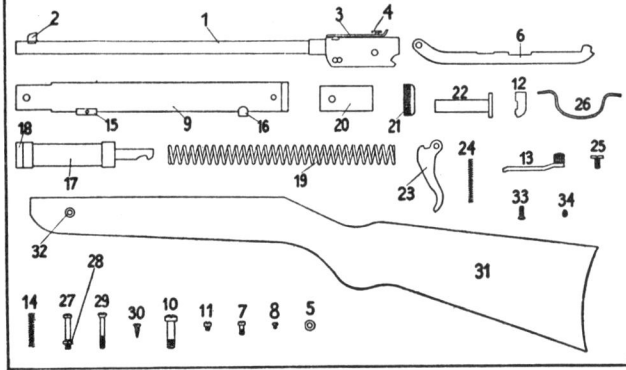

Part No.		Price	Part No.		Price
1	Barrel with base	$7.50	19	Piston Spring	$1.25
2	Front Sight	.50	20	Base Housing	.35
3	Rear Sight, Complete	.75	21	Base Cap	.60
4	Rear Sight Screw	.25	22	Spring Guide	.75
5	Barrel Washer	.25	23	Trigger	.75
6	Cocking Lever	1.25	24	Trigger Spring	.25
7	Cocking Rod Screw	.25	25	Piston Washer Screw	.25
8	Cocking Rod Screw Lock Screw	.25	26	Trigger Guard	.60
9	Housing	6.00	27	Trigger Guard Screw with Washer	.40
10	Joint Screw	.35	29	Front Trigger Guard Screw	.25
11	Joint Screw Lock Screw	.25	30	Rear Trigger Guard Screw	.25
12	Catch	.40	31	Stock	6.50
13	Catch Push Button	.75	32	Escutcheon for Retaining Plate Screw	.25
14	Catch Spring	.25	33	Retaining Plate Screw	.25
15	Retaining Plate	.60	34	Catch Lock Screw	.25
16	Support Plug	.50			
17	Piston, Complete	1.75			
18	Piston Washer	.25			

MODEL 3102-3 AIR RIFLE (HAENEL MOD. 3)

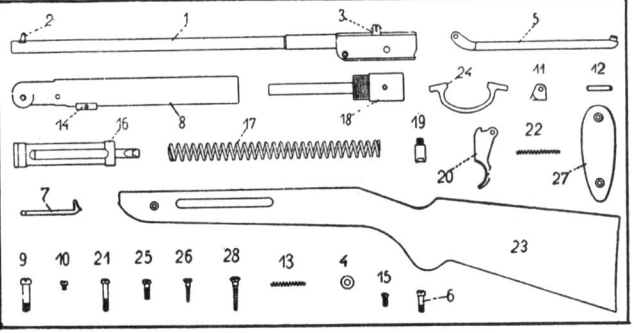

Part No.		Price	Part No.		Price
1	Barrel with base	$10.00	16a	Piston Washer	$ .25
2	Front Sight	.75	16b	Piston Washer Screw	.25
3	Rear Sight, Complete	1.75	17	Piston Spring	1.25
4	Leather Barrel Washer	.25	18	Base Plug	1.75
5	Cocking Rod	2.50	19	Support Plug	.50
6a	Cocking Rod Screw	.25	20	Trigger	1.25
6b	Cocking Rod Screw Lock Screw	.25	21	Trigger Pin	.30
7	Bolt Rod	1.25	22	Trigger Spring	.25
8	Piston Housing	4.50	22a	Regulating screw with nut	.50
9	Joint Screw	.35	23	Stock	10.00
10	Joint Screw Locking Screw	.25	24	Trigger Guard	1.00
11	Bolt	.50	25	Front Trigger Guard Screw	.25
12	Bolt Pin	.25	26	Rear Trigger Guard Screw	.25
13	Bolt Spring	.25	27	Butt Plate	1.00
14	Retaining Plate	.50	28	Butt Plate Screw	.25
15	Retaining Plate Screw	.25			
16	Piston, Complete	2.75			

ALL OTHER FOREIGN AIR GUN PARTS ON SPECIAL ORDER

WEBLEY AIR PISTOL PARTS

MARK 1 & 2 MODELS

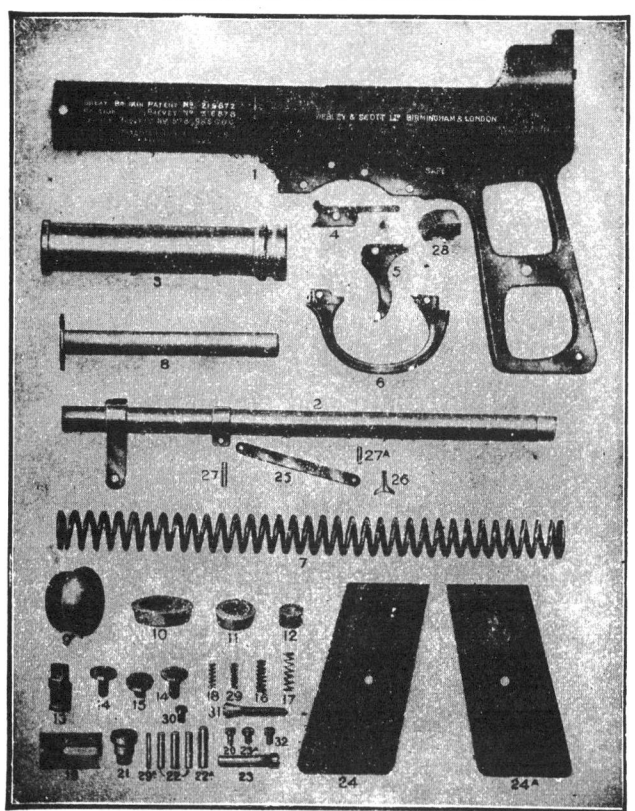

SENIOR MODEL

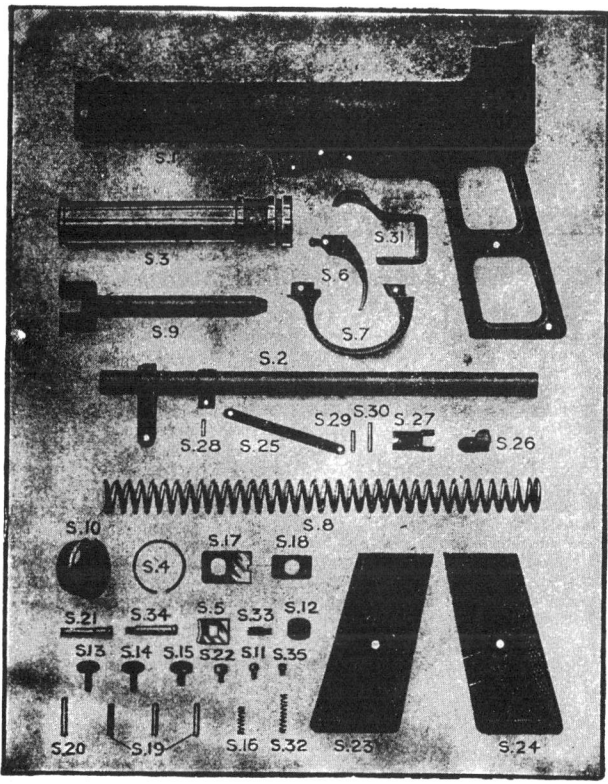

PARTS OF MARK I AND MARK II

No.		Price	No.		Price	No.		Price
1	Body Mark I.	$7.50	14	Stock Screw..	$.50	26A	Cup Washer Screw (not illustrated)	$.50
2A	Body Mark II.	7.50	15	Sight Screws..	.50			
2	Barrel Mark I (.177 or .22 cal.)	5.00	16	Sear Spring..	.50	27	Long Link Pin.	.50
			17	Safe Spring...	.50	27A	Small Link Pin	.50
			18	Trigger Spring.	.50	28	Top Catch....	1.50
2A	Barrel Mark II (.177 or .22 cal.)	6.00	19	Sight (Mark I)	.50	29	Top Catch Spring	.35
			20	Safe Screw...	.50	29A	Top Catch Pin	.50
3	Air Piston Complete (Mark I)	1.60	21	Piston Screw..	.50	30	Screw Retaining Breech Screw	.50
			22	Sear Trigger and Guard Pegs	.50	31	Screw Adjusting Screw..	.50
3A	Air Piston Complete (Mark II)	1.60	22A	Stock Side Positioning Pin.	.50	32	Screw Securing Trigger Adjusting Screw..	.50
4	Sear	.50	23	Barrel Joint Screw (Mark I)	.50	33	Brush	.25
5	Trigger	.50				34	Piston Rings (Mark II)..	.50
6	Trigger Guard.	1.25	23A	Barrel Joint Screw (Mark II)	.50	35	Back Sight (Mark II)..	.75
7	Main Spring.	1.00						
8	Spring Guide..	1.00	24	Stock Side (Mark I)	1.50	35A	Back Sight (Mark I)..	.75
9	Breech Screw..	.50						
10	Cup Washer (Mark I)	.50	24A	Stock Side (Mark II)	2.00	36	Trigger Adjusting Screw..	.50
11	Inside Cup Washer (Mark I)	.50	25	(Part of No. 2 Long Link)..	.50			
12	Barrel Joint Washer	.35	26	Small Cocking Lever Loop...	.75			
13	Safe	.50						

NOTE: Mark II has been discontinued and is replaced by the Senior.

The following Components of the Mark II. Air Pistol differ from the Mark I. Air Pistol:—

Body	$7.50	(Left)	$2.00	Top Catch	$1.50
Spring Guide..	.50	Piston	1.60	Top Catch Screw..	.50
Vulcanite Stocks (Right)	2.00	Piston Rings, each.	.50	Trigger	.50
Vulcanite Stocks		Horizontal Sights..	.50	Piston Complete with Rings..	1.60
		Vertical Sights....	.50		

When ordering, please state whether for the Mark I or Mark II Models.

PARTS FOR JUNIOR MODEL

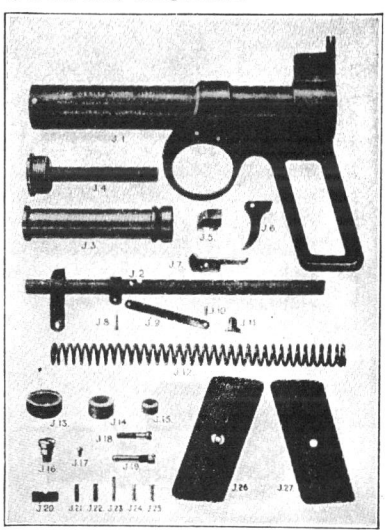

No.		Price
J 1	Body	$6.00
J 2	Barrel Complete (J2, 8, 9, 10 and 11)	4.00
J 3	Air Piston	7.50
J 4	Spring Guide	1.50
J 6	Trigger	.50
J 7	Sear	.50
J 8	Long Link Peg..	.25
J 9	Long Link	.50
J10	Small Link Peg..	.25
J11	Small Link	.50
J12	Main Spring	.75
J13	Cup Washer	.50
J14	Inside Washer	.50
J15	Barrel Joint Washer and Brush	.50
J16	Piston Screw	.25
J17	Sight Screw	.25
J18	Stock Screw	.25
J19	Barrel Screw	.50
J20	Sight	.25
J21	Sear Peg	.25
J22	Trigger Peg	.25
J23	Top Catch Peg	.25
J24	Sear Spring	.25
J25	Top Catch Spring	.25
J26	Stock Side Right (Wood or Metal)	.60
J27	Stock Side Left (Wood or Metal)	.60
J28	Brush	.25

PARTS OF SENIOR MODEL

No.		Price	No.		Price
S 1	Body	$7.50	S18	Sight, Horizontal	$.50
S 2	Barrel complete (S25, S26, S27, S28, S29, S30)	5.00	S19	Sear, Trigger and Guard Pin	.50
			S20	Stock Pins	.25
S 3	Piston	1.60	S21	Barrel Joint Screw..	.50
S 4	Piston Ring	.50	S22	Screw securing Joint Screw	.50
S 5	Sear (New Type as illustrated)	.50	S23	Stock Side, Right..	2.00
S 5a	Sear (Old Type not illustrated)	.50	S24	Stock Side, Left..	2.50
S 6	Trigger	.50	S25	Long Link	.75
S 7	Trigger Guard	1.25	S26	Small Link	.50
S 8	Main Spring	1.00	S27	Intermediate Link	.50
S 9	Spring Guide	1.00	S28 S29	Link Pins	.50
S10	Breech Screw	.50	S30	Intermediate Link Pin (Long)	.50
S11	Breech Screw Retainer	.50	S31	Barrel Catch	.50
S12	Barrel Joint Washer and Bush	.35	S32	Barrel Catch Pin	.50
	Screw	.50	S33	Barrel Catch Spring Plunger	.50
S13 S14	Stock Screw	.50	S34	Barrel Catch Joint Screw	.50
S15	Sight Screw	.50			
S16	Trigger Spring	.50	S35	Barrel Catch Stop Brush	.25
S17	Sight, Vertical	.50			

SEE PAGE 8, "HOW TO ORDER"

BROWNING OVER UNDER GRADE 1 PARTS

No.	Part	Price
OU-1	Barrel Plate Wood for Lightning Model (Right)	$0.35
OU-2	Barrel Plate Wood for Lightning Model (Left)	.35
OU-3	Barrel Plate Screws, each	.15
OU-4	Butt Plate	1.00
OU-5	Butt Plate Screws, each	.15
OU-6	Cocking Lever Lifter	.50
OU-7	Cocking Lever Lifter Pin	.15
OU-8	Cocking Lever	1.75
OU-9	Cocking Lever Pin	.15
OU-10	Connector	.65
OU-11	Connector Stop Pin	.15
OU-12	Ejector (Right)	1.05
OU-13	Ejector (Left)	1.05
OU-14	Ejector Extension (Right)	1.15
OU-15	Ejector Extension (Left)	1.15
OU-16	Ejector Extension Stop Screws, each	.15
OU-17	Ejector Stop Screws, each	.15
OU-18	Ejector Hammer (Right)	1.15
OU-19	Ejector Hammer (Left)	1.15
OU-20	Ejector Hammer Pin	.15
OU-21	Ejector Hammer Springs, each	.15
OU-22	Ejector Hammer Spring Guides, each	.15
OU-23	Ejector Hammer Catches, each	.20
OU-24	Ejector Hammer Catch Springs, each	.15
OU-25	Ejector Hammer Catch Pins, each	.15
OU-26	Firing Pin (Over Barrel)	.45
OU-27	Firing Pin (Under Barrel)	.45
OU-28	Firing Pin Spring for Under Barrel	.15
OU-29	Firing Pin Retaining Pins, each	.15
OU-30	Forearm, Full Grip with Escutcheons for Lightning Model	8.75
OU-31	Forearm Screw for OU-30	.25
OU-32	Forearm, Standard Grip for Standard Model	8.75
OU-33	Forearm Plate for OU-32 and OU-35	1.75
OU-34	Forearm Screw for OU-32 and OU-35	.65
OU-35	Forearm, Beavertail	17.45
OU-36	Forearm Bracket	4.10
OU-37	Hammer (Right)	1.25
OU-38	Hammer (Left)	1.25
OU-39	Hammer Pin	.15
OU-40	Inertia Block	1.25
OU-41	Inertia Block Spring	.15
OU-42	Inertia Black Spring Guide	.15
OU-43	Joint Pin	$0.65
OU-44	Locking Bolt	2.25
OU-45	Mainsprings, each	.25
OU-46	Mainspring Guides, each	.20
OU-47	Piston	.35
OU-48	Piston Spring	.15
OU-49	Piston Pin	.15
OU-50	Receiver	16.75
OU-51	Selector and Safety	1.25
OU-52	Selector Block	.15
OU-53	Selector Spring	.15
OU-54	Sear (Right)	.85
OU-55	Sear (Left)	.85
OU-56	Sear Springs, each	.15
OU-57	Sear Pin	.15
OU-58	Sight Base	.95
OU-59	Sight Bead	.15
OU-60	Stock Type field, 1⅝x2½x14⅛, Standard Pistol Grip as illustrated	17.50
OU-61	Stock Type Trap, 1½x1¾x14⅝, Standard Pistol Grip as illustrated	17.50
OU-62	Stock Bolt	.35
OU-63	Stock Bolt Washer	.15
OU-64	Take Down Lever	1.75
OU-65	Take Down Lever Pin	.15
OU-66	Take Down Lever Latch	1.35
OU-67	Take Down Lever Latch Spring	.15
OU-68	Take Down Lever Latch Pin	.15
OU-69	Tang Piece	1.50
OU-70	Tang Piece Screw (Over)	.15
OU-71	Tang Piece Screw (Under)	.15
OU-72	Top Lever	2.75
OU-73	Top Lever Spring	.15
OU-74	Top Lever Spring Retainer	.25
OU-75	Top Lever Dog	.55
OU-76	Top Lever Dog Screw	.15
OU-77	Top Lever Spring Retainer Screw	.15
OU-78	Trigger	2.50
OU-79	Trigger Pin	.15
OU-80	Trigger Guard Standard Pistol Grip	2.65
OU-81	Trigger Guard Straight Grip	2.95
OU-82	Trigger Guard Screws, each	.15
OU-83	Trip Rod (Right)	.95
OU-84	Trip Rod (Left)	.95

Prices for parts for grades other than our Grade 1 supplied on request.
When ordering parts please give serial number of gun and gauge.

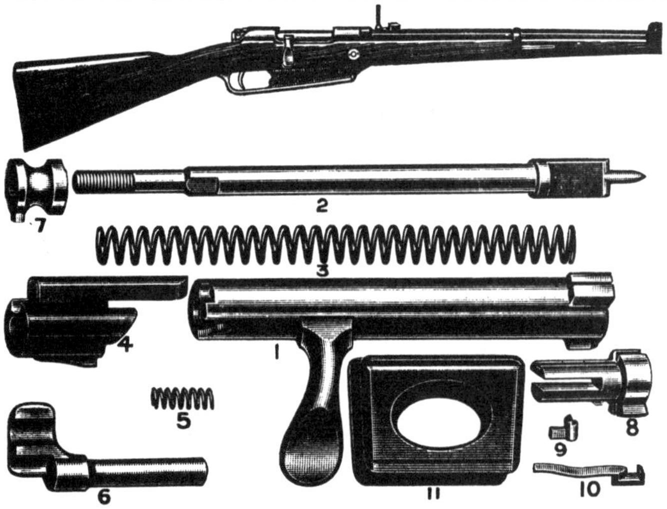

PARTS FOR THE MAUSER MODEL '88

The carbine shown here is the German Army Model '88 carbine, which was superseded in 1898 by the well-known Model '98 rifle and carbine. In spite of its obsolescence, many thousands were used in the world war, and large quantities eventually found their way to the U. S. A. As a result, there has been a demand for parts, which we carry in stock and on which prompt delivery can be made.

For best results, the Model '88 ammunition, listed on the upper right corner of this page is recommended. This rifle is a five shot repeater and requires the use of the box clip, (illustration No. 11). The clip and cartridges are inserted from the top of the magazine, and held in place by the charging arm or lever. After the last shell is worked into the chamber the empty clip drops out through the open magazine. This rifle is also known as the Mannlicher-Haenel or Schilling Mannlicher, but is not to be confused with the Mannlicher-Schoenauer.

No. 1.	Bolt	$7.50
No. 2.	Firing Pin	3.50
No. 3.	Firing Pin Spring	1.25
No. 4.	Cocking Piece	4.00
No. 5.	Safety Spring	.75
No. 6.	Safety	3.00
No. 7.	Firing Pin Nut	$2.50
No. 8.	Bolt Head	5.00
No. 9.	Ejector	1.25
No. 10.	Extractor	1.25
No. 11.	Box Clip	.50

Other Parts on Request.

MINIMUM SHIPPING ORDER $1.00

WALTHER AUTOMATIC RIFLE PARTS MODEL I AND II

No.	Part	Price
1-II	Action frame complete	$15.00
2-II	Barrel complete	35.00
3-II	Sights complete	1.75
4	Barrel sling Swivel complete	1.75
5	Hammer complete	1.75
6	Recoil Spring complete	1.25
7	Indicator and Spring complete	.75
8	Magazine catch plunger Spring	.75
9	Bolt head Plunger and Spring	1.00
10	Safety bar Plunger and Spring	1.00
11-II	Stock complete	25.00
12	5-shot Magazine complete	1.50
13	Breech case	7.50
14	Breech	6.00
15	Bolt Handle	5.50
16	Safety Bar	.75
17	Trigger	1.00
18	Trigger Spring	.50
19	Trigger axis Pin	.30
20	Sear	.75
21	Sear Spring	.50
22	Hammer Spring	.50
23	Hammer spring Stop	.50
24	Hammer spring Keeper	.50
25	Hammer axis Pin	.50
26	Ejector	$.50
27	Ejector fixing pin	.75
28	Striker	.75
29	Striker rebound Spring	.50
30	Striker Lever	1.00
31	Striker assembly Retainer	1.00
32	Extractor	.75
33	Main barrel fixing Screw	.50
34-II	Breech case Plunger	.50
35	Breech case plunger Spring	.50
36	Breech case plunger retaining Pin	.75
37	Magazine Catch	.50
38	Magazine catch Plunger	.50
39	Magazine catch Spring	.50
40	Rear stock fixing Screw	.50
41	Front stock fixing Screw	$.50
42	Escutcheon	.50
43	Butt swivel complete	1.00
44	Stock fixing screw Bush	.50
45-II	Safety	2.00
46-II	Safety Connector	.50
47-II	Safety cross Pin	.50
48-II	Wing safety Spring and Plunger	.75
49	Key for trigger adjustment	.75
50-II	Muzzle Protector	.75
51	9-shot Magazine complete	30.00

B.S.A. AIR RIFLE PARTS FOR ALL MODELS

B.S.A. AIR RIFLE SECTIONAL ILLUSTRATION. No. 2 MODEL

NOTE.—When ordering any replacement parts state whether for—
No. 1, .177" bore.
No. 4, Club Model, .177" bore.
No. 2, .22" bore.

FULL LISTS OF PARTS

A	Barrel	$25.00
B	Breech Plug	2.75
C	Cylinder	3.50
D	Piston	2.50
E	Piston Spring, Cal. .177, 2.25-.22	2.75
F	Trigger	1.50
G	Hand Lever	2.25
H	Link	1.75
I	Hand Lever Axis Pin	.75
J	Piston Rod	.75
K	Trigger Spring	.50
L	Trigger Axis Screw	.50
M	Hole in Breech (not strictly a part)	
N	Piston Rod Guide Tube	.75
O	Brass Washer	.50
P	Leather Washer (Large)	.75
P1	Leather Washer (Small)	$.50
Q	Leather Screw	.50
R	Link Axis Screw	.50
S	Sear Axis Screw	.50
T	Stock	7.50
U	Trigger Guard Screw	.50
V	Breech Plug Plate	1.75
W	Stock Bolt	1.75
X	Piston Rod Keeper Screw	.50
Y	Trigger Block	1.25
Z	Guard	1.75
1	Foresight Bead	1.00
2	Backsight Bed	2.25
3	Backsight Leaf	$.75
4	Elevating Screw	.50
5	Hand Lever Catch	.75
6	Hand Lever Catch Block	1.25
7	Hand Lever Catch Spring	.50
8	Hand Lever Catch Pin	.50
9	Breech Plate Screw	.50
11	Trigger Block Dowel Pin	.50
12	Butt Inlay Plate Screw	.50
13	Butt Trap	1.25
14	Butt Plate Inlay Plate Spring	.50
15	Stock Bolt Spring Washer	$.50
16	Breech Plate Plunger	.50
18	Sear	1.25
19	Trigger Spring Pin	.50
20	Backsight Spring	.50

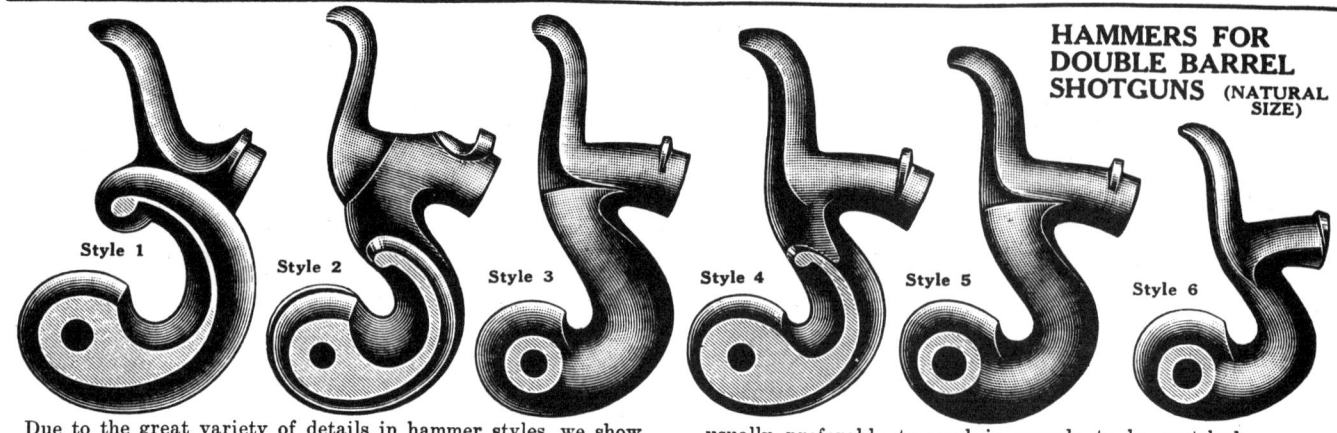

HAMMERS FOR DOUBLE BARREL SHOTGUNS (NATURAL SIZE)

Style 1 Style 2 Style 3 Style 4 Style 5 Style 6

Due to the great variety of details in hammer styles, we show here the six principal types in their natural standard sizes. In addition to the hammers illustrated, we carry a very large stock of assorted hammers. Most hammers are available in three finishes—rough forged, finished, finished and engraved. In many cases where the exact type can not be supplied, the gunsmith can take the nearest style, rough forged, and work it out. It is usually preferable to send in sample to be matched. When ordering without sample, specify following information: **1.** Style. **2.** Length from center of hole to center of hammer face. **3.** Whether rough forged, finished, or finished and engraved.

Price, forged .... $.50
Price, finished, polished with hole 1.25
Price, finished and engraved . $2.50
Hammer Screws, Each ...... .25

ACTION AND LEVER SPRINGS (Natural Size)

No. 1-9, inclusive $1.50
No. 10, Bonehill Spring 1.75
No. 11-14, inclusive 1.25

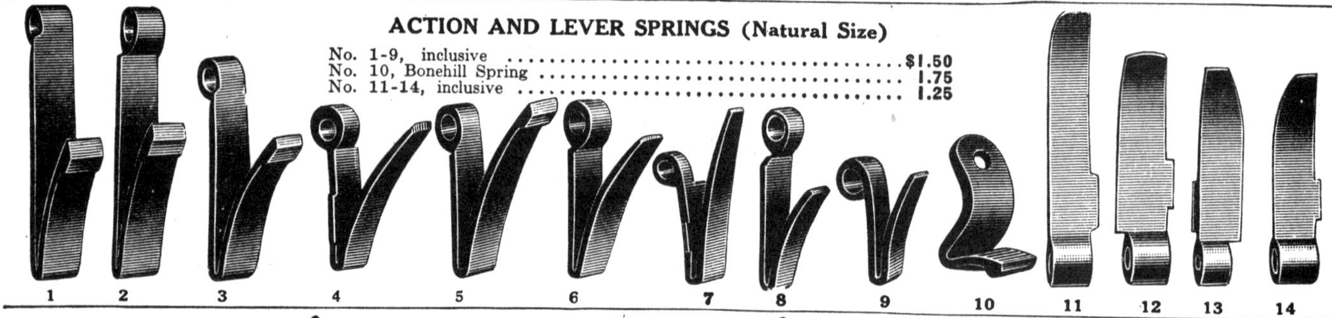

1 2 3 4 5 6 7 8 9 10 11 12 13 14

SHOTGUN MAIN SPRINGS (NATURAL SIZE)

Order by number, each $2.00

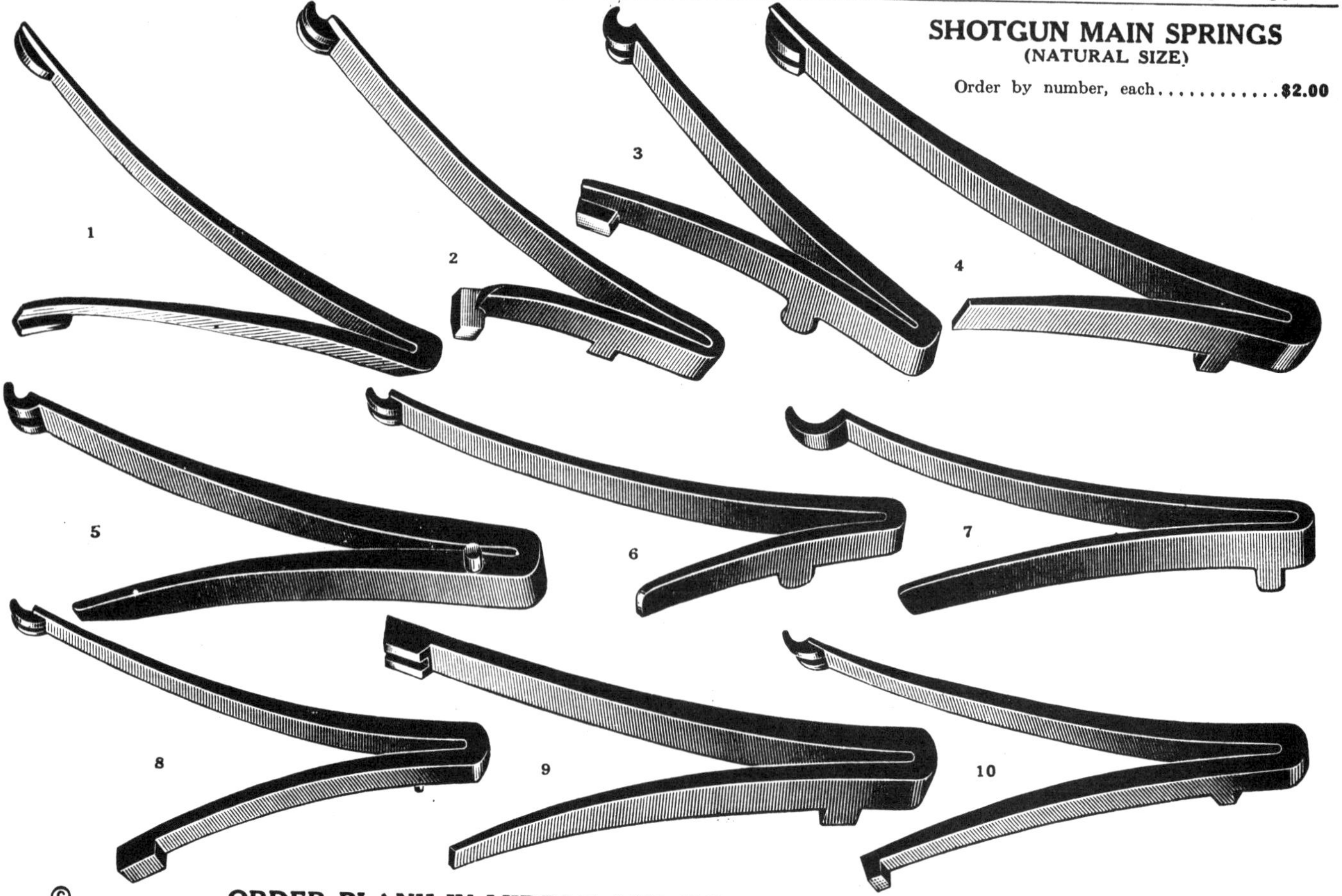

1 2 3 4 5 6 7 8 9 10

ORDER BLANK IN MIDDLE AND INDEX IN BACK OF CATALOG

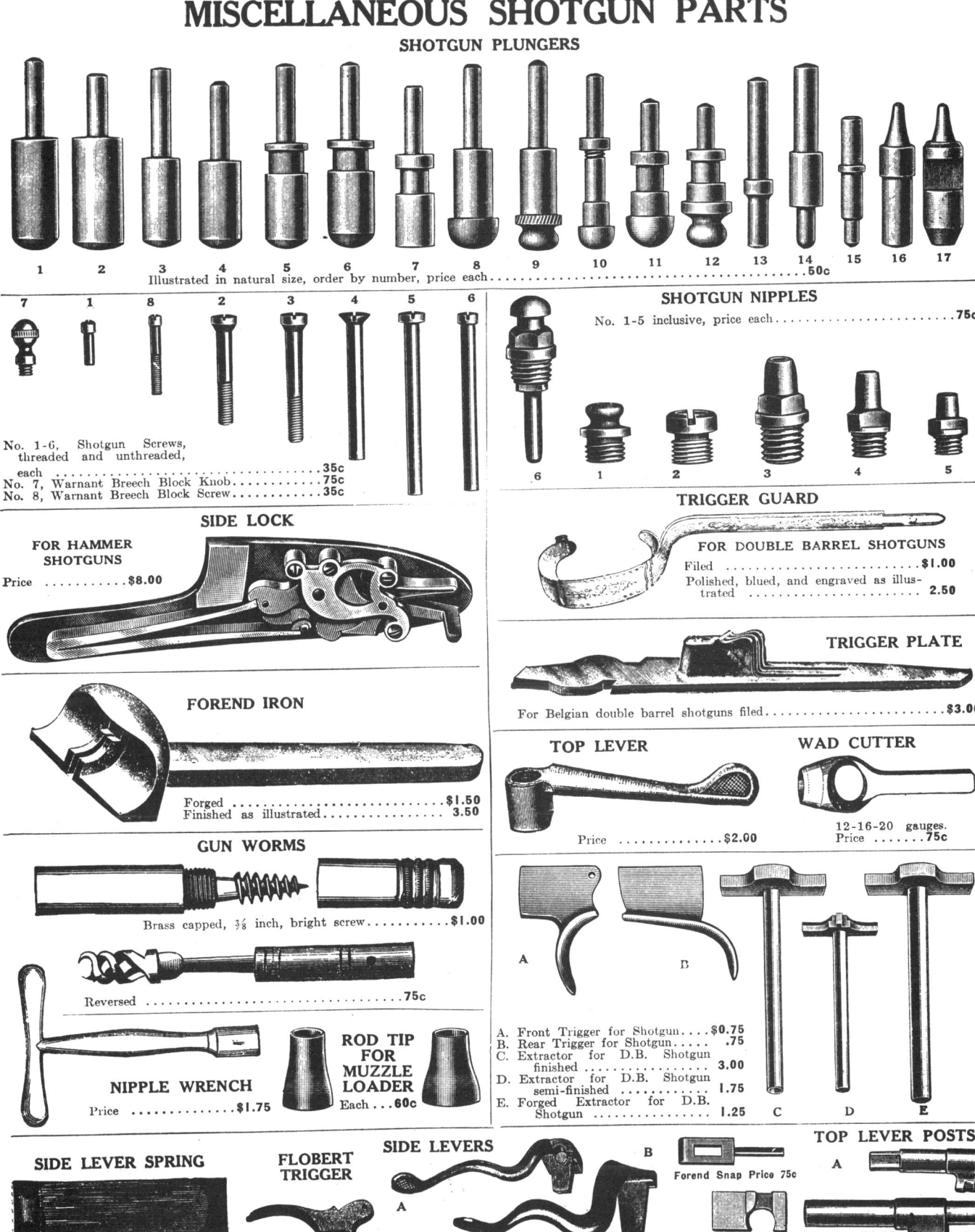

COMPONENT PARTS FOR OBSOLETE COLT REVOLVERS

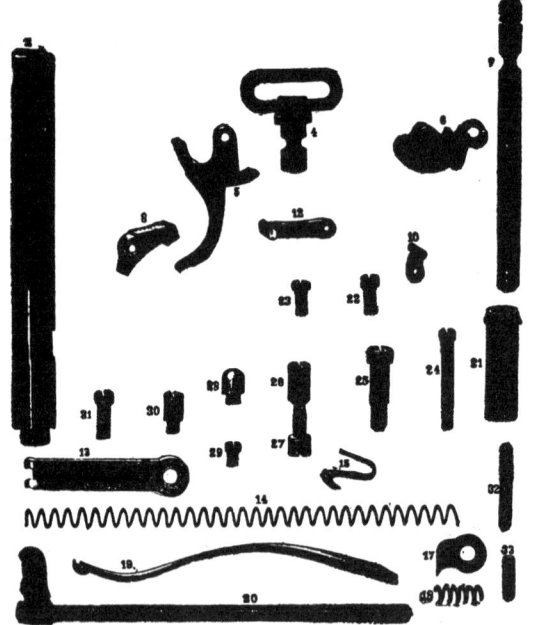

Only such parts as are listed can be supplied

"DOUBLE ACTION ARMY" REVOLVER

No.	Part	Price	No.	Part	Price
2	Ejector Tube	$3.00	23	Main Spring Set Screw	$.25
4	Swivel Ring and Stud	.40	24	Stock Screw	.25
5	Trigger	.90	25	Hammer Screw	.25
6	Saddle	1.50	26	Base Pin Catch Nut	.25
7	Base Pin	.35	27	Base Pin Catch Screw	.25
8	Sear	.75	28	Gate Screw	.25
10	Saddle Stirrup	.80	29	Gate Spring Screw	.25
12	Strut	.45	30	Ejector Tube Screw	.25
13	Trigger Spring	.75	31	Front Guard Screw	.25
14	Ejector Spring	.25	32	Trigger and Sear Pin	.25
15	Strut and Hand Spring	.25	33	Swivel Pin	.25
17	Sear Spring	.25		Barrel with Sight	4.50
18	Base Pin Catch Spring	.25		Recoil Plate	.25
19	Main Spring	.75		Stocks (rubber only), per pair	1.15
20	Ejector Rod and Head	1.20		Escutcheons, per set	.25
21	Cylinder Bushing	.60		Lock Frame Cap	1.00
22	Rear Guard Screw	.25			

"NEW ARMY", "NEW NAVY", "MARINE CORPS" AND "OFFICERS' MODEL" (OLD STYLE) REVOLVERS

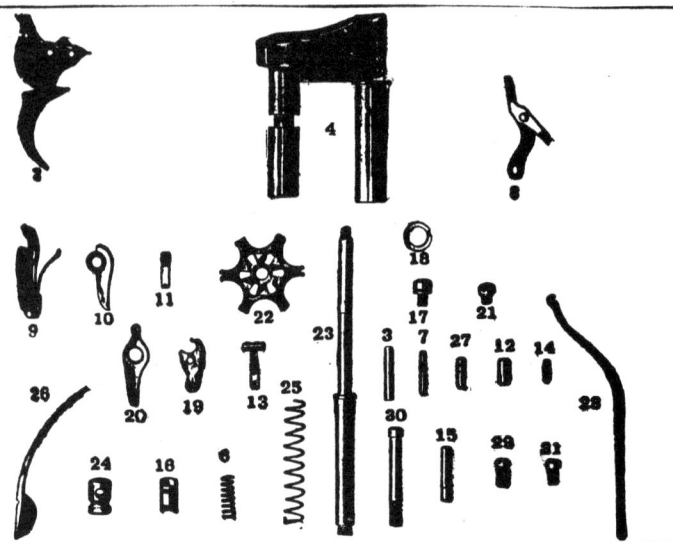

No.	Part	Price	No.	Part	Price
2	Trigger	$.90	21	Locking Lever Screw	$.25
3	Trigger Pin	.25	22	Ejector and Ratchet	1.20
4	Crane	3.75	23	Ejector Rod	.50
6	Latch Spring	.25	24	Ejector Head	.25
7	Latch Pin	.25	25	Ejector Spring	.25
8	Rebound Lever	.80	26	Rebound Spring	.50
9	Hand and Hand Spring	.60	27	Rebound Spring Pin	.25
	Hand Spring	.25	28	Main Spring	.75
10	Strut	.40	29	Main Spring Set Screw	.25
11	Strut Spring	.25	30	Stock Screw	.25
12	Strut Pin	.25	31	Side Plate Screw	.25
13	Hammer Stirrup	.30		Barrel, 4½" and 6" only	3.75
14	Hammer Stirrup Pin	.25		Cylinder	5.00
15	Hammer Pin	.25		Swivel, complete	.50
16	Crane Lock	.25		Stocks (rubber only), per pair	1.15
17	Crane Lock Screw	.25		Escutcheons, per set	.25
18	Crane Bushing	.25		Recoil Plate	.25
19	Bolt and Bolt Spring	.50		Side Plate	1.50
	Bolt Spring	.25			
20	Locking Lever	.25			

"DOUBLE ACTION" REVOLVERS
Calibers .38 and .41

No.	Part	Price	No.	Part	Price
3	Ejector Tube	$2.40	26	Sear Screw	$.25
6	Base Pin	.35	27	Gate Catch	.25
7	Hammer Stirrup	.40	28	Ejector Tube Screw	.25
8	Sear	.80	29	Front Strap Screw	.25
9	Strut	.40	30	Main Spring Set Screw	.25
10	Bolt	.90	31	Rear Guard Screw	.25
12	Sear and Bolt Spring	.30	32	Main Spring Screw	.25
13	Trigger Spring	.40	33	Trigger Roll	.25
14	Main Spring	.75	34	Latch Screw	.25
15	Ejector, Rod only	.30	35	Hand and Strut Spring Screw	.25
15	Ejector, Head only	.45	36	Trigger Spring Screw	.25
16	Ejector Spring	.25	37	Front Guard Screw	.25
17	Gate Spring	.25	38	Back Strap Screw	.25
18	Base Pin Catch Spring	.25		Cylinder	3.50
19	Strut Spring	.25		Barrel, 4½" and 6" only, with Sight	4.00
20	Hand Spring	.25		Lock Frame Gate	1.25
21	Stock Screw	.25		Stocks (rubber only), per pair	1.15
22	Hammer Screw	.25		Escutcheons, per set	.25
23	Trigger Screw	.25			
24	Base Pin Catch Nut	.25			
25	Base Pin Catch Screw	.25			

INSTRUCTIONS: In ordering parts always give name and number listed in catalog, also make, model, caliber and serial number of gun.

PAYMENTS: Parts will be sent only on advance payment. Parts cannot be returned for credit. A service charge of 25c must be added to every order under $1.00 to cover cost of handling. Do not forget to include postage.

SEE PAGE 8, "HOW TO ORDER"

COLT PARTS

COLT "SHOOTING MASTER" AND "NEW SERVICE TARGET" REVOLVERS

No.	Part	Price	No.	Part	Price
1	Hammer, complete	$3.75	26	Ejector Spring	$0.25
2	Hammer Pin	.25	27	Bolt	1.00
3	Hammer Stirrup	.30	28	Bolt Spring	.25
4	Hammer Stirrup Pin	.25	29	Bolt Screw	.25
5	Safety	.40	30	Rebound Lever	1.80
6	Safety Lever	.30	31	Rebound Lever Pin	.25
7	Strut	.40	32	Stock Pin	.25
8	Strut Spring	.25	33	Stock Screw	.25
9	Strut Pin	.25	34	Side Plate Screw	.25
10	Firing Pin	.25		Cylinder, complete	5.25
11	Firing Pin Rivet	.25		Cylinder, complete (for .357 Magnum)	8.50
12	Hand	1.00		Barrel (with sight)	7.50
13	Main Spring	1.50		Barrel (without sight)	6.00
14	Crane	4.00		Rear Sight	1.50
15	Crane Bushing	.25		Front Sight	1.50
16	Crane Lock	.25		Stocks, Checked Walnut, per pair:	
17	Crane Lock Screw	.25		Shooting Master	3.00
18	Latch	1.50		New Service Target	2.00
19	Latch Spring	.25		Escutcheons, per set	.25
20	Latch Pin	.25		Recoil Plate	.25
21	Trigger, Checked	1.90		Frame, complete	26.00
22	Trigger Pin	.25		Side Plate	1.95
23	Ejector and Ratchet	1.25			
24	Ejector Rod	.65			
25	Ejector Rod Head	.25			

"OFFICERS' MODEL" TARGET REVOLVER

Please specify whether Caliber .38 or .22

No.	Part	Price	No.	Part	Price
1	Hammer, complete	$3.40	26	Ejector Spring	$0.25
2	Hammer Pin	.25	27	Bolt	1.10
3	Hammer Stirrup	.30	28	Bolt Spring	.25
4	Hammer Stirrup Pin	.25	29	Bolt Screw	.25
5	Safety	.40	30	Rebound Lever	1.70
6	Safety Lever	.30	31	Rebound Lever Pin	.25
7	Strut	.40	32	Stock Pin	.25
8	Strut Spring	.25	33	Stock Screw	.25
9	Strut Pin	.25	34	Side Plate Screw	.25
10	Firing Pin	.30		Frame, complete	25.00
11	Firing Pin Rivet	.25		Side Plate	1.90
12	Hand	1.00		Cylinder, complete	5.50
13	Main Spring	1.30		Barrel, Standard (with sight)	6.75
14	Crane	3.75		Barrel, Heavy Type (with sight)	6.75
15	Crane Bushing	.25		Barrel, Standard (without sight)	5.25
16	Crane Lock	.25		Barrel, Heavy Type (without sight)	5.25
17	Crane Lock Screw	.25		Front Sight	1.50
18	Latch	1.30		Rear Sight	1.50
19	Latch Spring	.25		Walnut Stocks, pair	2.00
20	Latch Pin	.25		Escutcheons, per set	.25
21	Trigger, Checked	2.20		Recoil Plate	.25
22	Trigger Pin	.25			
23	Ejector and Ratchet	1.25			
24	Ejector Rod	.50			
25	Ejector Rod Head	.25			

In replacing parts marked thus (*) it will be necessary to send gun to us.

INSTRUCTIONS: In ordering parts always give name and number listed in catalog, also make, model, caliber and serial number of gun.

PAYMENTS: Parts will be sent only on advance payment. Parts cannot be returned for credit. A service charge of 25c must be added to every order under $1.00 to cover cost of handling. Do not forget to include postage.

COLT "NEW SERVICE" REVOLVER AND "NEW SERVICE .38" REVOLVER

No.	Part	Price	No.	Part	Price
1	Hammer, complete	$3.00	24	Ejector Rod	$0.65
2	Hammer Pin	.25	25	Ejector Rod Head	.25
3	Hammer Stirrup	.30	26	Ejector Spring	.25
4	Hammer Stirrup Pin	.25	27	Bolt	.75
5	Safety	.40	28	Bolt Spring	.25
6	Safety Lever	.25	29	Bolt Screw	.25
7	Strut	.40	30	Rebound Lever	1.30
8	Strut Spring	.25	31	Rebound Lever Pin	.25
9	Strut Pin	.25	32	Stock Pin	.25
10	Firing Pin	.25	33	Stock Screw	.25
11	Firing Pin Rivet	.25	34	Side Plate Screw	.25
12	Hand	.75		Cylinder, complete	5.25
13	Main Spring	.90		Cylinder, complete (for .357 Magnum)	8.50
14	Crane	4.00		Barrel	4.50
15	Crane Bushing	.25		Walnut Stocks, pair	2.00
16	Crane Lock	.25		Escutcheons, per set	.25
17	Crane Lock Screw	.25		Recoil Plate	.25
18	Latch	1.50		Swivel, complete	.40
19	Latch Spring	.25		Swivel Pin	.25
20	Latch Pin	.25		Frame, complete	19.00
21	Trigger, Checked	1.50		Side Plate	1.95
22	Trigger Pin	.25		Latch Spring Guide	.25
23	Ejector and Ratchet	1.25			

CAREFUL ATTENTION AND SAFE DELIVERY OF YOUR ORDER

COLT REVOLVER PARTS

COLT "OFFICIAL POLICE" REVOLVER CALIBER .38 SPECIAL AND .22 LONG RIFLE

"POLICE POSITIVE SPECIAL," "DETECTIVE SPECIAL," "POLICE POSITIVE" CALIBER .32 AND .38 AND "BANKER SPECIAL" COLT "POLICE POSITIVE TARGET"

Please specify whether Caliber .38 or .22

No.	Part	Price	No.	Part	Price
1	Hammer, complete	$2.70	23	Ejector and Ratchet	$1.20
2	Hammer Pin	.25	24	Ejector Rod	.50
3	Hammer Stirrup	.30	25	Ejector Rod Head	.25
4	Hammer Stirrup Pin	.25	26	Ejector Spring	.25
5	Safety	.40	27	Bolt	.75
6	Safety Lever	.25	28	Bolt Spring	.25
7	Strut	.40	29	Bolt Screw	.25
8	Strut Spring	.25	30	Rebound Lever	1.20
9	Strut Pin	.25	31	Rebound Lever Pin	.25
10	Firing Pin	.25	32	Stock Pin	.25
11	Firing Pin Rivet	.25	33	Stock Screw	.25
12	Hand	.75	34	Side Plate Screw	.25
13	Main Spring	.80		Frame, Complete	18.00
14	Crane	3.75		Side Plate	1.90
15	Crane Bushing	.25		Cylinder, complete	5.50
16	Crane Lock	.25		Barrel	3.75
17	Crane Lock Screw	.25		Stocks, Rubber, per pair	1.15
18	Latch	1.30		Stocks, Checked Walnut, per pair	2.00
19	Latch Spring	.25		Escutcheons, per set	.25
20	Latch Pin	.25		Recoil Plate	.25
21	Trigger, Checked	1.50			
22	Trigger Pin	.25			

No.	Part	Price	No.	Part	Price
1	Hammer, complete	$2.50	24	Ejector Rod	$0.45
2	Hammer Pin	.25	25	Ejector Rod Head	.25
3	Hammer Stirrup	.30	26	Ejector Spring	.25
4	Hammer Stirrup Pin	.25	27	Bolt	.75
5	Safety	.40	27a	Bolt Spring	.25
6	Safety Lever	.25	28	Bolt Screw	.25
7	Strut	.40	29	Rebound Lever	1.10
8	Strut Spring	.25	30	Rebound Lever Pin	.25
9	Strut Pin	.25	31	Stock Pin	.25
10	Firing Pin	.25	32	Stock Screw	.25
11	Firing Pin Rivet	.25	33	Side Plate Screw	.25
12	Hand	.60		Frame and Side Plate	17.00
13	Main Spring	.60		Frame (Target Model)	21.00
14	Crane	3.50		Side Plate	2.25
15	Crane Bushing	.25		Cylinder	5.50
16	Crane Lock	.25		Barrel	3.40
17	Crane Lock Screw	.25		Target Mod. Bbl. & Sgt.	5.25
18	Latch	1.15		Without Sight	3.75
19	Latch Spring	.25		Front Sgt., Target Mod.	1.50
20	Latch Pin	.25		Rear Sgt., Tar. Mod.	1.50
21	Trigger, Checked	1.40		Recoil Plate	.25
22	Trigger Pin	.25		Walnut Stocks, pair	2.00
23	Ejector and Ratchet	1.10		Escutcheons, per set	.25

"POCKET POSITIVE," "POLICE POSITIVE" CALIBER .32, AND "POLICE POSITIVE TARGET" REVOLVERS (LIGHT MODELS)

No.	Part	Price	No.	Part	Price
1	Hammer, complete	$2.50	26	Ejector Spring	$0.25
2	Hammer Pin	.25	27	Bolt	.75
3	Hammer Stirrup	.30	27a	Bolt Spring	.25
4	Hammer Stirrup Pin	.25	28	Bolt Screw	.25
5	Safety	.40	29	Rebound Lever	1.10
6	Safety Lever	.25	30	Rebound Lever Pin	.25
7	Strut	.40	31	Stock Pin	.25
8	Strut Spring	.25	32	Stock Screw	.25
9	Strut Pin	.25	33	Side Plate Screw	.25
10	Firing Pin	.25		Front Sgt. (Target Mod.)	1.50
11	Firing Pin Rivet	.25		Rear Sgt. (Target Mod.)	1.50
12	Hand	.60		Frame and Side Plate	17.00
13	Main Spring	.60		Frame (Target Model)	21.00
14	Crane	3.25		Side Plate	1.40
15	Crane Bushing	.25		Cylinder	5.30
16	Crane Lock	.25		Barrel, 2½ or 3½ ins.	2.75
17	Crane Lock Screw	.25		4, 5 or 6 ins.	3.25
18	Latch	1.15		Target Mod. Bbl. & Sgt.	5.25
19	Latch Spring	.25		Without Sight	3.75
20	Latch Pin	.25		Recoil Plate	.25
21	Trigger	.90		Walnut Stocks, pair	2.00
22	Trigger Pin	.25		Escutcheons, per set	.25
23	Ejector and Ratchet	1.00		"Police" models only:	
24	Ejector Rod	.45		Rubber Stocks for "Pocket Positive," pr.	1.15
25	Ejector Rod Head	.25			

In replacing parts marked thus (*) it will be necessary to send gun to us.

PLEASE TELL OTHERS ABOUT STOEGER'S CATALOG

COLT REVOLVER PISTOL PARTS

"SINGLE ACTION ARMY" REVOLVER

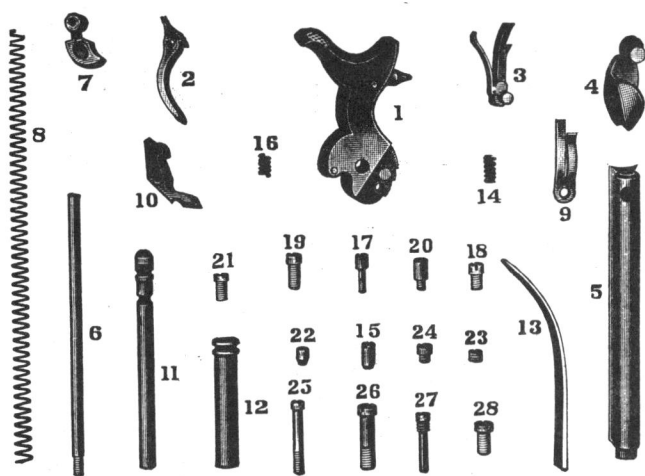

28	Main Spring Screw	$.25
	Lock Frame	15.00
	Barrel	4.50
	Cylinder	4.50
	Cylinder (for .357 Magnum)	7.75
	Firing Pin	.25
	Trigger Guard	$4.00
	Back Strap	3.00
	Stocks, Rubber, per pair	1.15
	Escutcheons, per set	.25
	Recoil Plate	.25
	Firing Pin Rivet	.25

THE COLT "CAMP PERRY" MODEL
CALIBER .22 SINGLE-SHOT TARGET PISTOL

In ordering parts, please give number of Pistol.

1	Hammer, complete	$2.70
2	Hammer Pin	.25
5	Rebound Lever	1.00
11	Firing Pin	.30
12	Firing Pin Rivet	.25
14	Main Spring	.25
16	Crane	3.75
18	Crane Lock	.25
19	Crane Lock Screw	.25
20	Latch	1.30
21	Latch Spring	.25
21a	Latch Spring Guide	.25
22	Latch Pin	.35
24	Trigger	2.20
25	Trigger Pin	.25
29	Ejector Rod	.50
30	Ejector Rod Head	.25
31	Ejector Rod Guide Bushing	.60
31½	Ejector Rod Guide Bushing Lock Screw	.25
33	Ejector Spring	.25
39	Stock Pin	.25
40	Stock Screw	.25
42	Side Plate Screws (2) each	.25
45	Barrel (less sight)	7.00
46	Recoil Plate	.25
52	Front Sight Blade	$1.50
54	Front Sight Pin	
55	Front Sight Adjusting Screw	1.50
56	Front Sight Spring	
57	Front Sight Locking Screw	
58	Rear Sight	
59	Rear Sight Adjusting Screw	1.50
60	Rear Sight Locking Screw	
71	Ejector	1.00
72	Barrel Block	4.00
73	Rebound Lever Connector	.30
74	Rebound Lever Connector Rivet	.25
75	Rebound Lever Connector Pivot	.25
76	Trigger Spring	.25
77	Trigger Spring Guide	.60
78	Main Spring Guide	.40
79	Main Spring Guide Pin	.25
80	Side Plate Upper Screw	.25
81	Main Spring Guide Collar	.25

These parts not shown in cut:
Frame, complete ... $28.00
Side Plate ... 1.90
Stocks, Checked Walnut, per pair ... 2.00
Escutcheons, per set ... .25

In ordering, give number of Revolver and part.

1	Hammer	$2.00
2	Trigger	.60
3	Hand and Hand Spring	.50
	Hand Spring	.25
4	Gate	1.25
5	Ejector Tube	3.00
6	Ejector Rod	.25
7	Ejector Head	.90
8	Ejector Spring	.25
9	Sear and Bolt Spring	.25
10	Bolt	.50
11	Base Pin	.35
12	Base Pin Bushing	.60
13	Main Spring	.35
14	Gate Spring	.25
15	Base Pin Catch	.25
16	Base Pin Catch Spring	$.25
17	Base Pin Catch Screw	.25
18	Front Guard Screw	.25
19	Rear Guard Screw (2) each	.25
20	Ejector Tube Screw	.25
21	Back Strap Screw (2) each	.25
	Front Strap Screw	.25
22	Gate Catch	.25
23	Gate Catch Screw	.25
24	Sear and Bolt Spring Screw	.25
25	Stock Screw	.25
26	Hammer Screw	.25
27	Trigger and Bolt Screw	.25

SMITH & WESSON PARTS

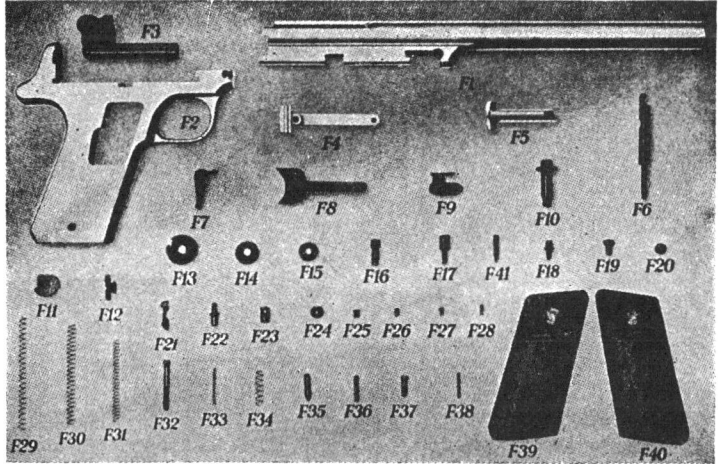

.22 STRAIGHT LINE SINGLE SHOT PISTOL

F 1	Barrel	$14.00
F 2	Frame	8.50
F 3	Hammer	3.00
F 4	Rear Sight Leaf	1.90
F 5	Extractor	1.50
F 6	Sear	.60
F 7	Trigger Lever	.70
F 8	Trigger	1.50
F 9	Locking Bolt	.70
F 10	Barrel Stud	.60
F 11	Front Sight	1.00
F 12	Rear Sight Slide	.60
F 13	Extractor Cam	.90
F 14	Bbl. Stud Wash.	.50
F 15	Bbl. Stud Nut.	.25
F 16	Main Spg. Plun.	.30
F 17	Strain Screw	.25
F 18	Hammer Nose	.25
F 19	Stop Lug	.25
F 20	Check Screw	.25
F 21	Ex. Cam Catch	$0.60
F 22	Main Spg. Arrest.	.25
F 23	Ex. Spg. Plunger	.25
F 24	Main Spg. Bush.	.25
F 25	Elevating Screw	.25
F 26	Windage Screw	.25
F 27	Sight Leaf Screw	.25
F 28	Hammer Nose P.	.25
F 29	Sear Spring	.25
F 30	Main Spring	.25
F 31	Extractor Spring	.25
F 32	Stk. Screw (long)	.25
F 33	Lock. Bolt Spg.	.25
F 34	Recoil Spring	.25
F 35	Hammer Pin	.25
F 36	Sear Pin	.25
F 37	Stk. Scr. (short)	.25
F 38	Locking Bolt Pin	.25
F 39	Stock, Right Hd.	1.25
F 40	Stock, Left Hand	1.25

INSTRUCTIONS: In ordering parts always give name and number listed in catalog, also make, model, caliber and serial number of gun.

PAYMENTS: Parts will be sent only on advance payment. Parts cannot be returned for credit. A service charge of 25c must be added to every order under $1.00 to cover cost of handling. Do not forget to include postage.

SEE PAGE 8, "HOW TO ORDER"

COLT AUTOMATIC PISTOL PARTS

Pocket Model, Hammerless, Caliber .25

Pocket Model, Hammerless, Cal. .32 and .380

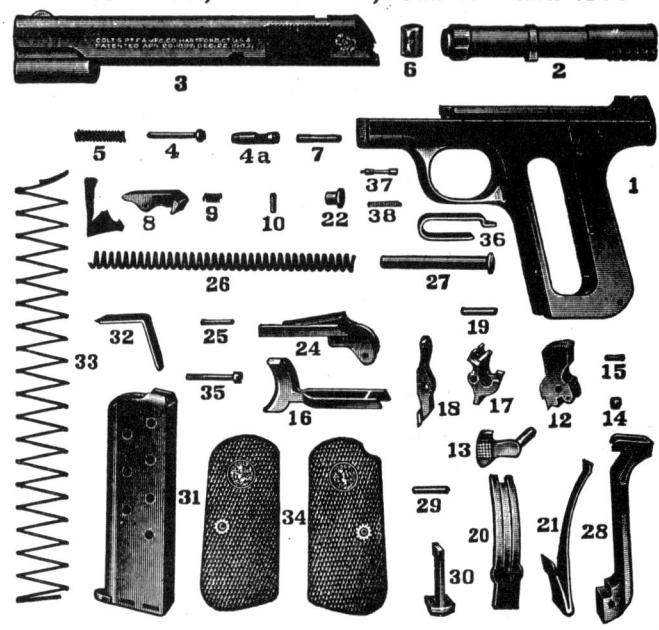

In ordering parts, please be sure to give number of Pistol, as improvements have been made since first issue.

1	Receiver	$9.00
2	Slide	5.00
3	Barrel	1.75
4	Extractor	.30
5	Extractor Spring	.25
6	Extractor Pin	.25
7	Firing Pin	.50
8	Main Spring	.25
9	Main Spring Guide	.25
10	Trigger	.35
11	Connector	.90
12	Trigger Pin	.25
13	Sear Stop Pin	.25
14	Sear	.60
15	Sear, Safety, Trigger & Mag. Catch Spg.	.25
16	Slide Lock Safety	.65
16A	Slide Lock Safety Plun.	.25
16B	Slide Lock Safety Plunger Spring	.25
17	Grip Safety	.90
18	Grip Safety Pin	.25
19	Sear Pin	.25
20	Retractor Spring	.25
21	Retractor Spring Guide (Complete with Safety Disconnector Plunger and Spring)	.35
22	Magazine Catch	.45
23	Magazine, complete	.85
24	Magazine Spring	.25
25	Magazine Follower	.25
26	Checked Stocks, pair	1.25
27	Stock Screw	.25
28	Safety Disconnector	.40
	Escutcheons, per set	.25

In ordering parts, please be sure to give number and caliber of Pistol, as improvements have been made since first issue.

1	Receiver	$12.75
2	Barrel	2.50
3	Slide	6.50
4	Front Firing Pin	.25
4a	Rear Firing Pin	.25
5	Firing Pin Spring	.25
6	Rear Sight	.40
7	Firing Pin Lock Pin	.25
8	Shell Extractor	.50
9	Shell Extractor Spring	.25
10	Shell Extractor Pin	.25
12	Hammer	.60
13	Slide Lock Safety	.60
14	Hammer Roll	.25
15	Hammer Roll Pin	.25
16	Trigger	1.20
17	Sear	.75
18	Safety	.60
19	Sear and Safety Pin	.25
20	Sear Sfty. & Trig. Spg.	.25
21	Main Spring	.60
22	Plug	.25
24	Ejector	$1.25
25	Ejector Pin	.25
26	Retractor Spring	.25
27	Retractor Spring Guide, complete with Safety Disconnector Plunger, and Spring	.35
28	Automatic Grip Safety	1.25
29	Automatic Safety Pin	.25
30	Magazine Catch	.40
31	Magazine, complete	1.00
32	Magazine Follower	.25
33	Magazine Spring	.25
34	Walnut Stocks, pair	1.25
35	Stock Screw	.25
36	Safety Disconnector	.40
37	Sfty. Discon. Plunger	.25
38	Safety Disconnector Plunger Spring	.25
	Safety Disconnector, Complete (36-37-38)	.60
	Escutcheons, per set	.25
	Front Sight	.25

"Woodsman" Automatic Pistol, Caliber .22

In ordering parts, please be sure to give number of Pistol.

1	Receiver	$15.00
2	Barrel, 6½" with sight	5.75
	Without sight	4.25
	Bbl. 4½" with fixed sight	4.25
3	Slide	5.00
4	Ejector	.35
5	Ejector Pin	.25
6	Extractor	.50
7	Extractor Plunger	.25
8	Extractor Spring	.25
9	Firing Pin	.40
10	Firing Pin Spring	.25
11	Firing Pin Stop Screw	.25
12	Hammer	.75
13	Hammer Strut	.25
14	Hammer Strut Pin	.25
15	Assembly Lock Plunger	.25
16	Housing Locking Pin	.25
17	Magazine Catch and Sear Spring, complete	.60
19	Magazine Follower	.25
20	Magazine Follower Pin	.25
22	Magazine Spring	.25
23	Magazine, complete	2.00
24	Main Spring	.25
25	Main Spring Cap	.25
26	Main Spring Cap Pin	$0.25
27	Main Spring Housing (New Type)	2.60
28	Assembly Lock	.25
30	Recoil Spring	.25
31	Recoil Spring Guide	.25
32	Safety Lock	1.00
33	Sear	.75
34	Sear Pin	.25
36	Side Plate	.40
37	Side Plate Screw	.25
38	Stock—right	1.25
39	Stock—left	1.25
40	Stock Screw	.25
41	*Escutcheons, per set	.25
43	Trigger, grooved	1.25
44	Trigger Bar	.60
45	Trigger Pivot	.25
46	Trigger Spring	.25
47	Rear Sight complete	1.50
53	Front Sight Blade	
54	Front Sight Pin	
55	Front Sgt. Adj. Screw	} 1.50
56	Front Sight Adj. Spg.	
57	Front Sgt. Lkg. Screw	

*These parts shown inserted in stocks.

In replacing parts marked thus (*) it will be necessary to send gun to us.

INSTRUCTIONS: In ordering parts always give name and number listed in catalog, also make, model, caliber and serial number of gun.

PAYMENTS: Parts will be sent only on advance payment. Parts cannot be returned for credit. A service charge of 25c must be added to every order under $1.00 to cover cost of handling. Do not forget to include postage.

EVERYTHING IN GUNS UNDER ONE COVER

COLT AUTOMATIC PISTOL PARTS
Colt Government Model Caliber .45 Automatic Pistol and Super .38 Automatic Pistol

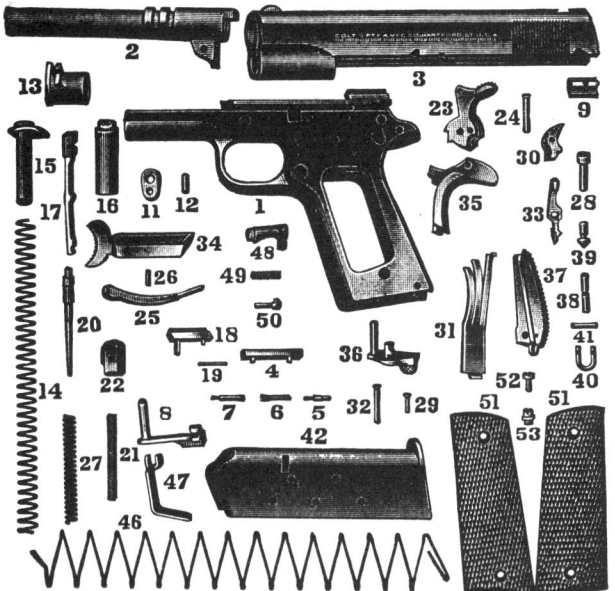

NOTE: When ordering parts, please be sure to give number of Pistol and state whether "Government Model", or "Super 38". "Government Model" parts are different from the previous caliber .45 Colt Automatic Pistol.

#	Part	Price	#	Part	Price
1	Receiver	$15.00	30	Sear	$1.00
2	Barrel	3.75	31	Sear Spring	.30
	Barrel, match type	4.50	32	Sear Pin	.25
3	Slide	9.00	33	Disconnector	.80
4	Plunger Tube	.75	34	Trigger	1.50
5	Slide Stop Plunger	.25	35	Grip Safety	1.70
6	Plunger Spring	.25	36	Safety Lock	1.50
7	Safety Lock Plunger	.25	37	Main Spring Housing	1.50
8	Slide Stop	1.20	38	Housing Pin	.25
9	Rear Sight	.50	39	Housing Pin Retainer	.25
10*	Front Sight	.25	40	Lanyard Loop	.25
11	Link	.25	41	Lanyard Loop Pin	.25
12	Link Pin	.25	42	Magazine Complete	1.50
13	Barrel Bushing	.75	46	Magazine Spring	.25
14	Recoil Spring	.25	47	Magazine Follower	.25
15	Recoil Spring Guide	.45	48	Magazine Catch	.60
16	Plug	.25	49	Magazine Catch Spring	.25
17	Extractor	.85	50	Magazine Catch Lock	.25
18	Ejector	.60	51	Stocks, right and left hand, pair	2.00
19	Ejector Pin	.25	52	Stock Screws (4), each	.25
20	Firing Pin	.35	53	Screw Bushings (4), each	.25
21	Firing Pin Spring	.25		* This part shown attached to Slide. Partridge Type Sights, Front $.75, Rear $1.00. Stevens Adjustable Rear Sight for all models 3.50 Ramp type front sight to match .75 Complete: Sights as above fitted 7.75	
22	Firing Pin Stop	.45			
23	Hammer	1.50			
24	Hammer Pin	.25			
25	Hammer Strut	.25			
26	Hammer Strut Pin	.25			
27	Main Spring	.25			
28	Main Spring Cap	.25			
29	Main Spring Cap Pin	.25			

The Colt Automatic Pistol, Caliber .38 "Military" and "Pocket" Models

In ordering, please give number of Pistol, and state whether Military or Pocket Model, as improvements have been made since that issue.

#	Part	Price	#	Part	Price	#	Part	Price
1	Receiver	$22.00	12	Hammer	$1.30	22	Main Spring Screw	$.25
2	Barrel	5.50	13	Hammer Screw	.25	23	Ejector	1.00
3	Slide	9.00	14	Hammer Roll	.25	24	Ejector Pin	.25
4	Firing Pin	.50	15	Hammer Roll Pin	.25	25	Recoil Plug	.25
5	Firing Pin Spring	.25	16	Trigger	1.90	26	Retractor Spring	.25
6	Rear Sight	.50	17	Sear	.85	27	Follower	.40
7	Firing Pin Lock Pin	.25	18	Safety	1.00	28	Plug (Take Down)	.50
8	Shell Extractor	.85	19	Sear and Safety Pin	.25	29	Plug and Link Pin	.25
9	Shell Extractor Spring	.25	20	Sear, Safety and Trigger Spring	.30	30	Links (2) each	.25
10	Shell Extractor Pin	.25	21	Main Spring	.50	31	Link Pin, short	.25
11	Slide Lock	.30				32	Magazine Catch	.75

33	Magazine Catch Pin	$.25
34	Magazine, complete	1.50
35	Magazine Follower	.25
36	Magazine Spring	.25
37	Stocks, per pair	1.15
38	Stock Screws, (4) each	.25
39	Slide Stop	1.00
40	Slide Stop Spring	.25
41	Swivel	.50
42	Swivel Pin	.25
	Escutcheons, per set (4)	.25
	Front Sight	.25

Colt "ACE" Automatic Pistol, Caliber .22 Long Rifle

NOTE: When ordering parts, please be sure to give number of pistol and state "New Ace Automatic."

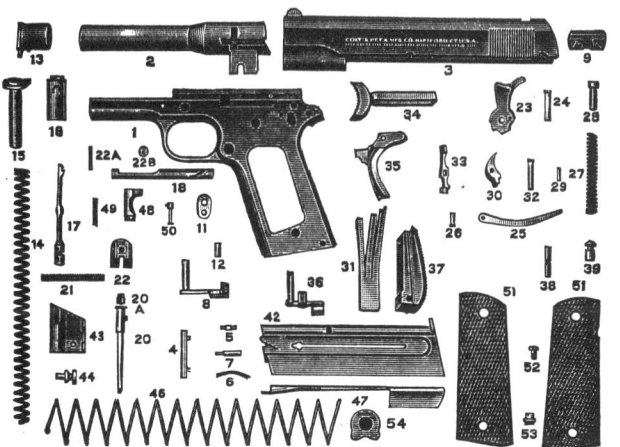

#	Part	Price	#	Part	Price
1	Receiver	$15.00	28	Main Spring Cap	$.25
2	Barrel	4.50	29	Main Spring Cap Pin	.25
3	Slide	12.00	30	Sear	1.25
4	Plunger Tube	.75	31	Sear Spring	.40
5	Slide Stop Plunger	.25	32	Sear Pin	.25
6	Plunger Spring	.25	33	Disconnector	1.00
7	Safety Lock Plunger	.25	34	Trigger	1.75
8	Slide Stop	1.20	35	Grip Safety	1.80
9	Rear Sight	2.50	36	Safety Lock	1.50
10*	Front Sight	.75	37	Main Spring Housing	1.75
13	Barrel Bushing	.75	38	Housing Pin	.25
14	Recoil Spring	.25	39	Housing Pin Retainer	.25
15	Recoil Spring Guide	.45	42	Magazine Complete	2.50
16	Plug	.25	43	Magazine Follower	.50
17	Extractor	1.00	44	Magazine Follower Stud	.25
18	Ejector	1.00	46	Magazine Spring	.25
20	Firing Pin	.60	48	Magazine Catch	.60
20a	Firing Pin Head	.25	49	Magazine Catch Spring	.25
21	Firing Pin Spring	.25	50	Magazine Catch Lock	.25
22	Firing Pin Stop		51	Stocks, right and left hand, pair	2.00
22a	Firing Pin Stop Roller Pin	.75	52	Stock Screws (4) each	.25
22b	Firing Pin Stop Roller		53	Screw Bushings (4) each	.25
23	Hammer	1.75	54	Buffers (8) per set	.40
24	Hammer Pin	.25		* This part shown attached to Slide.	
25	Hammer Strut	.45			
26	Hammer Strut Pin	.25			
27	Main Spring	.25			

In replacing parts marked thus (*) it will be necessary to send gun to us.

INSTRUCTIONS: In ordering parts always give name and number listed in catalog, also make, model, caliber and serial number of gun.

PAYMENTS: Parts will be sent only on advance payment. Parts cannot be returned for credit. A service charge of 25c must be added to every order under $1.00 to cover cost of handling. Do not forget to include postage.

A NEW GUN CARRIES A FACTORY GUARANTEE

SMITH & WESSON PARTS

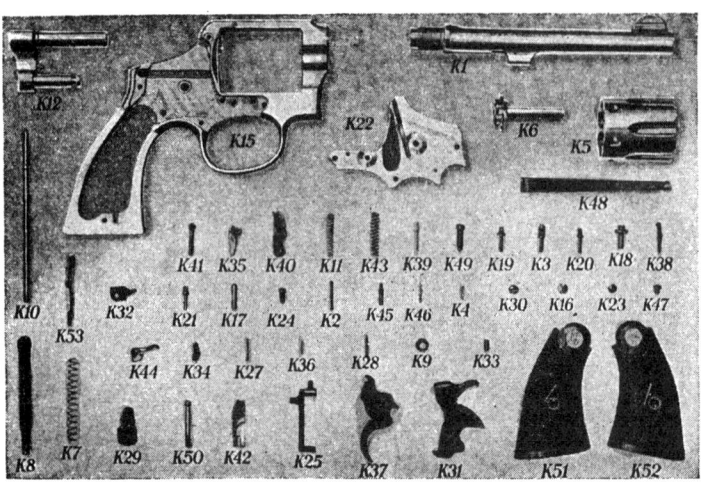

.38 & .32/20 MILITARY & POLICE, ALSO K-22

K 1	Barrel, 4" or 6"..$8.70	K 31	Hammer $2.00
K 2	Barrel Pin... .25	K 32	Hammer Nose.. .30
K 3	Locking Bolt... .60	K 33	Ham. Nose Riv. .25
K 4	Lock. Bolt Spg. .25	K 34	Stirrup .... .60
K 5	Cylinder 5.50	K 35	Sear .... .60
K 6	Extractor 1.20	K 36	Sear Spring.... .25
K 7	Extractor Spring .30	K 37	Trigger 1.70
K 8	Extractor Rod.. .60	K 38	Hand Lever.... .30
K 9	Extractor Collar .25	K 39	Hand Lever Spg. .25
K 10	Center Pin..... .60	K 40	Hand .... .80
K 11	Center Pin Spg. .25	K 41	Trigger Lever... .60
K 12	Yoke 2.50	K 42	Rebound Slide.. 1.20
K 15	Frame, 1905 M., Sq. Butt (as in cut) 11.00	K 43	Trigger Spring.. .60
		—	Rebound Sl. Spg. .60
K 15	Frame, 1902 M., Round Butt...11.00	K 44	Cylinder Stop... .60
		K 45	Cyl. Stop Plung. .25
K 16	Frame Lug..... .40	K 46	Cyl. Stop Spring .25
K 17	Stock Pin..... .25	K 47	Cyl. Stop Screw. .25
K 18	Hammer Stud... .30	K 48	Main Spring... 1.30
K 19	Trigger Stud... .30	K 49	Strain Screw... .25
K 20	Cylinder St. Stud .30	K 50	Stock Screw... .25
K 21	Reb. Slide Stud. .30	K 51	Rt. H. Stk., 1905 Mod., Sq. Butt. .70
K 22	Side Plate...... 1.20	K 52	Lt. H. Stk., 1905 Mod., Sq. Butt. .70
K 23	L. Hd. Pl. Screw .25		
K 24	S. Hd. Pl. Screw .25	K 51	Rt. H. Stk., 1902 Mod., Rd. Butt. .70
K 25	Bolt (assembled) 1.20		
K 27	Bolt Plung. Spg. .25	K 52	Lt. H. Stk., 1902 Mod., Rd Butt (wood only)... .70
K 28	Bolt Plunger... .25		
K 29	Thumb Piece... .60		
K 30	Thum. Pce. Nut. .25	K 53	Hammer Block.. .60

Following are the additional parts, for the K-22 are not found in the plate of the .38 M. & P.:

K 22—#53,	Ft. Sgt... $2.00	K 22—#57,	Fir. Pin S.$0.25
K 22—#54,	R. Sght S. .60	K 22—#58,	Fir. P. B. .30
K 22—#55,	R. Sgt. L. 1.90	K 22—#59,	F. P. B. P. .25
K 22—#56,	Firing Pin .25	In ordering, state model.	

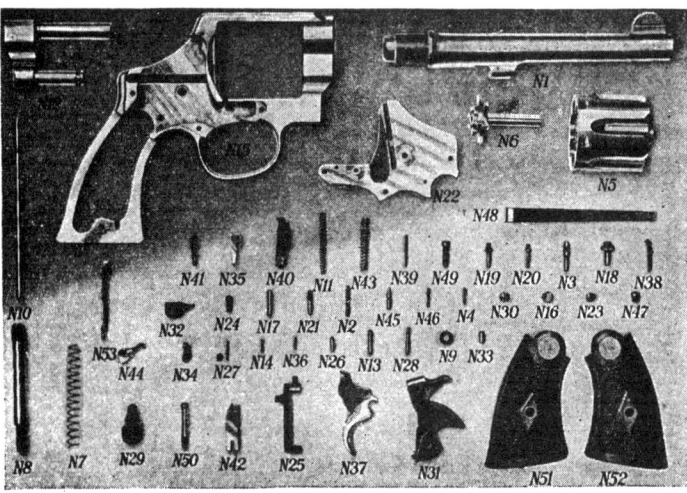

.44 MILITARY—.38/44 SUPER POLICE—.44/40 U. S. A. MOD. 1917—.455 BRITISH —.455 CANADIAN

N 1	Barrel $9.70	N 28	Bolt Plunger....$0.30
N 2	Barrel Pin...... .25	N 29	Thumb Piece... .60
N 3	Locking Bolt... .70	N 30	Thumb Pce. Nut .25
N 4	Lock. Bolt Spg.. .25	N 31	Hammer 2.50
N 5	Cylinder 6.50	N 32	Hammer Nose.. .40
N 6	Extractor 1.20	N 33	Ham. Nose Rivet .25
N 7	Extractor Spring .30	N 34	Stirrup .... .70
N 8	Extractor Rod.. .70	N 35	Sear .... .70
N 9	Ext. Rod Collar. .25	N 36	Sear Spring..... .25
N 10	Center Pin..... .70	N 37	Trigger 1.80
N 11	Center Pin Spg. .25	N 38	Hand Lever.... .40
N 12	Yoke 3.00	N 39	Hd. Lever Spg... .25
N 13	Yoke Stop...... .25	N 40	Hand 1.20
N 14	Yoke Stop Spg.. .25	N 41	Trigger Lever... .70
N 15	Frame 14.30	N 42	Rebound Slide.. 1.40
N 16	Frame Lug..... .40	N 43	Trigger Spring (reb. sld. spg.) 1.20
N 17	Stock Pin..... .25		
N 18	Hammer Stud... .40	N 44	Cylinder Stop... .70
N 19	Trigger Stud... .40	N 45	Cyl. Stop Plung. .25
N 20	Cyl. Stop Stud.. .40	N 46	Cyl. Stop Spring .25
N 21	Rebound S. Stud .40	N 47	Cyl. Stop Screw. .25
N 22	Sideplate 1.20	N 48	Main Spring... 1.40
N 23	Plate Scr., l. hd. .25	N 49	Strain Screw... .25
N 24	Plate Scr., s. hd. .25	N 50	Stock, Screw... .25
N 25	Bolt (plun. & sp.) 1.40	N 51	Stock, Rt. Hand. .80
N 26	Swivel Pin..... .25	N 52	Stock, Lt. Hand. .80
N 27	Bolt Plung. Spg. .25	N 53	Hammer Block.. .60

Note: In ordering barrels and cylinders, mention caliber and model.

.38 DOUBLE ACTION REVOLVER

D 1	Barrel. 3¼"–4"–5"–6" $8.70	D 20	Hammer Stud..$0.40
		D 21	Ham. Stud Nut .25
D 2	Barrel Catch... 1.30	D 22	Stirrup .... .60
D 3	Bbl. Catch Cam .40	D 23	Front Sight... .40
D 4	Bbl. Cth. C. Sp. .25	D 24	Front Sear.... 1.30
D 5	Bbl. Catch Scr. .25	*D 25	Rear Sear.....
*D 6	Base Pin......	D 26	Rear Sear Spg. .70
D 7	Cylinder 4.50	*D 27	Main Spring...
D 8	Extractor ..... .60	D 28	Strain Screw... .25
D 9	Extractor Stud. .60	D 29	Trigger 1.50
D 10	Extractor Post. .60	*D 30	Trigger Guard..
D 11	Extractor Cam. .40	D 31	Trigger Spring. .60
D 12	Ext. Cam Catch .30	*D 32	Cylinder Stop..
D 13	Extractor Scr. .25	D 33	Hand .... .60
*D 14	Fly and Spring.	D 34	Hand Spring... .25
*D 15	Frame	D 35	Stock Pin..... .25
D 16	Side Plate.... .70	D 36	Stock Screw... .25
D 17	Joint Pivot.... .25	D 37	Right Hd. Stk. .60
D 18	Joint Pivot Scr. .25	D 38	Left Hand Stk. .60
*D 19	Hammer	*Cannot be supplied.	

Note: Due to variations, sample must be sent in.

IMPORTANT NOTICE: All parts marked in front with an asterisk are out of stock and are not to be had. Please do not order.

SEND YOUR GUN TO STOEGER FOR EXPERT REPAIRING

SMITH & WESSON PARTS

.32 NEW DEPARTURE (SAFETY HAMMERLESS) REVOLVER

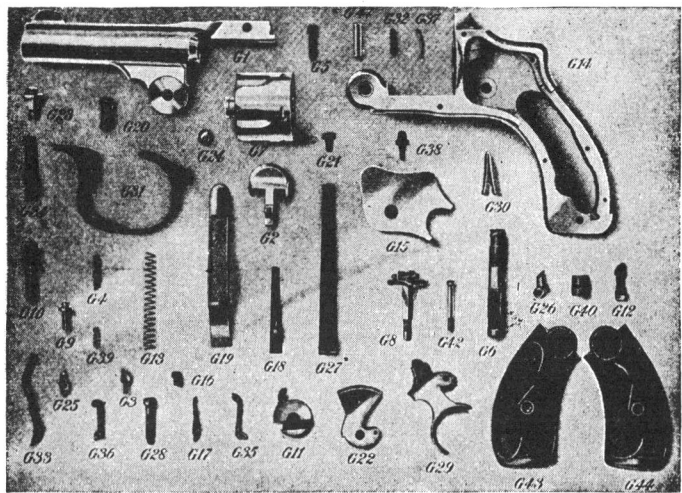

G 1	Bbl., 3″-3½″-6″	$8.00	G 23	Hammer Stud	$0.30
G 2	Barrel Catch	.90	G 24	Ham. Stud Nut	.25
G 3	Bar. Catch Cam	.40	G 25	Stirrup	.60
G 4	Bar. Catch Cam Spring	.25	G 26	Sear	1.00
			G 27	Main Spring	.60
G 5	Bar. Catch Screw	.25	G 28	Strain Screw	.25
G 6	Base Pin	.60	G 29	Trigger	1.50
G 7	Cylinder	3.50	G 30	Trigger Spring	.60
G 8	Extractor	.60	G 31	Trigger Guard	1.30
G 9	Extractor Stud	.30	G 32	Trigger Pin	.25
G 10	Extractor Post	.60	G 33	Cylinder Stop	1.00
G 11	Extractor Cam	.40	G 34	Cylind. Stop Spg.	.60
G 12	Ex. Cam Catch	.30	G 35	Split Spring	.60
G 13	Extractor Spg.	.25	G 36	Hand	.60
G 14	Frame	8.00	G 37	Hand Spring	.25
G 15	Side Plate	.70	G 38	Firing Pin	.25
G 16	Side Plate Screw	.25	G 39	Firing Pin Spg.	.25
G 17	Safety Latch	.30	G 40	Fring Pin Bush.	.30
G 18	Safety Latch Spg.	.60	G 41	Stock Pin	.25
G 19	Safety Lever	1.20	G 42	Stock Screw	.25
G 20	Joint Pivot	.25	G 43	Right Hand Stk.	.60
G 21	Joint Pivot Screw	.25	G 44	Left Hand Stock	.60
G 22	Hammer	.80			

Note: Due to variations, it is necessary to send in sample.

.38 NEW DEPARTURE (SAFETY HAMMERLESS) REVOLVER

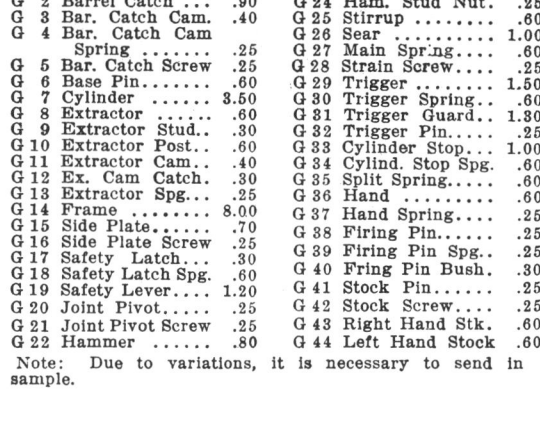

Y 1	Barrel, 3¼″-4″-5″-6″	$8.70	Y 22	Hammer	$0.80
			Y 23	Hammer Stud	.40
Y 2	Barrel Catch	1.30	Y 24	Ham. Stud Nut	.25
Y 3	Bbl. Catch Cam	.40	Y 25	Stirrup	.60
Y 4	Bbl. Catch Cam Spring	.25	Y 26	Sear	1.00
			Y 27	Main Spring	.60
Y 5	Bbl. Catch Screw	.25	Y 28	Strain Screw	.25
Y 6	Base Pin	.60	Y 29	Trigger	1.50
Y 7	Cylinder	4.50	Y 30	Trigger Spring	.60
Y 8	Extractor	.60	Y 31	Trigger Guard	1.30
Y 9	Extractor Stud	.30	Y 32	Trigger Pin	.25
Y 10	Extractor Post	.60	Y 33	Cylinder Stop	1.20
Y 11	Extractor Cam	.40	Y 34	Cylind. Stop Spg.	.60
Y 12	Ext. Cam Catch	.30	Y 35	Split Spring	.60
Y 13	Extractor Spring	.25	Y 36	Hand	.60
Y 14	Frame	8.50	Y 37	Hand Spring	.25
Y 15	Side Plate	.70	Y 38	Firing Pin	.25
Y 16	Side Plate Screw	.25	Y 39	Firing Pin Spg.	.25
Y 17	Latch	.30	Y 40	Firing Pin Bush.	.30
Y 18	Latch Spring	.60	Y 41	Stock Pin	.25
Y 19	Safety Lever	1.20	Y 42	Stock Screw	.25
Y 20	Joint Pivot	.25	Y 43	Right Hand Stk.	.60
Y 21	Joint Pivot Scr.	.25	Y 44	Left Hand Stock	.60

Note: Due to variations, it is necessary to send in sample.

.22/.32 HEAVY FRAME TARGET REVOLVER

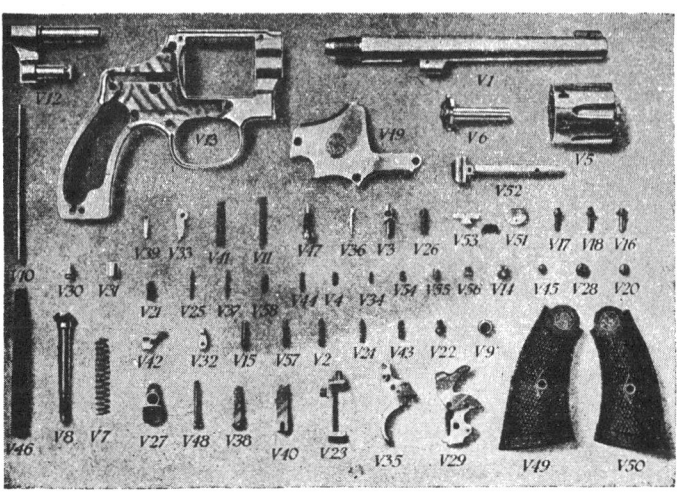

V 1	Barrel, 6-inch	$7.40	V 30	Firing Pin	$0.25
V 2	Barrel Pin	.25	V 31	Firing Pin Bush.	.30
V 3	Locking Bolt	.60	V 32	Stirrup	.60
V 4	Lock. Bolt Spg.	.25	V 33	Sear	.60
V 5	Cylinder	4.50	V 34	Sear Spring	.25
V 6	Extractor	.60	V 35	Trigger	1.20
V 7	Extractor Spring	.25	V 36	Hand Lever	.30
V 8	Extractor Rod	.60	V 37	Hd. Lever Spg.	.25
V 9	Ext. Rod Collar	.25	V 38	Hand	.60
V 10	Center Pin	.30	V 39	Trigger Lever	.40
V 11	Center Pin Spg.	.25	V 40	Rebound Slide	1.20
V 12	Yoke	2.50	V 41	Trigger Spring	.40
V 13	Frame	9.50	V 42	Cylinder Stop	.60
V 14	Frame Lug	.40	V 43	Cyl. Stop Plung.	.25
V 15	Stock Pin	.25	V 44	Cyl. Stop Spring	.25
V 16	Hammer Stud	.30	V 45	Cyl. Stop Screw.	.25
V 17	Trigger Stud	.30	V 46	Main Spring	.60
V 18	Stop Stud	.30	V 47	Strain Screw	.25
V 19	Side Plate	.70	V 48	Stock Screw	.25
V 20	L. Hd. Pl. Scre.	.25	V 49	Right Hand Stk.	1.20
V 21	S. Hd. Pl. Scre.	.25	V 50	Left Hand Stock	1.20
V 22	Yoke Screw	.25	V 51	Front Sight	1.40
V 23	Bolt (assembled)	1.20	V 52	Sight Leaf	1.90
V 24	Bolt Plunger	.25	V 53	Sight Slide	.60
V 25	Bolt Plunger Sp.	.25	V 54	Sight Leaf Screw	.25
V 26	Slide Stud	.30	V 55	Windage Screw.	.25
V 27	Thumb Piece	.60	V 56	Elevating Screw.	.25
V 28	Thum. Piece Nut	.25	V 57	Fir. P. Bush. P.	.25
V 29	Hammer	2.00	V 58	Firing Pin Spg.	.25

INSTRUCTIONS: In ordering parts always give name and number listed in catalog, also make, model, caliber and serial number of gun.

PAYMENTS: Parts will be sent only on advance payment. Parts cannot be returned for credit. A service charge of 25c must be added to every order under $1.00 to cover cost of handling. Do not forget to include postage.

PLEASE TELL OTHERS ABOUT STOEGER'S CATALOG

SMITH & WESSON PARTS

.32 HAND EJECTOR, ALSO .32 AND .38 REGULATION POLICE REVOLVERS

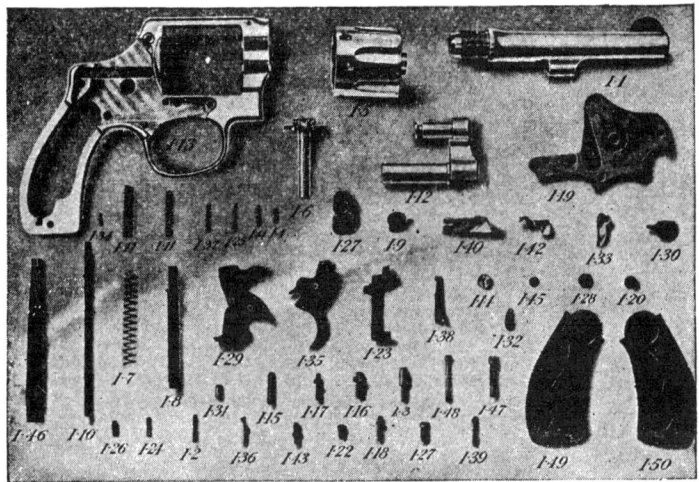

No.	Part	Price	No.	Part	Price
I 1	Bbl., 3¼"-4¼"-6".	$7.40	I 29	Hammer	$1.70
I 2	Barrel Pin	.25	I 30	Hammer Nose	.30
I 3	Locking Bolt	.60	I 31	Hammer Nose Riv.	.25
I 4	Locking Bolt Spg.	.25	I 32	Stirrup	.60
I 5	Cylinder	4.50	I 33	Sear	.60
I 6	Extractor	.60	I 34	Sear Spring	.25
I 7	Extractor Spring	.25	I 35	Trigger	1.20
I 8	Extractor Rod	.60	I 36	Hand Lever	.30
I 9	Extract. Rod Knob	.30	I 37	Hd. Lever Spring	.25
I 10	Center Pin	.30	I 38	Hand	.60
I 11	Center Pin Spring	.25	I 39	Trigger Lever	.40
I 12	Yoke	2.50	I 40	Rebound Slide	1.20
I 13	Frame	9.00	I 41	Trigger Spring	.40
I 14	Frame Lug	.40	—	Rebound Slide Spg.	.40
I 15	Stock Pin	.25	I 42	Cylinder Stop	.60
I 16	Hammer Stud	.30	I 43	Cyl. Stop Plunger	.25
I 17	Trigger Stud	.30	I 44	Cylinder Stop Spg.	.25
I 18	Cylinder Stop Stud	.30	I 45	Cylin. Stop Screw	.25
I —	Rebound Slide Stud	.30	I 46	Main Spring	.60
I 19	Side Plate	.70	I 47	Strain Screw	.25
I 20	L. Hd. Plate Screw	.25	I 48	Stock Screw	.25
I 21	S. Hd. Plate Screw	.25	I 49	Right Hand Stock	.60
I 22	Yoke Screw	.25	I 50	Left Hand Stock	.60
I 23	Bolt (assembled)	1.20		Hammer Block	.60
I 24	Bolt Plunger	.25		Hammer Block Plunger	.30
I 25	Bolt Plunger Spg.	.25		Hammer Bl. Plung. Spg.	.25
I 26	Bolt Plunger Screw	.25			
I 27	Thumb Piece	.60			
I 28	Thumb Piece Nut	.25			

Note: Send sample part if possible. State for which model part is wanted.

.32 CAL. AUTOMATIC PISTOL

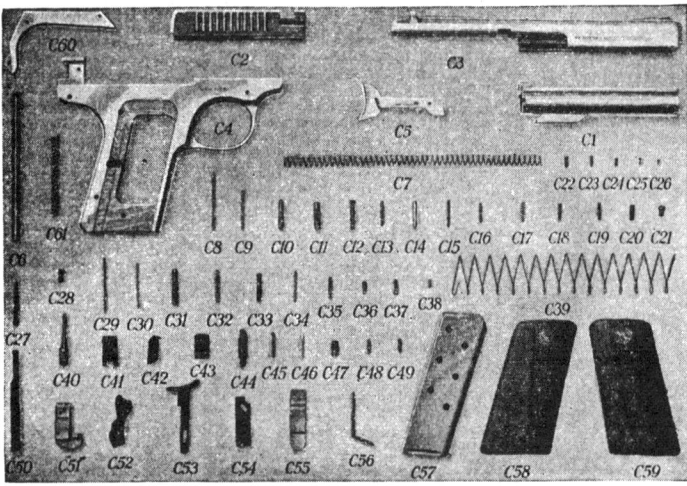

No.	Part	Price	No.	Part	Price
C 1	Barrel	$6.00	C 32	Firing Pin Spring	$0.25
C 2	Bolt	5.50	C 33	Insert Scr. Cr. Hd.	.25
C 3	Slide	9.00	C 34	Trigger Spring	.25
C 4	Frame	12.00	C 35	Sear Plunger	.25
C 5	Trigger	1.80	C 36	Mag. Catch Plun.	.25
C 6	Bolt Spring Rod	1.00	C 37	Stirrup	.60
C 7	Slide Spring	.80	C 38	Sear Latch Spring	.25
C 8	Ejector Spring	.25	C 39	Magazine Spring	.60
C 9	Bolt Re. Catch Sp.	.25	C 40	Firing Pin	.50
C 10	Barrel Pin	.25	C 41	Sear	.70
C 11	Slide Stop	1.00	C 42	Extractor	.40
C 12	Insert Scr., Fl. Hd.	.25	C 43	Magazine Catch	.60
C 13	Notch Plate Pin	.25	C 44	Main Spg. Plunger	.40
C 14	Hammer Pin Pin	.25	C 45	Mag. Catch Pin	.25
C 15	Extractor Spring	.25	C 46	Sear Plunger Spg.	.25
C 16	Firing Pin	.25	C 47	Trigger Spg. Plun.	.25
C 17	Slide Stop Spring	.25	C 48	Sear Pin	.25
C 18	Extractor Pin	.25	C 49	Ext. Spg. Plunger	.25
C 19	Slide Stop Pin	.25	C 50	Ejector	.60
C 20	Main Spg. Plun. P.	.25	C 51	Bolt Release Catch	1.00
C 21	Stock Screw	.25	C 52	Hammer	.75
C 22	Bolt Re. Catch Pl.	.25	C 53	Safety Lever	1.20
C 23	Trig. Spg. Plun Pin	.25	C 54	Safety Slide	.50
C 24	Ejec. Spg. Pl. Pin	.25	C 55	Notch Plate	.50
C 25	Sear Latch Pin	.25	C 56	Mag. Spg. Follower	.25
C 26	Safety Stop Rivet	.25	C 57	Magazine Complete	3.00
C 27	Safety Stop	.70	C 58	Stock Right	1.20
C 28	Sear Latch	.60	C 59	Stock Left	1.20
C 29	Safety Lev. Spg. P.	.25	C 60	Insert	2.50
C 30	Safety Lever Spg.	.25	C 61	Main Spring	.75
C 31	Ejector Spg. Plun.	.25			

Note: Send sample part if possible.

.35 CAL. AUTOMATIC PISTOL

No.	Part	Price	No.	Part	Price
A 1	Barrel	$8.00	A 26	Mag. Catch Nut	$0.60
A 2	Bolt	5.90	A 27	Mag. Catch Spg.	.25
A 3	Bolt Release Catch	.60	A 28	Magazine Spring	.60
A 4	Bolt Rel. Cth. Spg.	.25	A 29	Mag. Spg. Fol.	.25
A 5	Bolt Spring	1.00	A 30	Main Spring	.75
A 6	Bolt Spring Rod	1.00	A 31	Main Spg. Plun.	.40
A 7	Bolt Spg. Rod Nut	.40	A 32	Pivot	.25
A 8	Ejector	.60	A 33	Safety Cam	.60
A 9	Ejector Spring	.25	A 34	Safety Fin. Piece	.75
A 10	Extractor	.40	A 35	Sfty Lev. Spg, Coil	.25
A 11	Extractor Pin	.25	A 36	Sfty Lev Spg, Flat	.25
A 12	Extractor Plunger	.25	A 37	Safety Slide	.50
A 13	Extractor Spring	.25	A 38	Sear	.70
A 14	Firing Pin	.50	A 39	Sear Plunger	.25
A 15	Firing Pin Spg.	.25	A 40	Sear Plun. Pin	.25
A 16	Frame	12.00	A 41	Sear Plun. Spg.	.25
A 17	Frame Insert	2.50	A 42	Sear Spring	.50
A 18	Guard	1.20	A 43	Stirrup	.60
A 19	Guard Pin	.25	A 44	Stock, Left	1.20
A 20	Hammer	.70	A 45	Stock, Right	1.20
A 21	Hammer Pin	.25	A 46	Stock Screw	.25
A 22	Insrt. Scrw. F. Hd	.25	A 47	Trigger	1.80
A 23	Insrt. Scrw. C. Hd	.25	A 48	Trigger Plunger	.25
A 24	Magazine Case	2.10	A 49	Trigger Plun. Spg.	.25
A 25	Magazine Catch	.60		Magazine Complete	3.00

NOTE: Due to variations, sample parts must be sent in.

INSTRUCTIONS: In ordering parts always give name and number listed in catalog, also make, model, caliber and serial number of gun.

PAYMENTS: Parts will be sent only on advance payment. Parts cannot be returned for credit. A service charge of 25c must be added to every order under $1.00 to cover cost of handling. Do not forget to include **postage**.

CAREFUL ATTENTION AND SAFE DELIVERY OF YOUR ORDER

SMITH & WESSON PARTS

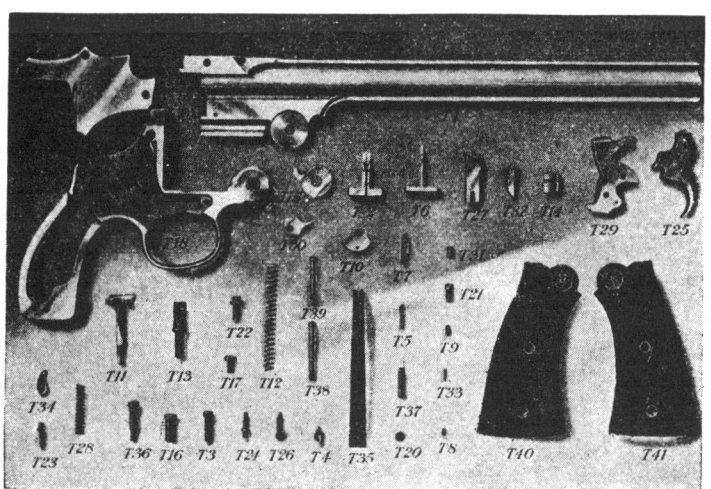

.22 PERFECTED SINGLE SHOT PISTOL

No.	Part	Price	No.	Part	Price
*T 1	Barrel, 10"	$14.30	T 24	Rebound Sl. St.	$0.30
*T 2	Barrel Catch	2.30	T 25	Trigger	1.20
T 3	Bbl. Catch Scr.	.25	T 26	Trigger Lever	.40
T 4	Bbl. Catch Cam	.40	T 27	Rebound Slide	1.20
T 5	Bbl. Catch Cam Spring	.25	T 28	Trigger Spring	.40
			—	Rebound S. Sp.	.40
*T 6	Bbl. Catch Cen. Piece	1.20	T 29	Hammer	1.70
T 7	Rear Sight Slide	.60	T 30	Hammer Nose	.25
T 8	Elevating Screw	.25	T 31	Ham. Nos. Riv.	.25
T 9	Windage Screw	.25	T 32	Sear	.60
T 10	Front Sight	1.40	T 33	Sear Spring	.25
T 11	Extractor	.60	T 34	Stirrup	.60
T 12	Extractor Spg.	.25	T 35	Main Spring	.60
T 13	Extractor Post	.60	T 36	Strain Screw	.25
T 14	Extractor Bush.	.30	T 37	Stock Pin	.25
T 15	Extractor Cam, Catch and Spg.	.80	T 38	Long Stock Scr.	.25
			T 39	S. Stock Screw.	.25
T 16	Joint Pivot	.25	T 40	Right Hand Stk. (wood only)	1.20
T 17	Joint Pivot Scr.	.25	T 41	Left Hand Stk. (wood only)	1.20
*T 18	Frame	8.50			
T 19	Side Plate	.70	*T 42	Target Barrel Catch, comp.	4.40
T 20	L. Hd. Plate Sc.	.25			
T 21	S. Hd. Plate Sc.	.25	*Stock exhausted. Impossible to furnish.		
T 22	Hammer Stud	.30			
T 23	Trigger Stud	.30			

Note: Due to variations in models, sample part must be sent in.

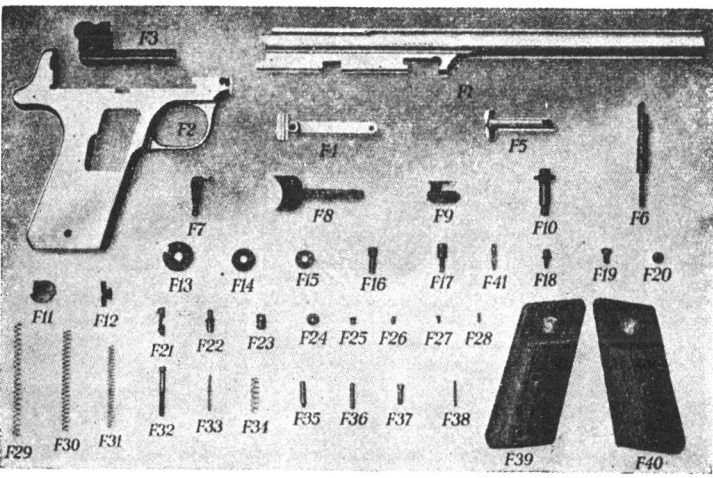

.22 STRAIGHT LINE SINGLE SHOT PISTOL

No.	Part	Price	No.	Part	Price
F 1	Barrel	$14.00	F 21	Ex. Cam Catch	$0.60
F 2	Frame	8.50	F 22	Main Spg. Arrest.	.25
F 3	Hammer	3.00	F 23	Ex. Spg. Plunger	.25
F 4	Rear Sight Leaf	1.90	F 24	Main Spg. Bush.	.25
F 5	Extractor	1.50	F 25	Elevating Screw	.25
F 6	Sear	.60	F 26	Windage Screw	.25
F 7	Trigger Lever	.70	F 27	Sight Leaf Screw	.25
F 8	Trigger	1.50	F 28	Hammer Nose P.	.25
F 9	Locking Bolt	.70	F 29	Sear Spring	.25
F 10	Barrel Stud	.60	F 30	Main Spring	.25
F 11	Front Sight	1.00	F 31	Extractor Spring	.25
F 12	Rear Sight Slide	.60	F 32	Stk. Screw (long)	.25
F 13	Extractor Cam	.90	F 33	Lock. Bolt Spg.	.25
F 14	Bbl. Stud Wash.	.50	F 34	Recoil Spring	.25
F 15	Bbl. Stud Nut	.25	F 35	Hammer Pin	.25
F 16	Main Spg. Plun.	.30	F 36	Sear Pin	.25
F 17	Strain Screw	.25	F 37	Stk. Scr. (short)	.25
F 18	Hammer Nose	.25	F 38	Locking Bolt Pin	.25
F 19	Stop Lug	.25	F 39	Stock, Right Hd.	1.25
F 20	Check Screw	.25	F 40	Stock, Left Hand	1.25

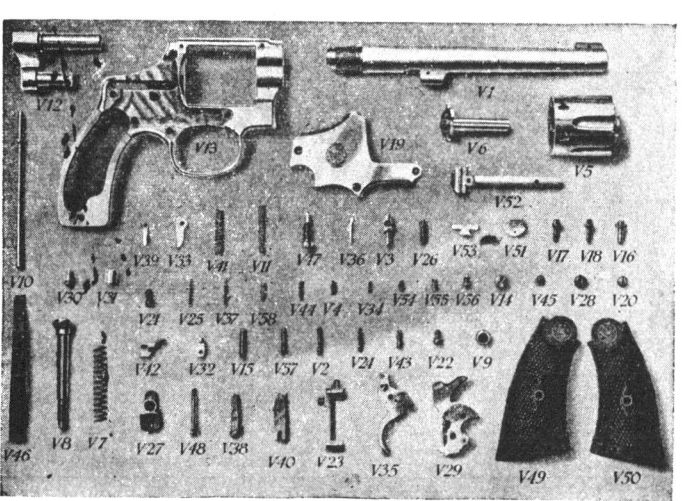

.22/.32 HEAVY FRAME TARGET REVOLVER

No.	Part	Price	No.	Part	Price
V 1	Barrel, 6-inch	$7.40	V 30	Firing Pin	$0.25
V 2	Barrel Pin	.25	V 31	Firing Pin Bush.	.30
V 3	Locking Bolt	.60	V 32	Stirrup	.60
V 4	Lock. Bolt Spg.	.25	V 33	Sear	.60
V 5	Cylinder	4.50	V 34	Sear Spring	.25
V 6	Extractor	.60	V 35	Trigger	1.20
V 7	Extractor Spring	.25	V 36	Hand Lever	.30
V 8	Extractor Rod	.60	V 37	Hd. Lever Spg.	.25
V 9	Ext. Rod Collar	.25	V 38	Hand	.60
V 10	Center Pin	.30	V 39	Trigger Lever	.40
V 11	Center Pin Spg.	.25	V 40	Rebound Slide	1.20
V 12	Yoke	2.50	V 41	Trigger Spring	.40
V 13	Frame	9.50	V 42	Cylinder Stop	.60
V 14	Frame Lug	.40	V 43	Cyl. Stop Plung.	.25
V 15	Stock Pin	.25	V 44	Cyl. Stop Spring	.25
V 16	Hammer Stud	.30	V 45	Cyl. Stop Screw	.25
V 17	Trigger Stud	.30	V 46	Main Spring	.60
V 18	Stop Stud	.30	V 47	Strain Screw	.25
V 19	Side Plate	.70	V 48	Stock Screw	.25
V 20	L. Hd. Pl. Scre.	.25	V 49	Right Hand Stk.	1.20
V 21	S. Hd. Pl. Scre.	.25	V 50	Left Hand Stock	1.20
V 22	Yoke Screw	.25	V 51	Front Sight	1.40
V 23	Bolt (assembled)	1.20	V 52	Sight Leaf	1.90
V 24	Bolt Plunger	.25	V 53	Sight Slide	.60
V 25	Bolt Plunger Sp.	.25	V 54	Sight Leaf Screw	.25
V 26	Slide Stud	.30	V 55	Windage Screw	.25
V 27	Thumb Piece	.60	V 56	Elevating Screw	.25
V 28	Thum. Piece Nut	.25	V 57	Fir. P. Bush. P.	.25
V 29	Hammer	2.00	V 58	Firing Pin Spg.	.25

INSTRUCTIONS: In ordering parts always give name and number listed in catalog, also make, model, caliber and serial number of gun.

PAYMENTS: Parts will be sent only on advance payment. Parts cannot be returned for credit. A service charge of 25c must be added to every order under $1.00 to cover cost of handling. Do not forget to include postage.

HARRINGTON & RICHARDSON REVOLVER PARTS

"PREMIER," "POLICE PREMIER" & "TARGET MODEL"   "AUTO. EJECTING," "POLICE" .22 SPL. & EXPERT

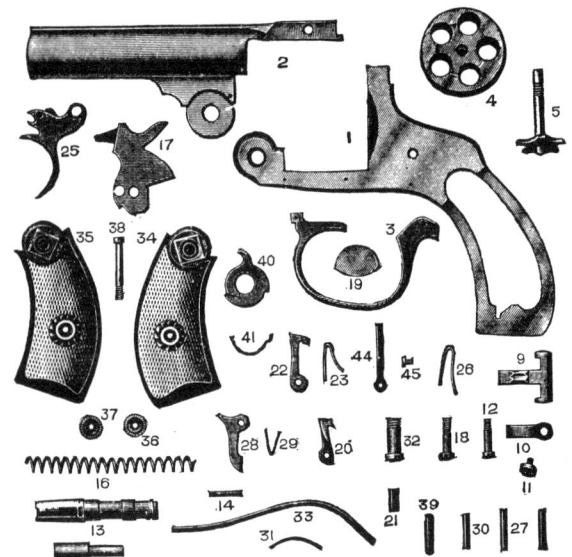

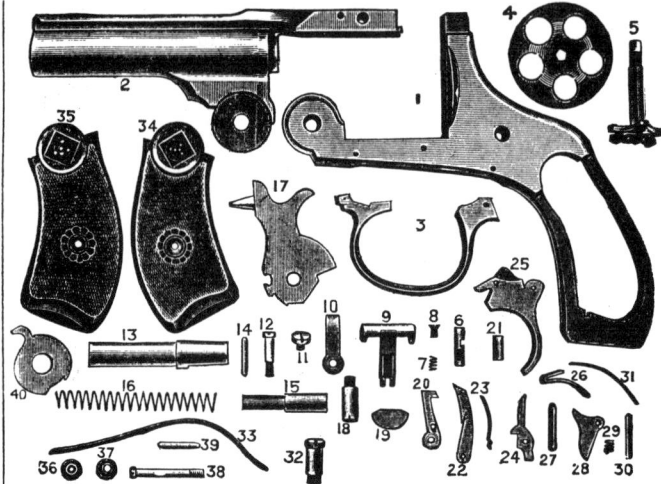

State caliber and number of shots and send broken or worn parts, if possible, and give number stamped on butt.

No.	Part	Price	No.	Part	Price
1	Frame	$2.75	22	Lever	$ .25
2	Barrel, 2 or 3 inch	2.50	23	Lever Spring	.25
	Barrel, 4 inch	2.90	25	Trigger	.55
	Barrel, 5 inch	3.25	26	Trigger Spring	.25
	Barrel, 6 inch	3.65	27	Trigger Pin	.25
3	Guard	.85	28	Sear	.25
4	Cylinder, complete	2.20	29	Sear Spring	.25
5	Extractor	.85	30	Guard Pin	.25
9	Barrel Catch	.45	31	Friction Spring	.25
10	Barrel Catch Spring	.25	32	Hinge Screw	.25
11	Barrel Catch Spring Screw	.25	33	Main Spring	.25
	Barrel Catch Spring Follower	.25	34	Stock, right	.25
			35	Stock, left	.25
12	Barrel Catch Screw	.25	36	Escutcheon Thread	.25
13	Quill	.25	37	Escutcheon Head	.25
14	Quill Pin	.25	38	Stock Screw	.25
15	Extractor Extension	.25	39	Stock Pin	.25
16	Extractor Spring	.25	40	Hook	.30
17	Hammer	.65	41	Hook Spring	.25
18	Hammer Screw	.25		Hook Slide	.25
19	Sight	.25	44	Cylinder Stop—Frame Part	.25
20	Lifter	.25	45	Frame Part Screw	.25
21	Lifter Pin	.25		Checked Walnut Target Grip Stocks	1.10

State caliber and number of shots and send broken or worn parts, if possible, and give number stamped on butt.

No.	Part	Price	No.	Part	Price
1	Frame	$2.75	19	Sight	$ .25
2	Barrel, 3¼ in	2.50	20	Lifter	.25
	Barrel, 4 in	2.85	21	Lifter Pin	.25
	Barrel, 5 in	3.25	22	Lever	.25
	Barrel, 6 in	3.65	23	Lever Spring	.25
	Barrel, 10 in. (Expert)	4.75	24	Cylinder Catch	.25
3	Guard	.85	25	Trigger	.55
4	Cylinder, complete	2.20	26	Trigger Spring	.25
5	Extractor	.85	27	Trigger Pin	.25
6	Cylinder Catch Bolt	.25	28	Sear	.25
7	Cylinder Catch Bolt Spring	.25	29	Sear Spring	.25
			30	Guard Pin	.25
8	Cylinder Catch Bolt Screw	.25	31	Friction Spring	.25
			32	Hinge Screw	.25
9	Barrel Catch	.45	33	Main Spring	.25
10	Barrel Catch Spring	.25	34	Stock, right	.25
11	Barrel Catch Spring Screw	.25	35	Stock, left	.25
	Barrel Catch Spring Follower	.25	36	Escutcheon Thread	.25
			37	Escutcheon Head	.25
12	Barrel Catch Screw	.25	38	Stock Screw	.25
13	Quill	.25	39	Stock Pin	.25
14	Quill Pin	.25	40	Hook	.35
15	Extractor Extension	.25	41	Hook Spring	.25
16	Extractor Spring	.25		Hook Slide	.25
17	Hammer	.65		Target Grip Stocks, walnut or hard rubber	1.10
18	Hammer Screw	.25			

.22, .32 & .38 CALIBER HAMMERLESS

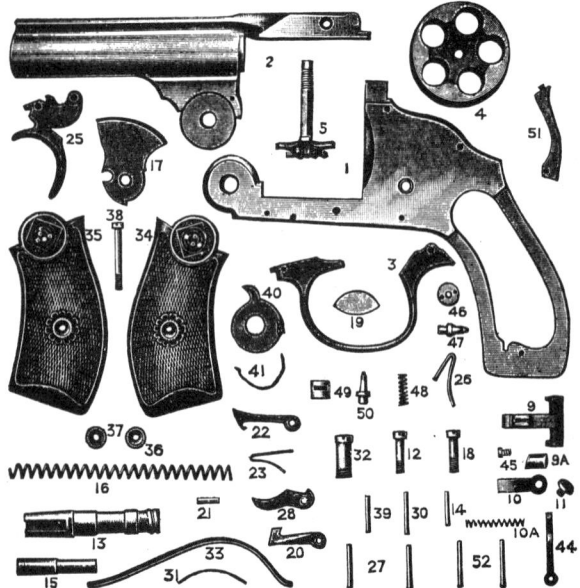

PARTS OF .22, .32 AND .38 CALIBER HAMMERLESS

No.	Part	Price	No.	Part	Price
1	Frame	$2.75	26	Trigger Spring	$ .25
2	Barrel, 3¼ inch or shorter	2.50	27	Trigger Pin	.25
			28	Rebounder	.25
	Barrel, 4 inch	2.85	30	Guard Pin	.25
	Barrel, 5 inch	3.25	31	Friction Spring	.25
	Barrel, 6 inch	3.65	32	Hinge Screw	.25
3	Guard	.85	33	Main Spring	.25
4	Cylinder, complete	2.20	34	Stock, right	.25
5	Extractor	.85	35	Stock, left	.25
9	Barrel Catch	.45	36	Escutcheon Thread	.25
10	Barrel Catch Spring	.25	37	Escutcheon Head	.25
11	Barrel Catch Spring Screw	.25	38	Stock Screw	.25
	Barrel Catch Spring Follower	.25	39	Stock Pin	.25
			40	Hook	.35
12	Barrel Catch Screw	.25	41	Hook Spring	.25
13	Quill	.25		Hook Slide	.25
14	Quill Pin	.25	44	Cylinder Stop—Frame Part	.25
15	Extractor Extension	.25	45	Frame Part Screw	.25
16	Extractor Spring	.25	46	Firing Pin Nut	.25
17	Hammer	.65	47	Firing Pin, old style	.25
18	Hammer Screw	.25	48	Firing Pin Spring	.25
19	Sight	.25	49	Firing Pin Plug	.25
20	Lifter	.25	50	Firing Pin, new style	.25
21	Lifter Pin	.25	51	Hammer Slot Cover	.25
22	Lever	.25	52	Hammer Slot Cover Pin	.25
23	Lever Spring	.25		Target Grip Stocks, walnut or hard rubber	1.10
25	Trigger	.55			

PAYMENTS: Parts will be sent only on advance payment. Parts cannot be returned for credit. A service charge of 25c must be added to every order under $1.00 to cover cost of handling. Do not forget to include postage.

INSTRUCTIONS: In ordering parts always give name and number listed in catalog, also make, model, caliber and serial number of gun.

SEE PAGE 8, "HOW TO ORDER"

HARRINGTON & RICHARDSON REVOLVER PARTS

Hunter Model, Trapper Model, & 922   "Sportsman," Single & Double Action, & New Defender

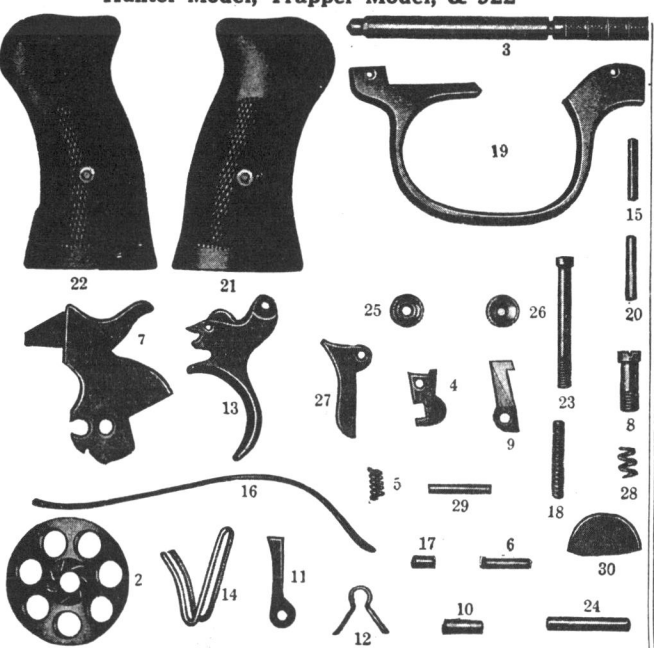
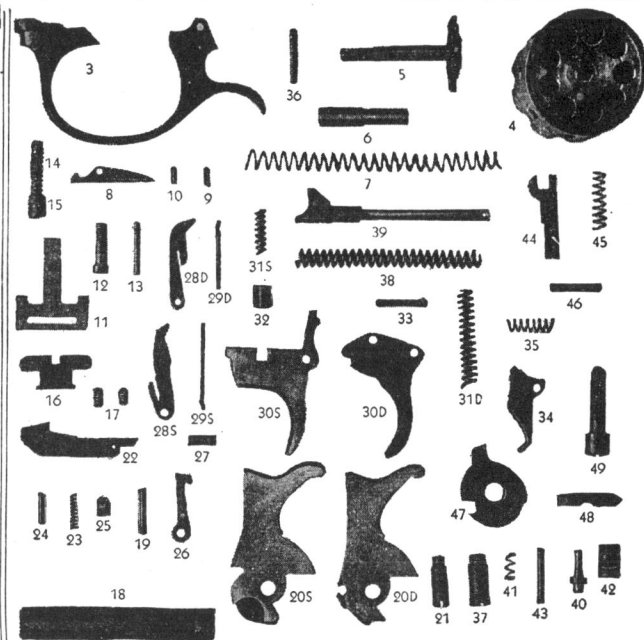

State caliber and number of shots and send broken or worn parts, if possible, and give number stamped on pistol butt.

1	Barrel, 6-inch	$1.90
	Barrel, 10-inch, Hunter	3.00
2	Cylinder	1.10
3	Center Pin	.25
4	Center Pin Catch	.25
5	Center Pin Catch Spring	.25
6	Center Pin Catch Pin	.25
7	Hammer	.50
8	Hammer Screw	.25
9	Lifter	.25
10	Lifter Pin	.25
11	Lever	.25
12	Lever Spring	.25
13	Trigger	.55
14	Trigger Spring	.25
15	Trigger Pin	.25
16	Main Spring	.25
17	Friction Pin	.25
18	Friction Pin Spring	.25
19	Guard	.55
20	Guard Pin	.25
21	Stock, right	.55
22	Stock, left	.55
23	Stock Screw	.25
24	Stock Pin (2), each	.25
25	Escutcheon, head	.25
26	Escutcheon, thread	.25
27	Sear	.25
28	Sear Spring	.25
29	Sear Pin	.25
30	Sight	.25
	Stocks, complete, Checked Walnut Target Grip	1.20

Parts of American Double Action, Safety Hammer Double Action, Young America Double Action, Young America Safety Hammer, Vest Pocket Safety Hammer, H. & R. Bulldog, Young America Bulldog and Victor

Be sure to mention NAME stamped on revolver

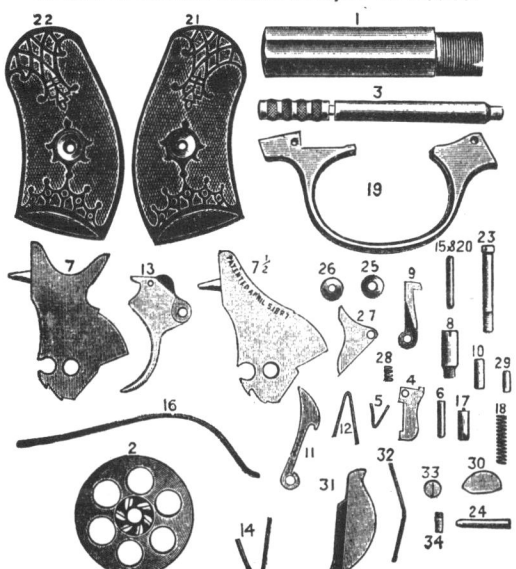

1	Barrel, 2½-inch	$1.20
	Barrel, 4½-inch	1.50
	Barrel, 6-inch	1.90
2	Cylinder	1.10
3	Center Pin	.25
4	Center Pin Catch	.25
5	Center Pin Catch Spring	.25
6	Center Pin Catch Pin	.25
7	Hammer	.55
7½	Safety Hammer	.55
8	Hammer Screw	.25
9	Lifter	.25
10	Lifter Pin	.25
11	Lever	.25
12	Lever Spring	.25
13	Trigger	.50
14	Trigger Spring	.25
15	Trigger Pin	.25
16	Main Spring	.25
17	Friction Pin	.25
18	Friction Pin Spring	.25
19	Guard	.50
20	Guard Pin	.25
21	Stock, right	.25
22	Stock, left	.25
23	Stock Screw	$0.25
24	Stock Pin	.25
25	Escutcheon Head	.25
26	Escutcheon Thread	.25
27	Sear	.25
28	Sear Spring	.25
29	Sear Pin	.25
30	Sight	.25
31	Gate	.25
32	Gate Spring	.25
33	Gate Spring Screw	.25
34	Gate Screw	.25

State caliber and number of shots and send broken or worn parts, if possible, and give number stamped on pistol butt.

1	Frame (not illustrated)	$3.85
2	Barrel (not illustrated)	6.05
3	Guard	1.10
4	Cylinder, complete (includes Nos. 5, 6 and 7)	3.30
5	Extractor	.90
6	Extractor Extension	.25
7	Extractor Spring	.25
8	Cylinder Catch	.45
9	Cylinder Catch Spring	.25
10	Cylinder Catch Screw	.25
11	Barrel Catch, complete (includes Nos. 16 and 17)	1.55
12	Barrel Catch Screw	.25
13	Barrel Catch Pin	.25
14	Barrel Catch Spring	.25
15	Barrel Catch Spring Follower	.25
16	Rear Sight	.55
17	Rear Sight Adjusting Screws (2) each	.25
18	Quill	.35
19	Quill Pin	.25
20S	Hammer (Single Action)	1.20
20D	Hammer (Double Action)	1.20
21	Hammer Screw	.25
22	Front Sight	.85
23	Front Sight Spring	.25
24	Front Sight Pin	.25
25	Front Sight Adjusting Screw	.25
26	Lifter (D)	.25
27	Lifter Pin (D)	.25
28S	Lever (Single Action)	.25
28D	Lever (Double Action)	.25
29S	Lever Spring (Single Action)	.25
29D	Lever Spring (Double Action)	.25
30S	Trigger (Single Action)	1.40
30D	Trigger (Double Action)	.85
31S	Trigger Spring (Single Action)	.25
31D	Trigger Spring (Double Action)	.25
32	Trigger Spring Follower (S)	.25
33	Trigger Pin	.25
34	Sear (D)	.25
35	Sear Spring (D)	.25
36	Guard Pin	.25
37	Hinge Screw	.25
38	Main Spring	.25
39	Main Spring Guide	.55
40	Firing Pin	.25
41	Firing Pin Spring	.25
42	Firing Pin Bushing	.25
43	Firing Pin Bushing Pin	.25
44	Cylinder Stop	.65
45	Cylinder Stop Spring	.25
46	Cylinder Stop Pin (S)	.25
47	Hook	.35
48	Hook Slide	.25
49	Stock Screw	.25
	Stocks (not illustrated) Interchangeable, Nos. 1-5, each	2.20

INSTRUCTIONS: In ordering parts always give name and number listed in catalog, also make, model, caliber and serial number of gun.

PAYMENTS: Parts will be sent only on advance payment. Parts cannot be returned for credit. A service charge of 25c must be added to every order under $1.00 to cover cost of handling. Do not forget to include postage.

Harrington & Richardson Shotgun and Revolver Parts

Models 1900, 1905, 1908, 1915; "Standard," Standard Light Wt., Heavy Breech, Top Rib, Folding Baystate, Handy Gun and Columbia

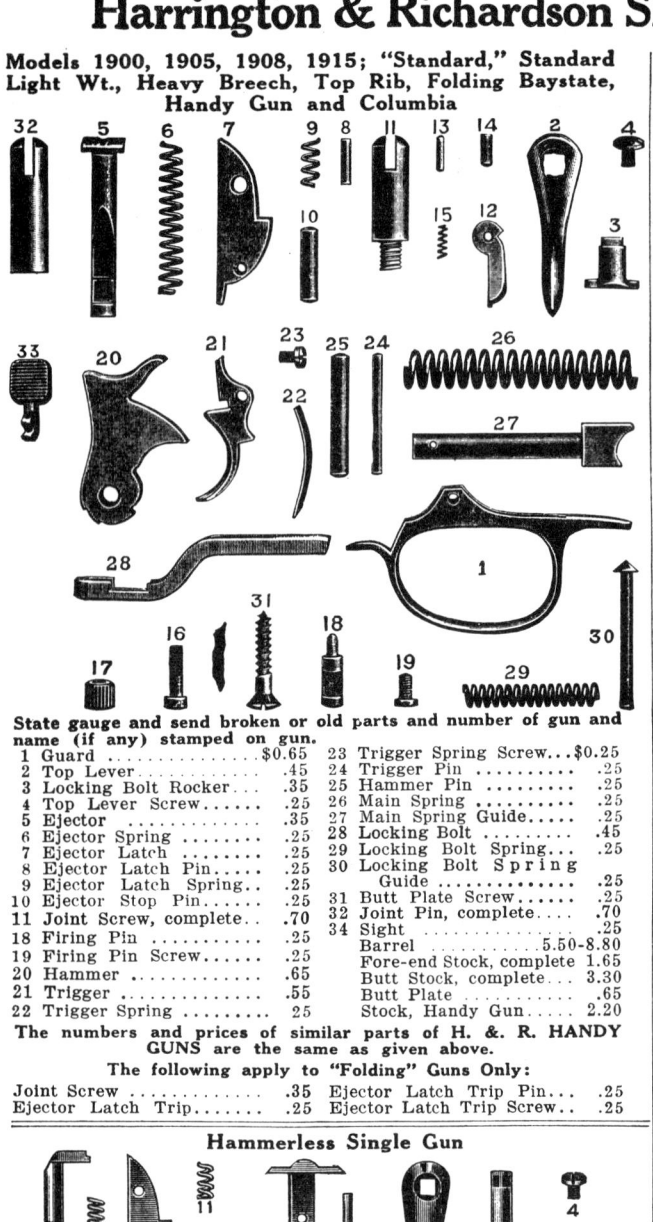

State gauge and send broken or old parts and number of gun and name (if any) stamped on gun.

No.	Part	Price	No.	Part	Price
1	Guard	$0.65	23	Trigger Spring Screw	$0.25
2	Top Lever	.45	24	Trigger Pin	.25
3	Locking Bolt Rocker	.35	25	Hammer Pin	.25
4	Top Lever Screw	.25	26	Main Spring	.25
5	Ejector	.35	27	Main Spring Guide	.25
6	Ejector Spring	.25	28	Locking Bolt	.45
7	Ejector Latch	.25	29	Locking Bolt Spring	.25
8	Ejector Latch Pin	.25	30	Locking Bolt Spring Guide	.25
9	Ejector Latch Spring	.25	31	Butt Plate Screw	.25
10	Ejector Stop Pin	.25	32	Joint Pin, complete	.70
11	Joint Screw, complete	.70	34	Sight	.25
18	Firing Pin	.25		Barrel	5.50-8.80
19	Firing Pin Screw	.25		Fore-end Stock, complete	1.65
20	Hammer	.65		Butt Stock, complete	3.30
21	Trigger	.55		Butt Plate	.65
22	Trigger Spring	.25		Stock, Handy Gun	2.20

The numbers and prices of similar parts of H. & R. HANDY GUNS are the same as given above.

The following apply to "Folding" Guns Only:
Joint Screw .35
Ejector Latch Trip .25
Ejector Latch Trip Pin .25
Ejector Latch Trip Screw .25

Hammerless Single Gun

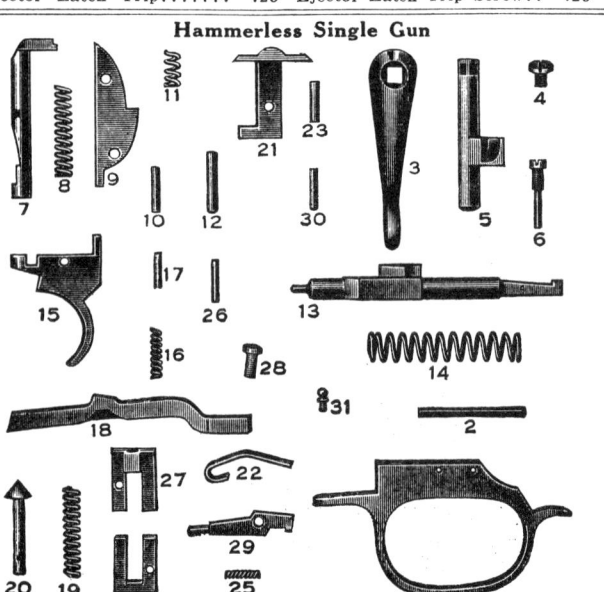

Single Shot Pistol U.S.R.A. Model

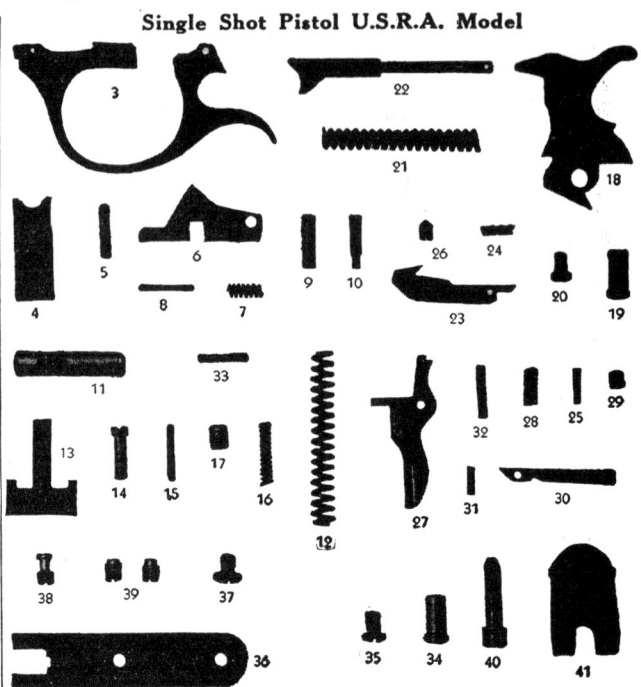

State name, caliber and send broken or worn part. Give number stamped on pistol butt.

No.	Part	Price	No.	Part	Price
1	Frame (not illustrated)	$5.50	25	Front Sight Pin	$0.25
2	Barrel (not illustrated)	9.35	26	Front Sight Adjusting Screw	.25
3	Guard	1.35	27	Trigger	1.95
4	Ejector	.85	28	Trigger Spring	.25
5	Ejector Pin	.25	29	Trigger Spring Adjusting Screw	.25
6	Ejector Latch	.85	30	Trigger Lever	.45
7	Ejector Latch Spring	.25	31	Trigger Lever Pin	.25
8	Ejector Latch Spring Pin	.25	32	Trigger Pin	.25
9	Ejector Latch Pin	.25	33	Guard Pin	.25
10	Ejector Latch Trip Screw	.30	34	Hinge Stud	.30
11	Ejector Plunger	.45	35	Hinge Stud Screw	.25
12	Ejector Spring	.25	36	Rear Sight	1.65
13	Barrel Catch	.85	37	Rear Sight Screw	.25
14	Barrel Catch Screw	.25	38	Rear Sight Elevation Screw	.25
15	Barrel Catch Pin	.25	39	Windage Adjustment Screws (2) each	.25
16	Barrel Catch Spring	.25	40	Stock Screw	.25
17	Barrel Catch Spring Follower	.30	41	Front Sight Guard	1.10
18	Hammer	1.95		Stocks (not illustrated) Interchangeable Nos. 1-5, each	2.20
19	Hammer Stud	.35			
20	Hammer Stud Screw	.25		Walnut Block for Stocks, slotted and drilled, but not turned or checked	1.10
21	Main Spring	.25			
22	Main Spring Guide	.55			
23	Front Sight	1.10			
24	Front Sight Spring	.25			

State gauge and send broken or old parts and number of gun and name, if any.

No.	Part	Price	No.	Part	Price
1	Guard	$0.85	21	Safety Slide	$0.45
2	Guard Pin	.25	22	Safety Slide Spring	.25
3	Top Lever	.55	23	Safety Slide Pin	.25
4	Top Lever Screw	.25	24	Safety Block	.25
5	Cocking Cam	.55	25	Safety Block Spring	.25
6	Cocking Cam Stop Screw	.25	26	Safety Block Pin	.25
7	Ejector	.35	27	Housing	.55
8	Ejector Spring	.25	28	Housing Screw	.25
9	Ejector Latch	.25	29	Sear	.55
10	Ejector Latch Pin	.25	30	Sear Pin	.25
11	Ejector Latch Spring	.25	31	Sight	.25
12	Ejector Stop Pin	.25		Frame	3.30
13	Firing Pin	1.10		Barrel	6.60
14	Firing Pin Spring	.25		Fore-end Stock, complete	1.65
15	Trigger	.55		Butt Stock, complete	3.30
16	Trigger Spring	.25		Butt Plate	.65
17	Trigger Pin	.25		Butt Plate Screws (2), each	.25
18	Locking Bolt	.55			
19	Locking Bolt Spring	.25			
20	Lkg. Bolt Spg. Guide	.25			

INSTRUCTIONS: In ordering parts always give name and number listed in catalog, also make, model, caliber and serial number of gun.

PAYMENTS: Parts will be sent only on advance payment. Parts cannot be returned for credit. A service charge of 25c must be added to every order under $1.00 to cover cost of handling. Do not forget to include postage.

A NEW GUN CARRIES A FACTORY GUARANTEE

America's Great Gun House

IVER JOHNSON AUTOMATIC SUPERSHOT AND SUPERSHOT SEALED EIGHT REVOLVERS

Part Name	22 Cal. 7 Shot	22 Cal. 9 Shot	22 Cal. 8 Shot	Price	Part Name	22 Cal. 7 Shot	22 Cal. 9 Shot	22 Cal. 8 Shot	Price
Frame	C601	C701	C801	$3.00	Cylinder — Complete Assembly	C653A	C753A	C853A	$2.15
Firing Pin	C602	C602	C802	.25	Extractor (Return cylinder for fitting)	C654	C754	C854	.40
Firing Pin Stop Pin	B587	B587	B587	.25	Extractor Stem	A555	A555	A555	.25
Firing Pin Spring	A105	A105	A105	.25	Extractor Spring	A556	A556	A556	.25
Stock Pin	C106	—	—	.25	Extractor Cam Assembly	C357A	C357A	C357A	.30
Stocks—					Extractor Cam	C357	C357	C357	.25
Western Walnut Checkered	C316	C316	C316	1.75	Extractor Cam Center	C158	C158	C158	.25
Hi-Hold Walnut Checkered	—	—	C816	1.75	Extractor Cam Center Spring	C159	C159	C159	.25
Target — Left — Checkered	C617	—	—	.90	Quill	C360	C360	C360	.25
Target — Right — Checkered	C618	—	—	.90	Cylinder Stop	C164	C164	C164	.25
Head Escutcheon for Target Stocks	A119	—	—	.25	Cylinder Stop Pin	B587	B587	B587	.25
Thread Escutcheon for Target Stocks	A121	—	—	.35	Cylinder Stop Spring	C166	C166	C166	.25
Stock Screw for Target Stocks	E523	—	—	.25	Hammer	C367	C367	C367	.40
Walnut Stock End Screw	C126	C126	C126	.25	Hammer Screw	A569	A569	A569	.25
Walnut Stock End Screw Escutcheon	C127	C127	C127	.25	Main Spring	C370	C370	C370	.25
Barrel — 6 inch	C638	C638	C838	3.25	Main Spring Tension Adjusting Bar	C171	C171	C171	.25
Sight, Gold Plated	C6402	C6402	C6402	.25	Main Spring Ball Plunger	C172	C172	C172	.25
Barrel Catch	C641	C641	C841	.40	Main Spring Ball Plunger Pin	C173	C173	C173	.25
Barrel Catch Plunger	C642	C642	C642	.35	Lever and Pin	A574	A574	A574	.25
Barrel Catch Spring	A543	A543	A543	.25	Lever Spring	A175	A175	A175	.25
Barrel Catch Screw	A544	A544	A544	.25	Lifter	C376	C376	C376	.25
Joint Screw	A548	A548	A548	.25	Sear	C378	C378	C378	.25
Guard	C349	C349	C349	.45	Sear Spring	C179	C179	C179	.25
Guard Pin, Front	A552	A552	A552	.25	Trigger	C380	C380	C880	.45
Guard Pin, Rear	A552	A552	A552	.25	Trigger Spring	C181	C181	C181	.25
Cylinder	C653	C753	C853	1.80	Trigger Pin	A552	A552	A552	.25

I. J. DOUBLE ACTION TARGET AND TARGET SEALED EIGHT REVOLVERS

Part Name	22 Cal. 7 Shot	22 Cal. 9 Shot	22 Cal. 8 Shot	Price	Part Name	22 Cal. 7 Shot	22 Cal. 9 Shot	22 Cal. 8 Shot	Price
Frame	E101	E701	E801	$2.35	Snap Pin	E147	E547	E547	$0.25
Stock Pin	A106			.25	Guard	E149	E549	E549	.45
Stocks —					Guard Pin, Front	E151	E551	E551	.25
Western Walnut Checkered		E316	E316	1.75	Guard Pin, Rear	E151	E551	E551	.25
Hi-Hold Walnut Checkered			E816	1.75	Cylinder	E153	E753	E853	1.00
Target, Left — Checkered	E117			.90	Center Pin	E161	E561	E561	.25
Target, Right — Checkered	E118			.90	Cylinder Friction Stud	E162	E162	E162	.25
Head Escutcheon for Target Stocks	A119			.25	Cylinder Friction Spring	E163	E563	E563	.25
Thread Escutcheon for Target Stocks	A121			.25	Hammer	E167	E767	E767	.40
Stock Screw for Target Stocks	A523			.25	Hammer Screw	E169	E569	E569	.25
Walnut Stock End Screw		C126	C126	.25	Main Spring	A170	A570	A570	.25
Walnut Stock End Screw Escutcheon		C127	C127	.25	Lever and Pin	A174	A574	A574	.25
Barrels —					Lever Spring	A175	A175	A175	.25
6 inch	E138	E738	E838	1.25	Lifter	E176	E576	E576	.25
9½ inch	E139			2.00	Sear	A178	A578	A578	.25
10 inch		E7391	E8391	2.00	Sear Spring	A179	A179	A179	.25
Sight, Gold Plated	E1402	C6402	C1402	.25	Trigger	E180	E580	E880	.45
Snap, 1926 Type	E1451	E5451	E5451	.25	Trigger Spring	E181	E581	E581	.25
Snap Spring, 1926 — Coil	E1461	E1461	E1461	.25	Trigger Pin	E151	E551	E551	.25

REVOLVER REFINISHING		REVOLVER BRUSHES	
Renickel or Reblue — any model —		Pure Bristle Brush in twisted wire, coppered —	
Revolver Complete	$2.50	22 caliber	PB22 $0.25
Frame	.95	32 caliber	PB22 .25
Barrel	.95	38 caliber	PB38 .25
Cylinder	.70	Firing Pin Nut Wrench	1.80
Note: Blued revolvers can be refinished either blue or nickel. Nickeled revolvers can only be refinished in nickel.		Firing Pin Nut Wrench for 22 caliber Hammerless	1.80

INSTRUCTIONS: In ordering parts always give name and number listed in catalog, also make, model, caliber and serial number of gun.

PAYMENTS: Parts will be sent only on advance payment. Parts cannot be returned for credit. A service charge of 25c must be added to every order under $1.00 to cover cost of handling. Do not forget to include postage.

PARTS FOR 1916 MODEL

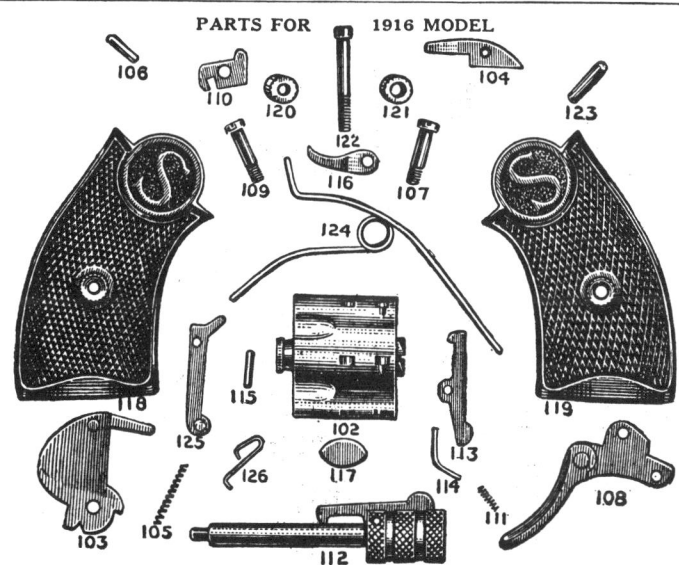

1916 MODEL BABY HAMMERLESS

101	Frame	$2.25
102	Cylinder	1.00
103	Hammer Complete	.80
104	Hammer Nose	.25
105	Hammer Nose Spg.	.25
106	Hammer Nose Pin	.25
107	Hammer Screw	.25
108	Trigger Complete	.80
109	Trigger Screw	.25
110	Cylinder Stop	.25
111	Cylinder Stop Spg.	.25
112	Base Pin Complete	.60
113	Base Pin Catch	.30
114	Base Pin Catch Sp.	.25
115	Base Pin Catch Pin	.25
116	Lifter or Cock. Lev.	.30
117	Sight	.25
118	Rubber Stock R. H.	.30
119	Rubber Stock L. H.	.30
120	Escutcheon (Thread)	.25
121	Escutcheon (Head)	.25
122	Stock Screw	.25
123	Stock Pin	.25
124	Combination Spring	.50
125	Lever or Hand	.30
126	Lever or Hand Spg.	.25

ALL SHIPMENTS ARE INSURED

IVER JOHNSON REVOLVER PARTS

OLD MODEL IVER JOHNSON SAFETY HAMMER AND SAFETY HAMMERLESS AUTOMATIC REVOLVERS

Part Name	Hammer 22 Cal.	Hammer 32 Cal.	Hammer 38 Cal.	H'Less 32 Cal.	H'Less 38 Cal.	Price	Part Name	Hammer 22 Cal.	Hammer 32 Cal.	Hammer 38 Cal.	H'Less 32 Cal.	H'Less 38 Cal.	Price
Frame	A101	A201	A501	B201	B501	$2.30	Barrel Catch	A141	A141	A541	A141	A541	$ .40
							Barrel Catch Plunger	A142	A142	A142	A142	A142	.25
Firing Pin	A102	A202	A202	A202	A202	.25	Barrel Catch Spring	A143	A143	A543	A143	A543	.25
Firing Pin Nut	—	A203	A203	A203	A203	.25	Barrel Catch Screw	A144	A144	A544	A144	A544	.25
Firing Pin Stop Pin	A104	—	—	—	—	.25							
Firing Pin Spring	A105	A205	A205	A205	A205	.25	Joint Screw	A148	A148	A548	A148	A548	.25
Stock Pin	A106	A106	A106	A106	A106	.25	Guard	A149	A149	A549	B249	B540	.35
Stocks—							Guard Screw	A150	A150	A150	A150	A150	.25
Rubber — Left	A107	A107	A507	A107	A507	.25	Guard Pin, Rear	A152	A152	A552	A152	A552	.25
Rubber — Right	A108	A108	A508	A108	A508	.25	Cylinder	A153	A253	A553	A253	A553	1.40
*Perfect — Left	A109	A109	A509	A109	A509	.60	Cylinder — Complete	A153A	A253A	A553A	A253A	A533A	1.75
*Perfect — Right	A110	A110	A510	A110	A510	.60	Extractor	A154	A254	A554	A254	A554	.25
Pearl — Left	A113	A113	A513	A113	A513	1.25	Extractor Stem	A155	A155	A555	A155	A555	.25
Pearl — Right	A114	A114	A514	A114	A514	1.25	Extractor Spring	A156	A156	A556	A156	A556	.25
Head Escutcheon for							Extractor Cam Assembly	C157A	C157A	C357A	C157A	C357A	.30
Rubber and Perfect Stocks	A119	A119	A119	A119	A119	.25	Extractor Cam Spring	A159	A159	A159	A159	A159	.25
Pearl Stocks	A120	A120	A120	A120	A120	.25	(For old type Cam)						
Thread Escutcheon for							Quill	A160	A160	A560	A160	A560	.30
Rubber and Perfect Stocks	A121	A121	A121	A121	A121	.25	Cylinder Friction Spring	A163	A163	A563	A163	A563	.25
Pearl Stocks	A122	A122	A122	A122	A122	.25	Hammer	A167	A167	A567	B267	B567	.40
Stock Screw for							Hammer Screw	A169	A169	A569	B269	B569	.25
Rubber Stocks	A123	A123	A523	A123	A523	.25	Main Spring	A170	A270	A570	A270	A570	.25
Perfect Stocks — Upper	A523	A523	E523	A523	E523	.25	Lever and Pin	A174	A174	A574	A174	A574	.25
Perfect Stocks — Lower	A124	A124	A524	A124	A524	.25	Lever Spring	A175	A175	A175	A175	A175	.35
Barrels—							Lifter	A176	A276	A576	B276	B576	.25
2 inch	—	A230	—	A230	—	2.50	Sear	A178	A178	A578	—	—	.25
3 inch	A132	A232	—	A232	—	2.70	Sear Spring	A179	A179	A179	—	—	.25
3¼ inch	—	—	A533	—	A533	2.75	Trigger	A180	A280	A580	B280	B580	.45
4 inch	A135	A235	A535	A235	A535	2.90	Trigger Spring	A181	A181	A581	A181	A581	.25
5 inch	A137	A237	A537	A237	A537	3.10	Trigger Pin	A152	A152	A552	A152	A552	.25
6 inch	A138	A238	A538	A238	A538	3.30	Safety Catch	—	—	—	B283	B583	.25
Sight	A140	A140	A540	A140	A540	.25	Safety Catch Pin	—	—	—	B284	B284	.25
							Safety Catch Spring	—	—	—	B285	B285	.25

* Perfect Stocks are of genuine hard rubber and are larger than Rubber Stocks

ORDER BY SYMBOL
Specify whether parts are wanted for a nickeled or blued revolver.

NEW MODEL IVER JOHNSON SAFETY HAMMER AUTOMATIC REVOLVERS

Part Name	22 Cal. 7 Shot	32 Cal. 5 Shot	32 Sp'l 6 Shot	38 Cal. 5 Shot	Price	Part Name	22 Cal. 7 Shot	32 Cal. 5 Shot	32 Sp'l 6 Shot	38 Cal. 5 Shot	Price
Frame	C101	C201	C301	C301	$3.00	Barrel Catch	C141	C141	C341	C341	$ .40
						Barrel Catch Plunger	A142	A142	A142	A142	.25
Firing Pin	A102	A202	A202	A202	.25	Barrel Catch Spring	A143	A143	A543	A543	.25
Firing Pin Nut and Washer	—	A203	A203	A203	.25	Barrel Catch Screw	A144	A144	A544	A544	.25
Firing Pin Stop Pin	A104	—	—	—	.25						
Firing Pin Spring	A105	A205	A205	A205	.25	Joint Screw	A148	A148	A548	A548	.25
Stock Pin	C106	C106	C106	C106	.25	Guard	A149	A149	C349	C349	.45
Stocks—						Guard Pin, Front	C151	C151	A552	A552	.25
Rubber — Left	C107	C107	C307	C307	.25	Guard Pin, Rear	A152	A152	A552	A552	.25
Rubber — Right	C108	C108	C308	C308	.25	Cylinder	C153	C253	C353	C553	1.40
*Perfect — Left	C109	C109	C309	C309	.60	Cylinder — Complete	C153A	C253A	C353A	C553A	1.75
*Perfect — Right	C110	C110	C310	C310	.60	Extractor (Return cylinder for fitting)	A154	A254	C354	A554	.25
Pearl — Left	C113	C113	C313	C313	1.25	Extractor Stem	A155	A155	A555	A555	.25
Pearl — Right	C114	C114	C314	C314	1.25	Extractor Spring	A156	A156	A556	A556	.25
Western Walnut	C115	C115	C315	C315	1.25	Extractor Cam Assembly	C157A	C157A	C357A	C357A	.30
Western Walnut Checkered	C116	C116	C316	C316	1.75	Extractor Cam	C157	C157	C357	C357	.25
Head Escutcheon for						Extractor Cam Center	C158	C158	C158	C158	.25
Rubber and Perfect Stocks	A119	A119	A119	A119	.25	Extractor Cam Center Spring	C159	C159	C159	C159	.25
Pearl Stocks	A120	A120	A120	A120	.25	Quill	C160	C160	C360	C360	.25
Thread Escutcheon for						Cylinder Stop	C164	C164	C164	C164	.25
Rubber and Perfect Stocks	A121	A121	A121	A121	.25	Cylinder Stop Pin	A104	A104	B587	B587	.25
Pearl Stocks	A122	A122	A122	A122	.25	Cylinder Stop Spring	C166	C166	C166	C166	.25
Stock Screw for						Hammer—					
Rubber Stocks	A123	A123	A523	A523	.25	Regular	C167	C267	C367	C367	.40
Perfect Stocks — Upper	A523	A523	E523	E523	.25	Semi-Hammerless	C168	C268	C368	C368	.45
Perfect Stocks — Lower	A124	A124	A524	A524	.25	Hammer Screw	A169	A169	A569	A569	.25
Pearl Stocks	A125	A125	A525	A525	.25	Main Spring	C170	C270	C370	C370	.25
Walnut Stock End Screw	C126	C126	C126	C126	.25	Main Spring Tension Adjusting Bar	C171	C171	C171	C171	.25
Walnut Stock End Screw Escutcheon	C127	C127	C127	C127	.25	Main Spring Ball Plunger	C172	C172	C172	C172	.25
Barrels—						Main Spring Ball Plunger Pin	C173	C173	C173	C173	.25
2 inch	C130	C230	C330	C530	2.50	Lever and Pin	A174	A174	A574	A574	.25
3 inch	C132	C232	—	—	2.50	Lever Spring	A175	A175	A175	A175	.25
3¼ inch	—	—	C333	C533	2.50	Lifter	C176	C276	C376	C376	.25
4 inch	C135	C235	C335	C535	2.75	Sear	C178	C178	C378	C378	.25
5 inch	C137	C237	C337	C537	3.00	Sear Spring	C179	C179	C179	C179	.25
6 inch	C138	C238	C338	C538	3.25	Trigger	C180	C180	C380	C380	.45
Sight for 2, 3, 3¼ and 4 inch	C140	C140	C340	C340	.25	Trigger Spring	C181	C181	C181	C181	.25
Sight for 5 and 6 inch	C640	C650	C640	C640	.25	Trigger Pin	A152	A152	A552	A552	.25

* Perfect Stocks are of genuine hard rubber and are larger than Rubber Stocks.

ORDER BY SYMBOL
Specify whether parts are wanted for a nickeled or blued revolver

SEND YOUR GUN TO STOEGER FOR EXPERT REPAIRING

IVER JOHNSON REVOLVER PARTS
NEW MODEL IVER JOHNSON SAFETY HAMMERLESS AUTOMATIC REVOLVERS

ORDER BY SYMBOL. Specify whether parts are wanted for a nickeled or blued revolver. Parts for rim and center fire Model 1900 are identical except where particularly designated. Unless order otherwise specified, parts for the center fire model will be supplied.
*Perfect Stocks are of genuine hard rubber and are larger than Rubber Stocks.

Part Name	22 Cal. 7 Shot	32 Cal. 5 Shot	32 Sp'l 6 Shot	38 Cal. 5 Shot	Price	Part Name	22 Cal. 7 Shot	32 Cal. 5 Shot	32 Sp'l 6 Shot	38 Cal. 5 Shot	Price
Frame	D101	D201	D301	D301	$3.25	Barrel Catch	C141	C141	C341	C341	$0.40
Firing Pin	D102	A202	A202	A202	.25	Barrel Catch Plunger	A142	A142	A142	A142	.25
Firing Pin Nut and Washer	D103	A203	A203	A203	.25	Barrel Catch Spring	A143	A143	A543	A543	.25
Firing Pin Spring	D105	205A	A205	A205	.25	Barrel Catch Screw	A144	A144	A544	A544	.25
Stock Pin	C106	C106	C106	C106	.25	Joint Screw	A148	A148	A548	A548	.25
Stocks —						Guard	D149	D149	D349	D349	.45
Rubber — Left	C107	C107	C307	C307	.25	Guard Pin, Front	C151	C151	A552	A552	.25
Rubber — Right	C108	C108	C308	C308	.25	Guard Pin, Rear	A152	A152	A552	A552	.25
*Perfect — Left	C109	C109	C309	C309	.60	Cylinder	C153	C253	C353	C553	1.40
*Perfect — Right	C110	C110	C310	C310	.60	Cylinder — Complete	C153A	C253A	C353A	C553A	1.75
Pearl — Left	C113	C113	C313	C313	1.25						
Pearl — Right	C114	C114	C314	C314	1.25	Extractor (Return cylinder for fitting)	A154	A254	C354	A554	.25
Western Walnut	C115	C115	C315	C315	1.25	Extractor Stem	A155	A155	A555	A555	.25
Western Walnut Checkered	C116	C116	C316	C316	1.75	Extractor Spring	A156	A156	A556	A556	.25
						Extractor Cam Assembly	C157A	C157A	C357A	C357A	.30
Head Escutcheon for						Extractor Cam	C157	C157	C357	C357	.25
Rubber and Perfect Stocks	A119	A119	A119	A119	.25	Extractor Cam Center	C158	C158	C158	C158	.25
Pearl Stocks	A120	A120	A120	A120	.25	Extractor Cam Center Spring	C159	C159	C159	C159	.25
Thread Escutcheon for						Quill	C160	C160	C360	C360	.25
Rubber and Perfect Stocks	A121	A121	A121	A121	.25	Cylinder Stop	C164	C164	C164	C164	.25
Pearl Stocks	A122	A122	A122	A122	.25	Cylinder Stop Pin	A104	A104	B587	B587	.25
						Cylinder Stop Spring	C166	C166	C166	C166	.25
Stock Screw for						Hammer	D167	D167	D367	D367	.40
Rubber Stocks	A123	A123	A523	A523	.25	Hammer Screw	B269	B269	B569	B569	.25
Perfect Stocks — Upper	A523	A523	E523	E523	.25						
Perfect Stocks — Lower	A124	A124	A524	A524	.25	Main Spring	C170	C270	C370	C370	.25
Pearl Stocks	A125	A125	A525	A525	.25	Main Spring Tension Adjusting Bar	C171	C171	C171	C171	.25
						Main Spring Ball Plunger	C172	C172	C172	C172	.25
Walnut Stock End Screw	C126	C126	C126	C126	.25	Main Spring Ball Plunger Pin	C173	C173	C173	C173	.25
Walnut Stock End Screw Escutcheon	C127	C127	C127	C127	.25	Lever and Pin	A174	A174	A574	A574	.25
						Lever Spring	A175	A175	A175	A175	.25
Barrels —											
2 inch	C130	C230	C330	C530	2.50	Lifter	D176	D176	D376	D376	.25
3 inch	C132	C232			2.50						
3½ inch			C333	C533	2.50	Trigger	C180	C180	C380	C380	.45
4 inch	C135	C235	C335	C535	2.75	Trigger Spring	C181	C181	C181	C181	.25
5 inch	C137	C237	C337	C537	3.00	Trigger Pin	A152	A152	A552	A552	.25
6 inch	C138	C238	C338	C538	3.25						
Sight for 2, 3, 3½ and 4 inch	C140	C140	C340	C340	.25	Frame Cap	D186	D186	D386	D386	.25
Sight for 5 and 6 inch	C640	C640	C640	C640	.25	Frame Cap Pin	A104	A104	B587	B587	.25

Specify whether parts are wanted for a nickled or blued revolver.

I. J. MODEL 1900 DOUBLE ACTION REVOLVERS

Part Name	22 Cal. 7 Shot	32 Cal. 5 Shot	32 Cal. 6 Shot	38 Cal. 5 Shot	Price	Part Name	22 Cal. 7 Shot	32 Cal. 5 Shot	32 Cal. 6 Shot	38 Cal. 5 Shot	Price
Frame	E101	E201	E501	E501	$2.35	Snap	E145	E145	E545	E545	$0.25
Frame (32 Rim Fire)		E401			2.35	Snap, 1926 Type	E1451	E1451	E5451	E5451	.25
Frame (Loading Gate)	E1012	E2012		E5012	2.50	Snap Spring — Flat	E146	E146	E546	E546	.25
Frame (32 Rim Fire Loading Gate)		E4012			2.50	Snap Spring, 1926 — Coil	E1461	E1461	E1461	E1461	.25
						Snap Pin	E147	E147	E547	E547	.25
Stock Pin	A106	A106	E551	E551	.25						
						Guard	E149	E249	E549	E549	.45
Stocks —						Guard Pin, Front	E151	A152	E549	E549	.25
Rubber — Left	C107	C107	C307	C307	.25	Guard Pin, Rear	E151	A152	E551	E551	.25
Rubber — Right	C108	C108	C308	C308	.25						
*Perfect — Left	C109	C109	C309	C309	.60	Cylinder	E153	E253	E353	E553	1.00
*Perfect — Right	C110	C110	C310	C310	.60	Center Pin	E161	E261	E561	E561	.25
Pearl — Left	C113	C113	C313	C313	1.25	Cylinder Friction Stud	E162	E162	E162	E162	.25
Pearl — Right	C114	C114	C314	C314	1.25	Cylinder Friction Spring	E163	E163	E563	E563	.25
Head Escutcheon for						Hammer	E167	E267	E567	E567	.40
Rubber and Perfect Stocks	A119	A119	A119	A119	.25	Hammer (32 Rim Fire)		E467			.40
Pearl Stocks	A120	A120	A120	A120	.25	Hammer Screw	E169	E169	E569	E569	.25
Thread Escutcheon for						Main Spring	A170	A270	A570	A570	.25
Rubber and Perfect Stocks	A121	A121	A121	A121	.25	Main Spring (32 Rim Fire)		A170			.25
Pearl Stocks	A122	A122	A122	A122	.25						
						Lever and Pin	A174	A174	A574	A574	.25
Stock Screw for						Lever Spring	A175	A175	A175	A175	.25
Rubber Stocks	A123	A123	E523	E523	.25						
Perfect Stocks — Upper	A523	A523	E523	E523	.25	Lifter	E176	E176	E576	E576	.25
Perfect Stocks — Lower	A124	A124	A524	A524	.25	Sear	A178	A178	A578	A578	.25
Pearl Stocks	A125	A125	A525	A525	.25	Sear Spring	A179	A179	A179	A179	.25
Barrels —						Trigger	E180	E280	E580	E580	.45
2½ inch	E131	E231	E331	E531	.75	Trigger Spring	E181	E181	E581	E581	.25
4½ inch	E136	E236	E336	E536	1.00	Trigger Pin	E151	A152	E551	E551	.25
6 inch	E138	E238	E338	E538	1.25	Loading Gate	E195	E195		E595	1.00
						Loading Gate Catch	E196	E196		E196	.25
Sight	E140	E140	E140	E140	.25	Loading Gate Spring	E197	E197		E197	.25

INSTRUCTIONS: In ordering parts always give name and number listed in catalog, also make, model, caliber and serial number of gun.

PAYMENTS: Parts will be sent only on advance payment. Parts cannot be returned for credit. A service charge of 25c must be added to every order under $1.00 to cover cost of handling. Do not forget to include postage.

ORDER BLANK IN MIDDLE AND INDEX IN BACK OF CATALOG

IVER JOHNSON SHOTGUN PARTS

Part Name	12 Ga.	16 Ga.	20 Ga.	.410 Bore Ga.	Price
FRAME GROUP					
*Frame, Non-Ejector	Y100	Y200	Y300	Y800	$12.00
*Frame, Ejector	Y101	Y201	Y301	Y801	12.00
Firing Pin (2)	Y102	Y102	Y102	Y802	.25
Firing Pin (2)	Y1022	Y1022	Y1022	Y1022	.25
*Top Lever — Fitted at Factory	Y104F	Y204F	Y204F	Y804F	1.50
Top Lever	Y104	Y204	Y204	Y804	.70
Top Lever Plunger	Y1043	Y1043	Y1043	Y1043	.25
Top Lever Plunger Spring	Y1044	Y1044	Y1044	Y1044	.25
Locking Bolt	Y105	Y105	Y105	Y105	.40
Safety Button	Y106	Y106	Y106	Y106	.35
Safety Button Pin, Short	Y1061	Y1061	Y1061	Y1061	.25
Safety Button Pin, Long	Y1062	Y1062	Y1062	Y1062	.25
Safety Button Spring	Y1063	Y1063	Y1063	Y1063	.25
Safety Button Spring Screw	Y1064	Y1064	Y1064	Y1064	.35
Safety Button Connecting Rod	Y1065	Y1065	Y1065	Y1065	.25
Safety Block	Y107	Y107	Y107	Y107	.25
Safety Block Pin	Y1071	Y1071	Y1071	Y1071	.25
Cocking Rod (2)	Y108	Y108	Y108	Y108	.25
Cocking Rod Screw (2)	Y1081	Y1081	Y1081	Y1081	.25
Hammer, Left	Y1091	Y1091	Y1091	Y1091	.50
Hammer, Right	Y1092	Y1092	Y1092	Y1092	.50
Hammer Pin	Y1095	Y1095	Y1095	Y1095	.25
Main Spring (2)	Y112	Y112	Y112	Y112	.25
Main Spring Plunger (2)	Y1122	Y1122	Y1122	Y1122	.25
Trigger, Left	Y1131	Y1131	Y1131	Y1131	.40
Trigger, Right	Y1132	Y1132	Y1132	Y1132	.40
Trigger Pin	Y1135	Y1135	Y1135	Y1135	.25
*Trigger Plate	Y1138	Y1138	Y1138	Y1138	3.00
Trigger Plate Screw	Y1139	Y1139	Y1139	Y1139	.25
Sear, Left	Y1141	Y1141	Y1141	Y1141	.30
Sear, Right	Y1142	Y1142	Y1142	Y1142	.30
Sear Pin	Y1145	Y1145	Y1145	Y1145	.25
Sear Spring (2)	Y1146	Y1146	Y1146	Y1146	.25
Guard	Y115	Y115	Y115	Y115	.50
Guard Screw	Y1151	Y1151	Y1151	Y1151	.25
Tang Screw, Front	Y1161	Y1161	Y1161	Y1161	.25
Tang Screw, Rear	Y1162	Y1162	Y1162	Y1162	.25

Part Name	12 Ga.	16 Ga.	20 Ga.	.410 Bore Ga.	Price
BARREL GROUP					
*Barrell, Non-Ejector (Complete)					
26 inch	—	—	—	Y826N	$16.00
28 inch	Y128N	Y228N	Y328N	—	16.00
30 inch	Y130N	Y230N	—	—	16.00
32 inch	Y132N	—	—	—	16.00
*Barrel, Ejector (Complete)					
26 inch	—	—	—	Y826E	19.00
28 inch	Y128E	Y228E	Y328E	—	19.00
30 inch	Y130E	Y230E	—	—	19.00
32 inch	Y132E	—	—	—	19.00
Sight, Front — Threaded	P140	P140	P140	P140	.25
Sight, Lyman Ivory Front	T140	T140	T140	T140	.50
Sight, Lyman Ivory Rear	T1401	T1401	T1401	T1401	.50
Non-Ejector Extractor	Y1411	Y2411	Y3411	Y8411	1.00
*Ejector Extractor, Left { Sold in pairs }	Y1412	Y2412	Y3412	Y8412	2.00
*Ejector Extractor, Right					
Non-Ejector Extractor Check Screw	Y1421	Y1421	Y1421	Y1421	.25
Ejector Extractor Check Screw	Y1422	Y1422	Y1422	Y1422	.25
FOREND GROUP					
*Forend, Non-Ejector (Complete)	Y150A	Y250A	Y350A	Y850A	6.00
*Forend, Ejector (Complete)	Y151A	Y251A	Y351A	Y851A	13.00
*Non-Ejector Forend Wood	Y150	Y250	Y350	Y850	3.00
*Ejector Forend Wood	Y151	Y251	Y351	Y851	5.00
*Non-Ejector Forend Iron	Y1521	Y1521	Y1521	Y1521	2.50
*Ejector Forend Iron	Y1522	Y1522	Y1522	Y1522	4.00
Non-Ejector Forend Front Screw	Y1531	Y1531	Y1531	Y1531	.25
Non-Ejector Forend Rear Screw	Y1532	Y1532	Y1532	Y1532	.25
Ejector Forend Screw (2)	Y1533	Y1533	Y1533	Y1533	.25
Non-Ejector Forend Escutcheon	Y1541	Y1541	Y1541	Y1541	.25
Ejector Forend Escutcheon	Y1542	Y1542	Y1542	Y1542	.25
Non-Ejector Forend Catch	Y157	Y157	Y157	Y157	.40
Non-Ejector Forend Catch Pin	Y1571	Y1571	Y1571	Y1571	.25
Non-Ejector Forend Catch Spring	Y1572	Y1572	Y1572	Y1572	.25
Non-Ejector Forend Catch Spring Screw	Y1573	Y1573	Y1573	Y1573	.25

DOUBLE GUN PARTS—CONTINUED

Part Name	12 Ga.	16 Ga.	20 Ga.	.410 Bore Ga.	Price
FOREND GROUP					
Cocking Rod Roller (2)	Y158	Y158	Y158	Y158	$0.25
Cocking Rod Roller Screw, Left	Y1581	Y1581	Y1581	Y1581	.25
Cocking Rod Roller Screw, Right	Y1582	Y1582	Y1582	Y1582	.25
*Ejector Forend Fastener	Y161	Y161	Y161	Y161	3.00
Ejector Forend Fastener Spring	Y1612	Y1612	Y1612	Y1612	.25
Ejector Forend Fastener Screw (2)	Y1613	Y1613	Y1613	Y1613	.25
Ejector Forend Fastener Plate	Y1614	Y1614	Y1614	Y1614	1.50
*Ejector Forend Fastener Lever	Y1615	Y1615	Y1615	Y1615	1.40
Ejector Forend Fastener Lever Pin	Y1616	Y1616	Y1616	Y1616	.25
Ejector Kicker, Left	Y1621	Y1621	Y1621	Y1621	.50
Ejector Kicker, Right	Y1622	Y1622	Y1622	Y1622	.50
Ejector Kicker Spring (2)	Y1623	Y1623	Y1623	Y1623	.25
Ejector Kicker Guide Rod (2)	Y1624	Y1624	Y1624	Y1624	.25
*Ejector Kicker Lock, Left	Y1626	Y1626	Y1626	Y1626	.40
*Ejector Kicker Lock, Right	Y1627	Y1627	Y1627	Y1627	.40
Ejector Kicker Lock Spring (2)	Y1628	Y1628	Y1628	Y1628	.25
*Ejector Sear	Y163	Y163	Y163	Y163	.40
Ejector Sear Pin	Y1631	Y1631	Y1631	Y1631	.25
Ejector Sear Spring	Y1628	Y1628	Y1628	Y1628	.25
BACK STOCK GROUP					
*Back Stock (Complete)	Y181A	Y181A	Y381A	Y881A	8.00
Back Stock Wood	Y181	Y181	Y381	Y881	6.00
Butt Plate	Y186	Y186	Y186	Y886	.75
Butt Plate Screw (2)	P1861	P1861	P1861	P1861	.25
Pistol Grip Cap	Y187	Y187	Y187	—	.40
Pistol Grip Cap Screw	R1871	R1871	R1871	—	.25
Recoil Pad with Screws	P1864	P1864	P1864	P8864	2.00

SUPERTRAP DOUBLE GUN PARTS

Parts not shown are the same as Ejector Double Gun parts.

Part Name	Symbol	Price
Frame	Z101	$14.00
*Top Lever — Fitted at Factory	Z104F	1.50
Top Lever	Z104	.70
Locking Bolt Trip	Y1045	.25
Locking Bolt Trip Spring	Y1046	.25
Locking Bolt Trip Screw	Y1047	.25
Locking Bolt	Z105	.40
Safety Button	Z106	.35
*Barrel, Supertrap — Complete — 32 inch	Z132E	28.00
*Forend, Supertrap — Complete	Z151A	16.00
*Forend Wood, Supertrap	Z151	8.00
*Back Stock, Supertrap — Complete	Z181A	14.00
*Back Stock Wood, Supertrap	Z181	12.00
Recoil Pad with Screws	P1864	2.00

DOUBLE GUN INFORMATION

Asterisk (*) preceding a part name indicates that complete gun must be returned to us to have that part fitted. List Price shown for such a part includes cost of part and labor cost of fitting same to gun.

The figure two (2) following a part name indicates that two of that particular piece are used on each gun. Prices quoted cover single pieces only.

DOUBLE GUN REFINISHING

Gun Complete	$8.75
Frame	1.75
Barrel	1.40
Forend	1.85
Back Stock	3.75

INSTRUCTIONS: In ordering parts always give name and number listed in catalog, also make, model, caliber and serial number of gun.

PAYMENTS: Parts will be sent only on advance payment. Parts cannot be returned for credit. A service charge of 25c must be added to every order under $1.00 to cover cost of handling. Do not forget to include postage.

CAREFUL ATTENTION AND SAFE DELIVERY OF YOUR ORDER

IVER JOHNSON SHOTGUN PARTS

SINGLE GUN INFORMATION

The Iver Johnson SEMI-HAMMERLESS and Old Model Iver Johnson CHAMPION TOP SNAP Single Barrel Shotguns are no longer manufactured. We will at all times endeavor to supply parts and make repairs on these models but advise customers to return complete gun to us when repair is necessary.

The manufacture of 24, 32, and 44 gauge guns has been discontinued but we will do our utmost to make such repairs as may be necessary on these gauges.

The manufacture of Iver Johnson CHAMPION SEMI-OCTAGON Single Barrel Shotguns has been discontinued. We will endeavor to supply parts and make such repairs as may be necessary.

SINGLE GUN REFINISHING

Champion
- Gun Complete...$3.75
- Frame .85
- Barrel .75
- Forend .90
- Back Stock 1.25

Matted Top Rib and Trap
- Gun Complete 5.50
- Frame .85
- Barrel .90
- Forend 1.50
- Back Stock 2.25

IVER JOHNSON CHAMPION SINGLE BARREL SHOTGUNS

Part Name	12 Ga.	16 Ga.	20 Ga.	23 Ga.	.410 Ga.	Price	Part Name	12 Ga.	16 Ga.	20 Ga.	28 Ga.	.410 Ga.	Price
FRAME GROUP							**BARREL GROUP**						
*Frame	P101	P201	P201	P201	P601	$4.00	Sight, Front—Threaded	P140	P140	P140	P140	P140	$0.25
Firing Pin	P102	P102	P102	P102	P102	.25	Sight, Lyman Ivory Front — Threaded	P1403	P1403	P1403	P1403	P1403	.50
Firing Pin Spring	P1021	P1021	P1021	P1021	P1021	.25	Non-Ejector Extractor	P1411	P2411	P3411	P5411	P7411	.25
Firing Pin Stop Screw	P1022	P2022	P2022	P2022	P2022	.25	Ejector Extractor	P1412	P2412	P3412	P5412	P7412	.25
Top Snap Lever	P104	P104	P104	P104	P104	.25	Ejector Spring	P143	P143	P143	P143	P143	.25
Top Snap Lever Yoke	P1041	P1041	P1041	P1041	P1041	.25	Ejector Stop Pin	P144	P144	P144	P144	P144	.25
Top Snap Lever Yoke Screw	P1042	P1042	P1042	P1042	P1042	.25	Ejector Lever and Stud — Old Type	P145	P245	P245	P545	P545	.30
Compensating Locking Bolt	P105	P105	P105	P105	P105	.25	Ejector Lever — 1929 Type	P1456	P1456	P1456	P5456	P5456	.25
Locking Bolt Pin	P1051	P1051	P1051	P1051	P1051	.25	Ejector Lever Tripping Pin — 1929 Type	P1457	P1457	P1457	P1457	P1457	.25
Locking Bolt Spring	P1052	P1052	P1052	P1052	P1052	.25	Ejector Lever Pin	P1451	P1451	P1451	P1451	P1451	.25
Locking Bolt Spring Screw	P1053	P1053	P1053	P1053	P1053	.25	Ejector Lever Spring	P1452	P1452	P1452	P1452	P1452	.25
Locking Bolt Connecting Rod	P1054	P1054	P1054	P1054	P1054	.25	Ejector Push Pin	P146	P146	P146	P146		.25
Hammer	P1091	P1091	P1091	P1091	P1091	.30	Barrel Stop Stud — Old Type	P147	P147	P147	P147	P147	.25
Hammer Pin	P1095	P1095	P1095	P1095	P1095	.25	Barrel Stop Pin — 1929 Type	P1457	P1457	P1457	P1457	P1457	.25
Main Spring Tension Adjusting Bar	P112	P112	P112	P112	P112	.25	Combination Bolt	P148	P148	P148	P148	P148	.25
Main Spring Plunger	P1121	P1121	P1121	P1121	P1121	.25	Band Swivel Assembly	P170A	P270A	P370A			.40
Main Spring Plunger Pin	P1122	P1122	P1122	P1122	P1122	.25	*Brazed Swivel Assembly	P171A	P171A	P171A	P171A	P171A	.70
	P1123	P1123	P1123	P1123	P1123	.25	Forend (Complete)	P151A	P251A	P251A	P451A	P651A	1.75
Trigger	P1131	P1131	P1131	P1131	P1131	.25	Forend Wood	P151	P251	P251	P451	P651	1.00
Trigger Pin	P1135	P1135	P1135	P1135	P1135	.25	Forend Iron	P1522	P1522	P1522	P1522	P1522	.35
Trigger Spring	P1136	P1136	P1136	P1136	P1136	.25	Forend Iron Screw (2)	P1533	P1533	P1533	P1533	P1533	.25
Trigger Spring Screw	P1137	P1137	P1137	P1137	P1137	.25	Forend Snap Plate	P155	P155	P155	P155	P155	.25
Guard	P115	P115	P115	P115	P115	.35	Forend Snap Plate Screw	P1551	P1551	P1551	P1551	P1551	.25
Guard Screw	P1151	P1151	P1151	P1151	P1151	.25	Forend Plunger	P156	P156	P156	P156	P156	.25
BARREL GROUP							Forend Plunger Pin	P1561	P1561	P1561	P1561	P1561	.25
Barrel, Non-Ejector (Complete)							Forend Plunger Spring	P1562	P1562	P1562	P1562	P1562	.25
26 inch				P326N	P526N	P826N	4.75	**BACK STOCK GROUP**						
28 inch	P128N	P228N	P328N	P528N	P828N	4.75	**Back Stock (Complete)	P181A	P181A	P181A	P181A	P681A	3.50
30 inch	P130N	P230N	P330N	P530N	P830N	4.75	**Back Stock Wood	P131	P131	P131	P131	P681	2.75
32 inch	P132N	P232N				4.75	Back Stock Screw	P185	P185	P185	P185	P185	.25
34 inch	P134N	P234N				5.25	Back Stock Screw Washer	P1851	P1851	P1851	P1851	P1851	.25
36 inch	P136N	P236N				5.75	Butt Plate	P186	P186	P186	P186	P686	.60
Barrel, Ejector (Complete)							Butt Plate Screw (2)	P1861	P1861	P1861	P1861	P1861	.25
26 inch			P326E	P526E	P826E	5.00	Recoil Pad with Screws	P1864	P1864	P1864	P1864	P8864	2.00
28 inch	P128E	P228E	P328E	P528E	P828E	5.00	Back Stock Loop Assembly	P172A	P172A	P172A	P172A	P172A	.30
30 inch	P130E	P230E	P330E	P530E	P830E	5.00							
32 inch	P132E	P232E				5.00							
34 inch	P134E	P234E				5.50							
36 inch	P136E	P236E				6.00							

Asterisk (*) preceding a part name indicates that complete gun must be returned to us to have that part fitted.

ORDER BY SYMBOL — Specify whether parts are wanted for case hardened, nickeled, or blued finish gun.

Double Asterisk (**) indicates that Back Stock only must be returned to us for correct duplication.

IVER JOHNSON MATTED TOP RIB AND TRAP VENTILATED RIB SINGLE BARREL SHOTGUNS
All parts not shown in this list are the same as those used on the Champion Models

Part Name	Matted Top Rib 12	16	20	.410	Price	Trap 12	Price	Part Name	Matted Top Rib 12	16	20	.410	Price	Trap 12	Price
FRAME GROUP								Ejector Lever — 1929 Type	P1456	P1456	P1456	P5456	.25	P1456	$0.25
*Frame	R101	R201	R201	R201	$4.25	T101	$4.25	Ejector Lever Tripping Pin 1929 Type	P1457	P1457	P1457	P1457	.25	P1457	.25
Firing Pin Stop Screw	P1022	P2022	P2022	P2022	.25	P1022	.25	Barrel Stop Stud — Old Type	P147	P147	P147	P147	.25	P147	.25
BARREL GROUP								Barrel Stop Pin — 1929 Type	P1457	P1457	P1457	P1457	.25	P1457	.25
Barrel, Ejector (Complete)								**FOREND GROUP**							
26 inch				R826E	7.50			Forend (Complete)	R151A	R251A	R251A	R851A	2.50	T151A	4.50
28 inch	R128E	R228E	R328E	R328E	7.50			Forend Wood	R151	R251	R251	R851	1.75	T151	3.75
30 inch	R130E	R230E	R330E	R830E	7.50			**BACK STOCK GROUP**							
32 inch	R132E	R232E			7.50	T132E	10.00	**Back Stock (Complete)	R181A	R181A	R181A	R881A	4.50	T181A	7.50
34 inch	R134E	R234E			8.00			**Back Stock Wood	R181	R181	R181	R881	3.75	T181	6.75
36 inch	R136E	R236E			8.50			Butt Plate	P186	P186	P186	P686	.60	P186	.60
Sight, Front — Threaded	P140	P140	P140	P140	.25			Pistol Grip Cap	R187	R187	R187	R187	.40	R187	.40
Sight, Lyman Ivory Front	T140	T140	T140	T140	.50	T140	.50	Pistol Grip Cap Screw	R1871	R1871	R1871	R1871	.25	R1871	.25
Sight, Lyman Ivory Rear	T1401	T1401	T1401	T1401	.50	T1401	.50	Recoil Pad with Screws	P1864	P1864	P1864	P8864	2.00	P1864	2.00
Ejector Extractor	P1412	P2412	P3412	P7412	.25	P1412	.25								
Ejector Lever and Stud — Old Type	P145	P245	P245	P545	.30	P145	.30								

In replacing parts marked thus (*) it will be necessary to send gun to us.

INSTRUCTIONS: In ordering parts always give name and number listed in catalog, also make, model, caliber and serial number of gun.

PAYMENTS: Parts will be sent only on advance payment. Parts cannot be returned for credit. A service charge of 25c must be added to every order under $1.00 to cover cost of handling. Do not forget to include postage.

© **PLEASE TELL OTHERS ABOUT STOEGER'S CATALOG**

SAVAGE RIFLE PARTS

Model '19 Rifle and M/22 Sporter

Our supply of M/19 and M/22 barrels is exhausted. We cannot obtain further production on these barrels

Prices on Component Parts for Model '19 and M/22 Sporter with Serial Numbers Below 25,000.

No.	Description	Price
4 N 29	Bolt only	$3.00
4 N 29½	Bolt complete	5.50
4 N 30	Bolt Sleeve and Handle	2.00
4 N 31	Bolt Sleeve Ret. Collar	.35
4 N 32	Bolt Pin	.25
1 N 1	Butt Stock, M 19 or M/22	8.00
1 N 2	Butt Plate	.50
1 N 3	Butt Plate Screws (2) each	.25
3 N 19	Barrel M/19	10.00
	Barrel, M/22—23 inches	9.00
4 N 38	Cocking Piece (Hammer)	1.50
4 N 39	Cocking Piece Head	.50
4 N 40	Cocking Piece Head Pin	.25
4 N 35	Extractor	.50
4 N 36	Extractor Spring	.25
4 N 37	Extractor Pin	.25
3 N 26	Ejector	.25
3 N 27	Ejector Pin	.25
3 N 28	Ejector Spring	.25
1 N 17	Front Barrel Band	.75
1 N 18	Front Barrel Band Screw	.25
1 N 11	Magazine Retainer	.25
1 N 12	Magazine Retainer Spring	.25
10 N 43½	Magazine complete	.65
4 N 41	Main Spring	.30
4 N 42	Main Spring Bushing	.25
1 N 13	Middle Barrel Band	.35
1 N 14	Middle Barrel Band Screw	.25
1 N 15	Middle Barrel Band Swivel	.25
1 N 16	Middle Bbl. Band Ret. Pin	.25
1 N 4	Stock Swivel Stud	.25
1 N 5	Stock Swivel Pin	.25
1 N 9	Assembling Screw, Front	.25
1 N 10	Assembling Screw, Rear	.25
3 N 20	Safety	.50
4 N 33	Striker	.50
4 N 34	Striker Pin	.25
1 N 6	Trigger Guard	1.00
1 N 7	Trigger Guard Screw	.25
1 N 8	Trigger Plate	.25
3 N 21	Trigger	1.50
3 N 22	Trigger Spring	.25
3 N 23	Trigger Spring Box	.25
3 N 24	Trigger Pin	.25
3 N 25	Trigger Adj. Screw	.25

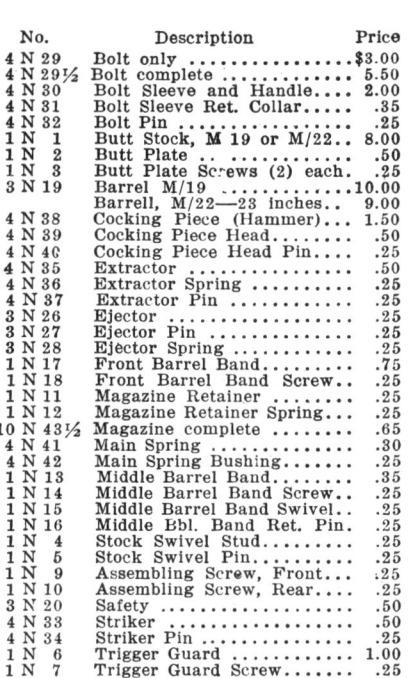
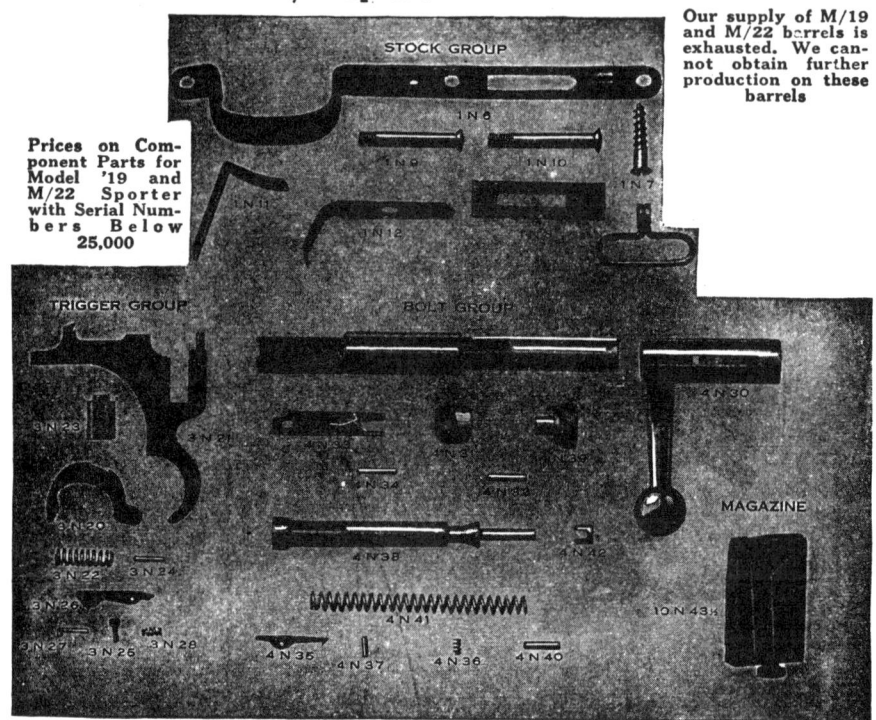

Parts for Model '19 NRA Match Rifle and M/23A Sportster Rifle with Serial Numbers Above 25,000; M/23A, 25,000 to 127,000; NRA 25,000 to 45,000

No.	Description	Price
4 N 60	Bolt only	$3.50
4 N 60½	Bolt complete	6.50
4 N 58	Bolt Sleeve and Handle	2.50
4 N 87	Bolt Sleeve Ret. Collar	.35
4 N 32	Bolt Pin	.25
1 N 1	Butt Stock (Military)	8.00
1 N 66	Butt Stock M/23-A	7.00
1 N 2	Butt Plate	.50
1 N 3	Butt Plate Screws (2), each	.25
3 N 89	Barrel, M/19NRA, 25 inch	10.00
3 N 64	Barrel, M/23-A, 23 inches	9.00
4 N 63	Cocking Piece (Hammer)	1.50
4 N 56	Cocking Pin	.25
4 N 59	Extractor (right)	.50
4 N 65	Extractor (left)	.50
4 N 90	Extractor Spring	.25
4 N 37	Extractor Pin	.25
1 N 17	Front Barrel Band, M/19	.75
1 N 18	Front Bbl. Bd. Screw, M/19	.25
3 N 61	Magazine Retainer	.35
1 N 12	Magazine Retainer Spring	.25
10 N 47½	Magazine complete	.65
3 N 73	Magazine Retainer Stud	.25
4 N 41	Main Spring	.30
1 N 13	Middle Barrel Band, M/19	.35
1 N 14	Middle Bbl. Bd. Screw, M/19	.25
1 N 15	Middle Barrel Band Swivel	.25
1 N 16	Middle Barrel Band Retainer	.25
1 N 4	Stock Swivel Stud	.25
1 N 5	Stock Swivel Pin	.25
1 N 9	Assembling Screw, Front	.25
1 N 76	Assembling Screw, Rear	.25
3 N 20	Safety	.50
4 N 62	Striker	.60
1 N 6	Trigger Guard	1.00
1 N 3	Trigger Guard Screw	.25
3 N 91	Trigger	1.50
3 N 22	Trigger Spring	.25
3 N 23	Trigger Spring Box	.35
3 N 24	Trigger Pin	.25
6	Front Sight	.75
5	Rear Sight	4.00
1 SP 5	Windgauge Screw	.25
1 SP 6	Elevating Screw	.25
	Click Springs, each	.25
	Elevation Slide (Aperture)	.75
20 SR	Rear Sight, M/23-A	1.25
28 SR	Front Sight, M/23-A	.65

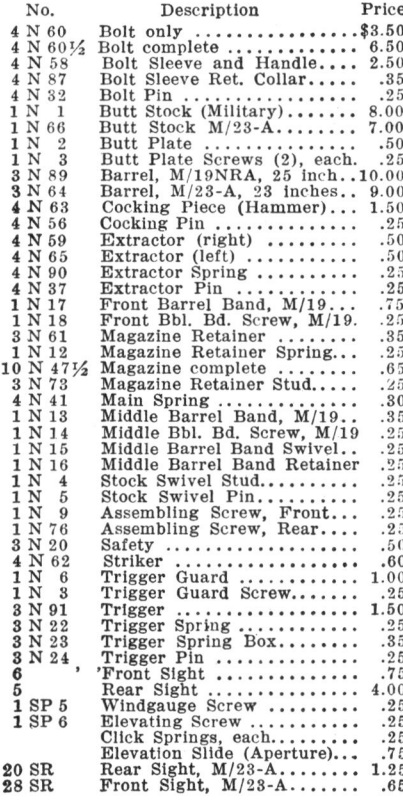
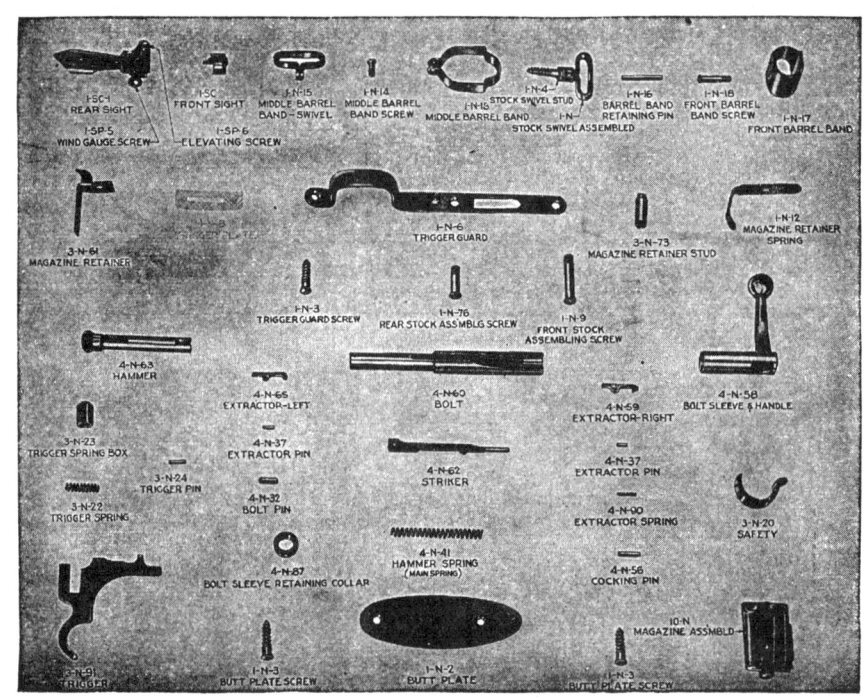

SEE PAGE 8, "HOW TO ORDER"

SAVAGE RIFLE PARTS

MODEL 29 RIFLE

No.	Description	Price
29-15	Action Slide	$2.00
29-14	Action Slide Handle	1.25
29-11 / 29-12	Act. S. Hdle. Scr. (2)	.25
29-13	Ac. Sl. Scr. W. (2)	.25
29-14	Action Slide Lock	.50
29-25	Action S. Lock Spg.	.25
29-26	Action S. Lock Scr.	.25
29-47	Assembling Screw	.35
29-48	Assem. Screw Bush.	.25
29-58	Barrel	7.00
29-57	Barrel Pin	.25
29-43*	Barrel Receiver	7.00
29-27	Bolt (Complete)	3.00
29-40	Butt Plate	.75
29-41	Butt Pl. Scr. (2) ea.	.25
29-59	Butt Stock, com.	4.50
29-56	Butt Stock Screw.	.25
29-44	Car. Cut-off, stl. ball	.25
29-60	Dead Screw, long.	.25
29-61	Dead Screw, short.	.25
29-31	Extractor, Left	.50
29-33	Extractor, Right	.50
29-32	Extractor Spring	.25
29-35	Extractor Sp. Bush.	.25
29-36	Extractor Pin, Rt.	.25
29-34	Extractor Pin, Left.	.25
29-19	Hammer	1.25
29-20	Hammer Bushing	.25
29-54	Hammer Lock	.50
29-55	Hammer Lock Spg.	.25
29-52	Lifter	1.25
29-53	Lifter Stud Screw	.25
29-17	Main Spring	.40
29-16	Main Spring Rod	.40
29-18	Main Spg. Washer	.25
29-3	Mag. Fol. Tube only	1.25
29-10	Mag. Fol. Tube Cpt.	2.00
29-10A	Magazine Grp. Cpt.	3.50
29-2	Magazine Fol. Spg.	.25
29-7	Mag. Fol. Tube Pl.	.25
29-1	Magazine Tube only	1.00
29-4	Magazine Tube Stud	.30
29-6	Mag. Tube. Re. Scr.	.25
29-5	Mag. T. Re. Scr. Bu.	.25
29-9	Mag. T. Thumb Pce.	.50
29-8	Mag. T. Th. Pce. Pin	.25
29-30	Operating Latch	.50
29-28	Operating Latch Pin	.25
29-29	Operating Latch Sp.	.25
29-22	Recoil Lock Plung.	.30
29-23	Recoil L. Plun. Pin	.25
29-25	Recoil L. Plun. Sp.	.25
29-50	Safety	.50
29-49	Safety Plunger	.25
29-51	Safety Plunger Spg.	.25
29-42*	Stock Receiver	8.00
29-37	Striker	.75
29-38	Striker Spring	.25
29-45	Trigger	.75
29-46	Trigger Pin	.25
29-39	Trunnion Pin	.25
20	S. R. Rear Sight	1.25
19	Gold Bead, Ft. Sgt.	.75

*Not supplied on order; must be sent to us.

MODEL '25 RIFLE

No.	Description	Price
3 T 32	Action Sl. Lock	$0.50
3 T 33	Action Sl. L. Pin	.25
3 T 34	Action Sl. L. Spg.	.25
3 T 35½	Action Slide	2.00
2 T 22	Action Stop	.35
2 T 23	Action Stop Pin	.25
2 T 24	Action Stop Spg.	.25
3 T 37	Action Slide Hdle.	1.00
3 T 38	Action Slide Hdle. Escutcheon (2).	.25
3 T 39	Ac. S. Hdle. Sc.(2)	.25
3 T 40	Ac. S. Hdle. Scw. Washer (2)	.25
2 T 26	Assem. Screw	.35
2 T 27	Assm. Screw Bus.	.25
3 T 30	Barrel	7.00
3 T 31*	Barrel Receiver	7.00
4 T 42½	Bolt complete	3.00
1 T 2	Butt Plate	.50
1 T 3	Butt P. Sc. (2) ea.	.25
1 T 1½	Butt Stock with Butt Plate	4.50
1 T 4	Butt Stock Screw.	.25
1 T 5	Butt Stk. Scr. W.	.25
2 T 7	Carrier only	1.25
2 T 7½	Carrier complete	2.00
2 T 9	Carrier Lifter	.60
2 T 10	Carrier Lifter Sp.	.25
2 T 8	Carrier Oper. Pin.	.25
2 T 25	Cartridge Guide	.25
4 T 44	Extractor, Left	.50
4 T 43	Extractor, Right	.50
4 T 47	Extractor Pin, Lt.	.25
4 T 46	Extractor Pin, Rt.	.25
4 T 45	Extractor Spring	.25
2 T 11	Hammer	1.25
2 T 12	Hammer Pin	.25
2 T 20	Indicator	.25
2 T 21	Indicator Spring	.25
2 T 28	Long Dead Screw	.25
2 T 15	Main Spring	.40
2 T 16	Main Spring Rod	.40
5 T 52	Mag. Fol. T. only.	1.25
5 T 52½	Mag. Fol. T. com.	2.00
5 T 50½	Mag. Group com.	3.50
5 T 53	Mag. Fol. T. Spg.	.30
5 T 54	Mag. Fol. T. Plun.	.30
5 T 50	Magazine Tube	1.00
3 T 41	Mag. Tube Clip	.25
5 T 51	Mag. T. Ret. Scr.	.25
5 T 55	Mag. T. Th. Piece	.50
5 T 56	Mag. T. Th. P. P.	.25
2 T 17	Safety	.50
2 T 18	Safety Plunger	.25
2 T 19	Safety Plun. Sp.	.25
2 T 6*	Stock Receiver	8.00
4 T 48	Striker	.75
4 T 57	Striker Pin	.25
2 T 13	Trigger	.75
2 T 14	Trigger Pin	.25
20 SR	Rear Sight com.	1.25
22 B	Front Sight com.	.65

*Not supplied on order. Rifle must be sent to factory to have this part fitted.

MODEL 29

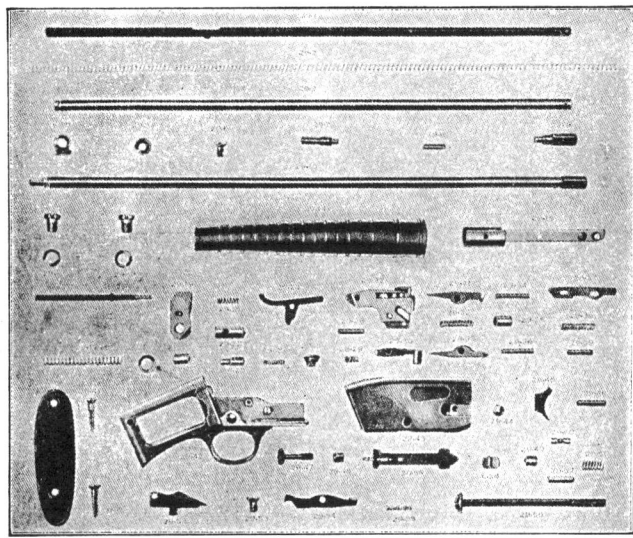

MODEL 25

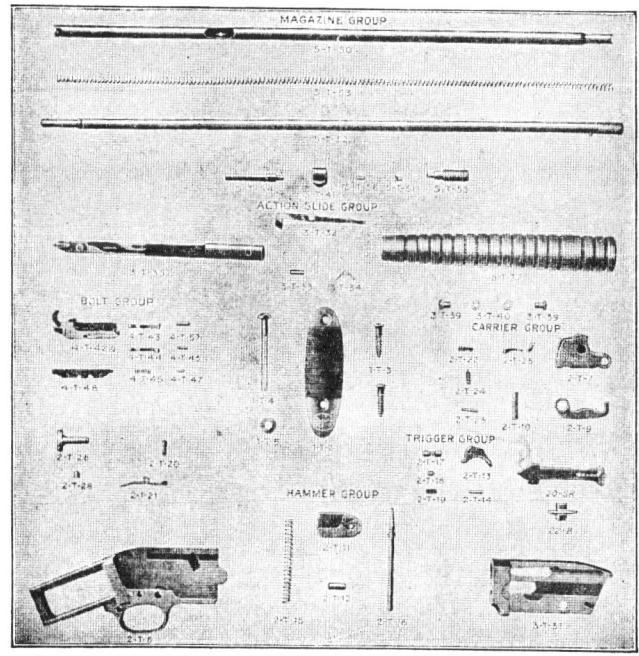

INSTRUCTIONS: In ordering parts always give name and number listed in catalog, also make, model, caliber and serial number of gun.

PAYMENTS: Parts will be sent only on advance payment. Parts cannot be returned for credit. A service charge of 25c must be added to every order under $1.00 to cover cost of handling. Do not forget to include postage.

IMPORTANT NOTICE

The following Savage Rifles are obsolete. We are listing the parts for same and shall continue to supply until supply is exhausted. Models 20, 03, 04, 11, 12, 14, 25, 19NRA, and Model 22 Sporter with serial numbers up to 127000. Models 23B, and 23C with serial numbers below 204048, Models 21 and 28 Repeating Shotguns. Also please note the old style N.R.A. peep sight on all old Models 19 has been discontinued and the No. 10 peep sight as illustrated with model 19-33 can be used instead.

SAVAGE RIFLE PARTS

MODELS 40 AND 45 SUPER SPORTER

No.	Name of Part	Price
3 S 23	*Barrel	$12.00
4 S 1	*Bolt complete	10.00
4 S 25	Bolt only	5.00
4 S 26	Bolt Sleeve and Handle	5.00
2 S 27	Bolt Sleeve Retaining Collar	.50
2 S 47	Bolt Sleeve Retaining Collar Pin	.25
2 S 22	Bolt Lock Plunger and Spring	.25
1 S 1	Butt Stock M/40	10.00
1 S 1	Butt Stock M/45	12.00
1 S 12	Butt Stock Assembling Screw (Front)	.25
1 S 11	Butt Stock Assembling Screw (Rear)	.25
1 S 2	Butt Plate	.60
1 S 36	Butt Plate Screws (2)	.25
4 S 30	Cocking Pin	.25
2 S 18	Ejector	.50
4 S 48	Ejector Screw	.25
4 S 33	Extractor (Right)	.50
4 S 34	Extractor (Left)	.50
4 S 35	Extractor Spring (Left and Right)	.25
4 S 36	Extractor Pin (Left and Right)	.25
4 S 31	Hammer	2.00
4 S 32	Hammer Spring	.50
5 S A	Magazine complete	1.75
5 S 37	Magazine Body	.75
5 S 38	Magazine Follower	.50
5 S 39	Magazine Spring	.30
1 S 7	Magazine Catch Body	.75
23 M 4	Magazine Catch Screws (2)	.25
1 S 8	Magazine Catch Lever	.25
1 S 9	Magazine Catch Lever Spring	.25
2 S 14-A	*Receiver	20.00
3 S 24	Recoil Clip	1.25
3 S 49	Recoil Clip Locating Pin	.25
2 S 20	Safety	.75
1 S 6	Safety Plunger and Spring	.50
4 S 29	Striker	.75
2 S 15	Trigger	1.25
2 S 16	Trigger Pin	.25
2 S 17	Trigger Spring	.25
1 S 4	Trigger Guard	1.25
1 B 36	Trig. Gd. Scr. (same as Butt Pl. Scws.)	.25
28 A	Front Sight M/40 and M/45	.65
M 95 H	Middle Sight for M/45	1.25
20 S R	Rear Sight for M/40	1.25
L 40	Peep Sight for M/45	4.50

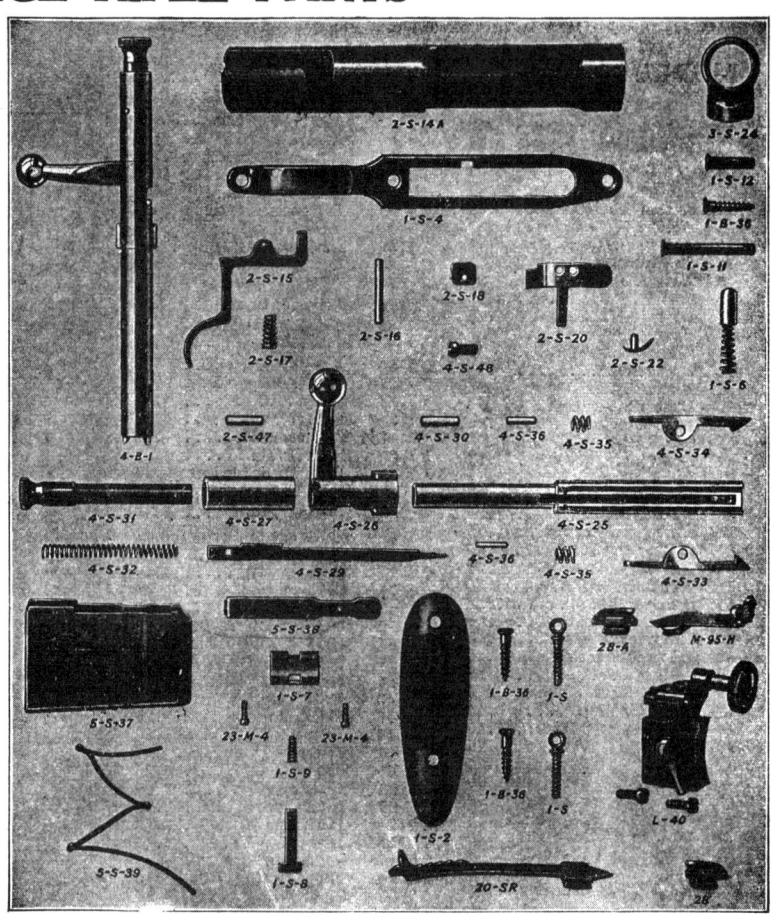

MODEL '03 RIFLE

No.		Description	Price	No.		Description	Price
10	A	Action Slide com.	$2.00	23	A	Mag. Catch Pin	$0.25
40	A	Action Slide Lock	.25	24	A	Mag. Catch Sp.	.25
42	A	Action Sl. Lk. Pin	.25			Magazine Spring	.25
41	A	Action Sl. Lk. Sp.	.25	36	A	Main Spring	.40
28	A	Assembling Screw	.35	39	A	Main Spring Pin	.25
1	A	Barrel Octagon	7.00	37	A	Main Spring Rod	.35
*55	A	Bbl. (M/09), Rd.	6.00	38	A	Main Spg. Washer	.25
2	A	Barrel Receiver	7.00	35	A	Safety Bar	.25
6	A	Barrel Stud	.40	33	A	Safety Slide	.50
7	A	Barrel Stud Screw	.25	34	A	Safety Slide Pin	.25
11	A	Breech Bolt com.	2.00	48	A	Short Dead Screw	.25
45	A	Butt Plate, Steel	.50	4	A	Slide Handle	1.00
46	A	Butt Plate Screw	.25	*54	A	Slide Hdle. (M/09)	.50
43	A	Butt Stock com.	4.00	8	A	Slide Hdle. Escut.	.25
*53	A	Butt S. co. (M/09)	3.50	5	A	Slide Handle Rod	.50
44	A	Butt Stock Screw	.25	9	A	Slide Hdle. Sc. (2)	.25
17	A	Ejector	.35	12	A	Striker	.50
21	A	Ejector Bear. Scr.	.25	13	A	Striker Pin	.25
18	A	Ejector Spring	.25	14	A	Striker Stop Pin	.25
		Ejector Plate	.50	3	A	Stock Receiver	8.00
		Ejector Pl. Screw	.25	44½	A	Stk. Screw Escut.	.25
15	A	Extractor	.40	29	A	Trigger	.75
16	A	Extractor Pin	.25	30	A	Trigger Pin	.25
19	A	Extractor Spring	.25	31	A	Trigger Spring	.25
25	A	Hammer	1.00	32	A	Trigger Sp. Screw	.25
26	A	Hammer Pin	.25	24	B	Front Sight	.50
27	A	Hammer Screw	.25	25	B	Rear Sight	1.25
47	A	Long Dead Screw	.25	*30	B	Front Sgt (M/09)	.50
52	A	Magazine complete	.50	*27	B	Rear Sight (M/09)	.60
22	A	Magazine Catch	.25				

Parts for Model '09 Rifle are same as for Model '03, except those marked (*).

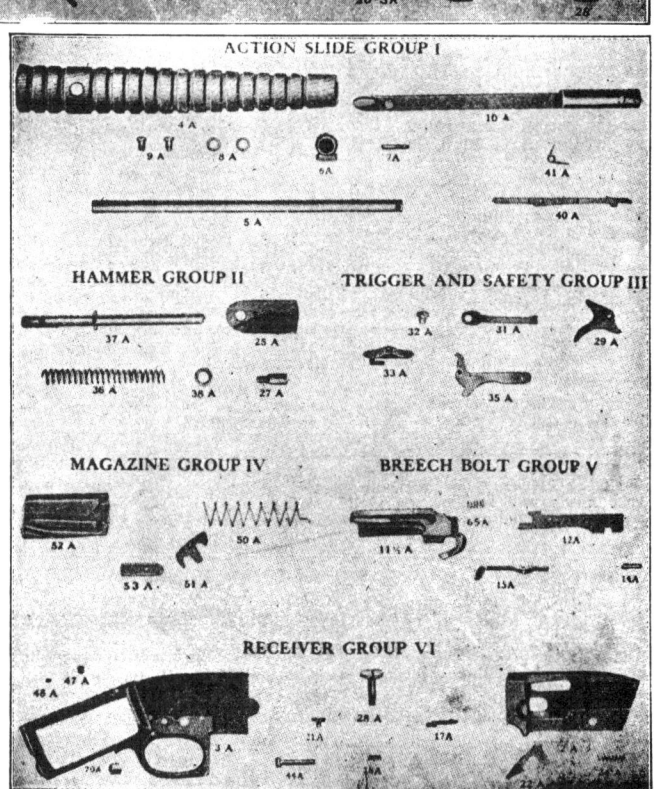

A NEW GUN CARRIES A FACTORY GUARANTEE

SAVAGE RIFLE PARTS

MODEL 99 RIFLE

No.	Description	Price
2 B 104	Automatic Cut-off	$3.00
2 B 16	Automatic Cut-off Spring	.30
*3 B 44	Barrel 20", 22" or 26" Rd.	12.00
3 B 115	Barrel Stud, T. D.	.75
3 R 20	Barrel Stud, Solid	.60
3 B 90	Barrel Stud Bushing	.25
*4 B 2	Breech Bolt	4.00
1 B 110	Butt Stock complete (Rifle Butt)	6.00
1 B 111	Butt Stock complete (Shot Gun Butt)	6.00
1 B 112	Butt Stock complete (Pistol Grip Checked)	10.00
1 B 51	Butt Stock Washers	.25
1 B 114	Butt Stock Screw	.40
1 B 66	Butt Plate S. G. B. Steel	.60
1 B 35	Butt Plate Reg. Rifle Steel	1.25
1 B 54	Butt Plate (Carbine Steel)	.60
1 B 36	Butt Plate Screws (2)	.25
	Butt Plate, Rubber	.75
2 B 31	Bolt Stop	.25
2 B 30	Bolt Stop Screw	.25
2 B 119	Cartridge Guide	.60
2 B 49	Cartridge Guide Pin	.25
	Cartridge Stop (Old Style)	.25
2 B 52	Dead Screws (2)	.25
4 B 99	Extractor	.50
4 B 28	Extractor Pin	.25
	Featherweight Front Sight Screw	.25
	In lots of a dozen	.25
4 B 4	Firing Pin	.50
4 B 29	Firing Pin Securing Pin	.25
*2 B 98	Finger Lever, Pistol Grip	4.00
*2 B 9	Finger Lever Straight Grip	4.00
2 B 10	Finger Lever Bushing	.40
2 B 60	Finger Lever Bushing Pin	.25
2 B 22	Finger Lever Bushing Screw	.25
3 B 75	Forearm (Wood only, checked)	4.00
*3 B 75½	Forearm complete (checked)	6.00
*3 B 117½	Forearm complete, T. D.	5.00
3 B 37½	Forearm, Solid or T. D.	3.00
	Forearm, Octagon	2.25
3 B 38	Forearm Screw	.25
3 B 39	Forearm Screw Escutcheon	.25
3 B 125	Forearm Clip Retaining Piece	.30
3 B 126	Forearm Clip Retaining Piece Screw	.25
3 B 83	Forearm, Clip, Forearm Key	1.50
1 B 76	Grip Cap (Rubber)	.25
1 B 77	Grip Cap Screw	.25
4 B 3	Hammer	1.00
5 B 6	Hammer Bushing	.25
4 B 23	Hammer Retaining Spring	.25
4 B 24	Hammer Bushing Screw	.25
4 B 3½	Hammer complete	2.00
2 B 40	Hammer Indicator	.60
2 B 41	Hammer Indicator Spring	.25
2 B 42	Hammer Indicator Pin	.25
5 B 14	Lever Lock (Safety)	.60
2 B 74	Lever Lock Pin	.25
5 B 73	Lever Lock Tension Spring	.25
10 B 102	Magazine Carrier	2.00
10 B 13	Magazine Spindle	.50
10 B 56	Magazine Spindle Head	.50
10 B 19	Magazine Spring	.45
10 B 57	Magazine Spindle Nut	.25
10 B 21	Magazine Spindle Screw	.25
10 B 102½	Magazine Carrier complete	3.00
4 B 17	Mainspring	.50
*2 B 87	Receiver	20.00
	Retractor Old Style	.40

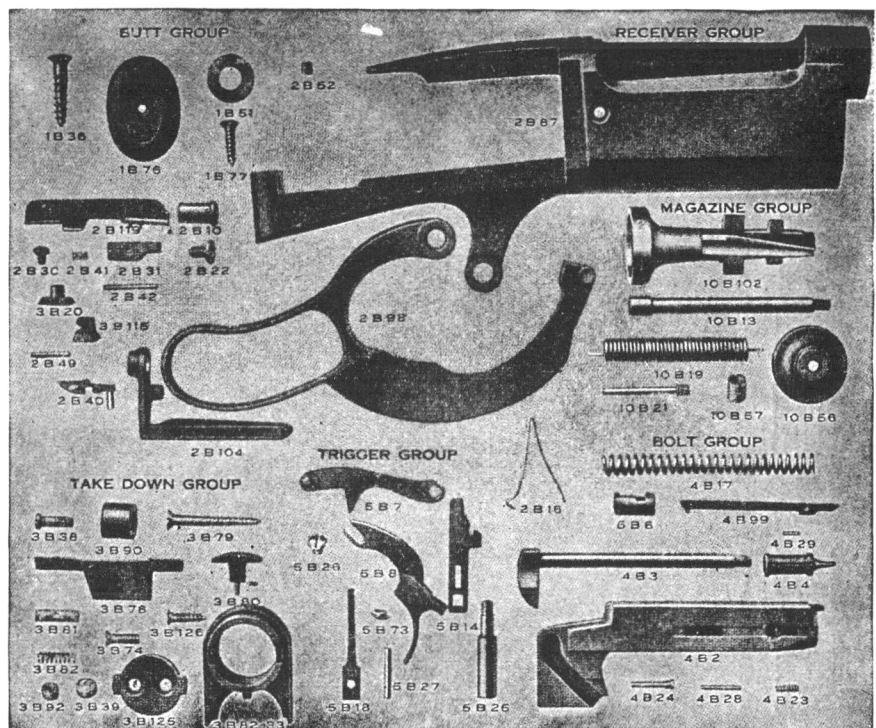

No.	Description	Price
	Retractor Spring	$0.25
5 B 7	Sear	
5 B 53	Sear Hub	.75
5 B 50	Sear Bushing	
2 B 25	Sear Screw	.40
4 B 5	Sear Screw Nut	.25
3 B 92	Snap Lock Block Machine Screw Nut	.25
3 B 78	Snap Lock Block	.75
3 B 80	Snap Lock Block Thumb Piece	.50
3 B 81	Snap Lock Locking Bolt	.35
3 B 82	Snap Lock Block Bolt Spring	.25
3 B 79	Snap Lock Block Wood Screw	$0.25
3 B 74	Snap Lock Block Machine Screw	.25
3 B 78½	Snap Lock Block complete	2.00
5 B 8	Trigger	1.00
5 B 18	Trigger Spring	.25
5 B 26	Trigger Spring Screw	.25
5 B 27	Trigger Pin	.25
20 SR	Rear Sight	1.25
31 B	Front Sight	.50
28	Front Sight	.65

MODEL '20 RIFLE

No.	Description	Price
1 U 45	Assembling Screw—Short	$0.25
1 U 45½	Assembling Screw—Long	.25
1 U 50	Assembling Screw—Escutcheon	.25
*3 U 1	Barrel	12.00
3 U 20	Barrel Stud	.50
*4 U 2	Bolt	8.00
*4 U 2½	Bolt complete	12.00
1 U 39	Butt Stock	12.00
1 U 3	Butt Plate	.60
1 B 36	Butt Plate Screw (2), each	.25
2 U 8	Butt Tang	1.50
2 U 11	Bolt Stop Plunger	.25
2 U 17	Bolt Stop Plunger Pin	.25
2 U 16	Bolt Stop Plunger Spring	.25
4 U 9	Cocking Piece	2.00
2 U 12	Ejector	.75
2 U 13	Ejector Pin	.25
4 U 14	Extractor	1.00
4 U 15	Extractor Ring	.25
3 B 38	Forearm Screw	.25
3 B 39	Forearm Screw Washer	.25
1 B 76	Grip Cap	.25
1 B 77	Grip Cap Screw	.25
4 U 22	Mainspring	.50
10 U 18	Magazine Follower	.50
10 U 19	Magazine Follower Spring	.25
10 U 20	Magazine Box	1.00
10 U 18½	Magazine complete	1.50
2 U 23	Rec. (not supplied on mail order)	25.00
2 U 24	Recoil Clip	1.25
2 U 25	Recoil Clip Locating Pin	.25
4 U 40	Striker	.50
2 U 27	Safety Bar	1.00
2 U 28	Safety Bar Catch	.25
2 U 29	Safety Bar Catch Spring	.35
2 U 30	Safety Bar Post	.50
2 U 31	Safety Bar Post Screw	.25
2 U 32	Safety Bar Post Pin	.25
2 U 33	Safety Thumb Piece	.75
2 U 34	Safety Thumb Piece Pin	.25
2 U 49	Safety Screw Washer	.25
5 U 35	Sear	2.00
5 U 36	Sear Pin	.25
5 U 37	Sear Spring	.25
1 U 43	Trigger Guard	1.50
2 U 26	Trigger Plate	.50
1 B 36	Trigger Guard Screw	.25
5 U 42	Trigger	1.00
5 U 46	Trigger Pin	.25
4 U 41	Tail Block	2.00

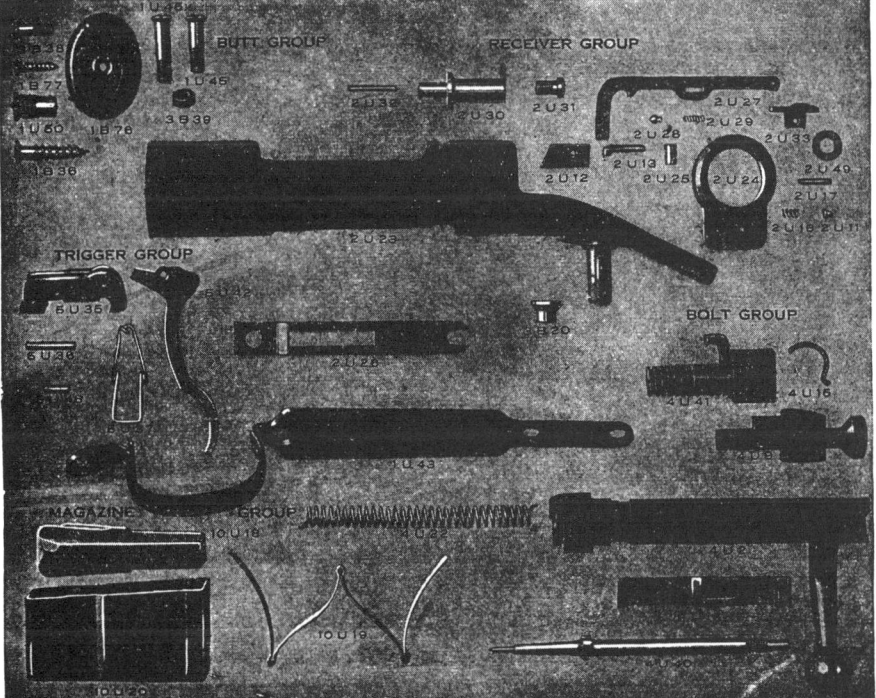

* Rifle must be sent to factory to have part fitted.

ALL SHIPMENTS ARE INSURED

SAVAGE RIFLE PARTS

Prices on Component Parts for Model 23-D Hornet Rifle, Model 23-B .25–20 and Model 23-C .32–20 Caliber Sporter Rifles

No.	Description	Price
3 N 67	Barrel, 25 inches	$11.50
3 N 237	Barrel, .25-20 or .32-20 Cal.	10.00
4 N 178	Bolt only	4.50
4 NA 113-A	Bolt complete	7.50
4 N 69	Bolt Sleeve and Handle	3.50
4 N 87	Bolt Sleeve Retain. Collar	.35
4 N 32-A	Bolt Pin	.25
1 NA 140	Butt Stock	9.00
1 B 321	Butt Plate	.50
1 B 36	Butt Plate Screw (2), each	.25
4 N 56	Cocking Pin	.25
4 N 70	Extractor (Right)	.50
4 N 71	Extractor (Left)	.50
4 N 37	Extractor Pin	.25
4 N 82	Extractor Spring	.25
3 N 173	Ejector	.40
8 B 88	Forearm Screw	.25
3 B 39	Forearm Screw Escutcheon	.25
4 N 123	Hammer (Cocking Piece)	1.50
4 N 41	Hammer Spring (M. Spg.)	.30
10 NA 180	Magazine complete	1.15
10 NA 242	.25-20 or .32-20 magazine cpt	1.10
10 N 175	Magazine Guide	.30
10 N 176	Magazine Retainer	.75
3 N 73-A	Mag. Retainer Stud (Rear)	.25
4 N 77	Recoil Lug	.25
3 N 20-A	Safety	.50
1 S 12	Stk. Assem. Screw (Rear)	.25
1 N 172	Stock Assm. Screw (Front)	.25
4 N 72	Striker	.75
3 N 81-A	Trigger	1.50
3 N 24	Trigger Pin	.25
3 N 22	Trigger Spring	.25
3 N 147	Trigger Spring Box	.25
3 N 116	Trigger Guard	1.00
1 B 36	Trig. Guard Screw (Front)	.25
1 B 36	Trig. Guard Screw (Rear)	.25
19	Gold Bead Front Sight	.60
	No. 20 Rear Sight	1.25
1 SR 4	No. 20 Elevator	.30
1 N 120	Dead Screw (Large)	.25
1 N 121	Dead Screw (Small)	.25

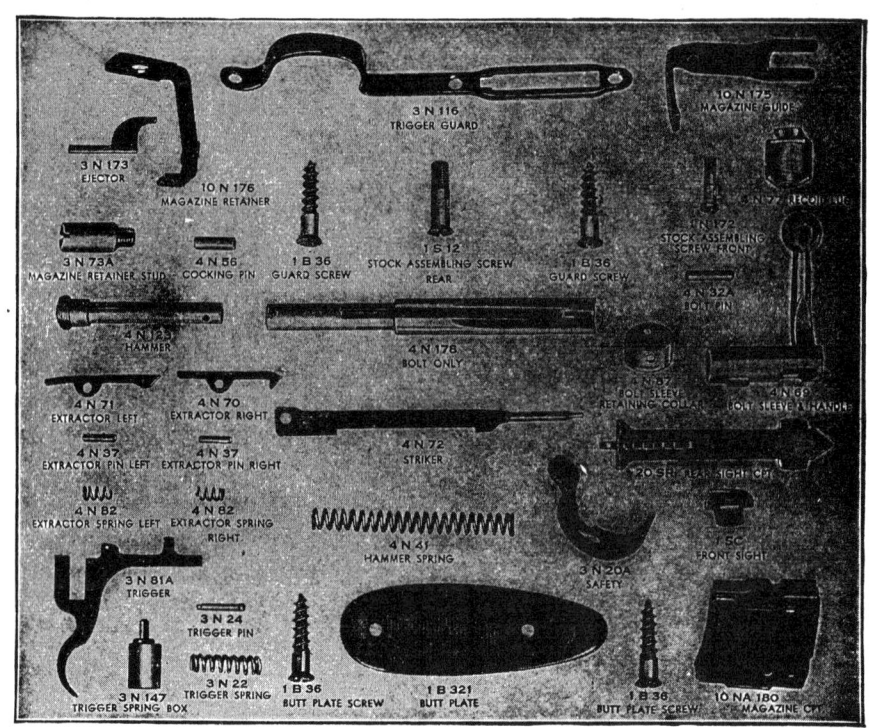

When ordering parts, please specify whether they are desired for the Model 23-D .22 Hornet rifle or the Model 23-B or Model 23-C sporter rifles.

MODEL 3, MODEL 3-A AND MODEL 3-B

No.	Description	Price
1	Barrel only	$3.00
2	Barrel Lug	.50
3	Barrel Pin	.25
4	Bolt only	1.40
5	Bolt complete	2.80
6	Butt Plate	.50
7	Butt Plate Screws (2)	.25
8	Butt Stock	3.00
9	Cocking Piece	.50
10	Ejector	.25
11	Extractor	.50
12	Extractor Spring	.25
13	Extractor Pin	.25
14	Extract Spring Plunger	.25
15	Firing Pin	.40
16	Guard	.40
17	Guard Screws (2)	.25
18	Main Spring	.40
19	Receiver	1.80
20	Striker	.45
21	Striker Bushing	.25
22	Striker Retaining Pin	.25
23	Trigger	.40
24	Trigger Spring	.25
25	Trigger Pin	.25
26	Take Down Screw	.40
27	Take Down Screw Bushing	.25
28	No. 112 Sporting Rear Sight	.75
29	No. 19 Gold Bead Front Sight	.60
30	Model 3-A Bolt complete	2.80
31	Model 3-A Striker	.45
32	Model 3-A Cocking Piece	.45

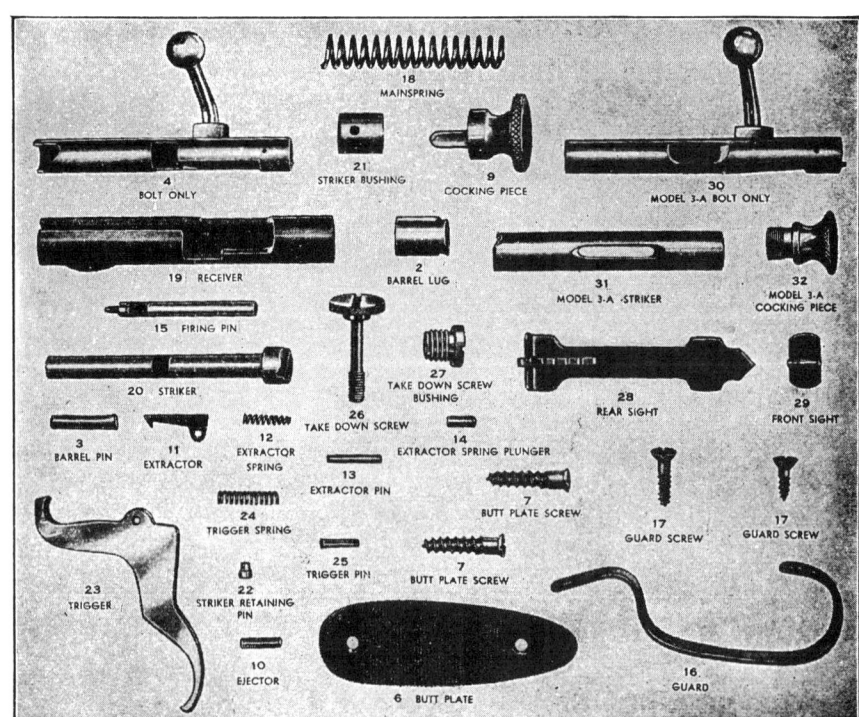

When ordering, please specify whether the parts are intended for a Model 3, Model 3-A, or Model 3-B Rifle.

INSTRUCTIONS: In ordering parts always give name and number listed in catalog, also make, model, caliber and serial number of gun.

PAYMENTS: Parts will be sent only on advance payment. Parts cannot be returned for credit. A service charge of 25c must be added to every order under $1.00 to cover cost of handling. Do not forget to include postage.

SEND YOUR GUN TO STOEGER FOR EXPERT REPAIRING

SAVAGE RIFLE PARTS

Prices on component parts for old style Model 23-B .25-20 and Model 23-C .32-20 caliber Sporter rifles having serial numbers below 204,048

No.	Description	Price
3 N 67	Barrel, 25-20 cal., 25"	$10.00
3 N 100	Barrel, 32-20 cal., 25"	10.00
4 N 68	Bolt only	4.00
4 N 68½	Bolt complete	7.00
4 N 69	Bolt Sleeve and Handle	3.50
4 N 87	Bolt Sleeve Retain. Collar	.35
4 N 32	Bolt Pin	.25
1 N 78	Butt Stock	8.00
1 N 2	Butt Plate	.50
1 N 3	Butt Plate Screw (2), each	.25
4 N 56	Cocking Pin	.25
4 N 70	Extractor (Right)	.50
4 N 71	Extractor (Left)	.50
4 N 82	Extractor Spring	.25
4 N 37	Extractor Pin	.25
3 B 38	Forearm Screw	.25
3 B 39	Forearm Screw Escutcheon	.25
4 N 88	Hammer (Cocking Piece)	1.50
4 N 41	Hammer Spg. (Main Spg.)	.30
10 N 2	Magazine complete	1.10
3 N 80	Magazine Retainer	.40
1 N 83	Magazine Ret. Sp. Screw	.25
1 N 85	Magazine Retainer Spring	.25
3 N 73	Magazine Retainer Stud	.25
1 N 76	Stock Assembling Screw	.25
4 N 77	Recoil Lug	.25
3 N 20	Safety	.50
4 N 72	Striker	.60
3 N 81	Trigger	1.50
1 N 86	Trigger Guard	1.00
1 N 3	Trigger Guard Screw (Frt.)	.25
1 N 3	Trigger Guard Screw (Rear)	.25
3 N 22	Trigger Spring	.25
3 N 23	Trigger Spring Box	.25
3 N 24	Trigger Pin	.25
1 SC	(22B) Front Sight	.50
1 SR	(20SR) Rear Sight	1.25
1 SP 13	Dead Screw	.25
1 SP 7	Dummy Screw	.25
1 SR 4	Rear Sight Elevator	.30

MODELS 19-33, 19 HORNET, 23-AA

No.	Description	Price
	Model 23AA Barrel, 23"	$9.00
	Model 19 Bbl., 22 cal., 25"	11.00
	Model 19 Bbl., .22 Hornet	12.00
4 N 158	Blt. only (M/23AA, M/19)	4.00
	Blt. only (M/19, .22 Hor.)	4.50
4 NA 113A	Bolt complete (M/23AA or M/19)	7.00
	Bolt com. (M/19, .22 Hor.)	7.50
4 N 69	Bolt Sleeve and Handle	3.00
4 N 87	Bolt Sleeve Retain. Collar	.40
4 N 32A	Bolt Pin	.25
	Model 23AA Butt Stock	7.00
	M/19 Stock (specify reg. or M/19, .22 Hornet)	11.00
1 B 321	Butt Plate	.50
1 B 36	Butt Plate Screws (2)	.25
4 N 219	Cocking Piece (Hammer)	1.50
4 N 56	Cocking Pin	.25
4 N 59A	Extractor (Right)	.50
4 N 65	Extractor (Left)	.50
4 N 37	Extractor Pin	.25
4 N 90	Extractor Spring	.25
3 N 205A	Ejector	.40
1 N 215	Guard Screw (Front)	.25
4 N 220	Main Spring	.30
10 N 203A	Magazine Retainer	.40
3 N 73	Mag. Retain. Stud (Front)	.25
3 N 73	Mag. Retain. Stud (Rear)	.25
10 NA 194	Mag. com., 23AA, M/19	.65
10 NA 180	Magazine com., .22 Hornet	1.25
10 N 202	Magazine Guide	.35
1 N 13	Middle Barrel Band	.25
1 N 15	Middle Barrel Band Swivel	.25
1 N 14	Middle Barrel Band Screw	.25
1 N 16	Middle Bbl. Bd. Ret. Pin	.25
1 NA 122	Stk Swivel and Stud com	.25
1 S 12	Stock Assembling Screw	.25
3 N 20A	Safety	.50
3 N 223	Sear	.60
4 N 160	Striker (M/23AA or M/19)	.90
	Striker (M/19, .22 Hornet)	
3 N 81A	Trigger	1.50
3 N 22	Trigger Spring	.25
3 N 24	Trigger Pin	.25
3 N 116	Trigger Guard	1.00
1 B 36	Trigger Guard Screw	.25
3 N 147	Trigger Spring Box	.40

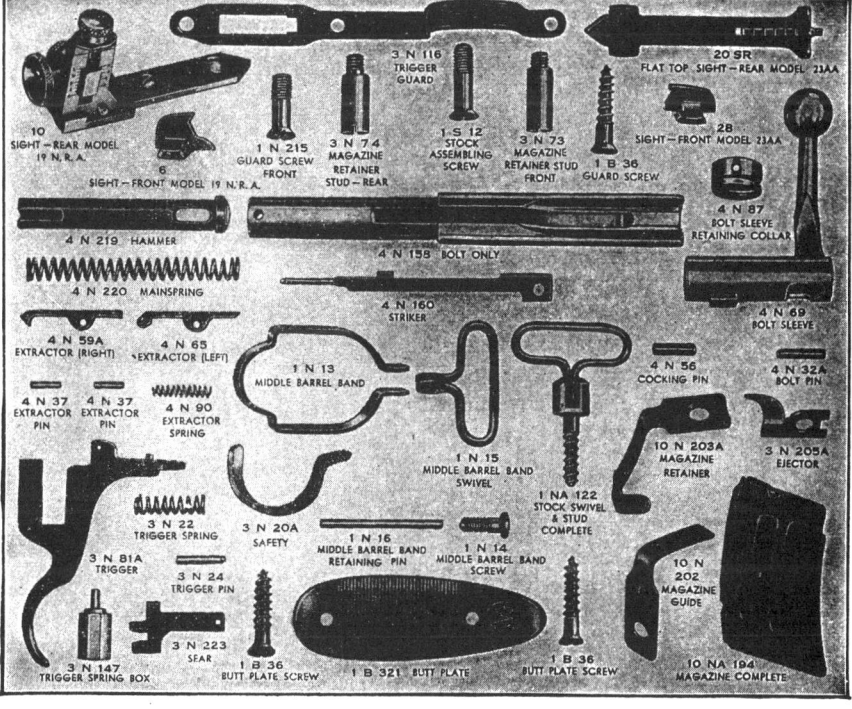

No.	Description	Price	No.	Description	Price
1 N 120	Dead Screw, Large	$0.25	20	Sight, Rear, Model 23AA	$1.25
1 N 121	Dead Screw, Small	.25	6	Sight, Frt., M/19-33 NRA	.75
28	Sight, Front, Model 23AA	.65	10	Sight, R., M/19-33 NRA	6.00

INSTRUCTIONS: In ordering parts always give name and number listed in catalog, also make, model, caliber and serial number of gun.

PAYMENTS: Parts will be sent only on advance payment. Parts cannot be returned for credit. A service charge of 25c must be added to every order under $1.00 to cover cost of handling. Do not forget to include postage.

ORDER BLANK IN MIDDLE AND INDEX IN BACK OF CATALOG

SAVAGE RIFLE PARTS

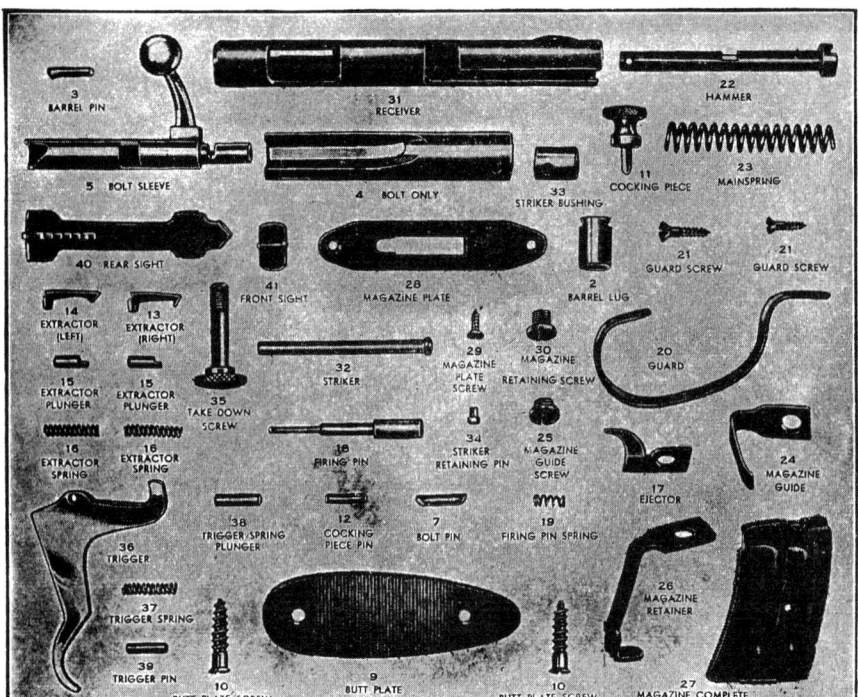

Model 4. .22 Bolt Action Rifle

No.	Description	Price
1	Barrel	$5.00
2	Barrel Lug	.60
3	Barrel Pin	.25
4	Bolt only	2.00
5	Bolt Sleeve	2.00
6	Bolt complete	4.00
7	Bolt Pin	.25
8	Butt Stock	4.00
9	Butt Plate	.50
10	Butt Plate Screws (2)	.25
11	Cocking Piece	.50
12	Cocking Piece Pin	.25
13	Extractor (Right)	.50
14	Extractor (Left)	.50
15	Extractor Plunger	.25
16	Extractor Spring	.25
17	Ejector	.30
18	Firing Pin	.60
19	Firing Pin Spring	.25
20	Guard	.40
21	Guard Screws (2)	.25
22	Hammer (sometimes called striker)	.45
23	Main Spring	.40
24	Magazine Guide	.35
25	Magazine Guide Screw	.25
26	Magazine Retainer	.35
27	Magazine complete	.65
28	Magazine Plate	.40
29	Magazine Plate Screw	.25
30	Magazine Retainer Screw	.25
31	Receiver	2.50
32	Striker (Firing Pin Extension)	.40
33	Striker Bushing	.25
34	Striker Retaining Pin	.25
35	Take Down Screw	.40
36	Trigger	.75
37	Trigger Spring	.25
38	Trigger Spring Plunger	.25
39	Trigger Pin	.25
40	No. 112 Sporting Rear Sight	.90
41	No. 19 Gold Bead Front Sight	.60

Model 21 Repeating Shotgun

No.	Description	Price
10-X-70	Action Bar	$3.00
10-X-69	Action Bar Handle	1.00
10-X-72	Action Bar Handle Escutcheon	
4-X-34	Action Bar Lock	1.25
4-X-33	Action Bar Lock Pin	.25
4-X-35	Action Bar Lock Spring	.25
10-X-71	Action Bar Sleeve Nut	.35
5-X-52	Action Lock	1.00
5-X-56	Action Lock Spring	.25
10-X-66	Assembling Clip	1.00
10-X-67	Assembling Clip Screw	.35
3-X-17	*Barrel	17.00
3-X-18	Barrel Clip	2.00
2-X-6	*Barrel Extension	1.00
2-X-7	Barrel Extension Screw	.25
4-X-23	Bolt complete	6.00
1-X-1	Butt Stock complete	7.50
1-X-4	Butt Plate	1.00
1-B-36	Butt Plate Screw (2)	.25
1-B-114	Butt Stock Screw	.35
1-B-51	Butt Stock Screw Washer	.25
5-X-30	Carrier	2.50
5-X-40	Carrier Pin	.25
5-X-41	Carrier Spring	.25
4-X-39	Carrier Latch	.75
4-X-78	Carrier Latch Pin	.25
2-X-8	*Cartridge Stop	1.00
3-X-19	Compensating Nut	1.00
3-X-20	Compensating Nut Retainer	.30
3-X-21	Compensating Nut Retainer Screw	.25
2-X-9	Ejector	.60
4-X-25	Extractor, Left	.50
4-X-24	Extractor, Right	.50
4-X-28	Extractor Pin, Left	.25
4-X-29	Extractor Spring, Left	.25
4-X-26	Extractor Plunger	.25
4-X-27	Extractor Plunger Spring	.25
4-X-30	Firing Pin	.90
4-X-31	Firing Pin Spring	.25
4-X-32	Firing Pin Retainer Pin	.25
3-X-22	Front Sight	.25
5-X-42	Hammer	1.50
5-X-43	Hammer Pin	.25
5-X-44	Hammer Spring	.25
5-X-45	Hammer Spring Abutment	.25
5-X-46	Hammer Spring Link	.40
5-X-47	Hammer Spring Link Pin	.25
	Magazine complete	8.00
10-X-57	Magazine Tube complete	3.00
10-X-58	Magazine Spring	.30
10-X-59	Magazine Follower	.30
10-X-60	Magazine Plug	.75
10-X-61	Magazine Plug Assembling Pin	.25
10-X-62	Magazine Plug Lever	1.50
10-X-63	Magazine Plug Lever Pin	.25
10-X-64	Magazine Plug Lever Plunger	.25
10-X-65	Magazine Plug Lever Plunger Spring	.25
2-X-5	*Receiver	20.00
5-X-53	Recoil Lock	.60

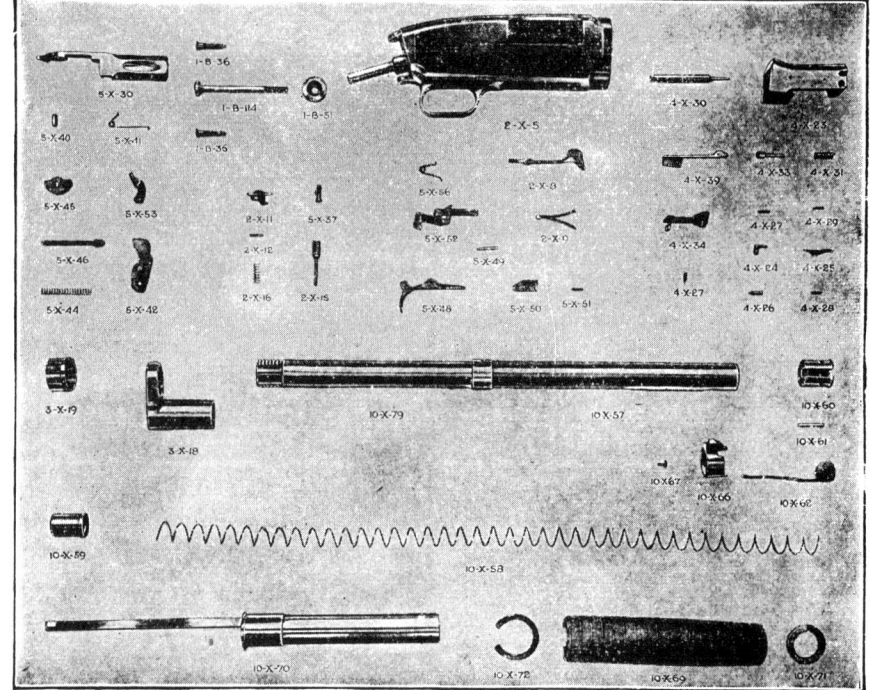

No.	Description	Price
5-X-54	Recoil Lock Pin	$0.25
5-X-55	Recoil Lock Spring	.25
5-X-75	Recoil Lock Spring Button	.25
2-X-11	Safety Thumb Piece	.50
2-X-12	Safety Thumb Piece Pin	.25
2-X-13	Safety Thumb Piece Plunger	.25
2-X-14	Safety Thumb Piece Plunger Spring	.25
2-X-15	Safety Post	.50
2-X-16	Safety Post Spring	.25

No.	Description	Price
5-X-48	Trigger	$1.00
5-X-49	Trigger Pin	.25
5-X-50	Trigger Lock	.50
5-X-51	Trigger Lock Spring	.25
5-X-36	*Trigger Guard	4.00
5-X-37	Trigger Guard Screw	.25
	*Extra Interchangeable Barrel with Magazine Group Assembled complete	22.00

INSTRUCTIONS: In ordering parts always give name and number listed in catalog, also make, model, caliber and serial number of gun.

PAYMENTS: Parts will be sent only on advance payment. Parts cannot be returned for credit. A service charge of 25c must be added to every order under $1.00 to cover cost of handling. Do not forget to include postage.

CAREFUL ATTENTION AND SAFE DELIVERY OF YOUR ORDER

SAVAGE AUTO. AND REPEATING SHOTGUNS

SAVAGE AND SPRINGFIELD AUTOMATIC SHOTGUN

No.	Name of Part	Price
A-26	Action Spring	$0.25
A-36	Action Spring Fol.	.25
A-25	Action Spring Plug	.25
A-24	Action Sp. Plug P.	.25
A-23	Action Spring Tube	.25
*A-75	Bbl. com. with ext.	18.50
*A-76	Bbl. com. with ext. (raised rib)	27.50
*A-18	Barrel Extension	4.00
*A-28	Breech Bolt (only)	4.00
*A-28A	Breech Bolt com.	7.00
A-69	Butt Plate	1.00
A-70	Butt Pl. Screws (2)	.25
A-78	Butt Stk. (includes stock screw)	7.50
A-96	740 Butt Stock includes grip and stock screw)	9.00
A-66	Butt Stk. Screw	.25
A-5A	Butt S. Scr. L. Scr.	.25
A-61	Carrier	2.00
A-68	Carrier Screw	.25
A-5A	Carrier Scr. L. Scr.	.25
A-27	Carrier Spring	.25
A-63	Carrier Dog	.40
A-44	Carrier Dog Fol.	.25
A-45	Carrier Dog Pin	.25
A-62	Carrier Dog Spring	.25
A-33	Carrier Latch	.75
A-46	Carrier Latch But.	.25
A-47	Carrier Lch. Screw	.25
A-48	Carrier Latch Spg.	.25
A-41	Cartridge Stop	.60
A-12	Cart. Stop Screw	.25
A-43	Cartridge Stop Spg.	.25
A-17	Ejector	.25
A-29	Extractor	.25
A-32	Extractor Pin	.25
A-30	Extractor Spring	.25
A-31	Extractor Spg. Fol.	.25
A-35	Firing Pin	.50
A-51	Fir. Pin. Ret. Spg.	$0.25
A-53	Fir. Pin Stop Pin	.25
A-7	Fore-end	3.50
	Fore-end 740 (Beavertail) specify gauge 3-shot or 5-shot	7.00
A-80	Fric. P. & Sp. com.	.40
A-10	Fric. P., Bron. only	.25
A-9	Friction Spring	.25
A-8	Friction Ring	.25
A-15	Front Sight	.25
	Front Sight Base	.25
A-39	Hammer, Assembly	1.00
A-56	Hammer Pin	.25
A-57	Hammer Roll	.25
A-40	Hammer Roll Pin	.25
A-20	Link	.80
A-21	Link Pin	.25
*A-22	Locking Block	1.25
A-49	Locking Bl. Latch	.40
A-52	Lock. Bl. Latch Pin	.25
A-50	Lock. Bl. Latch Sp.	.25
A-14	Magazine Cap	.40
A-79	Mag. Cap St. com.	.25
A-12	Mag. Cap. St. Plun.	.25
A-11	Mag. Cap Stop Spg.	.25
A-13	Mag. Cap St. Screw	.25
A-2	Magazine Follower	.25
A-3	Magazine Tube	1.50
A-5	Magazine Screw	.25
A-1	Magazine Spring	.25
A-4	Mag. Spg. Retainer	.25
A-59	Main Spring	.50
A-60	Main Spring Screw	.25
A-34	Operating Slide	1.00
*A-19	Receiver	16.00
A-6	Recoil Spring	.60
A-73	Safety	.30
A-74	Safety Ball	.25
*A-37	Safety Sear	.45

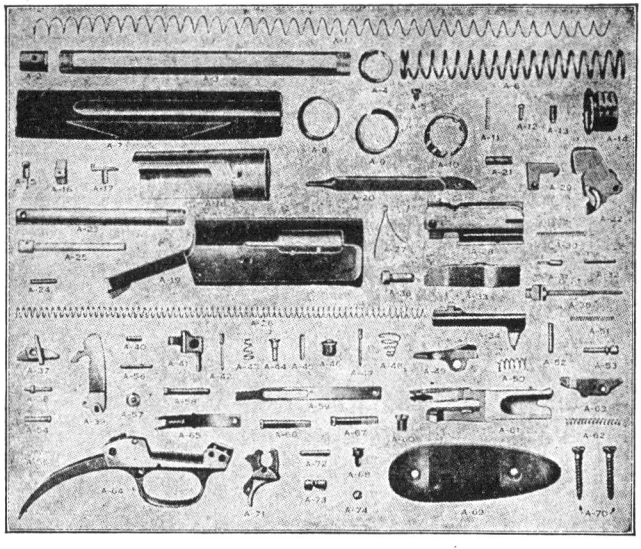

No.	Name of Part	Price	No.	Name of Part	Price
A-38	Safety Sear Fol.	$0.25	*A-64	Trigger Guard	$3.50
A-54	Safety Sear Pin	.25	A-58	Trigger Guard Pin	.25
A-55	Safety Sear Spring	.25	A-5A	Trig. Gd. Pin L. S.	.25
*A-71	Trigger	.80	A-67	Trig. Guard Screw	.25
A-72	Trigger Pin	.25	A-5A	Trig. Gd. S. L. S.	.25
A-65	Trigger Spring	.25			

MODEL 28 REPEATING SHOTGUN

No.	Name of Part	Price
10x68	Action Bar	$3.00
10x69	Action Bar Handle	1.00
10x135	Action Bar Handle Locking Spring	.25
10x136	Action Bar Sleeve	1.20
10x71A	Action Bar Sleeve Nut	.35
5x52A	Action Lock	1.00
5x56	Action Lock Spring	.25
3x162	*Barrel (regular)	17.00
3x162A	*Barrel (raised rib)	26.00
3x18	Barrel Clip	2.00
3x6	*Barrel Extension	1.00
2x7	Barrel Extension Screw	.25
4x121A	*Bolt, complete	6.00
4x122A	Bolt Retaining Latch	.25
4x120	Bolt Cartridge Guide	.50
4x33	Bolt Cartridge Guide Pin	.25
1x1	Buttstock (Reg.) complete	7.50
1x145	Buttstock (Trap Grade) complete	10.00
1B34	Buttstock Screw	.35
1x4	Buttplate	1.00
1B36	Buttplate Screws (2 each)	.25
5x38A	Carrier	2.50
5x41B	Carrier Spring	.25
5x138	Carrier Pin	.25
4x119	Carrier Latch	.75
4x118	Carrier Latch Spring	.25
4x124	Carrier Latch Pin	.25
4x123	*Cartridge Stop	1.00
3x19	Compensating Nut	1.00
3x20	Compensating Nut Retainer	$0.30
3x21	Compensating Nut Retainer Screw	.25
2x9	Ejector	.60
4x24	Extractor (right)	.50
4x26	Extractor Plunger (right)	.25
4x27	Extractor Plunger Spring (right)	.25
4x25	Extractor (left)	.50
4x28	Extractor Pin (left)	.25
4x29	Extractor Spring (left)	.25
4x140	Firing Pin	.90
4x31	Firing Pin Spring	.25
4x32	Firing Pin Retaining Pin	.25
3x22	Front Sight	.25
5x42	Hammer	1.50
5x160	Hammer Pin	.25
5x44	Hammer Spring	.25
5x45	Hammer Spring Abutment	.25
5x46	Hammer Spring Link	.40
4x84	Hammer Spring Link Washer	.25
5x47A	Hammer Spring Link Pin	.25
10x132	Magazine Group complete including action bar and handle	8.00
10x133	Magazine Tube	3.00
10x58	Magazine Spring	.30
10x59	Magazine Follower	.30
10x127	Magazine Tube Assem. Clip	2.00
10x128	Magazine Tube Clip Screw	.25
10x129	Magazine Plug	.60
10x130	Magazine Plug Stop	.30

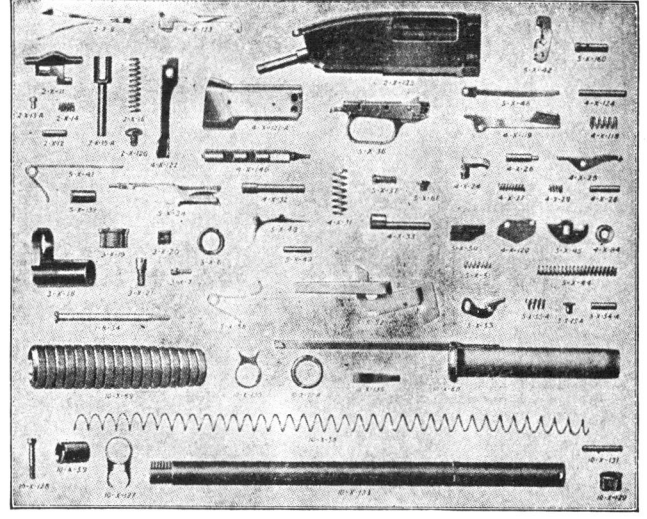

No.	Name of Part	Price	No.	Name of Part	Price
2x125	*Receiver	$20.00	2x126	Safety Post Retaining Screw	$0.25
5x53	Recoil Lock	.60	10x131	Takedown Pin	.25
5x54A	Recoil Lock Pin	.25	5x36A	*Trigger Guard	4.00
5x55A	Recoil Lock Spg.	.25	5x37	Trigger Guard Screw	.25
5x75A	Recoil Lock Spg. Button	.25	5x81	Trigger Guard Screw Locking Screw	.25
2x11	Safety Thumb Piece	.50	5x48	Trigger	1.00
2x12	Safety Thumb Piece Pin	.25	5x49	Trigger Pin	.25
2x13A	Safety Thumb Piece Plunger	.25	5x50	Trigger Lock	.50
2x14	Safety Thumb Piece Plunger Spring	.25	5x51	Trig. Lock Spg.	.25
2x15A	Safety Post	.50		*Extra Interchangeable Bbl. with Mag. Group Assembled Complete	22.00
2x16	Safety Post Spg.	.25			

In replacing parts marked thus (*) it will be necessary to send gun to us.

INSTRUCTIONS: In ordering parts always give name and number listed in catalog, also make, model, caliber and serial number of gun.

PAYMENTS: Parts will be sent only on advance payment. Parts cannot be returned for credit. A service charge of 25c must be added to every order under $1.00 to cover cost of handling. Do not forget to include postage.

STEVENS RIFLE PARTS

IMPORTANT NOTICE — For parts marked with a star (*) complete gun must be sent in to us.

"CRACK SHOT" RIFLES, NOS. 26 AND 26½

No.	Part	Each
1	Barrel with Sights	$2.25
1A	Barrel without Sights	2.00
2	Barrel Screw	.25
2A	Barrel Lug	.25
3	Butt Plate	.40
4	Butt Plate Screw	.25
5	Breech Block, .22	.80
6	Breech Block, .32	.80
7	Breech Block Screw	.25
8	Breech Block Plunger	.25
9	Breech Block Plun. Sp.	$0.25
10	Extractor, .22	.35
10A	Extractor, .32	.35
10B	Extractor Pin	.25
11	Frame	2.25
12	Fore-end	.60
13	Fore-end Screw	.25
14	Firing Pin	.25
15	Firing Pin Pin	.25
16	Hammer	$0.60
17	Hammer Screw	.25
18	Lever	.90
19	Lever Pin	.25
20	Lever Pin Roll	.25
21	Lever Pin Roll Screw	.25
22	Mainspring	.25
23	Mainspring Plunger	.25
24	Mainspring Plun. Sleeve	.25
25	Stock with Butt Plate	$2.00
26	Stock Bolt	.25
27	Stock Bolt Nut	.25
28	Take-Down Screw	.35
29	Trigger	.50
29A	Trigger Spring	.25
30	Trigger Screw	.25
31	Sight (Front)	.25
32	Sight (Rear)	.30

IDEAL RIFLES NOS. 44 AND 414

No.	Part	Each
0	*Barrel	$10.50
1	Barrel Screw	.35
2	Breech Block only	1.85
2A	Breech Block (complete)	2.00
3	Breech Block Pivot	.25
4	Breech Block Pivot Screw	.25
5	Butt Plate 44	1.50
5A	Butt Plate 414	1.15
6	Butt Plate Screw	.25
7	Dummy Screw	.25
8	Ejector, .22 Cal	1.00
9	Ejector Plunger	.25
10	Ejector Plunger Pin	$0.25
11	Ejector Spring	.25
12	Extractor	1.00
13	Firing Pin	.35
14	Firing Pin Screw	.25
15	Fore-end, No. 44	1.60
15A	Fore-end, No. 414	6.00
16	Fore-end Screw	.25
17	*Frame	7.85
18	Hammer	1.10
18A	Hammer N. S.	1.10
19	Hammer Screw	.25
20	Lever	2.10
21	Lever Pivot	.25
22	Lever Pivot Screw	$0.25
23	Lever Plunger	.25
24	Lever Plunger Spring	.25
25	Link	.30
26	Link Pin	.25
27	Mainspring (flat style)	.35
27A	Mainspring Coil	.35
27B	Mainspring Plunger	.35
27C	Mainspring Plunger Seat	.25
28	Mainspring Screw	.25
29	Trigger	.90
30	Trigger Screw	.25
31	Trigger Spring	.25
32	Trigger Spring Screw	.25
33	Stock without Butt Plate 44-414	$4.40
34	Front Sight Rocky Mountain	.80
35	Rear Sight, Sporting	1.00
36	Rear Sight Step	.25
40	Front Sight, Rocky Mountain, No. 414	1.00
41	Rear Sight, Receiver	2.00
42	Disc for Receiver Sight	.50
42A	Leaf for Receiver Sight	.40
43	Front Loop and Band, No. 414	.60
44	Rear Loop, No. 414	.40

"WALNUT HILL" RIFLES, NOS. 417 AND 417½

No.	Part	Each
1	*Barrel, No. 417—Tapped for Telescope Blocks	$18.50
2	*Barrel, No. 417½ Tapped for Telescope Blocks	14.80
3	Barrel Screw	.50
4	*Breech Block only	3.00
5	Breech Block complete	3.75
6	Breech Block Pivot	.50
7	Breech Block Pivot Screw	.25
8	Butt Plate	2.25
9	Butt Plate Screw	.25
10	Dummy Screw	.25
11	Ejector, .22 Cal	1.00
12	Ejector Plunger	$0.25
13	Ejector Plunger Pin	.25
14	Ejector Plunger Spring	.25
15	Extractor	1.00
16	Firing Pin	.50
17	Firing Pin Screw	.25
18	Fore-end, No. 417	8.25
19	Fore-end, No. 417½	6.50
20	Fore-end Checkered (extra)	4.50
21	Fore-end Screw, Front, No. 417	.25
22	Fore-end Screw, Front, No. 417½	.25
23	Fore-end Screw, Rear	.25
24	Fore-end Band and Loop, No. 417	1.00
25	*Frame, No. 417, 417½	$10.50
26	*Frame and Action complete	17.60
27	Hammer	1.50
28	Hammer Screw	.25
29	Lever	4.00
30	Lever Pivot	.50
31	Lever Screw	.25
32	Lever Plunger	.50
33	Lever Plunger Spring	.25
34	Link	.75
35	Link Pin	.25
36	Mainspring	.60
37	Mainspring Plunger	.50
38	Mainspring Plunger Seat	.25
39	Mainspring Screw	.25
39A	Sight, Lyman 144 Tang Peep with Click Adjustment for Elevation and Windage	$7.00
40	Stock (without Butt Plate)	12.00
41	Stock Screws	.25
42	Stock Checkered (extra)	4.50
43	Telescope Blocks and Screws for Lyman or Fecker	.80
44	Trigger	1.25
45	Trigger Screw	.25
46	Trigger Spring	.30
47	Trigger Spring Screw	.25
48	Trigger Stop Screw	.25

"WALNUT HILL" RIFLES, NOS. 418, 418½

No.	Part	Each
1	*Barrel only, No. 418	$8.00
2	*Barrel only, No. 418½	7.25
3	*Breech Block	1.75
4	Breech Block Screw	.25
5	Butt Plate	1.00
6	Butt Plate Screw	.25
7	Dummy Screw	.25
8	Ejector, .22 Cal	1.00
9	Ejector Spring	.25
10	Ejector Spring Plunger	.25
11	Extractor	$1.00
12	Firing Pin	.35
13	Firing Pin Pin	.25
14	Fore-end complete	3.60
15	Fore-end Screw	.25
16	*Frame	4.00
17	Hammer	1.00
18	Hammer Screw	.25
19	Lever	1.50
20	Lever Bushing	.25
21	Lever Screw	$0.25
22	Link	.40
23	Link Pin	.25
24	Mainspring	.50
25	Mainspring Plunger complete	.40
26	Mainspring Plunger Seat	.25
27	Mainspring Plunger Screw	.25
28	Mainspring Pin	.25
29	Stock with Butt Plate	$5.75
30	Sight, Front, Partridge Type No. 418	.60
32	Sight, Rear, Lyman No. 144 for No. 418	7.00
36	Takedown Screw	.40
37	Trigger	.80
38	Trigger Screw	.25
39	Trigger Spring	.25
40	Trigger Spring Screw	.25

MODELS 48, 49 AND 50

No.	Part	Each
	Bbl. & Sights Mod. 49	$3.00
	Bbl. & Sights Mod. 50	3.25
	Bbl. & Sights Mod. 50	2.50
	Barrel without Sights, Model 49	2.30
	Barrel without Sights, Model 50	2.60
	Barrel without Sights, Model 48	2.10
1	Barrel Lug	.35
2	Bolt Body	obsolete
3	Bolt Head	obsolete
4	Bolt Handle	obsolete
5	Bolt Head Complete	obsolete
6	Butt Plate 49-50	$0.65
7	Butt Plate Screw	.25
8	Cocking Piece	.45
9	Extractor	.50
10	Extractor Pin	.25
11	Firing Pin	.35
12	Main Spring	.25
13	Main Spring Nut	.25
14	Main Spring Stem	.25
15	Rebound Spring	.25
16	Receiver 49	1.10
17	Receiver 50	1.30
18	Receiver 48	$0.80
19	Receiver Pin	.25
20	Receiver Screw	.25
21	Sear	.35
22	Sear Spring with Trigger Stud	.65
23	Sear Spring Screw	.25
24	Sear Spring Complete	1.00
25	Sight Front Lyman Ivory Bead 49-50	1.00
26	Sight Front 48	.25
27	Sight Rear Sporting 49-50	.75
28	Sight Rear Sporting Step 49-50	$0.25
29	Sight Rear 48	.35
30	Stock & Butt Plate 49	2.75
31	Stock with Butt Plate 50	2.75
32	Stock 48	2.00
33	Take Down Screw 49-50	.25
34	Take Down Screw 48	.25
35	Trigger	.40
36	Trigger Guard	.45
37	Trigger Guard Screw	.25
38	Trigger Pin	.25

MODELS 51, 52 AND 53

No.	Part	Each
	Bbl. & Sights Mod. 51	$3.00
	Bbl. & Sights Mod. 52	4.80
	Bbl. & Sights Mod. 53	5.20
	Barrel without Sights, Model 51	2.80
	Barrel without Sights, Model 52	4.00
	Barrel without Sights, Model 53	4.40
1	Barrel Lug	.30
2	Barrel Pin	.25
3	Bolt	1.40
4	Bolt Complete	2.80
5	Butt Plate, 52-53 New Style	.50
6	Butt Plate, 52-53 Old Style	$0.50
7	Butt Plate Screw	.25
8	Cocking Piece	.50
9	Cocking Piece Spring	.25
10	Cocking Piece Pin	.25
11	Extractor	.50
12	Extractor Spring	.25
13	Extractor Pin	.25
14	Ejector	.25
15	Firing Pin New Style	.30
16	Firing Pin Old Style	.30
17	Firing Pin Spring	.25
18	Guard, 52-53 New Style	.30
19	Guard, 52-53 Old Style	.30
20	Guard, 51	.30
21	Guard Screw	$0.25
22	Mainspring	.30
23	Mainspring Bushing	.25
24	Receiver	1.40
25	Striker	.50
26	Striker Bushing	.25
27	Striker Bushing Pin	.25
28	Sleeve	.25
29	Sight Blade Front, 51	.25
30	Sight Open Rear, 51	.30
31	Sight Lyman Front, 52-53	.80
32	Sight Sporting Rear, 52-53	.70
33	Sight Sporting Rear Step, 52-53	.25
34	Stock, 51	$2.00
35	Stock with Plate, 52-53 New Style	2.80
36	Stock with Plate, 52-53 Old Style	2.80
37	Take Down Screw, 51	.50
38	Take Down Screw, 52-53 New Style	.50
39	Take Down Screw, 52-53 Old Style	.50
40	Trigger	.50
41	Trigger Pin	.25
42	Trigger Spring (Same as 17)	.25

In replacing parts marked thus (*) it will be necessary to send gun to us.

SEE PAGE 8, "HOW TO ORDER"

STEVENS RIFLE PARTS
LITTLE SCOUT RIFLE NO. 14½ AND STEVENS JUNIOR NO. 11

No.	Part	Each	No.	Part	Each	No.	Part	Each	No.	Part	Each	No.	Part	Each
1	Barrel with Sights	$2.00	17	Firing Pin	$.25	30	Stock Bolt Nut	$.25	33	Trigger	$.40	36	Trigger Screw	$.25
1A	Barrel without Sights	1.85	18	Guard	.35	32	Take Down Screw	.35	33A	Trigger, No. 11	.40	36A	Trigger Pin, No. 11	.25
2	Barrel Screw	.25	18A	Guard, No. 11	.35	32A	Take Down Screw, No. 11	.35	34	Trigger Plunger	.25	37	Front Sight	.25
2A	Barrel Lug	.25	18B	Guard Screw, No. 11	.25				35	Trigger Plunger Spring	.25	38	Rear Sight	.30
3	Butt Plate	.40	19	Guard Screw (front)	.25									
4	Butt Plate Screw	.25	20	Guard Screw (rear)	.25									
5	Breech Block	.70	21	Hammer	.50									
6	Breech Block Screw	.25	22	Hammer Screw	.25									
6A	Breech Block Screw, No. 11	.25	22A	Hammer Pin, No. 11	.25									
7	Breech Block Lever	.25	23	Mainspring	.25									
8	Breech Block Plunger	.25	24	Mainspring Sleeve	.25									
9	Breech Block Plunger Spring	.25	25	Mainspring Sleeve Pin	.25									
10	Escutcheon	.25	26	Mainspring Plunger	.25									
11	Extractor	.35	27	Mainspring Plunger Pin	.25									
13	Extractor Pin	.25	28	Stock with Butt Plate	1.85									
14	Frame	1.75	28A	Stock, No. 11	1.85									
14A	Frame, No. 11	1.15	29	Stock Bolt	.25									
15	Fore-end	.50												
16	Fore-end Screw	.25												

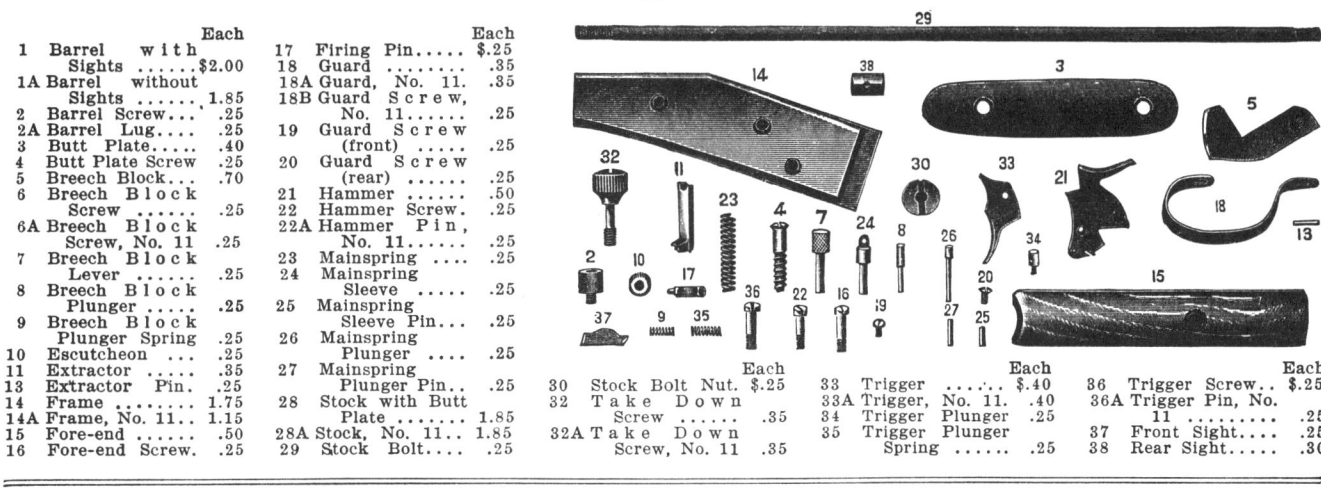

MARKSMAN RIFLE NO. 12

No.	Part	Each	No.	Part	Each	No.	Part	Each	No.	Part	Each	No.	Part	Each
1	Barrel only	$3.25	9	Extractor Pin	$.25	18	Joint Screw	$.25	26	Mainspring Plunger Screw	$.25	34	Rear Sight, O. S.	$.50
1A	Barrel with Sights	3.65	10	Firing Pin	.30	19	Lever	1.00	27	Stock with Butt Plate	2.75	35	Front Sight, Rocky Mountain	.70
2	Barrel Sleeve	1.50	11	Firing Pin Pin	.25	20	Lever Screw	.25	28	Stock Bolt	.25	36	Rear Sight Step	.25
4	Butt Plate	.60	12	Fore-end	.90	21	Link	.50	29	Stock Bolt Nut	.25	37	Rear Sight, Sporting, (complete)	.70
5	Butt Plate Screw	.25	13	Fore-end Screw	.25	22	Link Screw	.25	30	Trigger	.60	38	Take-Down Screw	.50
6	Cocking Plunger	.35	14	Fore-end Escutcheon	.25	23	Link Pin	.25	31	Trigger Spring	.25			
7	Cocking Plunger Spring	.25	15	Frame	2.75	24	Mainspring	.25	32	Trigger Screw	.25			
8	Extractor	.50	16	Hammer	.70	25	Mainspring Plunger	.25	33	Front Sight, O. S.	.50			
			17	Hammer Screw	.25									

"FAVORITE" RIFLES NOS. 17, 20 AND 27

No.	Part	Each
	Barrel with Sights:	
	For No. 17	$5.50
	For No. 20	4.50
	For No. 27	5.60
	Barrel without Sights:	
	For Nos. 17 and 20	4.50
	For No. 27	4.80
1	Breech Block	1.15
2	Breech Block Screw	.25
3	Butt Plate, Rubber	.60
4	Butt Plate Screw	.25
5	Dummy Screw	.25
6	Ejector	.90
7	Ejector Spring	.25
8	Ejector Spring Plunger	.25
9	Extractor	.90
10	Firing Pin	.30
11	Firing Pin Pin	.25
12	Fore-end (complete)	1.10
13	Fore-end Screw	.25
14	Frame	3.90
15	Hammer	.90
16	Hammer Screw	.25
17	Lever	1.40
18	Lever Bushing	.25
19	Lever Screw	.25
20	Link	.30
21	Link Pin	.25
22	Mainspring	.30
23	Mainspring Plunger (complete)	.35
24	Mainspring Plunger Seat	.25
25	Mainspring Plunger Screw	.25
26	Mainspring Plunger Pin	.25
26A	Stock with Butt Plate	3.90
27	Take-Down Screw	.50
28	Trigger	.70
29	Trigger Screw	.25
30	Trigger Spring	.25
31	Trigger Spring Screw	.25
32	Front Sight, Lyman Bead	.80
33	Rear Sight, Sporting (complete)	.70
34	Rear Sight Step only	.25

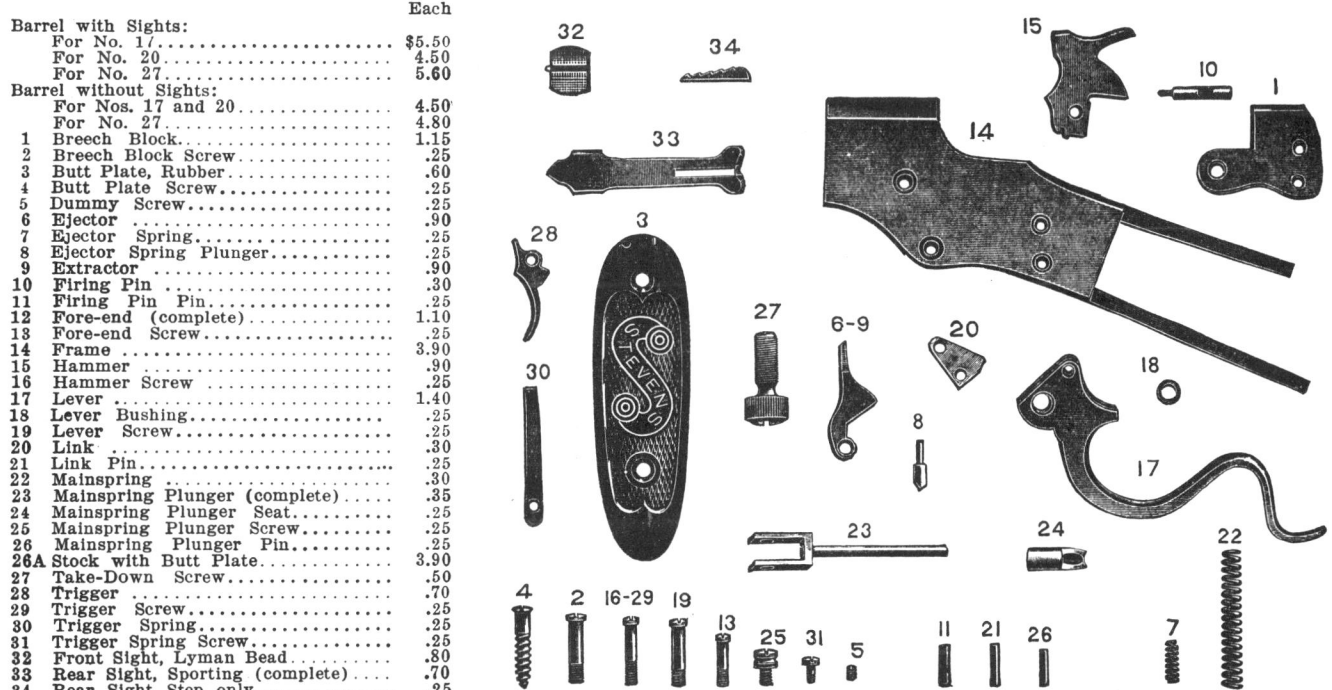

In replacing parts marked thus (*) it will be necessary to send gun to us.

INSTRUCTIONS: In ordering parts always give name and number listed in catalog, also make, model, caliber and serial number of gun.

PAYMENTS: Parts will be sent only on advance payment. Parts cannot be returned for credit. A service charge of 25c must be added to every order under $1.00 to cover cost of handling. Do not forget to include postage.

STEVENS RIFLE PARTS

NOS. 66A AND 066A RIFLES

No.	Part	Each
1	Barrel only	$5.00
2	Barrel with Sights	6.85
3	Barrel Pin	.25
4	Breech Block	2.25
5	Butt Plate	.60
6	Butt Plate Screw	.25
7	Bolt Handle	.90
8	Cocking Piece	.30
9	Cocking Piece Pin	.25
10	Extractor Left	.40
11	Extractor Right	.40
12	Extractor Spring Screw	.25
13	Extractor Spring	.25
14	Firing Pin	.25
15	Lifter	.40
16	Lifter Pin	.25
17	Lifter Trip	.25
18	Lifter Trip Screw	.25
19	Magazine Follower	.25
20	Magazine Mount Front	.50
21	Magazine Mount Rear	.50
22	Magazine Plug	.25
23	Magazine Plug Pin	.25
24	Magazine Spring	.30
25	Magazine Tube Inside Only	1.15
25A	Magazine Tube Inside Complete	1.70
26	Magazine Tube Outside	1.15
27	Main Spring	$0.30
28	Rebound Spring	.25
29	Receiver	2.00
30	Safety	.30
31	Safety Plunger	.25
32	Safety Plunger Bushing	.25
33	Safety Plunger Spring	.25
34	Sight, Gold Bead Front	.80
35	Sight, Sporting Rear	.70
36	Sight, Sporting Rear Step	.25
36A	Sight Front for 066	.80
36B	Sight Receiver for 066	.80
37	Sleeve	.90
38	Stock with Butt Plate	2.25
39	Striker	.60
40	Striker Complete with Firing Pin	1.20
41	Striker Retainer Pin	.25
42	Take Down Screw	.35
43	Trigger	.50
44	Trigger Pin	.25
45	Trigger Guard	.40
46	Trigger Guard Screw	.25

NOS. 70 AND 71 "VISIBLE LOADING" REPEATING RIFLES

No.	Part	Each
1	Action Pin	$.25
2	Action Pin Screw	.25
	Barrels Model 70 obsolete use Model 71 instead	
2C	Bbl. with't Sgt. No. 71	6.25
2D	Bbl. with Sgt. No. 71	7.00
3	Breech Block	2.30
4	Butt Plate	.60
5	Butt Plate Screw	.25
6	Ext'ctor (rt.) (2 styles)	.40
7	Ext'ctor (lt.) (2 styles)	.40
8	Extractor Screw	.25
9	Extractor Spring	.25
9A	Extractor Spring Pin	.25
10	Firing Pin	.60
11	Frame	5.20
12	Hammer	$1.00
13	Hammer Screw Nut	.25
14	Hammer Lock	.70
14A	Hammer Lock Spring	.25
14B	Hammer L. Spg. N.S.	.25
15	Hammer Lock Screw	.25
16	Hammer Lock Dummy Screw	.25
17	Lifter	.50
18	Lifter Pin	.25
19	Locking Cam	.60
20	Locking Cam Sleeve	.70
21	Magazine Mount (front)	.50
22	Magazine Mount (rear)	.50
23	Mag. Tube (outside)	1.15
24	Magazine Tube inside	$1.15
25	Magazine Follower — complete	.25 / $1.60
26	Mag. Spring	.30
27	Magazine Plug	.25
28	Mag. Plug Pin	
29	Mainspring	.30
30	Mainspring Plunger Bracket / Mainspring Plunger Wire / Mainspring Plunger Stud	.60
31	Mainspring Screw	.25
31A	Stock with Butt Plate	4.50
31B	Stock with Butt Plate No. 71	$4.80
32	Slide Handle Wood only	1.00
33	Slide Handle Bar	2.00
34	Slide Handle Screw	.25
35	Tang Screw	.25
36	Trigger	.70
37	Trigger Spring	.25
38	Trigger Spring Screw	.25
39	Trigger Pin	.25
40	Sporting Rear Sight	.70
41	Sptg. Rear Sight Step	.25
42	Front Sgt. Lyman Bead	.80
43	Mainspring Plunger Seat	.25
44	Dummy Screw	.25
45	Slide Handle Escutcheon	.25

NO. 75 REPEATING RIFLE

No.	Part	Each
1	Action Slide	$1.70
2	Action Slide Handle	1.00
3	Action Slide Hdle. Sc.	.25
3A	Action Slide Handle Screw Washers (2)	.25
4	Act. Slide Hdl. Stud	.25
5	Action Slide Handle Escutcheon	.25
6	Barrel Without Sights	6.50
7	Barrel With Sights	8.00
8	Barrel Pin	.25
9	Breech Block	3.00
10	Breech Block Complete	5.00
11	Butt Plate	.60
12	Butt Plate Screw	.25
13	Butt Stock	6.00
14	Butt Stock Bolt	.25
15	Dummy Screw	.25
16	Extractor Right	$0.50
17	Extractor Left	.50
18	Extractor Pin	.25
19	Extractor Spring	.25
20	Extractor Spg. Bushing	.25
21	Firing Pin	.70
22	Firing Pin Spring	.25
23	Firing Pin Spring Pin	.25
24	Frame or Bbl. Rec.	5.50
25	Hammer	1.00
26	Hammer Bushing	.25
27	Hammer Lock	.70
27A	Hammer Lock Washer	.25
28	Hammer Lock Stud	.25
29	Hammer Lock Spring	.25
30	Lifter	.50
31	Lifter Stud	.25
32	Mag. Group Complete	4.00
33	Magazine Follower Tube Complete	$2.25
34	Magazine Follower	.30
35	Magazine Follower Tube	1.15
36	Mag. Fol. Tube Spg.	.35
37	Magazine Stud	.30
38	Magazine Tube	1.60
39	Magazine Tube Retaining Screw	.25
40	Mag. Tube Th. Piece	.35
41	Magazine Tube Thumb Piece Pin	.25
42	Mainspring	.50
43	Mainspring Plunger	.40
44	Operating Latch	.50
45	Operating Latch Pin	.25
46	Operating Latch Spring	.25
47	Recoil Lock Plunger	.25
48	Recoil L. Plunger Spg.	$0.25
49	Recoil Lock Plunger Pin	.25
50	Safety	.50
51	Safety Plunger	.25
52	Safety Plunger Spring	.25
53	Slide Lock	.55
54	Slide Lock Screw	.25
55	Slide Lock Spring	.25
56	Sporting Rear Sight	.70
57	Sptg. Rear Sight Step	.25
58	Gold Bead Front Sight	.80
59	Takedown Screw	.35
60	Takedown Bushing	.25
61	Trigger	.65
62	Trigger Pin	.25
63	Trigger Guard or Stock Receiver	3.65
65	Trunion Pin	.25

NOS. 100 AND 105 FRONT AND REAR SIGHTS

No.	Part	Each
100	Hooded Ramp Front Sight	$0.80
1	Hood for same	.25
2	Post Insert	.25
3	Aperture Insert	.25
4	Bead Insert	$0.25
5	Ramp Base	.50
6	Ramp Base Screw	.25
105	Rear Peep Receiver Sight	.80
1	Sight Base	$0.50
2	Sight Base Screw	.25
3	Elevation Indicator	.25
4	Eye Disc Hunting	.25
5	Eye Disc Target	.25
6	Eye Disc Lock Nut	$0.25

The above mentioned sights can be fitted to the following models: 51, 52, 53, 56, 66.

In replacing parts marked thus (*) it will be necessary to send gun to us.

INSTRUCTIONS: In ordering parts always give name and number listed in catalog, also make, model, caliber and serial number of gun.

PAYMENTS: Parts will be sent only on advance payment. Parts cannot be returned for credit. A service charge of 25c must be added to every order under $1.00 to cover cost of handling. Do not forget to include postage.

A NEW GUN CARRIES A FACTORY GUARANTEE

AMERICA'S GREAT GUN HOUSE — 445

IMPORTANT NOTICE
For parts marked with a star (*) complete gun must be sent in to us.

STEVENS SHOTGUN PARTS

IMPORTANT NOTICE
For parts marked with a star (*) complete gun must be sent in to us.

SINGLE BARREL SHOTGUNS, NOS. 85, 89

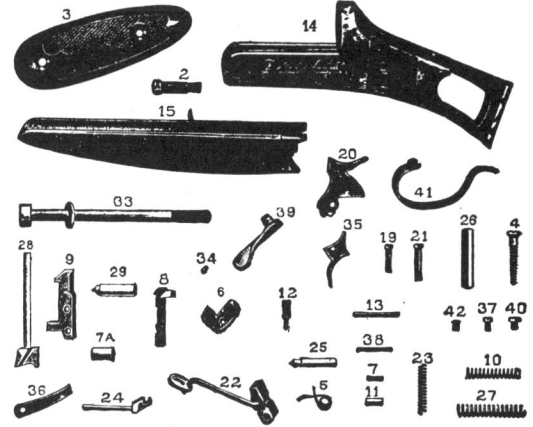

No.	Part	Each	No.	Part	Each	No.	Part	Each
1	*Barrel	$6.00	15	Fore-end, com.	$1.75	28	Mainspring Pl.	$0.30
2	Barrel Screw	.25	16	Fore-end wo'd only	1.20	29	Mainspring Pl. Seat	.25
3	Butt Plate	.60	17	Fore-end Iron	1.20	32	Stk., Butt Pl.	3.75
4	Butt Pl. Screw	.25	18	Fore-end Ir. S.	.40	33	Stk. Bolt com.	.35
5	Extr. Lev. Sp.	.25	18A	Fore-end S. S.	.25	34	Sight	.25
6	Extractor Lev.	.25	19	Fore-end Scw.	.25	35	Trigger	.60
7	Extr. Lev. Pin	.25	20	Hammer	.50	36	Trigger Spring	.25
7A	Extractor Stem	.25	21	Hammer Scw.	.25	37	Trigger Sp. Sc.	.25
8	Eject. or Extr.	.50	22	Lock. Bt. com.	.90	38	Trigger Pin	.25
9	Ejector Catch	.35	23	Lock. Bolt Sp.	.25	39	Top Snap	.50
10	Ejector Spring	.25	24	Lock. Bolt Pl.	.30	40	Top Snap Scw.	.25
11	Eject. St. Pin	.25	25	Lock. Bt. Seat	.25	41	Trigger Guard	.50
12	Firing Pin	.30	26	Lock. Bolt Pin	.25	42	Trig. Gd. Scw.	.25
13	Firing Pin Pin	.25	27	Mainspring	.30			
14	*Frame	4.75						

SINGLE BARREL SHOTGUNS NOS. 94, 95, 105, 107 AND 116

No.	Part	Each
1	*Barrel, Nos. 105-107	$4.00
1A	*Barrel, No. 94	4.00
2	*Barrel, No. 116	6.00
3	Barrel Screw	.25
4	Butt Plate, Nos. 94-95-105-107-116	.60
6	Butt Plate Screw	.25
7	Extractor	.50
8	Extractor Lever	.25
9	Extractor Lever Pin	.25
10	Extractor Lever Spring	.25
11	Extractor Stem	.25
12	Ejector	.50
13	Ejector Catch	.35
14	Ejector Catch Pin	.25
15	Ejector Spring	.25
16	Ejector Stop Pin	.25
17	Firing Pin	.30
18	Firing Pin Screw	.25
19	*Frame, No. 94	3.25
20	*Frame, Nos. 105-107	3.25
21	*Frame, No. 116	3.75
22	Fore-end (complete), No. 94	2.00
23	Fore-end (complete), No. 94	1.60
24	Fore-end (complete), No. 116	2.50
25	Fore-end Wood, No. 94	1.00
26	Fore-end Wood, Nos. 105-107	1.20
27	Fore-end Wood, No. 116	1.40
28	Fore-end Iron	1.20
29	Fore-end Spring	.40
30	Fore-end Spring Spring	.25
31	Fore-end Spring Pin	.25
32	Fore-end Screw	.25
33	Hammer	.50
34	Hammer Pin	.25
35	Locking Bolt, (complete)	.90
36	Locking Bolt Pin	.25
37	Locking Bolt Plunger	.30
38	Locking Bolt Plunger Spring	.25
39	Locking Bolt Plunger Seat	.25
40	Main Spring	.30
41	Main Spring Plunger	.30

No.	Part	Each	No.	Part	Each
42	Main Spring Plunger Seat	$.25	49B	Sight, Lyman Rear, No. 117	$.50
43	Pistol Grip Cap, No. 116	.30	50	Trigger	.60
44	Pistol Grip Cap Screw, No. 116	.25	51	Trigger Spring	.25
45	Stock with Butt Plate, No. 94	3.00	52	Trigger Spring Screw	.25
46	Stock with Butt Plate, Nos. 105-107	3.50	53	Trigger Pin	.25
47	Stock with Butt Plate, No. 116	4.25	54	Trigger Guard	.50
48	Stock Bolt Complete	.35	55	Trigger Guard Screw	.25
49	Sight	.25	56	Top Snap	.50
49A	Sight, Lyman Front, No. 117	.50	57	Top Snap Sleeve	.25
			58	Top Snap Screw	.25

DOUBLE BARREL HAMMER GUN, NO. 215

No.	Part	Each	No.	Part	Each	No.	Part	Each	No.	Part	Each
1	*Barrels, per pair	$8.00	13	Fore-end Screw (long)	$.25	26	Mainspring Plunger	$.30	37	Top Snap Trip Spring	$.25
2	Butt Stock with Butt Plate	7.00	14	Fore-end Screw (short)	.25	27	Mainspring Plunger Sleeve	.25	38	Trigger (left)	.50
3	Butt Plate	.60	15	Firing Pin	.30	28	Stock Bolt (complete)	.60	39	Trigger (right)	.50
4	Butt Plate Screw	.25	16	Firing Pin Screw	.25	29	Stock Bolt Washer	.25	40	Trigger Spring	.25
5	Extractor	1.00	17	Front Sight	.25	30	Top Snap	1.00	41	Trigger Spring Pin	.25
6	Extractor Screw	.25	18	*Frame	8.75	31	Top Snap Plunger	.25	42	Trigger Pin	.25
7	Fore-end Wood	2.00	19	*Frame and Action	11.50	32	Top snap Plunger Collar	.25	43	Tumbler (right)	.70
8	Fore-end Iron	1.85	20	Guard	1.00	33	Top Snap Plunger Spring	.25	44	Tumbler (left)	.70
9	Fore-end (complete)	3.65	21	Guard Screw	.25	34	Top Snap Plunger Screw	.25	45	Tumbler (collar)	.25
10	Fore-end Spring	.50	22	Hammer (right)	.90	35	Top Snap Screw	.25	46	Tumbler Collar Screw (long)	.25
11	Fore-end Spring Spring	.25	23	Hammer (left)	.90	36	Top Snap Trip	.30	47	Tumbler Collar Screw (short)	.25
12	Fore-end Spring Pin	.25	24	Hammer Screw	.25						
			25	Mainspring	.35						

In replacing parts marked thus (*) it will be necessary to send gun to us.

INSTRUCTIONS: In ordering parts always give name and number listed in catalog, also make, model, caliber and serial number of gun.

PAYMENTS: Parts will be sent only on advance payment. Parts cannot be returned for credit. A service charge of 25c must be added to every order under $1.00 to cover cost of handling. Do not forget to include postage.

ALL SHIPMENTS ARE INSURED

STEVENS SHOTGUN PARTS
DOUBLE BARREL HAMMER SHOTGUN, NO. 235

IMPORTANT NOTICE — For parts marked with a star (*) complete gun must be sent in to us.

No.	Part	Each
1	*Barrels—per pair	$10.00
2	Butt Stock with Plate	8.00
3	Butt Plate	.60
4	Butt Plate Screw	.25
5	Extractor	1.00
6	Extractor Lever	.30
7	Extractor Lever Pin	.25
8	Extractor Screw	.25
9	Fore-end Wood	2.00
9A	Fore-end (complete)	3.60
10	Fore-end Screw (long)	.25
11	Fore-end Screw (short)	.25
12	Fore-end Iron	2.00
13	Fore-end Spring	.40
14	Fore-end Spring Spring	.25
15	Fore-end Sp. Sp. Pin	$0.25
17	Firing Pin	.30
18	Firing Pin Screw	.25
19	Front Sight	.25
20	*Frame	9.60
20A	*Frame and Action	12.00
21	Guard	1.00
22	Guard Screw (long)	.25
23	Guard Screw (short)	.25
24	†Hammer (left)	1.00
25	†Hammer (right)	1.00
26	Hammer Screw	.25
27	Hammer Shaft	.25
28	Hammer Shaft Collar	.25
29	Mainspring	.35
30	Mainspring Plun. Seat	$0.25
31	Mainspring Plunger Head (right)	.35
32	M. S. P. Head (left)	.35
33	Sear (left)	.45
34	Sear (right)	.45
35	Sear Spring	.25
36	Sear Spring Screw	.25
37	Sear Screw	.25
38	Sear Stop	.25
39	Stock Bolt (complete)	.60
40	Stock Bolt Washer	.25
41	*Top Snap	1.50
42	Top Snap Plunger	.25
43	Top Snap Plunger Spg.	.25
44	Top Snap Nut	.25
45	Top Snap Nut Lock	$0.25
46	T. S. Nut Lock Screw	.25
47	Top Snap Stop Block	.35
48	Top Snap Trip	.30
49	Top Snap Trip Spring	.25
50	Trigger (right)	.55
51	Trigger (left)	.55
52	Trigger Spring	.25
53	Trigger Spring Screw	.25
54	*Trigger Plate	2.30
55	Trigger Pin	.25
56	Trigger Plate Screw	.25
57	Tang Screw Top	.25
58	Tumbler (right)	.85
59	Tumbler (left)	.85
60	Barrel Lug	.60

DOUBLE BARREL HAMMERLESS SHOTGUN, NOS. 311, 315, 3150, 3151 AND 330

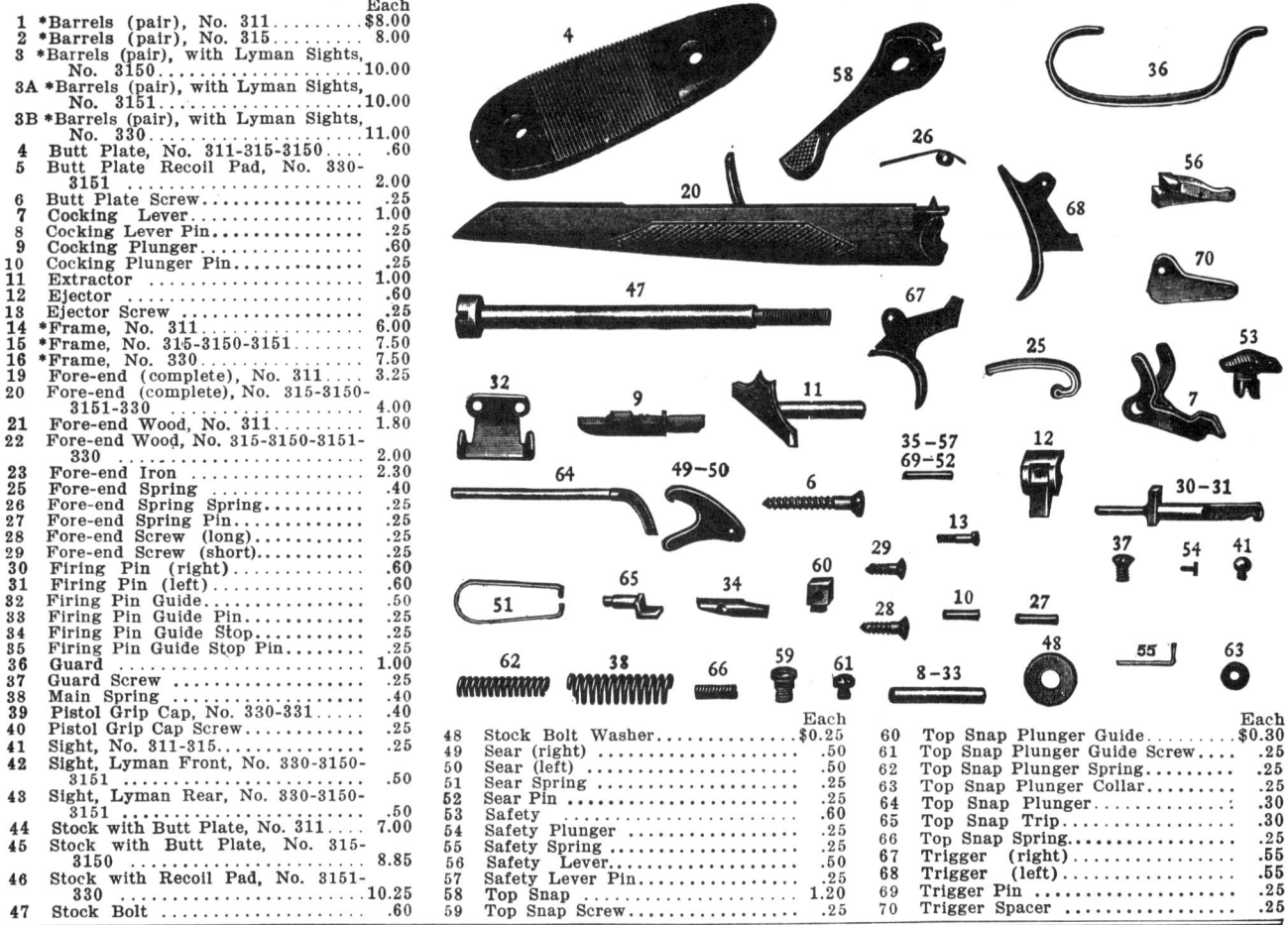

No.	Part	Each
1	*Barrels (pair), No. 311	$8.00
2	*Barrels (pair), No. 315	8.00
3	*Barrels (pair), with Lyman Sights, No. 3150	10.00
3A	*Barrels (pair), with Lyman Sights, No. 3151	10.00
3B	*Barrels (pair), with Lyman Sights, No. 330	11.00
4	Butt Plate, No. 311-315-3150	.60
5	Butt Plate Recoil Pad, No. 330-3151	2.00
6	Butt Plate Screw	.25
7	Cocking Lever	1.00
8	Cocking Lever Pin	.25
9	Cocking Plunger	.60
10	Cocking Plunger Pin	.25
11	Extractor	1.00
12	Ejector	.60
13	Ejector Screw	.25
14	*Frame, No. 311	6.00
15	*Frame, No. 315-3150-3151	7.50
16	*Frame, No. 330	7.50
19	Fore-end (complete), No. 311	3.25
20	Fore-end (complete), No. 315-3150-3151-330	4.00
21	Fore-end Wood, No. 311	1.80
22	Fore-end Wood, No. 315-3150-3151-330	2.00
23	Fore-end Iron	2.30
25	Fore-end Spring	.40
26	Fore-end Spring Spring	.25
27	Fore-end Spring Pin	.25
28	Fore-end Screw (long)	.25
29	Fore-end Screw (short)	.25
30	Firing Pin (right)	.60
31	Firing Pin (left)	.60
32	Firing Pin Guide	.50
33	Firing Pin Guide Pin	.25
34	Firing Pin Guide Stop	.25
35	Firing Pin Guide Stop Pin	.25
36	Guard	1.00
37	Guard Screw	.25
38	Main Spring	.40
39	Pistol Grip Cap, No. 330-331	.40
40	Pistol Grip Cap Screw	.25
41	Sight, No. 311-315	.25
42	Sight, Lyman Front, No. 330-3150-3151	.50
43	Sight, Lyman Rear, No. 330-3150-3151	.50
44	Stock with Butt Plate, No. 311	7.00
45	Stock with Butt Plate, No. 315-3150	8.85
46	Stock with Recoil Pad, No. 3151-330	10.25
47	Stock Bolt	.60
48	Stock Bolt Washer	$0.25
49	Sear (right)	.50
50	Sear (left)	.50
51	Sear Spring	.25
52	Sear Pin	.25
53	Safety	.60
54	Safety Plunger	.25
55	Safety Spring	.25
56	Safety Lever	.50
57	Safety Lever Pin	.25
58	Top Snap	1.20
59	Top Snap Screw	.25
60	Top Snap Plunger Guide	$0.30
61	Top Snap Plunger Guide Screw	.25
62	Top Snap Plunger Spring	.25
63	Top Snap Plunger Collar	.25
64	Top Snap Plunger	.30
65	Top Snap Trip	.30
66	Top Snap Spring	.25
67	Trigger (right)	.55
68	Trigger (left)	.55
69	Trigger Pin	.25
70	Trigger Spacer	.25

DOUBLE BARREL HAMMERLESS SHOTGUN NO. 335

No.	Part	Each
1	*Barrels—per pair	$10.00
2A	Butt Stock with Butt Plate	8.00
3	Butt Plate	.60
4	Butt Plate Screw	.25
5	Cocking Lever	.55
6	Extractor Lever	.30
7	Extractor	1.15
8	Extractor Screw	.25
9	Extractor Lever Pin	.25
10	*Frame	8.00
10A	*Frame and Action (complete)	14.00
11	Fore-end Wood	2.30
11A	Fore-end (complete)	4.00
12	Fore-end Iron	2.50
13	Fore-end Spring	.40
14A	Fore-end Spring Spring Coil (new style)	$0.25
16	Fore-end Spring Pin	.25
17	Fore-end Screw (long)	.25
18	Fore-end Screw (short)	.25
19	Firing Pin	.30
20	Firing Pin Screw	.25
21	Front Sight	.25
22	Guard	1.35
23	Guard Screw (long)	.25
24	Guard Screw (short)	.25
25	Hammer (right)	.90
26	Hammer (left)	.90
27	Hammer Rod	.30
28	Hammer Rod Pin	.25
29	Hammer Screw	.25
30	Joint Pin	.30
31	Joint Pin Screw	$0.25
32	Mainspring	.35
33	Mainspring Plunger	.30
33A	Pistol Grip Cap	.35
34	Stock Bolt (complete)	.60
35	Stock Bolt Washer	.25
36	Sear (right)	.60
37	Sear (left)	.60
38	Sear Spring	.25
39	Sear Spring Screw	.25
40	Sear Screw	.25
41	Safety Button Pin	.25
42	Safety Spring	.25
43	Safety Spring Screw	.25
44	Safety Lever	.40
45	Safety Lever Pin	.25
46	Safety Operating Lever	.60
47	Safety Button	$0.60
48	*Top Snap	1.85
49	Top Snap Plunger	.25
50	Top Snap Plun. Spg.	.30
51	Top Snap Nut	.30
52	Top Snap Nut Lock	.25
53	T. S. Nut Lock Screw	.25
54	Top Snap Trip	.30
55	Top Snap Trip Spring	.25
56	Trigger (right)	.70
57	Trigger (left)	.70
58	Trigger Spring	.25
59	Trigger Spring Screw	.25
60	*Trigger Plate	2.30
61	Trigger Plate Screw	.25
62	Tang Screw Top	.25
63	Top Snap Stop Block	.30

In replacing parts marked thus (*) it will be necessary to send gun to us.   † Use model 215 Hammers instead.

SEND YOUR GUN TO STOEGER FOR EXPERT REPAIRING

STEVENS SINGLE BARREL MODELS 944, 958, 106, 108, 102, 104

		Each				Each				Each				Each
1	*Barrel	$4.00	11	Ejector		$0.50	26	Fore-end Spring Spring	$0.25	39	Stock, Butt Plate 944	$3.00
2	Barrel Screw	.25	12	Ejector Catch		.35	27	Fore-end Spring Pin	.25	40	Stock with Butt Plate, other numbers	3.50
3	Butt Plate, Nos. 948-958	.60	13	Ejector Catch Pin		.25	28	Fore-end Screw	.25	41	Stock Bolt (complete)	.35
4	Butt Plate, Nos. 106-108, 102-104	.60	14	Ejector Spring		.25	29	Hammer	.50	42	Sight	.25
			15	Ejector Stop Pin		.25	30	Hammer Pin	.25	43	Trigger	.60
5	Butt Plate Screw	.25	16	Firing Pin		.30	31	Locking Bolt (complete)	.90	44	Trigger Spring	.25
6	Extractor	.50	17	Firing Pin Screw		.25	32	Locking Bolt Pin	.25	45	Trigger Spring Screw	.25
7	Extractor Lever	.25	18	*Frame		4.00	33	Locking Bolt Plunger	.30	46	Trigger Pin	.25
8	Extractor Lever Pin	.25	20	Fore-end (complete)		1.75	34	Lkg. Bolt Plunger Spg.	.25	47	Trigger Guard	.50
9	Extractor Lever Spring	.25	22	Fore-end Wood only		1.20	35	Lkg. Bolt Plunger Seat	.25	48	Trigger Guard Screw	.25
10	Extractor Stem	.25	24	Fore-end Iron		1.20	36	Mainspring	.30	49	Top Snap	.50
			25	Fore-end Spring		.40	37	Mainspring Plunger	.30	50	Top Snap Screw	.25
							38	Mainspring Plunger Seat	.25			

STEVENS SINGLE BARREL MODELS 948, 958, 106, 108

		Each			Each			Each			Each
1	*Barrel	$4.00	14	Ejector Spring	$.25	25	Fore-end Spring	$.25	38	Mainspring Plunger Seat	$.25
2	Barrel Screw	.25	15	Ejector Stop Pin	.25	26	Fore-end Spring Spring	.25	39	Stock with Butt Plate, No. 948	3.50
3	Butt Plate, Nos. 948-958	.60	16	Firing Pin	.30	27	Fore-end Spring Pin	.25	40	Stock with Butt Plate, Nos. 958-106-108	3.50
4	Butt Plate, Nos. 106-108	.60	17	Firing Pin Screw	.25	28	Fore-end Screw	.25	41	Stock Bolt (complete)	.35
5	Butt Plate Screw	.25	18	*Frame, Nos. 948-958	4.00	29	Hammer	.50	42	Sight	.25
6	Extractor	.50	19	*Frame, Nos. 106-108	4.00	30	Hammer Pin	.25	43	Trigger	.60
7	Extractor Lever	.25	20	Fore-end (complete), No. 948	1.75	31	Locking Bolt (complete)	.90	44	Trigger Spring	.25
8	Extractor Lever Pin	.25	21	Fore-end (complete), Nos. 958-106-108	1.75	32	Locking Bolt Pin	.25	45	Trigger Spring Screw	.25
9	Extractor Lever Spring	.25	22	Fore-end Wood only, No. 948	1.20	33	Locking Bolt Plunger	.30	46	Trigger Pin	.25
10	Extractor Stem	.25	23	Fore-end Wood only, Nos. 958-106-108	1.20	34	Locking Bolt Plunger Spring	.25	47	Trigger Guard	.50
11	Ejector	.50	24	Fore-end Iron	1.20	35	Locking Bolt Plunger Seat	.25	48	Trigger Guard Screw	.25
12	Ejector Catch	.35				36	Mainspring	.30	49	Top Snap	.50
13	Ejector Catch Pin	.25				37	Mainspring Plunger	.30	50	Top Snap Screw	.25

STEVENS NOS. 520, 521, 620 AND 621 REPEATING SHOTGUNS

1. *Barrel only, Nos. 520-620......$11.00
   *Barrel only, Nos. 521-621...... 14.00
   *Barrel with magazine operating handle complete, No. 520..... 15.00
   *Barrel with magazine operating handle complete, No. 620..... 15.00
   *Barrel with magazine operating handle complete, No. 521..... 18.50
   *Barrel with magazine operating handle complete, No. 621..... 18.50
2. Butt plate...... .45
3. Butt plate screw (2)...... .25
4. Cartridge stop O. S. 520-521.... .40
4b. Cartridge stop O. S. 620-621.... .40
5. Cartridge stop N. S. 520-521.... .40
5b. Cartridge stop N. S. 620-621.... .40
5a. Cartridge stop screw...... .25
6. Cartridge Stop bushing...... .25
7. Cartridge stop bushing screw.... .25
8. Cartridge stop screw front...... .25
9. Extractor right...... .40
10. Extractor spring right...... .25
11. Extractor plunger right...... .25
12. Extractor left...... .40
13. Extractor pin right...... .25
14. Extractor pin left...... .25
15. Extractor spring left...... .25
16. Ejector...... .40
17. Ejector Screw...... .25
18. Firing pin...... .45
19. Firing pin stop pin...... .25
20. Hammer complete, Nos. 520-521 1.00
21. Hammer complete, Nos. 620-621 1.00
22. Hammer pin...... .25
23. Hammer spacing collar...... .25
24. *Locking block...... 1.50
25. Lifter...... 2.00
26. Lifter pawl...... .30
27. Lifter pawl spring and plunger.. .25
28. Lifter pawl pin...... .25
29. Lifter spring...... .25
30. Lifter screw...... .25
31. Mainspring, Nos. 520-521...... .50
32. Mainspring, Nos. 620-621...... .50
33. Mainspring screw...... .25
34. Magazine tube...... 1.40
35. Magazine spring...... .25
36. Magazine follower...... .25
37. Magazine plug...... .45
38. Magazine plug screw...... .25
39. Magazine nut...... .90
40. Operating handle, wood only, Nos. 520-521...... 1.00
41. Operating handle, wood only, Nos. 620-621...... 1.50
42. Operating handle, complete, Nos. 520-521...... 5.00
43. Operating handle, complete, Nos. 620-621...... 6.75
44. Operating handle, collar front... .50
45. Operating handle, bar...... 3.00
46. Operating handle, bar only...... 1.00
47. Pistol grip cap, Nos. 620-621... .45
48. Pistol grip cap screw (2)...... .25
49. *Receiver Nos. 520-521...... 10.00
50. *Receiver Nos. 620-621......$11.75
51. Safety Nos. 520-521...... .40
52. Safety spring Nos. 520-521...... .25
53. Safety spring plunger Nos. 520-521 .25
54. Safety Nos. 620-621...... .40
55. Safety plunger Nos. 620-621.... .25
56. Safety plunger spring...... .25
57. Safety plunger screw...... .25
58. Sear Nos. 520-521...... .50
59. Sear spring Nos. 620-621...... .25
60. Sight Nos. 520-521...... .25
61. Sight Nos. 620-621...... .25
62. *Slide Nos. 520-521...... 2.00
63. *Slide Nos. 620-621...... 2.00
64. Slide lock...... 1.00
65. Slide lock pin...... .25
66. Slide lock spring...... .25
67. Slide lock release Nos. 520-521.. .40
68. Slide lock release Nos. 620-621.. .40
69. Slide lock release spring......... $0.25
70. *Sliding breech Nos. 520-521..... 3.00
71. *Sliding breech Nos. 620-621..... 3.50
72. Sliding breech stop screw....... .25
73. Stock with butt plate Nos. 520-521 5.50
74. Stock with butt plate and pistol grip cap Nos. 620-621........ 6.60
75. Stock tang screw Nos. 520-521.. .25
76. Stock tang screw Nos. 620-621.. .25
77. Trigger Nos. 520-521............ .70
78. Trigger Nos. 620-621............ .70
79. Trigger pin Nos. 520-521........ .25
80. Trigger pin Nos. 620-621........ .25
81. Trigger spring Nos. 520-521..... .25
82. Trigger spring Nos. 620-621..... .25
83. *Trigger plate Nos. 520-521..... 3.00
84. *Trigger plate Nos. 620-621..... 3.00
85. Trigger plate screw............. .25
86. Trigger plate pin............... .25

In replacing parts marked thus (*) it will be necessary to send gun to us.

STEVENS, ITHACA AND HI-STANDARD PARTS

STEVENS OFFHAND PISTOL NO. 35

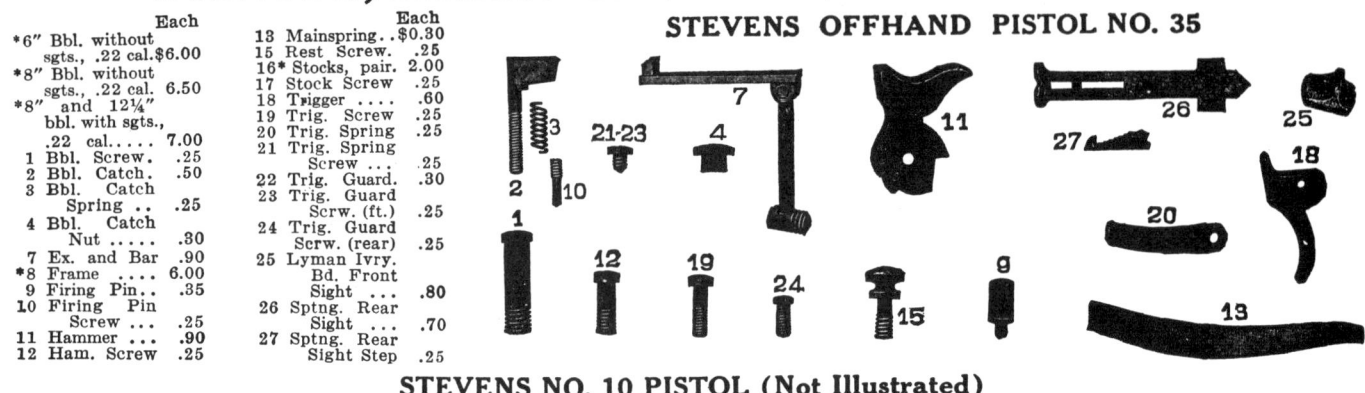

	Each		Each
*6" Bbl. without sgts., .22 cal.	$6.00	13 Mainspring	$0.30
*8" Bbl. without sgts., .22 cal.	6.50	15 Rest Screw	.25
*8" and 12¼" bbl. with sgts., .22 cal.	7.00	16* Stocks, pair	2.00
		17 Stock Screw	.25
1 Bbl. Screw	.25	18 Trigger	.60
2 Bbl. Catch	.50	19 Trig. Screw	.25
3 Bbl. Catch Spring	.25	20 Trig. Spring	.25
4 Bbl. Catch Nut	.30	21 Trig. Spring Screw	.25
7 Ex. and Bar	.90	22 Trig. Guard	.30
*8 Frame	6.00	23 Trig. Guard Scrw. (ft.)	.25
9 Firing Pin	.35	24 Trig. Guard Scrw. (rear)	.25
10 Firing Pin Screw	.25	25 Lyman Ivry. Bd. Front Sight	.80
11 Hammer	.90	26 Sptng. Rear Sight	.70
12 Ham. Screw	.25	27 Sptng. Rear Sight Step	.25

STEVENS NO. 10 PISTOL (Not Illustrated)

	Each		Each		Each		Each
* Bbl. without Sgts. complete with Extractor	$8.75	9 Cocking Rod Link Pins	$0.25	17 Hammer Screw	$0.25	26 Trigger Spring	$0.25
1 Barrel Screw	.30	10 Extractor Trip	.90	18 Mainspring	.30	27 Trigger Spring Plunger	.25
2 Barrel Lock	1.85	11 Extractor Trip Pin	.25	19 Mainspring Plunger	.50	28 Trigger Spring Plunger Screw	.25
3 Barrel Lock Plunger	.25	12 Extractor Trip Spring	.25	20 Mainspring Plun. Screw	.25	29 Trigger Pin	.25
4 Barrel Lock Plun. Spg.	.25	Extractor and Screw	.60	21 Stock (left)	.60	30 Sight (front)	.75
5 Barrel Lock Screw	.25	13 Firing Pin	.30	22 Stock (right)	.60	31 Sight (rear)	3.00
6 Cocking Rod	.60	14 Firing Pin Bushing	.25	23 Stock Screws	.25		
7 Cocking Rod Head	.30	15* Frame	8.75	24 Stock Separate	.25	* It will be necessary to return gun for fitting.	
8 Cocking Rod Link	.50	16 Hammer	1.00	25 Trigger	.90		

ITHACA SHOTGUN PARTS

Beavertail forend on Field, No. 1 or 2 (ship entire gun) $10.90
Beavertail forend on No. 3 or 4 (ship entire gun) .. 13.55
Beavertail forend on No. 5, 7, or Sousa (ship entire gun) 21.65
Bolt Spring .... .50
Butt plate 1.25
Chambering for longer shell, each barrel 1.50
Changing drop—send entire gun 5.00
Cocking cam .... .50
Cocking hook .... .75
Cocking Lever (old model) 1.00
Ejector kicker complete 1.50
Ejector kicker sear or retainer 1.00
Ejector kicker sear or retainer spring .... .25
Ejector kicker spring .... .35
Ejector extractors 2.50
(Must have entire gun if we fit extractors.)
Extractors plain 1.50
Extra barrels, one-half price of gun, net.
(Must have entire gun for about 4 weeks to fit barrels.)
Firing pin .... .50
Forend complete, Field or No. 1, 5.50; No. 2, 7.50; No. 3, 10.00; No. 4, 12.50; No. 5, 15.00; No. 6, 20.00; No. 7, 25.00; Sousa Grade, 40.00.
Forend escutcheon 1.50
Forend iron .... $3.50 to 20.00
Forend latch .... .75
Forend spring .... .50
Forend wood ... $3.50 to 20.00
Forend yoke .... .75
Add 50% if gun is an Ejector

Entire gun must be sent to be sure forend will fit but if serial number, gauge and grade are given we can usually send a forend which will fit well enough to work except that an ejector forend cannot be fitted without having the entire gun at factory.

Grip cap $0.50
Guard, plain 1.50
Hammer 1.00
Hammer rod complete 1.50
Indicator .... .25
Indicator lever .... .30
Indicator spring .... .25
Ivory sights, each .... .55
Main spring .... .65
Overhauling locks (send entire gun) 4.00
Overhauling ejector (send entire gun) 4.00
Overhauling locks on guns not Ithacas attempted at owner's risk for about $5.00 depending on time spent.
Pins .... .25
Reblue guard, triggers, forend iron and top lever 3.50
Reboring one barrel (ship barrels only), 2.50; two barrels $5.00
Reboring to remove choke (ship barrels only), per barrel 2.50
Reboring to put choke back (ship barrels only), per barrel 4.00

Rebrowning barrels (ship barrels only) $4.00
Rechambering for longer shells (ship barrels only), per barrel 1.50
Recoil Ithaca pad $2.25, fitting pad .... .75
Refinishing and rechecking stock on No. 2 or cheaper grades 4.00
Refinishing stocks and rechecking on higher grades 6.50
Refinishing forend wood on No. 1 or cheaper grades .. 2.00
Refinishing forend wood on higher grades 5.00
Reharden frame 7.50
Removing dents $2.50 per barrel (ship barrels only). If necessary to rebrown, extra $4.00. Everytime a barrel is fired with a dent in it a chance of blowing the barrel out is taken.
Repolishing one barrel (ship barrels only), $2.50; two barrels, $5.00.
Resetting ribs (ship barrels only) 1.50
Safety button .... .65
Safety, complete 2.50
Screw .... .25
Sear .... .50
Sear spring .... .25
Shortening stock and resetting butt plate 2.50

Single triggers fitted only to Ithacas numbered above 175,000, ship entire gun, Selective, $20.00; non-selective, $10.00.
Spring for Bolt $0.25
Spring Cap for Bolt .... .25
Stock, fitted and finished No. 1 or cheaper grades, 10.00; No. 2, 15.00; No. 3, 20.00; No. 4, 25.00; No. 5, 30.00; No. 6, 35.00; No. 7, 50.00; Sousa Grade, 75.00.
Restocking guns not Ithacas attempted at owner's risk at $20.00 for the Ithaca No. 1 grade stock, add $7.50 for each better grade of stock.
(Send entire gun—time required 2 weeks)
Stock, turned and milled, one-half price of finished stock.
Top lever nut .... .35
Top lever, plain 2.00
Top lever, post 2.00
Trigger .... 75c to 3.50
Trigger plate, plain 2.00
Trigger spring .... .30
Trip .... .25
Trip spring .... .35
Tumbler 1.00
Under bolt 1.00
When ordering parts or writing about gun give serial number of gun as stamped on barrels, frame and forend and state if hammer or hammerless. A rough drawing of part wanted helps.

HI-STANDARD .22 AUTOMATIC TARGET PISTOL

Part No.		Price	Part No.		Price	Part No.		Price	Part No.		Price
1	Barrel	$4.50	15	Hammer	$1.50	29	Retracting Rod spring plug	$0.25	40	Sideplate	$0.25
2	Barrel lock pin	.25	16	Hammer strut	.25	30	Retracting Rod spring plug pin	.25	41	Sight, front	1.50
3	Ejector	.25	17	Hammer strut pin	.25	31	Safety	1.10	42	Sight, rear	1.10
4	Extractor	.75	18	Magazine complete	2.25	32	Safety screw	.25	43	Slide	3.75
5	Extractor spring	.25	19	Magazine follower	.75	33	Safety lock spring	.25	44	Slide complete	6.00
6	Extractor pin	.25	20	Magazine spring	.40	34	Safety lock ball	.25	45	Stop Lug	.25
7	Firing Pin	.50	21	Magazine catch	.60	35	Sear	1.50	46	Take-down lever	1.10
8	Firing Pin spring	.25	22	Magazine catch spring	.25	36	Sear spring	.25	47	Take-down lever screw	.25
9	Firing Pin stop pin	.25	23	Magazine catch pin	.25	37	Sear pin	.25	48	Take-down lever pin	.25
10	Frame	15.00	24	Magazine button	.25	38	Sear bar	.45	49	Trigger	1.50
11	Grip, left side	1.10	25	Mainspring	.25	39	Sear bar spring	.25	50	Trigger plunger	.25
12	Grip, right side	1.10	26	Mainspring plunger	.25				51	Trigger plunger spring	.25
13	Grip screws (4)	.30	27	Retracting Rod	.50				52	Trigger pin	.25
14	Grip escutcheons (4)	.30	28	Retracting Rod spring	.25				53	Trigger pull pin	.25

ITHACA MODEL 37 REPEATER PARTS

1	Magazine Spring	$0.50
2	Magazine Spring Cup	.25
3	Magazine Cap	.65
4	Magazine Cap Pin	.25
5	Magazine Cap Pin Check Pin	.25
6	Magazine Cap Pin Check Pin Spg	.25
7	Magazine Cap Pin Check Pin Screw	.25
8	Magazine and Guide	5.00
9	Forend Tube Nut	.65
10	Action Bar and Tube (not including forend)	4.00
11	Butt Plate	1.25
12	Receiver	13.50
13	Action Bar Lock	.75
14	Action Bar Lock Spring (bottom)	.25
15	Action Bar Lock Spring (top)	.25
16	Trigger	1.00
17	Trigger Pin	.25
18	Trigger Spring	.25
19	Safety	.35
20	Hammer	1.00
21	Hammer Pin	.25
22	Hammer Bar	.35
23	Trigger Plate	5.00
24	Stock Bolt Lock Washer	.25
25	Stock Bolt Washer	.25
26	Stock Bolt	.50
27	Safety Plunger	.25
28	Magazine Cap Catch Spring (in lug on barrel)	.25
	Magazine Cap Catch (in lug on barrel) (Not illustrated)	.25
29	Safety Plunger Spring	.25
30	Main Spring Follower	.25
31	Main Spring	.65
32	Main Spring Retaining Plug	.25
33	Hammer Bar Pin	.25
34	Trigger Plate Screw	.25
35	Main Spring Stop Pin	.25
36	Carrier	3.00
37	Action Bar Lock	.75
38	Action Bar Lock Spring	.25
39	Action Bar Lock Retaining Pin	.25
40	Firing Pin	$0.50
41	Firing Pin Spring	.25
42	Firing Pin Retaining Pin	.25
43	Carrier Screw	.25
44	Carrier Screw Locking Screw	.25
45	Slide	4.00
46	Breech Block	5.00
47	Bottom Extractor	.75
48	Bottom Extractor Pin	.25
49	Bottom Extractor Spring	$0.25
	Top Extractor (not illustrated)	.75
	Top Extractor Spring (not illustrated)	.25
	Top Extractor Plunger (not illustrated)	.25
50	Cartridge Stop (left)	1.00
51	Cartridge Stop (right)	1.00
52	Cartridge Stop Screw	.25
53	Cartridge Stop Spring	.25
54	Grip Cap	.50

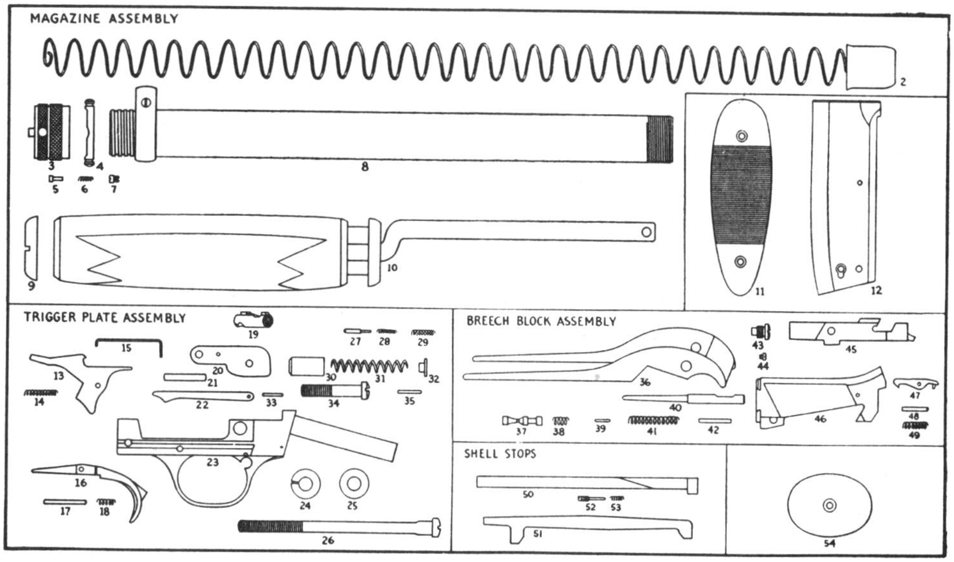

Changing drop (send entire gun) $5.60
Forend wood for Model 37 (will not fit 37S or 37T) 4.00
Large forend wood for Model 37S (will not fit 37 or 37T) 10.00
Large forend wood for Model 37T (will not fit 37 or 37S) 12.50
Extra barrel for Model 37 (send entire gun) (will not fit 37S or 37T) 18.70
Extra barrel including ventilated rib for Model 37S or 37T (send entire gun) (will not fit Model 37) 39.10
Lyman ivory sights, front and rear for Model 37S or 37T only..each .55
Lyman ivory front sight for Model 37 only 1.10
Brass sights .... each .25
Overhauling locks (send entire gun) 4.00
Reboring to remove choke 2.50
Rebluing barrel 4.00
Rebluing all metal parts except barrel 7.50

Recoil Pad (Ithaca) fitted $3.00
Refinishing and recheckering stock on Model 37 or 37S 4.00
Refinishing and recheckering stock on Model 37T 7.50
Refinishing and recheckering forend on Model 37 .... 2.50
Refinishing and recheckering forend on Model 37S or 37T 5.00
Removing dents (every time a barrel with a dent in it is fired a dangerous chance of blowing out the barrel is taken) 2.50
Repolishing inside of barrel 2.50
Shortening stock and resetting butt plate 3.35
New Stock for Model 37 or 37S (send entire gun) 10.00
New Stock for Model 37T (send entire gun) 20.00
Turned and milled stock for Model 37 or 37S 5.00
Turned and milled stock for Model 37T 10.00

WESTERN ARMS SHOTGUN PARTS

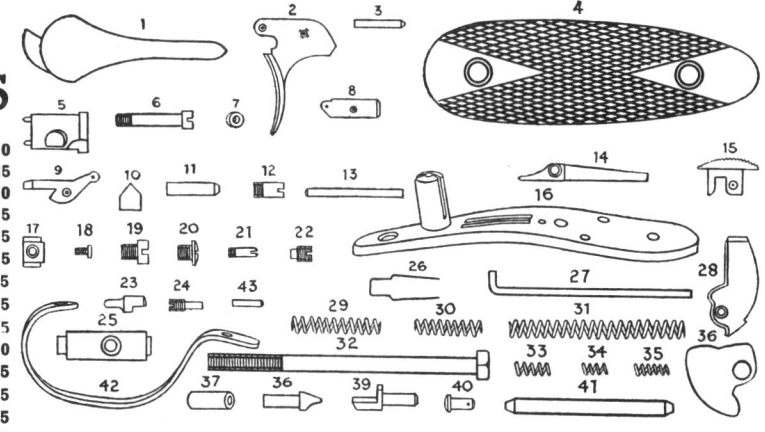

1	Top Lever	$1.50
2	Trigger, (front or rear)	.75
3	Trigger Pin	.25
4	Butt Plate	1.00
5	Top Lever Post	.75
6	Top Lever Post Screw	.25
7	Trigger Pin Collar	.35
8	Forend Fastener Bolt	.75
9	Safety Lever	.40
10	Safety Lever Catch	.25
11	Safety Lever Post Pin	.25
12	Trigger Screw	.25
13	Sear or Hammer Pin	.25
14	Sear, (right or left)	.40
15	Safety Button	.60
16	Trigger Plate	1.50
17	Trigger Bridge	.50
18	Trigger Bridge Screw	.25
19	Trigger Plate Screw	.25
20	Trigger Guard Screw	.25
21	Bolt Spring Stop Screw	.25
22	Extractor Check Screw	.25
23	Firing Pin	$0.40
24	Firing Pin Check Screw	.25
25	Tang Post	.50
26	Trigger Spring	.25
27	Safety Push Rod	.25
28	Hammer	.75
29	Forend Fastener Spring	.35
30	Bolt Spring	.35
31	Main Spring	.35
32	Stock Fastening Bolt	.50
33	Sear Spring	.25
34	Safety Lever Catch Sp'g	.25
35	Trip Spring	.25
36	Cocking Cam	.50
37	Sear Pin Collar	.35
38	Main Spring Cap	.35
39	Trip	.25
40	Bolt Spring Cap	.25
41	Cocking Rod	.35
42	Trigger Guard	1.00
43	Forend Fast'r Bolt Pin	.25

Note—Order By Number

Overhauling and cleaning locks—
Send frame and stock $3.50
Removing dents—per barrel 2.50
Removing dents—both barrels 5.00
Refinishing stock 2.25
Refinishing forearm 1.25
Restocking—send frame only 8.00
Rebrowning—send barrels only 3.00
Polishing out barrels and removing pits, send barrels only, per bbl. 2.50
Polishing out barrels and removing pits, send barrels only both bbls. 5.00

Reboring—send barrels only, per bbl. $2.50
Reboring—send barrels only, both barrels 5.00
Ivory sights, each .... .25
Soft rubber recoil pad 2.00
Refinishing all metal parts except barrels 6.00
Forearm complete 4.00
Forearm iron 2.25
Forearm wood 2.00
Shell extractor for barrels 1.25

DO NOT WAIT UNTIL THE LAST MINUTE TO HAVE YOUR GUN SERVICED

LEFEVER ARMS, SHOTGUN PARTS

PART PRICES FOR DISCONTINUED MODELS OF LEFEVER GUNS NUMBERED UNDER 100,000

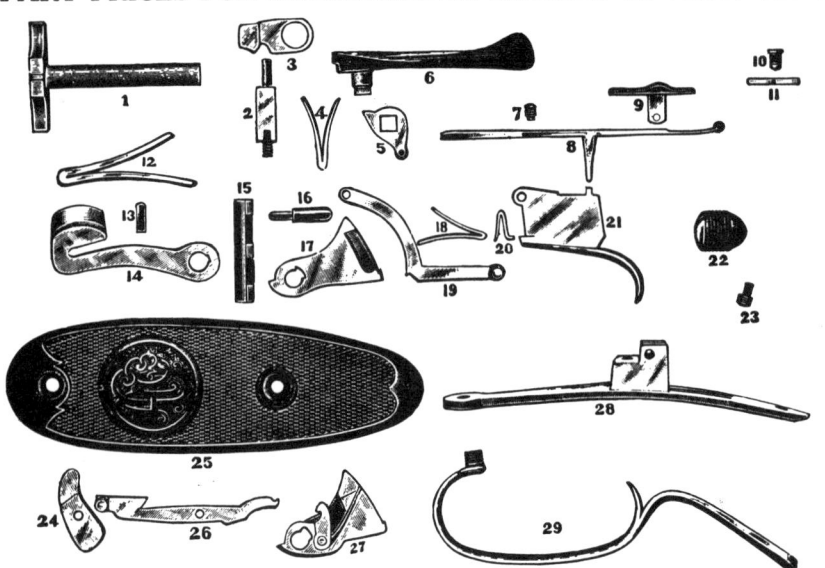

Parts Illustration for Lefever Guns Numbered Under 100,000

Number		Price
1	Extractor (Rough)	$2.00
2	Trip and Spring	1.00
3	Bolt	1.00
4	Top-Lever Spring	.75
5	Cam	1.50
6	Top-Lever (Plain)	3.00
7	Safety Adjustment-Screw	.25
8	Safety-Bar	1.50
9	Safety Slide	$1.00
10	Indicator Pin	.50
11	Indicator Springs	.50
12	Mainspring	1.00
13	Lug-Pin	.50
14	Cocking-Hook	2.00
15	Hammer-Pin	.50
16	Firing-Pin	.50
17	Hammer, non-ejector (right or left)	2.00
18	Sear-Spring	$0.50
19	Sear (right or left)	1.50
20	Trigger Spring	.50
21	Trigger (right or left)	1.50
22	Compensating Screw	.75
23	Trigger-Pull adjusting screw	.50
24	Ejector Kicker (right or left)	1.00
25	Butt-Plate	1.50
26	Ejector Frame-Lever (right or left)	2.00
27	Hammer, ejector (right or left)	2.50
28	Trigger-Plate	3.00
29	Guard (plain)	2.50
	Forend, complete	$15.00 to $25.00
	Forend, Wood	$5.00 to $12.50
	Forend, Iron	$12.00 to $20.00

An extra charge will be made for any parts which have to be made by hand.

Cleaning and overhauling locks $5.00, send whole gun. Overhauling ejector, send whole gun, $4.00.
Rebrowning barrels, $4.50; send barrels only.
Reboring barrels for pattern:—One barrel, $2.50; two barrels, $5.00; send barrels only.
Polishing out barrels and removing pits:— One barrel, $2.50; two barrels, $5.00; send barrels only.
Recoil pad fitted, $3.00. Grip Cap, $.50.
Ivory sights, $.55 each.
Removing dents from barrels:—$2.50 per barrel; send barrels only.
Refinishing and recheckering stock and forend on DS, H or G, $6.00. Better grades on application.

RESTOCKING

Send whole gun.

Durston Spec'l Grade	$14		C Grade	$40
H	"	16	B "	45
G	"	18	A "	50
F	"	22.50	AA "	55
E	"	27.50	Optimus	60
D	"	35	$1000 Grade	100

Parts for and work on very old models extra charge according to time spent.
Refinishing frame, forend iron, trigger guard, trigger, top lever and safety button, $10.

Note—Order parts by number and give number of gun. Always state whether right or left hand. Send old part, if possible.

PART PRICES FOR LEFEVER DOUBLE GUNS NUMBERED OVER 100,000

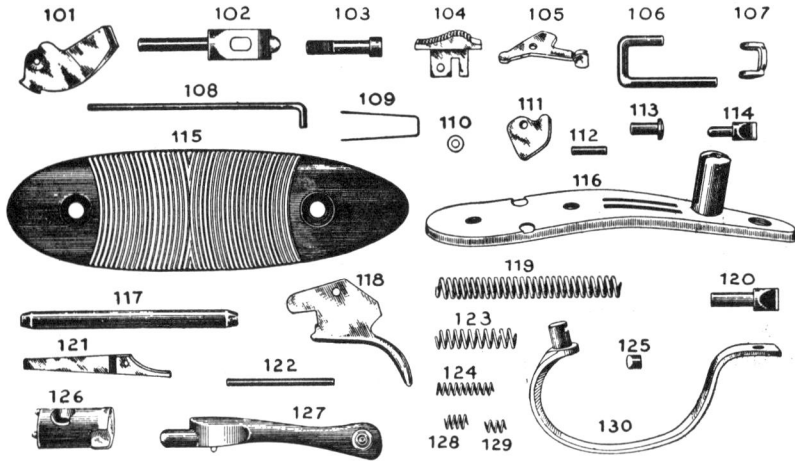

Parts for Lefever Double Guns Numbered Over 100,000

Number		Price
101	Hammer	$1.00
102	Forend Fastener Bolt	1.00
103	Forend Fastener Screw	.25
104	Safety Button	.75
105	Safet. Lever	.50
106	Trip	.25
107	Trigger Bridge	.50
108	Safety Rod	.25
109	Trigger Spring	.25
118	Trigger (front or rear)	1.00
110	Trigger Washer	$.25
111	Cocking Cam	.50
112	Trigger Pin	.25
113	Bolt Spring Cap	.25
114	Main Spring Cap	.25
115	Butt Plate	1.25
116	Trigger Plate	2.00
117	Cocking Rod	.25
119	Main Spring	$.50
120	Safety Post	.75
121	Sear (right or left)	.50
122	Sear or Hammer Pin	.25
123	Forend Spring	.50
124	Trip Spring	.50
125	Safety Lever Catch	.25
126	Top Lever Post	1.00
127	Top Lever	2.00
128	Trigger Spring	.25
129	Safety Spring	.25
130	Trigger Guard	1.50

Extra barrels cost ½ the price of the gun. Entire gun needed for about 3 weeks.
Cleaning and overhauling locks, $4.00; send stock and frame.
Rebrowning barrels, $4.00; send barrels only. Changing drop, $5.00; send entire gun.
Reboring barrels for pattern:—One barrel, $2.50; two barrels, $5.00; send barrels only.
Polishing out barrels and removing pits:— One barrel, $2.50; two barrels, $5.00; send barrels only.
Soft rubber recoil pad fitted, $3.00; not fitted, $2.25.
Ivory sights, $.55 each.
Removing dents from barrels:—$2.50 per barrel; send barrels only.
Refinishing and recheckering stock, $3.00; forend, $1.50.
Restocking—Send all except barrels and forearm. Nitro Special, double $8.50. Models 4 double trap, 5A or 6A $10.00.
Refinishing frame, forend iron, trigger guard, trigger, top lever and safety button, $7.50.
Single trigger can only be fitted to Lefever doubles numbered above 100,000. Stock and frame needed. Price, $6.00.

Note—Order parts by number and give number of gun. Send old part if possible.

In replacing parts marked thus (*) it will be necessary to send gun to us.

INSTRUCTIONS: In ordering parts always give name and number listed in catalog, also make, model, caliber and serial number of gun.

PAYMENTS: Parts will be sent only on advance payment. Parts cannot be returned for credit. A service charge of 25c must be added to every order under $1.00 to cover cost of handling. Do not forget to include postage.

A NEW GUN CARRIES A FACTORY GUARANTEE

L. C. SMITH & FULTON SHOTGUN PARTS

L. C. SMITH HAMMERLESS

Name	No.	Price	Name	No.	Price	Name	No.	Price	Name	No.	Price
Bolt	56R	$1.35	Extractor, Complete...	7-8R	$0.90	Kicker—Ejector, rt. or lt.	12E	$1.90	Selective Button—O. T.	148O	$1.75
Top Lever Spring	—	1.00	Firing Pin	67R	.35	Kicker Spring—Ej.	124E	.25	Sight—Brass	71R	.25
Bridle—rt. or lt.	38R	.80	Firing Pin Bushing and Screw	63R	.60	Leaf—Ejector, rt. or lt.	23R	.75	Swivels—per pair	85R	2.50
Butt Plate	54R	1.00	Fore-end Spring	32R	.90	Leaf Spring—Ejector	125E	.25	Top Lever and Screw	14R	2.50
Cocking Plate and Screw	39R	.35	Fore-end Spring Holder	40R	.25	Lifter—rt. or lt.	24R	.65	Trigger—rt. or lt.	6R	1.25
Cocking Rod	11R	1.60	Grip Cap	55R	.30	Main Spring	43R	1.10	Trigger Spring	49R	.25
Coupler and Screw	21R	1.50	Guard—one hole	5R	1.75	Safety Button	44-45R	.90	Trigger Plate and Bridge	4R	2.65
Cylinder Joint Check—Old	XR	1.75	Guard—two holes	5cR	1.75	Safety Link and Pins	42R	.75	Trip	69R	.25
Dog's Head	165R	.55	Guard—Straight Grip	5aR	1.90	Safety Push Rod	46R	.25	Trip Spring	123R	.25
Ejector	120R	.85	Guide Rod—Ejector	57E	.50	Safety Slide	X154R	.55	Any Screw	—	.25
Ejector Extractor and Pins—per pair	8R	2.50	Hammer and Pin—rt. or lt.	9R	1.25	Safety Spring	47R	.25	Any Pin not listed	—	.25
						Sear and Pin—rt. or lt.	13R	1.25			

L. C. SMITH HAMMER

Name	No.	Price	Name	No.	Price	Name	No.	Price	Name	No.	Price
Bolt	56R	1.35	Firing Pin	67H	.35	Sear and Pin—rt. or lt.	13H	1.60	Trigger Spring	49H	.25
Top Lever Spring	—	1.00	Fore-end Spring	32H	.90	Sear and Pin—Old	X13H	1.45	Trigger Plate	4H	2.40
Bridle—rt. or lt.	38R	.80	Fore-end Spring Holder	40H	.25	Sear Spring—Old	X33H	1.20	Trip	69R	.25
Butt Plate	54H	1.00	Guard—one hole	5R	1.75	Sight—Brass	71R	.25	Trip Spring	123R	.25
Coupler and Screw	21R	1.50	Guard—two holes	5cR	1.75	Stirrup—Old	X146H	.85	Tumbler—rt. or lt.	116H	1.35
Cylinder Joint Check	XR	1.75	Hammer—rt. or lt.	9H	1.20	Swivels—per pair	85R	2.50	Any Screw	—	.25
Ejector	120H	.85	Main Spring	43H	1.00	Top Lever and Screw	14H	2.30	Any Pin not listed	—	.25
Extractor, Complete	7-8R	.90	Main Spring—Old	X43H	1.00	Trigger—rt. or lt.	6R	1.25			

L. C. SMITH SINGLE-BARREL

Name	No.	Price	Name	No.	Price	Name	No.	Price	Name	No.	Price
Bolt	56S	1.50	Firing Pin	67S	.55	Kicker	12S	1.55	Sight—Brass	71R	.25
Bolt Spring	37S	.25	Fore-end Spring	32S	.90	Kicker Spring	124S	.25	Top Lever and Screw	14S	2.50
Bolt Spring Cap	66S	.25	Fore-end Spring Holder	40E	.25	Leaf	23S	1.10	Trigger	6S	1.25
Butt Plate	54R	1.00	Grip Cap	55R	.30	Leaf Spring	125E	.30	Trigger Plate	4S	3.20
Cocking Rod and Lifter	11S	2.00	Guard	5S	2.10	Main Spring	43S	.35	Trip	69S	.25
Coupler and Screw	21R	1.30	Guard—Straight Grip	5aS	2.10	Main Spring Cap	58S	.45	Trip Spring	123S	.25
Ejector Extractor and Pins	8S	1.75	Guide Rod	57S	.30	Sear	13S	2.10	Any Screw	—	.25
			Hammer	9S	3.30	Sear Spring	33S	.25	Any Pin not listed	—	.25

FULTON AND FULTON SPECIAL

Name	No.	Price	Name	No.	Price	Name	No.	Price	Name	No.	Price
Bolt	56F	1.00	Firing Pin	67F	.35	Safety Button	44-45F	.95	Top Lever and Screw	14F	2.25
Bolt Spring	37F	.25	Fore-end Spring	32F	.90	Safety Lever	151F	.65	Trigger—rt. or lt.	6F	1.00
Butt Plate	54F	1.00	Fore-end Spring Holder	40F	.25	Safety Push Rod	46F	.25	Trigger Plate and Bridge	4F	2.90
Cocking Hook	53F	1.20	Grip Cap	55F	.30	Safety Spring	47F	.25	Trip	69F	.55
Cocking Lever	20F	1.75	Guard	5R	1.75	Sear—rt. or lt.	13F	1.00	Trip Spring	123F	.25
Coupler	21F	.65	Hammer	9F	1.10	Sear Spring	33F	.25	Any Screw	—	.25
Ejector and Screw	120F	1.25	Main Spring	43F	.25	Sight—Brass	71R	.25	Any Pin not listed	—	.25
Extractor Complete	7-8F	.90	Main Spring Cap	58F	.25	Swivels—per pair	85R	2.50			

REPAIR PRICE LIST FOR L. C. SMITH AND FULTON GUNS

	Fulton and Hammer	Field No. 00	Field E No. 00E	Skeet	Skeet E	Ideal No. 0	Ideal E No. OE	Trap No. 1	Trap E No. 1E	Specialty No. 2-3	Spec. E No. 2-3E	Eagle E Pigeon E No. 4-E	Crown E No. 5-E	Monogram E Whitworth
*New or extra Set of Barrels	$17.00	$25.00	$34.00	$26.00	$35.00	$30.00	$40.50	$42.50	$54.75	$53.25	$66.50	$82.00	$100.00	$250.00
*New or extra Set of Ventilated Rib Barrels			30.00	54.00	63.00			77.50	89.75	89.25	102.50	124.00	144.00	290.00
*New or extra Set of Long Range Barrels		30.00	39.00	31.00	40.00	35.00	45.50	50.00	62.25	63.25	76.50	108.00	250.00	
*Restock (including Finishing)	11.00	13.00	13.00	13.50	13.50	15.75	16.75	22.00	22.00	27.50	27.50	34.50	51.50	75.00
Refinish and Rechecker	4.50	5.50	5.50	5.75	5.75	6.75	6.75	8.00	8.00	9.00	9.00	11.00	15.00	20.00
Rebrown Barrels	5.00	5.00	5.00	5.25	5.25	6.00	6.00	7.00	7.00	8.50	8.50	10.00	12.50	15.00
Fore-end Complete — not fitted	5.00	6.00		6.25		7.25		10.25		12.75				
*Ejector Fore-end Complete — fitted			12.00		12.50		14.25		19.50		23.50	25.00	29.00	45.00
*†Change from Non-Ejector to Ejector		17.00		17.50		19.00		22.50		25.00				
*Fore-end Wood — fitted	3.00	4.00	4.00	6.00	6.25	4.75	7.00	6.00	8.00	7.00	10.00	12.00	17.50	30.00
Safety Complete — fitted		6.00	6.00	6.00	6.00	6.00	6.00	7.00	7.00	8.00	8.00	9.25	11.00	
Trigger Plate — fitted and engraved	3.00	3.50	3.50	3.75	3.75	4.25	4.25	6.00	6.00	7.50	7.50			
Guard — fitted and engraved	3.00	3.00	3.00	3.25	3.25	3.75	3.75	5.00	5.00	6.50	6.50			
Top Lever — fitted and engraved	4.00	5.00	5.00	5.25	5.25	6.00	6.00	7.00	7.00	8.00	8.00			
Cut off Stock	2.50	2.50	2.50	2.50	2.50	3.00	3.00	3.00	3.00	3.50				

	Single-Barrel Trap Gun					Beaver-Tail Fore-end Gun			
	S Olympic	S Spec.	S Eagle	S Crown	S Mon.	B Spec.	B Eagle	B Crown	B. Mon. Whitworth
*New or extra Set of Barrels	$54.00	$65.00	$151.50	$151.50	$230.50	$76.00	$138.00	$138.00	$280.00
*New or extra Set of Ventilated Rib Barrels						105.00	180.00	180.00	320.00
*New or extra Set of Long Range Barrels						86.00	138.00	138.00	280.00
*Restock (including Finishing)	24.00	32.00	55.00	55.00	75.00	27.50	51.50	51.50	75.00
Refinish and Rechecker	7.50	10.00	18.00	18.00	22.00	10.00	18.00	18.00	22.00
Rebrown Barrels	6.75	9.00	14.00	14.00	17.00	8.50	12.50	12.50	15.00
Fore-end Complete — not fitted									
*Ejector Fore-end Complete — fitted	19.50	26.00	32.00	32.00	39.50	33.00	52.00	52.00	65.00
*†Change from Non-Ejector to Ejector									
*Fore-end Wood — fitted	7.50	10.00	28.50	28.50	41.00	21.00	27.00	27.00	48.00
Safety Complete — fitted						7.00			
Trigger Plate — fitted and engraved		6.50	8.75				7.50		
Guard — fitted and engraved		5.75	7.50				6.50		
Top Lever — fitted and engraved									
Cut off Stock		3.00					3.50		

Stocks of unusual size — extreme drop, Monte Carlo, Cheek Pieces, etc. $7.50 Net and up extra.
* Must have complete gun.
† Very old guns (about twenty years) with Cylinder Joint Check Roll in lug cannot be changed from Non-Ejector to Ejector

THESE PRICES ARE THE SAME FOR ALL GRADES OF GUNS

Bore Barrels — each	$2.50	SELECTIVE		Brass Sights — fitted — each		$0.35
Polish Barrels — each	2.00	HUNTER ONE-TRIGGER — fitted	$25.00	Grip Cap — fitted		.35
Chamber Barrels	3.00	NON-SELECTIVE		Ebony Tip — fitted		2.00
Cut off Barrels. (This will remove choke)	2.50	HUNTER ONE-TRIGGER — fitted	15.00	Target Gun		3.00
Recaseharden Frame and Parts	9.00	Any standard make Recoil Pad — fitted	5.00	Sling Strap Eyes — fitted — per set		1.00
Blue Guard and Parts	3.00	Butt Plate — fitted	2.75	Sling Straps — each		1.00
Remove Dents	2.50	Lyman Sights — fitted — each — net	.75	Cleaning, overhauling Locks and fitting small parts charged for according to the time required.		
If Barrels are rebrowned, extra charge necessary.		Marble Sights — fitted — each — net	1.00			
		Bradley Sights — fitted — each — net	1.50			

ALL SHIPMENTS ARE INSURED

BROWNING AUTO LOADING SHOTGUN PARTS

STATE GAUGE AND SERIAL NUMBER WHEN ORDERING

No.	Part	Price
A-1	Action spring	$0.25
A-2	Action spring follower	.25
A-3	Action spring plug and pin	.25
A-4	Action spring tube	.25
A-6	Barrel extension	4.00
A-7	Breech bolt	4.00
A-8	Butt plate	1.00
A-9	Butt plate screws, each	.25
A-10	Butt stock complete (Includes No. 8 and two screws No. 9)*	9.75
A-11	Butt stock swivel	.30
A-12	Carrier Assembled (Includes No. 13-14-15-16-17)	2.55
A-13	Carrier	2.00
A-14	Carrier dog	.40
A-15	Carrier dog follower	.25
A-16	Carrier dog pin	.25
A-17	Carrier dog spring	.25
A-18	Carrier latch assembled	1.00
A-19	Carrier latch button	.25
A-20	Carrier screws, each	.25
A-21	Carrier spring	.25
A-22	Carrier spring rivet	.25
A-23	Cartridge stop	.60
A-24	Cartridge stop spring	.25
A-25	Ejector	.25
A-26	Ejector rivet	.25
A-27	Extractor, left hand	.25
A-28	Extractor pin, left hand	.25
A-29	Extractor spring, left hand	.25
A-30	Extractor, right hand	.25
A-31	Extractor pin, right hand	.25
A-32	Extractor spring, right hand	.25
A-33	Firing pin	.60
A-34	Firing pin stop pin	.25
A-35	Forearm Standard Type (Specify 3- or 5-Shot)	3.80
A-35a	Forearm, Beavertail Type (5-Shot supplied unless otherwise Specified)	7.75
A-36	Friction piece bronze	.55
A-37	Friction ring	.25
A-38	Friction spring	.25
A-39	Hammer assembled (Includes No. 40-41-42-43)	.95
A-40	Hammer	.85
A-41	Hammer pin	.25
A-42	Hammer roll	.25
A-43	Hammer roll pin	.25
A-44	Link	1.50
A-45	Link pin	.25
A-46	Locking block	1.25
A-47	Locking block latch	.40
A-48	Locking block latch pin	.25
A-49	Locking block latch spring	.25
A-50	Lock screw	.25
A-51	Magazine cap without swivel	.75
A-52	Magazine cap with swivel	.90
A-53	Magazine cut-off	.60
A-54	Magazine cut-off spring	.25
A-55	Magazine cut-off spring screw	.25
A-56	Magazine follower	.25
A-57	Magazine spring	.25
A-58	Magazine spring retainer (5-Shot)	.25
A-58a	Magazine spring retainer shell eliminator (3-Shot)	.75
A-59	Magazine tube (Specify 3- or 5-Shot)	1.50
A-60	Mainspring	.60
A-61	Mainspring screw	.25
A-62	Operating slide	1.25
A-63	Receiver (Standard Grade 1)	16.00
A-64	Recoil spring	.75

No.	Part	Price
A-65	Safety	$.60
A-66	Safety lever	.25
A-67	Safety lever pin	.25
A-68	Safety spring	.25
A-69	Safety sear	.40
A-70	Safety sear follower	.25
A-71	Safety sear spring	.25
A-72	Screw for No. 18-23 or 53	.25
A-73	Sight base	$.85
A-74	Sight bead for plain barrel	.25
A-75	Sight bead for rib barrel	.25
A-76	Sling strap	1.75
A-77	Tang screw for pistol grip stock	.25
A-78	Tang screw for straight grip stock	.25
A-79	Trigger	$.80
A-80	Trigger pin	.25
A-81	Trigger spring	.25
A-82	Trigger plate	4.00
A-83	Trigger plate screw — front	.25
A-84	Trigger plate screw — rear	.25

INSTRUCTIONS: In ordering parts always give name and number listed in catalog, also make, model, caliber and serial number of gun.

PAYMENTS: Parts will be sent only on advance payment. Parts cannot be returned for credit. A service charge of 25c must be added to every order under $1.00 to cover cost of handling. Do not forget to include postage.

BE SURE AND SPECIFY GAUGE

FOX SHOTGUN PARTS

STERLINGWORTH

PRICES OF PARTS FOR FOX GUNS

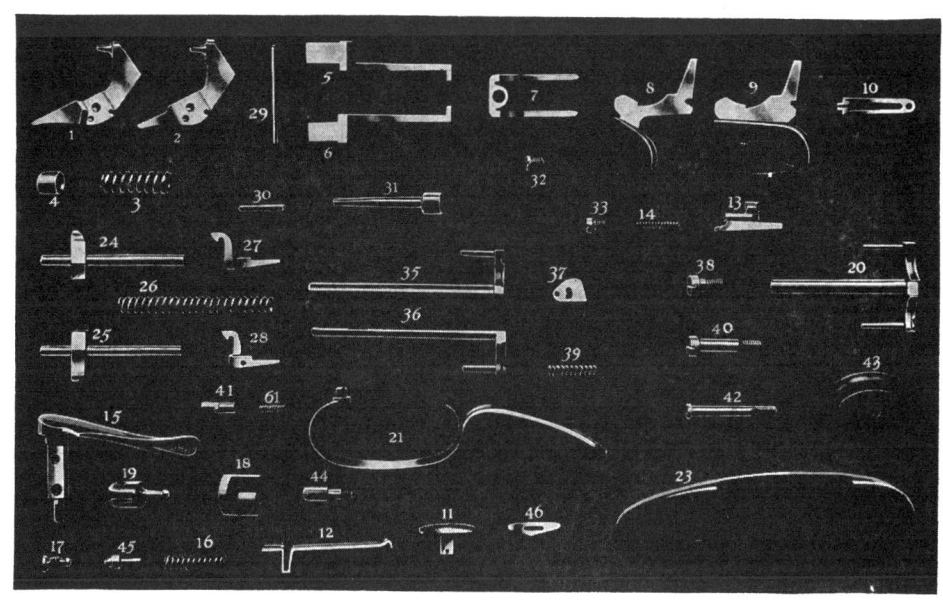

No.	Part	Price
1	Hammer, R.	$1.50
2	Hammer, L.	1.50
3	Mainspring	.65
4	Mainspring Follower	.25
5	Sear, R.	.75
6	Sear, L.	.75
7	Sear Spring	.40
8	Trigger, R.	.75
9	Trigger, L.	.75
10	Trigger Spring	.25
11	Safety Slide	.65
12	Safety Spring	.25
13	Cocking Slide	.75
14	Cocking Slide Spring	.25
15	Top Lever	1.75
16	Top Lever Spring	.50
17	Top Lever Ball Screw	.25
18	Bolt	1.25
19	Yoke	.70
20	Extractor	1.50
21	Trigger Guard	1.50
23	Butt Plate	.75
24	Ejector Hammer, R.	.75
25	Ejector Hammer, L.	.75
26	Ejector Spring	.50
27	Ejector Sear, L.	.75
28	Ejector Sear, R.	.75
29	Hammer and Sear Pin	.25
30	Ejector Sear Pin	.25
31	Ejector Mainspring Follower	.50
32	Sear Spring Screw	.25
33	Cocking Slide Screw	.25
35	Ejector Extractor, R.	.75
36	Ejector Extractor, L.	.75
37	Ejector Forend Latch	.25
38	Trigger Plate Screw	.25
39	Ejector Forend Latch Spring	.25
40	Front Tang Screw	.25
41	Trip	.25
42	Rear Tang Screw	.25
43	Grip Cap	$.25
44	Yoke Screw	.25
45	Top Lever Spring Follower	.25
46	Safety Tension Spring	.25
61	Trip Spring	.25
	Any other Spring, Pin or Screw in the gun	.25

REPAIRS AND REFINISHING

	STERLING-WORTH	STERLING-WORTH EJECTOR	A OR SP GRADE	AE OR SPE GRADE	HE GRADE	CE GRADE	XE GRADE	DE GRADE
Fitting New Forend, complete	$5.50	$15.00	$7.00	$17.00	$17.00	$22.00	$25.00	$30.00
" " " Wood only	3.50	3.50	3.75	3.75	3.75	5.00	6.50	9.00
Fitting Extra set barrels and new forend	21.50	30.00	30.00	36.50	37.50	58.00	100.00	150.00
Fitting new set of barrels when old forend is used	17.50	20.00	25.00	28.00	29.00	42.00	80.00	130.00
Restocking	12.00	12.00	15.00	15.00	15.00	25.00	35.00	50.00
Cutting off Stock	2.20	2.20	2.20	2.20	2.20	4.50	6.00	7.00
Refinished stock and forend	5.00	5.00	6.00	6.00	6.00	8.00	10.00	11.00
Changing drop 3/8" either way	4.75	4.75	6.00	6.00	6.00	7.00	8.50	10.00
Putting cast-off in stock	3.50	3.50	5.00	5.00	5.00	7.00	8.00	9.00
Re-casehardening frame and overhauling locks	10.00	10.00	11.00	11.00	11.00	13.00	15.00	17.00
Overhauling lock mechanism	5.00	5.00	5.00	5.00	5.00	8.00	10.00	12.00
Rebrowning barrels	4.00	4.00	4.00	4.00	4.00	6.00	7.00	9.00
Fitting Automatic Ejector to non-ejector gun	18.00		20.00					
Removing dents from barrels and rebrowning	8.00	8.00	8.00	8.00	8.00	9.00	10.00	12.00

	ANY GRADE
Fitting selective single trigger to any Fox Gun, old or new	$21.00
Removing dents without rebrowning	2.50

Note.— If the dent is sharp or deep it is usually necessary to rebrown.

Cutting off barrels	2.00
Reboring one barrel only	2.50
" both barrels	5.00
Repolishing barrels	5.00
Fitting Rubber Butt Plate	2.50
Extra for cast off stock	5.00

	ANY GRADE
Extra for Monte Carlo stock	$7.50
Fitting Recoil Pad	3.50
" Lyman or Marble's Sights, per pair	1.10
" and Engraving Gold Plate	7.00
" " " German Silver Plate	5.00
Engraving Monogram on trigger guard	2.50
Fitting Swivels	2.00
" Sling Strap and Swivels	3.50
" Safety to "No Safe" Gun	4.00

Note.— Old forend can only be used if old barrels are discarded or destroyed, as one forend cannot be made to fit two sets of barrels.

New or extra sets of barrels must be especially fitted to each individual gun. This requires hand word by expert gunsmiths. Such work requires four to five weeks for delivery.

The fitting of new stocks to old guns is carefully done by experts. A fine finish is the result of many operations and usually requires several weeks' time.

If new stocks or barrels are to be fitted, it is necessary that you send us the complete frame and action.

INSTRUCTIONS: In ordering parts always give name and number listed in catalog, also make, model, caliber and serial number of gun.

PAYMENTS: Parts will be sent only on advance payment. Parts cannot be returned for credit. A service charge of 25c must be added to every order under $1.00 to cover cost of handling. Do not forget to include postage.

SEE PAGE 8 "HOW TO ORDER"

454 STOEGER ARMS CORPORATION, 507 FIFTH AVENUE, NEW YORK, N. Y.

MARLIN SHOTGUN PARTS

MARLIN Models 93, 1894, 1895

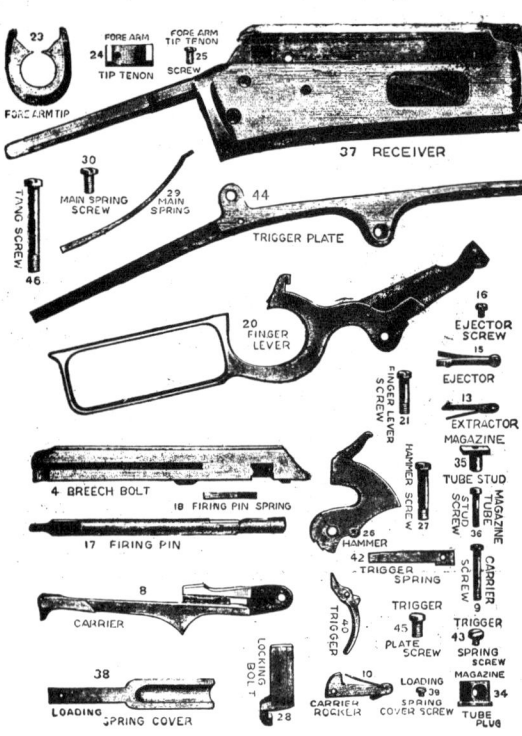

MARLIN Models 28, 31, 43 and 44

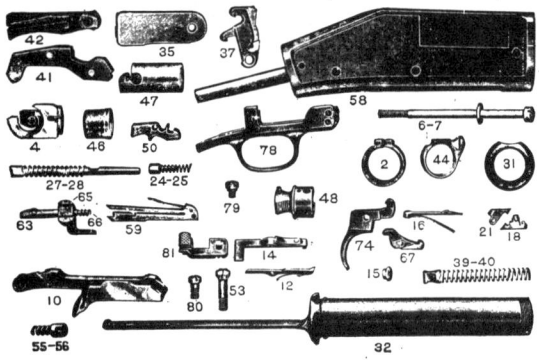

MODEL 31—16 AND 20 GAUGES

Action Rod (or Self-Starter in receiver shank)	$.40
Action Spring	.25
Action Spring Rod	.40
Action Spring Rod Bushing	.30
Action Spring Rod Bushing Pin	.25
Guard Plate Retaining Pin	.25
Trigger Plate Screw (left side, front)	.30
Trigger Plate Screw (left side, rear; right side, front)	.30
Trigger Plate Screw (bottom)	.30

MODELS 1893—1894—1895—410

Barrel 22" or 26", Mod. 410 only	$10.30
Barrel, Carbine, 20", Grade "B", Mod. 1894	7.00
Barrel, Carbine, 20", Smokls. Steel, Mod. 1893	9.50
Barrel, Round Rifle, 26", Grade "B", Mod. 1894	7.80
Barrel, Round Rifle, 26", Smokls. Steel, Mod. 1893	10.30
Barrel, Oct. or ½ Oct. Rifle, 26", Grade "B", Mod. 1893	10.00
Barrel, Oct. or ½ Oct. Rifle, 26", Smokls. Steel, Mod. 1893	12.50
Breech Bolt	3.75
Buttstock	3.00
Buttplate	1.00
Buttplate Screws (2), each	.25
Carrier	3.00
Carrier Screw	.30
Carrier Rocker	.90
Carrier Rocker Pin	.25
Carrier Rocker Spring	.25
Extractor	.60
Extractor Pin	.25
Ejector	.60
Firing Pin (2 pieces)	1.20
(a) Long Firing Pin	.80
(b) Short Firing Pin	.40
Firing Pin Spring	.25
Firing Pin Pin	.25
Finger Lever (with Plunger)	3.00
Finger Lever Screw	.30
Forearm	1.50
Forearm Tip	1.20
Forearm Tip Tenon	$.70
Forearm Tip Tenon Screw	.25
Hammer	1.20
Hammer Screw	.30
Locking Bolt	1.50
Mainspring	.70
Mainspring Screw	.25
Magazine Tube	2.40
Magazine Tube Spring	.60
Magazine Tube Spring Follower	.40
Magazine Tube Plug	.50
Magazine Tube Stud	.80
Magazine Tube Stud Screw	.30
Receiver	11.25
Loading Spring Cover	1.00
Loading Spring Cover Screw	.25
Trigger	.90
Trigger Pin	.25
Trigger Spring	.40
Trigger Spring Screw	.25
Trigger Plate	3.00
Trigger Plate Screw	.30
Trigger Plate Support Screw	.30
Tang Screw	.30
Dummy Screws (to fill Sight Screw Holes in tang or in top of Receiver), each	.25
Front Band for Carbines	1.80
Front Band Screw for Carbine	.30
Rear Band for Carbine	1.90
Rear Band Screw for Carbine	.30
Sling Ring and Staple for Carbine	.80
Stock Swivel and Screw	.80
Tip Swivel	.80

MODELS 28—31—43—44—53—63

No.	Part	Price
	Barrel, Special Rolled Steel, matted	16.50
2	Barrel Lock Nut	1.80
	Barrel Lock-Nut Screw	.25
4	Breech Block	3.75
	Buttstock, Grade "A"	4.50
6	Buttstock Bolt	.50
7	Buttstock Bolt Washers, each style	.25
	Buttplate	1.70
	Buttplate Screws (2) each	.25
10	Carrier	3.50
	Carrier Screw	.30
12	Cartridge Cut-Off	.80
	Cartridge Cut-Off Screw	.30
14	Cartridge Release	.80
15	Cartridge Release Button	.40
16	Ejector complete	.80
	Ejector Spring only	.25
	Ejector Retaining Screw	.30
18	Extractor (left side)	.80
	Extractor (left side) Spring	.25
	Extractor (left side) Pin	.25
21	Extractor (right side)	.80
	Extractor (right side) Spring	.25
	Extractor (right side) Pin	.25
24	Firing Pin (front)	.50
25	Firing Pin (front) Spring	.25
27	Firing Pin (rear)	1.00
28	Firing Pin (rear) Spring	.30
	Firing Pin (rear) Pin	.25
31	Foreend, Grade "A"	2.00
	Foreend Cap Nut	1.00
32	Foreend Slide and Tube	4.50
	Foreend Slide Spring	.25
	Foreend Slide Spring Rivet	.25
35	Guard Plate	1.50
	Guard Plate Screw	.25
37	Hammer	1.60
	Hammer Screw	.30
39	Hammer Spring (spiral)	.30
40	Hammer Spring Rod	.60
41	Link	2.00
42	Locking Bolt	2.25
	Magazine Tube	2.60
44	Magazine Tube Band (with foreend slide spring and rivet)	2.00
	Magazine Tube Spring	.80
46	Magazine Tube Spring Follower	1.00
47	Magazine Tube Plug (inside)	1.20
48	Magazine Tube Plug (outside)	1.50
	Magazine Tube Plug Screws (2), each	.25
50	Magazine Tube Plug Latch	1.50
	Magazine Tube Plug Latch Spring	.25
	Magazine Tube Plug Latch Pin	.25
53	Magazine Tube Stud Screw	.30
	Magazine Tube Stud Set Screw	.25
55	Magazine Tube Catch	.40
56	Magazine Tube Catch Spring	.30
	Magazine Tube Catch Screw	.25
58	Receiver with Sideplate	16.50
59	Safety Latch with Spring	1.00
	Safety Latch Pivot Pin	.25
	Safety Latch Stop Pin	.25
	Safety Latch Spring	.25
63	Safety Push Pin	.40
	Safety Push Pin Screw	.25
65	Safety Unlocking Block	1.00
66	Safety Push Pin Spring	.25
67	Sear	1.00
	Sear Spring	.25
	Sear Screw	.30
	Sight	.40
	Side plate	3.25
	Sideplate Screw (front)	.30
	Sideplate Screw (rear)	.30
74	Trigger	1.00
	Trigger Spring	.30
	Trigger Spring Screw	.30
	Trigger Pin	.25
78	Trigger Plate	3.40
79	Trigger Plate Screw (left side front)	.30
80	Trigger Plate Screw (left side, rear; and right side front and rear)	.30
81	Trigger and Hammer Safety	1.20
	Trigger Safety Spring	.50
	Trigger Safety Spring Screw	.30

MODEL 31—20 GAUGE ONLY

Carrier Cartridge Lifter	.80
Carrier Cartridge Lifter Spring	.25
Carrier Cartridge Lifter Pin	.25
Hammer Pin	.40
Safety Slide	.80
Safety Slide Pin	.25
Safety Latch only	.80
Safety Latch Pivot Pin	.25
Safety Latch Spring (spiral)	.25
Safety Latch Spring Rod	.25
Safety Recoil Block	1.00
Safety Recoil Block Pin	.25

In replacing parts marked thus (*) it will be necessary to send gun to us.

INSTRUCTIONS: In ordering parts always give name and number listed in catalog, also make, model, caliber and serial number of gun.

PAYMENTS: Parts will be sent only on advance payment. Parts cannot be returned for credit. A service charge of 25c must be added to every order under $1.00 to cover cost of handling. Do not forget to include postage.

PLEASE TELL OTHERS ABOUT STOEGER'S CATALOG

MARLIN RIFLE PARTS
MODEL 1898-19-19G-19N-19S-17-21-26-49

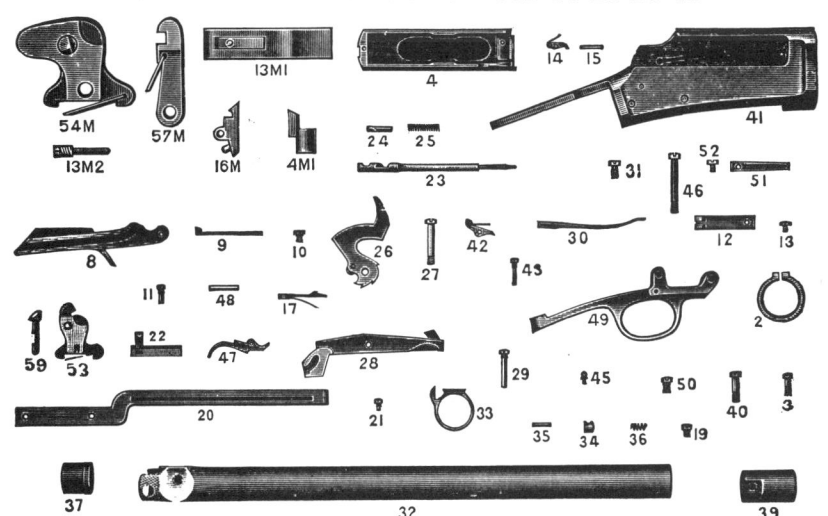

Number		Price
21M	Foreend Slide Screw in Band...	.20
22M	Foreend Slide Stop............	1.40
23M	Firing Pin....................	1.00
24M	Firing Pin Pin................	.25
25M	Firing Pin Spring.............	.30
26M	Hammer........................	1.60
27M	Hammer Screw..................	.30
28M	Locking Bolt..................	3.00
28M1	Locking Bolt Catch...........	.40
28M2	Locking Bolt Catch Spring.....	.30
29M	Locking Bolt Pin..............	.30
29M1	Locking Bolt Pin Screw.......	.25
30M	Mainspring....................	.80
31M	Mainspring Screw..............	.25
32M	Magazine Tube.................	3.00
33M	Magazine Tube Bank............	2.00
34M	Magazine Tube Catch...........	.40
35M	Magazine Tube Catch Pin.......	.25
36M	Magazine Tube Catch Spring....	.25
37M	Magazine Tube Follower........	1.00
38M	Magazine Tube Spring..........	.80
39M	Magazine Tube Plug............	1.50
40M	Magazine Tube Plug Screw......	.25
40M1	Magazine Tube Support Model 17-26..........	2.00
40M2	Magazine Tube Support Screw Model 17-26	.25
40M3	Magazine Tube Supporting Binding Screw M/17-26	.30
41M	Receiver......................	12.00
42M	Sear...........................	1.00
43M	Sear Screw....................	.30
44M	Sear Spring...................	.25
45M	Sight, Front..................	.40
46M	Tang Screw....................	.30
47M	Trigger.......................	1.00
48M	Trigger Pin...................	.25
49M	Trigger Plate or Guard........	3.50
50M	Trigger Plate Screws (2)..each	.30
51M	Trigger Spring................	.30
52M	Trigger Spring Screw..........	.30
53M	Recoil Safety Block (Old Style) Model 1898	1.80
54M	Recoil Block..................	1.80
55M	Recoil Safety Block Screw.....	.30
56M	Recoil Safety Block Spring....	.30
57M	Recoil Safety Hook............	.60
58M	Recoil Safety Hook Spring.....	.30
59M	Recoil Safety Push Pin........	.40
60M	Recoil Safety Push Pin Screw..	.25
61M	Recoil Safety Catch...........	.50
62M	Recoil Safety Catch Spring....	.30
63M	Recoil Safety Catch Pin.......	.25

Number		Price
1M	Barrel, Model 17 or Model 26..	$12.50
2M	Barrel Lock Nut...............	1.80
4M	Breech Bolt...................	4.50
4M1	Breech Bolt Spur.............	1.20
4M3	Breech Bolt Spur Screw or Spring, each	.30
5M	Buttstock, Grade "A"..........	4.50
6M	Buttplate.....................	1.70
8M	Carrier.......................	3.50
9M	Carrier Cartridge Stop........	.90
10M	Carrier Cartridge Stop Screw..	.25
11M	Carrier Screw.................	.30
12M	Cartridge Stop in Frame, Mod. 1898	.80
13M	Cartridge Stop in Frame Screw..	.30
13M1	Cartridge Stop in Frame......	.80
13M3	Cartridge Stop in Frame Spring.	.30
14M	Extractor (right side)........	.80
15M	Extractor (right side) Pin.....	.25
15M1	Extractor (right side) Spring..	.25
16M	Extractor (left side).........	.80
16M1	Extractor (left side) Pin....	.25
16M2	Extractor (left side) Spring..	.25
17M	Ejector.......................	.80
18M	Foreend, Grade "A"............	2.00
19M	Foreend Screws (2)......each	.30
19M1	Foreend Screw Escutcheons (2) each	.30
20M	Foreend Slide.................	2.40

MODEL 24-30-30G-42

Number		Price
24T	Firing Pin....................	1.00
25T	Firing Pin Pin................	.25
26T	Firing Pin Spring.............	.30
27T	Foreend, Grade "A"............	2.00
28T	Foreend Retaining Pins (2) ..each	.25
29T	Foreend Cap Nut...............	1.00
30T	Foreend Slide and Tube........	4.50
31T	Foreend Slide Spring..........	.25
32T	Foreend Slide Spring Rivet....	.25
33T	Hammer (with roller and pin)..	1.60
34T	Hammer Screw..................	.25
35T	Locking Bolt..................	3.00
36T	Locking Bolt Pin..............	.30
37T	Locking Bolt Pin Screw.......	.25
38T	Locking Bolt Catch............	.40
39T	Locking Bolt Catch Spring.....	.30
40T	Locking Bolt Catch Pin.......	.25
41T	Magazine Tube.................	2.60
42T	Magazine Tube Band (with Foreend Slide Spring and Rivet)..	2.00
43T	Magazine Tube Spring..........	.80
44T	Magazine Tube Spring Follower..	1.00
45T	Magazine Tube Plug (outside)..	1.50
46T	Magazine Tube Plug Screws (2) each	.25
47T	Magazine Tube Plug Latch......	1.50
48T	Magazine Tube Plug Latch Spring	.25
49T	Magazine Tube Plug Latch Pin..	.25
50T	Magazine Tube Plug (inside)...	1.20
51T	Magazine Tube Stud Screw......	.30
51T1	Magazine Tube Stud Set Screw...	.25
52T	Magazine Tube Catch...........	.40
53T	Magazine Tube Catch Spring....	.30
54T	Magazine Tube Catch Screw.....	.25
55T	Mainspring....................	.80
56T	Mainspring Screw..............	.25
57T	Receiver......................	12.00
58T	Recoil Safety Block with Spring.	1.80
59T	Recoil Safety Block Spring....	.30
60T	Recoil Safety Block Screw.....	.30
61T	Recoil Safety Block Plunger...	.50
62T	Recoil Safety Block Plunger Spring	.30
63T	Recoil Safety Block Plunger Pin.	.25
64T	Recoil Safety Hook with Spring..	.60
66T	Recoil Safety Push Pin........	.40
68T	Sear with Sear Spring.........	1.00
73T	Trigger.......................	1.00
74T	Trigger Pin or Spring....each	.25
77T	Trigger Plate or Guard........	3.50

Number		Price
1T	Barrel........................	$16.50
2T	Barrel Lock Nut...............	1.80
3T	Barrel Lock Nut Screw.........	.25
4T	Breech Bolt...................	4.50
5T	Buttstock, Grade "A"..........	4.50
6T	Buttplate.....................	1.70
7T	Buttplate Screws (2)......each	.25
8T	Carrier.......................	3.50
9T	Carrier Screw.................	.30
10T	Carrier Cartridge Stop........	.90
11T	Carrier Cartridge Stop Screw..	.25
12T	Cartridge Stop in Frame.......	.80
13T	Cartridge Stop in Frame Screw...	.30
14T	Cartridge Stop in Frame Spring..	.30
15T	Cartridge Stop in Frame Spring Rivet	.25
16T	Ejector Complete..............	.80
17T	Ejector Spring................	.25
18T	Extractor (right side) with Spring	.80
19T	Extractor (right side) Pin....	.25
20T	Extractor (right side) Spring..	.25
21T	Extractor (left side).........	.80
22T	Extractor (left side) Pin.....	.25
23T	Extractor (left side) Spring..	.25

WHEN ORDERING PARTS, STATE MODEL AND SERIAL NUMBER OF GUN.

MARLIN RIFLE PARTS

MARLIN Model 1892

	Price		Price
Bbl. (Round), 24", .32 cal.	$7.80	Finger Lever Spring	$0.50
Bbl. (Oct'an), 24", .22 and .32 caliber	10.00	Finger Lever Spring Screw	.25
		Finger Lever Screw	.30
Breech Bolt	3.00	Firing Pin, .22 cal. .32 cal. R.F., .32 cal. C.F.	1.20
Buttstock	2.40	Forearm	1.50
Buttstock Plate	1.00	Forearm Tip	1.20
Buttstock P. Screws, 2, ea.	.25	Forearm Tip Tenon	.70
Carrier	2.00	Forearm Tip Tenon Screws, 2, ea.	.25
Carrier Rocker	.70	Hammer	1.20
Carrier Rocker Spring	.30	Hammer Screw	.30
Carrier Rocker Sp. Screw	.25	Magazine Cartridge Cut-off.	.80
Carrier Block Pin	.25	Mag. Cart. Cut-off Screw.	.25
Carrier Pivot Pin	.25	Magazine Tube (outside)	2.25
Cartridge Guide (.22 cal. only)	.30	Magazine Tube (inside)	2.25
Cartridge Guide Spring.	.50	Magazine Tube Latch	.60
Cartridge Guide Sp. Screw.	.25	Mag. Tube Latch Spring.	.30
Cartridge Stop (.22 cal. only)	.50	Magazine Latch Pin	.25
		Mag. Tube Plug (inside)	.50
Cartridge Stop Screw (.22 cal. only)	.25	Mag. Tube Plug (outside)	.50
		Magazine Tube Spring	.50
Dummy Screw (to fill Sight screw Hole in tang and top of Receiver) each	.25	Mag. Tube Spg. Follower.	.60
		Magazine Tube Stud	.50
		Magazine Tube Stud Screw.	.30
Ejector, .32 caliber	.60	Main Spring	.70
Ejector, .22 caliber old style (like .32 caliber)	.60	Main Spring Screw	.25
		Receiver	8.75
Ejector, .22 caliber new style, complete	2.00	Side Plate	2.25
13A. Ejector Base	1.20	Side Plate Screw	.40
13B. Ejector Wing	.60	Side Plate Screw Collar.	.25
13C. Ejector Spring	.30	Tang Screw	.30
Ejector Sc., 2, ea.	.25	Trigger	.90
Ejector Pin	.25	Trigger Pin	.25
Extractor	.60	Trigger Spring	.40
Finger Lever	2.25	Trigger Spring Screw	.25

MODELS 32-38

	Price		Price
Action Slide	$2.50	*BB. Retain. Plunger Spg.	$0.25
Action Slide Handle	2.00	Buttplate	1.60
Action Slide Hdle. Screw, 2, ea.	.30	Buttplate Screw (2), each.	.25
		Buttstock	2.40
Action Slide Handle Screw Escutcheons, 2, each	.30	Carrier	1.50
		Carrier Plunger (Lower)	.30
Barrel, Octagon	10.00	Carrier Plunger (Upper)	.30
Barrel Round	7.80	Carrier Plunger Pin	.25
Breech Bolt	5.00	Carrier Plunger Spring	.25
Breech Bolt Binding Screw	.25	Cartridge Cut-off	.50
BB. Bind. Screw Washer	.25	Cartridge Cut-off Screw	.25
Breech B. Locking Latch	.60	Ejector	.60
BB. Locking Latch Pin	.25	*Ejector Lever	.50
BB. Locking Latch Spring	.25	*Ejector Lever Screw	.25
*Breech B. Retain. Plunger	.30	*Ejector Lever Spring	.25

MARLIN Model 27

Number		Price
	Barrel, Octagon	$10.00
	Barrel, Round, .25 R.F.	7.80
2	Breech Bolt	3.00
	Buttstock	2.40
	Buttplate	1.50
	Buttplate Screws, 2, ea.	.25
7	Carrier	3.00
	Carrier Pivot Pin	.25
9	Cartridge Cut-off	.90
	Cartridge Cut-off Screw	.25
	Dummy Screws (4), ea.	.25
12	Ejector Base	1.20
	Ej. Base Screws, 2 ea.	.25
14	Ejector Wing	.60
	Ejector Pin	.25
16	Ejector Spring	.30
18	Extractor	.60
	Extractor Screw	.25
20	Firing Pin	1.20
21	Firing Pin Plunger	.40
22	F. P. Plunger Spring	.30
	Firing Pin Plunger Pin	.25
	Fore-end (Wood)	2.00
	Fore-end Screws, each (short or long)	.30
	Fore-end Screws Escutcheons (2), each	.30
27	Fore-end Slide (action bar) new style	2.00
	Fore-end Slide, old style (without Forearm Extension)	1.50
28	Hammer (with roller and pin)	1.20
	Hammer Roller	.40
	Hammer Roller Pin	.25
31	Hammer Stud	.30
	Hammer Stud Re. Screw.	.25
33	Locking Bolt	1.50
34	Locking Bolt Plunger	.40
35	Lkg. Bolt Plunger Spg.	.30

Number		Price
	Lkg. Bolt Plunger Screw	$0.25
38	Main Spring	.60
	Main Spring Screw	.25
	Magazine Tube (inside)	2.25
	Magazine Tube (outside)	2.25
	Magazine Spring	.40
43	Magazine Plug (inside)	.50
44	Magazine Plug (outside)	.50
45	Mag. Latch (with Spg.)	.60
46	Magazine Latch Spring	.30
	Magazine Latch Pin	.25
48	Magazine Follower	.60
	Magazine Follower Pin	.25
50	Magazine Tube Stud	.50
51	Mag. Tube Stud Screw.	.25
53	Receiver (left side)	6.25
54	Receiver (right side)	6.25
55	Safety Block	1.00
56	Safety Block Plunger	.40
58	Safety Block Plg. Spring	.30
	Safety Block Plg. Pin.	.25
	Safety Block Stud	.40
61	Safety Latch	.70
	Safety Latch Spring	.30
63	Safety Latch Button	.40
64	Sear	.60
65	Sear Spring	.25
66	Sear Screw	.30
68	Tang Screw	.30
68	Thumb Lever Complete	1.00
	Thumb Lever Screw	.60
	Thb. Lev. Screw Collar.	.25
	Thb. Lev. Retain. Screw	.25
73	Thumb Nut (left side)	.40
	Thb. Nut Pl., 2, each	.25
	Thb. Nut Pl. Spg., 2, ea.	.25
76	Trigger	.90
	Trigger Pin	.25
78	Trigger Spring	.40
	Trigger Spring Screw	.25

	Price		Price
*Ejector Lever Spring Pin	$0.25	Magazine Tube Stud	$0.50
Ejector Screw	.25	Magazine Tube Stud Screw	.25
*Ejector Spring (Round)	.25	Rear Sgt. (Rocky Mount.)	1.60
§Ejector Spring (Flat)	.25	Rear Sight Elevator	.40
Ejector Spring Pin	.25	Receiver	6.50
Extractor R. H.	.60	Sear	1.00
Extractor L. H.	.60	Sear Pin	.25
Extractor Pin L. H.	.25	Sear Release	.30
Extractor Pin R. H.	.25	Sear Spring	.25
Extractor Spring R. H.	.25	Sear Spring Pin	.25
§Ext. Screw R. H. & L. H.	.25	Take Down Cam Lever	.40
Extractor Spring L. H.	.25	T.D. Cam Lever Axis Pin.	.25
Firing Pin	1.00	Take Down Cam Lever Pin	.25
Firing Pin Retaining Pin.	.25	Take Down Latch	1.60
Front Sight (Ivory Bead)	1.00	Take Down Latch Button	1.00
Guard	6.00	T.D. Latch Button Pin.	.25
Hammer	1.60	Take Down Latch Screw.	.30
Hammer Pin	.25	T.D. Latch Screw Re. Pin.	.25
Hammer Spring	.30	Take Down Latch Spring	.25
Hammer Spring Rod	1.00	T.D. Latch Spring Stud	.40
Hammer Spring Rod Pin	.25	Tang Screw	.30
Hammer Spg. Rod Washer	.25	Trigger	1.00
Hammer Spg. R'd W'h Pin	.25	Trigger Pin	.25
Locking Bolt	1.20	Trigger Safety Bolt	.40
Magazine Tube (Inside)	2.25	Trigger Safety Bolt Pin	.25
Magazine Tube (Outside)	2.25	Trigger Safety Slide	1.60
Magazine Tube Latch	.60	Trig. Safety Slide Plunger	.25
Magazine Tube Latch Pin.	.25	Trig. Safe. S'de Pl'ger Spg.	.25
Mag. Tube Latch Spring.	.30	Trigger Spring	.25
Mag. Tube Plug (Inside)	.50	Model 38 Breech Bolt Complete	10.90
Mag. Tube Plug (Outside)	.50	*Model No. 38 only.	
Magazine Tube Spring	.50	§Model No. 32 only.	
Mag. Tube Spg. Follower.	.60		

Note—When ordering parts state whether rifle is marked on upper tang "Model 27" or "Model 27-S." When ordering foreend or foreend slide, state whether or not old foreend slide has extension on front end. (See Instructions, etc., at bottom of preceding page.)

SEE PAGE 8, "HOW TO ORDER"

MARLIN RIFLE PARTS

MODELS 1897 AND 39

Number		Price
	Barrel (Octagon), 24"	$10.00
3	Breech Bolt	3.00
	Buttstock	2.40
	Buttplate	1.00
	Buttplate Screws (2), each	.25
7	Carrier	2.00
8	Carrier Rocker	.70
9	Carrier Rocker Spring	.30
	Carrier Pivot Screw	.30
	Cartridge Guide Spring	.50
	Cartridge Guide Spring Screw	.25
	Dummy Screw (to fill Sight Screw Hole in tang and top of Receiver), each	.25
	Extractor	.60
13	Ejector complete, old style	.60
	Ejector complete, new style	2.00
13A.	Ejector Base	1.20
13B.	Ejector Wing	.60
13C.	Ejector Spring	.30
	Ejector Screws (2), each	.25
	Ejector Pin	.25
14	Firing Pin	1.20
15	Finger Lever	2.25
	Finger Lever Screw	.30
	Finger Lever Spring	.50
	Finger Lever Spring Screw	.30
	Cartridge Stop	.50
	Cartridge Stop Screw	.25
	Forearm	1.50
	Forearm Tip	$1.20
	Forearm Tip Tenon	.25
	Forearm Tip Tenon Screws (2), each	.25
25	Hammer	1.20
	Hammer Screw	.80
	Magazine Cartridge Cut-Off	.80
	Magazine Cartridge Cut-Off Screw	.25
	Magazine Tube (outside)	2.25
	Magazine Tube (inside)	2.25
	Magazine Tube Latch Spring	.30
	Magazine Tube Latch	.60
	Magazine Latch Pin	.25
	Magazine Tube Plug (inside)	.50
	Magazine Tube Plug (outside)	.50
	Magazine Tube Spring	.50
	Magazine Tube Spring Follower	.60
	Magazine Tube Stud	.50
	Magazine Tube Stud Screw	.30
	Mainspring	.70
	Mainspring Screw	.25
39	Receiver (left side)	6.25
40	Receiver (right side)	6.25
	Tang Screw	.30
	Thumbscrew	.40
	Thumbscrew Collar	.25
	Trigger	.90
	Trigger Pin	.25
	Trigger Spring	.40
	Trigger Spring Screw	.25

MODELS 20, 20-S, 20-A, 29, 37, 47

Number		Price
	Barrel, Round, Mod. No. 29	$7.80
	Barrel, Octagon, Mod. No. 20	10.00
2	Breech Bolt	3.00
	Buttstock	2.25
	Buttplate	1.50
	Buttplate Screws (2), each	.25
6	Carrier	3.00
	Carrier Friction Spring	.40
	Carrier Pin	.25
	Carrier Stop Pin	.25
9	Cartridge Cut-Off	.90
	Cartridge Cut-Off Screw	.25
11	Cartridge Guard Base	.70
	Cartridge Guard Base Screw	.25
13	Cartridge Guard Leaf	.80
	Cartridge Guard Leaf Spring	.30
	Cartridge Guard Leaf Spring Rivet	.25
	Cartridge Guard Hinge Pin	.25
17	Cartridge Guide Spring	.70
	Cartridge Guide Spring Screw	.25
	Dummy Screw (to fill Sight Screw Hole in Tang and Receiver Top), each	.25
20	Ejector Base	1.20
21	Ejector Wing	.60
	Ejector Screws (2), each	.25
	Ejector Pin	.25
	Ejector Spring	.30
25	Extractor (old style)	.60
	Extractor Screw	.25
27	Firing Pin, old style 20 and 20-S	1.10
28	Firing Pin Spring, old style	.30
	Firing Pin, new style 20-A	1.10
	Firing Pin Plunger	.40
	Firing Pin Plunger Spring	.30
	Firing Pin Plunger Pin	.25
	Forearm	2.00
	Forearm Screws (2), each, short or long	$0.30
	Forearm Screw Escutcheons (2), each	.30
32	Hammer	1.20
	Hammer Roller	.40
	Hammer Roller Pin	.25
35	Hammer Screw	.40
36	Handle Slide	1.50
37	Locking Bolt	1.50
38	Locking Bolt Plunger	.40
39	Locking Bolt Plunger Spring	.30
	Locking Bolt Plunger Screw	.25
41	Mainspring	.60
42	Mainspring Screw	.25
	Magazine Tube (inside)	2.25
	Magazine Tube (outside)	2.25
	Magazine Spring	.50
46	Magazine Plug (inside)	.50
47	Magazine Plug (outside)	.50
48	Magazine Latch	.60
	Magazine Latch Pin	.25
50	Magazine Latch Spring	.30
51	Magazine Follower	.60
	Magazine Follower Pin	.25
53	Magazine Tube Stud	.50
54	Magazine Tube Screw	.25
55	Receiver, Left Side	5.00
56	Receiver, Right Side	5.00
	Receiver Dowell Stud	.40
59	Trigger	.90
58	Tang Screw	.30
	Trigger Pin	.25
61	Trigger Spring	.40
62	Trigger Spring Screw	.25
	Thumb Screw	.40
	Thumb Screw Collar	.25

Note—When ordering parts state whether rifle is marked on upper tang "Model 20," "Model 20-S," or "Model 20-A" and whether full or half magazine.

MODELS 18 AND 25

Number		Price
	Barrel, Round	$7.50
2	Breech Bolt	3.00
	Buttstock	2.25
	Buttplate	1.50
	Buttplate Screws, 2, ea.	.25
6	Carrier	3.00
	Carrier Friction Spring	.40
	Carrier Pin	.25
	Carrier Stop Pin	.25
	Cartridge Cut-Off	.90
	Cartridge Cut-Off Screw	.25
	Cartridge Guard Base	.70
	Cartridge Guard Base Screw	.25
	Cartridge Guard Leaf Spring	.80
	Cart. Gd. Leaf Spg. Rivet	.30
	Cart. Guard Hinge Pin	.25
11	Cartridge Guide Spring	.70
12	Cart. Gd. Spg. Screw	$0.25
13	Ejector Base	1.20
14	Ejector Wing	.60
	Ejector Screws (2) each	.25
	Ejector Pin	.25
17	Ejector Spring	.30
18	Extractor	.60
	Extractor Screw	.25
20	Firing Pin, old style	1.10
21	F. P. Spring, old style	.30
	Firing Pin, new style, Mod. 25-S only	1.10
	Firing Pin Plunger, Mod. 25-S only	.40
	Firing Pin Plunger Spring, Mod. 25-S only	.30
	Firing Pin Plunger Pin, Mod. 25-S only	.25
	Forearm	1.60
	Forearm Screw, 2, each	.30
	Forearm Screw Escutcheons (2), each	$0.30
25	Hammer	1.20
	Hammer Roller	.40
	Hammer Roller Pin	.25
28	Hammer Screw	.40
29	Handle Slide	1.50
30	Locking Bolt	1.50
31	Locking Bolt Plunger	.40
32	Lock. Bolt Plunger Spg.	.30
	Lock. Bolt Plunger Pin	.25
34	Mainspring	.60
	Mainspring Screw	.25
	Magazine Tube (inside)	2.10
	Magazine Tube (outside)	2.10
	Magazine Spring	.40
39	Magazine Plug (inside)	.50
40	Magazine Plug (outside)	.50
42	Magazine Latch	.60
	Magazine Latch Pin	$0.25
	Magazine Latch Spring	.30
44	Magazine Follower	.60
	Magazine Follower Pin	.25
46	Magazine Tube Stud	.50
	Mag. Tube Stud Screw	.25
48	Receiver	7.50
49	Sideplate	1.80
	Sideplate Screw	.40
	Sideplate Screw Collar	.25
52	Tang Thumbscrew	.40
53	Trigger	.90
	Trigger Pin	.25
55	Trigger Spring	.40
	Trigger Spring Screw	.25

When ordering parts state whether rifle is marked on upper tang "Model 25" or "Model 25-S."

PARKER HAMMERLESS SHOTGUN PARTS

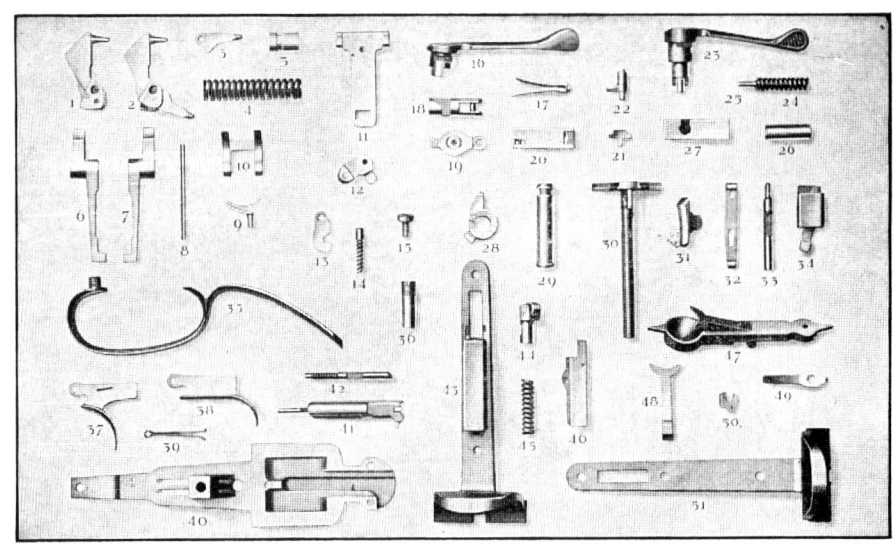

1	Left-hand Hammer	$1.50
2	Right-hand Hammer	1.50
3	Hammer Stirrup	.50
4	Main Spring	.40
5	Main Spring Plunger	.75
6	Left-hand Sear	1.50
7	Right-hand Sear	1.50
8	Sear Pin	.25
9	Sear Spring (Old Style)	.30
10	Sear Spring (Model 10)	.30
11	Cocking Slide	1.50
12	Cocking Crank	1.50
13	Cocking Hook	1.00
14	Cocking Hook Pin and Spring	.25
15	Cocking Hook Screw	.25
16	Top Lever (Old Style)	2.00
17	Top Lever Spring (Old Style)	1.00
18	Round, Top Bolt	.75
19	Bolt Lever, with Roll	1.00
20	Square Bolt	.75
21	Bolt Plate	.85
22	Trip, Spring and Pin	.35
23	Top Lever (Model 10)	2.50
24	Top Lever Spring (coiled) (Model 10)	.25
25	Top Lever Spring Plunger (Model 10)	.30
26	Top Lever Spring Shell (Model 10)	.30
27	Square Bolt (Model 10)	.85
28	Roll	1.25
29	Roll Pin	1.50
30	Extractor	2.00
31	Safety Slide	2.50
32	Safety Slide Spring	.25
33	Safety Pin	.25
34	Safety Lever and Jacket	1.00
35	Guard Bow (Blued only)	2.50
36	Bushing for Tang Screw	.25
37	Right-hand Trigger	1.50
38	Left-hand Trigger	1.50
39	Trigger Spring	.25
40	Trigger Plate (Machined only)	3.50
41	Unhooking Slide	1.50
42	Unhooking Pin and Spring	$0.25
43	Forend complete (Trojan Model)	5.00
44	Forend Plunger with Roll (Trojan Model)	.60
45	Forend Plunger Spring (Trojan Model)	.25
46	Forend Plunger Box (Trojan Model)	.50
47	Forend Lock complete	$4.00
48	Forend Lever	1.25
49	Forend Lever Spring	.25
50	Forend Tumbler	.50
51	Forend Iron Reg. Model (Machined only)	3.50

In replacing parts marked thus (*) it will be necessary to send gun to us.

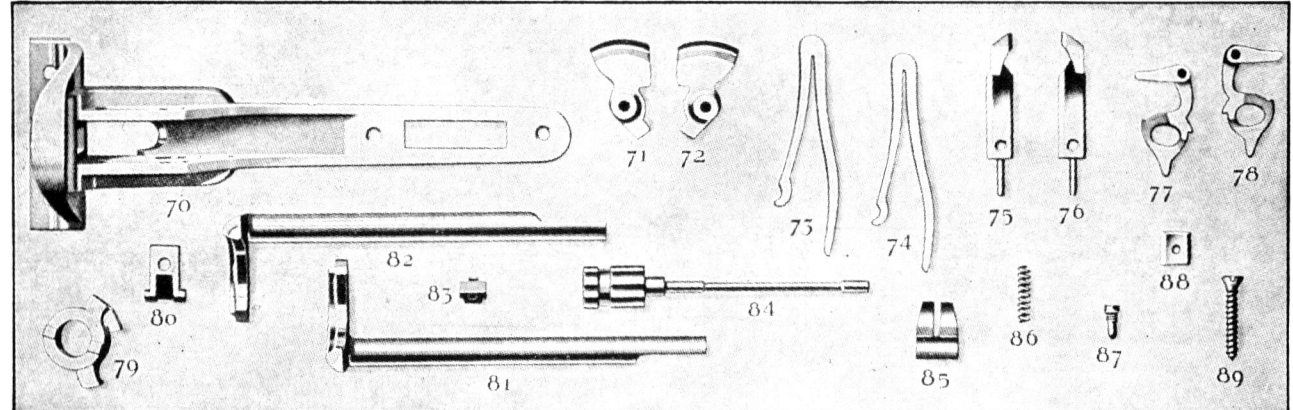

PARKER AUTOMATIC EJECTOR

70	Ejector Forend Iron (machined only)	$5.00
71	Right-hand Hammer	1.50
72	Left-hand Hammer	1.50
73	Right-hand Main Spring	1.00
74	Left-hand Main Spring	1.00
75	Right-hand Sear Slide	1.50
76	Left-hand Sear Slide	1.50
77	Right-hand Comb. Sear	1.50
78	Left-hand Comb. Sear	1.50
79	Joint Roll	1.25
80	Cocking Toggle	$1.00
81	Right-hand Ejector	2.00
82	Left-hand Ejector	2.00
83	Stop Plate for Sear Slide	.25
84	Ejector Plunger Pin & Main Spg. Plunger	1.00
85	Sear Spring	.25
86	Slide Spring	.25
87	Sear Slide Screw	.25
88	Extension Rib Stop Pl.	.25
89	Forend Wood Screw	.25

Net Prices for Fitting Automatic Ejectors to Finished Guns

Grade	Price
V. H.	$21.00
P. H.	21.00
G. H.	21.00
D. H.	24.00
C. H.	24.00
B. H.	25.00
A. H.	25.00

Cannot be applied to 8 gauge or Trojan grade.

Hard rubber butt plates, not fitted 1.00 net; fitted $2.25 Cushion recoil pads fitted to any grade of gun, $5.50 net each. Lyman white ivory sights fitted 75 cents net each.

GUN REPAIRS

BARRELS

Net Prices for Extra Barrels for Parker Guns, including New Forend

Grade	Price
A. 1. Special	$355.00
A. A. H. E.	293.50
A. H. E.	204.50
B. H. E.	159.00
C. H. E.	134.50
D. H. E.	100.00
D. H.	75.50
G. H. E.	75.50
G. H.	54.50
V. H. E.	65.50
V. H.	44.50
Trojan	34.50

Rebrowning Barrels, up to D. H. grade $8.25
Rebrowning Barrels, D. H. to A. A. H. gr. 9.25
Rebrowning Barrels, A. A. H. and A. 1 Special 10.00 & up
If necessary to remove dents previous to browning an extra charge will be made.
Reboring Barrel for patterning, per barrel 4.00
Removing Dents without rebrowning 2.50 up
Repolishing, per bbl. 2.50

STOCKS

Restocking Parker Guns

Grade	Price
A. 1 Special	$90.00
A. A. H. or A. A.	75.00
A. H. or A.	65.00
B. H. or B.	60.00
C. H. or C.	50.00
D. H. or D.	45.00
G. H. or G.	35.00
V. H.	30.00
Trojan	25.00

Cutting off Stock and refitting rubber butt plate 2.50 up
Redressing and rechecking stock and forend $7.50 up
Automatic Safety, fitted to old guns 5.00 up
Cleaning and repairing action and locks 3.50 up (Necessary new parts will be charged for.)
Cleaning and repairing Automatic Ejectors 3.50 up (Necessary new parts will be charged for.)
Recasehardening all iron parts 8.00 up (Includes cleaning and overhauling locks and action.)
Rebluing Trigger Guard and Butt Plate 1.00 ea.
Fitting Swivels to stock and barrel (include straps) 6.00

Fitting Non-Ejector Forends

Grade	Price
D. H. or D.	$15.00
G. H. or G.	11.00
P. H.	10.25
V. H.	9.85
Trojan	8.75

Parker Single Triggers

Grade	Price
V. H. to G. H. E. inc	$26.00
D. H. to C. H. E. inc	28.00
B. H. E. and A. H. E.	28.00
A. A. H. E.	37.00
A. 1 Special	46.00

SEND YOUR GUN TO STOEGER FOR EXPERT REPAIRING

WINCHESTER RIFLE PARTS
MODELS 94 AND 55 LEVER ACTION REPEATING RIFLES

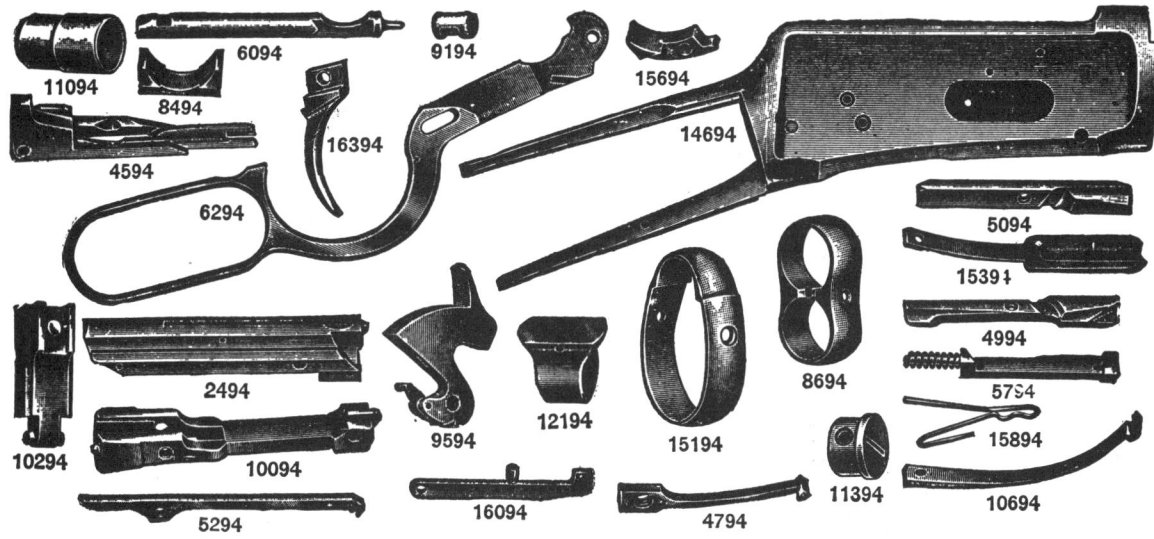

It is absolutely necessary that the numbers shown at the left of each item be specified when ordering.

In ordering any Pistol Grip part be sure to specify if gun number is higher than 1084891.

In ordering Barrels give length, caliber, round or octagon, solid frame, or take down, rifle or carbine.

No.	Description	Price
194	Barrel, round, full magazine, Solid-frame	$9.00
294	*Barrel, round, full magazine, Take-down	9.00
394	Barrel, round, ¾ magazine, Solid-frame	9.00
494	*Barrel, round, ¾ magazine, Take-down	9.00
594	Barrel, round, ⅔ magazine, Solid-frame	9.00
694	*Barrel, round, ⅔ magazine, Take-down	9.00
794	Barrel, round, ½ magazine, Solid-frame	9.00
894	*Barrel, round, ½ magazine, Take-down	9.00
994	Barrel, octagon, full magazine, Solid-frame	12.00
1094	*Barrel, octagon, full magazine, Take-down	12.00
1194	Barrel, octagon, ¾ magazine, Solid-frame	12.00
1294	*Barrel, octagon, ¾ magazine, Take-down	12.00
1394	Barrel, octagon, ⅔ magazine, Solid-frame	12.00
1494	*Barrel, octagon, ⅔ magazine, Take-down	12.00
1594	Barrel, octagon, ½ magazine, Solid-frame	12.00
1694	*Barrel, octagon, ½ magazine, Take-down	12.00
1794A	Barrel, carbine, full magazine, with ramp base	9.00
1894A	Barrel, carbine, ¾ magazine, with ramp base	9.00
1994A	Barrel, carbine, ⅔ magazine, with ramp base	9.00
2094A	*Interchangeable Round Barrels, Complete, Take-down	20.00
2094B	*Interchangeable Octagon Barrels, Complete, Take-down	23.00
2094C	Barrel, carbine, ½ magazine, with ramp base	9.00
2155	*Barrel, 30 W.C.F., light weight, round, ½ magazine, Take-down, model 55	9.00
2255	*Barrel, 25/35, light weight, round, ½ magazine, Take-down, model 55	9.00
2355	*Barrel, 32 W.S., light weight, round, ½ magazine, Take-down, model 55	9.00
2355A	Barrel, 30 W.C.F., light weight, round, ½ magazine, Solid-frame, model 55	9.00
2355B	Barrel, 25/35, light weight, round, ½ magazine, Solid-frame, model 55	9.00
2355C	Barrel, 32 W.S., light weight, round, ½ magazine, Solid-frame, model 55	9.00
2355½	*Interchangeable Barrels, light weight, ½ magazine, Take-down, model 55, round barrel	20.00
2494	Breech bolt with extractor and pin	3.30
2594	Breech bolt complete, comprising bolt with extractor and pin, firing pin, firing pin stop pin, ejector, ejector spring and ejector stop pin	4.60
2694	Butt stock, rifle	3.00
2794	Butt stock complete, rifle	4.25
2894	Butt stock, carbine	3.00
2994	Butt stock complete, carbine	4.05
3094	Butt stock, shot butt, for metal butt plate	3.00
3194	Butt stock complete, shot butt, metal butt plate	4.05
3294	Butt stock, shot butt for rubber butt plate	3.00
3394	Butt stock complete, shot butt, rubber butt plate. Stock complete comprises: stock with butt plate and (2) butt plate screws.	$3.80
3494	Butt stock, rifle, pistol grip (give gun number)	6.00
3594	Butt stock, complete, rifle, pistol grip (give gun number)	7.25
3694	Butt stock, shot butt, for metal butt plate, pistol grip (give gun number)	6.00
3794	Butt stock complete, shot butt, metal butt plate, pistol grip (give gun number)	7.05
3894	Butt stock, shot butt, for rubber butt plate, pistol grip (give gun number)	6.00
3994	Butt stock complete, shot butt, rubber butt plate, pistol grip (give gun number). Stock complete comprises: stock with butt plate and (2) butt plate screws, and pistol grip cap and screw.	6.80
4094	Butt plate, rifle	1.05
4194	Butt plate, carbine	.85
4294	Butt plate, shot butt, metal (give length)	.85
4394	Butt plate, shot butt, rubber (give length)	.60
4494	Butt plate screws (2) each	.25
4594	Carrier	1.40
4694	Carrier screw (2) each	.25
4794	Carrier spring	.35
4894	Carrier spring screw	.25
4994	Cartridge guide, right hand	.55
5094	Cartridge guide, left hand	.50
5194	Cartridge guide screws (2) each	.25
5294	Extractor	.40
5394	Extractor pin	.25
5494	*Extension, Take-down	2.25
5594	Extension adjusting screw, Take-down (3) each	.25
5694	Ejector	.65
5794	Ejector complete, comprising ejector with spring and pin	.85
5894	Ejector spring	.25
5994	Ejector stop pin	.25
6094	Firing pin	.35
6194	Firing pin stop pin	.25
6294	Finger lever	2.00
6394	Finger lever, pistol grip (give gun number)	2.25
6494	Finger lever pin	.25
6594	Finger lever pin stop screw	.25
6694	Finger lever link screw	.25
	In ordering Forearms give length.	
6794	Forearm, octagon, Solid-frame	1.40
6894	Forearm, octagon, Take-down	1.40
6994	Forearm, round, Solid-frame	1.40
7094	Forearm, round, Take-down	1.40
7194	Forearm, carbine, full magazine	1.40
7294	Forearm, carbine, ½ magazine	1.40
7355	Forearm, light weight, ½ magazine, Take-down, model 55	1.40

In replacing parts marked thus (*) when desired for Take-down Guns it is necessary to send gun to us.

(Continued on Next Page)

INSTRUCTIONS: In ordering parts always give name and number listed in catalog, also make, model, caliber and serial number of gun. (Parts marked with * cannot be supplied on Mail Order. It will be necessary to return arm to us for fitting.)

PAYMENTS: Parts will be sent only on advance payment. Parts cannot be returned for credit. A service charge of 25c must be added to every order under $1.00 to cover cost of handling. Do not forget to include postage.

© **ORDER BLANK IN MIDDLE AND INDEX IN BACK OF CATALOG**

WINCHESTER RIFLE PARTS

(Continued from Preceding Page)

No.	Description	Price
7494	Forearm tip, octagon, full magazine, Take-down.	$1.45
7594	Forearm tip, octagon, full magazine, Solid-frame	1.45
7694	Forearm tip, round, full magazine, Solid-frame	1.45
7794	Forearm tip, round, full magazine, Take-down	1.45
7894	Forearm tip, octagon, ½ magazine, Take-down	1.45
7994	Forearm tip, octagon, ½ magazine, Solid-frame	1.45
8094	Forearm tip, round, ½ magazine, Solid-frame	1.45
8194	Forearm tip, round, ½ magazine, Take-down	1.45
8255	Forearm tip, light weight, ½ magazine, model 55, Take-down	1.45
8394	Forearm tip screws (2) each	.25
8494	Forearm tip tenon	.40
8555	Forearm tip tenon, model 55	.40
8694	Front band, carbine	.65
8794	Front band screw, carbine	.25
8894	Friction stud	.25
8994	Friction stud spring	.25
9094	Friction stud stop pin	.25
9194	Firing pin striker	.25
9294	Firing pin striker stop pin	.25
9394	Hammer stirrup	.25
9494	Hammer stirrup pin	.25
9594	Hammer complete with stirrup and pin	1.25
9694	Hammer screw	.25
9794	Link	1.75
9894	Link pin	.25
9994	Link pin stop screw	.25
10094	Link complete, comprising link with friction stud, stud spring, and stud stop pin	2.10
10194	Locking bolt	.95
10294	Locking bolt complete, comprising locking bolt with striker and striker stop pin	1.20
10394	Lower tang	1.55
10494	Lower tang, pistol grip (give gun number)	1.85
10594	Lower tang complete, comprising tang with hammer complete, mainspring, mainspring screw, mainspring strain screw, trigger, sear, sear pin, sear and safety catch spring, sear and safety catch spring screw, safety catch, safety catch pin and hammer screw	5.15
10694	Mainspring	.50
10794	Mainspring, pistol grip (give gun number)	.60
10894	Mainspring screw	.25
10994	Mainspring strain screw	.25
11094	Magazine follower	.25
11194	Magazine follower stop ring, Take-down	.25
11294	Magazine spring, (give length of magazine tube)	.25
11394	Magazine plug, full magazine (No. 4) rifle and carbine, Solid-frame	.25
11494	Magazine plug, ½ magazine, (No. 5) rifle, Solid-frame	.25
11594	Magazine plug, ½ magazine, (No. 6) carbine	.25
11694	Magazine plug, full magazine, (No. 11) rifle, Take-down	.40
11794	Magazine plug, ½ magazine, (No. 12) rifle, Take-down	.40
11855	Magazine plug, ½ magazine, (No. 12) rifle, model 55, Take-down	.40
11994	Magazine plug screw, (B) Solid-frame	.25
12094	Magazine plug screw, (C) Take-down	.25
12194	Magazine ring, Solid-frame	.65
12294	Magazine ring, Take-down	.65
12394	Magazine ring pin, Solid-frame	.25
12494	Magazine tube, full magazine, rifle, Solid-frame	1.10
12594	Magazine tube, full magazine, rifle, Take-down	1.65
12694	Magazine tube, ¾ magazine, rifle, Solid-frame	1.10
12794	Magazine tube, ¾ magazine, rifle, Take-down	1.65
12894	Magazine tube, ⅔ magazine, rifle, Solid-frame	1.10
12994	Magazine tube, ⅔ magazine, rifle, Take-down	1.65
13094	Magazine tube, ½ magazine, rifle, Solid-frame	1.10
13194	Magazine tube, ½ magazine, rifle, Take-down	1.65
13255	Magazine tube, ½ magazine, rifle, model 55, Take-down	1.65
13394	Magazine tube, full magazine, carbine	1.10
13494	Magazine tube, ¾ magazine, carbine	1.10
13594	Magazine tube, ⅔ magazine, carbine	1.10
13694	Magazine tube, ½ magazine, carbine	1.10
13794	Magazine tube complete, rifle, Solid-frame, comprising magazine tube with mag. follower, mag. spring, mag. plug, mag. screw, mag. ring, and mag. ring pin	2.45
13894	Magazine tube complete, carbine, comprising magazine tube with mag. follower, mag. plug, mag. plug screw, and spring	1.70
13994	Magazine tube complete, rifle, Take-down	4.05
14055	Magazine tube complete, rifle, model 55, ½ magazine, Take-down	$4.05
	Magazine tube complete comprises: Magazine tube with magazine follower, magazine spring, magazine plug, magazine plug screw, magazine lever, magazine lever screw, magazine lever plunger and magazine lever plunger spring.	
14055½	Magazine tube complete, ½ magazine, Solid-frame, rifle	1.60
	Magazine tube complete, ½ magazine, Solid-frame, rifle, comprises: Tube, magazine plug, magazine spring and magazine follower.	
14194	Magazine lever, Take-down	.70
14294	Magazine lever screw, Take-down	.25
14394	Magazine lever plunger, Take-down	.25
14494	Magazine lever plunger spring, Take-down	.25
14594	Peep sight plug screw	.25
14694	Receiver, rifle, with lower tang and hammer screw, Solid-frame	10.15
14794	*Receiver, rifle, with lower tang and hammer screw, Take-down	10.15
14894	Receiver, carbine, with lower tang and hammer screw and carbine sling ring	10.15
14994	Receiver, rifle, complete with action, Solid-frame	28.15
15094	*Receiver, rifle, complete with action, Take-down	28.15
	Receiver, rifle, complete with action, comprises: Receiver with lower tang complete, breech bolt complete, right and left hand cartridge guides, cartridge guide screws (2), spring cover and screw, link complete, finger lever, link pin, link pin stop screw, carrier spring and screw, locking bolt complete, finger lever pin stop screw, carrier, carrier screw (2), and peep sight plug screw.	
15194	Rear band, carbine	.65
15294	Rear band screw	.25
15394	Spring cover	.70
15494	Spring cover screw	.25
15594	Sling ring hole plug screw	.25
15694	Sear	.40
15794	Sear pin	.25
15894	Sear and safety catch spring	.25
15994	Sear and safety catch spring screw	.25
16094	Safety catch	.25
16194	Safety catch, pistol grip (give gun number)	.25
16294	Safety catch pin	.25
16394	Trigger	.45
16494	Upper tang screw	.25
16594	Upper tang screw, pistol grip (give gun number)	.25
16694	Upper tang screw, peep sight	.25
16794	Upper tang screw, peep sight, pistol grip	.25

MODELS 94 AND 55

Parts necessary to change from plain to double set trigger straight grip 8.00 P. G. 8.35

No.	Description	Price
16894	Front trigger	.80
16994	Front trigger pin	.25
17094	Front trigger spring	.25
17194	Hammer complete, comprising hammer with fly, fly pin, stirrup and pin	1.95
17294	Hammer screw	.25
17394	Hammer fly	.30
17494	Hammer fly pin	.25
17594	Hammer stirrup	.35
17694	Hammer stirrup pin	.25
17794	Lower tang	1.75
17894	Lower tang, pistol grip (give gun number)	2.00
17994	Mainspring	.60
18094	Mainspring, pistol grip (give gun number)	.70
18194	Mainspring screw	.25
18294	Mainspring strain screw	.25
18394	Rear trigger	1.10
18494	Rear trigger pin	.25
18594	Rear trigger spring	.25
18694	Rear trigger stop pin	.25
18794	Sear	.60
18894	Sear spring	.25
18994	Sear spring screw	.25
19094	Trigger guide pin	.25
19194	Trigger adjusting screw	.25

In replacing parts marked thus (*) when desired for Take-down Guns it is necessary to send gun to us.

INSTRUCTIONS: In ordering parts always give name and number listed in catalog, also make, model, caliber and serial number of gun. (Parts marked with * cannot be supplied on Mail Order. It will be necessary to return arm to us for fitting.)

PAYMENTS: Parts will be sent only on advance payment. Parts cannot be returned for credit. A service charge of 25c must be added to every order under $1.00 to cover cost of handling. Do not forget to include postage.

CAREFUL ATTENTION AND SAFE DELIVERY OF YOUR ORDER

WINCHESTER RIFLE PARTS
MODELS 92 AND 53 LEVER ACTION REPEATING RIFLES

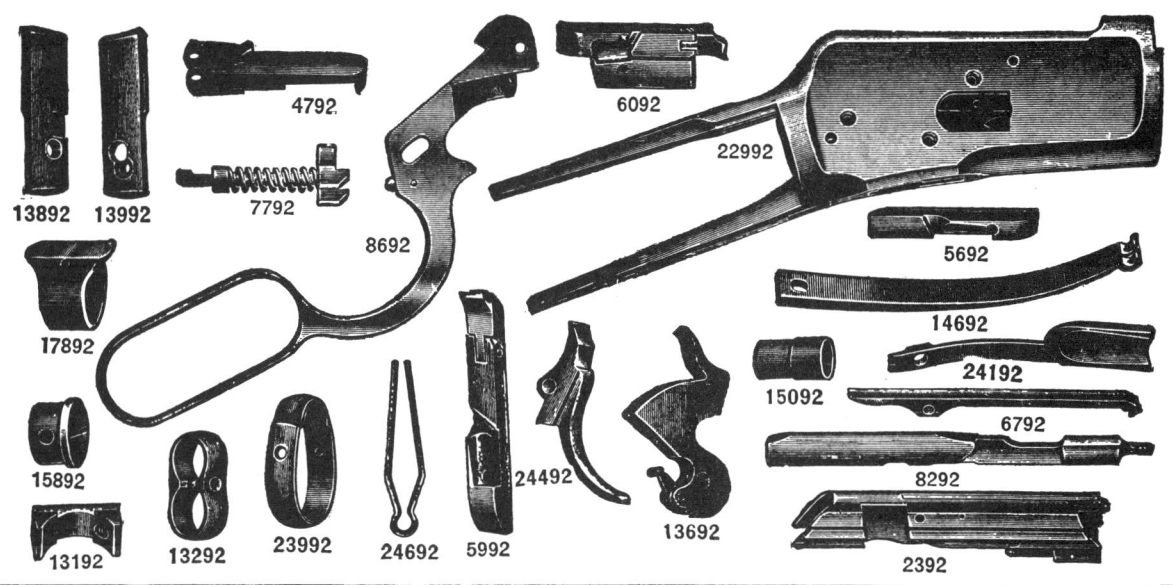

It is absolutely necessary that the numbers shown at the left of each gun part be specified when ordering.

In ordering any Pistol Grip part be sure and specify if gun number is higher than 1000219.

MODELS 92 AND 53

In ordering Barrels, give length, caliber, whether round or octagon, for rifle or carbine, and if for Solid-frame or Take-down rifle. Also specify if for ½, ⅔ or ¾ magazine.

192	Barrel, round, full magazine, Solid-frame	$7.00
292	*Barrel, round, full magazine, Take-down	7.00
392	Barrel, round, ¾ magazine, Solid-frame	7.00
492	*Barrel, round, ¾ magazine, Take-down	7.00
592	Barrel, round, ⅔ magazine, Solid-frame	7.00
692	*Barrel, round, ⅔ magazine, Take-down	7.00
792	Barrel, round, ½ magazine, Solid-frame	7.00
892	*Barrel, round, ½ magazine, Take-down	7.00
892A	*Interchangeable round barrel, 38 and 44 cal. only, complete Take-down	18.00
892B	*Interchangeable octagon barrel, 38 and 44 cal. only, complete Take-down	20.00
953	*Barrel, round, ½ magazine, light weight, Solid-frame, model 53	9.00
1053	*Barrel, round, ½ magazine, light weight, Take-down, model 53	9.00
1053A	*Front portion of gun, ½ magazine, extra light, Take-down, model 53	20.00
1192	Barrel, octagon, full magazine, Solid-frame	9.00
1292	*Barrel, octagon, full magazine, Take-down	9.00
1392	Barrel, octagon, ¾ magazine, Solid-frame	9.00
1492	*Barrel, octagon, ¾ magazine, Take-down	9.00
1592	Barrel, octagon, ⅔ magazine, Solid-frame	9.00
1692	*Barrel, octagon, ⅔ magazine, Take-down	9.00
1792	Barrel, octagon, ½ magazine, Solid-frame	9.00
1892	*Barrel, octagon, ½ magazine, Take-down	9.00
1992	Barrel, carbine, full magazine	7.00
1992A	Barrel, carbine, full magazine, with ramp base	7.00
2092	Barrel, carbine, ¾ magazine	7.00
2092A	Barrel, carbine, ¾ magazine, with ramp base	7.00
2192	Barrel, carbine, ⅔ magazine	7.00
2192A	Barrel, carbine, ⅔ magazine, with ramp base	7.00
2292	Barrel, carbine, ½ magazine	7.00
2292A	Barrel, carbine, ½ magazine, with ramp base	7.00
2392	Breech bolt, .38 and .44 cal., with extractor and pin	3.50
2492	Breech bolt, .25/20 and .32 cal., with extractor and pin	3.50
2592	Breech bolt, complete, .38 and .44 cal.	5.35
2692	Breech bolt, complete, .25/20 and .32 cal.	5.35

Breech bolt complete comprises: extractor and pin, firing pin, firing pin stop pin, ejector guide, ejector guide pin (2), ejector, ejector collar, and ejector spring.

2792	Butt stock, rifle	3.00
2892	Butt stock complete, rifle	4.25
2992	Butt stock, carbine	3.00
3092	Butt stock complete, carbine	$4.05
3192	Butt stock, shot butt for metal butt plate	3.00
3292	Butt stock, complete, shot butt, metal butt plate	4.05
3392	Butt stock, shot butt for rubber butt plate	3.00
3492	Butt stock complete, shot butt, rubber butt plate	3.80

Complete stocks take stocks with butt plate and (2) screws.

3592	Butt stock, pistol grip (give gun number)	6.00
3692	Butt stock complete, pistol grip (give gun number)	7.25
3792	Butt stock, pistol grip, shot butt, for metal butt plate (give gun number)	6.00
3892	Butt stock complete, pistol grip, shot butt, metal butt plate (give gun number)	7.05
3992	Butt stock, pistol grip, shot butt for rubber butt plate (give gun number)	6.00
4092	Butt stock, pistol grip complete, shot butt, rubber butt plate (give gun number)	6.80

Complete stocks take stock with butt plate, butt plate screws (2), pistol grip cap and screw.

4192	Butt plate, rifle	1.05
4292	Butt plate, carbine	.85
4392	Butt plate, shot butt, metal butt plate (give length of plate)	.85
4492	Butt plate, shot butt, rubber butt plate (give length of plate)	.60
4592	Butt plate screws (2) each	.25
4692	Carbine sling ring and staple	.30
4792	Carrier, .38 and .44 caliber	1.15
4892	Carrier, .25/20 and .32 caliber	1.15
4992	Carrier stop, .38 and .44 caliber	.25
5092	Carrier stop, .25/20 and .32 caliber	.25
5192	Carrier stop pin	.25
5292	Carrier stop spring	.25
5392	Carrier complete, .38 and .44 caliber	1.50
5492	Carrier complete, .25/20 and .32 caliber	1.50

Carrier complete comprises: carrier with carrier stop, pin and spring.

5592	Carrier screws (2) each	.25
5692	Cartridge guide, right hand, .38 and .44 caliber	.50
5792	Cartridge guide, right hand, .25/20 caliber	.50
5892	Cartridge guide, right hand, .32 caliber	.50
5992	Cartridge guide, left hand, .38 and .44 caliber, complete	1.10
6092	Cartridge guide, left hand, .25/20 caliber, complete	1.40
6192	Cartridge guide, left hand, .32 caliber, complete	1.40

Cartridge guide complete comprises: cartridge guide with cartridge stop and joint pin.

6292	Cartridge guide screws (2) each	.25
6392	Cartridge stop, .38 and .44 caliber	.40
6492	Cartridge stop, .25/20 and .32 caliber	.40
6592	Cartridge stop joint pin	.25
6692	Cartridge stop spring	.25

In replacing parts marked thus (*) when desired for Take-down Guns it is necessary to send gun to us.

(Continued on Next Page)

INSTRUCTIONS: In ordering parts always give name and number listed in catalog, also make, model, caliber and serial number of gun. (Parts marked with * cannot be supplied on Mail Order. It will be necessary to return arm to us for fitting.)

PAYMENTS: Parts will be sent only on advance payment. Parts cannot be returned for credit. A service charge of 25c must be added to every order under $1.00 to cover cost of handling. Do not forget to include postage.

PLEASE TELL OTHERS ABOUT STOEGER'S CATALOG

WINCHESTER RIFLE PARTS
MODEL 92 AND 53 LEVER ACTION REPEATING RIFLES
(Continued from Preceding Page)

No.	Description	Price
6792	Extractor, .38 and .44 caliber	$0.40
6892	Extractor, .25/20 and .32 caliber	.40
6992	Extractor pin	.25
7092	Ejector, .38 and .44 caliber	.65
7192	Ejector, .25/20 and .32 caliber	.65
7292	Ejector guide, .38 and .44 caliber	.25
7392	Ejector guide, .25/20 and .32 caliber	.25
7492	Ejector guide pins (2) each	.25
7592	Ejector collar	.25
7692	Ejector spring	.25
7792	Ejector complete, .38 and .44 caliber	.85
7892	Ejector complete, .25/20 and .32 caliber	.85
	Ejector complete comprises: ejector with collar and spring.	
7992	*Extension, .38 and .44 caliber, Take-down	2.25
8092	*Extension, .25/20 and .32 caliber, Take-down	2.25
8192	Extension adjusting screws, (3) each, Take-down	.25
8992	Firing pin	.45
8392	Firing pin stop pin	.25
8492	Finger lever (only), .38 and .44 caliber	2.50
3592	Finger lever (only), .25/20 and .32 caliber	2.50
8692	Finger lever complete, .38 and .44 caliber	2.85
8792	Finger lever complete, .25/20 and .32 caliber	2.85
8892	Finger lever complete, .38 and .44 caliber, pistol grip (give gun number)	2.95
8992	Finger lever complete, .25/20 and .32 caliber, pistol grip (give gun number)	2.95
	Finger lever complete comprises: finger lever, with friction stud, spring and stop pin.	
9092	Finger lever pin	.25
9192	Finger lever pin stop screw	.25
9292	Friction stud	.25
9393	Friction stud spring	.25
9492	Friction stud stop pin	.25
	In ordering Forearms give the length.	
9592	Forearm, octagon, rifle, .38 and .44 caliber, Solid-frame	1.40
9692	Forearm, octagon, rifle, .38 and .44 caliber, Take-down	1.40
9792	Forearm, octagon, rifle, .25/20 and .32 caliber, Solid-frame	1.40
9892	Forearm, octagon, rifle, .25/20 and .32 caliber, Take-down	1.40
9992	Forearm, round, rifle, .38 and .44 caliber, Solid-frame	1.40
10092	Forearm, round, rifle, .38 and .44 caliber, Take-down	1.40
10192	Forearm, round, rifle, .25/20 and .32 caliber, Solid-frame	1.40
10292	Forearm, round, rifle, .25/20 and .32 caliber, Take-down	1.40
10353	Forearm, round, rifle, model 53, Solid-frame	1.40
10453	Forearm, round, rifle, model 53, Take-down	1.40
10592	Forearm, carbine, full mag., .38 and .44 caliber	1.40
10692	Forearm, carbine, ½ magazine, .38 and .44 caliber	1.40
10792	Forearm, carbine, full magazine, .25/20 and .32 caliber	1.40
10892	Forearm, carbine, ½ magazine, .25/20 and .32 caliber	1.40
10992	Forearm tip, octagon, full magazine, .38 and .44 caliber, Solid-frame	1.45
11092	Forearm tip, octagon, full magazine, .38 and .44 caliber, Take-down	1.45
11192	Forearm tip, octagon, ½ magazine, .38 and .44 caliber, Solid-frame	1.45
11292	Forearm tip, octagon, ½ magazine, .38 and .44 caliber, Take-down	1.45
11392	Forearm tip, octagon, full magazine, .25/20 and .32 caliber, Solid-frame	1.45
11492	Forearm tip, octagon, full magazine, .25/20 and .32 caliber, Take-down	1.45
11592	Forearm tip, octagon, ½ magazine, .25/20 and .32 caliber, Solid-frame	1.45
11692	Forearm tip, octagon, ½ magazine, .25/20 and .32 caliber, Take-down	1.45
11792	Forearm tip, round, full magazine, .38 and .44 caliber, Solid-frame	1.45
11892	Forearm tip, round, full magazine, .38 and .44 caliber, Take-down	1.45
11992	Forearm tip, round, ½ magazine, .38 and .44 caliber, Solid-frame	1.45
12092	Forearm tip, round, ½ magazine, .38 and .44 caliber, Take-down	1.45
12192	Forearm tip, round, full magazine, .25/20 and .32 caliber, Solid-frame	1.45
12292	Forearm tip, round, full magazine, .25/20 and .32 caliber, Take-down	1.45
12392	Forearm tip, round, ½ magazine, .25/20 and .32 caliber, Solid-frame	1.45
12492	Forearm tip, round, ½ magazine, .25/20 and .32 caliber, Take-down	1.45
12553	Forearm tip, round, .44 caliber, model 53, Solid-frame	$1.45
12653	Forearm tip, round, .44 caliber, model 53, Take-down	1.45
12753	Forearm tip, round, .25/20 and .32 caliber, model 53, Solid-frame	1.45
12853	Forearm tip, round, .25/20 and .32 caliber, model 53, Take-down	1.45
12992	Forearm tip screw (2) each	.25
13092	Forearm tip tenon, .38 and .44 caliber	.40
13153	Forearm tip tenon, .25/20 and .32 caliber, model 53 and model 92	.40
13292	Front band, carbine, .38 and .44 caliber	.65
13392	Front band screw, carbine, .38 and .44 caliber	.25
13492	Hammer stirrup	.25
13592	Hammer stirrup pin	.25
13692	Hammer complete	1.25
	Hammer complete comprises hammer with stirrup and pin.	
13792	Hammer screw	.25
13892	Locking bolt, right hand	.75
13992	Locking bolt, left hand	.70
14092	Locking bolt pin	.25
14192	Locking bolt pin stop screw	.25
14292	Lower tang	1.50
14392	Lower tang pistol grip (give gun number)	1.60
14492	Lower tang complete	4.50
14592	Lower tang complete, pistol grip (give gun number)	4.60
	Lower tang complete comprises: lower tang with hammer complete, mainspring, mainspring screw, mainspring strain screw, trigger, trigger pin, trigger spring, trigger spring screw and hammer screw.	
14692	Mainspring	.50
14792	Mainspring, pistol grip (give gun number)	.60
14892	Mainspring screw	.25
14992	Mainspring strain screw	.25
15092	Magazine follower, .38 and .44 caliber	.25
15192	Magazine follower, .25/20 and .32 caliber	.25
15292	Magazine follower stop ring, .38 and .44 caliber, Take-down	.25
15392	Magazine follower stop ring, .25/20 and .32 caliber, Take-down	.25
15492	Magazine spring, .38 and .44 caliber (give length of magazine tube)	.25
15592	Magazine spring, .25/20 and .32 caliber (give length of magazine tube)	.25
15692	Magazine plug, rifle, .38 and .44 caliber, full magazine, No. 4, Solid-frame	.25
15792	Magazine plug, rifle, .38 and .44 caliber, full magazine, No. 11, Take-down	.40
15892	Magazine plug, rifle, .38 and .44 caliber, ½ magazine, No. 5, Solid-frame	.25
15992	Magazine plug, rifle, .38 and .44 caliber, ½ magazine, No. 12, Take-down	.40
16092	Magazine plug, rifle, .25/20 and .32 caliber, full magazine, No. 24, Solid-frame	.25
16192	Magazine plug, rifle, .25/20 and .32 caliber, full magazine, No. 9, Take-down	.40
16292	Magazine plug, rifle, .25/20 and .32 caliber, ½ magazine, No. 2, Solid-frame	.25
16392	Magazine plug, rifle, .25/20 and .32 caliber, ½ magazine, No. 10, Take-down	.40
16453	Magazine plug, rifle, .44 caliber, ½ magazine, No. 5, model 53, Solid-frame	.25
16553	Magazine plug, rifle, .44 caliber, ½ magazine, No. 12, model 53, Take-down	.40
16653	Magazine plug, rifle, .25/20 and .32 caliber, ½ magazine, No. 29, model 53, Solid-frame	.25
16753	Magazine plug, rifle, .25/20 and .32 caliber, ½ magazine, No. 10, model 53, Take-down	.40
16892	Magazine plug, carbine, .38 and .44 caliber, full magazine, No. 4	.25
16992	Magazine plug, carbine, .38 and .44 caliber, ½ magazine, No. 6	.25
17092	Magazine plug, carbine, .25/20 and .32 caliber, full magazine, No. 24	.25
17192	Magazine plug, carbine, .25/20 and .32 caliber, ½ magazine, No. 3	.25
17292	Magazine plug screw, (B) .38 and .44 caliber, rifle and carbine, Solid-frame	.25
17392	Magazine plug screw, (A) .25/20 and .32 caliber, rifle and carbine, Solid-frame	.25
17492	Magazine plug screw, (C) .38 and .44 caliber, rifle, Take-down	.25
17592	Magazine plug screw, (E) .25/20 and .32 caliber, rifle, Take-down	.25

In replacing parts marked thus (*) when desired for Take-down Guns it is necessary to send gun to us.
(Continued on Next Page)

INSTRUCTIONS: In ordering parts always give name and number listed in catalog, also make, model, caliber and serial number of gun. (Parts marked with * cannot be supplied on Mail Order. It will be necessary to return arm to us for fitting.)

PAYMENTS: Parts will be sent only on advance payment. Parts cannot be returned for credit. A service charge of 25c must be added to every order under $1.00 to cover cost of handling. Do not forget to include postage.

SEE PAGE 8 "HOW TO ORDER"

WINCHESTER RIFLE PARTS
MODELS 92 AND 53 LEVER ACTION REPEATING RIFLES
(Continued from Preceding Page)

No.	Description	Price
17692	Magazine ring, .38 and .44 caliber, Solid-frame..	$0.65
17792	Magazine ring, .25/20 and .32 caliber, Solid-frame	.65
17892	Magazine ring, .38 and .44 caliber, Take-down...	.65
17992	Magazine ring, .25/20 and .32 caliber, Take-down	.65
18092	Magazine, ring pin	.25
18192	Magazine tube, rifle, .38 and .44 caliber, full magazine, Solid-frame	1.10
18292	Magazine tube, rifle, .38 and .44 caliber, full magazine, Take-down	1.65
18392	Magazine tube, rifle, .38 and .44 caliber, ¾ magazine, Solid-frame	1.10
18492	Magazine tube, rifle, .38 and .44 caliber, ¾ magazine, Take-down	1.65
18592	Magazine tube, rifle, .38 and .44 caliber, ⅔ magazine, Solid-frame	1.10
18692	Magazine tube, rifle, .38 and .44 caliber, ⅔ magazine, Take-down	1.65
18792	Magazine tube, rifle, .38 and .44 caliber, ½ magazine, Solid-frame	1.10
18892	Magazine tube, rifle, .38 and .44 caliber, ½ magazine, Take-down	1.65
18992	Magazine tube, rifle, .25/20 and .32 caliber, full magazine, Solid-frame	1.10
19092	Magazine tube, rifle, .25/20 and .32 caliber, full magazine, Take-down	1.65
19192	Magazine tube, rifle, .25/20 and .32 caliber, ¾ magazine, Solid-frame	1.10
19292	Magazine tube, rifle, .25/20 and .32 caliber, ¾ magazine, Take-down	1.65
19392	Magazine tube, rifle, .25/20 and .32 caliber, ⅔ magazine, Solid-frame	1.10
19492	Magazine tube, rifle, .25/20 and .32 caliber, ⅔ magazine, Take-down	1.65
19592	Magazine tube, rifle, .25/20 and .32 caliber, ½ magazine, Solid-frame	1.10
19692	Magazine tube, rifle, .25/20 and .32 caliber, ½ magazine, Take-down	1.65
19753	Magazine tube, rifle, .44 caliber, ½ magazine, model 53, Solid-frame	1.10
19853	Magazine tube, rifle, .25/20 and .32 caliber, ½ magazine, model 53, Solid-frame	1.10
19953	Magazine tube, rifle, .44 caliber, ½ magazine, model 53, Take-down	1.65
20053	Magazine tube, rifle, .25/20 and .32 caliber, ½ magazine, model 53, Take-down	1.65
20192	Magazine tube, carbine, .38 and .44 caliber, full magazine	1.10
20292	Magazine tube, carbine, .25/20 and .32 caliber, full magazine	1.10
20392	Magazine tube, carbine, .38 and .44 caliber, ¾ magazine	1.10
20492	Magazine tube, carbine, .25/20 and .32 caliber, ¾ magazine	1.10
20592	Magazine tube, carbine, .38 and .44 caliber, ⅔ magazine	1.10
20692	Magazine tube, carbine, .25/20 and .32 caliber, ⅔ magazine	1.10
20792	Mag. tube, carbine, .38 and .44 cal., ½ mag...	1.10
20892	Mag. tube, carbine, .25/20 and .32 cal., ½ mag...	1.10
20992	Magazine tube, complete, rifle, .38 and .44 caliber, Solid-frame	2.45
21092	Magazine tube, complete, rifle, .25/20 and .32 caliber, Solid-frame	2.45
	Magazine tube complete comprises: magazine tube, with mag. spring, follower, plug, plug screw, ring and ring pin.	
21192	Mag. tube complete, .38; .44 cal., Take-down..	4.05
21292	Mag. tube complete, .25/20; .32 cal., Take-down	4.05
	Magazine tube complete comprises: magazine tube, with mag. spring, follower, plug, plug screws, mag. lever, mag. lever screw, plunger and plunger spring and mag. ring.	
21353	Magazine tube complete, rifle, .44 caliber, model 53, ½ magazine, Solid-frame	1.60
21453	Magazine tube complete, rifle, .25/20 and .32 caliber, model 53, ½ magazine, Solid-frame...	1.60
	Magazine tube complete comprises: magazine tube with mag. spring, follower and plug.	
21553	Magazine tube complete, rifle, .44 caliber, model 53, ½ magazine, Take-down	4.05
21653	Magazine tube complete, rifle, .25/20 and .32 caliber, model 53, ½ magazine, Take-down....	4.05
	Magazine tube complete comprises: magazine tube with magazine spring, follower, plug, plug screw, magazine lever, lever screw, plunger and plunger spring.	
21792	Mag. tube complete, carbine, .38 and .44 cal....	1.70
	Magazine tube complete comprises: magazine tube with mag. spring, follower, plug and plug screw.	
21892	Mag. tube complete, carbine, .25/20 and .32 cal. Magazine tube complete comprises: magazine tube with mag. spring, follower, plug, plug screw, ring and ring pin.	2.45
21992	Magazine lever, .38 and .44 caliber, Take-down..	$0.70
22092	Magazine lever, .25/20 and .32 caliber, Take-down	.70
22192	Mag. lever screw, .38 and .44 cal., Take-down..	.25
22292	Mag. lever screw, .25/20; .32 cal., Take-down.	.25
22392	Mag. lever plunger, .38; .44 cal., Take-down	.25
22492	Mag. lever plunger, .25/20; .32 cal., Take-down	.25
22592	Mag. lever plunger spring, .38; ... cal. Take-down	.25
22692	Magazine lever plunger spring, .25/20 and .32 caliber, Take-down	.25
22792	Receiver, rifle, with lower tang and hammer screw, .38 and .44 caliber, Solid-frame	11.00
22892	*Receiver, rifle, with lower tang and hammer screw, .38 and .44 caliber, Take-down	11.00
22992	Receiver, rifle, with lower tang and hammer screw, .25/20 and .32 caliber, Solid-frame	11.00
23092	*Receiver, rifle, with lower tang and hammer screw, .25/20 and .32 caliber, Take-down....	11.00
23192	Receiver, carbine, with lower tang and hammer screw and sling ring, .38 and .44 caliber	11.00
23292	Receiver, carbine, with lower tang and hammer screw and sling ring, .25/20 and .32 caliber	11.00
	All above Receivers can be furnished with pistol grip tangs.	
23392	Receiver complete with action, rifle, .38 and .44 caliber, Solid-frame	29.10
23492	*Receiver complete with action, rifle, .38 and .44 caliber, Take-down	29.10
23592	Receiver complete with action, rifle, .25/20 and .32 caliber, Solid-frame	29.10
23692	*Receiver complete with action, rifle, .25/20 and .32 caliber, Take-down	29.10
23792	Receiver complete with action, carbine, .38 and .44 caliber	29.10
23892	Receiver complete with action, carbine, .25/20 and .32 caliber	29.10
	Receiver complete comprises: receiver with lower tang complete, breech bolt complete, carrier complete, finger lever complete, right and left hand cartridge guide, cartridge guide screw (2), spring cover, spring cover screw, right and left hand locking bolt, locking bolt pin stop screw, locking bolt pin, carrier screw (2), finger lever pin, finger lever pin stop screw and peep sight plug screw.	
23992	Rear band, carbine	.65
24092	Rear band screw, carbine	.25
24192	Spring cover, .38 and .44 caliber	.75
24292	Spring cover, .25/20 and .32 caliber	.75
24392	Spring cover screw	.25
24492	Trigger	.75
24592	Trigger pin	.25
24692	Trigger spring	.25
24792	Trigger spring screw	.25
24892	Upper tang screw	.25
24992	Upper tang screw, pistol grip (give gun number)	.25
25092	Upper tang screw, peep sight	.25
25192	Upper tang screw, peep sight, pistol grip	.25

MODELS 92 AND 53 DOUBLE SET TRIGGER

Parts necessary to change from plain to double set trigger, straight grip, $8.00; P. G., $8.35.

No.	Description	Price
25292	Front trigger	.80
25392	Front trigger pin	.25
25492	Front trigger spring	.25
25592	Hammer complete, comprising hammer with fly, fly pin, stirrup and stirrup pin	1.95
25692	Hammer screw	.25
25792	Hammer fly	.30
25892	Hammer fly pin	.25
25992	Hammer stirrup	.35
26092	Hammer stirrup pin	.25
26192	Lower tang	1.75
26292	Lower tang, pistol grip (give gun number)	2.00
26392	Mainspring	.60
26492	Mainspring, pistol grip (give gun number)	.70
26592	Mainspring screw	.25
26692	Mainspring strain screw	.25
26792	Rear trigger	1.10
26892	Rear trigger pin	.25
26992	Rear trigger spring	.25
27092	Rear trigger stop pin	.25
27192	Sear	.60
27292	Sear spring	.25
27392	Sear spring screw	.25
27492	Trigger guide pin	.25
27592	Trigger adjusting screw	.25

In replacing parts marked thus (*) when desired for Take-down Guns it is necessary to send gun to us.

INSTRUCTIONS: In ordering parts always give name and number listed in catalog, also make, model, caliber and serial number of gun. (Parts marked with * cannot be supplied on Mail Order. It will be necessary to return arm to us for fitting.)

PAYMENTS: Parts will be sent only on advance payment. Parts cannot be returned for credit. A service charge of 25c must be added to every order under $1.00 to cover cost of handling. Do not forget to include postage.

WINCHESTER RIFLE PARTS
MODEL 86 LEVER ACTION REPEATING RIFLE

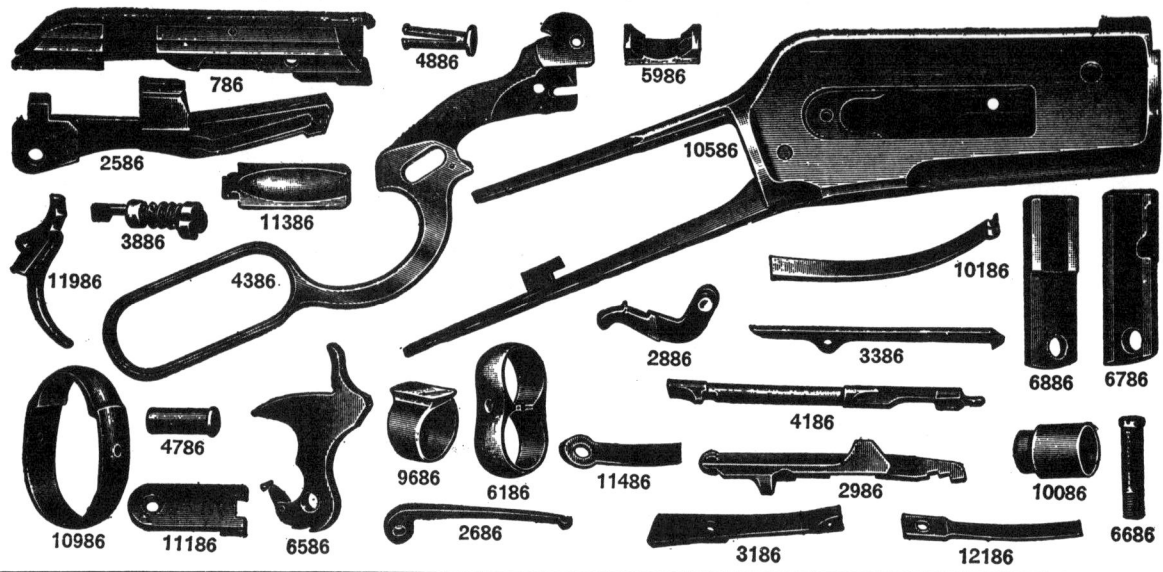

It is absolutely necessary that the numbers shown at the left of each gun part be specified when ordering.

MODEL 86 SOLID-FRAME AND TAKE-DOWN

In ordering barrels give length, round or octagon, full, ¾, ⅔, or ½ magazine, Solid-frame or Take-down, rifle or carbine.

No.	Description	Price
186	Barrel, .33 caliber, round, light weight, Solid-frame	$14.25
286	*Barrel, .33 caliber, round, light weight, Take-down	14.25
386	*Barrel, .45-70 caliber, round, light weight, Take-down, ½ mag. only	14.25
486	Barrel, round	9.00
686	Barrel, octagon	10.75
786	Breech bolt with extractor and pin	4.40
886	Breech bolt complete comprising bolt with extractor and pin, firing pin, firing pin stop pin, ejector, ejector spring and ejector collar	6.00
986	Butt stock, rifle	3.00
1086	Butt stock complete, rifle	4.25
1186	Butt stock, rifle, pistol grip	6.00
1286	Butt stock, rifle, complete, pistol grip	7.25
1386	Butt stock, shot butt for metal butt plate	3.00
1486	Butt stock, shot butt, metal butt plate complete	4.05
1586	Butt stock, shot butt for rubber butt plate	3.00
1686	Butt stock, shot butt, rubber butt plate complete	3.80

The above stocks that are complete take stock with butt plate, and (2) butt plate screws.

1786	Butt stock, shot butt for rubber butt plate, pistol grip	6.00
1886	Butt stock, shot butt, rubber butt plate, pistol grip, complete	6.80
1986	Butt stock, shot butt for metal butt plate, pistol grip	6.00
2086	Butt stock, shot butt, metal butt plate, pistol grip, complete	7.05

The above stocks that are complete take stock with butt plate, butt plate screws (2) and pistol grip cap and screw.

2186	Butt plate, rifle	1.05
2286	Butt plate, shot butt, metal, give length	.85
2386	Butt plate, shot butt, rubber, give length	.60
2486	Butt plate, screws, (2) each	.25
2586	Carrier	3.60
2686	Carrier spring	.35
2786	Carrier spring screw	.25
2886	Carrier hook	.50
2986	Cartridge guide	1.00
3086	Cartridge guide screw	.25
3186	Cartridge stop	.50
3286	Cartridge stop screw	.25
3386	Extractor	.40
3486	Extractor pin	.25
3586	Ejector	.65
3686	Ejector collar	.25
3786	Ejector spring	.25
3886	Ejector complete comprising ejector with spring and collar	$.85
3986	*Extension Take-down	2.25
4086	Extension adjusting screw, Take-down (3) each	.25
4186	Firing pin (give number of gun or send in old firing pin)	.65
4286	Firing pin stop pin	.25
4386	Finger lever	2.75
4486	Finger lever, pistol grip	3.00
4586	Finger lever complete	3.10
4686	Finger lever complete, pistol grip	3.35

Finger lever complete comprises: finger lever with friction stud, friction stud spring and stop pin.

4786	Finger lever bushing	.25
4886	Finger lever bushing pin	.25
4986	Finger lever connecting pin	.25
5086	Forearm, rifle, round, Solid-frame	1.50
5186	Forearm, rifle, octagon, Solid-frame	1.50
5286	Forearm, rifle, .33 caliber light weight, round, Solid-frame	1.50
5386	Forearm, rifle, .33 caliber and .45-70 light, weight, round, Take-down	1.50
5486	Forearm tip, octagon	1.65
5586	Forearm tip, round	1.65
5686	Forearm tip, .33 caliber, light weight, Solid-frame	1.65
5786	Forearm tip, .33 caliber and .45-70 light weight, Take-down	1.65
5886	Forearm tip screw (2) each	.25
5986	Forearm tip tenon	.40
6086	Forearm tip tenon, light weight, .33 and .45/70	.40
15186	Friction stud	.25
15286	Friction stud spring	.25
15386	Friction stud stop pin	.25
6186	Front band, carbine	.60
6286	Front band screw, carbine	.25
6386	Hammer stirrup	.25
6486	Hammer stirrup pin	.25
6586	Hammer complete comprising hammer with stirrup and pin	1.25
6686	Hammer screw	.25
6786	Locking bolt, right hand	.75
6886	Locking bolt, left hand	.65
6986	Lower tang	2.75
7086	Lower tang, pistol grip	3.00
7186	Lower tang complete, comprising lower tang with hammer complete, mainspring, mainspring strain screw, trigger, trigger spring, trigger spring screw, trigger pin, and hammer screw	5.90
7286	Lower tang complete, pistol grip	6.15

Lower tang complete comprises: lower tang with hammer complete, mainspring, mainspring strain screw, trigger, trigger spring, trigger spring screw, trigger pin, and hammer screw.

(Continued on Next Page)

In replacing parts marked thus (*) when desired for Take-down Guns it is necessary to send gun to us.

INSTRUCTIONS: In ordering parts always give name and number listed in catalog, also make, caliber and serial number of gun. (Parts marked with * cannot be supplied on Mail Order. It will be necessary to return arm to us for fitting.)

PAYMENTS: Parts will be sent only on advance payment. Parts cannot be returned for credit. A service charge of 25c must be added to every order under $1.00 to cover cost of handling. Do not forget to include postage.

© A NEW GUN CARRIES A FACTORY GUARANTEE

WINCHESTER RIFLE PARTS
MODEL 86 LEVER ACTION
(Continued from Preceding Page)

No.	Description	Price
7386	Lower tang screw	$ .25
7486	Magazine tube, rifle, full magazine, Solid-frame	1.50
7586	Magazine tube, rifle, ¾ magazine, Solid-frame	1.50
7686	Magazine tube, rifle, ⅔ magazine, Solid-frame	1.50
7786	Magazine tube, rifle, ½ magazine, Solid-frame	1.50
7886	Magazine tube, carbine, full magazine	1.50
7986	Magazine tube, .33 caliber, light weight, ½ magazine, Solid-frame	1.50
8086	Magazine tube, complete, Solid-frame	2.95
	Magazine complete comprises: magazine tube with magazine spring, magazine follower, magazine plug, magazine plug screw, ring and ring pin.	
8186	Magazine tube, rifle, full magazine, Take-down	1.75
8286	Magazine tube, rifle, ¾ magazine, Take-down	1.75
8386	Magazine tube, rifle, ⅔ magazine, Take-down	1.75
8486	Magazine tube, rifle, ½ magazine, Take-down	1.75
8586	Magazine tube, .33 caliber, light weight, ½ magazine, Take-down	1.75
8686	Magazine tube, complete, Take-down	3.55
	Magazine complete comprises: Take-down magazine tube with magazine follower, magazine spring, magazine plug, magazine plug screw, magazine lever, magazine lever plunger, magazine lever plunger spring, magazine lever screw.	
8786	Magazine lever, Take-down	.70
8886	Magazine lever plunger, Take-down	.25
8986	Magazine lever plunger spring, Take-down	.25
9086	Magazine lever screw, Take-down	.25
9186	Magazine plug, full and ½ magazine (No. 13) Take-down	.40
9286	Magazine plug, full magazine, rifle and carbine (No. 7) Solid-frame	.25
9386	Magazine plug, ½ magazine, rifle (No. 8) Solid-frame	.25
9486	Magazine plug screw, Solid-frame	.25
9586	Magazine plug screw, Take-down	.25
9686	Magazine ring, Take-down	.70
9786	Magazine ring, Solid-frame	.70
9886	Magazine ring pin, Solid-frame	.25
9986	Magazine spring (give length of magazine tube)	.25
10086	Magazine follower	.25
10186	Mainspring	.65
10286	Mainspring, pistol grip	.75
10386	Mainspring strain screw	.25
10486	Peep sight plug screw	.25
10586	Receiver with lower tang and hammer screw, Solid-frame	17.45
10686	*Receiver with lower tang and hammer screw, Take-down	17.45
10786	Rubber pistol grip tip (small size) with screw	.40
10886	Rubber pistol grip cap screw	$ .25
10986	Rear band, carbine	.65
11086	Rear band screw, carbine	.25
11186	Spring cover base	.65
11286	Spring cover base screw	.25
11386	Spring cover leaf	.70
11486	Spring cover leaf spring	.25
11586	Spring cover leaf joint pin	.25
11686	Spring cover leaf stop pin	.25
11786	Spring cover complete, comprising base with leaf, leaf spring, leaf joint pin, leaf stop pin and base screw	1.85
11886	Sling ring hole plug screw	.25
11986	Trigger	.70
12086	Trigger pin	.25
12186	Trigger spring	.25
12286	Trigger spring screw	.25
12386	Upper tang screw	.25
12486	Upper tang screw, pistol grip	.25
12586	Upper tang screw, peep sight	.25
12686	Upper tang screw, peep sight, pistol grip	.25
	All parts necessary to change from plain to double set trigger, model 86	7.30
12786	Front trigger	.70
12886	Front trigger pin	.25
12986	Front trigger spring	.25
13086	Hammer screw	.25
13186	Hammer stirrup	.35
13286	Hammer stirrup pin	.25
13386	Hammer fly	.25
13486	Hammer fly pin	.25
13586	Lower tang	1.75
13686	Lower tang, pistol grip	2.00
13786	Mainspring	.50
13886	Mainspring, pistol grip	.50
13986	Mainspring, strain screw	.25
14086	Rear trigger	1.00
14186	Rear trigger pin	.25
14286	Rear trigger spring	.25
14386	Rear trigger stop pin	.25
14486	Sear	.50
14586	Sear spring	.25
14686	Sear spring screw	.25
14786	Trigger guide pin	.25
14886	Trigger adjusting screw	.25
14986	Hammer complete, comprising hammer with hammer stirrup, hammer stirrup pin, hammer fly, hammer fly pin	1.75

In replacing parts marked thus (*) when desired for Take-down Guns it is necessary to send gun to us.

WINCHESTER CANNON—10 GAUGE

It is absolutely necessary that the numbers shown at the left of each gun part be specified when ordering.

No.	Description	Chromium	Black
1	Axle	$ 1.10	$ .80
2	Axle nut	.30	.25
3	Axle pin	.25	.25
4	Barrel with trunnion ring	17.00	10.00
5	Breech bolt	2.00	1.60
6	Breech bolt complete comprising breech bolt with handle, stop pin, breech hinge and pin, and hammer complete	5.00	4.00
7	Breech bolt handle	.30	.25
8	Breech bolt stop pin	.25	.25
9	Breech hinge	1.75	1.25
10	Breech hinge pin	.25	.25
11	Cross bar	1.00	.60
12	Cross bar screw (2) each	.25	.25
13	Elevating screw	$ .40	$ .25
14	Extractor	1.00	.75
15	Extractor stop screw	.25	.25
16	Frame, right side	2.50	1.50
17	Frame, left side	2.50	1.50
18	Hammer complete, (hammer with roll and pin)	1.00	.75
19	Hammer roll	.25	.25
20	Hammer roll pin	.25	.25
21	Lanyard	.25	.25
22	Mainspring	.75	.50
23	Mainspring screw	.30	.25
24	Tie rod	.25	.25
25	Tie rod nut	.25	.25
26	Tie rod sleeve	.30	.25
27	Trunnion ring	3.00	2.00
28	Wheel (2) each	4.00	.50

INSTRUCTIONS: In ordering parts always give name and number listed in catalog, also make, model, caliber and serial number of gun. (Parts marked with * cannot be supplied on Mail Order. It will be necessary to return arm to us for fitting.)

PAYMENTS: Parts will be sent only on advance payment. Parts cannot be returned for credit. A service charge of 25c must be added to every order under $1.00 to cover cost of handling. Do not forget to include postage.

WINCHESTER RIFLE PARTS
MODEL 95 LEVER ACTION REPEATING RIFLE

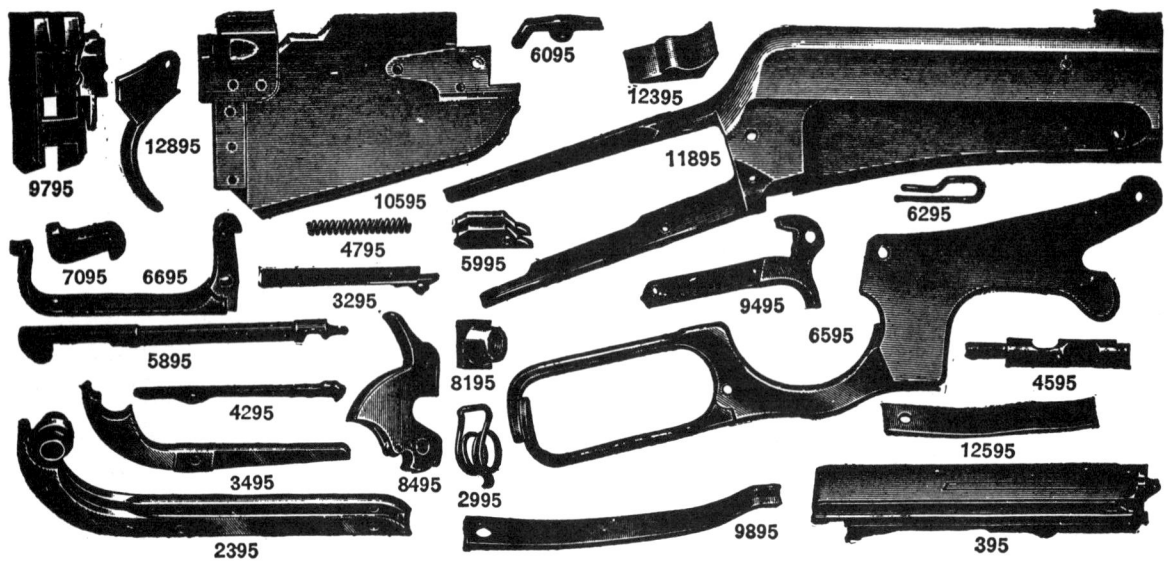

MODEL 95 RIFLE

In ordering barrels, give length, caliber, whether for Solid-frame or Take-down rifle or for carbine.

No.	Description	Price
195	*Barrel, round, rifle, Take-down	$12.00
195A	Barrel, round, rifle, Solid-frame	12.00
295	Barrel, round, carbine	12.00
395	Breech bolt, A, with extractor and pin, .30 Army, .35, .405 and .303 British	4.50
495	Breech bolt, C, with extractor and pin, .30 Gov't, '03 and '06	4.50
595	Breech bolt, A, complete, .30 Army, .35, .405 and .303 British	7.30
695	Breech bolt, C, complete, .30 Gov't, '03 and '06. Bolt complete comprises: bolt with extractor and pin, firing pin, firing pin lock, firing pin recoil lock, recoil lock pin, firing pin lock spring, lock spring screw, ejector, ejector spring and pin.	7.30
795	Butt stock, rifle	3.25
895	Butt stock, rifle, complete	4.50
995	Butt stock, carbine	3.25
1095	Butt stock, carbine, complete	4.95
	Butt stock complete comprises: butt plate and (2) butt plate screws.	
1195	Butt stock N. R. A. Musket	3.25
1295	Butt stock N. R. A. musket complete	4.90
	Butt stock complete comprises: stock with butt plate, butt plate screws (2), and stock swivel base complete with bow and (2) screws.	
1395	Butt stock, shot butt for metal butt plate	3.00
1495	Butt stock shot butt metal butt plate complete	4.00
1595	Butt stock shot butt for rubber butt plate	3.00
1695	Butt stock shot butt rubber butt plate complete	4.00
	Butt stock complete comprises: stock with butt plate and (2) butt plate screws.	
1795	Butt plate, rifle	1.05
1895	Butt plate, carbine	1.50
1995	Butt plate, N. R. A. musket	.85
2095	Butt plate, shot butt, metal	.85
2195	Butt plate, shot butt, rubber	.50
2295	Butt plate screw (2) each	.25
2395	Carrier (A) .30 Army and .303 British	1.10
2495	Carrier (B) .38-72 and .40-72 caliber	1.10
2595	Carrier (E) .405, .30 Gov't '03 and '06	1.10
2695	Carrier (F) .35 caliber	1.10
2795	Carrier complete (give caliber, see above)	3.00
	Carrier complete comprises: carrier with carrier stop pin, carrier cradle, carrier spring, cradle pin, cam lever and pin.	
2895	Carrier spring (flat spring) old style	.50
2995	Carrier spring (coil spring)	.55
3095	Carrier screw	.25
3195	Carrier stop pin	.25
3295	Carrier cradle, A, .303 British, .35-405 and .30 Army	.60
3295A	Carrier cradle, B, .30 Gov't '06 and .30 Gov't '03	.60
3395	Carrier cradle pin	$0.25
3495	Carrier cam lever, A, .30 Army, .35 and .303 British	.45
3595	Carrier cam lever, B, .38-72 and .40-72	.45
3695	Carrier cam lever, C, .30 Gov't '03 and '06 and .405	.45
3795	Carrier cam lever pin	.25
3895	Cartridge stop and (2) pins, A, .30 Army and .303 British	.50
3995	Cartridge stop and (2) pins, B, .35, .405, .30 Gov't '03 and '06	.50
4095	*Cartridge guide, right hand with (2) rivets	.25
4195	*Cartridge guide, left hand with (2) rivets	.25
4295	Extratcor, A, .30 Gov't '03 and '06	.45
4395	Extractor, B, .30 Army, .35, .405 and .303 British	.45
4495	Extractor pin	.25
4595	Ejector, A, .30 Army, .35, .405 and .303 British	.60
4695	Ejector, B, .30 Gov't '03 and '06	.60
4795	Ejector spring	.25
4895	Ejector stop pin	.25
4995	Ejector A complete, .30 Army, .35, .405 and .303 British	.80
5095	Ejector B complete, .30 Gov't '03 and '06	.80
	(Ejector with spring and pin)	
5195	*Extension, Take-down	2.25
5295	Extension adjusting screw, Take-down	.25
5395	Extension adjusting screw lock, Take-down	.30
5495	Extension adjusting screw lock screw, Take-down	.25
5595	Extension lock	.75
5695	Extension lock plunger	.25
5795	Extension lock plunger spring	.25
5895	Firing pin	1.05
5995	Firing pin lock	.45
6095	Firing pin recoil lock	.25
6195	Firing pin lock pin or firing pin recoil lock pin	.25
6295	Firing pin lock spring or firing pin recoil lock spring	.25
6395	Firing pin lock spring screw or firing pin recoil lock spring screw	.25
6495	Finger lever only	5.60
6595	Finger lever complete	7.45
	Finger lever complete comprises: lever with lock, lock joint pin, lock plunger and lock plunger spring.	
6695	Finger lever lock	1.50
6795	Finger lever lock joint pin	.25
6895	Finger lever lock plunger	.25
6995	Finger lever lock plunger spring	.25
7095	Finger lever catch	.35
7195	Finger lever catch plunger	.25
7295	Finger lever catch plunger spring	.25

(Model 95 Parts Continued on Page 485)

In replacing parts marked thus (*) when desired for Take-down Guns it is necessary to send gun to us.

INSTRUCTIONS: In ordering parts always give name and number listed in catalog, also make, model, caliber and serial number of gun. (Parts marked with * cannot be supplied on Mail Order. It will be necessary to return arm to us for fitting.)

PAYMENTS: Parts will be sent only on advance payment. Parts cannot be returned for credit. A service charge of 25c must be added to every order under $1.00 to cover cost of handling. Do not forget to include postage.

SEND YOUR GUN TO STOEGER FOR EXPERT REPAIRING

AMERICA'S GREAT GUN HOUSE

WINCHESTER RIFLE PARTS
MODEL 71 LEVER ACTION REPEATING RIFLE

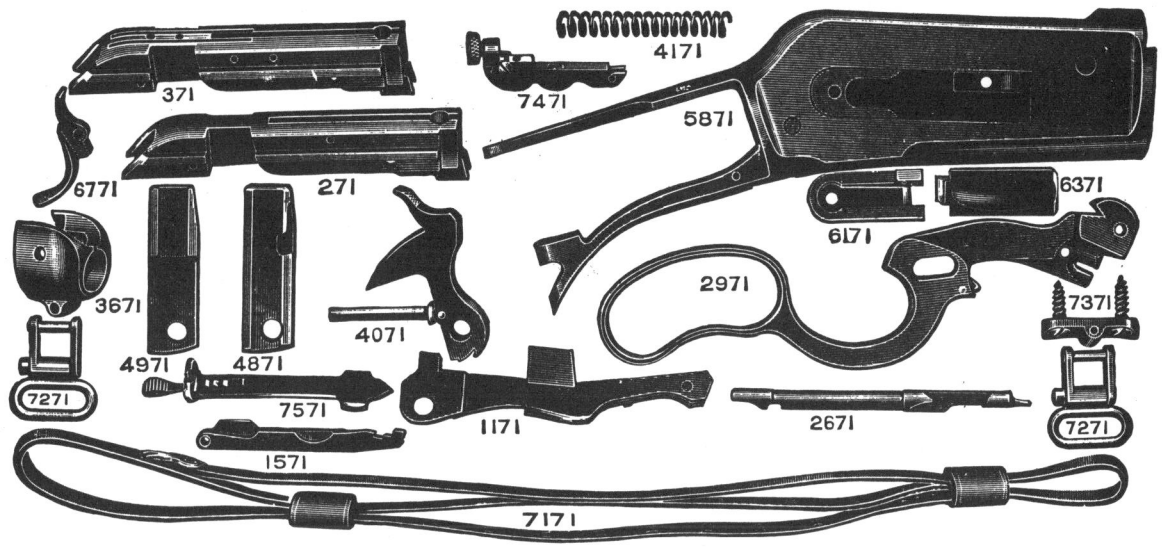

It is absolutely necessary that the numbers shown at the left of each gun part be specified when ordering.

No.	Description	Price
171	Barrel 24" Round with ramp Front Sight Base	$15.00
171A	Barrel 20" Round with Ramp	15.00
271	Breech Bolt with Extractor and Pin	4.40
371	Breech Bolt for Peep Sight with Extractor and Pin	4.60
471	Breech Bolt Complete Comprises Bolt, with Extractor and Pin, Firing Pin, Firing Pin Stop Pin, Ejector, Collar, and Ejector Spring	6.20
571	Butt Stock—Checked Pistol Grip Cap for Shot Butt Metal Butt Plate	6.00
671	Butt Stock Complete Comprises Stock, Butt Plate, Butt Plate Screws (2), P. G. Cap and Screw, Snap Swivel Base and (2) Screws	7.75
771	Butt Stock (not Checked) Semi P. G. (No. P. G. Cap) for Shot Butt Metal Butt Plate	4.45
871	Butt Stock Complete less P. G. Cap and Checking for the above	5.50
971	Butt Plate Steel Checked Shot Butt	.85
1071	Butt Plate Screws (2) each	.25
1171	Carrier	3.60
1271	Carrier Plunger	.25
1371	Carrier Plunger Spring	.25
1471	Carrier Plunger Pin	.25
1571	Cartridge Guide	1.00
1671	Cartridge Guide Screw	.25
1771	Cartridge Guide Screw Bushing	.25
1871	Cartridge Stop	.50
1971	Cartridge Stop Screw	.25
2071	Ejector	.65
2171	Ejector Collar	.25
2271	Ejector Spring	.25
2371	Ejector Complete Comprises Ejector with Spring and Collar	.85
2471	Extractor	.40
2571	Extractor Pin	.25
2671	Firing Pin	.65
2771	Firing Pin Stop Pin	.25
2871	Finger Lever	3.00
2971	Finger Lever Complete Comprises Finger Lever, with Friction Stud, Spring and Stop Pin	3.35
3071	Finger Lever Bushing	.25
3171	Finger Lever Bushing Pin	.25
3271	Finger Lever Connecting Pin	.25
3371	Friction Stud	.25
3471	Friction Stud Spring	.25
3571	Friction Stud Stop Pin	.25
3671	Forearm Tip Fitted with Swivel Base	2.00
3671A	Forearm Tip without Swivel Base	1.65
3771	Forearm Checked	2.10
3771A	Forearm—not Checked	1.50
3871	Forearm Tip Screws (2) each	.25
3971	Forearm Tip Tenon	.40
4071	Hammer Complete Comprises Hammer, Hammer Spring Guide Rod and Pin	$1.20
4171	Hammer Spring	.25
4271	Hammer Spring Guide Rod	.25
4371	Hammer Spring Guide Rod Pin	.25
4471	Hammer Spring Abutment	.45
4571	Hammer Spring Abutment Pin	.25
4671	Hammer Screw	.25
4771	Hammer Screw Bushing	.25
4871	Locking Bolt, R. Hand	.75
4971	Locking Bolt, L. Hand	.75
5071	Lower Tang P. G.	3.00
5171	Lower Tang P. G. Complete Comprises Tank, Hammer Complete, Hammer Spring, Trigger, Trigger Spring, Trigger Pin, Hammer Screw, Abutment, Abutment Pin and Hammer Screw Bushing	6.05
5271	Magazine Tube No. 39A	1.50
5371	Magazine Spring	.25
5471	Magazine Plug No. 8	.25
5571	Magazine Plug Screw	.25
5671	Magazine Follower	.25
5771	Magazine Tube Complete Comprises Magazine Spring, Magazine Follower, Magazine Plug and Magazine Plug Screw	2.20
5871	Receiver with Lower Tang, Hammer Screw and Bushing	18.00
5971	Rubber P. G. Cap (large size) with Screw	.75
6071	Rubber P. G. Cap Screw	.25
6171	Spring Cover Base	.65
6271	Spring Cover Base Screw	.25
6371	Spring Cover Leaf	.70
6471	Spring Cover Leaf Spring	.25
6571	Spring Cover Leaf Point Pin	.25
6671	Spring Cover Stop Pin	.25
6671A	Spring Cover Complete Comprises Base, Leaf, Leaf Spring, Leaf Joint Pin, Leaf Stop Pin and Base Screw	1.85
6771	Trigger	.70
6871	Trigger Pin	.25
6971	Trigger Spring	.25
7071	Upper Tang Screw P. G.	.25
7171	Sling Strap No. 3268	2.00
7271	Sling Strap Snap Swivel Fig. No. 8 (2) each	.50
7371	Snap Swivel Base Complete for Stock Fig. 28	.70
7471	Rear Peep Sight 98A	4.00
7471A	Rear Sight Body 98A	1.50
7471B	Rear Sight Elevation Screw 98A	.25
7471C	Rear Sight Elevation Screw 98A	.25
7471D	Rear Sight Elevation Screw Spring 98A	.25
7471E	Rear Sight Stop Screw 98A	.25
7471F	Rear Sight Disc 7/16 aperture .081—98A	.50
7471G	Rear Sight Disc 5/8 aperture .052—98A	.50
7471H	Rear Sight Windage Screw 98A	1.00
7471J	Rear Sight Windage Slide 98A	1.00
7471K	Rear Sight Windage Screw Nut 98A	.25
7571	Rear Sight 22H with 1-C Elevator	.95
7671	Front Sight Lyman No. 31W	1.00
7771	Front Sight Cover No. 3278	.25
7871	Rear Sight Blank	.50

INSTRUCTIONS: In ordering parts always give name and number listed in catalog, also make, model, caliber and serial number of gun.

PAYMENTS: Parts will be sent only on advance payment. Parts cannot be returned for credit. A service charge of 25c must be added to every order under $1.00 to cover cost of handling. Do not forget to include postage.

ORDER BLANK IN MIDDLE AND INDEX IN BACK OF CATALOG

WINCHESTER RIFLE PARTS
MODELS 05, 07 AND 10 SELF LOADING RIFLES

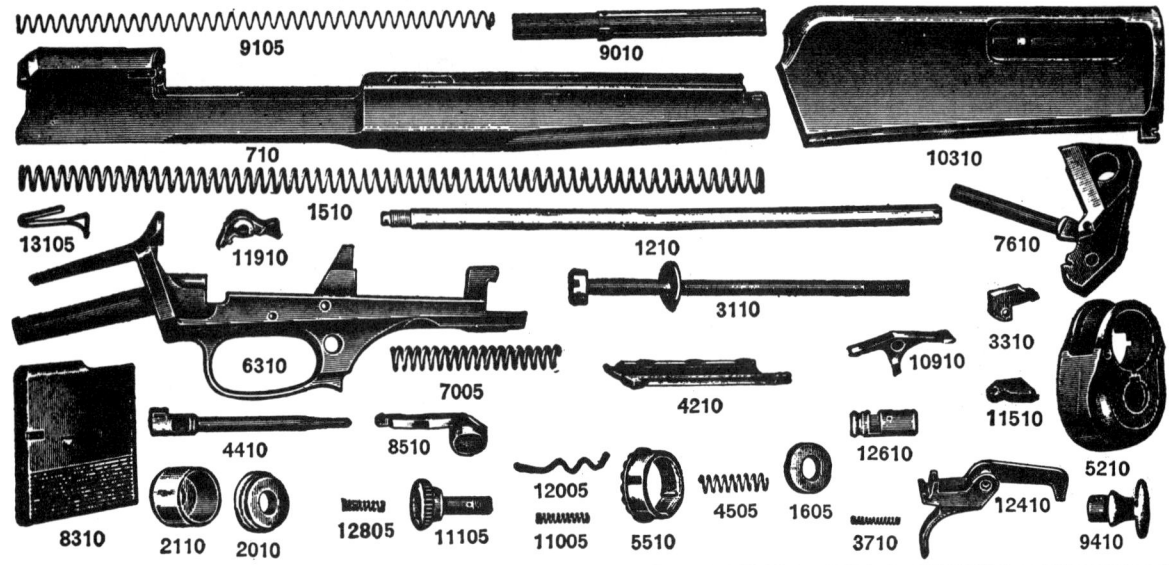

MODELS 05, 07 AND 10

	MODELS				
105	05			Barrel .32 caliber	$11.00
205	05			Barrel .35 caliber	11.00
307		07		Barrel .351 caliber	13.00
410			10	Barrel .401 caliber	13.00
505	05			Bolt	8.00
607		07		Bolt	14.00
710			10	Bolt	14.00
805	05			Bolt complete	9.80
907		07		Bolt complete	15.80
1010			10	Bolt complete	15.80

Bolt complete comprises: bolt with with firing pin, firing pin spring, firing pin stop pin, extractor, extractor plunger, extractor spring, and extractor plunger stop screw.

1105	05	07		Bolt guide rod	.65
1210			10	Bolt guide rod	.65
1305	05			Bolt spring	.30
1407		07		Bolt spring	.30
1510			10	Bolt spring	.30
1605	05		10	Buffers (2) each	.40
1707		07		Buffers (2) each	.40
1805	05			Buffer washers (2) each	.20
1907		07		Buffer washers (2) each	.25
2010			10	Buffer washers (2) each	.25
2110			10	Buffer pocket	.30
2205	05	07		Butt plate	.30
2310			10	Butt plate	.55
2405	05	07	10	Butt plate screw (2) each	.25
2505	05	07		Butt stock complete	4.75
2610			10	Butt stock complete	4.75

Butt stock complete comprises: stock with butt plate and (2) butt plate screws.

5705	05	07		Butt stock bolt	.25
2810			10	Butt stock bolt	.25
2905	05	07	10	Butt stock bolt washer	.25
3005	05	07		Butt stock bolt complete (bolt with washer)	.25
3110			10	Butt stock bolt complete (bolt with washer)	.25
3205	05	07		Extractor	.40
3310			10	Extractor	.40
3405	05	07		Extractor plunger	.25
3510			10	Extractor pin	.25
3605	05	07		Extractor plunger spring	.25
3710			10	Extractor spring	.25
3805	05	07		Extractor plunger stop screw	.25
3905	05			Ejector, .32 caliber	.85
4005	05			Ejector, .35 caliber	.85
4107		07		Ejector, .351 caliber	.95
4210			10	Ejector, .401 caliber	.80
4305	05	07		Firing pin	.55
4410			10	Firing pin	$0.55
4505	05	07	10	Firing pin stop pin	.25
4605	05	07	10	Firing pin stop pin	.25
4705	05			Forearm	1.90
4807		07		Forearm	2.50
4910			10	Forearm	2.10
5005	05			Forearm tip	2.20
5107		07		Forearm tip	2.30
5210			10	Forearm tip	2.50
5305	05			Forearm tip screw	.25
5407		07		Forearm tip nut	.45
5510			10	Forearm tip nut	.50
5607		07	10	Forearm tip nut plunger	.25
5707		07	10	Forearm tip nut plunger spring	.25
5807		07	10	Forearm tip key	.25
5907		07		Forearm tip complete comprising tip with forearm tip nut plunger and spring	2.50
6010			10	Forearm tip complete comprising tip with forearm tip nut plunger and spring	2.70
6105	05			Guard with shank	7.00
6207		07		Guard with shank	8.50
6310			10	Guard with shank	8.60
6405	05			Guard complete	15.50
6507		07		Guard complete	17.00
6610			10	Guard complete	17.10

Guard complete comprises: guard with shank, hammer complete, hammer spring, hammer pin, Take-down screw, Take-down screw stop pin, Take-down screw lock, timing lever, timing lever spring, timing lever spring screw, trigger, trigger lock, trigger lock plunger, trigger lock plunger spring, trigger pin, trigger spring, magazine lock, magazine lock spring, magazine lock screw and (2) peep sight plug screws, sear and sear spring.

6705	05	07		Guard shank	.25
6805	05	07		Hammer pin	.25
6910			10	Hammer pin	.25
7005	05	07	10	Hammer spring	.25
7105	05	07		Hammer spring guide rod	.25
7210			10	Hammer spring guide rod	.25
7305	05	07	10	Hammer spring guide rod pin	.25
7405	05			Hammer complete	1.75
7507		07		Hammer complete	1.75
7610			10	Hammer complete	1.85

Hammer complete comprises: hammer with hammer spring guide rod and hammer spring guide rod pin.

7705	05			†Magazine complete, .32 caliber, 5 cartridge	2.50

(Models 05, 07 and 10 Continued on Page 485)

INSTRUCTIONS: In ordering parts always give name and number listed in catalog, also make, model, caliber and serial number of gun. (Parts marked with * cannot be supplied on Mail Order. It will be necessary to return arm to us for fitting.)

PAYMENTS: Parts will be sent only on advance payment. Parts cannot be returned for credit. A service charge of 25c must be added to every order under $1.00 to cover cost of handling. Do not forget to include postage.

WINCHESTER RIFLE PARTS
MODEL 64 AND 64 DEER—LEVER ACTION RIFLES

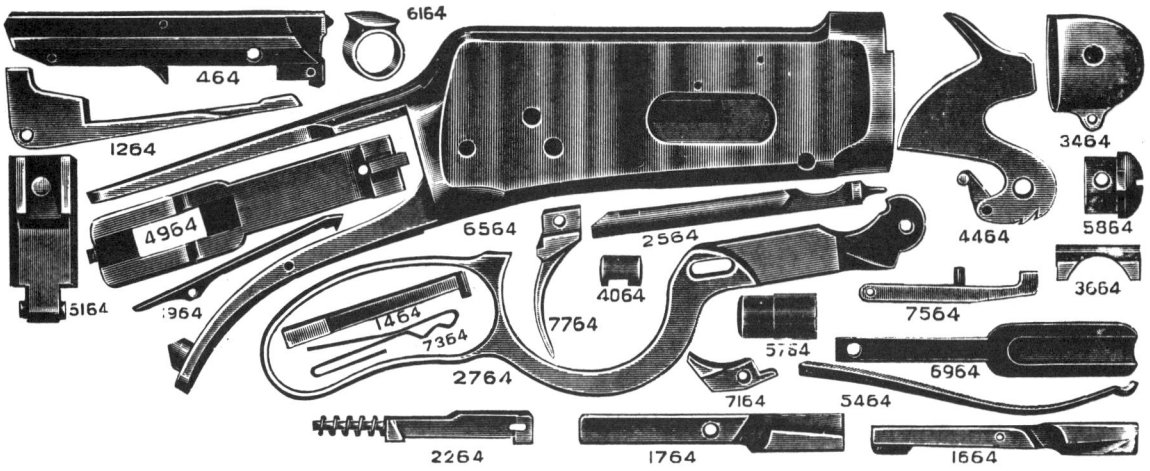

It is absolutely necessary that the numbers shown at the left of each item be specified when ordering.

No.	Description	Price
164	Barrel, .25/35, 24" round, tapered with ramp	$9.00
164A	Barrel, 25/35-20" round with ramp	9.00
264	Barrel, .30 W.C.F., 24" round, tapered with ramp	9.00
264A	Barrel, 30 W.C.F. 20" round with ramp	9.00
364	Barrel, .32 Win. Special, 24" round, tapered with ramp	9.00
364A	Barrel, 32 W.S. 20" round with ramp	9.00
464	Breech bolt with extractor and pin	3.30
564	Breech bolt complete comprises: bolt with extractor and pin, firing pin, firing pin stop pin, ejector, ejector spring and ejector stop pin	4.60
664	Butt stock, P.G. only	6.00
764	Butt stock, P.G. only complete comprises: stock, butt plate shot butt metal and (2) butt plate screws	7.05
864 Deer Rifle	Butt stock, P.G. only, with rubber P.G. tip and screw	8.00
964 Deer Rifle	Butt stock, P.G. only complete comprises: stock, butt plate shot butt metal, (2) butt plate screws, stock swivel base and (2) screws, rubber P.G. tip and screw	9.75
1064	Butt plate shot butt metal	.85
1164	Butt plate screws (2) each	.25
1264	Carrier	1.40
1364	Carrier screws (2) each	.25
1464	Carrier spring	.35
1564	Carrier spring screw	.25
1664	Cartridge guide, right hand	.55
1764	Cartridge guide, left hand	.50
1864	Cartridge guide screws (2) each	.25
1964	Extractor	.40
2064	Extractor pin	.25
2164	Ejector	.65
2264	Ejector complete comprises: ejector, spring and pin	.85
2364	Ejector spring	.25
2464	Ejector stop pin	.25
2564	Firing pin	.35
2664	Firing pin stop pin	.25
2764	Finger lever, P.G. only	2.25
2864	Finger lever pin	.25
2964	Finger lever pin stop screw	.25
3064	Finger lever link screw	.25
3164	Forearm	1.40
3264 Deer Rifle	Forearm	3.00
3364	Forearm tip	1.45
3464 Deer Rifle	Forearm tip fitted with snap swivel base	2.00
3564	Forearm tip screw (2) each	.25
3664	Forearm tip tenon	.40
3764	Friction stud	.25
3864	Friction stud spring	.25
3964	Friction stud stop pin	.25
4064	Firing pin striker	.25
4164	Firing pin striker stop pin	.25
4264	Hammer stirrup	.25
4364	Hammer stirrup pin	.25
4464	Hammer complete with stirrup and pin	1.25
4564	Hammer screw	$0.25
4664	Link	1.75
4764	Link pin	.25
4864	Link pin stop screw	.25
4964	Link complete comprises: link, friction stud, stud spring and stud stop pin	2.10
5064	Locking bolt	.95
5164	Locking bolt complete comprises: locking bolt, striker and striker stop pin	1.20
5264	Lower tang, P.G. only	1.85
5364	Lower tang complete comprises: tang with hammer complete, mainspring, mainspring screw, strain screw, trigger, sear, sear pin, sear and safety catch spring, spring screw, safety catch, safety catch pin, and hammer screw	5.15
5464	Mainspring, P.G. only	.60
5564	Mainspring screw	.25
5664	Mainspring strain screw	.25
5764	Magazine follower	.25
5864	Magazine plug No. 27	.25
5964	Magazine plug screw	.25
6064	Magazine spring	.25
6164	Magazine ring	.65
6264	Magazine ring pin	.25
6364	Magazine tube 38A	1.10
6464	Magazine tube 38A complete comprises: magazine tube, magazine follower, magazine spring, magazine plug, magazine plug screw, magazine ring and magazine ring pin	2.45
6564	Receiver with pistol grip, lower tang and hammer screw	10.45
6664	Receiver complete with action comprises: receiver with lower tang complete, breech bolt complete, right and left hand cartridge guides, cartridge guide screws (2), spring cover and screw, link complete, finger lever, link pin, link pin stop screw, carrier spring and screw, locking bolt complete, finger lever pin stop screw, carrier, carrier screws (2), and peep sight plug screw.	28.45
6764 Deer Rifle	Rubber P.G. tip	.40
6864 Deer Rifle	Rubber P.G. tip screw	.25
6964	Spring cover	.70
7064	Spring cover screw	.25
7164	Sear	.40
7264	Sear pin	.25
7364	Sear and safety catch spring	.25
7464	Sear and safety catch spring screw	.25
7564	Safety catch, P.G.	.25
7664	Safety catch pin	.25
7764	Trigger	.45
7864	Upper tang screw, P.G.	.25
7964	Upper tang screw, peep sight, P.G.	.25
8064	Front sight 31W Lyman 5/64 gold bead	1.00
8164	Rear sight 22H with 2C elevator	.95

(Continued on Next Page)

In replacing parts marked thus (*) when desired for Take-down Guns it is necessary to send gun to us.

INSTRUCTIONS: In ordering parts always give name and number listed in catalog, also make, model, caliber and serial number of gun. (Parts marked with * cannot be supplied on Mail Order. It will be necessary to return arm to us for fitting.)

PAYMENTS: Parts will be sent only on advance payment. Parts cannot be returned for credit. A service charge of 25c must be added to every order under $1.00 to cover cost of handling. Do not forget to include postage.

CAREFUL ATTENTION AND SAFE DELIVERY OF YOUR ORDER

WINCHESTER RIFLE PARTS
MODEL 03 RIFLE

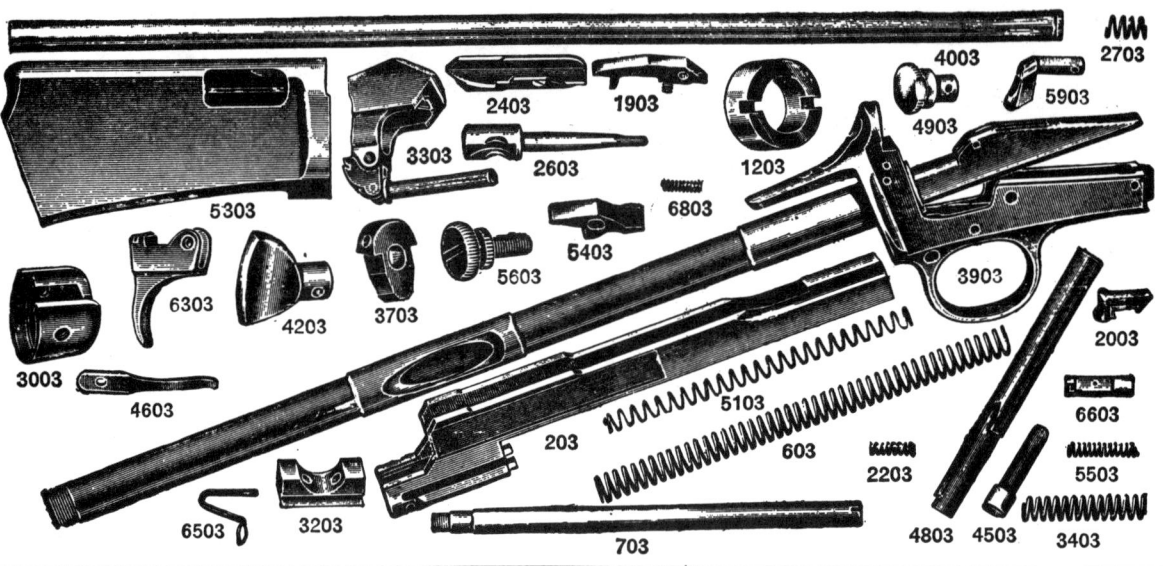

It is absolutely necessary that the numbers shown at the left of each gun part be specified when ordering.

103	Barrel 20"	$6.50
203	Bolt	6.25
303	Bolt complete comprising: bolt with firing pin and spring, firing pin stop pin, bolt roll, extractor, extractor plunger, extractor plunger spring and extractor plunger stop screw	8.00
403	Bolt roll	.25
503	Bolt roll pin (same as firing pin stop pin)	.25
603	Bolt spring	.25
703	Bolt guide rod	.30
803	Butt stock	3.00
903	Butt stock complete	4.10
	Stock complete comprises: stock with butt plate and (2) butt plate screws.	
1003	Butt stock, pistol grip	3.00
1103	Butt stock complete, pistol grip comprising: stock with butt plate, butt plate screws (2) pistol grip cap and screw	4.60
1203	Butt stock nut	.25
1303	Butt stock nut washer	.25
1403	Butt plate	.90
1503	Butt plate screw (2) each	.25
1603	Cartridge cut off	.45
1703	Cartridge cut off spring	.25
1803	Cartridge cut off pin	.25
1903	Cartridge cut off complete comprising: cartridge cut off and spring	.55
2003	Extractor	.65
2103	Extractor plunger	.25
2203	Extractor plunger spring	.25
2303	Extractor plunger stop screw	.25
2403	Ejector	.60
2503	Ejector screw	.25
2603	Firing pin	.50
2703	Firing pin spring	.25
2803	Firing pin stop pin	.25
2903	Forearm	1.40
3003	Forearm tip	1.40
3103	Forearm tip screw (2) each	.25
3203	Forearm tip tenon	.25
3303	Hammer with hammer spring guide rod and pin	2.10
3303½	Hammer pin	$0.25
3403	Hammer spring	.25
3503	Hammer spring guide rod	.25
3603	Hammer spring guide rod pin	.25
3703	Hammer spring abutment	.45
3803	Hammer spring abutment pin	.25
3903	*Magazine tube outside, with throat and tang	9.55
4003	Magazine tube inside	1.10
4103	Magazine tube inside complete comprising: tube with magazine plug, magazine plug pin, magazine spring and magazine follower	2.15
4203	Magazine plug	.65
4303	Magazine plug pin	.25
4403	Magazine spring	.25
4503	Magazine follower	.25
4603	Magazine friction spring	.25
4703	Magazine charger	.75
4803	Operating sleeve	.85
4903	Operating sleeve tip	.25
5003	Operating sleeve tip pin	.25
5103	Operating sleeve spring	.25
5203	Peep sight plug screw (2) each	.25
5303	Receiver with take down screw bushing, ejector and screw	14.75
5403	Sear	.50
5503	Sear spring	.25
5603	Take down screw and stop pin	.30
5703	Take down screw bushing	.25
5803	Take down screw stop pin	.25
5903	Take down screw lock	.75
6003	Take down screw lock pin	.25
6103	Take down screw lock spring	.25
6203	Throat pin	.25
6303	Trigger	.85
6403	Trigger pin	.25
6503	Trigger spring	.25
6603	Trigger lock	.30
6703	Trigger lock plunger	.25
6803	Trigger lock plunger spring	.25
6903	Wiping rod	.25
7003	Pistol grip cap	.40
7103	Pistol grip cap screw	.25

In replacing parts marked thus (*), it will be necessary to send receiver and tang to us

MODEL 64—(Continued from Preceding Page)

	Parts necessary to change from Plain to Double Set Trigger	$8.35
8564	Front trigger	.80
8664	Front trigger pin	.25
8764	Front trigger spring	.25
8864	Hammer complete comprises: hammer with fly, fly pin, stirrup and pin	1.95
8964	Hammer screw	.25
9064	Hammer fly	.30
9164	Hammer fly pin	.25
9264	Hammer stirrup	.35
9364	Hammer stirrup pin	.25
9464	Lower tang, P.G. only	2.00
9564	Mainspring, P.G. only	$0.70
9664	Mainspring screw	.25
9764	Mainspring strain screw	.25
9864	Rear trigger	1.10
9964	Rear trigger pin	.25
10064	Rear trigger spring	.25
10164	Rear trigger stop pin	.25
10264	Sear	.60
10364	Sear spring	.25
10464	Sear spring screw	.25
10564	Trigger guide pin	.25
10664	Trigger adj. screw	.25

PLEASE TELL OTHERS ABOUT STOEGER'S CATALOG

WINCHESTER RIFLE PARTS
MODEL 65—LEVER ACTION REPEATING RIFLE

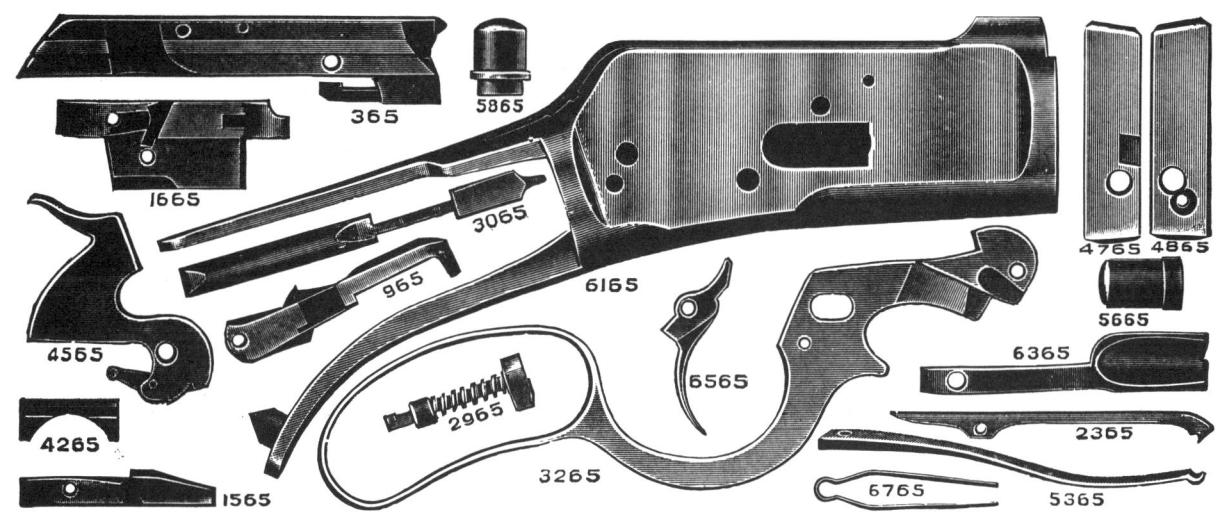

It is absolutely necessary that the numbers shown at the left of each item be specified when ordering.

No.	Description	Price
165	Barrel, 22″ round, .25/20 cal., tapered with ramp	$9.00
265	Bbl., 22″ rd., .32 W.C.F. cal., tapered with ramp	9.00
365	Breech bolt with extractor and p.n.	3.50
465	Breech bolt complete comprises bolt, extractor, extractor pin, firing pin, firing pin stop pin, ejec. guide, 2 pins, ejec., ejec. collar, ejec. spg.	5.35
565	Butt stock, P.G. only	6.00
665	Butt stock, P.G. only complete comprises: stock, butt plate and (2) screws	7.05
765	Butt plate shot butt, metal	.85
865	Butt plate screws (2) each	.25
965	Carrier	1.15
1065	Carrier stop	.25
1165	Carrier stop pin	.25
1265	Carrier stop spring	.25
1365	Carrier screws (2) each	.25
1465	Carrier complete comprises: carrier, carrier stop, carrier stop pin and spring	1.50
1565	Cartridge guide, right hand, .25/20 cal.	.50
1665	Cartridge guide, left hand, .25/20 cal., complete	1.40
1765	Cartridge guide, right hand, .32 W.C.F. cal.	.50
1865	Cartridge guide, left hand, .32 W.C.F. cal. com. Cartridge guide complete comprises: cartridge guide, cartridge stop and joint pin	1.40
1965	Cartridge guide screws (2) each	.25
2065	Cartridge stop	.40
2165	Cartridge stop joint pin	.25
2265	Cartridge stop spring	.25
2365	Extractor	.40
2465	Extractor pin	.25
2565	Ejector	.65
2665	Ejector guide and (2) pins	.25
2765	Ejector collar	.25
2865	Ejector spring	.25
2965	Ejector com. comprises: ejector, collar and spring	.85
3065	Firing pin	.45
3165	Firing pin stop pin	.25
3265	Finger lever, P.G. only complete comprises: finger lever, friction stud, spring and stop pin	2.95
3465	Finger lever pin	.25
3565	Finger lever pin stop screw	.25
3665	Friction stud	.25
3765	Friction stud spring	.25
3865	Friction stud stop pin	.25
3965	Forearm	1.40
4065	Forearm tip	1.45
4165	Forearm tip screws (2) each	.25
4265	Forearm tip tenon	.40
4365	Hammer stirrup	.25
4465	Hammer stirrup pin	.25
4565	Hammer complete comprises: hammer, hammer stirrup, and pin	1.25
4665	Hammer screw	.25
4765	Locking bolt, right hand	.75
4865	Locking bolt, left hand	.70
4965	Locking bolt pin	.25
5065	Locking bolt pin stop screw	.25
5165	Lower tang, P.G. only	1.60
5265	Lower tang, P.G. only complete comprises: lower tang, hammer complete, mainspring, screw, mainspring strain screw, trigger, trigger pin, trigger spring, trigger spring screw and hammer screw	$4.60
5365	Mainspring, P.G. only	.60
5465	Mainspring screw	.25
5565	Mainspring strain screw	.25
5665	Magazine follower	.25
5765	Magazine spring	.25
5865	Magazine plug No. 29	.25
5965	Magazine tube, 25E	1.10
6065	Magazine tube complete comprises: magazine tube, mag. follower, mag. spring and mag. plug	1.70
6165	Receiver with P.G. lower tang and hammer screw	11.10
6265	Receiver complete with action comprises: Receiver with P.G. lower tang complete, breech bolt complete, carrier complete, finger lever complete, right and left hand cartridge guides, cartridge guide screws (2), spring cover, spring cover screw, right and left hand locking bolt, locking bolt pin stop screw, locking bolt pin, carrier screws (2), finger lever pin, finger lever pin stop screw, and peep sight plug screw	29.65
6365	Spring cover	.75
6465	Spring cover screw	.25
6565	Trigger	.75
6665	Trigger pin	.25
6765	Trigger spring	.25
6865	Trigger spring screw	.25
6965	Upper tang screw, P.G.	.25
7065	Upper tang screw, P.G., peep sight	.25
7165	Front sgt. Lyman 31W, 5/64, Gold Bead .260 high	1.00
7265	Rear sight, 22H Rocky Mt. with 1C elevator	.95
	Parts necessary to change from Plain to Double Set Trigger	8.35
7465	Front trigger	.80
7565	Front trigger pin	.25
7665	Front trigger spring	.25
7765	Hammer complete comprises: hammer with fly, fly pin, stirrup and stirrup pin	1.95
7865	Hammer screw	.25
7965	Hammer fly	.30
8065	Hammer fly pin	.25
8165	Hammer stirrup	.35
8265	Hammer stirrup pin	.25
8365	Lower tang, P.G. only	2.00
8465	Mainspring, P.G. only	.70
8565	Mainspring screw	.25
8665	Mainspring strain screw	.25
8765	Rear trigger	1.10
8865	Rear trigger pin	.25
8965	Rear trigger spring	.25
9065	Rear trigger stop pin	.25
9165	Sear	.60
9265	Sear spring	.25
9365	Sear spring screw	.25
9465	Trigger guide pin	.25
9565	Trigger adj screw	.25

In replacing parts marked thus (*) when desired for Takedown Guns it is necessary to send gun to us.

INSTRUCTIONS: In ordering parts always give name and number listed in catalog, also make, model, caliber and serial number of gun. (Parts marked with * cannot be supplied on Mail Order. It will be necessary to return arm to us for fitting.)

PAYMENTS: Parts will be sent only on advance payment. Parts cannot be returned for credit. A service charge of 25c must be added to every order under $1.00 to cover cost of handling. Do not forget to include postage.

SEE PAGE 8 "HOW TO ORDER"

WINCHESTER RIFLE PARTS
MODEL 54 BOLT ACTION REPEATING RIFLE

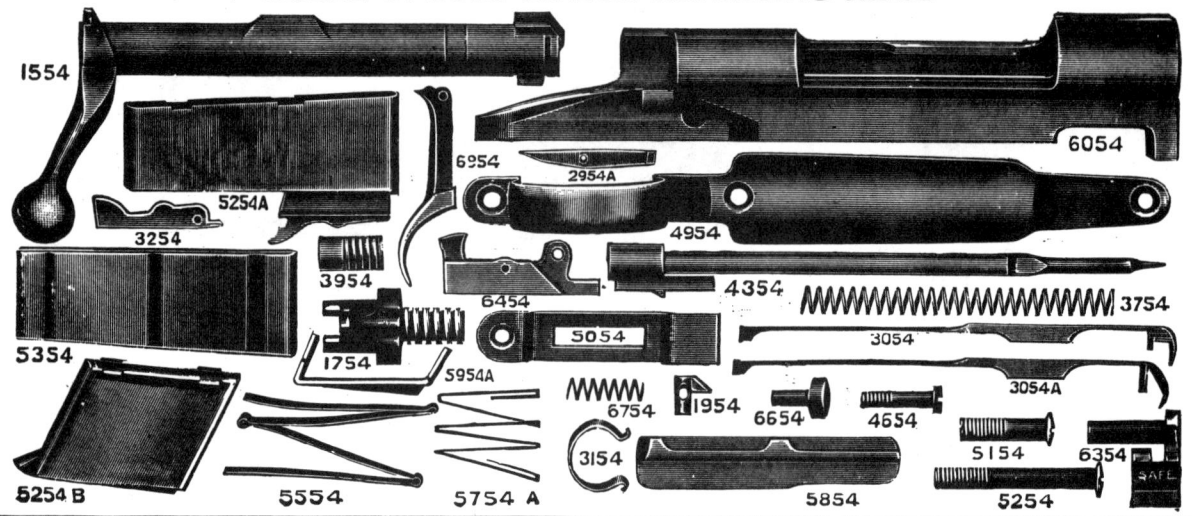

Be sure to specify if Plain or Speed Lock Parts are wanted. All Barrels have the Ramp Base for front sight, except Sniper.

It is absolutely necessary that the numbers shown at the left of each gun part be specified when ordering.

When ordering be sure to specify the caliber of rifle.

054	*Barrel, regular .22 Hornet, 24"	$10.00
154	*Barrel, regular .270 caliber, rifle, 20" or 24"	10.00
254	*Barrel, regular .270 caliber, carbine, 20"	10.00
354	*Barrel, regular .30 Gov't. '06, rifle, 20" or 24"	10.00
454	*Barrel, regular .30 Gov't. '06, carbine, 20"	10.00
554	*Barrel, regular 7 M/M, rifle, 20" or 24"	10.00
654	*Barrel, regular 7 M/M, carbine, 20"	10.00
1354	*Barrel, regular 9 M/M, rifle, 20" or 24"	10.00
1454	*Barrel, regular 9 M/M, carbine, 20"	10.00
1454½	*Barrel, regular .250/3000 Savage, rifle, 20" or 24"	10.00
1454A	*Barrel, regular .250/3000 Savage, carbine, 20"	10.00
1454B	*Barrel, regular .257 Roberts, 24"	10.00
1454C	*Barrel, regular .220 Swift, 26" only	10.00
254AA	*Barrel, regular National Match 30/06, 24"	10.00
354AA	*Barrel, heavy 22 Hornet, 24"	20.00
354AB	*Barrel, heavy .270 caliber, 24"	20.00
354AC	*Barrel, heavy 30/06, 24"	20.00
354AD	*Barrel, heavy 7 M/M, 24"	20.00
354AE	*Barrel, heavy 250/3000 Savage, 24"	20.00
354AF	*Barrel, heavy .257 Roberts, 24"	20.00
354AG	*Barrel, heavy .220 Swift, 26"	20.00
454AA	*Barrel, Sniper 30/06, 26"	30.00

Heavy and Sniper Barrels have the Tel Sight bases on them

1554	*Breech bolt, No. 1, .270 Winchester, .30 Gov't. '06, 7 M/M, 7.65 M/M and 9 M/M	8.50
1554A	*Breech bolt, No. 1 for above cals. (Speed Lock)	8.50
1654½	*Breech bolt, No. 3, 250/3000 Savage (Speed Lock)	8.50
1654B	*Breech bolt, .22 Hornet (Speed Lock)	8.50
1654C	*Breech bolt, No. 4, .220 Swift and .257 Roberts	8.50
1754	Breech bolt sleeve	2.25
1854	Breech bolt sleeve complete comprising breech bolt sleeve with breech bolt sleeve lock, breech bolt sleeve lock spring, breech bolt sleeve lock pin, safety lock, plunger, spring and F.P. stop screw	4.50
1954	Breech bolt sleeve lock	.50
2054	Breech bolt sleeve lock spring	.25
2154	Breech bolt sleeve lock pin	.25
2254	*Breech bolt, No. 1 complete comprising bolt with firing pin, firing pin sleeve, firing pin spring, breech bolt sleeve, breech bolt sleeve lock, breech bolt sleeve lock spring and pin, safety lock, safety lock plunger, safety lock plunger spring, extractor, ring and firing pin stop screw	17.80
2254A	Butt stock, Super grade, with forearm tip, cheek piece and fancy checking on stock and forearm, pistol grip cap and screw	24.00
2254B	Butt stock complete, Super grade, comprises: butt stock, pistol grip cap and screw, butt plate and (2) screws, forearm tip black plastic material, snap swivel base complete with (2) screws for forearm, snap swivel base complete with screws and forearm stud screw escutcheon	28.05
2254C	Let in stock blank for Super grade thick enough for check piece	24.00
2454	Butt stock, carbine	13.25
2454A	Butt stock, wood only	17.80
2454B	Butt stock with butt plate and two screws	18.50
2654	Butt stock, carbine, complete comprising stock with butt plate and (2) butt plate screws, and forearm stud screw escutcheon	14.40
2654½	Butt stock, N. R. A. complete	19.30
	Butt stock, N. R. A. complete comprises stock, butt plate, butt plate screws (2), stock screw eye swivel bow and forearm screw eye swivel complete with escutcheon and forearm stud screw escutcheon.	
2654B	Butt stock, National Match Model, for reg. barrel	$32.50
2654C	Butt stock, Target Model, for heavy barrel	32.50
2654D	Butt stock, Sniper Match Model, for extra heavy barrel	32.50
2654E	Above stocks complete (including butt plate & swivel bases, and screws)	34.65
2654F	Let in stock blank for above National Match, Target and Sniper	32.50
2654A	Let in stock blank for regular gun	17.50
	The above blank comprises forearm stud screw escutcheon, butt plate and (2) screws	
2654G	Butt plate for matchstock	.65
2654H	Butt plate screw for match stock (2) each	.25
2754	Butt plate, rifle	.85
2854	Butt plate, carbine	.85
2854A	Butt plate, N. R. A.	.80
2954	Butt plate screw (2) each	.25
2954A	Cartridge pusher, Hornet (Speed Lock)	.30
2954B	Cartridge pusher pin, Hornet (Speed Lock)	.25
2954C	Cartridge pusher spring, Hornet (Speed Lock)	.25
3054	Extractor (specify if letter A is on receiver)	2.00
3054A	Extractor, .22 Hornet (Speed Lock)	2.00
3154	Extractor ring	.40
3254	Ejector No. 1, .270 Winchester, .30 Gov't. '06, 7 M/M, 7.65 M/M and 9 M/M	.30
3354	Ejector, No. 2, .30 W. C. F. and .250/3000 Savage (Speed Lock on 250/3000)	.30
3354A	Ejector, .22 Hornet (Speed Lock)	.30
3354B	Ejector rivet, .22 Hornet (Speed Lock)	.25
3354C	Ejector No. 4, .220 Swift and .257 Roberts	.30
3454	Ejector pin	.25
3554	Ejector spring	.25
3654	Ejector complete with ejector spring and pin	.50
	For parts marked thus (*) gun must be sent us	
3754	Firing pin spring, .270 Winchester, .30 Gov't. '06, 7 M/M, 7.65 M/M and 9 M/M	.25
3854A	*Firing pin spring (Speed Lock) .270 Win., .30 Gov't. '06*, 7 M/M, 7.65 M/M, 9 M/M, .220 Swift and .257 Roberts	.25
3854B	*Firing pin spring, Hornet (Speed Lock)	.25
3954	Firing pin sleeve (for two-piece firing pin)	.25
3954A	Firing pin sleeve (for one-piece firing pin)	.25
4054	Firing pin striker (for two piece firing pin)	.50
4054A	Firing pin stop screw	.25
4154	Firing pin rod (for two piece firing pin)	2.35
4254	Firing pin complete comprising firing pin rod with striker, sleeve and spring	3.25
4354	Firing pin (one piece)	2.85
4354A	*Firing pin (Speed Lock)	2.85
4454	Firing pin, complete (one piece) consisting of firing pin, sleeve and spring	3.25
4454A	Forearm tip (blank). Not fitted. Made of black plastic material, regular barrel	.75
4554	Forearm stud	.25
4654	Forearm stud screw	.25
4754	Forearm stud screw escutcheon	.25
4854	Forearm screw eye and escutcheon	.25
4954	Guard	2.00
4954A	Guard (Super Grade)	2.25
5054	Guard plate	.50
5154	Guard screw front, short	.25
5254	Guard screw rear, long, (2) each	.25
5254A	Magazine, .22 Hornet with ejector, spring, holder and rivets (Speed Lock)	1.80
5254B	Mag. adapter, .22 Hornet with Back (Speed Lock)	.40
5354	Magazine, No. 1, .30 Gov't. '06, 7 M/M, 7.65 M/M and 9 M/M	1.25

(Continued on Page 485)

AMERICA'S GREAT GUN HOUSE

WINCHESTER RIFLE PARTS

MODEL 70 BOLT ACTION RIFLE

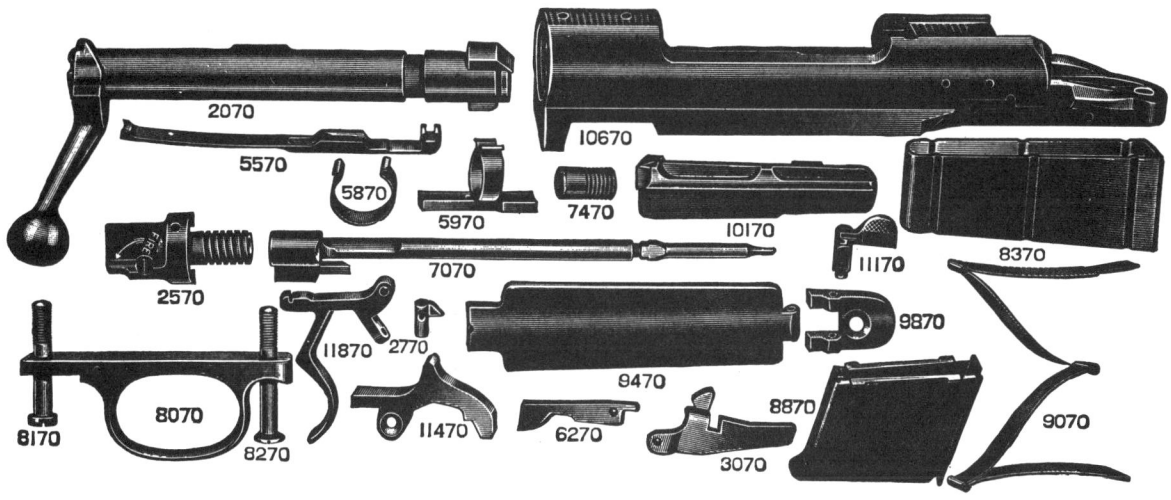

It is absolutely necessary that the numbers shown at the left of each gun part be specified when ordering.

170	*Barrel, .22 cal. Hornet, 20" and 24".............	$15.00
270	*Barrel, .270 cal., 20" and 24"..................	15.00
370	*Barrel, .30 Gov't '06 cal., 20" and 24".........	15.00
470	*Barrel, 7 m/m, 20" and 24"......................	15.00
570	*Barrel, 250/3000 Savage, 20" and 24"............	15.00
670	*Barrel, .257 Winchester Roberts, 20" and 24"....	15.00
770	*Barrel, .220 Swift, 26" only....................	15.00
970	*Barrel, .300 Magnum, 26"........................	15.00
1070	*Heavy barrel, .22 cal. Hornet, 24".............	20.00
1170	*Heavy barrel, .270 cal., 24"...................	20.00
1270	*Heavy barrel, .30 Gov't '06 cal., 24"..........	20.00
1370	*Heavy barrel, 7 m/m, 24".......................	20.00
1470	*Heavy barrel, .250/3000 Savage, 24"............	20.00
1570	*Heavy barrel, .257 Winchester Roberts, 24".....	20.00
1670	*Heavy barrel, .220 Swift, 26" only.............	20.00
1870	*Heavy barrel, .300 Magnum, 26".................	20.00
1870A	*Heavy barrel, .375 Magnum, 24"................	20.00
1870B	*Swivel butt barrel, .375 Magnum, 25"..........	20.00
1970	*Bull barrel, .30 Gov't '06 cal., 28"...........	20.00
1970A	*Bull barrel, .300 Magnum, 28".................	30.00
2070	*Breech bolt, .270 cal., .30 Gov't '06 cal., 7 m/m, .220 Swift, .257 Winchester Roberts and .250/3000 Savage..	8.50
2270	*Breech bolt, .375 and .300 Magnum..............	8.50
2370	*Breech bolt, .22 cal. Hornet...................	8.50
2470	*Breech bolt complete, .270 Win., .30 Gov't '06, 7 m/m. Comprises bolt, with firing pin, firing pin sleeve, firing pin spring, breech bolt sleeve, breech bolt sleeve lock, breech bolt sleeve lock pin and spring, safety lock, safety lock plunger, safety lock plunger spring, extractor, ring and firing pin stop screw...................	16.55
2470A	*Breech bolt complete for .375 and .300 Magnum. Same as above...................................	16.55
2470B	*Breech bolt complete for .220 Swift, .257 Roberts and .250/3000 Savage. Same as above only add bolt stop extension........................	16.90
2470C	*Breech bolt complete for .22 cal. Hornet. Same as above only add bolt stop extension, cartridge pusher, pin and spring.................................	17.60
2570	Breech bolt sleeve..............................	2.25
2670	Breech bolt sleeve complete comprises sleeve, sleeve lock, sleeve lock spring, sleeve lock pin, safety lock, plunger, plunger spring and firing pin stop screw.............	4.50
2770	Breech bolt sleeve lock.........................	.50

In replacing parts marked thus (*) it is necessary to send Gun.

2870	Breech bolt sleeve lock spring..................	$.25
2970	Breech bolt sleeve lock pin.....................	.25
3070	Bolt stop	.40
3170	Bolt stop plunger..............................	.25
3270	Bolt stop plunger spring.......................	.25
3370	Butt stock, wood only, for regular barrel......	15.00
3470	Butt stock, wood only, for heavy barrel........	15.00
3570	Butt stock, wood only, for Bull barrel.........	15.00
Above three for all Cal. except .300 and .375 Magnum		
3570A	Butt stock, wood only, for regular barrel.....	15.00
3570B	Butt stock, wood only, for heavy barrel.......	15.00
3570C	Butt stock, wood only, for Bull barrel........	15.00
Above three for .300 and .375 Magnum		
3670	Butt stock complete for all Cals. except .300 Magnum regular, heavy and Bull barrel comprises butt stock, butt plate and (2) screws, stock screw eye swivel bow Fig. 7, and forearm screw eye swivel complete Fig. 12, with 1" or 1¼" bow.............	16.70
3670AA	Butt stock complete for .300 Magnum regular, heavy and Bull barrel comprises butt stock, butt plate and (2) screws, stock screw eye swivel bow Fig. 7 and forearm screw eye swivel complete Fig. 12, with 1" or 1¼" bow......	16.70
3670A	Butt stock complete, Reg. Gun, .375 Magnum with Reg. barrel comprises butt stock, Win. recoil pad (large) and (2) screws, stock screw eye swivel bow Fig. 7, 1" or 1¼" bow and forearm screw eye swivel complete Fig. 12 with 1" or 1¼" bow............................	21.20
3770	Butt stock, Super grade, Reg. barrel...........	24.00
3870	Butt stock, Super grade, Heavy barrel..........	24.00
3970	Butt stock, Super grade, Bull barrel...........	24.00
Above Three for Cal. except .300 and .375 Magnum		
3970A	Butt stock, Super grade, Reg. barrel, with recoil pad....	26.00
3970B	Butt stock, Super grade, Heavy barrel.........	24.00
3970C	Butt stock, Super grade, Bull barrel..........	24.00
Above for .300 and .375 Magnum		
4070	Butt stock, Super grade, complete for Reg., Heavy and Bull barrels comprises stock, P. G. cap and screw, butt plate and (2) screws, forearm tip made of black plastic material, snap swivel base complete with (2) screws for stock, Fig. 28, snap swivel base complete with (2) screws for forearm, Fig. 11, and forearm stud screw escutcheon	28.05

(Continued on next page)

INSTRUCTIONS: In ordering parts always give name and number listed in catalog, also make, model, caliber and serial number of gun.

PAYMENTS: Parts will be sent only on advance payment. Parts cannot be returned for credit. A service charge of 25c must be added to every order under $1.00 to cover cost of handling. Do not forget to include postage.

A NEW GUN CARRIES A FACTORY GUARANTEE

WINCHESTER RIFLE PARTS MODEL 70

(Continued from preceding page)

No.	Description	Price
4070A	Butt stock complete, Super grade gun, .300 and .375 Magnum, with Reg. barrel, comprises butt stock, Win. recoil pad (large) and (2) screws, P. G. cap and screw, forearm tip made of black plastic material, snap swivel base complete with (2) screws for stock Fig. 28, snap swivel base complete with (2) screws for forearm Fig. 11, and forearm stud screw escutcheon	$30.05
4170	Butt stock, Marksman, Reg. barrel, .30 Gov't '06	32.50
4270	Butt stock, Marksman, Heavy barrel, .30 Gov't '06	32.50
4370	Butt stock, Marksman, Bull barrel, .30 Gov't '06	32.50
4370A	Butt stock, Marksman, Reg. barrel, .300 Magnum	32.50
4370B	Butt stock, Marksman, Heavy barrel, .300 Magnum	32.50
4370C	Butt stock, Marksman, Bull barrel, .300 Magnum	32.50
4470	Butt stock, Marksman, complete for Reg., Heavy and Bull barrel comprises stock, butt plate and (2) screws, stock swivel base complete with (2) screws, Fig. 2 with 1¼" bow, used on rear end of stock. Front end use Part No. 7970M	34.65
4570	Let in butt stock blank, Reg. gun. Specify if wanted for Reg., Heavy or Bull barrel	17.50
4670	Let in butt stock blank, Super grade gun. Specify if wanted for Reg., Heavy or Bull barrel	24.00
4770	Let in butt stock blank, Marksman stock. Specify if wanted for Reg., Heavy or Bull barrel	32.50
4870	Butt plate metal for Reg. and Super Grade stock	.80
4970	Butt plate screws for above (2) each	.25
5070	Butt plate metal for Marksman stock	.65
5170	Butt plate screws for Marksman stock (2) each	.25
5170A	Win. recoil pad (large)	2.00
5270	Cartridge pusher, .22 cal. Hornet	.30
5370	Cartridge pusher pin, .22 cal. Hornet	.25
5470	Cartridge pusher spring, .22 cal. Hornet	.25
5570	Extractor, .30 Gov't '06 cal., .270 Win., 7 m/m, .220 Swift, .257 Win. Roberts and .250/3000 Savage	2.00
5670	Extractor, .375 and .300 Magnum	2.00
5770	Extractor, .22 cal. Hornet	2.00
5870	Extractor ring for cal. .270 Win., .30 Gov't '06, 7 m/m, .375 and .300 Magnum	.40
5970	Extractor ring and bolt stop extension, .22 cal. Hornet	.75
6070	Extractor ring and bolt stop extension, .250/3000 Savage	.75
6170	Extractor ring and bolt stop extension, .220 Swift and .257 Win. Roberts	.75
6270	Ejector, .270 Win., .30 Gov't '06, 7 m/m, .375 and .300 Magnum	.30
6370	Ejector No. 5, .250/3000 Savage	.30
6470	Ejector No. 4, .220 Swift and .257 Winchester Roberts	.30
6470A	Ejector, .22 cal. Hornet	.30
6570	Ejector rivet, .22 cal. Hornet	.25
6670	Ejector pin, all cal. except .22 Hornet	.25
6770	Ejector spring, all cal. except .22 Hornet	.25
6870	Ejector spring, .22 cal. Hornet	.25
6970	Ejector complete (specify cal.) comprises ejector, ejector spring and pin	.50
7070	Firing pin	2.85
7170	Firing pin complete comprises firing pin, sleeve and spring	3.25
7270	Firing pin spring, all cal. except .22 Hornet	.25
7370	Firing pin spring, .22 cal. Hornet	.25
7470	Firing pin sleeve	.25
7570	Firing pin stop screw	.25
7670	Forearm tip blank, not fitted, made of black plastic material	.75
7770	Forearm stud	.25
7870	Forearm stud screw	.25
7970	Forearm stud screw escutcheon	.25
7970A	Forearm adjustment base	.75
7970B	Forearm adjustment base screw (Flat Head)	.25
7970C	Forearm adjustment base screw escutcheon	.25
7970D	Forearm adjustment swivel base (Bakelite)	.75
7970E	Forearm adjustment swivel bow complete	.25
7970G	Forearm adjustment swivel bow base screw (Round Head)	.25
7970H	Forearm adjustment swivel bow base with bow (Base for Bakelite)	.60
7970L	Forearm adjustment bow screw escutcheon	.25
7970M	Forearm adjustment base complete	2.85
8070	Guard bow	1.50
8170	Guard bow screw, front, thick head	.25
8270	Guard bow screw, rear, thin head	.25
8370	Magazine, .30 Gov't '06, .270 Win. and 7 m/m	$1.50
8470	Magazine No. 7, .250/3000 Savage	1.50
8570	Magazine No. 6, .220 Swift	1.50
8670	Magazine No. 5, .257 Win. Roberts	1.50
8770	Magazine, .375 and .300 Magnum	1.50
8870	Magazine adapter with black, .22 cal. Hornet	.75
8970	Magazine complete, .22 cal. Hornet	1.80
9070	Magazine spring, .30 Gov't '06, .375 and .300 Magnum and .270 Win.	.50
9170	Magazine spring, .250/3000 Savage, .257 Win. Roberts and .220 Swift	.50
9270	Magazine spring, 7 m/m	.50
9370	Magazine spring, .22 cal. Hornet	.50
9470	Magazine cover	1.25
9570	Magazine cover catch	.25
9670	Magazine cover catch pin	.25
9770	Magazine cover catch spring	.25
9870	Magazine cover hinge plate	.50
9970	Magazine cover hinge plate screw	.25
10070	Magazine cover hinge pin	.25
10170	Magazine follower, .30 Gov't '06, .270 Win. and 7 m/m	1.50
10270	Magazine follower, .250/3000 Savage, .257 Roberts and .220 Swift	1.50
10370	Magazine follower, .22 cal. Hornet	1.50
10570	Magazine follower, .375 and .300 Magnum	1.50
10670	*Receiver, .30 Gov't '06, .270 Win., 7 m/m, .22 Hornet, .250/3000 Savage, .220 Swift, .257 Win. Roberts	12.35
10970	*Receiver, .375 and .300 Magnum	12.35
11070	Rubber P. G. cap and screw, large size, Super grade only	.75
11170	Safety lock	1.25
11270	Safety lock plunger	.25
11370	Safety lock plunger spring	.25
11370A	Safety lock slot pin	.25
11470	Sear	1.25
11570	Sear pin	.25
11670	Sear spring	.25
11870	Trigger	1.20
11970	Trigger pin	.25
12070	Trigger spring	.25
12170	Trigger stop screw	.25
12270	Trigger stop screw nut	.25
12370	Trigger spring adjusting nut (2) each	.25
12470	Front sight cover 3277 for 7 m/m	.25
12570	Front sight cover 3278 for .22 Hornet, .250/3000 Savage, .270 Win. and 30 Gov't '06	.25
12570A	Redfield 5/64" full Gold Bead front sight for Super Grade	1.50
12670	Lyman front sight 31W, Reg. barrel	1.00
12770	Lyman front sight 77 or Redfield 63, Target Model, National Match	2.50
12870	Lyman front sight 77 or Redfield 63, Bull barrel	2.50
12970	Lyman receiver sight No. 48WJS for Super Grade, Reg.	13.00
12970D	National Match, Target Model and Bull Gun Lyman 48WH rear sight	11.50
12970A	Lyman receiver sight No. 57W for above	6.00
12970B	Lyman receiver sight plug screw (2) each	.25
12970C	Lyman telescope sight base plug screw (2) each	.25
13070	Rear sight 22G, Reg. Barrel on Reg. Gun and Super Grade	.95
13170	Sling strap 3256—for 1¼" bows, National Match, Target Model and Bull Gun	1.50
13270	Sling strap 3269—for 1" bows, Super Grade	2.00
13470	Stock screw eye with swivel bow Fig. 7 for 1" or 1¼" bows, for Reg. Gun	.25
13470A	Forearm screw eye escutcheon	.25
13570	Forearm screw eye swivel complete Fig. 12 for 1" or 1¼" bows, for Reg. Gun	.50
13670	Sling strap snap swivel Fig. 8 for 1" or 1¼" bows	.50
13770	Snap swivel base complete—Fig. 28 for stock	.70
13870	Snap swivel base complete—Fig. 11 for forearm, for Super Grade	.70
13970	Stock swivel base complete—Fig. 2 for 1¼" bows; for stock and front end use Part No. 7970M	.60
14070	Telescope sight base complete front (long) National Match .470 high	.75
14170	Telescope sight base complete front (long) Target Heavy Barrel .360 high	.75
14270	Telescope sight base complete front (long) Bull Barrel .262 high	.75
14370	Albree Keeper	1.50

In replacing parts marked thus (*) it is necessary to send Gun.

INSTRUCTIONS: In ordering parts always give name and number listed in catalog, also make, model, caliber and serial number of gun.

PAYMENTS: Parts will be sent only on advance payment. Parts cannot be returned for credit. A service charge of 25c must be added to every order under $1.00 to cover cost of handling. Do not forget to include postage.

PLEASE TELL OTHERS ABOUT STOEGER'S CATALOG

WINCHESTER RIFLE PARTS
MODEL 52 BOLT ACTION RIFLE

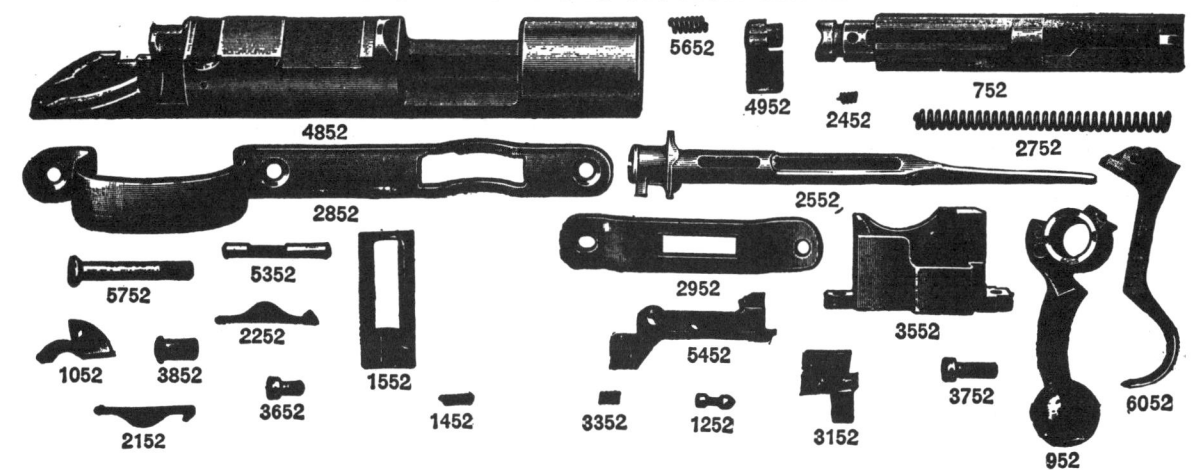

Be sure and specify if Plain or Speed Lock Parts are wanted.
It is absolutely necessary that the numbers shown at the left of each gun part be specified when ordering.

No.	Description	Price
052	Abutment plate	$0.25
152	Barrel, round, 28"	15.00
152A	Barrel (Sporting Rifle), 24" with ramp front sight base	17.50
352	Barrel, heavy, round, 28"	25.00
552	Band complete (band with bow, bow pin and band screw)	1.50
552½	Band complete for heavy barrel (band with bow, bow pin and band screw)	1.75
652	Band screw	.25
752	Breech bolt	5.05
852	Breech bolt complete	14.85
	Breech bolt complete comprises: bolt with bolt handle, retainer, retainer pin, extractor right hand, extractor left hand, extractor pins (2), extractor springs (2), firing pin, firing pin spring and firing pin plug.	
952	Breech bolt handle	4.30
952A	Breech bolt handle (Speed Lock)	4.30
1052	Breech bolt handle retainer	.40
1152	Breech bolt handle retainer pin	.25
1252	Breech bolt handle locking plunger	.25
1352	Breech bolt handle locking plunger pin	.25
1452	Breech bolt handle locking plunger spring	.25
1552	Breech bolt guide	1.10
1552A	Butt stock	10.00
1552B	Butt stock, heavy barrel	11.00
1552C	Butt stock complete	11.90
1552D	Butt stock complete, heavy barrel	12.90
	Butt stock complete comprises: stock with bushing, magazine release plunger and escutcheon, butt plate, butt plate screws (2), abutment plate and stock swivel complete.	
1752A	Butt stock (Sporting Rifle) with cheek piece, selected wood, fancy checking on pistol grip and forearm, has tip of black moulded material on forearm	32.50
1752B	Butt stock complete (Sporting Rifle) comprises stock, butt plate, butt plate screws (2), bushing, magazine release plunger and escutcheon, abutment plate, sling strap snap swivel complete, Fig. 9 and 10 for 1" strap, pistol grip, cap and screw and forearm stud screw escutcheon	36.15
1852	Butt stock screw bushing	.25
1952	Butt plate	.65
1952A	Butt plate (Sporting Rifle)	.85
1952B	Butt plate (Special Target)	.65
2052	Butt plate screws (2) each	.25
2152	Extractor, right hand	.50
2252	Extractor, left hand	.50
2352	Extractor pins (2) each	.25
2452	Extractor spring, right hand	.25
2452½	Extractor spring, left hand	.25
2552	Firing pin and firing pin plug	3.00
2552A	Firing pin and firing pin plug (Speed Lock)	3.00
2652	Firing pin plug	.25
2752	Firing pin spring	.25
2752A	Firing pin spring (Speed Lock)	.25
2752½	Firing pin guide pin	.25
2752B	Forearm tip (blank) not fitted, made of black moulded material	.75
2852	Guard	1.15
2852A	Guard (Sporting)	1.25
2952	Guard plate	.30
2952A	Guard plate (Speed Lock)	.30
3052	Guard screw, rear, (2) each	$0.25
3152	Magazine catch	.60
3252	Magazine catch pin	.25
3352	Magazine catch spring	.25
3452	Magazine holder	2.25
3552	Magazine holder complete	3.05
	Magazine holder complete comprises: holder with magazine catch, magazine catch pin, and magazine catch spring	
3652	Magazine holder screw, front (short screw)	.25
3752	Magazine holder screw, rear (long screw)	.25
3852	Magazine release plunger	.25
3852A	Magazine release plunger (Sporting rifle)	.25
3952	Magazine release plunger escutcheon	.25
3952A	Magazine release plunger escutcheon (Sporting rifle)	.25
4052	†Magazine complete, 5 cartridge	1.00
4152	†Magazine complete, 10 cartridge	1.25
	Magazine complete comprises: magazine case with magazine follower, magazine spring and magazine bottom.	
4252	Magazine case and bottom, 5 cartridge	.45
4352	Magazine case and bottom, 10 cartridge	.50
4452	Magazine bottom	.25
4552	Magazine follower, 5 cartridge	.25
4552½	Magazine follower, 10 cartridge	.25
4652	Magazine spring, 5 cartridge	.45
4752	Magazine spring, 10 cartridge	.45
4852	Receiver	10.10
4852B	Receiver (Sporting rifle)	10.10
4852A	Rubber P.G. Cap (large size) with screw	.75
4952	Safety lock	1.00
4952A	Safety lock (Speed Lock)	1.00
5052	Safety lock pin	.25
5152	Safety lock plunger	.25
5252	Safety lock plunger spring	.25
5352	Safety lock stem	.30
5452	Sear	1.25
5452A	Sear assembly (Speed Lock)	1.35
5552	Sear pin	.25
5552A	Sear pin (Speed Lock)	.25
5652	Sear spring	.25
5752	Stock screw (front end of guard)	.25
5852	Stock swivel base, complete with bow and 2 base screws	.60
5952	Stock swivel base screw (2) each	.25
6052	Trigger	.95
6052A	Trigger (Speed Lock)	.95
6152	Trigger pin	.25
6152A	Trigger pin (Speed Lock)	.25
6152B	Trigger spring (Speed Lock)	.25
6152C	Trigger holder (Speed Lock)	1.50
6152D	Trigger holder screw (Speed Lock)	.25
6152E	Trigger adjusting screw (Speed Lock)	.25
6152F	Sight cover, style B. H. No. 3279 (Sporting Rifle)	.25
6152G	Front sight (Lyman No. 31W 5/64 Gold Bead) (Sporting rifle)	1.00
6152H	Rear sight (Lyman No. 48F Receiver Sight) (Sporting rifle)	11.50
3264	Leather sling strap, dark russet, 1" wide (Sporting rifle)	2.00
6152J	Snap swivel base, complete with (2) screws for stock, (Sporting rifle)	.70
6152K	Snap swivel base, complete with (2) screws for forearm, (Sporting rifle)	.70

In ordering parts marked thus (*) gun must be sent us.

(†) For dealer and jobber net prices see Gun Price List.   See foot of page 478 for special speed lock parts.

WINCHESTER RIFLE PARTS
MODEL 52-B—STANDARD WEIGHT—HEAVY WEIGHT BARREL AND SPORTING RIFLE

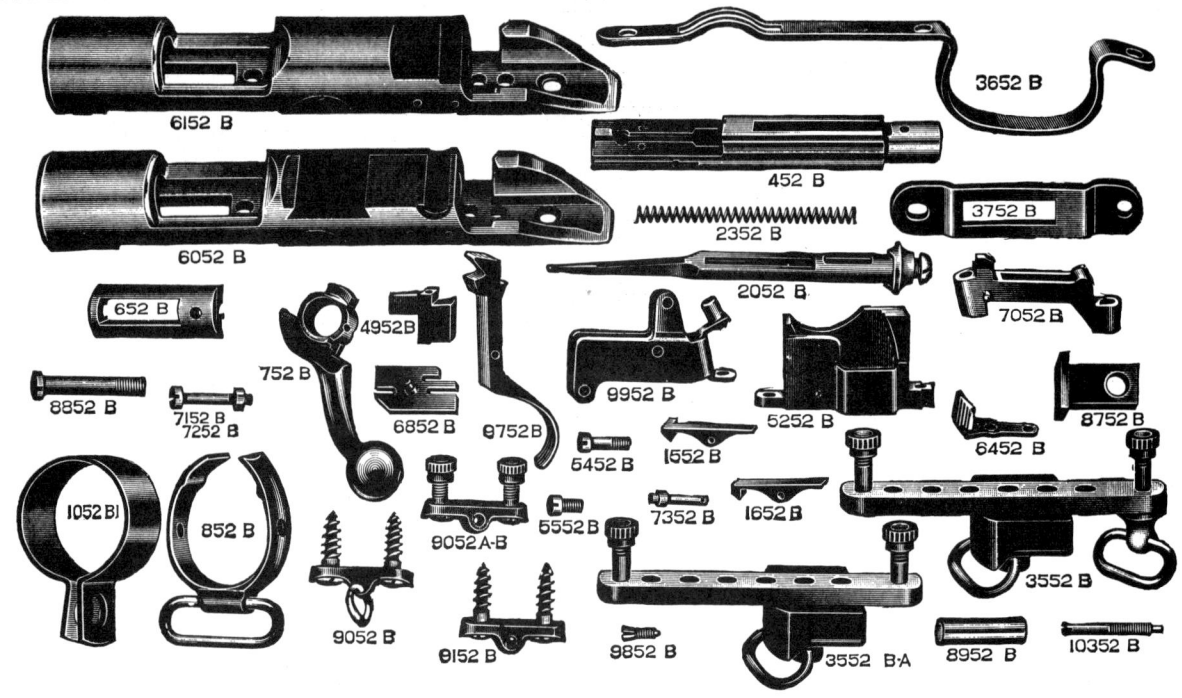

Be sure and specify which of the above Guns the parts are wanted for. It is absolutely necessary that the numbers shown with each Gun part be specified when ordering.

No.	Description	Price
152B	Barrel, regular, 28"	$15.00
252B	Barrel, heavy, 28"	25.00
352B	Barrel, sporting rifle, 24"	17.50
452B	Breech Bolt	5.05
552B	Breech Bolt complete comprises Breech Bolt, Firing Pin and Plug, Bolt Handle, R. H. Extractor, L. H. Extractor, Firing Pin Spring, Extractor Pins (2), Extractor Spring R. H., Extractor Spring L. H. and Firing Pin Guide Pin.	13.95
652B	Breech Bolt Guide	1.10
752B	Breech Bolt Handle	4.30
852B	Band, complete regular barrel	1.50
952B	Band, complete heavy barrel	1.75
	Band complete comprises Band, Bow, Bow Pin and Band Screw.	
1052B	Band Screw, Regular Stock	.25
1752A	Buttstock (Sporting Rifle) with cheek piece, selected wood, fancy checking on pistol grip and forearm, has tip of black moulded material on forearm	32.50
1752B	Butt stock complete (Sporting Rifle) comprises stock, butt plate, butt plate screws (2), bushing, magazine release plunger and escutcheon, abutment plate, sling strap snap swivel complete, Fig. 28 and 11 for 1" strap, pistol grip, cap and screw and forearm stud screw escutcheon	36.15
1852	Butt stock screw bushing	.25
1952	Butt plate	.65
1952A	Butt plate (Sporting Rifle)	.85
1952B	Butt plate (Special Target)	.65
2052	Butt plate screws (2) each	.25
2152	Extractor, right hand	.50
2252	Extractor, left hand	.50
2352	Extractor pins (2) each	.25
1952B	Extractor Spring, left hand	.25
2052B	Firing Pin and Plug	3.00
2152B	Firing Pin Guide Pin	.25
2252B	Firing Pin Plug	.25
2352B	Firing Pin Spring	.25
2452B	Forearm Stud (sporting rifle)	.25
2552B	Forearm Stud Screw (sporting rifle)	.25
2552AB	Forearm Stud Screw Escutcheon (sporting rifle)	$.25
2652B	Forearm Tip Blank, not fitted, made of Black Plastic material (for sporting rifle)	.75
2752B	Forearm Adjustment Base	.75
2852B	Forearm Adjustment Base Screw	.25
2952B	Forearm Adjustment Base Screw Escutcheon	.25
3052B	Forearm Adjusting Swivel Base	.75
3152B	Forearm Adjusting Swivel Bow Complete	.25
3252B	Forearm Adjusting Swivel Bow Base Screw	.25
3352B	Forearm Adjusting Bow Complete	.60
3452B	Forearm Adjusting Bow Screw Escutcheon	.25
3552B	Forearm Adjusting Base Complete for Marksman Stock	2.85
3552BA	Forearm Adjusting Base Complete for Reg. Stock	2.25
3652B	Guard	1.15
3752B	Guard Plate	.30
3852B	Guard Screw, rear (2) each	.25
3952B	Magazine complete, 5 cartridge	1.00
4052B	Magazine complete, 10 cartridge	1.25
4152B	Single Loading Adapter can be substituted for Regular Magazine	1.00
4252B	Magazine Case and Bottom, 5 cartridge	.45
4352B	Magazine Case and Bottom, 10 cartridge	.50
4452B	Magazine Bottom	.25
4552B	Magazine Follower, 5 cartridge	.25
4652B	Magazine Follower, 10 Cartridge	.25
4752B	Magazine Spring, 5 cartridge	.45
4852B	Magazine Spring, 10 cartridge	.45
4952B	Magazine Catch	.60
5052B	Magazine Catch Pin	.25
5152B	Magazine Catch Spring	.25
5252B	Magazine Holder	2.25
5352B	Magazine Holder complete comprises Holder with Mag. Catch, Mag. Catch Pin, and Mag. Catch Spring	3.05
5452B	Magazine Holder Screw, long rear	.25
5552B	Magazine Holder Screw, short front	.25
5652B	Magazine Release Plunger (regular)	.25
5752B	Magazine Release Plunger (sporting rifle)	.25

(Continued on next page)

INSTRUCTIONS: In ordering parts always give name and number listed in catalog, also make, model, caliber and serial number of gun. (Parts marked with * cannot be supplied on Mail Order. It will be necessary to return arm to us for fitting.)

PAYMENT: Parts will be sent only on advance payment. Parts cannot be returned for credit. A service charge of 25c must be added to every order under $1.00 to cover cost of handling. Do not forget to include postage.

SEE PAGE 8, "HOW TO ORDER"

WINCHESTER RIFLE PARTS MODEL 52-B

(Continued from preceding page)

5852B	Magazine Release Plunger Escutcheon (regular)	$.25
5952B	Magazine Release Plunger Escutcheon (sporting rifle)	.25
6052B	Receiver for 82A, Rear Sight only	10.10
6152B	Receiver with two holes drilled on left side	10.10
6152AB	Receiver for the 82A, Rear Sight and Receiver Sight	10.10
6252B	Rubber P. G. Cap (large size) with Screw (sporting rifle)	.75
6352B	Safety Washer	.25
6452B	Safety Lever	.30
6552B	Safety Lever Screw	.25
6652B	Safety Lever Screw Nut	.25
6752B	Safety Lever Spring	.25
6852B	Safety Slide with Stud	.25
6952B	Safety Slide Pin (2) each	.25
7052B	Sear and Pin	1.35
7152B	Sear Screw	.25
7252B	Sear Screw Nut	.25
7352B	Sear Plunger	.25
7452B	Sear Plunger Spring	.25
7552B	Sear Plunger Pin	.25
7652B	Sear Spring	.25
7752B	Stock for Regular Barrel	10.00
7852B	Stock for Heavy Barrel	10.00
7952B	Stock for Regular Barrel (marksman) Type No. 1 or High Comb	32.50
7952B1	Stock for Reg. Barrel Marksman Type No. 2 or Low Comb	32.50
8052B	Stock for Heavy Barrel (marksman) Type No. 1 or High Comb	32.50
8052B1	Stock for Heavy Barrel Marksman Type No. 2 or Low Comb	32.50
8152B	Stock complete for Regular Barrel	14.30
8252B	Stock complete for Heavy Barrel	14.30
8352B	Stock complete for Regular Barrel (marksman) Type No. 2 or Low Comb	37.40
8352B1	Stock complete for Reg. Barrel Marksman Type No. 2 or Low Comb	37.40
8452B	Stock complete for Heavy Barrel (marksman) Type No. 1 or High Comb	37.40
8452B1	Stock complete for Heavy Barrel Marksman Type No. 1 or High Comb	$37.40

Above Complete Stock comprises Stock with Bushing, Mag. Release, Plunger and Escutcheon, Butt Plate, Butt Plate Screw (2), Abutment Plate, Stock Swivel Complete, Forearm Adjusting Base Complete and Tang Screw Escutcheon.

8452BA	Let in Butt Stock Blank for Reg. Barrel	10.00
8452BB	Let in Butt Stock Blank for Heavy Barrel	10.00
8452BC	Let in Butt Stock Blank for Reg. Barrel Marksman	32.50
8452BD	Let in Butt Stock Blank for Heavy Barrel Marksman	32.50
8552B	Stock for (sporting rifle) with Cheek Piece Selected Wood, fancy checking on Pistol Grip and Forearm, has Tip of Black Plastic material on Forearm	18.00
8652B	Stock Complete for (sporting rifle)	21.75

Comprises Stock, Butt Plate, Butt Plate Screws (2), Bushing, Mag. Release, Plunger and Escutcheon, Abutment Plate, Sling Strap Snap Swivels Complete, both Fig. 11 and 28 for 1" Strap, Pistol Grip Cap and Screw and Forearm Stud Screw Escutcheon.

8752B	Stock Abutment Plate	.25
8852B	Stock Screw (front end of guard)	.25
8952B	Stock Screw Bushing	.25
9052B	Snap Swivel Base Complete—Fig. 2 1¼" Bow	.60
9052AB	Snap Swivel Base Complete—Fig. 11 (sporting rifle)	.70
9152B	Snap Swivel Base Complete—Fig. 28 (sporting rifle)	.70
9252B	Snap Swivel Base Screws (2) each	.25
9352B	Tank Screw	.25
9452B	Tang Screw Escutcheon	.25
9552B	Telescope Sight Bases Complete for regular Barrel, low rear and medium front (2) each	.50
9652B	Telescope Sight Bases Complete for heavy Barrel, low rear and low front (2) each	.50
9752B	Trigger	.95
9852B	Trigger Adjusting Screw	.25
9952B	Trigger Holder and Bushing	1.50
10052B	Trigger Holder Screw	.25
10152B	Trigger Pin	.25
10252B	Trigger Spring	.25
10352B	Trigger Spring Adjusting Screw	.25

PARTS FOR CRESCENT DOUBLE BARREL GUNS

NEW MODEL NO. 9 AND EMPIRE NOS. 60 AND 88

N 6*	Barrel fore-end loop	$1.00
N 23	Bridle	.40
N 67	Bridle Screw	.25
N 3	Butt Plate	.60
N 54	Butt Plate Screw	.25
N 24	Cocking Rod	.60
N 45	Cocking Rod Screw	.25
N 46	Cocking Pin	.25
N 5	D & E Catch Comp.	1.60
N X	D & E Catch large part	1.00
N 6	D & E Catch small part	.70
N 7	D & E Catch spring	.25
N 75	D & E Catch spring screw	.25
N 74	D & E Catch pin	.25
N 56	D & E Catch screw	.25
N 6X	Extractor	1.00
N 53	Extractor screw	.25
N 25	Firing Pin	.40
N 26	Firing pin screw	.25
N 77	Fore-end complete for No. 6	4.50
N 99	Fore-end wood for No. 6	2.00
N 78	Fore-end wood screw	$.25
N 69	Fore-end Iron	2.30
N 677	Fore-end Comp. for No. 60 Empire	3.25
N 699	Fore-end wood for No. 60 Empire	1.80
N 669	Fore-end Iron for No. 60 Empire	2.40
N 690*	Frame only	8.75
N XXX*	Frame complete with action	10.50
N 28	Hammer & Pin	.90
N XX	Lock Complete, each	3.20
N X	Lock plate	1.00
N 51	Lock Plate screw (front)	.25
N 63	Lock Plate screw (rear)	.25
N 31	Locking Bolt	.50
N 35	Main spring	.50
N 36	Main spring post	.25
N 38	Main spring screw	.25
N 82	Pistol grip cap	.40
N 61	Pistol grip cap screw	.25
N 40	Safety Thumb slide	.60
N 40½	Safety Thumb slide pin	.25
N 50	Safety Thumb slide spring	.25
N 39	Safety Rod and Post	$.60
N 39½	Safety push rod	.20
N 60¼	Safety push rod screw	.25
N 37	Sear	.50
N 37½	Sear pin	.25
N 85	Sight	.25
N 71*	Stock finished with butt plate, No. 60 fitted at factory	8.25
N 671*	Stock, 9 (fitted at factory)	9.25
N 65	Tang screw	.25
N 44	Trigger plate	1.85
N 44½	Trigger plate screw	.25
N 10	Trigger guard	1.25
N 10½	Trigger guard screw	.25
N 42	Trigger (right hand)	.50
N 42½	Trigger (left hand)	.50
N 142	Trigger pin	.25
N 43	Trigger spring	.25
N 32	Top lever	1.20
N 60	Top lever screw	.25
N 33	Top lever post	.40
N 615	Top lever spring	.25

INSTRUCTIONS: In ordering parts always give name and number listed in catalog, also make, model, caliber and serial number of gun. (Parts marked with * cannot be supplied on Mail Order. It will be necessary to return arm to us for fitting.)

PAYMENT: Parts will be sent only on advance payment. Parts cannot be returned for credit. A service charge of 25c must be added to every order under $1.00 to cover cost of handling. Do not forget to include postage.

SEND YOUR GUN TO STOEGER FOR EXPERT REPAIRING

WINCHESTER RIFLE PARTS

MODEL 72 BOLT ACTION TUBULAR MAGAZINE—69A BOX MAGAZINE
75 TARGET AND SPORTING RIFLE

It is absolutely necessary that the numbers shown at the left of each gun part be specified when ordering.

Model	Model		
172	72	Barrel Round 25" Straight Taper with Dovetail	$7.00
172A	72	Barrel Round 25" Straight Taper without Dovetail	7.00
172B	72	Barrel 25" 22 Short only	7.00
269A	69A	Barrel Round 25" Tapered	6.00
375	75	Barrel Round 28" L.R. Tapered	12.00
375A	75	Barrel Round 24" Tapered (Sporter)	17.50
475	75	Barrel Band	.30
575	75	Barrel Band Screw	.25
675	75	Barrel Band Screw Escutcheon	.25
775	75	Barrel Band Screw Bushing	.25
872	72	Breech Bolt	2.00
972	72	Breech Bolt Complete	5.45
1069A	69A-75	Breech Bolt	2.00
1169A	69A-75	Breech Bolt Complete comprises Bolt, Handle with Cocking Sleeve, Breech Bolt Plug, Breech Bolt Sleeve, Sleeve Pin, Extractor Left Hand, Extractor Right Hand, Extractor Pin (2), Extractor Spring (2), Firing Pin, Firing Pin Stop Pin and Firing Pin Spring	5.45
1272	72-69A-75	Breech Bolt Handle with Cocking Sleeve	.85
1372	72-69A-75	Breech Bolt Plug	.25
1472	72-69A-75	Breech Bolt Sleeve	.25
1572	72-69A-75	Breech Bolt Sleeve Pin	.25
1672	72-69A	Butt Plate	.30
1775	75	Butt Plate	.65
1775A	75	Butt Plate Shot Butt Metal (Sporter)	.85
1872	72-69A-75	Butt Plate Screw (2) each	.25
1972	72	Carrier	.50
2072	72	Carrier Spring	.25
2172	72	Carrier Pin	.25
2272	72	Carrier Lever	.25
2372	72	Carrier Lever Pin (2) each	.25
2472	72	Carrier Lever Spring	.25
2572	72	Carrier Complete comprises Carrier, Carrier Lever, Carrier Lever Pin (2) and Carrier Lever Spring	.90
2672	72	Cartridge Retainer	.25
2769A	69A-75	Ejector	.50
2872	72-69A-75	Extractor Right Hand	.50
2972	72-69A-75	Extractor Left Hand	.50
3072	72-69A-75	Extractor Pin (2) each	.25
3172	72-69A-75	Extractor Spring (2) each	.25
3272	72-69A-75	Firing Pin	.50
3372	72-69A-75	Firing Pin Stop Pin	.25
3472	72-69A-75	Firing Pin Spring	.25
3575	75	Forearm Adjustment Base Complete	1.65
3675	75	Forearm Adjustment Base Screw (2) each	.25
3775	75	Forearm Adjustment Swivel Bow Complete	.60
3875	75	Forearm Adjustment Swivel Bow Base Screw	.25
3875A	75	Forearm Screw Eye Swivel (Fig. 12) for 1" Strap (Sporter)	.50
3972	72-69A	Guard Bow	.25
4072	72-69A	Guard Bow Screw (2) each	.25
4175	75	Guard Bow	1.15
4175A	75	Guard Bow Stamped (Sporter)	1.25
4275	75	Guard Bow Screw (2) each	.25
4372	72	Magazine Outside Tube No. 40B	1.50
4472	72	Magazine Inside Tube No. 40A	1.10
4572	72	Magazine Inside Tube Complete comprises Tube, Plug, Plug Pin, Mag. Spring and Follower	1.70
4672	72	Magazine Plug No. 14	.25
4772	72	Magazine Plug Pin	.25
4872	72	Magazine Spring	.25
4972	72	Magazine Follower	.25
5072	72	Magazine Throat	.50
5172	72	Magazine Throat Pin	.25
5272	72	Magazine Throat Pin Bushing	.25
5372	72	Magazine Ring	.50
5472	72	Magazine Ring Pin	.25
5569A	69A-75	Magazine Complete .22 Long Rifle 5 Cartridge	1.00
5569AB	69A-75	Single Loading adapter can be substituted for the reg. mag.	1.00
5669A	69A-75	Magazine Complete .22 Long Rifle 10 Cartridge	1.25
5769A	69A	Magazine Complete .22 Short 5 Cartridge	1.00
5869A	69A	Magazine Complete .22 Short 10 Cartridge	1.25
5969A	69A-75	Magazine Catch	.25
6069A	69A-75	Magazine Catch Screw	.25
6169A	69A-75	Magazine Holder	1.00
6269A	69A-75	Magazine Holder Screw (2) each	.25
6369A	69A-75	Magazine Release Plunger	.25
6469A	69A-75	Magazine Release Plunger Escutcheon	.15
6569A	69A	Magazine Release Plunger Spring	.25
6669A	69A-75	Magazine Release Plunger Stop	.25

(Continued on Next Page)

MINIMUM SHIPPING ORDER $1.00

WINCHESTER RIFLE PARTS
MODEL 72 - 69A - 75—(Continued from Preceding Page)

Part No.	Model	Description	Price
6769A	69A-75	Magazine Release Plunger Complete comprises Plunger, Escutcheon and Stop	.40
6869A	69A	Magazine Plate	.25
6869A	69A	Magazine Plate Screw (2) each	.25
7072	72	Receiver	6.00
7172	72	Receiver for 80A Rear Sight	6.50
7269A	69A	Receiver for 80A Rear Sight	6.50
7369A	69A	Receiver	6.50
7475	75	Receiver	6.00
7475A	75	Rubber P.G. Cap and Screw (Sporter)	.75
7572	72-69A-75	Safety Lever	.20
7572A	69A-75	Safety Lever Stop Pin	.25
7672	72	Safety Lock	.25
7769A	69A-75	Safety Lock	.25
7872	72-69A-75	Safety Lock Screw	.25
7972	72-69A-75	Safety Lock Plunger	.25
8072	72-69A-75	Safety Lock Plunger Spring	.25
8172	72	Stock with Butt Plate and 2 Screws	5.00
8272	72	Stock Complete comprises Stock, Butt Plate and 2 Screws, Guard Bow and 2 Screws, Stock Stud Screw and Escutcheon	5.90
8369A	69A	Stock with Butt Plate, 2 Screws, Mag., Release Plunger and Escutcheon	3.50
8469A	69A	Stock Complete comprises Stock, Butt Plate and 2 Screws, Guard Bow and 2 Screws, Mag. Plate and 2 Screws, Stock Stud Screw and Escutcheon, Mag. Release Plunger and Escutcheon	4.75
8575	75	Stock with Release Plunger and Escutcheon	10.00
8675	75	Stock Complete comprises Stock, Butt Plate and 2 Screws, Guard Bow and 3 Screws, Mag. Release Plunger and Escutcheon, Fig. No. 2 and Forearm Adj. Base complete, Barrel Band Screw Escutcheon, Barrel Band Screw Bushing	13.85
8675A	75	Stock with Mag. Release Plunger and Escutcheon (Sporter)	12.00
8675B	75	Stock Complete (Sporter) comprises Stock, Butt Plate, and (2) Screws, Release Plunger and Escutcheon (Fig. 7 and 12), Guard Bow and 3 Screws	15.30
8772	72	Stock Stud	.35
8869A	69A-75	Stock Stud	.25
8972	72	Stock Stud Screw	.25
9069A	69A	Stock Stud Screw	.25
9175	75	Stock Stud Screw	.25
9272	72-69A	Stock Stud Screw Escutcheon	.25
9375	75	Stock Swivel Base Complete No. 2 with 1¼" Bow	.60
9472	72	Trigger	1.00
9569A	69A-75	Trigger	.80
9672	72	Trigger Assembly	1.45
9769A	69A-75	Trigger Assembly	1.25
9872	72-69A-75	Trigger Base	.25
9972	72-69A-75	Trigger Pin	.25
10069A	69A-75	Trigger Spring	.25
10169A	69A-75	Trigger Spring Adj. Screw	.25
10275	75	Sling Strap No. 3256 Light Color	1.25
		Front Sight	
10372	72-69A	Front Sight No. 75C .330 high used with No. 32B Rear Sight	.25
10475	75	Front Sight No. 99A Complete	1.50
10575	75	Front Sight Base No. 99A	.40
10675	75	Front Sight Binding Screw No. 99A	.25
10775	75	Front Sight Hood No. 99A	.30
10875	75	Front Sight inserts Aperture .07-.093—.110 for No. 99A (3) ea.	.25
10975	75	Front Sight inserts Post, for No. 99A	.25
10975A	75	Front Sight 103B (Sporter)	.50
10975B	75	Front Sight Cover 3278 (Sporter)	.25
11172	72-69A	Front Sight No. 97B with Ramp Complete and Sight Cover No. 3280	.85
11272	72-69A	Front Sight Key for No. 97B	.25
11372	72-69A	Front Sight Ramp for No. 97B	.25
11472	72-69A	Front Sight Cover No. 3280	.25
11572	72-69A	Front Sight No. 97B Sight only .525 high to be used with 80A Rear Sight	.30
		Rear Sight	
11672	72-69A	Rear Sight No. 32B with 2C Elevator used with No. 75C	.75
11675A	75	Rear Sight 32D with 2C Elevator (Sporter)	.75
11772	72-69A	Rear Sight Elevator 2C	.25
11872	72-69A	Rear Sight No. 80A Complete used with No. 97B Front Sight	2.10
11972	72-69A	Rear Sight Disc for No. 80A (.080, Standard also .052, and .0225 Aperture)	.30
12072	72-69A	Rear Sight Disc Nut for No. 80A	.25
12172	72-69A	Rear Sight Base Washer for No. 80A	.25
12272	72-69A	Rear Sight Pivot Screw for No. 80A	.25
12372	72-69A	Rear Sight Index Plate for No. 80A	.25
12472	72-69A	Rear Sight Index Plate Screw for No. 80A	.25
12572	72-69A	Rear Sight Binding Screw for No. 80A	.25
12672	72-69A	Rear Sight Binding Screw Washer for No. 80A	.25
12772	72-69A	Rear Sight Base for No. 80A	.70
12872	72-69A	Rear Sight Base Stop Screw for No. 80A	.25
12975A	75	Lyman Rear Sight No. 57E (Sporter)	6.00
13075	75	Rear Sight No. 84A Complete	4.50
13175	75	Rear Sight Base No. 84A	.30
13275	75	Rear Sight Base Screw for No. 84A (2) each	.25
13375	75	Rear Sight Binding Screw for No. 84A	.25
13475	75	Rear Sight Extension Base and Rod for No. 84A	.40
13575	75	Rear Sight Elevating Screw for No. 84A	.30
13675	75	Rear Sight Elevating Screw Knob and Screw for No. 84A	.25
13775	75	Rear Sight Elevating Screw Knob Ball and Spring for No. 84A	.25
13875	75	Rear Sight Elevating Screw Knob Binding Screw for No. 84A	.25
13975	75	Rear Sight Elevating Slide for No. 84A	.30
13975A	75	Rear Sight Elevating Slide Spring	.25
14075	75	Rear Sight Elevating Slide Binding Screw for No. 84A	.25
14175	75	Rear Sight Elevating Slide Stop Screw for No. 84A	.25
14275	75	Rear Sight Elevating Slide Friction Washer for No. 84A	.25
2372	72	Carrier Lever Pin (2) each	.25
2472	72	Carrier Lever Spring	.25
2572	72	Carrier Complete comprises Carrier, Carrier Lever, Carrier Lever Pin (2) and Carrier Lever Spring	.90
2672	72	Cartridge Retainer	.25
2769A	69A-75	Ejector	.50
2872	72-69A-75	Extractor Right Hand	.50
2972	72-69A-75	Extractor Left Hand	.50
3072	72-69A-75	Extractor Pin (2) each	.25
3172	72-69A-75	Extractor Spring (2) each	.25
3272	72-69A-75	Firing Pin	.50
3372	72-69A-75	Firing Pin Stop Pin	.25
3472	72-69A-75	Firing Pin Spring	.25
3575	75	Forearm Adjustment Base Complete	1.65
3675	75	Forearm Adjustment Base Screw (2) each	.25
3775	75	Forearm Adjustment Swivel Bow Complete	.60
3875	75	Forearm Adjustment Swivel Bow Base Screw	.25
3875A	75	Forearm Screw Eye Swivel (Fig. 12) for for 1" Strap (Sporter)	.50
3972	72-69A	Guard Bow	.25
4072	72-69A	Guard Bow Screw (2) each	.25
4175	75	Guard Bow	1.15
4175A	75	Guard Bow Stamped (Sporter)	1.25
4275	75	Guard Bow Screw (2) each	.25
4372	72	Magazine Outside Tube No. 40B	1.50
4472	72	Magazine Inside Tube No. 40A	1.10
4572	72	Magazine Inside Tube Complete comprises Tube, Plug, Plug Pin, Mag. Spring and Follower	1.70
4672	72	Magazine Plug No. 14	.25
4772	72	Magazine Plug Pin	.25
4872	72	Magazine Spring	.25
4972	72	Magazine Follower	.25
5072	72	Magazine Throat	.50
5172	72	Magazine Throat Pin	.25
5272	72	Magazine Throat Pin Bushing	.25
5372	72	Magazine Ring	.50
5472	72	Magazine Ring Pin	.25
5569A	69A	Magazine Complete .22 Long Rifle 5 Cartridge	1.00
5569AB	69A-75	Single loading adapter can be substituted for the reg. mag.	1.00
5669A	69A-75	Magazine Complete .22 Long Rifle	

MINIMUM SHIPPING ORDER $1.00

WINCHESTER RIFLE PARTS
MODELS 56 AND 57 BOLT ACTION RIFLES

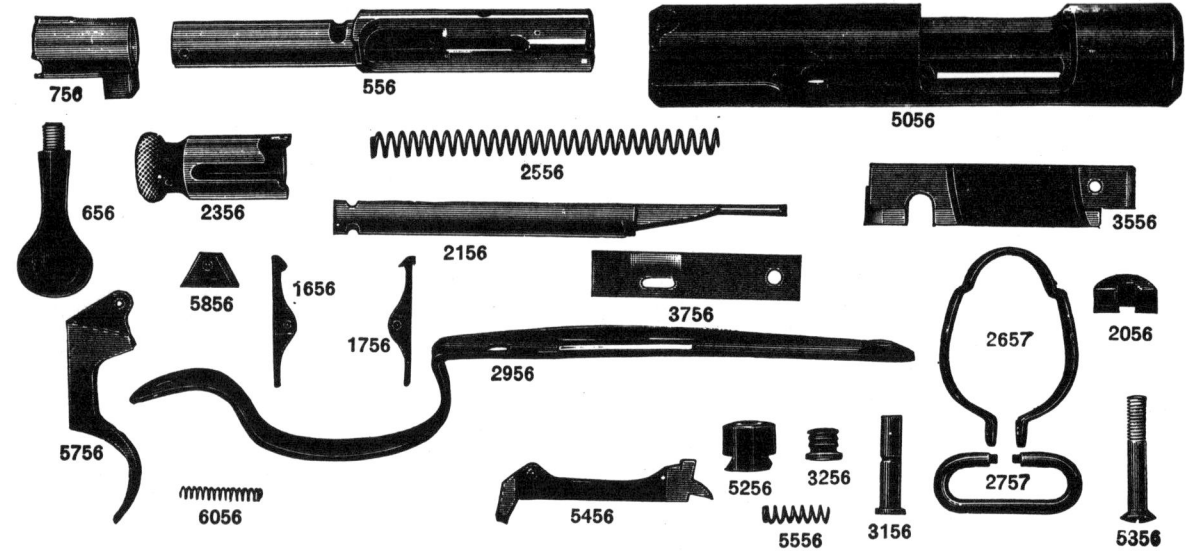

It is absolutely necessary that the numbers shown at the left of each gun part be specified when ordering.

MODELS 56 AND 57 BOLT ACTION

No.	MODEL	MODEL	Description	Price
256	56		Barrel, .22 Long rifle	$8.00
457		57	Barrel, .22 Long rifle	8.00
556	56	57	Breech bolt	3.50
556A	56	57	Breech bolt stop spring	.25
656	56	57	Breech bolt handle	1.00
756	56	57	Breech bolt sleeve	1.25
856	56	57	Breech bolt stop	.25
956	56	57	Breech bolt complete comprising bolt with handle, sleeve, extractor right hand, extractor left hand, extractor pins (2), extractor springs (2), firing pin, guide pin, firing pin head, head pin, and firing pin spring	10.20
1056	56		Butt stock	5.50
1157		57	Butt stock	5.50
1256	56		Butt stock complete comprising stock with butt plate and (2) butt plate screws, magazine release plunger, magazine release plunger escutcheon, magazine release plunger stop	6.65
1357		57	Butt stock complete comprising: stock with butt plate and (2) butt plate screws, magazine release plunger, magazine release plunger escutcheon, magazine release plunger stop, and stock screw eye swivel bow	6.85
1456	56	57	Butt plate	.50
1556	56	57	Butt plate screw (2) each	.25
1656	56	57	Extractor left hand	.50
1756	56	57	Extractor right hand	.50
1856	56	57	Extractor pins (2) each	.25
1956	56	57	Extractor springs (2) each	.25
2056	56	57	Ejector	.50
2156	56	57	Firing pin	2.00
2256	56	57	Firing pin guide pin	.25
2356	56	57	Firing pin head	.75
2456	56	57	Firing pin head pin	.25
2556	56	57	Firing pin spring	.75
2657		57	Front band	.25
2757		57	Front band bow 1″ or 1¼″	.25
2857		57	Front band stop pin	.25
2956	56	57	Guard	1.15
3056	56	57	Guard screws (2) each (rear screws)	.25
3156	56	57	Magazine release plunger	.25
3256	56	57	Magazine release plunger escutcheon	$0.25
3356	56	57	Magazine release plunger stop	.25
3456	56	57	Magazine release plunger complete (Plunger with escutcheon and stop)	.40
3556	56	57	Magazine holder	1.00
3656	56	57	Magazine holder screw (2) also ejector screw, each	.25
3756	56	57	Magazine catch	.25
3856	56	57	Magazine catch screw	.25
3956	56	57	†Magazine complete, .22 Short, 5 cartridge	1.00
4056	56	57	†Magazine complete, .22 Short, 10 ctg.	1.25
4156	56	57	†Magazine complete, .22 Long rifle, 5 cartridge	1.00
4256	56	57	†Magazine complete, .22 Long rifle, 10 cartridge	1.25
			Magazine complete comprises: magazine case with magazine follower, magazine spring and magazine bottom.	
4256A	56	57	†Single loading adapter	1.00
4356	56	57	Magazine case and bottom, 5 shot, Short	.45
4356A	56	57	Magazine case and bottom, 5 shot, L.R.	.45
4456	56	57	Magazine case and bottom, 10 shot, Short	.50
4456A	56	57	Magazine case and bottom, 10 shot, L.R.	.50
4556	56	57	Magazine case bottom	.25
4656	56	57	Magazine follower, 5 shot, Short	.25
4656A	56	57	Magazine follower, 5 shot, Long rifle	.25
4756	56	57	Magazine follower, 10 shot, Short	.25
4756A	56	57	Magazine follower, 10 shot, Long rifle	.25
4856	56	57	Magazine spring, 5 cartridge, Short	.45
4956	56	57	Magazine spring, 10 cartridge, Short	.45
4956A	56	57	Magazine spring, 5 shot, Long rifle	.45
4956B	56	57	Magazine spring, 10 shot, Long rifle	.45
5056	56	57	Receiver with breech bolt stop	8.15
5156	56	57	Receiver sight plug screw	.25
5256	56	57	Stock stud	.25
5356	56	57	Stock stud screw	.25
5456	56	57	Sear	1.25
5556	56	57	Sear spring	.25
5657		57	Stock screw eye swivel bow	.25
5756	56	57	Trigger	1.20
5856	56	57	Trigger base	.25
5956	56	57	Trigger pin	.25
6056	56	57	Trigger spring	.25

In replacing parts marked thus (*) when desired for Take-down Guns it is necessary to send gun to us.

PARTS FOR WIN. 52 SPEED LOCK—Continued from page 475
*Special parts necessary to change Model 52 from Standard Lock to Speed Lock

Breech bolt handle $4.30, firing pin and plug 3.00, firing pin spring .10, sear and adjusting screw 1.35, sear pin .10, trigger .95, trigger pin .10, trigger spring .10, trigger holder 1.50, trigger holder screw .10, safety lock 1.00, guard plate .30, tap .50 Total.................. $13.30

6252	"Let In" Stock Blanks including bushing, abutment plate, butt plate and (2) screws	10.00
6252A	"Let In" Stock Blanks including bushing, abutment plate, butt plate and (2) screws for heavy barrel	$11.00
6252B	"Let In" Stock Blanks including bushing, abutment plate, butt plate and (2) screws for (Special Target)	10.00
6252C	"Let In" Stock Blanks including bushing, abutment plate, butt plate and (2) screws for (Special Target) heavy barrel	11.00

INSTRUCTIONS: In ordering parts always give name and number listed in catalog, also make, model, caliber and serial number of gun. (Parts marked with * cannot be supplied on Mail Order. It will be necessary to return arm to us for fitting.)

PAYMENTS: Parts will be sent only on advance payment. Parts cannot be returned for credit. A service charge of 25c must be added to every order under $1.00 to cover cost of handling. Do not forget to include postage.

ALL SHIPMENTS ARE INSURED

WINCHESTER RIFLE PARTS
MODELS 90 AND 06 REPEATING RIFLES

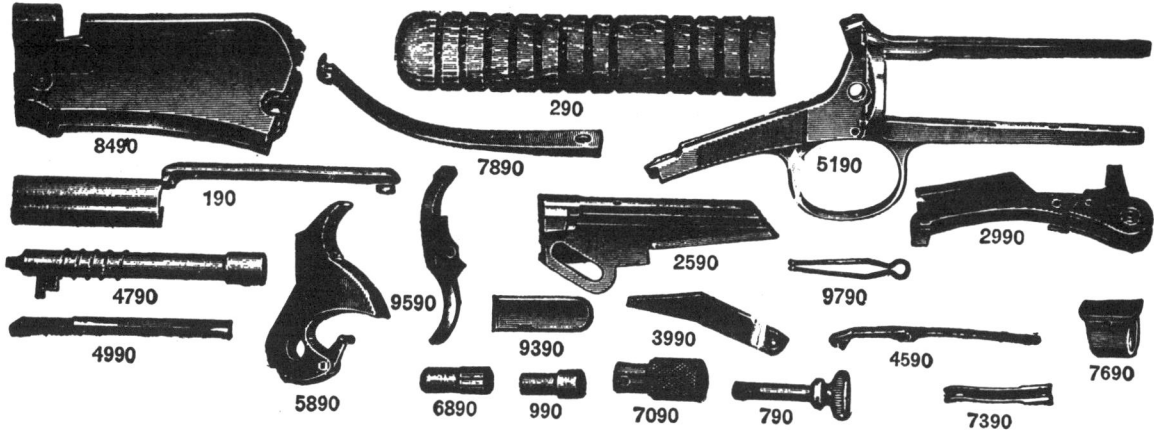

It is absolutely necessary that the numbers shown at the left of each gun part be specified when ordering.

No.	Models		Description	Price
190	90	06	Action slide	$2.00
290	90		Action slide handle with (2) escutcheons	.60
306		06	Action slide handle with (2) escutcheons	.60
406		06	Action slide handle with (2) escutcheons, expert grade	1.00
590	90	06	Action slide handle escutcheons (2) each	.25
690	90	06	Action slide handle screw (2) each	.25
790	90	06	Assembling screw and stop pin	.25
890	90	06	Assembling screw stop pin	.25
990	90	06	Assembling screw bushing	.25
1090	90		Barrel, .22 short, 24"	5.00
1190	90		Barrel, .22 long, 24"	5.00
1290	90		Barrel, .22 long rifle, 24"	5.00
1390	90		Barrel, .22 W. R. F., 24"	5.00
1406		06	Barrel, 20"	3.60
1590	90		Butt stock	3.00
1690	90		Butt stock complete	4.25
1706		06	Butt stock complete	2.75
1806		06	Butt stock complete, expert grade	3.50

Butt stock complete comprises: stock with butt plate and (2) butt plate screws.

1990	90		Butt stock, pistol grip	6.00
2090	90		Butt stock, pistol grip, complete comprising stock with butt plate and (2) butt plate screws, pistol grip cap and screw	7.25
2190	90		Butt plate	1.05
2290	90		Butt plate screw (2) each	.25
2306		06	Butt plate	.25
2406		06	Butt plate screw (2) each	.25
2590	90	06	Breech bolt .22 short, long and long rifle	3.00
2690	90		Breech bolt .22 W. R. F.	3.00
2790	90		Breech bolt .22 W. R. F., complete	4.60
2890	90	06	Breech bolt .22 short, long and long rifle, complete	4.60

Breech bolt complete comprises: bolt with extractor, extractor pin, firing pin and spring, firing pin stop, and firing pin stop screws (2).

2990	90		Carrier, .22 short, with trigger stop pin	1.75
3090	90		Carrier, .22 long, with trigger stop pin	1.75
3190	90		Carrier, .22 long rifle, with trigger stop pin	1.75
3290	90		Carrier, .22 W. R. F., with trigger stop pin	1.75
3390	90		Carrier, complete, .22 short	2.25
3490	90		Carrier, complete, .22 long	2.25
3590	90		Carrier, complete, .22 long rifle	2.25
3690	90		Carrier, complete, .22 W. R. F.	2.25

Carrier complete comprises: carrier with carrier lever, carrier lever pin, carrier lever spring, carrier lever spring screw and trigger stop pin.

| 3706 | | 06 | Carrier, with cartridge stop and pin and trigger stop pin, .22 short, long and long rifle | 2.30 |
| 3806 | | 06 | Carrier complete, .22 short, long and long rifle | 2.80 |

Carrier complete comprises: carrier with carrier lever, carrier lever pin, carrier lever spring, carrier lever spring screw, trigger stop pin, cartridge stop and cartridge stop pin.

3990	90	06	Carrier lever	$.25
4090	90	06	Carrier lever pin	.25
4190	90	06	Carrier lever spring	.25
4290	90	06	Carrier lever spring screw	.25
4306		06	Cartridge stop	.25
4406		06	Cartridge stop pin	.25
4590	90	06	Extractor, .22 short, long and long rifle	.45
4590½	90		Extractor, .22 W. R. F.	.45
4690	90	06	Extractor pin	.25
4790	90	06	Firing pin and spring	.60
4890	90	06	Firing pin spring	.25
4990	90	06	Firing pin stop	.25
5090	90	06	Firing pin stop screw (2) each	.25
5190	90	06	Guard	3.75
5290	90	06	Guard pistol grip	3.85
5390	90		Guard complete, .22 short	9.10
5490	90		Guard complete, .22 long	9.10
5590	90		Guard complete, .22 long rifle	9.10
5690	90		Guard complete, .22 W. R. F.	9.10

Guard complete comprises: guard with carrier complete, hammer complete, mainspring, mainspring screw, mainspring strain screw, trigger, trigger pin, trigger spring, trigger spring screw, assembling screw, assembling screw stop pin and assembling screw bushing.

5706		06	Guard complete, .22 short, long and long rifle, comprising guard with carrier complete, hammer complete, mainspring, mainspring screw, mainspring strain screw, trigger, trigger pin, trigger spring, trigger spring screw, assembling screw and stop pin, and assembling screw bushing	9.65
5890	90	06	Hammer complete comprising hammer with stirrup and pin	1.25
5990	90	06	Hammer stirrup	.25
6090	90	06	Hammer stirrup pin	.25
6190	90	06	Magazine tube outside, .22 short, long and long rifle	1.50
6290	90		Magazine tube outside, .22 W. R. F.	1.50
6390	90	06	Magazine tube inside, .22 short and long rifle	1.10
6490	90		Magazine tube inside, .22 W. R. F.	1.10
6590	90	06	Magazine tube inside complete, .22 short, long and long rifle	1.70
6690	90		Magazine tube inside, complete, .22 W. R. F.	1.70

Magazine tube inside complete comprises: tube with mag. plug, mag. plug pin, mag. spring and mag. follower.

6790	90	06	Magazine spring	.25
6890	90	06	Magazine follower, short, long and long rifle	.25
6990	90		Magazine follower, .22 W. R. F.	.25
7090	90	06	Magazine plug, .22 short, long or long rifle	.25
7190	90		Magazine plug, .22 W. R. F.	.25

In replacing parts marked thus (*) when desired for Takedown Guns it is necessary to send gun to us.

(Continued on Next Page)

INSTRUCTIONS: In ordering parts always give name and number listed in catalog, also make, model, caliber and serial number of gun. (Parts marked with * cannot be supplied on Mail Order. It will be necessary to return arm to us for fitting.)

PAYMENTS: Parts will be sent only on advance payment. Parts cannot be returned for credit. A service charge of 25c must be added to every order under $1.00 to cover cost of handling. Do not forget to include postage.

SEND YOUR GUN TO STOEGER FOR EXPERT REPAIRING

WINCHESTER RIFLE PARTS
MODEL 63—.22 AUTOMATIC RIFLE

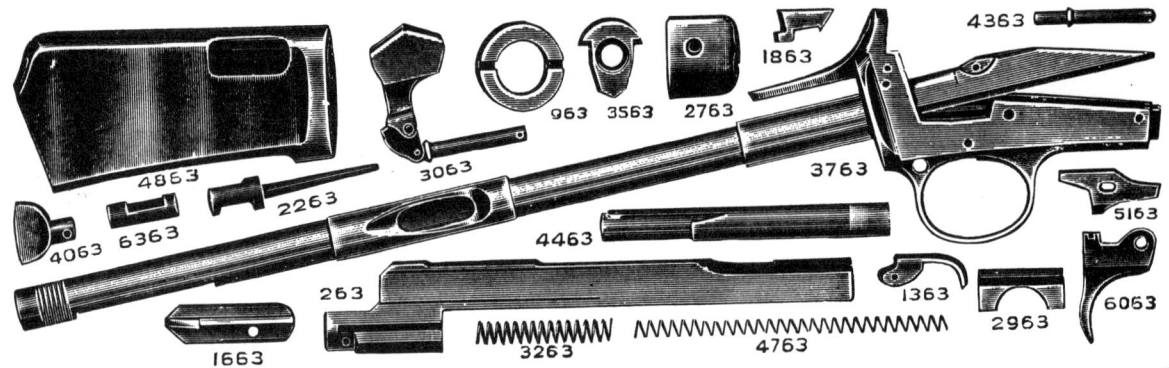

It is absolutely necessary that the numbers shown at the left of each gun part be specified when ordering.

163	Barrel, round tapered, 20"	$6.50
163A	Barrel round tapered 23"	6.50
263	Bolt	6.25
363	Bolt complete comprises bolt, firing pin, firing pin spring, firing pin stop pin, extractor, extractor plunger, extractor plunger spring and stop screw	8.00
463	Bolt spring	.25
563	Bolt guide rod	.30
663	Butt stock, pistol grip	3.00
763	Butt stock pistol grip complete comprises: stock with butt plate and (2) screws	4.10
863	Butt stock pistol grip complete fancy checked with P. G. rubber tip and screw	7.75
863A	Butt stock P. G. complete fancy wood fancy checked with P. G. rubber cap and screw	19.75
963	Butt stock nut	.25
1063	Butt stock nut washer	.25
1163	Butt plate (steel)	.90
1263	Butt plate screw (2) each	.25
1363	Cartridge cut off	.45
1463	Cartridge cut off spring	.25
1563	Cartridge cut off pin	.25
1663	Ejector	.60
1763	Ejector screw	.25
1863	Extractor	.65
1963	Extractor plunger	.25
2063	Extractor plunger stop screw	.25
2163	Extractor plunger spring	.50
2263	Firing pin	.25
2363	Firing pin spring	.25
2463	Firing pin stop pin	.25
2563	Forearm	1.40
2663	Forearm fancy checked	11.00
2763	Forearm tip	1.40
2863	Forearm tip screws (2) each	.25
2963	Forearm tip tenon	.25
3063	Hammer with guide rod and pin. Give gun number	2.10
3163	Hammer pin	.25
3265	Hammer spring	.25
3363	Hammer spring guide rod	$0.25
3463	Hammer spring guide rod pin	.25
3563	Hammer spring abutment	.45
3663	Hammer spring abutment pin	.25
3763*	Magazine tube outside 35B with throat and tang	9.55
3863	Magazine tube inside 35A (holds 10 ctgs.)	1.10
3963	Magazine tube inside complete comprises tube, magazine plug, magazine plug pin, magazine spring and magazine follower	1.90
4063	Magazine plug No. 31	.40
4163	Magazine plug pin	.25
4263	Magazine spring	.25
4363	Magazine follower	.25
4463	Operating sleeve	.85
4563	Operating sleeve tip	.25
4663	Operating sleeve tip pin	.25
4763	Operating sleeve spring	.25
4863	Receiver with take-down screw bushing, ejector and screw	14.75
4963	Rubber pistol grip tip	.40
5063	Rubber pistol grip tip screw	.25
5163	Sear	.50
5263	Sear spring	.25
5363	Take down screw and stop pin	.30
5463	Take down screw stop pin	.25
5563	Take down screw lock	.75
5663	Take down screw lock pin	.25
5763	Take down screw lock spring	.25
5863	Take down screw bushing	.25
5963	Throat pin	.25
6063	Trigger	.85
6163	Trigger pin	.25
6263	Trigger spring	.25
6363	Trigger lock	.30
6463	Trigger lock plunger	.25
6563	Trigger lock plunger spring	.25
6663	Front sight Lyman No. 3W 5/64 gold bead	.00
6763	Rear sight 32B with 2C elevator	.75
6863	Peep sight plug screw (2) each	.25
6963	Wiping rod	.25

In replacing parts marked thus (*) it will be necessary to send rear portion of gun to us.

MODELS 90 and 06—(Continued from Preceding Page)

No.	Model	Model	Part	Price
7290	90	06	Magazine plug pin	$0.25
7390	90	06	Magazine friction spring, .22 short, long and long rifle	.25
7490	90		Magazine friction spring, .22 W. R. F.	.25
7590	90	06	Magazine ring front	.50
7690	90	06	Magazine ring rear	.50
7790	90	06	Magazine ring pin (rear)	.25
7890	90	06	Mainspring, .22 short, long and long rifle	.50
7990	90		Mainspring, .22 W. R. F.	.50
8090	90	06	Mainspring, pistol grip	.60
8190	90	06	Mainspring screw	.25
8290	90	06	Mainspring strain screw	.25
8390	90	06	Peep sight plug screw	.25
8490	90	06	Receiver, .22 short, long and long rifle	6.00
8590	90		Receiver, .22 W. R. F.	6.00
8690	90	06	Receiver and guard, .22 short, long and long rifle	10.10
8790	90		Receiver and guard, .22 W. R. F.	10.10
8890	90	06	Receiver and guard, pistol grip, .22 short, long and long rifle	10.20
8990	90		Receiver and guard, pistol grip, .22 W. R. F.	10.20
			Receiver and guard comprises: receiver with guard, assembling screw, assembling screw stop pin and bushing.	
9090	90		Receiver and guard complete with action, .22 short	20.00
9090A	90		Receiver and guard complete with action, .22 long	20.00
9090B	90		Receiver and guard complete with action, .22 long rifle	$20.00
9190		06	Receiver and guard complete with action, .22 short, long and long rifle	20.55
9290	90		Receiver and guard complete with action, .22 W. R. F.	20.00
			Receiver complete with guard comprises: receiver with guard, hammer complete, carrier complete, breech bolt complete, mainspring, main spring screw, mainspring strain screw, peep sight plug screw, trigger, trigger pin, trigger spring, trigger spring screw, assembling screw, assembling screw bushing, assembling screw stop pin, slide cover, and slide cover stop screw.	
9390	90	06	Slide cover	.25
9490	90	06	Slide cover stop screw	.25
9590	90	06	Trigger	.50
9690	90	06	Trigger pin	.25
9790	90	06	Trigger spring	.25
9890	90	06	Trigger spring screw	.25
9990	90	06	Upper tang screw	.25
10090	90	06	Upper tang screw, pistol grip	.25
10190	90	06	Upper tang screw, pistol grip, peep sight	.25
10290	90	06	Upper tang screw, peep sight	.25
10390	90	06	Wiping rod	.25

ORDER BLANK IN MIDDLE AND INDEX IN BACK OF CATALOG

WINCHESTER RIFLE PARTS
MODEL 61—.22 CAL. HAMMERLESS REPEATING RIFLE

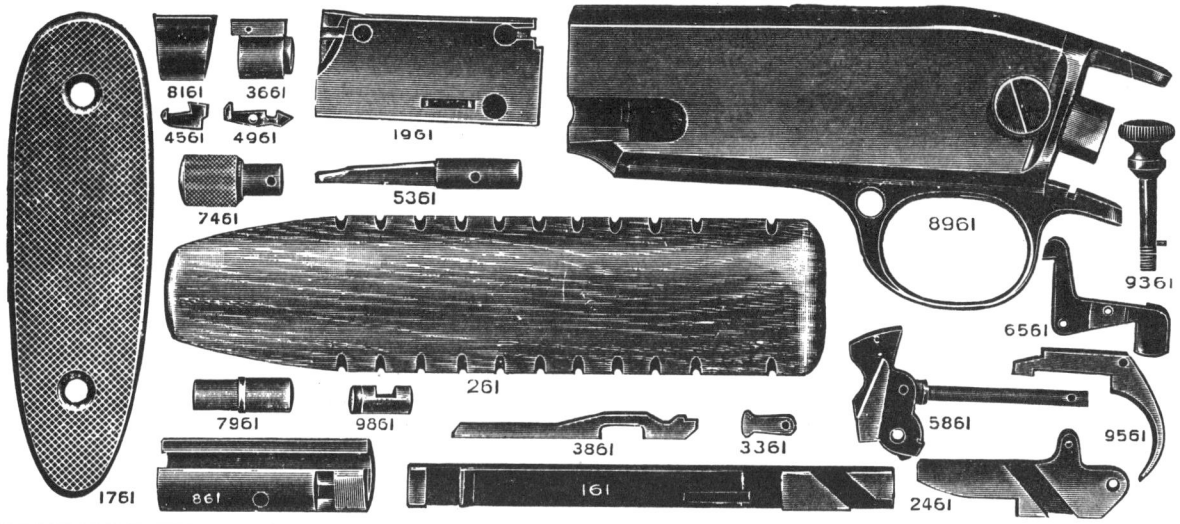

It is absolutely necessary that the numbers shown at the left of each gun part be specified when ordering.

161	Action Slide Bar	$0.35
261	Escutcheon Slide Handle	1.25
361	Action Slide Handle Screw (2) each	.25
461	Action Slide Handle Escutcheon (2) each	.25
561	Action Slide Lock	.25
661	Action Slide Lock Pivot	.25
761	Action Slide Lock Spring	.25
861	Action Slide Sleeve	.30
961	Barrel Round, .22 Short, Long or Long Rifle	4.00
1061	Barrel Oct., .22 Short	5.00
1161	Barrel Oct., .22 Long Rifle	5.00
1261	Barrel Oct., .22 W. R. F.	5.00
1361	Butt Stock Pistol Grip, wood only	3.00
1461	Butt Stock P. G. Complete	3.70
	Butt Stock Complete comprises Butt Stock, Butt Plate and Butt Plate Screw (2).	
1561	Butt Stock Bolt	.25
1661	Butt Stock Bolt Washer	.25
1761	Butt Plate	.60
1861	Butt Plate Screw (2) each	.25
1961	Breech Bolt, .22 Short, Long or Long Rifle	2.50
2061	Breech Bolt, .22 W. R. F.	2.50
2161	Breech Bolt Complete, .22 Short, Long or Long Rifle	5.70
2261	Breech Bolt Complete, .22 W. R. F.	5.70
	Breech Bolt Complete comprises: Breech Bolt, Ejector, Ejector Spring, Ejector Pin, Carrier Plunger, Carrier Plunger Pin, Carrier Plunger Spring, Extractor Upper, Extractor Upper Plunger, Extractor Upper Plunger Spring, Firing Pin, Firing Pin Stop Pin, Firing Pin Retracting Spring and Plunger, Extractor Lower, Extractor Lower Pin, and Extractor Lower Spring.	
2361	Breech Bolt Retaining Spring	.25
2461	Carrier, .22 Short, Long or Long Rifle	.50
2561	Carrier, .22 W. R. F.	.50
2661	Carrier Plunger	.25
2761	Carrier Plunger Pin	.25
2861	Carrier Plunger Spring	.25
2961	Carrier Spring	.25
3061	Carrier Spring Pin	.25
3161	Carrier Stop Pin	.25
3261	Carrier Stop Screw	.25
3361	Ctge. Cut-off, .22 Short, Long or Long Rifle	.25
3461	Ctge. Cut-off, .22 W. R. F.	0.25
3561	Ctge. Cut-off Pin	.25
3661	Ctge. Cut-off Retainer, .22 Short, Long or Long Rifle	.40
3761	Ctge. Cut-off Retainer, .22 W. R. F.	.40
3861	Ejector, .22 Short, Long or Long Rifle	.30
3961	Ejector, .22 W. R. F.	.30
4061	Ejector Spring	.25
4161	Ejector Pin	.25
4261	Ejector Stop	.25
4361	Ejector Stop Pin	.25
4461	Ejector Stop Spring	.25
4561	Extractor (upper) .22 Short, Long or Long Rifle	.40
4661	Extractor (upper) .22 W.R.F.	.40
4761	Extractor (upper) Plunger	.25
4861	Extractor (upper) Plunger Spring	.25
4961	Extractor (lower) .22 Short, Long or Long Rifle	.40
5061	Extractor (lower) .22 W.R.F.	.40
5161	Extractor (lower) Pin	.25
5261	Extractor (lower) Spring	.25
5361	Firing Pin	.50
5461	Firing Pin Stop Pin	.25
5561	Firing Pin Retracting Spring	.25
5661	F. P. Retracting Plunger	.25
5761	Front Sight No. 3W Lyman Gold Bead	.60
5861	Hammer Complete	1.25
	Hammer Complete comprises Hammer, Hammer Spg. Guide Rod and Pin.	
5961	Hammer Pin	.25
6061	Hammer Spring, .22 Short, Long or Long Rifle	.25
6161	Hammer Spring, .22 W. R. F.	.25
6261	Hammer Spring Guide Rod	.25
6361	Ham. Spg. Guide Rod Pin	.25
6461	Hammer Spring Abutment	.25
6561	Hammer Catch	.50
6661	Hammer Catch Stud	.25
6761	Magazine Tube Inside No. 27A, to hold 20 Short, 16 Long or 14 Long Rifle ctge.	1.10
6861	Mag. Tube Inside No. 29A, to hold 15 W. R. F. ctge	1.10
6961	Magazine Tube Inside Complete No. 27A, .22 Short, Long or Long Rifle	1.70
7061	Magazine Tube Inside Complete No. 29A, W. R. F.	1.70
	Magazine Tube Inside Complete comprises Magazine Tube, Magazine Spring, Magazine Plug, Magazine Plug Pin and Magazine Follower.	
7161	Mag. Tube Outside 27B, .22 Short, Long or L. R.	1.50
7261	Magazine Tube Outside 29B, .22 W. R. F.	1.50
7361	Magazine Tube Outside 28B, .22 Short only	1.50
7461	Magazine Plug No. 14, .22 Short, Long or Long Rifle	.25
7561	M. Plug No. 15, .22 W. R. F.	.25
7661	Magazine Plug Pin	.25
7761	Magazine Spring, .22 Short, Long or Long Rifle	.25
7861	Magazine Spring, .22 W.R.F.	.25
7961	Magazine Follower, .22 Short, Long or Long Rifle	.25
8061	Mag. Follower, .22 W. R. F.	.25
8161	Magazine Ring, front	.50
8261	Magazine Ring, rear	.50
8361	Magazine Ring Pin	.25
8461	Peep Sight Plug Screw (2) each	.25
8561	Rear Sight No. 32B	.75
8661	Rear Sight Elevator No. 2C	.25
8761	Receiver .22 Short, Long or Long Rifle	4.50
8861	Receiver, .22 W. R. F.	4.50
8961	Receiver and Guard, .22 Short, Long or Long Rifle	7.75
9061	Receiver Guard, .22 W. R. F.	7.75
	Receiver and Guard comprises Receiver, Guard, Take-Down Screw and Stop Pin.	
9161	Guard	3.00
9261	Guard Complete	8.75
	Guard Complete comprises Guard, Action Slide Lock, Action Slide Lock Pivot, Action Slide Lock Spring, Carrier, Carrier Spring, Carrier Spring Pin, Carrier Stop Pin, Carrier Stop Screw, Ejector Stop Ejector Stop Pin, Ejector Stop Spring, Hammer Complete, Hammer Pin, Hammer Spring Abutment, Hammer Catch, Hammer Catch Stud, Take-Down Screw and Stop Pin, Trigger, Trigger Pin, Trigger Spring, Trigger Lock, Trigger Lock Plunger, Trigger Lock Plunger Spring and 2 Peep Sight Plug Screws.	
9361	T. D. Screw and Stop Pin	.25
9461	Take-Down Screw Stop Pin	.25
9561	Trigger, Short, Long or Long Rifle	.75
9561A	Trigger, W. R. F.	.75
9661	Trigger Pin	.25
9761	Trigger Spring	.25
9861	Triger Lock	.40
9961	Trigger Lock Plunger	.25
10061	Trigger Lock Plunger Spring	.25

In replacing parts marked thus (*) when desired for Take-down Guns it is necessary to send gun to us.

WINCHESTER RIFLE PARTS
MODEL 62—.22 CAL. HAMMER REPEATING RIFLE

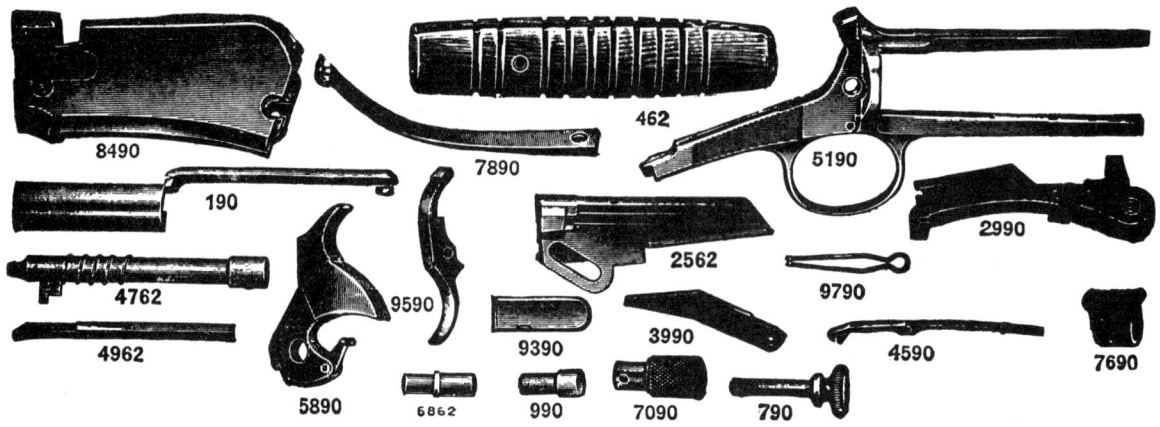

It is absolutely necessary that the numbers shown at the left of each gun part be specified when ordering.

190	Action slide	$2.00
462	Action slide handle with (2) escutcheons	1.25
562	Action slide handle escutcheon (2) each	.25
662	Action slide handle screws (2) each	.25
662A	Action slide lock	.25
790	Assembling screw and stop pin	.25
890	Assembling screw stop pin	.25
990	Assembling screw bushing	.25
1462	Barrel, short, long and long rifle, 23"	4.00
1462A	Barrel, short only, 23"	4.00
2062A	Butt stock, wood only, shot butt	2.50
2062B	Butt stock complete, shot butt	3.00

Butt stock complete comprises: stock, butt plate and (2) screws.

2362A	Butt plate, composition	.60
2462A	Butt plate screws (2) each	.25
2562	Breech bolt, short, long and long rifle	3.00
2862	Breech bolt complete	4.60

Breech bolt complete comprises: bolt with extractor, extractor pin, firing pin and spring, firing pin stop and firing pin stop pins (2).

2990	Carrier, short only	1.75
3390	Carrier complete, short only	2.25

Carrier complete comprises: carrier, carrier lever, carrier lever pin, carrier lever spring, carrier lever spring screw and trigger stop pin.

3706	Carrier, short, long and long rifle	2.30
3806	Carrier, complete, short, long and long rifle	2.80

Carrier complete comprises: carrier, carrier lever, carrier lever pin, carrier lever spring, carrier lever spring screw, trigger stop pin, cartridge stop and pin.

3990	Carrier lever	.25
4090	Carrier lever pin	.25
4190	Carrier lever spring	.25
4290	Carrier lever spring screw	.25
4306	Cartridge stop	.25
4406	Cartridge stop pin	.25
4590	Extractor	.45
4690	Extractor pin	.25
4762	Firing pin and spring	.60
4890	Firing pin spring	.25
4962	Firing pin stop	.25
5062	Firing pin stop pins (2) each	.25
5062A	Firing pin guide pin	.25
5190	Guard	3.75
5390	Guard complete, short only	9.10

Guard complete comprises guard, carrier complete, hammer complete, mainspring, mainspring screw, mainspring strain screw, trigger, trigger pin, trigger spring, trigger spring screw, assembling screw, assembling screw stop pin and assembling screw bushing.

5706	Guard complete, short, long or long rifle	9.65

Guard complete for S. L. & L. R. comprises guard, carrier complete, hammer complete, mainspring, mainspring screw, mainspring strain screw, trigger, trigger pin, trigger spring, trigger spring screw, assembling screw, assembling screw stop pin and assembling screw bushing.

5890	Hammer complete comprises hammer, stirrup and pin	$1.25
5990	Hammer stirrup	.25
6090	Hammer stirrup pin	.25
6162	Magazine tube outside, 30B short	1.50
6162A	Magazine tube outside, 32B short, long and long rifle	1.50
6362	Magazine tube inside, 27A short, long and long rifle	1.10
6662	Magazine tube inside, complete 27A short, long and long rifle	1.70

Mainspring tube inside complete comprises magazine tube, magazine spring, magazine plug, magazine plug pin and magazine follower.

6762	Magazine spring short, long and long rifle	.25
6862	Magazine follower short, long and long rifle	.25
7090	Magazine plug short, long and long rifle	.25
7290	Magazine plug pin	.25
7562	Magazine ring, front	.50
7690	Magazine ring, rear	.50
7790	Magazine ring pin, rear	.25
7890	Mainspring	.50
8190	Mainspring screw	.25
8290	Mainspring strain screw	.25
8390	Peep sight plug screw	.25
8490	Receiver, short, long and long rifle	6.00
8690	Receiver and guard, short, long and long rifle	10.10

Receiver and guard comprises receiver, guard, assembling screw, assembling screw stop pin and bushing.

9090	Receiver and guard complete with action, short	20.00
9190	Receiver and guard complete with action, short, long and long rifle	20.55

Receiver and guard complete with action comprises receiver with guard, hammer complete, carrier complete, breech bolt complete, mainspring, mainspring screw, mainspring strain screw, peep sight plug screw, trigger, trigger pin, trigger spring, trigger spring screw, assembling screw, assembling screw bushing, assembling screw stop pin, slide cover and slide cover stop screw.

9390	Slide cover	.25
9490	Slide cover stop screw	.25
9590	Trigger	.50
9690	Trigger pin	.25
9790	Trigger spring	.25
9890	Trigger spring screw	.25
9990	Upper tang screw	.25
10062	Front sight, 75C	.25
10162	Rear sight No. 32B with 2C elevator	.75

In replacing parts marked thus (*) it will be necessary to send guns to us.

INSTRUCTIONS: In ordering parts always give name and number listed in catalog, also make, model, caliber and serial number of gun. (Parts marked with * cannot be supplied on Mail Order. It will be necessary to return arm to us for fitting.)

PAYMENTS: Parts will be sent only on advance payment. Parts cannot be returned for credit. A service charge of 25c must be added to every order under $1.00 to cover cost of handling. Do not forget to include postage.

AMERICA'S GREAT GUN HOUSE   485

WINCHESTER MODEL 95—CONTINUED FROM WINCHESTER PARTS PAGE 466

Part No.	Description	Price
7395	Finger lever pin	$0.25
7495	Finger lever pin stop screw	.25
7595	Finger lever link pin	.25
7695	Forearm (Rifle) with escutcheon .38-72 and .40-72 caliber	2.00
7795	Forearm (Rifle) with escutcheon .30 Army and .303 British	2.00
7895	Forearm (Rifle) with escutcheon, .35 .405 .30 Gov't '03 and '06	2.00
7995	Forearm (Carbine) all calibers	2.00
8095	Forearm (Musket) N. R. A.	4.00
8195	Forearm stud	.25
8295	Forearm stud screw	.25
8395	Forearm stud screw escutcheon	.25
8495	Hammer complete (hammer with roll and pin)	1.25
8595	Hammer roll	.25
8695	Hammer roll pin	.25
8795	Hammer screw	.25
8895	Hand guard rivet, front (2) each (carbine)	.25
8995	Hand guard rivet, rear (2) each (carbine)	.25
9095	Hand guard spring, front	.25
9195	Hand guard spring, rear	.25
9295	Hand guard complete (carbine) (guard with front and rear springs and rivets)	1.65
9395	Hand guard complete (Musket) N. R. A.	1.65
	Hand guard complete comprises: guard with front and rear springs and (4) rivets.	
9495	Link	1.50
9595	Link pin	.25
9695	Locking bolt	1.75
9795	Locking bolt complete (give caliber)	2.45
	Locking bolt complete comprises: bolt with cartridge stop and (2) pins.	
9895	Mainspring	.45
9995	Mainspring screw	$0.25
10095	Mainspring strain screw	.25
10195	Musket front band N. R. A.	1.50
10295	Musket front band screw N. R. A.	.25
10395	Musket rear band N. R. A.	1.00
10495	Musket rear band screw N. R. A.	.25
10595	Magazine, two cartridge guides and 4 rivets	4.75
11095	Magazine complete	7.85
	Magazine complete comprises: right and left hand cartridge guide and 4 rivets, carrier, carrier screw, carrier spring, stop pin, cradle, cradle pin, cam lever and pin.	
11595	Magazine tip screw (2) each	.25
11695	Rear band (carbine)	.65
11795	Rear band screw (carbine)	.25
11895	Receiver (rifle) .38-72, .40-72, .30 Army and .303 British, Solid-frame	12.00
11995	*Receiver (rifle) .30 Army and .303 British T.D.	12.00
12095	Receiver (rifle) .405, .35, .30 Gov't '03 and '06, Solid-frame	12.00
12195	*Receiver (rifle) .405, .35, .30 Gov't '03 and '06, Take-down	12.00
12295	Receiver (carbine) .30 Army and .303 British	12.00
12395	Sear	.40
12495	Sear pin	.25
12595	Sear spring	.25
12695	Sear spring screw	.25
12795	Sling ring hole plug screw	.25
12895	Trigger	.40
12995	Trigger pin	.25
13095	Upper tang screw	.25
13195	Stock swivel base with bow and 2 base screws	.60

WINCHESTER 05, 07 & 10—CONTINUED FROM WINCHESTER PARTS PAGE 468

Part No.	05	07	10	Description	Price
7805	05			*Mag. complete, .35 cal., 5 ctg.	$2.50
7905	05			*Mag. complete, .32 cal., 10 ctg.	4.00
8005	05			*Mag. complete, .35 cal., 10 ctg.	4.00
8107		07		*Mag. complete, .351 cal., 5 ctg.	2.50
8207		07		*Mag. complete, .351 cal., 10 ctg.	4.00
8310			10	*Mag. complete, .401 cal., 4 ctg.	2.50
				Magazine complete comprises: magazine case with magazine spring, magazine follower, magazine follower roll and magazine follower roll pin.	
8405	05	07		Magazine lock	.65
8510			10	Magazine lock	.65
8605	05	07		Magazine lock screw	.25
8710			10	Magazine lock screw	.25
8805	05	07	10	Magazine lock spring	.25
8905	05	07		Operating sleeve	1.20
9010			10	Operating sleeve	1.20
9105	05	07	10	Operating sleeve spring	.25
9205	05			Operating sleeve tip	.25
9307		07		Operating sleeve tip	.35
9410			10	Operating sleeve tip	.35
9505	05	07	10	Operating sleeve tip pin	.25
9605	05			Operating sleeve tip complete, (Tip with pin)	.35
9707		07		Operating sleeve tip complete, (Tip with pin)	.45
9810			10	Operating sleeve tip complete, (Tip with pin)	.45
9905	05	07	10	Peep sight plug screw (2) each	.25
10005	05			Receiver, .32 caliber with ejector and Take-down screw bushing	11.75
10105	05			Receiver, .35 caliber with ejector and Take-down screw bushing	11.75
10207		07		Receiver, .351 caliber with ejector and Take-down screw bushing	15.30
10310			10	Receiver, .401 caliber with ejector and Take-down screw bushing	14.60
10405	05			Receiver, .32 caliber, complete	20.30
10505	05			Receiver, .35 caliber, complete	$20.30
10607		07		Receiver, .351 caliber, complete	25.35
				Receiver complete comprises: receiver with guard, shank, ejector, Take-down screw, Take-down screw bushing, Take-down screw stop pin and Take-down screw lock.	
10710			10	Receiver, .401 complete, comprising receiver with guard, shank, ejector, Take-down screw, Take-down screw bushing, Take-down screw stop pin, Take-down screw lock, Take-down screw lock pin and Take-down screw lock spring	24.95
10805	05	07		Sear	.55
10910			10	Sear	.55
11005	05	07	10	Sear spring	.25
11105	05	07		Take-down screw	.75
11205	05	07		Take-down screw bushing	.30
11305	05	07		Take-down screw stop pin	.25
11405	05	07		Take-down screw lock	.70
11510			10	Take-down screw lock	.70
11610			10	Take-down screw lock pin	.25
11710			10	Take-down screw lock spring	.25
11805	05	07		Timing lever	.75
11910			10	Timing lever	.75
12005	05	07		Timing lever spring	.25
12105	05	07		Timing lever spring screw	.25
12210			10	Timing lever spring screw	.25
12305	05	07		Trigger	1.40
12410			10	Trigger	1.40
12505	05	07		Trigger lock	.40
12610			10	Trigger lock	.40
12705	05	07	10	Trigger lock plunger	.25
12805	05	07	10	Trigger lock plunger spring	.25
12905	05	07		Trigger pin	.25
13010			10	Trigger pin	.25
13105	05	07	10	Trigger spring	.25

WINCHESTER MODEL 54—CONTINUED FROM WINCHESTER PARTS PAGE 472

Part No.	Description	Price
5454	Magazine, No. 2 and .250/3000 Savage (Speed Lock on .250/3000)	$1.50
5454A	Magazine #4, .257 Roberts	1.50
5454B	Magazine #3, .220 Swift	1.50
5554	Magazine spring, No. 1, .270 Winchester, 30 Gov't '06 and 9 M/M	.50
5654	Magazine spring, No. 2, and .250/3000 Savage (Speed Lock on .250/3000); also .220 Swift and .257 Roberts	.50
5754	Magazine spring, No. 3, 7 M/M and 7.65 M/M	.50
5754A	Magazine spring, .22 Hornet (Speed Lock)	.50
5854	Magazine follower, No. 1, .270 Winchester, .30 Gov't '06, 7 M/M, 7.65 M/M and 9 M/M	1.50
5954	Magazine follower (No. 2) and .250/3000 Savage (Speed Lock on .250/3000; also .257 Roberts	1.50
5954A	Magazine follower, .22 Hornet (Speed Lock)	1.50
5954B	Magazine follower, .220 Swift	1.50
6054	*Receiver, No. 1, .270 Winchester, .30 Gov't. '06, 7 M/M, 7.65 M/M, 9 M/M and Hornet; also .250/3000 Savage	12.35
6154A	Rubber P.G. cap and screw (large size)	.75
6154B	*Receiver, .257 Roberts	12.35
6154C	*Receiver, .220 Swift	12.35
6254	Lyman Receiver sight plug screw (2) each	.25
6354	Safety lock	1.25
6354A	Safety lock plunger	.25
6354B	Safety lock plunger spring	.25
6454	Sear	$1.25
6454A	*Sear (Speed Lock) including stop screw and nut	1.45
6454B	Sear stop screw	.25
6454C	Sear stop screw nut	.25
6554	Sear (Speed Lock) complete comprising sear, trigger, trigger spring, trigger pin, sear stop screw and nut	2.65
6654	Sear pin	.25
6754	Sear spring	.25
6854	Stock screw eye	.25
6854A	Snap swivel base complete with 2 screws for forearm	.70
6854B	Snap swivel base complete with 2 screws for stock	.70
6954	Trigger, Regular and Hornet	1.20
6954A	*Trigger (Speed Lock)	1.20
7054	Trigger pin	.25
7154	Trigger spring	.25
7254	*Special parts necessary to change Model 54 from plain lock to speed lock are as follows: sear 1.25, firing pin 2.85, breech bolt 8.50, firing pin spring .20 and trigger 1.20. Total 14.00.	

SIGHT COVER

Part No.	Description	Price
7254A	Sight cover No. 3277—7 m/m, 7.65 m/m, 9 m/m. Style BL	.25
7254B	Sight cover No. 3278—.22 Hornet, .250-3000 Savage, .270 W.C.F. & .30 Gov't '06. Style BM	.25

In replacing part marked thus (*) gun must be sent us.

SEE PAGE 8 "HOW TO ORDER"

WINCHESTER SHOTGUN PARTS
MODEL 12 REPEATING SHOTGUN

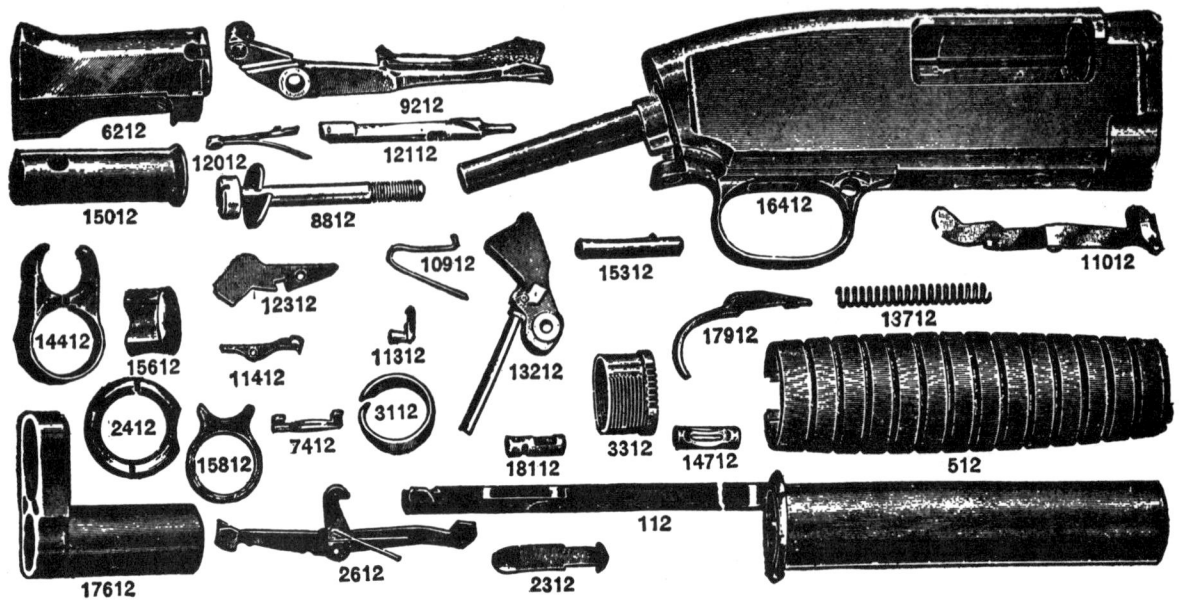

It is absolutely necessary that the numbers shown at the left of each gun part be specified when ordering.

No.	Description	Price
112	Action slide 12 Ga. Standard grade	$4.80
212	Action slide 16 and 20 Ga. Standard grade	4.80
212A	Action slide 12 Ga. (for Duck Gun)	5.00
212½	Action slide complete	6.05

Action slide complete comprises Action slide, Action slide handle and Action slide sleeve screw cap.

No.	Description	Price
312	Action slide 12 Ga. Special Trap or Pigeon grade	5.75
412	Action slide 16 and 20 Ga. Special Trap or Pigeon grade	5.75
412A	Action slide extension style, 12 Ga.	5.00
412B	Action slide extension style, 16 and 20 Ga.	5.00
512	Action slide handle, 12 Ga. Standard grade	.75
612	Action slide handle, 16 and 20 Ga. Standard grade	.75
712	Action slide handle, 12 Ga. Standard Trap	2.50
812	Action slide handle, 16 and 20 Ga. Standard Trap	2.50
912	Action slide handle, 12 Ga. Special Trap and Pigeon grade	5.00
1012	Action slide handle, 16 and 20 Ga. Special Trap and Pigeon grade	5.00
1312A	Action slide handle, extension style, 12 Ga. Standard Trap	8.00
1412A	Action slide handle, extension style, 16 and 20 Ga. Standard Trap	8.00
1512A	Action slide handle, extension style, 12 Ga. Special Trap or Pigeon grade	12.00
1612B	Action slide handle, extension style, 16 and 20 Ga. Special Trap or Pigeon grade	12.00
2312	Action slide handle retaining spring, 12-16-20 Ga.	.25
2412	Action slide sleeve screw cap, 12 Ga.	.40
2512	Action slide sleeve screw cap, 16 and 20 Ga.	.40
2612	*Action slide lock with spring, 12 Ga.	1.85
2712	*Action slide lock with spring, 16 and 20 Ga.	1.85
2812	Action slide lock pivot, 12 Ga.	.25
2912	Action slide lock pivot, 16 and 20 Ga.	.25
3012	Action slide lock spring, 12-16-20 Ga. (2) each	.25
3112	Action slide spring, 12 Ga.	.25
3212	Action slide spring, 16 and 20 Ga.	.25
3312	Adjusting sleeve, 12 Ga.	1.00
3412	Adjusting sleeve, 16 and 20 Ga.	1.00

If the barrel and extension are loose on receiver and the adjusting sleeve has been turned back to the last notch and are still loose, order heavy draw or extra heavy draw adjusting sleeve.

No.	Description	Price
3512	Adjusting sleeve lock, 12-16-20 Ga.	.30
3612	Adjusting sleeve lock screw, 12-16-20 Ga.	.25

In ordering barrels, give length, choke and gauge also style, whether Standard, Trap, Pigeon or Ventilated Rib.

Barrels can be furnished in our three (3) Standard chokes, full choke, modified choke and cylinder bore, also two (2) new chokes, improved modified choke and improved cylinder bore. We can also furnish either of our Skeet Chokes, No. 1 (Killing Pattern at 20 yards) or No. 2 (Killing Pattern at 30 yards) at an additional cost of $2.50 per barrel. No cancellation can be accepted on orders for improved modified, improved cylinder bores or Skeet Chokes, as barrels with these chokes are made on special order only.

No.	Description	Price
3712	*Barrel, 12 Ga.	$15.00
3712A	*Barrel, 16 Ga.	15.00
3712B	*Barrel, 20 Ga.	15.00
3712C	*Barrel, 30 and 32" full choke (for Duck Gun) 12 Ga. only	20.00
3712D	*Barrel, 30 and 32" with raised matted rib, full choke (for Duck Gun) 12 Ga. only	27.00
3812	*Barrel with raised matted rib, 12 Ga.	22.00
3812A	*Barrel with raised matted rib, 16 Ga.	22.00
3812B	*Barrel with raised matted rib, 20 Ga.	22.00
3812C	*Barrel with raised matted rib, 12 Ga. (Skeet No. 1)	22.00
3812F	*Barrel with raised matted rib, 12 Ga. (Skeet No. 2)	22.00
3812D	*Barrel with raised matted rib, 16 Ga. (Skeet No. 1)	22.00
3812G	*Barrel with raised matted rib, 16 Ga. (Skeet No. 2)	22.00
3812E	*Barrel with raised matted rib, 20 Ga. (Skeet No. 1)	22.00
3812H	*Barrel with raised matted rib, 20 Ga. (Skeet No. 2)	22.00
3912	*Barrel with ventilated rib, 12 Ga. only, 30"	45.00
3912A	*Barrel with ventilated rib, 12 Ga. only, Skeet 26¾"	45.00

*INTERCHANGEABLE BARREL COMPLETE
Give Length, Choke and Gauge

No.	Description	Price
4012F	Standard grade, plain barrel	20.00
4112G	Standard grade, matted rib barrel	27.25
4112B-1	Standard trap, matted rib barrel	29.00
4112C-2	Special trap or pigeon grade, matted rib barrel	43.00
4112H-3	Skeet gun, matted rib barrel	29.00
5112D-4	Standard trap, ventilated rib barrel	60.00
5112E-5	Special trap or pigeon grade, ventilated rib barrel	75.00
5112K	Standard grade, 12 Ga. only (for Duck Gun)	25.00
5112L	Standard grade, 12 Ga. only (for Duck Gun) matted rib	32.25
5112M	Standard trap, 12 Ga. only (for Duck Gun)	34.00
5112N	Special trap, 12 Ga. only (for Duck Gun)	48.00
5112O	Pigeon grade, 12 Ga. only (for Duck Gun)	48.00
5812	*Barrel chamber ring, 12 Ga.	.45
5912	*Barrel chamber ring, 16 Ga.	.45
6012	*Barrel chamber ring, 20 Ga.	.45
6112	Barrel chamber ring screw (2) each	.25
6212	Breech bolt, 12 Ga. Standard grade	5.25
6312	Breech bolt, 16 Ga. Standard grade	5.25
6412	Breech bolt, 20 Ga. Standard grade	5.25
6512	Breech bolt, 12 Ga., Special Trap or Pigeon grade	6.00
6612	Breech bolt, 16 Ga. Special Trap or Pigeon grade	6.00
6712	Breech bolt, 20 Ga. Special Trap or Pigeon grade	6.00
6712A	Breech bolt, 12 Ga. only (for Duck Gun)	5.50
6812	Breech bolt, 12 Ga. complete	8.65
6912	Breech bolt, 16 Ga. complete	8.65
7012	Breech bolt, 20 Ga. complete	8.65

In replacing parts marked thus (*) it will be necessary to send guns to us.

(Continued on Next Page)

EVERYTHING IN GUNS UNDER ONE COVER

WINCHESTER SHOTGUN PARTS
MODEL 12 SHOTGUN—CONTINUED FROM PRECEDING PAGE

No.	Description	Price
7112	Breech bolt, 12 Ga. complete, Special Trap or Pigeon grade	$9.25
7212	Breech bolt, 16 Ga., complete, Special Trap or Pigeon grade	9.25
7312	Breech bolt, 20 Ga. complete, Special Trap or Pigeon grade	9.25
	Breech bolt complete comprises: bolt with extractor right hand, extractor left hand, extractor spring right hand, extractor spring left hand, extractor spring plunger right hand, extractor pin left hand, breech bolt retaining lever and pin, firing pin, firing pin retractor, retractor screw and retractor spring.	
7412	Breech bolt retaining lever	.70
7512	Breech bolt retaining lever pin	.25
7612	Butt stock complete, Standard grade, 12 Ga. Standard dimensions	5.50
7612½	Butt stock complete, Standard grade, 12 Ga. Customer's dimensions	20.50
7712	Butt stock complete, Standard grade, 16 and 20 Ga. Standard dimensions	5.50
7712½	Butt stock complete, Standard grade, 16 and 20 Ga. Customer's dimensions	20.50
7812½	Butt stock complete, Standard Trap, Straight grip with recoil pad, 12 Ga. only	13.50
7912	Butt stock complete, Standard Trap, Straight grip with recoil pad, 16 and 20 Ga. only	13.50
8012	Butt stock complete, Standard Trap, Pistol grip with recoil pad, 12 Ga.	13.50
8112	Butt stock complete, Standard Trap, Pistol grip with recoil pad, 16 and 20 Ga.	13.50
8212	Butt stock complete, Pigeon or Special Trap, Straight grip, 12 Ga. Ask for customer's dimensions before filling order	40.50
8312	Butt stock complete, Pigeon or Special Trap, Straight grip, 16 and 20 Ga.	40.50
8412	Butt stock complete, Pigeon or Special Trap, Pistol grip, 12 Ga. Ask for customer's dimensions before filling order	40.50
8512	Butt stock complete, Pigeon or Special Trap, Pistol grip, 16 and 20 Ga.	40.50
8512A	Butt stock complete, Standard Trap Ventilated Rib, Straight grip, 12 Ga. only with recoil pad.	13.50
8512B	Butt stock complete, Standard Trap Ventilated Rib, Pistol grip, 12 Ga. only with recoil pad.	13.50
8712	Butt stock complete, Pigeon or Special Trap Ventilated Rib, 12 Ga. only with recoil pad. Ask for customer's dimensions before filling order	40.50
	Butt stock complete comprises: stock with butt plate and (2) butt plate screws.	
8712C	Butt stock complete with recoil pad (for Duck Gun) 12 Ga. only	8.00
8812	Butt stock bolt and washer	.25
8912	Butt stock bolt washer	.25
9012	Butt plate, rubber	.60
9112	Butt plate screws (2) each	.25
9212	Carrier, 12 Ga. Standard and Standard Trap	2.75
9312	Carrier, 16 Ga. Standard and Standard Trap	2.75
9412	Carrier, 20 Ga. Standard and Standard Trap	2.75
9512	Carrier, 12 Ga. Special Trap and Pigeon grade.	3.25
9612	Carrier, 16 Ga. Special Trap and Pigeon grade.	3.25
9712	Carrier, 20 Ga. Special Trap and Pigeon grade.	3.25
9712A	Carrier (for Duck Gun) 12 Ga. only	3.00
9812	Carrier plunger	.25
9912	Carrier plunger spring	.25
10012	Carrier plunger screw	.25
10112	Carrier complete, 12 Ga. Standard and Standard Trap grade	3.05
10212	Carrier complete, 16 Ga. Standard and Standard Trap grade	3.05
10312	Carrier complete, 20 Ga. Standard and Standard Trap grade	3.05
10412	Carrier complete, 12 Ga. Special Trap and Pigeon grade	3.55
10512	Carrier complete, 16 Ga. Special Trap and Pigeon grade	3.55
10612	Carrier complete, 20 Ga. Special Trap and Pigeon grade	3.55
	Carrier complete comprises: carrier with carrier plunger, carrier plunger spring, and carrier plunger screw.	
10712	Carrier pivot, 12 Ga.	.25
10812	Carrier pivot, 16 and 20 Ga.	.25
10912	Carrier spring	.25
11012	Cartridge cut off, 12 Ga.	1.00
11112	Cartridge cut off, 16 Ga.	1.00
11212	Cartridge cut off, 20 Ga.	1.00
11312	Extractor, right hand, 12-16-20 Ga.	.40
11412	Extractor, left hand, 12-16 Ga.	.50
11512	Extractor, left hand, 20 Ga.	.50
11612	Extractor spring, right hand	.25
11712	Extractor spring plunger, right hand	.25
11812	Extractor spring, left hand	.25
11912	Extractor pin, left hand	.25
12012	Ejector with spring	.75
12012A	Ejector spring	.25
12012B	Ejector with spring (for Duck Gun)	.75
12112	Firing pin, 12 Ga.	.50
12212	Firing pin, 16 and 20 Ga.	.50
12312	Firing pin retractor, 12 Ga.	.40
12412	Firing pin retractor, 16 and 20 Ga.	.40
12512	Firing pin retractor screw	.25
12612	Firing pin retractor spring	$0.25
12712	Guard, 12 Ga.	4.50
12812	Guard, 16 and 20 Ga.	4.50
12812A	Guard, 12 Ga. only (for Duck Gun)	5.00
12912	Guard, complete 12 Ga.	13.10
13012	Guard, complete 16 and 20 Ga.	13.10
	Guard complete comprises: guard, carrier complete, action slide lock and spring, action slide lock pivot, carrier pivot, carrier spring, trigger, trigger spring, trigger pin, hammer complete, hammer pin, hammer spring, trigger lock, trigger lock plunger and trigger lock plunger spring.	
13112	Guard screw	.25
13212	*Hammer with hammer spring guide rod and pin, Standard grade	1.40
13312	*Hammer with hammer spring guide rod and pin, Special Trap or Pigeon grade	1.50
13412	Hammer spring guide rod	.25
13512	Hammer spring guide rod pin	.25
13612	Hammer pin	.25
13712	Hammer spring	.25
13812	Magazine tube, 12 Ga.	5.25
13912	Magazine tube, 16 Ga.	5.25
14012	Magazine tube, 20 Ga.	5.25
14112	Magazine tube complete, 12 Ga.	9.80
14212	Magazine tube complete, 16 Ga.	9.80
14312	Magazine tube complete, 20 Ga.	9.80
	Magazine tube complete comprises: magazine with magazine spring, magazine follower, magazine plug, magazine plug screw (2), magazine locking pin complete, mag. band bushing, magazine band bushing screw (2), magazine band, magazine plug stop, action slide handle retaining spring and action slide spring.	
14412	Magazine band, 12 Ga.	1.50
14512	Magazine band, 16 Ga.	1.50
14612	Magazine band, 20 Ga.	1.50
14612A	Magazine band, 12 Ga. only (for Duck Gun)	2.00
14712	Magazine band bushing, 12 Ga.	.60
14812	Magazine band bushing, 16 and 20 Ga.	.60
14812A	Magazine band bushing, 12 Ga. only (for Duck Gun)	.60
14912	Magazine band bushing screw (2) each	.25
15012	Magazine follower, 12 Ga.	.35
15112	Magazine follower, 16 Ga.	.35
15212	Magazine follower, 20 Ga.	.35
15312	Magazine locking pin and spring, 12 Ga.	.50
15412	Magazine locking pin and spring, 16 and 20 Ga.	.50
15512	Magazine locking pin spring	.25
15612	Magazine plug, 12 Ga. No. 25	.70
15712	Magazine plug, 16 and 20 Ga. No. 26	.70
15812	Magazine plug stop, 12 Ga.	.30
15912	Magazine plug stop, 16 Ga.	.30
16012	Magazine plug stop, 20 Ga.	.30
16012A	Magazine plug stop, 12 Ga. only (for Duck Gun)	.30
16112	Magazine plug screw (2) each	.25
16212	Magazine spring, 12 Ga.	.25
16312	Magazine spring, 16 and 20 Ga.	.25
16412	*Receiver, guard, guard screw and shank, 12 Ga. Standard and Standard Trap grade	20.00
16512	*Receiver, guard, guard screw and shank, 16 Ga. Standard and Standard Trap grade	20.00
16612	*Receiver, guard, guard screw and shank, 20 Ga. Standard and Standard Trap grade	20.00
16612A	*Receiver, guard, guard screw and shank (for Duck Gun)	22.00
16712	*Receiver, guard, guard screw and shank, 12 Ga. Special Trap	24.75
16812	*Receiver, guard, guard screw and shank, 16 Ga. Special Trap	24.75
16912	*Receiver, guard, guard screw and shank, 20 Ga. Special Trap	24.75
17012	*Receiver, guard, guard screw and shank, 12 Ga. Pigeon grade, engraved	130.00
17112	*Receiver, guard, guard screw and shank, 16 Ga. Pigeon grade, engraved	130.00
17212	*Receiver, guard, guard screw and shank, 20 Ga. Pigeon grade, engraved	130.00
17312	*Receiver, guard, guard screw and shank, 12 Ga. Tournament grade, (ventilated rib model) with receiver rib	35.00
17412	*Receiver, guard, guard screw and shank, 12 Ga. Standard Trap grade, (ventilated rib model) with receiver rib	35.00
17512	*Receiver, guard, guard screw and shank, 12 Ga. Pigeon grade, (ventilated rib model) with receiver rib, engraved	135.00
17612	*Receiver extension, 12 Ga.	2.50
17712	*Receiver extension, 16 and 20 Ga.	2.50
17812	Receiver shank	.25
17812½	Spanner wrench for 12, 16 and 20 Ga.	1.00
17912	Trigger 12 Ga.	.75
18012	Trigger 16 and 20 Ga.	.75
18112	Trigger lock	.40
18212	Trigger lock plunger	.25
18312	Trigger lock plunger spring	.25
18412	Trigger lock complete comprises: lock with plunger and spring.	.60
18512	Trigger spring	.25
18612	Trigger pin	.25

In replacing parts marked thus (*) it will be necessary to send guns to us.

WINCHESTER SHOTGUN PARTS
MODEL 97 REPEATING SHOTGUN

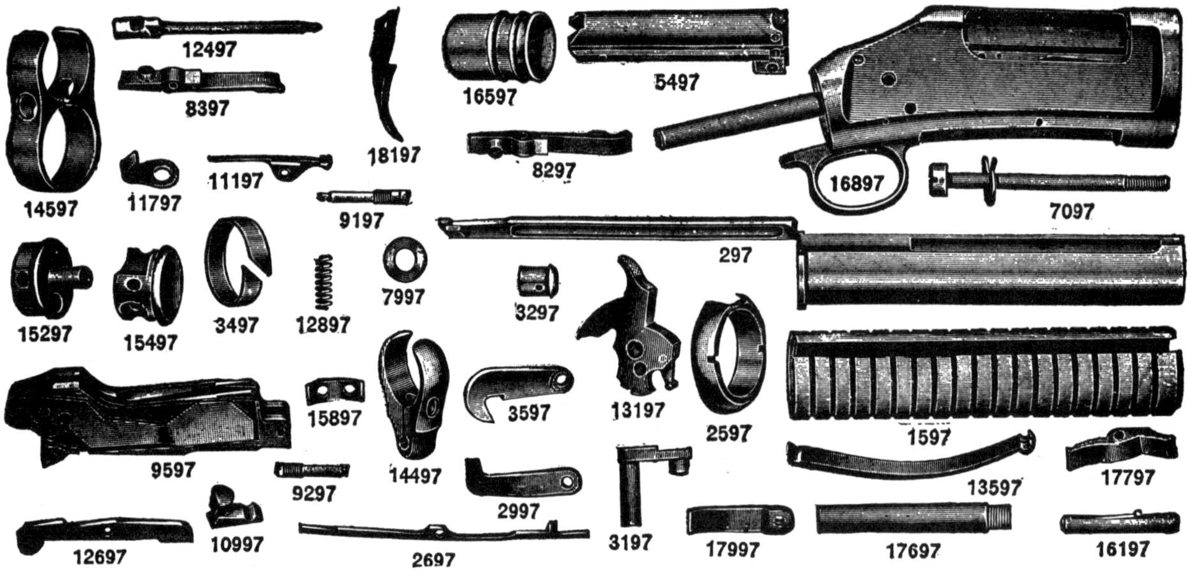

It is absolutely necessary that the numbers shown at the left of each gun part be specified when ordering.

MODEL 97 SHOTGUN

No.	Description	Price
197	Action slide, Solid-frame, 12 Ga.	$2.40
297	Action slide, Take-down, 12 and 16 Ga.	2.40
397	Action slide, Solid-frame, Style C (old style) with (3) screw holes, 12 Ga.	3.75
597	Action slide complete, Solid-frame, 12 Ga.	3.55
697	Action slide complete, Take-down, 12 and 16 Ga.	3.55
997	Action slide com., Solid-frame, Stand. Trap, 12 Ga.	5.30
1097	Action slide com., T. D., Stand. Trap, 12 & 16 Ga.	5.30
1197	Action slide com., Solid-fr., Pigeon gr., 12 Ga.	7.80
1297	Action slide com., T. D., Pigeon gr., 12 & 16 Ga.	7.80

Action slide complete comprises: action slide, action slide handle, and action slide sleeve screw cap.

| 1397 | Action slide complete, Solid-frame, Style "C" (old style) with (3) screw holes, 12 Ga. | 5.30 |

Action slide complete, Style "C" comprises: action slide, action slide handle, action slide handle screws (3), and action slide handle escutcheons (3).

1597	Action slide handle, Stand. grade, 12 & 16 Ga.	.75
1797	Action slide handle, Trap, 12 & 16 Ga.	2.50
1997	Act. slide hdle., Sp. Trap or Pgn. gr., 12 & 16 Ga.	5.00
2397	Action slide handle, Style "C" (old style) with (3) screw holes, 12 Ga.	1.25
2497	Action slide handle screw, Style "C" (old style) 12 Ga. (3) each	.40
2597	Action slide sleeve screw cap, 12 and 16 Ga.	.40
2697	Action slide lock, 12 and 16 Ga.	.25
2797	Action slide lock joint pin, 12 and 16 Ga.	.25
2897	Act. slide lock joint pin stop screw, 12 & 16 Ga.	.25
2997	Action slide lock spring, 12 and 16 Ga.	.25
3097	Action slide lock spring screw, 12 and 16 Ga.	.25
3197	Action slide lock release plunger, 12 and 16 Ga.	.40
3297	Action slide lock release plunger pin, 12 and 16 Ga.	.25
3397	Act. slide lock release plun. p.n spg., 12 & 16 Ga.	.25
3497	Action slide spring, 12 and 16 Ga.	.25
3597	Action slide hook, 12 and 16 Ga.	.35
3697	Action slide hook screw, 12 and 16 Ga.	.25
3797	Adjusting sleeve, Take-down	1.00

If barrel and extension are loose on receiver and adjusting sleeve has been turned back to last notch and are still loose, order heavy draw or extra heavy draw adjusting sleeve.

| 3897 | Adjusting sleeve lock, Take-down, 12 & 16 Ga. | .30 |
| 3997 | Ad. sleeve lock screw, Take-down, 12 & 16 Ga. | $0.25 |

In ordering barrels give length, choke and gauge, Solid-frame or Take-down.
Barrels can be furnished in our three (3) Standard Chokes, full choke, modified choke and cylinder bore, also two (2) new chokes, improved modified choke and improved cylinder bore. **Also we can furnish either of our Skeet Chokes, No. 1 (Killing Pattern at 20 yards) or No. 2 (Killing Pattern at 30 yards) at an additional cost of $2.50 per barrel.** No cancellation can be accepted on orders for improved modified, improved cylinder bores or Skeet Chokes as barrels with these chokes are made on special order only.

4097	Barrel, plain, Solid-frame, 12 Ga.	7.50
4197	*Barrel, plain, Take-down, 12 Ga.	7.50
4297	*Barrel, plain, Take-down, 16 Ga.	7.50
4397	*Barrel, matted, Take-down, Standard Trap, Special Trap or Pigeon grade, 12 Ga.	15.00
4497	*Barrel, matted, Take-down, Standard Trap, Special Trap or Pigeon grade, 16 Ga.	15.00
4597	Barrel chamber ring, Take-down, 12 Ga.	.25
4697	Barrel chamber ring, Take-down, 16 Ga.	.25
4797	Barrel cham. ring ret. screw, Take-down, (2) ea.	.25

*INTERCHANGEABLE BARRELS COMPLETE
Specify if 12 or 16 Ga.

4897H	Standard Grade Plain Barrel	18.00
5297F-2	Standard Trap Matted Top Barrel	23.00
5297G-3	Special Trap or Pigeon Grade Matted Top Barrel	35.00
5497	Breech bolt, 12 Ga.	3.50
5597	Breech bolt, 16 Ga.	3.50
5697	Breech bolt, Trap grade, 12 Ga.	4.00
5797	Breech bolt, Trap grade, 16 Ga.	4.00
5897	Breech bolt complete, 12 Ga.	6.00
5997	Breech bolt complete, 16 Ga.	6.00
6097	Breech bolt complete, Trap grade, 12 Ga.	6.50
6197	Breech bolt complete, Trap grade, 16 Ga.	6.50

Breech bolt complete comprises: bolt with right hand extractor, plunger and spring, left hand extractor and pin, firing pin, firing pin lock, firing pin lock screw, firing pin lock spring, and firing pin stop pin.

In replacing parts marked thus (*) when desired for Take-down Guns it is necessary to send gun to us.

(Continued on Next Page)

INSTRUCTIONS: In ordering parts always give name and number listed in catalog, also make, model, caliber and serial number of gun. (Parts marked with * cannot be supplied on Mail Order. It will be necessary to return arm to us for fitting.)

PAYMENTS: Parts will be sent only on advance payment. Parts cannot be returned for credit. A service charge of 25c must be added to every order under $1.00 to cover cost of handling. Do not forget to include postage.

ALL SHIPMENTS ARE INSURED

WINCHESTER SHOTGUN PARTS
MODEL 97 REPEATING SHOTGUN
(Continued from Preceding Page)

No.	Description	Price
6297	Butt stock com., Stand. gr., 12 Ga., Stand. dimen.	$5.00
6297½	Butt stock com., Stand. gr., 12 Ga. Cus. dimen.	20.00
6397	Butt stock com., Stand. gr., 16 Ga., Stand. dimen.	5.00
6397½	Butt stock com., Stand. gr., 16 Ga., Cus. dimen.	20.00
6397A	Butt stock complete, Standard Trap, 12 Ga., Standard dimensions with recoil pad	12.50
6397B	Butt stock complete, Standard Trap, 16 Ga., Standard dimensions with recoil pad	12.50
6697	Butt stock complete, Special Trap or Pigeon grade, 12 Ga. Ask for customer's dimensions before filling order	40.00
6797	Butt stock complete, Special Trap or Pigeon grade, 16 Ga. Ask for customer's dimensions before filling order	40.00
6897	Butt stk. com., Stand. gr., 12 Ga., met. butt plate	5.20
6997	Butt stk. com., Stand. gr., 16 Ga., met. butt plate	5.20
	Butt stock complete comprises: stock, butt plate and (2) butt plate screws.	
7097	Butt stk. bolt and wa., (give length), 12 & 16 Ga.	.25
7197	Butt stock bolt washer, 12 and 16 Ga.	.25
7397	Butt plate, rubber, 12 and 16 Ga.	.60
7497	Butt plate, rubber for Trap stock, 12 and 16 Ga.	.70
7597	Butt plate, metal, 12 and 16 Ga.	.85
7697	Butt plate screw, 12 and 16 Ga. (2) each	.25
7797	Cartridge guide, 12 Ga.	.25
7897	Cartridge guide, 16 Ga.	.25
7997	Cartridge guide friction spring, 12 and 16 Ga.	.25
8097	Cartridge guide rivet, 12 and 16 Ga.	.25
8197	Cartridge guide stop screw, 12 and 16 Ga.	.25
8297	Cartridge stop and spring, right hand, 12 Ga.	.60
8397	Cartridge stop and spring, left hand, 12 Ga.	.60
8497	Cartridge stop and spring, right hand, 16 Ga.	.60
8597	Cartridge stop and spring, left hand, 16 Ga.	.60
8697	Cartridge stop and spring, r. h., Style C (old style), with screw on side of receiver, 12 Ga.	.60
8797	Cartridge stop and spring, r. h., Style C (old style), with screw on side of receiver, 16 Ga.	.60
8897	Cartridge stop and spring, l. h., Style C (old style), with screw on side of receiver, 12 Ga.	.60
8997	Cartridge stop and spring, l. h., Style C (old style), with screw on side of receiver, 16 Ga.	.60
9097	Cartridge stop spring, 12 and 16 Ga.	.25
9197	Cartridge stop screw, right hand, 12 and 16 Ga.	.25
9297	Cartridge stop screw, left hand, 12 and 16 Ga.	.25
9397	Cartridge stop screw, right hand, Style "C" 12 and 16 Ga. (old style through side of receiver)	.25
9497	Cartridge stop screw, left hand, Style "C" 12 and 16 Ga. (old style through side of receiver)	.25
9597	Carrier, 12 Ga. Standard grade	5.00
9697	Carrier, 16 Ga. Standard grade	5.00
9797	Carrier, 12 Ga. Trap grade	6.00
9897	Carrier, 16 Ga. Trap grade	6.00
9997	Carrier, 12 Ga. Pigeon grade	6.00
10097	Carrier, 16 Ga. Pigeon grade	6.00
	Carrier comprises: ctge. guide, friction spring, ctge. guide rivet, and action slide lock release plunger.	
10197	Carrier complete, Standard grade, 12 Ga.	9.20
10297	Carrier complete, Standard grade, 16 Ga.	9.20
10397	Carrier complete, Trap grade, 12 Ga.	9.95
10497	Carrier complete, Trap grade, 16 Ga.	9.95
10597	Carrier complete, Pigeon grade, 12 Ga.	9.95
10697	Carrier complete, Pigeon grade, 16 Ga.	9.95
	Carrier complete comprises: carrier with cartridge guide, friction spring, rivet, hammer comp. hammer pin, sear, sear spring, sear spring screw, action slide lock, action slide lock joint pin, and stop screw, action slide lock spring, and screw, release plunger, mainspring, strain screw, and pin.	
10797	Carrier pin, 12 and 16 Ga.	.25
10897	Carrier pin stop screw, 12 and 16 Ga.	.25
10997	Extractor right hand, 12 Ga.	.40
11097	Extractor right hand, 16 Ga.	.40
11197	Extractor left hand, 12 Ga.	.40
11297	Extractor left hand, 16 Ga.	.40
11397	Extractor plunger right hand, 12 and 16 Ga.	.25
11497	Extractor plunger spring, r. h., 12 and 16 Ga.	.25
11597	Extractor pin, left hand, 12 Ga.	.25
11697	Extractor pin, left hand, 16 Ga.	.25
11797	Ejector spring, 12 Ga.	.25
11897	Ejector spring, 16 Ga.	.25
11997	Ejector spring screw, 12 and 16 Ga.	.25
12097	Ejector pin, 12 Ga.	.25
12197	Ejector pin, 16 Ga.	.25
12297	*Extension, Take-down, 12 and 16 Ga.	2.25
12397	Extension stop screw, Take-down, 12 and 16 Ga.	.25
12497	Firing pin, 12 Ga.	.60
12597	Firing pin, 16 Ga.	.60
12697	Firing pin lock, 12 and 16 Ga.	.30
12797	Firing pin lock screw, 12 and 16 Ga.	.25
12897	Firing pin lock spring, 12 and 16 Ga.	.25
12997	Firing pin stop pin, 12 and 16 Ga.	$0.25
13097	Guard bow, 12 and 16 Ga.	1.25
13197	Hammer complete (Hammer with stirrup and pin), 12 and 16 Ga.	1.25
13297	Hammer pin, 12 and 16 Ga.	.25
13397	Hammer stirrup, 12 and 16 Ga.	.25
13497	Hammer stirrup pin, 12 and 16 Ga.	.25
13597	Mainspring, 12 and 16 Ga.	.40
13697	Mainspring strain screw, 12 and 16 Ga.	.25
13797	Mainspring pin, 12 and 16 Ga.	.25
13897	Magazine tube, Solid-frame, 12 Ga.	1.50
13997	Magazine tube, Solid-frame, complete, 12 Ga.	3.25
	Magazine tube complete comprises: mag. tube, with mag. spring, mag. follower, mag. plug, mag. plug screw, mag. band, band screw and action slide spring.	
14097	Magazine tube, Take-down, 12 Ga.	2.00
14197	Magazine tube, Take-down, 16 Ga.	2.00
14297	Magazine tube complete, Take-down, 12 Ga.	5.40
14397	Magazine tube complete, Take-down, 16 Ga.	5.40
	Magazine tube complete comprises: mag. tube, with mag. follower, mag. spring, mag. plug, mag. plug screws (2), mag. plug stop, mag. band, mag. band bushing screws (2), mag. band bushing, magazine locking pin complete and action slide spring.	
14497	Magazine band, Solid-frame, 12 Ga.	.75
14597	Magazine band, Take-down, 12 Ga.	1.25
14697	Magazine band, Take-down, 16 Ga.	1.25
14797	Magazine band screw, Solid-frame, 12 Ga.	.25
14897	Magazine band bushing screw, Take-down, 12 Ga. (2) each	.25
14997	Magazine band bushing screw, Take-down, 16 Ga. (2) each	.25
15097	Magazine band bushing, Take-down, 12 Ga.	.50
15197	Magazine band bushing, Take-down, 16 Ga.	.50
15297	Magazine plug, Solid-frame, 12 Ga.	.40
15397	Magazine plug screw, Solid-frame, 12 Ga.	.25
15497	Magazine plug, Take-down, 12 and 16 Ga.	.60
15597	Mag. plug screw, Take-down, 12 & 16 Ga. (2) ea.	.25
15697	Magazine plug stop, Take-down, 12 Ga.	.25
15797	Magazine plug stop, Take-down, 16 Ga.	.25
15897	Magazine stop, Take-down, 12 Ga. and (2) screws.	.25
16097	Magazine stop screw, Solid-frame, 12 Ga.	.25
16197	Magazine locking pin and spring, Take-down, 12 and 16 Ga.	.50
16297	Mag. locking pin spring, Take-down, 12 & 16 Ga.	.25
16397	Magazine spring, 12 and 16 Ga.	.25
16497	Magazine follower, Solid-frame, 12 Ga.	.25
16597	Magazine follower, Take-down, 12 Ga.	.25
16697	Magazine follower, Take-down, 16 Ga.	.25
16797	Receiver, Solid-frame, Standard grade, 12 Ga.	12.00
16897	*Receiver, Take-down, Standard grade, 12 Ga.	14.00
16997	*Receiver, Take-down, Standard grade, 16 Ga.	14.00
17297	*Receiver, Take-down, Trap grade, 12 Ga.	15.00
17397	*Receiver, Take-down, Trap guide, 16 Ga.	15.00
17497	*Receiver, Take-down Pigeon gr. (engrav.), 12 Ga.	117.85
17597	*Receiver, Take-down, Pigeon gr. (engrav.), 16 Ga.	117.85
	Receiver comprises: receiver with guard, trigger pin, cartridge stop r. and l. hand, cartridge stop springs (2), ctge. stop screws (2), and receiver shank.	
17697	Receiver shank (give length), 12 and 16 Ga.	.25
17697½	Spanner wrench for 12 and 16 Ga.	1.00
17797	Sear, 12 and 16 Ga.	.30
17897	Sear pin, 12 and 16 Ga.	.25
17997	Sear spring, 12 and 16 Ga.	.25
18097	Sear spring screw, 12 and 16 Ga.	.25
18197	Trigger, 12 and 16 Ga.	.40
18297	Trigger pin, 12 and 16 Ga.	.25
18397	Trigger spring, 12 and 16 Ga.	.25
18497	Trigger stop screw, 12 and 16 Ga.	.25
18597	Receiver, complete with action, Solid-frame, 12 Ga. Standard grade	29.50
18697	*Receiver, complete with action, Take-down, 12 Ga. Standard grade	31.90
18797	*Receiver, complete with action, Take-down, 16 Ga.	31.90
	Receiver complete with action comprises: Receiver with breech bolt complete, carrier complete, action slide hook, action slide hook screw, ejector spring, ejector pin, ejector spring screw, trigger, trigger pin, trigger spring trigger stop screw, cartridge stop complete r. h., cartridge stop complete l. h., cartridge stop screw (2), guard bow, receiver shank, release plunger, release plunger spring, carrier pin stop screw, and cartridge guide stop screw.	

In replacing parts marked thus (*) it will be necessary to send guns to us.

INSTRUCTIONS: In ordering parts always give name and number listed in catalog, also make, model, caliber and serial number of gun. (Parts marked with * cannot be supplied on Mail Order It will be necessary to return arm to us for fitting.)

PAYMENTS: Parts will be sent only on advance payment. Parts cannot be returned for credit. A service charge of 25c must be added to every order under $1.00 to cover cost of handling. Do not forget to include postage.

© **SEND YOUR GUN TO STOEGER FOR EXPERT REPAIRING**

WINCHESTER SHOTGUN PARTS
MODEL 21 DOUBLE BARREL HAMMERLESS SHOTGUN

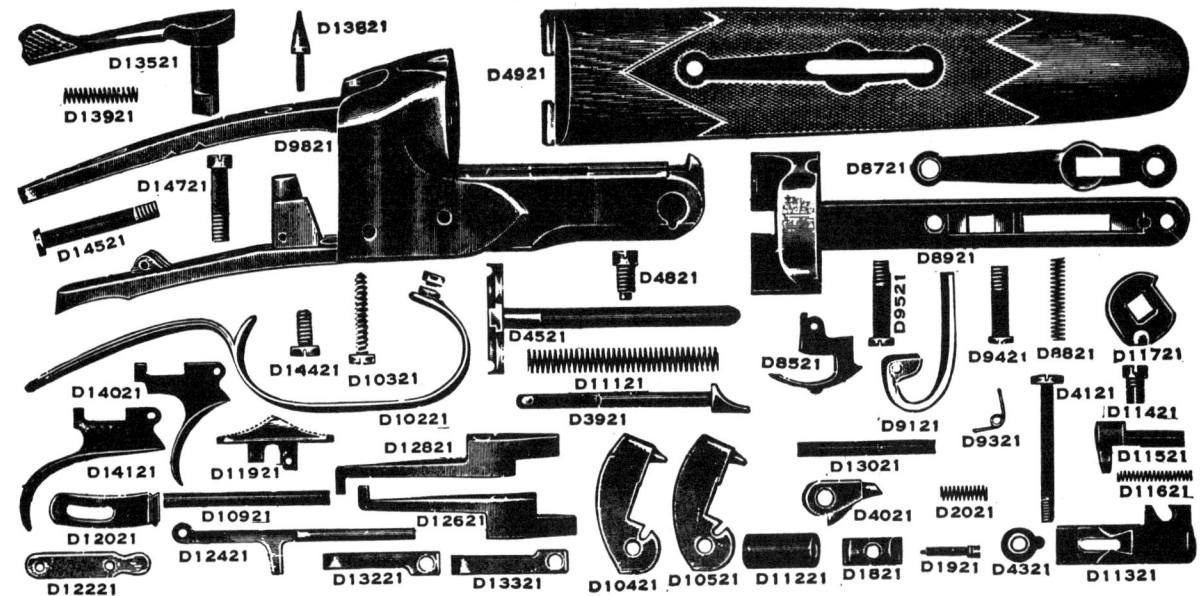

DOUBLE TRIGGER STANDARD COMPONENT GUN PARTS

It is absolutely necessary that the numbers shown at the left of each gun part be specified when ordering. Selective double trigger and single trigger component parts on following pages.

		List Each
	Set of Barrels without Fore-end.	
D1621*	Set of Barrels Standard	$40.00
D1721*	Set of Barrels Ventilated Rib, 26", 30" and 32".	70.00
	Set of Barrels comprises: 2 Barrels, Barrel Stop, Barrel Stop Screw, Barrel Stop Spring, Extractor, Extractor Stop Screw, Front Sight, and Locking Bolt Stop Screw.	
D1821	Barrel Stop, 12-16-20 Ga.	.25
D1921	Barrel Stop Screw, 12-16-20 Ga. (Same as Locking Bolt Lever Screw)	.25
D2021	Barrel Stop Spring, 12-16-20 Ga.	.25
D2121*	Butt Stock Complete, 12 Ga., Standard Grade Pistol Grip	10.00
D2221*	Butt Stock Complete, 16 Ga., Standard Grade Pistol Grip	10.00
D2321*	Butt Stock Complete, 20 Ga., Standard Grade Pistol Grip	10.00
D2321A*	Butt Stock Complete, 12 Ga., Standard Grade Straight Grip	10.00
D2321B*	Butt Stock Complete, 16 Ga., Standard Grade Straight Grip	10.00
D2321C*	Butt Stock Complete, 20 Ga., Standard Grade Straight Grip	10.00
	Butt Stock Complete Comprises Stock, Butt Plate and (2) Butt Plate Screw.	
D2921A*	Butt Stock Complete, made in 12, 16 and 20 Ga., Standard Grade Pistol Grip and Straight Grip, made to customer's dimensions	25.00
D2921B*	Butt Stock, 12 Ga., Straight Grip, Skeet Gun, Standard Grade	$25.00
D2921C*	Butt Stock, 16 Ga., Straight Grip, Skeet Gun, Standard Grade	25.00
D2921D*	Butt Stock, 20 Ga., Straight Grip, Skeet Gun, Standard rade	25.00
D2921E*	Butt Stock Complete, 12 Ga., Pistol Grip, Skeet Gun, Standard Grade	25.00
D2921F*	Butt Stock Complete, 16 Ga., Pistol Grip, Skeet Gun, Standard Grade	25.00
D2921G*	Butt Stock Complete, 20 Ga., Pistol Grip, Skeet Gun, Standard Grade	25.00
D2921H*	Butt Stock, 12 Ga., Straight Grip, Skeet Gun, Trap Grade	40.00
D2921J*	Butt Stock, 16 Ga., Straight Grip, Skeet Gun, Trap Grade	40.00
D2921K*	Butt Stock, 20 Ga., Straight Grip, Skeet Gun, Trap Grade	40.00
D2921L*	Butt Stock Complete, 12 Ga., Pistol Grip, Skeet Gun, Trap Grade	40.00
D2921M*	Butt Stock Complete, 16 Ga., Pistol Grip, Skeet Gun, Trap Grade	40.00
D2921N*	Butt Stock Complete, 20 Ga., Pistol Grip, Skeet Gun, Trap Grade	40.00
	Butt Stock Skeet has no butt plate (wood checked)	
	Butt Stock Skeet Pistol Grip Complete comprises: Pistol Grip Cap and Screw.	

		List Each
D3021*	Butt Stock Complete, 12 Ga., Trap Grade Straight Grip	40.00
D3121*	Butt Stock Complete, 12 Ga., Trap Grade Pistol Grip	40.00
D3221*	Butt Stock Complete, 16 Ga., Trap Grade Straight Grip	40.00
D3321*	Butt Stock Complete, 16 Ga., Trap Grade Pistol Grip	40.00
D3421*	Butt Stock Complete, 20 Ga., Trap Grade Straight Grip	40.00
D3521*	Butt Stock Complete, 20 Ga., Trap Grade Pistol Grip	40.00
	Butt Stock Complete comprises: Stock, Butt Plate and (2) Butt Plate Screws.	
D3621	Butt Plate, 12-16 Ga.	$0.60
D3721	Butt Plate, 20 Ga.	.60
D3821	Butt Plate Screws, 12-16-20 Ga. (2) each	.25
D3921	Cocking Rod, 12-16-20 Ga. (2) each	.75
D4021	Cocking Lever, 12-16-20 Ga. (2) each	.75
D4121	Cocking Lever Screw and Nut, 12 Ga.	.30
D4221	Cocking Lever Screw and Nut, 16-20 Ga.	.30
D4321	Cocking Lever Screw Nut, 12 Ga.	.25
D4421	Cocking Lever Screw Nut, 16-20 Ga.	.25
D4521	Extractor, 12 Ga.	1.00
D4621	Extractor, 16 Ga.	1.00
D4721	Extractor, 20 Ga.	1.00
D4821	Extractor Top Screw, 12-16-20 Ga.	.25
D4921*	Fore-end, 12 Ga., Standard Grade	4.00
D5021*	Fore-end, 16 Ga., Standard Grade	4.00
D5121*	Fore-end, 20 Ga., Standard Grade	4.00
D5521*	Fore-end, 12 Ga., Trap Grade	9.00
D5621*	Fore-end, 16 Ga., Trap Grade	9.00
D5721*	Fore-end, 20 Ga., Trap Grade	9.00
D5821*	Fore-end, 12 Ga., Beavertail Standard Grade	12.00
D5921*	Fore-end, 16 Ga., Beavertail Standard Grade	12.00
D6021*	Fore-end, 20 Ga., Beavertail Standard Grade	12.00
D6421*	Fore-end, 12 Ga., Beavertail Trap Grade	23.00
D6521*	Fore-end, 16 Ga., Beavertail Trap Guide	23.00
D6621*	Fore-end, 20 Ga., Beavertail Trap Guide	23.00
D6721*	Fore-end, Complete, 12 Ga., Standard Grade	9.10
D6821*	Fore-end, Complete, 16 Ga., Standard Grade	9.10
D6921*	Fore-end, Complete, 20 Ga., Standard Grade	9.10
D7321*	Fore-end, Complete, 12 Ga., Trap Grade	14.10
D7421*	Fore-end, Complete, 16 Ga., Trap Grade	14.10
D7521*	Fore-end, Complete, 20 Ga., Trap Grade	14.10
D7621*	Fore-end, Complete, 12 Ga., Beavertail Standard Grade	17.10
D7721*	Fore-end, Complete, 16 Ga., Beavertail Standard Grade	17.10
D7821*	Fore-end, Complete, 20 Ga., Beavertail Standard Grade	17.10

(Continued on page 494)

INSTRUCTIONS: In ordering parts always give name and number listed in catalog, also make, model, caliber and serial number of gun. (Parts marked with * cannot be supplied on Mail Order. It will be necessary to return arm to us for fitting.)
When ordering parts marked thus (*) it is necessary to send gun to factory.

PAYMENTS: Parts will be sent only on advance payment. Parts cannot be returned for credit. A service charge of 25c must be added to every order under $1.00 to cover cost of handling. Do not forget to include postage.

WINCHESTER SHOTGUN PARTS
MODEL 21 DOUBLE BARREL HAMMERLESS SHOTGUN
DOUBLE TRIGGER SELECTIVE EJECTION COMPONENTS
(All Other Parts Same as Standard Gun)

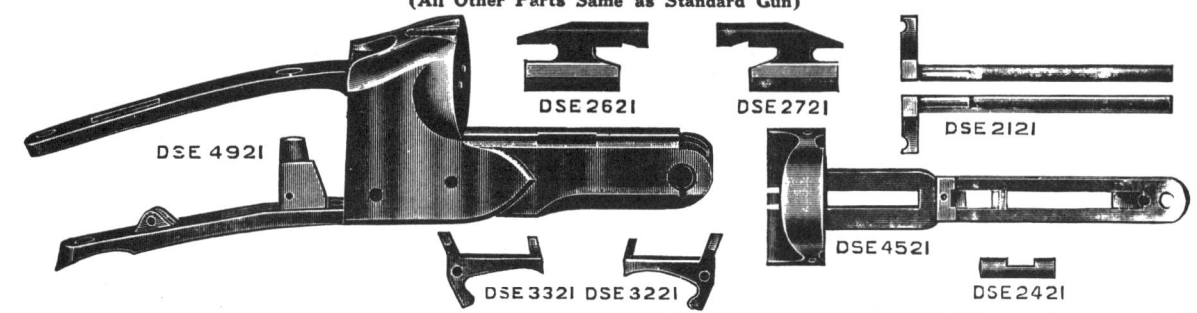

In ordering Barrels, give Length, Choke, Bore, Gauge and also state whether Selective Ejection or Selective Ejection Ventilated Rib.

Barrels can be furnished in our three (3) standard chokes, full choke, modified choke and cylinder bore, and two (2) new chokes, improved modified choke and improved cylinder bore. We can also furnish either of our Skeet chokes, No. 1 (killing pattern at 20 yards) or No. 2 (killing pattern at 30 yards). No cancellation can be accepted on orders for improved modified, improved cylinder bore or Skeet chokes as barrels with these chokes are made on special order only.

SET OF BARRELS WITHOUT FORE-END — Each
- DS1621A* Set of Barrels, Selective Ejection............. $50.00
- DS1721A* Set of Barrels, Selection Ejection Vent. Rib..... 80.00

* All butt stocks on single trigger guns it will be necessary to send gun to factory.

- DS1821* Cocking Lever, Left Hand, 12-16-20 Ga., Selective Ejection 1.00
- DS1921* Cocking Lever, Right Hand, 12-16-20 Ga., Selective Ejection 1.00
- DS2021* Cocking Rod, Left Hand, 12-16-20 Ga., Selective Ejection .... .75
- DS2121* Cocking Rod, Right Hand, 12-16-20 Ga., Selective Ejection .... .75
- DS2221 Extractor, Right and Left Hand, 12 Ga., Selective Ejection 2.50
- DS2321 Extractor, Right and Left Hand, 16 Ga., Selective Ejection 2.50
- DS2421 Extractor, Right and Left Hand, 20 Ga., Selective Ejection 2.50
- DS2521 Extractor Plunger, 12-16-20 Ga., Selective Ejection .25
- DS2621 Extractor Plunger Stop Pin, 12-16-20 Ga., Selective Ejection .... .25
- DS2721* Fore-end, 12 Ga., Selective Ejection................ 4.00
- DS2821* Fore-end, 16 Ga., Selective Ejection................ 4.00
- DS2921* Fore-end, 20 Ga., Selective Ejection................ 4.00
- DS3021* Fore-end, 12 Ga., Complete, Selective Ejection.. 13.20
- DS3121* Fore-end, 16 Ga., Complete, Selective Ejection... $13.20
- DS3221* Fore-end, 20 Ga., Complete, Selective Ejection.. 13.20
- DS3621* Fore-end, 12 Ga., Trap Grade, Selective Ejection 9.00
- DS3721* Fore-end, 16 Ga., Trap Grade, Selective Ejection. 9.00
- DS3821* Fore-end, 20 Ga., Trap Grade, Selective Ejection. 9.00
- DS3621A* Fore-end, Complete, 12 Ga., Trap Grade, Selective Ejection 18.20
- DS3721A* Fore-end, Complete, 16 Ga., Trap Grade, Selective Ejection 18.20
- DS3821A* Fore-end, Complete, 20 Ga., Trap Grade, Selective Ejection 18.20
- DS3921* Fore-end, 12 Ga., Beavertail, Selective Ejection... 12.00
- DS4021* Fore-end, 16 Ga., Beavertail, Selective Ejection... 12.00
- DS4121* Fore-end, 20 Ga., Beavertail, Selective Ejection.. 12.00
- DS3921A* Fore-end, Complete, 12 Ga., Beavertail, Selective Ejection 21.20
- DS4021A* Fore-end, Complete, 16 Ga., Beavertail, Selective Ejection 21.20
- DS4121A* Fore-end, Complete, 20 Ga., Beavertail, Selective Ejection 21.20
- DS4521* Fore-end, 12 Ga., Beavertail, Trap Grade, Selective Ejection 23.00
- DS4621* Fore-end, 16 Ga., Beavertail, Trap Grade, Selective Ejection 23.00
- DS4721* Fore-end, 20 Ga., Beavertail, Trap Grade, Selective Ejection 23.00
- DS4521A* Fore-end, Complete, 12 Ga., Beavertail, Trap Grade, Selective Ejection.................... 32.20
- DS4621A* Fore-end, Complete, 16 Ga., Beavertail, Trap Grade, Selective Ejection.................... 32.20
- DS4721A* Fore-end, Complete, 20 Ga., Beavertail, Trap Grade, Selective Ejection.................... 32.20

Fore-end complete comprises: Fore-end, catch, catch pin, catch plate, catch spring, shoe, retainer, retainer pin, retainer spring, screw front, screw rear, ejection hammer, right hand, ejection hammer, left hand, ejection hammer roll, roll pin, ejection hammer spring guide rod (2), ejection hammer spring (2), ejection sear, right and left hand, ejection sear spring (2) and ejection sear pin.

- DS4821 Fore-end Screw Rear 12-16-20 Ga., Selective Ejection $0.25
- DS4921* Fore-end Shoe 12 Ga., Selective Ejection....... 3.75
- DS5021* Fore-end Shoe 12 Ga., Selective Ejection, Beavertail 4.00
- DS5121* Fore-end Shoe 16-20 Ga., Selective Ejection... 4.00
- DS5221* Fore-end Shoe 16-20 Ga., Selective Ejection, Beavertail 4.00
- DS5321* Frame and Trigger Plate 12 Ga., Selective Ejection 18.00
- DS5421* Frame and Trigger Plate 12 Ga., Selective Ejection, Vent Rib 19.00
- DS5521* Frame and Trigger Plate 16 Ga., Selective Ejection 18.00
- DS5521A* Frame and Trigger Plate 16 Ga., Selective Ejection, Vent Rib 19.00
- DS5621* Frame and Trigger Plate 20 Ga., Selective Ejection 18.00
- DS5621A* Frame and Trigger Plate 20 Ga., Selective Ejection, Vent Rib 19.00
- DS5721* Ejection Hammer Left Hand 12-16-20 Ga., Selective Ejection .... .50
- DS5821* Ejection Hammer Right Hand 12-16-20 Ga., Selective Ejection .... .50
- DS6021 Ejection Hammer Roll Pin 12-16-20 Ga., Selective Ejection .... .25
- DS6021 Ejection Hammer Roll Pin 12-16-20 Ga., Selective Ejection .... .25
- DS6121 Ejection Hammer Spring 12-16-20 Ga., (2) each Selective Ejection .... .25
- DS6221 Ejection Hammer Spring Guide Rod (2) each, 12-16-20 Ga., Selective Ejection........... .25
- DS6321* Ejection Sear Left Hand 12-16-20 Ga., Selective Ejection .... .60
- DS6421* Ejection Sear Right Hand 12-16-20 Ga., Selective Ejection .... .60
- DS6521 Ejection Sear Pin 12 Ga., Selective Ejection..... .25
- DS6621 Ejection Sear Pin 16-20 Ga., Selective Ejection.. .25
- DS6721 Ejection Sear Spring (2) each, Selective Ejection. .25
- DS6821* Guard Bow, Selective Ejection P.G............. 1.25
- DS6921* Guard Bow, Straight Grip, Selective Ejection.... 1.50

*M/21 SINGLE TRIGGER COMPONENTS
All Other Parts Are the Same as Standard

- S121* Hammer Left Hand 12 Ga., Single Trigger....... 1.00
- S121A* Guard Bow, Pistol Grip, 12-16-20 Ga.......... 1.25
- S121B* Guard Bow, Straight Grip, 12-16-20 Ga....... 1.50
- S221* Hammer Right Hand 12 Ga., Single Trigger..... 1.00
- S321* Hammer Right and Left Hand 16 Ga., Single Trigger each 1.00
- S421* Hammer Left Hand 20 Ga., Single Trigger...... $1.00
- S521* Hammer Right Hand 20 Ga., Single Trigger..... 1.00
- S621* Safety Lever Auto Safety 12-16-20 Ga., Single Trigger .... .25
- S721* Safety Lever Non Auto Safety 12-16-20 Ga., Single Trigger .... .25
- S821* Safety Lever Pin 12-16-20 Ga., Single Trigger.. .25
- S921* Safety Lever Operating Rod 12-16-20 Ga., Single Trigger .... .60
- S1021 Safety Lever Operating Rod Returning Spring Non Auto Safety, Single Trigger................. .25
- S1121 Safety Lever Operating Rod Returning Spring Pin, Single Trigger .... .25
- S1221* Sear Left Hand 12 Ga., Single Trigger......... .75
- S1321* Sear Left Hand 16-20 Ga., Single Trigger...... .75
- S1421* Sear Right Hand 12 Ga., Single Trigger....... .75
- S1521* Sear Right Hand 16-20 Ga., Single Trigger..... .75
- S1621* Shift Lever 12-16-20 Ga., Single Trigger...... .60
- S1721* Shift Lever Button 12-16-20 Ga., Single Trigger. .25
- S1821* Shift Lever Spring 12-16-20 Ga., Single Trigger. .25
- S1921* Timing Weight 12-16-20 Ga., Single Trigger.... .30
- S2021* Timing Weight Pin 12-16-20 Ga., Single Trigger. .25
- S2121* Timing Weight Plunger 12-16-20 Ga., Single Trigger .... .25
- S2221* Timing Weight Plunger Spring, Single Trigger.... .25
- S2321* Trigger 12-16-20 Ga., Single Trigger........... 1.50
- S2421* Trigger Spring, Single Trigger................ .25
- S2521* Trigger Spring Plunger, Single Trigger......... .25
- S2621* Trigger Blade 12-16-20 Ga., Single Trigger..... .25
- S2621A* Trigger Blade Pin (2) each, Single Trigger..... .25

(Continued on following page)

INSTRUCTIONS: In ordering parts always give name and number listed in catalog, also make, model, caliber and serial number of gun. (Parts marked with * cannot be supplied on Mail Order. It will be necessary to return arm to us for fitting.)

PAYMENTS: Parts will be sent only on advance payment. Parts cannot be returned for credit. A service charge of 25c must be added to every order under $1.00 to cover cost of handling. Do not forget to include postage.

CAREFUL ATTENTION AND SAFE DELIVERY OF YOUR ORDER

WINCHESTER SHOTGUN PARTS

MODEL 21 DOUBLE BARREL HAMMERLESS SHOTGUN

DOUBLE TRIGGER SELECTIVE EJECTION COMPONENTS (All Other Parts Same as Standard Gun)
(Continued from Preceding Page)

		List
S2721*	Trigger Plate 12-16-20 Ga., Single Trigger	$3.75
S2821	Upper Tang Screw Bushing 12-16-20 Ga., Single Trigger	.25
S2921*	Butt Stock 12 Ga., Complete, Single Trigger	10.00
S3021*	Butt Stock 16 Ga., Complete, Single Trigger	10.00
S3121*	Butt Stock 20 Ga., Complete, Single Trigger	10.00
	Note—Above Butt Stock also used on Single Trigger Selective Ejection.	
S3321*	Frame 12 Ga., Reg., Single Trigger	13.20
S3221*	Frame 16 Ga., Reg., Single Trigger	13.20
S3421*	Frame 20 Ga., Reg., Single Trigger	13.20
S3521*	Frame 12 Ga., Reg., Ventilated Rib, Single Trigger	14.20
S3521A*	Frame 16 Ga., Reg. Vent Rib, Single Trigger	14.20
S3521B*	Frame 20 Ga., Reg. Vent Rib, Single Trigger	$14.20
SS3621*	Frame 12 Ga., Selective Ejection, Single Trigger	13.20
SS3721*	Frame 16 Ga., Selective Ejection, Single Trigger	13.20
SS3821*	Frame 20 Ga., Selective Ejection, Single Trigger	13.20
SS3921*	Frame 12 Ga., Selective Ejection, Vent Rib, Single Trigger	14.20
SS3921A*	Frame 16 Ga., Selective Ejection, Vent Rib, Single Trigger	14.20
SS3921B*	Frame 20 Ga., Selective Ejection, Vent Rib, Single Trigger	14.20
SS4021*	Fore-end 12 Ga., Selective Ejection, Single Trigger	3.00
SS4121*	Fore-end 16 Ga., Selective Ejection, Single Trigger	3.00
SS4221*	Fore-end 20 Ga., Selective Ejection, Single Trigger	3.00

MODEL 21 DOUBLE BARREL HAMMERLESS SHOTGUN
(Continued from page 492)

		List
D8221*	Fore-end, Complete, 12 Ga., Beavertail Trap Grade	$28.10
D8321*	Fore-end, Complete, 16 Ga., Beavertail Trap Grade	28.10
D8421*	Fore-end, Complete, 20 Ga., Beavertail Trap Grade	28.10
	Fore-end Complete comprises: Fore-end, catch, catch pin, catch plate, catch spring, shoe, retainer, retainer pin, retainer spring, screw front and screw rear.	
NOTE—All of the above fore-ends are also used on Standard Single Trigger Guns.		
D8521	Fore-end Catch, 12-16-20 Ga.	.75
D8621	Fore-end Catch Pin, 12-16-20 Ga.	.25
D8721	Fore-end Catch Plate, 12-16-20 Ga.	.50
D8821	Fore-end Catch Spring, 12-16-20 Ga.	.25
D8921	Fore-end Shoe, 12 Ga.	2.75
D9021	Fore-end Shoe, 16 and 20 Ga.	2.75
D9121	Fore-end Retainer, 12-16-20 Ga.	.50
D9221	Fore-end Retainer Pin, 12-16-20 Ga.	.25
D9321	Fore-end Retainer Spring, 12-16-20 Ga.	.25
D9421	Fore-end Screw Fronts, 12-16-20 Ga.	.25
D9521	Fore-end Screw Rear, 12-16-20 Ga.	.25
D9621	Fore-end Recoil Nut, 12-16-20 Ga., for Beavertail Fore-end	.25
D9721	Fore-end Recoil Screw, 12-16-20 Ga., for Beavertail Fore-end	.25
D9821*	Frame and Trigger Plate, 12 Ga.	18.00
D9921*	Frame and Trigger Plate, 12 Ga., for Ventilated Rib	19.00
D10021*	Frame and Trigger Plate, 16 Ga.	18.00
D10021A*	Frame and Trigger Plate, 16 Ga., for Vent Rib	19.00
D10021B*	Frame and Trigger Plate, 20 Ga., for Vent Rib	19.00
D10121*	Frame and Trigger Plate, 20 Ga.	18.00
D10121A*	Frame, 12 Ga.	14.25
D10121B*	Frame, 16 Ga.	14.25
D10121C*	Frame, 20 Ga.	14.25
D10221*	Guard Bow, 12-16-20 Ga. (Pistol Grip)	1.25
D10321	Guard Bow Screw, 12-16-20 Ga.	.25
D10321A*	Guard Bow, Straight Grip	1.50
D10321B	Guard Bow Screws (2) each	.25
D10421	Hammer Left Hand, 12 Ga.	1.00
D10521	Hammer Right Hand, 12 Ga.	1.00
D10621	Hammer Right and Left Hand, 16 Ga., (2) each	1.00
D10721	Hammer Right Hand, 20 Ga.	1.00
D10821	Hammer Left Hand, 20 Ga.	1.00
D10921	Hammer Pin, 12 Ga.	.25
D11021	Hammer Pin, 16 and 20 Ga.	.25
D11121	Hammer Spring, 12-16-20 Ga., (2) each	.25
D11221	Joint Pin, 12-16-20 Ga.	.25
D11321	Locking Bolt, 12-16-20 Ga.	.60
D11421	Locking Bolt Stop Screw, 12-16-20 Ga.	$0.25
D11521	Locking Bolt Catch, 12-16-20 Ga.	.50
D11621	Locking Bolt Catch Spring, 12-16-20 Ga.	.25
D11721	Locking Bolt Lever, 12-16-20 Ga.	.75
D11821	Locking Bolt Lever Screw, 12-16-20 Ga.	.25
D11921	Safety Slide, 12-16-20 Ga.	.50
D12021	Safety Slide Spring, 12-16-20 Ga.	.25
D12121	Safety Slide Spring Stop Pin, 12-16-20 Ga.	.25
D12221	Safety Lever, 12-16-20 Ga.	.25
D12321	Safety Lever, Pivot Pin, 12-16-20 Ga.	.25
D12421	Safety Lever Operating Rod, 12-16-20 Ga.	.60
D12521	Safety Lever Operating Rod Pin, 12-16-20 Ga.	.25
D12621	Sear Right Hand, 12 Ga.	.75
D12721	Sear Right Hand, 16-20 Ga.	.75
D12821	Sear Left Hand, 12 Ga.	.75
D12921	Sear Left Hand, 16-20 Ga.	.75
D13021	Sear Pin, 12 Ga.	.25
D13121	Sear Pin, 16-20 Ga.	.25
D13221	Sear Spring Right Hand, 12-16-20 Ga.	.25
D13321	Sear Spring Left Hand, 12-16-20 Ga.	.25
D13421	Sear Spring Screw, 12-16-20 Ga. (2) each	.25
D13521	Top Lever, 12 Ga.	1.25
D13621	Top Lever, 12 Ga., Vent. Rib	1.25
D13721	Top Lever, 16-20 Ga.	1.25
D13721A	Top Lever, 16 and 20 Ga., Vent. Rib	1.25
D13821	Top Lever Plunger, 12-16-20 Ga.	.25
D13921	Top Lever Spring, 12-16-20 Ga.	.25
D14021	Trigger Right Hand, 12-16-20 Ga.	.75
D14121	Trigger Left Hand, 12-16-20 Ga.	.75
D14221	Trigger Pin, 12-16-20 Ga.	.25
D14321*	Trigger Plate	3.75
D14421	Trigger Plate Screw, 12-16-20 Ga.	.25
D14521	Trigger Plate Tang Screw, 12-16-20 Ga.	.25
D14521A	Trigger Plate Tang Screw for large grip	.25
D14621	Trigger Spring, 12-16-20 Ga. (2) each	.25
D14721	Upper Tang Screw, 12-16-20 Ga.	.25

SIGHT EQUIPMENT

D14821	Front Sight for Material Rib 81A .123 Bead	.25
D14921	Middle Sight for Matted Rib 94B .067 Bead	.25
D15021	Front Sight for Ventilated Rib 81B .140 Bead	.25
D15121	Middle Sight for Ventilated Rib 72A .10 Bead	.25

COLORED SIGHTS

D15221	Bradley 1/8" or 5/32" Ivory or Red Bead Front Sight	1.00
D15321	Winchester White Metal Middle Sight 94B	.25

* When ordering guns marked (*) gun must be sent us.

PARTS FOR B. S. A. AIR RIFLE MODEL NO. 2

Piston Washer with Screw, Complete Set	$1.50
Main Spring, Cal. 177 (One Piece)	2.25
Main Spring, Cal. 22 (Two Pieces)	2.75
Front Sight	1.00
Rear Sight, Complete	2.25
Sear	1.75

When ordering Main Springs state whether for No. 1 Cal. 177, No. 4 Club Model 177 or No. 2 Cal. 22.

When in need of any other parts send in broken or worn samples for duplication.

INSTRUCTIONS: In ordering parts always give name and number listed in catalog, also make, model, caliber and serial number of gun. (Parts marked with * cannot be supplied on Mail Order. It will be necessary to return arm to us for fitting.)

PAYMENTS: Parts will be sent only on advance payment. Parts cannot be returned for credit. A service charge of 25c must be added to every order under $1.00 to cover cost of handling. Do not forget to include postage.

CAREFUL ATTENTION AND SAFE DELIVERY OF YOUR ORDER

WINCHESTER REPEATING SHOTGUN PARTS
MODEL 42—.410 BORE REPEATING SHOTGUN

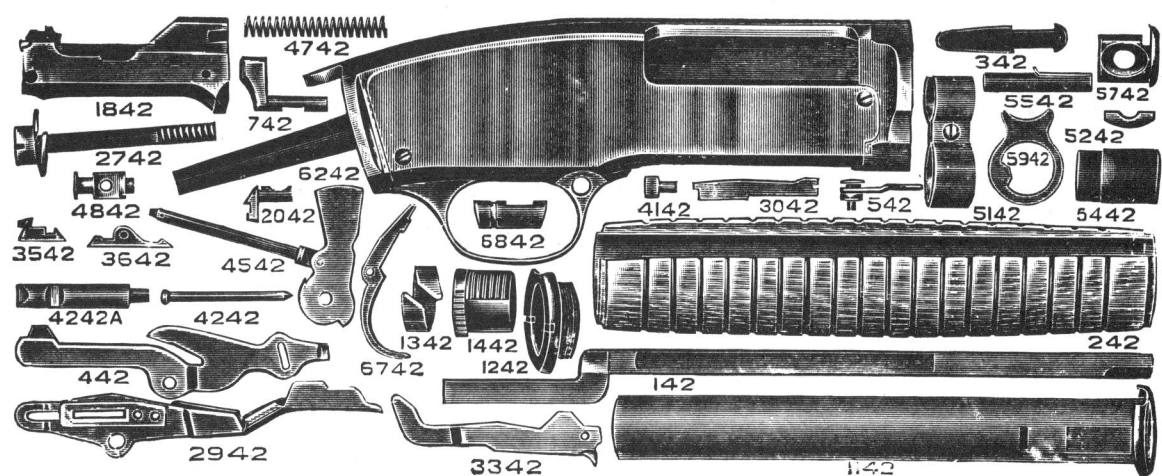

It is absolutely necessary that the numbers shown at the left of each gun part be specified when ordering.

142	Action slide bar	$1.00
242	Action slide handle	.75
242A	Extension action slide handle	5.75
242B	Action Slide Handle Trap, fancy wood checked	3.50
242C	Extension Action Slide Handle, fancy wood checked	11.75
342	Action slide handle retaining spring	.25
442	Action slide lock	.50
542	Action slide lock link	.25
642	Action slide lock link pin	.25
742	Action slide lock plunger	.40
842	Action slide lock plunger retaining screw	.25
942	Action slide lock screw	.25
1042	Action slide lock spring	.25
1142	Action slide sleeve	1.25
1242	Action slide sleeve cap	.50
1342	Action slide spring	.25
1442	Adjusting sleeve	.75
1542	Adjusting sleeve lock	.25
1642	Adjusting sleeve lock screw	.25
1742	*Barrel, 26″ Full Choke	10.00
1742A	*Barrel, 26″ Mod. Choke	10.00
1742B	*Barrel, 26″ Cyl. Bore	10.00
1742C	*Barrel, 28″ Full Choke	10.00
1742D	*Barrel, 28″ Mod. Choke	10.00
1742E	*Barrel, 28″ Cyl. Bore	10.00
1742F	*Barrel, 26″ Skeet Choke	10.00
1742G	*Barrel, 28″ Skeet Choke	10.00
1742K	*Barrel, 26″ Full Choke Matted Rib	17.00
1742L	*Barrel, 26″ Mod. Matted Rib	17.00
1742M	*Barrel, 26″ Cyl. Matted Rib	17.00
1742N	*Barrel, 26″ Skeet Matted Rib	17.00
1742O	*Barrel, 28″ Full Choke Matted Rib	17.00
1742P	*Barrel, 28″ Mod. Matted Rib	17.00
1742R	*Barrel, 28″ Cyl. Matted Rib	17.00
1742S	*Barrel, 28″ Skeet Matted Rib	17.00
1742H	*Interchangeable barrel complete with standard action slide handle	12.70
1742J	*Interchangeable barrel complete with extension action slide handle (checked)	17.70

Interchangeable barrel complete comprises: Barrel with extension, magazine tube complete, action slide bar, action slide handle, action slide sleeve, action slide sleeve cap, magazine band key and action slide handle retaining spring.

1842	Breech bolt	3.75
1942	Breech bolt complete	6.35

Breech bolt complete comprises: Breech bolt, breech bolt retainer, breech bolt retainer spring, cartridge guide pin, extractor R.H., extractor L.H., extractor plunger R.H., extractor spring R.H., extractor pin L.H., extractor spring L.H., firing pin, firing pin retracting spring, firing pin stop pin and firing pin striker.

2042	Breech bolt retainer	.30
2142	Breech bolt retainer spring	.25
2242	Butt plate (rubber)	.50
2342	Butt plate screw (2) each	.25
2442	Butt stock complete (Straight Grip) for Skeet Gun	6.00
2542	Butt stock complete (Pistol Grip) for Standard Gun	4.25

Butt stock complete comprises: Stock, butt plate and butt plate screw (2).

2642	Butt stock bolt	$0.25
2742	Butt stock bolt complete	.25

Butt stock bolt complete comprises: Butt stock bolt and washer.

2842	Butt stock bolt washer	.25
2942	Carrier	.75
3042	Carrier cam lever	.25
3142	Carrier screw	.25
3242	Carrier spring	.25
3342	Cartridge cut off	.50
3442	Cartridge guide pin	.25
3542	Extractor, right hand	.60
3642	Extractor, left hand	.50
3742	Extractor pin, left hand	.25
3842	Extractor plunger, right hand	.25
3942	Extractor spring, right hand	.25
4042	Extractor spring, left hand	.25
4142	Ejector	.25
4242	Firing pin	.25
4242A	Firing pin striker	.30
4342	Firing pin retracting spring	.25
4442	Firing pin stop pin	.25
4542	Hammer with hammer spring guide rod and pin	1.40
4642	Hammer pin	.25
4742	Hammer spring	.25
4842	Hammer spring abutment	.25
4942	Hammer spring guide rod	.25
5042	Hammer spring guide rod pin	.25
5142	Magazine band	1.00
5242	Magazine band key	.25
5342	Magazine band screw	.25
5442	Magazine follower	.25
5542	Magazine locking pin and spring	.40
5642	Magazine locking pin spring	.25
5742	Magazine plug	.50
5842	Magazine plug screw	.25
5942	Magazine plug stop	.30
6042	Magazine spring	.25
6142	Magazine tube (capacity 5—3″ shells; 6—2½″)	3.00
6142A	Magazine tube complete	5.80

Magazine tube complete comprises: Tube, spring, follower, plug, plug screw, plug stop, band, band screw, magazine locking pin and spring, and action slide spring.

6242	*Receiver (matted top)	15.00

Receiver comprises: Receiver, receiver shank, side plate and side plate screws (2).

6342	*Receiver complete	27.00
6442	*Receiver extension	1.50
6542	Receiver shank	.25
6642	*Side plate	1.25
6942	Side plate screws (2) each	.25
6742	Trigger	.75
6842	Trigger lock	.40
7042	Trigger lock complete	.60

Trigger lock complete comprises: Trigger lock, trigger lock plunger and spring.

7142	Trigger lock plunger	.25
7242	Trigger lock plunger spring	.25
7342	Trigger screw	.25
7442	Trigger spring	.25
7542	Front sight 81A	.25

In replacing parts marked thus (*) gun must be sent us.

SEE PAGE 8 "HOW TO ORDER"

WINCHESTER SHOTGUN PARTS
MODEL 37 SINGLE BARREL SINGLE SHOT SHOTGUN

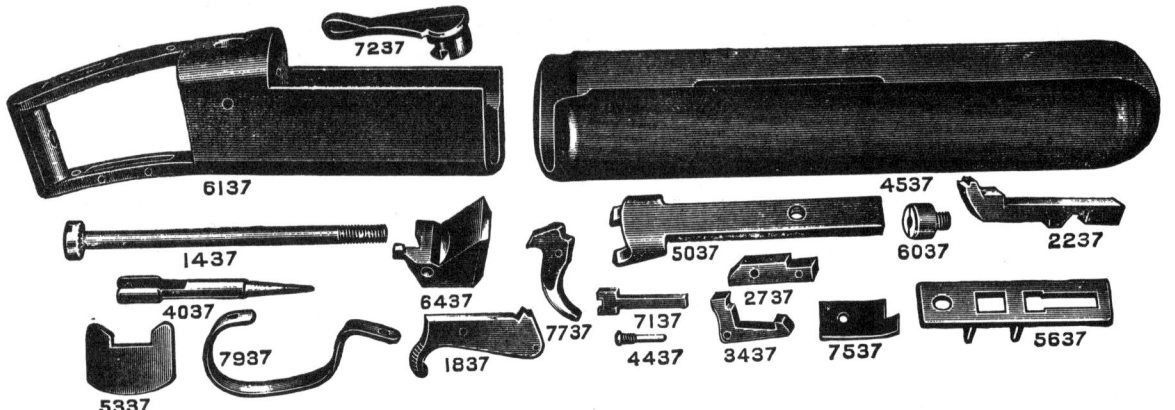

It is absolutely necessary that the numbers shown at the left of each gun part be specified when ordering.

No.	Description	Price
137	*Barrel, 12 Ga., 32" Full Choke, 2¾ Shell	$6.00
237	*Barrel, 12 Ga., 30" Full Choke, 2¾ Shell	6.00
337	*Barrel, 12 Ga., 28" Full Choke, 2¾ Shell	6.00
337A	*Barrel, 16 Ga., 32" Full Choke, 2¾ Shell	6.00
437	*Barrel, 16 Ga., 30" Full Choke, 2¾ Shell	6.00
537	*Barrel, 16 Ga., 28" Full Choke, 2¾ Shell	6.00
537A	*Barrel, 20 Ga., 32" Full Choke, 2¾ Shell	6.00
637	*Barrel, 20 Ga., 30" Full Choke, 2¾ Shell	6.00
737	*Barrel, 20 Ga., 28" Full Choke, 2¾ Shell	6.00
837	*Barrel, 28 Ga., 30" Full Choke, 2⅞ Shell	6.00
937	*Barrel, 28 Ga., 28" Full Choke, 2⅞ Shell	6.00
1037	*Barrel, .410 Bore, 26" Full Choke, 3" Shell	6.00
1037A	*Barrel, .410 Bore, 28" Full Choke, 3" Shell	6.00

Above Barrels Are Plain. Order Will Not Be Accepted for Solid Raised Matted Rib Barrel.

No.	Description	Price
1137	Butt Stock Complete, 12 and 16 Ga.	2.00
1237	Butt Stock Complete, 20 and 28 Ga.	2.00
1337	Butt Stock Complete, .410 Bore	2.00

Butt Stock Complete Comprises Stock, Butt Plate and Butt Plate Screw (2)

No.	Description	Price
1437	Butt Stock Bolt and Washer	.25
1537	Butt Stock Bolt Washer	.25
1637	Butt Plate, Hard Rubber	.30
1737	Butt Plate Screw (2) each	.25
1837	Cocking Lever, 12 and 16 Ga.	.40
1937	Cocking Lever, 20 and 28 Ga. and .410 Bore	.40
2037	Cocking Lever Pin, 12 and 16 Ga.	.25
2137	Cocking Lever Pin, 20 and 28 Ga. and .410 Bore	.25
2237	Extractor, 12 Ga.	.35
2337	Extractor, 16 Ga.	.35
2437	Extractor, 20 Ga.	.35
2537	Extractor, 28 Ga.	.35
2637	Extractor, .410 Bore	.35
2737	Extractor Guide	.25
2837	Extractor Guide Pin Front	.25
3037	Extractor Guide Pin Rear	.25
3437	Extractor Sear	.30
3537	Extractor Sear Pin, 12 and 16 Ga.	.25
3637	Extractor Sear Pin, 20 and 28 Ga.	.25
3737	Extractor Sear Pin, .410 Bore	.25
3837	Extractor Spring, 12-16-20-28 Gauge and .410 Bore	.25
4037	Firing Pin	.25
4137	Firing Pin Connecting Pin	.25
4237	Firing Pin Spring	.25
4237A	Firing Pin Spring Washer	.25
4337	Firing Pin Spring Pin	.25
4437	Firing Pin Spring Stop Screw	.25
4537	Forearm with Escutcheon, 12 and 16 Ga.	$1.25
4637	Forearm with Escutcheon, 20 and 28 Ga.	1.25
4727	Forearm with Escutcheon, .410 Bore	1.25
4837	Forearm Escutcheon	.25
4937	Forearm Escutcheon Screw	.25
5037	Forearm Shoe, 12 and 16 Ga.	.40
5137	Forearm Shoe, 20 and 28 Ga.	.40
5237	Forearm Shoe, .410 Bore	.40
5337	Forearm Shoe Liner, 12 and 16 Ga.	.25
5437	Forearm Shoe Liner, 20 and 28 Ga.	.25
5537	Forearm Shoe Liner, .410 Bore	.25
5637	Forearm Shoe Retainer	.25
5737	Forearm Shoe Retainer Plunger	.25
5837	Forearm Shoe Retainer Plunger Pin	.25
5937	Forearm Shoe Retainer Plunger Spring	.25
6037	Forearm Shoe Stud	.25
6037A	Forearm Complete Comprises Forearm with Escutcheon and Screw, Forearm Shoe, Liner, Retainer, Retainer Plunger, Plunger Pin, Plunger Spring and Stud	2.40
6137	*Frame, 12 and 16 Ga.	4.00
6237	*Frame, 20 and 28 Ga.	4.00
6337	*Frame, .410 Bore	4.00
6437	Lock, 12 and 16 Ga.	.50
6537	Lock, 20 and 28 Ga.	.50
6637	Lock, .410 Bore	.50
6737	Lock Pin, 12 and 16 Ga.	.25
6837	Lock Pin, 20 and 28 Ga.	.25
6937	Lock Pin, .410 Bore	.25
7037	Lock Spring	.25
7137	Lock Spring Guide Rod	.25
7137A	Lock Spring Guide Rod Stop Pin	.25
7237	Top Lever, 12 and 16 Ga.	.25
7337	Top Lever, 20 and 28 Ga.	.25
7437	Top Lever, .410 Bore	.25
7537	Top Lever Retainer	.25
7537A	Top Lever Retaining Screw 12-16-20 and 28 Gauge are the same	.25
7637	Top Lever Retainer Screw, .410 Bore	.25
7737	Trigger, 12 and 16 Ga.	.25
7837	Trigger, 20 and 28 Ga. and .410 Bore	.25
7937	Trigger Guard	.25
8037	Trigger Guard Screw (2) each	.25
8137	Trigger Pin, 12 and 16 Ga.	.25
8237	Trigger Pin, 20 and 28 Ga. and .410 Bore	.25
8237A	Trigger Spring	.25
8337	Front Sight 81A	.25

In replacing parts marked thus (*) when desired for Take-Down Guns it will be necessary to send Gun to Factory

INSTRUCTIONS: In ordering parts always give name and number listed in catalog, also make, model, caliber and serial number of gun. (Parts marked with * cannot be supplied on Mail Order. It will be necessary to return arm to us for fitting.)

PAYMENT: Parts will be sent only on advance payment. Parts cannot be returned for credit. A service charge of 25c must be added to every order under $1.00 to cover cost of handling. Do not forget to include postage.

SEE PAGE 8 "HOW TO ORDER"

REMINGTON RIFLE PARTS

MODEL 12 RIFLE

Part			Price
W	1	Action Bar	$2.00
W	2	Action Bar Plunger	.25
W	3	Action Bar Plunger Pin	.25
W	4	Action Bar Spring	.25
W	5A	Barrel, Grade A	5.00
W	5B	Barrel, Grade B	6.00
W	5C	Barrel, Grade C	6.00
W	5CS	Barrel, Grade CS	6.00
W	5D	Barrel, Grade D	12.00
W	5E	Barrel, Grade E	16.00
W	5F	Barrel, Grade F	20.00
W	7	Breech Block	2.00
W	7½	Breech Block Complete	3.00
W	8	Butt Plate, Rubber, 12A	.60
W	9	Butt Plate Metal	1.25
W	10	Butt Plate Screw	.25
W	11	Carrier	1.00
W	11S	Carrier 22 Special	1.00
W	12	Carrier Dog	.40
W	13	Carrier Dog Pin	.25
W	14	Carrier Dog Spring	.25
*W	15	Cartridge Stop	.30
W	16	Ejector Pin	.25
W	36	Ejector Spring	.25
W	37	Ejector Spring Plunger	.25
W	17	Extractor	.40
W	18	Extractor Plunger	.25
W	19	Extractor Spring	.25
W	20	Firing Pin	.40
W	21	Firing Pin Pin	.25
W	22	Firing Pin Spring	.25
W	23	Firing Pin Spring Guide	.25
W	24A, B, C, CS	Fore-end, Grades A, B, C and CS	1.00
W	24D	Fore-end, Grade D	5.00
W	24E	Fore-end, Grade E	7.00
W	24F	Fore-end, Grade F	8.00
W	26	Fore-end Escutcheon	.25
W	27	Fore-end Screw	.25
W	28	Front Sight	.25
W	29A, B, C, CS	Guard, Grades A, B, C and CS	4.00
W	29D	Guard, Grade D	12.00
W	29E	Guard, Grade E	16.00
W	29F	Guard, Grade F	20.00
W	30	Hammer	.75
W	31	Hammer Bushing	.25
W	32	Hammer Pin	.25
W	42	Magazine Tube, Inner (specify whether round or octagon barrel)	.50
W	42½	Magazine Tube, Inner, Complete (specify whether round or octagon barrel)	1.50
W	33	Magazine Follower	.25
W	78	Magazine Lever	.25
W	80	Magazine Lever Pin	.25
W	79	Magazine Lever Spring	.25
W	34	Magazine Pin	.25
W	35	Magazine Plug	.30
W	38	Magazine Ring	.40
W	39	Magazine Screw	.25
W	40	Magazine Spring	.25
W	46	Main Spring	.25
W	47	Main Spring Rod	.40
W	44	Magazine Tube, Outer (specify whether round or octagon barrel)	1.00

Part		Price	Part		Price
W	75 Plug Screw	$ .25	W	59 Safety Plunger	$ .25
W	48 Rear Sight Leaf	.40	W	60 Safety Plunger Pin	.25
W	49 Rear Sight Base	.25	W	61 Safety Spring	.25
W	50 Rear Sight Elevating Screw	.25	W	62 Stock, Grades A, B, C and CS	2.00
W	51 Rear Sight Screw	.25	W	62D Stock, Grade D	24.00
W	48-51 Rear Sight, Complete	.80	W	62E Stock, Grade E	30.00
W	52A, B, C, CS Receiver, Grades A, B, C and CS	5.00	W	62F Stock, Grade F	40.00
W	52D Receiver, Grade D	25.00	W	64 Stock Bolt	.25
W	52E Receiver, Grade E	30.00	W	66 Take Down Screw	.25
W	52F Receiver, Grade F	40.00	W	85 Take Down Screw Retainer	.25
W	53 Receiver Bushing, Plain	.25	W	68 Trigger	.75
W	54 Receiver Bushing, Threaded	.25	W	70 Trigger Spring	.25
W	57 Retainer	.25	W	71 Trigger Spring Case	.25
W	58 Safety	.25	W	83-84 Wiping Rod	.25

In replacing parts marked thus (*) it will be necessary to send gun to us.   * Not used on No. 12CS.

MODELS 8 AND 81 HIGH POWER AUTOLOADING RIFLES

Part		Price	Part		Price	Part		Price	Part		Price
2	Action Spring	$ .25	25	Butt Stock, grade 8A	$6.00	59	Main Spring	$ .50	88	Trigger Plate Screw	$ .25
1	Action Spring Follower	.25	209	Butt Plate, Steel Rifle Shape	1.50	60	Main Spring Screw	.25	69	Rear Sight, Complete	2.00
3 & 4	Action Spring Plug with Pin	.25	91	Butt Plate Screw	.25	61	Operating Handle	1.00	39	Front Sight	.50
5	Action Spring Tube	.25	110	Carrier Latch Screw	.25	62	Operating Handle Bushing	.25	298	Clips, specify caliber, each	.25
6	Barrel	12.00	27	Ejector	.25	63	Operating Handle Plunger	.25	107	Spanner Wrench	.25
8	Barrel Jacket, grade A	8.00	29	Ejector Pin	.25	64	Operating Handle Plunger Spring	.25	221	Take-down Screw Washer	.25
9	Barrel Jacket Bushing	.25	28	Ejector Spring	.25	65	Peep Sight Plug Screw	.25	122	Barrel Jacket Plug Screw	.25
10	Barrel Nut (give cal.)	.25	30	Escutcheon	.25	66	Receiver, grade 8A	16.00		**Parts for Model 81 only**	
295	Barrel Nut Washer (give Caliber)	.25	31	Extractor (give cal.)	.80	67	Recoil Spring (give caliber)	.25	825	Butt Stock (Pistol Grip)	$6.00
130	Barrel Lock	.60	32	Firing Pin	.40	68	Recoil Spring Case (give caliber)	.25	309	Butt Plate (Steel, Shotgun Shape)	1.50
12	Barrel Lock Screw	.25	33	Firing-pin Pin	.25	75	Safety	1.20	334	Fore-end	2.00
131	Barrel Lock Spring	.25	34	Fore-arm, grade 8A	2.00	77	Safety Rocker	1.00	330	Fore-end Escutcheon	.25
14	Bolt	2.50	119	Fore-arm Screw and Swivel	.25	78	Safety Rocker Stop Screw	.25	335	Fore-end Screw	.25
26	Bolt Cam Pin	.25	42	Hammer	.80	80	Take-Down Screw, Lever and Pin	.40	348	Link	.80
15	Bolt Lock	.25	43	Hammer Roll	.25	83	Tang Screw (give length)	.25	359	Main Spring	.50
17	Bolt Lock Spring	.25	44	Hammer Roll Pin	.25	84	Trigger	.80	466	Receiver (Pistol Grip)	16.00
18	Bolt Lock Pin	.25	45	Hammer Pin	.25	85	Trigger Spring	.25	483	Tang Screw (Pistol Grip)	.25
19	Bolt Carrier	5.00	46	Hammer Bushing	.25	87	Trigger Pin	.25	341	Trigger Plate (Pistol Grip)	4.00
20	Bolt Carrier Latch	.30	48	Link	.80	41	Trigger Plate, grade A	*4.00			
21	Bolt Carrier Latch Spring	.25	49	Link Pin	.25						
24	Buffer Spring (give caliber)	.50	134	Magazine	3.50						
			134½	Magazine Complete	4.00						
			55	Magazine Indicator Comp.	1.00						
			135	Magazine Follower	.25						
			57	Magazine Spring	.40						
			103	Magazine Side Spring	.25						

* Unless otherwise specified, straight grip will be furnished.

REMINGTON RIFLE PARTS
MODEL 25 SLIDE ACTION REPEATING RIFLE

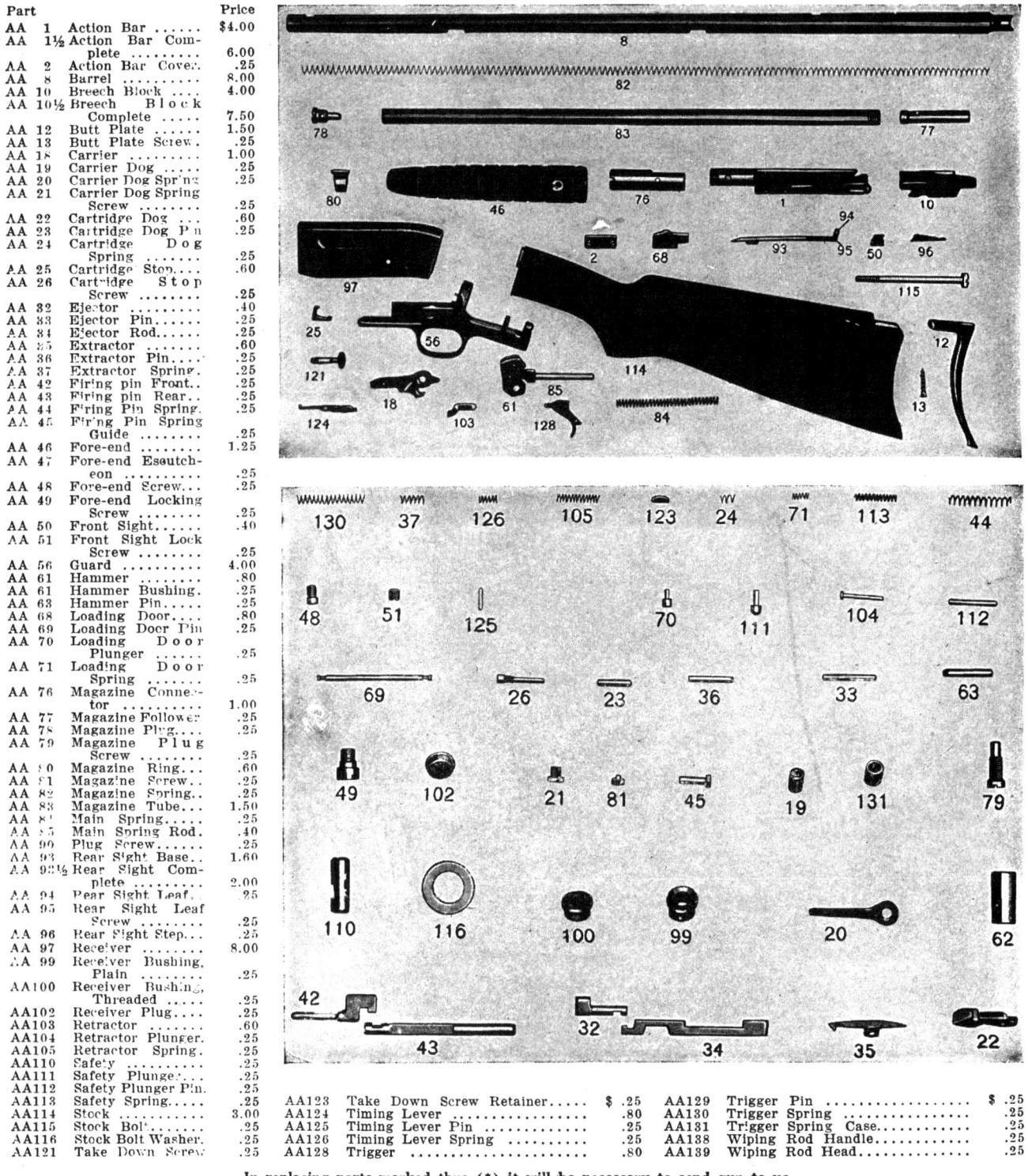

Part			Price
AA	1	Action Bar	$4.00
AA	1½	Action Bar Complete	6.00
AA	2	Action Bar Cover	.25
AA	8	Barrel	8.00
AA	10	Breech Block	4.00
AA	10½	Breech Block Complete	7.50
AA	12	Butt Plate	1.50
AA	13	Butt Plate Screw	.25
AA	18	Carrier	1.00
AA	19	Carrier Dog	.25
AA	20	Carrier Dog Spring	.25
AA	21	Carrier Dog Spring Screw	.25
AA	22	Cartridge Dog	.60
AA	23	Cartridge Dog Pin	.25
AA	24	Cartridge Dog Spring	.25
AA	25	Cartridge Stop	.60
AA	26	Cartridge Stop Screw	.25
AA	32	Ejector	.40
AA	33	Ejector Pin	.25
AA	34	Ejector Rod	.25
AA	35	Extractor	.60
AA	36	Extractor Pin	.25
AA	37	Extractor Spring	.25
AA	42	Firing pin Front	.25
AA	43	Firing pin Rear	.25
AA	44	Firing Pin Spring	.25
AA	45	Firing Pin Spring Guide	.25
AA	46	Fore-end	1.25
AA	47	Fore-end Escutcheon	.25
AA	48	Fore-end Screw	.25
AA	49	Fore-end Locking Screw	.25
AA	50	Front Sight	.40
AA	51	Front Sight Lock Screw	.25
AA	56	Guard	4.00
AA	61	Hammer	.80
AA	62	Hammer Bushing	.25
AA	63	Hammer Pin	.25
AA	68	Loading Door	.80
AA	69	Loading Door Pin	.25
AA	70	Loading Door Plunger	.25
AA	71	Loading Door Spring	.25
AA	76	Magazine Connector	1.00
AA	77	Magazine Follower	.25
AA	78	Magazine Plug	.25
AA	79	Magazine Plug Screw	.25
AA	80	Magazine Ring	.60
AA	81	Magazine Screw	.25
AA	82	Magazine Spring	.25
AA	83	Magazine Tube	1.50
AA	84	Main Spring	.25
AA	85	Main Spring Rod	.40
AA	90	Plug Screw	.25
AA	93	Rear Sight Base	1.60
AA	93½	Rear Sight Complete	2.00
AA	94	Rear Sight Leaf	.25
AA	95	Rear Sight Leaf Screw	.25
AA	96	Rear Sight Step	.25
AA	97	Receiver	8.00
AA	99	Receiver Bushing, Plain	.25
AA	100	Receiver Bushing, Threaded	.25
AA	102	Receiver Plug	.25
AA	103	Retractor	.60
AA	104	Retractor Plunger	.25
AA	105	Retractor Spring	.25
AA	110	Safety	.25
AA	111	Safety Plunger	.25
AA	112	Safety Plunger Pin	.25
AA	113	Safety Spring	.25
AA	114	Stock	3.00
AA	115	Stock Bolt	.25
AA	116	Stock Bolt Washer	.25
AA	121	Take Down Screw	.25
AA	123	Take Down Screw Retainer	.25
AA	124	Timing Lever	.80
AA	125	Timing Lever Pin	.25
AA	126	Timing Lever Spring	.25
AA	128	Trigger	.80
AA	129	Trigger Pin	.25
AA	130	Trigger Spring	.25
AA	131	Trigger Spring Case	.25
AA	138	Wiping Rod Handle	.25
AA	139	Wiping Rod Head	.25

In replacing parts marked thus (*) it will be necessary to send gun to us.

INSTRUCTIONS: In ordering parts always give name and number listed in catalog, also make, model, caliber and serial number of gun.

PAYMENTS: Parts will be sent only on advance payment. Parts cannot be returned for credit. A service charge of 25c must be added to every order under $1.00 to cover cost of handling. Do not forget to include postage.

A NEW GUN CARRIES A FACTORY GUARANTEE

America's Great Gun House 497

REMINGTON RIFLE PARTS
MODEL 30, EXPRESS, BOLT ACTION RIFLE

No.	Part Name	Price
317	Barrel (state caliber)	$12.00
318	Receiver (state caliber)	10.00
319	Bolt (state caliber)	8.00
20	Bolt Plug	.60
321	Bolt Stop	.80
22	Bolt Stop Axis Screw	.25
36	Bolt Stop Spring	.60
37	Bolt Stop Spring Rest	.25
162	Butt Plate	1.50
163	Butt Plate Screw (2)	.25
340	Cocking Piece	1.00
58	Ejector	.25
359	Extractor (state caliber)	2.00
60	Extractor Ring	.25
365	Front Sight Band Block	2.00
266	Band Block Fixing Key	.25
267	Band Block Fixing Pin	.25
193	Front Sight Blade	1.00
194	Front Sight Blade Pin	.25
272	Front Guard Screw	.25
73	Front Guard Screw Collar	.25
195	Front Swivel Nut	.25
196	Front Swivel Screw	.25
87	Locking Bolt	.25
88	Locking Bolt Spring	.25
298	Magazine Assembled	2.00
99	Magazine Bottom	.60
100	Magazine Catch	.25
101	Magazine Catch Pin	.25
102	Magazine Catch Spring	.25
305	Magazine Follower	.60
106	Magazine Follower Spring	.25
172	Mag. Follower Stop Pin	.25
110	Main Spring	.25
237	Rear Guard Screw	.25
238	Rear Guard Screw Collar	.25
202	Rear Sight Base	2.00
203	Rear Sgt. Base Lk. Screw	.25
205	Rear Sight Complete	2.00
206	Rear Sight Step	.25
142	Safety Catch	.60
143	Safety Hole Plug	.25
144	Safety Hole Plug Screw	.25
345	Sear	.60
146	Sear Axis Pin	.25

No.	Part Name	Price
117	Sear Pin	$0.25
148	Sear Spring	.25
189	Strap Hook (2)	.50
449	Stock (state caliber)	20.00
188	Stock Swivel Screw	.25

No.	Part Name	Price
150	Firing Pin	$0.40
458	Trigger	.80
159	Trigger Axis Pin	.25
460	Trigger Guard	6.00
538	Cartridge Clip (state caliber)	.25

MODEL 33—AF—RIFLE

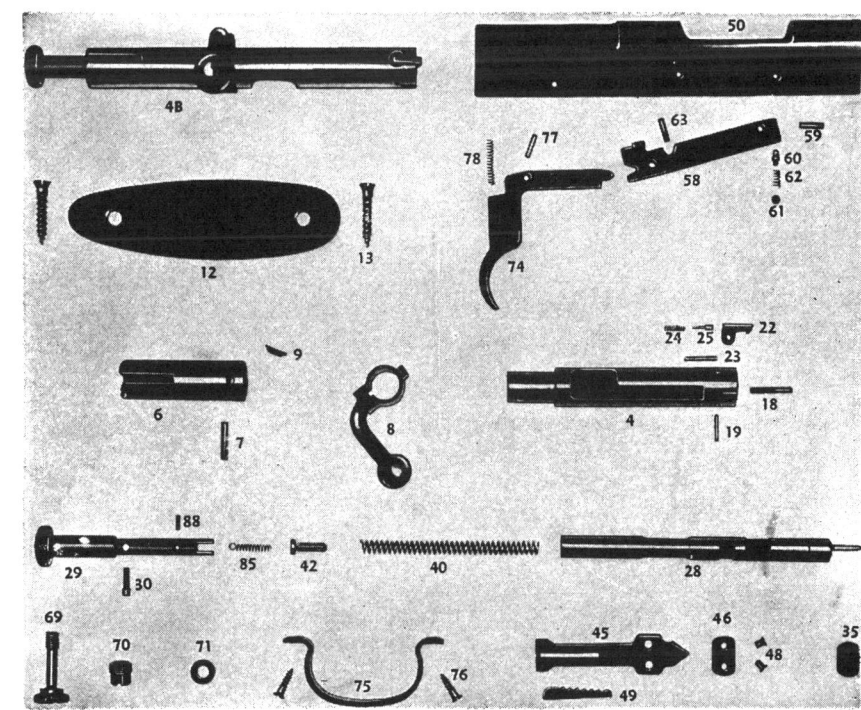

Part No.		List Price
1	Barrel	$3.00
4	Bolt	1.50
4A	Bolt assem. com. without fir. pin	2.00
4B	Bolt assem. com. with firing pin	3.00
7	Bolt Extension Pin	.25
6	Bolt Extension Sleeve	.40
8	Bolt Handle	.60
9	Bolt Handle Key	.25
12	Butt Plate	.30
13	Butt Plate Screw (2)	.25
18	Ejector	.25
19	Ejector Pin	.25
22	Extractor	.40
23	Extractor Pin	.25
24	Extractor Spring	.25
25	Extractor Spring Plunger	.25
28	Firing Pin complete with sleeve	.70
29	Firing Pin Extension complete with Retractor Spring Case	.40
30	Firing Pin Extension Pin	.25
35	Front Sight	.25
40	Main Spring	.25
42	Main Spring Plunger	.25
46	Rear Sight Base	.25
45	Rear Sight Leaf	.40
48	Rear Sight Screw (2)	.25
49	Rear Sight Step	.25
50	Receiver complete	2.00
85	Retractor Spring	.25
88	Retractor Spring Pin	.25
58	Sear	.50
59	Sear Pin	.25
60	Sear Plunger	.25
61	Sear Plunger Screw	.25
62	Sear Plunger Spring	.25
63	Sear Stop Pin	.25
65	Stock	3.00
69	Take Down Screw	.25
70	Take Down Screw Bushing	.25
71	Take Down Screw Escutcheon	.25
74	Trigger	.30
75	Trigger Guard	.25
76	Trigger Guard Screw (2)	.25
77	Trigger Pin (Same as 59)	.25
78	Trigger Spring	.25

In replacing parts marked thus (*) it will be necessary to send gun to us.

INSTRUCTIONS: In ordering parts always give name and number listed in catalog, also make, model, caliber and serial number of gun.

PAYMENTS: Parts will be sent only on advance payment. Parts cannot be returned for credit. A service charge of 25c must be added to every order under $1.00 to cover cost of handling. Do not forget to include postage.

ALL SHIPMENTS ARE INSURED

REMINGTON RIFLE PARTS
MODELS 24 AND 241 .22 CALIBER AUTOLOADING RIFLES
See foot of page 500 for certain special parts for Model 241 only

Part No.	Name of Part	Price
1	Barrel, .22 Short	$6.00
1½	Barrel, .22 long rifle	6.00
2	Barrel Adjustment Ring	.25
3	Barrel Take Up Ring	1.00
4	Barrel Take Up Lock	.50
5	Barrel Take Up Lock Spring	.25
6	Barrel Take Up Lock Plunger	.25
7	Barrel Lug	.30
8	Breech Block, .22 short	3.50
8½	Breech Block, .22 long rifle	3.50
106	Breech Block Button	.25
107	Breech Block Button Pin	.25
108	Breech Block Button Spring	.25
9	Breech Block Spring	.25
10	Breech Block Spring Plug	.25
11	Breech Block Stop Pin	.25
12	Butt Plate	.40
14	Butt Plate Screw	.25
19	Cartridge Carrier, .22 short	.25
19½	Cartridge Carrier, .22 long rifle	.25
20	Cartridge Guide, .22 short	.80
20½	Cartridge Guide, .22 long rifle	.80
22	Cartridge Stop	.60
113	Cartridge Stop Plunger Left	.25
114	Cartridge Stop Plunger Left Spring Screw	.25
115	Cartridge Stop Plunger Left Spring	.25
112	Deflector	1.50
26	Disconnector	.25
27	Disconnector Pin	.25
28	Disconnector Spring	.25
33	Extractor	.60
30	Extractor Detent Spring	.25
31	Extractor Detent Spring Pin	.25
37	Extractor Spring	.25
38	Extractor Spring Plunger	.25
41	Firing Pin, .22 short	.80
41½	Firing Pin, .22 long rifle	.80
42	Fore End	1.00
43	Fore End Escutcheon	.25
44	Fore End Screw	.25
145	Front Sight	.25
49	Inner Magazine Tube	.50
49½	Inner Magazine Tube complete	1.00
53	Locating Hole Plug Screw (Front)	.25
54	Locating Hole Plug Screw (Rear)	.25
59	Magazine Follower	.25
60	Magazine Follower Plug Front End	.25
61	Magazine Follower Plug Rear End	.25
62	Magazine Spring	.25
63	Magazine Plug	.25
64	Magazine Plug Pin	.25
69	Outer Magazine Tube	1.00
71	Peep Sight Plug Screw	.25
173	Rear Sight complete	.80
74	Rear Sight Base	.25
75	Rear Sight Elevating Screw	.25
76	Rear Sight Screw	.25
77	Receiver, .22 short	6.00
77½	Receiver, .22 long rifle	6.00
78	Receiver and Stock Dowel	.25
79	Recoil Spring	.25
80	Recoil Spring Plug, .22 short	.25

Part No.	Name of Part	Price
80½	Recoil Spring Plug, .22 long rifle	$ .25
85	Safety	.25
86	Safety Detent Plunger	.25
87	Safety Detent Spring	.25
88	Sear	.40
89	Sear Pin	.25
90	Sear Spring	.25
91	Sear Pin Retaining Pin	$ .25
92	Stock	3.00
93	Stock Bolt Nut	.25
94	Stock Bolt Washer	.25
98	Trigger	1.00
99	Trigger Plate	6.00
100	Trigger Pin	.25

In replacing parts marked thus (*) it will be necessary to send gun to us.

INSTRUCTIONS: In ordering parts always give name and number listed in catalog, also make, model, caliber and serial number of gun.

PAYMENTS: Parts will be sent only on advance payment. Parts cannot be returned for credit. A service charge of 25c must be added to every order under $1.00 to cover cost of handling. Do not forget to include postage.

SEND YOUR GUN TO STOEGER FOR EXPERT REPAIRING

AMERICA'S GREAT GUN HOUSE 499

REMINGTON RIFLE PARTS
MODELS 14, 14½ AND 141 SLIDE ACTION REPEATING RIFLES

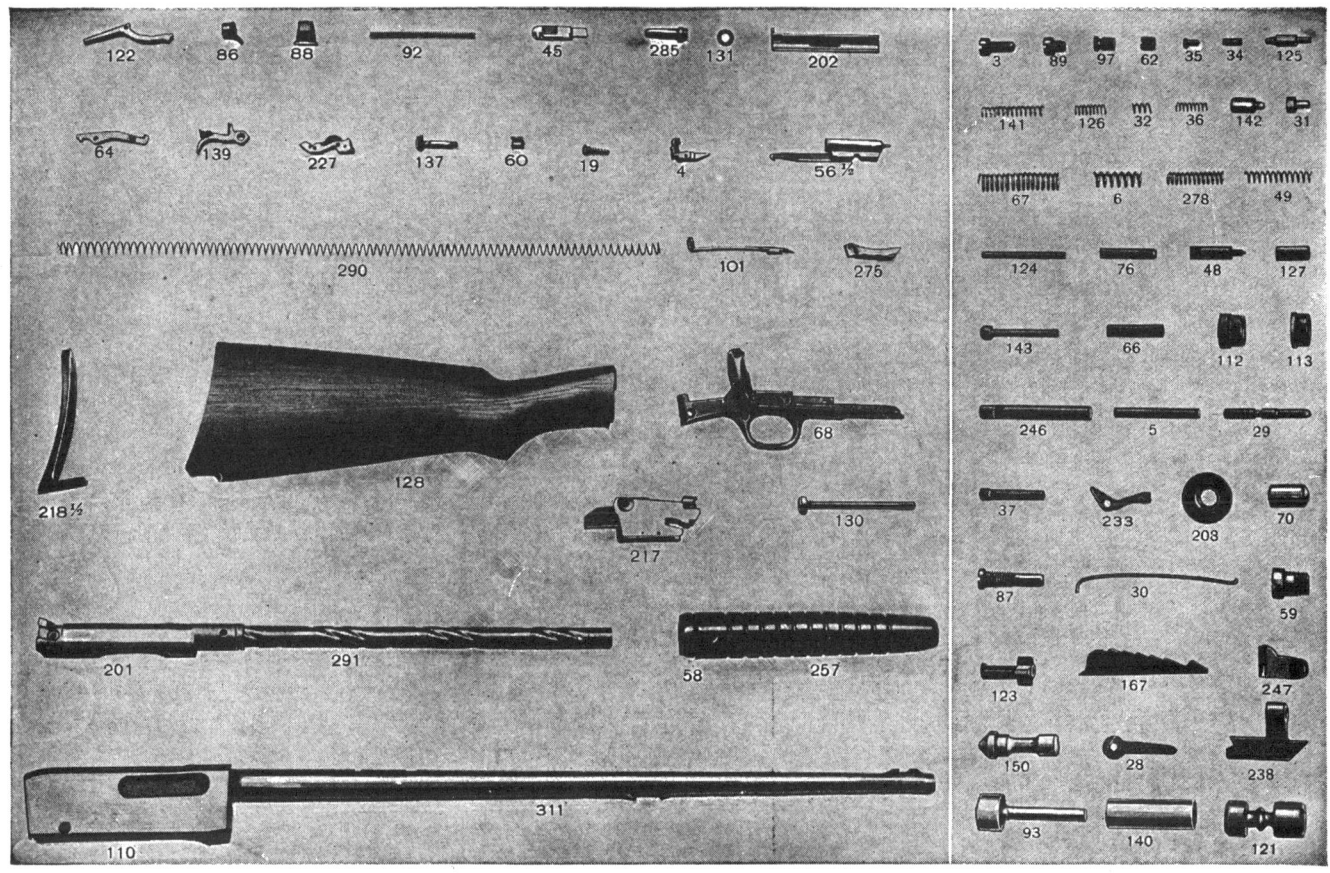

Part		Price
C 201	Action Bar	$6.00
C 202	Action Bar Cover	.30
C 3	Action Bar Cover Screw	.25
C 4	Action Bar Lock	.80
C 5	Action Bar Lock Pin	.25
C 6	Action Bar Lock Spring	.25
C 7	Action Bar Lock Spring Case	.25
C 208	Ammunition Indicator	.25
C 311	Barrel, Grade A and C	12.00
	Grade D	20.00
	Grade F	40.00
C 217	Breech Block	6.00
C 217½	Breech Block Complete	7.50
C 218S	Butt Plate, Steel Shotgun Shape	1.00
C 218½	Butt Plate, Steel Rifle Shape	1.50
C 19	Butt Plate Screw	.25
C 227	Carrier	1.00
C 28	Carrier Dog	.30
C 29	Carrier Dog Pin	.25
C 30	Carrier Dog Spring	.25
C 31	Carrier Friction Plunger	.25
C 32	Carrier Friction Spring	.25
C 233	Carrier Lever	.25
C 34	Carier Lever Pin	.25
C 35	Carrier Lever Plunger	.25
C 36	Carrier Lever Spring	.25
C 37	Carrier Pin	.25
C 238	Cartridge Stop	.60
C 45	Ejector	.60
C 246-346	Ejector Rod (give cal.)	.25
C 247	Extractor	.40
C 48	Extractor Plunger	.25
C 49	Extractor Spring	.25
C 56	Firing Pin and Extension	1.50
C 64	Firing Pin Catch	.25
C 66	Firing Pin Catch Pin	.25

Part		Price
C 70	Firing Pin Catch Plunger	$.25
C 67	Firing Pin Catch Spring	.25
C 257A	Fore-end, Grade A	1.00
C 257C	Fore-end, Grade C	8.00
C 257D	Fore-end, Grade D	9.00
C 257F	Fore-end, Grade F	12.00
C 58	Fore-end Escutcheon	.25
C 59	Fore-end Screw	.25
C 60	Front Sight	.50
C 61	Front Sight Bead	.25
C 68A & C	Guard, Grade A & C	6.00
C 68D	Guard, Grade D	16.00
C 68F	Guard, Grade F	20.00
C 275	Loading Door, No. 14	1.50
C 375	Loading Door, No. 14½	1.50
C 76	Loading Door Pin	.25
C 277	Loading Door Plunger	.25
C 278	Loading Door Spring	.25
C 285	Magazine Follower	.25
C 86	Magazine Plug	.40
C 87	Magazine Plug Screw	.25
C 88	Magazine Ring	.60
C 89	Magazine Screw	.25
C 290	Magazine Spring	.25
C 291	Magazine Tube, No. 14	2.50
C 391	Magazine Tube, No. 14½	2.50
C 92	Main Spring	.25
C 93	Main Spring Plug	.25
C 701½	Rear Sight Complete	2.00
C 701	Rear Sight Base	1.60
C 203	Rear Sight Leaf	.25
C 167	Rear Sight Slip	.25
C 169	Rear Sight Leaf Screw	.25
C 110A & C	Receiver, Grade A & C	14.00
C 110D	Receiver, Grade D	50.00
C 110F	Receiver, Grade F	100.00

Part		Price
C 112	Receiver Bushing, Plain	$.25
C 113	Receiver Bushing, Threaded	.25
C 121	Safety	.25
C 122	Sear	.75
C 123	Sear Lock	.25
C 124	Sear Lock Pin	.25
C 125	Sear Lock Plunger	.25
C 126	Sear Lock Spring	.25
C 127	Sear Pin	.25
C 128A	Stock, Grade A	6.00
C 128C	Stock, Grade C	20.00
C 128D	Stock, Grade D	30.00
C 128F	Stock, Grade F	60.00
C 130	Stock Bolt	.25
C 137	Take-Down Screw	.25
C 139	Trigger	.60
C 140	Trigger Bushing	.25
C 141	Trigger Spring	.25
C 142	Trigger Spring Cap	.25
C 143	Trigger Spring Rod	.25
C 150	Unlocking Plunger	.25
Parts for Model 141 only		
502	Action Bar Cover (State caliber)	$.30
611	Barrel (State caliber) A Grade	12.00
718	Butt Plate (Steel Shotgun type)	1.50
557A	Fore-end, A Grade	1.50
258	Fore-end Escutcheon (2) each	.25
259	Fore-end Screw (2) each	.25
268A	Guard, A Grade	6.00
277	Loading Door Plunger	.25
288	Magazine Ring	.60
2288	Stock, A Grade	6.00

In replacing parts marked thus (*) it will be necessary to send gun to us.

INSTRUCTIONS: In ordering parts always give name and number listed in catalog, also make, model, caliber and serial number of gun.

PAYMENTS: Parts will be sent only on advance payment. Parts cannot be returned for credit. A service charge of 25c must be added to every order under $1.00 to cover cost of handling. Do not forget to include postage.

© **ORDER BLANK IN MIDDLE AND INDEX IN BACK OF CATALOG**

REMINGTON RIFLE PARTS
MODEL 341-A AND 341-P CAL. 22 REPEATING BOLT ACTION RIFLE

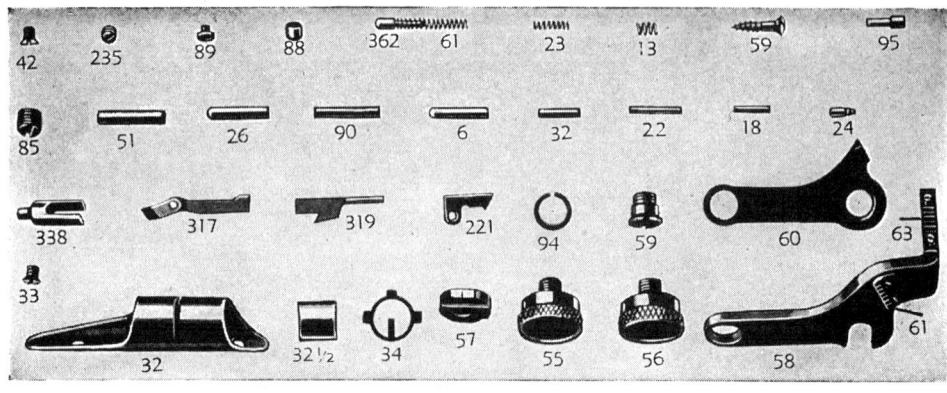

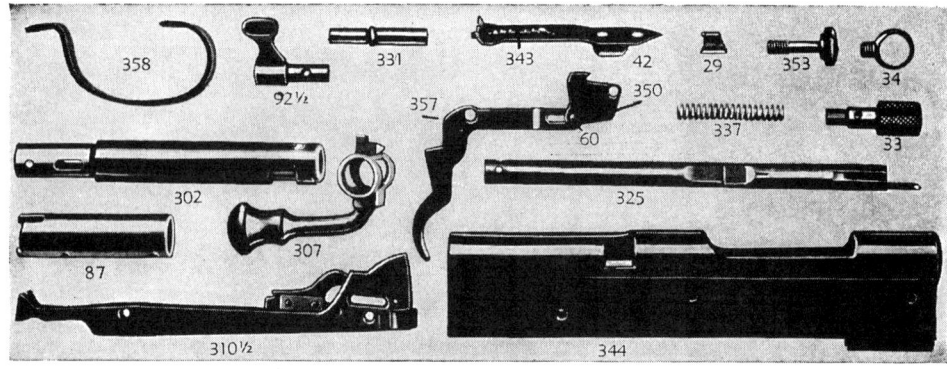

It is absolutely necessary that the numbers shown at the left of each gun part be specified when ordering.

Part No.		Price
401	*Barrel	$4.00
501	*Barrel (341-P and 341-NRA)	4.00
302	*Bolt	1.50
6	Bolt Extension Sleeve Pin	.25
87	Bolt Sleeve	.50
307	*Bolt Handle	1.25
308	Buttplate	.30
309	Buttplate Screw (2)	.25
310½	Carrier (complete)	2.50
13	Carrier Friction Spring	.25
88	Carrier Friction Spring Case	.25
89	Carrier Friction Spring Plunger	.25
14	Carrier Pin	.25
317	Cartridge Stop	.40
18	Cartridge Stop Pin	.25
319	Ejector	.25
221	Extractor	.40
22	Extractor Pin	.25
23	Extractor Spring	.25
24	Extractor Spring Plunger	.25
325	Firing Pin	1.00
26	Firing Pin Cam Pin	.25
29	Front Sight	.25
73	Front Swivel Screw (341-NRA)	.25
74	Front Swivel Screw Nut (341-NRA)	.25
75	Front Swivel Screw Washer (341-NRA)	.25
330	Inner Magazine Tube	.50
331	Magazine Follower	.25
32	Magazine Pin	.25

Part No.		Price
33	Magazine Plug	$.25
34	Magazine Ring	.30
35	Magazine Screw	.25
36	Magazine Spring	.25
85	Magazine Tube Support Screw	.25
337	Main Spring	.25
90	Main Spring Abutment Pin	.25
338	Main Spring Plunger	.25
339	Outer Magazine Tube	1.00
341	Rear Sight Leaf	.40
42	Rear Sight Screw (2)	.25
343	Rear Sight Step	.25
344½	Receiver (complete)	3.00
444½	Receiver (341-P and 341-NRA)	3.00
92½	Safety	.80
94	Safety Shaft Friction Washer	.25
95	Safety Shaft Pin	.25
350	Sear	.50
51	Sear Pin	.25
77½	Sling Strap (341-NRA) complete	2.35
352	Stock	4.00
452	Stock (341-P and 341-NRA)	4.00
76	Stock Swivel Screw (341-NRA)	.25
453	Take-Down Screw	.25
454	Take-Down Screw Escutcheon	.25
357	Trigger	.40
358	Trigger Guard	.40
59	Trigger Guard Screw (2)	.25
60	Trigger Pin	.25
61	Trigger Spring	.25

Part No.		Price
362	Trigger Spring Plunger	$.25
	Globe Front Sight (341-P and 341-NRA)	
329	Front Sight Hood	.40
329½	Front Sight (complete)	.85
98	Front Sight Screw (2), (341-P and 341-NRA)	.25
99	Front Sight Reticule .070" aperture (341-P and 341-NRA)	.25
100	Front Sight Reticule .110" aperture (341-P and 341-NRA)	.25
101	Front Sight Reticule .050" Blade (341-P and 341-NRA)	.25
102	Front Sight Reticule .100" Blade (341-P and 341-NRA)	.25
	Rear Peep Sight (341-P and 341-NRA)	
103	Rear Peep Sight Disc (small aperture)	.25
104	Rear Peep Sight Disc (large aperture)	.25
105	Rear Peep Sight Nut	.25
106	Rear Peep Sight Base	.50
107	Rear Peep Sight Base Screw	.25
108	Rear Sight Elevating Indicator	.25
109	Rear Sight Elevating Plate	.25
110	Rear Sight Elevating Plate Screw (2)	.25
111	Rear Sight Windage Plate	.25
112	Rear Sight Windage Plate Screw (2)	.25
103½	Rear Peep Sight (complete)	1.50

PARTS FOR MODEL 241 ONLY (Continued from page 498)

Part		Price
601	Barrel (State ctg.)	$6.00
116	Barrel Adjusting Bushing	.60
117	Barrel Adjusting Bushing Lock	.25
118	Barrel Adjusting Bushing Lock Screw	.25
119	Barrel Lock	.25
120	Barrel Lock Button	.25
121	Barrel Lock Spring	.25
122	Barrel Lock Spring Plunger	.25
123	Barrel Stop Screw	.80
124	Barrel Yoke	.80
225	Breech Block (Short ctg.)	4.00

Part		Price
125	Breech Block (Long Rifle ctg.)	$4.00
2126	Breech Block Button	.25
127	Breech Block Button Pin	.25
128	Breech Block Button Spring	.25
212	Butt Plate	.40
219	Cartridge Carrier (Short ctg.)	.25
319	Cartridge Carrier (Long Rifle ctg.)	.25
220	Cartridge Guide (Short ctg.)	.80
320	Cartridge Guide (Long Rifle ctg.)	.80

Part		Price
2112	Deflector (Special)	$.25
2129	Extractor	.60
132	Extractor Pin, Lower	.25
131	Extractor Pin, Upper	.25
137	Extractor Plunger	.25
2130	Extractor Spring	.25
241	Firing Pin (Short ctg.)	.80
341	Firing Pin (Long Rifle ctg.)	.80
242	Fore-end	4.00
138	Fore-end Dowel	.25
243	Fore-end Escutcheon	.25
244	Fore-end Screw	.25
362	Magazine Spring (Short ctg.)	.25

Part		Price
262	Magazine Spring (Long Rifle ctg.)	$.25
263	Magazine Plug	.25
140	Rear Sight Leaf	.40
141	Rear Sight Leaf Screw (2) each	.25
142	Rear Sight Step	.25
177	Receiver (Short ctg.)	6.00
577	Receiver (Long ctg.)	6.00
143	Recoil Stud	.25
285	Safety	.25
292	Stock	4.00
134	Stock Bolt Nut	.25
135	Stock Bolt Washer	.25
136	Stock Bolt Lock Washer	.25
299	Trigger Plate	6.00

INSTRUCTIONS: In ordering parts always give name and number listed in catalog, also make, model, caliber and serial number of gun.

PAYMENTS: Parts will be sent only on advance payment. Parts cannot be returned for credit. A service charge of 25c must be added to every order under $1.00 to cover cost of handling. Do not forget to include postage

SEND YOUR GUN TO STOEGER FOR EXPERT REPAIRING

America's Great Gun House

REMINGTON MODEL 41 RIFLE PARTS

Part No.		Price
1	Barrel	$3.00
3	Bolt only (with handle)	1.50
11	Bolt Assembled	3.00
12	Bolt Plug	.30
13	Bolt Plug Lock Screw	.25
7	Butt Plate	.30
8	Butt Plate Screw (2)	.25
14	Cocking Head (with safety and mainspring abutment)	.70
20	Ejector	.25
21	Extractor	.40
22	Extractor Pin	.25
323	Extractor Spring	.25
24	Extractor Spring Plunger	.25
30	Firing Pin	.40
31	Front Sight—Regular	.25
32	Front Sight Hood—P grade	.40
32½	Front Sight Complete—P grade (with screws and reticules)	.85
33	Front Sight Screw—P grade (2)	.25
34	Front Sight Reticule .070" aperture—P grade	.25
334	Front Sight Reticule .110" aperture—P grade	.25
434	Front Sight Reticule .050" blade—P grade	.25
534	Front Sight Reticule .100" blade—P grade	.25
37	Grip Cap	.25
38	Grip Cap Screw	.25
40	Main Spring	.25
342	Main Spring Rod	.25
344	Main Spring Rod Pin	.25
45	Main Spring Washer	.25
52	Rear Sight Leaf—Regular	.40
352	Rear Sight Leaf—Special	.40
53	Rear Sight Screw—Regular	.25
54	Rear Sight Step—Regular	.25
55	Rear Peep Sight Disc (small aperture)—P grade	.25
56	Rear Peep Sight Disc (large aperture)—P grade	.25
57	Rear Peep Sight Nut—P grade	.25
58	Rear Peep Sight Base—P grade	.50
59	Rear Peep Sight Base Screw—P grade	.25
60	Rear Peep Sight Elevating Indicator—P grade	.25
61	Rear Peep Sight Elevating Plate—P grade	$.25
62	Rear Peep Sight Elevating Plate Screw (2)—P grade	.25
63	Rear Peep Sight Windage Plate—P grade	.25
64	Rear Peep Sight Windage Plate Screw (2)—P grade (same as 62)	.25
65	Rear Peep Sight Complete—P grade	1.50
51	Retractor Spring	.25
71	Stock only	3.00
71½	Stock Complete (with butt plate, trigger guard, bushing and escutcheon)	$3.50
73	Stock Bushing	.25
380	Take Down Screw	.25
81	Take Down Screw Bushing	.25
382	Take Down Screw Escutcheon	.25
83	Trigger	.30
384	Trigger Guard	.25
85	Trigger Guard Screw (2)	.25
86	Trigger Pin	.25
87	Trigger Spring	.25
88	Trigger Stud	.25

CROSMAN AIR RIFLE PARTS

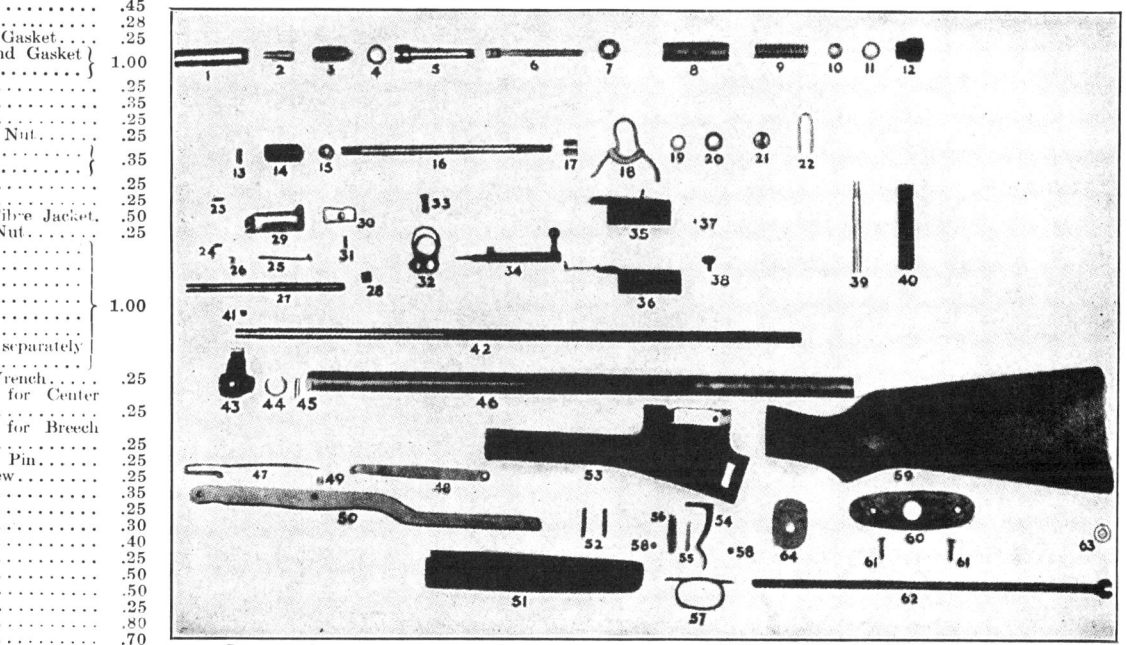

Part No.		Price
1	Compression Chamber	$.40
2	Check Valve	.45
3	Check Valve Spring	.28
4	Exhaust Valve Body Gasket	.25
5	Exhaust Valve Body and Gasket	1.00
6	Exhaust Valve Stem	
7	Body Lock Nut	.25
8	Hammer Sleeve	.35
9	Hammer Spring	.25
10	Hammer Spring Lock Nut	.25
11	Hammer Plug Spring	.35
12	Hammer Plug	
12A	Hammer Plug	.25
13	Plunger Guide Pin	.25
14	Plunger Guide with Fibre Jacket	.50
15	Plunger Guide Lock Nut	.25
16	Plunger Rod	
17	Compression Body	
18	Lubricating Felt	1.00
21	Compression Head	
19	Leather Compression Ring and Expander. May be purchased separately for 20¢	
22	Compression Head Wrench	.25
23	Magazine Set Screw for Center Strap, ¼ inch long	.25
24	Magazine Set Screw for Breech Block, ⅜ inch long	.25
25	Separator Spring and Pin	.25
26	Separator Spring Screw	.25
27	Magazine Tubing	.35
28	Magazine Cover	.25
29	Swinging Cam	.30
30	Cross Feed	.40
31	Cross Feed Pin	.25
32	Center Strap	.50
32A	Center Strap	.50
33	Center Strap Screw	.25
34	Breech Bolt	.80
34A	Breech Bolt	.70
35	Rear Sight, Peep	1.00
35A	Rear Sight, Peep	.50
36	Rear Sight, Open	1.00
37	Rear Sight Set Screw	.25
38	Knurled Set Screw for Cover	.25
39	Dismounting Wrench	.50
40	Dismounting Wrench Handle	
41	Barrel Set Screw	.25
42	Barrel	4.00
43	Front Sight Block	1.00
43A	Front Sight Block	1.00
44	Front Sight Pin Spring	.25
45	Front Sight Pin	.25
46	Compression Tube	2.00

In most instances parts for both the Repeater and the Single Shot Rifles are interchangeable. Wherever such is not the case, Single Shot Rifle part numbers are signified by "A" which follows part numbers in the list below:

Part No.		Price
47	Pump Lever Spring	$.25
48	Pump Lever Link	.35
49	Pump Lever Link Rivet	.05 / 1.25
50	Pump Lever	.85
51	Fore End	2.00
51A	Fore End	1.75
52	Fore End Pin	.25
53	Breech Block	3.50
53A	Breech Block	2.50
54	Trigger	.25
55	Trigger Pin	.25
56	Trigger Spring	$.25
57	Trigger Guard	.50
58	Trigger Guard Screws	.25
59	Stock with Butt Plate	4.00
59A	Stock with Butt Plate	3.00
60	Butt Plate	.30
61	Butt Plate Screws	.25
62	Stock Bolt	.50
63	Stock Bolt Washer	.25
64	Cork Packing for Stock	.25

PLEASE TELL OTHERS ABOUT STOEGER'S CATALOG

REMINGTON SHOTGUN PARTS
MODEL 11 AND SPORTSMAN AUTOLOADING SHOTGUNS

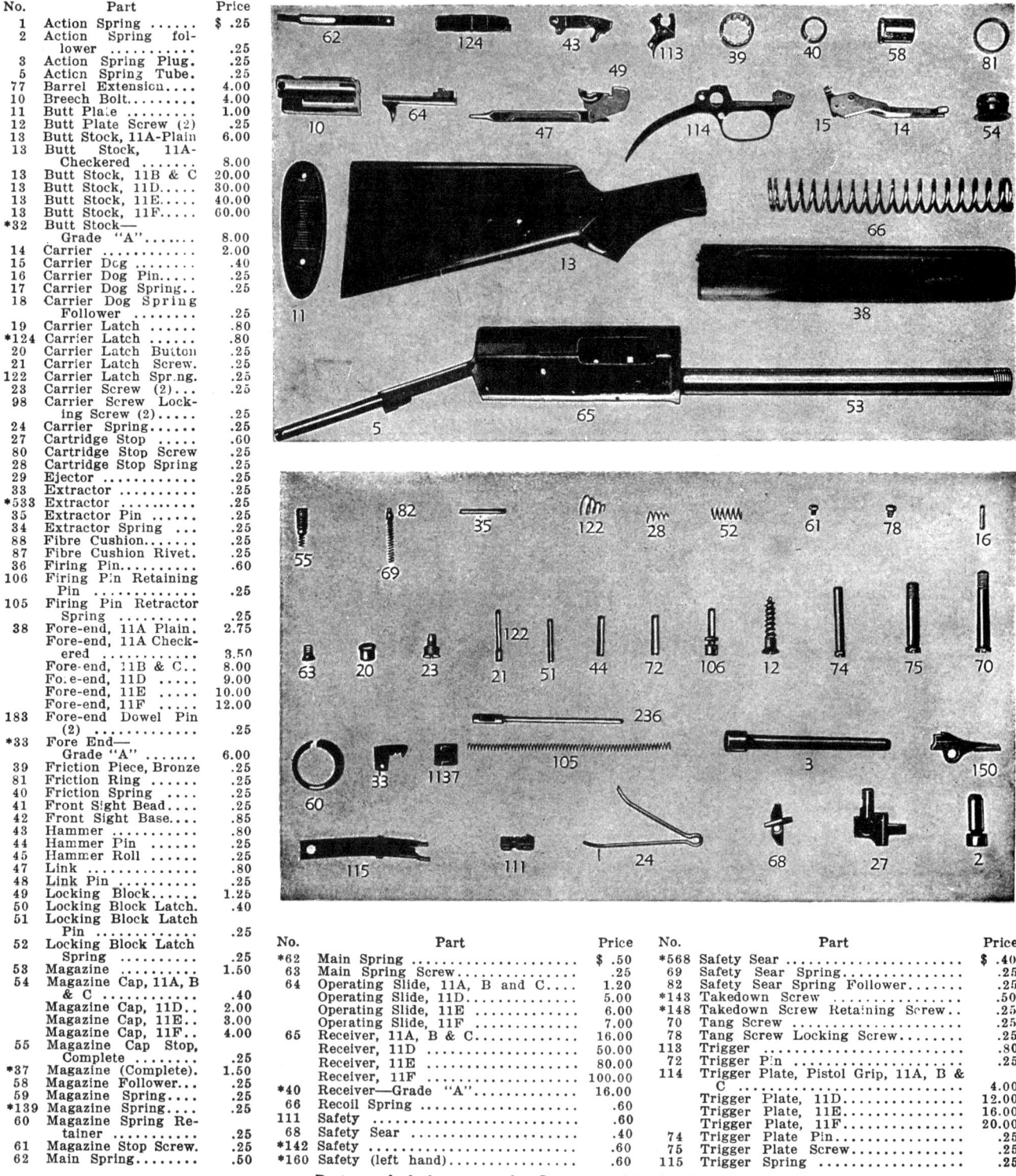

No.	Part	Price
1	Action Spring	$ .25
2	Action Spring follower	.25
3	Action Spring Plug.	.25
5	Action Spring Tube.	.25
77	Barrel Extension	4.00
10	Breech Bolt	4.00
11	Butt Plate	1.00
12	Butt Plate Screw (2)	.25
13	Butt Stock, 11A-Plain	6.00
13	Butt Stock, 11A-Checkered	8.00
13	Butt Stock, 11B & C	20.00
13	Butt Stock, 11D	30.00
13	Butt Stock, 11E	40.00
13	Butt Stock, 11F	60.00
*32	Butt Stock—Grade "A"	8.00
14	Carrier	2.00
15	Carrier Dog	.40
16	Carrier Dog Pin	.25
17	Carrier Dog Spring	.25
18	Carrier Dog Spring Follower	.25
19	Carrier Latch	.80
*124	Carrier Latch	.80
20	Carrier Latch Button	.25
21	Carrier Latch Screw	.25
122	Carrier Latch Spring	.25
23	Carrier Screw (2)	.25
98	Carrier Screw Locking Screw (2)	.25
24	Carrier Spring	.25
27	Cartridge Stop	.60
80	Cartridge Stop Screw	.25
28	Cartridge Stop Spring	.25
29	Ejector	.25
33	Extractor	.25
*533	Extractor	.25
35	Extractor Pin	.25
34	Extractor Spring	.25
88	Fibre Cushion	.25
87	Fibre Cushion Rivet	.25
36	Firing Pin	.60
106	Firing Pin Retaining Pin	.25
105	Firing Pin Retractor Spring	.25
38	Fore-end, 11A Plain	2.75
	Fore-end, 11A Checkered	3.50
	Fore-end, 11B & C	8.00
	Fore-end, 11D	9.00
	Fore-end, 11E	10.00
	Fore-end, 11F	12.00
183	Fore-end Dowel Pin (2)	.25
*33	Fore End—Grade "A"	6.00
39	Friction Piece, Bronze	.25
81	Friction Ring	.25
40	Friction Spring	.25
41	Front Sight Bead	.25
42	Front Sight Base	.85
43	Hammer	.80
44	Hammer Pin	.25
45	Hammer Roll	.25
47	Link	.80
48	Link Pin	.25
49	Locking Block	1.25
50	Locking Block Latch	.40
51	Locking Block Latch Pin	.25
52	Locking Block Latch Spring	.25
53	Magazine	1.50
54	Magazine Cap, 11A, B & C	.40
	Magazine Cap, 11D	2.00
	Magazine Cap, 11E	3.00
	Magazine Cap, 11F	4.00
55	Magazine Cap Stop, Complete	.25
*37	Magazine (Complete)	1.50
58	Magazine Follower	.25
59	Magazine Spring	.25
*139	Magazine Spring	.25
60	Magazine Spring Retainer	.25
61	Magazine Stop Screw	.25
62	Main Spring	.50

No.	Part	Price
*62	Main Spring	$ .50
63	Main Spring Screw	.25
64	Operating Slide, 11A, B and C	1.20
	Operating Slide, 11D	5.00
	Operating Slide, 11E	6.00
	Operating Slide, 11F	7.00
65	Receiver, 11A, B & C	16.00
	Receiver, 11D	50.00
	Receiver, 11E	80.00
	Receiver, 11F	100.00
*40	Receiver—Grade "A"	16.00
66	Recoil Spring	.60
111	Safety	.60
68	Safety Sear	.40
*142	Safety	.60
*160	Safety (left hand)	.60

No.	Part	Price
*568	Safety Sear	$ .40
69	Safety Sear Spring	.25
82	Safety Sear Spring Follower	.25
*143	Takedown Screw	.50
*148	Takedown Screw Retaining Screw	.25
70	Tang Screw	.25
78	Tang Screw Locking Screw	.25
113	Trigger	.80
72	Trigger Pin	.25
114	Trigger Plate, Pistol Grip, 11A, B & C	4.00
	Trigger Plate, 11D	12.00
	Trigger Plate, 11E	16.00
	Trigger Plate, 11F	20.00
74	Trigger Plate Pin	.25
75	Trigger Plate Screw	.25
115	Trigger Spring	.25

Parts marked thus * are for Sportsman Model only.

INSTRUCTIONS: In ordering parts always give name and number listed in catalog, also make, model, caliber and serial number of gun.

PAYMENTS: Parts will be sent only on advance payment. Parts cannot be returned for credit. A service charge of 25c must be added to every order under $1.00 to cover cost of handling. Do not forget to include postage.

© **CAREFUL ATTENTION AND SAFE DELIVERY OF YOUR ORDER**

REMINGTON SHOTGUN PARTS
MODEL 31 SIDE EJECTION SHOTGUN, SERIES 1931 AND 1934

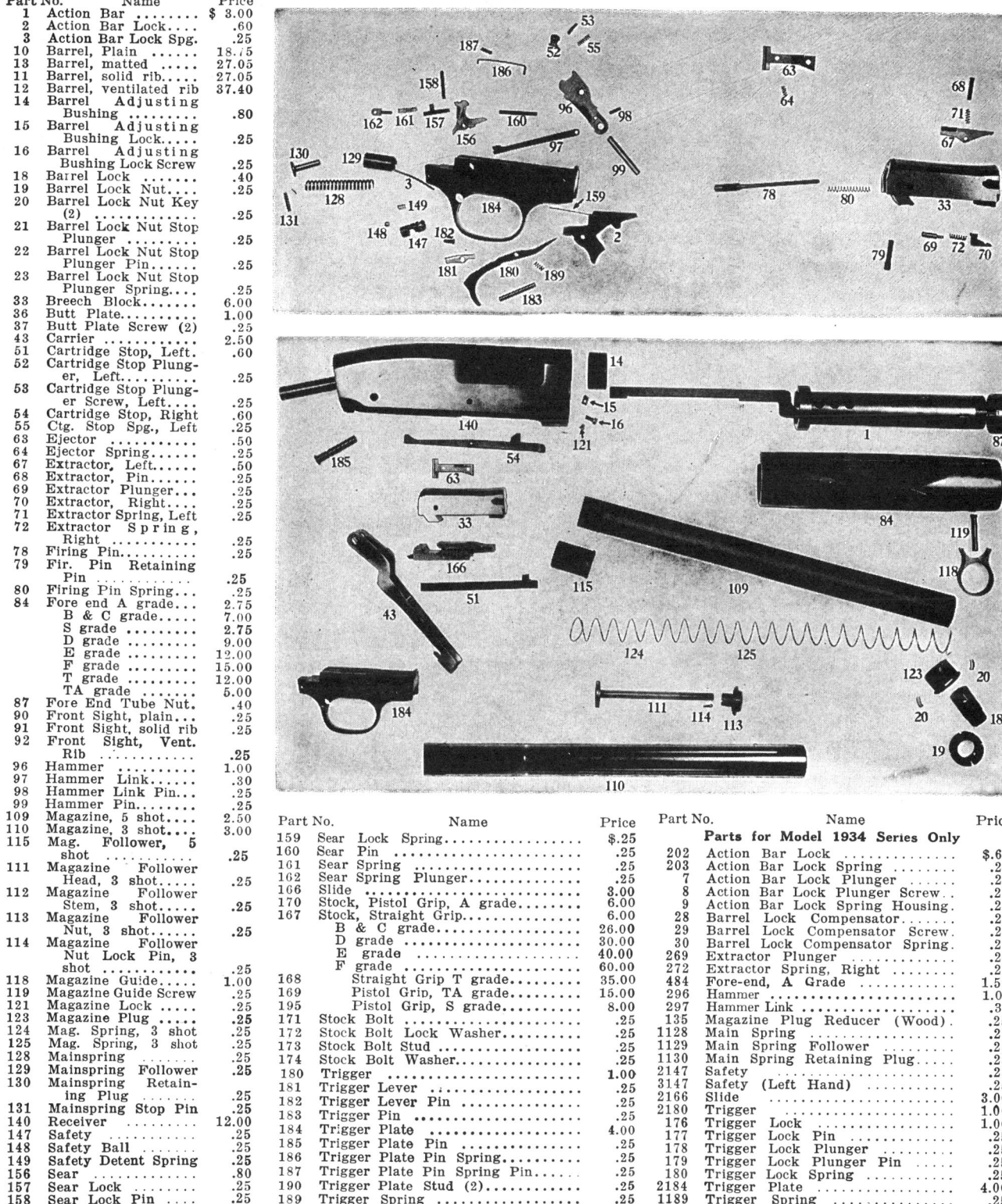

Part No.	Name	Price
1	Action Bar	$3.00
2	Action Bar Lock	.60
3	Action Bar Lock Spg.	.25
10	Barrel, Plain	18.75
13	Barrel, matted	27.05
11	Barrel, solid rib	27.05
12	Barrel, ventilated rib	37.40
14	Barrel Adjusting Bushing	.80
15	Barrel Adjusting Bushing Lock	.25
16	Barrel Adjusting Bushing Lock Screw	.25
18	Barrel Lock	.40
19	Barrel Lock Nut	.25
20	Barrel Lock Nut Key (2)	.25
21	Barrel Lock Nut Stop Plunger	.25
22	Barrel Lock Nut Stop Plunger Pin	.25
23	Barrel Lock Nut Stop Plunger Spring	.25
33	Breech Block	6.00
36	Butt Plate	1.00
37	Butt Plate Screw (2)	.25
43	Carrier	2.50
51	Cartridge Stop, Left	.60
52	Cartridge Stop Plunger, Left	.25
53	Cartridge Stop Plunger Screw, Left	.25
54	Cartridge Stop, Right	.60
55	Ctg. Stop Spg., Left	.25
63	Ejector	.50
64	Ejector Spring	.25
67	Extractor, Left	.50
68	Extractor, Pin	.25
69	Extractor Plunger	.25
70	Extractor, Right	.25
71	Extractor Spring, Left	.25
72	Extractor Spring, Right	.25
78	Firing Pin	.25
79	Fir. Pin Retaining Pin	.25
80	Firing Pin Spring	.25
84	Fore end A grade	2.75
	B & C grade	7.00
	S grade	2.75
	D grade	9.00
	E grade	12.00
	F grade	15.00
	T grade	12.00
	TA grade	5.00
87	Fore End Tube Nut	.40
90	Front Sight, plain	.25
91	Front Sight, solid rib	.25
92	Front Sight, Vent. Rib	.25
96	Hammer	1.00
97	Hammer Link	.30
98	Hammer Link Pin	.25
99	Hammer Pin	.25
109	Magazine, 5 shot	2.50
110	Magazine, 3 shot	3.00
115	Mag. Follower, 5 shot	.25
111	Magazine Follower Head, 3 shot	.25
112	Magazine Follower Stem, 3 shot	.25
113	Magazine Follower Nut, 3 shot	.25
114	Magazine Follower Nut Lock Pin, 3 shot	.25
118	Magazine Guide	1.00
119	Magazine Guide Screw	.25
121	Magazine Lock	.25
123	Magazine Plug	.25
124	Mag. Spring, 3 shot	.25
125	Mag. Spring, 3 shot	.25
128	Mainspring	.25
129	Mainspring Follower	.25
130	Mainspring Retaining Plug	.25
131	Mainspring Stop Pin	.25
140	Receiver	12.00
147	Safety	.25
148	Safety Ball	.25
149	Safety Detent Spring	.25
156	Sear	.80
157	Sear Lock	.25
158	Sear Lock Pin	.25
159	Sear Lock Spring	.25
160	Sear Pin	.25
161	Sear Spring	.25
162	Sear Spring Plunger	.25
166	Slide	3.00
170	Stock, Pistol Grip, A grade	6.00
167	Stock, Straight Grip	6.00
	B & C grade	26.00
	D grade	30.00
	E grade	40.00
	F grade	60.00
168	Straight Grip T grade	35.00
169	Pistol Grip, TA grade	15.00
195	Pistol Grip, S grade	8.00
171	Stock Bolt	.25
172	Stock Bolt Lock Washer	.25
173	Stock Bolt Stud	.25
174	Stock Bolt Washer	.25
180	Trigger	1.00
181	Trigger Lever	.25
182	Trigger Lever Pin	.25
183	Trigger Pin	.25
184	Trigger Plate	4.00
185	Trigger Plate Pin	.25
186	Trigger Plate Pin Spring	.25
187	Trigger Plate Pin Spring Pin	.25
190	Trigger Plate Stud (2)	.25
189	Trigger Spring	.25

Parts for Model 1934 Series Only

Part No.	Name	Price
202	Action Bar Lock	$.60
203	Action Bar Lock Spring	.25
7	Action Bar Lock Plunger	.25
8	Action Bar Lock Plunger Screw	.25
9	Action Bar Lock Spring Housing	.25
28	Barrel Lock Compensator	.25
29	Barrel Lock Compensator Screw	.25
30	Barrel Lock Compensator Spring	.25
269	Extractor Plunger	.25
272	Extractor Spring, Right	.25
484	Fore-end, A Grade	1.50
296	Hammer	1.00
297	Hammer Link	.30
135	Magazine Plug Reducer (Wood)	.25
1128	Main Spring	.25
1129	Main Spring Follower	.25
1130	Main Spring Retaining Plug	.25
2147	Safety	.25
3147	Safety (Left Hand)	.25
2166	Slide	3.00
2180	Trigger	1.00
176	Trigger Lock	1.00
177	Trigger Lock Pin	.25
178	Trigger Lock Plunger	.25
179	Trigger Lock Plunger Pin	.25
180	Trigger Lock Spring	.25
2184	Trigger Plate	4.00
1189	Trigger Spring	.25

In replacing parts marked thus (*) it will be necessary to send gun to us.

INSTRUCTIONS: In ordering parts always give name and number listed in catalog, also make, model, caliber and serial number of gun.

PAYMENTS: Parts will be sent only on advance payment. Parts cannot be returned for credit. A service charge of 25c must be added to every order under $1.00 to cover cost of handling. Do not forget to include postage.

PLEASE TELL OTHERS ABOUT STOEGER'S CATALOG

REMINGTON SHOTGUN PARTS
MODEL 29

Name	Component No.	Price
Action Bar, Complete		
Grade A, B, C	140	$3.00
Grade 29-D	140	10.00
Grade 29-E	140	11.00
Grade 29-F	140	12.00
Act. Bar Lock Button	168	.25
Act. Bar L. But. Nut	169	.25
Act. Bar Lk. But. Spg.	170	.25
Action Bar Lock Lever	141	.60
Act. Bar Lk. Lev. Pl.	130	.25
Action Bar Lock Pin	5	.25
Action Bar Lock Shoe	69	.40
Act. Bar Lk. Sh. Pl.	103	.25
Act. Bar Lk. Sh. Riv.	134	.25
Act. Bar Lock Spring	6	.25
Action Bar Stud	7	.25
Bbl. Adjstg. Bushing	10	.80
Bbl. Adj. Bushing Lk.	83	.25
Barrel Adjusting Bushing Lock Screw	85	.25
Barrel Lug (should be fitted at factory)	43	2.00
Barrel Lug Screw (should be fitted at factory)	45	.25
Barrel Lug Stop (should be fitted at factory)	86	.25
Barrel Yoke (should be fitted at factory)		
Grade A, B, C	12	2.00
Grade D	12	6.00
Grade E	12	8.00
Grade F	12	10.00
Breech Block, Complete	143½	12.00
Breech Block Supporting Pins (2)	90	.25
Butt Plate	15	1.00
Butt Plate Screws (2)	16	.25
Butt Stock	143	
Grade A		8.00
Grade B. and C.		26.00
Grade S		12.00
Grade 29-D		30.00
Grade 29-E		40.00
Grade 29-F		60.00
Grade 29-T		45.00
Butt Stock Bolt	18	.25
Butt St. Bolt Bushing	84	.25
Butt St. Bolt Washer	19	.25
Butt Stock Bolt Lock Washer	132	.25
Carrier (Complete)	144½	3.00
Carrier Friction Spring	82	.25
Carrier Stop	23	.30
Carrier Thrust Stud	82	.25
Cocking Head	146	1.50
Cocking Head Pin	26	.25
Ejector	180	.50
Ejector Pin	181	.25
Ejector Plunger	182	.25
Ejector Plunger Spring	183	.25
Extractor Spring	150	.25
Extractor Link	185	.50
Extractor Pin	186	.25
Extractor, Lower	147	.50
Extractor, Upper	148	.50
Extractor Pin	149	.25
Extractor Spring	150	.25
Firing Pin	151	.40
Firing Pin Bushing	152	.25
Firing Pin Bush. Pin	33	.25
Fore-end	153	
Grade 29-A	153	2.75
Grade 29-B and C	153	7.00
Grade 29-S	153	2.75
Grade 29-D	153	9.00
Grade 29-E	153	12.00
Grade 29-F	153	
Grade 29-T	434	12.00
Fore-end Nut	237	.40
Fore-end Screw (2) (29-T)	277	.25
Fore-end Screw Lock Screw (2) (29-T)	131	.25
Front Sight	275	.25
Guard	154	4.00
Guard Screw	74	.25
Guard Screw Check Screw	105	.25
Latch (Breech Block)	106	.25
Latch Pin	107	.25
Latch Spring	108	.25
Magazine Lever	40	.80
Magazine Lever Detent	44	.25
Mag. Lever Det. Rivet	128	.25
Magazine Lever Pin	41	.25

Name	No.	Price
Magazine Lever Spring	42	$0.25
Magazine Plug Screw Lock Screw	127	.25
Magazine Tube (Complete)	155½	3.00
Magazine Tube Follower	51	.40
Magazine Tube Plug	50	.40
Magazine Tube Plug Screw (2)	46	.25
Magazine Tube Spring	52	.25
Main Spring	39	.25
Receiver:		
Grade A, B, C, S	157	17.00
*Grade D	157	50.00
*Grade E	157	80.00
*Grade F	157	100.00

*These parts must be sent in.

Name	No.	Price
Safety	159	$0.40
Safety Ball	54	.25
Safety Spring	160	.25
Safety Spring Pin	161	.25
Sear	162	.80
Sear Pin	60	.25
Sear Spring	163	.25
Sear Spring Plunger	164	.25
Tang Screw	63	.25
Tang Screw Check Screw	268	.25
Trigger	165	1.20
Trigger Pin	166	.25
Trigger Spring	167	.25

SEE PAGE 8 "HOW TO ORDER"

REMINGTON SHOTGUN PARTS
MODEL 32 OVER AND UNDER

Part No.		Price Ea.
20	Butt Plate	$1.00
21	Butt Plate Screw	.25
26	Cocking Lever	.50
27	Cocking Lever Pin	.25
28	Cocking Rod, Left	.40
29	Cocking Rod, Right	.40
30	Cocking Rod Pin	.25
35	Ejector, Left	1.50
36	Ejector, Right	1.50
37	Ejector Hammer, Left	.50
38	Ejector Hammer, Right	.50
39	Ejector Hammer Stop Pin	.25
40	Ejector Main Spring	.25
41	Ejector Retaining Screw	.25
42	Ejector Sear, Left	.40
43	Ejector Sear, Right	.40
44	Ejector Sear Pin	.25
45	Ejector Sear Spring	.25
52	Firing Pin	.25
53	Firing Pin Housing	1.00
54	Firing Pin Housing Pin	.25
55	Firing Pin Housing Plug	.25
56	Firing Pin Retaining Pin	.25
57	Firing Pin Spring	.25
60	Fore-end (wood only)	7.50
60½	Fore-end Complete	15.00
260	Fore-end Complete, T. C. Grade	17.50
61	Fore-end Catch	.60
62	Fore-end Catch Pin	.25
63	Fore-end Catch Spring	.25
64	Fore-end Catch Spring Screw	.25
67	Fore-end Iron	7.00
68	Fore-end Screw, Front	.25
69	Fore-end Screws, Rear	.25
74	Frame	20.00
78	Front Sight for Plain Barrels	.25
278	Front Sight for Ribbed Barrels	.25
80	Guard Bow	2.00
81	Guard Bow Screw	.25
86	Hammer, Left	1.00
87	Hammer, Right	1.00
88	Hammer Pin	.25
91	Hammer Pin Locking Screw	.25
89	Hammer Pin Stud	.25
90	Hammer Pin Stud Check Screw	.25
95	Joint Pin, Left	.60
96	Joint Pin, Right	.60
97	Joint Pin Check Screw	.25
107	Main Bolt for Plain Barrel	3.50
1107	Main Bolt for Ribbed Barrels	3.50
108	Main Bolt Lock	.40
109	Main Bolt Lock Spring	.25
110	Main Bolt Stop	.25
111	Main Bolt Stop Pin	.25
114	Main Spring	.25
115	Main Spring Rod	.50
118	Middle Sight Ribbed Barrels	.25
124	Safety Detent	.25
125	Safety Detent Screw	.25
126	Safety Plunger	.75
127	Safety Plunger Pin	.25
128	Safety Slide	.80
129	Safety Slide Adjusting Screw	.25
132	Safety Spring	.25
135	Sear, Left	.75
136	Sear, Right	.75
137	Sear Housing	.50
138	Sear Housing Pin	.25
139	Sear Housing Rivet	.25
140	Sear Pin	.25
141	Sear Spring	.25
143	Sear Spring Plunger	.25
147	Stock A Grade	15.00
1147	Stock S Grade	20.00
3147	Stock T. C. Grade	35.00
148	Stock Bolt	.25
149	Stock Bolt Bushing	.25
150	Stock Bolt Lock Washer	.25

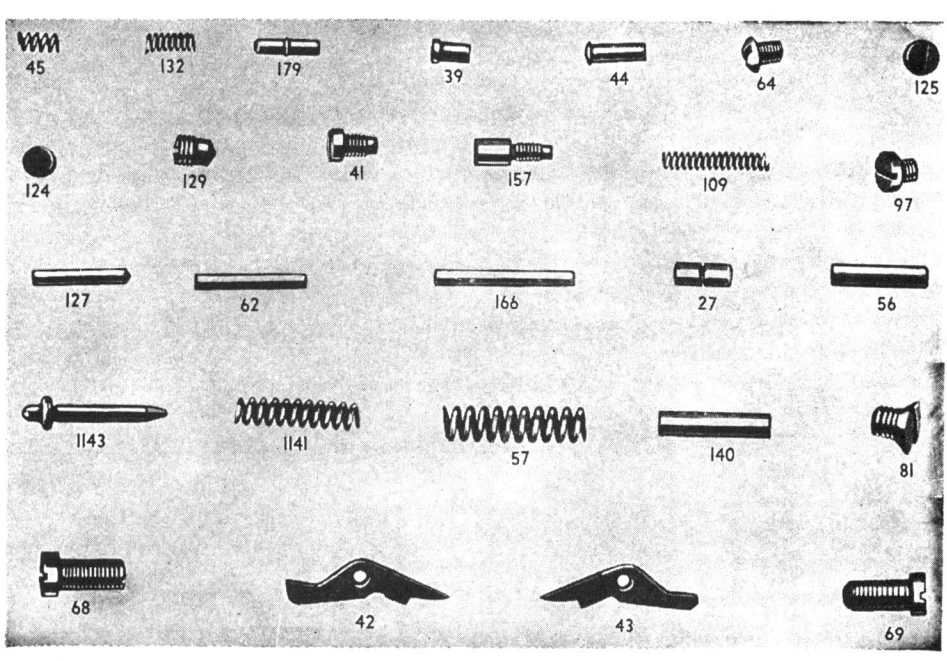

In replacing parts marked thus (*) it will be necessary to send gun to us.

INSTRUCTIONS: In ordering parts always give name and number listed in catalog, also make, model, caliber and serial number of gun.

PAYMENTS: Parts will be sent only on advance payment. Parts cannot be returned for credit. A service charge of 25c must be added to every order under $1.00 to cover cost of handling. Do not forget to include postage.

ALL SHIPMENTS ARE INSURED

INDEX

★

IMPORTANT NOTICE—Due to the present unstable and fluctuating conditions, all prices in this catalog are subject to change or correction without notice. Merchandise will be charged for at the prevailing established prices.

★

FOR HANDY REFERENCE, THE MERCHANDISE IS ARRANGED IN SECTIONS

How to Order 8	Shooter's Accessories 184–189
Rifles 10–50	Sights & Telescopes 190–229
Shotguns 51–92	Ammunition & Ballistics 230–267
Trap Equipment 82–87	Camp Equipment . . . . . . {268–273 / 309–317}
Muzzle Loaders 94–97	
Pistols & Revolvers 98–135	Walnut Stocks & Remodeling . . 274–294
Police Equipment 136–139	Hunting Clothing & Shoes . . . 296–307
Air Guns 140–145	Reloading Equipment 318–339
Targets. 146–151	Dog Accessories 340–341
Cleaning Accessories 154–161	Trophies & Medals 342–349
Books 162–170	Cameras 350–351
Holsters, Cabinets, Gun Cases, etc. 172–183	Gunsmith's Tools 352–404

A

	Page
Abrasives	382
Adaptors (Stoeger-Parker)	159
Adaptors for Revolvers	115, 186-188, 207
Aim Corrector	209
Airguide Barometers & Thermometers	221
Airguide Fieldglasses	227
Air-Gun Pellets	140–141, 144–145
Air Gun Slug	142
Air Pistols:	
Benjamin	143
Haenel	140
Tell	140
Webley	141
Air Rifles:	
Benjamin	143
Crosman	145
Daisy	142
Haenel	144
Stoeger	144, 145
Ajack Rifle Scopes	211
Alaskan Scope	216
Allscope	228
Alphabetical Dies	394
Aluminum Rifle Rests	294
American Game	6–7
Ammunition:	
Blank, Shot, Rim Fire, etc.	242
Brenneke	247
Foreign	243–247
Gas Cartridges	137
Metalics (American)	236–241, 232–234
Shot Shells	248–252
.22 Caliber	230–231
Very or Flare Shells	132, 137
Animal Heads, Miniature	315
Anti-Fudge Shothole Gauge	189

	Page
Antique Model Guns	93–97
Anti-Rust Ropes	157
Arkansas Stones	383
Articles:	
Development of the Springfield	235
Discovery & History of Gunpowder	318
Elementary Ballistics	235
Foreign Proofmarks	52
History of Colt Firearms	99
History of Lefever & Ithaca Shotguns	68
History of L. C. Smith Shotgun	59
History of Remington Arms Co.	28
History of Savage Arms Co.	34
History of Smith & Wesson	110
History of Win. Repeating Arms Co.	11
Introduction to Gunsmithing	352
Introduction to Muzzle Loaders	93
Mossberg Features	48
Notes on Reloading Foreign Cartridges	323
On Springfield	235
Pistol & Revolver Shooting	98
Principle Foreign Proof Marks	52
Regarding 8mm. Cartridges	265
The Making of the Marlin Gun	41
The Rifle	10
The Shotgun	53
This Reloading Game	319
Atlas: Lathes	354–355
Lathe Attachments	355
Austrian Proofmarks	52
Auto Gun Clip	188
Automatic Pistols:	
Colt	100–103
Harrington & Richardson	125
Hi-Standard	120, 121
Luger	132
Mauser	130, 134

	Page
Automatic Rifles:	
Marlin	42
Mossberg	50
Remington	30
Savage	40
Springfield	44
Stevens	46
Winchester	15, 25
Automatic Shotguns:	
Browning	54
Remington	81
Savage	76
Winchester	75
Auxiliary Barrels:	
Semper	154
Auxiliary Cartridges: Marble	154
Winchester	154
Axes	268

B

	Page
Bags:	
Shell	172, 174
Balar Field Glass	225
Ballistics:	
Article	235
English	262–264
German	266–267
Peters	256–257
Remington	253–255
Western	258–259
Winchester	260–261
Balls, Lead	97, 252, 339
Band Saws	356
Barometers	221

YOU FIND WHAT YOU WANT AT STOEGER'S

AMERICA'S GREAT GUN HOUSE

	Page
Barrels: Dent Raiser	395
Peerless Blanks	291
Standard Factory	290
Winchester Blanks	291
Barrel Bands	284–285
Barrel Vise	390
Basin, Blueing	286
Basin, Canvas	309
Bausch & Lomb: Binoculars	225
Shooting Glasses	229
Spotting Scopes	223
Bean's Twisters & Handcuffs	139
Bed Roll	309
Behind the Scenes	4–5
Belding & Mull: Cleaning Rods	158
Handbook	326
Reloading Tools	326
Belgian: Muzzleloaders	93–97
Proofmarks	52
Belgian Shotgun Parts	416–417
Belts: Cartridge	172, 174, 177
Heiser	172
Lawrence	177
Money	309
Sam Brown	138, 176
Shell	172, 174, 177
Bench Blocks	365, 371, 377
Bending Apparatus, Stocks	395
Benjamin Air Guns	143
Berdan Primers	323
Berloque Miniature Blank Pistols	129
Biascope	228
Billets	138
Billies	138
Binoculars: Bausch & Lomb	225
Wollensak	228
Zeiss	224
Bird & Star Target	151
Bird Calls	152, 153
Bird of Prey Call	153
Black Bird Call	153
Black Diamond Lightning Bluer	286
Black Powder (see powder)	
Blank Cartridges	128, 129, 242
Blank Guns	128, 129
Blood Test Equipment	171
Blue Rock Targets	86
Blueing: Basin	286
Blueing Salts	286
Circular Brushes	286
Damascus Browner	286
Gunsmith's Bluer	286
Handbrushes	287
Lightning Bluer	286
Oil	286
Old Connecticut	287
Peerless Blueing Kit	287
Spray Blue	287
Blueing Salts	286
Bolt-Action Shotgun Parts, Geha	135
Books	162–170
Art of Shooting	162, 163
Big Game & Adventure	167
Camp & Game Cooking	167
Collectors	166
Fencing	166
Forests	166
Game Preservation	166
Game Prints	167
Gunsmithing	164
Handling of Your Dog	169
Historical	164
Hunting Stories	168
Military & Technical	163
Natural History	167
Pistols & Revolvers	165
Rifles	165
Shotguns	166
Trapping — Furs — Camping — Taxidermy	170
Woodworking	166
Boots	306–307
Bore-Polishing Paste	158
Brass Shot Cases	252
Brenneke Shotgun Slugs	247
Broilers	317
Broken Shell Extractor	390
Browner	286
Browning Shotguns	54, 55

	Page
Browne & Sharpe Tools:	
Calipers, Vernier	368
Center Gages	370
Center Punches	371
Combination Squares	368
Depth Gages	369
Dial Indicator	371
Micrometers	366–367
Rules	367–368
Screw Pitch Gage	370
Surface Gages	370
Telescoping Gages	369
Thickness Gages	370
Twist Drill Gage	370
V Blocks & Clamps	371
Brushes: Blueing	287
Cleaning	156–159
Dog	341
B. S. A.:	
Bore Polishing Paste	158
Cunirid	158
Safety Paste	160
Buckets, Canvas	309
Buckhorn Rifles (Stevens)	46
Buckshot Shells (see ammunition)	
Buckshot Sizes	252
Buff Barrel Polishers	159
Buffer Shells	181
Bullet Moulds:	
Belding & Mull	326
Cramer	334
Ideal	324
Modern Bond	325
Peerless	332
Bullets	322, 333, 335
Bullet Trap	151
Burred Slugs	142
Bulls Eye Rubber Band Pistol	142
Burke Milling Machine	353
Burners, Gas	363
Butt Plates	188, 292–293, 284
Buzzard Owl Call	153

C

	Page
Cabinets:	
Steel Gun Cabinets	182
Tool Chests	404
Tools & Parts Cabinets	185
Walnut Gun Cabinets	183
Calipers, Toolmakers	380
Calipers, Vernier:	
Brown & Sharpe	366–367
Keilpart	364
Mauser	395
Calls, Game	152, 153
Cameras: Keystone Movie	350–351
Camp Equipment: Axe, Safety	268
Basins	309
Boots	306–307
Compasses	269
Duffle Bags	309
Flashlights	272, 273, 309
Knives	268–271
Match Boxes	269
Money Belt	309
Pack Cloth	309
Primus Stoves	316
Rucksacks	308
Shooting Coats & Shirts	296–305
Sleeping Robes	309
Tents	310–313
Water Bags	309
Cannon, Blank	128
Canvas Gun Cases	172, 175
Caps, Pistol Grip	284
Carbide Lamp	188
Carbine Stocks & Remodeling	281
Cartridges: Foreign	243–247
Auxiliary	154
Flare	132, 137
Gas	137
Supplemental	154
Metalics	232–234, 236–241
Shot Shells	248–252
.22 Cal.	230–231
Cartridge: Bags	172, 174
Belts	172, 174, 177

	Page
Boxes	173, 174, 177, 187, 184, 189
Box Holder	331
Carriers	139
Clip Boxes	173, 177
Magazines	395
Carving Sets	386, 388
Cases, Brass Shot	252
Cases: Canvas	172, 175
English Trunk	175
Leather	172–175
Leg of Mutton	172
Sheepskin	173
Center Punches	371, 378, 380
Chamber Sizes (Shotgun)	252
Charcoal Stoves	317
Checkering Tools	389
Cheek Pads	292–292
Cheek Piece, Walnut	293
Chisels: Cold	387
Die Sinkers	389
Inletting	386
Stockmakers	386
Wood	386, 389
Chokes:	
Cutts	82
Poly	82
Weaver	83
Circular Brushes	286
Circular Saws	356
Clamps	371, 377
Clay Targets	84–87
Cleaning Kits	160
Cleaning Rods:	
Belding & Mull	158
Marble	156–157
Parker-Hale	158–159
Tripak	155
Union Hdwe.	156–157
Cleaning Rod Stops	159
Clips for Foreign Cartridges	246
Clothing (see Camp Equipment)	
Clubs, Police	137, 138
Collars, Dog	341
Colt:	
"A Century of Achievement" (article)	99
Automatic Pistols	100–103
Engraving	109
Grips	109
Revolvers	104–108
Combination Case	186
Combination Guns:	
Marble	127
Marlin	65
Savage	35
Stevens	64
Stoeger	51
Combs, Dog	341
Compasses	269
Compensators, Cutts	82
Connecticut Bluer	287
Connecting Screw Reamer	277
Conservation	6, 7
Conversion Tables	265
Core-Lokt Ammunition	236
Corner Gun Racks	180
Corrector, Aim	209
Counterbores	372
Countersinks	375
Countersinks, Muzzle	390
Cramer Bullet Moulds	334
Crime Detection Equipment	171
Crosman Air Rifles	145
Crossbows	97
Crow Calls	152, 153
Crow Decoys	150
Crystal Cleaner	160
Cunirid	158
Cups, Prize	342–347
Cutts Compensator	82

D

	Page
Daisy Air Rifles	142
Dart Puller	141
Darts	141
Damascus Browner	286

BUY FROM STOEGER WITH CONFIDENCE

Page
Dead Black 189
Dead Center 6 Hole Eye Piece...... 189
Decoys 150
Deer Call 153
Dent Raiser 395
Depth Gages 369, 376
Detachable Swivels 284–285
Deutsche Werke (Ortgies) Parts.... 135
Dial Indicator 371
Dick Files 396–397
Dies, Numerical and Alphabetical..... 394
Die Sinkers Chisels................ 389
Die Sinkers Files................ 402
Die Stocks 373–374
Dishes, Dog 341
Dividers 379, 380
Dog: Brushes 341
Call 153
Collars 341
Combs 341
Dishes 341
Leads 341
Medicine 340
Nail Nippers 341
Whistles 153, 341
Double Barrel Rifles:
Powell 91
Zephyr 89
Draw Knives 392
Drill Bit & Tap Cabinet............ 185
Drill Blocks & Clamps............371, 377
Drill Presses 357
Drill Rod, Round & Square.......... 289
Drillings 51
Drills 374, 375
Driver Power Tools:
Band Saws 356
Belt Sanders 356
Drill Presses 357
Grinders 356
Jig Saws 357
Driving Rod, .22 Cal............. 395
Drop Measurer 395
Duck Calls 152, 153
Duck Decoys 150
Duffle Bags 309
Du Pont Powders 320–321
Duvrock Trap 86
Dynamo Pocket Lamp.............. 309

E

Ear Stoppers 188
Ebony Forend Blocks................ 284
Elastic Finger Guard................ 189
Elbow Pads 189
Electric Furnace 331
Elementary Ballistics (article)...... 235
Emery Cloth 382
Emergency Kit 295
Empty Cases 322, 339
Enfield Remodeling 276, 280, 281
English Ammunition 243
English Cases 174, 175
English:
Ammunition 243
Ballistics 262–264
Shotguns 90, 91
Rifles 91
Proofmarks 52
Engraving:
Colt 109
Engraving Tools 389
Eureka Shotgun Loading Set........ 338
Express Rifles (see Double Barrel Rifles)
Extractor, Broken Shell............. 390
Extras:
for Fox Guns 63
for Ithaca Guns 70
for L. C. Smith Shotguns.......... 61
for Remington Rifles.............. 33
for Remington Shotguns.......... 79
for Winchester Rifles.............. 19
Eye Piece:
Mico-Iris 186

Page

F

Fancy Pearl & Ivory Grips....109, 118, 119
Featherweight Telescope Mount...... 188
Fecker:
Rifle Scope 215
Sporting Scopes 222
Felted Slugs 142
Field Cleaners 156
Field Glasses 224–228
Field Repair Kit................... 385
Files:
Dick 396–397
Rotary 362
Swiss 398
Nicholson 389–393
Finger Guard 189
Finger Print Outfit................. 171
Firing Pins, Shotguns.............. 415
First Aid Kit........................ 295
Fitemal Nipple Wrench............. 181
Flannel Patches 156
Flare Cartridges 137
Flare Gun 132, 136
Flashlights and Batteries......272–273, 309
Flashlight Carrier 139
Flat Stock, Ground................. 381
Flexible Shafts:
Handee 358
Utility 362
Flintlock Guns 96, 97
Flintlocks 93
Flints 97
Flobert Triggers 415
Fluid White 209
Folding Shotguns 58
Food:
Dog 340
Pheasant 341
Quail 341
Foreign Cartridges 243–247
Foreign Parts (see Parts, Foreign)
Foreign Proof Marks............... 52
Foreign Shot Shells................ 245
Forend Parts 415
Four Barrel Guns................... 51
Fox Shotguns 62, 63
French:
Ammunition 245, 246
Lebel Rifle Stocks................ 279
French Proofmarks 52
French Walnut 274
Fulton Shotguns 67
Furnace, Soldering 363

G

Gages:
Center 370, 379
Depth 364, 376
Screw Pitch 370
Screw and Wire.................. 378
Surface 370
Tap and Drill 378
Telescoping 369
Thickness 370
Twist Drill 370
Game, American 6–7
Game Calls 152, 153
Game Carrier 303
Game Getter 127
Game Targets 149
Garnet Paper 382
Gas Checks 326
Gas Equipment 363
Ammunition 137
Billies 137
Gasmasks 136
Grenades 137
Guns 136
Revolvers 136
Gauges:
Cartridge Case 337
Headspace 337
Shothole 189

Page
Geha Parts 135
Gem Reloading Tool 330
German:
Air Rifles 144–145
Ammunition 244–247
Ballistics 266–267
Files 396–397
Proofmarks 52
Shotgun Springs 135
German Shotgun Springs............ 135
Glasses, Shooting 229
Gloves, Shooters 173, 187
Goose Decoys 150
Gouges, Wood 386–388
Grain Weights 323
Grease, Gun 160
Gridirons 317
Grills 317
Grinders 356
Grinding Wheels 382
Grip Adaptors ......115, 186—188, 207, 293
Grips:
Arthorn 119
Colt 109
Forfit 207
Handful 207
Harrington & Richardson........123, 125
Ivory 109, 119
Olympic 187
Pachmayr 187
Pearl 109, 119
Spur 186
Stag 119
Tenite 118
Ten Point 186
Wesson Adaptor 115
Ground Flat Stock 381
Grouse Call 153
Gull and Goose Call................ 153
Gun Cabinets 182–183
Gun Cases 172–175
Gun Grease 160
Gun Oil 160, 161
Gun Powder (see Powder)
Gun Racks 180
Gun Room Requisites.............. 181
Gunslick 160
Gun Slings 294
Gunsmith's Bluer 286
Gunstocks 274–282

H

Hack Saws & Blades..............381, 393
Haenel: Air Pistols 140
Air Rifles 144
Parts 410
Model 88 Rifle Parts.............. 412
Hammers, Gunsmith's 390
Hammers, Shotgun 414
Hammer Key, Anson 390
Hand Brushes, Metal.............. 287
Handcuffs & Cases 139
Handee Power Tools 358–361
Hand Protectors 181
Hand Traps 86, 87
Harrington & Richardson:
Flare Gun 132
Pistols 125
Recoil Pads 293
Revolvers 122–125
Shotguns 58
Haversacks 308
Hawk Calls 153
Hawkins Recoil Pads.............. 292
Heads, Miniature Animal.......... 315
Headspace Gauges 337
Heater 316
Heath Hen Call 153
Heavy Duty Lead Solvent.......... 160
Heiser Holsters 178–179
Henckel's Hunting Knives.......... 269
Henckel's Pocket Knives.......... 270
Hensoldt Rifle Scopes.............. 210
Hercules Powder 320–321
Hi-Standard 120, 121

AMERICA'S GREAT GUN HOUSE

	Page
History:	
Colt	99
Gun Powder	318
Lefever & Ithaca	68
Marlin	41
Remington	28
Savage	34
Smith, L. C.	59
Smith & Wesson	110
Winchester	11
Hook Saw	381
Holsters, Pistol and Revolver	173, 176, 178–179
Hoppe's Nitro Solvent	160
Hornet Darts	141
Hornet Pellets	140, 141, 144, 145
How to Order	8
Hump Back Hammer	115
Hunter Shotguns	67
Hunting Clothing:	
Boots	306–307
Breeches	297, 298, 301, 303
Caps	300, 303
Coats	294–305
Moccasin	306
Pants	297–298, 301, 303
Socks	300
Shirts	296

I

	Page
Ideal Handbook	324
Ideal Reloading Tools	324, 329, 339
India Stones	383
Ingot Mould	331
Inletting Chisels	386, 387
Inletting Rasp	389
Inletting Saw	393
Inner-Belted Ammunition	236
Introduction to Gunsmithing	352
Italian Cartridges	245
Italian Proofmarks	52
Ithaca:	
History	68
Ithaca Recoil Pads	293
Ithaca Shotguns	70, 71
Iver Johnson:	
Revolvers	126–127
Shotguns	66, 67
Ivory Grips	109, 119

J

	Page
Jackets	297–305
Jags	158, 159
Jaws, Vise	390
Jig Saws	357
Jordan Reloading Tools	327
Jostam Recoil Pads	292

K

	Page
Keepers for Gun Sling	294
Keys:	
Anson	390
Nipple	181, 415
Keilpart Precision Tools:	
Calipers	364
Micrometers	365
Keystone Movie Cameras	350–351
King:	
Detachable Swivels	207
Iron Sights	205–207
Formfit Grips	207
Handful Grips	207
King Semi-Smokeless Powder	321
Kit Boxes, Metal	184, 185, 189
Kits:	
Blueing	287
Cleaning Kit	158, 160
Field Repair Kit	395
First Aid Kit	295
Knives: Draw	395
Hunting	268–269
Pocket	270–271
Krag Remodeling	278
Kynoch Cartridges	243

L

	Page
Lanters, Call	188, 272, 316
Lapwing, Call	153
Lark Call	153
Lathes: Atlas	354–355
Lawrence: Holsters	176
Cartridge Belt	177
Sam Browne Belts	176
L. C. Smith:	
Extras	61
History	59
Shotguns	60, 61
Lead Balls & Shot	97, 252, 339
Lead Solvent	160
Lead Tester	331
Leads, Dog	341
Leather Cleaning Solution	294
Leather Gun Cases	172–175
Leather Gun Racks	180
Leather Gunslings	294
Lebel: Clips & Cartridges	246
Remodeling	279
Rifle	246
Stocks	279
Lee Enfield:	
Remodeling	279
Lefever:	
History	68
Lefever Shotguns	69
Leg Irons	139
Lens Holder	189
Levels	377
Lightning Bluer, Black Diamond	286
Lightning Metalite Cloth	382
Lock	309
London Oil Finish	277
Lubricant, Bullet	324, 326
Luger: Barrels	132
Parts	133
Reconditioned Pistols	132
Lyman: Ideal Handbook	324
Iron Sights	190–192
Polaroid Tube Sight	190
Reloading Tools, Ideal	324, 329, 339
Rifle Scopes	216

M

	Page
Mallard Call	153
Mauser Model 88 Parts	412
Mannlicher Schoenauer Rifles:	
Parts	408, 409
Marble:	
Auxiliary Cartridges	154
Axes	268
Broken Shell Extractor	390
Compasses	269
Game Getter	127
Iron Sights	200–204
Knives	268
Match Box	269
Nitro Solvent	160
Rods	156–157
Marlin:	
History	41
Rifles	42–43
Shot Guns	65
Marlin Rifles:	
Models 80, 81, A1, 100	42
Models 36, 39	43
Mauser:	
Automatic Pistols	130, 134
Model 88 Parts	412
Model 98 Remodeling	278
Pistol Parts	131, 134
Rifle Parts	406, 407
Mauser Actions:	
F.N. (Belgian)	288
Match Box	269
Mechanical Owl Decoys	150
Mechanical Targets	151
Medals	348–349
Medicine, Dog	340
Meepos Reloading Tools	336
Melting Pots	324, 331
Merit:	
Melting Pot	331
Sights	193

	Page
Metal Oil Bottles	181
Metal Targets	151
Metal Wool	287
Metalics (see Ammunition)	
Mico-Iris Eyepiece	186
Micrometer for Springfield	189
Micrometers:	
Brown & Sharpe	366–367
Keilpart	365
Starrett	376
Milling Machine	353
Miniature Animal Heads	315
Miniature Blank Pistols	129
Miniature Revolvers	128
Mirror	294
Modern Bond Reloading Tools	325
Money Belts	309
Moore Hen Call	153
Morse:	
Adjustable Round Split Dies	374
Counterbores	372
Die Stocks	373
Drills	374, 375
Drill Sets	374
Reamers	372
Taps	373
Tap Wrenches	373
Mo-Skeet-O	84
Mossberg:	
Features	48
Rifles:	
Models 26, 42, 44, 45, 46	49
Models 42, 46, 50 & 51	50
Targo	85
Rifle Scopes	220
Shotguns:	
Models 83, 85	50
Spotting Scopes	222
Mossin (Russian) Rifle	246
Remodeling	276
Motty Rifle Paste	158
Moulded Lead Balls	84
Moulds, Bullet (see Reloading)	
Mounts, Telescope: Featherweight	188
Redfield	217
Stoeger Side	210
Mounts for Telescopes:	
Lyman	216
Mossberg	220
Weaver	219
Moving Picture Cameras	350–351
Musket Caps	323
Muzzle Countersink	390
Muzzle Loading: Guns	94, 97
Pistols	97
Rod Tips, etc.	415
Muzzle Stops	181

N

	Page
Needle Files	397, 398, 402
Nevarust Gun Grease	160
Newton Rifle Stocks	275
Nicholson Files	399–403
Nippers: Cutting	381
Dog	341
Nipples: Gun	415
Keys	181, 415
Nitro Solvent Oil	160, 161
Noshine	160
Noshoe Recoil Pad	293
Noske Rifle Scopes	212
Numerical Dies	394

O

	Page
Oigee Rifle Scopes	210
Oil Bottles, Metal	181
Oil Cans, Valve Spout	189
Oil Finish	277
Oils: Blueing	286
Gun Cleaning	160, 161
Stoegerol	160
Oilstones	383
Old Connecticut Bluer	287
Olympic Pistol Grips	187

SEE PAGE 405 BEFORE ORDERING PARTS

	Page
Olympic Stocks	280
Oper Glass	227
Optical Attachment	1
Order, How to	8
Ortgies Pistol Parts	135
Over & Under Guns:	
Browning	55
Marlin	65
Remington	80
Savage	77
Stevens	64
Stoeger	51
Zephyr	92
Owl Decoys	150
Owl Decoys, Stuffed Mechanical	150
Oyster Catcher Call	153

P

	Page
Pachmayr Adaptor	187
Pacific:	
Iron Sights	208–209
Reloading Equipment	328
Pack Cloth	309
Paper Shot Shells	339
Paper Targets	146–149
Parachute Flares	137
Parallels	365, 377
Parker Hale; Cleaning Rods	158, 159
Cushion Ring Elbow Pads	189
Dead Black	189
Fluid White	209
Iron Sights	209
Peep Sight Reamers	189
Six Hole Eye Pieces	189
Parker Iron Sights	209
Parker Shotguns	56–57
Partridge Call	153
Parts, Domestic:	
Baby Hammerless Revolvers	429
Colt Automatics	420–421
Colt Revolvers	416–419
Crescent Shotguns	477
Empire Shotguns	477
Fox Shotguns	453
Fulton Shotguns	451
Harrington & Richardson Revolvers	426–428
Harrington & Richardson Shotguns	428
Hi-Standard Pistols	448
Ithaca Shotguns	448–449
Iver Johnson Revolvers	429–431
Iver Johnson Shotguns	432–433
Lefever Shotguns	450
Marlin Rifles	455–457
Marlin Shotguns	454
Parker Shotguns	458
Remington Rifles	495–501
Remington Shotguns	502–505
Savage Rifles	434–440
Savage Shotguns	440–441
Smith, L. C., Shotguns	451
Smith & Wesson Pistols	419, 424, 425
Smith & Wesson Revolvers	422–425
Stevens Pistols	448
Stevens Rifles	442–444
Stevens Shotguns	445–447
Western Shotguns	449
Winchester Cannon	465
Winchester Rifles	459–485
Winchester Shotguns	486–494
Parts, Foreign:	
B. S. A. Airrifle	413
Belgian Shotgun Parts	414, 415
Browning Shotguns	412, 452
Geha	135
German Shotgun Springs	135
Haenel Air Guns	410
Luger	133
Mannlicher Schoenauer Rifle	408, 409
Mauser Pistols	131, 134
Mauser Rifle	406, 407
Model 88 Rifle	412
Ortgies	135
Rheinmetall	135
Spanish Revolver	135

	Page
Walther Automatic Rifle	413
Walther Pistol	117
Webley Air Pistol	411
Patches, Cleaning	156
Pearl Grips	109, 119
Peep Sight Reamer	189
Peerless Action & Barrel	288
Peerless Barrel Blanks	291
Peerless Blueing Kit	287
Peerless Bullet Moulds	332
Peerless Ramps	284
Peerless Steel	289
Peerless Stocks	275–281
Pellets	140, 141, 144, 145
Percussion Caps	323
Percussion Guns	94, 97
Percussion Pistols	97
Peters: Ballistics	256–257
Duvrock Trap	86
Metalics (see Ammunition)	
Shot Shells	249
Pheasant Call	153
Pheasant Food	341
Picnic Stoves	317
Pin Vises	378
Pistol Grip Attachments	293
Pistol Grip Caps	284
Pistol and Revolver Cases	186, 187
Pistol and Revolver Shooting (article)	98
Pistols:	
Percussion	97
Pistols, Air:	
Benjamin	143
Haenel	140
Tell	140
Webley	141
Pistols, Automatic:	
Blank	128, 129
Colt	100–103
Hi-Standard	120, 121
Luger	132, 133
Mauser	130, 131
Pistols, Single Shot:	
Colt	108
Harrington & Richardson	125
Harrington & Richardson Flare Pistol	132
Stevens	127
Plugs:	
Ear	188
Plungers, Shotgun	415
Pliers	384, 385
Pockescope	228
Polaroid Glasses	229
Polaroid Tube Sight	190
Police Equipment	136–139, 171
Polisher, Leather	158–159
Polishing Preparations	382
Poly, Choke, Super	82
Potter Reloading Tools	330–331
Powder Flasks	93
Powder, Gun:	
Dupont	320–321
Hercules	320–321
History (Article)	318
King	321
Powder Measures	324, 325, 326, 328
Powder Scales	323, 328
Powell & Son:	
Double Barrel Rifles	91
Double Barrel Shotguns	90, 91
Power Tools (See Driver and Handee)	
Pres-To-Oiler	181
Primed Shells	322
Primers	323
Primer Tray	331
Prize Cups and Trophies	342–347
Prize Medals	348–349
Projectors, Movie	351
Proofmarks of Foreign Guns	52
Propert's Saddle Soap	294
Protractor	376
Pull Through	156, 157
Pump-Shotguns:	
Ithaca	70, 71
Remington	78, 79
Stevens	77
Winchester	72, 73
Put-A-Way Plan	9

Q

	Page
Quackenbush Slugs	142
Quail Call	153
Quail Food	341

R

	Page
Rabbit Call	152
Racks for Guns	180
Radius Stoves	316
Ramps	284, 197, 205–206
Rasps	414
Ray-Ban Shooting Glasses	229
Reamers: Center	372
Hand	372
Inside Neck	337
Peepsight	189
Taper	372
Reamer Connecting Screw	277
Reblueing (See Blueing)	
Recoil Pads	292–293
Rectifying Cylinders	395
Redfield:	
Iron Sights	197–199
Telescope Mounts	217
Reloading Components:	
Article "This Reloading Game"	319
Brass Shotshells	252
Bullets	322, 333, 335
Gas Checks	326
Lead Shot	339
Lubricant	324, 326
Paper Shells	322, 339
Percussion Caps	323
Powder	320, 321
Primed Cases	322
Primers	323
Wads and Cardboards	322, 339
Reloading Tools: Belding & Mull	326
Cramer	334–335
Eureka	338
Ideal (Lyman)	324, 338–339
Jordan	327
Meepos	336
Modern Bond	325
Pacific	328
Peerless Moulds	332–333
Potter	330, 331
Schmitt	328, 329
Wilson	337
Remington: Ballistics	253–255
Blue Rock Targets	86
Cleaning and Lubrication Preparations	160
Metalics (See Ammunition)	
Pocket Knives	271
Remodeling Model 30	275
Rifles	29–33
Shotguns	78–81
Shot Shells	248
Remington Rifles:	
Models 30 & 141	29
Models 81, 121 & 241	30
Model 37 Rangemaster	31
Models 341, 510 & 511	32
Model 513	33
Extras for Remington Rifles	33
History	28
Remington Shells	248
Remodeling: Accessories	281, 284–285
Enfield	276, 280–281
Lebel	279
Newton	275
Remington Model 30	275
Russian	276
Springfield	277, 280–281
Winchester Model 52	275
Winchester Model 54	275
Repair Kit	395
Replacement Stocks	282
Restocking	274–283
Rest, Rifle	294
Revolver Cases	186, 187
Revolvers, Gas	136

SEE PAGE 8, "HOW TO ORDER"

	Page
Revolver Sights (see Sights)	
Revolver Spring Plyer	390
Revolvers: Blanks	128
Colt	104–108
Harrington & Richardson	122–125
Iver Johnson	126, 127
Miniature	128
Smith & Wesson	111–116
Rheinmetall Shotgun Parts	135
Rifflers	403
Rifle Kit, Metal Box	184–185, 189
Rifle Rest	294
Rifles, Air:	
Benjamin	143
Crosman	145
Daisy	142
Haenel	144
Stoeger	144, 145
Rifles:	
Marlin	42–43
Mossberg	49, 50
Powell, Wm. & Co.	91
Remington	29–33
Savage	35–40
Springfield (Stevens)	44, 47
Stevens-Springfield	44, 47
Winchester	12–27
Zephyr	89
Rifle Sights, see Sights	
Rifle Vise	181
Rig	160
Riot Equipment:	
Ammunition	137
Guns	73, 87, 136
Roaster	317
Rods, Cleaning	155–159
Rooster, Target	151
Rotary Files	362
Rubber Band Pistols	142
Rubber Boots	306
Rucksacks	308
Rules	367, 368, 379
Rumanian:	
Rifle	246
Cartridge	246
Russian (Mossin) Rifle	246
Russian Rifle Remodeling	276
Rust Remover	160, 161

S

Saddle Soap	294
Safety Paste, B. S. A.	160
Sam Browne Belts	138, 176
Sanders	356
Sand Paper	382
Sandpiper Call	153
Savage:	
History	34
Rifles	35–40
Shotguns	36, 76, 77
Savage Rifles:	
Models 219 & 221	35
Model 99	36–37
Models 23 B, C, & D, 29 & 40	38
Models 3, 4, 19 & 23AA	39
Models 5, 6 & 7	40
Savage Shotguns:	
Models 220, 221	35
Model 99, .410 Ga. Barrel	36
Saws:	
Band	356
Dovetail	393
Inletting	393
Gunstockers	393
Scales, Powder	323, 328
Schmitt Reloading Tools	328–329
Schutzentype Butt Plate	293
Scrapers	403
Screw Chest	395
Screw Drivers:	
Gunsmith's	181, 394
Parker Hale	394
Starrett	378
Utica	386
Screw Drivers, English	181

	Page
Screws: Sets	395
Shotgun	415
Scribers	380
Searchlight, Brilliant	188
Semi Rib	204
Semper Auxiliary Barrel	154
Sharpshooter Rubber Band Pistol	142
Sheepskin Cases, etc.	173
Shell Bags and Belts	172–174, 177
Shell Boxes, English	174
Shell Extractors	390
Shells (See Ammunition)	
Shirts	296
Shooter's Gloves	173, 187
Shooting Coats & Jack..ets	297–305
Shooting Glasses	229
Shooting Prizes and Medals	342–349
Shooting Spectacles	239
Shop Pictures	4, 5
Shotguns:	
Article	55
Browning	54, 55
Folding Guns	58
Fox	62, 63
Fulton	67
Harrington & Richardson	58
Hunter	67
Ithaca	70, 71
Iver Johnson	66, 67
Lefever	69
Marlin	65
Parker	56–57
Powell	90, 91
Remington	78–81
Savage	35, 36, 76–77
Smith, L. C.	60, 61
Stevens	64, 67
Western	69
Winchester	72–75
Zephyr	88, 89
Shotgun, Miscellaneous Parts	414, 415
Shotgun Reloading	338, 339
Shotgun Shells (See Ammunition)	
Shotgun Sights	192, 204, 207
Shotgun Springs	135, 414
Shotgun Stocks	282
Shotgun Wads	322, 339
Shothole Gauges	189
Shot, Lead	252
Shot Sizes	252
Shoulder Holsters	176, 178, 179
Showroom Pictures	2, 3
Sickening Gas	137
Side Lever:	
Lever	415
Spring	415
Sight Gauge	188
Sights, Iron: King	205–207
Lyman	190–192
Marble	200–204
Merit	193
Pacific	208–209
Parker Hale	209
Parker Skylight	193
Redfield	197–199
Vaver	194–196
Wittek (See Vaver)	
Sight Spanner	390
Signal Pistol	132
Silent Dog Call	153, 341
Silver-Tip Ammunition	236
Single Shot Pistol:	
Colt	108
Harrington & Richardson	125
Stevens	127
Six-Hole Eye Pieces	189
Skeet Equipment	84–87
Sleeping Bags	309
Sleeping Robes	309
Slings, Gun	294
Sling Strap Keeper	294
Sling Swivels	207, 284, 285
Slot Blanks	192, 197, 204
Slugs, Quackenbush	142
Slugs, Shotgun	247, 248–251
Smith, L. C., Shotguns	60, 61
Smith & Wesson:	
History (article)	110
Revolvers	111–116

	Page
Smokeless Powder (See Powder)	
Smoke Shells	137
Snake Bite Kit	295
Snap Shells	181
Sneezing Gas	137
Snips: Dog	341
Tinner's	387
Soap, Saddle	294
Soldering Furnace	363
Soldering Iron	363
Sound & Voice Detector	171
Spacers, White Lined	188
Spanish Proofmarks	52
Spanish Revolver Parts	135
Spanners	390
Spectacles, Shooting	229
Spinning Bird Target	151
Spotting Scopes:	
Bausch & Lomb	223
Fecker	222
Mossberg	222
Unertl	222
Wollensak	223
Spratt's Dog Equipment	340–341
Springfield Rifle:	
Headspace Gage	337
History (Article)	235
Springfield Micrometer	189
Springfield Remodeling	277, 280, 281
Springfield (Stevens):	
Models 85, 87, 872	44
Models, 83, 84, 86	47
Springs: Belgian	414
German	135
Plier	390
Spanish	135
Spanner	390
Steel For	289
Spring Steel	289
Springwire	289
Spur Grip Adaptor	186
Squares	365, 368, 376
Stag Call	153
Stag Grips	119
Stag Horn Gun Racks	180
Stamps, Numerical and Alphabetical	394
Starrett Tools:	
Bench Block	365, 373, 377
Center Gages	379
Center Punches	378
Combination Hand Vises	378
Cutting Nippers	381
Depth Gages	376
Dividers	380
Drill Blocks and Clamps	377
Drill Point Gage	380
Ground Flat Stock	381
Hack Saws and Blades	381
Hermaphrodite Calipers	380
Hook Saw	381
Levels	377
Micrometers	376
Parallels	377
Pin Vises	378
Protractor	376
Rules	379
Screw Drivers	378
Screw Pitch Gage	379
Screw and Wire Gages	378
Scribers	380
Squares	376
Surface Gage	380
Tap and Drill Gages	368
Tap Wrench	377
Toolmaker's Calipers	380
Trammel Points	380
Starter Guns	128
Steel for Gunsmiths	289, 381
Steel Gun Cabinets	182
Steel Shooter Boxes	184
Steel Tool Chests	184, 185
Steel Tool & Parts Cabinets	185
Stevens: Pistol	127
Rifles	45, 47
Shotgun	64, 77
Stevens Rifles:	
Models 417, 417½, 418, 418½	45
Models 53, 56, 66, 76	46

	Page
Stevens-Springfield:	
Models 85, 87, 872	44
Models 83, 84, 86	47
Steyr:	
Rifle	246
Pistol	246
Cartridge	246
Stock Bending Apparatus	390
Stocking	274–283
Stoeger:	
Air Rifles	144, 145
Blueing Accessories	286–287
Camp Equipment	308–317
Carbine Stocks	281
Cleaning Kit	160
Cross Bows	97
Combination Over and Unders	51
Dural Lightweight Guns	51
Four Barrel Guns	51
First Air Kit	295
Gunsmithing, Introduction to	352
Inletted Stocks	274–282
Mounts	210
Olympic Grips	187
Olympic Stocks	280
Patches	156
Peerless Remodeling	275–281
Pellets	140, 141, 144, 145
Pistol Shooter's Case	187
Shooting Glasses	229
Stoegerol	161
Three Barrel Guns	51
Stoeger Oil Finish	277
Stoegerol	161
Stop, for Cleaning Rod	159
Storm Lantern	316
Stoves	316, 317
Sub-Caliber Barrels:	
Semper	151
Sun Glasses	229
Super Nitro Solvent	160
Super Poly Choke	82
Supplemental Chambers	154
Sure Sight Gauge	188
Surface Plates	365
Swedish:	
Carving Knives	388
Plyers	385
Radius Stoves	316
Saws	393
Wood Gouges	387
Swivels	207, 284–285

T

	Page
Tables, Conversion	265
Tapes, Steel	379
Taps	373
Tap Wrench	373, 377
Targets: Clay	84–87
Game	149
Mechanical	151
Metal	151
Paper	146–148
Targo	85
Tatem's Shot Sizes	252
Telescope Mounts:	
Featherweight	188
Redfield	217
Stoeger Side	210
Telescopes, Rifle: Ajack	211
Fecker	215
Hensoldt	210
Lyman	216
Mossberg	220
Noske	212
Oigee	210
Unertl	214
Weaver	218–219
Zeiss	213
Telescopes, Spotting:	
Bausch & Lomb	223
Fecker	222
Mossberg	222
Wollensak	223
Unertl	222
Tell Air Pistols	140

	Page
Tell Target Pistol	154
Tenite Grips	118
Ten Point Grip	186
Tents	310–313
Ten X:	
Glove	187
Gun Case	173
Ten X Shooting Coat	305
Three Barrel Guns	51
Thermometers	221, 286
Time Payment Plan	9
Tomlinson Cleaner	157
Tool Steel	289, 381
Top, Lever:	
Lever	417
Parts	417
Springs	417, 153
Torches, Gas	363
Trap Equipment:	
Mo-Skeet-O	84
Remington, Peters	86
Targo	85
Western	87
Trigger Guard	417
Triggers	417
Triggers, Double Set	320
Trigger Shoe	186
Trigger Tester, "Truwait"	181
Tripak Cleaning Rod	155
Trojan Binoculars & Fieldglasses	226–227
Trophies	342–347
True Weight Trigger Tester	181
Trunk Cases, English	197
Tubascope	229
Tubes for Parkerifling	326
Turkey Call	152
Turn Screws	181
Twisters, Bean's	139

U

	Page
Unertl Rifle Scopes	214
Unertl Spotting Scope	222
Union Hardware Cleaning Equipment	156–157
Universal Apperture:	
Shooting Glasses	229
Utica: Cold Chisels	387
Pliers	387
Screw Drivers	394
Steel Chisels	387
Tinner Ships	387
Utility Power Tool	362

V

	Page
"V" Blocks and Clamps	371, 377
Valve Spout Oil Can	189
Van-Au-Matic Target	151
Vari-Power Scopes	223
Vaver	194–196
Vernier Calipers	364
Very Pistols and Cartridges	132, 136–137
Vests	305
Vests: Shell	347
Vickers	38
Vienna Cases	174
Vises: Barrel	390
Gunsmiths	391
Hand	390
Jaws	390
Milling Machine	353
Pin	378
Rifle Vise	181

W

	Page
Wads	322, 339
Wall Gun Racks	180
Walnut Cheek Piece	293
Walnut Gun Cabinets	183
Walnut Hill (Stevens Rifles)	45
Walnut Stock Blanks	274
Walther: Pistol Parts	117
Water Bags	309

	Page
Water Hen Call	153
Waterproofing Compound	314
Water Proof Match Boxes	269
Weaver:	
Choke	83
Shotgun Scope	83
Weaver Telescopes	218–219
Webley: Air Pistols	141
Weights, Grain	323
Wesson Grip Adaptor	115
Western: Ballistics	258–259
Metalics (see Ammunition)	
Shot Shells	250
Traps and Targets	87
Western Recoil Pad	293
Western Shotguns	69
Whistles: Dog	153, 341
Game	152, 153
White Flyer Targets	87
White Line Recoil Pad	293
Whitelined Spacers	188
Wigeon Call	152, 153
Wild Fowl Call	152, 153
Wilson Reloading Tool	337
Winchester: Barrel Blanks	291
Ballistics	260–261
Cannon Blank	128
Cleaning & Lubricating Preparations	160
Flashlights (see Ammunition)	272–273
Metalics (see Ammunition)	
Models 52 & 54 Remodeling	275
Rifles	12–27
Shotguns	72–75
Shot Shells	251
Supplemental Chambers	154
Winchester Rifles:	
Model 70	12–14
Model 71	15
Model 07	15
Model 65 (.218 Bee)	16
Model 64 (Deer)	17
Model 64 (.219 Zipper)	18
Model 94 Carbine	18
Model 52 Sporter	19
Model 52 Target	20–21
Model 75 Sporter	22
Model 75 Target	23
Model 61 & 62	24
Model 74 & 63	25
Model 69, 72	26
Model 67 & 677 & 68	27
Extras for Winchester Rifles	19
History	11
Winchester Shotguns:	
Model 12	72, 73
Model 42, 97	73
Model 21, 24, 37	74
Model 30	75
Shells	251
Wire for Springs	289
Wittek Sights (See Vaver)	
Wollensak:	
Binoculars	228
Spotting Scopes	223
Wood Carving	386–388
Wood Chisels	383–389
Woodcock Call	153
Wool Clothing, see Hunting Clothes	
Wool, Metal Cleaning	287
Wool Mops	158, 159
Worms, Gun	415
Wrenches, Nipple	181, 415
Wrist Compasses	269

X

	Page
X-Ring Bullet Trap	151

Z

	Page
Zeiss: Binoculars	224
Rifle Scopes	213
Zephyr: Double Barrel Rifles	89
Double Barrel Shotguns	88–89
Over & Under	92

WE APPRECIATE YOUR PATRONAGE